Pro Basketball Prospectus 2010-11

THE ESSENTIAL GUIDE TO THE 2010-11 NBA SEASON

by Bradford Doolittle and Kevin Pelton

Cover by Amanda Bonner

Layout by Vince Verhei

Copyright 2010 Prospectus Entertainment Ventures LLC

ISBN 1453868992

All rights reserved

Without limiting the rights under copyright reserved above, no part of this publication may be reproduced, stored in or introduced into a retrieval system, or transmitted, in any form, or by any means (electronic, mechanical, photocopying, recording, or otherwise), without the prior written permission of both the copyright owner and the above publisher of this book.

Table of Contents

Introduction	iv
Statistical Toolbox	v
SCHOENE Explained	x
WARP2: Explaining Our Updated WARP	xiii

NBA TEAMS

Atlanta Hawks	1
Boston Celtics	12
Charlotte Bobcats	23
Chicago Bulls	35
Cleveland Cavaliers	47
Dallas Mavericks	57
Denver Nuggets	67
Detroit Pistons	77
Golden State Warriors	87
Houston Rockets	97
Indiana Pacers	109
Los Angeles Clippers	119
Los Angeles Lakers	130
Memphis Grizzlies	141
Miami Heat	152
Milwaukee Bucks	163
Minnesota Timberwolves	174
New Jersey Nets	187
New Orleans Hornets	199
New York Knicks	208
Oklahoma City Thunder	219
Orlando Magic	232
Philadelphia 76ers	243
Phoenix Suns	253
Portland Trail Blazers	264
Sacramento Kings	275
San Antonio Spurs	286
Toronto Raptors	296
Utah Jazz	306
Washington Wizards	315

OTHER ESSAYS

Fantasy 2010-11	326
Fantasy Rankings	330
A Primer on the CBA Crisis	334
Second Best: Ranking the Other Leagues	337
The WARP Hall of Fame	340
2010-11 NBA Schedule	345
Acknowledgments	350
Author Bios	351
Player Index	352

Introduction

Usually, this introduction is a place for us to talk about the value of statistical analysis and how it has helped NBA teams win. This year calls for a slightly different tack. The moral of the 2010 postseason, after all, was more about misleading statistics. By no measure did the Boston Celtics look like an elite team after limping into the playoffs with an 11-11 record in March and April. The defending champion Los Angeles Lakers claimed the Western Conference's top seed, meanwhile, but did so with a point differential that ranked third in the West.

Ultimately, those numbers did not matter during the playoffs. The Celtics and Lakers both found additional gears, demonstrating that their regular-season performance painted an inaccurate picture of their ability. While we weren't fooled by the Lakers' middling numbers, both of us picked against Boston prior to the Celtics' upset wins over Cleveland and Orlando.

The lesson here is not to abandon statistics entirely. After all, the Celtics' run was noteworthy precisely because it was so unlikely and unexpected. The NBA's grueling seven-game series leave relatively little room for the kind of fluke outcomes that are commonplace in the MLB and NFL postseasons; more often than not teams perform to their regular-season level during the playoffs. Instead, the takeaway is a healthy humility about the limitations of statistical analysis, which cannot account for every external factor like health or even motivation.

Because there is so much in the sport of basketball that still defies easy quantification, the APBRmetrics community has always been open to incorporating the scouting process. The battle lines have been drawn much less sharply between basketball's traditional thinkers and the progressive-minded newcomers who champion analytics. Often, statistical research has backed up the game's conventional wisdom. Long before he was the Michael Lewis-approved face of basketball's answer to *Moneyball*, Shane Battier was simply the kind of player a coach loved to have on his team.

That kind of common ground has made it easy for statistical analysts to infiltrate NBA front offices in increasing numbers. In March, the *Wall Street Journal* reported that half of the league's teams now have at least one person responsible for statistical analysis. Some, like the Houston Rockets and the Portland Trail Blazers, boast much larger teams of analysts working together. For new general mangers like Portland's Rich Cho, an understanding of the numbers has become a selling point.

At Basketball Prospectus, we strive to bring the same level of insight and detail to covering and analyzing the NBA game. After a successful debut edition of the *Pro Basketball Prospectus*, we're back with improvements to our core statistic, Wins Above Replacement Player (WARP), and our SCHOENE projection system. With the addition of D-League Translations to our arsenal, we have 2010-11 projections for more than 500 players as well as every team.

In addition to team essays and player capsules, you'll also find a variety of essays in the back of the book. Fantasy players will want to check out our SCHOENE fantasy projections, which account for player development and some measure of team context, as well as an essay highlighting where those projections differ from conventional wisdom. We also compare the level of play in the best leagues in the world outside the NBA and consider what might be the most important story of the upcoming season--the looming possibility of a lockout next summer.

If you're new to Basketball Prospectus, get ready to enhance your understanding of the NBA game and statistical analysis with detailed information about every player who took the floor in 2009-10 and this year's newcomers. For veteran readers, we hope the quality of our analysis continues to live up to our high standards.

Thanks for reading and enjoy!

Bradford Doolittle
Kevin Pelton
September 25, 2010

Statistical Toolbox

While we may not be quite as fond of acronyms as our Baseball Prospectus counterparts, new readers will find some unfamiliar metrics in the pages that follow. Here's a how-to guide on the statistics we use.

HOW TO READ THE TEAM BOXES

HAWKS IN A BOX

Last year's record	53-29
Last year's Offensive Rating	113.5 (3)
Last year's Defensive Rating	108.3 (14)
Last year's point differential	4.7 (7)
Team pace	89.6 (27)
SCHOENE projection	35-47 (10)
Projected Offensive Rating	107.1 (24)
Projected Defensive Rating	109.6 (14)
Projected team weighted age	27.5 (14)
Projected '10-11 payroll	$68.9 (12)
Est. payroll obligations, '11-12	$60.6 (10)

Each team essay features a box summarizing the team's 2009-10 performance and looking ahead to 2010-11. Besides record, the most important information about last season is the team's **Offensive and Defensive Ratings, pace** and **point differential**.

The first three metrics rely on the building block of NBA analysis: the possession. As baseball teams have just 27 outs with which to score runs, teams have a certain number of possessions. We define possessions as ending only when the other team gets the ball, meaning that two teams generally have the same number of possessions in a game (the totals can differ by up to two per game if the same team has the final shot in all four quarters).

Over the long term, however, teams have very different possession totals because of the paces at which they play. Last year, the difference between the league's fastest team (the Golden State Warriors) and its slowest (the Portland Trail Blazers) was more than 12 possessions per game. Because offenses and defenses are judged primarily by points scored and allowed per game, a fast or slow pace can badly skew perceptions. For example, the Phoenix Suns under Mike D'Antoni had a bad defensive reputation in part because of how fast the team played. That is why statistical analysts consider it critical to rate offenses and defenses on a per-possession basis (actually per 100 possessions, which is easier to understand and similar to per-game averages).

Basketball Prospectus estimates possessions with this formula: .96 * (FGA + (.44*FTA) - OR + TO). The .44 multiplier on free throws reflects the fact that they are not always shot in pairs. "And one" free throws do not add a possession (already reflected in the made field goal); nor do technical or flagrant foul shots. Three-shot fouls also mean fewer than two free throws per possession. Multiple studies have confirmed the .44 ratio of free throw attempts to possessions. As for the .96 multiplier on the entire term, that accounts for team offensive rebounds, as when a defensive player blocks a shot out of bounds. The NBA does not track these second chances in any meaningful sense, which means possessions are slightly overstated without the adjustment.

Offensive Ratings and Defensive Ratings, then, are simply points scored and allowed per 100 estimated possessions. The best and worst in 2009-10:

Best/Worst Offenses and Defenses, 2009-10

Best Offenses	ORTG	Worst Offenses	ORTG
Phoenix	117.4	New Jersey	102.1
Orlando	114.0	Minnesota	103.0
Atlanta	113.5	Chicago	105.0
Cleveland	113.3	L.A. Clippers	105.1
Denver	113.3	Indiana	105.5

Best Defenses	DRTG	Worst Defenses	DRTG
Charlotte	104.4	Toronto	114.8
Orlando	104.4	Golden State	113.9
Milwaukee	105.1	Minnesota	113.8
Miami	105.1	New York	113.7
Boston	105.3	Detroit	113.4

Pace is calculated by the average of the team's possessions and its opponents' possessions per 48 minutes. The league's fastest and slowest teams:

Fastest and Slowest Teams, 2009-10

Fastest Teams	Pace	Slowest Teams	Pace
Golden State	98.6	Portland	86.6
Indiana	95.4	Detroit	87.3
Minnesota	94.5	Miami	88.2
Phoenix	94.0	Atlanta	88.8
Denver	93.5	Charlotte	89.1

The last bit of 2009-10 data is point differential. As in baseball, differential tends to predict future results slightly better than actual win-loss record because of the role of randomness in the outcome of close games.

2010-11 projections are generated using our SCHOENE projection system, as described in detail in the next chapter. In addition to a record, based on projected differential, we also project each team's Offensive and Defensive Rating and league rankings. Note that the rank for projected record is within each conference, giving an idea of whether we project a playoff season or not.

We also include the projected weighted age for each team. Each player's age is weighted by projected minutes played, meaning players on the end of the bench have little impact on team age. Note that age is calculated as of the end of the 2010-11 regular season.

Lastly, we include financial data on each team--their projected payroll for this season and their commitments for the summer of 2011 and the 2011-12 season based on the most likely outcome of team and player options. This gives an early look at which teams will have money to spend in free agency next summer, though negotiations on a new Collective Bargaining Agreement may fundamentally change salary-cap rules by then.

All financial data in the book is unofficial and was compiled through numerous media reports and with the help of the salary data at storytellerscontracts.com.

HOW TO READ THE FIVE-YEAR TABLES

At the conclusion of each team's essay, you'll find a table summarizing team performance over the last five years. In addition to final records and seed in the postseason, each season's finish in our **NBAPET power rankings (POW)** and the team's **Pythagorean win totals (PYTH)** are included to give a better idea of performance, while the information included in the team box is put in a five-year context.

Digging deeper, the second table looks at each team's offense and defense using the Four Factors created by Denver Nuggets analyst Dean Oliver. These break down a team's performance at each end of the floor into four categories:

• Shooting, as measured by **effective field-goal percentage (eFG)**, which counts each three-pointer as 1.5 field goals to account for their added value.

• Rebounding, as measured by **rebound percentage (oREB/dREB)**, the percentage of available rebounds captured by the team, either on offense or defense.

• Free Throws, as measured by made **free throws**

HAWKS FIVE-YEAR TRENDS

Season	AGE	W-L	POW	PYTH	SEED	ORTG	DRTG	PT DIFF	PACE
05_06	22.7	26_56	25.5 (28)	27.8	---	108.1 (12)	112.8 (26)	-4.8 (28)	90.2 (17)
06_07	24.1	30_52	27.5 (27)	27.3	---	104.3 (29)	109.8 (23)	-4.8 (29)	89.7 (24)
07_08	24.7	37_45	35.1 (20)	35.9	8	109.1 (16)	111.0 (18)	-1.8 (19)	90.1 (18)
08_09	25.8	47-35	46.8 (12)	45.6	4	111.1 (10)	109.0 (10)	1.6 (12)	88.4 (24)
09_10	27.3	53-29	53.8 (5)	54.0	3	113.5 (3)	108.3 (14)	4.7 (7)	89.6 (27)

		OFFENSE				DEFENSE			
Season	PAY	eFG	oREB	FT/FGA	TO	eFG	oREB	FT/FGA	TO
05_06	$36.6	.486 (20)	.314 (3)	.255 (14)	.174 (27)	.513 (27)	.695 (28)	.275 (26)	.166 (6)
06_07	$47.8	.471 (30)	.292 (5)	.263 (9)	.178 (26)	.503 (21)	.709 (26)	.268 (25)	.170 (8)
07_08	$58.5	.483 (21)	.297 (4)	.263 (6)	.158 (26)	.501 (15)	.717 (26)	.217 (13)	.146 (15)
08_09	$68.2	.504 (10)	.260 (19)	.238 (13)	.144 (6)	.494 (11)	.716 (24)	.210 (5)	.154 (12)
09_10	$65.1	.506 (11)	.282 (5)	.213 (23)	.133 (1)	.496 (16)	.727 (24)	.208 (8)	.154 (17)

(league rankings in parenthesis)

STATISTICAL TOOLBOX

per field-goal attempt (FT/FGA) to capture both getting to the line and making shots when there.

• Turnovers, as measured by **turnover percentage (TO)** the percentage of plays that end in turnovers - note that an offensive rebound starts a new play, so there can be multiple plays within a single possession.

HOW TO READ THE PLAYER TABLES

Each player table includes four different sections: biographical information, skill ratings, statistics for the last three seasons plus a 2010-11 projection and, lastly, the information SCHOENE used to generate that projection.

The bio information includes player contract data--both salary for this season and status for the 2011-12 campaign. Also note the player's jersey number underneath their primary position.

SKILL RATINGS

Skill ratings are derived from data compiled in our **NBAPET (NBA P**rojection, **E**valuation and **T**racking**)** system, which tracks player and team performance at the box score level. The heart of the system is an estimate of both offensive and defensive possessions used by each player in each game and how efficiently those possessions are used. Because the output of NBAPET is so similar to the data used to generate our SCHOENE projections and other per-possession metrics, we have translated its results to Skill Ratings. These ratings serve as a handy reference for each player's strengths, weaknesses and bottom-line value.

Each of the skill ratings is expressed as an integer between +5 (the best) and -5 (the worst). The rating is based on the player's percentile ranking in each statistical category *at his position*. The percentile groups are assigned ratings according to the following table:

Skill Ratings By Percentile

Rating	Percentile	Rating	Percentile
+5	96th to 100th	-1	31st to 42nd
+4	88th to 95th	-2	21st to 30th
+3	79th to 87th	-3	12th to 20th
+2	69th to 78th	-4	4th to 11th
+1	57th to 68th	-5	0 to 3rd
0	43rd to 56th		

It's important to note that each player is compared only to others that play the same position. Keep these positional differences in mind as you read the player tables. When Pau Gasol is rated +5 for his passing ability, that doesn't mean he passes as well as Steve Nash. It just means he's one of the best passing centers in the game.

Finally, the Skill Ratings are forecasts for the coming season. In other words, we've used past data, aging factors and projected role in 2010-11 to generate the results. Here is an explanation of each rating, and the criteria used to calculate it:

TOT: Total. The player's bottom-line value, based on Wins Produced. Note that this is both a rate statistic (a measure of efficiency) and a counting statistic (results are accumulated over the course of a season). As such, this rating is highly influenced by a player's projected playing time.

OFF: Offensive value. Based on NBAPET's estimated points per possession as well as the player's usage rate. These figures are combined to estimate how many points a player is worth per 100 team possessions.

DEF: Defensive value. Calculated exactly the same as OFF, except the data is based on the statistics each player's opponents have compiled. As mentioned, this is done at the box score level. In each game, every point created and possession used by a team's opponent is assigned to one of the defenders. In other words, for every offensive "debit" there is a defensive

SF	LeBron James	Hght: 6'8" Exp: 7 Salary: $14.5 million		SKILL RATINGS						
		Wght: 250 From: St. Vincent-St. Mary HS (OH)		TOT	OFF	DEF	REB	PAS	HND	SHT	ATH
6		2011-12 status: guaranteed contract for $16.0 million		+5	+5	+5	+2	+5	+5	+3	+5

Year	Team	Age	G	MPG	Usg	3PA%	FTA%	INS	2P%	3P%	FT%	TS%	Reb%	Ast%	TO%	BLK%	STL%	PF%	oRTG	dRTG	Win%	WARP
07-08	CLE	23.3	75	40.4	.338	.160	.152	.991	.531	.315	.712	.568	.114	.081	.114	.021	.021	.026	112.8	103.3	.773	22.5
08-09	CLE	24.3	81	37.7	.341	.175	.153	.978	.535	.344	.780	.591	.117	.091	.110	.024	.024	.022	115.7	102.8	.839	26.9
09-10	CLE	25.3	76	39.0	.337	.182	.160	.978	.560	.333	.767	.604	.107	.103	.123	.020	.022	.019	115.5	103.3	.828	25.4
10-11p	MIA	26.3	75	38.0	.303	.229	.152	.923	.553	.315	.752	.584	.101	.099	.118	.022	.020	.020	112.7	103.4	.769	21.0

Most similar to: Dwyane Wade (93.1), Grant Hill, Michael Jordan, Kobe Bryant   **IMP:** 43%   **BRK:** 0%   **COP:** 9%

"credit." Also, keep in mind that the traditional box score defensive statistics a player accumulates (rebounds, steal, blocks, fouls) are not included in this rating. It's strictly an estimate of how effectively a player limits his opponents' production.

REB: Rebounding. Based on SCHOENE's projected rebound percentage for the player.

PAS: Passing. Based on SCHOENE's projected assist percentage for the player.

HND: Ballhandling. Based on SCHOENE's projected assist-to-turnover ratio (A/TO) for the player. This statistic has been the subject of much debate in the analysis community. Many analysts dismiss A/TO altogether, and the statistic does have its flaws. However, we feel that comparing players only to others at the same position alleviates some of the problems with A/TO and allows it to serve as a reasonable estimate of a player's ballhandling ability.

SHT: Shooting. Based on SCHOENE's projected effective field-goal percentage.

ATH: Athleticism. This recent addition to our statistical toolbox attempts to quantify the "applied" athleticism of a player. In other words, we're not interested in how high a player jumps, how quickly he can do a shuttle run or how fast he backpedals. We're interested in how he turns his skills into production. ATH is based upon height-adjusted ratings for foul-drawing ability, rebounding, steals and blocks.

STAT LINES

The stat lines rely heavily on per-play metrics. The first step for NBA analysts was using player stats on a per-minute basis to account for heavy discrepancies in playing time. However, pace can still color per-minute stats, so per-play numbers do the best job possible of placing player performance in a neutral context.

The player's age for each season is reported through the end of the regular season.

After games and minutes per game--the only per-game stat you'll find in these stat tables--we start with a group of statistics describing how the player plays on offense. **Usage rate (Usg)** is the percentage of team plays a player uses while on the floor. With five players per game, an average usage rate is 20.0 percent. Dwyane Wade played a larger role in his team's offense than any other player in the league last year, using 35.2 percent of Miami's plays while on the floor. His two-year stranglehold on this statistic figures to end this season.

Next, we look at what percentage of the possessions a player ended were used on three-point attempts **(3PA%)** and trips to the foul line **(FTA%**, again using the .44 multiplier to convert free throws to possessions). We subtract three-attempt percentage from free throw-attempt percentage and add one to get the **"Inside" rating**, which measures how much time a player spends in the paint as compared to on the perimeter. Miami's Jamaal Magloire had the league's highest inside rating a year ago (1.262), while Steve Novak of the L.A. Clippers (0.412) repeated as the most perimeter-bound player.

The next group of stats deals with how well players shot. You won't find field-goal percentage because that statistic is influenced by how often a player shoots threes. Instead, we separate shooting from the field into **two-point percentage (2P%)** and **three-point percentage (3P%)**. **Free throw percentage (FT%)** is, of course, standard. To summarize a player's efficiency, we use **True Shooting Percentage (TS%)**, which can be thought of as what a player's field-goal percentage would be if he maintained the same level of efficiency while shooting only two-pointers. True Shooting Percentage is calculated by points divided by two times shooting possessions used, which is FGA + (.44*FTA). Portland rookie Jeff Pendergraph led the league last season with a .705 True Shooting Percentage. Tyson Chandler (.643) was tops among players with at least 1,000 minutes.

Moving on from offense, we have **rebound percentage (Reb%), assist percentage (Ast%)** and **turnover percentage (TO%)**. Rebound percentage is an average of the player's offensive and defensive rebound percentage, accounting for the fact that some teams have relatively more defensive rebounds available, which would artificially inflate players' rebound percentages. Offensive and defensive rebound percentages are not listed in the table, but will be referenced from time to time. Marcus Camby's 22.3 percent total rebound rate led the NBA last season. Camby was also best in defensive rebound percentage (32.0 percent), while Sacramento's Jon Brockman had the league's best offensive rebound percentage (18.2 percent). Assist percentage is calculated as the percentage of team plays on which the player records an assist. Steve Nash handed out assists on 14.9 percent of Phoenix's plays to pace the NBA. Turnover percentage is, like 3PA% and FTA%, a percentage of the plays used by the player. Fabricio Oberto was the league's most turnover-prone player, turning the ball

STATISTICAL TOOLBOX

over on an incredible 36.2 percent of his possessions, while the aforementioned Novak was the most sure-handed, with a miniscule 1.8 percent turnover rate.

The stats table continues with defensive metrics. **Steal percentage (Stl%)** and **personal foul percentage (PF%)** are calculated per team plays; **block percentage (Blk%)** is calculated per opponent two-point attempts. While steals and blocks can indicate a player who is taking risks that hurt his team, they are still positives--especially for players who record plenty of both. Tony Allen beat out teammate Rajon Rondo to lead the league in thievery, posting a 3.4 steal percentage. The best block rate in the league was Washington's JaVale McGee at 8.0 percent. Meanwhile, the league's most foul-prone regular was Amir Johnson, who fouled on 8.1 percent of Toronto's possessions.

The final four columns relate to our WARP rating system, which calculates **Wins Above Replacement Player** in the same spirit as Baseball Prospectus' metric. In concept, the system seeks to create a team of the player plus four average teammates--similar to the Marginal Lineup Value used by Baseball Prospectus. Because of team interaction, this is much more challenging in basketball. WARP draws upon Oliver's work on individual player ratings while accounting for a player's role using usage rate.

Offensive (oRTG) and **Defensive Ratings (dRTG)** are calculated for this imaginary "team." Those ratings are translated into a **win percentage (Win%)** for the team, which serves as the per-minute player rating. The last step is to subtract replacement level from that win percentage and multiply by minutes played divided by 82 games to determine how many wins above a replacement-level contributor the player has created for his team over the course of the season. Replacement level is set using the assumption that a team of replacement players would win 10 games over the course of the season. The NBA's leaders in WARP last season generally mirror the top candidates for MVP:

Most WARP, 2009-10

Player	Team	Win%	WARP
LeBron James	cle	0.828	25.4
Dwyane Wade	mia	0.761	20.0
Kevin Durant	okl	0.687	18.3
Dwight Howard	orl	0.724	18.2
Jason Kidd	dal	0.673	15.4

SCHOENE DETAILS

Below the projected statistics is the rest of the output from the SCHOENE projection system. The four most similar players are listed, with the level of similarity (out of 100) listed for the most comparable player to give a general idea of how unique the player is. At the bottom right are the percentage of the comparables used (generally just over 50 per player) who improved the following season, who broke out (improved by at least 20 percent) and coppaged (declined by at least 20 percent).

Besides those in the player tables, there are two other important statistics you'll often see in the player capsules. Net plus-minus is a concept borrowed from hockey that measures how teams fare with a given player on the court as opposed to on the bench, expressed on a per-100 possession basis. This can also be separated into net offensive and net defensive plus-minus. Adjusted plus-minus attempts to take this a step further by accounting for the quality of a player's teammates and opponents. However, this adjustment tends to be unreliable over the course of a single season, which means adjusted plus-minus must be used with care.

Capsules for players currently on each team, including training-camp invitees, are listed in alphabetical order. After current players are capsules for unsigned draft picks, followed by free agents who played in the NBA in 2009-10, listed with their last team.

SCHOENE Explained

When Nate Silver unveiled his PECOTA method for projecting player performance at our sister site Baseball Prospectus in 2004, it set the template for future projection systems on two counts--the use of similarity scores to identify development paths and the use of a former fringe player's name as an acronym. On both counts, Basketball Prospectus' SCHOENE projection system follows in PECOTA's footsteps.

SCHOENE is named for former NBA forward Russ Schoene, who spent four seasons in the NBA in the 1980s, most prominently playing for the Seattle SuperSonics. Like PECOTA, SCHONE is technically an acronym, standing for Standardized Comparable Heuristic Optimizing Empirical NBA Evolution.

We first introduced SCHOENE to project the results of the 2008-09 NBA season. While the player projection aspect is not entirely unique--ESPN Insider's John Hollinger independently developed a similar projection system--SCHOENE goes a step further by beginning to consider team context. For each team, player usage rates are adjusted (along with efficiency) to replicate the interactions between players in divvying up offensive possessions. Another adjustment handles defensive rebounding because of the tendency for good rebounders to cannibalize defensive boards from their teammates and vice versa.

While SCHOENE's default output is per-possession or per-shot rate stats, it also incorporates team pace to produce complete, realistic stat lines for each player. This is especially useful for creating fantasy projections, since a player's per-game averages will depend in part upon the pace at which his team plays.

Finally, SCHOENE brings it all together to create team stat lines, unprecedented for an NBA projection system. This gives us an idea not only of a bottom-line projection for each team's win-loss record but also how they will get there and projected strengths and weaknesses.

At the heart of the SCHOENE system are similarity scores for each player based on 13 statistical categories, standardized for league norms: height, weight, a "shooting" rating (based on 3P%, 3PM/Min and FT%), two-point percentage, "inside" rating (FTA-3PA)/possessions, usage rate, rebound percentage, assist percentage, steal percentage, block percentage, turnover percentage and player winning percentage, the per-minute component of the WARP system.

Like many similarity scores, SCHOENE's are calculated out of 100, that being an identical match. A score of 95 means two highly similar players, while 90 is reasonable similarity and anything below that starts to get dicey. The closest match for any player in this year's projections is Houston Rockets forward Jordan Hill and Kris Humphries, at 99.2. A handful of players, most notably Shaquille O'Neal, did not have a single match of 90 or better.

In general, at least the 50 most similar players of the same age--within six months of the player's age during the season, as with PECOTA--were used to generate each player's 2010-11 forecast, though the smaller pool of players in the NBA--the similarity database dates back only through 1979-80, the first year of the three-point line--means very young and very old players have a smaller group. For eight players whose comparable pools were far too small, an average age adjustment has been applied to their statistics.

In addition to using this group of comparable players to project the improvement or decline in each of 14 statistical categories, we also follow PECOTA's lead in generating summary statistics that reflect the variation in each player's projection. Recreated with each player's projection are the familiar Improve/Breakout/Decline percentages, a breakout or coppage (our term for a steep decline) being defined as at least 20 percent improvement or drop-off.

The only noticeable change to the player projections this year is the use of D-League Translations, as established by a study published on the website last season, to create projections for players who have not seen at least 250 minutes of action at the NBA level but have seen more action in the D-League. In addition to translations for rookies based on NCAA stats and for European players who played in either Euroleague or the EuroCup, this further increases the size of the pool of player projections. This year's book features more than 500 individual projections.

SCHOENE EXPLAINED

TEAM PROJECTIONS

After projections were generated for each player, these were incorporated into a team context. Games played are projected for each player using a baseline estimate of 76 games played. From there, players are penalized one game for each six missed last season (up to a maximum of 10 for players who missed the entire season) and one for each 20 missed two years ago, based upon research done by Houston Rockets analyst Ed Küpfer on projecting games played. We also account for preexisting injuries and suspensions. Playing-time projections are strictly subjective based on each team's projected depth chart.

On offense, the only step between individual projections and team totals is the aforementioned usage adjustment. Each player's usage rate is adjusted so that the team as a whole uses only the number of possessions projected based on team pace. There is also a corresponding adjustment to the player's shooting percentages and turnover rates to reflect the inverse relationship statistical analysts have found between usage and efficiency. One percentage point of usage is approximately equal to a point of Offensive Rating.

For now, assists are essentially ignored in calculating a team's offensive efficiency based on the sum of player shooting percentages, free throw rates, offensive rebounding and turnover rates.

The projection is more complicated at the defensive end because of the paucity of tracked individual defensive stats. Defensive rebounding, blocks, steals and personal fouls are projected from individual statistics. Defensive rebounding is regressed significantly to league average, a notion supported by studies done by another Rockets analyst, Eli Witus.

Two-point percentage on unblocked shots and non-steal turnovers (as well as other descriptive factors like ratio of three-point attempts to twos) are based on past team performance regressed to league average (by a factor of 25 percent for two-point shots and about 45 percent for non-steal turnovers, which also factor in projected steal rate). This can be problematic in the case of teams that change a high percentage of their personnel or defensive schemes.

After making significant changes to the individual projections last season, this year's focus was on revisiting the team projections. The APBRmetrics message board tracked the accuracy of several statistical projections during the 2009-10 season, with SCHOENE placing second in terms of root mean squared error--the average squared error of the projections, which heavily penalizes wildly inaccurate projections (Table 1).

Table 1: SCHOENE vs. Other Metrics

System	MSE	RMSE
Component Score (Jon Nichols)	7.21	8.73
SCHOENE	7.84	9.44
Simple Rating System (B-R.com)	7.72	9.55
Statistical Plus-Minus (B-R.com)	7.87	9.73
Win Shares (B-Reference.com)	8.33	10.08
eWins (Mike Goodman)	8.48	10.48
NBAPET (Bradford Doolittle)	8.70	11.30

Unquestionably, there is room for improvement. While SCHOENE's stunningly optimistic assessment of the Memphis Grizzlies proved fairly accurate and the Eastern Conference race shaped up largely as projected (Cleveland and Orlando at the top, with Boston in the rear-view mirror--at least during the regular season), SCHOENE was too bullish on New Orleans and failed to foresee the rises of the Atlanta Hawks and Oklahoma City Thunder.

Breaking down SCHOENE's accuracy at projecting each of the Four Factors in terms of the correlation between the projection and actual performance provided some interesting results (Table 2).

Table 2: SCHOENE Accuracy By Category

Offense	ORtg	eFG%	OR%	FTM/FGA	TO%
Correlation to actual	0.74	0.82	0.33	0.58	0.58

Defense	DRtg	eFG%	DR%	FTM/FGA	TO%
Correlation to actual	0.59	0.49	0.49	0.63	0.55

As you might expect, SCHOENE does a better job of predicting offense than defense, where the lack of individual defensive statistics is a major limitation. What is surprising is how good SCHOENE is at projecting team shooting (as measured by eFG%), given that it does not include adjustments for passing or teams' ability to stretch the floor with three-point shooting. While we know these traits are valuable at the team level, adding them to the equation did not significantly improve SCHOENE's accuracy.

On the other hand, SCHOENE was unexpectedly poor at projecting team offensive rebounding in 2009-

10. There was no clear pattern along the lines of defensive rebounding, where each team must be brought toward average to account for diminishing returns (that is, good defensive rebounders take some boards away from their teammates in addition to the opposition). Re-running the 2009-10 projection with actual minutes played shed some light on the issue (Table 3).

Table 3: SCHOENE Accuracy By Category, With Minutes

Offense	eFG%	OR%	FTM/FGA	TO%
Correlation to actual	0.82	0.33	0.58	0.58
Correlation w/minutes	0.79	0.51	0.69	0.57

Defense	eFG%	DR%	FTM/FGA	TO%
Correlation to actual	0.49	0.49	0.63	0.55
Correlation w/minutes	0.50	0.60	0.53	0.69

On both sides of the ball, knowing minutes played made a substantial difference in terms of projecting rebounding. Elsewhere, it provided no improvement and actually hurt projections of team shooting. This might be explained by the way smaller or bigger lineups can affect rebounding. For example, Golden State's projected defensive rebounding was strong because it was assumed that Brandan Wright and Anthony Randolph would be sharing minutes at power forward. Instead, both players were hurt and Don Nelson played smallball much of the year, using Corey Maggette at the four. The Warriors' rebounding tanked as a result.

Ultimately, the only noticeable adjustment made to SCHOENE at the team level was increasing the strength of the regression to the mean on defensive rebounding. Nothing else helped improve SCHOENE's accuracy in predicting what actually transpired in 2009-10. That may change next season. SCHOENE has served up some more surprising results, as you'll see over the following pages, and whether they hit or miss will help determine future alterations to SCHOENE.

Kevin Pelton

WARP2: Explaining Our Updated WARP

How do you rate a rating system? That thorny question has been problematic for statistical analysts. The oldest method is the "laugh test," which simply compares the results to conventional wisdom. In the early 2000s, the "Shaq test" held that any good rating system would rank Shaquille O'Neal as the league's best player. Something similar could be applied now with LeBron James. However, there is nothing scientific about this method, which is nothing more than a first cut.

Dave Berri has argued in favor of his Win Score metric on the basis of how successfully it explains team performance. While this might be a necessary condition for a good rating system, it is not a sufficient one. Any rating system that utilizes a "team adjustment" to account for the aspects of defense that are not captured by individual statistics will equate to team wins. At the extreme, team wins could simply be allocated on the basis of minutes played. This easy rating system correlates perfectly with team performance, but it does a poor job of crediting individual players for their contributions.

Dan Rosenbaum first came up with the notion of using adjusted plus-minus to evaluate rating systems. In this role, adjusted plus-minus--traditional plus-minus adjusted for a player's teammates and opponents--is objective and unbiased. The noise that makes adjusted plus-minus problematic at the individual level evens out over the sample of hundreds of players, leaving adjusted plus-minus as a capable measure of how different types of players help their teams win.

To calibrate the WARP rating system, we compared results from the 2007-08 season to adjusted plus-minus data from that season. Why 2007-08? For that season alone, Eli Witus of CountTheBasket.com compiled adjusted plus-minus data split up into its offensive and defensive components. This allowed us to focus specifically on improving the Offensive and Defensive Ratings that go into player win percentages and WARP.

Among regular players, here are the correlations between adjusted plus-minus and WARP components (Table 1):

Table 1: Correlations Between Adjusted Plus-Minus and WARP Components

	Win%	ORtg	DRtg
Net +/-	0.450	0.369	0.351
Off +/-	0.487	0.567	-
Def +/-	0.081	-	0.413

Correlation measures the strength of a relationship between two variables, with 1 or -1 indicating a perfect relationship and 0 indicating none at all. In this case, we've made all the correlations positive. Again, the noisiness in adjusted plus-minus means the correlations inevitably are not very high. What stands out here is that Offensive Rating measures offensive adjusted plus-minus much better than Defensive Rating measures defensive adjusted plus-minus. Given the limited number of individual defensive statistics we have to work with, this is no surprise.

The bigger question is where WARP has room for improvement. Here, we focused on the differences between how WARP and adjusted plus-minus rated each player on offense and defense. For example, Kobe Bryant's adjusted offensive plus-minus in 2007-08 was +10.4 points per 100 possessions. His Offensive Rating was +6.4 points per 100 possessions compared to league average. Thus, adjusted plus-minus rated Bryant as 4.0 points better on offense. Are there shared traits among players who are overrated or underrated by WARP? (Table 2)

For the most part, these correlations are close to zero, indicating that WARP is properly valuing each statistic. The most notable differences share a common theme--three-point shooting. The correlations indicate that players with higher three-point percentages and especially three-attempt percentages tend to

WARP2: EXPLAINING OUR UPDATED WARP

Table 2: WARP Accuracy, by Statistic

Statistic	Correlation	Statistic	Correlation
2P%	-0.087	FTA%	-0.185
3P%	0.269	TO%	-0.139
FT%	0.153	PF%	-0.124
TS%	0.006	**Defense**	
OR%	-0.236	Statistic	Correlation
Ast%	0.059	Stl%	-0.091
Usage	0.054	Blk%	0.094
2A%	-0.277	DR%	0.147
3A%	0.318	PF%	0.198

Table 4: WARP vs. WARP2 by Position

	WARP		WARP2	
Pos	ORtg	DRtg	ORtg	DRtg
PG	105.7	0.467	106.1	0.479
SG	104.3	0.431	105.0	0.453
SF	104.1	0.437	104.6	0.454
PF	105.3	0.487	104.7	0.470
C	104.9	0.508	103.9	0.476

rate better by adjusted plus-minus than by WARP. Essentially, there appears to be a value to spacing the floor that is not captured by the individual statistics of three-point shooters.

The correlation between Offensive Rating and adjusted offensive plus-minus is maximized by adding a term that multiplies the difference between the player's three-attempt percentage and the league three attempt percentage by seven. Here are the correlations between various offensive statistics and this new Offensive Rating (Table 3):

Table 3: New WARP Accuracy, by Offensive Statistic

Statistic	Correlation	Statistic	Correlation
2P%	0.009	Usage	0.049
3P%	0.061	2A%	0.015
FT%	0.013	3A%	0.003
TS%	0.001	FTA%	-0.014
Shoot	0.049	TO%	-0.045
OR%	-0.032	PF%	-0.016
Ast%	-0.008		

Now, it looks like Offensive Rating accurately captures what is helping teams win. This change increases the correlation with adjusted offensive plus-minus from .567 to .625. It also does a better job of valuing players at the wing positions, who previously lagged behind their peers at point guard and in the frontcourt (Table 4).

For whatever reason, wings still have less value statistically than other positions, but we're closer to seeing descending offensive value by position, which is what adjusted plus-minus shows. Defensive value increases the closer players get to the basket.

Almost all of the players who benefit the most from the change are wing players. Most of them were near or below replacement level despite helping their teams with their shooting (Table 5).

Table 5: Most Improved Players by WARP2

Player	Team	WARP	WARP2	Change
Quentin Richardson	mia	1.8	5.6	3.8
Jason Kidd	dal	11.8	15.4	3.5
Shane Battier	hou	0.7	4.2	3.5
Danilo Gallinari	nyk	3.2	6.4	3.2
Rasual Butler	lac	-3.7	-0.4	3.2
James Posey	nor	-2.2	1.0	3.2
Channing Frye	pho	4.1	7.3	3.1
Anthony Parker	cle	-1.8	1.2	3.0
Rashard Lewis	orl	2.5	5.4	2.9
Steve Blake	lac	0.6	3.4	2.8

Channing Frye is a good poster boy for WARP2. The Suns' offense was 6.8 points better per 100 possessions with Frye on the floor. Under the old WARP, he rated as below average on offense. His new rating is much more appropriate.

Table 6: Players with Biggest Losses by WARP2

Player	Team	WARP	WARP2	Change
Brook Lopez	njn	11.1	8.7	-2.4
Al Horford	atl	11.0	8.8	-2.2
LaMarcus Aldridge	por	7.3	5.0	-2.2
David Lee	nyk	13.8	11.6	-2.2
Luis Scola	hou	5.0	2.9	-2.2
David West	nor	7.5	5.4	-2.2
Amar'e Stoudemire	pho	11.7	9.5	-2.2
Nenê Hilario	den	11.0	8.8	-2.1
Chris Kaman	lac	2.7	0.6	-2.1
Carlos Boozer	uta	11.6	9.5	-2.1

WARP2: EXPLAINING OUR UPDATED WARP

No single player loses as much value as the most frequent three-point shooters gain from WARP2. Since many players attempted no threes all season, the biggest losers are simply the big men who played the most minutes and generally had the most value (Table 6).

Going forward, we will use WARP2 everywhere you are used to seeing WARP, including throughout this book as part of the past and projected player stat lines. Despite the potential for Star Trek puns, we will only refer to WARP2 as part of discussions comparing the two incarnations. Generally speaking, the term WARP will mean the updated version.

Kevin Pelton

Atlanta Hawks

Before last season, we interviewed the Hawks' Rick Sund. The general manager was emphatic in his belief that his team still had room to grow. He was so insistent that even over the phone you could almost picture him pounding on his desk as he spoke. Dammit, his team was going to grow from within. And so it did.

A year-by-year reading of the Hawks' regular-season win totals gives you the picture, one that suggests the team's upward mobility is interminable: 13, 26, 30, 37, 47 and, finally, 53. Last season's victory count was Atlanta's highest since 1996, landed the Hawks the Eastern Conference's third playoff seed, and came after a relatively quiet 2009 offseason during which the only major acquisition was sixth man Jamal Crawford. The team could still get better, Sund said, because so many of the key components were on the upswing. Growth from within was his meme.

Turned out, he was right and the state-of-the-art, well-oiled analytical machines of Basketball Prospectus were wrong. Indeed, there may not have been a team that we misread as drastically as we did the Hawks. Kudos to Sund and his staff.

Still, despite another regular season of progress, the Hawks lost for the second straight season in the conference semifinals. This time, the ouster came in a sweep at the hands of Orlando. The listless defeat punctuated a lackadaisical postseason run for the Hawks, who were fortunate to outlast a depleted Milwaukee squad in the first round. Worse, it apparently signaled to Sund that stagnation was setting in, because the man who oversaw Atlanta's gradual, but persistent, development was canned. Out with Mike Woodson, in with his former assistant Larry Drew, who will log his first season as an NBA head coach in 2010-11.

The coaching change turned out to be the extent of Sund's plan to keep the wheels of progress turning. During a summer in which several of the Hawks' Eastern Conference competitors made sweeping changes, Sund repeated the as-is policy in 2010- -all of the major components are back. That sounds almost like apathy until you consider that to keep the roster intact, Sund had to dole out a fully-guaranteed six-year, $123.7 million contract to his top player, Joe Johnson. The deal was widely panned by those deep in the quantitative pool, and by plenty more of those who just wade in the shallows. The reasons for this are pretty basic. Even if you consider Johnson to be a max-caliber player now, which is debatable, the chances of him remaining so for more than a season or two are basically nil considering the history of players of his age and type. In a league where bloated, ill-conceived contracts can set a franchise back for a half-decade or more, this type of a commitment is anathema to efficient franchise management.

So it would seem that the seeds for decay have been sewn in Atlanta. Last year's catch phrase of "growth from within" has been replaced by platitudes about the

HAWKS IN A BOX

Last year's record	53-29
Last year's Offensive Rating	113.5 (3)
Last year's Defensive Rating	108.3 (14)
Last year's point differential	4.7 (7)
Team pace	88.8 (27)
SCHOENE projection	35-47 (10)
Projected Offensive Rating	107.0 (24)
Projected Defensive Rating	109.5 (14)
Projected team weighted age	27.5 (15)
Projected '10-11 payroll	$68.9 (11)
Est. payroll obligations, '11-12	$60.4 (10)

Head coach: Larry Drew

An assistant coach for 17 years, including the last six in Atlanta under Mike Woodson, Drew will get his first opportunity to be a head coach after replacing Woodson at the helm of the Hawks. Since Atlanta's roster has remained largely the same, the Hawks are counting on the coaching change to help spur them forward. Drew plans significant changes at both ends of the floor. He will emphasize ball movement on offense while trying to improve the defense with more size in the frontcourt. Drew must be careful not to lose the strengths that made Atlanta a 53-win team in 2009-10.

sanctity of continuity. To others, the Hawks' plan reeks of stagnation. Indeed, Sund needs to be careful, because in the rapid evolution state of professional athletics, the growth from within can eventually turn into cancer.

With little further development anticipated from its roster, the Hawks have turned to Drew, who is replete with Ideas of His Own. The perception is that the Hawks fired Woodson because the team was underachieving when, in fact, the opposite is likely true. That's not to say the coaching swap can't or won't work. Teams do tend to tune out coaches after a period of time, and new ideas, if they're sound, are never a bad thing. Drew has set to work installing a new, motion-based offense in which the ball will always be moving and players will be cutting, screening and passing. That sounds all well and good, though this may turn out to be an attempt to tweak something that seemingly does not need tweaking.

The Hawks are an unusual group in that they have the reputation of a young, athletic team (which they are, though less so with each passing season), yet their actual playing style is more akin to an old team. The offense is prone to isolations and buzzer-beating jump shots, which isn't the formula for offensive efficiency. Still, the Hawks were tremendously efficient last season, ranking third in the league in Offensive Rating (113.5). The seven-place improvement on offense more than offset the four-place drop on the defensive end and fueled the Hawks' six-win improvement. This is the facet of the team that, initially, Drew seems most intent to change. And he might be right.

As good as the Hawks' offense was during the season, the postseason was a different story. Atlanta's two opponents, Orlando and Milwaukee, ranked second and third, respectively, in regular-season Defensive Rating. As a result, the Hawks dropped eight points per 100 possessions in offensive efficiency, and scored 84 points or fewer in three of their four losses to the Magic. There was widespread criticism of the predictability of Woodson's sets, suggesting that against high-caliber competition and in a format that allows for a little game-planning and preparation, Atlanta's stuff doesn't work.

We haven't seen Drew's offense in action yet, but descriptions provided by *Atlanta Journal-Constitution* beat writer Michael Cunningham bring to mind the base attack long deployed by Jazz coach Jerry Sloan. There are sure to be differences in the details. Plus, it's a heck of a lot easier for Sloan, a Hall of Famer with 25 seasons under his belt, to get his players to buy what he's selling than Drew, whose won-loss ledger stands at 0-0. However, the concepts are sound and the proliferation of back-cuts would be well suited to the Hawks' frontline.

Johnson is no longer going to be able to dominate possessions by holding the ball out top, but now that he's been enabled with a ridiculously fat megadeal, we'll have to see how he adapts to the change in emphasis. According to Synergy, the Hawks ranked third in shots coming off of isolations last season; they were 14th in shots off cuts. They were effective in both (seventh in points per play off isos, fourth on cuts). However, the league standard on isolations is 0.86 points per play; on cuts it's 1.24. Of course, it's not anything like a straight-forward transition, but if Drew can leverage the physical abilities of Josh Smith, Al Horford and Marvin Williams to get more easy baskets, the almost-certain overall regression in offensive efficiency might not be too severe. But if his players don't buy in, or Drew isn't well-equipped to install such a system at the NBA level, then it could get ugly.

The cornerstone of the Hawks' offensive success last season was a terrific ability to protect the basketball. Atlanta posted the lowest turnover percentage in the NBA, which more than offset the passive approach that too infrequently resulted in free throw attempts. Drew is messing with that dynamic by installing his new offense. Turnovers will certainly go up, and if they get out of control, it would be a very bad sign.

All of this discussion sidesteps that which most stands in the way of Atlanta making the leap from good to great: defense. The steady improvement of Atlanta over the last six years has been accompanied by a corresponding climb in Defensive Rating, going from 26th to 23rd to 18th to 10th over the four seasons previous to 2009-10. However, last season saw a four-place drop as the defensively-challenged Crawford became a fixture in the lineup, aging spot shooter Mike Bibby slowed down a bit more and Woodson put a greater emphasis on offensive rebounding. The latter of those items resulted in Atlanta ranking in the bottom third in the league in both transition opportunities allowed and in the rate as which those plays were converted.

A few weeks before teams were due to start filtering into training camp, Drew told reporters that the Hawks would likely abandon the rampant defensive switching that was standard operating procedure under Woodson. Woodson believed that the mix-and-match possibilities on his roster gave him an edge in pick-and-roll situations--most of his players could guard multiple positions, so why let the opposition get a step by trying to fight through picks? Perhaps he even thought this strategy was working, because the Hawks were ninth in the league by giving up just 97.0 points per game. However, most readers of this book already know that the per-game figure was warped by Woodson's mind-numbingly slow tempo and that, in reality, the Hawks were a middling-to-poor defense squad. If you have to be wary of Drew's decision to change offensive philosophies because of an "if it ain't broke, don't fix it" attitude, then you have to give him credit for recognizing the underachieving ways of Atlanta's defense and trying to do something about it.

Among other changes Drew wants to make is to have perennially-undersized center Al Horford to play more four, with Josh Smith sliding over to three and Zaza Pachulia presumably logging more playing time at center. Does that also mean Williams spends some time at two? We'll have to see, but Drew's reasoning for all of this re-shaping is that he has a versatile roster and he needs to have a system that exploits that interchangeability. Again, the logic is sound. It remains to be seen how well that logic will be executed.

While the biggest item on Sund's offseason docket was the disposition of Johnson, there were a few other dramas during the Hawks' summer vacation. First was the team's quest for another viable center, which could be important given Drew's desire to go more with Horford and Smith as his forwards. For much of July, Atlanta was mentioned as a leading candidate for the services of Shaquille O'Neal. There was even a rumor at one point that a potential Williams-for-Shaq sign-and-trade fell through. In the end, Sund settled for former Lakers center Josh Powell and was courting Erick Dampier at press time after he was released by Charlotte. Sund also finally settled matters with forward Josh Childress, who spent the last two seasons in Greece after failing to come to terms with the Hawks. Ultimately, he was shipped to Phoenix for the Suns' 2012 second-round draft pick--a disappointing return for a very good player. Part, or all, of the problem is an ownership group that is reportedly unwilling to go into luxury-tax territory. Depending on what happens with the negotiations for the next Collective Bargaining Agreement, that may be a wise stance. However, if you look at the payrolls of the league's upper crust, paying the tax is almost compulsory for team that genuinely wants to win a championship.

Late in the summer, rumors emerged that the softspoken Crawford was going to request a trade. Crawford reportedly is perturbed that the Hawks have not

> **From the Blogosphere**
>
> **Who:** Bret Lagree
> **What:** Hoopinion
> **Where:** http://www.hoopinionblog.com/
>
> Josh Smith deserved all the positive attention he received for his long-overdue decision to renounce the three-point shot in 2009-10. A career 26.6 percent shooter from beyond the arc, Smith stubbornly launched at least 87 three-pointers in each of the previous four seasons but attempted only seven in 2009-10. Yet Smith's eFG% fell (very) slightly last season. Why? Smith traded an obvious flaw for one without its own column in the box score--long two-point jumpers. Smith attempted 80 fewer threes, but he also attempted 65 more two-point jumpers at least 16-feet from the basket and made just 29 percent of them. Renouncing the three wasn't entirely a cosmetic change. By occupying space on the floor where he commanded defensive attention, Smith took greater advantage of his passing skills, setting a career high in assists. If he can expand his self-control to encompass all manner of jump shots, expect Smith to make a similar leap forward as a scorer.

offered him a contract extension as he enters the last year of his current deal. On one hand, it's easy to understand Crawford's desire for a multi-year contract. No one knows what next summer will bring. In this case, you can also appreciate the Hawks' position. Crawford has had an up-and-down career and his spike in shooting percentage last season will be difficult to retain. He's also a defensive liability and is at an age when you don't want to be handing out long-term contracts to mono-skilled guards. Besides, the Hawks already have one of those on the ledger in Mike Bibby. Nevertheless, this situation is touchy because in the short term, the Hawks are better off with Crawford than without him.

Last year, we wrote that if the Hawks were to make a leap, it would be due to the light coming on for Smith. It did, as he played smarter and more gregariously than ever before. Still, the second-round loss reaffirmed our belief that the gap between Atlanta and the top tier teams in its conference is too great to overcome, and now the Hawks have likely been leap-frogged by two or three other squads in their own circuit. Crawford played the best ball of his career. Smith improved his shot selection and had a career season. Horford continued his development into an All-Star caliber player and perhaps has yet to hit his ceiling. Johnson stayed steady, but has nowhere to go but down. Overall, with the lack of new blood, where is further growth going to come from?

Williams' upward arc didn't continue last season, as he devolved into an even lower-usage player and not a particularly efficient one at that. There was little to separate him from backup Maurice Evans, who had arthroscopic knee surgery after the season. Bibby's downward arc steepened; he's little more than a spot-up shooter who doesn't defend very well. Pachulia had an off year and now could play a larger role. Fellow frontcourt reserve Joe Smith fell below replacement level at the age of 35. Overall, the Hawks lacked depth. They were mediocre, even passive, on defense and once again did not do a good job of cleaning off the defensive glass. Horford (restricted) and Crawford (unrestricted) want extensions or else they'll be free agents, though Horford will almost certainly get his deal before the Oct. 31 deadline. This looks like it's going to be a crossroads kind of season in Atlanta. What could slow or prevent this fraying process is a rousing success of Drew's new approach. The opposite could hasten the slide.

The numbers still don't like this group. Either there is something systematically unique about the way Atlanta plays that causes them to be underestimated by advance metrics (doubtful) or there are a number of players due for a correction (probable). Is there something to which we can trace the root of the disconnect between Atlanta's win total and their statistical profile? Perhaps, and you'll never see us claim that numbers always tell the whole story. That said, it's tough to construct an objective argument that the Hawks will be better in the coming season.

The biggest challenge is for the roster to take to the new offensive philosophy without a loss of efficiency. The extent to which the Hawks buy into what Drew is trying to accomplish on offense will determine the initial direction of the team. The ultimate direction will depend upon how well those new schemes were conceived in the first place. Perhaps the development of jet-fast, second-year guard Jeff Teague can compensate for the rapidly aging Bibby. Perhaps a bounceback season from Williams can keep the win total steady. Perhaps the depth will improve, important because with the increased motion and a greater emphasis on conditioning, the thin Hawks need more capable hands than the past few seasons.

If the Hawks have peaked, it means that Atlanta cannot compete for a title, especially in the newly energized Eastern Conference, and Sund has made a huge error in giving a max contract to Johnson, a player whom the numbers suggest should never have received such a commitment. If that turns out to be true, it dooms this group to a prolonged period of decline and decay. The projected win total spit out by the SCHOENE machinery may be overly pessimistic, but it should be seen as a read flag for the Hawks. Atlanta may not fall off a cliff, but a step towards the precipice is a likely outcome for this season.

Bradford Doolittle

HAWKS FIVE-YEAR TRENDS

Season	AGE	W-L	POW	PYTH	SEED	ORTG	DRTG	PT DIFF	PACE
05-06	22.7	26-56	25.5 (28)	27.8	—	108.1 (12)	112.8 (26)	-4.8 (28)	89.3 (17)
06-07	24.1	30-52	27.5 (27)	27.3	—	104.3 (29)	109.8 (23)	-4.8 (29)	88.8 (24)
07-08	24.7	37-45	35.1 (20)	35.9	8	109.1 (16)	111.0 (18)	-1.8 (19)	89.3 (18)
08-09	25.8	47-35	46.8 (12)	45.6	4	111.1 (10)	109.0 (10)	1.6 (12)	88.4 (24)
09-10	27.3	53-29	53.8 (5)	54.0	3	113.5 (3)	108.3 (14)	4.7 (7)	88.8 (27)

		OFFENSE				DEFENSE			
Season	PAY	eFG	oREB	FT/FGA	TO	eFG	oREB	FT/FGA	TO
05-06	$36.6	.486 (20)	.314 (3)	.255 (14)	.174 (27)	.513 (27)	.695 (28)	.275 (26)	.166 (6)
06-07	$47.8	.471 (30)	.292 (5)	.263 (9)	.178 (26)	.503 (21)	.709 (26)	.268 (25)	.170 (8)
07-08	$58.5	.483 (21)	.297 (4)	.263 (6)	.158 (26)	.501 (15)	.717 (26)	.217 (13)	.146 (15)
08-09	$68.2	.504 (10)	.260 (19)	.238 (13)	.144 (6)	.494 (11)	.716 (24)	.210 (5)	.154 (12)
09-10	$65.1	.506 (11)	.282 (5)	.213 (23)	.133 (1)	.496 (16)	.727 (24)	.208 (8)	.154 (17)

(league rankings in parenthesis)

ATLANTA HAWKS

PG 10 — Mike Bibby

Hght: 6'2"	Exp: 12	Salary: $5.8 million
Wght: 195	From: Arizona	
2011-12 status: guaranteed contract for $6.4 million		

SKILL RATINGS

TOT	OFF	DEF	REB	PAS	HND	SHT	ATH
+1	+3	-3	0	0	+3	+1	-3

Year	Team	Age	G	MPG	Usg	3PA%	FTA%	INS	2P%	3P%	FT%	TS%	Reb%	Ast%	TO%	BLK%	STL%	PF%	oRTG	dRTG	Win%	WARP
07-08	ATL	29.9	47	33.4	.223	.325	.057	.732	.438	.373	.780	.515	.059	.085	.155	.002	.016	.028	106.9	106.4	.517	3.3
08-09	ATL	30.9	79	34.7	.208	.354	.062	.708	.468	.390	.789	.544	.059	.067	.106	.003	.019	.025	108.8	106.6	.568	8.7
09-10	ATL	31.9	80	27.4	.162	.421	.045	.624	.444	.389	.861	.538	.049	.065	.117	.001	.016	.033	107.1	107.2	.496	3.6
10-11p	ATL	32.9	76	25.0	.169	.369	.050	.680	.449	.387	.812	.534	.053	.069	.128	.002	.016	.032	106.3	106.8	.484	2.7

Most similar to: Rafer Alston (98.2), Mike James, Derek Fisher, Terry Porter   IMP: 39%   BRK: 7%   COP: 12%

As long as Mike Bibby can continue to hit his annual three-point percentage of 37-39 percent, he's going to have a role in the league. He's at the age where that role is going to continue to shrink with each passing season. This year, he'll try to stave off the challenge of Jeff Teague, who is inevitably going to take his job. You can see the shift in Bibby's game by looking at his usage rates (fallen from .223 to .162 in two years) and the percentage of his field goals that have been assisted (up from .597 to .795). He's strictly a stand-still shooter at this point, but a good one. His ability to protect the basketball was also a key part of Atlanta's league-best turnover rate last season. It will be interesting to see what kind of shape Bibby can get into, as conditioning will be a key to keeping up with the new motion offense being installed by Hawks coach Larry Drew. Bibby's defense may keep him from getting the court time to which he has grown accustomed, though his metrics weren't terrible last year, and the Hawks were actually better defensively with him on the floor. Teague was pretty raw as a rookie, so Bibby may hold on to his spot in Atlanta's first unit, for continuity's sake as much as anything. If Jamal Crawford ends up getting traded, the Hawks may be forced to overexpose their aging point guard.

C 34 — Jason Collins

Hght: 7'0"	Exp: 9	Salary: $0.9 million
Wght: 255	From: Stanford	
2011-12 status: free agent		

SKILL RATINGS

TOT	OFF	DEF	REB	PAS	HND	SHT	ATH
-5	-2	+2	-5	-4	-1	-5	-2

Year	Team	Age	G	MPG	Usg	3PA%	FTA%	INS	2P%	3P%	FT%	TS%	Reb%	Ast%	TO%	BLK%	STL%	PF%	oRTG	dRTG	Win%	WARP
07-08	NJN	29.4	74	15.8	.076	.005	.168	1.163	.473	.000	.459	.481	.088	.010	.248	.017	.009	.076	99.0	107.7	.235	-4.4
08-09	MIN	30.4	31	13.6	.101	.000	.131	1.131	.314	.000	.464	.346	.098	.012	.127	.024	.011	.078	99.3	108.0	.237	-1.6
09-10	ATL	31.4	24	4.8	.116	.035	.030	.996	.364	.000	.000	.335	.071	.016	.173	.013	.014	.084	97.3	108.3	.183	-0.6
10-11p	ATL	32.4	76	5.0	.082	.011	.135	1.124	.369	.000	.455	.392	.090	.011	.172	.022	.010	.082	98.7	107.6	.231	-1.5

Most similar to: Paul Mokeski (92.7), Greg Kite, Marc Iavaroni, Greg Foster   IMP: 44%   BRK: 15%   COP: 24%

The Hawks cited the locker-room presence of Jason Collins when they re-signed the veteran center in July. He's your basic roster filler who keeps his career alive by being a good guy and a positive influence. Is that worth the veteran's minimum for a nine-year player? Must be, because teams always keep guys like this around. His measurables once again are nil. His defense does rate as positive, underscoring his reputation as a solid one-on-one defender in the post, albeit one without the athleticism to be a factor as a shot-blocker. Collins used to draw a lot of charges, but hasn't even done that the last couple of years. Perhaps he's getting timid in his old age.

SG 11 — Jamal Crawford

Hght: 6'5"	Exp: 10	Salary: $10.1 million
Wght: 200	From: Michigan	
2011-12 status: free agent		

SKILL RATINGS

TOT	OFF	DEF	REB	PAS	HND	SHT	ATH
+1	+3	-4	-4	+3	+2	0	-2

Year	Team	Age	G	MPG	Usg	3PA%	FTA%	INS	2P%	3P%	FT%	TS%	Reb%	Ast%	TO%	BLK%	STL%	PF%	oRTG	dRTG	Win%	WARP
07-08	NYK	28.1	80	39.9	.248	.282	.096	.814	.439	.356	.864	.528	.038	.056	.110	.004	.012	.021	107.1	107.2	.498	5.4
08-09	GSW	29.1	65	38.1	.229	.298	.115	.816	.441	.360	.872	.545	.042	.050	.112	.004	.011	.016	107.5	107.9	.486	3.6
09-10	ATL	30.1	79	31.1	.260	.309	.100	.791	.491	.382	.857	.573	.048	.045	.099	.004	.013	.025	108.6	107.2	.546	6.6
10-11p	ATL	31.1	75	32.0	.235	.296	.097	.801	.464	.370	.854	.549	.045	.048	.104	.004	.011	.022	106.5	107.2	.478	3.1

Most similar to: Joe Dumars (99.1), Mitch Richmond, Allan Houston, Rex Chapman   IMP: 32%   BRK: 8%   COP: 5%

ATLANTA HAWKS

Jamal Crawford had a breakout year last season, winning the NBA's Sixth Man Award at age 30. Now, he wants to cash in, and it remains to be seen if he'll stick around Atlanta for an encore. Because Crawford has a reputation for on-court selfishness, and because his name pops up in ominous-sounding stories about trade demands, there is a perception of him that he's a bad locker-room guy. In fact, Crawford is one of the most soft-spoken, well-liked players in the NBA. He handled a significant cut in his playing time with aplomb last season and simply produced more when he was out there. With the Hawks, Crawford became even less of a playmaker and more of a gunner. He was perhaps the league's most dangerous instant offense threat off the bench and was also Atlanta's go-to player in game-winning situations. His usage rate climbed to .260, yet his True Shooting Percentage soared, as Crawford saw spikes in his success rate from sectors all over the court. How sustainable is it? That's hard to say. How does a player go from .460 in shots at the rim to .643 two years later? You have to expect his percentages to regress, but as long as he's surrounded by the same personnel and asked to play the same role, Crawford should continue to be one of the league's best bench players. He's entering a contract year and Hawks fans are holding their breath that his concerns for his future don't bleed over to the action on the court.

SG 55	Jordan Crawford	Hght: 6'4" Exp: R Salary: $1.0 million										
		Wght: 195 From: Xavier (Ohio)										
		2011-12 status: guaranteed contract for $1.1 million										

SKILL RATINGS

TOT	OFF	DEF	REB	PAS	HND	SHT	ATH
-4	-1	-2	0	0	-1	-3	-2

Year	Team	Age	G	MPG	Usg	3PA%	FTA%	INS	2P%	3P%	FT%	TS%	Reb%	Ast%	TO%	BLK%	STL%	PF%	oRTG	dRTG	Win%	WARP
10-11p	ATL	22.5	76	15.0	.224	.221	.070	.849	.412	.337	.756	.470	.067	.038	.119	.003	.015	.032	102.3	106.8	.355	-1.4

Most similar to: Ben Gordon (97.2), J.J. Redick, Sonny Weems, Casey Jacobsen   IMP: -   BRK: -   COP: -

Jordan Crawford turned a lot of heads with his string of big shots in Xavier's overtime loss to Kansas State in last spring's NCAA Tournament, which turned out to be his final college game. He looked like a microwave kind of player, capable of hitting shots from just about any range when he's hot. In the pros, he's going to have to diversify his arsenal, because there are plenty of guys that fit that description and do it better, including his new teammate and near namesake, Jamal Crawford. As a collegian, Jordan Crawford tended to dominate the ball and his shooting percentages were unimpressive, as was his foul-drawing rate. A tweener in size, he's going to have to improve his defense and ballhandling if he hopes to get the opportunity to showcase his potentially explosive scoring ability. Barring a Jamal Crawford trade, Jordan Crawford looks to be the Hawks' fifth guard this season and will struggle to find minutes. He's athletic enough to play some three, but the Hawks have depth there in Marvin Williams and Maurice Evans, plus Josh Smith may be spending more time at the position this season.

SF 1	Maurice Evans	Hght: 6'5" Exp: 7 Salary: $2.5 million
		Wght: 220 From: Texas
		2011-12 status: free agent

SKILL RATINGS

TOT	OFF	DEF	REB	PAS	HND	SHT	ATH
-1	+2	-4	-3	-3	+3	+3	-4

Year	Team	Age	G	MPG	Usg	3PA%	FTA%	INS	2P%	3P%	FT%	TS%	Reb%	Ast%	TO%	BLK%	STL%	PF%	oRTG	dRTG	Win%	WARP
07-08	ORL	29.5	75	22.9	.167	.336	.059	.722	.539	.388	.711	.571	.073	.022	.064	.004	.012	.037	107.0	107.0	.501	3.0
08-09	ATL	30.5	80	23.0	.143	.445	.058	.613	.470	.395	.822	.558	.077	.014	.077	.004	.014	.042	106.4	107.7	.455	1.5
09-10	ATL	31.5	79	16.7	.154	.384	.061	.677	.527	.337	.754	.539	.068	.017	.045	.010	.014	.044	105.8	107.3	.453	1.0
10-11p	ATL	32.5	75	5.0	.145	.403	.060	.657	.517	.368	.775	.546	.071	.016	.064	.006	.012	.044	105.2	107.4	.427	0.1

Most similar to: Wesley Person (96.6), Lucious Harris, Jud Buechler, Scott Wedman   IMP: 43%   BRK: 6%   COP: 2%

Should be status quo this season for Maurice Evans, health permitting. He had arthroscopic surgery to patch up some knee cartilage in early August. Evans is a stand-still shooter off the bench, with the added benefit of being a good finisher at the rim. Last season, his three-point percentage dropped from his career baseline and you can expect it to rebound some this year. More troublesome are Evans' defensive metrics, which were shaky. The Hawks consistently get worse defensively when Evans comes onto the floor; a guy with such a low usage rate has to defend to help his team. If he's not healthy, or shows declining defensive ability--and he's at an age when that could happen--Evans' time could be usurped by rookie Jordan Crawford.

ATLANTA HAWKS

C 15	Al Horford	Hght: 6'10" Exp: 3 Salary: $5.4 million
		Wght: 245 From: Florida
		2011-12 status: due qualifying offer of $7.1 million

SKILL RATINGS

TOT	OFF	DEF	REB	PAS	HND	SHT	ATH
+3	+2	+3	+2	+4	+4	+3	0

Year	Team	Age	G	MPG	Usg	3PA%	FTA%	INS	2P%	3P%	FT%	TS%	Reb%	Ast%	TO%	BLK%	STL%	PF%	oRTG	dRTG	Win%	WARP
07-08	ATL	21.9	81	31.3	.162	.006	.104	1.098	.503	.000	.731	.540	.180	.022	.153	.022	.011	.048	103.7	104.6	.471	2.9
08-09	ATL	22.9	67	33.5	.165	.001	.115	1.113	.526	.000	.727	.565	.163	.034	.131	.033	.012	.040	105.1	104.0	.534	5.5
09-10	ATL	23.9	81	35.1	.177	.001	.109	1.108	.551	1.000	.789	.594	.164	.031	.112	.024	.011	.037	106.5	104.5	.565	8.8
10-11p	ATL	24.9	75	35.0	.173	.006	.111	1.105	.541	.500	.771	.585	.166	.033	.125	.025	.011	.039	105.1	104.2	.532	6.4

Most similar to: Andrew Bogut (98.7), Vin Baker, Buck Williams, David Greenwood **IMP: 47% BRK: 3% COP: 2%**

The big early season storyline for the Hawks, assuming the Jamal Crawford situation is settled before camp breaks, will be whether or not Atlanta offers a contract extension to Horford, and whether or not he accepts it. Horford was excellent as a rookie and has improved markedly in each of his two subsequent seasons. He's clearly a player the Hawks have to keep around, and if he maintains, or even builds upon, his progress of the last two years, he'll be worth a near-max deal. Ordinarily, it might be worth it to let Horford hit the restricted free-agent market, especially since you're likely to give him something close to the max anyway. If the market ends up bearing less than that, perhaps you can retain him at a number that is friendlier to the cap. However, with the CBA crisis looming, we don't know what the RFA market is going to look like, or if it will even exist. Given his qualities on and off the court, the Hawks would do well to just keep Horford in the fold and let him play out this season happy and secure in his future. He's an excellent player across the board who shot a vastly improved percentage on long twos last season. That will serve him well if he indeed spends more time at power forward his season.

SG 2	Joe Johnson	Hght: 6'7" Exp: 9 Salary: $16.3 million
		Wght: 240 From: Arkansas
		2011-12 status: guaranteed contract for $18.0 million

SKILL RATINGS

TOT	OFF	DEF	REB	PAS	HND	SHT	ATH
+3	+4	-2	0	+4	+4	+1	-2

Year	Team	Age	G	MPG	Usg	3PA%	FTA%	INS	2P%	3P%	FT%	TS%	Reb%	Ast%	TO%	BLK%	STL%	PF%	oRTG	dRTG	Win%	WARP
07-08	ATL	26.8	82	40.7	.258	.235	.088	.853	.453	.381	.834	.534	.064	.065	.118	.004	.012	.023	107.6	106.9	.523	7.4
08-09	ATL	27.8	79	39.5	.267	.233	.090	.856	.468	.360	.826	.534	.065	.069	.110	.005	.014	.027	108.8	107.1	.556	9.1
09-10	ATL	28.8	76	38.0	.264	.212	.072	.860	.488	.369	.818	.538	.072	.059	.088	.001	.015	.023	108.3	106.6	.554	8.2
10-11p	ATL	29.8	75	38.0	.249	.282	.075	.794	.468	.373	.822	.536	.066	.062	.101	.002	.013	.024	107.6	106.7	.528	6.7

Most similar to: Jamal Mashburn (98.6), Steve Smith, Michael Finley, Purvis Short **IMP: 30% BRK: 5% COP: 5%**

With a little rough sketching using WARP and projected salaries, you can estimate that Johnson will be overpaid by about $2.1 million this season. When you consider that his salary goes up in each of the five years beyond this one, topping out at $24.9 million for the 2015-16 season, and his WARP totals figure to keep going down, you can see how the max contract the Hawks gave Johnson in July has albatross written all over it. Unlike other teams willing to overpay for Johnson last summer, you can't say the Hawks didn't know what they were getting themselves into. However, even though there is an extreme likelihood that Johnson's deal is a boondoggle, the outcry that has followed loses track of the fact that Johnson is a very good player. Last season was a mirror image of the season before for Johnson, and if he maintains that level of play for a few years, the Hawks will feel somewhat justified in giving him the contract. This season will be interesting for Johnson in that no player will be more affected by Larry Drew's new scheme of player movement and ball sharing. During the late summer, Johnson said that he'd like to see second-year guard Jeff Teague become more assertive when playing alongside him, so perhaps he's ready to accept the role of a traditional two-guard. Of course, if Johnson becomes less a part of the attack, then the contract looks even worse.

ATLANTA HAWKS

C 27	Zaza Pachulia	Hght: 6'11" Wght: 275 2011-12 status: guaranteed contract for $4.8 million	Exp: 7 From: Tbilisi, Georgia	Salary: $4.3 million		SKILL RATINGS						
					TOT	OFF	DEF	REB	PAS	HND	SHT	ATH
					-2	0	+3	+1	-1	-2	-1	+4

Year	Team	Age	G	MPG	Usg	3PA%	FTA%	INS	2P%	3P%	FT%	TS%	Reb%	Ast%	TO%	BLK%	STL%	PF%	oRTG	dRTG	Win%	WARP
07-08	ATL	24.2	62	15.2	.184	.008	.177	1.169	.442	.000	.706	.515	.153	.017	.181	.010	.012	.068	102.6	106.5	.374	-0.8
08-09	ATL	25.2	77	19.1	.164	.006	.198	1.192	.502	.000	.709	.571	.174	.018	.178	.014	.012	.067	105.7	106.7	.466	1.5
09-10	ATL	26.2	78	14.0	.156	.011	.171	1.161	.496	.000	.650	.539	.157	.018	.158	.021	.018	.079	104.2	105.9	.446	0.7
10-11p	ATL	27.2	76	16.3	.157	.013	.177	1.164	.489	.003	.681	.542	.158	.017	.172	.015	.014	.073	103.4	106.1	.410	-0.2

Most similar to: Vitaly Potapenko (97.6), Danny Schayes, Evan Eschmeyer, Charles Shackleford IMP: 43% BRK: 2% COP: 11%

The next logical step for Zaza Pachulia is to develop a three-point shot. His offensive skill set continues to move towards that of a face-up center, with the exception of his still-excellent offensive rebound rate. Last season, Pachulia bumped his percentage on long twos up to 51 percent, 10 percent better than league average and 20 percent better than he posted the season before. In the paint, Pachulia is a poor finisher at the rim and gets his shot blocked twice as often as the league norm. One thing we don't know about Larry Drew's system is how much emphasis it puts on offensive rebounding, so we can't say if Pachulia will be allowed to roam the perimeter. However, he is projected to play beside Al Horford more this season; since Horford is the superior post player, Pachulia's face-up game could help space the floor. The key for getting Drew's projected Pachulia/Horford/Josh Smith frontline to work will be Pachulia's ability to defend the post and protect the rim. He showed improved abilities at both last season and now rates as an above-average overall defender. His shot-block rate crawled above the league mean last season, a trend the Hawks would love to see continue.

PF 12	Josh Powell	Hght: 6'9" Wght: 240 2011-12 status: free agent	Exp: 5 From: North Carolina State	Salary: $0.9 million		SKILL RATINGS						
					TOT	OFF	DEF	REB	PAS	HND	SHT	ATH
					-5	-2	-5	0	+1	-1	-4	-4

Year	Team	Age	G	MPG	Usg	3PA%	FTA%	INS	2P%	3P%	FT%	TS%	Reb%	Ast%	TO%	BLK%	STL%	PF%	oRTG	dRTG	Win%	WARP
07-08	LAC	25.2	64	19.2	.158	.007	.092	1.084	.465	.000	.724	.500	.156	.018	.155	.014	.005	.048	102.1	106.3	.363	-1.4
08-09	LAL	26.2	60	11.7	.196	.000	.071	1.071	.444	.000	.760	.479	.141	.017	.163	.019	.006	.061	102.2	107.6	.326	-1.3
09-10	LAL	27.2	63	9.2	.186	.066	.057	.990	.360	.438	.645	.407	.111	.027	.137	.008	.008	.055	100.7	107.7	.280	-1.7
10-11p	ATL	28.2	76	10.0	.172	.047	.065	1.018	.423	.253	.701	.449	.126	.024	.152	.012	.007	.056	100.8	107.3	.296	-1.9

Most similar to: Greg Foster (97.8), Larry Krystkowiak, Eddie Lee Wilkins, Bob Thornton IMP: 57% BRK: 11% COP: 15%

It will be a homecoming for Atlanta native Josh Powell, who comes to the Hawks with the championship rings he picked up during his last two seasons with the Lakers. Powell was a bit player in L.A., but has the chance to be more than that with the Hawks as he battles a diminished Etan Thomas for minutes behind Al Horford and Zaza Pachulia. That role is more important than you'd ordinarily think it would be because of Larry Drew's plan to play Horford and Pachulia together. Unfortunately, Powell has limited game, as evidenced by his .469 shooting percentage in shots at the rim. That's why the Hawks continue to search for another capable center.

PF 5	Josh Smith	Hght: 6'9" Wght: 240 2011-12 status: guaranteed contract for $12.5 million	Exp: 6 From: Oak Hill Academy (Mouth of Wilson, VA)	Salary: $11.7 million		SKILL RATINGS						
					TOT	OFF	DEF	REB	PAS	HND	SHT	ATH
					+4	+1	+4	+1	+5	+4	-1	+5

Year	Team	Age	G	MPG	Usg	3PA%	FTA%	INS	2P%	3P%	FT%	TS%	Reb%	Ast%	TO%	BLK%	STL%	PF%	oRTG	dRTG	Win%	WARP
07-08	ATL	22.4	81	35.5	.252	.062	.130	1.068	.477	.253	.710	.520	.135	.043	.155	.059	.020	.043	104.2	101.4	.593	10.6
08-09	ATL	23.4	69	35.1	.227	.074	.135	1.061	.514	.299	.588	.533	.121	.033	.138	.035	.020	.036	104.8	103.8	.536	6.0
09-10	ATL	24.4	81	35.4	.223	.005	.134	1.129	.508	.000	.618	.536	.144	.055	.143	.046	.024	.039	106.5	102.1	.642	13.5
10-11p	ATL	25.4	75	35.0	.230	.041	.136	1.095	.504	.149	.631	.525	.136	.050	.141	.045	.021	.039	104.8	102.2	.588	9.4

Most similar to: Gerald Wallace (95.4), Kevin Garnett, Chris Webber, Shawn Kemp IMP: 37% BRK: 0% COP: 2%

ATLANTA HAWKS

People can change. Josh Smith enjoyed the best of his six NBA seasons last year. Part of the progress stemmed from his widely reported improved shot selection. Smith's three-point attempts dropped from 87 in 2008-09 to seven in 2009-10, and he didn't make any of them. His percentage of shots at the rim jumped from 43 percent to 54 percent. Overall, Smith's True Shooting Percentage held steady because his accuracy on two-point shots dropped a bit, particularly on the long twos that were still a bit too much a part of his game. The shot selection was only part of his heightened efficiency. Smith's assist rate climbed to career-best levels and he became more of a force on the boards. His trademark help defense was as dynamic as ever, and his on-ball metrics were improved, too. Despite all of this, the Hawks reportedly considered putting Smith on the trade market over the summer. As far as we know, that didn't happen--good thing, too, because he's one of the league's top players, with a contract that makes him a solid value. As we note throughout the Hawks chapter, Smith is slated to play the three more this season, allowing Horford to slide over to four. Smith has played sporadically at five through his career and Drew may find that is an increasingly attractive option. He defends interior players better than perimeter players, has an average back-to-the-basket game and put up one of the league's best finishing rates on the few pick-and-rolls that called for him to be the screener. Horford is a better face-up shooter than Smith, so the configuration makes sense, especially when the Hawks are playing teams without an elite pivot.

SF	Pape Sy	Hght: 6'7"	Exp: R	Salary: $0.5 million	SKILL RATINGS							
7		Wght: 225	From: France		TOT	OFF	DEF	REB	PAS	HND	SHT	ATH
		2011-12 status: due qualifying offer of $1.0 million			--	--	--	--	--	--	--	--

French guard Pape Sy was taken at No. 53 in this year's draft by Atlanta. He's headed to training camp with the team after the Hawks agreed to a buyout deal with Sy's team in France. He was a bit of an unknown quantity at the time he was taken, and he showed little in a couple of brief appearances in summer league. Sy is a project at best at this point, and his NBA audition may be best saved for a couple of years down the line.

PG	Jeff Teague	Hght: 6'2"	Exp: 1	Salary: $1.5 million	SKILL RATINGS							
0		Wght: 180	From: Wake Forest		TOT	OFF	DEF	REB	PAS	HND	SHT	ATH
		2011-12 status: team option for $1.6 million			0	0	-1	0	+2	+2	-4	+4

Year	Team	Age	G	MPG	Usg	3PA%	FTA%	INS	2P%	3P%	FT%	TS%	Reb%	Ast%	TO%	BLK%	STL%	PF%	oRTG	dRTG	Win%	WARP
09-10	ATL	21.9	71	10.1	.192	.107	.072	.965	.426	.219	.837	.459	.055	.078	.167	.012	.025	.053	102.7	105.9	.393	-0.4
10-11p	ATL	22.9	76	15.0	.193	.152	.076	.924	.441	.225	.869	.473	.056	.085	.157	.016	.024	.050	103.7	105.2	.451	0.8

Most similar to: Kenny Anderson (97.9), Terrell Brandon, Rob Williams, Rodney Stuckey   IMP: 76%   BRK: 24%   COP: 8%

When looking for potential breakout players, it's always a good idea to start with those entering their second NBA seasons. This may be a campaign when talent meets opportunity for Jeff Teague. With Teague and Mike Bibby headed in opposite directions along the aging spectrum, their paths may intersect a lot sooner than many people realize. New coach Larry Drew suggests the chance is there for Teague to move into the Hawks' starting lineup, but he must clearly beat out Bibby with his play on the court. In a vacuum, Teague has already passed Bibby, but he has to prove to be a better complement to a starting unit that has been together in Atlanta for a long time now. Teague needs to find an offensive identity. He doesn't have the jump shot to be a starting two-guard yet, but isn't a prolific playmaker, either. Despite his lack of accuracy from the perimeter, Teague settled for those shots far too often. The raw ability is there and the point guard job in Atlanta is there for Teague to take. If can do so, he'd be a big upgrade for Atlanta's soft perimeter defense. In the short term, he would do well to seize command of the Hawks' second unit, Jamal Crawford's presence notwithstanding.

ATLANTA HAWKS

C 36	Etan Thomas	Hght: 6'10" Wght: 260 2011-12 status: free agent	Exp: 8 From: Syracuse	Salary: $0.9 million							
					SKILL RATINGS						
					TOT	OFF	DEF	REB	PAS	HND	SHT	ATH
					-4	--	0	--	--	--	--	--

Year	Team	Age	G	MPG	Usg	3PA%	FTA%	INS	2P%	3P%	FT%	TS%	Reb%	Ast%	TO%	BLK%	STL%	PF%	oRTG	dRTG	Win%	WARP
08-09	WAS	31.1	26	11.8	.141	.000	.108	1.108	.485	.000	.696	.525	.128	.009	.191	.048	.005	.052	101.7	105.9	.364	-0.3
09-10	OKC	32.1	23	14.0	.135	.000	.101	1.101	.456	--	.591	.483	.113	.001	.188	.037	.006	.055	99.1	105.7	.288	-0.9
10-11p	ATL	33.1	76	--	.132	.001	.092	1.091	.463	.000	.651	.494	.111	.004	.185	.036	.005	.054	--	--	.331	--

Most similar to: Brian Skinner (96.8), Francisco Elson, Sean Rooks, Andrew Lang — IMP: 35% BRK: 9% COP: 26%

Before Serge Ibaka solidified his spot in the Thunder's rotation, Etan Thomas got some early minutes as the team's backup center. Predictably, Thomas struggled in that role, and he totaled just 61 minutes from December onward. The NBA's poet laureate, Thomas has not been the same player since missing the 2007-08 season because of open-heart surgery. A variety of injuries have severely hampered his mobility, leaving Thomas to rely solely on throwing his weight around in the paint. Thomas went to Atlanta, where old centers go to finish their careers as third-stringers. The Hawks would be mistaken to count on Thomas for any kind of rotation role.

SF 24	Marvin Williams	Hght: 6'9" Wght: 240 2011-12 status: guaranteed contract for $8.1 million	Exp: 5 From: North Carolina	Salary: $7.3 million							
					SKILL RATINGS						
					TOT	OFF	DEF	REB	PAS	HND	SHT	ATH
					+1	+1	-2	+1	-2	-1	0	+1

Year	Team	Age	G	MPG	Usg	3PA%	FTA%	INS	2P%	3P%	FT%	TS%	Reb%	Ast%	TO%	BLK%	STL%	PF%	oRTG	dRTG	Win%	WARP
07-08	ATL	21.8	80	34.6	.203	.008	.147	1.139	.466	.100	.822	.540	.096	.023	.104	.009	.013	.037	103.2	106.2	.403	-0.8
08-09	ATL	22.8	61	34.3	.183	.191	.148	.957	.493	.355	.806	.569	.107	.018	.086	.014	.014	.029	106.5	105.9	.520	4.5
09-10	ATL	23.8	81	30.5	.156	.159	.114	.955	.492	.303	.819	.540	.099	.017	.087	.014	.014	.030	103.8	105.7	.439	1.1
10-11p	ATL	24.8	75	30.0	.177	.214	.133	.919	.499	.315	.840	.559	.097	.020	.091	.014	.014	.030	104.8	105.6	.472	2.7

Most similar to: Kenny Walker (98.6), Danny Granger, Derrick McKey, Horace Grant — IMP: 59% BRK: 12% COP: 2%

It was a banner season for most of Atlanta's frontline players in 2009-10, but that did not include Marvin Williams, who was reportedly on the trading block over the summer. Five years into his career, Williams continues to hover right around average in terms of across-the-board skills. After displaying an improved three-point shot in 2008-09, he regressed to well below average, and it remains to be seen where his baseline will fall. With the outside shots going down less frequently, Williams became even more passive on the offensive end, though he did put the ball on the floor more often when he decided to become a part of the attack. He's an excellent finisher at the rim and could be a premier foul-drawer with his build and athleticism. Williams remains very much a finisher rather than a play-creator, not really what you want from a small forward who doesn't provide premium defense. This is an important season for Williams. If his lack of production last season was a result of him being the odd man out in Atlanta's frequent isolation plays, then perhaps he will make strides in the high-motion, share-the-ball scheme being installed by new coach Larry Drew. The Hawks may feel stuck with Williams at this point because if they really did shop him over the summer, they likely found limited demand for a player who barely produces more than replacement level and still has four years and $32 million left on his contract.

PF 50	Othello Hunter	Hght: 6'8" Wght: 225 2011-12 status: free agent	Exp: 2 From: Ohio State	Salary: --							
					SKILL RATINGS						
					TOT	OFF	DEF	REB	PAS	HND	SHT	ATH
					--	--	--	--	--	--	--	--

Year	Team	Age	G	MPG	Usg	3PA%	FTA%	INS	2P%	3P%	FT%	TS%	Reb%	Ast%	TO%	BLK%	STL%	PF%	oRTG	dRTG	Win%	WARP
08-09	ATL	22.9	16	5.8	.124	.000	.091	1.091	.550	.000	.000	.495	.153	.005	.083	.042	.011	.056	102.6	105.0	.423	0.0
09-10	ATL	23.9	7	4.7	.235	.000	.105	1.105	.333	--	.750	.400	.212	.000	.179	.023	.000	.070	101.1	107.2	.305	-0.1

The NBA jig is up for Othello Hunter, a long-armed, undersized power forward with limited offensive skills. After getting into just seven NBA games last season, he parlayed a solid summer-league showing into a contract to play in Italy with Dinamo Sassari.

ATLANTA HAWKS

C	Randolph Morris	Hght: 6'11"	Exp: 4	Salary: --	SKILL RATINGS							
33		Wght: 275	From: Kentucky		TOT	OFF	DEF	REB	PAS	HND	SHT	ATH
		2011-12 status: free agent			--	--	--	--	--	--	--	--

Year	Team	Age	G	MPG	Usg	3PA%	FTA%	INS	2P%	3P%	FT%	TS%	Reb%	Ast%	TO%	BLK%	STL%	PF%	oRTG	dRTG	Win%	WARP
07-08	NYK	22.3	18	10.1	.199	.000	.160	1.160	.362	.000	.483	.396	.118	.005	.113	.009	.010	.094	98.4	108.0	.212	-0.8
08-09	ATL	23.3	23	3.9	.136	.000	.068	1.068	.412	.000	1.000	.480	.132	.011	.272	.009	.012	.132	98.4	109.4	.186	-0.4
09-10	ATL	24.3	28	4.4	.242	.000	.183	1.183	.561	-	.593	.586	.179	.007	.185	.018	.021	.127	103.7	106.3	.415	0.0

Randolph Morris' per-minute numbers actually shot up last season, but that means little when you only get 124 minutes over the course of a year. Last season, Morris showed glimpses of a developing touch beyond the immediate vicinity of the rim. He's a space eater in the lane and a solid rebounder. He'll ply those trades overseas this year, as he signed on to play in China.

SG	Sergiy Gladyr	Hght: 6'5"	Exp: --	Salary: --	SKILL RATINGS							
--		Wght: 190	From: Ukraine		TOT	OFF	DEF	REB	PAS	HND	SHT	ATH
		2011-12 status: free agent			--	--	--	--	--	--	--	--

The Hawks took a flyer on the teenaged Sergiy Gladyr in the second round of the 2009 Draft. A good, raw athlete, Gladyr moved up in overseas competition from the Ukrainian League last season, playing in Liga ACB, the top circuit in Spain. He averaged 9.4 points in 20 minutes per game in the ACB, a solid showing for his age. Gladyr also played for the Hawks' 2010 summer-league team, but struggled with some pretty sad shooting performances. With his length and athleticism, he could help the Hawks if he becomes more consistent as a catch-and-shoot player, but there is a lot of progress to be made and no guarantee he will ever become NBA-ready.

Boston Celtics

One half of one quarter. That's how close the Celtics came to winning their second championship in three years and the 18th title in franchise history, which would have given Boston a little bit of a historical buffer over the Minneapolis/Los Angeles Lakers.

During the waning days of last spring, the Celtics led the Lakers through three quarters in Game 7. They still maintained a 64-61 lead when L.A.'s perennially pesky Derek Fisher drained a three-pointer with 6:12 left to play, tying the game. Then Rajon Rondo missed a shot for Boston. Kobe Bryant rebounded, was fouled, and put the Lakers up with two free throws. Ray Allen missed, Bryant rebounded and nailed a fadeaway jumper. After a Doc Rivers timeout, during which Paul Pierce somehow got the idea to take over the Celtic offense, Pierce missed a jumper. Bryant rebounded again, the Lakers worked the clock down and the ball in to Pau Gasol, who was fouled by Kevin Garnett. Two free throws later, the Lakers were up by six. The Celtics recovered enough to keep the heat on the Lakers all the way into the final seconds of the game, but they never caught up and never again had the ball with a chance for a lead or a tie. Pierce went 1-of-4 during that crucial stretch and committed a turnover before the Celtics went back to running the attack through Rondo during the last minute.

It was a bad half-quarter that came on the heels of nearly nine months of up-and-down basketball, but it was a stretch that defined the season for both the Celtics and Lakers, and one that defines how we view the immediate futures of the league's marquee franchises. The Lakers have now closed to within 17-16 on the championship count in the race for bragging rights in the NBA history book. The Lakers appear to be a team poised to remain in title contention for the foreseeable future. The Celtics spent the summer desperately keeping their creaky roster mostly intact while adding a couple of pieces in a desperate attempt to stave off the apparent rise of several prime challengers to their Eastern Conference throne. These Celtics aren't dead yet, and as we saw during their spirited run to the Finals last spring, you can never count this group out. But the end of this Boston mini-dynasty is coming fast. It may be here already.

Last year's storyline ultimately ran pretty much as expected. We thought that if the roster was healthy, the talent was there for another championship run. When playing his full hand, Rivers certainly had a title-caliber team on his hands. The journey to the Finals had some unusual tangents, such as a 23-5 sprint to the start of the season, then an extended malaise: Boston went 27-27 over its final 54 games, blew a gaggle of fourth-quarter leads and had fallen so far in the good graces of NBA pundits that several analysts picked the Miami Heat to knock the Celtics out in the first round of the postseason.

Rivers did a masterful job of getting his roster ready

CELTICS IN A BOX

Last year's record	50-32
Last year's Offensive Rating	109.8 (13)
Last year's Defensive Rating	105.3 (5)
Last year's point differential	3.7 (9)
Team pace	90.1 (23)
SCHOENE projection	42-40 (5)
Projected Offensive Rating	109.2 (21)
Projected Defensive Rating	108.7 (10)
Projected team weighted age	30.9 (2)
Projected '10-11 payroll	$76.9 (6)
Est. payroll obligations, '11-12	$70.1 (4)

Head coach: Doc Rivers

He's been a Coach of the Year and an NBA champion before, but Doc Rivers might have put together his best campaign on the sidelines in 2009-10. Rivers got the most of his unique group of veterans by willingly taking some lumps during the second half of the regular season. When the playoffs rolled around, Boston was rested and ready. Rivers reportedly contemplated retirement before deciding to return. With several aging veterans and chemistry risks added to the roster, Rivers' task will get no easier. He also must deal with a significant change to his coaching staff. Long-time New Jersey coach Lawrence Frank replaces defensive specialist Tom Thibodeau as Rivers' lead assistant.

for the playoffs. He eased off the reins of his horses halfway through the season and was rewarded with success when it mattered most. Rivers appeared to learn from the fade of Allen and, to a lesser extent, Pierce in the 2009 playoffs, and was careful with his handling of Garnett, who wasn't available for the postseason the season before. At some point, Rivers weighed his team's chances of landing the top seed in the East and decided it wasn't likely to happen and not wise to try. Instead, he allowed his veteran core to regenerate and the worries over his team to mount. It's a risky strategy, but Rivers knows his team and you can't argue with the results.

One would expect more of the same in 2010-11. With little choice, Celtics honcho Danny Ainge kept his window for contention open for another season by retaining most of the aging core on hand, while adding a pair of veteran big men named O'Neal: Shaquille and Jermaine. The acquisitions were necessary. Kendrick Perkins, Boston's starting center for the better part of the last five seasons, tore the ACL in his right knee during Game Six of the Finals. His absence in Game Seven may have been enough to put the Lakers over the top in a contest with razor-thin margins. Perkins isn't likely to be back until the second half of the season, and even then it's unclear how much of a load he's going to be able to carry. Also, mercurial big man Rasheed Wallace decided to retire after a topsy-turvy season in Boston as the team's top frontcourt reserve. He was waived in early August after coming to a buyout agreement with Ainge for the last two seasons of his contract.

Ainge also retained Allen, whose spot-up shooting would have been a big hit on the open market, and Pierce, who opted out of the last year of his deal to sign an extension for three guaranteed years plus a player option that would take him close to his 37th birthday. Reserve free agents Nate Robinson and Marquis Daniels were also retained. Tony Allen and Shelden Williams were lost on the free-agent market. Williams wasn't much of a factor during his one season in Boston, but Tony Allen's athleticism and perimeter defense will be missed. Free-agent guard Von Wafer was added after spending a year overseas, but he's not the same kind of a player as Allen. The absence of the defensive specialist leaves a void, especially as Ray Allen invariably manifests the all-too-familiar symptoms of advancing age.

Late in August, Ainge rounded out his 15-man roster by signing talented but troubled guard Delonte West. This is a good situation for West, who was a popular and productive player during his first stint playing under Rivers in Boston before Ainge included him in the mega-package sent to Seattle for Allen. West's deal is non-guaranteed, but even this doesn't ensure max effort and focus from a player whose particular brand of crazy can have tangible effects on his availability. He'll miss the first 10 games of the coming season as part of the fallout from the weapons charges he was slapped with a year ago. The upside of the signing was considerable, however, as West can provide everything Boston got from Tony Allen and perhaps a little more, particularly if Rivers needs a stand-in for Ray Allen for any length of time. West can also serve as the primary backup for Rondo at point guard.

What are the keys for the Celtics in their effort to stave off the challenge of rising Eastern Conference contenders all around them? They must get better production from their offseason acquisitions than they did last year's additions. The O'Neals, West and maybe even Wafer could end up serving as four-fifths of Boston's postseason second unit. The newbies will also go a long way towards determining what seed the Celtics eventually secure, a reality stemming from Perkins' injury and Rivers' customary lack of faith in rookies. Boston will likely carry three first-year players on its roster--Avery Bradley, Luke Harangody and Semih Erden--and if recent history is any guide, you won't see any of them performing much more than mop-up duty. The holdovers from last season's bench--Nate Robinson, Marquis Daniels and Big Baby Davis--will be looked upon to provide greater and more consistent production in the coming year. Truly, the Celtics are going to need a solid effort from at least 12 players to position themselves for another postseason run, because it's not likely last season's rise from a No. 4 seed can be replicated. The competition in the East has just gotten too fierce, but it's still incumbent upon Rivers to balance wins and rest.

What effect will the departure of former assistant Tom Thibodeau have on the team's defense? Boston must prove that system can excel without the team's defensive architect, now the head coach in Chicago, and it will have to do so while working in a number of new players. Perhaps the most important part of that is to recognize when O'Neal works on that end of the court, and when he doesn't, which is all too often at this stage of his Hall-of-Fame career.

In a way, this reminds you of the fading Celtics dynasties in the '60s and '80s. This group can't really be considered a dynasty because there was only one title,

BOSTON CELTICS

> ### From the Blogosphere
>
> **Who:** Zach Lowe
> **What:** CelticsHub
> **Where:** http://www.celticshub.com/
>
> The Celtics were one of the worst offensive teams ever advance to the Finals. It's a tribute to their defense that they came within a few minutes of winning the title, but if they are going to challenge the Heat and Lakers, the C's will must score more efficiently. There is evidence to suggest they might. New Celtics Jermaine O'Neal and Von Wafer rarely turn the ball over--Boston's biggest offensive weakness. Shaquille O'Neal is old and declining, but he still grab an occasional offensive board--something only Glen Davis did regularly last season. Delonte West is a decent three-point shooter capable of creating his own shot. Improvement from roster holdovers will also be necessary. Rajon Rondo's shooting remains a liability, and Paul Pierce's midrange game took a step back in 2010. Davis must hit from midrange and be a force inside; he's never done both in the same season. Kendrick Perkins must stop committing so many turnovers.

injury of winning it all. Perhaps nothing changed. Boston's early season charge and its strong road record (26-15) may have been the key indicators of the team's real strength, indicators that most of us missed once the postseason rolled around and all we could see was the 27-27 finish. There probably isn't a good objective way to evaluate a team that lets up on the accelerator, then punches it once the playoffs begin. It's happened before. The Shaq/Kobe Lakers won a title that way. The second Rockets title team in the '90s was similar. However, it's not really a sustainable practice.

Ainge didn't stand pat, but did he do enough in light of what's happened in Miami and Chicago? He certainly seems to have done the best he could once it was decided to retain the team's veteran core. Unless Ainge was ready to start a rebuild, he really didn't have an alternative. That he was able to add what he did with the funds Boston had available is a testament to how attractive this Boston group is to players around the league. Still, can this team maintain, or even grow? Rivers can make some small changes as well, such as trusting Rondo to become the decision-maker with the game on the line in place of Pierce, even in the playoffs.

This season, it sure looks like age and heightened competition will catch up with the Celtics in too many places. The slippage will be readily apparent on the defensive end in particular. The offseason could have gone very differently for Boston. In a few months, Celtics fans may wish it had.

but this was still a dynastic core. The problem was that the Allen/Pierce/Garnett core didn't play together until well into their respective careers. We're seeing the final phase of a group that never got to grow up together.

There was a lot of analysis over what changed in the postseason to catapult Boston to within a Perkins

Bradford Doolittle

CELTICS FIVE-YEAR TRENDS

Season	AGE	W-L	POW	PYTH	SEED	ORTG	DRTG	PT DIFF	PACE
05-06	25.3	33-49	33.6 (25)	36.6	---	106.8 (19)	108.4 (18)	-1.5 (19)	90.9 (8)
06-07	23.5	24-58	26.8 (29)	31.1	---	104.3 (28)	108.9 (18)	-3.4 (24)	90.7 (13)
07-08	27.9	66-16	65.2 (1)	67.1	1	113.1 (9)	100.8 (1)	10.3 (1)	88.9 (19)
08-09	27.8	62-20	61.8 (2)	61.3	2	112.6 (5)	103.5 (2)	7.5 (3)	89.0 (18)
09-10	30.2	50-32	49.7 (12)	51.5	4	109.8 (13)	105.3 (5)	3.7 (9)	90.1 (23)

		OFFENSE				DEFENSE			
Season	PAY	eFG	oREB	FT/FGA	TO	eFG	oREB	FT/FGA	TO
05-06	$52.6	.504 (4)	.255 (23)	.263 (8)	.181 (29)	.490 (16)	.728 (14)	.282 (27)	.161 (13)
06-07	$53.6	.479 (28)	.270 (18)	.259 (10)	.180 (28)	.502 (20)	.738 (12)	.280 (28)	.167 (14)
07-08	$73.8	.523 (5)	.266 (17)	.267 (3)	.161 (29)	.457 (1)	.744 (8)	.253 (23)	.172 (1)
08-09	$78.7	.528 (2)	.279 (9)	.251 (7)	.173 (28)	.470 (3)	.756 (3)	.253 (23)	.162 (9)
09-10	$84.1	.522 (5)	.228 (28)	.248 (6)	.164 (26)	.487 (9)	.738 (13)	.251 (25)	.173 (2)

(league rankings in parenthesis)

BOSTON CELTICS

SG 20	**Ray Allen**	Hght: 6'5" Wght: 205 2011-12 status: guaranteed contract for $10.0 million	Exp: 14 From: Connecticut	Salary: $10.0 million	

SKILL RATINGS

TOT	OFF	DEF	REB	PAS	HND	SHT	ATH
+1	+3	+4	-2	0	+1	+4	-3

Year	Team	Age	G	MPG	Usg	3PA%	FTA%	INS	2P%	3P%	FT%	TS%	Reb%	Ast%	TO%	BLK%	STL%	PF%	oRTG	dRTG	Win%	WARP
07-08	BOS	32.8	73	35.9	.218	.371	.086	.715	.484	.398	.907	.583	.060	.040	.104	.005	.011	.026	108.3	105.9	.578	8.8
08-09	BOS	33.8	79	36.4	.209	.379	.085	.707	.542	.409	.952	.624	.057	.036	.104	.004	.012	.026	109.4	106.9	.579	9.7
09-10	BOS	34.8	80	35.2	.204	.329	.092	.763	.556	.363	.913	.601	.054	.035	.106	.007	.012	.031	107.1	106.9	.506	5.2
10-11p	BOS	35.8	76	34.0	.182	.381	.084	.703	.535	.379	.912	.596	.057	.035	.107	.007	.011	.028	106.5	107.0	.485	3.7

Most similar to: Reggie Miller (97.7), Mitch Richmond, Joe Dumars, Eddie Jones   IMP: 45%   BRK: 6%   COP: 15%

The Celtics, understandably, are still trying to win with the core group that they've had in place the last couple of years. That makes the two-year, $20 million deal Ray Allen signed with Boston this summer a no-brainer. He's 35 years old as the season opens, and the years are going to catch up with him sooner rather than later. That process may have gotten a jumpstart last year, when Allen's Offensive Rating dropped because of a decline in three-point percentage and an increase in turnover rate. His athletic markers also continued to dwindle. Boston can hope the three-point accuracy will bounce back, but everything else should be expected to keep heading in the wrong direction. Allen's defensive numbers remain solid, as they've been since he arrived in Boston, but we have to see if he can continue to thrive without the protection of Tom Thibodeau's scheme. All age-related concerns aside, there is no one the Celtics would rather have at shooting guard. At $10 million per season, he may be overpaid, but not so much so that Boston will have any regrets about bringing him back for another championship run.

PG 0	**Avery Bradley**	Hght: 6'2" Wght: 180 2011-12 status: guaranteed contract for $1.5 million	Exp: R From: Texas	Salary: $1.4 million	

SKILL RATINGS

TOT	OFF	DEF	REB	PAS	HND	SHT	ATH
-4	--	--	--	--	--	--	--

Year	Team	Age	G	MPG	Usg	3PA%	FTA%	INS	2P%	3P%	FT%	TS%	Reb%	Ast%	TO%	BLK%	STL%	PF%	oRTG	dRTG	Win%	WARP
10-11p	BOS	20.4	76	-	.148	.194	.048	.854	.380	.329	.536	.418	.044	.028	.114	.008	.015	.048	-	-	.316	-

Most similar to: Dajuan Wagner (95.1), Keyon Dooling, Russell Westbrook   IMP: -   BRK: -   COP: -

Celtics coach Doc Rivers has been reluctant to play rookies, especially since Boston rose to contending status a couple of years ago. That pattern may change after Texas' Avery Bradley was taken with the 19th pick in the draft. In a preseason survey, Bradley was voted by his fellow rookies as the best defender in this year's class. If he lives up to that billing, Bradley will earn minutes in a crowded backcourt rotation that includes Ray Allen, Rajon Rondo, Von Wafer, Delonte West and Nate Robinson. We didn't get the usual summer sneak peek of his skills, as Bradley sat out the Orlando Summer League after having his ankle scoped. He's expected to be ready for the start of the season. Early on, Bradley projects to derive almost all of his value from the defensive end of the floor, with a very low usage rate, especially for a guard. That could change if he flashes some yet-to-be-seen point guard skills. If so, there are minutes to be had behind Rondo. It might be more realistic in the short term for him to just demonstrate an ability to hit the three-point shot.

SF 8	**Marquis Daniels**	Hght: 6'6" Wght: 200 2011-12 status: free agent	Exp: 7 From: Auburn	Salary: $2.4 million	

SKILL RATINGS

TOT	OFF	DEF	REB	PAS	HND	SHT	ATH
-4	-1	+1	-3	+3	+1	-1	-1

Year	Team	Age	G	MPG	Usg	3PA%	FTA%	INS	2P%	3P%	FT%	TS%	Reb%	Ast%	TO%	BLK%	STL%	PF%	oRTG	dRTG	Win%	WARP
07-08	IND	27.3	74	20.9	.207	.139	.083	.944	.467	.265	.698	.488	.075	.039	.153	.009	.022	.034	102.3	105.1	.405	-0.4
08-09	IND	28.3	54	31.5	.216	.107	.068	.960	.489	.200	.721	.491	.081	.029	.112	.011	.018	.031	103.2	106.4	.395	-0.8
09-10	BOS	29.3	51	18.4	.159	.089	.078	.989	.534	.214	.607	.526	.061	.033	.133	.005	.015	.046	102.1	107.3	.332	-1.7
10-11p	BOS	30.3	70	15.0	.171	.122	.071	.949	.496	.238	.667	.500	.070	.035	.133	.008	.017	.039	101.8	106.4	.352	-1.4

Most similar to: Willie Anderson (98.2), Mike Sanders, Blue Edwards, Malik Sealy   IMP: 53%   BRK: 12%   COP: 5%

BOSTON CELTICS

It was a bit of a surprise that the Celtics' push to keep their core intact included bringing back Marquis Daniels for another season as the primary backup to Paul Pierce. Once again, Daniels finished below replacement level. Once again, he struggled with injuries and was not part of the Celtics' playoff rotation, logging just 37 minutes in 11 appearances. Doc Rivers says that, when healthy, Daniels is a "$5 or $6 million player." Except, he's not. A below-replacement player is worth the league minimum, no more. So in that respect, the Celtics overpaid to bring him back at $2.4 million. If Daniels can fill a role, which is to play solid defense and chip in with 6-8 efficient points per game, then he's fine. His defense grades out as decent, but this may still be an area where the Celtics need to upgrade, especially if the injuries quicken the erosion of Daniels' athleticism.

PF 11	Glen Davis	Hght: 6'9" Wght: 289 2011-12 status: free agent	Exp: 3 From: Louisiana State	Salary: $3.0 million			**SKILL RATINGS**							
							TOT	OFF	DEF	REB	PAS	HND	SHT	ATH
							-2	0	-3	0	-1	-2	-2	+1

Year	Team	Age	G	MPG	Usg	3PA%	FTA%	INS	2P%	3P%	FT%	TS%	Reb%	Ast%	TO%	BLK%	STL%	PF%	oRTG	dRTG	Win%	WARP
07-08	BOS	22.3	69	13.6	.175	.000	.188	1.188	.484	.000	.660	.545	.131	.014	.185	.017	.015	.079	103.5	106.4	.404	-0.2
08-09	BOS	23.3	76	21.5	.172	.008	.131	1.122	.443	.400	.730	.502	.111	.020	.118	.009	.017	.066	103.3	107.2	.373	-1.5
09-10	BOS	24.3	54	17.3	.199	.010	.155	1.144	.444	.000	.696	.500	.135	.018	.135	.012	.012	.067	104.1	107.4	.393	-0.5
10-11p	BOS	25.3	71	22.0	.177	.014	.153	1.139	.468	.121	.710	.524	.127	.019	.135	.013	.013	.066	103.7	106.9	.394	-0.7

Most similar to: J.R. Reid (97.6), Zaza Pachulia, Vitaly Potapenko, Kevin Duckworth — IMP: 60% BRK: 17% COP: 3%

If it surprises you that Big Baby Davis projects as below replacement level, you've likely been swayed by his playoff performances, and for good reason. Davis has played prominent roles in each of the last two postseasons for the Celtics. In 2009, his increased time was a product of necessity, as Kevin Garnett's knee injury left the Celtics shorthanded. Last year, Davis played his way into the rotation--once again not just playing more, but better. Part of this phenomenon may stem from his eschewing the perimeter shot in the playoffs, but he did that in the regular season as well in 2009-10. In 2008-09, nearly 44 percent of Davis' shots were long twos; that fell to less than 20 percent last season. That helped make Davis more accurate, if not exactly efficient. His True Shooting Percentage still lags well below league average because of his inability to finish around the basket, where he gets shot blocked at three times the league rate. It's becoming a chicken-or-egg thing for Davis. He gets too many shots blocked in the paint, but his face-up shot is too erratic to be an attractive option on the perimeter. Perhaps he should focus his energies on his fine rebounding skills, setting screens with his wide body, keeping the ball moving and limiting his offense to open putbacks. With an expiring contract, he's not likely going to be happy in a reduced role, especially because he's said that he still considers himself to be a future All-Star. Davis will probably be too expensive to retain after this year once you consider what he offers for what he's likely to command on the open market. However, he's very popular in Boston, and it will be tough for the team to cut ties with him.

C 86	Semih Erden	Hght: 6'11" Wght: 240 2011-12 status: guaranteed contract for $0.8 million	Exp: R From: Turkey	Salary: $0.5 million			**SKILL RATINGS**							
							TOT	OFF	DEF	REB	PAS	HND	SHT	ATH
							-2	--	--	--	--	--	--	--

Year	Team	Age	G	MPG	Usg	3PA%	FTA%	INS	2P%	3P%	FT%	TS%	Reb%	Ast%	TO%	BLK%	STL%	PF%	oRTG	dRTG	Win%	WARP
10-11p	BOS	24.7	76	-	.148	.010	.168	1.158	.465	.004	.598	.505	.140	.021	.206	.035	.008	.064	-	-	.411	-

Most similar to: Curtis Borchardt (97.3), Hilton Armstrong, Jim Petersen, Jason Collins — IMP: 62% BRK: 16% COP: 8%

The Celtics project as one of the biggest teams in the league. Their collection of giants now includes Turkish center Semih Erden, who was taken with the last pick of the 2008 draft. Erden is an impressive physical specimen, with a long wingspan, chiseled arms and good leaping ability. He's relatively unskilled, which you can tell from the wildly different projections SCHOENE gives Erden and fellow Turkish big man Omer Asik. Erden should be a solid rebounder and shot blocker right off the bat, but will battle Shaquille O'Neal, Jermaine O'Neal, Kevin Garnett, Glen Davis and fellow rookie Luke Harangody for minutes in the big-man rotation,

BOSTON CELTICS

and that's not even considering the eventual return of Kendrick Perkins. It should be a developmental season for Erden, but if injury problems set in for the gaggle of old guys in the Celtics' frontcourt, he may provide more than that.

SF	**Tony Gaffney**	Hght: 6'8"	Exp: R	Salary: $0.8 million	SKILL RATINGS						
		Wght: 205	From: Massachusetts		TOT	OFF	DEF	REB	PAS	HND	SHT	ATH
27		2011-12 status: non-guaranteed contract for $1.1 million		--	--	--	--	--	--	--	--

Tony Gaffney was one of several young players to latch on with teams towards the end of the 2009-10 season, signing a make-good deal with the Celtics. He played for Boston's summer-league team, but wasn't impressive. He's a defense-first type, but lacks an offensive calling card. He'll go to camp with the Celtics, but there doesn't appear to be any room for Gaffney in their crowded frontcourt.

PF	**Kevin Garnett**	Hght: 6'11"	Exp: 15	Salary: $18.8 million	SKILL RATINGS						
		Wght: 253	From: Farragut Academy HS (IL)		TOT	OFF	DEF	REB	PAS	HND	SHT	ATH
5		2011-12 status: guaranteed contract for $21.2 million		+3	+1	+5	+2	+5	+5	+2	+4

Year	Team	Age	G	MPG	Usg	3PA%	FTA%	INS	2P%	3P%	FT%	TS%	Reb%	Ast%	TO%	BLK%	STL%	PF%	oRTG	dRTG	Win%	WARP
07-08	BOS	31.9	71	32.8	.257	.009	.116	1.107	.545	.000	.801	.588	.162	.049	.107	.032	.020	.032	108.4	101.3	.721	14.7
08-09	BOS	32.9	57	31.1	.235	.009	.065	1.056	.534	.250	.841	.563	.162	.038	.101	.031	.018	.034	105.8	102.7	.603	6.9
09-10	BOS	33.9	69	29.9	.223	.005	.100	1.095	.523	.200	.837	.569	.148	.042	.104	.022	.017	.039	105.4	103.6	.561	6.2
10-11p	BOS	34.9	73	30.0	.211	.007	.086	1.078	.524	.173	.833	.562	.147	.042	.106	.025	.017	.037	104.5	103.4	.539	5.6

Most similar to: Bob Lanier (96.4), Vlade Divac, Robert Parish, Moses Malone — IMP: 19% BRK: 0% COP: 4%

It's apparent now that Kevin Garnett will never return to his pre-injury form, which means he is not going to be the elite player he was during his first season in Boston. He's still pretty darn good. Garnett recovered enough of his mobility last season to move his foul-drawing rate back towards his career baseline. However, he's still becoming ever-more perimeter-oriented, with nearly 43 percent of his shots coming as long twos. Luckily, he shoots very well from there. His usage rate has also fallen, and 82 percent of his field goals were assisted last year, a 14 percent increase over his first year in Boston. Garnett just can't be counted upon to create as much offense for himself. That will at least allow him to save some energy for the other end, where he is still the kingpin of the Celtics' defense and one of the best in the game. His steal and block rates continued to fall last season, as did his rebound rate, all evidence of his waning athleticism. However, his on-ball metrics are still excellent. If we see a significant change in that area this season, it may be because Garnett won't have Kendrick Perkins to help cover for mistakes made because of his aggressiveness.

PF	**Luke Harangody**	Hght: 6'7"	Exp: R	Salary: $0.5 million	SKILL RATINGS						
		Wght: 251	From: Notre Dame		TOT	OFF	DEF	REB	PAS	HND	SHT	ATH
55		2011-12 status: due qualifying offer of $1.0 million		-4	-1	-2	+1	0	0	-4	-3

Year	Team	Age	G	MPG	Usg	3PA%	FTA%	INS	2P%	3P%	FT%	TS%	Reb%	Ast%	TO%	BLK%	STL%	PF%	oRTG	dRTG	Win%	WARP
10-11p	BOS	23.3	76	5.3	.241	.100	.089	.989	.418	.262	.769	.460	.134	.022	.086	.010	.005	.049	101.7	106.8	.335	-0.7

Most similar to: Brian Cook (96.8), Leon Powe, Ronald Dupree, Hakim Warrick — IMP: - BRK: - COP: -

As an undersized power forward with limited athleticism, Luke Harangody sets about trying to translate his impressive college productivity to the NBA level. He's strong and a solid rebounder, though he may not play inside enough to be much of a factor on the offensive glass. He played well in summer league, displaying eye-opening range and accuracy with this three-point shot. That continues a gradual evolution from a paint player to a face-up player, one Harangody had to make to have a chance in the NBA. He's known as a hard worker, and whatever ceiling he has a professional player, you can be pretty sure he'll reach it.

BOSTON CELTICS

C 7 — Jermaine O'Neal

Hght: 6'11"	Exp: 14	Salary: $5.8 million	
Wght: 255	From: Eau Claire HS (SC)		
2011-12 status: guaranteed contract for $6.2 million			

SKILL RATINGS

TOT	OFF	DEF	REB	PAS	HND	SHT	ATH
-2	-1	+1	-2	+3	+1	-1	-2

Year	Team	Age	G	MPG	Usg	3PA%	FTA%	INS	2P%	3P%	FT%	TS%	Reb%	Ast%	TO%	BLK%	STL%	PF%	oRTG	dRTG	Win%	WARP
07-08	IND	29.5	42	28.7	.248	.007	.104	1.097	.444	.000	.742	.489	.129	.033	.154	.054	.007	.046	102.0	103.7	.443	0.7
08-09	MIA	30.5	68	29.8	.233	.001	.097	1.096	.475	.000	.788	.522	.126	.028	.142	.055	.007	.049	103.5	104.8	.457	1.7
09-10	MIA	31.5	70	28.4	.231	.002	.102	1.100	.530	.000	.720	.563	.143	.022	.129	.039	.007	.051	104.7	104.6	.503	3.6
10-11p	BOS	32.5	73	28.0	.215	.005	.093	1.088	.492	.000	.738	.526	.126	.027	.138	.043	.007	.051	102.1	104.8	.412	-0.2

Most similar to: Rony Seikaly (97.3), Sam Bowie, John Hot Rod Williams, Zydrunas Ilgauskas

IMP: 38% BRK: 4% COP: 11%

Jermaine O'Neal's decade-long run as a starter in the NBA is going to come to an end this season. We just don't know when. It seems likely that Jermaine will start over Shaquille O'Neal at center to begin the season because he's the better defensive player. At some point, Kendrick Perkins will return from his knee injury and when he does, Jermaine O'Neal will become a full-time reserve for the first time since he ended his post-prep apprenticeship in Portland. Knee problems have sapped much of his once-impressive athleticism, but O'Neal has settled onto a nice plateau as a supporting player. Last season, he shot the ball well from every distance inside the three-point line, including a .697 mark in shots at the rim. He can't get his own shot like he used to, but he's more efficient. O'Neal remains an above-average defender, though his blocked-shot rate is declining. He plays solid post defense and annually ranks among the league leaders in charges drawn.

C 36 — Shaquille O'Neal

Hght: 7'1"	Exp: 18	Salary: $0.9 million	
Wght: 325	From: Louisiana State		
2011-12 status: free agent			

SKILL RATINGS

TOT	OFF	DEF	REB	PAS	HND	SHT	ATH
-1	-1	-1	+1	+2	-2	+4	+2

Year	Team	Age	G	MPG	Usg	3PA%	FTA%	INS	2P%	3P%	FT%	TS%	Reb%	Ast%	TO%	BLK%	STL%	PF%	oRTG	dRTG	Win%	WARP
07-08	PHX	36.1	61	28.7	.228	.000	.168	1.168	.593	.000	.503	.589	.174	.024	.204	.033	.008	.056	104.3	104.4	.500	3.0
08-09	PHX	37.1	75	30.0	.243	.001	.185	1.184	.610	.000	.595	.623	.162	.025	.136	.035	.011	.050	108.5	105.1	.610	9.1
09-10	CLE	38.1	53	23.4	.253	.001	.149	1.147	.567	.000	.496	.565	.167	.030	.157	.039	.006	.064	105.2	104.8	.515	2.5
10-11p	BOS	39.1	71	18.0	.216	.002	.153	1.152	.565	.000	.498	.565	.155	.024	.178	.035	.010	.069	103.1	105.0	.435	0.5

Most similar to: Artis Gilmore (88.9), Hakeem Olajuwon, Patrick Ewing, Robert Parish

IMP: 14% BRK: 0% COP: 14%

Shaquille O'Neal isn't done with us yet. Last year, he went to Cleveland to try to get LeBron James over the championship hump. That failed, so he jumps to Boston, one of the teams standing in the way of James getting a ring now that he's in Miami. Shaq has fallen behind teammate/nemesis Kobe Bryant in rings, so you can be sure he's going to be motivated for the season in which he turns 39 years old. Sometimes, it's almost painful to watch O'Neal, as he looks so old and slow. Then you look at his numbers and see a player that still he has some positive attributes. He's at the age, or well past it, when you don't know when he's going to run out of bullets altogether, or if he can stay healthy. O'Neal is also well past the point when he raises the level of his teammates. In a vacuum, however, he put up 20.5 points and 11.5 boards per 40 minutes while posting an above-average True Shooting Percentage. That in itself is amazing for a player of his age and experience who has both taken and dished out so much abuse over the last two decades. Last year, he played in just 53 games and the Celtics will need more than that from him as they await the return of injured Kendrick Perkins. O'Neal is still a good finisher at the rim, though his percentage dropped seven percent last year and he got more shots blocked. He remains a solid defensive rebounder. On offense, he's better suited to finishing off the pick-and-roll, despite his lack of mobility, than he is playing in straight post-ups. He's still above average there, but gets worse with each season and he becomes more and more of a black hole when the ball goes in to him. As everyone knows by now, O'Neal is a defensive liability. That is most true on pick-and-roll defense, where he ranked in just the 14th percentile of the league last season. His post defense was also below average, though he now has the luxury of playing alongside either Jermaine O'Neal or Kevin Garnett for the majority of his minutes.

BOSTON CELTICS

C 43 — Kendrick Perkins

Hght: 6'10"	Exp: 7	Salary: $4.6 million
Wght: 280	From: Clifton J. Ozen HS (TX)	
2011-12 status: free agent		

SKILL RATINGS

TOT	OFF	DEF	REB	PAS	HND	SHT	ATH
0	-1	+4	+1	+1	-3	+5	-2

Year	Team	Age	G	MPG	Usg	3PA%	FTA%	INS	2P%	3P%	FT%	TS%	Reb%	Ast%	TO%	BLK%	STL%	PF%	oRTG	dRTG	Win%	WARP
07-08	BOS	23.4	78	24.5	.136	.002	.145	1.143	.615	.000	.623	.631	.145	.021	.225	.048	.007	.059	103.1	103.8	.477	2.4
08-09	BOS	24.4	76	29.6	.149	.003	.099	1.096	.580	.000	.600	.591	.165	.020	.231	.053	.005	.053	103.5	104.1	.479	2.9
09-10	BOS	25.4	78	27.6	.178	.004	.152	1.148	.605	.000	.582	.613	.167	.018	.204	.048	.006	.048	103.4	103.5	.494	3.5
10-11p	BOS	26.4	26	20.0	.160	.003	.137	1.134	.593	.001	.599	.607	.155	.021	.212	.048	.006	.050	102.8	104.1	.455	0.4

Most similar to: Samuel Dalembert (95.7), Darryl Dawkins, Jahidi White, Alton Lister

IMP: 44%   BRK: 4%   COP: 4%

We'll never know for sure whether the Celtics would have won another title had Kendrick Perkins not been injured in Game 6 of last year's Finals, but it makes for a nice bit of what-if debating. Perkins hopes to be back from his torn ACL by January; the team is expecting more like February, and covered themselves for the regular season by bringing in Shaquille O'Neal, Jermaine O'Neal and Semih Erden. Perkins is just entering his prime years and enjoyed his best season yet in 2009-10. He became more of a factor on the offensive end, with an improved foul-drawing rate and an outstanding .747 percentage on shots at the rim. He's polished his post game to the point where the Celtics can dump the ball in to him if the matchups favor doing so. He's one of the best post defenders and basket protectors in the league, a vital part of a Celtics defense that may lag in his absence. With his contract expiring after the season, it will be important for Perkins to show he's whole before the season and playoffs run their course.

SF 34 — Paul Pierce

Hght: 6'7"	Exp: 12	Salary: $13.9 million
Wght: 235	From: Kansas	
2011-12 status: guaranteed contract for $14.8 million		

SKILL RATINGS

TOT	OFF	DEF	REB	PAS	HND	SHT	ATH
+3	+4	+4	-2	+4	+1	+4	+2

Year	Team	Age	G	MPG	Usg	3PA%	FTA%	INS	2P%	3P%	FT%	TS%	Reb%	Ast%	TO%	BLK%	STL%	PF%	oRTG	dRTG	Win%	WARP
07-08	BOS	30.5	80	35.9	.250	.238	.139	.901	.499	.392	.843	.599	.082	.059	.144	.010	.016	.032	108.7	104.3	.639	13.3
08-09	BOS	31.5	81	37.5	.255	.184	.147	.963	.480	.391	.830	.582	.089	.045	.138	.007	.014	.033	107.4	105.9	.549	8.4
09-10	BOS	32.5	71	34.0	.240	.215	.156	.941	.497	.414	.852	.613	.077	.043	.136	.010	.018	.038	107.7	105.6	.568	7.6
10-11p	BOS	33.5	74	34.0	.218	.299	.142	.843	.493	.410	.838	.612	.077	.045	.141	.008	.015	.037	107.4	106.0	.545	6.8

Most similar to: Chris Mullin (97.4), Toni Kukoc, Detlef Schrempf, Clyde Drexler

IMP: 22%   BRK: 0%   COP: 12%

The lingering images from Paul Pierce's 2009-10 season were of him trying to take over the Celtics' offense down the stretch of Game Seven and being unable to answer the call. It was a disappointing end to another excellent year from the Celtics' longest-tenured player. After the campaign, he opted out of the last year of his contract and signed a new one that will keep him in Celtic green for at least three more seasons and probably four, with a player option tacked onto the end of the deal. He's earned the right to be overpaid, but Pierce is aging so well, his contract may turn out to be a solid value. He's become a little more perimeter oriented now that he's into his 30s, and a lot of Pierce's offensive value is derived from two areas: foul-drawing and three-point shooting. Pierce's midrange game suffered last season, as he shot below the league average in the sectors between the rim and the three-point line. He made up for that with a .414 success rate on treys and a .640 percentage at the rim, all while posting a higher foul-drawing rate than in recent seasons. Add it all up and you have an outstanding .613 True Shooting Percentage, a showing that SCHOENE expects him to repeat in 2010-11. Pierce doesn't rebound as much as he once did, but he's still an excellent defender, especially a team defender, and is a fine passer for his position. Pierce remains the Celtics' on-court leader and will continue to be for the foreseeable future.

BOSTON CELTICS

PG 4	Nate Robinson	Hght: 5'9"	Exp: 5	Salary: $4.2 million	SKILL RATINGS								
		Wght: 180	From: Washington		TOT	OFF	DEF	REB	PAS	HND	SHT	ATH
		2011-12 status: guaranteed contract for $4.5 million			+4	+5	0	+3	0	0	+2	0

Year	Team	Age	G	MPG	Usg	3PA%	FTA%	INS	2P%	3P%	FT%	TS%	Reb%	Ast%	TO%	BLK%	STL%	PF%	oRTG	dRTG	Win%	WARP
07-08	NYK	23.9	72	26.1	.233	.301	.089	.788	.478	.332	.786	.526	.069	.051	.106	.000	.015	.046	107.2	107.2	.502	3.3
08-09	NYK	24.9	74	29.9	.257	.297	.100	.804	.504	.325	.841	.549	.073	.060	.107	.002	.021	.041	110.2	107.2	.596	8.3
09-10	BOS	25.9	56	19.9	.246	.374	.050	.675	.474	.390	.746	.543	.058	.067	.123	.003	.022	.048	108.9	106.8	.568	3.5
10-11p	BOS	26.9	76	15.0	.233	.347	.072	.726	.495	.362	.787	.547	.067	.063	.111	.003	.019	.045	108.2	106.6	.553	3.3

Most similar to: Chris Whitney (95.3), Mahmoud Abdul-Rauf, Mike Bibby, Jameer Nelson — IMP: 44% BRK: 0% COP: 2%

After not showing much during his first few weeks as a Celtic, Nate Robinson turned it on during the latter stages of the playoffs and earned a new two-year contract in the process. Robinson's streak-shooting and chest-thumping actually fit in well with a veteran Boston team that can look a little methodical at times. Robinson had a rough last few months in New York, but seems to be reborn in Celtic green. Robinson displayed a greater willingness to share the ball in 2009-10, and an improved ability to play a catch-and-shoot role. His True Shooting Percentage was more or less flat from the season before, but only because his percentage at the rim (.500) cratered. If he gets that back to previous levels, he'll have the full shot arsenal working. Robinson's defense was impressive during the playoffs. For him to earn the consistent minutes he needs to keep his fine shooting stroke humming, he's going to have to maintain his effort on that end.

PG 9	Rajon Rondo	Hght: 6'1"	Exp: 4	Salary: $9.1 million	SKILL RATINGS								
		Wght: 171	From: Kentucky		TOT	OFF	DEF	REB	PAS	HND	SHT	ATH
		2011-12 status: guaranteed contract for $10.0 million			+5	+5	+4	+4	+4	+4	+3	+4

Year	Team	Age	G	MPG	Usg	3PA%	FTA%	INS	2P%	3P%	FT%	TS%	Reb%	Ast%	TO%	BLK%	STL%	PF%	oRTG	dRTG	Win%	WARP
07-08	BOS	22.2	77	30.0	.190	.020	.082	1.062	.499	.263	.611	.515	.081	.080	.157	.005	.026	.037	104.8	104.1	.525	5.2
08-09	BOS	23.2	80	33.0	.193	.044	.109	1.064	.518	.313	.642	.543	.094	.117	.192	.003	.029	.034	108.7	104.6	.630	11.7
09-10	BOS	24.2	81	36.6	.203	.063	.097	1.035	.536	.213	.621	.540	.074	.127	.193	.003	.033	.032	108.7	104.4	.637	13.6
10-11p	BOS	25.2	76	37.0	.193	.065	.092	1.027	.541	.278	.649	.553	.076	.119	.178	.003	.028	.031	108.2	104.6	.616	11.7

Most similar to: Brevin Knight (95.8), Johnny Moore, Maurice Cheeks, John Stockton — IMP: 61% BRK: 0% COP: 0%

Last season was the year in which the Celtics became Rajon Rondo's team. Paul Pierce is the scoring leader and franchise flag-bearer, Kevin Garnett the spiritual leader and Ray Allen the steadying influence, but Rondo is the team's best player. He's made progress in all four of his NBA seasons and, at 25, is just now entering his peak seasons. His five-year, $55 million extension kicks in this year and looks like it's going to be one of the best values of any deal in the league. Rondo took on an even greater portion of the Boston offense last season, increasing both his usage and assist rates. He became a deadly scorer from 15 feet and in, though he still struggles beyond that distance. Perhaps the long-range shooting doesn't matter so much, because the Celtics are at their best when Rondo has the ball in his hands, creating for himself and his veteran teammates. He is perhaps the game's best rebounding guard and becomes a greater disruptive force on defense with each passing season. Perhaps most impressive is the fact that Rondo very nearly cracked double digits in assists per game despite playing on a slow-paced team. When the Celtics do excel in transition, it's almost entirely due to Rondo's ability to push the ball down the floor with jet-like speed.

SG 12	Von Wafer	Hght: 6'5"	Exp: 4	Salary: $0.9 million	SKILL RATINGS								
		Wght: 209	From: Florida State		TOT	OFF	DEF	REB	PAS	HND	SHT	ATH
		2011-12 status: free agent			-1	+1	0	-3	-2	-1	+2	-1

Year	Team	Age	G	MPG	Usg	3PA%	FTA%	INS	2P%	3P%	FT%	TS%	Reb%	Ast%	TO%	BLK%	STL%	PF%	oRTG	dRTG	Win%	WARP
07-08	POR	22.8	29	5.4	.242	.328	.067	.739	.371	.154	.667	.347	.071	.021	.164	.015	.006	.021	95.8	106.0	.194	-0.7
08-09	HOU	23.8	63	19.4	.238	.263	.083	.819	.474	.390	.752	.541	.052	.027	.095	.005	.017	.027	105.7	106.9	.460	1.1
10-11p	BOS	25.8	69	5.0	.224	.259	.081	.822	.481	.390	.756	.550	.052	.028	.092	.005	.016	.026	104.5	106.5	.433	0.1

Most similar to: Morris Peterson (98.4), Terry Teagle, Butch Carter, Anthony Peeler — IMP: 42% BRK: 8% COP: 8%

BOSTON CELTICS

It's a happy time for Von Wafer, who went overseas for more money last season, then returned home from Greece before the campaign in Europe ended. He was close to signing with either Houston or Memphis, but failed a physical because of a bulging disc. He landed in Dallas on a 10-day contract in February, but never saw the court. Wafer was a revelation in 2008-09, his last NBA season, when he averaged nearly 20 points per 40 minutes. He's another good outside shooter for the Celtics to deploy, but also has the one-on-one skills to get his own shot. For him to work in Boston, Wafer is going to have to share the ball more willingly than he did in his previous NBA stints. He also has to show that he can hold his own on defense, or Doc Rivers will forget he's on the bench.

Delonte West — SG #13

Hght: 6'4" | Wght: 180 | Exp: 6 | From: Saint Joseph's | Salary: $1.1 million
2011-12 status: free agent

SKILL RATINGS

TOT	OFF	DEF	REB	PAS	HND	SHT	ATH
+2	+2	+5	-1	+4	+3	+2	0

Year	Team	Age	G	MPG	Usg	3PA%	FTA%	INS	2P%	3P%	FT%	TS%	Reb%	Ast%	TO%	BLK%	STL%	PF%	oRTG	dRTG	Win%	WARP
07-08	CLE	24.7	61	25.1	.189	.214	.063	.850	.437	.356	.736	.493	.074	.069	.185	.015	.018	.032	103.9	105.0	.464	1.5
08-09	CLE	25.7	64	33.6	.169	.299	.062	.764	.490	.399	.833	.559	.055	.050	.120	.005	.023	.028	106.4	105.8	.521	4.7
09-10	CLE	26.7	60	25.0	.184	.131	.106	.975	.471	.325	.810	.530	.065	.061	.153	.014	.019	.027	104.5	105.4	.472	1.7
10-11p	BOS	27.7	62	20.0	.175	.276	.080	.803	.474	.384	.792	.547	.063	.060	.149	.014	.018	.029	105.2	105.4	.492	2.0

Most similar to: Bimbo Coles (98.7), Winston Garland, Frank Johnson, Alvin Williams

IMP: 49% BRK: 4% COP: 10%

Delonte West has danced beyond the line between eccentric and something more ominous during the last calendar year, but his decision to return the Celtics could save his career. West will miss the first 10 games of the coming season as part of the fallout from his weapons charges last year. He is returning to the city where he was first drafted into the NBA and will be playing for a coach in Doc Rivers with whom he feels comfortable. If Rivers can keep West focused on basketball, he's a great fit in Boston. His long-range shooting, which slipped last season, fits anywhere, but he also can handle playmaking duties for stretches, important because Boston lacks backcourt depth. West is a good defensive player, if not quite the +5 our skill rating system assigns, and serves as a hedge against an injury or severe decline from the aging Ray Allen. West has a lot to prove and Boston is the perfect place for him to get back on the right track.

Mario West — SG #47

Hght: 6'5" | Wght: 210 | Exp: 3 | From: Georgia Tech | Salary: --
2011-12 status: free agent

SKILL RATINGS

TOT	OFF	DEF	REB	PAS	HND	SHT	ATH
-1	0	0	+5	-1	0	0	+4

Year	Team	Age	G	MPG	Usg	3PA%	FTA%	INS	2P%	3P%	FT%	TS%	Reb%	Ast%	TO%	BLK%	STL%	PF%	oRTG	dRTG	Win%	WARP
07-08	ATL	23.8	64	4.5	.111	.058	.165	1.107	.467	.000	.654	.488	.098	.021	.130	.010	.019	.098	102.9	107.8	.344	-0.4
08-09	ATL	24.8	53	5.1	.105	.017	.219	1.203	.394	1.000	.467	.456	.122	.033	.216	.011	.035	.061	102.7	105.0	.425	0.0
09-10	ATL	25.8	39	3.6	.106	.031	.136	1.105	.600	.000	.600	.591	.111	.029	.216	.000	.029	.081	102.4	106.4	.371	-0.1
10-11p	AVG	26.8	76	3.6	.108	.060	.181	1.120	.424	.767	.554	.520	.108	.031	.181	.014	.027	.076	103.1	105.7	.416	0.0

Most similar to: Pete Myers (94.1), Randy Brown, Johnny High, Chris McNealy

IMP: 68% BRK: 18% COP: 0%

The minutes have been so sporadic for Mario West during his three NBA seasons that it's tough to get a solid read from his numbers. He profiles as a good athlete and possibly a plus defender. There just isn't much court time to be had for a wing player who not only can't shoot accurately from the outside, but is so rarely willing to try. During his garbage-time minutes last season, he was 12-of-17 at the rim, and 0-of-4 everywhere else. He caught on with the Celtics for training camp, but unless namesake Delonte West proves an issue, there does not appear to be an opening on the Boston roster.

BOSTON CELTICS

Michael Finley — SF

Hght: 6'7" Exp: 15 Salary: --
Wght: 225 From: Wisconsin
2011-12 status: free agent

SKILL RATINGS

TOT	OFF	DEF	REB	PAS	HND	SHT	ATH
-4	-1	-4	-5	-1	+3	+1	-5

Year	Team	Age	G	MPG	Usg	3PA%	FTA%	INS	2P%	3P%	FT%	TS%	Reb%	Ast%	TO%	BLK%	STL%	PF%	oRTG	dRTG	Win%	WARP
07-08	SAS	35.1	82	27.0	.186	.419	.041	.622	.453	.370	.800	.519	.067	.025	.066	.003	.006	.020	104.7	106.5	.440	1.1
08-09	SAS	36.1	81	28.8	.162	.410	.035	.625	.459	.411	.823	.547	.068	.024	.078	.005	.008	.017	105.3	106.9	.446	1.4
09-10	BOS	37.1	46	15.4	.139	.388	.031	.644	.480	.390	.533	.530	.059	.028	.099	.006	.007	.022	103.5	107.1	.381	-0.5
10-11p	AVG	38.1	70	15.4	.136	.349	.029	.680	.451	.392	.637	.513	.059	.022	.094	.006	.007	.023	102.6	107.2	.351	-1.5

Most similar to: Dale Ellis (96.9), Bruce Bowen, Johnny Newman, Eddie A. Johnson

IMP: 21% BRK: 4% COP: 29%

Michael Finley was still waiting for a call from an NBA team at press time, not surprising for a guy who will be 38 before the 2010-11 season ends. His athleticism has diminished to the point where he's strictly a spot-up shooter, and his defense is nowhere close to the level it was a few years ago. If he does get one more shot, it will be because he continues to shoot a high percentage from behind the three-point arc. If he doesn't and 15 years is it, it's been an outstanding career for the two-time All-Star.

Oliver Lafayette — PG

Hght: 6'2" Exp: 1 Salary: $0.8 million
Wght: 190 From: Houston
2011-12 status: non-guaranteed contract for $1.1 million

SKILL RATINGS

TOT	OFF	DEF	REB	PAS	HND	SHT	ATH
-1	--	0	--	--	--	--	--

Year	Team	Age	G	MPG	Usg	3PA%	FTA%	INS	2P%	3P%	FT%	TS%	Reb%	Ast%	TO%	BLK%	STL%	PF%	oRTG	dRTG	Win%	WARP
09-10	BOS	26.0	1	22.0	.150	.286	.000	.714	.500	.500	-	.583	.110	.043	.143	.000	.000	.000	106.0	107.0	.465	0.0
10-11p	BOS	27.0	76	-	.184	.384	.080	.695	.414	.346	.744	.503	.068	.060	.155	.002	.024	.046	-	-	.421	-

Most similar to: Winston Garland (97.3), Derek Fisher, Sedale Threatt, Greg Anthony

IMP: 56% BRK: 10% COP: 8%

Signed at the same time as Tony Gaffney during the waning days of the 2009-10 regular season, Oliver Lafayette got in one game for the Celtics. He hung around the roster until just before training camp, when Boston waived him. He was a distant long shot to make the team, but the timing was bad for Lafayette because it was too late for him to join another team's camp.

Rasheed Wallace — C

Hght: 6'10" Exp: 15 Salary: $6.3 million
Wght: 225 From: North Carolina
2011-12 status: guaranteed contract for $6.8 million

SKILL RATINGS

TOT	OFF	DEF	REB	PAS	HND	SHT	ATH
0	--	+2	--	--	--	--	--

Year	Team	Age	G	MPG	Usg	3PA%	FTA%	INS	2P%	3P%	FT%	TS%	Reb%	Ast%	TO%	BLK%	STL%	PF%	oRTG	dRTG	Win%	WARP
07-08	DET	33.6	77	30.5	.206	.309	.065	.756	.477	.356	.767	.524	.130	.028	.084	.043	.019	.044	105.1	101.9	.607	9.3
08-09	DET	34.6	66	32.2	.186	.387	.054	.667	.471	.354	.772	.520	.138	.021	.072	.031	.016	.045	105.4	103.8	.554	6.1
09-10	BOS	35.6	79	22.5	.204	.378	.072	.694	.511	.283	.768	.504	.110	.021	.082	.031	.023	.059	104.0	103.7	.509	3.4
10-11p	AVG	36.6	75	-	.179	.399	.055	.657	.474	.307	.757	.492	.114	.024	.096	.035	.019	.054	-	-	.442	-

Most similar to: Robert Horry (94.9), Sam Perkins, Clifford Robinson, Ron Harper

IMP: 12% BRK: 0% COP: 18%

Say it ain't so, 'Sheed! Rasheed Wallace has hung up the headband after 15 years of giving NBA officials the business. He'll always be known for his tempestuous behavior, but he was an awfully good player, too. He played in four All-Star games and won a ring with the 2004 Detroit Pistons. It's a debate for another day, but you know what? There are worse players in the Hall of Fame. The league will be poorer for Wallace's absence.

Charlotte Bobcats

If crusty-but-clever hoops scribe Sam Smith were to pen a 21st century opus on Michael Jordan, his most famous subject, he might recycle *Jordan Rules* as a title, because the game's greatest player is now the unchallenged king of his basketball fiefdom in Carolina. Whether or not that's good news for fans of the Bobcats remains to be seen.

Jordan became the majority owner of the Charlotte Bobcats on March 17, 2010 after nearly four years of serving as the team's head of basketball operations under former owner Bob Johnson. Jordan is following in the footsteps of hockey's Mario Lemieux, who parlayed a Hall of Fame NHL career, some huge contracts and hometown-hero worship into an ownership gig with the Pittsburgh Penguins. Lemieux has only enhanced his reputation in Pittsburgh as the team's owner, having purchased the team out of bankruptcy in 1999, leveraging a faux relocation flirtation with Kansas City into a yet-to-open new arena and overseeing a Stanley Cup champion in 2009. The Bobcats weren't bankrupt when Jordan took control the team, but the franchise's fortunes were flagging. He didn't make his NBA fortune in Charlotte, but Jordan is undoubtedly a Carolina legend and is considered a hometown guy. Nevertheless, he will be lucky to do as well as his hockey counterpart.

Jordan quickly set about repairing some of the damaged relationships between the team and the business community in Charlotte, which never quite saw eye-to-eye with Johnson. To this day, it's hard to discern whether or not the Bobcats' nickname was selected due the vanity of its original owner--the story may be apocryphal--but when Jordan took over, there was almost immediately an outcry that he give the franchise a new brand. (Charlotte Flight seems to be a popular choice.) Jordan told reporters that if there seems to be enough support in the city to make the change, he'll go through the lengthy process with the league to make it happen. That process would take a couple of years and, according to Jordan, $8 to $10 million. Whether or not the name switch happens, it had to be refreshing for Charlotte basketball fans to hear some conciliatory words coming from the steward of their NBA franchise.

According the *Charlotte Observer*'s David Scott, season-ticket renewals for the coming season stand at 91 percent, and the team has sold nearly 1,600 new tickets for the campaign. Charlotte team president Fred Whitfield says those figures place the Bobcats in the top 10 of the league, after previously never cracking the top 20. To be sure, the team's success on the court last season has fueled part of the excitement around the team. However, it's not like the Bobcats were knocking on the door of a championship. The team won 44 games in a weak conference and was swept out of the first round in a mismatch with the Orlando Magic. There are no impact young players on the roster. During the offseason, Charlotte lost starting point guard Ray Felton, replaced him

BOBCATS IN A BOX

Last year's record	44-38
Last year's Offensive Rating	105.7 (24)
Last year's Defensive Rating	104.4 (1)
Last year's point differential	1.5 (15)
Team pace	89.1 (26)
SCHOENE projection	32-50 (12)
Projected Offensive Rating	104.3 (29)
Projected Defensive Rating	108.2 (7)
Projected team weighted age	28.3 (11)
Projected '10-11 payroll	$66.7 (15)
Est. payroll obligations, '11-12	$60.4 (11)

Head coach: Larry Brown

It took two years, but Larry Brown managed to pilot Charlotte into the playoffs for the first time in franchise history in 2009-10. In typical Brown fashion, the Bobcats did it with defense. Charlotte narrowly edged out Orlando for the league's best Defensive Rating and excelled at keeping teams off the free throw line and forcing turnovers. Despite his trademark wandering eye, Brown is back for his third season at the helm. He will have to deal with significant personnel losses at point guard (Raymond Felton) and center (Tyson Chandler). If Brown can cobble together another playoff squad, he'll deserve Coach of the Year consideration.

with no one and did nothing to address the team's gaping hole at center. Wins always help, but a great deal of the growing goodwill towards the Bobcats in their hometown can be attributed to the monumental charisma of one Michael Jeffrey Jordan. Whatever the reason, it's about time Bobcats fans turned out. Since coming into the league, Charlotte has filled their home venues to just 75.9 percent capacity, the lowest figure in the league.

Going into last season, we expected the Bobcats to be better and, quite possibly, be headed for their first postseason appearance. That's what happened. We thought the Bobcats would struggle for points for stretches at a time, but would again be strong defensively under the insistent guidance of head coach Larry Brown. We thought these things and were more or less correct, but the route Charlotte took to its best finish ever wasn't quite the one we thought they'd take. It was believed that Tyson Chandler would more than fill the shoes of former center Emeka Okafor. He didn't. Chandler looked like a player whose healthy days were in the past and provided less value in the pivot than journeyman backup Nazr Mohammed. In addition, the Bobcats weren't hungry for points early in the season--they were starved. Charlotte scored 59 points in its opener at Boston and scored 81 points or fewer in seven of their first nine games.

At that point, Jordan took advantage of Stephen Jackson's inevitable wanderlust out in the Bay Area, dealing Raja Bell and Vladimir Radmanovic to Golden State for the mercurial wing man and throw-in Acie Law. Jackson is entering the decline phase of his career and is far from efficient on the offensive end of the floor, but he gave Brown's attack a focal point and teamed with super-athletic forward Gerald Wallace to give the Bobcats a wing tandem that could guard anybody. In the big picture, Charlotte may come to rue the day it brought Jackson into the fold, given his controversial past, ball-dominating ways and the $19.3 million left on his contract over the two years after this season. In the short term, however, the benefit was obvious: Jackson was the fuel that got the Bobcats into the playoffs.

Bringing in Jackson allowed Brown to improve his offense without hurting his defense. Quite the opposite, in fact. The Bobcats improved from 22nd to seventh in Defensive Rating in their first season under Brown. Last season, they jumped all the way up to the top spot in the league. The players currently on the Charlotte roster have really bought into the Larry Brown style of defense. They put a high degree of pressure on the opposition without fouling, ranking third in forced turnover percentage and tops in the NBA in lowest rate of fouls committed. The other key indicators were also solid--12th in limiting effective field-goal percentage and 10th in defensive rebound rate. Charlotte was also fifth in the league in blocked-shot rate, even though Chandler didn't help out in that area nearly as much as hoped.

The stingy defense mitigated a dreadful offense that ranked 24th in Offensive Rating, leaving one to wonder just where the Bobcats would have finished without Jackson's .277 usage rate and 105.0 Offensive Rating. The team's only real positive offensive trait was its collective ability to hurl itself into defenders and draw fouls. Wallace and Jackson both finished in the league's top 50 in foul-drawing and the team ranked third. No team turned the ball over more than the Bobcats. The disparity in offensive and defensive efficiency was apropos for a Larry Brown team. Of the 30 coaches who will be leading NBA teams at the beginning of this season, only Jim O'Brien, Kurt Rambis and Scott Skiles have posted a lower composite Offensive Rating than Brown's 106.0. On the flip side, only Skiles and Gregg Popovich have better career Defensive Ratings than Brown's 104.5. With 29 years of coaching professional basketball under his belt, it's safe to say Brown will emphasize a defense-first philosophy once again this season.

The Bobcats appear to be a team entering into the tenuous holding pattern between boom and bust. As mentioned, Jackson has two more years left on his deal and would do well to maintain his performance from last season. Wallace has two more years at $10.5 million per annum, plus an additional season under a player option for the same amount. He's younger than Jackson and far more likely to retain his value through the length of his deal. There is always the risk of an injury-related decline in athleticism with Wallace, because he's a player that derives a more-than-usual portion of his value from superior physical abilities. His is not a bad contract and Wallace is a solid core player, but on a championship team, Wallace would be no better than the third-best player. Right now, the Bobcats don't have any candidates to assume those first two slots.

Part of that is because of apparent misses in the last two drafts. D.J. Augustin, the ninth pick of the 2008 Draft, took a big step back last season and faces a pivotal campaign in his career. Augustin has withered under Brown's trademark stern handling of point guards and struggled with his shot in 2009-10. The best hope for adding an alternative option to Augustin at the point disappeared when Jordan couldn't find a taker for Erick Dampier's non-guaranteed contract and the center was released in mid-September.

That the Bobcats don't have a starting point guard is partly because of their surprisingly gun-shy owner and their crotchety coach. No one has gone on the record about it, but Jordan and Brown reportedly experienced cold feet after a trade that would have sent Chandler and Boris Diaw to the Toronto Raptors for Jose Calderon was in place. Really, that's probably for the best, because Calderon's pay-to-performance ratio isn't a pretty one and the Bobcats really can't afford to be taking on major chunks of unproductive dollars at this point. However, if Augustin starts the season as the starting point guard and struggles, that will stir the ire of the Charlotte fan base. This would all have been moot if Jordan had parlayed Dampier into a starting lead guard. The Bobcats are left to hope that Augustin blossoms in a full-time role.

It's easy to use hindsight to look back at past drafts and say, "This team could have had super-productive Player X." In Charlotte's case, you can really pick at the selection of Augustin. At the time, the Bobcats had Felton on the roster, entrenched as the starting point guard. Meanwhile, Okafor manned the center position after moving over from power forward. The player picked one selection after Augustin was Brook Lopez. Taking Augustin was a head-scratcher at the time. Two years later, the pick doesn't look any better. If the Bobcats select Lopez ... well, you can go on and on about this. Last year, we wrote how the Bobcats had been unlucky on lottery night. Well, they haven't always been too good on draft night, either. Even given the slots Charlotte ended up in after the lottery balls fell, they could have had a lineup last season of Felton, Wallace, Okafor, Lopez and Brandon Roy. Oh well.

With better drafts, perhaps last year's reach for Gerald Henderson Jr. doesn't happen. Henderson failed to earn court time last season and was woeful when he did manage to play. Yes, he was a rookie, but he'll be 23 in December and given that he grew up around the NBA game his father played so well, you would think he'd be a little more polished at this point. He's an excellent athlete and that part of his makeup did shine through during his limited opportunities a season ago, but the skill part of the game sure didn't. He shot 21 percent from three-point range, which is bad enough,

> ### From the Blogosphere
>
> **Who:** Brett Hainline
> **What:** QueenCityHoops
> **Where:** http://www.queencityhoops.com/
>
> Charlotte is going to take a step back defensively this year--it just remains to be seen how big that step back will be. The switch from Tyson Chandler and Raymond Felton starting at center and point guard to Nazr Mohammed and D.J. Augustin improves the Bobcats' ability to put the ball in the basket, but severely weakens them at the other end of the court, where the team forged its identity last season. Will the improvement offensively offset the defensive adjustment? Spoiler alert: no. As seen in last season's playoffs, Mohammed is not up for the task of defending the post and assisting on the pick-and-roll--you can have one but not both. And while Felton does not have the prototypical size for a point, he still dwarfs Augustin, who also needs to rediscover his shot to hope to overcome his disadvantages on defense. The Bobcats' time as a playoff team may be short-lived.

but in that wide expanse between shots at the rim and the three-point line, he was 12-of-46 from the floor. His assist rate was less than half the league average and his turnover rate was above the league average even though he was rarely asked to handle the ball. If Henderson was two or three years younger, you might be willing to squint through these numbers and, to be fair, they were posted in bits and pieces of garbage time. However, at this point, it sure looks like Henderson was another draft miss. The No. 12 pick was an awkward place to be drafting in 2009 as there was a drop-off after the top seven or eight players. The Bobcats could have taken Tyler Hansbrough, who isn't a sure thing himself; Ty Lawson, another local product who shined in statistically informed draft previews; or even Austin Daye, who would have given them a high-upside player.

No worries on this year's draft: the Bobcats didn't have a pick. Instead, Jordan and general manager Rod Higgins set out to improve the team by bringing in plenty of end-of-the-roster fodder. Rookie Sherron Collins, a point guard from Kansas, was added after he went unselected on draft night. Shaun Livingston, another season and a couple of more teams removed from his horrific knee injury, signed on. Charlotte also added Dominic McGuire and old Jordan favorite Kwame Brown. All of these players project at below replacement level. If any of them turn out to be prominent players in Brown's rotation, it will be a sign that the season isn't going very well.

The team's handling of Chandler was also puzzling. Even in his diminished state, Chandler had value as a defender and a rebounder off the bench. The value wasn't enough to justify the $12.6 million he'll make this season, but at least he was entering the last season of his contract. Bringing back Dampier's non-guaranteed contract in the trade that sent Chandler to Dallas was fine, but to make that happen, the Bobcats also took on Matt Carroll and Eduardo Najera. Najera's contract isn't a back-breaker and if he shows further signs of decline, his deal for next season is only partially guaranteed. He's the kind of player and the kind of salary that is always handy in filling out trades. However, the six-year, $26.9 million contract Carroll signed in 2007 was one of the more befuddling transactions of recent years. The Bobcats were, of course, the team responsible for that folly, but managed to escape the deal by sending Carroll and Ryan Hollins to the Mavs for DeSagana Diop. And now they *bring him back*? Ah, well.

Charlotte bolstered its roster during last season by sending Law, Flip Murray and a future No. 1 pick to the Bulls for talented, but underachieving, forward Tyrus Thomas. Thomas played his best basketball so far as a professional under Brown. There was plenty of interest in Thomas as he hit the restricted free agent market this summer, given his progress and high ceiling. Charlotte managed to bring him back at the cost of five years, $37.2 million. The eventual outcome of this deal is hard to predict. It could turn out to be a fantastic bargain; it could also turn out to be an ugly bit of sunk cost. Thomas probably doesn't have the offensive skill to ever be a real core player, but his ability to run the floor, finish at the basket, defend both forward positions and erase defensive mistakes with awe-inspiring shot blocks should make him a useful player in a playoff-caliber team's rotation. If he sulks or falls back into his old habit of trying to do more on offense than he's capable, the contract could turn sour. He should be fine this season, but what happens when Brown leaves?

That's just one of the questions facing the Bobcats, whose honeymoon after a breakthrough season proved to be short-lived. Can Augustin and Henderson become what they were hoping they would become when they were drafted? If slippage becomes apparent in the roster, what can be done to change direction? For Charlotte to stay at last season's level, it must find solid point guard play, and using Dampier's contract seemed like the best bet, but it takes two teams to tango. Also, Jackson can't drop off, even though he's at an age when that seems inevitable. The center position is a potential mess as well, and Charlotte missed out on former Suns reserve Louis Amundson, who signed with the Warriors.

The Bobcats can be expected to cling to mediocrity, much to the consternation of their new owner who likely will remain just a little bit too hands-on in the basketball opps department. They were lucky to get Brown back this year, so the chances of getting him back in 2011 have to be considered slim. Unless one of the point guards on hand overachieves, the offense will probe even deeper depths than last season, rendering a return trip to the postseason unlikely. The Bobcats' first-round sweep last spring seems to be the high-water mark for this group.

Bradford Doolittle

CHARLOTTE BOBCATS

BOBCATS FIVE-YEAR TRENDS

Season	AGE	W-L	POW	PYTH	SEED	ORTG	DRTG	PT DIFF	PACE
05-06	25.2	26-56	26.6 (27)	29.7	---	103.7 (28)	108.5 (19)	-4.0 (27)	92.1 (3)
06-07	25.5	33-49	30.5 (26)	30.4	---	104.9 (27)	109.2 (20)	-3.7 (26)	90.8 (12)
07-08	26.5	32-50	29.0 (23)	28.7	---	107.3 (21)	111.9 (22)	-4.4 (22)	89.6 (15)
08-09	25.8	35-47	35.7 (20)	37.1	---	105.8 (27)	107.7 (7)	-1.3 (20)	87.2 (26)
09-10	28.2	44-38	44.5 (15)	45.4	7	105.7 (24)	104.4 (1)	1.5 (15)	89.1 (26)

		OFFENSE				DEFENSE			
Season	PAY	eFG	oREB	FT/FGA	TO	eFG	oREB	FT/FGA	TO
05-06	$30.3	.464 (29)	.271 (13)	.233 (23)	.153 (7)	.514 (28)	.707 (27)	.263 (22)	.192 (1)
06-07	$42.0	.480 (25)	.264 (19)	.236 (19)	.162 (11)	.500 (18)	.716 (22)	.279 (27)	.171 (6)
07-08	$51.7	.492 (16)	.257 (20)	.230 (12)	.153 (18)	.505 (21)	.710 (28)	.235 (16)	.152 (9)
08-09	$68.0	.494 (19)	.277 (12)	.231 (19)	.177 (30)	.498 (13)	.730 (17)	.230 (15)	.167 (5)
09-10	$68.4	.490 (24)	.265 (17)	.260 (3)	.175 (30)	.491 (12)	.742 (10)	.194 (1)	.170 (3)

(league rankings in parenthesis)

PG 14 — D.J. Augustin
Hght: 6'0" Wght: 180 Exp: 2 From: Texas Salary: $2.5 million
2011-12 status: team option for $3.2 million

SKILL RATINGS: TOT +2, OFF +4, DEF -1, REB -4, PAS 0, HND 0, SHT -1, ATH 0

Year	Team	Age	G	MPG	Usg	3PA%	FTA%	INS	2P%	3P%	FT%	TS%	Reb%	Ast%	TO%	BLK%	STL%	PF%	oRTG	dRTG	Win%	WARP
08-09	CHA	21.4	72	26.5	.210	.292	.122	.830	.424	.439	.893	.587	.043	.062	.141	.001	.012	.035	108.4	108.3	.504	3.5
09-10	CHA	22.4	80	18.4	.180	.314	.102	.788	.381	.393	.779	.516	.039	.061	.131	.003	.016	.040	105.6	107.4	.442	0.8
10-11p	CHA	23.4	75	25.0	.214	.336	.120	.785	.405	.392	.833	.551	.042	.064	.136	.002	.014	.036	107.3	107.5	.495	3.1

Most similar to: Nick Van Exel (96.3), Chauncey Billups, Sebastian Telfair, Nate Robinson
IMP: 54% BRK: 4% COP: 7%

D.J. Augustin enters training camp as the Bobcats' projected starter at point guard. That has as much do with the fact that the team was unable to acquire somebody else to play there as it has to does how much they value Augustin's production. Hey, an opportunity is an opportunity. To hold off the challenge of free-agent signee Shaun Livingston, Augustin needs to gain confidence in his ability to run the offense and distribute the basketball. He's a very good outside shooter, at least from three-point range, but really struggles inside the arc, hitting just 38 percent of two-point shots last season. Fifty-one percent of his field goals were assisted, the kind of rate you expect more from a catch-and-shoot two-guard than a lead guard. Augustin does protect the basketball fairly well and isn't terrible as an on-ball defender. If he doesn't embrace this chance to be a starting point guard, he may forever after be cast as a 20-minute, off-the-bench gunner.

SF 4 — Derrick Brown
Hght: 6'8" Wght: 227 Exp: 1 From: Xavier (Ohio) Salary: $0.8 million
2011-12 status: due qualifying offer of $1.1 million

SKILL RATINGS: TOT -1, OFF 0, DEF 0, REB -1, PAS -3, HND -2, SHT -1, ATH +4

Year	Team	Age	G	MPG	Usg	3PA%	FTA%	INS	2P%	3P%	FT%	TS%	Reb%	Ast%	TO%	BLK%	STL%	PF%	oRTG	dRTG	Win%	WARP
09-10	CHA	22.6	57	9.4	.173	.035	.160	1.125	.471	.286	.667	.520	.088	.017	.096	.015	.020	.046	103.2	105.9	.411	-0.1
10-11p	CHA	23.6	76	10.0	.179	.043	.152	1.110	.478	.366	.700	.535	.084	.019	.099	.019	.020	.044	103.3	105.5	.427	0.2

Most similar to: Jared Dudley (96.8), Anthony Bonner, Gerald Wallace, Jerome Kersey
IMP: 57% BRK: 10% COP: 6%

As the Bobcats work on transitioning him from a college power forward to a pro quick forward, rangy Derrick Brown shows promise as a wing defender. Right now, the best thing he has going for him is his athleticism. On offense, he put up a sparkling foul-drawing rate during his limited minutes but needs to develop a semblance of a jump shot or opponents are simply going to sag back off of him. In any event, it appears the Bobcats did well for themselves by getting Brown at No. 40 in the 2009 draft.

CHARLOTTE BOBCATS

C 54 — Kwame Brown

Hght: 6'11" | Exp: 9 | Salary: $1.2 million
Wght: 270 | From: Glynn Academy HS (GA)
2011-12 status: free agent

SKILL RATINGS

TOT	OFF	DEF	REB	PAS	HND	SHT	ATH
-4	-2	+2	+1	0	-2	0	+3

Year	Team	Age	G	MPG	Usg	3PA%	FTA%	INS	2P%	3P%	FT%	TS%	Reb%	Ast%	TO%	BLK%	STL%	PF%	oRTG	dRTG	Win%	WARP
07-08	LAL	26.1	38	18.8	.146	.000	.183	1.183	.507	.000	.408	.497	.143	.028	.216	.023	.013	.050	100.9	104.6	.378	-0.6
08-09	DET	27.1	58	17.2	.131	.000	.197	1.197	.533	.000	.516	.546	.173	.015	.183	.019	.013	.066	103.2	105.9	.411	-0.1
09-10	DET	28.1	48	13.8	.148	.005	.205	1.200	.504	.000	.337	.470	.167	.015	.205	.015	.012	.065	100.6	105.9	.325	-1.3
10-11p	CHA	29.1	75	5.0	.149	.005	.196	1.192	.512	.001	.387	.488	.161	.019	.203	.020	.012	.063	100.9	105.4	.351	-0.5

Most similar to: Corie Blount (96.6), Eric Leckner, Vitaly Potapenko, Felton Spencer | IMP: 56% | BRK: 9% | COP: 7%

After releasing Erick Dampier to get under the luxury-tax threshold, the Bobcats are desperate for center play. Desperate, thy name is Kwame. If the reunion of Michael Jordan and Kwame Brown doesn't bring a tear to your eye, you've got a heart of stone. Brown has never developed as an offensive player and really should probably quit trying. His usage rate is low at less than 15 percent, but it should probably be closer to the 10 percent range of the Ben Wallace types. Brown ranked 33rd in the league in percent of post-ups per overall plays, but averaged just .6 points on those plays, putting him in the league's 24th percentile. He's nine years into his career, so let's just bag the offense. If he doesn't continue to try to be a force, then perhaps his annually horrific turnover rate would improve. Brown can rebound, and he can defend the post. That's going to have to be enough, and it doesn't matter that Jordan once took him with the No. 1 overall pick. Also, you see references to Kwame being brought in for his shot-blocking prowess, but he's unspectacular in that regard. He blocked shots at exactly the league rate last season, and his percentage drops with each season.

SG 33 — Matt Carroll

Hght: 6'6" | Exp: 7 | Salary: $4.3 million
Wght: 212 | From: Notre Dame
2011-12 status: guaranteed contract for $3.9 million

SKILL RATINGS

TOT	OFF	DEF	REB	PAS	HND	SHT	ATH
-4	-1	-2	0	-4	-4	-2	-3

Year	Team	Age	G	MPG	Usg	3PA%	FTA%	INS	2P%	3P%	FT%	TS%	Reb%	Ast%	TO%	BLK%	STL%	PF%	oRTG	dRTG	Win%	WARP
07-08	CHA	27.6	80	25.1	.163	.340	.086	.746	.422	.436	.804	.554	.065	.017	.083	.007	.010	.042	104.2	107.2	.404	-0.5
08-09	DAL	28.6	55	11.2	.165	.247	.051	.805	.441	.245	.840	.451	.068	.021	.153	.007	.018	.051	100.2	107.1	.282	-1.7
09-10	DAL	29.6	25	4.8	.228	.319	.044	.726	.452	.211	1.000	.437	.057	.023	.117	.000	.021	.050	101.1	98.3	.598	0.5
10-11p	CHA	30.6	76	5.0	.164	.365	.057	.692	.426	.325	.850	.494	.068	.020	.129	.007	.014	.047	102.0	106.8	.343	-0.6

Most similar to: Jaren Jackson (98.6), Mike Sanders, Gordan Giricek, Tony Brown | IMP: 57% | BRK: 16% | COP: 2%

What comes around goes around. The Bobcats signed backup shooting guard Matt Carroll to a six-year, $27 million contract in 2007 because "they wanted to retain depth at the position," according to Michael Jordan. Then the depth didn't matter, but the long contract did, so Carroll was included in the trade along with Ryan Hollins to acquire DeSagana Diop. Then the Bobcats need payroll flexibility, so they traded for the non-guaranteed contract of Dallas' Erick Dampier. To get that, they had to take Carroll back. Carroll still has two more years plus a player option left on that contract he signed with Charlotte three years ago, and it gets more onerous the worse he gets. Carroll has really struggled to get on the court the last two seasons, as his three-point stroke has all but disappeared. During his last two seasons in Charlotte, Carroll shot nearly 43 percent on more than 500 three-point attempts. In Dallas the last two years, he was 17-of-72. The Bobcats can definitely use the outside shooting touch of the younger version of Carroll, and he'll get a chance to carve out a regular role for himself. Whether he does or not, he'll be one of the most overpaid players in the league.

PG 11 — Sherron Collins

Hght: 5'11" | Exp: R | Salary: $0.5 million
Wght: 205 | From: Kansas
2011-12 status: non-guaranteed contract for $1.0 million

SKILL RATINGS

TOT	OFF	DEF	REB	PAS	HND	SHT	ATH
-3	--	--	--	--	--	--	--

Year	Team	Age	G	MPG	Usg	3PA%	FTA%	INS	2P%	3P%	FT%	TS%	Reb%	Ast%	TO%	BLK%	STL%	PF%	oRTG	dRTG	Win%	WARP
10-11p	CHA	24.1	76	-	.181	.256	.077	.821	.383	.315	.835	.461	.028	.058	.148	.001	.012	.033	-	-	.374	-

Most similar to: Lionel Chalmers (97.8), Dan Dickau, Willie Solomon, Chris Quinn | IMP: - | BRK: - | COP: -

CHARLOTTE BOBCATS

Former Kansas guard Sherron Collins earned an invitation to Bobcats camp on the strength of a 32-point performance in a summer-league game, when he drained 7-of-11 three-pointers. He was a shoot-first point guard at KU, capable of carrying the Jayhawks for long stretches but also prone to the occasional disappearing act. A strong, bowling ball type of player with a low center of gravity, Collins impressed during pre-draft workouts with better conditioning than he had in college. He also showed some good NBA point guard traits as far as directing the pick-and-roll, yet still went undrafted. If there is an NBA point guard in here somewhere, Larry Brown will find it.

Boris Diaw — PF #32

Hght: 6'8" Exp: 7 Salary: $9.0 million
Wght: 235 From: Cormeille-en-Parisis, France
2011-12 status: player option or ETO for $9.0 million

SKILL RATINGS

TOT	OFF	DEF	REB	PAS	HND	SHT	ATH
0	+2	+3	-4	+5	+4	+3	-3

Year	Team	Age	G	MPG	Usg	3PA%	FTA%	INS	2P%	3P%	FT%	TS%	Reb%	Ast%	TO%	BLK%	STL%	PF%	oRTG	dRTG	Win%	WARP
07-08	PHX	26.0	82	28.2	.167	.049	.066	1.017	.487	.310	.744	.514	.089	.062	.181	.011	.011	.031	103.1	106.0	.406	-0.5
08-09	CHA	27.0	81	34.0	.199	.156	.056	.900	.531	.414	.687	.565	.096	.057	.185	.016	.012	.034	106.0	106.5	.483	3.8
09-10	CHA	28.0	82	35.4	.164	.203	.064	.861	.541	.320	.769	.552	.087	.052	.175	.016	.011	.035	105.4	106.3	.470	3.2
10-11p	CHA	29.0	76	32.0	.180	.192	.060	.868	.524	.377	.726	.556	.088	.051	.172	.017	.011	.035	105.1	106.2	.463	2.4

Most similar to: Derrick McKey (98.1), Mike Bantom, Luke Walton, Billy Owens   IMP: 57% BRK: 10% COP: 2%

Boris Diaw was nearly traded to the Raptors during the offseason in a deal that would have brought Jose Calderon back to the Queen City. The Bobcats got cold feet, and Diaw is back for another season. His productivity was impacted by Stephen Jackson's arrival in Charlotte last season. Jackson teamed with Gerald Wallace as the top two options in Larry Brown's offense. Meanwhile, Diaw lapsed back into the passive role in which he seems to feel more comfortable. His usage rate dropped by 35 points and his rate of assisted field goals soared. He became more of a spot-up shooter, but hit just .320 from behind the arc. Diaw is still one of the better passing forwards in the game, but simply had the ball in his hands less last season. He's a decent defender, but certainly not a game-changing one. He needs to pack more of an offensive punch to justify the $9 million he's got coming the next two seasons. With the Bobcats lacking at the point, Diaw's playmaking could move back to the forefront of the Charlotte attack.

DeSagana Diop — C #7

Hght: 7'0" Exp: 9 Salary: $6.5 million
Wght: 280 From: Oak Hill Academy (Mouth of Wilson, VA)
2011-12 status: guaranteed contract for $6.9 million

SKILL RATINGS

TOT	OFF	DEF	REB	PAS	HND	SHT	ATH
0	--	+1	--	--	--	--	--

Year	Team	Age	G	MPG	Usg	3PA%	FTA%	INS	2P%	3P%	FT%	TS%	Reb%	Ast%	TO%	BLK%	STL%	PF%	oRTG	dRTG	Win%	WARP
07-08	NJN	26.2	79	16.5	.095	.000	.115	1.115	.522	.000	.543	.536	.175	.014	.216	.053	.009	.052	102.5	103.3	.473	1.5
08-09	CHA	27.2	75	13.8	.109	.000	.121	1.121	.433	.000	.333	.425	.158	.015	.163	.045	.015	.058	102.0	104.7	.408	-0.2
09-10	CHA	28.2	27	9.7	.080	.000	.088	1.088	.517	-	.222	.485	.149	.009	.267	.044	.010	.055	100.5	104.7	.360	-0.3
10-11p	CHA	29.2	76	-	.092	.003	.107	1.104	.503	.000	.317	.482	.155	.012	.227	.044	.010	.056	-	-	.441	-

Most similar to: Greg Kite (94.9), Joel Przybilla, Corie Blount, Jerome James   IMP: 49% BRK: 11% COP: 7%

Did you know that DeSagana Diop has been in the NBA for nine seasons? Of course you know--it's right there in the table above this paragraph--but had you contemplated that on a conscious level? Diop seems like the classic big man project that's just sort of lying around unfinished in the garage. He played sparingly in 2009-10, in part because of an MCL sprain but also because Larry Brown sees no particular use for him. Yet, Diop has three years and $20.8 million left on his contract, so perhaps a use needs to be found. When he did get on the court, he took just 29 shots in 27 games and did not make anything other than a layup or dunk. His blocked-shot rate was still at the elite level, which is why he got that contract in the first place. He'll never be anything more than a shot-blocking specialist, but will likely see some regular minutes this season as Charlotte has so few options at the center position. Diop is the epitome of the concept of sunk cost.

CHARLOTTE BOBCATS

SG 15	Gerald Henderson Jr.	Hght: 6'4" Wght: 215 2011-12 status: team option for $2.3 million	Exp: 1 From: Duke	Salary: $2.1 million		**SKILL RATINGS**						
						TOT	OFF	DEF	REB	PAS	HND	SHT	ATH
						-2	-1	+2	+4	-4	-3	-5	+4

Year	Team	Age	G	MPG	Usg	3PA%	FTA%	INS	2P%	3P%	FT%	TS%	Reb%	Ast%	TO%	BLK%	STL%	PF%	oRTG	dRTG	Win%	WARP
09-10	CHA	22.4	43	8.3	.183	.137	.149	1.012	.388	.211	.745	.453	.093	.017	.101	.021	.015	.033	101.6	105.5	.372	-0.3
10-11p	CHA	23.4	76	15.0	.191	.124	.146	1.022	.408	.248	.787	.480	.094	.020	.102	.027	.015	.031	102.2	104.8	.410	-0.1

Most similar to: Jud Buechler (97.8), Kirk Snyder, Arron Afflalo, Bernard Thompson   IMP: 63%   BRK: 31%   COP: 4%

It might be too soon to write off Gerald Henderson Jr. as a bust, but he's entering a pivotal season as he tries to justify his selection at No. 12 in the 2009 Draft. Henderson saw painfully little court time last season, as he was lost behind Stephen Jackson, Flip Murray and Larry Hughes at the two-guard position. Jackson is the only one back, so Henderson needs to impress Larry Brown early to prevent the Bobcats from bringing in another veteran stopgap like Hughes (perhaps even Hughes himself). Henderson's athleticism is unquestioned. He has a nice crossover and a quick first step, then explosive leaping ability that lets him finish at the rim. However, he's not strong enough to be strictly a slasher. He needs a jump shot to keep defenders from sagging, and last season he was painfully bad away from the hoop. Henderson also needs to get a better feel for passing the ball within the structure of an offense. He's got potential as a defender, and if he can start hitting some jumpers, he may turn into something. He's a smart kid--and not just because he went to Duke--and spent the summer working the many rough edges of his game. We'll know in preseason if the work paid off and whether or not he's going to carve out a regular niche in Brown's exacting system.

SG 1	Stephen Jackson	Hght: 6'8" Wght: 215 2011-12 status: guaranteed contract for $9.3 million	Exp: 10 From: Oak Hill Academy (Mouth of Wilson, VA)	Salary: $8.5 million		**SKILL RATINGS**						
						TOT	OFF	DEF	REB	PAS	HND	SHT	ATH
						+1	+1	-1	+1	+3	-1	-1	+2

Year	Team	Age	G	MPG	Usg	3PA%	FTA%	INS	2P%	3P%	FT%	TS%	Reb%	Ast%	TO%	BLK%	STL%	PF%	oRTG	dRTG	Win%	WARP
07-08	GSW	30.0	73	39.1	.231	.321	.104	.783	.436	.363	.832	.536	.061	.044	.126	.007	.014	.025	106.4	106.4	.501	5.0
08-09	GSW	31.0	59	39.6	.253	.221	.113	.893	.448	.338	.826	.530	.070	.070	.166	.009	.018	.028	107.4	106.7	.522	5.1
09-10	CHA	32.0	81	38.6	.277	.210	.102	.892	.460	.328	.779	.518	.076	.045	.139	.011	.022	.029	105.0	105.1	.497	5.2
10-11p	CHA	33.0	75	39.0	.249	.253	.101	.849	.446	.342	.795	.521	.069	.051	.150	.010	.017	.030	105.1	105.8	.477	3.7

Most similar to: Latrell Sprewell (96.9), James Worthy, Reggie Theus, Chris Mullin   IMP: 36%   BRK: 2%   COP: 13%

Stephen Jackson has always been nothing if not adaptable. He's been a role player on a great team. He's been the big cheese on a bad team. He's been just about everything in between, with the ability to play just about every position on the court. Last season, the Bobcats needed him to score, and that's what he did. Going forward, you'd like to see him ease up on his own offense, shoot a better percentage and get his teammates more involved. Jackson's three-point percentage has been down for two straight years, which is an issue for him because he's a below-average shooter at all distances inside the arc. Charlotte needed Jackson to be aggressive, even selfish, last season. While the Bobcats haven't exactly added a ton of firepower over the summer, to keep the momentum they need Jackson to raise the play of his teammates more so than himself. He's certainly capable of doing just that.

PG 2	Shaun Livingston	Hght: 6'7" Wght: 185 2011-12 status: guaranteed contract for $3.5 million	Exp: 5 From: Peoria Central HS (IL)	Salary: $3.5 million		**SKILL RATINGS**						
						TOT	OFF	DEF	REB	PAS	HND	SHT	ATH
						-2	0	-2	0	+1	0	0	-3

Year	Team	Age	G	MPG	Usg	3PA%	FTA%	INS	2P%	3P%	FT%	TS%	Reb%	Ast%	TO%	BLK%	STL%	PF%	oRTG	dRTG	Win%	WARP
08-09	OKC	23.6	12	19.3	.143	.000	.060	1.060	.517	.000	.900	.551	.071	.039	.123	.006	.015	.024	102.5	106.5	.369	-0.2
09-10	WAS	24.6	36	22.1	.160	.021	.075	1.054	.533	.000	.875	.563	.057	.074	.207	.011	.011	.035	104.3	107.2	.405	-0.2
10-11p	CHA	25.6	76	25.0	.169	.027	.074	1.047	.520	.000	.882	.548	.054	.073	.196	.015	.012	.036	103.7	106.7	.402	-0.6

Most similar to: Boris Diaw (96.2), Jalen Rose, Jarrett Jack, Jose Calderon   IMP: 45%   BRK: 9%   COP: 4%

CHARLOTTE BOBCATS

It's great to see Shaun Livingston with some job security. He was one of the game's more promising young players when he suffered a catastrophic knee injury in Feb. 2007. He's been slowly working his way back since, going from the Clippers to the Heat to the Thunder to the Wizards before finally landing some guaranteed money from the point guard-starved Bobcats. This doesn't mean Charlotte views Livingston as the starter at the position, though he could beat out D.J. Augustin for the job. Livingston is probably never going to be durable, and his lateral movement is still weak enough that he's too much of a defensive liability to hold down a full-time role. The good news is that his once-elite playmaking skills began to resurface during his time with the Wizards, and he shot the ball extremely well for the second straight season. Livingston may never be the All-Star he once had the potential to become, but he can be one of the better second-unit guards in the NBA and stay employed as a professional basketball player for a long time to come. That's great news because, after all, the kid is still only 25 years old.

SF 5	Dominic McGuire	Hght: 6'9" Exp: 3 Salary: $0.9 million										
		Wght: 220 From: Fresno State				**SKILL RATINGS**						
		2011-12 status: free agent				TOT	OFF	DEF	REB	PAS	HND	SHT	ATH
						-4	-2	-4	+5	+1	-1	-4	-2

Year	Team	Age	G	MPG	Usg	3PA%	FTA%	INS	2P%	3P%	FT%	TS%	Reb%	Ast%	TO%	BLK%	STL%	PF%	oRTG	dRTG	Win%	WARP
07-08	WAS	22.5	70	10.0	.104	.038	.090	1.051	.392	.167	.438	.397	.118	.027	.255	.031	.013	.051	99.8	105.1	.327	-1.3
08-09	WAS	23.5	79	26.2	.102	.009	.097	1.089	.431	.500	.725	.483	.123	.044	.200	.029	.016	.034	102.3	105.3	.399	-0.7
09-10	SAC	24.5	51	6.0	.107	.000	.043	1.043	.365	-	.000	.345	.149	.016	.236	.010	.008	.052	98.2	106.5	.245	-1.1
10-11p	CHA	25.5	76	5.0	.109	.016	.069	1.053	.418	.120	.309	.405	.134	.029	.211	.024	.013	.044	99.7	105.1	.321	-0.7

Most similar to: Bob Thornton (95.4), Byron Houston, Jerome Whitehead, Alvin Scott   IMP: 77% BRK: 28% COP: 2%

The Bobcats have a chance to either look really smart or really dumb for their offseason acquisitions. Dominic McGuire may be the litmus test for how that cookie crumbles. McGuire has almost no offensive ability whatsoever, consistently using around 10 percent of his team's plays despite playing the majority of his minutes at small forward. The only bullet in his belt is a stand-still jumper from 19 feet or so, but he doesn't even hit that at the league average rate. Inside of that distance, he has no touch whatsoever, and his thin build makes him a poor finisher at the hoop. He also can't step back behind the three-point line or draw fouls, which kills his chance to at least be efficient per possession used. Sure, he can be an adequate wing defender, but Charlotte already has a long, defense-first reserve wing in Derrick Brown, who has considerably more upside than McGuire.

SF 24	Darius Miles	Hght: 6'9" Exp: 7 Salary: $0.9 million										
		Wght: 210 From: East Saint Louis HS				**SKILL RATINGS**						
		2011-12 status: free agent				TOT	OFF	DEF	REB	PAS	HND	SHT	ATH
						+3	--	+1	--	--	--	--	--

Year	Team	Age	G	MPG	Usg	3PA%	FTA%	INS	2P%	3P%	FT%	TS%	Reb%	Ast%	TO%	BLK%	STL%	PF%	oRTG	dRTG	Win%	WARP
08-09	MEM	27.5	34	8.8	.212	.045	.102	1.057	.505	.167	.742	.533	.118	.027	.157	.055	.019	.051	104.2	103.6	.521	0.6
10-11p	CHA	29.5	76	-	.206	.035	.096	1.062	.493	.132	.718	.518	.111	.029	.160	.050	.017	.050	-	-	.527	-

Most similar to: Aaron Williams (95.8), Benoit Benjamin, Edgar Jones, Dan Gadzuric   IMP: 38% BRK: 4% COP: 13%

The long, winding journey of Darius Miles next takes him to Bobcats training camp. His small-sample-size numbers two years ago weren't bad, but it would be an upset to see him in an NBA uniform come opening night.

CHARLOTTE BOBCATS

C 13 — Nazr Mohammed

Hght: 6'10" Exp: 12 Salary: $6.9 million
Wght: 250 From: Kentucky
2011-12 status: free agent

SKILL RATINGS

TOT	OFF	DEF	REB	PAS	HND	SHT	ATH
-1	0	-4	+1	-2	-4	0	-2

Year	Team	Age	G	MPG	Usg	3PA%	FTA%	INS	2P%	3P%	FT%	TS%	Reb%	Ast%	TO%	BLK%	STL%	PF%	oRTG	dRTG	Win%	WARP
07-08	CHA	30.6	82	20.1	.196	.001	.102	1.101	.515	.000	.583	.532	.173	.020	.144	.027	.013	.063	104.5	104.9	.487	2.4
08-09	CHA	31.6	39	8.7	.197	.000	.124	1.124	.406	.000	.550	.438	.143	.011	.162	.039	.008	.088	101.1	107.2	.306	-0.8
09-10	CHA	32.6	58	17.0	.214	.000	.122	1.122	.553	-	.648	.578	.185	.013	.118	.036	.008	.050	106.8	104.6	.573	3.2
10-11p	CHA	33.6	72	25.0	.193	.003	.111	1.108	.499	.000	.592	.521	.162	.014	.150	.037	.008	.069	103.3	105.6	.423	0.3

Most similar to: Alton Lister (96.6), Aaron Williams, Antonio McDyess, Joe Smith

IMP: 30% BRK: 2% COP: 14%

It looks like 12-year veteran Nazr Mohammed is going to be the opening-night starter at center for the Bobcats, not a career path you would have predicted for him a couple of years ago. Mohammed has never played more than 26 minutes per game, and probably won't log more than 20-22 for Charlotte, which means he's going to need plenty of help. Mohammed is still good as a shot blocker and was a beast on the glass last season. He's also a surprisingly effective shooter who can get you 15-18 efficient points for every 40 minutes he plays. He's got the reputation as a defense-first center, but he's actually statuesque in that regard, one of the reasons he never caught on as a full-time starter.

PF 21 — Eduardo Najera

Hght: 6'8" Exp: 10 Salary: $3.0 million
Wght: 235 From: Oklahoma
2011-12 status: partially-guaranteed contract for $2.8 million

SKILL RATINGS

TOT	OFF	DEF	REB	PAS	HND	SHT	ATH
-1	0	+3	-3	+1	+2	-1	0

Year	Team	Age	G	MPG	Usg	3PA%	FTA%	INS	2P%	3P%	FT%	TS%	Reb%	Ast%	TO%	BLK%	STL%	PF%	oRTG	dRTG	Win%	WARP
07-08	DEN	31.8	78	21.3	.119	.315	.086	.771	.548	.361	.714	.571	.109	.024	.126	.017	.017	.050	105.1	105.5	.486	2.4
08-09	NJN	32.8	27	11.8	.150	.246	.095	.849	.571	.200	.364	.472	.126	.028	.177	.010	.016	.074	102.7	107.1	.356	-0.4
09-10	DAL	33.8	46	14.9	.123	.353	.058	.706	.524	.297	.583	.501	.097	.020	.138	.015	.019	.063	103.1	106.2	.399	-0.3
10-11p	CHA	34.8	76	10.0	.127	.404	.070	.666	.529	.292	.562	.497	.106	.023	.148	.014	.019	.066	103.5	106.0	.415	0.0

Most similar to: George Lynch (95.9), Tom Gugliotta, Corie Blount, Mark Bryant

IMP: 54% BRK: 8% COP: 5%

Considering the $31 million Eduardo Najera has earned in his career, it seems like there are worse things to be than tall and scrappy. Najera is roster filler at this point in his career, which will likely end this year or next. He can still hold his own defensively in snippets, but he has no offensive value.

PF 12 — Tyrus Thomas

Hght: 6'10" Exp: 4 Salary: $6.6 million
Wght: 225 From: Louisiana State
2011-12 status: guaranteed contract for $7.0 million

SKILL RATINGS

TOT	OFF	DEF	REB	PAS	HND	SHT	ATH
+3	-1	+2	+2	+1	-3	-2	+5

Year	Team	Age	G	MPG	Usg	3PA%	FTA%	INS	2P%	3P%	FT%	TS%	Reb%	Ast%	TO%	BLK%	STL%	PF%	oRTG	dRTG	Win%	WARP
07-08	CHI	21.7	74	17.9	.199	.010	.129	1.119	.426	.167	.741	.486	.148	.030	.130	.043	.016	.058	102.7	103.2	.484	1.9
08-09	CHI	22.7	79	27.5	.195	.010	.141	1.132	.453	.333	.783	.525	.133	.016	.136	.051	.021	.045	103.3	102.8	.514	4.4
09-10	CHA	23.7	54	22.6	.222	.005	.131	1.126	.465	.000	.686	.511	.157	.021	.156	.055	.026	.049	102.3	101.1	.541	3.2
10-11p	CHA	24.7	71	28.1	.226	.012	.141	1.129	.475	.131	.740	.530	.147	.023	.145	.050	.023	.047	103.1	101.9	.540	5.2

Most similar to: Stromile Swift (96.5), Gerald Wallace, Marcus Camby, Paul Millsap

IMP: 55% BRK: 11% COP: 5%

Tyrus Thomas showed enough during his two months in Charlotte to convince Michael Jordan to give him a five-year, $38.3 million deal. Thomas was once viewed as a potential franchise player, and through that prism it's easy to scratch your head over the Bobcats' investment. However, when you look at the cost of wins in the NBA and how hard they are to come by, Thomas' deal should be a solid value. If the light comes on for Thomas in a couple of key areas of his game, the contract could be a downright steal. He could also go into the tank. As it is, SCHOENE sees a breakout season for Thomas, who is just on the threshold of his peak seasons. He still needs to develop his game close to the basket. He hit a solid .447 on long twos last year, but that may only encourage his worst habits. On defense, he's one of the more spectacular playmakers in the league and even looks like he's improving as a position defender. For now, that's where his value lies.

CHARLOTTE BOBCATS

SF 3	Gerald Wallace	Hght: 6'7" Wght: 220 2011-12 status: guaranteed contract for $10.5 million	Exp: 9 From: Alabama	Salary: $10.5 million							
					SKILL RATINGS						
					TOT	OFF	DEF	REB	PAS	HND	SHT	ATH
					+4	+2	+5	+4	+1	-2	+2	+4

Year	Team	Age	G	MPG	Usg	3PA%	FTA%	INS	2P%	3P%	FT%	TS%	Reb%	Ast%	TO%	BLK%	STL%	PF%	oRTG	dRTG	Win%	WARP
07-08	CHA	25.7	62	38.4	.247	.173	.148	.974	.491	.321	.731	.548	.091	.042	.141	.019	.025	.036	105.2	103.7	.548	6.5
08-09	CHA	26.7	71	37.6	.206	.113	.172	1.059	.515	.298	.804	.585	.128	.034	.128	.021	.024	.037	106.6	103.9	.587	9.5
09-10	CHA	27.7	76	41.0	.204	.103	.176	1.073	.503	.371	.776	.586	.146	.024	.131	.022	.020	.029	105.7	103.2	.584	10.8
10-11p	CHA	28.7	74	40.0	.216	.153	.166	1.013	.506	.365	.773	.585	.123	.031	.138	.021	.019	.033	105.9	103.8	.569	9.4

Most similar to: Kenyon Martin (97.7), Jerome Kersey, Tom Gugliotta, Caron Butler   IMP: 37%   BRK: 2%   COP: 3%

With Gerald Wallace, you have to start on defense, where he is the total package. He blocks shots, draws charges, gets steals and plays excellent one-on-one defense. He's been in the upper crust for a while, but he was finally recognized as one of the NBA's best defenders with a First Team All-Defensive selection in 2009-10. Wallace is so good on defense, it's easy to underrate his solid offensive game. He uses his freakish athleticism to put up an outstanding foul-drawing rate, and while he's got a shaky midrange game, he added a solid three-point shot to his arsenal last season. Unfortunately, his .371 percentage on threes screams for a regression. That won't matter as long as Wallace continues to play elite defense and get to the line. If he can stay healthy, he'll remain an excellent player through the duration of the three years remaining on his contract.

C --	Erick Dampier	Hght: 6'11" Wght: 265 2011-12 status: free agent	Exp: 14 From: Mississippi State	Salary: --							
					SKILL RATINGS						
					TOT	OFF	DEF	REB	PAS	HND	SHT	ATH
					+1	0	+1	+2	-3	-2	+5	-3

Year	Team	Age	G	MPG	Usg	3PA%	FTA%	INS	2P%	3P%	FT%	TS%	Reb%	Ast%	TO%	BLK%	STL%	PF%	oRTG	dRTG	Win%	WARP
07-08	DAL	32.8	72	24.4	.113	.000	.153	1.153	.643	.000	.575	.645	.176	.017	.190	.044	.006	.060	105.0	104.0	.534	4.3
08-09	DAL	33.8	80	23.0	.105	.000	.149	1.149	.650	.000	.638	.664	.176	.019	.178	.038	.007	.048	106.0	105.1	.529	4.3
09-10	DAL	34.8	55	23.3	.115	.009	.140	1.130	.629	.333	.604	.637	.178	.011	.192	.045	.006	.055	103.8	104.2	.487	1.9
10-11p	AVG	35.8	71	23.3	.099	.004	.156	1.152	.648	.088	.627	.658	.162	.013	.202	.043	.006	.058	103.9	104.9	.466	1.7

Most similar to: Mark West (95.4), Ervin Johnson, Dikembe Mutombo, Robert Parish   IMP: 50%   BRK: 11%   COP: 6%

Erick Dampier went from outcast to popular the day the Bobcats waived him in September to avoid getting locked into the $13.5 million, non-guaranteed year he had left on his contract. At the veteran's minimum, Dampier looks a whole lot more attractive to contending teams, and he was reportedly weighing offers from multiple teams as camps were set to open. Dampier is still a good-defending, good-rebounding big man who can protect the basket. He's got little offensive utility, but is extremely efficient on the opportunities that come his way, making him an excellent option as a role player. Knee trouble limited Dampier to 55 games last season and he's at an age when he has to be considered a yellow-light injury risk to whichever team signs him.

SG --	Larry Hughes	Hght: 6'5" Wght: 185 2011-12 status: free agent	Exp: 12 From: St. Louis	Salary: --							
					SKILL RATINGS						
					TOT	OFF	DEF	REB	PAS	HND	SHT	ATH
					-1	-1	-3	0	+2	0	-4	+2

Year	Team	Age	G	MPG	Usg	3PA%	FTA%	INS	2P%	3P%	FT%	TS%	Reb%	Ast%	TO%	BLK%	STL%	PF%	oRTG	dRTG	Win%	WARP
07-08	CHI	29.2	68	29.7	.220	.194	.083	.889	.393	.345	.798	.468	.066	.040	.116	.007	.022	.031	102.2	105.1	.403	-0.6
08-09	NYK	30.2	55	26.9	.207	.279	.092	.813	.409	.389	.807	.515	.061	.036	.103	.007	.024	.029	104.9	105.8	.470	1.6
09-10	CHA	31.2	45	24.8	.210	.272	.097	.825	.381	.309	.832	.472	.074	.056	.147	.010	.024	.029	104.6	105.1	.484	1.6
10-11p	AVG	32.2	75	24.8	.199	.259	.085	.826	.387	.331	.793	.470	.067	.046	.138	.009	.021	.031	102.8	105.4	.416	0.0

Most similar to: Ron Harper (97.0), Derek Fisher, Doug Christie, Pooh Richardson   IMP: 31%   BRK: 6%   COP: 15%

Larry Hughes was unemployed at press time, but it's likely that he'll log some NBA minutes at some point in the coming season--perhaps for Charlotte, with whom he finished the 2009-10 campaign. Hughes still has a lot to offer. He can create his own shot, is an underrated passer and is a defensive playmaker, if not exactly disciplined on that end of the floor. The knock against him has always been a low shooting percentage and if he's yet to find a couple of hot spots on the floor by now, you can't expect that it's ever going to happen.

Chicago Bulls

The madness is back on Madison, and not just because of the Blackhawks. During a crucial year in the organization's development, the Bulls charted a course, kept to it and have been rewarded with one of the brightest futures of any franchise in the NBA.

Like the Knicks, Nets and Heat, the Bulls played the 2009-10 season in a sort of limbo. Like the Heat, but unlike the New York-area franchises, the Bulls managed to set themselves up for the wild free-agent summer without punting the season. Chicago projected to a win total ranging from the high-30s to the mid-40s. Despite a couple of bad stretches and injuries that came in bunches, the Bulls closed the season with 41 wins for the third time in five years. In fact, the Bulls' composite regular-season record over that last half-decade is .500 on the nose. It's one thing to be mediocre on the downward arc--that's the time to tear down. It's also a common and undesirable NBA malady to be middling and stagnant, especially if your payroll strangles your flexibility. The Bulls were mediocre with a bullet, if that makes any sense, because of a terrific core of young talent that is only going to improve. Even better, Chicago's braintrust of general manager Gar Forman and basketball operations vice president John Paxson maneuvered the franchise into a position in which it could have landed two elite free-agent talents. In simple terms, Chicago could have signed two of the LeBron/Wade/Bosh mother lode and was one more salary-shedding move from being able to do what Miami did: sign all three.

The Bulls turned out to be bridesmaids in the hunt for the big game in the free-agent safari, but the whiff may have been a blessing in disguise. When Plan A failed, the Bulls sidestepped the landmine Plan B, which would have been to throw max-type dollars at players that didn't deserve it. The young group of Joakim Noah, Derrick Rose, Luol Deng and Taj Gibson gave GarPax another option. Methodically, throughout the summer, the Bulls were able to piece by piece build a roster of complementary talents and establish some of the NBA's best depth. It's not a perfect roster--the team still needs to add a shooter or two--but it's a talented group with room to grow, and they haven't yet spent up to the salary cap. With a few more sound decisions, the Bulls can continue to massage the middle and back end of the roster, explore extensions with Noah and Rose and still have a financial prospectus that is sustainable after the possible harsh turns taken with the next Collective Bargaining Agreement.

How much of an advantage will Chicago's revamped depth be over most of the league? It could be significant, and let's explore the issue by comparing the projected rosters of the Heat and the Bulls (Table 1).

Right after the Heat landed LeBron James, thus locking up the greatest free-agent haul in NBA history, detractors noted that the team would have little money left to build a competitive roster around their

BULLS IN A BOX

Last year's record	41-41
Last year's Offensive Rating	105.0 (28)
Last year's Defensive Rating	106.9 (10)
Last year's point differential	-1.6 (18)
Team pace	91.7 (12)
SCHOENE projection	49-33 (3)
Projected Offensive Rating	110.6 (13)
Projected Defensive Rating	107.5 (3)
Projected team weighted age	27.2 (17)
Projected '10-11 payroll	$55.4 (25)
Est. payroll obligations, '11-12	$56.3 (14)

Head coach: Tom Thibodeau

One of the league's most respected assistant coaches thanks to his role as architect of the Boston Celtics' defense, Tom Thibodeau was overdue for a promotion to head coach. The Chicago Bulls will give him the opportunity, and Thibodeau has the luxury of better talent than most first-time head men. As his mentor Jeff Van Gundy has emphasized, Thibodeau is more than just a one-dimensional defensive expert. Adjusting Chicago's offensive attack may be his most important task. The Bulls have the talent to run an effective motion offense, but must compensate for a lack of shooting in the starting five.

CHICAGO BULLS

Table 1: Projected Value, Starters vs. Bench, Heat vs. Bulls

Miami Heat			Chicago Bulls		
Player	Win%	WARP2	Player	Win%	WARP2
LeBron James	.770	21.0	Carlos Boozer	.572	8.1
Dwyane Wade	.697	15.8	Joakim Noah	.551	6.2
Chris Bosh	.591	9.7	Derrick Rose	.522	6.2
Stars Total	--	46.6	*Stars Total*	--	20.4
Mario Chalmers	.492	3.3	Ronnie Brewer	.487	3.0
Mike Miller	.467	2.1	Luol Deng	.472	2.9
Eddie House	.412	-0.1	Kyle Korver	.495	2.8
James Jones	.410	-0.1	C.J. Watson	.505	2.4
Zydrunas Ilgauskas	.402	-0.3	Omer Asik	.662	2.0
Joel Anthony	.394	-0.7	Keith Bogans	.458	1.0
Jamaal Magloire	.316	-0.8	Taj Gibson	.437	0.8
Carlos Arroyo	.363	-1.0	James Johnson	.442	0.2
Udonis Haslem	.365	-2.2	Kurt Thomas	.380	-0.7
Da'Sean Butler	.438	-	John Lucas III	--	--
Dexter Pittman	.453	-	*Depth Total*	--	14.5
Juwan Howard	.303	-			
Kenny Hasbrouck	--	--			
Patrick Beverley	--	--			
Shavlik Randolph	--	--			
Depth Total	--	0.3			

superstars. Then Miami went about filling out its roster with a lot of relatively familiar names. Many of those naysayers, such as ABC/ESPN commentator Jeff Van Gundy, fell over themselves lauding the supporting roster Pat Riley put together in South Beach. In reality, the initial, kneejerk reactions were probably closer to the truth. Miami's supporting cast beyond the big three is a baby's whisker above replacement level. This is key to the hopes of fans in Chicago, Orlando, Boston and other outposts in the Eastern Conference. No one is going to be able to match the star power of the Heat, but from roster spots four to 15, the competitors will be able to make up a lot of ground.

For the Bulls, it's striking to see the disparity in the WARP totals of each team's core trio, but in fact there is some good news there. Wade is a star-caliber player to be sure, but he's already had one down season due to physical problems. Given his helter-skelter style and the fact that he's in his late 20s, there is no guarantee that Wade is going to remain an elite player. Bosh is an All-Star but, for a couple of years at least, isn't likely to be more than a win or two better than Carlos Boozer. There is no real answer for James--he may remain the NBA's best player for the next decade. But Rose is a dynamic talent still three years away from beginning his peak seasons and who is doggedly smoothing out the rough edges in his game.

There remains a disconnect between the way you evaluate Rose statistically and the way you might view him through the eyes of a scout. The Bulls are banking that Rose, who is actually a lot more deferential by nature than he's given credit for, will become more efficient with better surrounding talent and in a better offensive system. Don't be surprised if Rose's metrics take a sharp turn for the better in the 2010-11 season. If that happens, the WARP gap between James and Rose will narrow. Rose will never challenge James in terms of overall value. Only Oklahoma City's Kevin Durant seems capable of that. But Rose doesn't have to be James. If he can get within hailing distance, then the ebbs and flows elsewhere on the team's respective rosters will do the rest. Chicago can, should and likely will compete with Miami and Orlando for the top spot in the East, as soon as this season, and those already planning their Miami-to-Los Angeles flights for next spring's Finals would do well to hold off until we actually see these revamped teams in action.

In the Bulls' case, the wait will be longer than than expected. Boozer had his share of injury problems in Utah, with seasons of 31, 49 and 45 games missed over six years. Just before the Bulls started their preseason schedule, Boozer broke the fifth metacarpal in his right hand. The injury required surgery, and was expected to keep him out of action until at least early December. For a team already under the gun to integrate a lot of new parts, this was an especially unwelcome setback.

Last season went more or less as expected. The team won about as often as it lost and squeezed into the playoffs once again. Rose improved and the team not only foreswore making short-term decisions to improve its 2009-10 standing but managed to prune the payroll while remaining competitive on the court. The defense was expected to be in the top 10 and it was, just barely, while the offense projected to be near the league's bottom, and it was. It also seemed likely that raw coach Vinny Del Negro would remain on shaky ground. That certainly turned out to be the case.

On the court, the Bulls often seemed disorganized on

offense and Del Negro's substitution patterns ranged from erratic to bizarre, but to his credit, the team played hard and demonstrated a lot of resilience. With Rose slightly hobbled early in the season, the Bulls got off to a 10-17 start. Gradually, the Bulls climbed back into the playoff chase, and a 21-10 stretch put them a season-best four games over .500. Then the injuries hit. Gibson and Noah battled plantar faciitis, with the latter's recovery and minutes eventually leading to a ballyhooed blowout between Paxson and Del Negro. Hinrich missed time. Rose missed time. On March 16 in Memphis, the Bulls started Flip Murray, Jannero Pargo and Acie Law. Chicago lost 10 straight right after its high-water mark, a slump that came not long after Forman dealt John Salmons to Milwaukee and Tyrus Thomas to Charlotte in cap-clearing deals.

At that point, no one would really have been too worked up about the Bulls missing the postseason, as they were clearly positioning themselves for the future. Instead, Chicago finished 10-4, got back to break-even and passed the tanking Raptors to earn a first-round matchup against James' Cavaliers. As in 2009, the Bulls were competitive in their first-round series, but eventually fell to Cleveland in five games. In the grand scheme of things, it might seem like the playoff appearance didn't mean much and, probably, it didn't. However, the manner in which the Bulls got to the postseason derby spoke volumes about the competitiveness of its young talent and caught the attention of free agents like Boozer once the offseason kicked into high gear. The Bulls went 23-18 in the games when Deng, Gibson, Rose and Noah were all in the starting lineup. That 46-win pace was more indicative of the roster's quality than its actual final record. And it's that foundation from which Forman set out to build upon.

When the Bulls made the crucial decision to cut bait on Thomas, the team's direction became clear. Entering last season, it was still uncertain whether Thomas was going to be part of the team's future. Thomas remained as unreliable as ever, regularly flopping between the spectacular and the grotesque. He became a problem in the locker room and few tears were shed at the United Center when he was ultimately unloaded on the Bobcats. It's not easy to give up on such a talented player who still may yet turn out to be something. However, the Bulls assessed the odds of that happening and pulled the plug when they had the chance. After the summer played out, it was clear that Forman and Paxson made the right decision.

All of this talk of roster reshaping ignores what could

From the Blogosphere

Who: Matt Bernhardt
What: Blog a Bull
Where: http://www.blogabull.com/

Derrick Rose has superlative quickness and plays his game near (and often above) the rim. So why can't he get to the line more? With his average of four free throw attempts a game, Rose lags behind other star guards in that department, which suppresses his overall offensive efficiency. Rose's stock should be rising to where he gets more 'star' treatment from officials, but there's more to getting to the free throw line than reputation. Rose is almost too fast and athletic; he can dance through the lane and adjust in midair, but that can lead to a difficult layup attempt (or his favorite finish, the floater) instead of two free throws. Rose expanded his game last season by dramatically improving his midrange shooting, and there's the tease of an improved three-point shot to come, but also look to see if he unleashes his inner Dwyane Wade to become even more unstoppable.

turn out to be just as big of an upgrade as anything done with the playing roster. Del Negro often seemed overmatched and there was obviously a disconnect between the coaching staff and the front office. Rumors of Del Negro's impending demise first surfaced in December, which makes the team's late-season turnaround that much more impressive. You can't pick at Del Negro's game and roster management without giving him credit for the fact that his players played hard and overcame long odds just to get into the playoffs when it would have been so easy to cruise into an early offseason. It's likely that the Bulls' perceived overachievement landed Del Negro a second chance at coaching long before anyone thought possible. Of course, he took the Clippers' job, so it's anyone's guess what led to that decision.

In any event, Bulls fans generally rejoiced when Del Negro was fired and rejoiced anew when his replacement turned out to be longtime NBA assistant Tom Thibodeau. Thibodeau was one of the league's best-known assistants by the time he took the Chicago job. If you can believe the reports about the Bulls' recruiting strategy during free agency, it sounds as if Thibodeau's presence was a strong selling point, not something typical of a first-time NBA head coach. Fans are familiar with Thibodeau as the architect of the great Celtics defenses of the last three years, but he was just as successful prior to that when working under Jeff Van Gundy in Houston. There is no easy way to quantify how much of an uptick in wins a team can expect from changing a subpar coach to an above-average coach. It's not even clear that Thibodeau is really an upgrade. After all, he's never sat in the big chair. Perhaps Del Negro has been underrated and Thibodeau doesn't have the qualities it takes to be the top guy on an NBA bench. We don't know--there isn't enough to go on. However, heading into the season, the consensus is that the Bulls have improved themselves more than a little at the head coaching position.

The first challenge for Thibodeau will be to find a workable offensive system for the new roster. Last year's attack was far too reliant on long two-point jumpers and maintained an inconsistent tempo. Del Negro was hesitant to go all-out in pushing the pace, though he coached the league's fastest player in Rose. After this summer's acquisitions, the Bulls have the pieces to be a premier running team, but will Thibodeau let them play fast? He initially hinted at a drive-and-kick attack that would take full advantage of Rose's talents, but the Bulls don't have the shooters to make that style work as a base offense. Boozer is a great pick-and-roll and pick-and-pop player and there will likely be a lot of two-man action going on between him and Rose. Thibodeau also has athletic, active talents filling out his starting lineup in Deng, Noah and Ronnie Brewer, which would suggest a Jerry Sloan-style offense with a lot of movement, back screening and cuts along the baseline. Kyle Korver, signed away from Utah, gives the Bulls the NBA's top three-point shooter and will help spread the floor. Rose continues to work on his perimeter game, but his strength will remain working in the lane. Deng's ability as a mid-range jump shooter has often hindered his efficiency and he's not reliable from beyond the arc and, anyway, would be wasted as a stand-in-the-corner three-point shooter. Noah is excellent diving to the hoop on the pick-and-roll and even developed a not-horrible midrange shot last season, but Boozer's presence may limit his opportunities to further develop his offensive arsenal. So there are a lot of pieces here, but also a lot of questions, and it's a big challenge for a first-time head coach to make it all work.

Thibodeau will need to craft a defense that is again greater than the sum of its parts. It's easy to note that the Bulls finished 10th in the league in Defensive Rating and then went out and hired one of the league's best defensive minds as its head coach. However, the drop-off in defense from Gibson to Boozer as the full-time power forward is significant, and while Brewer works hard as a perimeter defender and holds his own, he's a clear downgrade from Kirk Hinrich, the longtime Bulls combo guard dealt to Washington just before the draft to clear cap space. Deng is underrated--he may be one of the league's five best defensive small forwards--but there is a distinct possibility that the Bulls' best lineup will include Korver, whose defense isn't as bad as its reputation but is a couple of notches below Deng. If Thibodeau could deploy NFL-style platoons, he'd be in good shape. As it is, the Bulls will try to leverage Noah, Brewer, an improving Rose and Thibodeau's tactical skills to hold down opposing first units.

There are other questions for Thibodeau to work through. How big of a factor can Omer Asik become in his first stateside season? The Bulls won't have a very deep big-man rotation. Given the injury histories of Noah and Boozer, as well as the age of Kurt Thomas, it's likely that Asik is going to be counted on for extended stretches this season. He's a skilled, mobile big man with a long reach that could make him a quality help defender. He's also underweight and was easily bounced out of position in international play. In the NBA, he may spend much of his first season laying on the laps of the patrons sitting courtside. Ideally, Asik would spend a year learning the NBA game, putting on weight and gaining strength, but he'll probably have to do all of that while also making regular contributions on the court. SCHOENE is really excited about his translated Euroleague production, so perhaps he'll prove to be more league ready than he appeared during the FIBA World Championship in late summer.

The Bulls might not have hit the jackpot this summer, but they nevertheless enjoyed the best offseason of any team this side of Miami and are extremely well positioned for the future. While Chicago fans would have embraced the LeBron/Wade superstar combo at the United Center, they may come to love this group just as much as they build a rivalry with the potential dynasty in Miami. The projections for this season are optimistic, and they only promise to get better from here. If the Heat is to become the league's biggest villains, the Bulls may become the team that everybody wants to topple them.

Bradford Doolittle

CHICAGO BULLS

BULLS FIVE-YEAR TRENDS

Season	AGE	W-L	POW	PYTH	SEED	ORTG	DRTG	PT DIFF	PACE
05-06	24.1	41-41	41.0 (15)	42.9	7	105.5 (23)	104.4 (6)	0.6 (14)	91.8 (5)
06-07	26.0	49-33	51.3 (7)	55.3	5	106.7 (20)	101.1 (1)	5.0 (4)	92.2 (6)
07-08	25.1	33-49	31.4 (21)	32.2	---	105.8 (26)	109.3 (13)	-3.1 (21)	91.3 (10)
08-09	24.9	41-41	40.6 (16)	40.2	7	109.5 (19)	110.3 (18)	-0.3 (16)	91.9 (9)
09-10	26.9	41-41	38.5 (18)	36.2	8	105.0 (28)	106.9 (10)	-1.6 (18)	91.7 (12)

Season	PAY	OFFENSE eFG	oREB	FT/FGA	TO	DEFENSE eFG	oREB	FT/FGA	TO
05-06	$37.7	.487 (16)	.263 (19)	.216 (27)	.161 (18)	.464 (3)	.747 (5)	.295 (29)	.161 (12)
06-07	$54.7	.493 (17)	.286 (9)	.229 (22)	.172 (24)	.473 (3)	.743 (10)	.252 (19)	.188 (2)
07-08	$62.8	.470 (28)	.289 (8)	.223 (19)	.153 (19)	.496 (12)	.731 (17)	.258 (26)	.159 (5)
08-09	$67.7	.493 (21)	.280 (6)	.239 (12)	.156 (18)	.493 (9)	.709 (28)	.238 (18)	.154 (13)
09-10	$67.0	.477 (28)	.266 (16)	.217 (21)	.154 (15)	.484 (7)	.748 (8)	.212 (9)	.143 (24)

(league rankings in parenthesis)

C 3 — Omer Asik
Hght: 7'0" Exp: R Salary: $1.7 million
Wght: 255 From: Turkey
2011-12 status: guaranteed contract for $1.9 million

SKILL RATINGS: TOT +5, OFF +2, DEF +5, REB +2, PAS -2, HND -4, SHT +4, ATH +5

Year	Team	Age	G	MPG	Usg	3PA%	FTA%	INS	2P%	3P%	FT%	TS%	Reb%	Ast%	TO%	BLK%	STL%	PF%	oRTG	dRTG	Win%	WARP
10-11p	CHI	24.8	76	5.0	.186	.019	.175	1.157	.568	.018	.551	.571	.170	.014	.168	.088	.013	.039	105.6	100.6	.664	2.0

Most similar to: Sam Bowie (91.8), Samuel Dalembert, Alonzo Mourning, Andrew Lang

IMP: 48% BRK: 0% COP: 3%

It's true that the Bulls and Omer Asik love one another, and SCHOENE loves Asik like a little brother. Realistically, Asik is not going to be a +5 defender out of the gate, nor is he going to be a +5 overall player. However, even if you temper Asik's translations--based on a strong 279-minute run in Euroleague during 2007-08, when he was 21--he looks awfully good. Asik had an uneven performance in the FIBA World Championship. His length and athleticism will make him a premier shot blocker no matter where he plays. If he's a low-usage player at the start, you hope that he can finish at the high percentage projected for him. That's not a given, because he needs to get a whole lot stronger to avoid getting bumped off the court. However, his active body and reckless style give him a projected foul rate that brings to mind a young Pau Gasol. Unfortunately, Asik is a really bad free-throw shooter, something that he's going to have to iron out. Asik is a wild card and ideally you'd give him a year to percolate on the bench. However the Bulls don't have an abundance of bigs and Carlos Boozer's early-season injury may press Asik into regular minutes before he's ready. If SCHOENE is right about him, Asik will continue to be a key part of why the Bulls' future looks so bright.

SF 6 — Keith Bogans
Hght: 6'5" Exp: 7 Salary: $1.3 million
Wght: 215 From: Kentucky
2011-12 status: guaranteed contract for $1.3 million

SKILL RATINGS: TOT 0, OFF +2, DEF +1, REB -3, PAS 0, HND +2, SHT +2, ATH -4

Year	Team	Age	G	MPG	Usg	3PA%	FTA%	INS	2P%	3P%	FT%	TS%	Reb%	Ast%	TO%	BLK%	STL%	PF%	oRTG	dRTG	Win%	WARP
07-08	ORL	27.9	82	26.9	.144	.592	.070	.478	.520	.364	.736	.560	.068	.022	.077	.003	.012	.034	106.1	106.4	.492	3.4
08-09	MIL	28.9	65	19.6	.140	.559	.064	.505	.425	.339	.912	.521	.091	.023	.105	.003	.017	.038	105.5	106.5	.465	1.3
09-10	SAS	29.9	79	19.7	.110	.525	.059	.534	.490	.357	.740	.542	.065	.028	.142	.006	.015	.046	104.0	106.9	.406	-0.3
10-11p	CHI	30.9	75	15.0	.129	.667	.061	.394	.459	.350	.799	.541	.070	.026	.125	.004	.015	.043	105.6	106.8	.461	1.1

Most similar to: Bobby Hansen (97.1), James Posey, Ime Udoka, Walter McCarty

IMP: 42% BRK: 2% COP: 4%

As the free-agent wing options dwindled during the summer, the Bulls were kind of stuck with Keith Bogans. Chicago is counting on him to be an above-average defender and a high-percentage stand-still shooter. He can help on the defense part, though he's not quite as good as his reputation. As a shooting specialist, he was miscast the last two seasons in Milwaukee and San Antonio. However, he was solid in that role when playing in the floor-spacing scheme in Orlando. As with so many players of his type, his usefulness is very much tied into how frequently he hits three-point shots. How much the Bulls get out of Bogans may depend on what kind of scheme new coach Tom Thibodeau hatches.

PF 5 — Carlos Boozer

Hght: 6'9" | Exp: 8 | Salary: $14.4 million
Wght: 266 | From: Duke
2011-12 status: guaranteed contract for $13.5 million

SKILL RATINGS

TOT	OFF	DEF	REB	PAS	HND	SHT	ATH
+4	+3	-4	+4	+4	+1	+2	+3

Year	Team	Age	G	MPG	Usg	3PA%	FTA%	INS	2P%	3P%	FT%	TS%	Reb%	Ast%	TO%	BLK%	STL%	PF%	oRTG	dRTG	Win%	WARP
07-08	UTA	26.4	81	34.9	.267	.001	.103	1.102	.547	.000	.738	.581	.181	.037	.125	.012	.016	.047	106.6	104.0	.586	9.9
08-09	UTA	27.4	37	32.4	.245	.000	.094	1.094	.490	.000	.698	.523	.192	.030	.121	.005	.016	.050	105.2	105.5	.492	1.9
09-10	UTA	28.4	78	34.3	.250	.000	.114	1.114	.562	–	.742	.599	.191	.042	.143	.011	.016	.046	106.8	104.1	.588	9.5
10-11p	CHI	29.4	59	34.0	.262	.004	.102	1.098	.532	.001	.730	.565	.174	.038	.134	.009	.016	.048	106.8	104.5	.575	6.6

Most similar to: Tom Gugliotta (96.6), Shawn Kemp, Brad Miller, Christian Laettner | IMP: 44% BRK: 4% COP: 4%

The Bulls have been searching for a prolific low-post scorer since Artis Gilmore was traded to San Antonio in 1982. Carlos Boozer may be the closest thing to a top-notch post player that the team has had in a long, long time. This point is arguable, of course. Bill Cartwright was a solid post option during Chicago's first three-peat in the '90s. Michael Jordan was outstanding in the post, but he wasn't a post player per se; he could score from anywhere. Boozer is not a classic back-to-the-basket player. He faces up with a nice little jumper from 15 feet and in, with the range to move back a little further. He's especially effective at finishing in the pick-and-roll, a necessity for elite big men in today's game. However you want to slot Boozer, he gives the Bulls an inside scoring threat that simply hasn't been there in recent seasons, and he frees up jack-of-all-trades Joakim Noah to go about taking care of all the little things. Boozer is also a dominant defensive rebounder because he's so strong and has such a low center of gravity that it's impossible to move him once he's established position. The chink in Boozer's armor is his defense. He's too short-armed to guard centers and doesn't move his feet well enough to effectively guard power forwards. Part of his defensive shortcomings in Utah may well be traced to playing alongside Mehmet Okur. If so, we'll be able to tell this season now that he's teamed with Noah. In any event, the Jazz consistently got 5-6 points better per 100 possessions on defense when Boozer went to the bench. A broken bone in Boozer's right hand will delay his Bulls' debut, which at least gives us the chance to compare their defense with and without the chiseled but oft-injured forward.

SG 11 — Ronnie Brewer

Hght: 6'7" | Exp: 4 | Salary: $4.8 million
Wght: 227 | From: Arkansas
2011-12 status: guaranteed contract for $4.7 million

SKILL RATINGS

TOT	OFF	DEF	REB	PAS	HND	SHT	ATH
+1	+1	-4	-2	0	+2	+1	+4

Year	Team	Age	G	MPG	Usg	3PA%	FTA%	INS	2P%	3P%	FT%	TS%	Reb%	Ast%	TO%	BLK%	STL%	PF%	oRTG	dRTG	Win%	WARP
07-08	UTA	23.1	76	27.5	.176	.061	.139	1.077	.587	.220	.759	.612	.064	.029	.085	.007	.028	.024	105.7	104.6	.537	5.2
08-09	UTA	24.1	81	32.2	.189	.078	.142	1.064	.537	.259	.702	.565	.069	.031	.101	.009	.027	.022	105.0	105.4	.487	3.8
09-10	MEM	25.1	58	30.0	.140	.057	.108	1.051	.505	.258	.639	.524	.063	.040	.098	.007	.026	.021	102.6	105.0	.419	0.1
10-11p	CHI	26.1	72	28.0	.175	.087	.128	1.042	.519	.278	.699	.547	.059	.036	.097	.007	.025	.021	104.5	104.9	.488	3.0

Most similar to: Sonny Parker (97.0), Marquis Daniels, Robert Reid, Josh Howard | IMP: 50% BRK: 4% COP: 11%

It's been a whirlwind 12 months for Ronnie Brewer, who likely began last season pretty secure in his future as Utah's starting shooting guard. First, he got off to a slow start, as his midrange game--which has been receding for two years--fell off a cliff. Brewer was still finishing at the rim, which he does as well as any guard in the league, but his foul rate dropped and his usage rate tumbled. Suddenly Brewer's averageish usage and high efficiency turned into low usage and below-average efficiency. His reputation for solid defense, which might be overstated, can't make up for that. Making matters worse, Brewer was getting outplayed by undrafted rookie Wesley Matthews. When the Jazz needed to trim its luxury-tax bill, Brewer was shipped to Memphis for a conditional first-round pick. He promptly tore his hamstring in his first game with the Grizzlies, who subsequently

CHICAGO BULLS

opted against submitting him a qualifying offer after the season. After shopping himself to several teams, including the Celtics and his old team in Utah, Brewer landed a three-year, $13.8 deal with the rising Bulls. It's a win-win deal for both sides. Brewer won't give the Bulls the floor spacer they could use, but he'll team with Luol Deng on the wing to give Chicago a pair of capable perimeter defenders. He'll also be a good running mate for Derrick Rose in transition while serving his old Jazz role of cutting to the hoop and finishing along the baseline as the fourth or fifth option in Chicago's half-court attack.

SF 9	Luol Deng	Hght: 6'9" Wght: 220 2011-12 status: guaranteed contract for $12.3 million	Exp: 6 From: Duke	Salary: $11.3 million		**SKILL RATINGS**							
						TOT	OFF	DEF	REB	PAS	HND	SHT	ATH
						+1	+1	+2	+2	0	-1	-1	+1

Year	Team	Age	G	MPG	Usg	3PA%	FTA%	INS	2P%	3P%	FT%	TS%	Reb%	Ast%	TO%	BLK%	STL%	PF%	oRTG	dRTG	Win%	WARP
07-08	CHI	23.0	63	33.7	.237	.019	.103	1.084	.482	.364	.770	.529	.105	.032	.106	.011	.012	.025	104.5	105.6	.465	2.1
08-09	CHI	24.0	49	34.0	.201	.027	.112	1.086	.450	.400	.796	.511	.101	.025	.096	.011	.018	.023	103.6	105.6	.436	0.7
09-10	CHI	25.0	70	37.9	.220	.064	.112	1.048	.474	.386	.764	.531	.107	.024	.104	.018	.013	.022	104.2	105.0	.471	3.0
10-11p	CHI	26.0	72	35.0	.229	.057	.108	1.051	.469	.407	.796	.529	.100	.026	.101	.014	.013	.022	104.3	105.2	.471	2.9

Most similar to: Clarence Weatherspoon (98.6), Antawn Jamison, Reggie Lewis, Lionel Simmons   IMP: 53%   BRK: 5%   COP: 7%

Luol Deng is in an unfortunate situation in that he's so maligned as overpaid--and he is--that he doesn't get credit for how good he is. The problem is that Deng is a three-win player. He's paid like a six-win player. That's not his fault. He's been more or less the same player his entire career. Maybe perceptions of Deng will shift this year, as his offensive burden is lightened by the addition of Carlos Boozer. Deng is at his best at the basket, where he finishes well and draws fouls, and behind the three-point line, where he shoots a much better percentage than for which he's given credit. The problem in his game under Vinny Del Negro, as with many Bulls, was that he spent too much time in between, where he shoots right about league average. Instead of taking 46 percent of his shots from 16-23 feet, Deng needs to cut that to about 25 percent while moving the missing portion of his shots back a few feet. His ability to put the ball on the floor against close-outs will make him more than a typical spot-up shooter. A better offensive scheme is the best bet for Deng to take his offense to another level of efficiency. On the other end of the floor, Deng's above-average athleticism and exceptional reach make him a top-notch defensive small forward.

PF 22	Taj Gibson	Hght: 6'9" Wght: 225 2011-12 status: team option for $1.2 million	Exp: 1 From: USC	Salary: $1.1 million		**SKILL RATINGS**							
						TOT	OFF	DEF	REB	PAS	HND	SHT	ATH
						0	0	+1	+2	-3	-4	-1	0

Year	Team	Age	G	MPG	Usg	3PA%	FTA%	INS	2P%	3P%	FT%	TS%	Reb%	Ast%	TO%	BLK%	STL%	PF%	oRTG	dRTG	Win%	WARP
09-10	CHI	24.8	82	26.9	.168	.000	.094	1.094	.494	-	.646	.521	.154	.014	.139	.036	.011	.058	103.3	104.8	.451	1.5
10-11p	CHI	25.8	76	25.0	.183	.000	.097	1.097	.484	.000	.655	.513	.145	.015	.137	.034	.011	.056	103.1	104.9	.438	0.9

Most similar to: Cadillac Anderson (98.6), Roy Hinson, James Bailey, Chris Kaman   IMP: 40%   BRK: 9%   COP: 6%

Taj Gibson was one of the surprise rookies in the NBA last season. Now the question is how much better he can get given that he was old for a rookie. Gibson supplied the shot blocking that his college translations suggested he would bring. He also was a better rebounder than anticipated and was surprisingly effective as a one-on-one defender. On offense, he was better in some respects, with a face-up jumper that proved dependable as long as he didn't venture outside of 12 feet or so, which he did a little too frequently. His post-up game was also much more polished than everyone thought it would be. Gibson's transition to super sub will be pushed back a few weeks. With Carlos Boozer sitting out with a broken bone in his right hand, Gibson will be starting alongside Joakim Noah early in the season just like last year. Once Boozer returns, Gibson will be the top reserve at the big man positions, and still should see 22-23 minutes per game. If Gibson doesn't improve from here, the Bulls still have a keeper and one of the league's better reserve bigs. If he improves his offensive efficiency, he'll be even more than that.

CHICAGO BULLS

PF 16 — James Johnson

Hght: 6'9"	Exp: 1	Salary: $1.7 million
Wght: 245	From: Wake Forest	
2011-12 status: team option for $1.8 million		

SKILL RATINGS

TOT	OFF	DEF	REB	PAS	HND	SHT	ATH
0	0	0	-4	+3	-1	0	+2

Year	Team	Age	G	MPG	Usg	3PA%	FTA%	INS	2P%	3P%	FT%	TS%	Reb%	Ast%	TO%	BLK%	STL%	PF%	oRTG	dRTG	Win%	WARP
09-10	CHI	23.2	65	11.6	.181	.152	.102	.950	.488	.326	.729	.532	.093	.029	.205	.043	.014	.075	102.4	105.4	.400	-0.3
10-11p	CHI	24.2	76	6.2	.194	.109	.111	1.002	.499	.320	.753	.544	.092	.030	.179	.044	.014	.068	103.3	105.1	.440	0.2

Most similar to: Brad Lohaus (97.1), James Hardy, Viktor Khryapa, Brian Skinner   IMP: 76%   BRK: 28%   COP: 4%

James Johnson was a bit of a reach at No. 16 in the 2009 Draft. He's a tweener forward, is old for a prospect considering his lack of polish and lacks that one offensive skill you'd like him to be able to build around. The Bulls reportedly have tried to trade him for everybody from Rudy Fernandez to Carmelo Anthony, and that Johnson and a bundle of draft picks wasn't a good enough bounty probably says a lot about Johnson's perceived upside around the league. His rookie season was a disappointment. He couldn't find regular minutes under Vinny Del Negro, who admitted that he bungled Johnson's development. Johnson did get better as the season progressed, so hope is not lost. He's a good athlete, with surprisingly good upcourt speed and passing ability. He's got all the qualities a player needs to be a good defender, if he can improve his footwork enough to handle small forwards. Johnson doesn't have the worst three-point stroke in the world, but he probably needs to become more proficient inside the arc before he falls in love with the area behind it.

SG 26 — Kyle Korver

Hght: 6'7"	Exp: 7	Salary: $5.0 million
Wght: 212	From: Creighton	
2011-12 status: guaranteed contract for $5.0 million		

SKILL RATINGS

TOT	OFF	DEF	REB	PAS	HND	SHT	ATH
+2	+3	+4	0	0	0	+4	-3

Year	Team	Age	G	MPG	Usg	3PA%	FTA%	INS	2P%	3P%	FT%	TS%	Reb%	Ast%	TO%	BLK%	STL%	PF%	oRTG	dRTG	Win%	WARP
07-08	UTA	27.1	75	23.1	.183	.419	.081	.662	.516	.375	.915	.585	.060	.026	.106	.014	.011	.051	105.6	106.9	.455	1.4
08-09	UTA	28.1	78	24.0	.170	.378	.079	.701	.485	.386	.882	.572	.082	.033	.128	.013	.013	.041	105.7	106.9	.463	1.8
09-10	UTA	29.1	52	18.3	.163	.320	.063	.743	.465	.536	.796	.620	.068	.042	.122	.010	.014	.036	106.1	106.5	.489	1.4
10-11p	CHI	30.1	71	24.0	.177	.373	.067	.694	.468	.437	.837	.584	.065	.036	.124	.012	.012	.042	106.4	106.5	.495	2.8

Most similar to: Eric Piatkowski (98.1), Kelly Tripucka, Tracy Murray, Brian Winters   IMP: 35%   BRK: 5%   COP: 9%

The Bulls signed Kyle Korver to be the floor-spacing three-point shooter that they so desperately needed. Nobody does it better. One of the things that makes Korver a cut above other shooting specialists is his ability to step inside the arc when the close-outs get too aggressive. He shoots 46-49 percent on long twos, and while you wouldn't want that to be the basis for an offense, he's one of the few players who make that shot a good idea. Korver is not going to create a lot of his own offense, as generally 90 percent of his field goals come off of assists. However, he makes himself available by working tirelessly without the ball. Korver is also more than capable of putting the ball on the floor and finishing at the rim if a lane comes open. On defense, our metrics suggest he's better than his reputation, though +4 is probably a reach. He's closer to average than he is to terrible, and until last year, could be counted to rank high in the league in charges drawn. Korver is an ideal role player who will play under a very cap-friendly deal for the next three years in Chicago.

PG 15 — John Lucas III

Hght: 5'11"	Exp: 2	Salary: $0.5 million
Wght: 165	From: Oklahoma State	
2011-12 status: free agent		

SKILL RATINGS

TOT	OFF	DEF	REB	PAS	HND	SHT	ATH
--	--	--	--	--	--	--	--

John Lucas III hasn't graced NBA courts since 2007, but he heads to the Bulls' camp with a chance to win a job as end-of-the-bench depth behind Derrick Rose and C.J. Watson. Lucas probably earned that invite with a sterling performance in the NBA Summer League, where he shot 10-of-14 from behind the arc. If he can prove to be a 40 percent three-point shooter, he might well stick.

CHICAGO BULLS

C 13	**Joakim Noah**	Hght: 6'11" Wght: 232	Exp: 3 From: Florida	Salary: $3.1 million							
		2011-12 status: guaranteed contract for $12 million									

SKILL RATINGS

TOT	OFF	DEF	REB	PAS	HND	SHT	ATH
+4	+2	0	+3	+4	+3	0	+2

Year	Team	Age	G	MPG	Usg	3PA%	FTA%	INS	2P%	3P%	FT%	TS%	Reb%	Ast%	TO%	BLK%	STL%	PF%	oRTG	dRTG	Win%	WARP
07-08	CHI	23.2	74	20.7	.157	.002	.158	1.156	.484	.000	.691	.539	.154	.024	.164	.033	.020	.051	104.2	103.5	.524	3.4
08-09	CHI	24.2	80	24.2	.124	.002	.150	1.148	.558	.000	.676	.594	.179	.025	.154	.041	.013	.055	106.4	104.4	.566	6.0
09-10	CHI	25.2	64	30.1	.172	.000	.131	1.131	.504	--	.744	.557	.203	.031	.160	.040	.008	.046	105.8	103.4	.579	6.5
10-11p	CHI	26.2	73	30.0	.168	.004	.142	1.138	.508	.004	.729	.560	.174	.030	.155	.037	.011	.048	105.5	103.9	.553	6.3

Most similar to: Antonio Davis (97.6), Dale Davis, LaSalle Thompson, Emeka Okafor — IMP: 52% BRK: 4% COP: 2%

Joakim Noah was one of the NBA's most improved players last season and was rewarded with a five-year, $60 million extension just before the start of preseason that will keep him in a Bulls uniform for the foreseeable future. He's worth the investment, and the Bulls think so highly of their defensive anchor that they reportedly fell out of the running for Carmelo Anthony because of their unwillingness to part with Noah. He's an excellent shot blocker, a solid one-on-one defender who improves as he gets stronger and is a decent bet to lead the NBA in rebounding one of these seasons. Noah is also useful on the offensive end, more so last year than ever before. He's a willing and gifted passer, though he needs to improve his hands and cut his turnover rate. Noah has been developing a nice little jump hook as a go-to move on the block, and is dangerous, if inconsistent, finishing on the pick-and-roll. Noah is in the league's upper crust of big men when it comes to running the floor. Last season, he even added a midrange jumper that he hit at a better-than-average rate, and improved his free-throw shooting. His offensive role could diminish this season with the addition of Carlos Boozer, but his efficiency could soar. A tireless worker and a good bet to keep getting better, Noah is a solid foundation player for a contending team.

PF 35	**Chris Richard**	Hght: 6'9" Wght: 270	Exp: 2 From: Florida	Salary: --							
		2011-12 status: free agent									

SKILL RATINGS

TOT	OFF	DEF	REB	PAS	HND	SHT	ATH
-3	--	+1	--	--	--	--	--

Year	Team	Age	G	MPG	Usg	3PA%	FTA%	INS	2P%	3P%	FT%	TS%	Reb%	Ast%	TO%	BLK%	STL%	PF%	oRTG	dRTG	Win%	WARP
07-08	MIN	23.3	52	10.7	.100	.000	.097	1.097	.471	.000	.593	.496	.142	.015	.189	.017	.008	.069	101.4	106.7	.328	-1.0
09-10	CHI	25.3	18	12.4	.097	.000	.101	1.101	.517	--	.636	.547	.146	.014	.293	.014	.018	.101	100.7	106.9	.302	-0.5
10-11p	CHI	26.3	76	--	.107	.015	.089	1.075	.470	.014	.616	.487	.132	.017	.175	.016	.008	.067	--	--	.377	--

Most similar to: Mark Madsen (98.0), Eric Leckner, Tom LaGarde, Mike Brown — IMP: 54% BRK: 10% COP: 6%

Joakim Noah's former teammate on two national title teams at Florida found the going tough in a reunion with his college pal. Richard is a banger who can help on the glass, but he's got limited athletic ability, which inhibits his performance on the defensive end. On offense, he's going to give you little more than the occasional garbage bucket. He returns to Chicago for training camp with no guarantees on a roster spot.

PG 1	**Derrick Rose**	Hght: 6'3" Wght: 190	Exp: 2 From: Memphis	Salary: $5.5 million							
		2011-12 status: team option for $7.0 million									

SKILL RATINGS

TOT	OFF	DEF	REB	PAS	HND	SHT	ATH
+3	+4	-2	0	+2	0	0	-1

Year	Team	Age	G	MPG	Usg	3PA%	FTA%	INS	2P%	3P%	FT%	TS%	Reb%	Ast%	TO%	BLK%	STL%	PF%	oRTG	dRTG	Win%	WARP
08-09	CHI	20.5	81	37.0	.227	.047	.072	1.025	.491	.222	.788	.516	.060	.077	.133	.004	.011	.019	106.5	107.5	.465	3.1
09-10	CHI	21.5	78	36.8	.274	.035	.086	1.051	.500	.267	.766	.532	.056	.074	.125	.007	.010	.015	106.8	106.7	.503	5.1
10-11p	CHI	22.5	75	37.0	.280	.049	.080	1.031	.500	.259	.780	.530	.054	.081	.126	.006	.010	.015	107.5	106.7	.525	6.3

Most similar to: Tony Parker (97.0), Stephon Marbury, Mike Bibby, Kobe Bryant — IMP: 64% BRK: 6% COP: 3%

Derrick Rose has everything you'd want in a cornerstone player for a championship team except the objective record to indicate he's really that good. If he's not now, there is little doubt he's going to get there. One of the league's hardest-working and most humble young stars, Rose spent the offseason developing his three-point shot before becoming a key piece of the U.S. squad that won gold in the FIBA World Championship. He's one of the quickest, fastest and most explosive players in a league full of those types. Why then, does he draw the skill rating of a below-average athlete? First off, Rose is a conservative defender who doesn't gamble or read passing lanes well enough to pick up a lot of steals. He doesn't help out much on the boards and is a little too good at avoiding contact when he drives the lane. This latter aspect is most germane to Rose improving his efficiency. He gets into the lane, then hangs and twists to throw up miraculous-looking shots and avoid defenders. That looks good on the highlight reel, but Rose would be better off just attacking the rim, something he's become more adept at doing. He did improve his midrange shooting percentages last season, so a three-point shot would give him the full arsenal. Rose has taken a higher share of the scoring load than he prefers, as he's a willing passer who still has work to do in learning how to read the floor. New Bulls coach Tom Thibodeau should install a system that takes better advantage of Rose's developing playmaking skills. Perhaps most importantly, Rose will have better talent around him and will be able to focus on improving his all-around game. This should be the season Rose's metrics fall in line his reputation.

PF 24 — Brian Scalabrine

Hght: 6'9" Wght: 235 Exp: 9 From: USC Salary: --
2011-12 status: free agent

SKILL RATINGS

TOT	OFF	DEF	REB	PAS	HND	SHT	ATH
-4	0	-1	-5	+2	+4	-2	-5

Year	Team	Age	G	MPG	Usg	3PA%	FTA%	INS	2P%	3P%	FT%	TS%	Reb%	Ast%	TO%	BLK%	STL%	PF%	oRTG	dRTG	Win%	WARP
07-08	BOS	30.1	48	10.7	.118	.357	.068	.711	.292	.326	.750	.428	.090	.037	.202	.013	.008	.057	102.3	107.1	.343	-0.8
08-09	BOS	31.1	39	12.9	.125	.455	.059	.604	.453	.393	.889	.558	.058	.017	.090	.016	.007	.068	104.4	108.7	.364	-0.6
09-10	BOS	32.1	52	9.1	.105	.468	.025	.557	.361	.327	.667	.445	.061	.027	.162	.007	.010	.059	101.9	108.2	.303	-1.1
10-11p	CHI	33.1	73	5.0	.114	.518	.050	.531	.362	.355	.772	.497	.063	.026	.144	.011	.008	.062	103.7	108.2	.356	-0.5

Most similar to: Sean Elliott (91.6), Scott Wedman, Danny Ferry, Jeff Turner

IMP: 61% BRK: 9% COP: 17%

Brian Scalabrine's good work ethic and willingness to do the dirty work for a team are positive traits that may no longer offset his limited skill set. Perhaps they never did. In a pinch, he's capable enough as a defender to fill in for a few minutes here and there as a floor-spacing four. He's headed to training camp with the Bulls, who would no doubt like Scalabrine to help Chicago adapt to the systems of former Celtics assistant Tom Thibodeau. That he's lasted nine years in the NBA already is a testament to … something. If Scalabrine is going to find a foothold in Chicago, he'll need to take advantage of Carlos Boozer's early absence because of a broken bone in his hand.

C 40 — Kurt Thomas

Hght: 6'9" Wght: 230 Exp: 15 From: Texas Christian Salary: $1.8 million
2011-12 status: free agent

SKILL RATINGS

TOT	OFF	DEF	REB	PAS	HND	SHT	ATH
-3	-2	+3	0	+1	+3	-2	-2

Year	Team	Age	G	MPG	Usg	3PA%	FTA%	INS	2P%	3P%	FT%	TS%	Reb%	Ast%	TO%	BLK%	STL%	PF%	oRTG	dRTG	Win%	WARP
07-08	SAS	35.5	70	22.6	.145	.002	.074	1.072	.494	.000	.663	.514	.188	.020	.096	.027	.017	.057	103.1	102.8	.510	3.1
08-09	SAS	36.5	79	17.8	.127	.005	.054	1.049	.507	.000	.822	.530	.171	.023	.115	.031	.013	.059	104.3	104.8	.485	2.0
09-10	MIL	37.5	70	15.0	.114	.000	.025	1.025	.476	-	.800	.489	.161	.020	.183	.034	.013	.069	101.0	104.5	.383	-0.7
10-11p	CHI	38.5	76	12.0	.117	.003	.036	1.034	.470	.000	.788	.484	.150	.020	.156	.028	.014	.067	101.4	105.0	.380	-0.7

Most similar to: Buck Williams (97.3), Caldwell Jones, Kevin Willis, Otis Thorpe

IMP: 38% BRK: 0% COP: 14%

One of Kurt Thomas' teammates his rookie year was 14-year veteran Danny Schayes, who was once teammates with Dan Issel, who played with Paul Silas, who played with Bob Pettit, was born in the early years of the Great Depression. This is an exaggerated way of saying that Thomas has been around a long, long time. He's still a rock-solid defender at 38 who closes off the defensive glass and picks up a few blocks in help defense. On offense, he sets screens and stands around, but if you double off him, Thomas will drill the open jump shot. Thomas fell below replacement level last season, mostly because his success from 10 feet and in waned. If that's a matter of declining athleticism, then he may not be much help to the Bulls except in short stints. If he can get back some of that ability to finish putbacks and score off the occasional pick-and-roll, he'll be a solid option as the primary backup to Joakim Noah. Thomas will see key minutes early in the season while Carlos Boozer recovers from a broken bone in his right hand.

CHICAGO BULLS

PG	**C.J.**	Hght: 6'2"	Exp: 3	Salary: $3.6 million		**SKILL RATINGS**						
	Watson	Wght: 175	From: Tennessee			TOT	OFF	DEF	REB	PAS	HND	SHT	ATH
32		2011-12 status: guaranteed contract for $3.4 million				+2	+3	+3	-2	-3	0	+1	+2

Year	Team	Age	G	MPG	Usg	3PA%	FTA%	INS	2P%	3P%	FT%	TS%	Reb%	Ast%	TO%	BLK%	STL%	PF%	oRTG	dRTG	Win%	WARP
07-08	GSW	24.0	32	11.4	.152	.197	.097	.900	.453	.346	.793	.519	.047	.039	.137	.000	.017	.022	103.7	106.6	.404	-0.1
08-09	GSW	25.0	77	24.5	.168	.162	.115	.953	.473	.400	.870	.564	.055	.047	.125	.001	.024	.031	105.8	106.8	.468	2.0
09-10	GSW	26.0	65	27.5	.161	.216	.109	.893	.527	.310	.771	.555	.053	.043	.103	.003	.027	.030	105.1	105.7	.479	2.3
10-11p	CHI	27.0	73	18.0	.175	.268	.109	.841	.490	.365	.814	.561	.049	.044	.111	.002	.023	.028	106.0	105.9	.505	2.4

Most similar to: Sedale Threatt (97.2), Smush Parker, Steve Colter, Tony Smith — IMP: 51% BRK: 9% COP: 7%

As the Bulls' roster began taking shape in the offseason, it became apparent that they needed a backup for Derrick Rose, as well as a scoring focal point for its second unit. C.J. Watson fills both needs. He's been a low-usage player for most of his career, but will likely become more of a designated gunner in the Bulls' rotation. Watson is a good percentage shooter with limited range, which is something he needs to improve. Watson's ability to shoot closer to .400 on three-pointers, which he did in 2008-09, than the .310 mark he posted last season will determine just how effective he ends up being. Watson is quick off the dribble and an excellent finisher, with an above-average foul-drawing rate. He also posted high steal rates the last two seasons in Golden State, though he probably won't be allowed to gamble as much in Chicago. Watson will be an ideal third guard for the Bulls because he can run the offense, create shots for himself and play off the ball alongside Derrick Rose for stretches. His streak shooting will give the Bulls the element they lost when Ben Gordon left before last season.

SG	**Kyle**	Hght: 6'6"	Exp: 2	Salary: --		**SKILL RATINGS**						
	Weaver	Wght: 201	From: Washington State			TOT	OFF	DEF	REB	PAS	HND	SHT	ATH
25		2011-12 status: free agent				-1	--	+2	--	--	--	--	--

Year	Team	Age	G	MPG	Usg	3PA%	FTA%	INS	2P%	3P%	FT%	TS%	Reb%	Ast%	TO%	BLK%	STL%	PF%	oRTG	dRTG	Win%	WARP
08-09	OKC	22.4	56	20.8	.130	.273	.075	.802	.529	.344	.707	.551	.065	.039	.203	.016	.020	.031	103.7	106.0	.424	0.2
09-10	OKC	23.4	12	12.0	.124	.479	.067	.587	.357	.368	.833	.505	.070	.035	.101	.031	.021	.041	104.4	104.3	.504	0.3
10-11p	CHI	24.4	75	--	.142	.310	.069	.758	.518	.348	.707	.544	.062	.040	.195	.020	.019	.030	-	-	.417	-

Most similar to: Michael Cooper (97.2), Blue Edwards, Francisco Garcia, Tom Garrick — IMP: 54% BRK: 11% COP: 5%

Kyle Weaver was a victim of the numbers game in Oklahoma City. He actually started much of his rookie season before Thabo Sefolosha pushed him to the bench. The addition of James Harden knocked Weaver out of the rotation entirely. Add in a separated shoulder that kept him out half the season and Weaver played just 144 minutes in 2009-10.

Weaver showed promise as a rookie thanks to his versatility. He's a good passer for the wing and has the ability to develop into a quality one-on-one defender. A lack of scoring punch is holding Weaver back. He's only average as an outside shooter, and the driving lanes he thrived in at Washington State just aren't open in the pros. Still, Weaver belongs on a roster somewhere as a fifth wing. Waived in July, Weaver spent the summer holding out hope for an NBA offer and passed up a deal to join Maccabi Tel Aviv. He is headed to training camp with the Bulls, but doesn't appear to be a good fit since Chicago needs shooting on the wing.

SG	**Devin**	Hght: 6'5"	Exp: 8	Salary: --		**SKILL RATINGS**						
	Brown	Wght: 220	From: Texas-San Antonio			TOT	OFF	DEF	REB	PAS	HND	SHT	ATH
--		2011-12 status: free agent				-2	0	+4	+2	-1	-3	-3	-1

Year	Team	Age	G	MPG	Usg	3PA%	FTA%	INS	2P%	3P%	FT%	TS%	Reb%	Ast%	TO%	BLK%	STL%	PF%	oRTG	dRTG	Win%	WARP
07-08	CLE	29.3	78	22.6	.180	.211	.090	.879	.447	.308	.754	.494	.086	.045	.142	.003	.014	.039	103.8	106.5	.412	-0.1
08-09	NOH	30.3	63	13.8	.230	.236	.107	.871	.384	.289	.780	.459	.083	.030	.131	.005	.020	.045	102.9	106.9	.370	-0.8
09-10	CHI	31.3	50	21.2	.200	.356	.082	.726	.396	.354	.802	.500	.069	.028	.135	.004	.016	.031	103.9	106.8	.404	-0.3
10-11p	AVG	32.3	71	21.2	.185	.303	.091	.788	.409	.344	.772	.497	.075	.031	.141	.004	.016	.039	103.4	106.6	.397	-0.6

Most similar to: Kevin Edwards (98.3), Blue Edwards, Derek Anderson, Mike Sanders — IMP: 53% BRK: 17% COP: 3%

Devin Brown's run as a below-replacement, quasi-defensive specialist may have come to an end. He was traded to the Bulls last winter, but despite the team's desperate needs for a solid off-the-bench wing player, Brown found himself inactive more often than not. He played just two minutes in the postseason.

PG --	Lindsey Hunter		Hght: 6'2" Wght: 170 2011-12 status: free agent		Exp: 17 From: Texas		Salary: --				**SKILL RATINGS**							
											TOT	OFF	DEF	REB	PAS	HND	SHT	ATH
											--	--	--	--	--	--	--	--

Year	Team	Age	G	MPG	Usg	3PA%	FTA%	INS	2P%	3P%	FT%	TS%	Reb%	Ast%	TO%	BLK%	STL%	PF%	oRTG	dRTG	Win%	WARP
07-08	DET	37.4	24	9.0	.178	.321	.049	.728	.395	.269	.778	.427	.036	.072	.161	.007	.029	.067	103.3	106.1	.406	0.0
08-09	CHI	38.4	28	9.5	.174	.465	.021	.556	.324	.333	.600	.433	.026	.062	.184	.003	.038	.047	103.7	106.0	.425	0.0
09-10	CHI	39.4	13	9.4	.129	.373	.025	.653	.235	.077	1.000	.210	.063	.033	.115	.000	.004	.044	97.5	108.6	.181	-0.6

Lindsey Hunter made a natural transition from a veteran player who only saw the court in an emergency to a job as an assistant coach/player development specialist with Chicago. Hunter's 17-year playing career stretched all the way back to the days when he was Isiah Thomas' last backup in Detroit. He won two championship rings and earned a reputation as one of the most respected personalities in the game.

SG --	Ronald Murray		Hght: 6'4" Wght: 190 2011-12 status: free agent		Exp: 8 From: Shaw		Salary: --				**SKILL RATINGS**							
											TOT	OFF	DEF	REB	PAS	HND	SHT	ATH
											-1	0	0	-2	+2	-1	-2	+1

Year	Team	Age	G	MPG	Usg	3PA%	FTA%	INS	2P%	3P%	FT%	TS%	Reb%	Ast%	TO%	BLK%	STL%	PF%	oRTG	dRTG	Win%	WARP
07-08	IND	28.7	42	20.8	.246	.127	.087	.960	.441	.317	.694	.483	.053	.072	.170	.003	.019	.025	103.6	106.0	.421	0.1
08-09	ATL	29.7	80	24.7	.245	.236	.100	.864	.485	.360	.760	.543	.050	.038	.125	.007	.023	.041	105.5	106.6	.461	1.8
09-10	CHI	30.7	75	22.3	.237	.257	.099	.842	.431	.312	.727	.485	.063	.037	.106	.008	.014	.035	103.8	106.6	.405	-0.4
10-11p	AVG	31.7	75	22.3	.227	.275	.089	.815	.439	.335	.710	.498	.056	.044	.134	.008	.017	.036	103.8	106.4	.416	0.0

Most similar to: Mike Woodson (98.5), Blue Edwards, John Long, Jim Paxson   IMP: 36%   BRK: 6%   COP: 9%

Flip Murray gave the Bulls some scoring punch after coming over from Charlotte last season. He doesn't really play defense and can't run the point, and his streak shooting appears unlikely to attract another significant NBA contract. At press time, he was reportedly shopping his services overseas.

Cleveland Cavaliers

There is no playbook for what the Cleveland Cavaliers are attempting to do in 2010-11. Only the 1996-97 Orlando Magic can truly empathize with losing one of the league's top players in his prime in free agency with nothing in return, but the Magic had the luxury of retaining another young star in Anfernee Hardaway when Shaquille O'Neal bolted for Los Angeles. When LeBron James announced he was taking his talents to South Beach, Cleveland was left with a group of role players built to surround James that now must stand on its own.

The lingering question is just how big a role the shortcomings of that supporting cast played in James' decision to leave. General manager Danny Ferry put better pieces around James the last two seasons, and the addition of Mo Williams made the Cavaliers one of the league's elite teams. Cleveland posted the league's top regular-season record each of the last two seasons, as well as its best point differential in 2008-09, yet the mix that was so successful in the regular season crumbled in playoff series losses to Orlando in the 2009 Eastern Conference Finals and to Boston in last year's semifinals.

The collapse against the Celtics was stunning in its swiftness; after blowing out Boston in Game Three, the Cavaliers seemed to be well on their way to a rematch with Orlando, even when the Celtics evened the series at home. Game Five may be seen in hindsight as the turning point for an entire franchise. Cleveland followed the listless lead of James and was blown out on its home floor in what turned out to be James' last home game at Quicken Loans Arena. James' triple-double wasn't enough to keep the Cavaliers alive in an elimination game in Boston.

Removing the storyline of James' odd behavior during the series, however, the result was largely similar to what happened to Cleveland the previous year in the Eastern Conference Finals. An elite defense held James in check (lest you believe this a personal failing on James' part, compare his performance to Kobe Bryant's in the NBA Finals) and the team's other scorers were unable to pick up the slack. Williams shot 21.1 percent from three-point range in the series and was held to single digits twice, while trade-deadline pickup Antawn Jamison was thoroughly outplayed by Kevin Garnett at both ends of the floor. Only Shaquille O'Neal really troubled the Celtics besides James.

Without the hope of a championship keeping him at home, majority owner Dan Gilbert shifted into desperation mode to try to convince James to re-sign with the Cavaliers. Head coach Mike Brown was the first casualty, getting a pink slip 10 days after the season ended--just before his salary for 2010-11 became guaranteed. The 2008-09 Coach of the Year had Cleveland among the league's top defenses even when the team's talent was substandard (you'll recall Sasha Pavlovic starting throughout the surprise run to the 2007 NBA Finals), but Brown had a difficult time

CAVALIERS IN A BOX

Last year's record	61-21
Last year's Offensive Rating	113.3 (4)
Last year's Defensive Rating	105.7 (7)
Last year's point differential	6.5 (2)
Team pace	89.8 (25)
SCHOENE projection	**39-43 (8)**
Projected Offensive Rating	110.0 (17)
Projected Defensive Rating	110.7 (20)
Projected team weighted age	29.0 (8)
Projected '10-11 payroll	$52.8 (26)
Est. payroll obligations, '11-12	$49.3 (22)

Head coach: Byron Scott

Scott was fired nine games into the 2009-10 season, when the Hornets' 3-6 start had made clear what was suspected after New Orleans flamed out in the 2009 postseason: Despite maintaining the ear of Chris Paul, Scott had lost the team. Something similar happened in New Jersey, though in this case Scott did himself no favors with his inability to develop young talent. The last straw for Scott might have been his unwillingness to use rookies Darren Collison and Marcus Thornton; he preferred the inferior Bobby Brown and Devin Brown. Still, Scott gets another chance in Cleveland.

making adjustments when the Cavaliers struggled in the playoffs.

Next out was Ferry, who chose to resign rather than watch Gilbert take on a larger role in running the team's basketball operations and was replaced by deputy Chris Grant. Make no mistake, though, the decision on a replacement for Brown was all Gilbert's. The Michigan State grad put on a full-court press to lure Tom Izzo to the NBA only to see Izzo pass when James was unwilling to meet with him. After flirting with Lakers assistant Brian Shaw, Cleveland ultimately settled on veteran Byron Scott, the most accomplished coach on the market.

Eventually, the Cavaliers had nothing to do but wait on the decision by James. It's not clear they ever had a chance. Reporting by Yahoo!'s Adrian Wojnarowski and Brian Windhorst of *The Plain Dealer* since "The Decision" has indicated that James had toyed with the notion of teaming up with Chris Bosh and Dwyane Wade since the three played together for the U.S. National Team in the 2006 FIBA World Championship and decided to sign extensions that would allow them to opt out in the summer of 2010.

The scenario surely became more palatable as each playoff exit made Cleveland's limitations clearer to James. The Cavaliers would never realistically have the chance to pair him with another superstar short of sacrificing a season or two to clear room under the cap. Their last best chance came at the deadline, when they passed on a possible Amar'e Stoudemire trade in favor of Jamison, seemingly a better fit in the Cleveland frontcourt.

The Cavaliers would have been left with a vicious cycle of chasing short-term upgrades like Jamison and O'Neal, players their former teams were willing to jettison because of their contracts. That might have been enough for James to win a championship or two, but his best chance of building a legacy as a winner always meant leaving Cleveland.

So now, after seven seasons of James being the focal point of everything the Cavaliers did, they are forced to contemplate life without him. The cupboard is hardly bare. Cleveland had talent under contract at every position and a pair of players (Jamison and Williams) capable of stepping into larger roles on offense. Still, the Cavaliers will make some adjustments. Scott has said he wants to push the pace, which was one of the NBA's slowest under Brown, who favored half-court execution on both ends. Scott's Hornets were even slower, but his New Jersey teams were faster than league average.

A faster pace is ideal for J.J. Hickson, Cleveland's most promising youngster. Hickson made major strides during his second season, and holding on to him was a major factor in the Cavaliers electing to trade for Jamison instead of other, more valuable targets. Buried after the Jamison trade, Hickson was effective in his postseason cameos and is now due for a larger role. It appears he could even start ahead of Jamison, who would shift to a sixth man role.

Scott has options in the frontcourt, if not a tremendous amount of size. Anderson Varejao will likely step into the starting role at center after emerging as one of the league's most valuable reserves. The only other true center under contract is newcomer Ryan Hollins, which means the 6'9" Hickson could end up playing the middle in certain smaller, quicker lineups. Cleveland could go the other direction by giving Jamison spot minutes at small forward against slower, bigger three-men. Leon Powe is also in the mix for playing time in the frontcourt, having successfully returned from ACL surgery during the second half of last season. With O'Neal and Zydrunas Ilgauskas in the picture, the Cavaliers' frontcourt was far too crowded for Powe to break into the rotation last season, but he's too good not to play this year.

Cleveland turned its main offseason attention to the backcourt. The Cavaliers signed restricted free agent Kyle Lowry to a four-year offer sheet the Houston Rockets quickly matched. To add creativity at the point, Cleveland ultimately dealt for Ramon Sessions, the odd man out in Minnesota. A terrible fit for the Timberwolves' triangle offense, Sessions thrived as a pick-and-roll point guard with the Bucks and has the size and ability to team with Williams in a quick backcourt that would allow Williams to play off the ball and focus on scoring.

The Cavaliers also offered their mid-level exception to free agent small forward Matt Barnes, who decided to take less money in order to have a better chance of winning a championship with the Los Angeles Lakers. Instead, Cleveland went with a lower-rent option in Joey Graham. Graham will figure into the rotation at the three along with Jamario Moon and Anthony Parker, who will probably start at shooting guard and split time between both wing positions.

The Cavaliers' goals will have to shift dramatically. Without James, the team is no longer competing for championships. Still, there's no reason this Cleveland group should not reasonably aspire to reach the playoffs. SCHOENE sees this group as essentially league average on both ends of the floor, which would be enough to be one of the East's top eight teams. Depth is a strength, as the team boasts a nine-man rotation with every player solidly above replacement level.

The bigger question is where the Cavaliers go from here. They have a year to use the enormous trade exception generated by signing-and-trading James to Miami, which could bring in a big name or be used to take on salary from a team over the luxury tax in exchange for picks and other assets. The latter seems more likely, since Cleveland needs to rebuild its core with young talent. Sessions was a good start in that regard. He and Hickson give the Cavaliers a pair of possible building blocks in their 20s. Cleveland will have its own first-round pick next June and brought over its 2009 first-round selection, Congolese forward Christian Eyenga, to begin his development in the U.S., most likely in the D-League.

Looking ahead, the Cavaliers will be able to get under the cap by the summer of 2012, when Jamison's contract will end. Depending on whether Williams opts out of the final two years of his contract next summer, Varejao could be left as the team's only player making more than $5 million. Between now and then, Cleveland has the opportunity to pursue a soft rebuild. Starting over is probably not advisable with a fan base that is impatient after the departure of their once beloved hometown star, but the Cavaliers can remain competitive while developing young talent and making decisions that maintain flexibility.

The silliest of the reactions to James' departure was the suggestion that the NBA might be in trouble in Cleveland. Hard as it may be to believe, the Cavaliers were around for three-plus decades before James' arrival on the scene. While they have certainly contributed to the Cleveland sports curse, the Cavaliers have put together competitive teams in the past (most notably in the early '90s under Lenny Wilkens) and will do so again, with or without James.

Kevin Pelton

From the Blogosphere

Who: John Krolik
What: Cavs: The Blog
Where: http://www.cavstheblog.com/

Well, LeBron James is gone, and the Cavaliers won't be title contenders again for a while. However, Dan Gilbert and Co. aren't ready to go into rebuilding mode just yet. Instead, the team is going to try and sneak into the playoffs with a new point guard, a new coach and a new philosophy. Replacing LeBron is impossible, and Byron Scott recognizes that. Instead of playing the conservative style that defined Mike Brown's Cleveland teams, the Cavaliers will run and gun. They have the tools to do it: New acquisition Ramon Sessions is the best pure point guard Cleveland has had since Andre Miller. Mo Williams will cause mismatches as a two-guard. J.J. Hickson, Jamario Moon, and Anderson Varejao all run the floor extremely well. Will the Cavaliers be contenders next season? No. But they should be fun to watch, and could surprise any team who thinks the Cavaliers are just going to spend the season in mourning.

CLEVELAND CAVALIERS

CAVALIERS FIVE-YEAR TRENDS

Season	AGE	W-L	POW	PYTH	SEED	ORTG	DRTG	PT DIFF	PACE
05-06	27.1	50-32	48.3 (7)	47.6	4	109.5 (10)	106.9 (14)	2.2 (8)	88.5 (18)
06-07	26.9	50-32	50.2 (8)	52.3	2	106.8 (19)	103.0 (4)	3.8 (7)	89.5 (18)
07-08	27.0	45-37	41.5 (14)	39.9	4	108.4 (18)	108.5 (10)	-0.4 (16)	88.2 (22)
08-09	26.6	66-16	65.3 (1)	64.5	1	114.3 (4)	103.5 (3)	8.9 (1)	87.6 (25)
09-10	28.7	61-21	59.2 (2)	58.7	1	113.3 (4)	105.7 (7)	6.5 (2)	89.8 (25)

		OFFENSE				DEFENSE			
Season	PAY	eFG	oREB	FT/FGA	TO	eFG	dREB	FT/FGA	TO
05-06	$51.8	.492 (13)	.284 (10)	.263 (7)	.156 (12)	.490 (18)	.757 (4)	.226 (5)	.148 (28)
06-07	$63.0	.484 (22)	.297 (3)	.223 (24)	.159 (9)	.480 (7)	.758 (2)	.243 (14)	.169 (10)
07-08	$84.2	.480 (26)	.304 (2)	.221 (20)	.148 (13)	.494 (10)	.759 (2)	.240 (18)	.144 (20)
08-09	$90.8	.519 (4)	.277 (11)	.236 (14)	.145 (8)	.468 (2)	.746 (9)	.226 (12)	.158 (10)
09-10	$84.7	.532 (3)	.251 (22)	.246 (8)	.154 (14)	.482 (3)	.772 (2)	.218 (13)	.141 (27)

(league rankings in parenthesis)

SF 8 — Christian Eyenga
Hght: 6'6" Exp: R Salary: $1.0 million
Wght: 210 From: Kinshasa, DRC
2011-12 status: guaranteed contract for $1.1 million

SKILL RATINGS: TOT — OFF — DEF — REB — PAS — HND — SHT — ATH —

The Cavaliers' 2009 first-round pick, Christian Eyenga comes to the NBA this season after playing for Cleveland's entry in the NBA Summer League. An athletic wing from the Democratic Republic of the Congo, Eyenga has room to grow into his game, having turned 21 in June. A product of the same DKV Joventut squad that introduced the world to Ricky Rubio, Eyenga graduated to the senior team last season, playing about 10 minutes a night off the bench. His performance in that role suggests he's a long way from contributing in the NBA. That raises the question of why the Cavaliers were so eager to bring him over. They will be able to control his development this way; look for it to include a heavy dose of the D-League.

PG 1 — Daniel Gibson
Hght: 6'2" Exp: 4 Salary: $4.0 million
Wght: 200 From: Texas
2011-12 status: guaranteed contract for $4.4 million

SKILL RATINGS: TOT +2 OFF +4 DEF +2 REB -3 PAS -4 HND -2 SHT +4 ATH -2

Year	Team	Age	G	MPG	Usg	3PA%	FTA%	INS	2P%	3P%	FT%	TS%	Reb%	Ast%	TO%	BLK%	STL%	PF%	oRTG	dRTG	Win%	WARP
07-08	CLE	22.1	58	30.5	.152	.456	.079	.622	.421	.440	.810	.592	.044	.038	.129	.006	.013	.044	106.5	107.4	.471	2.0
08-09	CLE	23.1	75	23.9	.166	.452	.060	.608	.402	.382	.767	.519	.050	.035	.097	.007	.013	.043	106.0	107.7	.445	1.1
09-10	CLE	24.1	56	19.1	.143	.458	.066	.609	.454	.477	.694	.613	.040	.031	.111	.005	.012	.035	106.3	107.6	.456	0.9
10-11p	CLE	25.1	71	22.3	.169	.462	.072	.611	.432	.429	.742	.576	.043	.037	.111	.007	.013	.038	107.2	107.4	.495	2.6

Most similar to: Luther Head (96.3), Sasha Vujacic, Steve Alford, Hubert Davis   IMP: 58% BRK: 18% COP: 2%

Cleveland's talent and Daniel Gibson's playing time have gone in opposite directions since he played a key role in the team's run to the 2007 NBA Finals, a trend that culminated in him playing fewer than 20 minutes a night last season. Nonetheless, the Cavaliers' step backward this season is unlikely to translate into more action for Gibson. A classic complementary piece, he was assisted on 77.6 percent of his shot attempts last season, per Hoopdata.com. Without James around to create those kind of open looks from beyond the arc, Gibson can expect to see his three-point percentage fall. The arrival of Ramon Sessions also means Gibson will be back to shooting guard after backing up Mo Williams the last two seasons. A Sessions-Gibson backcourt is big enough to handle most second units, so look for the two to play heavy minutes together.

CLEVELAND CAVALIERS

SF 12 — Joey Graham

Hght: 6'7"	Exp: 5	Salary: $1.0 million
Wght: 225	From: Oklahoma State	
2011-12 status: team option for $1.1 million		

SKILL RATINGS

TOT	OFF	DEF	REB	PAS	HND	SHT	ATH
-4	0	+3	+2	-4	-5	+1	-1

Year	Team	Age	G	MPG	Usg	3PA%	FTA%	INS	2P%	3P%	FT%	TS%	Reb%	Ast%	TO%	BLK%	STL%	PF%	oRTG	dRTG	Win%	WARP
07-08	TOR	25.9	38	8.7	.222	.019	.127	1.108	.427	.667	.844	.520	.120	.021	.148	.000	.004	.067	102.1	108.2	.305	-0.8
08-09	TOR	26.9	78	19.8	.188	.026	.113	1.087	.491	.188	.825	.542	.111	.014	.119	.006	.012	.057	103.4	107.9	.355	-2.0
09-10	DEN	27.9	63	12.0	.162	.047	.116	1.069	.545	.154	.740	.568	.093	.013	.155	.007	.015	.061	102.4	107.3	.343	-1.2
10-11p	CLE	28.9	76	5.0	.201	.052	.116	1.064	.498	.280	.793	.554	.100	.015	.146	.006	.011	.063	103.2	107.5	.359	-0.4

Most similar to: Jeff Grayer (97.8), Carl Herrera, Fred Roberts, Tom Hammonds   IMP: 49%   BRK: 12%   COP: 10%

Joey Graham heads to training camp with hopes of competing for the starting spot at small forward, which would be a big promotion after spending a good chunk of last season out of Denver's rotation. The more likely possibility has Graham backing up Jamario Moon and Anthony Parker, a scenario he should be familiar with after doing the same in Toronto. Graham posted a career-best 56.8 percent True Shooting Percentage while with the Nuggets, but that was his only contribution to the team. Despite tremendous athleticism, Graham is a below-average rebounder and nothing special as a defender. Denver was 7.8 points per 100 possessions worse with Graham on the floor, and while part of that can be explained by the fact that he mostly saw playing time when Carmelo Anthony was out of the lineup (Graham started to keep J.R. Smith in his familiar role as sixth man), it's fairly consistent with the rest of his career.

SG 14 — Daniel Green

Hght: 6'6"	Exp: 1	Salary: $0.8 million
Wght: 210	From: North Carolina	
2011-12 status: due qualifying offer of $1.1 million		

SKILL RATINGS

TOT	OFF	DEF	REB	PAS	HND	SHT	ATH
--	--	--	--	--	--	--	--

Year	Team	Age	G	MPG	Usg	3PA%	FTA%	INS	2P%	3P%	FT%	TS%	Reb%	Ast%	TO%	BLK%	STL%	PF%	oRTG	dRTG	Win%	WARP
09-10	CLE	22.8	20	5.8	.191	.472	.057	.585	.529	.273	.667	.480	.088	.020	.107	.020	.027	.037	105.6	104.7	.531	0.3

A second-round selection by the Cavaliers last year, Daniel Green found himself behind another North Carolina product (Jawad Williams) on a small forward depth chart that was already squeezed by a certain No. 23. With LeBron James' departure, Green might have more opportunity to earn playing time this season. His numbers as a Tar Heel suggest that he will make an ideal role player. Green was an excellent defender at the NCAA level and has the tools to fill the same kind of niche in the NBA once he adds experience. He's also got legitimate three-point range, as he demonstrated by making half of his threes in two D-League appearances, during which he averaged 25.5 points per game.

PF 21 — J.J. Hickson

Hght: 6'9"	Exp: 2	Salary: $1.5 million
Wght: 242	From: North Carolina State	
2011-12 status: team option for $2.4 million		

SKILL RATINGS

TOT	OFF	DEF	REB	PAS	HND	SHT	ATH
0	0	-5	+1	-4	-5	+3	0

Year	Team	Age	G	MPG	Usg	3PA%	FTA%	INS	2P%	3P%	FT%	TS%	Reb%	Ast%	TO%	BLK%	STL%	PF%	oRTG	dRTG	Win%	WARP
08-09	CLE	20.6	62	11.4	.181	.000	.110	1.110	.515	.000	.672	.548	.137	.006	.168	.034	.010	.055	102.4	105.5	.398	-0.3
09-10	CLE	21.6	81	20.9	.191	.001	.105	1.103	.555	.000	.681	.580	.138	.011	.134	.018	.011	.037	103.4	105.2	.439	0.8
10-11p	CLE	22.6	76	28.0	.222	.005	.111	1.105	.536	.006	.706	.567	.137	.011	.145	.023	.011	.040	103.7	105.0	.458	1.9

Most similar to: Chris Wilcox (98.1), Kwame Brown, Nenad Krstic, Johan Petro   IMP: 65%   BRK: 17%   COP: 2%

The Cavaliers have anointed J.J. Hickson their future at the power forward position and their go-to guy in the frontcourt. Hickson showed signs of being that kind of player in year two. While his individual numbers improved, particularly because he boosted his two-point percentage by hitting the occasional shot outside the paint, the bigger difference was at the defensive end of the floor. Hickson was a sieve during his rookie season. His on-court impact during 2009-10 was still very negative--Cleveland allowed 7.4 more points per 100 possessions with him on the floor, per BasketballValue.com--but vastly improved over the previous year. Visually, Hickson seemed to be out of position less frequently and created fewer breakdowns in the Cavaliers' team defense.

CLEVELAND CAVALIERS

If Hickson can even be average at the defensive end, he's got the ability to be a pretty good player. He sprints the floor end to end and finishes above the rim. Now, the challenge will be creating more of his own offense. Continuing to develop his midrange game will help him by allowing him to face up and use his quickness to beat slower defenders. SCHOENE sees Hickson making a big usage jump this season, so Cleveland will need him to be effective in a larger role.

C 5 — Ryan Hollins

Hght: 7'1" Exp: 4 Salary: $2.3 million
Wght: 230 From: UCLA
2011-12 status: player option or ETO for $2.5 million

SKILL RATINGS

TOT	OFF	DEF	REB	PAS	HND	SHT	ATH
-3	0	-2	-4	-1	-4	+1	+1

Year	Team	Age	G	MPG	Usg	3PA%	FTA%	INS	2P%	3P%	FT%	TS%	Reb%	Ast%	TO%	BLK%	STL%	PF%	oRTG	dRTG	Win%	WARP
07-08	CHA	23.5	60	8.9	.134	.000	.233	1.233	.489	.000	.671	.565	.116	.012	.161	.043	.009	.082	103.6	106.3	.413	0.0
08-09	DAL	24.5	45	9.9	.157	.000	.212	1.212	.532	.000	.597	.569	.129	.007	.160	.053	.008	.082	104.5	106.1	.447	0.3
09-10	MIN	25.5	73	16.8	.167	.002	.149	1.147	.560	.000	.690	.600	.095	.018	.203	.023	.008	.071	103.0	107.8	.347	-1.8
10-11p	CLE	26.5	74	5.0	.178	.007	.182	1.175	.520	.006	.655	.563	.105	.015	.180	.034	.008	.072	103.1	106.6	.387	-0.2

Most similar to: Jake Tsakalidis (97.2), Carl Herrera, Carlos Rogers, Brian Skinner

IMP: 49% BRK: 6% COP: 8%

When he signed in Minnesota, Ryan Hollins figured to get regular playing time as the long, athletic center who could complement undersized big men Al Jefferson and Kevin Love. Hollins failed to seize the opportunity, taking a major step back as compared to a solid 2008-09 season split between Charlotte and Dallas. Hollins stopped rebounding the basketball--his 9.5 percent rebound percentage was below average for any player, let alone a center--and saw his block rate decline by more than half. Then again, Hollins had previously played limited NBA minutes, so maybe he just never was that good. The Timberwolves didn't wait around to find out. Darko Milicic replaced Hollins as David Kahn's 7-footer of the month, and Minnesota dumped Hollins' contract on Cleveland as the price for getting Ramon Sessions. His length is unique in the Cavaliers' frontcourt, so he might find his way into the rotation, but the other options are a lot better than they were in Minnesota.

PG 9 — Cedric Jackson

Hght: 6'3" Exp: 1 Salary: --
Wght: 190 From: Cleveland State
2011-12 status: free agent

SKILL RATINGS

TOT	OFF	DEF	REB	PAS	HND	SHT	ATH
+1	--	0	--	--	--	--	--

Year	Team	Age	G	MPG	Usg	3PA%	FTA%	INS	2P%	3P%	FT%	TS%	Reb%	Ast%	TO%	BLK%	STL%	PF%	oRTG	dRTG	Win%	WARP
09-10	WAS	24.1	12	6.2	.225	.165	.146	.980	.357	.167	.583	.396	.063	.087	.303	.020	.021	.043	99.6	105.6	.307	-0.2
10-11p	CLE	25.1	76	-	.230	.211	.141	.930	.413	.250	.676	.464	.082	.079	.173	.008	.030	.050	-	-	.477	-

Most similar to: Darrell Walker (96.9), Gary Grant, Speedy Claxton, Gary Payton

IMP: 63% BRK: 11% COP: 9%

Cedric Jackson made the rounds as a 10-day player and enjoyed the thrill of playing on the same team as LeBron James in the city where he went to college. Jackson showed a nice range of skills in his very limited minutes, and earned a camp invite from the Cavaliers. It's probably back to the D-League for Jackson, who nevertheless should be on the list of point guards to get a call once the injuries start to hit.

PF 4 — Antawn Jamison

Hght: 6'9" Exp: 12 Salary: $13.4 million
Wght: 235 From: North Carolina
2011-12 status: guaranteed contract for $15.1 million

SKILL RATINGS

TOT	OFF	DEF	REB	PAS	HND	SHT	ATH
+3	+3	-4	0	-1	0	-1	+2

Year	Team	Age	G	MPG	Usg	3PA%	FTA%	INS	2P%	3P%	FT%	TS%	Reb%	Ast%	TO%	BLK%	STL%	PF%	oRTG	dRTG	Win%	WARP
07-08	WAS	31.9	79	38.8	.260	.206	.112	.906	.469	.339	.760	.525	.156	.018	.066	.009	.016	.030	107.2	104.6	.584	10.7
08-09	WAS	32.9	81	38.2	.261	.181	.113	.932	.501	.351	.754	.549	.139	.023	.071	.007	.016	.032	108.3	106.6	.557	9.1
09-10	CLE	33.9	66	36.5	.241	.196	.105	.909	.498	.344	.647	.529	.134	.016	.072	.007	.015	.034	106.0	105.4	.519	5.1
10-11p	CLE	34.9	73	32.0	.262	.200	.101	.901	.477	.338	.700	.519	.128	.018	.074	.007	.015	.033	106.1	105.3	.526	5.4

Most similar to: Clifford Robinson (94.5), Dominique Wilkins, Tom Chambers, Grant Hill

IMP: 23% BRK: 0% COP: 3%

CLEVELAND CAVALIERS

A stretch four was Cleveland's white whale for a year and a half. The Cavaliers finally filled the role at the trade deadline by acquiring Antawn Jamison from Washington only to be let down by Jamison's performance. In part, Jamison wasn't ideal for the role. He's a good shooter, not a great one, having shot 34.4 percent from downtown last season. But he also suffered because he was judged largely on his performance and the team's in the playoff loss to Boston. Going up against Kevin Garnett, one of the greatest defensive power forwards of all time, is hardly an ideal matchup, and Garnett silenced Rashard Lewis in much the same manner in the next round.

Whether it was the right move at the deadline or not, Cleveland has Jamison now, and his scoring ability will be valuable for the post-LeBron Cavaliers. The biggest problem is that Jamison's minutes will be limited because he plays the same position as J.J. Hickson. The only alternative is Jamison stepping out and defending small forwards, which seems unlikely at age 34. Byron Scott will have to make time for Jamison somehow, because he's the best scorer on the roster. Jamison thrived as a sixth man in 2003-04 in Dallas, and might settle into that role in the latter stages of his career.

SF #15 Jamario Moon

Hght: 6'8" Wght: 200 Exp: 3 From: Meridian CC (MS) Salary: $3.0 million
2011-12 status: free agent

SKILL RATINGS

TOT	OFF	DEF	REB	PAS	HND	SHT	ATH
+2	+1	+3	+3	-2	+2	0	0

Year	Team	Age	G	MPG	Usg	3PA%	FTA%	INS	2P%	3P%	FT%	TS%	Reb%	Ast%	TO%	BLK%	STL%	PF%	oRTG	dRTG	Win%	WARP
07-08	TOR	27.9	78	27.8	.145	.185	.056	.871	.529	.325	.741	.540	.133	.020	.077	.040	.017	.033	103.3	102.4	.531	5.2
08-09	MIA	28.9	80	25.9	.125	.331	.064	.732	.540	.355	.850	.567	.104	.021	.078	.024	.021	.030	104.9	104.4	.515	4.2
09-10	CLE	29.9	61	17.2	.129	.345	.068	.723	.558	.320	.800	.555	.104	.022	.079	.022	.017	.031	104.3	104.4	.497	1.8
10-11p	CLE	30.9	72	28.0	.138	.398	.062	.664	.516	.318	.809	.526	.106	.020	.082	.024	.016	.032	104.4	104.2	.509	3.9

Most similar to: Ime Udoka (94.8), Shane Battier, Maurice Evans, Lucious Harris
IMP: 27% BRK: 0% COP: 15%

Jamario Moon might have been the only person in Cleveland to benefit from LeBron James' decision to sign in Miami. During the walk year of his contract, Moon goes from being the backup to the league's best player to the frontrunner to start at small forward for the Cavaliers. It's a role for which he's perfectly qualified. Moon is best at the defensive end of the floor, using his athleticism to generate both steals and blocks regularly. The book on Moon is that he takes too many chances going for those impact defensive plays, but his history of strong plus-minus ratings suggests he's coming out ahead on the exchange.

An excellent transition player, Moon would benefit from a faster pace to get out and run the wings. He's less effective in the half court because of an inconsistent jumper. He made 35.5 percent of his three-pointers in 2008-09, but has been around 32 percent in his other two NBA seasons.

Random note: Moon might be the NBA's only player who played with all three of Miami's stars--James in Cleveland, Chris Bosh in Toronto and Dwyane Wade in Miami.

SG #18 Anthony Parker

Hght: 6'6" Wght: 215 Exp: 7 From: Bradley Salary: $2.9 million
2011-12 status: free agent

SKILL RATINGS

TOT	OFF	DEF	REB	PAS	HND	SHT	ATH
+1	+2	-1	0	0	+2	+2	-3

Year	Team	Age	G	MPG	Usg	3PA%	FTA%	INS	2P%	3P%	FT%	TS%	Reb%	Ast%	TO%	BLK%	STL%	PF%	oRTG	dRTG	Win%	WARP
07-08	TOR	32.8	82	32.1	.175	.313	.057	.743	.499	.438	.816	.580	.076	.033	.089	.005	.014	.028	105.7	106.0	.491	4.1
08-09	TOR	33.8	80	33.0	.164	.259	.068	.810	.442	.390	.834	.524	.070	.047	.122	.004	.019	.025	104.9	106.5	.446	1.6
09-10	CLE	34.8	81	28.3	.121	.444	.071	.627	.458	.414	.789	.576	.058	.032	.121	.006	.014	.031	104.9	106.6	.442	1.2
10-11p	CLE	35.8	76	30.0	.147	.421	.064	.642	.438	.390	.778	.541	.064	.036	.122	.007	.015	.030	105.3	106.3	.468	2.5

Most similar to: Bruce Bowen (97.8), Tyrone Corbin, Anthony Peeler, Jim Jackson
IMP: 40% BRK: 6% COP: 23%

Signed away from the Raptors as a free agent, Anthony Parker proved to be an ideal wingman for LeBron James. After Parker played a more versatile role in Toronto, the Cavaliers essentially asked him to do two things--defend the opposition's best scorer and shoot three-pointers. Check and check. Parker was an upgrade defensively on Delonte West, and his size allows him to match up at either wing position. He's somewhere below the level of great stopper and doesn't put up a lot of measurable statistics, but his ability to check star players without fouling is a positive.

On offense, Parker attempted far more threes than twos and knocked them down at a 41.4 percent clip. Since returning to the NBA after a stellar Euroleague career, he's been over 40 percent beyond the arc three times in four years. He was also the only Cleveland player who was effective from downtown in the loss to the Celtics, making 11 threes in 21 attempts. The danger is that Parker will have to do more ballhandling and shot creation this season. At 35, those are no longer his strengths. Less is more for Parker on offense.

PF 44 — Leon Powe
Hght: 6'8" Wght: 240 Exp: 4 From: California Salary: $0.9 million
2011-12 status: free agent

SKILL RATINGS
TOT	OFF	DEF	REB	PAS	HND	SHT	ATH
+3	+4	+2	+3	-2	-4	+2	+3

Year	Team	Age	G	MPG	Usg	3PA%	FTA%	INS	2P%	3P%	FT%	TS%	Reb%	Ast%	TO%	BLK%	STL%	PF%	oRTG	dRTG	Win%	WARP
07-08	BOS	24.2	56	14.4	.230	.003	.214	1.212	.577	.000	.710	.630	.166	.009	.109	.016	.009	.073	109.3	106.5	.591	2.9
08-09	BOS	25.2	70	17.5	.203	.000	.221	1.221	.524	.000	.689	.591	.170	.018	.143	.025	.010	.073	107.9	106.6	.542	3.2
09-10	CLE	26.2	20	11.8	.175	.000	.316	1.316	.429	-	.587	.515	.151	.000	.125	.007	.013	.072	102.9	106.9	.369	-0.2
10-11p	CLE	27.2	67	19.5	.228	.009	.211	1.202	.533	.006	.708	.594	.155	.015	.132	.019	.008	.072	108.1	106.9	.537	3.3

Most similar to: Chris Gatling (97.4), Reggie Slater, Etan Thomas, Brad Miller

IMP: 41% BRK: 2% COP: 7%

The Celtics' loss was the Cavaliers' gain when Boston cut loose Leon Powe after he tore his ACL in the 2009 postseason. Several teams were interested in signing Powe, but he signed a two-year minimum contract with Cleveland to have a chance to win. Powe returned right around schedule in late February. He played spot minutes the rest of the way and predictably struggled before being buried in the playoffs.

Because of the injury, signing Powe was always about 2010-11. He now finds himself in a crowded battle for playing time at power forward, but his talent demands he find some opportunities. Coming off the bench for the Celtics, Powe was highly productive, averaging 17.6 points and 11.3 rebounds per 40 minutes. A high-percentage shooter, Powe has consistently been excellent in terms of True Shooting Percentage when healthy.

PF 24 — Samardo Samuels
Hght: 6'9" Wght: 260 Exp: R From: Louisville Salary: $0.5 million
2011-12 status: due qualifying offer of $1.0 million

SKILL RATINGS
TOT	OFF	DEF	REB	PAS	HND	SHT	ATH
-3	--	--	--	--	--	--	--

Year	Team	Age	G	MPG	Usg	3PA%	FTA%	INS	2P%	3P%	FT%	TS%	Reb%	Ast%	TO%	BLK%	STL%	PF%	oRTG	dRTG	Win%	WARP
10-11p	CLE	22.3	76	-	.216	.000	.138	1.138	.421	.000	.692	.481	.115	.017	.163	.019	.008	.059	-	-	.381	-

Most similar to: Troy Murphy (97.2), Ike Diogu, Joe Alexander, Marreese Speights

IMP: - BRK: - COP: -

An elite prospect entering Louisville (DraftExpress.com's Recruiting Service Consensus Index had him ranked fourth in the 2008 class, just ahead of DeMar DeRozan and Greg Monroe), Samuels was unable to turn that potential into production. He unexpectedly entered the draft after a solid but hardly spectacular sophomore season that saw him average 15.3 points and 7.4 rebounds per game, and went undrafted. Samuels was able to redeem himself with a solid NBA Summer League performance for Chicago and landed a three-year contract from Cleveland. Per ShamSports.com, $200,000 of his salary is guaranteed this season. Since the Cavaliers are already flush with power forwards, Samuels is unlikely to see any playing time this season, and his translation doesn't suggest he's ready for the league anyway. Samuels needs to spend the year working to broaden his game and develop his shooting range to compensate for the fact that he's somewhat undersized for an NBA power forward.

CLEVELAND CAVALIERS

PG 3	Ramon Sessions	Hght: 6'3"	Exp: 3	Salary: $4.0 million	SKILL RATINGS							
		Wght: 190	From: Nevada-Reno		TOT	OFF	DEF	REB	PAS	HND	SHT	ATH
		2011-12 status: guaranteed contract for $4.3 million			+2	+3	-1	+4	+3	0	-3	+2

Year	Team	Age	G	MPG	Usg	3PA%	FTA%	INS	2P%	3P%	FT%	TS%	Reb%	Ast%	TO%	BLK%	STL%	PF%	oRTG	dRTG	Win%	WARP
07-08	MIL	22.0	17	26.3	.172	.041	.106	1.065	.436	.429	.780	.507	.079	.128	.206	.005	.018	.027	106.6	105.4	.540	1.2
08-09	MIL	23.0	79	27.5	.224	.031	.144	1.112	.457	.176	.794	.525	.075	.094	.140	.003	.019	.033	107.7	106.4	.541	5.6
09-10	MIN	24.0	82	21.1	.200	.019	.129	1.110	.467	.067	.717	.513	.070	.065	.172	.002	.016	.035	104.0	107.2	.396	-0.7
10-11p	CLE	25.0	76	25.0	.230	.040	.130	1.090	.461	.197	.774	.517	.070	.087	.165	.003	.017	.031	106.1	106.2	.499	3.3

Most similar to: Ronnie Lester (97.9), Robert Pack, Antonio Daniels, Bimbo Coles — IMP: 67% BRK: 9% COP: 7%

Ramon Sessions is the latest example of why fit matters in the NBA. Last season, Sessions went from a point guard-friendly offense in Milwaukee to Kurt Rambis' triangle offense in Minnesota. According to Synergy Sports, Sessions spent just 30 percent of the time playing to his strength, running the pick-and-roll. As a result, Sessions' numbers suffered across the board. Most notably, his assist rate dropped from being one of the league's best to below average for a point guard. Sessions also saw his usage rate drop since he was spending more time playing off the ball, exposing his limited shooting range.

The trade to Cleveland was a godsend for Sessions, who has a shot at emerging as a starter in a small backcourt with Mo Williams. That would allow Sessions to run pick-and-rolls with J.J. Hickson or Anderson Varejao with Williams as a dangerous spot-up shooter. Whatever his role, Sessions will have the ball in his hands in a position to create in Cleveland, which is what he needs. At 24, Sessions still has room to grow, and while SCHOENE is no longer quite as excited about his upside, there are some solid point guards among his comparables. He could prove one of the summer's best value pickups.

C 50	Greg Stiemsma	Hght: 6'11"	Exp: R	Salary: $0.8 million	SKILL RATINGS							
		Wght: 260	From: Wisconsin		TOT	OFF	DEF	REB	PAS	HND	SHT	ATH
		2011-12 status: free agent			+1	--	--	--	--	--	--	--

Year	Team	Age	G	MPG	Usg	3PA%	FTA%	INS	2P%	3P%	FT%	TS%	Reb%	Ast%	TO%	BLK%	STL%	PF%	oRTG	dRTG	Win%	WARP
10-11p	CLE	25.6	76	-	.126	.002	.072	1.069	.467	.000	.766	.500	.136	.017	.148	.078	.011	.072	-	-	.477	-

Most similar to: Jim McIlvaine (98.4), Kelvin Cato, Calvin Booth, Andrew Lang — IMP: 40% BRK: 3% COP: 3%

The Timberwolves signed Greg Stiemsma at the end of last season to a contract that covered 2010-11. According to ShamSports.com, $100,000 of the contract became guaranteed on Sept. 15, and Stiemsma was waived ahead of that date because of the team's depth in the frontcourt. Stiemsma had the chance to find a new home for training camp and landed in Cleveland, though the Cavaliers' roster is likely already full with 15 players under contract.

A career backup at Wisconsin, Stiemsma has proven a late bloomer. He's become the D-League's premier shot blocker, and his competent rebounding and occasional scoring suggests he might be good enough to be a third center in the NBA.

PF 17	Anderson Varejao	Hght: 6'11"	Exp: 6	Salary: $7.3 million	SKILL RATINGS							
		Wght: 260	From: Santa Teresa, Brazil		TOT	OFF	DEF	REB	PAS	HND	SHT	ATH
		2011-12 status: guaranteed contract for $8.0 million			+1	+1	+5	+3	0	+1	+2	+3

Year	Team	Age	G	MPG	Usg	3PA%	FTA%	INS	2P%	3P%	FT%	TS%	Reb%	Ast%	TO%	BLK%	STL%	PF%	oRTG	dRTG	Win%	WARP
07-08	CLE	25.6	48	27.4	.136	.005	.092	1.087	.464	.000	.598	.485	.175	.018	.151	.016	.013	.048	102.2	104.7	.417	0.0
08-09	CLE	26.6	81	28.5	.143	.003	.159	1.156	.538	.000	.616	.565	.148	.017	.115	.023	.017	.049	104.3	104.6	.491	3.6
09-10	CLE	27.6	76	28.5	.133	.008	.126	1.118	.576	.200	.663	.598	.157	.019	.110	.024	.017	.048	105.1	104.4	.523	4.8
10-11p	CLE	28.6	75	28.0	.152	.008	.117	1.109	.531	.094	.633	.553	.153	.020	.127	.022	.016	.049	104.3	104.6	.489	3.2

Most similar to: Scot Pollard (98.4), Michael Cage, Jeff Foster, Brian Skinner — IMP: 42% BRK: 7% COP: 4%

2009-10 finally saw Anderson Varejao get recognized as the unique and valuable contributor he is. It was nearly impossible to miss how much more effective the Cavaliers were with the floppy-haired Brazilian on the floor.

Varejao's +12.8 net plus-minus rating was fifth in the league, per BasketballValue.com, and all four players ahead of him (Kobe Bryant, Kevin Durant, LeBron James and Dwyane Wade) were selected to the All-NBA First Team. Varejao settled for an overdue third-place finish in Sixth Man Award voting.

Surprisingly, part of Varejao's strong season was eliminating the flopping that had once been his trademark. According to Hoopdata.com, Varejao took 28 charges, down from 51 the previous season. The upshot was that Varejao did a better job of playing solid fundamental defense and denying shot attempts. When it comes to defending the pick-and-roll, Varejao is as good as anyone in the NBA. He's also a better offensive player than most people realize. Varejao shot a career-best 57.6 percent on two-pointers last season and is an athletic finisher in the paint.

SF 31	Jawad Williams	Hght: 6'9" Wght: 218 2011-12 status: free agent	Exp: 2 From: North Carolina	Salary: $1.0 million	SKILL RATINGS TOT OFF DEF REB PAS HND SHT ATH -2 +1 -2 -4 -1 +3 -2 -5

Year	Team	Age	G	MPG	Usg	3PA%	FTA%	INS	2P%	3P%	FT%	TS%	Reb%	Ast%	TO%	BLK%	STL%	PF%	oRTG	dRTG	Win%	WARP
08-09	CLE	26.2	10	2.0	.309	.462	.000	.538	.500	.333	.000	.500	.060	.000	.077	.000	.026	.048	105.5	107.3	.440	0.0
09-10	CLE	27.2	54	13.7	.154	.381	.081	.700	.451	.323	.711	.496	.065	.022	.074	.005	.008	.046	103.7	108.0	.363	-0.8
10-11p	CLE	28.2	76	10.0	.168	.455	.075	.619	.449	.323	.687	.494	.063	.023	.078	.006	.008	.046	104.7	107.9	.396	-0.3

Most similar to: Sam Mack (95.7), Rasual Butler, Jarvis Hayes, Don Ford — IMP: 40% BRK: 8% COP: 10%

Before the Cavaliers dealt for Antawn Jamison, they gave Jawad Williams a brief audition as their stretch four. The native of the Cleveland suburbs, seeing his first extended NBA action, proved lacking in that role. He knocked down just 32.3 percent of his three-point attempts and was atrocious on the glass. Nonetheless, the Cavaliers extended Williams a qualifying offer, making him a restricted free agent. He signed the offer just before training camp and returns as part of a crowded battle for forward minutes.

PG 2	Maurice Williams	Hght: 6'1" Wght: 190 2011-12 status: player option or ETO for $8.5 million	Exp: 7 From: Alabama	Salary: $9.3 million	SKILL RATINGS TOT OFF DEF REB PAS HND SHT ATH +4 +5 -3 -1 0 -2 +3 -1

Year	Team	Age	G	MPG	Usg	3PA%	FTA%	INS	2P%	3P%	FT%	TS%	Reb%	Ast%	TO%	BLK%	STL%	PF%	oRTG	dRTG	Win%	WARP
07-08	MIL	25.3	66	36.5	.223	.195	.072	.877	.512	.385	.856	.566	.058	.079	.153	.003	.015	.036	107.6	107.1	.517	5.0
08-09	CLE	26.3	81	35.0	.236	.299	.071	.773	.486	.436	.912	.588	.057	.055	.127	.003	.013	.036	109.2	107.3	.561	8.5
09-10	CLE	27.3	69	34.2	.222	.333	.078	.745	.452	.429	.894	.580	.050	.073	.155	.007	.015	.034	108.6	106.7	.561	7.1
10-11p	CLE	28.3	74	34.0	.249	.340	.071	.731	.468	.412	.903	.574	.050	.068	.150	.005	.013	.034	109.3	107.1	.573	8.2

Most similar to: Mike Bibby (97.2), Chauncey Billups, Kirk Hinrich, Jason Terry — IMP: 47% BRK: 2% COP: 7%

Somewhere between the two extreme schools of thought on Mo Williams lies the truth about his game. Williams' supporters saw him as the difference-maker for Cleveland during two stellar regular seasons, the team's second-best player and a deserving All-Star in 2008-09. Critics see Williams' success as a function of playing alongside LeBron James and believe his true ability was revealed during the Cavaliers' postseason series losses, both of which saw Williams come up short.

The overwhelming amount of evidence suggests that Williams is an above-average point guard, though not an All-Star one. Certainly, the pairing with James was an ideal one for both Williams and the Cavaliers, who needed Williams' ability to handle the basketball and keep defenses honest. With James gone, Cleveland will need more scoring from Williams, who will almost certainly see his shooting percentages suffer to compensate. How much playmaking he'll do depends on how much he plays alongside Ramon Sessions. If Williams and Anthony Parker again start in the backcourt, Williams will have the ball in his hands the vast majority of the time and will have to make plays for his teammates. For better or worse, Williams looks like Cleveland's go-to starter this season.

Dallas Mavericks

At this point, the Dallas Mavericks' reputation as perennial contenders in the Western Conference might have as much to do with legacy as recent performance. Since the Mavericks lost in the 2006 NBA Finals, five teams have reached the Western Conference Finals, and Dallas isn't among them. In fact, the Mavericks have won but a single playoff series in that four-year span, upsetting a short-handed San Antonio Spurs team playing without Manu Ginobili in 2009 before being summarily dispatched by Denver in five games.

Dallas did finish second in the West during the 2009-10 regular season, winning 55 games. However, the impressive record was not matched by an equally strong point differential. The Mavericks outscored opponents by just 2.7 points per game, which ranked them last among the eight West playoff teams. The difference between their expected and actual record, 6.7 games, was the largest in the NBA.

The discrepancy can be explained by this: Dallas padded its record by going 16-7 (.739) in games decided by five points, the league's highest number of close wins and best winning percentage in close games. The success in close games was nothing new for the Mavericks, who have done something similar three of the last four years (Table 1).

Better teams tend to win close games more often than poor teams, though the difference is muted as compared to their overall winning percentage. The expected close win percentage (xCW% in the table) uses this historical relationship and the Mavericks' record in all other games to show how the typical team would have performed in close games. The 2006-07, 2008-09 and 2009-10 Dallas teams all outperformed their expected record in close games by enough to rank among the top 12 NBA overachievers of the last nine seasons.

To the extent the Mavericks have found the recipe for close games--and it is interesting to note that owner Mark Cuban has been a major proponent of clutch statistics--it has not paid off in the postseason. In fact, last year's series against the Spurs reversed the regular-season trends. Dallas won the most lopsided game in the series, but suffered two close losses by three and four points in San Antonio and fell in six games. It's hard to really call the outcome an upset. Statistically, the Spurs were the better of the two teams, and throughout the series the talent appeared even.

To escape from the pack of second-tier teams in the West and have a legitimate chance to win the conference, the Mavericks needed an infusion of star talent. They hoped adding Shawn Marion in a sign-and-trade deal last summer might accomplish the task, but Marion is on the decline and had the worst season of his career in terms of WARP. Dallas went shopping again at the trade deadline, using expiring contracts to land Caron Butler and Brendan Haywood from the Washington Wizards. The additions helped--the Mavericks' point differential, adjusted for schedule, went from +2.1 before the trade to +3.7 the remainder of the way--but not enough to really push Dallas into the West elite.

MAVERICKS IN A BOX

Last year's record	55-27
Last year's Offensive Rating	111.6 (10)
Last year's Defensive Rating	107.5 (12)
Last year's point differential	2.7 (12)
Team pace	91.0 (17)
SCHOENE projection	**48-34 (7)**
Projected Offensive Rating	110.7 (13)
Projected Defensive Rating	107.8 (5)
Projected team weighted age	31.3 (1)
Projected '10-11 payroll	$83.5 (3)
Est. payroll obligations, '11-12	$59.4 (12)

Head coach: Rick Carlisle

Is it time to wonder whether Carlisle is a better coach during the regular season than the playoffs? His teams have averaged 48.3 wins a year and won 50-plus games five times in his eight seasons as a head coach, but four times in seven postseason runs Carlisle's teams have fallen despite the benefit of home-court advantage. Two others saw Carlisle's team pull an upset, so only once in seven trips to the playoffs has Carlisle's team done as expected. Perhaps he's just a fan of unexpected outcomes?

Table 1: Dallas Mavericks In Close Games, 2006-10

Season	CW	CL	CW%	xCW%	Diff
2006-07	20	4	0.833	0.606	0.227
2007-08	9	12	0.429	0.565	-0.137
2008-09	17	5	0.773	0.519	0.253
2009-10	17	6	0.739	0.548	0.191

That left one last opportunity prior to the 2010-11 season. For a year, the Mavericks had been selling the possibility of sign-and-trade deals this summer as their way to add a superstar player like LeBron James or hometown favorite Chris Bosh despite being over the salary cap. Dallas had a compelling asset to complete such a trade in the contract of center Erick Dampier, which was fully non-guaranteed in its final year. The Mavericks also hoped they could sell free agents on the Dallas market and the ability to compete more quickly by joining a roster that was already full of talent.

Instead, none of the top free agents on the market showed much interest in going to a team over the cap via the sign-and-trade route. Shut out there, the Mavericks could only use Dampier's contract in a trade with a team looking to clear salary. They ended up dealing Dampier to Charlotte for centers Alexis Ajinca and Tyson Chandler, shedding the dead-weight deals of guard Matt Carroll and forward Eduardo Najera in the process. The move was a good one for Dallas, which saved money, created a trade exception and added a useful player, but it was hardly the blockbuster deal the Mavericks hoped to swing.

Outside of the Dampier deal, Dallas enjoyed a fairly quiet offseason. Star forward Dirk Nowitzki opted out of the final year of his contract and became a free agent, but he showed little interest in going anywhere else before quickly re-signing with the Mavericks for $80 million over four years. The team also brought back Haywood, an unrestricted free agent, giving him a generous and lengthy six-year, $55 million deal to be their starting center.

Besides Chandler, Dallas added a couple of young pieces to the mix. Having lost their first-round pick to New Jersey in the Jason Kidd trade, the Mavericks bought their way back into the draft, taking South Florida guard Dominique Jones with the pick purchased from Memphis. Dallas also made a very smart value signing up front, locking up promising but unproven center Ian Mahinmi to a two-year deal at the minimum.

The final product is a Dallas team that seems to be in about the same place as last season and the few before that. The Mavericks have a superstar in Nowitzki surrounded by a number of players who are good, but not great. That describes the team as a whole. They will quite possibly win 50 games once again, but given the talent in the rest of the conference, it's hard to see Dallas as a favorite to win a round in the playoffs. Upgrading almost any position would require adding a star with no easy avenue to do so. Expiring contracts (Butler and Chandler are both in the final season of their deals) are unlikely to be as valuable at this year's trade deadline because few teams are worried about clearing cap space and several contenders can use trade exceptions to make deals.

Looking ahead, the most likely path out of the status quo is the Mavericks taking a step backward as their key players age. In terms of effective age, Dallas was a year and a half older than any other team in the league a year ago, and that doesn't figure to change this season. Kidd will turn 38 during the year, and no matter how well he has aged, he won't be able to run

From the Blogosphere

Who: Rob Mahoney
What: The Two Man Game
Where: http://www.thetwomangame.com/

Dirk Nowitzki is still an elite offensive player and can create shots in one-on-one situations with ease. Behind him, Caron Butler and Rodrigue Beaubois can also generate quality attempts on their own. Yet aside from Nowitzki, Butler, and Beaubois, the Mavericks are short on shot creation. Jason Terry just isn't as skilled or as efficient in that regard as he once was, and Shawn Marion's post-Phoenix offensive effectiveness has never quite lived up to his billing. Both Terry and Marion are *contributors*, but they're no longer offensive focal points. That puts more pressure on Jason Kidd to make sense of a roster with plenty of theoretical offensive options, but a limited number of avenues in which to reach them. It's no longer as simple as finding Terry on the perimeter and letting him go to work or dumping it off to Marion in the high post; Kidd now has to feed points to most of the Mavs' cast.

DALLAS MAVERICKS

the point forever. Meanwhile, the clock is ticking on Nowitzki's time as a superstar now that he's 32. All of the Mavericks' most important players are on the wrong side of 30.

SCHOENE sees age being a major problem on the offensive end of the floor, where Dallas is projected to drop from 10th in the league in Offensive Rating to 13th. The defensive upgrade provided by the tandem of Chandler and Haywood in the middle will help offset that this season. From a long-term perspective, the Mavericks need to develop new weapons on offense.

Dallas' best hope for the future is second-year guard Rodrigue Beaubois. Just 21 for most of his rookie season, Beaubois was a revelation, averaging 22.7 points per 40 minutes. Unfortunately, he looks more like a combo guard or an undersized two rather than a replacement for Kidd at the point. Beaubois could start at shooting guard this season, and the Mavericks may need him to break out to keep 2010-11 from following what has become a familiar script.

Kevin Pelton

MAVERICKS FIVE-YEAR TRENDS

Season	AGE	W-L	POW	PYTH	SEED	ORTG	DRTG	PT DIFF	PACE
05-06	27.5	60-22	61.1 (3)	58.0	4	113.2 (2)	106.2 (11)	6.1 (3)	86.7 (27)
06-07	28.1	67-15	66.1 (1)	60.7	1	113.0 (2)	104.7 (5)	7.2 (3)	88.2 (28)
07-08	28.9	51-31	54.8 (9)	53.8	7	113.9 (7)	108.2 (8)	4.5 (10)	88.2 (23)
08-09	29.0	50-32	48.2 (9)	46.6	6	112.6 (6)	109.7 (16)	2.0 (10)	90.1 (16)
09-10	31.5	55-27	51.3 (9)	48.7	2	111.6 (10)	107.5 (12)	2.7 (12)	91.0 (17)

		OFFENSE				DEFENSE			
Season	PAY	eFG	oREB	FT/FGA	TO	eFG	oREB	FT/FGA	TO
05-06	$68.3	.495 (10)	.318 (2)	.285 (3)	.155 (11)	.475 (8)	.722 (17)	.257 (19)	.160 (14)
06-07	$64.8	.509 (5)	.287 (8)	.256 (11)	.157 (7)	.477 (4)	.750 (5)	.265 (22)	.164 (18)
07-08	$88.4	.502 (12)	.267 (16)	.259 (7)	.136 (5)	.474 (4)	.750 (5)	.252 (22)	.131 (30)
08-09	$93.2	.504 (11)	.266 (16)	.224 (23)	.140 (4)	.493 (10)	.746 (8)	.225 (11)	.143 (26)
09-10	$87.8	.506 (13)	.243 (26)	.226 (15)	.141 (2)	.495 (15)	.737 (15)	.206 (6)	.159 (11)

(league rankings in parenthesis)

C 8 — Alexis Ajinca Hght: 7'0" Exp: 2 Salary: $1.5 million Wght: 220 From: Saint Etienne, France 2011-12 status: team option for $2.3 million

SKILL RATINGS

TOT	OFF	DEF	REB	PAS	HND	SHT	ATH
+2	--	+1	--	--	--	--	--

Year	Team	Age	G	MPG	Usg	3PA%	FTA%	INS	2P%	3P%	FT%	TS%	Reb%	Ast%	TO%	BLK%	STL%	PF%	oRTG	dRTG	Win%	WARP
08-09	CHA	21.0	31	5.9	.244	.021	.132	1.111	.373	.000	.714	.430	.102	.008	.129	.027	.021	.089	98.9	106.7	.257	-0.6
09-10	CHA	22.0	6	5.0	.194	.000	.035	1.035	.500	-	.000	.479	.080	.000	.161	.027	.017	.078	97.2	106.5	.220	-0.1
10-11p	DAL	23.0	76	-	.203	.012	.141	1.129	.492	.000	.682	.534	.144	.006	.187	.080	.008	.081	-	-	.514	-

Most similar to: Darko Milicic (94.2), Sean Williams, Shawn Bradley, Benoit Benjamin   IMP: 59% BRK: 11% COP: 4%

A behemoth Frenchman whose reported 7'9" wingspan remains the biggest recorded by the NBA in pre-draft measurements, Alexis Ajinca played sparingly in two seasons with the Charlotte Bobcats before arriving in Dallas as the throw-in to this summer's Tyson Chandler-Erick Dampier trade. His projection, and any statistical evaluation of his career to date, is based on his 22 games with Maine in the D-League last season, which saw him reject 4.8 shots per 40 minutes against hopelessly overmatched opponents. Ajinca is no longer eligible to be sent down and is buried on the Dallas depth chart (he's not even the team's best French center; that honor belongs to Ian Mahinmi), so a trade might be best for him and the team. If the Mavericks can't complete one before the end of training camp, there's no guarantee they will pick up the option on the last year of Ajinca's rookie contract.

DALLAS MAVERICKS

PG 11	Jose Juan Barea	Hght: 6'0" Wght: 175 2011-12 status: free agent	Exp: 4 From: Northeastern	Salary: $1.8 million	SKILL RATINGS TOT OFF DEF REB PAS HND SHT ATH 0 +2 -2 0 +1 +1 +1 -3

Year	Team	Age	G	MPG	Usg	3PA%	FTA%	INS	2P%	3P%	FT%	TS%	Reb%	Ast%	TO%	BLK%	STL%	PF%	oRTG	dRTG	Win%	WARP
07-08	DAL	23.8	44	10.5	.224	.245	.070	.825	.431	.389	.800	.515	.057	.059	.159	.002	.014	.049	104.3	107.1	.409	-0.1
08-09	DAL	24.8	79	20.3	.203	.219	.058	.839	.474	.357	.753	.516	.063	.078	.149	.002	.012	.035	106.7	108.0	.457	1.4
09-10	DAL	25.8	78	19.8	.200	.235	.059	.824	.476	.357	.844	.526	.054	.077	.153	.003	.012	.036	105.8	107.5	.444	0.9
10-11p	DAL	26.8	75	15.0	.201	.219	.063	.843	.480	.384	.810	.537	.056	.071	.142	.003	.012	.036	105.9	107.4	.449	0.8

Most similar to: Troy Hudson (99.1), Larry Wright, Tyronn Lue, Darrick Martin   IMP: 57% BRK: 9% COP: 6%

Undrafted out of Northeastern (not exactly a basketball hotbed) and generously listed at 6'0", Barea has carved out a nice little career for himself as a backup point guard in Dallas. Despite the slight drop in winning percentage, Barea essentially put up a carbon copy of his 2008-09 effort, coming eerily close to duplicating his performance in terms of two- and three-point shooting and assist percentage. Barea tends to call his own number quite a bit despite middling efficiency, but he's also capable of setting up teammates.

Barea's height works against him at the defensive end of the floor, and Dallas defended considerably worse when he was on the court last season. Barea's low center of gravity helps him compete physically, but opponents can still see over him and get by him off the dribble. Barea makes up for this slightly by taking charges. According to Hoopdata.com, only Nick Collison drew more offensive fouls on a per-minute basis last season.

PG 3	Rodrigue Beaubois	Hght: 6'0" Wght: 170 2011-12 status: team option for $1.2 million	Exp: 1 From: Pointe-a-Pitre, Guadeloupe	Salary: $1.2 million	SKILL RATINGS TOT OFF DEF REB PAS HND SHT ATH +5 +5 0 +3 -2 -3 +5 +4

Year	Team	Age	G	MPG	Usg	3PA%	FTA%	INS	2P%	3P%	FT%	TS%	Reb%	Ast%	TO%	BLK%	STL%	PF%	oRTG	dRTG	Win%	WARP
09-10	DAL	22.2	56	12.5	.248	.293	.061	.768	.582	.409	.808	.617	.063	.049	.144	.013	.021	.055	108.3	106.2	.567	2.2
10-11p	DAL	23.2	76	20.0	.269	.283	.069	.786	.575	.414	.822	.619	.065	.053	.130	.017	.020	.053	109.5	105.7	.620	6.5

Most similar to: Leandro Barbosa (91.9), Devin Harris, Delonte West, Gilbert Arenas   IMP: 76% BRK: 5% COP: 5%

Like a French version of Leandro Barbosa, Rodrigue Beaubois instantly became one of the league's most exciting players as a rookie. Relying on breathtaking end-to-end speed and surprising range, Beaubois was consistently effective and sensational at times, most notably in a 40-point outing at Golden State that saw him shoot 15-of-22 from the field. After inexplicably playing sporadic minutes down the stretch, Beaubois proved to be a spark when he got a chance late in the series with San Antonio.

Like Barbosa, his top comparable, Beaubois appears to be more of an off guard than the lead ballhandler he was advertised as before being drafted. Still, Rick Carlisle has no choice but to find more time for Beaubois this season, and he could start at shooting guard. Playing heavy minutes could be a challenge for Beaubois, who at this point in his career still relies more on his athleticism than a well-rounded game. Still, Beaubois has a bright future.

While training with the French National Team, Beaubois suffered a stress fracture of the fifth metatarsal in his right foot. The injury might sideline him for training camp and slow his ascent to the starting lineup, but it should not cost him much if any of the regular season.

SF 4	Caron Butler	Hght: 6'7" Wght: 228 2011-12 status: free agent	Exp: 8 From: Connecticut	Salary: $10.6 million	SKILL RATINGS TOT OFF DEF REB PAS HND SHT ATH 0 0 -2 0 +3 0 -2 +3

Year	Team	Age	G	MPG	Usg	3PA%	FTA%	INS	2P%	3P%	FT%	TS%	Reb%	Ast%	TO%	BLK%	STL%	PF%	oRTG	dRTG	Win%	WARP
07-08	WAS	28.1	58	39.9	.241	.153	.095	.942	.492	.357	.901	.558	.099	.057	.124	.008	.026	.032	107.8	104.5	.609	9.3
08-09	WAS	29.1	67	38.6	.260	.143	.120	.977	.487	.310	.858	.552	.095	.051	.143	.006	.021	.029	107.6	106.6	.532	6.2
09-10	DAL	30.1	74	37.6	.222	.107	.103	.995	.450	.290	.838	.507	.096	.026	.119	.007	.021	.032	103.0	105.3	.422	0.3
10-11p	DAL	31.1	74	32.0	.221	.140	.101	.961	.468	.305	.848	.524	.092	.036	.127	.007	.020	.034	103.9	105.4	.451	1.7

Most similar to: Ron Harper (97.9), Kendall Gill, Marques Johnson, Tony Campbell   IMP: 26% BRK: 5% COP: 11%

DALLAS MAVERICKS

Still just three years removed from making the All-Star team, Caron Butler already appears to be on the downside of his NBA career. The product of troubled teenage years, he did not arrive at UConn until age 20, so he has always seemed younger than he really was. He's now 30, and slipped badly last season. Exacerbating the problem, Butler didn't seem to realize he was no longer the same player, as detailed in a sober, definitive takedown by Mike Prada of BulletsForever.com.

In February, Butler was sent packing as part of Washington's rebuilding effort. He fit in perfectly with Dallas' cast of just-past-their-prime stars. His production, however, was little different after the trade. The biggest problem was Butler's declining efficiency. Among rotation regulars who used at least 22 percent of their team's possessions, just eight players had lower True Shooting Percentages. Entering the last year of his contract, Butler will need to bounce back in a big way before hitting the free-agent market. Because Butler declined so much from the previous season, ordinarily a return to form would be in order. However, the poor history of semi-star wings in their early 30s serves to dampen those expectations.

PF 35	Brian Cardinal	Hght: 6'8" Wght: 240 2011-12 status: free agent	Exp: 10 From: Purdue	Salary: --		SKILL RATINGS TOT OFF DEF REB PAS HND SHT ATH -4 -- +2 -- -- -- -- --
Year	Team	Age	G	MPG	Usg	3PA%	FTA%	INS	2P%	3P%	FT%	TS%	Reb%	Ast%	TO%	BLK%	STL%	PF%	oRTG	dRTG	Win%	WARP
07-08	MEM	31.0	37	11.9	.160	.515	.053	.538	.400	.309	.684	.461	.123	.022	.146	.003	.010	.062	104.3	107.1	.406	-0.1
08-09	MIN	32.0	64	14.2	.116	.396	.066	.670	.455	.326	.857	.515	.093	.038	.207	.011	.021	.067	104.4	107.0	.414	0.0
09-10	MIN	33.0	29	9.2	.083	.177	.156	.979	.407	.333	.944	.546	.061	.039	.137	.008	.017	.092	103.3	108.5	.334	-0.5
10-11p	DAL	34.0	76	-	.104	.334	.103	.769	.412	.351	.871	.528	.077	.034	.159	.008	.015	.077	-	-	.323	-
Most similar to: M.L. Carr (96.8), Bryon Russell, Tom Gugliotta, David Wingate																			IMP: 50%	BRK: 4%	COP: 11%	

Indianapolis Star reporter Mark Montieth has told a great story about Brian Cardinal's contract, and while it might be apocryphal, it's entertaining at minimum. Quoting Montieth: "Seems Memphis owner Michael Heisley, frustrated by general manager Jerry West's lack of activity, walked into West's office one day and asked why he hadn't signed anyone yet. So an exasperated West picked up his phone, called Cardinal's agent and offered the mid-level on the spot. Then he turned to Heisley and said something along the lines of 'There, you happy now?'"

Whatever the origin of Cardinal's six-year deal, it finally reached its conclusion at the end of the season. Over that span, Cardinal produced just 4.7 WARP and was at or below replacement level four times in six seasons. Credit Cardinal for continuing to work for his money. He was useful in the locker room and ready when called upon, but injuries robbed him of his meager skills. Cardinal is headed to Dallas for training camp with a chance to compete against Steve Novak for the backup power forward position. If he doesn't stick, the career of the player fondly known as The Custodian might be over.

C 6	Tyson Chandler	Hght: 7'1" Wght: 235 2011-12 status: free agent	Exp: 9 From: Dominguez HS (CA)	Salary: $12.6 million		SKILL RATINGS TOT OFF DEF REB PAS HND SHT ATH -1 0 +2 +1 -5 -5 +5 -2
Year	Team	Age	G	MPG	Usg	3PA%	FTA%	INS	2P%	3P%	FT%	TS%	Reb%	Ast%	TO%	BLK%	STL%	PF%	oRTG	dRTG	Win%	WARP
07-08	NOH	25.6	79	35.3	.146	.001	.149	1.148	.624	.000	.593	.632	.196	.014	.156	.024	.008	.041	105.6	104.4	.542	7.3
08-09	NOH	26.6	45	32.1	.138	.000	.142	1.142	.565	.000	.579	.581	.164	.007	.170	.033	.006	.048	104.5	106.0	.450	1.0
09-10	CHA	27.6	51	22.8	.141	.000	.197	1.197	.574	-	.732	.643	.165	.006	.260	.039	.008	.056	103.3	104.9	.447	0.7
10-11p	DAL	28.6	70	20.0	.138	.003	.161	1.158	.584	.003	.661	.614	.162	.008	.207	.032	.007	.053	103.3	105.2	.434	0.5
Most similar to: Mark West (95.4), Will Perdue, Brendan Haywood, Steve Johnson																			IMP: 42%	BRK: 9%	COP: 9%	

A change of scenery failed to revitalize Tyson Chandler's career like it did when he went from Chicago to New Orleans. He was limited by injuries and inconsistent on the floor during his final year with the Hornets, and the same was true of his lone season in Charlotte. Both Chandler's rebounding and his two-point percentage have fallen dramatically the last two years, and SCHOENE isn't optimistic about his chances to return to peak form. Chandler is only 28, but similar players were already starting to decline at the same age.

DALLAS MAVERICKS

Expected to play a backup role behind Brendan Haywood, Chandler has little chance of being worth the $12.6 million he'll make during the final season of his contract. Still, he can help Dallas as a defensive-minded backup. Never a great shot blocker, Chandler relies more on defensive positioning and takes relatively few chances. His size will always make him an effective paint defender when he is healthy. Chandler looked good over the summer with the U.S. National Team and was the only true center the team took to the FIBA World Championship.

C 33	Brendan Haywood	Hght: 7'0"	Exp: 9	Salary: $6.9 million		SKILL RATINGS							
		Wght: 263	From: North Carolina			TOT	OFF	DEF	REB	PAS	HND	SHT	ATH
		2011-12 status: guaranteed contract for $7.6 million				+1	+1	+4	+1	-4	-4	+3	-2
Year	Team	Age	G	MPG	Usg	3PA%	FTA%	INS	2P%	3P%	FT%	TS%	Reb%	Ast%	TO%	BLK%	STL%	PF%	oRTG	dRTG	Win%	WARP
07-08	WAS	28.4	80	27.8	.174	.000	.155	1.155	.528	.000	.735	.582	.152	.015	.129	.050	.007	.046	106.3	104.7	.552	6.3
08-09	WAS	29.4	6	29.2	.178	.000	.135	1.135	.480	.000	.476	.490	.149	.021	.132	.070	.012	.037	102.6	102.4	.505	0.3
09-10	DAL	30.4	77	30.6	.136	.001	.154	1.153	.563	.000	.620	.588	.175	.008	.142	.051	.006	.041	104.8	103.7	.537	5.9
10-11p	DAL	31.4	71	27.0	.143	.002	.146	1.145	.540	.000	.659	.575	.157	.010	.143	.046	.006	.042	104.2	104.5	.489	2.9
Most similar to: Erick Dampier (98.5), Ervin Johnson, Kelvin Cato, Dale Davis																IMP: 40%	BRK: 0%		COP: 15%			

Brendan Haywood stepped in as Dallas' starting center after being acquired with Caron Butler from Washington at the trade deadline, and played well enough for the Mavericks to give him a six-year contract worth up to $55 million over the summer. Because the last year is non-guaranteed, the deal is not as bad as the total numbers make it look. This is a matter of degree, however. The team is still on the hook for $10 million to Haywood during his age-35 season, which is unappealing.

Salary aside, Haywood is a very nice fit in the middle for a team in need of defense and rebounding, not scoring, from its center. Like Erick Dampier, his predecessor, Haywood is a high-percentage shooter who is judicious with his shot attempts. According to Hoopdata.com, more than 70 percent of Haywood's shots last season were at the rim. Defensively, Haywood is an upgrade over Dampier. He moves well for a player his size and does an excellent job of contesting shots without fouling. Though Butler was the biggest name in the deadline deal, Haywood should end up being the most valuable.

SG 20	Dominique Jones	Hght: 6'4"	Exp: R	Salary: $1.1 million		SKILL RATINGS							
		Wght: 215	From: South Florida			TOT	OFF	DEF	REB	PAS	HND	SHT	ATH
		2011-12 status: guaranteed contract for $1.2 million				-3	-1	-1	+2	+2	-1	-4	+3
Year	Team	Age	G	MPG	Usg	3PA%	FTA%	INS	2P%	3P%	FT%	TS%	Reb%	Ast%	TO%	BLK%	STL%	PF%	oRTG	dRTG	Win%	WARP
10-11p	DAL	22.5	76	5.0	.225	.189	.128	.939	.427	.267	.725	.474	.077	.045	.137	.008	.017	.052	102.8	106.6	.378	-0.3
Most similar to: Chris Douglas-Roberts (96.9), Tarence Kinsey, Sonny Weems, Antoine Wright																IMP: -	BRK: -		COP: -			

The Mavericks bought their way into the first round, purchasing Memphis' No. 25 overall pick (reportedly for the maximum $3 million, the usual going rate) to draft Dominique Jones. As a junior at South Florida, Jones ranked second in the Big East at 21.4 points per game, so his scoring pedigree is strong. Jones was a volume scorer at the NCAA level, however, and his translations suggest he'll need to improve his efficiency to become a useful NBA contributor. His comparisons are not particularly encouraging in this regard. One thing that would help Jones is ditching the three-pointer, at least until he improves his accuracy. He attempted five threes a night last season and made them at just a 31.1 percent clip with the shorter college line.

Working in Jones' favor is that he's more than just a one-dimensional player. He's got solid size for an off-guard and was a contributor on the glass, but can also handle the ball well enough to potentially become a combo guard down the road or share these duties with a scoring-minded point guard like Beaubois. Much like Beaubois, Jones will likely be limited to spot minutes as a rookie before moving into a larger role.

DALLAS MAVERICKS

PG 2	Jason Kidd	Hght: 6'4"	Exp: 16	Salary: $8.6 million	SKILL RATINGS						
		Wght: 210	From: California		TOT	OFF	DEF	REB	PAS	HND	SHT	ATH
		2011-12 status: guaranteed contract for $8.6 million			+5	+4	+3	+5	+4	+4	0	+2

Year	Team	Age	G	MPG	Usg	3PA%	FTA%	INS	2P%	3P%	FT%	TS%	Reb%	Ast%	TO%	BLK%	STL%	PF%	oRTG	dRTG	Win%	WARP
07-08	DAL	35.1	80	36.4	.182	.276	.064	.788	.387	.381	.818	.499	.117	.130	.234	.007	.022	.026	108.3	103.5	.654	14.4
08-09	DAL	36.1	81	35.6	.136	.380	.054	.674	.427	.406	.819	.550	.099	.112	.218	.010	.028	.027	109.4	104.4	.657	14.5
09-10	DAL	37.1	80	36.0	.146	.455	.048	.593	.420	.425	.808	.577	.088	.116	.214	.009	.026	.023	109.8	104.3	.673	15.4
10-11p	DAL	38.1	76	32.0	.132	.400	.046	.646	.400	.381	.797	.518	.089	.115	.227	.009	.024	.028	107.9	104.4	.612	10.0

Most similar to: Mark Jackson (92.6), Scottie Pippen, Darrell Armstrong, John Stockton — IMP: - BRK: - COP: -

If you're ever transported back to the year 1995 by a Hot Tub Time Machine, bet as many people as possible that by the end of his career Jason Kidd will become one of the league's best three-point shooters. Free money! Kidd was third in the league in three-pointers a year ago, making them at a career-best 42.3 percent clip. As his quickness has waned, Kidd has become progressively more reliant on the outside shot, improving his True Shooting Percentage in the process.

NBA fans from the mid-90s will be less surprised to hear that Kidd remains one of the league's best distributors. He passed Mark Jackson last November to move into second place on the career assists leaderboard and ranked fifth in the league in assist percentage last season. Fewer of Kidd's assists are of the drive-and-dish variety now, but he still runs a mean fast break and sees the court better than most of his peers. At the defensive end, Kidd struggles badly with quicker point guards. He tends to be more effective cross-matching and taking shooting guards, where his size and strength allow him to hold his own. Kidd's excellent defensive rebounding means calling him a liability at that end is a mistake.

WARP aside, Kidd was an unexpected All-Star pick--at best, a nod to the hometown fans at Cowboys Stadium or, at worst, simply the only substitute available because a snowstorm shut down airports throughout the East Coast. Still, he is aging with remarkable grace and figures to have a couple more years as a high-level starter ahead of him.

C 28	Ian Mahinmi	Hght: 6'11"	Exp: 2	Salary: $0.9 million	SKILL RATINGS						
		Wght: 230	From: Rouen, France		TOT	OFF	DEF	REB	PAS	HND	SHT	ATH
		2011-12 status: team option for $0.9 million			+4	+1	0	-2	0	-3	+3	+5

Year	Team	Age	G	MPG	Usg	3PA%	FTA%	INS	2P%	3P%	FT%	TS%	Reb%	Ast%	TO%	BLK%	STL%	PF%	oRTG	dRTG	Win%	WARP
07-08	SAS	21.5	6	3.8	.377	.000	.220	1.220	.500	.000	1.000	.658	.127	.021	.111	.132	.000	.084	110.7	99.3	.820	0.2
09-10	SAS	23.5	26	6.3	.253	.000	.228	1.228	.636	-	.660	.667	.183	.006	.165	.035	.009	.089	107.4	105.0	.577	0.5
10-11p	DAL	24.5	72	5.1	.194	.014	.148	1.134	.552	.023	.723	.592	.132	.018	.165	.057	.024	.071	104.2	102.5	.558	1.1

Most similar to: Vlade Divac (95.4), Stromile Swift, Joakim Noah, Gerald Wallace — IMP: 50% BRK: 5% COP: 3%

Over the course of three years in San Antonio, Ian Mahinmi totaled just 188 minutes. A variety of factors conspired to keep him off the court. Mahinmi spent nearly his entire rookie season playing in the D-League as a 21 year old. An ankle injury that ultimately required surgery cost Mahinmi the entire 2008-09 campaign. By the time he returned last year, the Spurs had loaded up in the frontcourt with little room left for him.

Physically, Mahinmi is intriguing. He's athletic for his size and runs the floor well. However, due to his lack of NBA playing time, Mahinmi is still very raw. He played well in the D-League, shooting a high percentage and blocking a high number of shots, which generated his remarkably optimistic SCHOENE projection for this season. As a lottery ticket, Mahinmi cost the Mavericks virtually nothing--a two-year minimum contract with the second season at team option. If Mahinmi provides even a fraction of the production his projection calls for, he'll be one of the league's best bargains.

DALLAS MAVERICKS

SF	Shawn Marion	Hght: 6'7"	Exp: 11	Salary: $7.1 million	SKILL RATINGS						
0		Wght: 228	From: UNLV		TOT	OFF	DEF	REB	PAS	HND	SHT	ATH
		2011-12 status: guaranteed contract for $7.7 million			0	0	+4	+4	-1	0	0	+1

Year	Team	Age	G	MPG	Usg	3PA%	FTA%	INS	2P%	3P%	FT%	TS%	Reb%	Ast%	TO%	BLK%	STL%	PF%	oRTG	dRTG	Win%	WARP
07-08	MIA	30.0	63	36.7	.194	.211	.070	.859	.567	.333	.707	.570	.168	.028	.092	.029	.025	.030	106.6	101.5	.667	12.1
08-09	TOR	31.0	69	35.8	.182	.055	.068	1.012	.506	.189	.796	.522	.142	.027	.110	.021	.018	.025	104.5	104.4	.505	4.5
09-10	DAL	32.0	75	31.8	.182	.020	.065	1.045	.516	.158	.755	.535	.114	.021	.106	.019	.015	.027	103.2	105.1	.437	1.0
10-11p	DAL	33.0	74	30.0	.177	.089	.064	.975	.518	.209	.759	.523	.126	.024	.108	.021	.017	.029	103.2	104.2	.465	2.3

Most similar to: Horace Grant (97.5), Kurt Thomas, Clarence Weatherspoon, P.J. Brown   IMP: 37%   BRK: 2%   COP: 8%

Someday, somewhere NBA historians will gather to figure out exactly how Shawn Marion fell so far so quickly. Within a two-year span, Marion went from All-Star to barely better than replacement level. Signing with Dallas last summer as a free agent did nothing to arrest Marion's freefall.

Naturally, Marion's biggest issue has been going from a perfect scenario in the up-tempo Phoenix offense to playing more half-court basketball in his last three stops (Miami, Toronto and now Dallas). That helps explain why Marion's two-point percentage is no longer stellar. Other drop-offs are more mysterious. Most players become better outside shooters as they age. Marion is going the wrong direction, having made less than 20 percent of his three-pointers the last two seasons. Never a great shooter, and always an awkward-looking one, Marion used to be much more accurate beyond the arc.

More troubling than the offensive losses were the hits Marion took to his defensive statistics last season. Playing more on the perimeter could have caused Marion's rebounding percentage to drop, but his steal and block percentages also both fell. Marion has always relied heavily on his athleticism. Now that he's in his mid-30s, that simply may not be an option any longer.

SF	Steve Novak	Hght: 6'10"	Exp: 4	Salary: --	SKILL RATINGS						
21		Wght: 240	From: Marquette		TOT	OFF	DEF	REB	PAS	HND	SHT	ATH
		2011-12 status: free agent			-4	--	-2	--	--	--	--	--

Year	Team	Age	G	MPG	Usg	3PA%	FTA%	INS	2P%	3P%	FT%	TS%	Reb%	Ast%	TO%	BLK%	STL%	PF%	oRTG	dRTG	Win%	WARP
07-08	HOU	24.9	35	7.6	.186	.659	.016	.357	.484	.479	.750	.651	.073	.010	.037	.008	.003	.030	109.7	107.1	.584	0.9
08-09	LAC	25.9	71	16.4	.169	.666	.024	.357	.518	.416	.913	.606	.064	.016	.054	.003	.009	.028	108.6	108.1	.516	2.4
09-10	LAC	26.9	54	6.7	.143	.623	.035	.412	.541	.310	.778	.505	.053	.008	.018	.004	.010	.026	103.9	107.3	.388	-0.2
10-11p	DAL	27.9	75	-	.154	.674	.025	.351	.515	.372	.804	.556	.060	.011	.036	.004	.007	.027	-	-	.345	-

Most similar to: Rasual Butler (90.7), Sam Mack, James Jones, Hubert Davis   IMP: 32%   BRK: 11%   COP: 14%

The ultimate shooting specialist, Steve Novak annually puts together bizarre statistics. Last year, Novak was off the charts in terms of turnovers, committing just two miscues all season in 361 minutes. The next-lowest turnover percentage among players with at least 100 minutes was 4.5 percent of plays, two and a half times higher than Novak's.

Alas, a reduced role was hardly ideal for Novak to get his shooting stroke going. Add in a smaller sample of three-point attempts and he ended up shooting a fluky low percentage from beyond the arc. Prospective new teams should judge Novak based on his 2008-09 season, when he was super-efficient from downtown and even managed a respectable usage rate. In limited minutes off the bench, especially if paired with big men who can mask his horrendous rebounding, Novak can be useful. He's headed to training camp with Dallas, which has an opening for a backup to Dirk Nowitzki.

DALLAS MAVERICKS

PF 41	Dirk Nowitzki	Hght: 7'0" Wght: 245 2011-12 status: guaranteed contract for $19.1 million	Exp: 12 Salary: $17.3 million From: Wurzburg, Germany		**SKILL RATINGS**						
					TOT	OFF	DEF	REB	PAS	HND	SHT	ATH
					+4	+4	+4	-2	+4	+3	+1	+3

Year	Team	Age	G	MPG	Usg	3PA%	FTA%	INS	2P%	3P%	FT%	TS%	Reb%	Ast%	TO%	BLK%	STL%	PF%	oRTG	dRTG	Win%	WARP
07-08	DAL	29.8	77	35.9	.290	.128	.140	1.011	.504	.359	.879	.585	.135	.045	.093	.019	.009	.033	109.6	104.2	.670	14.6
08-09	DAL	30.8	81	37.7	.304	.084	.119	1.035	.493	.359	.890	.564	.127	.030	.078	.015	.010	.027	107.7	105.4	.575	10.0
09-10	DAL	31.8	81	37.5	.290	.064	.136	1.072	.487	.421	.915	.578	.116	.033	.078	.020	.012	.032	107.5	104.9	.585	10.7
10-11p	DAL	32.8	76	37.0	.286	.105	.125	1.019	.488	.419	.892	.576	.113	.033	.082	.018	.010	.032	107.3	105.3	.568	8.9

Most similar to: Dominique Wilkins (96.7), Dan Issel, Tom Chambers, Chris Webber   IMP: 35% BRK: 0% COP: 7%

Dirk Nowitzki remains one of the toughest matchups in the NBA. At 6'11", Nowitzki can shoot over nearly any defender he encounters, and as a pure shot-maker he is as good as they come. Slowly, Nowitzki's game has migrated away from both the three-point line and the post, making him primarily a midrange jump shooter. Nowitzki manages to make this suboptimal strategy work with sheer brilliance. According to Hoopdata.com, he led the league in both makes and attempts from 16-23 feet, knocking down 46.0 percent of his attempts from a distance where the NBA average was just 40.0 percent.

Every so often, a writer will call Nowitzki the league's "forgotten superstar" and favorably compare his stats to his prime, including his 2006-07 MVP campaign. There are two primary reasons why Nowitzki is no longer that valuable. First, shooting fewer three-pointers has caused his efficiency to go down while the league as a whole has improved on offense. Second, Nowitzki has declined significantly as a rebounder. He rarely gets any offensive boards anymore and is below average overall on the glass for a power forward. These are minor quibbles, however. Nowitzki remains an All-Star and should hold his value through his new contract--especially if he mixes in a few more three-pointers.

SG 92	DeShawn Stevenson	Hght: 6'5" Wght: 218 2011-12 status: free agent	Exp: 10 Salary: $4.2 million From: Washington Union HS (CA)		**SKILL RATINGS**						
					TOT	OFF	DEF	REB	PAS	HND	SHT	ATH
					-3	-1	-1	-3	+1	+4	-5	-5

Year	Team	Age	G	MPG	Usg	3PA%	FTA%	INS	2P%	3P%	FT%	TS%	Reb%	Ast%	TO%	BLK%	STL%	PF%	oRTG	dRTG	Win%	WARP
07-08	WAS	27.1	82	31.2	.175	.426	.090	.664	.390	.381	.797	.528	.055	.046	.105	.005	.012	.020	106.3	106.9	.481	3.4
08-09	WAS	28.1	32	27.7	.149	.446	.091	.645	.363	.271	.533	.410	.051	.051	.111	.002	.012	.022	103.8	107.9	.368	-0.9
09-10	DAL	29.1	64	13.8	.108	.417	.074	.656	.355	.218	.714	.381	.060	.029	.144	.005	.009	.038	101.1	107.6	.293	-2.3
10-11p	DAL	30.1	73	5.0	.127	.546	.073	.527	.369	.278	.669	.423	.052	.039	.131	.004	.011	.029	103.0	107.4	.357	-0.4

Most similar to: Bruce Bowen (94.7), Clint Richardson, Brian Scalabrine, Fred Jones   IMP: 56% BRK: 26% COP: 4%

DeShawn Stevenson returned from a back injury that ended his 2008-09 campaign with a tattoo of Abe Lincoln on his neck surrounded by two No. 5s, which would have made more sense had Stevenson in fact wore the No. 5. (He was No. 2 in Washington before switching to No. 92 when he was involved in the Wizards' deadline deal with Dallas.) Alas, the tattoo might have been the most interesting aspect of Stevenson's season. Never a favorite of the numbers, Stevenson went into the tank last year, posting a 38.1 percent True Shooting Percentage. No one in the league who played more than 500 minutes was less efficient as a shooter.

To justify regular minutes while scoring so poorly, Stevenson would have to be our day's answer to Bill Russell on defense. He isn't. Despite a reputation as a stopper, Stevenson is an average defender. Last year, opponents produced almost exactly at their typical level against Stevenson. With the addition of Jones and more minutes for Beaubois, Stevenson should be regarded as a desperation option this season.

DALLAS MAVERICKS

SG 31	Jason Terry	Hght: 6'2" Wght: 180	Exp: 11 From: Arizona	Salary: $9.9 million							
		2011-12 status: partially-guaranteed contract for $10.7 million									

SKILL RATINGS

TOT	OFF	DEF	REB	PAS	HND	SHT	ATH
+2	+3	-1	-5	+3	+4	+1	0

Year	Team	Age	G	MPG	Usg	3PA%	FTA%	INS	2P%	3P%	FT%	TS%	Reb%	Ast%	TO%	BLK%	STL%	PF%	oRTG	dRTG	Win%	WARP
07-08	DAL	30.6	82	31.5	.218	.303	.082	.779	.519	.375	.857	.574	.046	.048	.077	.005	.016	.031	108.1	106.1	.565	8.0
08-09	DAL	31.6	74	33.7	.257	.329	.071	.742	.525	.366	.880	.571	.041	.046	.086	.006	.020	.026	109.4	107.0	.577	8.4
09-10	DAL	32.6	77	33.0	.231	.294	.093	.799	.479	.365	.866	.552	.031	.053	.086	.005	.019	.026	107.5	106.7	.524	5.6
10-11p	DAL	33.6	75	32.0	.215	.327	.078	.751	.489	.358	.850	.547	.035	.050	.091	.005	.017	.029	106.7	106.8	.496	4.0

Most similar to: Calvin Murphy (98.3), Jeff Hornacek, Randy Smith, David Wesley — IMP: 25% BRK: 0% COP: 15%

The NBA's Sixth Man Award winner in 2008-09, Jason Terry took a step backward last season, his worst performance in six years in Dallas. Terry's usage rate dropped from 25.7 percent in 2008-09, which tied his career high, to 23.1 percent of the Mavericks' plays. Meanwhile, he shot below 50 percent on two-pointers for the first time since arriving in Dallas, a drop attributable largely to worse accuracy from 10-15 feet out, according to Hoopdata.com.

Dangerous as a shooter and off the dribble, Terry creates problems for opposing reserves when he comes off the bench looking to score. He was most effective last season in isolation situations--Synergy Sports has him ranked sixth in the league, scoring an average of 1.06 points per play on isos. Terry can beat slower shooting guards one-on-one and regularly got to the free throw line in these situations. Still, the drop in his two-point percentage might be the first sign of Terry slowing slightly, as is to be expected at age 32. Since his 2011-12 contract is only partially guaranteed through mid-July, Dallas will have to keep a close eye on how Terry plays this season as well as the progress made by youngsters Rodrigue Beaubois and Dominique Jones before deciding how to proceed at shooting guard.

PF 7	Tim Thomas	Hght: 6'10" Wght: 240	Exp: 13 From: Villanova	Salary: $1.4 million							
		2011-12 status: free agent									

SKILL RATINGS

TOT	OFF	DEF	REB	PAS	HND	SHT	ATH
-1	--	+3	--	--	--	--	--

Year	Team	Age	G	MPG	Usg	3PA%	FTA%	INS	2P%	3P%	FT%	TS%	Reb%	Ast%	TO%	BLK%	STL%	PF%	oRTG	dRTG	Win%	WARP
07-08	LAC	31.2	63	30.8	.208	.311	.077	.767	.479	.307	.752	.506	.097	.041	.113	.011	.009	.045	104.9	106.4	.448	1.3
08-09	NYK	32.2	64	19.5	.200	.337	.095	.758	.446	.413	.736	.555	.092	.024	.125	.006	.012	.051	105.9	107.6	.446	0.8
09-10	DAL	33.2	18	15.8	.212	.329	.081	.752	.524	.372	.875	.579	.082	.023	.107	.005	.018	.050	106.9	106.9	.502	0.5
10-11p	DAL	34.2	75	-	.196	.339	.077	.738	.482	.365	.782	.543	.081	.027	.119	.007	.014	.051	-	-	.414	-

Most similar to: George McCloud (96.9), Rodney Rogers, Ron Anderson, Steve Smith — IMP: 42% BRK: 3% COP: 8%

A history of good adjusted plus-minus ratings helped sell former Dallas consultant Wayne Winston on Tim Thomas, and Thomas signed with the Mavericks for the veteran minimum last summer. Thomas was effective off the bench in spot minutes as a power forward during the first half of the season before real life intervened, as he missed the remainder of the year caring for his sick wife. Thomas hoped to return this season and re-signed with Dallas in August, but decided before training camp he could not leave his wife.

Denver Nuggets

Health issues derailed the Denver Nuggets' 2009-10 season, which isn't exactly an original story. What made the Nuggets unique was that their biggest loss was not a player but their head coach, George Karl.

Days after coaching the Western Conference in the All-Star Game, Karl held a press conference to announce he had been diagnosed with throat and neck cancer. Karl continued coaching for the next couple of weeks while beginning chemotherapy. Ultimately, the physical toll of the treatment was too much, and he had to take a leave of absence. The hope was that Karl would be able to return by the postseason, but blood clots slowed his recovery and he was nowhere close to full health when the Nuggets began their playoff run, which ended quickly with a six-game loss to the Utah Jazz.

In the bigger picture, the far more important news is this: Karl is recovering nicely. He returned to the public eye in July, making a poignant appearance at the fundraising dinner for the St. Jude Research Hospital in Memphis. Shortly thereafter, he accepted the fitting Jimmy V Award at the ESPY awards. In early September, Karl was cleared to return to the sidelines.

From a basketball-centric perspective, Karl's return is big news. His departure was costly down the stretch for a Nuggets team that was as good as any in the Western Conference through the start of March. Under Karl, Denver outscored opponents by 5.0 points per game, which would have put the Nuggets fifth in the league over the course of the full season. In the 19 games coached by acting replacement Adrian Dantley, Denver's point differential dropped to +1.1 points per game, worse than any other West playoff team.

More interesting than the fact that the Nuggets saw a drop-off without Karl is just how the change played out: suddenly, they found referees' whistles far less favorable. Credit ESPN's Chris Broussard for noticing the trend and his colleague John Hollinger for confirming it with advanced statistics. Denver's ratio of free throw attempts per field goal attempt went down from .391 under Karl to .326. Meanwhile, at the other end of the floor, opponents saw their FTA/FGA ratio increase from .315 to .345 when Dantley replaced Karl on the sidelines. Even accounting for the slight difference attributable to the Nuggets playing 11 of their 19 games under Dantley on the road, it's hard to write off that difference.

A comparison of players' rates of free throw attempts per field goal attempt under Karl and Dantley shows that Denver's stars, Carmelo Anthony and Chauncey Billups, suffered heavily from the coaching change in terms of their ability to get to the line (Table 1).

The loss of the points at the charity stripe was a huge factor in Denver struggling down the stretch. We can imagine a game without free throws and simulate this possibility by taking away the points scored at the line and the possessions used there in the formulas for Offensive and Defensive Rating. Comparing these theoretical foul-free Offensive and Defensive Ratings to what the Nuggets actually did under Dantley and Karl shows how much Denver was hurt by less favorable refereeing.

NUGGETS IN A BOX

Last year's record	53-29
Last year's Offensive Rating	113.3 (5)
Last year's Defensive Rating	109.1 (16)
Last year's point differential	4.1 (8)
Team pace	93.5 (5)
SCHOENE projection	49-33 (3)
Projected Offensive Rating	113.5 (5)
Projected Defensive Rating	110.1 (17)
Projected team weighted age	29.0 (7)
Projected '10-11 payroll	$82.4 (4)
Est. payroll obligations, '11-12	$61.6 (9)

Head coach: George Karl

George Karl will return to the sidelines this season, which is great news for his health and for the Nuggets. Sometime this season, Karl will win his 1,000th game as an NBA head coach, putting him in elite company--just six other coaches are in the 1,000 club. To secure his legacy as one of the league's best coaches, a championship remains missing from his resume. With Chauncey Billups aging, this might be Karl's last best shot to win one.

Table 1: Denver Nuggets' Free Throw Rates, Karl vs. Dantley

Player	Karl	Dantley	Diff
Anthony	0.460	0.278	-0.182
Lawson	0.375	0.211	-0.164
Petro	0.294	0.164	-0.130
Billups	0.562	0.456	-0.107
Graham	0.381	0.286	-0.096
Carter	0.090	0.000	-0.090
Smith	0.211	0.152	-0.059
Afflalo	0.172	0.152	-0.020
Andersen	0.932	0.977	0.045
Allen	0.087	0.149	0.062
Hilario	0.528	0.769	0.242

This remarkably crude measure suggest that more than 40 percent in the difference between how Denver played under Dantley and Karl was attributable to the way the team was refereed under each coach. Some part of this is probably explained by personnel. The Nuggets largely played without Kenyon Martin down the stretch due to left patella tendinitis. Martin's absence did not affect the team's ability to get to the free throw line on offense, but replacements Malik Allen and Johan Petro were far more prone to fouling at the other end of the floor.

Alas, getting Martin back in the lineup was not enough to save Denver from falling victim to fouls in the playoffs. The Nuggets-Jazz matchup may as well have been a free throw shooting contest at times. Both teams averaged more than 35 free throw attempts per game during the series, and Utah shot a ridiculous 51 foul shots during a series-ending Game Six victory. Denver tried seven fewer free throws over the course of the series, and the Nuggets' most favorable game at the line (Game Five, when they attempted 42 free throws to the Jazz's 25) came, coincidentally or not, later on the day Hollinger wrote about the team's difficulty getting calls under Dantley.

Whatever the explanation for the foul phenomenon, it

Table 2: Referees' Effect on Nuggets Games, Karl vs. Dantley

	Net Rating	Foul-Free Net Rating	Refereeing Factor
Karl	5.0	3.6	1.4
Dantley	1.4	1.5	-0.1
Difference	3.6	2.1	1.5

should be a thing of the past with a healthy Karl at the helm. The question now becomes whether Denver can return to the level at which the team was playing before Karl's departure. They'll try to do so with virtually the same mix as last season. The Nuggets' top eight players in terms of minutes played are all under contract for 2010-11. Denver also brought back experienced point guard Anthony Carter, leaving reserves Joey Graham and Petro as the biggest departures.

Still, the Nuggets had a major issue to address in the health of the frontcourt. Martin's status going forward is something of a question mark after he missed 24 games last season and underwent offseason knee surgery. Already, Martin has undergone microfracture surgery on both knees, so nagging injuries are basically a given for him. He's missed at least 11 games during every season of his seven-year contract that expires at the end of 2010-11. Surgery this summer on his left patella tendon is expected to cost Martin at least part of the season.

That being the case, Denver needed a fourth big man capable of playing rotation minutes and stepping into the starting lineup in Martin's absence--especially with backup post Chris Andersen returning from his own patella surgery. The Nuggets found a well-qualified option in Al Harrington, a coveted option among teams dangling the mid-level exception. Harrington's three-point range and effectiveness at spacing the floor give Denver a different dimension in the frontcourt, and his ability to sop up minutes (he's averaged at least 30 mpg in seven of the last eight years) is valuable insurance should Harrington be able to accept the fact that he might not be a starter when the team is at full strength.

Harrington didn't come cheaply. Denver was already over the luxury-tax limit, so the team will be paying double Harrington's $5.8 million salary. But he's not especially old (he'll be 31 in February) and the Nuggets protected themselves down the road by guaranteeing only part of the fourth year of Harrington's contract and none of the fifth and final year.

The addition of Harrington turned out to be the last move made by vice president of basketball operations Mark Warkentien, whose contract--along with that of vice president of player personnel Rex Chapman--was allowed to expire in August. The move was surprising because Warkentien was the NBA's Executive of the Year in 2008-09, but Denver never had much centralized power in a front-office structure that included multiple voices.

The front office by committee will now be led by new executive vice president of basketball operations Masai Ujiri, a native of Nigeria who made his name in the league as an international scout. Ujiri served the Nuggets in a scouting role before leaving for a promotion to assistant general manager in Toronto. Josh Kroenke is taking a larger role as he assumes ownership of the team from his father, Stan, who withdrew from day-to-day operations after purchasing the NFL's St. Louis Rams. Advisor Bret Bearup is also influential in Denver's basketball decisions.

The first order of business for the new front office is figuring out what to do with Anthony. Growing whispers over the summer suggested that the team's leading scorer wants to be traded. Denver has a standing max extension offer for Anthony on the table, but scuttle has it that he would rather not stay in the Mile High City for the long term. Anthony could leave as an unrestricted free agent at season's end, but doing so would put him at the mercy of changes in the NBA's Collective Bargaining Agreement, which is up for renewal next summer. Anthony would be better off locking in his new contract now by using his possible departure as leverage to force a trade.

Fanhouse.com reported in August that reserve guard J.R. Smith is also on the trade block. Smith, who has clashed at times with Karl and his previous coaches, lost a key ally with Warkentien's departure and now might be vulnerable.

For all the turmoil, the Nuggets look like a pretty good basketball team if they keep their core together and get healthy. Whether he pushes Martin to a reserve role or comes off the bench himself, Harrington strengthens what might be the league's best second unit, at least in terms of a core nine-man rotation. The addition of Arron Afflalo as a defensive specialist and outside shooter at shooting guard allowed Denver to keep Smith in a super-sixth man role in 2009-10. Smith and Andersen are both energizers, a role they played to perfection en route to the 2009 Western Conference Finals. The Nuggets also boast second-year guard Ty Lawson, who could start for many teams but continues to serve an apprenticeship under Billups, pushing a pace that is already fast even higher when he replaces the veteran.

Where Denver could run into issues is going deeper into the bench, which was the case last year when injuries forced Allen and Graham into regular roles. This year's group is better with the addition of Shelden Williams and the subtraction of Graham, which might force Karl into using front-office favorite Renaldo Balkman at small forward. In the backcourt, Carter is aging but remains adequate for spot minutes.

Besides an injury, the biggest potential problem for the Nuggets would be slippage by Billups. Fortunately, SCHOENE sees a relatively gentle aging curve for the veteran point guard, who will be 34 by the time the season starts. Gradually, Denver should start shifting some of Billups' minutes to Lawson, aiding the youngster's development and keeping the starter fresh.

Anthony might be wise to reconsider his desire to leave given that the Nuggets have been much more successful in recent years than most of the teams that might pursue him in free agency. A healthy Denver squad with Karl on the sidelines stands the chance of being as good as anyone in the Western Conference. SCHOENE sees the Nuggets returning to the level of play they reached during the 2009 playoffs and the first half of the 2009-10 season. It's not far-fetched to imagine Denver winning the West if the team can simply hold everything together for one more year.

Kevin Pelton

From the Blogosphere

Who: Jeremy Wagner
What: Roundball Mining Company
Where: http://www.roundballminingcompany.com

Last year, Chauncey Billups began to fall victim to the subtle attack of physical deterioration. After producing the best stretch of basketball of his career from January through mid-March, following a three-week vacation due to a strained groin, Billups appeared to hit a wall. Over the Nuggets' final 15 games, Billups converted better than 40 percent of his shots a meager four times and his defense suffered as well.

Billups had a similar experience in the 2009 Western Conference Finals, and it is a red flag that fatigue hit two months earlier in 2010. His stamina could be further compromised by spending the summer playing for the U.S. in the FIBA World Championship. Billups may produce another one- or two-month stretch of spectacular play, but if he is going to avoid a similar meltdown come the Ides of March, his minutes must decrease significantly.

DENVER NUGGETS

NUGGETS FIVE-YEAR TRENDS

Season	AGE	W-L	POW	PYTH	SEED	ORTG	DRTG	PT DIFF	PACE
05-06	27.4	44-38	43.9 (12)	41.7	3	107.1 (18)	106.3 (12)	0.2 (15)	92.7 (2)
06-07	26.5	45-37	46.4 (9)	45.4	6	109.3 (9)	107.0 (9)	1.6 (9)	96.2 (2)
07-08	28.5	50-32	52.4 (10)	50.6	8	112.4 (11)	108.3 (9)	3.7 (11)	97.7 (1)
08-09	27.7	54-28	52.2 (7)	50.4	2	112.0 (7)	107.9 (8)	3.4 (8)	93.1 (5)
09-10	28.3	53-29	53.6 (7)	52.0	4	113.3 (5)	109.1 (16)	4.1 (8)	93.5 (5)

Season	PAY	OFFENSE eFG	oREB	FT/FGA	TO	DEFENSE eFG	oREB	FT/FGA	TO
05-06	$53.8	.488 (15)	.268 (16)	.258 (12)	.158 (14)	.493 (20)	.720 (20)	.227 (6)	.172 (4)
06-07	$65.0	.501 (12)	.289 (7)	.268 (8)	.171 (21)	.499 (15)	.718 (21)	.203 (2)	.169 (9)
07-08	$81.2	.510 (9)	.255 (21)	.269 (2)	.146 (10)	.499 (14)	.721 (22)	.203 (5)	.159 (6)
08-09	$67.1	.512 (7)	.275 (15)	.290 (1)	.164 (24)	.485 (5)	.717 (23)	.259 (25)	.165 (7)
09-10	$75.3	.509 (10)	.261 (19)	.290 (1)	.147 (8)	.495 (14)	.724 (26)	.251 (24)	.160 (9)

(league rankings in parenthesis)

SG 6 — Arron Afflalo
Hght: 6'5" Exp: 3 Salary: $2.0 million
Wght: 215 From: UCLA
2011-12 status: due qualifying offer of $2.9 million

SKILL RATINGS
TOT	OFF	DEF	REB	PAS	HND	SHT	ATH
-1	+1	+4	+1	-2	+1	+3	-2

Year	Team	Age	G	MPG	Usg	3PA%	FTA%	INS	2P%	3P%	FT%	TS%	Reb%	Ast%	TO%	BLK%	STL%	PF%	oRTG	dRTG	Win%	WARP
07-08	DET	22.5	75	13.0	.152	.153	.122	.969	.461	.208	.782	.494	.084	.025	.109	.006	.015	.041	102.3	106.1	.375	-0.8
08-09	DET	23.5	74	16.7	.146	.286	.083	.798	.456	.402	.817	.548	.065	.017	.115	.008	.012	.056	103.8	108.1	.362	-1.4
09-10	DEN	24.5	82	27.2	.140	.355	.061	.707	.488	.434	.735	.576	.065	.028	.105	.010	.010	.045	105.4	107.5	.430	0.6
10-11p	DEN	25.5	76	27.0	.143	.358	.082	.724	.474	.392	.764	.556	.070	.026	.108	.011	.012	.047	104.8	107.0	.429	0.6

Most similar to: Rod Higgins (98.1), Al Wood, Eric Washington, Kelenna Azubuike
IMP: 47% BRK: 12% COP: 2%

Picked up from Detroit last summer for a second-round pick as a cost-effective replacement for Dahntay Jones, Afflalo proved an upgrade as the Nuggets' perimeter defensive specialist. As a stopper, Afflalo was a slight step down. He's not as physical as Jones, who made his reputation by refusing to give an inch to Kobe Bryant in the 2009 Western Conference Finals. Afflalo lacks the size to match up with many of the league's better small forwards and relies more on moving his feet defensively. He was very strong in terms of defending the pick-and-roll.

Afflalo was, however, a pleasant surprise on offense, where he demonstrated that his 40.2 percent three-point shooting during his last year with the Pistons was no fluke. Taking advantage of the good looks created by Chauncey Billups and Carmelo Anthony, Afflalo shot 43.4 percent, good for eighth in the league. A heavy percentage of Afflalo's offense came from the perimeter. He has yet to show the ability as a pro to create for himself on a consistent basis--a bit of a surprise because he was a go-to scorer at UCLA.

C 11 — Chris Andersen
Hght: 6'10" Exp: 8 Salary: $4.5 million
Wght: 228 From: Blinn Junior College (TX)
2011-12 status: guaranteed contract for $4.9 million

SKILL RATINGS
TOT	OFF	DEF	REB	PAS	HND	SHT	ATH
+4	0	+4	+2	-4	-3	+4	+3

Year	Team	Age	G	MPG	Usg	3PA%	FTA%	INS	2P%	3P%	FT%	TS%	Reb%	Ast%	TO%	BLK%	STL%	PF%	oRTG	dRTG	Win%	WARP
07-08	NOH	29.8	5	6.8	.134	.000	.180	1.180	.286	.000	.500	.342	.157	.000	.102	.092	.000	.083	97.5	102.5	.333	-0.1
08-09	DEN	30.8	71	20.6	.135	.023	.181	1.158	.560	.200	.718	.608	.175	.009	.157	.093	.014	.053	105.6	101.2	.644	6.9
09-10	DEN	31.8	76	22.3	.109	.007	.251	1.244	.573	.000	.695	.631	.164	.009	.143	.063	.012	.045	104.3	102.2	.570	5.4
10-11p	DEN	32.8	64	20.0	.103	.007	.235	1.228	.576	.023	.695	.631	.165	.009	.155	.067	.013	.048	104.0	102.0	.565	4.0

Most similar to: Ervin Johnson (94.9), Dikembe Mutombo, Marcus Camby, Adonal Foyle
IMP: 41% BRK: 0% COP: 6%

The Birdman received less attention than he had during his first season back in Denver, but Chris Andersen was nearly as effective as the Nuggets' top frontcourt reserve. The biggest difference between Andersen's two stat lines was a drop in block percentage. While his league-leading block rate from 2008-09 was probably unsustainable, he still ranked third in the league a year ago. Otherwise, Andersen remained effective on the glass and highly efficient as a scorer thanks to his strict regimen of easy attempts at the rim.

It's easy to see Andersen's tattoos and hair (all part of the Birdman persona) and think he is nothing more than a curiosity, but his strong individual statistics are backed up by a positive impact at the team level. Denver played much better with Andersen and other reserves on the floor in the 2009 postseason (especially at home, where the crowd fed off the energy provided by Andersen and J.R. Smith), and that trend continued last season. Andersen's +13.5 adjusted plus-minus ranked sixth in the league, trailing only superstars. He doesn't belong in that class, but he changes the game in a positive way when he comes off the bench, which is one of the highest compliments possible for a reserve. As a result, the Nuggets can't get Andersen back from surgery on his right patella tendon quickly enough. Unfortunately, he may not be back in time for the start of the season.

SF 15 — Carmelo Anthony

Hght: 6'8" Exp: 7 Salary: $17.1 million
Wght: 230 From: Syracuse
2011-12 status: player option or ETO for $18.5 million

SKILL RATINGS

TOT	OFF	DEF	REB	PAS	HND	SHT	ATH
+4	+4	-4	+2	+3	-1	0	+4

Year	Team	Age	G	MPG	Usg	3PA%	FTA%	INS	2P%	3P%	FT%	TS%	Reb%	Ast%	TO%	BLK%	STL%	PF%	oRTG	dRTG	Win%	WARP
07-08	DEN	23.9	77	36.4	.303	.082	.130	1.048	.509	.354	.786	.568	.109	.039	.126	.010	.015	.038	107.7	106.0	.557	8.2
08-09	DEN	24.9	66	34.5	.316	.105	.128	1.022	.455	.371	.793	.532	.113	.044	.123	.008	.016	.038	106.9	106.1	.525	5.1
09-10	DEN	25.9	69	38.2	.335	.094	.136	1.042	.478	.316	.830	.548	.099	.038	.106	.009	.017	.038	108.5	106.2	.574	8.6
10-11p	DEN	26.9	73	38.0	.305	.131	.128	.997	.481	.356	.811	.552	.099	.041	.116	.008	.015	.038	107.9	106.1	.559	8.3

Most similar to: Dominique Wilkins (98.3), Xavier McDaniel, Glenn Robinson, Corey Maggette   IMP: 43% BRK: 0% COP: 9%

Now in his prime, Carmelo Anthony has established a fairly steady level of performance. He can be counted on to use somewhere just over 30 percent of the Nuggets' plays with an efficiency right around the league average. He's an average to slightly above rebounder and a quality defender when committed. Is that package worth the max salary? Probably, and there's no question that's what Anthony is going to command next season, whether in Denver or somewhere else. At the same time, grouping him in with LeBron James and Dwyane Wade, his peers from the 2003 draft class, flatters Anthony. This isn't solely a statistical perspective; last year was the first time Anthony made an All-NBA Second Team. He's a second-tier star.

The big upgrade Anthony made to his game last season was cutting down on his miscues, posting his lowest turnover percentage since 2005-06. That translated into career highs in both Win% and WARP. Anthony's numbers might have looked even better if not for the decline in trips to the free throw line under Adrian Dantley. Those free throws are a crucial part of Anthony's offensive game, which can use the high-percentage scores generated by his isolations on the wing.

PF 32 — Renaldo Balkman

Hght: 6'8" Exp: 4 Salary: $1.7 million
Wght: 208 From: South Carolina
2011-12 status: guaranteed contract for $1.7 million

SKILL RATINGS

TOT	OFF	DEF	REB	PAS	HND	SHT	ATH
+1	0	+1	+1	0	+1	+3	+4

Year	Team	Age	G	MPG	Usg	3PA%	FTA%	INS	2P%	3P%	FT%	TS%	Reb%	Ast%	TO%	BLK%	STL%	PF%	oRTG	dRTG	Win%	WARP
07-08	NYK	23.8	65	14.6	.126	.045	.158	1.113	.517	.083	.432	.492	.131	.019	.140	.025	.021	.064	102.5	104.6	.431	0.3
08-09	DEN	24.8	53	14.7	.149	.027	.110	1.083	.568	.286	.646	.585	.151	.019	.134	.023	.030	.056	106.1	104.4	.557	2.3
09-10	DEN	25.8	13	7.0	.130	.263	.099	.836	.545	.000	.333	.339	.145	.034	.225	.017	.044	.078	99.5	102.5	.396	0.0
10-11p	DEN	26.8	76	5.0	.131	.049	.120	1.071	.543	.203	.575	.546	.138	.021	.136	.022	.022	.057	103.8	104.5	.477	0.5

Most similar to: Andrew DeClercq (96.8), Ryan Bowen, Jerome Williams, Eduardo Najera   IMP: 38% BRK: 2% COP: 7%

The Denver front office is fond of Renaldo Balkman, who was signed to a three-year contract extension for very reasonable money that kicks in this season. Alas, George Karl hasn't been won over, and Balkman spent most of last season glued to the Denver bench. The Nuggets moved him to small forward from power forward, yet Balkman found fewer minutes behind Joey Graham in the Denver rotation. With Graham in Cleveland, Karl may have no choice but to use Balkman at times behind Carmelo Anthony this season.

DENVER NUGGETS

As a three-man, Balkman's lack of range is a major issue. He's made just eight three-pointers in his four-year NBA career, and his poor shooting from the foul line suggests improvement is not in the offing. The tradeoff is the activity Balkman brings to the floor, especially at the defensive end. As a small forward, his rebounding is excellent, and he has piled up steals and blocks whenever he has seen regular action.

PG 1	Chauncey Billups	Hght: 6'3" Exp: 13 Salary: $13.2 million					
		Wght: 202 From: Colorado					
		2011-12 status: partially-guaranteed contract for $14.2 million					

SKILL RATINGS

TOT	OFF	DEF	REB	PAS	HND	SHT	ATH
+5	+5	-3	-2	+1	+1	+1	+3

Year	Team	Age	G	MPG	Usg	3PA%	FTA%	INS	2P%	3P%	FT%	TS%	Reb%	Ast%	TO%	BLK%	STL%	PF%	oRTG	dRTG	Win%	WARP
07-08	DET	31.6	78	32.4	.231	.278	.156	.878	.479	.401	.918	.619	.050	.099	.130	.005	.019	.025	112.8	105.4	.721	16.0
08-09	DEN	32.6	79	35.3	.218	.292	.148	.856	.425	.408	.913	.592	.049	.081	.130	.005	.017	.026	110.7	107.0	.617	11.7
09-10	DEN	33.6	73	34.1	.244	.298	.165	.867	.441	.386	.910	.601	.052	.073	.130	.003	.016	.027	111.0	106.7	.632	11.2
10-11p	DEN	34.6	74	34.0	.214	.289	.146	.857	.452	.392	.905	.594	.048	.077	.133	.004	.017	.029	109.9	106.5	.606	10.0

Most similar to: John Lucas (97.3), Tim Hardaway, Mark Price, Sam Cassell   IMP: 46% BRK: 0% COP: 0%

Chauncey Billups put together a carbon copy of his first season in Denver, an encouraging sign for a player who turned 33 just before the start of training camp. About the only negative to be found in Billups' 2009-10 campaign were the nine games he missed in late December and early January due to a groin injury.

Billups' game is ideal for aging well. He has excellent size and strength for a point guard and is also a fine outside shooter, allowing him to compensate for declining quickness. SCHOENE comparable Sam Cassell is a good comparison in that regard, and Cassell remained effective through age 37 and made his first All-Star Game at the age of 34. One significant point of similarity between the two? With Cassell retired, Billups is probably the best post-up point guard in the league, with an honorable mention to Andre Miller.

Billups has suffered a bit more with age at the defensive end, and the Nuggets were better defensively as a team with backup Ty Lawson on the court last season. However, Billups' size works to his advantage on the other end as well, as he's been able to trade assignments at times with first Dahntay Jones and now Arron Afflalo.

PG 25	Anthony Carter	Hght: 6'2" Exp: 11 Salary: $0.9 million					
		Wght: 195 From: Hawaii					
		2011-12 status: free agent					

SKILL RATINGS

TOT	OFF	DEF	REB	PAS	HND	SHT	ATH
-1	0	-3	+1	+1	+2	-1	+1

Year	Team	Age	G	MPG	Usg	3PA%	FTA%	INS	2P%	3P%	FT%	TS%	Reb%	Ast%	TO%	BLK%	STL%	PF%	oRTG	dRTG	Win%	WARP
07-08	DEN	32.8	70	28.0	.138	.203	.059	.856	.497	.349	.753	.530	.055	.084	.195	.010	.023	.037	104.8	105.4	.480	2.6
08-09	DEN	33.8	78	22.9	.144	.153	.060	.907	.490	.239	.731	.490	.066	.091	.269	.006	.027	.036	104.0	105.9	.436	0.7
09-10	DEN	34.8	54	15.9	.127	.257	.023	.766	.500	.270	.846	.482	.059	.083	.237	.011	.023	.037	104.1	105.7	.446	0.5
10-11p	DEN	35.8	71	1.6	.119	.212	.035	.823	.492	.272	.744	.482	.059	.077	.235	.007	.024	.040	103.4	105.8	.419	0.0

Most similar to: Frank Johnson (94.4), Rickey Green, Maurice Cheeks, Dennis Johnson   IMP: 43% BRK: 0% COP: 9%

The addition of Ty Lawson through the draft relegated Anthony Carter to the role of third point guard last season, yet Carter still ended up playing more than 850 minutes as a fill-in at both backcourt spots and briefly moved ahead of Lawson as the backup point guard. Carter is a favorite of the coaching staff because he's an excellent defender and a good passer who understands his role. Still, Carter's limited playoff action (seven minutes all series) ought to be more indicative of his role in 2010-11.

Other than a fluky 2007-08, Carter has been highly inefficient as a scorer. The big problem is Carter's insistence on regularly shooting threes despite having made them at better than a 27.0 percent clip just once in his career (2007-08, natch). The combination of a poor True Shooting Percentage and a very low usage rate makes Carter one of the league's weaker scorers. At 35, that's unlikely to change.

DENVER NUGGETS

PF 7 — Al Harrington

Hght: 6'9" Exp: 12 Salary: $5.8 million
Wght: 250 From: St. Patrick's HS (Elizabeth, NJ)
2011-12 status: guaranteed contract for $6.2 million

SKILL RATINGS

TOT	OFF	DEF	REB	PAS	HND	SHT	ATH
+1	+2	-2	-3	0	-1	+1	+1

Year	Team	Age	G	MPG	Usg	3PA%	FTA%	INS	2P%	3P%	FT%	TS%	Reb%	Ast%	TO%	BLK%	STL%	PF%	oRTG	dRTG	Win%	WARP
07-08	GSW	28.2	81	27.0	.212	.371	.076	.705	.481	.376	.774	.547	.110	.026	.082	.005	.014	.051	107.3	106.3	.534	5.4
08-09	NYK	29.2	73	34.9	.258	.313	.086	.774	.487	.364	.793	.547	.100	.017	.107	.006	.017	.039	106.5	106.5	.497	4.3
09-10	NYK	30.2	72	30.5	.269	.314	.107	.793	.496	.342	.757	.546	.106	.023	.101	.009	.014	.043	106.9	106.4	.517	4.6
10-11p	DEN	31.2	74	29.3	.228	.343	.088	.744	.490	.350	.761	.539	.105	.020	.098	.008	.014	.046	105.9	106.2	.488	3.2

Most similar to: Chris Morris (97.1), Antoine Walker, Clifford Robinson, Scott Wedman   IMP: 28% BRK: 2% COP: 19%

As players in their early 30s go, Al Harrington might be one of the most reliable bets. He last missed more than nine games in a season way back in 2004-05, has averaged more than 30 minutes a night seven times in the last eight years and has put up virtually identical stat lines the last three seasons, right down to True Shooting Percentages within a thousandth of each other. His three-point range should help Harrington remain effective as he ages. All of that is to say Harrington was a good choice as a target in free agency.

The downside to Harrington's 2009-10 campaign, which is not reflected in his individual statistics, was a distinct lack of effort at the defensive end. In fairness to Harrington, he was not alone among last season's Knicks, especially after the trade deadline. On a winning team where the coach has more freedom to cut his minutes, Harrington should provide much more energy in Denver.

C 31 — Nenê Hilario

Hght: 6'11" Exp: 8 Salary: $11.4 million
Wght: 250 From: Sao Carlos, Brazil
2011-12 status: player option or ETO for $11.6 million

SKILL RATINGS

TOT	OFF	DEF	REB	PAS	HND	SHT	ATH
+3	+2	+3	-1	+4	+4	+4	+5

Year	Team	Age	G	MPG	Usg	3PA%	FTA%	INS	2P%	3P%	FT%	TS%	Reb%	Ast%	TO%	BLK%	STL%	PF%	oRTG	dRTG	Win%	WARP
07-08	DEN	25.6	16	16.6	.182	.009	.190	1.181	.414	.000	.551	.459	.176	.024	.185	.037	.014	.072	102.0	104.1	.429	0.1
08-09	DEN	26.6	77	32.6	.181	.005	.159	1.154	.607	.200	.723	.645	.137	.019	.144	.031	.019	.049	106.4	104.6	.559	7.4
09-10	DEN	27.6	82	33.6	.166	.002	.179	1.177	.589	.000	.704	.631	.131	.033	.122	.022	.021	.045	106.5	104.3	.571	8.8
10-11p	DEN	28.6	76	34.0	.163	.005	.169	1.164	.569	.058	.677	.605	.138	.030	.145	.025	.017	.052	105.3	104.5	.527	6.0

Most similar to: Scot Pollard (96.5), Brad Miller, Horace Grant, Tyrone Hill   IMP: 40% BRK: 0% COP: 4%

Nenê represents the limitations of the term "athletic." The Brazilian center looks like a lumbering block-to-block player, yet he's got tremendous quickness for his size. At the same time, Nenê is not a leaper at all. This contradiction is revealed by the fact that Nenê's steal rate was nearly as good as his block rate last season. So is he athletic or not? The multiple components of what we consider athleticism make a single word insufficient to capture them all.

As for Nenê himself, he enjoyed another solid season as a starting center, playing all 82 games for the first time in his career. Given that he topped out at 64 games over the span from 2004-05 through 2007-08 (when he dealt with a ruptured ACL in the season opener and testicular cancer, among other ailments), this fact deserves to be celebrated. The full campaign helped Nenê finish sixth among centers in WARP. He might just sneak into an All-Star Game at some point, especially if Denver plays well in the first half of this season; lesser players have certainly been rewarded with an All-Star trip.

The strength of Nenê's game is his play in the post. He can overpower smaller defenders and possesses nice touch around the basket. Defensively, Nenê is only average because he struggles in the most important areas for a center--contesting shots in the paint and controlling the defensive glass.

DENVER NUGGETS

PG 3	Ty Lawson	Hght: 5'11" Wght: 195 2011-12 status: team option for $1.7 million	Exp: 1 From: North Carolina	Salary: $1.5 million						

SKILL RATINGS

TOT	OFF	DEF	REB	PAS	HND	SHT	ATH
+4	+5	+2	-1	+1	+2	+5	+1

Year	Team	Age	G	MPG	Usg	3PA%	FTA%	INS	2P%	3P%	FT%	TS%	Reb%	Ast%	TO%	BLK%	STL%	PF%	oRTG	dRTG	Win%	WARP
09-10	DEN	22.5	65	20.2	.180	.156	.115	.960	.544	.410	.757	.600	.054	.069	.154	.001	.018	.030	107.9	107.0	.529	3.1
10-11p	DEN	23.5	73	20.0	.187	.178	.127	.949	.546	.433	.776	.619	.052	.074	.144	.001	.018	.028	109.1	106.8	.576	4.9

Most similar to: Allen Leavell (96.9), Kyle Lowry, Terrell Brandon, Kevin Johnson IMP: 62% BRK: 4% COP: 4%

While statistical analysts loved Ty Lawson prior to last year's draft, scouts were a little less certain about Lawson's NBA prospects because of his size and the up-tempo system in which he played at North Carolina. Lawson landed in a perfect scenario for his talents in Denver, which not only valued his strong NCAA numbers but also saw him fitting in with a fast-paced second unit. Lawson rarely disappointed as a rookie, strengthening the Nuggets' bench and effectively filling in for Chauncey Billups when the starter was briefly sidelined.

Lawson has virtually all the tools you'd want in an elite point guard. His quickness proved even more valuable at the NBA level because of limitations on hand-checking on the perimeter. Opponents could not back off because of Lawson's shooting ability. He's also a good passer with strong court vision. Lawson's assist percentage was held down somewhat during his rookie season because he occasionally split ballhandling duties as part of backcourts with Billups or Anthony Carter. Statistically, Lawson was also a positive presence at the defensive end. He is very strong for his size and has exceptionally quick hands, allowing him to put pressure on opposing point guards.

With Billups going strong, Lawson has another season or two as a backup as part of his apprenticeship. By the time he graduates to a starting position, he might be ready to make a run at the All-Star Game.

PF 4	Kenyon Martin	Hght: 6'9" Wght: 240 2011-12 status: free agent	Exp: 10 From: Cincinnati	Salary: $16.8 million						

SKILL RATINGS

TOT	OFF	DEF	REB	PAS	HND	SHT	ATH
-1	-1	+2	0	+1	+2	-1	+3

Year	Team	Age	G	MPG	Usg	3PA%	FTA%	INS	2P%	3P%	FT%	TS%	Reb%	Ast%	TO%	BLK%	STL%	PF%	oRTG	dRTG	Win%	WARP
07-08	DEN	30.3	71	30.5	.174	.012	.106	1.093	.544	.182	.580	.553	.114	.018	.103	.028	.017	.046	102.4	104.3	.435	0.8
08-09	DEN	31.3	66	32.0	.178	.045	.103	1.058	.498	.368	.604	.523	.107	.028	.124	.027	.023	.043	102.8	104.4	.444	1.2
09-10	DEN	32.3	58	34.2	.176	.037	.094	1.057	.465	.276	.557	.481	.158	.024	.116	.023	.018	.042	102.6	103.9	.456	1.6
10-11p	DEN	33.3	62	24.0	.159	.045	.095	1.050	.490	.321	.584	.508	.128	.023	.119	.025	.017	.045	102.1	104.3	.428	0.4

Most similar to: Kurt Thomas (97.0), John Hot Rod Williams, Horace Grant, Tyrone Hill IMP: 31% BRK: 2% COP: 13%

In the ongoing battle between Kenyon Martin and his troublesome knees, 2009-10 would have to be scored in favor of the knees. On the positive side, Martin was effective when he was on the floor, substantially improving his rebound percentage and posting his best win percentage since 2005-06. However, Martin missed 19 key games late in the regular season and was limited in the playoffs. Martin told the *Denver Post* that he did additional damage to his left knee by coming back. He had surgery on his patella tendon after the season and could miss extensive time in 2010-11 due to his rehabilitation.

It's easy to root for Martin as he comes back from another surgery after he has worked so valiantly to get back to something approaching 100 percent following microfracture surgery on both knees. Once a high flyer, he has remade himself into a garbage man who is valued for his tough, physical defense. That may not be worth the $16.8 million Martin will make this season in the last year of his contract, but the Nuggets need him on the floor.

DENVER NUGGETS

SG 5	J.R. Smith	Hght: 6'6" Wght: 220 2011-12 status: free agent	Exp: 6 From: St. Benedict's Prep (Newark, NJ)	Salary: $6.8 million							
					SKILL RATINGS						
					TOT	OFF	DEF	REB	PAS	HND	SHT	ATH
					+3	+4	+4	0	+1	-1	+2	+2

Year	Team	Age	G	MPG	Usg	3PA%	FTA%	INS	2P%	3P%	FT%	TS%	Reb%	Ast%	TO%	BLK%	STL%	PF%	oRTG	dRTG	Win%	WARP
07-08	DEN	22.6	74	19.2	.259	.451	.091	.639	.542	.403	.719	.603	.057	.038	.130	.006	.018	.042	109.6	106.6	.595	5.3
08-09	DEN	23.6	81	27.7	.243	.371	.098	.727	.491	.397	.754	.576	.075	.045	.123	.005	.017	.038	108.7	106.8	.561	6.8
09-10	DEN	24.6	75	27.7	.270	.371	.070	.700	.477	.338	.706	.515	.065	.039	.110	.007	.024	.037	105.9	105.7	.508	3.9
10-11p	DEN	25.6	75	28.0	.248	.404	.089	.685	.500	.359	.732	.551	.067	.041	.114	.007	.019	.037	107.5	106.0	.547	5.8

Most similar to: Billy Ray Bates (97.2), Paul Graham, John Long, Jamal Crawford   IMP: 47%   BRK: 4%   COP: 6%

It was a down season for J.R. Smith, who saw his three-point percentage tumble and take his True Shooting Percentage and overall efficiency with it. Though Smith's shot selection has been questionable at times, this appears to be largely a fluke. According to Hoopdata.com, Smith's accuracy was also down on long twos, but he shot as well or better from every other area of the court. SCHOENE more or less splits the difference on Smith's last two seasons, and that's enough to make him one of the league's better sixth men.

Trade rumors started swirling around Smith about the same time news broke that he was involved in a scuffle at the Nuggets' training facility that resulted in a police investigation. According to Fanhouse.com, Smith got frustrated with the physical defense of a local D-League player during pick-up games and ended up attempting to choke the other player. Fights during practice are nothing new in the NBA, but Smith needs to be on good behavior given his track record. He previously served jail time for a reckless driving charge stemming from a traffic accident in June 2007 that killed one of his close friends.

PF 13	Shelden Williams	Hght: 6'9" Wght: 250 2011-12 status: free agent	Exp: 4 From: Duke	Salary: $0.9 million							
					SKILL RATINGS						
					TOT	OFF	DEF	REB	PAS	HND	SHT	ATH
					0	0	+3	+3	-3	-3	-1	+2

Year	Team	Age	G	MPG	Usg	3PA%	FTA%	INS	2P%	3P%	FT%	TS%	Reb%	Ast%	TO%	BLK%	STL%	PF%	oRTG	dRTG	Win%	WARP
07-08	SAC	24.5	64	12.1	.170	.007	.158	1.151	.438	.000	.676	.494	.155	.011	.116	.021	.013	.064	102.8	105.4	.414	0.0
08-09	MIN	25.5	45	11.4	.193	.009	.127	1.118	.452	.000	.730	.503	.176	.011	.155	.027	.022	.057	102.9	104.1	.457	0.4
09-10	BOS	26.5	54	11.1	.154	.005	.222	1.217	.525	.000	.765	.612	.149	.017	.155	.028	.011	.067	104.9	105.6	.476	0.7
10-11p	DEN	27.5	76	10.0	.152	.006	.173	1.167	.497	.002	.737	.558	.154	.014	.148	.027	.013	.061	103.5	105.1	.448	0.5

Most similar to: Nazr Mohammed (98.5), Cadillac Anderson, Scott Williams, Adam Keefe   IMP: 35%   BRK: 4%   COP: 8%

Shelden Williams' season would have been a lot more pleasant had the Boston Celtics not advanced deep into the postseason. As the stat line above indicates, Williams was effective during the regular season. He spent the first two months of the year as Boston's backup power forward in place of the injured Glen Davis and helped the Celtics get off to a good start with his solid rebounding and the most efficient scoring of his NBA career to date.

Williams was an afterthought the rest of the way before unexpectedly getting key minutes on the big stage of the NBA Finals. He played four minutes in Game Two, turning the ball over twice and committing a pair of fouls, and was scoreless with a pair of turnovers and fouls in 14 minutes of action after Kendrick Perkins was injured in Game Six. Williams managed to look even worse than the numbers, which is understandable given it was his most meaningful basketball in weeks.

The Nuggets signed Williams for the minimum over the summer, and he will likely start the season in the rotation while Chris Andersen and Kenyon Martin rehab. As a third power forward, he's a major upgrade from Malik Allen. Denver just has to remember not to use Williams in the NBA Finals.

DENVER NUGGETS

PF	Brian Butch	Hght: 6'11"	Exp: --	Salary: --	SKILL RATINGS						
		Wght: 240	From: Wisconsin		TOT	OFF	DEF	REB	PAS	HND	SHT	ATH
--		2011-12 status: free agent			+1	--	--	--	--	--	--	--

Year	Team	Age	G	MPG	Usg	3PA%	FTA%	INS	2P%	3P%	FT%	TS%	Reb%	Ast%	TO%	BLK%	STL%	PF%	oRTG	dRTG	Win%	WARP
10-11p	AVG	26.3	76	-	.180	.557	.091	.535	.481	.304	.639	.490	.173	.017	.106	.019	.013	.060	-	-	.474	-

Most similar to: Donyell Marshall (96.7), Loy Vaught, Richard Washington, Pete Chilcutt — IMP: 38% BRK: 2% COP: 13%

The Nuggets were one of several teams to jump on the NBA's new trend last season--calling players up from the D-League after its regular season ended and signing them to contracts that extended into 2010-11 with token guaranteed money at most. This gives teams an extended opportunity to get the player in their facility throughout the offseason and take a look at them before training camp. The downside? If the player gets hurt while under contract, the team is on the hook whether the contract is guaranteed or not.

Such was the case with Brian Butch, who ruptured his patella tendon during the NBA Summer League and will be sidelined for much of next season. Denver waived Butch before his contract became guaranteed on Aug. 15, but must continue to pay him until he is able to return to action. The timing worked poorly for Butch. He actually would have been better off had his guarantee date been later, since he could have stayed with the team for the rehab process. The early guarantee date is supposed to give the player a chance to shop for another offer for training camp, but no one is going to invite an injured player, so Butch will likely have to hope for a call-up after he demonstrates he is healthy.

SF	Coby Karl	Hght: 6'5"	Exp: 2	Salary: --	SKILL RATINGS						
		Wght: 215	From: Boise State		TOT	OFF	DEF	REB	PAS	HND	SHT	ATH
--		2011-12 status: free agent			0	+2	0	-4	+4	+2	-1	0

Year	Team	Age	G	MPG	Usg	3PA%	FTA%	INS	2P%	3P%	FT%	TS%	Reb%	Ast%	TO%	BLK%	STL%	PF%	oRTG	dRTG	Win%	WARP
07-08	LAL	25.1	17	4.1	.227	.367	.124	.757	.385	.308	.800	.493	.110	.058	.141	.021	.025	.025	106.5	102.8	.620	0.3
09-10	GSW	27.1	7	16.1	.170	.246	.059	.813	.429	.182	.667	.404	.089	.057	.224	.006	.013	.053	101.1	107.2	.305	-0.3
10-11p	AVG	28.1	76	16.0	.168	.442	.110	.668	.476	.312	.721	.514	.065	.044	.150	.009	.016	.046	105.2	106.6	.453	0.9

Most similar to: Fred Jones (98.9), Keith Bogans, Bob Wilkerson, Clint Richardson — IMP: 55% BRK: 11% COP: 11%

The coach's son, Coby Karl, was the other D-Leaguer signed by the Nuggets near the end of the regular season. Karl too was waived on Aug. 15. Karl did get seven NBA games last season, shooting the ball poorly for the Golden State Warriors. His projection is based on translated D-League statistics from the last two seasons, which suggest he's a borderline NBA player thanks to his versatility. Karl has a tough time defending anyone at the NBA level, however. Karl signed to play with CB Granada in the Spanish ACB this season.

Detroit Pistons

What is Joe Dumars' plan? The Pistons were primed to take a step back in 2009-10 during a transitional season in which Dumars, the head of the Pistons' basketball operations department, finished clearing away the last vestiges of his championship team. The Pistons didn't take a step back. They took about three, and the direction of the franchise is still unclear. What Dumars has done runs contrary to the maximum and minimum strategy of NBA roster building.

An explanation: There is a school of thought that the way you build a contending roster in the NBA that is healthy in both win totals and in payroll, you invest the bulk of your dollars in two or three impact talents worthy of maximum, or near-maximum, contracts. The rest of the roster is filled out by players making either the rookie scale or the veteran's minimum, with the ideal being the former—young players who are bound by the Collective Bargaining Agreement to be compensated at a rate less than what is commensurate with their on-court production. There is, of course, more than one way to build a team and much of it depends where your franchise resides in the success cycle. Ordinarily, building a team by paying the going rate for average talents is a death sentence for a club's championship hopes. If you have a team close to contention or already at championship level, then you might have to dip into the luxury-tax waters for these average talents that can fill roles. It's all about recognizing what level your team is at and where it can be expected to go, and it requires some deft planning and fortunate timing.

No matter what approach you take to building a championship team, it starts with finding those impact talents, which is awfully tough to do and too often is a result of lottery luck more so than careful planning. That's life in the NBA. No matter how well you scout, draft and manage your salary cap, if you don't fall into a Tim Duncan, Kobe Bryant or LeBron James, you're not going to win a title unless, well, you're Dumars, who built a title team out of excellent but non-elite players. That accomplishment buys Dumars a lot of credibility in the NBA, but unless one of the young players on the Pistons' roster unexpectedly develops into a foundation player, it's tough to see how he's going to repeat the success of a half-decade ago. During the offseason, Dumars reportedly flirted with the Nets and the Hornets, rumors that he vehemently denied.

We saw several rebuilding projects unfold this summer, with a couple of different variations. You had the Miami/New York/New Jersey strategy of clearing the decks in hopes of landing an elite free-agent bundle, with Miami being a bit different because of the presence of top-five talent Dwyane Wade. Then you had the Bulls, who did more or less the same thing but had the additional advantage of having their two best players still playing under rookie contracts in Derrick Rose and Joakim Noah. That allowed Chicago's front office the luxury of having a playoff-caliber young core of players to build around and remain competitive while still clearing the necessary cap space for a summer

PISTONS IN A BOX

Last year's record	27-55
Last year's Offensive Rating	106.7 (21)
Last year's Defensive Rating	113.4 (26)
Last year's point differential	-5.1 (27)
Team pace	87.3 (29)
SCHOENE projection	27-55 (14)
Projected Offensive Rating	106.3 (25)
Projected Defensive Rating	112.1 (27)
Projected team weighted age	28.3 (12)
Projected '10-11 payroll	$65.5 (16)
Est. payroll obligations, '11-12	$51.5 (19)

Head coach: John Kuester

For the first time since 2007, the Pistons will have a returning coach calling the shots during training camp. John Kuester will surely appreciate the opportunity to continue installing his system during his second season at the helm. Health might be the most important factor for Kuester. Because of a series of injuries, he had to start 14 of the 15 players on the roster. Only rookie Jonas Jerebko started more than 67 games. Kuester's most important decisions in terms of playing time will come in the backcourt, where one of Ben Gordon, Rip Hamilton and Rodney Stuckey must come off the bench. Will Bynum and newcomer Tracy McGrady also demand playing time at guard.

splash. When Dumars set out to remake the Pistons, he didn't follow either of these paths. Instead, he has gone after middling free agents and drafted with middling picks while more than a few pieces of the franchise's last-decade surge remain on the roster.

The expected ascension of Pistons guard Rodney Stuckey was really at the forefront of Dumars' strategy when he began tearing down his six-time Eastern Conference finalist by trading Chauncey Billups to Denver just after the start of the 2008-09 season. Stuckey wasn't bad last season. His defense is excellent and he can be a dynamic force on the offensive end at times, putting the ball on the floor against longer defenders and muscling up against smaller players. However, he's got to become a better shooter in order for the Pistons' offense to become more efficient. Last season, during which Stuckey more or less split time evenly between the two backcourt positions, his usage rage jumped near the 27 percent mark, too high for a player whose effective field-goal percentage limped in at .413. He's also got to overcome lingering concerns about his heart, which came to the forefront when he collapsed on the Pistons' bench during a game in early March. Stuckey can hit the market as a restricted free agent after the season (CBA pending), so this is a key campaign for him.

First-time head coach John Kuester arrived in Detroit last year with a bag full of hyperbole because of the offense he installed in Cleveland, which in part helped make the Cavaliers an elite-level team. However, Kuester also had a reputation as a fine defensive coach and it was hoped that when he replaced overmatched Michael Curry, he would return the Pistons' defense to a Dumars-friendly level. On offense, Kuester found the going is rough without LeBron James, as the Pistons finished 21st in the league. The other end was even more troubling. The end result of all of Dumars' changes was 55 losses and a defense that plummeted to 26th in the league on a per-possession basis. That's not Pistons basketball.

One area in which Kuester was consistent with his predecessors is tempo, as the Pistons ranked 29th in possessions per game, the fifth straight season Detroit ranked in the bottom two of the league. The miserable pace allowed the Pistons to hang in the middle of the pack in points allowed per game, but Kuester can't hide his team's poor defense so easily. Detroit's rank in Defensive Rating was its worst since 1994-95.

Perhaps the most disappointing aspect of the Pistons season was that Kuester failed to use the rebuilding campaign to get extended minutes for rookies Austin Daye and DaJuan Summers. Too many minutes went to players who aren't going to be a part of the next contending Pistons team. The team got younger, but is still far from young. Veterans Wallace, Prince and Hamilton all remained on hand, mostly because last year was not the time to be unloading multi-year contracts. The first year of last year's free-agent signings was a bust, as Ben Gordon, Charlie Villunueva and Chris Wilcox all turned out to be major disappointments.

On the bright side, Wallace played better than expected, though he was still not an impact player. Offensive rebounding was the team's one strength among the Four Factors and Wallace was a big part of that. After once again contemplating retirement after the season, Wallace instead signed on for two more years in Detroit. If he continues to play like he did last season, he's a bargain. Wallace may not be the solution, but he certainly isn't the problem, either. He also serves as a codifying presence for a team in transition and a symbol for a city's distinctive style of hoops.

If the foundation of a contending team does begin to emerge, you have to think it's going to come from the development of the club's quartet of young forwards. The jury is still out on last year's rookies. Daye and Summers were very raw, while unheralded overseas import Jonas Jerebko flashed a surprising degree of promise. Daye and Jerebko are intriguing players, though one has to wonder if their talents are redundant. Daye needs to make a second-season leap and push Prince to the wayside. In any event, this year's first-round pick, Greg Monroe, appears to have the potential to be the best of them all.

What would be a great sign is if Monroe emerged as the starter at the pivot. That could happen considering his competition, which includes the overaged Wallace and the undersized Jason Maxiell. Monroe looked really good in NBA Summer League action and, on a team lacking playmaking skills, his passing abilities from the high post could give Kuester's squad an offensive identity. Detroit needs to improve its distance shooting while becoming more aggressive off the dribble. The team also needs much better ball movement and fewer isolations.

If you are a believer in the Pistons' young talent, then you might have been content in the direction Dumars is taking the franchise. Then he went out and signed Tracy McGrady.

Kuester must keep McGrady from becoming a disrupting force for development of his young players while still giving the veteran a chance to show he's got something left. A productive McGrady would give Dumars an added trading chip to go along with Prince's expiring contract. The Pistons are hoping that highly respected strength and conditioning coach Arnie Kander will re-energize McGrady, just as he supposedly did last season with Wallace. But would it really be a good thing for McGrady to emerge as the Pistons' best player? That's the double-edged Sword of Damocles hanging over the team as the season opens.

Point guard play was a disaster for Detroit last season, which is to say the functions of a traditional lead guard were mostly lacking in the Pistons' attack. Kuester was able to put together an effective offensive design in Cleveland without a traditional point guard initiating the offense. Can he put together something similar in Detroit, given that he doesn't have a franchise player as a starting point? Increasing the pace would be a good start and would take advantage of the young legs on his roster. The Pistons were actually a very capable defensive transition team last season, so an up-tempo game might work to their advantage. Last season, the Pistons' offense featured lots of screens, cuts and handoffs and a decentralized attack might work best for this group. Kuester has said he's excited about allowing Monroe to handle the ball on the elbow and make plays, so pure point guard play could become irrelevant if it all works out. Will Bynum may not be a starting-caliber NBA point guard, but he was again an offensive spark plug for the Pistons.

The big off-court story in Detroit entering this season is the ownership situation. Former owner Bill Davidson died last year and left the team to his wife, Karen, who wants to unload the team. Relocation was briefly bandied about the rumor mill during the summer, but that outcome seems very unlikely. Tom Gores, a celebrity in the finance world and a Michigan native, is a contender to land the team, as is Mike Ilitch, owner of baseball's Tigers and hockey's Red Wings. Ilitch has hinted at moving the team into a new arena in downtown Detroit and doing so could give him a near monopoly on entertainment dollars in Detroit. The charismatic Gores could give the franchise a Mark Cuban-type of presence and would likely be more committed to building a basketball team than an entertainment empire. There are other curious groups as well, and it will be interesting to see how it all plays out.

The depths to which the Pistons sunk last season can at least in part be explained away by injuries, as Hamilton, Prince and Gordon were all hobbled. The overall team health will be something to watch when training camp opens; there was a lot of rehab going on over the summer involving Monroe, Gordon, Prince, Hamilton and Stuckey, among others. What appears to lie ahead in the immediate future is another transitional season of dubious success, with another trip to the lottery a good possibility. Right now, the Pistons are a hodgepodge of redundant parts, with players on the downside of their careers blocking players on the upswing. Another 55 losses or so could be in the offing unless the young players get on the court and make an impact.

Dumars needs to find a way to dispense of Prince and Hamilton to really turn the page for this franchise. He's got younger options at the positions of those stalwarts and he's already cast his lot with Wallace as the flag bearer of franchise continuity.

Right now, it just seems like Dumars is aimlessly collecting talent, but a few positive trends could emerge this season. More than anything, the team defense needs to make a quantum leap. After all, lockdown defense is what defines professional basketball in the Motor City.

Bradford Doolittle

From the Blogosphere

Who: Matt Watson
What: Detroit Bad Boys
Where: http://www.detroitbadboys.com/

Last year was ugly--I won't bore you with details about the imbalanced roster, double-digit losing streaks or how ankle sprains and pulled muscles suddenly turned contagious. Instead, I'll point out what went right, since it was so easy to overlook if you weren't watching every game. Ben Wallace's "Benaissance" kept this team out of the cellar--he played nearly as well as he did before leaving Detroit in 2006. Even if he slows down, simply having him around to toughen up lottery pick Greg Monroe in practice is a blessing. Second, Jonas Jerebko was an absolute steal, jumping from the second round to the starting lineup. Jerebko averaged 9.3 points without plays being called for him. At worst, he's a serviceable energy player, but if his EuroBasket performance for Sweden's national team (25 points, 12.3 rebounds) in August is any indication, he's just scratching the surface of his potential.

DETROIT PISTONS

PISTONS FIVE-YEAR TRENDS

Season	AGE	W-L	POW	PYTH	SEED	ORTG	DRTG	PT DIFF	PACE
05-06	28.5	64-18	61.8 (2)	59.9	1	112.2 (3)	104.3 (5)	6.7 (2)	85.7 (29)
06-07	29.0	53-29	51.6 (6)	53.3	1	110.6 (6)	105.3 (6)	4.2 (6)	86.1 (30)
07-08	27.6	59-23	59.4 (4)	61.6	2	113.3 (8)	105.1 (4)	7.4 (2)	85.7 (30)
08-09	28.2	39-43	39.3 (17)	39.5	8	108.9 (21)	109.8 (17)	-0.5 (17)	85.4 (30)
09-10	27.6	27-55	26.4 (27)	26.5	--	106.7 (21)	113.4 (26)	-5.1 (27)	87.3 (29)

		OFFENSE				DEFENSE			
Season	PAY	eFG	oREB	FT/FGA	TO	eFG	oREB	FT/FGA	TO
05-06	$57.9	.497 (7)	.289 (7)	.216 (26)	.131 (1)	.477 (11)	.712 (25)	.191 (1)	.162 (10)
06-07	$75.5	.488 (21)	.283 (11)	.237 (18)	.140 (1)	.477 (5)	.709 (25)	.234 (10)	.169 (11)
07-08	$66.6	.495 (15)	.293 (6)	.230 (13)	.129 (3)	.470 (3)	.737 (12)	.244 (19)	.149 (14)
08-09	$71.1	.483 (26)	.279 (8)	.212 (27)	.137 (2)	.485 (6)	.740 (12)	.248 (20)	.134 (29)
09-10	$58.6	.474 (29)	.303 (2)	.220 (19)	.153 (13)	.526 (30)	.734 (19)	.264 (28)	.163 (6)

(league rankings in parenthesis)

PG 12 — Will Bynum
Hght: 6'0" Exp: 3 Salary: $3.3 million
Wght: 185 From: Georgia Tech
2011-12 status: guaranteed contract for $3.3 million

SKILL RATINGS

TOT	OFF	DEF	REB	PAS	HND	SHT	ATH
-1	+1	-5	0	+2	0	-3	+1

Year	Team	Age	G	MPG	Usg	3PA%	FTA%	INS	2P%	3P%	FT%	TS%	Reb%	Ast%	TO%	BLK%	STL%	PF%	oRTG	dRTG	Win%	WARP
08-09	DET	26.3	57	14.1	.281	.040	.111	1.071	.474	.158	.798	.520	.056	.094	.162	.002	.023	.051	107.2	107.4	.494	1.3
09-10	DET	27.3	63	26.5	.203	.076	.108	1.032	.470	.218	.798	.513	.054	.079	.158	.004	.018	.040	104.9	107.2	.425	0.3
10-11p	DET	28.3	73	14.9	.220	.087	.106	1.019	.474	.208	.802	.511	.055	.081	.153	.004	.018	.042	104.9	106.8	.436	0.5

Most similar to: Carlos Arroyo (97.6), Darnell Valentine, Bobby Jackson, Travis Best
IMP: 46% BRK: 12% COP: 6%

Will Bynum has carved out a nice little place for himself as a third guard in the NBA, but he continues to fancy himself a starting-caliber player and is vocal in saying so. The Pistons signed Bynum to a three-year, $9.75 million deal in the offseason, so it's obvious they think highly of his abilities. Bynum's loss in usage rate last season can partially be chalked up to the injury storm that swept the Pistons last year. Part of it may also have been that new coach John Kuester kept a closer rein on the shot-happy point guard. There appears to be a disconnect between how good Bynum believes he is and how good he actually is, and Kuester will have to monitor that as he doles out backcourt minutes. One thing that would help Bynum's cause would be to improve his lousy defense.

SF 5 — Austin Daye
Hght: 6'11" Exp: 1 Salary: $1.8 million
Wght: 200 From: Gonzaga
2011-12 status: team option for $1.9 million

SKILL RATINGS

TOT	OFF	DEF	REB	PAS	HND	SHT	ATH
0	--	-1	--	--	--	--	--

Year	Team	Age	G	MPG	Usg	3PA%	FTA%	INS	2P%	3P%	FT%	TS%	Reb%	Ast%	TO%	BLK%	STL%	PF%	oRTG	dRTG	Win%	WARP
09-10	DET	21.9	69	13.3	.187	.258	.067	.809	.540	.305	.821	.546	.120	.017	.131	.024	.015	.058	103.9	105.5	.446	0.6
10-11p	DET	22.9	76	-	.187	.290	.070	.781	.553	.328	.838	.565	.126	.020	.127	.023	.015	.056	-	-	.445	-

Most similar to: Jumaine Jones (96.6), Hedo Turkoglu, Derrick McKey, Rasheed Wallace
IMP: 63% BRK: 8% COP: 4%

Not much has changed in our opinion of Austin Daye after one season in the NBA. He still needs to add strength, but he can shoot the ball and is a potentially disruptive wing defender. For this season, you'd like to see Daye become more of a playmaker, both for himself off the dribble and for others, and to extend his range so he can be more consistent from beyond the arc. More than anything, you'd like to see Daye take over most of the minutes that might otherwise go to Tayshaun Prince. Daye is still fairly raw, but he still looks like a keeper.

DETROIT PISTONS

PF 50	Ike Diogu	Hght: 6'9" Exp: 4 Salary: --									SKILL RATINGS						
		Wght: 250 From: Arizona State									TOT	OFF	DEF	REB	PAS	HND	SHT	ATH
		2011-12 status: free agent									+1	--	-2	--	--	--	--	--

Year	Team	Age	G	MPG	Usg	3PA%	FTA%	INS	2P%	3P%	FT%	TS%	Reb%	Ast%	TO%	BLK%	STL%	PF%	oRTG	dRTG	Win%	WARP
07-08	IND	24.6	30	10.3	.247	.000	.118	1.118	.478	.000	.851	.543	.151	.014	.114	.007	.010	.061	105.9	106.9	.466	0.3
08-09	SAC	25.6	29	7.4	.233	.018	.213	1.195	.528	.500	.755	.611	.155	.006	.110	.010	.007	.049	109.4	107.6	.560	0.6
10-11p	DET	27.6	63	-	.226	.018	.112	1.094	.484	.010	.868	.539	.146	.014	.117	.007	.010	.063	-	-	.489	-

Most similar to: Mitch Kupchak (97.4), Gary Trent, Scott May, James Bailey — IMP: 35% BRK: 2% COP: 7%

The Hornets hoped Ike Diogu would compete for backup minutes at the four and the five. Instead, he never even made it to training camp. Diogu injured his left knee while working out over the summer, and when it failed to respond to time off he was forced to undergo microfracture surgery in December, ending his season. It's going to be a tough road back for Diogu, who never has been able to carve out a consistent role in the NBA and needs every bit of athleticism as an undersized big man. Diogu's hometown Mavericks showed some interest before declining to invite him to training camp. He landed in Detroit. The Pistons are unlikely to have any openings on their roster, but will give Diogu the chance to prove to other teams that he is healthy.

SG 7	Ben Gordon	Hght: 6'3" Exp: 6 Salary: $10.8 million									SKILL RATINGS						
		Wght: 200 From: Connecticut									TOT	OFF	DEF	REB	PAS	HND	SHT	ATH
		2011-12 status: guaranteed contract for $11.6 million									0	+2	-5	-4	+2	0	0	-1

Year	Team	Age	G	MPG	Usg	3PA%	FTA%	INS	2P%	3P%	FT%	TS%	Reb%	Ast%	TO%	BLK%	STL%	PF%	oRTG	dRTG	Win%	WARP
07-08	CHI	25.0	72	31.8	.262	.257	.096	.838	.445	.409	.908	.557	.056	.041	.112	.003	.011	.034	106.8	107.2	.488	3.4
08-09	CHI	26.0	82	36.6	.252	.251	.100	.849	.476	.410	.864	.573	.054	.042	.119	.005	.012	.028	107.8	107.6	.506	5.6
09-10	DET	27.0	62	27.9	.246	.255	.110	.855	.465	.321	.861	.534	.043	.045	.129	.003	.015	.039	105.8	107.9	.433	0.6
10-11p	DET	28.0	73	28.0	.233	.280	.101	.821	.462	.364	.865	.549	.047	.045	.122	.004	.013	.035	105.8	107.5	.442	1.1

Most similar to: Cuttino Mobley (98.4), Jamal Crawford, Rex Chapman, Allan Houston — IMP: 43% BRK: 2% COP: 12%

Ben Gordon's first season in Detroit didn't go very well. Like so many of his teammates, Gordon struggled with injuries. On the floor, he lost confidence in his outside shot, which pretty much drained his offensive value-- which is to say all of his value. Gordon has sworn to become more aggressive attacking the basket this season, but there really isn't anything in his numbers to suggest there was a problematic change in his approach or demeanor. He simply didn't shoot the ball very well. He did get off to a fast start, but as the injuries mounted, the players around Gordon changed on a day-by-day basis before he joined the walking wounded by hurting his ankle. The result was lost confidence and a lost season. Chances are Gordon will bounce back closer to the player he was in Chicago, but it's unlikely he's going to produce enough to justify even half of what he's getting paid.

SG 32	Richard Hamilton	Hght: 6'7" Exp: 11 Salary: $12.5 million									SKILL RATINGS						
		Wght: 193 From: Connecticut									TOT	OFF	DEF	REB	PAS	HND	SHT	ATH
		2011-12 status: guaranteed contract for $12.7 million									-1	+2	+2	-3	+4	+3	-1	-3

Year	Team	Age	G	MPG	Usg	3PA%	FTA%	INS	2P%	3P%	FT%	TS%	Reb%	Ast%	TO%	BLK%	STL%	PF%	oRTG	dRTG	Win%	WARP
07-08	DET	30.2	72	33.6	.247	.112	.077	.965	.492	.440	.833	.552	.058	.059	.105	.003	.015	.034	107.0	106.5	.516	5.0
08-09	DET	31.2	67	34.0	.272	.147	.090	.942	.464	.368	.848	.529	.054	.063	.103	.001	.010	.037	107.5	108.4	.471	2.6
09-10	DET	32.2	46	33.7	.281	.147	.113	.966	.435	.297	.846	.505	.049	.060	.123	.002	.010	.034	105.7	108.2	.417	0.0
10-11p	DET	33.2	70	32.0	.240	.181	.093	.912	.450	.365	.836	.523	.050	.061	.118	.001	.011	.036	105.7	108.0	.424	0.4

Most similar to: Reggie Theus (98.5), Jalen Rose, Rolando Blackman, Bernard King — IMP: 35% BRK: 2% COP: 10%

It's been a great career for 11-year veteran Rip Hamilton, but last season showed a decline in performance that can only be partially explained away by injury. He will likely be one of the most overpaid players in the NBA over the next two or three seasons. Hamilton has become increasingly perimeter oriented, and his once-deadly midrange game has really ebbed. He's actually started to shoot more three-pointers, but the shot is out of his range. The Pistons will be crossing their fingers that a happy and healthy Hamilton starts the season on a roll and thus showcases himself for a contender. He enters the season as the Pistons' best option at two-guard, but that's strictly a short-term designation.

SF 33	Jonas Jerebko	Hght: 6'10" Exp: 1 Salary: $0.8 million						**SKILL RATINGS**							
		Wght: 231 From: Kinna, Sweden						TOT	OFF	DEF	REB	PAS	HND	SHT	ATH
		2011-12 status: free agent						+1	+1	-1	+4	-4	-4	+2	+3

Year	Team	Age	G	MPG	Usg	3PA%	FTA%	INS	2P%	3P%	FT%	TS%	Reb%	Ast%	TO%	BLK%	STL%	PF%	oRTG	dRTG	Win%	WARP
09-10	DET	23.1	80	27.9	.159	.151	.102	.951	.520	.313	.710	.545	.132	.012	.108	.011	.019	.048	104.9	106.0	.463	2.1
10-11p	DET	24.1	76	24.0	.159	.214	.100	.885	.527	.333	.735	.554	.127	.013	.108	.011	.019	.045	104.9	105.5	.478	2.4

Most similar to: George Lynch (97.4), Jared Dudley, Josh Childress, Danny Granger IMP: 54% BRK: 5% COP: 2%

One of the bright lights of a dark Pistons season was the emergence of Swedish rookie Jonas Jerebko as a possible long-term solution as a combo forward. Jerebko has a chance to be a better-rebounding Rashard Lewis if he can improve his three-point percentage. He has the stroke to do it. Last season, 72.6 percent of his shots came either at the rim or from the three-point line, which is exactly what you want. Even though he shot just .313 from behind the arc, he still posted an above-average True Shooting Percentage because of his prowess in the lane, where he drew fouls at an above-average rate. He needs to improve his on-ball defense, but looks like he can become a plus player on that end of the floor with an excellent block-plus-steal rate and a lot of drawn charges. More than anything, Jerebko needs to learn how to move the ball within the flow of an NBA offense. Pistons fans should be excited about this guy. He looks like a good one.

C 54	Jason Maxiell	Hght: 6'7" Exp: 5 Salary: $5.0 million						**SKILL RATINGS**							
		Wght: 260 From: Cincinnati						TOT	OFF	DEF	REB	PAS	HND	SHT	ATH
		2011-12 status: guaranteed contract for $5.0 million						0	+1	-3	0	-3	-2	+3	0

Year	Team	Age	G	MPG	Usg	3PA%	FTA%	INS	2P%	3P%	FT%	TS%	Reb%	Ast%	TO%	BLK%	STL%	PF%	oRTG	dRTG	Win%	WARP
07-08	DET	25.2	82	21.5	.171	.002	.187	1.185	.539	.000	.633	.576	.147	.012	.112	.042	.006	.050	105.2	104.5	.524	3.9
08-09	DET	26.2	78	18.1	.148	.002	.160	1.158	.577	.000	.532	.580	.136	.008	.104	.035	.010	.054	106.0	106.2	.496	2.3
09-10	DET	27.2	76	20.4	.165	.002	.124	1.122	.512	.000	.574	.531	.159	.012	.123	.021	.012	.052	103.9	105.8	.435	0.6
10-11p	DET	28.2	75	20.0	.157	.005	.140	1.135	.542	.003	.585	.559	.148	.012	.115	.032	.010	.053	104.2	105.5	.454	1.2

Most similar to: Brian Skinner (97.9), Cliff Levingston, Nick Collison, Etan Thomas IMP: 40% BRK: 5% COP: 3%

Among the million summertime rumors that never turned into actual news was the story that the Pistons were shopping Jason Maxiell. He's still in Detroit, but it's easy to understand why Joe Dumars would want to move him. Maxiell is a nice enough player. He's a beast in the lane and his long reach allows him to compensate for being undersized. However, he's lacking in skill to the extent that he can't be counted up to do much more than dunk off of putbacks and defensive lapses. He attempted to become more active in the midrange last season, but the results there weren't great and the approach ate into his foul-drawing rate, which sapped much of his prior efficiency. He's still a useful player for somebody, but with plenty of options at the big man positions in Detroit, the Pistons really don't want to pay $5 million a year for a player who may not see a whole lot of the court in coming seasons.

DETROIT PISTONS

SG 1	Tracy McGrady	Hght: 6'8" Wght: 223 2011-12 status: free agent	Exp: 13 Salary: $1.4 million From: Mount Zion Christian Acad. HS (NC)				SKILL RATINGS						
							TOT	OFF	DEF	REB	PAS	HND	SHT	ATH
							+1	+1	+3	+3	+4	+3	-3	-1

Year	Team	Age	G	MPG	Usg	3PA%	FTA%	INS	2P%	3P%	FT%	TS%	Reb%	Ast%	TO%	BLK%	STL%	PF%	oRTG	dRTG	Win%	WARP
07-08	HOU	28.9	66	37.0	.306	.182	.097	.915	.457	.292	.684	.487	.077	.073	.098	.009	.013	.017	106.5	104.9	.552	6.9
08-09	HOU	29.9	35	33.7	.247	.188	.110	.922	.391	.376	.801	.492	.074	.069	.111	.009	.019	.015	106.5	105.4	.535	2.9
09-10	NYK	30.9	30	22.4	.207	.209	.090	.882	.439	.250	.746	.466	.080	.067	.143	.015	.011	.027	104.5	106.2	.444	0.4
10-11p	DET	31.9	66	15.0	.215	.254	.090	.836	.426	.310	.741	.484	.079	.065	.133	.015	.013	.023	104.7	105.6	.470	1.1

Most similar to: Jerry Stackhouse (97.7), Reggie Theus, Penny Hardaway, Jalen Rose   IMP: 35% BRK: 7% COP: 4%

No matter how you frame it, Detroit's decision to try to resurrect the career of Tracy McGrady is one of the more head-scratching choices of the summer. To be fair, the financial investment is minimal. However, the Pistons are a rebuilding team and if the best-case scenario for McGrady comes to pass, he's only going to be using up possessions that would better go to Detroit's developing youngsters. What is that best-case scenario anyway? There is virtually no chance that McGrady is going to be what he was 5-6 years ago. What you would hope to see instead is a player who can at least rediscover his jump shot. That won't be easy, because he's simply not a threat to break down a defense off the dribble, which means he's always going to have a hand in his face. McGrady is an excellent passer and can probably put up 12-15 points per game, with questionable efficiency. It's really unclear why the Pistons would want that skill set.

C 10	Greg Monroe	Hght: 6'11" Wght: 250 2011-12 status: guaranteed contract for $3.0 million	Exp: R Salary: $2.8 million From: Georgetown				SKILL RATINGS						
							TOT	OFF	DEF	REB	PAS	HND	SHT	ATH
							0	-1	+2	+1	+5	+4	-3	+3

Year	Team	Age	G	MPG	Usg	3PA%	FTA%	INS	2P%	3P%	FT%	TS%	Reb%	Ast%	TO%	BLK%	STL%	PF%	oRTG	dRTG	Win%	WARP
10-11p	DET	20.9	76	25.0	.196	.038	.117	1.079	.458	.231	.648	.494	.154	.051	.186	.024	.014	.051	103.0	104.7	.442	1.0

Most similar to: J.J. Hickson (95.8), Andrew Bogut, Julian Wright, Brandon Bass   IMP: - BRK: - COP: -

Greg Monroe could turn out to be a steal as the ninth pick of the most recent draft, and may be the long-term solution for Detroit in the pivot. He's a skilled offensive player, with playmaking skills from the high post and elbow that Pistons coach John Kuester has already sworn will be used to the team's advantage. Monroe should hold his own on the glass right away, but will have to prove he can defend the league's better post players. On offense, he has to concentrate on getting high-percentage opportunities and leverage his mobility to get to the line. If his shooting percentages end up higher than his projection, Monroe will be on the All-Rookie Team. He may be there anyway. After an impressive summer-league showing, Monroe had surgery for a nagging problem with a toe in late July and wasn't able to resume full workouts until early September, so it remains to be seen what kind of shape he's going to be in when camp opens.

SF 22	Tayshaun Prince	Hght: 6'9" Wght: 215 2011-12 status: free agent	Exp: 8 Salary: $11.1 million From: Kentucky				SKILL RATINGS						
							TOT	OFF	DEF	REB	PAS	HND	SHT	ATH
							0	+1	0	+1	+3	+5	0	-4

Year	Team	Age	G	MPG	Usg	3PA%	FTA%	INS	2P%	3P%	FT%	TS%	Reb%	Ast%	TO%	BLK%	STL%	PF%	oRTG	dRTG	Win%	WARP
07-08	DET	28.1	82	32.9	.200	.128	.093	.965	.463	.363	.768	.516	.088	.047	.080	.010	.008	.016	105.4	105.8	.488	4.0
08-09	DET	29.1	82	37.3	.193	.115	.087	.972	.458	.397	.778	.516	.093	.040	.082	.013	.008	.016	105.4	106.3	.468	3.3
09-10	DET	30.1	49	34.0	.191	.107	.063	.956	.503	.370	.714	.530	.093	.045	.088	.011	.011	.021	105.6	106.4	.476	2.0
10-11p	DET	31.1	70	32.0	.178	.135	.074	.939	.479	.384	.732	.523	.095	.041	.085	.012	.009	.020	104.5	106.2	.445	1.4

Most similar to: Chris Mills (98.0), Marques Johnson, Rolando Blackman, Clifford Robinson   IMP: 37% BRK: 6% COP: 8%

It seems like Tayshaun Prince has been around forever, but he's actually got just eight years of NBA service time--one more than the likes of LeBron James, Dwyane Wade and Chris Bosh. Prince looked like an old player last season. The one-time bastion of durability missed 33 games, most of them due to a balky back. As a result, he became more stationary and deferential as an offensive player. The limited mobility also sapped his signature prowess on defense. He's entering the last year of his contract, and if he proves that his back can hold up, Prince will be a coveted player on the trade market. That's really his remaining value to the Pistons, who may try to leverage Prince's expiring contract to entice a team to also take on Rip Hamilton's more onerous deal.

PG 3	Rodney Stuckey	Hght: 6'5" Wght: 205 2011-12 status: due qualifying offer of $3.9 million	Exp: 3 From: Eastern Washington	Salary: $2.8 million		**SKILL RATINGS**							
					TOT	OFF	DEF	REB	PAS	HND	SHT	ATH
					0	+1	+4	+3	+1	0	-4	+2

Year	Team	Age	G	MPG	Usg	3PA%	FTA%	INS	2P%	3P%	FT%	TS%	Reb%	Ast%	TO%	BLK%	STL%	PF%	oRTG	dRTG	Win%	WARP
07-08	DET	22.0	57	18.9	.232	.030	.130	1.100	.411	.188	.814	.485	.072	.070	.148	.004	.022	.050	103.7	105.9	.428	0.3
08-09	DET	23.0	79	31.9	.231	.064	.105	1.041	.453	.295	.803	.508	.065	.074	.143	.003	.017	.041	105.7	107.3	.447	1.6
09-10	DET	24.0	73	34.2	.266	.055	.110	1.055	.418	.228	.833	.479	.071	.065	.114	.004	.021	.038	104.6	106.6	.436	1.0
10-11p	DET	25.0	74	34.0	.237	.076	.117	1.041	.440	.272	.837	.505	.068	.069	.124	.004	.019	.039	105.0	106.5	.451	1.8

Most similar to: Kendall Gill (98.2), Ricky Davis, Derek Anderson, Larry Hughes   IMP: 72%   BRK: 4%   COP: 4%

Self-awareness is an important trait for a player and a team. Rodney Stuckey declared late in the summer that the Pistons were the NBA's best team on paper. We're currently trying to obtain his e-mail address so that we can send him a copy of *Pro Basketball Prospectus 2010-11*.

Stuckey was the victim of a scary incident in March, when he collapsed on the Pistons bench with a faulty heart rate, but he's been given a clean bill of health going forward. On the court, Stuckey struggled with being a full-time point guard and ended up splitting time between the two backcourt positions. His assist rate actually fell by nine points over 2008-09. Stuckey became more passive, as many of his former shots at the rim turned into jump shots--not that he finishes well at the rim anyway. Adding to the trouble was that his touch between the rim and long range seemed to disappear. You could chalk it up as just a bad year. However, much of what plagued Stuckey last season was present when he was a rookie. No worries on the other end of the court, where Stuckey is on his way to becoming an elite defender who can take on just about any guard you want to throw his way.

PF 35	DaJuan Summers	Hght: 6'8" Wght: 240 2011-12 status: free agent	Exp: 1 From: Georgetown	Salary: $0.8 million		**SKILL RATINGS**							
					TOT	OFF	DEF	REB	PAS	HND	SHT	ATH
					-4	--	0	--	--	--	--	--

Year	Team	Age	G	MPG	Usg	3PA%	FTA%	INS	2P%	3P%	FT%	TS%	Reb%	Ast%	TO%	BLK%	STL%	PF%	oRTG	dRTG	Win%	WARP
09-10	DET	22.2	44	9.2	.187	.258	.103	.845	.352	.357	.711	.457	.069	.018	.098	.015	.011	.060	102.3	107.8	.325	-0.8
10-11p	DET	23.2	76	-	.183	.220	.111	.891	.384	.394	.755	.493	.074	.020	.099	.016	.011	.056	-	-	.353	-

Most similar to: Kirk Snyder (97.2), Marcus Liberty, Randy White, Keith Edmonson   IMP: 86%   BRK: 47%   COP: 6%

DaJuan Summers never really got a chance to get into the flow of an NBA season, so we're still not sure to make of the former Georgetown star. Summers loves the three-point shot, and he's got potential from that range. However, he's got to become more physical. His rebound rate would barely be acceptable even if Summers was a guard, and he drew just one charge in 405 minutes. He doesn't have much of a midrange game, but at this juncture, that's the least of his worries. Summers has good raw talent and has the chance to be a plus defender if he can guard more mobile players. With no guarantees beyond this season, it's a key campaign for Summers to take a step forward.

DETROIT PISTONS

PF 31	Charlie Villanueva																				

Hght: 6'11" Exp: 5 Salary: $7.0 million
Wght: 232 From: Connecticut
2011-12 status: guaranteed contract for $7.5 million

SKILL RATINGS
TOT	OFF	DEF	REB	PAS	HND	SHT	ATH
+3	+2	-5	+1	0	0	0	0

Year	Team	Age	G	MPG	Usg	3PA%	FTA%	INS	2P%	3P%	FT%	TS%	Reb%	Ast%	TO%	BLK%	STL%	PF%	oRTG	dRTG	Win%	WARP
07-08	MIL	23.7	76	24.1	.244	.187	.070	.883	.475	.297	.783	.502	.152	.019	.107	.015	.008	.044	104.6	105.9	.456	1.5
08-09	MIL	24.7	78	26.9	.287	.194	.079	.886	.479	.345	.838	.529	.150	.029	.104	.022	.012	.055	107.4	105.6	.561	6.3
09-10	DET	25.7	78	23.7	.241	.294	.060	.765	.484	.351	.815	.526	.124	.013	.077	.025	.014	.056	105.6	105.6	.501	3.2
10-11p	DET	26.7	75	25.0	.243	.295	.065	.770	.494	.347	.819	.535	.138	.021	.092	.022	.012	.052	105.8	105.3	.519	4.0

Most similar to: Donyell Marshall (98.2), Keith Van Horn, Austin Croshere, Thurl Bailey

IMP: 56% BRK: 0% COP: 6%

Charlie Villanueva demonstrated why he's played for three teams in five seasons and why Milwaukee opted not to extend him a qualifying offer after the 2008-09 season. He bickered with coaches, underperformed on the court, missed team flights and ran into trouble with the law. These are not the reasons why Joe Dumars gave him a five-year, $35 million contract to come to Detroit. Simply put, Villanueva needs to grow up, because the talent is there. There is more to life than jacking up three-point shots and being a pain in the ass. Villanueva reportedly worked hard in the summer, dropped some weight and set his sights on winning a starting job.

C 6	Ben Wallace																				

Hght: 6'9" Exp: 14 Salary: $2.1 million
Wght: 240 From: Virginia Union
2011-12 status: guaranteed contract for $1.9 million

SKILL RATINGS
TOT	OFF	DEF	REB	PAS	HND	SHT	ATH
+1	-1	+5	+1	+1	+5	-2	+3

Year	Team	Age	G	MPG	Usg	3PA%	FTA%	INS	2P%	3P%	FT%	TS%	Reb%	Ast%	TO%	BLK%	STL%	PF%	oRTG	dRTG	Win%	WARP
07-08	CLE	33.6	72	30.7	.102	.008	.151	1.143	.397	.000	.426	.408	.157	.022	.136	.042	.019	.026	101.7	102.1	.486	3.2
08-09	CLE	34.6	56	23.5	.079	.000	.130	1.130	.445	.000	.422	.450	.163	.016	.157	.045	.019	.030	102.6	102.6	.503	2.4
09-10	DET	35.6	69	28.6	.100	.005	.165	1.160	.545	.000	.406	.526	.186	.025	.150	.036	.023	.031	104.5	102.5	.566	6.1
10-11p	DET	36.6	73	20.0	.081	.007	.130	1.123	.477	.000	.402	.470	.157	.022	.171	.040	.020	.031	102.0	102.7	.477	1.9

Most similar to: Michael Cage (93.1), Kurt Thomas, John Hot Rod Williams, Vlade Divac

IMP: 21% BRK: 0% COP: 21%

Ben Wallace reached back and pulled the fork out of his back last season, and now he's signed on for two more years. Wallace's performance in his 14th season put the efforts of his mostly underachieving teammates to shame. Wallace put up his best overall rebound rate in five years and led NBA regulars in offensive rebound percentage. His defense was back to the elite level it seemed like he left behind a couple of years back. Amazingly enough, Wallace even turned into an efficient offensive player, finishing more than 60 percent of his chances at the basket and handing out more assists. At his age, health is always going to be a concern, but Wallace continues to serve as a reminder of when all was good with Detroit basketball.

PG 23	Terrico White																				

Hght: 6'5" Exp: R Salary: $0.5 million
Wght: 213 From: Mississippi
2011-12 status: non-guaranteed contract for $0.8 million

SKILL RATINGS
TOT	OFF	DEF	REB	PAS	HND	SHT	ATH
-4	--	--	--	--	--	--	--

Year	Team	Age	G	MPG	Usg	3PA%	FTA%	INS	2P%	3P%	FT%	TS%	Reb%	Ast%	TO%	BLK%	STL%	PF%	oRTG	dRTG	Win%	WARP
10-11p	DET	21.1	76	-	.169	.255	.070	.815	.398	.295	.701	.441	.065	.020	.086	.003	.010	.035	-	-	.352	-

Most similar to: Bill Walker (92.3), Daequan Cook, Jamal Crawford, Wilson Chandler

IMP: - BRK: - COP: -

The Pistons took Mississippi's Terrico White with the sixth pick of the second round and will try to develop him as a swing guard off the bench. White is an impressive athlete and his length makes him an intriguing prospect if he can handle point guard duties. His projections suggest that is going to be a long process. If he can't shoot a better percentage than SCHOENE foresees, White won't play more than 250 minutes or so during his rookie season.

DETROIT PISTONS

PF 9 — **Chris Wilcox**

Hght: 6'10" Wght: 235
Exp: 8 From: Maryland
Salary: $3.0 million
2011-12 status: free agent

SKILL RATINGS

TOT	OFF	DEF	REB	PAS	HND	SHT	ATH
0	--	-1	--	--	--	--	--

Year	Team	Age	G	MPG	Usg	3PA%	FTA%	INS	2P%	3P%	FT%	TS%	Reb%	Ast%	TO%	BLK%	STL%	PF%	oRTG	dRTG	Win%	WARP
07-08	SEA	25.6	62	28.1	.213	.004	.128	1.125	.526	.000	.645	.554	.135	.019	.121	.015	.012	.044	104.1	105.4	.454	1.4
08-09	NYK	26.6	62	16.9	.213	.008	.122	1.114	.501	.000	.564	.517	.151	.020	.148	.011	.012	.058	103.7	106.8	.398	-0.4
09-10	DET	27.6	34	13.0	.190	.000	.126	1.126	.525	--	.500	.532	.164	.014	.210	.023	.016	.067	102.2	105.5	.391	-0.2
10-11p	DET	28.6	75	--	.194	.008	.122	1.114	.529	.002	.547	.538	.153	.018	.173	.019	.014	.060	--	--	.443	--

Most similar to: Kurt Thomas (97.8), Andrew DeClercq, Ike Austin, Jason Caffey

IMP: 54% BRK: 9% COP: 9%

The Pistons couldn't realistically expect much from Chris Wilcox after a below-replacement season, and they didn't get much. Wilcox's year was wrecked by injuries and ineffectiveness. Wilcox was brought in to be an option in the post, but his success rate on the blocks was in the lower fifth of the league. Wilcox remained effective around the rim, but still has a frustrating tendency to stray from there. He's back in the mix for Detroit this season. If he is healthy, he could prove to be trade bait, though the return on a deal wouldn't be anything to get excited about.

Golden State Warriors

When Peter Guber and Joe Lacob are formally approved as the new owners of the Golden State Warriors, they're unlikely to proclaim a long regional nightmare to be over. For long-suffering Warriors fans, however, the ownership transition is at worst a close second to the "We Believe!" run in the 2007 Playoffs in terms of highlights of the last decade and a half.

Under the 16-year stewardship of Chris Cohan, who purchased the team in the fall of 1994, Golden State made one playoff appearance and averaged 30.6 wins per season. Cohan hired a series of inept general managers and coaches who kept the team in the lottery and squandered whatever talent the Warriors did have.

Golden State only found success when Don Nelson returned to the Bay Area more than a decade after being Cohan's first head coach. But the Nellie era quickly descended into turmoil if not farce despite seeing him become the NBA's all-time winningest coach late in the season, surpassing Lenny Wilkens. 2009-10 saw Nelson's hand-picked captain, Stephen Jackson, demand and ultimately receive a trade less than a year after signing a new contract extension. It saw the Warriors suit up a remarkable 20 players, 18 of whom started at least one game. It also saw, repeatedly, some of the most bizarre rotations in NBA history.

In part, Nelson's hand was forced by a series of crippling injuries. At one point, Golden State had to petition the league for not one but two exemptions to exceed the 15-player roster limit in order to have enough healthy bodies to play. First on Jan. 15 against Milwaukee and again in the season finale at Portland, the Warriors' depth was so limited that they invoked a little-known provision in the league rulebook allowing a player to continue with six fouls if no one else is available on the bench.

Even when Golden State had more reserves available, Nelson frequently decided to make leading scorer Monta Ellis a marathon man. Like a starting pitcher from the 1970s, Ellis played an entire game 13 times, including one 53-minute overtime effort at Denver. By contrast, Charlotte's Gerald Wallace--the only other player to average more than 40 minutes per game last season--played just four complete games.

It was Keith Smart, acting as head coach when Nelson himself hit the injured list with pneumonia, who presided over the Warriors' unique win in Dallas in November. With nine players sidelined, Smart used just six of the seven players available to him in an entire game, sending three starters (Ellis, Anthony Morrow and Vladimir Radmanovic) out for the full 48 minutes. The last time that happened for the Warriors? According to the *San Jose Mercury News*, it was Nov. 25, 1964--when one of the three players was Wilt Chamberlain.

If Golden State ever had any hope of contending for a playoff berth in 2009-10, the injuries ended that. The Warriors lost 503 total games to injuries, the second-highest total in the 25 years the league has been tracking games lost. Only one player--rookie Stephen

WARRIORS IN A BOX

Last year's record	26-56
Last year's Offensive Rating	109.8 (14)
Last year's Defensive Rating	113.9 (29)
Last year's point differential	-3.6 (22)
Team pace	98.6 (1)
SCHOENE projection	**49-33 (4)**
Projected Offensive Rating	112.3 (7)
Projected Defensive Rating	109.1 (12)
Projected team weighted age	25.6 (23)
Projected '10-11 payroll	$67.3 (14)
Est. payroll obligations, '11-12	$55.0 (16)

Head coach: Keith Smart

Smart takes over under unusual circumstances, replacing Don Nelson on media day. Compared to Nelson, Smart is a bit of a blank slate. He predated Nelson as an assistant for the Warriors, so it's not entirely clear that he will maintain the status quo in terms of style. Smart does seem to prefer an up-tempo game. When he served as interim head coach in Cleveland during the second half of the 2002-03 season, the Cavaliers ranked third in the league in pace. The Cavaliers played slightly faster after Smart replaced John Lucas.

Curry--played in more than 70 games. Starter Andris Biedrins and second-year forward Anthony Randolph missed 49 games apiece, sharpshooter Kelenna Azubuike saw his season end after nine games and promising young forward Brandan Wright never set foot on the court after shoulder surgery.

Improbably, the injuries might have done some good for the Warriors going forward. Notably, they ensured Curry a chance to go out and play his game as a rookie. Turned loose and given the keys to the Golden State offense, Curry responded with an impressive season that saw him make a run at Rookie of the Year honors. He actually posted the most Wins Above Replacement Player of any rookie, demonstrating that his shooting and ballhandling would translate from Davidson College to the NBA.

Because of the need for healthy contributors, the Warriors became the unofficial 17th D-League franchise, calling up five players over the course of the season. Some quickly returned, but Golden State hung on to big men Chris Hunter and Anthony Tolliver and swingman Reggie Williams. Williams, who went undrafted out of non-basketball hotbed Virginia Military Institute and spent his first season after college playing overseas, proved to be the real hidden gem of the group. He averaged 15.2 points in 24 late-season games and now figures to be a big part of the Warriors' future, like D-Leaguers Azubuike and C.J. Watson before him.

The additional depth allowed Golden State to do some consolidating during the offseason. First, the Warriors offloaded the contract of forward Corey Maggette, made expendable in part by Williams' emergence. Golden State sent Maggette, who never fit in with a young team out of contention, to the Milwaukee Bucks for a pair of players with expiring contracts--guard Charlie Bell and center Dan Gadzuric.

The big move of the offseason came in free agency. Well over the salary cap, the Warriors struck via a sign-and-trade deal, landing one of the better players on the market in former Knicks big man David Lee. The price in terms of talent was steep. Golden State gave up the enigmatic but promising Randolph, as well as useful role player Azubuike and backup center Ronny Turiaf to make the salaries match. Add in Lee's new six-year, $80 million contract and the Warriors are wagering a lot on him. At least they've done so for a good player, and one who is young enough that he will likely hold his value through the deal.

Golden State's selection in the draft was more difficult to explain. Uncertain which big men would be available at the sixth pick, the Warriors honed in on Baylor forward Ekpe Udoh in the final days before the draft. The 23-year-old Udoh may never be a good scorer in the NBA and lacks the upside of players like Ed Davis and Greg Monroe who were still on the board. Even Udoh's best attribute--his ability to contribute right away, especially as a defender--was partially negated when he underwent wrist surgery in July that will sideline him up to half his rookie season.

After signing athletic Dorell Wright from the Miami Heat to replace Azubuike and see action at both wing positions, the last hole for Golden State to fill was backup point guard. The team never seemed enamored with Watson despite two years of solid play off the bench, and he was allowed to walk to Chicago as a free agent. Rookie Jeremy Lin is the leading contender for the position. Lin might already be Golden State's most popular player. The Palo Alto product returns to the Bay after being passed over by local colleges. He ended up at Harvard, becoming the top Ivy League prospect in recent memory. Lin also happens to be a hero to Asian-Americans as the first American of fully Asian descent to play in the league since Wat Misaka suited up for the New York Knicks in 1947-48.

The Warriors' impressive SCHOENE projection reflects the talent the team has amassed, which is much better than last year's performance would suggest. A frontcourt of Lee and Biedrins would be stout on the glass, and Biedrins' shot blocking will help cover for Lee's biggest weakness. At the other end, Golden State has two creators in the backcourt in Curry and Ellis. A small forward rotation of Williams and Dorell Wright offers a great deal of upside. Don't sleep on Williams, whose translated college and D-League statistics suggested he could play in the league and play well.

The Warriors could be especially dangerous on offense, where their projection places them second in the league in effective field-goal percentage. Other than Ellis, a volume scorer, every other player in the primary rotation is above average in terms of efficiency and is projected for a .567 True Shooting Percentage or better. At the other end of the floor, defensive rebounding and interior defense can help make up for Golden State's other weaknesses. If nothing else, the Warriors should be far more competitive on defense.

Still, there are a couple of big asterisks that need to be slapped onto that projection. The first of them is the risk of injuries. After all, last year's Golden State essay suggested that improved health would help the Warriors bounce back. At this point, Biedrins has to be consid-

GOLDEN STATE WARRIORS

ered prone to injury, while Ellis must prove he can last a full season after his ankle surgery. Udoh, meanwhile, is already out of the lineup. The upside is Golden State has improved its depth, adding NBA veterans Louis Amundson and Rodney Carney as free agents during the month of September. The newcomers push replacement-level talents like Bell and Gadzuric to the end of the bench.

On the eve of training camp, Nelson resigned as the Warriors' head coach, a move that was officially termed a mutual decision but has the fingerprints of the new ownership group all over it. Long-time assistant Smart will replace Nelson on the sidelines, completing the fresh start by the Bay. Smart's strongest attribute right now might be that he is not Nelson. The coach and his inconsistent rotations represented the biggest wild card in Golden State's projection.

Smart figures to play things more traditionally and he takes over a roster set up for that style of play with several new additions in the frontcourt. The Warriors might be a year away from making the kind of noise SCHOENE predicts, but all the changes mean Golden State's future looks as bright as it has in the last 15 years. For fans, sustained success can't come a moment too soon.

Kevin Pelton

From the Blogosphere

Who: Q McCall
What: Swish Appeal
Where: http://www.swishappeal.com/

Stephen Curry seems to stand in direct opposition to everything that has defined the Warriors throughout the unmitigated disaster that was the Chris Cohan era. Drafted as a combo guard with somewhat uncertain point guard skills, he earned Don Nelson's trust and actually exceeded expectations, clearly overcoming any uncertainty about his ability to run a team. There were times were it appeared that Curry was just the new kid on the block who didn't realize that things like deliberatively and patiently running an offense just weren't done here. So if we are to characterize the way forward, the acquisition of players like David Lee and Ekpe Udoh could be interpreted as building a foundation of players who might best perform with defined roles in a structure rather than the unorthodox insanity of the past. Though it's unreasonable to believe the Warriors can make a sudden turnaround, it's a respite from chaos.

WARRIORS FIVE-YEAR TRENDS

Season	AGE	W-L	POW	PYTH	SEED	ORTG	DRTG	PT DIFF	PACE
05-06	25.6	34-48	36.0 (18)	37.1	---	106.2 (20)	107.8 (17)	-1.4 (18)	92.0 (4)
06-07	24.6	42-40	42.2 (12)	40.1	8	109.1 (10)	108.9 (17)	-0.3 (13)	97.6 (1)
07-08	25.6	48-34	48.8 (12)	46.7	---	113.9 (6)	111.8 (21)	2.2 (13)	96.9 (2)
08-09	25.0	29-53	29.5 (24)	31.5	---	111.0 (11)	114.7 (28)	-3.7 (24)	96.9 (1)
09-10	25.7	26-56	29.0 (23)	31.8	--	109.8 (14)	113.9 (29)	-3.6 (22)	98.6 (1)

		OFFENSE				DEFENSE			
Season	PAY	eFG	oREB	FT/FGA	TO	eFG	oREB	FT/FGA	TO
05-06	$57.5	.479 (24)	.269 (14)	.232 (24)	.152 (6)	.492 (19)	.716 (22)	.243 (14)	.166 (7)
06-07	$62.1	.512 (3)	.256 (23)	.215 (29)	.163 (13)	.506 (24)	.696 (29)	.264 (21)	.190 (1)
07-08	$70.3	.511 (7)	.272 (12)	.208 (25)	.133 (4)	.509 (23)	.703 (30)	.258 (25)	.166 (4)
08-09	$63.3	.497 (18)	.261 (18)	.268 (3)	.150 (12)	.508 (20)	.682 (30)	.251 (22)	.153 (16)
09-10	$66.5	.514 (8)	.209 (30)	.230 (13)	.149 (10)	.525 (28)	.685 (30)	.260 (27)	.178 (1)

(league rankings in parenthesis)

GOLDEN STATE WARRIORS

PF 19 — Louis Amundson

Hght: 6'9"	Exp: 4	Salary: $2.5 million
Wght: 238	From: Nevada-Las Vegas	
2011-12 status: guaranteed contract for $2.5 million		

SKILL RATINGS

TOT	OFF	DEF	REB	PAS	HND	SHT	ATH
+1	+1	+3	+3	-4	-4	+3	+2

Year	Team	Age	G	MPG	Usg	3PA%	FTA%	INS	2P%	3P%	FT%	TS%	Reb%	Ast%	TO%	BLK%	STL%	PF%	oRTG	dRTG	Win%	WARP
07-08	PHI	25.4	16	3.9	.152	.000	.146	1.146	.500	.000	.286	.472	.113	.000	.095	.013	.007	.096	102.0	109.1	.282	-0.2
08-09	PHX	26.4	76	13.7	.152	.003	.147	1.144	.538	.000	.442	.530	.151	.012	.156	.046	.015	.065	104.5	105.2	.475	1.3
09-10	PHX	27.4	79	14.8	.147	.003	.140	1.137	.553	.000	.545	.562	.165	.012	.147	.044	.010	.064	104.3	104.5	.493	1.9
10-11p	GSW	28.4	76	10.0	.150	.004	.134	1.130	.545	.001	.524	.551	.151	.012	.149	.044	.011	.064	104.1	104.9	.473	0.9

Most similar to: Etan Thomas (98.3), Aaron Williams, Keon Clark, Tim Perry   IMP: 46%   BRK: 6%   COP: 6%

Louis Amundson was a key part of the Suns' bench brigade during 2009-10 before being deemed replaceable. Amundson spent most of the summer looking for a team that would meet his rational salary demands after Phoenix signed Hakim Warrick as his replacement. The Warriors finally signed him two weeks before the start of training camp, and Amundson ended up getting a reasonable two-year contract worth up to $5 million.

Amundson emerged last season as sort of a lesser Chris Andersen, an energy big man with more than a modicum of skill. A big-time leaper, Amundson has always been a positive presence on the glass and is especially dangerous on the offensive boards. He's lacking in range, but good shot selection and regular finishes at the rim helped him shoot a career-best 55.3 percent on twos. Defensively, Amundson gives up strength in the post, but the trade-off is his plus shot-blocking. Because he is more a four than a five, Amundson would be best paired with a physical post defender who struggles as a help defender.

SG 34 — Charlie Bell

Hght: 6'3"	Exp: 6	Salary: $4.4 million
Wght: 200	From: Michigan State	
2011-12 status: player option or ETO for $4.1 million		

SKILL RATINGS

TOT	OFF	DEF	REB	PAS	HND	SHT	ATH
-2	+1	+2	-4	0	+3	-1	-4

Year	Team	Age	G	MPG	Usg	3PA%	FTA%	INS	2P%	3P%	FT%	TS%	Reb%	Ast%	TO%	BLK%	STL%	PF%	oRTG	dRTG	Win%	WARP
07-08	MIL	29.1	68	24.0	.166	.361	.064	.703	.413	.341	.805	.490	.062	.058	.128	.001	.015	.034	105.0	107.0	.435	0.6
08-09	MIL	30.1	70	25.5	.160	.378	.055	.678	.458	.363	.825	.525	.046	.038	.120	.003	.014	.035	105.0	107.7	.412	-0.2
09-10	MIL	31.1	71	22.7	.149	.380	.056	.676	.395	.365	.716	.486	.048	.029	.103	.006	.012	.038	103.4	107.3	.374	-1.4
10-11p	GSW	32.1	74	5.4	.151	.397	.054	.657	.418	.364	.742	.500	.048	.037	.114	.004	.013	.038	104.3	107.6	.393	-0.2

Most similar to: Bruce Bowen (97.3), Blue Edwards, Anthony Peeler, Rory Sparrow   IMP: 41%   BRK: 7%   COP: 0%

Charlie Bell hasn't been a particularly effective NBA player since 2006-07, but the combination of a long-term contract and Michael Redd's series of injuries allowed him to continue to see regular playing time in Milwaukee. His minutes will surely drop after this summer's trade to Golden State, which makes him the oldest player on the Warriors' roster.

Bell's big issue has been making enough two-pointers to lift his True Shooting Percentage above 50 percent. He generates few easy shots and is a very poor finisher in the paint, having made just 46.3 percent of his attempts at the rim last season (per Hoopdata.com). Bell is better from the perimeter, so ramping up his three-point attempts to fit in with the Warriors' offense might help him. He is solid at the defensive end of the floor despite being undersized for a two-guard. He competes and can defend either backcourt position.

C 15 — Andris Biedrins

Hght: 6'11"	Exp: 6	Salary: $9.0 million
Wght: 240	From: Riga, Latvia	
2011-12 status: guaranteed contract for $9.0 million		

SKILL RATINGS

TOT	OFF	DEF	REB	PAS	HND	SHT	ATH
+2	+1	-1	+3	+4	+4	+5	+2

Year	Team	Age	G	MPG	Usg	3PA%	FTA%	INS	2P%	3P%	FT%	TS%	Reb%	Ast%	TO%	BLK%	STL%	PF%	oRTG	dRTG	Win%	WARP
07-08	GSW	22.1	76	27.3	.144	.000	.116	1.116	.628	.000	.620	.639	.194	.015	.120	.033	.011	.053	106.4	103.8	.585	7.3
08-09	GSW	23.1	62	30.0	.170	.001	.129	1.127	.579	.000	.551	.585	.202	.028	.149	.036	.016	.054	106.9	103.9	.601	7.2
09-10	GSW	24.1	33	23.1	.101	.000	.061	1.061	.591	-	.160	.561	.190	.032	.178	.041	.012	.066	103.1	103.5	.483	1.1
10-11p	GSW	25.1	68	22.0	.139	.005	.089	1.084	.588	.004	.382	.569	.177	.031	.160	.036	.013	.055	104.2	103.9	.511	3.0

Most similar to: Dale Davis (97.1), Tyson Chandler, Michael Smith, Samuel Dalembert   IMP: 36%   BRK: 0%   COP: 4%

GOLDEN STATE WARRIORS

2009-10 was a lost season for Andris Biedrins, who played just 33 games due to a hernia injury that ultimately required surgery. In an interview with website sportacentrs.com in his native Latvia, as translated by WarriorsWorld.net, Biedrins said he felt surgery was the right option from the beginning but team doctors tried to convince him to play through the injury.

Ultimately, that worked for no one. Biedrins was a shell of himself when he did play. His usage rate plummeted, and Biedrins was down in pretty much every category save shot blocking. The most notable number in his stat line was Biedrins' 16.0 percent shooting from the free throw line. His free throws have always been an adventure; last season took this to an extreme, whether for mechanical reasons or simply out of a lack of confidence. It's telling that Biedrins' rate of free throw attempts also dropped by more than half; the last thing he wanted to do was go to the line.

Biedrins should be healthy to start this season, which is great news for Golden State. A Biedrins-David Lee frontcourt stands the chance to be very effective, since each addresses the other's weakness. Biedrins' shot-blocking efforts often leave him out of position to rebound, so having another glass-cleaner alongside him will help. Meanwhile, Biedrins' help defense will help Lee look better in one-on-one situations.

SG 25	Rodney Carney	Hght: 6'7" Wght: 205 2011-12 status: free agent	Exp: 4 From: Memphis	Salary: $0.9 million			SKILL RATINGS						
							TOT	OFF	DEF	REB	PAS	HND	SHT	ATH
							+3	+3	+2	+3	-4	-3	+1	+3

Year	Team	Age	G	MPG	Usg	3PA%	FTA%	INS	2P%	3P%	FT%	TS%	Reb%	Ast%	TO%	BLK%	STL%	PF%	oRTG	dRTG	Win%	WARP
07-08	PHI	24.0	70	14.9	.202	.260	.077	.817	.441	.317	.679	.478	.085	.014	.074	.017	.017	.043	103.4	105.5	.428	0.3
08-09	MIN	25.0	67	17.9	.187	.457	.059	.602	.492	.350	.758	.532	.063	.010	.087	.019	.019	.036	105.3	106.2	.469	1.3
09-10	PHI	26.0	68	12.6	.177	.408	.084	.676	.490	.304	.825	.515	.095	.020	.063	.018	.015	.042	105.3	105.8	.484	1.2
10-11p	GSW	27.0	75	9.9	.189	.489	.077	.589	.485	.337	.798	.533	.077	.017	.074	.020	.018	.041	106.2	105.4	.526	1.7

Most similar to: Mickael Pietrus (97.6), Tim Legler, Lucious Harris, Eric Piatkowski — IMP: 66% BRK: 17% COP: 7%

Rodney Carney needs to figure out what he does well and cut out the rest. Unfortunately, he has proven to be too inconsistent to stick in a team's rotation. He's much more athletic than he is skilled, a description that can be applied to most failed lottery picks. Carney hasn't ironed out the wrinkles in his game, and as he approaches age 27 it's unlikely that he ever will. Thus he remains in a team-hopping phase. Golden State will be his latest stop. Carney signed a one-year contract for the minimum and will battle for a rotation spot on the wing.

Carney's love affair with the three-point line continues unabated, though he barely cracked a 30 percent success rate from there. He is pretty effective in isolations, when he is less prone to settle for the outside shot, and also runs the floor well. Defensively, Carney's teams have been consistently better when he's on the floor. His other metrics are solid on that end, even though he drew only one charge in 857 minutes last season.

PG 30	Stephen Curry	Hght: 6'3" Wght: 185 2011-12 status: guaranteed contract for $3.1 million	Exp: 1 From: Davidson	Salary: $2.9 million			SKILL RATINGS						
							TOT	OFF	DEF	REB	PAS	HND	SHT	ATH
							+5	+5	-5	+3	+1	-1	+4	+4

Year	Team	Age	G	MPG	Usg	3PA%	FTA%	INS	2P%	3P%	FT%	TS%	Reb%	Ast%	TO%	BLK%	STL%	PF%	oRTG	dRTG	Win%	WARP
09-10	GSW	22.1	80	36.2	.219	.258	.060	.802	.474	.437	.885	.568	.069	.070	.165	.005	.025	.037	107.4	105.9	.549	7.9
10-11p	GSW	23.1	76	36.0	.240	.264	.067	.804	.476	.452	.885	.581	.068	.074	.150	.005	.024	.037	108.9	105.5	.610	11.1

Most similar to: Gilbert Arenas (97.5), Isiah Thomas, Steve Francis, Chauncey Billups — IMP: 75% BRK: 4% COP: 4%

Stephen Curry was a revelation during his rookie season, and SCHOENE's prediction of further improvement ahead this season suggests he could play his way into the ranks of the league's better point guards in a hurry. A starter from the very early stages of the season, Curry made the transition from college to pro look easy. The time he spent playing on the ball as Davidson's point guard as a junior translated into an ability to balance setting up teammates and looking for his own offense. This rare combination figures to be Curry's calling card.

GOLDEN STATE WARRIORS

Curry can also shoot the rock. He finished in the league's top 10 in three-point percentage, free throw percentage and three-pointers. According to Synergy Sports, Curry was the league's most efficient shooter in spot-up situations, posting a True Shooting Percentage of nearly 70 percent on these attempts. Curry's improvement should come from a few areas. First, he could stand to cut down on his turnovers. The Warriors' television broadcast team of Jim Barnett and Bob Fitzgerald pointed out that many of Curry's miscues came when he attempted one-handed passes, something he could pull off against NCAA opponents but not at this level. Second, he has work to do at the defensive end. While his -5 defensive skill rating is fluky--Synergy shows his defensive performance near average--improved strength would allow him to deal with bigger, more physical opponents.

SG 8 — Monta Ellis

Hght: 6'3" Exp: 5 Salary: $11.0 million
Wght: 180 From: Lanier HS (Jackson, MS)
2011-12 status: guaranteed contract for $11.0 million

SKILL RATINGS

TOT	OFF	DEF	REB	PAS	HND	SHT	ATH
+1	+2	-4	-2	+3	-1	0	+4

Year	Team	Age	G	MPG	Usg	3PA%	FTA%	INS	2P%	3P%	FT%	TS%	Reb%	Ast%	TO%	BLK%	STL%	PF%	oRTG	dRTG	Win%	WARP
07-08	GSW	22.5	81	37.9	.218	.033	.116	1.083	.544	.231	.767	.580	.072	.043	.109	.006	.017	.027	106.4	106.0	.511	6.1
08-09	GSW	23.5	25	35.7	.259	.048	.077	1.029	.460	.308	.830	.503	.066	.045	.124	.006	.021	.032	103.3	106.5	.395	-0.4
09-10	GSW	24.5	64	41.4	.295	.125	.094	.969	.470	.338	.753	.517	.055	.055	.134	.007	.025	.031	105.0	105.8	.471	3.0
10-11p	GSW	25.5	70	40.0	.273	.111	.097	.986	.486	.328	.794	.533	.056	.050	.122	.008	.021	.030	105.3	105.9	.481	3.8

Most similar to: Larry Hughes (97.5), Ricky Davis, Kendall Gill, Latrell Sprewell   IMP: 60% BRK: 3% COP: 6%

It was, to say the least, an odd season for Monta Ellis. A year removed from ankle surgery, Ellis appeared fully healthy, bouncing back from his poor, abbreviated 2008-09 campaign. Inexplicably, Don Nelson took this as an excuse to play Ellis into the ground. Because he had to try to conserve energy, Ellis neglected his defensive responsibilities after playing reasonably well at that end of the floor early in the season. When he wants to be, and has the energy to do so, Ellis can be a good defender who battles bigger players. His rebounding also suffered.

The bigger changes in Ellis' production had to do with the way he was used. Ellis took over the role of leading man, using plays at a career-high rate. As expected, Ellis' efficiency numbers took a major hit. His two-point percentage dropped dramatically because he was attempting so many long jumpers, frequently off the dribble, and he turned the ball over more often. Ellis is more effective when sharing the scoring load. The growth of Stephen Curry and the addition of David Lee should give Ellis the necessary talent around him; now it's a matter of whether he is willing to take more of a backseat. His attitude last season, starting with his declaration at media day that he and Curry would be unable to play together in the backcourt, is not encouraging in this regard.

C 50 — Dan Gadzuric

Hght: 6'11" Exp: 8 Salary: $7.2 million
Wght: 245 From: UCLA
2011-12 status: free agent

SKILL RATINGS

TOT	OFF	DEF	REB	PAS	HND	SHT	ATH
-3	-1	0	0	-1	-1	-3	+4

Year	Team	Age	G	MPG	Usg	3PA%	FTA%	INS	2P%	3P%	FT%	TS%	Reb%	Ast%	TO%	BLK%	STL%	PF%	oRTG	dRTG	Win%	WARP
07-08	MIL	30.2	51	10.4	.183	.005	.128	1.124	.418	.000	.524	.443	.160	.009	.158	.036	.017	.072	101.4	104.5	.396	-0.2
08-09	MIL	31.2	67	14.0	.151	.006	.095	1.089	.483	.000	.544	.495	.162	.019	.130	.038	.017	.078	103.3	105.1	.438	0.4
09-10	MIL	32.2	32	9.8	.167	.000	.096	1.096	.438	-	.400	.440	.168	.017	.130	.033	.015	.091	102.1	105.7	.382	-0.2
10-11p	GSW	33.2	76	5.0	.164	.005	.101	1.096	.454	.000	.476	.457	.148	.016	.141	.034	.015	.087	101.9	105.7	.376	-0.3

Most similar to: Andrew Lang (96.0), Corie Blount, Brian Skinner, Francisco Elson   IMP: 43% BRK: 7% COP: 9%

It's been years now since Dan Gadzuric was a favorite of statistical analysts for his strong numbers in a reserve role. When the Bucks signed him to a six-year mid-level contract, it seemed like a reasonable risk on a promising player. It ended up an albatross, both because of length and because Gadzuric turned out to not be very good. He's played a limited role in recent seasons, and only saw action last year when Andrew Bogut was out of the lineup.

Gadzuric is still athletic enough that he might appeal to the Warriors as a neo-Ronny Turiaf. He remains a solid rebounder and shot blocker, but has been very poor as a scorer in his 30s, which has limited his value. Gadzuric's size will keep him around as a third center for a while, though this will be his last season cashing big paychecks.

GOLDEN STATE WARRIORS

C 10	**David Lee**	Hght: 6'9" Wght: 250 2011-12 status: guaranteed contract for $11.9 million	Exp: 5 From: Florida	Salary: $10.8 million								
					SKILL RATINGS							
					TOT	OFF	DEF	REB	PAS	HND	SHT	ATH
					+4	+3	-5	+2	+4	+4	+4	+1

Year	Team	Age	G	MPG	Usg	3PA%	FTA%	INS	2P%	3P%	FT%	TS%	Reb%	Ast%	TO%	BLK%	STL%	PF%	oRTG	dRTG	Win%	WARP
07-08	NYK	25.0	81	29.1	.157	.002	.127	1.125	.554	.000	.819	.607	.177	.018	.119	.010	.011	.041	106.1	105.2	.528	5.5
08-09	NYK	26.0	81	34.9	.193	.002	.117	1.114	.551	.000	.755	.590	.187	.027	.120	.006	.014	.040	106.8	105.4	.545	7.6
09-10	NYK	27.0	81	37.3	.240	.005	.091	1.086	.549	.000	.812	.584	.180	.044	.119	.010	.014	.039	108.0	104.9	.601	11.6
10-11p	GSW	28.0	76	36.0	.210	.007	.101	1.094	.552	.003	.796	.588	.165	.035	.115	.008	.012	.040	106.9	105.4	.551	7.7

Most similar to: Brad Miller (98.1), Tyrone Hill, Otis Thorpe, Shareef Abdur-Rahim | IMP: 37% | BRK: 2% | COP: 0%

You could have gotten pretty good odds a few years ago that David Lee would end a Knicks drought in the All-Star Game that dated all the way back to Allan Houston and Latrell Sprewell in 2001. Lee did just that, making last year's Eastern Conference team as a replacement for Allen Iverson. Lee earned the honor, putting together his best season as a pro. Serving as the roll man in Mike D'Antoni's pick-and-roll and also creating his own shots out of face-up situations, Lee became a much bigger factor in the New York offense without sacrificing anything in terms of efficiency. Another unexpected development was Lee becoming one of the league's leading assisters among big men. When operating out of the high post, he saw the floor well and was able to feed cutters.

The tradeoff was at the other end of the floor. Lee will never be a good individual defender because he does not move well laterally and can get overpowered in the paint. Since Lee is not a shot blocker either, playing center only exacerbated his defensive issues. Moving to power forward in Golden State will be a much better scenario for Lee, who has developed enough of a midrange jump shot to pull off the floor spacing required from the position. Lee will help the Warriors' defense with his rebounding, which has been a strength throughout his NBA career.

PG 7	**Jeremy Lin**	Hght: 6'3" Wght: 200 2011-12 status: non-guaranteed contract for $0.8 million	Exp: R From: Harvard	Salary: $0.5 million								
					SKILL RATINGS							
					TOT	OFF	DEF	REB	PAS	HND	SHT	ATH
					-2	-1	+1	0	-1	-3	-4	+5

Year	Team	Age	G	MPG	Usg	3PA%	FTA%	INS	2P%	3P%	FT%	TS%	Reb%	Ast%	TO%	BLK%	STL%	PF%	oRTG	dRTG	Win%	WARP
10-11p	GSW	22.7	76	15.0	.170	.154	.126	.972	.450	.269	.739	.504	.053	.058	.213	.016	.026	.057	102.8	105.6	.410	-0.1

Most similar to: Earl Watson (97.4), Kyle Weaver, Jarrett Jack, Chris Duhon | IMP: - | BRK: - | COP: -

Undrafted rookie Jeremy Lin will be one of the Warriors' most popular players, but that should not overshadow the fact that he's good enough to play at this level. Lin's numbers are impressive even when adjusted for the relatively low level of play in the Ivy League, and he backed them up with strong outings against Boston College and UConn, the latter of which drew plaudits from Jim Calhoun. It took NBA scouts a little longer to embrace Lin. That happened after he succeeded for the Dallas Mavericks in Las Vegas at the NBA Summer League. The performance was enough to earn Lin some guaranteed money from the Warriors.

Lin has good size for a point guard, which helps produce some unusual statistical markers. He blocks shots on a regular basis and was also excellent in reading the passing lanes and coming up with steals. The big question mark in how Lin's game will translate is in terms of his finishing. He shot a high percentage around the rim against NCAA defenders and will be more challenged to do so in the NBA. Lin needs those scores because he is not a pure shooter. The big weakness to watch is that Lin was very prone to turnovers at Harvard. To take advantage of his other skills, he'll need to keep his efficiency up.

GOLDEN STATE WARRIORS

PF 77 — Vladimir Radmanovic

Hght: 6'10" Exp: 9 Salary: $6.9 million
Wght: 235 From: Belgrade, Serbia
2011-12 status: free agent

SKILL RATINGS

TOT	OFF	DEF	REB	PAS	HND	SHT	ATH
-1	0	-3	-4	+2	+1	-2	0

Year	Team	Age	G	MPG	Usg	3PA%	FTA%	INS	2P%	3P%	FT%	TS%	Reb%	Ast%	TO%	BLK%	STL%	PF%	oRTG	dRTG	Win%	WARP
07-08	LAL	27.4	65	22.8	.161	.434	.053	.619	.507	.406	.800	.583	.079	.037	.136	.006	.014	.044	106.5	106.6	.497	2.5
08-09	CHA	28.4	78	18.5	.187	.444	.043	.599	.446	.401	.741	.549	.090	.026	.166	.009	.016	.035	105.1	106.5	.455	1.2
09-10	GSW	29.4	41	21.7	.161	.328	.036	.708	.442	.278	.741	.449	.113	.022	.134	.006	.016	.047	102.7	106.5	.375	-0.8
10-11p	GSW	30.4	70	10.0	.167	.402	.038	.636	.440	.339	.771	.490	.094	.026	.142	.006	.015	.044	103.9	106.5	.413	0.0

Most similar to: Devean George (97.3), Walter McCarty, James Posey, Jaren Jackson

IMP: 47% BRK: 15% COP: 6%

Vladimir Radmanovic is the canary in the coal mine for the Warriors' season. If he plays heavy minutes, whether because of injuries or as a smallball option at the four, things have gone wrong. That's not so much a knock on Radmanovic's game as it is a statement about the players he's behind in the Golden State rotation, who are either better, younger or both.

It's hard to believe that Radmanovic is just three years removed from starting in the 2008 NBA Finals. He posted a career-best True Shooting Percentage that season for Los Angeles and has been unable to sustain that level of efficiency. Last year, Radmanovic's poor three-point shooting made him a liability on offense and dropped his overall performance below replacement level. Always a weak rebounder, Radmanovic's effort has been inconsistent at the defensive end of the floor. He's actually better defensively against power forwards, since he can deal with their strength better than he can the quickness of small forwards on the wing.

C 20 — Ekpe Udoh

Hght: 6'10" Exp: R Salary: $3.1 million
Wght: 240 From: Baylor
2011-12 status: guaranteed contract for $3.3 million

SKILL RATINGS

TOT	OFF	DEF	REB	PAS	HND	SHT	ATH
0	-1	+3	-2	+4	+4	-4	-1

Year	Team	Age	G	MPG	Usg	3PA%	FTA%	INS	2P%	3P%	FT%	TS%	Reb%	Ast%	TO%	BLK%	STL%	PF%	oRTG	dRTG	Win%	WARP
10-11p	GSW	23.9	35	20.0	.166	.037	.096	1.059	.416	.230	.669	.449	.128	.034	.159	.053	.008	.046	102.7	104.4	.443	0.4

Most similar to: Loren Woods (96.6), Ryan Humphrey, Shelden Williams

IMP: - BRK: - COP: -

A role player at Michigan who didn't fit into John Beilein's system, Ekpe Udoh transferred to Baylor and transformed himself into an NBA lottery pick with a strong season. Though he'll never be a go-to guy, Udoh showed more scoring ability in a featured role in Waco. The concern is that his two-point percentage still was not very good for a post player. Udoh is mechanical in the post and will have a difficult time scoring one-on-one against NBA defenders. He might be better off in the high post, where he can find teammates and has a decent midrange jumper.

Udoh should be an instant contributor on defense. He's a plus shot blocker, especially as a power forward (he's athletic enough to defend fours). Udoh would help himself by improving on the glass. His projection suggests he'll be below-average in that regard. The whole package sounds awfully similar to former Warrior Ronny Turiaf. Unfortunately, the Warriors are expecting more from the sixth pick. Udoh's age--he'll be 23 to start his rookie season--suggests they're likely to be disappointed, especially since he will miss much of his rookie season after summer wrist surgery.

SF 55 — Reggie Williams

Hght: 6'6" Exp: 1 Salary: $0.8 million
Wght: 210 From: Virginia Military Inst.
2011-12 status: free agent

SKILL RATINGS

TOT	OFF	DEF	REB	PAS	HND	SHT	ATH
+4	+4	-3	-3	+3	+4	+4	-1

Year	Team	Age	G	MPG	Usg	3PA%	FTA%	INS	2P%	3P%	FT%	TS%	Reb%	Ast%	TO%	BLK%	STL%	PF%	oRTG	dRTG	Win%	WARP
09-10	GSW	23.6	24	32.6	.186	.271	.080	.809	.560	.359	.839	.588	.079	.036	.085	.005	.013	.027	107.0	106.5	.517	1.6
10-11p	GSW	24.6	76	25.0	.199	.330	.083	.753	.557	.371	.855	.594	.071	.040	.087	.006	.014	.025	108.2	106.4	.558	5.6

Most similar to: Michael Finley (96.9), Rashard Lewis, Wally Szczerbiak, Byron Scott

IMP: 59% BRK: 4% COP: 6%

No, the Warriors did not resurrect the former Georgetown small forward. This Reggie Williams, who plays the same position, hails from Virginia Military Institute, where he led the nation in scoring his last two seasons in college. Williams' translated statistics indicated he could contribute, but he drew little interest in the draft and spent a year playing in France before trying his hand at the D-League last season. Again, he put up excellent numbers, and this time the NBA started paying attention. Williams was the fifth player Golden State called up from the D-League but the most successful of the group, quickly claiming a starting spot that he has a good chance of maintaining this season.

Watching Williams play, it's easy to see why scouts were skeptical. He's not much of an athlete for a wing; instead, he deceptively manages to get where he wants on the floor. Williams was especially effective in the paint last year, making 69.7 percent of his attempts at the rim according to Hoopdata.com. Teams will likely contain Williams somewhat better this season with improved scouting reports. Defenders will try to force him to his weaker right hand. That will make it important for Williams to develop his ballhandling; he's already very good for a small forward and rarely turned the ball over. At the defensive end, Williams competed, which was more than could be said of a lot of his teammates. His lateral quickness can be an issue in certain matchups.

PF 32	Brandan Wright	Hght: 6'10" Exp: 2 Salary: $3.4 million										**SKILL RATINGS**							
		Wght: 210 From: North Carolina										TOT	OFF	DEF	REB	PAS	HND	SHT	ATH
		2011-12 status: due qualifying offer of $4.6 million										+3	+2	0	-1	-2	0	+3	+1
Year	Team	Age	G	MPG	Usg	3PA%	FTA%	INS	2P%	3P%	FT%	TS%	Reb%	Ast%	TO%	BLK%	STL%	PF%	oRTG	dRTG	Win%	WARP
07-08	GSW	20.5	38	9.9	.160	.000	.123	1.123	.554	.000	.675	.583	.142	.010	.091	.043	.007	.040	104.9	104.3	.519	0.8
08-09	GSW	21.5	39	17.6	.191	.013	.122	1.109	.537	.000	.741	.570	.124	.013	.075	.037	.015	.046	106.4	105.1	.543	1.8
10-11p	GSW	23.5	61	22.0	.188	.016	.112	1.096	.548	.019	.737	.573	.121	.015	.083	.037	.010	.038	105.4	104.8	.521	2.9

Most similar to: Kenny Williams (97.1), Travis Knight, Jermaine O'Neal, Rasheed Wallace   IMP: 48%   BRK: 5%   COP: 5%

Brandan Wright's left shoulder cost him a season and a half of prime development time. Wright initially dislocated the shoulder in January 2009 and missed 37 games that season. Wright then re-injured the shoulder last fall in training camp, and surgery kept him out the entire 2009-10 campaign. Besides depriving the Warriors of a rotation regular, the injury also meant Wright was unable to get the experience he needs to improve, especially at the defensive end of the floor, where his awareness is a work in progress.

On offense, Wright should be fine. A long-limbed southpaw (one of four on the Golden State roster and three up front--Andris Biedrins, David Lee and Reggie Williams are the others), he's an excellent finisher with a dangerous jump hook. The presence of Curry as a pick-and-roll partner should create good looks for Wright in the paint. If Wright can improve his help defense, it will make it easier for the Warriors to play him together with Lee in a frontcourt that will create some problems for opposing defenses.

SF 1	Dorell Wright	Hght: 6'9" Exp: 6 Salary: $3.5 million										**SKILL RATINGS**							
		Wght: 210 From: South Kent Prep HS (Lawndale, CA)										TOT	OFF	DEF	REB	PAS	HND	SHT	ATH
		2011-12 status: guaranteed contract for $3.7 million										+3	+2	+1	0	+1	+2	+4	+2
Year	Team	Age	G	MPG	Usg	3PA%	FTA%	INS	2P%	3P%	FT%	TS%	Reb%	Ast%	TO%	BLK%	STL%	PF%	oRTG	dRTG	Win%	WARP
07-08	MIA	22.4	44	25.1	.152	.031	.086	1.055	.493	.364	.826	.537	.119	.026	.082	.029	.012	.033	103.0	104.2	.459	1.0
08-09	MIA	23.4	6	12.2	.185	.000	.092	1.092	.400	.000	.333	.398	.165	.013	.209	.000	.014	.052	96.1	105.8	.208	-0.3
09-10	MIA	24.4	72	20.8	.159	.313	.060	.748	.508	.389	.884	.567	.092	.029	.106	.017	.018	.030	105.9	104.8	.534	3.6
10-11p	GSW	25.4	74	25.0	.162	.263	.069	.807	.505	.401	.890	.573	.091	.028	.103	.022	.016	.029	105.5	104.9	.520	4.0

Most similar to: Scott Burrell (98.6), Danny Granger, Shane Battier, James Posey   IMP: 59%   BRK: 9%   COP: 5%

The Miami Heat was forced to sacrifice Dorell Wright in its pursuit of the max trio and veterans Mike Miller and Udonis Haslem. Golden State wisely pounced, signing Wright to a three-year, $11.1 million contract that stands the chance to be a steal. Wright has been solid in a reserve role two of the last three years and won't turn 25 until midway through the season, so he's a nice replacement for Kelenna Azubuike in the role of marksman on the wing.

The big key for Wright will be maintaining his three-point percentage. SCHOENE optimistically suggests he'll make better than 40 percent of his triples this season. He's hardly a specialist, however. Wright is a terrific athlete who can defend either wing position and will thrive in a faster-paced system than Miami's. Look for Wright to become one of Stephen Curry's favorite targets on the break.

GOLDEN STATE WARRIORS

SF	Devean George	Hght: 6'8"	Exp: 11	Salary: --	SKILL RATINGS						
		Wght: 235	From: Augsburg		TOT	OFF	DEF	REB	PAS	HND	SHT	ATH
--		2011-12 status: free agent			-2	0	-2	-2	-3	+2	0	-1

Year	Team	Age	G	MPG	Usg	3PA%	FTA%	INS	2P%	3P%	FT%	TS%	Reb%	Ast%	TO%	BLK%	STL%	PF%	oRTG	dRTG	Win%	WARP
07-08	DAL	30.6	53	15.5	.141	.276	.061	.784	.374	.324	.706	.437	.095	.020	.098	.012	.011	.051	101.5	106.3	.344	-1.2
08-09	DAL	31.6	43	16.5	.110	.451	.057	.607	.485	.289	.773	.485	.063	.010	.101	.011	.017	.037	103.1	107.0	.373	-0.6
09-10	GSW	32.6	45	16.9	.131	.532	.044	.512	.494	.390	.696	.560	.084	.018	.065	.009	.025	.050	105.7	105.5	.507	1.4
10-11p	AVG	33.6	69	16.9	.122	.432	.048	.617	.461	.341	.726	.505	.078	.016	.084	.012	.017	.048	103.4	106.2	.407	-0.2

Most similar to: Jud Buechler (96.7), Bryon Russell, Robert Reid, M.L. Carr   IMP: 42% BRK: 4% COP: 15%

Injuries forced Devean George into the Golden State rotation much of last season, and he responded with his best performance since leaving the L.A. Lakers. In fact, by win percentage, it was the best year of George's entire career. The key was that George, who has become almost strictly a three-point shooter in his waning years, made them at a career-best clip. Expecting that to continue is like expecting multiple paydays at the same slot machine. NBA teams have not been fooled, and George has found little interest on the market. He'll probably have to settle for a camp invite or wait for some team to call him at midseason.

C	Chris Hunter	Hght: 6'11"	Exp: 1	Salary: --	SKILL RATINGS						
		Wght: 240	From: Michigan		TOT	OFF	DEF	REB	PAS	HND	SHT	ATH
--		2011-12 status: free agent			-3	-1	-1	-3	+1	+3	-1	-2

Year	Team	Age	G	MPG	Usg	3PA%	FTA%	INS	2P%	3P%	FT%	TS%	Reb%	Ast%	TO%	BLK%	STL%	PF%	oRTG	dRTG	Win%	WARP
09-10	GSW	25.8	60	13.1	.152	.014	.109	1.095	.512	.000	.754	.546	.119	.020	.108	.032	.008	.072	103.6	106.6	.403	-0.2
10-11p	AVG	26.8	76	13.1	.150	.023	.112	1.089	.498	.000	.753	.532	.115	.021	.114	.030	.008	.071	102.9	106.5	.382	-0.7

Most similar to: Cherokee Parks (99.1), Rasho Nesterovic, Jake Tsakalidis, Melvin Ely   IMP: 46% BRK: 2% COP: 12%

The first player called up from the D-League by the Warriors, Chris Hunter stuck around for the entire year and played rotation minutes much of the way. Ultimately, he provided a pretty good example of replacement level (his per-minute win percentage was about .014 below what we calculate as replacement, which also includes the superior level of talent available for the minimum prior to training camp). Hunter blocked the occasional shot, hit better than 50 percent of his shot attempts and was careful with the basketball. His biggest negative was surprisingly poor rebounding for a big, athletic center. Vladimir Radmanovic nearly outrebounded him last season. Hunter has done enough to land in a training camp this fall. He'll probably look for a team with more openings in the frontcourt than Golden State currently has.

PF	Mikki Moore	Hght: 7'0"	Exp: 12	Salary: --	SKILL RATINGS						
		Wght: 225	From: Nebraska		TOT	OFF	DEF	REB	PAS	HND	SHT	ATH
--		2011-12 status: free agent			-4	-1	-2	-3	+3	+3	+4	-5

Year	Team	Age	G	MPG	Usg	3PA%	FTA%	INS	2P%	3P%	FT%	TS%	Reb%	Ast%	TO%	BLK%	STL%	PF%	oRTG	dRTG	Win%	WARP
07-08	SAC	32.5	82	29.0	.128	.003	.118	1.115	.579	.000	.736	.613	.122	.016	.162	.015	.007	.058	103.3	107.0	.379	-1.9
08-09	BOS	33.5	70	17.2	.107	.000	.096	1.096	.553	.000	.787	.593	.127	.020	.171	.013	.007	.079	103.0	108.4	.327	-2.2
09-10	GSW	34.5	23	17.7	.123	.000	.042	1.042	.600	-	.636	.606	.095	.038	.181	.023	.006	.064	103.7	107.6	.375	-0.4
10-11p	AVG	35.5	75	17.7	.113	.002	.068	1.065	.569	.000	.695	.584	.100	.027	.182	.021	.006	.076	102.3	107.8	.325	-2.5

Most similar to: Aaron Williams (95.9), Mark Bryant, Caldwell Jones, Corie Blount   IMP: 43% BRK: 4% COP: 13%

Mikki Moore took advantage of the Warriors' injury-plagued frontcourt to see regular action before succumbing to the injury bug himself. Moore underwent surgery to remove bone spurs from his heel in the middle of December and was waived in January so that Golden State could keep Chris Hunter around. Even in a limited sample, Moore provided his typical production--a high shooting percentage, poor rebounding and plenty of fouls. Moore has posted a win percentage above replacement level once in his last four seasons, and at some point teams are going to stop giving him chances. Now might be that time.

Houston Rockets

To borrow a line from former NFL coach Denny Green, the 2009-10 Houston Rockets both were and were not who we thought they were. The expectation that the Rockets would take a significant step back proved correct, as Houston sunk into the lottery without injured star center Yao Ming. Yet it wasn't for lack of scoring, as was feared, that the Rockets struggled. Instead, their issues cropped up at the other end of the floor, shedding new light on Yao's value as a defender.

The 2009 postseason run, which saw Houston get out of the first round for the first time since 1997, came at a heavy price. During Game Three of a competitive seven-game series against the Lakers, Yao suffered a hairline fracture of the tarsal navicular bone of his left foot. With the bone healing slowly, Yao underwent surgery in July to reduce pressure on the injured area. Subsequently, he was ruled out for the entire 2009-10 season.

Yao joined teammate Tracy McGrady (recovering from February 2009 microfracture surgery) on the most expensive inactive list in NBA history. Without their two stars, the Rockets faced the difficult question of where to find scoring from a group of players previously expected to play supporting roles. Most of the preseason analysis about Houston, including the team essay in last year's *Pro Basketball Prospectus*, focused on this thorny issue. The Rockets lost more of their possession creation than any other team in the NBA.

The upside for Houston was that neither McGrady nor Ron Artest (who left as a free agent) was an efficient option. After all, the Rockets were just a middle-of-the-pack offensive team at full strength; this wasn't exactly equivalent to the Cleveland Cavaliers trying to replace LeBron James. The situation played out largely as SCHOENE projected. Several players, including Trevor Ariza, Aaron Brooks and Luis Scola, stepped into larger roles. Their efficiency declined from where it had been, but they had enough room to drop off and still be just as effective overall as the Yao-McGrady-Artest core. In the end, Houston went from 16th in the league in Offensive Rating in 2008-09 to 18th in 2009-10.

The Rockets' real issues were at the defensive end of the floor, which speaks well to Yao's defense. At 7'6", Yao's limitations are easy to see. Like other behemoths, he has a tough time when asked to defend on the perimeter or step out against the pick-and-roll. Still, Yao has made strides in these regards since entering the league (no less an authority than Tom Thibodeau, an assistant in Houston under Jeff Van Gundy before going to Boston, has praised his improvement) and it's impossible to duplicate his size in the paint.

Exacerbating the issue was the Rockets' lack of size behind Yao. 6'6" Chuck Hayes replaced him in the starting lineup, becoming the shortest starting center in NBA history according to the Elias Sports Bureau via Fanhouse.com. Hayes is a phenomenal post defender capable of stonewalling far bigger players, but

ROCKETS IN A BOX

Last year's record	42-40
Last year's Offensive Rating	108.9 (18)
Last year's Defensive Rating	109.9 (17)
Last year's point differential	-0.4 (16)
Team pace	92.7 (6)
SCHOENE projection	**36-46 (13)**
Projected Offensive Rating	109.9 (19)
Projected Defensive Rating	111.8 (25)
Projected team weighted age	28.6 (10)
Projected '10-11 payroll	$72.3 (8)
Est. payroll obligations, '11-12	$43.4 (27)

Head coach: Rick Adelman

Last season was just the third time in Adelman's 19 years as a head coach that his team missed the postseason, and the first non-playoff season he's ever had outside of Golden State (where his coaching wasn't nearly good enough to make up for years of ineptitude). Adelman's steady approach doesn't resonate with fans who want more fire from their coaches, and his record once in the playoffs is mixed at best. Still, it's hard to argue with the success he's enjoyed at multiple stops. He is two strong seasons or three average ones away from joining the 1,000-win club.

his help defense is limited to taking charges. Houston's other options were even worse. David Andersen, brought over from Europe to back up the middle, was a disappointment. The tallest player on the roster, Andersen was soft defensively. Rockets coach Rick Adelman was forced to use 6'9" Luis Scola, a power forward by trade, in the middle much of the time.

Houston opponents went from making 46.5 percent of their two-point attempts in 2008-09, the league's fifth-lowest mark, to hitting them at a cool 50.3 percent clip in 2009-10, eighth-highest in the NBA. The Rockets' Defensive Rating skyrocketed along with the shooting percentages, falling all the way from fourth in the league to 17th.

Houston actually got off to an impressive start to the season, playing above-.500 basketball despite a torturous slate of early games. The expectation, at least at Rockets HQ, was that the team would take off as soon as the schedule evened out. That never came to pass; after peaking at 24-18, Houston lost 11 of its next 16 games to slip back to even and never again got more than four games over .500. In a Western Conference where 50 wins were needed to make the postseason, the Rockets were not nearly good enough.

By the trade deadline, Houston was already starting to look ahead to 2010-11. The Rockets owned one of the league's most valuable chips in McGrady's enormous expiring contract. Ahead of schedule in his rehab, McGrady had briefly rejoined the team in December, but it quickly became clear he did not figure into Houston's plans for either the short or long term. He went back to Chicago to continue his rehab under the guidance of trainer Tim Grover while Daryl Morey sought to turn his contract into useful assets.

Desperate to shed salary and clear space for the summer of 2010, the New York Knicks emerged as the most obvious suitor. Morey refused to budge on his offer to Knicks president of basketball operations Donnie Walsh. He'd take back the final season of Jared Jeffries' contract, but only if New York gave up its 2009 lottery pick (forward Jordan Hill), the right to swap first-round picks in 2011 and its 2012 first-round pick (protected only through the top five picks). The price was steep, but on the morning of the deadline Walsh agreed to the deal.

In the interim, Morey had already worked out a related deal with the Sacramento Kings. The Rockets sent forward Carl Landry, enjoying a breakout season in a sixth-man role, to Sacramento in exchange for shooting guard Kevin Martin. Filler was included on both sides as part of the eventual three-way trade. The move was a bold one for Houston, sending out a proven performer with a bargain contract. In return, the Rockets got the efficient scorer they had coveted at the two-guard to replace the inefficient McGrady.

Having made the trade and sacrificed cap space, Houston was not a player in free agency. The Rockets hoped to get in on the bidding for free agent Chris Bosh via a sign-and-trade deal and had the assets to make a compelling offer to Toronto, but Bosh showed only cursory interest. Instead, the Rockets focused on bringing back their own restricted free agents, Scola and backup guard Kyle Lowry. They matched a four-year, $23.5 million offer sheet from the Cavaliers to Lowry and came to terms with Scola on a deal that guarantees him $30 million over the next four years (a fifth year can become guaranteed depending on performance clauses, per ShamSports.com).

With the mid-level exception to spend, Houston went shopping for a big man to provide insurance for Yao and settled on former Chicago center Brad Miller, who will be a strong backup if Yao is healthy and is capable of stepping into the starting lineup and providing size and skill if not. Miller was expensive on a per-year basis (about $4.5 million annually), but the Rockets limited their exposure by guaranteeing only $800,000 of the third and final season, again per ShamSports.

The Martin trade also had an impact on Houston's offseason trade. Getting Martin created a logjam at small forward, where the Rockets had not only two starting-caliber players in Ariza and Shane Battier but also Chase Budinger, who was effective as a rookie. Houston solved it by dealing Ariza to New Orleans in a four-team trade that brought back third-year shooting guard Courtney Lee. Lee is a better fit as a backup to Martin. More importantly his rookie contract is much cap-friendlier than Ariza's deal, which had four years and $28 million left to go. The team also created a $6.3 million trade exception that Morey can put to use.

Because the Rockets are in luxury-tax territory, they saved nearly $10 million by swapping Ariza for Lee, having already cut their bill by paying Toronto to take Andersen off their hands. Despite the moves, the team still has enviable depth. Houston's third unit includes Hill, Jeffries and rookie Patrick Patterson, while the second group is stocked with solid young contributors. Lowry might be the best backup point guard in the league.

Still, a surplus of capable contributors won't be enough for the Rockets if they're lacking in star power. That's where Yao comes in, and as the season approaches it is not entirely clear whether he'll be back on the court for the start of training camp. Houston can't count on a full season from Yao, and his minutes will be limited to no more than 24 in any game all season long to preserve his health. There's also the question of just how effective Yao will be after missing a full season, and even if he had been entirely healthy, he's at an age (30) where he might be showing the early signs of decline. Comparable players, per SCHOENE, saw their per-minute production decline by 6.0 percent at the same age.

Those caveats help explain a projection that is surprising in its pessimism. Could the Rockets actually be worse in 2010-11 despite Yao's return and a full season with Martin? In particular, SCHOENE sees Houston failing to improve on defense. The Rockets' projected shot blocking is even worse than it was a year ago because Yao is the team's only consistent shot-blocking threat. A starting frontcourt of Miller and Scola might be the league's worst in terms of blocking shots, since Miller is a weaker shot blocker than Hayes despite his superior height. A full season from Yao would help Houston beat its defensive projection.

There's also the fact that the Rockets outplayed their point differential a year ago, winning nearly two more games than expected. An apparent offensive decline is really just an issue of how the teams are distributed. SCHOENE projects Houston to be right at league average in terms of per-possession offense, with several other teams bunched in the same area. That's better than the Rockets was a year ago, though not dramatically so.

Houston stands an excellent chance of outplaying their projection if things break right, though the downside risk is also worth mentioning. As with Yao, Martin is also prone to injury--he's missed at least 21 games each of the last three seasons, making him a fitting replacement for McGrady. If those two players go down, the Rockets are left with more or less the same group as last year. Houston has proven it can be competitive without its stars, but will need them healthy to really make some noise.

Kevin Pelton

From the Blogosphere

Who: Jason Friedman
What: Rockets.com
Where: http://www.rockets.com

9.1 points and 4.5 rebounds per game don't exactly leap off the page. Paying $5.75 million per year for that production, however, does--especially when the team writing the checks is the perpetually value-conscious Houston Rockets. So what's the deal? Put simply, Kyle Lowry is a fast-breaking, playmaking, foul-drawing, board-gobbling dynamo who stands at the center of the Rockets' turbocharged second unit. The per-minute numbers tell the true tale: Lowry ranks among the game's top point guards in terms of both rebounds snagged and fouls drawn, racking up plenty of both thanks to an in-your-face physical tenacity that belies his rather limited stature. Watch the energy rise the second he steps on the floor. Watch him doggedly defend opposing ones *and* twos. Watch the way he grabs three straight rebounds to help knock off the supersized Lakers. Then it quickly becomes evident why the Rockets feel the Philly native earns every penny.

HOUSTON ROCKETS

ROCKETS FIVE-YEAR TRENDS

Season	AGE	W-L	POW	PYTH	SEED	ORTG	DRTG	PT DIFF	PACE
05-06	28.8	34-48	35.9 (19)	36.0	---	103.0 (29)	104.8 (7)	-1.6 (20)	86.8 (25)
06-07	28.2	52-30	55.1 (4)	55.1	4	108.3 (14)	101.6 (3)	4.9 (5)	89.3 (22)
07-08	28.1	55-27	56.8 (7)	54.7	5	109.0 (17)	103.4 (2)	4.7 (9)	88.6 (20)
08-09	27.9	53-29	53.1 (6)	52.6	5	109.7 (16)	105.6 (4)	4.0 (6)	89.0 (19)
09-10	26.7	42-40	42.0 (16)	40.0	--	108.9 (18)	109.9 (17)	-0.4 (16)	92.7 (6)

Season	PAY	OFFENSE eFG	oREB	FT/FGA	TO	DEFENSE eFG	oREB	FT/FGA	TO
05-06	$52.4	.471 (27)	.255 (24)	.240 (21)	.166 (23)	.472 (6)	.746 (7)	.247 (16)	.153 (25)
06-07	$62.6	.499 (15)	.257 (22)	.220 (26)	.157 (8)	.466 (1)	.770 (1)	.230 (8)	.157 (24)
07-08	$77.6	.492 (17)	.291 (7)	.200 (27)	.147 (12)	.465 (2)	.748 (7)	.214 (10)	.146 (18)
08-09	$68.8	.501 (13)	.264 (17)	.235 (16)	.158 (20)	.479 (4)	.753 (4)	.192 (2)	.138 (27)
09-10	$69.1	.494 (20)	.269 (12)	.225 (16)	.155 (16)	.511 (21)	.738 (12)	.215 (12)	.157 (12)

(league rankings in parenthesis)

SG 3 — Antonio Anderson
Hght: 6'6" Exp: 1 Salary: --
Wght: 215 From: Memphis
2011-12 status: free agent

SKILL RATINGS: TOT -4, OFF --, DEF 0, REB --, PAS --, HND --, SHT --, ATH --

Year	Team	Age	G	MPG	Usg	3PA%	FTA%	INS	2P%	3P%	FT%	TS%	Reb%	Ast%	TO%	BLK%	STL%	PF%	oRTG	dRTG	Win%	WARP
09-10	OKC	24.9	1	15.0	.120	.000	.000	1.000	.333	-	-	.333	.039	.000	.250	.000	.000	.030	96.2	110.2	.129	-0.1
10-11p	HOU	25.9	76	-	.167	.171	.099	.928	.453	.234	.704	.473	.051	.054	.162	.011	.015	.038	-	-	.357	-

Most similar to: Cedric E. Henderson (98.1), Alvin Williams, Mardy Collins, Mitchell Butler   IMP: 59% BRK: 17% COP: 2%

Antonio Anderson got his name in the NBA history books with a 15-minute appearance during a 10-day contract with the Thunder. He spent the rest of the year with the Rio Grande Valley Vipers, winning the D-League championship. The Memphis product has developed into a capable ballhandler as a pro, averaging 6.1 assists per game from his two-guard spot last season. That's the only notable aspect of Anderson's game, however. In particular, he'll have to improve his three-point shooting to have a chance to stick in the NBA. The Rockets will give Anderson a look during training camp.

SF 31 — Shane Battier
Hght: 6'8" Exp: 9 Salary: $7.4 million
Wght: 220 From: Duke
2011-12 status: free agent

SKILL RATINGS: TOT +2, OFF +2, DEF +4, REB -1, PAS +1, HND +4, SHT +2, ATH -3

Year	Team	Age	G	MPG	Usg	3PA%	FTA%	INS	2P%	3P%	FT%	TS%	Reb%	Ast%	TO%	BLK%	STL%	PF%	oRTG	dRTG	Win%	WARP
07-08	HOU	29.6	80	36.3	.117	.498	.060	.562	.504	.377	.743	.561	.079	.025	.105	.023	.012	.031	105.5	104.8	.523	6.5
08-09	HOU	30.6	60	33.9	.100	.548	.068	.520	.462	.384	.821	.568	.080	.032	.113	.019	.012	.026	105.9	105.7	.506	3.8
09-10	HOU	31.6	67	32.4	.114	.500	.084	.583	.458	.362	.726	.541	.084	.034	.115	.026	.012	.029	105.5	105.2	.509	4.2
10-11p	HOU	32.6	72	30.0	.110	.520	.072	.552	.470	.363	.763	.545	.080	.030	.123	.023	.012	.031	105.2	105.5	.489	3.3

Most similar to: James Posey (96.3), Bruce Bowen, Dan Majerle, Craig Ehlo   IMP: 43% BRK: 6% COP: 3%

It's a big season for Shane Battier, who is entering the final year of his deal and will likely get his last big contract next summer. Battier will hope to show the same kind of consistent production he's had the last three campaigns. An increase in usage rate last season offset a drop in Battier's three-point percentage, and his per-minute win percentage was in the same neighborhood as it has been for a while--slightly better than league average.

Battier is better than his statistics indicate because of his contributions at the defensive end of the floor. He continued to frustrate opposing wings with his size, footwork and intimate knowledge of the detailed scouting reports prepared by Houston's extensive analytics department. Battier's defense will be even more important

HOUSTON ROCKETS

this season. After two years of playing alongside another quality defender on the wing (first Ron Artest, then Trevor Ariza), Battier will have to take the tougher matchup every night now that he is paired with the weaker Kevin Martin.

PG	Aaron Brooks	Hght: 6'0"	Exp: 3	Salary: $2.0 million	SKILL RATINGS							
0		Wght: 161	From: Oregon		TOT	OFF	DEF	REB	PAS	HND	SHT	ATH
		2011-12 status: due qualifying offer of $3.0 million			+3	+5	-4	-3	-1	-2	+1	-1

Year	Team	Age	G	MPG	Usg	3PA%	FTA%	INS	2P%	3P%	FT%	TS%	Reb%	Ast%	TO%	BLK%	STL%	PF%	oRTG	dRTG	Win%	WARP
07-08	HOU	23.3	51	12.0	.219	.375	.074	.699	.491	.330	.857	.535	.051	.066	.151	.006	.010	.053	107.1	107.8	.478	0.8
08-09	HOU	24.3	80	25.0	.231	.314	.077	.763	.428	.366	.866	.521	.045	.056	.127	.003	.012	.036	106.8	108.0	.459	1.8
09-10	HOU	25.3	82	35.6	.258	.310	.077	.768	.454	.398	.822	.549	.043	.066	.137	.003	.012	.030	108.2	107.7	.519	6.2
10-11p	HOU	26.3	76	34.0	.249	.328	.083	.755	.466	.384	.856	.555	.045	.060	.130	.004	.011	.034	108.3	107.7	.521	5.7

Most similar to: Mahmoud Abdul-Rauf (97.9), Chucky Atkins, Sleepy Floyd, Nick Van Exel   IMP: 63%   BRK: 4%   COP: 2%

The league's Most Improved Player, Aaron Brooks had a successful first full season as a starter. Brooks was one of several players who helped replace Yao Ming by playing an increased role in the Rockets' offense. Of them, Brooks was the most effective, as he also boosted his True Shooting Percentage at the same time. Brooks improved his three-point shooting and was also more successful at using his jets to get to the rim, helping him shoulder the additional load.

The Rockets have to be careful not to overrate Brooks, who is eligible for a contract extension through Oct. 31 and will become a restricted free agent next summer if he can't come to a deal with the team. Brooks will be 26 this season and SCHOENE doesn't see him growing much more. He's overcome his small stature to become a capable starting point guard, but it still affects him in the paint (where he is one of the league's worst finishers) and at the defensive end of the floor. Brooks also tends to think about scoring rather than distributing when he gets into the paint. The entire package suggests Brooks is an average starting point guard, not a future star.

SF	Chase Budinger	Hght: 6'7"	Exp: 1	Salary: $0.8 million	SKILL RATINGS							
10		Wght: 218	From: Arizona		TOT	OFF	DEF	REB	PAS	HND	SHT	ATH
		2011-12 status: partially-guaranteed contract for $0.9 million			+3	+3	-2	+1	+1	+4	+3	-3

Year	Team	Age	G	MPG	Usg	3PA%	FTA%	INS	2P%	3P%	FT%	TS%	Reb%	Ast%	TO%	BLK%	STL%	PF%	oRTG	dRTG	Win%	WARP
09-10	HOU	21.9	74	20.1	.195	.382	.059	.676	.497	.369	.770	.545	.087	.026	.074	.005	.011	.025	106.1	106.4	.491	2.3
10-11p	HOU	22.9	75	20.0	.206	.407	.062	.656	.502	.369	.775	.552	.093	.030	.075	.005	.011	.025	107.0	106.1	.529	3.5

Most similar to: Mike Miller (97.9), Peja Stojakovic, J.R. Smith, Quentin Richardson   IMP: 62%   BRK: 5%   COP: 3%

Chase Budinger beat out fellow second-round pick Jermaine Taylor for the right to play backup minutes on the wing and had a solid rookie campaign, suggesting good things in store. A complete small forward at Arizona, Budinger transformed into a perimeter specialist in the pros. Budinger has a quick release and has demonstrated the ability to make contested shots. He knocked down threes at a good clip and almost never turned the ball over.

Going forward, Budinger would do well to show off more of the athleticism that made him the Mizuno National High School Volleyball Player of the Year before he chose to focus on hoops. Budinger has the talent to contribute more on the glass and as a shot blocker. He was only passable defensively, and improvement at that end of the floor will help convince the Rockets that Budinger can become Battier's heir apparent at small forward.

HOUSTON ROCKETS

SF **Mike Harris** 33	Hght: 6'6" Wght: 235 2011-12 status: free agent	Exp: 2 From: Rice	Salary: $0.9 million	**SKILL RATINGS** TOT +3 OFF -- DEF 0 REB -- PAS -- HND -- SHT -- ATH --

Year	Team	Age	G	MPG	Usg	3PA%	FTA%	INS	2P%	3P%	FT%	TS%	Reb%	Ast%	TO%	BLK%	STL%	PF%	oRTG	dRTG	Win%	WARP
07-08	HOU	24.9	17	9.4	.199	.029	.083	1.054	.519	.000	.615	.519	.191	.009	.131	.014	.018	.047	105.1	104.4	.523	0.4
09-10	WAS	26.9	13	7.4	.204	.023	.110	1.088	.379	.000	.636	.416	.144	.014	.205	.008	.026	.065	99.3	105.5	.301	-0.2
10-11p	HOU	27.9	76	-	.241	.101	.100	.999	.524	.244	.723	.539	.144	.018	.096	.011	.014	.060	-	-	.526	-

Most similar to: Loy Vaught (97.3), Alan Henderson, Kenny Carr, Bill Robinzine   IMP: 32% BRK: 2% COP: 8%

If you're ever in need of directions from the Rio Grande Valley to Houston, Mike Harris is your man. Harris rode the D-League shuttle back and forth from the Rockets to their affiliate last season. Houston has long been intrigued by the undersized power forward, though not enough to keep him on the roster for an extended period of time. He played eight games for the Rockets and five for the Wizards last season. Late in the year, Houston signed Harris and assigned him to the D-League, where he won MVP and led the Vipers to the league championship.

Harris' translated D-League statistics suggest he's capable of handling a heavy possession load at reasonable efficiency. He's also very solid on the glass. The biggest issue is just how undersized Harris is for the power forward position that his skills indicate he ought to play, which makes teams reluctant to trust him on the floor. Harris is likely capable of providing solid minutes if he ever got a real NBA opportunity. However, that's not going to happen with the Rockets because of the team's frontcourt depth, and no one else seems particularly interested.

C **Chuck Hayes** 44	Hght: 6'6" Wght: 238 2011-12 status: free agent	Exp: 5 From: Kentucky	Salary: $2.0 million	**SKILL RATINGS** TOT -2 OFF -2 DEF +4 REB 0 PAS +4 HND +5 SHT -3 ATH +2

Year	Team	Age	G	MPG	Usg	3PA%	FTA%	INS	2P%	3P%	FT%	TS%	Reb%	Ast%	TO%	BLK%	STL%	PF%	oRTG	dRTG	Win%	WARP
07-08	HOU	24.9	79	20.0	.086	.010	.036	1.026	.518	.000	.458	.512	.152	.027	.211	.020	.025	.062	101.6	103.3	.442	0.8
08-09	HOU	25.9	71	12.1	.080	.027	.057	1.030	.385	.000	.368	.375	.167	.023	.171	.016	.021	.073	101.4	105.4	.367	-0.9
09-10	HOU	26.9	82	21.6	.108	.000	.067	1.067	.489	-	.545	.500	.152	.035	.171	.018	.021	.055	102.7	104.6	.434	0.6
10-11p	HOU	27.9	76	20.0	.098	.014	.053	1.039	.468	.003	.505	.466	.145	.031	.181	.017	.021	.061	101.5	104.7	.393	-0.7

Most similar to: George Lynch (94.9), Kurt Rambis, Andrew DeClercq, Jared Jeffries   IMP: 45% BRK: 2% COP: 9%

While Michael Lewis latched on to Shane Battier as the storyline for his NBA *Moneyball* follow-up, Chuck Hayes might have been the better choice. Battier is a former lottery pick who has started throughout his career, so he's not exactly obscure. Hayes, a 6'6" center, is the logical equivalent to an overweight third baseman. Individual statistics struggle to capture Hayes' value. He's posted an above-average winning percentage just once, and that took a fluky performance during his rookie season. Yet Hayes had the best adjusted plus-minus on the Rockets last season, per BasketballValue.com.

Hayes is a uniquely skilled defender. His low center of gravity helps him keep taller players from establishing position and forces them to settle for difficult shot attempts. He also contributes as a help defender by taking charges on a regular basis. Last season did show that Hayes needs a longer player next to him in the frontcourt to help with contesting shots. Brad Miller has the height for that role, though not the shot-blocking chops. A Hayes-Jordan Hill pairing might be more optimal.

PF **Jordan Hill** 27	Hght: 6'10" Wght: 235 2011-12 status: team option for $2.9 million	Exp: 1 From: Arizona	Salary: $2.7 million	**SKILL RATINGS** TOT 0 OFF +1 DEF 0 REB +3 PAS -2 HND -2 SHT -1 ATH 0

Year	Team	Age	G	MPG	Usg	3PA%	FTA%	INS	2P%	3P%	FT%	TS%	Reb%	Ast%	TO%	BLK%	STL%	PF%	oRTG	dRTG	Win%	WARP
09-10	HOU	22.7	47	13.3	.188	.008	.115	1.107	.497	.000	.676	.528	.161	.014	.115	.025	.011	.066	105.0	106.0	.467	0.7
10-11p	HOU	23.7	76	8.0	.194	.008	.110	1.102	.492	.000	.701	.525	.154	.017	.117	.025	.011	.063	104.5	105.7	.459	0.5

Most similar to: Kris Humphries (99.2), Horace Grant, Jon Koncak, Brandon Bass   IMP: 52% BRK: 5% COP: 9%

HOUSTON ROCKETS

A disappointed Knicks fan base casting about for villains settled, among other targets, on rookie Jordan Hill. It was easy to mock Hill for what he wasn't--namely, one of the elite point guards taken after him, like Brandon Jennings. It certainly didn't help matters that Mike D'Antoni largely refused to play Hill other than during garbage time even though New York's alternatives in the frontcourt were lacking. The midseason trade that sent Hill to Houston gave him a fresh start and an opportunity to shed the excess baggage.

In the limited minutes he did play, Hill demonstrated some useful skills. He's an above-average rebounder who runs the floor very well for a big man. Over the course of his time at Arizona, Hill emerged as a go-to scorer (alongside Rockets teammate Chase Budinger), and he has the ability to become a bigger part of the offense. Hill also blocks enough shots to play some minutes at center and be an asset as a help defender when he's at power forward. The biggest thing Hill needs to develop is his strength. He got pushed around a bit in the post and could stand to put more weight on his frame without sacrificing quickness.

PF 20	Jared Jeffries	Hght: 6'11" Exp: 8 Salary: $6.9 million Wght: 240 From: Indiana 2011-12 status: free agent	**SKILL RATINGS** TOT OFF DEF REB PAS HND SHT ATH -3 -- +3 -- -- -- -- --
Year	Team	Age G MPG Usg 3PA% FTA% INS 2P% 3P% FT% TS% Reb% Ast% TO% BLK% STL% PF% oRTG dRTG Win% WARP
07-08	NYK	26.4 73 18.1 .128 .067 .109 1.042 .423 .160 .527 .431 .105 .023 .170 .014 .013 .046 101.4 106.6 .334 -2.3
08-09	NYK	27.4 56 23.4 .126 .032 .105 1.073 .456 .083 .611 .473 .096 .027 .172 .018 .018 .051 102.9 107.0 .366 -1.4
09-10	HOU	28.4 70 25.6 .112 .160 .119 .959 .481 .296 .625 .507 .092 .025 .172 .029 .017 .051 103.1 105.7 .412 -0.2
10-11p	HOU	29.4 73 -- .120 .098 .113 1.015 .456 .183 .577 .462 .090 .024 .175 .022 .015 .052 -- -- .380 --
Most similar to: Jon Koncak (97.4), Earl Cureton, Marc Iavaroni, Jim Petersen			IMP: 44% BRK: 3% COP: 8%

The Knicks finally got some return on their investment in Jared Jeffries just before they dumped the last year and a half of his contract to clear cap space. Jeffries moved into New York's starting lineup in early December to provide some measure of defensive intensity, and the Knicks immediately went on a winning streak. That wasn't entirely because of Jeffries, but he did help. In New York's post-positional revolution lineup, Mike D'Antoni deployed him largely against point guards. Jeffries has the quickness to keep up on the perimeter, and his length smothered these guards, rendering them unable to find teammates.

At the offensive end, Jeffries was better than in years past, which is to say he still wasn't very good. If his defensive skills are more suited to the backcourt, Jeffries is a big man on offense because he has very limited range. The 21 three-pointers he made last year were a career high. Basically, Jeffries' best offense is staying out of the way, which often leaves his team playing 4-on-5. That's why he's likely to see his minutes dwindle as the fifth wing in the Rockets' rotation this season. His contract will mercifully end next summer, and Jeffries will sign a more appropriate deal to be the defensive specialist for a contender.

PF 30	Alexander Johnson	Hght: 6'9" Exp: 3 Salary: $0.9 million Wght: 240 From: Florida State 2011-12 status: free agent	**SKILL RATINGS** TOT OFF DEF REB PAS HND SHT ATH -4 -- -2 -- -- -- -- --
Year	Team	Age G MPG Usg 3PA% FTA% INS 2P% 3P% FT% TS% Reb% Ast% TO% BLK% STL% PF% oRTG dRTG Win% WARP
07-08	MIA	25.2 43 12.8 .176 .000 .179 1.179 .488 .000 .687 .554 .103 .011 .206 .014 .011 .068 101.1 107.0 .310 -1.2
10-11p	HOU	28.2 76 -- .179 .012 .177 1.165 .496 .008 .700 .556 .099 .011 .206 .014 .011 .068 -- -- .348 --
Most similar to: Frank Brickowski (97.8), Charlie Pittman, Fred Roberts, Jake Voskuhl			IMP: 48% BRK: 13% COP: 17%

Houston also plucked Alexander Johnson from the D-League late in the season. Johnson averaged 23.0 points and 11.1 rebounds in Sioux Falls, and his translated statistics indicate more ability than Johnson showed in his last NBA campaign, three years ago in Miami. (His projection is based on his time with the Heat.) A burly rebounder who can score in the paint, Johnson is weak defensively. That combination of skills might help some teams; unfortunately, the Rockets only have one spot open on the roster and Johnson doesn't really fill a need for them.

HOUSTON ROCKETS

SG 5 — Courtney Lee

Hght: 6'5" Wght: 200 Exp: 2 From: Western Kentucky Salary: $1.4 million
2011-12 status: team option for $2.2 million

SKILL RATINGS

TOT	OFF	DEF	REB	PAS	HND	SHT	ATH
0	+1	-4	-2	-3	-1	+1	0

Year	Team	Age	G	MPG	Usg	3PA%	FTA%	INS	2P%	3P%	FT%	TS%	Reb%	Ast%	TO%	BLK%	STL%	PF%	oRTG	dRTG	Win%	WARP
08-09	ORL	23.6	77	25.2	.155	.312	.064	.751	.478	.404	.830	.556	.051	.022	.106	.005	.020	.038	104.2	106.6	.424	0.3
09-10	NJN	24.6	71	33.5	.179	.245	.073	.828	.476	.338	.869	.525	.063	.024	.083	.006	.020	.025	104.1	106.2	.432	0.7
10-11p	HOU	25.6	74	18.9	.181	.293	.071	.778	.471	.370	.846	.536	.057	.024	.093	.007	.019	.031	104.2	106.0	.439	0.7

Most similar to: Todd Lichti (98.4), Tyrone Nesby, Morris Peterson, Ron Brewer

IMP: 51% BRK: 11% COP: 4%

Few first-round picks end up playing for three teams in their first three years, and usually that's a sign of a bust. Not so for Courtney Lee, who was the carrot in last year's trade that sent Vince Carter to Orlando before landing in Houston as part of this summer's four-team deal. The changes in Lee's statistics from his first and second seasons reflect his very different circumstances. He increased his usage rate with the Nets and saw his efficiency take a corresponding hit. The lack of overall improvement tends to hint at what was already suspected: Lee's ceiling is pretty limited.

For now, Lee is a useful contributor, and this year's trade put him in a more appropriate reserve role. He'll be the Rockets' ace perimeter defender off the bench, teaming with Chase Budinger for one of the league's better second-unit wing duos. Lee's playing time might be affected by matchups. He can step in for longer outings to help Kevin Martin against teams with two top scorers on the wing. Houston would love to see Lee shoot somewhere closer to the 40.4 percent of threes he made during his rookie season than last year's pedestrian 33.8 percent.

PG 7 — Kyle Lowry

Hght: 6'0" Wght: 205 Exp: 4 From: Villanova Salary: $5.8 million
2011-12 status: guaranteed contract for $5.8 million

SKILL RATINGS

TOT	OFF	DEF	REB	PAS	HND	SHT	ATH
+4	+4	+3	+4	+2	0	-3	+4

Year	Team	Age	G	MPG	Usg	3PA%	FTA%	INS	2P%	3P%	FT%	TS%	Reb%	Ast%	TO%	BLK%	STL%	PF%	oRTG	dRTG	Win%	WARP
07-08	MEM	22.1	82	25.5	.186	.161	.176	1.015	.486	.257	.698	.530	.068	.064	.146	.007	.020	.039	105.5	106.0	.484	2.9
08-09	HOU	23.1	77	21.8	.182	.151	.153	1.002	.488	.255	.801	.547	.067	.077	.180	.007	.021	.041	106.4	106.5	.499	2.9
09-10	HOU	24.1	68	24.3	.187	.196	.165	.969	.448	.272	.827	.536	.087	.082	.167	.004	.018	.047	108.1	106.8	.544	4.4
10-11p	HOU	25.1	73	24.0	.200	.207	.168	.961	.473	.285	.800	.550	.074	.081	.164	.007	.019	.042	107.9	106.2	.557	5.2

Most similar to: Terrell Brandon (98.3), Dee Brown, Bimbo Coles, Luke Ridnour

IMP: 64% BRK: 6% COP: 6%

Kyle Lowry's restricted free agency was a mixed blessing. Lowry got a big new contract, but not a chance at a starting job. He might have had that opportunity in Cleveland, where he signed an offer sheet and could have pushed Mo Williams to shooting guard. The Rockets quickly dashed any such hopes by matching the Cavaliers' offer and making Lowry one of the league's better-paid backup point guards.

His performance merits such compensation. Lowry was arguably more effective than Brooks last season. Houston played better with Lowry at the controls. He's much more of a true point guard with the ability to set up teammates. As a scorer, Lowry has always been average at best; he's limited by his lack of three-point range, though regular trips to the free throw line do help boost his True Shooting Percentage. It's on defense that Lowry truly shines. He uses his strength to hound opposing point guards.

Despite being four years into his career, Lowry will not turn 25 until late this season. If he makes strides again this season, the Rockets may be forced to trade Lowry to a team that can offer him a bigger role.

HOUSTON ROCKETS

SG 12 — Kevin Martin

Hght: 6'7" Exp: 6 Salary: $10.6 million
Wght: 185 From: Western Carolina
2011-12 status: guaranteed contract for $11.5 million

SKILL RATINGS

TOT	OFF	DEF	REB	PAS	HND	SHT	ATH
+2	+4	-5	-2	-1	-3	-1	+3

Year	Team	Age	G	MPG	Usg	3PA%	FTA%	INS	2P%	3P%	FT%	TS%	Reb%	Ast%	TO%	BLK%	STL%	PF%	oRTG	dRTG	Win%	WARP
07-08	SAC	25.2	61	36.4	.263	.205	.196	.991	.478	.402	.869	.618	.071	.026	.101	.002	.012	.030	109.5	106.7	.588	7.9
08-09	SAC	26.2	51	38.2	.275	.233	.195	.962	.423	.415	.867	.601	.055	.032	.123	.003	.016	.027	109.2	107.6	.552	5.5
09-10	HOU	27.2	46	35.5	.255	.225	.160	.935	.453	.333	.876	.561	.059	.030	.098	.003	.014	.026	106.9	106.9	.499	2.8
10-11p	HOU	28.2	69	35.0	.266	.238	.170	.932	.447	.363	.868	.576	.058	.032	.109	.002	.013	.027	107.5	107.0	.517	5.1

Most similar to: Cuttino Mobley (98.4), Michael Redd, Latrell Sprewell, Purvis Short

IMP: 38% BRK: 0% COP: 2%

Kevin Martin suffered a hairline fracture in his left wrist five games into last season. By the time he returned, rookie Tyreke Evans had settled in as a shooting guard and taken over Martin's spot as the Kings' go-to scorer. The two struggled to mesh their talents for the next month before Sacramento pulled the plug on the Speedracer era, dealing Martin to Houston for Carl Landry and expiring contracts.

The wrist injury was the latest malady to befall Martin, who has missed at least 21 games each of the last three seasons. At this point, it's fair to wonder whether the series of injuries Martin has dealt with have hampered his game. His win percentage has dropped the last two seasons, and took a major tumble a year ago. The counter-argument is that the biggest change in Martin's statistics was his poor three-point shooting, which is liable to correct itself next season. At his best, Martin is one of the league's most efficient lead scorers because so many of his points come from the two most efficient methods of scoring--the three and the free throw line. The Rockets haven't had a guard who scored frequently and efficiently since Steve Francis' early days, so Martin certainly fills a need.

C 52 — Brad Miller

Hght: 7'0" Exp: 12 Salary: $4.4 million
Wght: 261 From: Purdue
2011-12 status: guaranteed contract for $4.8 million

SKILL RATINGS

TOT	OFF	DEF	REB	PAS	HND	SHT	ATH
0	+1	+1	-3	+5	+5	-2	+2

Year	Team	Age	G	MPG	Usg	3PA%	FTA%	INS	2P%	3P%	FT%	TS%	Reb%	Ast%	TO%	BLK%	STL%	PF%	oRTG	dRTG	Win%	WARP
07-08	SAC	32.0	72	34.9	.184	.088	.132	1.045	.484	.311	.848	.558	.158	.047	.160	.023	.012	.044	106.2	104.4	.560	7.5
08-09	CHI	33.0	70	30.0	.185	.065	.139	1.074	.482	.411	.824	.566	.151	.050	.151	.013	.012	.048	107.3	106.2	.535	5.2
09-10	CHI	34.0	82	23.8	.182	.168	.123	.955	.474	.280	.827	.530	.113	.036	.136	.011	.011	.044	104.5	106.1	.447	1.2
10-11p	HOU	35.0	75	26.0	.174	.114	.120	1.006	.466	.314	.831	.533	.123	.042	.150	.014	.012	.049	104.4	105.8	.454	1.5

Most similar to: Christian Laettner (97.2), Armon Gilliam, Charles Oakley, Bill Cartwright

IMP: 31% BRK: 2% COP: 8%

Brad Miller's game changed for the worse last season. The "inside" rating conveniently points to the cause--always capable in the high post, Miller drifted to the perimeter much more last season. The Rockets will have to hope that it came as a result of Miller trying to coexist with Joakim Noah and Taj Gibson in Chicago. Otherwise, Houston has badly overpaid for a declining center.

Of course, regression is to be expected for a player in his mid-30s. What made the changes in Miller's game so difficult to understand was that they occurred so suddenly. Attempting far more threes did not work out, as Miller had an effective field-goal percentage of 42.0 percent beyond the arc. At the same time, Miller's rebounding dropped off at both ends of the floor. Paired with either Chuck Hayes or Luis Scola, Miller will surely see plenty of the high post again in Houston. He can be an asset to the Rockets with his passing from that spot, a strength of his game that stood out when he played for Rick Adelman in Sacramento.

PF 54 — Patrick Patterson

Hght: 6'9" Exp: R Salary: $1.8 million
Wght: 235 From: Kentucky
2011-12 status: guaranteed contract for $2.0 million

SKILL RATINGS

TOT	OFF	DEF	REB	PAS	HND	SHT	ATH
0	--	--	--	--	--	--	--

Year	Team	Age	G	MPG	Usg	3PA%	FTA%	INS	2P%	3P%	FT%	TS%	Reb%	Ast%	TO%	BLK%	STL%	PF%	oRTG	dRTG	Win%	WARP
10-11p	HOU	22.1	76	-	.138	.115	.089	.973	.506	.295	.678	.524	.101	.012	.088	.019	.008	.031	-	-	.453	-

Most similar to: D.J. White (95.1), Malik Hairston, Josh Boone, Marreese Speights

IMP: - BRK: - COP: -

HOUSTON ROCKETS

Patrick Patterson saw his role at Kentucky change substantially during his junior year with the additions of DeMarcus Cousins and John Wall. Patterson was the steady veteran leader of the group headlined by talented freshmen, willingly accepting a backseat in terms of media coverage. He still ended up being picked in the lottery by the Rockets.

Patterson enters the NBA primarily as a power forward, though it's possible he could play small forward down the line as he develops his perimeter game. Right now, his translations suggest he should probably lay off the threes, especially because he's an effective scorer down low. To play the four, Patterson will have to rebound much better than he did last season. He had been stronger on the glass in the past, and playing alongside Cousins in the frontcourt explains some of his decline. While he's much too old to be part of the pool of NCAA players used to draw comparables, the best match for Patterson's game might be another burly No. 54 who could play both forward positions, Rodney Rogers.

PF 4	Luis Scola	Hght: 6'9" Wght: 245 2011-12 status: guaranteed contract for $8.6 million	Exp: 3 From: Buenos Aires, Argentina	Salary: $7.8 million		**SKILL RATINGS**						
					TOT	OFF	DEF	REB	PAS	HND	SHT	ATH
					-1	0	-1	+2	+1	0	0	0

Year	Team	Age	G	MPG	Usg	3PA%	FTA%	INS	2P%	3P%	FT%	TS%	Reb%	Ast%	TO%	BLK%	STL%	PF%	oRTG	dRTG	Win%	WARP
07-08	HOU	28.0	82	24.7	.200	.003	.118	1.114	.517	.000	.668	.548	.146	.024	.120	.007	.014	.054	104.7	105.5	.474	2.4
08-09	HOU	29.0	82	30.3	.195	.003	.110	1.107	.533	.000	.760	.572	.166	.023	.119	.003	.014	.049	105.9	105.9	.499	4.3
09-10	HOU	30.0	82	32.6	.228	.004	.086	1.082	.515	.200	.779	.550	.154	.028	.119	.007	.012	.041	104.6	105.6	.468	2.9
10-11p	HOU	31.0	76	30.0	.213	.006	.090	1.084	.506	.110	.713	.535	.150	.024	.118	.005	.013	.050	103.8	105.9	.432	0.8

Most similar to: Matt Harpring (98.6), Kurt Thomas, Truck Robinson, Tom Gugliotta   IMP: 40%   BRK: 2%   COP: 9%

Of the candidates to become Houston's new go-to player on offense, Luis Scola actually saw the least change in his statistics last season. His usage did increase somewhat, while his efficiency dropped. Add in more minutes in a thinner frontcourt and Scola saw his scoring average go from 12.7 points per game to 16.2. That change was well-timed before Scola hit the market as a restricted free agent, and as a proven starter at power forward he cashed in with a big new contract.

Is Scola worth the money? The advanced numbers suggest he is nothing more than an average contributor, a solid scorer and good rebounder who is a bit of a drag at the defensive end of the floor. Scola's net plus-minus ratings have generally hovered right around zero, and the Rockets were 3.8 points worse per 100 possessions with him on the floor last season, per BasketballValue.com. On top of that, Scola's age is an issue. He seems younger than he is because he has played just three years in the NBA. Scola hit 30 last season, and SCHOENE foresees a big decline. Ideally, Daryl Morey would surely love to flip Scola as part of a deal for a star power forward. If such a trade doesn't come together quickly, Houston could be left with an ugly contract on the books that pays Scola until he's 35.

PG 13	Ishmael Smith	Hght: 6'0" Wght: 165 2011-12 status: non-guaranteed contract for $1.0 million	Exp: R From: Wake Forest	Salary: $0.5 million		**SKILL RATINGS**						
					TOT	OFF	DEF	REB	PAS	HND	SHT	ATH
					-4	--	--	--	--	--	--	--

Year	Team	Age	G	MPG	Usg	3PA%	FTA%	INS	2P%	3P%	FT%	TS%	Reb%	Ast%	TO%	BLK%	STL%	PF%	oRTG	dRTG	Win%	WARP
10-11p	HOU	22.8	76	-	.181	.076	.053	.977	.369	.191	.484	.373	.058	.068	.172	.008	.016	.031	-	-	.335	-

Most similar to: Royal Ivey (95.8), Acie Law, Dee D. Brown, Aaron Brooks   IMP: -   BRK: -   COP: -

It was fated that Houston would sign Wake Forest product Ishmael Smith after he went undrafted, allowing him to become Rocket Ishmael. Smith played well for Houston in the NBA Summer League and earned a two-year contract. He's the favorite to serve as the Rockets' third point guard this season.

A super-quick water bug, Smith is capable of getting to the rim. The problem is finishing there. Add in the fact that Smith is a complete non-shooter and it's going to be difficult for him to maintain any level of efficiency in the NBA. If Smith can square the shooting aspect away, the rest of his game is sound. He's a heady point guard who runs a team well and can distribute the basketball. Defensively, his quickness helps make up for his lack of size.

HOUSTON ROCKETS
107

SG 8	Jermaine Taylor	Hght: 6'4"	Exp: 1	Salary: $0.8 million	SKILL RATINGS						
		Wght: 210	From: Central Florida || TOT	OFF	DEF	REB	PAS	HND	SHT	ATH
		2011-12 status: partially-guaranteed contract for $0.9 million		-2	--	-1	--	--	--	--	--

Year	Team	Age	G	MPG	Usg	3PA%	FTA%	INS	2P%	3P%	FT%	TS%	Reb%	Ast%	TO%	BLK%	STL%	PF%	oRTG	dRTG	Win%	WARP
09-10	HOU	23.4	31	9.8	.232	.139	.128	.989	.412	.227	.717	.460	.087	.024	.120	.007	.017	.022	102.7	106.2	.385	-0.2
10-11p	HOU	24.4	76	--	.232	.271	.128	.856	.420	.251	.744	.468	.084	.025	.117	.008	.016	.021	--	--	.407	--

Most similar to: Tariq Abdul-Wahad (98.1), Lucious Harris, Ronald Dupree, Bernard Thompson   IMP: 65%   BRK: 18%   COP: 12%

A big-time scorer at Central Florida for whom the Rockets had high hopes, Jermaine Taylor never managed to break into the rotation during his rookie season and was ineffective in the action he did see. As his brief foray into the D-League (where he scored 158 points in 223 minutes) reinforced, Taylor is a volume scorer. The question marks about his game right now are twofold--can he score those points efficiently and can he provide anything else? Adding NBA three-point range would help Taylor in the first regard. He also needs to show more commitment at the defensive end, though he is a good rebounder. Taylor will turn 24 this season, so he needs to show something more or risk falling out of Houston's plans entirely.

C 11	Yao Ming	Hght: 7'6"	Exp: 8	Salary: $17.7 million	SKILL RATINGS						
		Wght: 310	From: Shanghai, China || TOT	OFF	DEF	REB	PAS	HND	SHT	ATH
		2011-12 status: free agent		+4	+2	+5	+1	+2	-3	+2	-1

Year	Team	Age	G	MPG	Usg	3PA%	FTA%	INS	2P%	3P%	FT%	TS%	Reb%	Ast%	TO%	BLK%	STL%	PF%	oRTG	dRTG	Win%	WARP
07-08	HOU	27.6	55	37.2	.273	.002	.147	1.146	.508	.000	.850	.587	.163	.029	.151	.040	.006	.039	106.9	103.3	.618	8.6
08-09	HOU	28.6	77	33.6	.264	.001	.133	1.132	.548	1.000	.866	.618	.168	.025	.160	.042	.006	.046	107.7	104.0	.620	11.0
10-11p	HOU	30.6	63	24.0	.267	.004	.126	1.121	.530	.309	.855	.596	.159	.023	.164	.040	.005	.045	105.8	104.3	.551	4.3

Most similar to: Zydrunas Ilgauskas (93.8), Rik Smits, Alonzo Mourning, Erick Dampier   IMP: 31%   BRK: 0%   COP: 7%

Yao Ming's absence for all of last season was a loss not just for the Rockets, but to the NBA in general. He is one of the league's most unique stars, a curiosity because of his height who is also an exceptionally skilled basketball player. Until Yao returns to the court, his long-term future will worry fans both in his native China and stateside. Foot injuries have stolen some of the game's best behemoths, and it would be a shame for the same to happen with Yao.

It will be interesting to see if Houston uses Yao any differently after his season away from the team. The additions of former Kings Kevin Martin and Brad Miller may make it more realistic for Rick Adelman to incorporate Princeton-style elements into the Rockets' offense. Yao certainly has the skills to make his role in such an attack work. His assist rate would be substantially better if the NBA tracked hockey-style assists. When he's double-teamed, Yao does a good job of working the basketball out to the perimeter, a process that often features multiple passes before a shot. His size makes him lethal against double-teams because he can almost always see over them to find the open man. At the same time, playing Yao one-on-one guarantees he'll be able to pile up points in an efficient manner, leaving defenses with no good option.

PG --	Will Conroy	Hght: 6'2"	Exp: 2	Salary: --	SKILL RATINGS						
		Wght: 195	From: Washington || TOT	OFF	DEF	REB	PAS	HND	SHT	ATH
		2011-12 status: free agent		+1	+3	-1	+4	+1	-1	0	+1

Year	Team	Age	G	MPG	Usg	3PA%	FTA%	INS	2P%	3P%	FT%	TS%	Reb%	Ast%	TO%	BLK%	STL%	PF%	oRTG	dRTG	Win%	WARP
09-10	HOU	27.4	5	7.2	.184	.202	.059	.858	.429	.000	.000	.276	.050	.087	.269	.000	.000	.062	97.0	110.0	.146	-0.2
10-11p	AVG	28.4	76	7.2	.178	.310	.109	.799	.483	.330	.698	.534	.070	.071	.185	.001	.018	.037	106.1	106.6	.485	0.8

Most similar to: Bimbo Coles (98.5), Jacque Vaughn, Winston Garland, Wes Matthews   IMP: 48%   BRK: 13%   COP: 6%

Will Conroy is basketball's Crash Davis. He's the D-League's all-time leader in assists and ranks second in scoring as well as fifth in games played. Conroy keeps plugging away, looking for 10-day contracts. Last season saw him get back to the NBA for the first time since 2006-07, playing briefly with the Rockets before returning to help lead

Rio Grande Valley to the D-League championship. Conroy's translated production suggests he has the ability to be a competent backup point guard in the NBA. A pure point guard at Washington, Conroy has improved as a scorer; he has even operated as a score-first point at times when his D-League team has needed points.

Indiana Pacers

At least there now appears to be a future. The Pacers have struggled to escape the shadow of the Reggie Miller years and to leave behind the baggage of the Stephen Jackson/Jamaal Tinsley era, both on the court and off. Now, at last, team honcho and local legend Larry Bird is on the verge of a clean slate. Unfortunately, while the Pacers have collected some nice, young pieces, there is more urgency to the team's turnaround than in most NBA locations. With a possible lockout looming next summer, the future of professional basketball in Indianapolis is far from assured.

The attendance at Conseco Fieldhouse has become a growing problem since patronage began to decline a few years ago. During the span of 2004-05 to 2007-08, the Pacers lost about 4,700 fans per game off of their nightly ticket sales. In 2008-09, they regained nearly 2,000 of those fans, but last season that figure was flat. Of course, raw attendance only tells you so much about how well a city is supporting a team. We use a rough attendance metric called Loyalty Factor (LOY) that, in fact, probably doesn't measure loyalty at all; you have to call a metric something. LOY simply looks at the percentage of capacity to which a team fills its arena, adjusts for the league average to account for national economic trends and measures this adjusted figure against an expected capacity percentage based on team victories. The main problem with this metric is the listed capacities for each arena. For instance, the Mavericks and Spurs routinely sell more than 100 percent of available seats, which leads one to believe that in Texas, they don't define the term "capacity" quite like the rest of us. Also, as with all sports, it would be great to have actual turnstile counts, but professional sports teams simply don't make those figures available. So you can have a game listed as a sellout, yet still sit in the arena on game night and have half of it all to yourself.

For the Pacers, the team's LOY is surprisingly low given Indiana's reputation as the hoops answer to football in Texas. Then again, that distinction has always applied more to the college and prep level than the pros, and the Pacers' fan support has fluctuated with team success just like in most cities (Table 1).

LOY doesn't necessarily dovetail exactly with success, though the teams at the bottom certainly haven't been helped by their collective struggles. Indiana has been pretty mediocre over the span covered by the data in this table, but still has drawn about 1,000 fans fewer per game than you'd expect, with that figure growing larger during the last three seasons. It doesn't have to be that way. The Knicks and Bulls have the clear advantage in population base and that is something which is not accounted for here, with the assumption being that the NBA wouldn't put a team in a market without enough fans to support it. Besides, the New York market hasn't done a whole lot to help the Nets, which is why they're planning a new

PACERS IN A BOX

Last year's record	32-50
Last year's Offensive Rating	105.5 (26)
Last year's Defensive Rating	108.6 (15)
Last year's point differential	-3.0 (21)
Team pace	95.4 (2)
SCHOENE projection	**29-53 (13)**
Projected Offensive Rating	106.1 (26)
Projected Defensive Rating	110.5 (18)
Projected team weighted age	26.6 (19)
Projected '10-11 payroll	$59.6 (21)
Est. payroll obligations, '11-12	$35.6 (29)

Head coach: Jim O'Brien

With so many young players on O'Brien's roster, it's an important season for the Pacers to show that their development is heading in the right direction. In 2011, Indiana will be positioned for its most important offseason in some time, with plenty of cap space available with which to build around the team's emergent core, so they want to put their best foot forward this season. O'Brien enters his fourth campaign with the Pacers still looking for his first .500 season with the team, and he's four games under .500 (286-290) overall in eight years on an NBA bench. O'Brien is known as an offensive coach, and his teams have almost always ranked in the top five of the league in tempo. However, six of his eight teams have had a higher ranking in Defensive Rating than Offensive Rating.

Table 1: NBA Loyalty Factors, 2002-2010

TEAM	AVG	%CAP	LOY	TEAM	AVG	%CAP	LOY
1. Knicks	19,233	99.2%	1.168	16. Pistons	21,028	95.2%	1.012
2. Bulls	20,592	95.5%	1.092	17. Celtics	17,194	92.3%	1.005
3. Mavericks	20,053	104.4%	1.073	18. Suns	17,484	92.6%	0.989
4. Raptors	18,404	92.9%	1.067	19. Bucks	16,188	86.5%	0.988
5. Thunder*	16,053	92.6%	1.055	20. Nuggets	16,943	88.4%	0.977
6. Jazz	19,206	96.5%	1.051	21. Cavaliers	18,250	88.7%	0.974
7. Clippers	17,033	89.6%	1.048	22. T'wolves	16,066	84.2%	0.961
8. Lakers	18,955	98.6%	1.039	23. 76ers	17,067	83.8%	0.946
9. Spurs	18,754	101.1%	1.036	24. Pacers	15,420	84.2%	0.935
10. Heat	17,899	91.6%	1.024	25. Rockets	15,611	85.1%	0.929
11. Kings	15,952	92.4%	1.021	26. Hornets^	15,308	83.2%	0.927
12. Blazers	18,238	91.3%	1.019	27. Hawks	14,842	79.2%	0.919
13. Warriors	17,280	88.2%	1.019	28. Grizzlies	14,502	76.8%	0.891
14. Wizards	17,793	88.2%	1.016	29. Bobcats	15,102	75.9%	0.861
15. Magic	15,927	92.1%	1.014	30. Nets	15,188	76.4%	0.856

* Includes Seattle SuperSonics
^ Includes Charlotte Hornets

venue in Brooklyn. Also, as an aside, it's awesome that the Clippers rank better in this metric than the Lakers. Ralph Lawler would be proud.

According to 2008 estimates of the top 100 metropolitan areas put together by the Brookings Institute, Indianapolis ranks 22nd of the NBA's 28 markets in population. (Note: 2006 census figures were added to the data for the Toronto area.) Of the markets smaller than Indy, New Orleans, Memphis and Charlotte rank lower in LOY. Not surprisingly, all have had their viability as NBA markets questioned to various degrees. There are about a dozen U.S. markets with a higher population count than Indianapolis that do not currently have an NBA franchise. Some of these cities are unlikely to be candidates for franchise relocation. St. Louis, San Diego, Tampa, Pittsburgh, Cincinnati and Baltimore all either have too many competing professional franchises, a general lack of interest in the NBA, proximity to an adjacent NBA market or all the above.

Other cities are more of a threat. Seattle has to be considered the most attractive of these markets given that basketball fans there proved that they can support a team over the span of more than four decades. Working against the city are the limitations of KeyArena and a progressive citizenry not keen on the idea of using public funds to build another sports arena. Kansas City is larger than Indianapolis by a whisker and built a state-of-the-art arena just a few years ago, a venue built with public funds approved under the guise that the city would get an anchor tenant from either the NBA or NHL. Kansas City's problems are the two competing professional teams (yes, the Royals count) in a market that may not be able to support a third, as well as a general apathy regarding the NBA. Las Vegas has long been rumored as a potential NBA city and fits the league's strategy of placing teams in smaller cities without major-league competition, a model that has worked so well in Orlando, Salt Lake City, Sacramento, San Antonio and, most recently, Oklahoma City. Those cities were all added to the league after Portland, the first of these types of smallish towns to define its professional sports identity through professional basketball. The only city where this strategy has failed to date has been Memphis, and even that is not a lost cause. However, Vegas presents its own unique set of problems for the NBA. Nevertheless, the Seattle/Kansas City/Las Vegas triumvirate will continue to be linked to the league as long as there are franchises in distress and voters unwilling to subsidize facilities for billionaires.

Indianapolis, of course, fit that NBA-exclusive definition of NBA markets until 1984, when the Colts moved to town. That didn't really have too much effect on the Pacers until Peyton Manning joined the fun in 1998. Since then, the fervor in Indianapolis over the Colts seems to have grown by the year. That enthusiasm culminated last year, when Lucas Oil Stadium was opened. According to the *Indianapolis Business Journal*, the Pacers "fell through the cracks" during the negotiations between the city and state over who would pay for the Colts' new home. The Pacers had subsidized their NBA revenue with non-NBA events held at Conseco, many of which went away when Lucas Oil Stadium opened its doors. To help offset the losses, Pacers owner Herb Simon, who assumed sole control of the franchise after his brother Mel died last year, went to the city-operated Capital Improvement Board with a request to assume operating costs of Conseco Fieldhouse. Pacers officials gave the city a June 30 deadline for a deal while hinting at relocation as an alternative.

Finally, a deal was struck, ensuring a tenuous marriage between the Pacers and Indianapolis for the next three years or so. Here are some highlights of the deal, according to the *Indianapolis Star*:

- The CIB will give $30 million over the next three seasons to the Pacers
- The CIB will make a minimum of $3.5 million in capital improvements to Conseco Fieldhouse
- The Pacers will continue to operate the Fieldhouse and keep revenues from game and non-game events
- If the Pacers move before the 2013-14 season, they will repay $30 million to the CIB by June 30, 2013
- The amount the Pacers repay will be reduced for each season that they continue to play at Conseco: If they play the 2013-14 season, they'll repay $28 million; by 2018-19, that would fall to $1 million

So the Pacers are likely to hang in for three years, at least. However, there is no guarantee that, given the uncertain state of the economy, the CIB will continue to contribute to the operation of the arena beyond the $30 million already committed. If that happens, then the net cost of moving the team begins to shrink, and if the franchise thinks they can make more money elsewhere, a shift becomes that much more likely. Complicating these issues is the fact that Herb Simon is 75 years old and it is unclear what happens when he is gone, though he has stated that the franchise will remain within his family. A final, ominous factor is the possibility of a lockout of players for the 2011-12 season, something that could kill professional basketball in a handful of NBA markets, Indianapolis included.

The best thing Bird can do to keep the Pacers in his home state is to draw more fans to Conseco and thus render the operating costs of the arena a moot point. For that, he needs to win on the court in a big way. To get to that point, he needed to clear the decks of some bad payroll, and he's on the verge of doing just that. While doing so, he's accumulated a nice group of young, inexpensive talents to build around in Darren Collison, Roy Hibbert, Brandon Rush and Tyler Hansbrough, not to mention franchise cornerstone Danny Granger. So the on-court future is much brighter than it was a couple of years ago, but will it come together fast enough? The Pacers need to show some upward mobility because with an eroding fan base in a city that grows ever-more Colts crazy (and Big Ten hoops crazy) each year, they have no time to waste.

To that end, this stands as a key season in the franchise's history. If the young core can coalesce into an overachieving, exciting squad that is viewed as a coming power in the Eastern Conference, that will go a long way towards energizing the fan base. Then, after the season, Bird will have just $35 million on the books, a figure that could go lower if he finds a taker for aging forward James Posey, whom he was forced to take back as part of the deal bringing Collison to Indianapolis. While the Pacers are unlikely to land any of the top-tier free agents that might be on the market next summer, the financial flexibility will allow Bird to add to his emergent core or swap some of those pieces and bring back an impact talent to complement Granger. For this to be perceived as the logical next step in the organization's evolution, the young core must prove itself as a worthy group to build around.

The possibilities are intriguing. Hansbrough showed signs of becoming an effective banger despite physical problems that hampered his efficiency. Overall, he showed a good range of skills, save for an inability to score from the floor. That is a problem, as is the vertigo caused by his inner ear problems that hampered his activity into September. Hibbert emerged as one of the more prolific post scorers in the league and as an effective finisher on the pick-and-roll. He's big and skilled. However, his lack of athleticism, particularly foot speed, has a crippling effect on the defense. He's poor against the pick-and-roll, though his size makes him an adequate post defender. His help defense isn't

---

From the Blogosphere

Who: Tom Lewis
What: Indy Cornrows
Where: http://www.indycornrows.com/

The Indiana Pacers have to play better than the sum of their parts to make a successful run to the playoff in the 2010-11 season. The direction the team dynamic takes could ultimately make the difference. If the season starts poorly and attitudes sour, the locker room could quickly become a soap opera entitled The Young and The Expirings. Larry Bird and David Morway have been beating the drum for some time now about their efforts to put together a young core of talented players while looking ahead to next summer and the big chunk of cap space they'll have thanks to several expiring contracts. Well, those expiring deals have faces attached to them, and they'll be in the Pacers locker room until the season ends or they are dealt. In the meantime, seeing how Jim O'Brien deals with the varying interests on his roster will be must-see TV.

great and a player his size ought to block more shots--if only he could get off the floor. And he can't stop fouling. At the same time, Hibbert has an excellent work ethic and reportedly slimmed down over the summer in an effort to address the shortcomings in his game.

Of these young players, Rush's development is the murkiest. His performance was flat last season, though he did manage to creep above replacement level. He remains passive, with results that fall well short of his natural physical ability. Compounding these problems is the fact that he's been suspended for the first five games of the season for violating the NBA's drug policy. That means he tested positive at least three times *in season*. It's not a good sign for a player whose game is in serious need of maturation.

Granger was again the team's best player, but didn't improve as much as he has in past seasons. Then again, he couldn't maintain that rate of progress forever and missed 20 games due to injury. By the end of the season, he was back to putting up big numbers. His deficiencies in defense and ballhandling still need to be addressed.

Added to this group are rookies Paul George, taken in this year's lottery, and Lance Stephenson, a potential second-round steal provided he can get his rather serious off-court issues ironed out. With Collison, the Pacers now have a potential young rotation going 7-8 players deep. It will be incumbent upon head coach Jim O'Brien to see how the young pieces fit together while the team positions for the next phase in its rebuilding. Bird has to figure out what is to be done with T.J. Ford, who rejected a buyout offer in favor of another season of discontent. He must also determine if Posey can be moved, or whether can he help facilitate the development of Indiana's young wing players. Will there be a taker for Mike Dunleavy Jr., who enters the final year of his contract? Does he have a comeback season in him? Will he have to be showcased even if he doesn't play well and thus block a younger player? There are a lot of terrific possibilities for the Pacers right now, but also plenty of questions.

SCHOENE foresees another 50-loss season for Indiana, but there is the potential to surprise given the number of young players in featured roles. This could not only kickstart a flagging franchise and energize a shrinking fan base, but the likelihood of a continually evolving roster could make things downright exciting in Indy. With all the money coming off the books, things are looking up, but the clock is ticking.

Bradford Doolittle

PACERS FIVE-YEAR TRENDS

Season	AGE	W-L	POW	PYTH	SEED	ORTG	DRTG	PT DIFF	PACE
05-06	27.3	41-41	42.9 (14)	46.8	6	105.8 (21)	104.0 (4)	1.9 (9)	88.4 (19)
06-07	27.2	35-47	33.2 (20)	33.8	---	104.2 (30)	107.3 (11)	-2.4 (20)	91.1 (9)
07-08	27.0	36-46	35.4 (19)	37.2	---	108.4 (19)	109.8 (15)	-1.4 (18)	95.6 (3)
08-09	26.5	36-46	37.4 (18)	38.0	---	109.8 (15)	111.0 (19)	-1.1 (19)	95.0 (3)
09-10	27.3	32-50	31.5 (21)	32.7	---	105.5 (26)	108.6 (15)	-3.0 (21)	95.4 (2)

		OFFENSE				DEFENSE			
Season	PAY	eFG	oREB	FT/FGA	TO	eFG	oREB	FT/FGA	TO
05-06	$66.6	.487 (19)	.271 (12)	.254 (16)	.173 (26)	.464 (2)	.726 (15)	.232 (8)	.153 (24)
06-07	$61.5	.474 (29)	.284 (10)	.246 (14)	.178 (27)	.491 (11)	.727 (16)	.271 (26)	.171 (5)
07-08	$66.9	.498 (14)	.244 (23)	.224 (18)	.153 (20)	.498 (13)	.739 (10)	.271 (28)	.157 (8)
08-09	$69.6	.501 (15)	.254 (21)	.215 (25)	.151 (14)	.499 (14)	.745 (10)	.271 (28)	.147 (22)
09-10	$66.9	.491 (23)	.216 (29)	.229 (14)	.157 (19)	.490 (10)	.730 (22)	.258 (26)	.157 (13)
(league rankings in parenthesis)									

INDIANA PACERS

PG 2 — Darren Collison

Hght: 6'0"	Exp: 1	Salary: $1.4 million
Wght: 160	From: UCLA	
2011-12 status: team option for $1.5 million		

SKILL RATINGS

TOT	OFF	DEF	REB	PAS	HND	SHT	ATH
+4	+4	-3	0	+3	0	+1	+1

Year	Team	Age	G	MPG	Usg	3PA%	FTA%	INS	2P%	3P%	FT%	TS%	Reb%	Ast%	TO%	BLK%	STL%	PF%	oRTG	dRTG	Win%	WARP
09-10	NOH	22.7	76	27.8	.233	.108	.072	.964	.490	.400	.851	.546	.054	.094	.189	.001	.019	.020	106.8	106.6	.504	3.8
10-11p	IND	23.7	75	30.0	.236	.117	.077	.960	.493	.411	.866	.556	.056	.097	.176	.002	.018	.019	107.9	105.9	.563	6.9

Most similar to: T.J. Ford (97.1), Mike Bibby, Allen Leavell, Jason Terry — IMP: 54% BRK: 3% COP: 5%

After a one-year apprenticeship behind Chris Paul, Darren Collison now has a team to call his own. Collison fills a huge void in the Indiana rebuilding plan, offering hope at a position the Pacers once believed T.J. Ford would be able to fill. Collison put up impressive basic numbers last year, averaging 17.9 points and 8.2 assists per 40 minutes. That paints over the work he still needs to do on his game. The first thing is to take better care of the ball. Collison turned the ball over on five percent more of his plays than the league rate as a rookie, and that was already a weak area for the Pacers last season. He looks like he's going to be an above-average outside shooter, but he needs to do better around the rim, where he didn't make the best decisions on the pick-and-roll and drew few fouls. More than anything, he needs to up his game on defense. These quibbles aside, Collison looks like he's going to be a fine NBA point guard and the Pacers seem to have that spot filled for the foreseeable future.

SF 17 — Mike Dunleavy Jr.

Hght: 6'9"	Exp: 8	Salary: $10.6 million
Wght: 230	From: Duke	
2011-12 status: free agent		

SKILL RATINGS

TOT	OFF	DEF	REB	PAS	HND	SHT	ATH
+1	+2	0	-1	+2	0	0	0

Year	Team	Age	G	MPG	Usg	3PA%	FTA%	INS	2P%	3P%	FT%	TS%	Reb%	Ast%	TO%	BLK%	STL%	PF%	oRTG	dRTG	Win%	WARP
07-08	IND	27.6	82	36.0	.218	.262	.119	.857	.503	.424	.834	.604	.079	.042	.128	.008	.013	.031	107.5	105.9	.552	8.3
08-09	IND	28.6	18	27.5	.264	.301	.096	.794	.430	.356	.815	.520	.076	.039	.127	.013	.012	.032	106.2	106.9	.478	0.6
09-10	IND	29.6	67	22.2	.209	.337	.099	.762	.478	.318	.842	.531	.087	.031	.103	.007	.012	.031	105.2	106.1	.471	1.7
10-11p	IND	30.6	70	22.0	.211	.361	.099	.738	.469	.345	.823	.541	.081	.033	.115	.009	.011	.034	105.6	106.3	.478	2.0

Most similar to: Tim Thomas (98.4), Danny Ferry, Stephen Jackson, Keith Van Horn — IMP: 30% BRK: 2% COP: 6%

Mike Dunleavy Jr.'s game has hit the skids the last two seasons and he enters the last year of his contract hoping to win himself a few admirers for the next offseason. Dunleavy was once a solid outside shooter, but he's suddenly weak outside of 15 feet. His playmaking skills have also declined, though part of that may be because he doesn't play as big a part in the Indiana offense as he once did. Defensively, Dunleavy isn't terrible and is always willing to give up his body to take a charge, but he's not going to win a lot of games on that end of the floor--especially when he plays the two-guard, which is his best bet for big minutes on the Pacers' current depth chart.

PG 5 — T.J. Ford

Hght: 6'0"	Exp: 6	Salary: $8.5 million
Wght: 165	From: Texas	
2011-12 status: free agent		

SKILL RATINGS

TOT	OFF	DEF	REB	PAS	HND	SHT	ATH
+2	--	-2	--	--	--	--	--

Year	Team	Age	G	MPG	Usg	3PA%	FTA%	INS	2P%	3P%	FT%	TS%	Reb%	Ast%	TO%	BLK%	STL%	PF%	oRTG	dRTG	Win%	WARP
07-08	TOR	25.1	51	23.5	.269	.075	.081	1.006	.488	.294	.880	.533	.049	.124	.150	.001	.021	.036	109.5	106.3	.601	4.6
08-09	IND	26.1	74	30.5	.236	.085	.102	1.016	.467	.337	.872	.533	.063	.076	.148	.005	.019	.035	106.9	106.9	.498	3.9
09-10	IND	27.1	47	25.3	.212	.088	.105	1.017	.484	.160	.770	.507	.069	.067	.159	.007	.018	.038	104.6	106.4	.441	0.6
10-11p	IND	28.1	76	--	.219	.108	.092	.984	.487	.256	.822	.523	.063	.079	.151	.005	.017	.036	--	--	.496	--

Most similar to: Luke Ridnour (97.1), Sam Vincent, Bobby Jackson, Pooh Richardson — IMP: 48% BRK: 7% COP: 10%

The Pacers can finally cut ties with T.J. Ford after this season if they can't find a taker for him before the trade deadline. Ford's game seems to slip with each passing season. Entering 2009-10, the Pacers were hopeful that Ford would become more of a pure point guard, but instead his assist rate dropped, his turnovers increased and his three-point shot went bye-bye. Ford was once projected as an excellent all-around point guard and a potential All-Star. During his time with the Pacers, he's only proven that he lacks the ability to make his team better at either end of the floor. There is talent in there somewhere. At some point soon, somebody outside of Indiana is going to get a chance to make it emerge.

C 10 — Jeff Foster

Hght: 6'11" Exp: 11 Salary: $6.7 million
Wght: 250 From: Texas State
2011-12 status: free agent

SKILL RATINGS

TOT	OFF	DEF	REB	PAS	HND	SHT	ATH
-2	0	+2	+2	+4	+5	-1	-2

Year	Team	Age	G	MPG	Usg	3PA%	FTA%	INS	2P%	3P%	FT%	TS%	Reb%	Ast%	TO%	BLK%	STL%	PF%	oRTG	dRTG	Win%	WARP
07-08	IND	31.3	77	24.5	.115	.006	.128	1.122	.554	.000	.593	.568	.194	.030	.124	.013	.013	.051	106.0	104.9	.537	4.7
08-09	IND	32.3	74	24.7	.121	.014	.127	1.113	.506	.286	.658	.542	.153	.031	.174	.020	.014	.055	105.1	106.2	.463	1.8
09-10	IND	33.3	16	15.9	.111	.016	.062	1.046	.489	.000	.556	.490	.173	.037	.219	.011	.006	.078	103.9	107.6	.380	-0.2
10-11p	IND	34.3	66	5.0	.102	.011	.091	1.080	.504	.040	.568	.508	.167	.035	.191	.014	.009	.070	103.8	106.8	.402	-0.1

Most similar to: Fabricio Oberto (97.4), Corie Blount, Kurt Rambis, Alan Henderson

IMP: 39% BRK: 4% COP: 9%

Hard-working Jeff Foster was limited to 16 games in 2009-10 because of back surgery. Foster is getting up in years and there is no guarantee he'll be able to regain his defense and rebounding skills, at least not at their past levels. When healthy, Foster is one of the game's best offensive rebounders and a solid man-on-man defender who flops with the best of them. The little face-up jumper that Foster had once added to his arsenal was missing for the second straight season last year and his ability to finish inside is in decline. Because of the uncertainty surrounding Tyler Hansbrough and the Pacers' lack of proven depth at the four-spot, Foster could end up battling Josh McRoberts for playing time at the position.

SG 24 — Paul George

Hght: 6'8" Exp: R Salary: $2.2 million
Wght: 210 From: Fresno State
2011-12 status: guaranteed contract for $2.4 million

SKILL RATINGS

TOT	OFF	DEF	REB	PAS	HND	SHT	ATH
-1	-1	+2	+5	+1	-3	-4	+5

Year	Team	Age	G	MPG	Usg	3PA%	FTA%	INS	2P%	3P%	FT%	TS%	Reb%	Ast%	TO%	BLK%	STL%	PF%	oRTG	dRTG	Win%	WARP
10-11p	IND	21.0	76	10.0	.185	.255	.079	.824	.383	.294	.891	.464	.099	.040	.190	.013	.024	.056	102.5	105.1	.413	0.0

Most similar to: Joe Johnson (94.9), Andre Iguodala, Kenny Satterfield, Rudy Gay

IMP: - BRK: - COP: -

Paul George soared up the prospect rankings on the basis of elite athletic ability. With his long legs and straight-line speed, he can really get down the floor and should prove to be one of the most exciting finishers in the game. If the Pacers can get stops and get out on the break, George will make a breathtaking running mate for Darren Collison. In the half-court offense, he still needs to improve his shot selection and decision-making to become more efficient. He's a terrific foul shooter, which offers hope that his touch can be translated to the floor. George also has the physical attributes to become an elite defender. He looked raw in summer league, so Pacers fans shouldn't expect too much, too soon. However, the ceiling is extremely high for George.

SF 33 — Danny Granger

Hght: 6'8" Exp: 5 Salary: $11.0 million
Wght: 228 From: New Mexico
2011-12 status: guaranteed contract for $12.0 million

SKILL RATINGS

TOT	OFF	DEF	REB	PAS	HND	SHT	ATH
+5	+4	-3	-1	+2	-1	+2	+4

Year	Team	Age	G	MPG	Usg	3PA%	FTA%	INS	2P%	3P%	FT%	TS%	Reb%	Ast%	TO%	BLK%	STL%	PF%	oRTG	dRTG	Win%	WARP
07-08	IND	25.0	80	36.0	.233	.274	.108	.834	.467	.404	.852	.571	.093	.025	.111	.022	.014	.044	106.3	105.0	.542	7.5
08-09	IND	26.0	67	36.2	.297	.274	.123	.849	.470	.404	.878	.584	.078	.033	.100	.030	.014	.037	109.6	105.6	.626	10.6
09-10	IND	27.0	62	36.7	.289	.295	.127	.832	.471	.361	.848	.564	.082	.033	.106	.016	.020	.036	108.4	105.0	.610	9.2
10-11p	IND	28.0	72	37.0	.265	.311	.118	.807	.480	.370	.855	.571	.082	.033	.106	.023	.016	.037	107.9	104.8	.599	10.2

Most similar to: Jason Richardson (98.0), Vince Carter, Rashard Lewis, Paul Pierce

IMP: 42% BRK: 0% COP: 4%

INDIANA PACERS

For the first time in his career, Danny Granger didn't get better. He didn't get worse, either, which means he was still awfully good. Injuries played a part in Granger settling on a plateau. Towards the end of the season, when he was healthy, Granger really went on a tear. Last year, he turned more of his midrange jumpers into three-point attempts, but his accuracy behind the arc dipped. If he can get back up to the 40 percent mark while keeping the shot selection and foul-drawing steady, he'll have his most efficient season yet. Beyond that, Granger still needs to become a more willing and skilled playmaker as the focal point of the Indiana offense. He also needs to batten down the hatches on the defensive end of the floor, a shortcoming that kept him from getting many minutes for the U.S. team in the FIBA World Championship. Granger is an All-Star-level player on a mediocre team. He needs to make these further refinements in his game in order to become an All-Star-level player on a good team.

PF 50 — Tyler Hansbrough

Hght: 6'9" Exp: 1 Salary: $2.0 million
Wght: 250 From: North Carolina
2011-12 status: team option for $2.1 million

SKILL RATINGS

TOT	OFF	DEF	REB	PAS	HND	SHT	ATH
+1	+1	0	+3	+1	+3	-5	+5

Year	Team	Age	G	MPG	Usg	3PA%	FTA%	INS	2P%	3P%	FT%	TS%	Reb%	Ast%	TO%	BLK%	STL%	PF%	oRTG	dRTG	Win%	WARP
09-10	IND	24.5	29	17.6	.257	.014	.168	1.155	.367	.000	.743	.448	.147	.024	.071	.011	.016	.061	104.8	106.3	.453	0.4
10-11p	IND	25.5	68	24.0	.254	.019	.166	1.147	.377	.000	.756	.455	.154	.023	.071	.014	.016	.061	104.9	105.7	.473	1.9

Most similar to: Alan Henderson (93.4), Clifford Robinson, Doug Smith, Randy White   IMP: 65% BRK: 22% COP: 13%

Twenty-nine games isn't much to go on, but it looks like Tyler Hansbrough can be a solid NBA power forward. That's pending some refinements to his game and the status of his health. On the plus side, Hansbrough proved to be active on the boards, especially on the offensive glass. His strength is his ability to draw contact, which led to an outstanding foul-drawing rate. He also passed the ball well without committing many turnovers. On the downside, his shooting from the floor was abominable. Hansbrough had shots blocked at more than twice the league rate and barely cracked break-even in his shots at the rim. Two-thirds of his shots came from midrange, where he hit an almost unbelievably bad 29 percent of his jumpers. Hansbrough isn't the +5 athlete we have him slotted as; the rating is a result of the extreme foul-drawing rate. However, he looks like a player who can get a shot off when he needs to. Whether or not he can make them is another story. You'd like to think his shooting touch will improve as he gains more experience, but vertigo caused by an inner ear infection has plagued Hansbrough for months and he still wasn't cleared for full workouts until late September. By the time he returns, it will be just like starting over.

C 55 — Roy Hibbert

Hght: 7'2" Exp: 2 Salary: $1.7 million
Wght: 278 From: Georgetown
2011-12 status: guaranteed contract for $2.6 million

SKILL RATINGS

TOT	OFF	DEF	REB	PAS	HND	SHT	ATH
+2	+1	-1	-2	+4	+3	0	0

Year	Team	Age	G	MPG	Usg	3PA%	FTA%	INS	2P%	3P%	FT%	TS%	Reb%	Ast%	TO%	BLK%	STL%	PF%	oRTG	dRTG	Win%	WARP
08-09	IND	22.4	70	14.4	.234	.000	.120	1.120	.471	.000	.667	.510	.133	.021	.102	.056	.010	.093	105.8	106.3	.485	1.4
09-10	IND	23.4	81	25.1	.224	.006	.096	1.090	.495	.500	.754	.537	.125	.034	.141	.046	.007	.062	105.1	105.1	.498	3.4
10-11p	IND	24.4	76	28.0	.221	.005	.105	1.100	.497	.219	.709	.532	.128	.032	.128	.048	.008	.071	105.0	105.2	.491	3.4

Most similar to: Stanley Roberts (97.6), Brian Grant, Rik Smits, Erick Dampier   IMP: 50% BRK: 6% COP: 13%

Roy Hibbert made a lot of progress in his second NBA season and if you believe offseason hype, he's due for another leap in his third. Hibbert became a solid post option in the Pacers' offense, ranking sixth among all players in percentage of shots coming off post-ups. He finished in the 66th percentile on those plays; he was in the 90th percentile in finishing pick-and-rolls. His True Shooting Percentage was dragged down by a couple of categories that can both be traced back to Hibbert's limited athleticism. He shot below the league average at the rim, hitting 59 percent there, a disappointing figure for a skilled 7-footer. He also had a below-average foul-drawing rate, which may also have stemmed from a 10 percent increase in shots from midrange. Hibbert actually took 129 long twos last year, hitting those at just a 33 percent success rate. That portion of his game needs to be excised. Hibbert's rebound rate is way too low for someone of his size, but is a reflection of his limited leaping ability. That same trait holds him back on the defense, where he is a good shot blocker but only an average defender overall. Hibbert spent the summer working with Bill Walton and reportedly reduced his body fat to 10 percent. He was called "noticeably quicker." If that's true, the Pacers will have themselves a top-10 center.

SF 1	Dahntay Jones	Hght: 6'6" Exp: 7 Salary: $2.5 million
		Wght: 210 From: Duke
		2011-12 status: guaranteed contract for $2.7 million

SKILL RATINGS

TOT	OFF	DEF	REB	PAS	HND	SHT	ATH
-4	-1	-2	-3	+2	0	-1	0

Year	Team	Age	G	MPG	Usg	3PA%	FTA%	INS	2P%	3P%	FT%	TS%	Reb%	Ast%	TO%	BLK%	STL%	PF%	oRTG	dRTG	Win%	WARP
07-08	SAC	27.3	25	8.4	.184	.070	.263	1.192	.468	.167	.667	.537	.098	.026	.117	.022	.017	.059	103.9	105.3	.454	0.2
08-09	DEN	28.3	79	18.1	.147	.036	.141	1.105	.448	.647	.728	.533	.068	.024	.145	.010	.017	.062	102.5	107.9	.329	-2.6
09-10	IND	29.3	76	24.9	.203	.037	.131	1.094	.479	.125	.770	.527	.066	.035	.149	.015	.010	.056	102.4	107.3	.342	-3.0
10-11p	IND	30.3	75	14.3	.166	.040	.129	1.089	.472	.350	.758	.536	.068	.032	.149	.014	.013	.059	102.3	107.2	.342	-1.7

Most similar to: Doug West (98.8), Mike Sanders, Stacey Augmon, Willie Anderson   IMP: 56%   BRK: 15%   COP: 5%

Dahntay Jones moved over from Denver before last season and was probably overexposed by playing 25 minutes per night. Jones became more assertive on offense without really hurting his efficiency. He's strictly a slasher, but the Indiana system requires jump shots and the portion of Jones' attempts coming from midrange jumped by 14 percent even though he's below average in accuracy from 10 feet and out. He can't shoot three-pointers at all, which led to late-summer rumors that he was going to be traded to make room for second-round pick Magnum Rolle. Jones' calling card is solid positional defense, but that aspect of his game lagged during his first season in Indianapolis. Jones' improvements were merely superficial and, overall, he was just slightly less bad. His deal isn't a huge albatross, but he does have $8.1 million left on his contract, too much for a player of minimum-salary quality.

C 44	Solomon Jones	Hght: 6'10" Exp: 4 Salary: $1.5 million
		Wght: 245 From: South Florida
		2011-12 status: free agent

SKILL RATINGS

TOT	OFF	DEF	REB	PAS	HND	SHT	ATH
-3	-1	-2	-3	0	0	0	-1

Year	Team	Age	G	MPG	Usg	3PA%	FTA%	INS	2P%	3P%	FT%	TS%	Reb%	Ast%	TO%	BLK%	STL%	PF%	oRTG	dRTG	Win%	WARP
07-08	ATL	23.8	35	4.3	.152	.040	.177	1.137	.429	.000	.550	.451	.163	.000	.221	.025	.009	.086	100.8	106.6	.313	-0.3
08-09	ATL	24.8	63	10.7	.119	.012	.191	1.179	.606	.500	.716	.655	.123	.010	.158	.039	.005	.087	104.6	107.4	.411	-0.1
09-10	IND	25.8	52	13.0	.163	.012	.126	1.114	.451	.000	.718	.499	.117	.021	.162	.039	.010	.082	101.9	106.0	.364	-0.7
10-11p	IND	26.8	76	8.0	.140	.012	.149	1.136	.505	.083	.711	.555	.119	.018	.162	.038	.009	.081	102.5	106.2	.378	-0.5

Most similar to: Carl Herrera (98.0), Jake Tsakalidis, Brian Skinner, Eric Mobley   IMP: 46%   BRK: 2%   COP: 10%

Solomon Jones is your basic below-replacement banger who isn't really good at anything in particular. Two years ago, he put up an unsustainable .604 field-goal percentage that was propped up by a .700 success rate at the rim. Last year, that dropped to .590 and the solid midrange percentage he posted in a small 2008-09 sample size also fell. His portion of shots at the rim dropped from 61 percent to 35 percent. Add it all up, and you have a tumbling True Shooting Percentage and a very inefficient player. Jones' blocked shot rate is nothing special; nor is any other aspect of his defense and rebounding. He's got another guaranteed season this year, and then it will be life on the fringe for Jones.

INDIANA PACERS

PF	Josh McRoberts	Hght: 6'10"	Exp: 3	Salary: $0.9 million	SKILL RATINGS						
32		Wght: 240	From: Duke		TOT	OFF	DEF	REB	PAS	HND	SHT	ATH
		2011-12 status: free agent			+2	+1	+1	+1	+4	+5	0	+3

Year	Team	Age	G	MPG	Usg	3PA%	FTA%	INS	2P%	3P%	FT%	TS%	Reb%	Ast%	TO%	BLK%	STL%	PF%	oRTG	dRTG	Win%	WARP
07-08	POR	21.1	8	3.8	.191	.083	.000	.917	.667	.000	.000	.600	.196	.032	.167	.000	.016	.016	104.6	103.2	.546	0.1
08-09	IND	22.1	33	8.5	.158	.099	.057	.958	.479	.000	.769	.451	.146	.025	.119	.043	.021	.064	103.2	104.1	.470	0.3
09-10	IND	23.1	42	12.5	.154	.127	.092	.965	.553	.348	.500	.550	.133	.037	.105	.022	.016	.063	105.9	105.5	.514	1.1
10-11p	IND	24.1	76	15.0	.149	.137	.081	.944	.533	.193	.610	.511	.133	.035	.107	.027	.016	.061	104.6	104.9	.489	1.7

Most similar to: Brian Cook (98.4), Danny Granger, Terry Mills, Travis Knight IMP: 42% BRK: 7% COP: 7%

In one of the more fascinating stat lines from summer-league action, Josh McRoberts launched 12 three-pointers in a single game. He made two, so he's not going the Jack Sikma route just yet. McRoberts has to work for his shots on putbacks and defensive breakdowns, but he converts his chances at the rim at a very high rate. In Jim O'Brien's system, power forwards have to be able to face up a little bit, so that's likely why McRoberts was honing that three-point stroke over the summer. He tried 23 threes last year, and that number may go way up. McRoberts has a solid skill set across the board and may be developing into a rotation player. He's a particularly good passer for his size, gets steals and blocks, and plays decent one-on-one defense. With Tyler Hansbrough still battling vertigo, Jeff Foster recovering from back problems and Troy Murphy in New Jersey, McRoberts has a chance at playing big minutes at the beginning of the season. He may turn some heads.

SF	James Posey	Hght: 6'8"	Exp: 11	Salary: $7.1 million	SKILL RATINGS						
41		Wght: 217	From: Xavier (Ohio)		TOT	OFF	DEF	REB	PAS	HND	SHT	ATH
		2011-12 status: guaranteed contract for $7.6 million			0	0	-1	+3	0	+3	-1	-1

Year	Team	Age	G	MPG	Usg	3PA%	FTA%	INS	2P%	3P%	FT%	TS%	Reb%	Ast%	TO%	BLK%	STL%	PF%	oRTG	dRTG	Win%	WARP
07-08	BOS	31.3	74	24.5	.137	.527	.096	.569	.496	.380	.809	.587	.101	.029	.123	.009	.018	.046	105.7	104.5	.540	4.7
08-09	NOH	32.3	75	28.5	.151	.471	.096	.626	.476	.369	.822	.568	.102	.019	.118	.008	.015	.049	105.6	106.6	.466	2.2
09-10	NOH	33.3	77	22.5	.115	.561	.082	.520	.437	.335	.825	.525	.113	.031	.118	.008	.012	.054	104.8	106.5	.445	1.0
10-11p	IND	34.3	75	22.0	.121	.506	.088	.582	.451	.332	.810	.528	.111	.026	.122	.009	.015	.050	104.1	105.6	.450	1.2

Most similar to: Bryon Russell (97.6), George McCloud, Bruce Bowen, Rick Fox IMP: 53% BRK: 8% COP: 8%

James Posey was part of the price tag for bringing Darren Collison to Indiana. Posey's game is in decline, though he kept himself a win better than replacement last season. He's got two years and $14.7 million left on his contract, which included a 10 percent trade kicker, and said that he's not going to seek a buyout from Indiana. It seems unlikely that any team is going to trade for Posey at that salary, even though his skill set remains useful. His three-point shooting has been declining, as is his ability to get shots at all. Defensively, he's still adequate, with his calling card being an ability to draw charges as frequently as any player in the league. Posey may not provide much bang for his buck at this stage of his career, but he should be a solid mentor on a team full of developing players.

PG	A.J. Price	Hght: 6'2"	Exp: 1	Salary: $0.8 million	SKILL RATINGS						
22		Wght: 181	From: Connecticut		TOT	OFF	DEF	REB	PAS	HND	SHT	ATH
		2011-12 status: non-guaranteed contract for $0.9 million			+3	+4	+3	0	-1	-1	+1	+1

Year	Team	Age	G	MPG	Usg	3PA%	FTA%	INS	2P%	3P%	FT%	TS%	Reb%	Ast%	TO%	BLK%	STL%	PF%	oRTG	dRTG	Win%	WARP
09-10	IND	23.5	56	15.4	.229	.390	.074	.684	.472	.345	.800	.530	.056	.054	.132	.002	.020	.027	106.7	106.2	.516	1.8
10-11p	IND	24.5	56	15.0	.220	.396	.072	.677	.484	.352	.807	.540	.056	.058	.124	.003	.019	.024	107.2	105.9	.543	2.2

Most similar to: Steve Colter (98.3), Jamal Crawford, Dell Curry, Wes Matthews IMP: 65% BRK: 11% COP: 6%

A.J. Price had a promising rookie season before going down with a fractured patella that required surgery. He was still working himself into shape as training camp approached. Price flashed a solid ability to get to the rim as a rookie and showed a decent three-point stroke. His playmaking is a work in progress, but his defense was very solid. One-year plus-minus figures can be misleading, but it is worth noting that the Pacers were 7.2 points better per 100 possessions with Price on the floor. If healthy, Price should combine with Darren Collison to give the Pacers a solid one-two punch at point guard.

PF 15	Magnum Rolle	Hght: 6'11" Exp: R Salary: -- Wght: 225 From: Louisiana Tech 2011-12 status: free agent								**SKILL RATINGS**						
										TOT	OFF	DEF	REB	PAS	HND	SHT	ATH
										-4	-2	0	-1	-4	-4	-4	-2
Year	Team	Age	G	MPG	Usg	3PA%	FTA%	INS	2P%	3P%	FT%	TS%	Reb%	Ast%	TO%	BLK%	STL%	PF%	oRTG	dRTG	Win%	WARP
10-11p	IND	25.2	76	5.0	.152	-.001	.085	1.086	.425	.000	.625	.455	.120	.010	.153	.031	.009	.057	100.7	106.1	.325	-0.7
Most similar to: Dan Gadzuric (97.0), Britton Johnsen, Melvin Ely														IMP: -	BRK: -	COP: -

The Pacers still don't have a spot on the roster for second-round pick Magnum Rolle, but their decision to sign him to a two-year contract indicates they expect Rolle to make the team. Rolle is an athletic, raw, shot-blocking type who will be strictly a development player and will likely spend a chunk of time in the D-League.

SG 25	Brandon Rush	Hght: 6'6" Exp: 2 Salary: $2.1 million Wght: 210 From: Kansas 2011-12 status: team option for $3.0 million								**SKILL RATINGS**						
										TOT	OFF	DEF	REB	PAS	HND	SHT	ATH
										-1	0	+3	+3	-4	-2	+2	-3
Year	Team	Age	G	MPG	Usg	3PA%	FTA%	INS	2P%	3P%	FT%	TS%	Reb%	Ast%	TO%	BLK%	STL%	PF%	oRTG	dRTG	Win%	WARP
08-09	IND	23.8	75	24.0	.165	.308	.043	.735	.451	.373	.697	.505	.072	.016	.110	.015	.010	.031	102.8	106.9	.365	-1.9
09-10	IND	24.8	82	30.4	.149	.362	.047	.685	.433	.411	.629	.522	.076	.020	.111	.019	.011	.028	103.1	105.6	.417	0.0
10-11p	IND	25.8	71	25.0	.152	.381	.046	.665	.443	.407	.655	.530	.080	.021	.106	.020	.011	.029	103.5	105.5	.433	0.6
Most similar to: Chris Mills (98.0), Tyrone Nesby, Sasha Pavlovic, Jarvis Hayes														IMP: 50%	BRK: 20%	COP: 6%

Brandon Rush continues to be an enigma on and off the floor. On the court, he became even more passive in his second NBA season. His foul-drawing rate was still miniscule. Fewer of his field goals came off his own work and his three-point attempts soared. He's a solid shooter from distance--long-range shooting is his best attribute right now--but he's got too much physical ability to be a stand-still shooter with a .149 usage rate. Rush's defensive metrics were solid, and it looks like he at least puts his athleticism to use on that end of the floor. Off the court, Rush was suspended by the league for five games for violating the league's substance abuse policy. Rush turned 25 in July. It's time for him to mature.

SG 6	Lance Stephenson	Hght: 6'5" Exp: R Salary: $0.8 million Wght: 210 From: Cincinnati 2011-12 status: guaranteed contract for $0.8 million								**SKILL RATINGS**						
										TOT	OFF	DEF	REB	PAS	HND	SHT	ATH
										-5	-2	-2	+4	+1	-2	-5	-2
Year	Team	Age	G	MPG	Usg	3PA%	FTA%	INS	2P%	3P%	FT%	TS%	Reb%	Ast%	TO%	BLK%	STL%	PF%	oRTG	dRTG	Win%	WARP
10-11p	IND	20.6	76	12.0	.189	.115	.078	.962	.412	.194	.652	.427	.094	.038	.160	.003	.013	.047	101.0	107.2	.303	-2.1
Most similar to: Joe Johnson (95.3), Jamal Crawford, Daequan Cook, Derrick Rose														IMP: -	BRK: -	COP: -

Lance Stephenson slid into the second round of the draft after a subpar showing in his one college season at Cincinnati. Then he turned heads in the NBA Summer League in Orlando, shooting over 70 percent from the floor in four games. So Indiana handed him a four-year contract that is fully guaranteed the first two seasons. Then Stephenson went back to New York and was hit with some very serious domestic abuse charges. That's still all getting sorted out at press time, but the unhappy Pacers weren't letting Stephenson use their facilities to work out. Because his one college season was poor, he projects as two wins below replacement even in limited minutes. Stephenson is a physical player who isn't as quick and explosive as you'd think given his age. Right now, it's hard to know what kind of career Stephenson is going to have, or if he's even going to have a career.

Los Angeles Clippers

The injury that ended No. 1 overall pick Blake Griffin's rookie season before it even began might just have been the most quintessential Los Angeles Clippers moment of all time. When Griffin was drafted, numerous jokes and an entire column by ESPN's Bill Simmons suggested he was sure to become the next victim of the so-called "Clippers curse." Surely not even the most cynical observer imagined Griffin would be struck down so quickly.

In L.A.'s last preseason game, which was nationally televised, Griffin threw down a monster dunk. Having already dealt with patella tendinitis, Griffin came down awkwardly and suffered what was diagnosed as a stress fracture of his left patella. The Clippers initially set an aggressive timetable for Griffin, hoping to get their prized rookie back within six weeks at the latest. That date came and went with no sign of Griffin, and by January the lack of progress forced doctors to perform surgery.

The Griffin injury was an obvious stroke of bad luck. At the same time, the Clippers may not have helped their own cause. When Griffin first went down, *Carroll Guide to Sports Injuries* author Dr. Bill Carroll suggested they were being overly optimistic to hope that the injury would heal without surgery, even with the use of platelet-rich plasma (PRP) treatment. Simmons later alleged the team knew all along he would need to have surgery.

While every injury is unique, the Clippers' treatment of Griffin's injury certainly stood in contrast to how the Portland Trail Blazers have dealt with the knee injuries suffered by their own No. 1 pick, Greg Oden. After Oden underwent microfracture knee surgery before his rookie season, the Blazers announced he was out for the season, precluding any thought he might rush back too quickly. Portland took the same conservative course when Oden fractured his patella last year.

Griffin is now back on the court and is expected to be fine for the start of the 2010-11 season, but delaying the surgery set back his rehab efforts. He still has yet to take part in a competitive game since his injury, having sat out this year's NBA Summer League schedule.

There was more business as usual for the Clippers off the court--or, rather, in it. They spent the summer battling former coach Mike Dunleavy over his salary. Dunleavy entered the season in full control of Los Angeles' basketball operations as head coach and general manager. He was relieved of the coaching duties in February. A little over a month later, Dunleavy was also out as GM, leaving him to join his coaching predecessors in trying to recoup the money owed to him by the organization.

On the court, the Clippers were typically desultory. The highlight of the season came in January, when four straight wins pushed the team to the precipice of the .500 mark. On Jan. 12, Los Angeles led the Memphis Grizzlies when a water main burst at the FedExForum, forcing the evacuation of the building and delaying the game for more than a half hour. When the teams re-

CLIPPERS IN A BOX

Last year's record	29-53
Last year's Offensive Rating	105.1 (27)
Last year's Defensive Rating	111.6 (20)
Last year's point differential	-6.4 (28)
Team pace	91.2 (15)
SCHOENE projection	27-55 (15)
Projected Offensive Rating	106.1 (27)
Projected Defensive Rating	111.9 (26)
Projected team weighted age	26.3 (20)
Projected '10-11 payroll	$52.6 (27)
Est. payroll obligations, '11-12	$51.1 (21)

Head coach: Vinny Del Negro

Twice in three years, Del Negro and Dwane Casey have been the finalists for a head-coaching job. Both times, Del Negro has secured the position on the strength of his interviews, which raises the question of just what exactly he's saying behind closed doors. Del Negro was a punchline for most of his two years in Chicago, including a bizarre altercation initiated by his boss, John Paxson. However, Del Negro wrung decent results out of a good team, and the Bulls were strong at the defensive end of the floor. He'll have to improve his offensive creativity with the Clippers.

sumed play, Marc Gasol took over in the paint and led the Grizzlies to a come-from-behind victory. Two days later, Griffin was shelved for the season, and any Clipper hopes of making the postseason were dashed.

The loss in Memphis has been described as a turning point in the Clippers' season, but in truth the team never played that well. Entering that game, L.A.'s schedule-adjusted point differential of -2.3 points per game put the Clippers a distant 13th in the Western Conference, and with the West's eighth seed winning 50 games, they would have been hard-pressed to get back in the playoff race even had Griffin been able to return.

As it was, the Clippers tanked down the stretch. Veteran assistant Kim Hughes, who replaced Dunleavy on the sidelines on an interim basis, appeared unprepared to be a head coach. He had less talent with which to work after Los Angeles dealt steady big man Marcus Camby (in the final year of his contract) to Portland in exchange for reserves Steve Blake and Travis Outlaw. Hughes lost the first five games he coached and finished with an 8-25 record.

Still, the Clippers had reasons to be optimistic entering the summer. Before his departure, Dunleavy set the team up with an opportunity for free agency, shedding the contracts of lottery bust Al Thornton and Sebastian Telfair in a three-way trade with the Cleveland Cavaliers and Washington Wizards that netted the Clippers expiring contracts. The deal sacrificed little in terms of talent while putting L.A. far enough under the salary cap to have room to make a max contract offer.

The Clippers could offer free agents the prospect of a blank slate, with no head coach in place, as well as a solid core of talent between veterans Baron Davis and Chris Kaman and youngsters Griffin and Eric Gordon. However, the Clippers were weighed down by their heavy organizational baggage. They got the chance to pitch LeBron James, but never really had any hope of signing him and basically approached the experience like a young actor who's happy just to be nominated for an award.

When the Clippers moved on to the second tier of free agents, that same group of incumbent starters limited their options. L.A.'s glaring need for a small forward contrasted with the quality talent available, most of it in the frontcourt. Restricted free agent Rudy Gay was an obvious fit, but that only helped convince Memphis to pay up for Gay on the opening day of free agency, taking him off the market.

His options limited, new vice president of basketball operations Neil Olshey went shopping at a lower price range. Filling out their roster, the Clippers signed Ryan Gomes to compete for the starting spot at small forward and added depth in the backcourt with combo guard Randy Foye. They re-signed a pair of their own free agents in Rasual Butler, last year's starter at small forward, and Craig Smith, and also added journeyman big man Brian Cook.

The free agents will compete for playing time with the Clippers' draft picks. The long-term answer to the hole at small forward is Wake Forest product Al-Farouq Aminu, Los Angeles' lottery pick. Aminu played primarily in the paint in college and will have to transition out to the perimeter as a pro. He's got the athleticism to make it work; it's the skills of a small forward that Aminu is going to need to refine. During the NBA Summer League, he appeared very much a work in progress, spending too much time shooting shaky jump shots and too little attacking the basket.

The Clippers traded for a second pick in the first round, taking Kentucky point guard Eric Bledsoe with the 19th overall selection. Bledsoe benefited from the thin crop of point guards available in the draft, emerging as the second-best prospect after his Wildcats backcourt-mate John Wall. At one point, it looked as if Bledsoe might even be a lottery pick, which would have been a reach given how far he is from becoming an NBA contributor. The Clippers were a good landing spot. Foye can handle backup minutes at the point, allowing Bledsoe to develop at his own pace, but the rookie will become the designated successor for Davis.

The Clippers completed the heavy lifting of their offseason by hiring Vinny Del Negro as their new head coach in mid-July, less than two months after he was fired by the Chicago Bulls. Del Negro did a good job of incorporating a No. 1 overall pick into a veteran core in Chicago, but his challenge will be more difficult with the Clippers. The first order of business is finding a small forward, with defensive specialist Butler and the more physical Gomes providing contrasting options. Aminu is a long shot to start as a rookie.

By far, the most important addition for the Clippers will be Griffin. He was the odds-on favorite to win Rookie of the Year before his injury and should immediately be a contributor on the glass and in the post. Griffin may have more difficulty at the defensive end of the floor, where he was less impactful at Oklahoma and will have to deal with superior athletes at the NBA level. Griffin is a capable shot blocker, but the Clippers are taking a step back defensively with him effectively replacing Camby.

LOS ANGELES CLIPPERS

Even with Griffin's return, the Clippers are unlikely to improve dramatically. Their newly-signed free agents have middling track records and a history of being inefficient scorers. The $13 million they spent in free agency (including re-signing Butler and Smith) bought a total of just 2.1 projected Wins Above Replacement in 2010-11, which is a dismal rate of return even by the standards of the inflated market.

Add in a group of young rookies (Aminu, Bledsoe and second-round pick Willie Warren), all of whom project below replacement level, and the Clippers have not apparently helped themselves much, at least not for this season. SCHOENE's projections call for the four Clippers cornerstones to combine for 21.5 Wins Above Replacement, but no one else on the roster is projected to be worth even one WARP.

The final two months of last season showed how much work the Clippers have to do to get back into contention in the Western Conference. Their summer won't get them there. Owner Donald Sterling's criticism of his team's signings ("If I really called the shots we wouldn't have signed Gomes and what's the other guy's name?" he told the *Los Angeles Times*, referring to Foye) was embarrassing, but it wasn't inaccurate. Consider this yet another missed opportunity for L.A.'s other team.

Kevin Pelton

From the Blogosphere

Who: Kevin Arnovitz
What: ClipperBlog
Where: http://www.clipperblog.com/

During Mike Dunleavy's six-and-a-half-year tenure as the Clippers' head coach, none of his squads ranked in the top half of the league in offensive efficiency. Baron Davis, in particular, bristled at Dunleavy's commandeering style. With Vinny Del Negro now at the controls, Davis will have considerably more freedom as the conductor of the offense. Davis has always been a gifted distributor and his pure point skills have maintained themselves even as the Clippers struggled. Last season, Davis established a nice on-court rapport with Chris Kaman in the pick-and-pop game. This fall, Davis will inherit one of the best potential roll men to come into the league in a while, rookie Blake Griffin. Davis will also have Eric Gordon as a trusty kick-out option and perimeter counterweight. For Davis, the more options, the less likely he is to heave up ill-advised jumpers off the dribble. 94 players attempted more than 200 three-pointers, and Davis' .277 clip ranked him 93rd.

CLIPPERS FIVE-YEAR TRENDS

Season	AGE	W-L	POW	PYTH	SEED	ORTG	DRTG	PT DIFF	PACE
05-06	26.8	47-35	47.5 (9)	45.7	6	107.2 (17)	104.8 (8)	1.6 (11)	90.3 (11)
06-07	27.5	40-42	40.7 (13)	39.6	---	106.7 (21)	107.1 (10)	-0.5 (14)	89.5 (19)
07-08	28.4	23-59	22.7 (25)	21.8	---	103.6 (28)	111.1 (19)	-7.0 (28)	90.1 (12)
08-09	26.6	19-63	18.9 (29)	18.5	---	103.7 (30)	113.3 (26)	-8.8 (30)	90.8 (13)
09-10	28.1	29-53	25.9 (28)	23.7	--	105.1 (27)	111.6 (20)	-6.4 (28)	91.2 (15)

		OFFENSE				DEFENSE			
Season	PAY	eFG	oREB	FT/FGA	TO	eFG	oREB	FT/FGA	TO
05-06	$51.3	.487 (18)	.254 (25)	.263 (9)	.159 (15)	.471 (5)	.759 (3)	.240 (11)	.141 (30)
06-07	$58.2	.481 (24)	.272 (17)	.280 (4)	.168 (17)	.488 (9)	.747 (6)	.249 (17)	.154 (28)
07-08	$63.2	.465 (30)	.232 (28)	.264 (5)	.152 (15)	.502 (18)	.729 (19)	.236 (17)	.145 (19)
08-09	$61.9	.481 (28)	.251 (23)	.202 (29)	.162 (23)	.512 (24)	.712 (27)	.227 (14)	.145 (24)
09-10	$59.2	.491 (21)	.271 (11)	.206 (26)	.172 (29)	.509 (20)	.740 (11)	.214 (11)	.141 (25)

(league rankings in parenthesis)

LOS ANGELES CLIPPERS

SF 3	Al-Farouq Aminu	Hght: 6'9" Wght: 215 2011-12 status: guaranteed contract for $2.8 million	Exp: R From: Wake Forest	Salary: $2.6 million		**SKILL RATINGS**						
					TOT	OFF	DEF	REB	PAS	HND	SHT	ATH
					-3	-1	+1	+5	-3	-5	-5	+3

Year	Team	Age	G	MPG	Usg	3PA%	FTA%	INS	2P%	3P%	FT%	TS%	Reb%	Ast%	TO%	BLK%	STL%	PF%	oRTG	dRTG	Win%	WARP
10-11p	LAC	20.6	76	20.0	.202	.096	.117	1.021	.405	.242	.686	.453	.149	.018	.174	.021	.016	.059	102.2	105.5	.390	-0.8

Most similar to: Luol Deng (96.7), Julian Wright, Shawne Williams, J.J. Hickson   IMP: -   BRK: -   COP: -

Al-Farouq Aminu's college statistics show his promise as well as the development he'll need to make to be a contributor at the NBA level. Aminu's athleticism markers are strong across the board. He was a very good rebounder and should be a major plus on the glass as a small forward. Aminu also racked up both steals and blocks at good rates, and he was effective at getting to the free throw line.

The biggest problem for Aminu is putting the ball in the hoop. His translated two-point percentage of 40.5 percent is very poor for a small forward. Aminu's athleticism should have produced far better finishing around the rim. At this point, he lacks NBA three-point range, which will allow opponents to help off him. In addition, Aminu rarely handled the ball in college. It will take a couple of years for Aminu to improve his skills to the point where he can be a contributor. He's only 20, so time is on his side. However, similar players have not always panned out.

PG 12	Eric Bledsoe	Hght: 6'1" Wght: 190 2011-12 status: guaranteed contract for $1.6 million	Exp: R From: Kentucky	Salary: $1.5 million		**SKILL RATINGS**						
					TOT	OFF	DEF	REB	PAS	HND	SHT	ATH
					-5	-2	-2	-3	-3	-4	-3	-2

Year	Team	Age	G	MPG	Usg	3PA%	FTA%	INS	2P%	3P%	FT%	TS%	Reb%	Ast%	TO%	BLK%	STL%	PF%	oRTG	dRTG	Win%	WARP
10-11p	LAC	21.4	76	10.0	.147	.213	.083	.871	.425	.333	.655	.485	.043	.040	.234	.005	.016	.046	100.8	107.4	.291	-2.0

Most similar to: Jordan Farmar (93.6), Russell Westbrook, Kenny Satterfield, Keyon Dooling   IMP: -   BRK: -   COP: -

Scouts flocked to Kentucky games for DeMarcus Cousins, John Wall and Patrick Patterson, but Eric Bledsoe managed to capture their attention as well with his play. That confounded Basketball Prospectus' college analysts, who focused on his unimpressive stat line. Bledsoe's numbers were colored by playing shooting guard opposite Wall, a role that left him primarily a spot-up jump shooter. However, that makes it all the more troubling that he turned the ball over so frequently, and his projection suggests he'll be one of the league's most turnover-prone players.

Bledsoe's quickness will work in his favor. Like many young point guards, he will be more difficult to defend as a pro because of the limitations on hand-checking on the perimeter. Bledsoe's NBA Summer League experience suggests he will be able to get into the paint. Now, it's a matter of finishing those shots against bigger defenders. Bledsoe also must improve his playmaking. He's got the chance to earn the backup role behind Baron Davis if he plays well, though Randy Foye's presence means Bledsoe can watch and learn if he struggles.

SF 45	Rasual Butler	Hght: 6'7" Wght: 205 2011-12 status: free agent	Exp: 8 From: La Salle	Salary: $2.4 million		**SKILL RATINGS**						
					TOT	OFF	DEF	REB	PAS	HND	SHT	ATH
					-1	+1	+2	-5	-3	+2	+1	-4

Year	Team	Age	G	MPG	Usg	3PA%	FTA%	INS	2P%	3P%	FT%	TS%	Reb%	Ast%	TO%	BLK%	STL%	PF%	oRTG	dRTG	Win%	WARP
07-08	NOH	28.9	51	17.2	.151	.469	.048	.579	.370	.331	.839	.460	.068	.019	.035	.019	.008	.036	103.6	106.3	.408	-0.1
08-09	NOH	29.9	82	31.9	.169	.394	.053	.659	.468	.390	.782	.541	.063	.014	.065	.020	.010	.030	105.2	106.8	.448	1.7
09-10	LAC	30.9	82	33.0	.171	.427	.063	.636	.482	.336	.841	.524	.052	.020	.078	.019	.007	.020	104.3	107.1	.409	-0.5
10-11p	LAC	31.9	76	24.2	.147	.516	.054	.538	.453	.356	.796	.523	.056	.017	.067	.019	.008	.026	104.5	106.7	.427	0.4

Most similar to: Dennis Scott (97.1), Raja Bell, Morris Peterson, Wesley Person   IMP: 38%   BRK: 11%   COP: 2%

Picked up from New Orleans in a salary dump last summer, Rasual Butler quickly beat out incumbent Al Thornton for the starting job at small forward. He'll compete with Al-Farouq Aminu and Ryan Gomes to maintain the position this season. Butler is by far the best defensive option of the three, which makes him the best fit with the rest of the Clippers' starting lineup. He's very strong for a defensive specialist, more of a Ron Artest than a Bruce Bowen, and uses his long wingspan to contest shots. These tools have done less to help Butler on the glass, where he's a total non-factor.

On offense, Butler's value is pretty closely tied to his three-point percentage. When he's been around 33 percent, as in 2007-08 and last season, he's rated below replacement level. In between, Butler made 39 percent of his threes and was much more useful to the Hornets. SCHOENE sees Butler settling in between those two marks. According to Hoopdata.com, Butler was assisted on more than three-fourths of his field goals last season, so he's rarely doing any creating or almost any ballhandling. His role is strictly to hang around the perimeter and wait for open shots.

C #31 Jarron Collins

Hght: 6'11" Exp: 9 Salary: --
Wght: 249 From: Stanford
2011-12 status: free agent

SKILL RATINGS

TOT	OFF	DEF	REB	PAS	HND	SHT	ATH
-5	--	+3	--	--	--	--	--

Year	Team	Age	G	MPG	Usg	3PA%	FTA%	INS	2P%	3P%	FT%	TS%	Reb%	Ast%	TO%	BLK%	STL%	PF%	oRTG	dRTG	Win%	WARP
07-08	UTA	29.4	70	10.0	.087	.007	.238	1.231	.444	.000	.622	.515	.101	.024	.161	.007	.007	.069	101.5	108.2	.289	-1.9
08-09	UTA	30.4	26	7.7	.109	.000	.099	1.099	.457	.000	.727	.502	.110	.016	.184	.004	.005	.078	102.4	110.2	.265	-0.6
09-10	PHX	31.4	34	7.6	.089	.000	.212	1.212	.387	-	.400	.405	.133	.010	.192	.008	.004	.072	100.2	108.3	.251	-0.9
10-11p	LAC	32.4	76	-	.083	.006	.203	1.196	.394	.000	.469	.425	.112	.014	.177	.009	.005	.074	-	-	.278	-

Most similar to: Greg Kite (94.2), Marc Iavaroni, Paul Mokeski, Joe Wolf

IMP: 38% BRK: 12% COP: 27%

Because Alvin Gentry wanted to keep Channing Frye in a sixth man role when Robin Lopez was sidelined, Jarron Collins earned the distinction of being one of the worst players to start playoff games in league history. Lopez's return to the lineup pushed Collins back to the end of the bench, a more appropriate role at this stage of his career.

In fairness to Collins, our individual metrics fail to pick up his biggest strengths. He's excellent at defending the post and very good at taking charges. Still, the rest of Collins' game is so weak that he is a liability. He rarely shoots the basketball yet is still an inaccurate shooter. Collins is also a poor rebounder; last year's rebound percentage was the best of his career. As a result, Phoenix was 7.0 points worse per 100 possessions with Collins on the floor. If basketball offered a platoon system, he would have value, but it is too difficult to score playing 4-on-5 at the NBA level. Collins will attend training camp with the Los Angeles Clippers, where he will battle Jake Voskuhl for a possible spot for a third center.

PF #34 Brian Cook

Hght: 6'9" Exp: 7 Salary: $1.1 million
Wght: 250 From: Illinois
2011-12 status: player option or ETO for $1.3 million

SKILL RATINGS

TOT	OFF	DEF	REB	PAS	HND	SHT	ATH
-4	--	0	--	--	--	--	--

Year	Team	Age	G	MPG	Usg	3PA%	FTA%	INS	2P%	3P%	FT%	TS%	Reb%	Ast%	TO%	BLK%	STL%	PF%	oRTG	dRTG	Win%	WARP
07-08	ORL	27.4	51	12.4	.206	.407	.033	.625	.378	.374	.905	.489	.098	.020	.138	.014	.009	.067	103.7	107.0	.392	-0.3
08-09	HOU	28.4	30	5.7	.249	.327	.029	.701	.326	.433	.833	.470	.104	.014	.142	.013	.009	.071	102.4	107.9	.323	-0.3
09-10	HOU	29.4	15	2.9	.324	.281	.096	.815	.357	.222	.714	.403	.121	.010	.187	.033	.000	.051	95.6	105.8	.195	-0.2
10-11p	LAC	30.4	76	-	.194	.404	.028	.624	.371	.360	.926	.473	.088	.019	.140	.012	.010	.070	-	-	.314	-

Most similar to: Tracy Murray (96.1), Matt Bullard, Pat Garrity, Brian Scalabrine

IMP: 37% BRK: 14% COP: 11%

Brian Cook was a curious signing by the Clippers. He barely got off the bench in 2009-10 in Houston, yet still ended up with two years' worth of guaranteed money from L.A. (his second season is a player option). Cook's sole NBA-caliber skill is his shooting. He's developed NBA three-point range, which has helped him offer slightly more value. Still, Cook's lack of strength and athleticism make him a turnstile defensively and a major liability on the glass. The Clippers might have been better off bringing back Steve Novak, a superior shooter with similar weaknesses.

LOS ANGELES CLIPPERS

PG 1	Baron Davis	Hght: 6'3" Wght: 215 2011-12 status: guaranteed contract for $13.9 million	Exp: 11 From: UCLA	Salary: $13.0 million			SKILL RATINGS						
						TOT	OFF	DEF	REB	PAS	HND	SHT	ATH
						+4	+5	-2	+1	+3	+2	-3	+4

Year	Team	Age	G	MPG	Usg	3PA%	FTA%	INS	2P%	3P%	FT%	TS%	Reb%	Ast%	TO%	BLK%	STL%	PF%	oRTG	dRTG	Win%	WARP
07-08	GSW	29.0	82	39.0	.257	.270	.096	.826	.477	.330	.750	.523	.066	.082	.119	.010	.025	.033	109.2	104.9	.637	14.7
08-09	LAC	30.0	65	34.6	.254	.264	.074	.811	.406	.302	.757	.460	.062	.102	.155	.012	.025	.039	107.0	106.3	.521	4.9
09-10	LAC	31.0	75	33.6	.245	.219	.095	.876	.459	.277	.821	.501	.061	.108	.156	.013	.025	.038	108.2	105.6	.583	8.7
10-11p	LAC	32.0	74	34.0	.231	.298	.083	.785	.452	.310	.784	.499	.058	.099	.145	.014	.024	.039	108.2	105.4	.591	9.2

Most similar to: Isiah Thomas (96.7), Ray Williams, Derek Harper, Terrell Brandon   IMP: 46%   BRK: 3%   COP: 3%

Baron Davis bounced back from a forgettable first season with the L.A. Clippers, providing a solid season at the point. Davis' efficiency was good enough to be acceptable after his True Shooting Percentage was among the league's lowest in 2008-09. That allowed Davis' other contributions to shine through. His assist percentage ranked sixth in the NBA and his steal percentage made him useful at the defensive end of the floor despite inconsistent effort.

Davis is getting to the point in his career where he is going to have to begin adjusting. SCHOENE sees his game holding up well this season, but in the near future Davis will have to think about taking a backseat in the offense and focusing on his playmaking. Last year's reduced number of three-point attempts was also a positive. Davis is one of the few players in the league who shoots a lower effective field-goal percentage on threes (.416 last season) than twos. It's not just the threes off the dribble that are a problem; Davis is a very poor spot-up jump shooter.

PG 4	Randy Foye	Hght: 6'4" Wght: 213 2011-12 status: guaranteed contract for $4.3 million	Exp: 4 From: Villanova	Salary: $4.3 million			SKILL RATINGS						
						TOT	OFF	DEF	REB	PAS	HND	SHT	ATH
						0	+2	-4	-2	-1	0	-2	-3

Year	Team	Age	G	MPG	Usg	3PA%	FTA%	INS	2P%	3P%	FT%	TS%	Reb%	Ast%	TO%	BLK%	STL%	PF%	oRTG	dRTG	Win%	WARP
07-08	MIN	24.6	39	32.3	.205	.260	.050	.790	.436	.412	.815	.520	.060	.059	.139	.002	.013	.037	105.2	107.0	.440	0.6
08-09	MIN	25.6	70	35.6	.227	.246	.096	.849	.428	.360	.846	.517	.052	.055	.120	.008	.015	.037	106.1	107.7	.451	1.8
09-10	WAS	26.6	70	23.8	.213	.234	.082	.848	.442	.346	.890	.516	.045	.062	.121	.005	.010	.034	105.9	107.8	.441	0.8
10-11p	LAC	27.6	73	20.0	.206	.282	.078	.796	.438	.357	.871	.521	.046	.061	.124	.005	.012	.036	105.8	107.5	.443	0.8

Most similar to: DeShawn Stevenson (98.4), Johnny Davis, Gerald Wilkins, Bob Wilkerson   IMP: 43%   BRK: 7%   COP: 12%

The Washington Wizards became the second team to cut bait on Randy Foye within the last year and a half. When Minnesota did so, it was to get value in return--the Timberwolves acquired the No. 5 overall pick, which turned into Ricky Rubio, for Foye and Mike Miller. The Wizards merely decided to let Foye walk after one season in D.C., opting against making him a $4.8 million qualifying offer. Foye landed in Los Angeles, where he figures to be the Clippers' third guard and back up both spots in the backcourt.

Foye will turn 27 this season, so the potential that made him a lottery pick has expired. He hasn't made any progress in the last three seasons, settling in as a backup guard. While his shooting percentages have fluctuated, the resulting True Shooting Percentages have been consistently mediocre. That makes Foye the worst kind of tweener. He is a liability at either position (because of his playmaking as a point guard and his size as a two) who lacks the other skills to compensate.

LOS ANGELES CLIPPERS

SF 15	Ryan Gomes	Hght: 6'7" Wght: 245 2011-12 status: guaranteed contract for $4.0 million	Exp: 5 From: Providence	Salary: $4.0 million					
					SKILL RATINGS				
					TOT	OFF	DEF	REB	PAS	HND	SHT	ATH
					-1	+1	-4	0	0	0	0	-3

Year	Team	Age	G	MPG	Usg	3PA%	FTA%	INS	2P%	3P%	FT%	TS%	Reb%	Ast%	TO%	BLK%	STL%	PF%	oRTG	dRTG	Win%	WARP
07-08	MIN	25.6	82	29.7	.196	.170	.096	.926	.491	.330	.830	.539	.115	.027	.091	.003	.012	.029	105.6	106.1	.482	3.3
08-09	MIN	26.6	82	31.9	.205	.241	.067	.826	.456	.372	.807	.518	.089	.023	.108	.006	.012	.032	104.6	107.3	.413	-0.2
09-10	MIN	27.6	76	29.1	.175	.226	.063	.837	.475	.372	.825	.528	.089	.025	.108	.005	.014	.031	104.0	106.7	.413	-0.2
10-11p	LAC	28.6	75	23.0	.182	.263	.067	.804	.472	.368	.804	.528	.088	.025	.106	.005	.012	.031	104.1	106.6	.418	0.1

Most similar to: Tim Thomas (98.1), Lonnie Shelton, Lamond Murray, Chris Mills   IMP: 44%   BRK: 4%   COP: 6%

Ryan Gomes was the Clippers' other big addition in free agency as part of their effort to reunite the 2008-09 Timberwolves. Minnesota used Gomes' contract, which guaranteed him just $2.75 million over the next three seasons, as trade bait this summer. He landed temporarily in Portland before being waived. The Blazers effectively decided Gomes wasn't worth $11.6 million over the next three years, the difference between his total contract and the guaranteed portion. Naturally, the Clippers almost immediately offered Gomes $12 million over the same span.

An undersized four in college, Gomes has seen his game slowly drift to the perimeter since he entered the NBA. That's caused his free throw attempts to drop steadily. He got to the line on 13.8 percent of his plays as a rookie, and less than half of that (6.3 percent) a year ago. Without the freebies, Gomes has seen his True Shooting Percentage head downward, and he's also less effective as a rebounder. As a sophomore at Providence, Gomes nearly averaged a double-double. Now, he's not even an average rebounder for a small forward. The sum package makes Gomes nothing more than a stopgap as a starter. He'll likely back up Rasual Butler this season, with the future of the small forward position dependent on how quickly Al-Farouq Aminu gets up to speed.

SG 10	Eric Gordon	Hght: 6'3" Wght: 222 2011-12 status: guranteed contract for $3.8 million	Exp: 2 From: Indiana	Salary: $3.0 million					
					SKILL RATINGS				
					TOT	OFF	DEF	REB	PAS	HND	SHT	ATH
					+2	+3	-2	-5	+1	-1	+3	+2

Year	Team	Age	G	MPG	Usg	3PA%	FTA%	INS	2P%	3P%	FT%	TS%	Reb%	Ast%	TO%	BLK%	STL%	PF%	oRTG	dRTG	Win%	WARP
08-09	LAC	20.3	78	34.3	.209	.276	.126	.850	.496	.389	.854	.593	.044	.037	.135	.010	.015	.029	107.0	107.8	.474	3.2
09-10	LAC	21.3	62	36.0	.217	.303	.124	.821	.503	.371	.742	.571	.042	.038	.136	.005	.016	.020	105.8	107.0	.460	2.0
10-11p	LAC	22.3	72	36.0	.219	.259	.145	.886	.505	.377	.784	.588	.041	.042	.137	.008	.015	.023	106.7	106.8	.496	4.3

Most similar to: Jason Richardson (97.1), Ray Allen, Deron Williams, Jerry Stackhouse   IMP: 57%   BRK: 4%   COP: 4%

Eric Gordon essentially dropped a carbon copy of his rookie season in year two. The slight decline in his True Shooting Percentage and per-minute productivity can be traced largely to the difference in his free throw percentage. Otherwise, Gordon's first two seasons were highly similar. There are worse fates, but that makes it important that Gordon takes a step forward in his development this season. SCHOENE remains very optimistic about his future because of his combination of youth and shooting ability.

Gordon has the chance to be one of the league's best two-way shooting guards. On offense, he's got a diverse game and is effective scoring in a variety of manners--isolation plays, coming off of screens and spotting up on the perimeter. Gordon even handles the ball well enough that he could be a threat in pick-and-roll plays down the road. Defensively, Gordon is on the small side for a shooting guard. He's tough, however, and likes to get up in his man. His defensive numbers haven't quite caught up to his tools, but that should come with experience. It would also help if he grabbed a rebound every once in a while.

LOS ANGELES CLIPPERS

PF 32	Blake Griffin	Hght: 6'10" Wght: 251 2011-12 status: guranteed contract for $5.7 million	Exp: R From: Oklahoma	Salary: $5.4 million			**SKILL RATINGS**					
					TOT	OFF	DEF	REB	PAS	HND	SHT	ATH
					+4	+3	+3	+5	+3	-1	+4	+4

Year	Team	Age	G	MPG	Usg	3PA%	FTA%	INS	2P%	3P%	FT%	TS%	Reb%	Ast%	TO%	BLK%	STL%	PF%	oRTG	dRTG	Win%	WARP
10-11p	LAC	22.1	63	30.0	.221	.009	.156	1.146	.543	.325	.577	.564	.209	.029	.159	.017	.014	.049	106.4	104.3	.569	6.1

Most similar to: Kevin Love (96.7), Andrew Bogut, Carlos Boozer   IMP: -   BRK: -   COP: -

The upside of the timing of Blake Griffin's injury was that it gave him the entire offseason to ease his way back into live action, which should allow him to be ready to go by the time training camp begins. As a result, Griffin deserves to be considered the favorite for Rookie of the Year honors. Even a conservative projection in terms of playing time suggests he'll be the rookie leader in WARP next season, ahead of DeMarcus Cousins.

Griffin might see the lingering effect of his season away from the court in terms of his midrange jumper, which was already a work in progress before the injury. In time, Griffin should be able to develop reliable range out to the high post, which will allow him to operate more comfortably with Chris Kaman, but the perimeter shot is more likely to gather rust with the time off. The other area of Griffin's game worth watching is his defense, which was a weakness at Oklahoma. The Sooners asked Griffin to back off rather than risk foul trouble; the Clippers will want him to be more aggressive, within reason.

C 9	DeAndre Jordan	Hght: 6'11" Wght: 250 2011-12 status: free agent	Exp: 2 From: Texas A&M	Salary: $0.9 million			**SKILL RATINGS**					
					TOT	OFF	DEF	REB	PAS	HND	SHT	ATH
					0	-1	-4	+3	-4	-5	+5	0

Year	Team	Age	G	MPG	Usg	3PA%	FTA%	INS	2P%	3P%	FT%	TS%	Reb%	Ast%	TO%	BLK%	STL%	PF%	oRTG	dRTG	Win%	WARP
08-09	LAC	20.8	53	14.5	.140	.000	.203	1.203	.633	.000	.385	.585	.180	.007	.174	.057	.007	.057	103.3	103.7	.486	1.1
09-10	LAC	21.8	70	16.2	.148	.005	.152	1.147	.610	.000	.375	.571	.180	.008	.203	.040	.007	.061	102.8	104.7	.435	0.4
10-11p	LAC	22.8	76	18.0	.150	.005	.170	1.164	.617	.001	.375	.573	.173	.009	.189	.046	.007	.058	102.5	104.1	.443	0.8

Most similar to: Sean Williams (95.1), Tyson Chandler, Andris Biedrins, Kendrick Perkins   IMP: 52%   BRK: 9%   COP: 6%

Two years into his career, DeAndre Jordan remains all potential and no polish. After playing more minutes than the Clippers anticipated during his rookie season, Jordan was the team's third center much of last season. He ramped up his playing time after Marcus Camby was dealt to Portland and enters this year as the team's backup center, the first time he will be counted on to play a role for an extended period. Jordan will have to be more consistent than he has been thus far.

If Jordan can put it together mentally, the tools are there. He's demonstrated that in spurts during the regular season and on a more regular basis during NBA Summer League action. Thanks to a steady diet of dunks, Jordan should always be a high-percentage shooter. He made just four shots all season away from the rim, which was actually a major improvement after he did not make a single such shot in his entire rookie campaign. Defensively, Jordan tries to block everything, and this approach is about as effective as you'd imagine. The Clippers' Defensive Rating has been significantly worse with Jordan on the floor each of the last two seasons.

Jordan turned 22 over the summer and will be a free agent after this year, so it's about time he started to convert more of his potential into production.

C 35	Chris Kaman	Hght: 7'0" Wght: 265 2011-12 status: guaranteed contract for $12.2 million	Exp: 7 From: Central Michigan	Salary: $11.3 million			**SKILL RATINGS**					
					TOT	OFF	DEF	REB	PAS	HND	SHT	ATH
					0	-1	+4	+1	+2	-2	+1	-1

Year	Team	Age	G	MPG	Usg	3PA%	FTA%	INS	2P%	3P%	FT%	TS%	Reb%	Ast%	TO%	BLK%	STL%	PF%	oRTG	dRTG	Win%	WARP
07-08	LAC	26.0	56	37.2	.219	.004	.119	1.115	.486	.000	.762	.538	.197	.024	.167	.056	.007	.039	103.3	101.7	.552	5.9
08-09	LAC	27.0	31	29.7	.210	.000	.078	1.078	.528	.000	.680	.552	.157	.023	.199	.036	.009	.046	103.0	104.9	.434	0.3
09-10	LAC	28.0	76	34.3	.273	.004	.087	1.083	.492	.000	.749	.527	.157	.021	.143	.027	.007	.037	102.9	105.1	.428	0.6
10-11p	LAC	29.0	72	34.0	.223	.004	.086	1.082	.512	.001	.736	.542	.156	.023	.164	.036	.008	.041	103.0	104.4	.453	1.9

Most similar to: Herb Williams (97.4), Rony Seikaly, Jamaal Magloire, Dino Radja   IMP: 51%   BRK: 5%   COP: 4%

LOS ANGELES CLIPPERS

Someday, analysts will look back and wonder how Chris Kaman was an All-Star last season. Playing more than 36 minutes a night during the first half, Kaman put up 19.3 points and 9.8 rebounds per game, averages that looked impressive on paper. Yet he really wasn't much different as a player than the year before. Kaman's emergence as a go-to option on offense had predictable results. His usage went up while his True Shooting Percentage went down. To Kaman's credit, he also cut down on his turnovers, which was significant given how much more often he was handling the basketball. Playing alongside Marcus Camby, Kaman has grabbed fewer rebounds and blocked fewer shots the last two seasons, which explains a decline in his defensive value.

Kaman does have a very nice post game. He not only can score with either hand but is actually better with his off hand, the left, using strong footwork to create hooks and other makeable attempts in the paint. Blake Griffin's return should push Kaman to a more appropriate role after he got his chance to be a star. While the All-Star nod was a stretch, Kaman deserves a lot of credit for overcoming what was misdiagnosed as ADHD to become a consistent presence for the Clippers.

PF 5	Craig Smith	Hght: 6'7" Exp: 4 Salary: $2.3 million Wght: 250 From: Boston College 2011-12 status: free agent	SKILL RATINGS						
			TOT	OFF	DEF	REB	PAS	HND	SHT	ATH
			0	+2	+1	-1	+3	0	+4	+1

Year	Team	Age	G	MPG	Usg	3PA%	FTA%	INS	2P%	3P%	FT%	TS%	Reb%	Ast%	TO%	BLK%	STL%	PF%	oRTG	dRTG	Win%	WARP
07-08	MIN	24.4	77	20.1	.207	.013	.125	1.112	.572	.000	.665	.590	.134	.018	.126	.009	.011	.065	105.5	106.9	.452	1.1
08-09	MIN	25.4	74	19.7	.226	.001	.150	1.148	.563	.000	.677	.599	.115	.025	.144	.010	.011	.057	106.1	107.8	.447	0.9
09-10	LAC	26.4	75	16.4	.213	.009	.159	1.150	.574	.200	.635	.599	.135	.031	.153	.015	.014	.072	106.2	106.8	.482	1.7
10-11p	LAC	27.4	74	16.0	.202	.009	.147	1.138	.565	.102	.667	.596	.120	.028	.145	.011	.011	.065	105.4	107.1	.444	0.7

Most similar to: Reggie Slater (98.7), Kenny Gattison, Kenny Carr, J.R. Reid IMP: 37% BRK: 5% COP: 8%

Craig Smith was a nice value pickup for the Clippers last season and was the team's best reserve. The Rhino is a gifted scorer who uses his girth to power his way to the basket, where he finishes well. He's capable of using plays at an above-average rate, and his high field-goal percentages ensure his efficiency will stay high. Smith is limited to a part-time role because it is difficult to find good defensive matchups for him. Smith simply gives up too much size, which also hurts him on the defensive glass.

The Clippers ended up getting Smith back on a very reasonable one-year, $2.3 million deal to back up Blake Griffin. SCHOENE isn't optimistic about him aging well, but for now Smith remains the anchor of the young Los Angeles bench.

SG 13	Willie Warren	Hght: 6'4" Exp: R Salary: $0.5 million Wght: 203 From: Oklahoma 2011-12 status: non-guaranteed contract for $0.8 million	SKILL RATINGS						
			TOT	OFF	DEF	REB	PAS	HND	SHT	ATH
			-4	-1	-3	-4	+4	-2	-4	-2

Year	Team	Age	G	MPG	Usg	3PA%	FTA%	INS	2P%	3P%	FT%	TS%	Reb%	Ast%	TO%	BLK%	STL%	PF%	oRTG	dRTG	Win%	WARP
10-11p	LAC	21.5	76	5.0	.208	.207	.110	.903	.436	.271	.779	.491	.050	.057	.210	.000	.012	.048	102.5	108.2	.320	-0.8

Most similar to: Ramon Sessions (96.0), Maurice Williams, Jamal Crawford, Kirk Snyder IMP: - BRK: - COP: -

Until and unless he becomes a successful NBA player, Willie Warren will be the new poster child for players making a mistake by returning to college. Warren had lottery buzz after a strong freshman season that saw him serve as the perimeter counterpunch alongside Blake Griffin. With Griffin in the NBA, Warren had a disastrous sophomore campaign as the Sooners' leading man. He battled injuries, clashed at times with coach Jeff Capel and saw his efficiency fall across the board.

Warren has been advertised at times as a point guard, but his attack mindset is not ideal for the position. His skill set is better suited for a role handling the ball frequently while playing alongside a pass-first player. To make that work, Warren will have to shoot the ball more like he did as a freshman than as a sophomore, when his three-point percentage declined from 37.2 percent to 30.6 percent. Warren's comparables are impressive, but a more likely scenario sees him repeating Flip Murray's career.

LOS ANGELES CLIPPERS

PG	Bobby Brown	Hght: 6'2"	Exp: 2	Salary: --	SKILL RATINGS							
		Wght: 175	From: Cal State-Fullerton		TOT	OFF	DEF	REB	PAS	HND	SHT	ATH
--		2011-12 status: free agent			-2	+1	0	-4	0	-1	-3	-4

Year	Team	Age	G	MPG	Usg	3PA%	FTA%	INS	2P%	3P%	FT%	TS%	Reb%	Ast%	TO%	BLK%	STL%	PF%	oRTG	dRTG	Win%	WARP
08-09	MIN	24.6	68	13.7	.214	.294	.043	.749	.417	.346	.791	.476	.033	.057	.143	.002	.011	.046	104.5	109.1	.352	-1.3
09-10	LAC	25.6	45	11.5	.256	.338	.023	.684	.446	.265	.867	.441	.043	.078	.159	.001	.015	.037	103.9	107.8	.375	-0.4
10-11p	AVG	26.6	76	11.5	.233	.303	.031	.728	.455	.309	.843	.477	.038	.068	.143	.003	.013	.038	104.7	107.8	.400	-0.3

Most similar to: Jannero Pargo (98.7), Troy Hudson, Michael Holton, James Robinson   IMP: 62%   BRK: 11%   COP: 2%

During two NBA seasons, Bobby Brown has proven cruel to rims everywhere. Year two saw Brown actually manage to decline from one of the league's worst True Shooting Percentages, all the while using more than a quarter of his teams' plays while on the court. Brown inexplicably began the season ahead of Darren Collison in the New Orleans rotation before sanity was restored. He was dealt to his hometown Clippers in January, playing sparingly the rest of the way. Brown did show some improved playmaking in year two, but he has no hope of contributing in the NBA unless he makes dramatic strides in terms of his shot selection. Even then, he'd have to be far more efficient just to get to replacement level. Brown passed on a camp invite from Toronto to sign with Polish club Asseco Prokom.

SG	Mardy Collins	Hght: 6'6"	Exp: 4	Salary: --	SKILL RATINGS							
		Wght: 220	From: Temple		TOT	OFF	DEF	REB	PAS	HND	SHT	ATH
--		2011-12 status: free agent			-4	-2	+2	-1	+3	+1	-4	0

Year	Team	Age	G	MPG	Usg	3PA%	FTA%	INS	2P%	3P%	FT%	TS%	Reb%	Ast%	TO%	BLK%	STL%	PF%	oRTG	dRTG	Win%	WARP
07-08	NYK	23.7	46	13.8	.176	.129	.067	.938	.343	.250	.605	.378	.068	.063	.226	.010	.017	.041	99.8	106.0	.299	-1.6
08-09	LAC	24.7	48	18.5	.167	.095	.062	.967	.426	.419	.609	.470	.070	.057	.178	.008	.018	.041	102.7	107.2	.356	-1.1
09-10	LAC	25.7	43	10.9	.164	.100	.055	.954	.387	.235	.619	.404	.062	.043	.189	.002	.025	.044	99.3	106.4	.274	-1.4
10-11p	AVG	26.7	76	10.9	.162	.142	.058	.916	.402	.360	.628	.446	.063	.051	.184	.007	.021	.041	101.2	106.1	.338	-1.3

Most similar to: Milt Palacio (96.4), Anthony Johnson, Mitchell Butler, Scott Roth   IMP: 66%   BRK: 20%   COP: 0%

Mardy Collins is evidence that Isiah Thomas occasionally struck out on his draft picks in New York. At the completion of his rookie contract, Collins has yet to make any real progress or establish an NBA position. He's too slow and too weak a distributor to handle the point on a full-time basis, yet doesn't score or shoot well enough to justify minutes on the wing. Getting sucker-punched by Carmelo Anthony is likely to remain the defining moment of Collins' NBA career. A calf injury prevented him from accepting an invitation to the Wizards' training camp.

PG	JamesOn Curry	Hght: 6'3"	Exp: 1	Salary: --	SKILL RATINGS							
		Wght: 190	From: Oklahoma State		TOT	OFF	DEF	REB	PAS	HND	SHT	ATH
--		2011-12 status: free agent			-3	--	--	--	--	--	--	--

Year	Team	Age	G	MPG	Usg	3PA%	FTA%	INS	2P%	3P%	FT%	TS%	Reb%	Ast%	TO%	BLK%	STL%	PF%	oRTG	dRTG	Win%	WARP
09-10	LAC	24.3	1	1.0	.000	.000	.000	1.000	-	-	-	.000	.000	.000	.000	.000	.000	.000	97.4	109.2	.168	0.0
10-11p	AVG	25.3	76	--	.160	.385	.058	.673	.433	.379	.725	.521	.049	.050	.152	.009	.017	.040	-	-	.375	-

Most similar to: Sedale Threatt (98.7), Keyon Dooling, Michael Holton, Alvin Williams   IMP: 71%   BRK: 24%   COP: 5%

JamesOn Curry has the league's most unique 2009-10 stat line, since he was credited with playing zero minutes. Curry made his NBA debut on Jan. 25 at Boston and played just four seconds, which fits with a career that already has seen Curry spend an entire year on the roster of the Chicago Bulls without seeing action. In more extensive playing time at the D-League level, Curry has operated as a combo guard, but his translated statistics are nothing special. He may not make it back to the NBA.

LOS ANGELES CLIPPERS

Ricky Davis — SF

Hght: 6'6" | Exp: 12 | Salary: --
Wght: 196 | From: Iowa
2011-12 status: free agent

SKILL RATINGS

TOT	OFF	DEF	REB	PAS	HND	SHT	ATH
-3	0	-4	-4	+3	+2	-1	-4

Year	Team	Age	G	MPG	Usg	3PA%	FTA%	INS	2P%	3P%	FT%	TS%	Reb%	Ast%	TO%	BLK%	STL%	PF%	oRTG	dRTG	Win%	WARP
07-08	MIA	28.6	82	36.1	.201	.267	.069	.803	.447	.405	.787	.534	.072	.044	.153	.004	.014	.029	104.4	106.5	.431	0.9
08-09	LAC	29.6	36	21.8	.175	.370	.053	.683	.358	.315	.861	.445	.045	.048	.130	.005	.012	.037	103.4	108.2	.346	-1.1
09-10	LAC	30.6	36	13.9	.170	.226	.073	.847	.455	.381	.581	.504	.066	.036	.156	.004	.011	.036	102.3	107.4	.338	-0.8
10-11p	AVG	31.6	74	13.9	.169	.335	.061	.726	.427	.372	.678	.503	.063	.040	.153	.005	.012	.036	103.4	107.1	.379	-0.8

Most similar to: Tony Brown (97.0), Mike Sanders, Jaren Jackson, Bruce Bowen

IMP: 41% | BRK: 11% | COP: 13%

This looks like the end for Ricky Davis, who was waived by the Clippers at the trade deadline to make room for their new additions. Davis is just 30, but his game has declined noticeably the last couple of seasons, which saw him playing a bit role for the Clippers off the bench. A knee injury robbed Davis of what remained of the explosive athleticism that once made him special, forcing him to unsuccessfully rely on a shaky jumper. Davis finished the season in Turkey and is probably headed to Europe for good, since he carries too much baggage to be worth having around at the end of an NBA bench.

Kareem Rush — SG

Hght: 6'6" | Exp: 7 | Salary: --
Wght: 215 | From: Missouri
2011-12 status: free agent

SKILL RATINGS

TOT	OFF	DEF	REB	PAS	HND	SHT	ATH
-2	0	-3	-1	-3	-1	0	-5

Year	Team	Age	G	MPG	Usg	3PA%	FTA%	INS	2P%	3P%	FT%	TS%	Reb%	Ast%	TO%	BLK%	STL%	PF%	oRTG	dRTG	Win%	WARP
07-08	IND	27.5	71	21.2	.187	.404	.028	.624	.412	.389	.714	.501	.062	.026	.096	.010	.012	.031	103.5	106.3	.407	-0.3
08-09	PHI	28.5	25	8.0	.161	.473	.025	.552	.400	.303	1.000	.452	.046	.035	.143	.004	.013	.023	102.7	107.4	.347	-0.3
09-10	LAC	29.5	7	8.3	.110	.214	.000	.786	.375	.333	-	.409	.060	.031	.214	.038	.017	.063	99.4	105.3	.308	-0.1
10-11p	AVG	30.5	64	8.3	.182	.463	.023	.560	.407	.386	.721	.506	.062	.026	.101	.009	.012	.032	104.0	106.7	.412	0.0

Most similar to: Tracy Murray (98.2), Kevin Grevey, Dennis Scott, Matt Bullard

IMP: 40% | BRK: 12% | COP: 2%

Kareem Rush won a spot on the Clippers' roster in training camp, but before his season could get going he tore his right ACL in the middle of November. He was waived in January and should be back in time for the start of the season. Given that he was already fighting for his NBA life on year-to-year contracts, the injury might push Rush out of the league. It's hard to justify giving him a spot over a younger prospect, especially since Rush has never been an effective scorer. In seven NBA seasons, he's yet to manage a True Shooting Percentage of better than 50.5 percent. If Rush is to find a new home in the league, his best hope is the Phoenix Suns, who have shown a fondness for signing lesser NBA siblings (Jarron Collins, Taylor Griffin, Robin Lopez).

Los Angeles Lakers

For basketball fans who came of age in the late 1980s and 1990s, repeat NBA champions seem like something of a given. The '80s closed with the Los Angeles Lakers and Detroit Pistons each winning a pair of championships. The next decade saw the Chicago Bulls win their six titles three at a time, with the Houston Rockets interrupting the run to win back-to-back championships of their own, aided by Michael Jordan's efforts to hit curveballs.

The Los Angeles Lakers kicked off the 2000s with another Phil Jackson-helmed three-peat, but that was followed by seven years of teams failing to defend their titles, a stretch that reminded us that once upon a time repeating was an unthinkable prospect. From the end of the Boston Celtics' run in 1968-69 through the Lakers' title in 1987-88, the NBA never saw a single back-to-back champion. Before that drought of nearly two decades could be threatened, the Lakers successfully retained their title last June, outlasting Boston in a hard-fought seven-game NBA Finals for their second consecutive championship and the 16th in franchise history.

Even before the Finals, it wasn't always easy for the Lakers, who needed key offensive rebounds to finish three of their four playoff series. As has been typical for defending champions under Jackson, who has more experience with the task of repeating than any coach in pro sports history, the Lakers were not as effective during the regular season the second time around. In this case, L.A.'s eight-win drop from 65 victories in 2008-09 to just 57 in 2009-10 actually understated the magnitude of the team's decline.

To get to 57 wins, the Lakers needed a series of heroic scores in the closing seconds from star guard Kobe Bryant, who made six game-winning shots in the final 10 seconds of regulation or overtime. According to the Elias Sports Bureau, that was the most in a season for any player in the last decade. Los Angeles' point differential of +4.7 points per game ranked third in the conference and fifth in the league, yet the Lakers claimed the No. 1 seed in the West and wound up with home-court advantage throughout the playoffs when the Celtics bounced the two East teams with superior records.

During the first half of the season, the Lakers dealt with injuries, most notably the 17 games Pau Gasol missed with separate injuries to each of his hamstrings. The Lakers went 11-6 in those games, compensating for the hit to their offense by playing stout defense. That would be the theme throughout the regular season, even with Gasol healthy. The Lakers' Offensive Rating dropped from third in the league in 2008-09 to 11th in 2009-10, but they shaved nearly a point per 100 possessions off their Defensive Rating.

Still, the Lakers were underwhelming at best in the second half of the season. 32-9 at the turn, they won just 25 out of their last 41 games. More noteworthy was the complete absence of easy victories. After the All-Star break, just two of the Lakers' 16 wins were by double-digits, and one of those was by exactly 10 points.

LAKERS IN A BOX

Last year's record	57-25
Last year's Offensive Rating	110.4 (11)
Last year's Defensive Rating	105.3 (6)
Last year's point differential	4.7 (6)
Team pace	91.4 (14)
SCHOENE projection	46-36 (8)
Projected Offensive Rating	110.1 (16)
Projected Defensive Rating	108.2 (6)
Projected team weighted age	30.8 (3)
Projected '10-11 payroll	$93.2 (2)
Est. payroll obligations, '11-12	$93.3 (2)

Head coach: Phil Jackson

We've said this before, but 2010-11 looks like it could be the final lap of Jackson's legendary NBA coaching career. Jackson is hardly easing into retirement. With the departure of long-time assistant Kurt Rambis, he took on greater defensive responsibility last season, which was a factor in the Lakers' improvement at that end of the floor. As usual, Jackson's patient managerial style resulted in a few bumps along the road, but was ultimately rewarded with his record 11th NBA championship as a head coach.

It took Los Angeles four playoff games to shake the malaise and find a sense of urgency. That required the Oklahoma City Thunder tying the teams' first-round series at two wins apiece with an embarrassing 21-point smackdown at the Ford Center. The Lakers responded with their first blowout win in months, beating Oklahoma City by 24 points at home, and then closed out the series on Gasol's putback in the closing seconds of Game Six.

Starting with the last two games against the Thunder, the Lakers would play against type the rest of the postseason. Not only did they actually put some games away early, they went from being a defense-first squad to one that relied largely on its offense. This was especially true in the Western Conference Finals. After a four-game sweep of a Utah team that had no answer for Bryant, the Lakers and the Phoenix Suns engaged in an entertaining six-game shootout that saw both teams unable to stop each other. The Lakers got another key second-chance score, with Ron Artest rebounding Bryant's miss and connecting at the buzzer to win Game Five, then rode Bryant to a series-clinching road win.

The victory set up a rematch of the 2008 NBA Finals against a Boston team that had proven its mettle in series wins against Cleveland and Orlando. The teams traded victories through the first six games, setting up an epic deciding Game Seven at the Staples Center. Their nerves clearly affected by the game's magnitude, the Lakers came out erratic and only stayed in the game thanks to their rebounding dominance over the Celtics, who were playing without starting center Kendrick Perkins. When Boston went cold in the fourth quarter, the Lakers seized the opportunity. Another offensive rebound, this time by Gasol in the final minute, helped Los Angeles preserve an 83-79 victory and made the Lakers repeat champions.

Now, the Lakers go for three in a row, which would match Jackson's previous championship teams in Chicago and Los Angeles. Conventional wisdom holds that the biggest obstacle to another Lakers championship is the Miami Heat and its trio of star players. However, an equally problematic threat could be emerging from within: the Lakers' age. Since winning their first championship, the Lakers have systematically been replacing the younger players in their line-up with older ones.

At the start of the 2008-09 season, the Lakers had four young prospects: guards Jordan Farmar and Sasha Vujacic, small forward Trevor Ariza and center Andrew Bynum. Two are gone, while Vujacic no longer figures prominently in the Lakers' plans, leaving Bynum as the only one who panned out and stuck around. Despite their youth, Farmar and Vujacic both went backwards in their development after solid 2007-08 campaigns, and Farmar was not even tendered a qualifying offer by the Lakers this summer. He left for New Jersey and was replaced by veteran Steve Blake. The summer before, the Lakers were unwilling to accede to Ariza's desire for a lengthy contract at the full mid-level exception and instead signed Artest to serve as their small forward and top wing defender.

The Lakers added another 30-something later in free agency, signing Matt Barnes to back up Artest and Bryant. He'll take most of the minutes played by younger wings Vujacic and Shannon Brown. As a result, Los Angeles enters the season with only one player under 30 (Bynum) among the top eight in its rotation. Amazingly, the Lakers project as the league's third-oldest team in terms of effective age, trailing the Dallas Mavericks and the Celtics (Table 1).

Table 1: Oldest Projected Teams

Team	Age
Dallas Mavericks	31.5
Boston Celtics	30.9
L.A. Lakers	30.7
Phoenix Suns	30.2
Miami Heat	29.1

Other than Fisher, none of the players in the Lakers' rotation is ready to start thinking about retirement, but the moves do seem to be limiting their window. As core players inevitably start to decline due to age in their early 30s, the Lakers may see their talent base slowly but steadily erode. A pessimistic SCHOENE projection suggests that age may be a factor as soon as this season. Surprisingly, this is not because of Bryant, who turned 32 over the summer. Comparable players saw relatively little loss of production at the same age, though Bryant could be in for a sharper decline in years to come.

Instead, it's the Lakers' forwards whose projections are worrisome. Players similar to Artest, Gasol and Lamar Odom all saw their win percentage decline by at least 5.8 percent the next season. At the individual level, that may not make a huge difference--all three players will remain quality contributors, and Gasol should still be All-Star caliber--but when combined

From the Blogosphere

Who: Kurt Helin
What: Pro Basketball Talk
Where: http://probasketballtalk.nbcsports.com/

On a team loaded with veterans even your grandmother can name, a rookie could see real minutes for the Lakers this season. Derrick Caracter was drafted in the second round because of his NBA size and four-man skills, but there were questions about attitude and conditioning. During the NBA Summer League, the positives came through--he has good footwork and impressive scoring instincts inside. He rebounded and showed polish. He also brought the consistent effort, hanging with DeMarcus Cousins for three quarters in one game. With the Lakers looking to rest Andrew Bynum, Pau Gasol, Lamar Odom and others, Caracter could step into what was the Josh Powell role--getting mop-up minutes, but with the chance to earn some quality run if he plays well. He'll have to improve his conditioning--basically carve out a new body--but on a stacked Lakers team he could get more minutes than you would expect for a rookie.

---

with the fact that the Lakers have few players on the upswing, it's problematic.

The second important bit of context for the Lakers' projection is their aforementioned poor point differential. Start the Lakers at the baseline of 53.7 games they would have been expected to win based on their differential rather than the 57 they actually won and a low projection is much more reasonable.

The last issue facing the Lakers is one of regression to the mean. Specifically, they can't expect to defend the three-point line as well as they did a year ago. One of the league's worst teams at stopping threes in 2008-09 (when Rambis' defense called for aggressive ball pressure on the strong side and left shooters open if teams were able to successfully reverse the ball), the Lakers allowed the league's lowest three-point percentage in 2009-10 at 32.8 percent. Only one other team (Charlotte) kept opponents below 34 percent on threes.

This sounds like something to be celebrated, but in terms of projecting how the Lakers will play this season it is actually a negative. There is virtually no carry-over from year to year in terms of how teams defend three-pointers. Elite teams like the Lakers are little more likely than their ineffective counterparts to fare well in terms of opponent three-point percentage the following season. As a result, SCHOENE assumes everyone will defend threes equally. Had the Lakers been league average in terms of opponent three-point percentage a year ago, it would have cost them about a point and a half per game--a difference of four wins over the course of the season.

The more optimistic perspective holds that the Lakers finished last season as poorly as they did in large part because they wrapped up the top seed in the Western Conference early and had little incentive to play well down the stretch. Certainly, the Lakers team we saw for much of the postseason bore little resemblance to the one shown by the regular-season statistics. In particular, the Lakers were much more committed to moving the basketball and executing their triangle offense. Along with Fisher snapping out of a slump that started in the 2009 postseason and extended throughout the entire 2009-10 regular season, that made the Lakers a much more dangerous offensive outfit.

Under Jackson, the Lakers have a well-earned reputation for turning their effort level off and on within games and over the course of the season. What we might see in 2010-11 is a Lakers team that no longer has the same margin for error during the regular season and has to play closer to postseason level for all 82 games. Even before getting to a much-anticipated battle with the Heat in the NBA Finals, the Lakers will be tested--and just might see their bid for a three-peat come to an early end.

Kevin Pelton

LOS ANGELES LAKERS

LAKERS FIVE-YEAR TRENDS

Season	AGE	W-L	POW	PYTH	SEED	ORTG	DRTG	PT DIFF	PACE
05-06	25.1	45-37	47.8 (8)	48.2	7	109.8 (8)	106.9 (15)	2.5 (7)	89.8 (14)
06-07	25.3	42-40	42.5 (11)	40.8	7	110.0 (7)	110.5 (24)	-0.1 (12)	92.1 (7)
07-08	26.9	57-25	59.9 (2)	59.4	1	115.4 (3)	107.7 (6)	7.3 (3)	93.6 (6)
08-09	27.4	65-17	61.4 (3)	60.6	1	114.5 (3)	106.1 (5)	7.7 (2)	93.0 (6)
09-10	29.0	57-25	56.5 (3)	54.2	1	110.4 (11)	105.3 (6)	4.7 (6)	91.4 (14)

		OFFENSE				DEFENSE			
Season	PAY	eFG	oREB	FT/FGA	TO	eFG	oREB	FT/FGA	TO
05-06	$54.2	.495 (11)	.288 (8)	.245 (19)	.154 (10)	.486 (12)	.736 (9)	.242 (13)	.156 (21)
06-07	$62.3	.511 (4)	.261 (20)	.249 (13)	.166 (16)	.500 (17)	.723 (18)	.262 (20)	.157 (25)
07-08	$71.3	.525 (4)	.263 (19)	.256 (8)	.145 (9)	.485 (7)	.734 (15)	.214 (9)	.146 (17)
08-09	$78.2	.513 (6)	.294 (3)	.230 (20)	.142 (5)	.490 (8)	.729 (18)	.213 (6)	.166 (6)
09-10	$91.3	.496 (15)	.276 (7)	.221 (18)	.145 (5)	.484 (6)	.744 (9)	.195 (2)	.153 (19)

(league rankings in parenthesis)

SF 15 Ron Artest

Hght: 6'7" Exp: 11 Salary: $6.3 million
Wght: 260 From: St. John's
2011-12 status: guaranteed contract for $6.8 million

SKILL RATINGS

TOT	OFF	DEF	REB	PAS	HND	SHT	ATH
+1	+1	+5	-2	+3	+2	-1	+3

Year	Team	Age	G	MPG	Usg	3PA%	FTA%	INS	2P%	3P%	FT%	TS%	Reb%	Ast%	TO%	BLK%	STL%	PF%	oRTG	dRTG	Win%	WARP
07-08	SAC	28.4	57	38.1	.257	.178	.105	.926	.474	.380	.719	.534	.089	.041	.119	.014	.027	.033	106.8	104.0	.590	7.8
08-09	HOU	29.4	69	35.5	.247	.296	.089	.793	.402	.399	.748	.512	.083	.044	.108	.007	.022	.030	106.6	105.4	.540	6.3
09-10	LAL	30.4	77	33.8	.163	.314	.087	.773	.453	.355	.688	.514	.071	.040	.128	.006	.021	.028	105.1	105.7	.480	3.4
10-11p	LAL	31.4	75	32.0	.196	.321	.086	.765	.431	.372	.707	.513	.075	.039	.122	.008	.021	.032	104.9	105.4	.482	3.3

Most similar to: Bryon Russell (95.8), Doug Christie, Greg Ballard, Doc Rivers

IMP: 29% BRK: 3% COP: 13%

Ron Artest's entire career--his entire life, in fact--was just an elaborate setup for his reaction to winning a championship. Artest thanked his psychiatrist on national television before delivering an entertaining soliloquy on the postgame press conference dais. He then spent the night partying in full uniform. Artest deserved to celebrate after accepting a smaller role to help fit in with the Lakers. His usage rate was far and away the lowest of his career, and Artest rarely made news for the wrong reasons. Phil Jackson questioned Artest's fondness for three-point shots during the playoffs, but Artest responded with improved play and redeemed his bad shot selection in the final minute of Game Five of the Western Conference Finals with the game-winning putback.

The downside to Artest's subordinate place in the Lakers' offense was that it failed to help his efficiency. Artest saw his three-point percentage drop after two strong seasons, and his True Shooting Percentage remained well below league average. He'll likely see a rebound in his long-range shooting, but it's tempered by his age. Artest proved an upgrade over Trevor Ariza at the defensive end of the floor, where he delivered an outstanding season. Artest has compensated for losing a little quickness with his immense strength. He doesn't get enough credit for his ability to play tough, physical defense while rarely fouling. One odd Artest weakness: his rebounding has dropped off as he's aged, making him a liability on the glass.

LOS ANGELES LAKERS

SF 9 — Matt Barnes

Hght: 6'7" Exp: 7 Salary: $1.8 million
Wght: 226 From: UCLA
2011-12 status: guaranteed contract for $1.9 million

SKILL RATINGS

TOT	OFF	DEF	REB	PAS	HND	SHT	ATH
+1	+1	-3	+4	+3	+1	+1	-2

Year	Team	Age	G	MPG	Usg	3PA%	FTA%	INS	2P%	3P%	FT%	TS%	Reb%	Ast%	TO%	BLK%	STL%	PF%	oRTG	dRTG	Win%	WARP
07-08	GSW	28.1	72	19.5	.168	.323	.062	.739	.515	.293	.747	.511	.125	.042	.152	.019	.014	.048	105.4	105.1	.511	2.8
08-09	PHX	29.1	77	27.0	.183	.395	.069	.675	.505	.343	.743	.537	.115	.045	.150	.009	.012	.044	106.7	106.9	.494	3.4
09-10	ORL	30.1	81	25.9	.163	.282	.088	.805	.586	.319	.740	.576	.121	.030	.153	.011	.014	.041	105.7	105.5	.508	4.0
10-11p	LAL	31.2	76	20.0	.162	.382	.072	.690	.537	.318	.734	.535	.115	.034	.152	.012	.013	.046	104.9	105.9	.467	1.6

Most similar to: Rick Fox (97.7), Mario Elie, Vincent Askew, Ken Norman

IMP: 33% BRK: 0% COP: 15%

The NBA's small forward for hire, Matt Barnes will play for his fourth team in as many seasons, though a two-year contract will help Barnes get a little more comfortable in Los Angeles than he was in his previous stops. Barnes was very effective for the Orlando Magic as a starting small forward a year ago, posting a career-high True Shooting Percentage and providing consistently solid play. However, the Magic chose not to offer Barnes part of its mid-level exception, which was split between Chris Duhon and Barnes' replacement, Quentin Richardson. Barnes thought he was going to cash in as a free agent when he agreed to sign with Toronto for two years and $10 million before everyone realized the deal was impossible under the Collective Bargaining Agreement. That option off the table, Barnes chose the Lakers' offer over what was likely a more lucrative one from the Cleveland Cavaliers.

Barnes is an ideal role player because he's solid across the board. He's enough of a three-point shooter to keep defenses honest, is very effective in transition and is strong on the glass. Capable of defending either wing position, Barnes took the toughest defensive assignments for the Magic last season. He should fit in well for the Lakers. Phil Jackson's biggest challenge will be finding enough minutes for Barnes, who could see action at shooting guard or as a stretch power forward in addition to serving as Ron Artest's backup.

PG 5 — Steve Blake

Hght: 6'3" Exp: 7 Salary: $4.0 million
Wght: 172 From: Maryland
2011-12 status: guaranteed contract for $4.0 million

SKILL RATINGS

TOT	OFF	DEF	REB	PAS	HND	SHT	ATH
+2	+3	-1	-1	+2	+2	+1	-4

Year	Team	Age	G	MPG	Usg	3PA%	FTA%	INS	2P%	3P%	FT%	TS%	Reb%	Ast%	TO%	BLK%	STL%	PF%	oRTG	dRTG	Win%	WARP
07-08	POR	28.2	81	29.9	.154	.380	.036	.656	.408	.407	.766	.518	.048	.081	.145	.001	.011	.026	106.7	107.0	.492	3.8
08-09	POR	29.2	69	31.7	.171	.417	.042	.625	.429	.427	.840	.557	.050	.075	.136	.001	.017	.027	108.8	107.3	.545	5.9
09-10	LAC	30.2	80	27.0	.146	.438	.031	.593	.443	.395	.750	.539	.053	.083	.191	.002	.014	.027	106.8	107.1	.492	3.4
10-11p	LAL	31.2	75	28.0	.161	.451	.032	.581	.426	.391	.767	.528	.049	.078	.159	.003	.014	.027	106.8	106.9	.499	3.6

Most similar to: Howard Eisley (98.9), Sleepy Floyd, Chris Whitney, Sarunas Jasikevicius

IMP: 45% BRK: 6% COP: 9%

Dealt from Portland to the L.A. Clippers at the trade deadline, Steve Blake moved across town as a free agent, signing with the Lakers. Blake is a sound fit for a triangle offense and brings similar skills to those Derek Fisher has utilized in the triangle for the better part of the last decade. Blake is one of the league's better spot-up shooters, and he'll love the open looks opponents will be forced to give him at times because of the defensive attention drawn by the Lakers' stars.

The one red flag for Blake on offense is his turnover rate. He's never been a particularly sure ballhandler, and last season his turnovers jumped because Blake spent more time creating off the dribble while playing a traditional point guard role with the Clippers. Blake also won't solve the Lakers' issues defending point guards, though he should be an upgrade from Fisher in this role. The incumbent veteran might still start this season, but Blake will likely end up playing more minutes as the Lakers ease Fisher into retirement.

LOS ANGELES LAKERS

SG 12	Shannon Brown	Hght: 6'4"	Exp: 4	Salary: $2.3 million	SKILL RATINGS						
		Wght: 210	From: Michigan State || TOT	OFF	DEF	REB	PAS	HND	SHT	ATH
		2011-12 status: guaranteed contract for $2.3 million			0	+1	-1	-2	-1	-2	+1	+2

Year	Team	Age	G	MPG	Usg	3PA%	FTA%	INS	2P%	3P%	FT%	TS%	Reb%	Ast%	TO%	BLK%	STL%	PF%	oRTG	dRTG	Win%	WARP
07-08	CHI	22.4	21	11.5	.300	.184	.078	.894	.365	.300	.586	.411	.047	.031	.147	.010	.021	.054	98.0	106.5	.238	-0.9
08-09	LAL	23.4	48	9.9	.215	.168	.078	.910	.500	.378	.821	.554	.055	.037	.173	.011	.024	.041	103.9	106.3	.419	0.0
09-10	LAL	24.4	82	20.7	.188	.265	.075	.809	.474	.328	.818	.517	.060	.029	.094	.014	.017	.034	104.0	105.9	.436	0.7
10-11p	LAL	25.4	76	10.0	.201	.269	.077	.808	.482	.368	.822	.542	.057	.034	.125	.016	.018	.036	104.2	105.7	.452	0.6

Most similar to: Dion Glover (98.7), Todd Lichti, Mike Woodson, Lucious Harris IMP: 56% BRK: 12% COP: 7%

Shannon Brown parlayed his breakout effort in the 2009 playoffs into a spot in the rotation in 2009-10, more than tripling his previous career high in minutes played. Brown saw time at both guard positions and regularly finished games when Phil Jackson slid Kobe Bryant to small forward. At season's end, Brown opted out of his contract and ended up signing a new deal for similar money to stay with the Lakers.

Brown is the primary source of athleticism for the Lakers on the perimeter. He's a big-time leaper and one of the league's best in-game dunkers (a skill that did not translate when Brown participated in the Sprite Slam Dunk during All-Star Weekend), making him effective in transition. Brown is less dangerous in the half-court offense; he's a mediocre three-point shooter who lacks the ability to create easy shots for himself off the dribble. Brown was the Lakers' best defender off the bench and the team's best answer for big point guards.

Newcomers Steve Blake and Matt Barnes may usurp much of Brown's playing time. He'll be the ninth man in a rotation that may go just eight deep on some nights.

SG 24	Kobe Bryant	Hght: 6'6"	Exp: 14	Salary: $24.8 million	SKILL RATINGS						
		Wght: 205	From: Lower Merion HS (PA) || TOT	OFF	DEF	REB	PAS	HND	SHT	ATH
		2011-12 status: guaranteed contract for $25.2 million			+4	+5	+5	+1	+3	0	+1	+3

Year	Team	Age	G	MPG	Usg	3PA%	FTA%	INS	2P%	3P%	FT%	TS%	Reb%	Ast%	TO%	BLK%	STL%	PF%	oRTG	dRTG	Win%	WARP
07-08	LAL	29.7	82	38.9	.315	.183	.144	.961	.490	.361	.840	.576	.088	.061	.113	.009	.021	.031	111.3	104.7	.702	19.0
08-09	LAL	30.7	82	36.1	.323	.155	.114	.960	.496	.351	.856	.561	.081	.059	.097	.010	.020	.028	110.4	105.8	.647	14.2
09-10	LAL	31.7	73	38.8	.324	.148	.117	.969	.487	.329	.811	.545	.077	.058	.114	.005	.020	.030	108.4	105.5	.595	10.5
10-11p	LAL	32.7	74	39.0	.313	.161	.121	.960	.497	.352	.838	.565	.071	.056	.108	.008	.018	.030	108.8	105.8	.597	10.9

Most similar to: Vince Carter (97.5), Clyde Drexler, Alex English, Scottie Pippen IMP: 26% BRK: 0% COP: 0%

Kobe Bryant continues to build a résumé that will see him start to make some important history over the next few years. In February, Bryant passed Jerry West to become the all-time leading scorer in Lakers history. He's sure to move into the top 10 on the NBA scoring list this season if he stays healthy, and a 2,000-point season would push him to sixth in league history.

It's odd to speak of Bryant in such historic terms because he's still in the tail end of his prime. Bryant has seen his regular-season numbers fall since his MVP 2007-08 campaign. Bryant has had bigger goals in sight, though, and he's delivered exemplary postseason performances en route to a pair of championships and Finals MVP honors. Bryant was phenomenal in the middle two rounds of last year's Lakers run, torching Utah and Phoenix with better than 50 percent shooting from the field in both rounds. His matchup with the Boston defense in the NBA Finals was more even, and the Celtics held him to 6-of-24 shooting in Game Seven.

The second half of the season might have provided a preview of how Bryant will age. Bryant took fewer shots after the All-Star break and was more of a playmaker. This might be explained by the fact that he was playing through an avulsion fracture of the index finger on his shooting hand. Still, that ability to adapt his game will serve Bryant well as he begins to feel the gentle effects of aging.

LOS ANGELES LAKERS

C 17	Andrew Bynum	Hght: 7'0" Wght: 285	Exp: 5 From: St. Joseph HS (NJ)	Salary: $13.7 million							
		2011-12 status: guaranteed contract for $14.9 million									

SKILL RATINGS

TOT	OFF	DEF	REB	PAS	HND	SHT	ATH
+4	+3	+3	0	+2	0	+5	+1

Year	Team	Age	G	MPG	Usg	3PA%	FTA%	INS	2P%	3P%	FT%	TS%	Reb%	Ast%	TO%	BLK%	STL%	PF%	oRTG	dRTG	Win%	WARP
07-08	LAL	20.5	35	28.8	.176	.000	.130	1.130	.636	.000	.695	.659	.193	.027	.130	.051	.005	.043	107.9	102.7	.665	5.2
08-09	LAL	21.5	50	28.9	.208	.000	.139	1.139	.560	.000	.707	.598	.155	.022	.125	.048	.006	.048	107.1	104.8	.575	4.8
09-10	LAL	22.5	65	30.4	.209	.001	.125	1.124	.571	.000	.739	.608	.153	.015	.125	.036	.009	.044	106.4	104.4	.566	6.2
10-11p	LAL	23.5	72	30.0	.217	.006	.127	1.121	.584	.013	.729	.615	.152	.023	.125	.041	.008	.041	106.7	104.0	.587	7.7

Most similar to: Yao Ming (96.6), Al Jefferson, Hakeem Olajuwon, Stanley Roberts   IMP: 63%   BRK: 0%   COP: 3%

A healthy Andrew Bynum in the middle was a key reason the Lakers were improved at the defensive end in 2009-10, and the meniscus tear that limited him in the postseason helps explain why the team slipped on defense. Bynum doesn't block a ton of shots--his block rate was equal to Pau Gasol's last season--but his sheer size is a deterrent to opponents in the paint. Bynum commits few fouls for a center and is strong on the defensive glass.

Bynum's size is also an asset on the offensive end, where smaller defenders can be overmatched trying to keep him out of the paint. Bynum has used plays at an above-average rate on a team with multiple other offensive options, and he's done it while shooting high percentages from the field. It helps Bynum that he's a good free throw shooter, cashing in when opponents have to resort to fouling him.

The big issue for Bynum remains health. He's suffered a variety of injuries to his knees, and behemoths of Bynum's size often have a tough time staying in the lineup. The tear of his lateral meniscus is the latest injury to sideline Bynum. He underwent arthroscopic surgery in late July, but because of the location of the meniscus injury, Bynum's recovery will be slow. On media day, he told reporters that he hopes to be back on the court by late November. The Lakers will badly miss him during his absence.

PF 45	Derrick Caracter	Hght: 6'9" Wght: 265	Exp: R From: Texas-El Paso	Salary: $0.5 million							
		2011-12 status: non-guaranteed contract for $0.7 million									

SKILL RATINGS

TOT	OFF	DEF	REB	PAS	HND	SHT	ATH
-5	-2	-2	0	-1	-5	-2	0

Year	Team	Age	G	MPG	Usg	3PA%	FTA%	INS	2P%	3P%	FT%	TS%	Reb%	Ast%	TO%	BLK%	STL%	PF%	oRTG	dRTG	Win%	WARP
10-11p	LAL	23.0	76	2.8	.192	.030	.095	1.065	.459	.219	.658	.497	.129	.018	.207	.018	.013	.071	100.8	106.7	.311	-0.5

Most similar to: David Lee (96.3), Jamaal Magloire, Paul Davis, Brandon Hunter   IMP: -   BRK: -   COP: -

A big-time recruit, Derrick Caracter washed out at Louisville when he was ruled academically ineligible after a series of suspensions. Caracter landed at UTEP, where he became eligible midway through last season. Producing far more consistently than he ever had at Louisville, Caracter helped lead the Miners into the NCAA Tournament. Having already spent four years in college, Caracter opted for the draft and was taken by the Lakers in the second round.

The opportunity is there for Caracter in L.A. He'll battle Theo Ratliff for the role of fourth big man, and while the Lakers are covered up front with their three-man rotation of Andrew Bynum, Pau Gasol and Lamar Odom, Bynum's late start to the season means the Lakers will need another big man to step into the rotation. Caracter's translation is hardly encouraging. He'll need to improve his efficiency around the basket and become more effective as a rebounder. The more optimistic perspective comes from the NBA Summer League, where Caracter used his enormous frame to control the paint.

SF 3	Devin Ebanks	Hght: 6'9" Wght: 215	Exp: R From: West Virginia	Salary: $0.5 million							
		2011-12 status: non-guaranteed contract for $0.7 million									

SKILL RATINGS

TOT	OFF	DEF	REB	PAS	HND	SHT	ATH
-4	-1	0	+4	+2	0	-5	-1

Year	Team	Age	G	MPG	Usg	3PA%	FTA%	INS	2P%	3P%	FT%	TS%	Reb%	Ast%	TO%	BLK%	STL%	PF%	oRTG	dRTG	Win%	WARP
10-11p	LAL	21.5	76	5.0	.156	.053	.110	1.057	.413	.089	.754	.457	.120	.032	.162	.010	.012	.033	101.7	106.0	.357	-0.5

Most similar to: Marcus A. Williams (96.7), Bill Walker, Jeff Green, Mike Miller   IMP: -   BRK: -   COP: -

LOS ANGELES LAKERS

Despite helping his West Virginia team to the Final Four, Devin Ebanks saw his draft stock plummet during his sophomore season. Ebanks' lack of development on offense troubled scouts, and he went from possible lottery pick to eventual second-round selection when he declared for the draft. It's easy to see how Ebanks could fail in the NBA. He was challenged by the college three-point line, which means defenses will be able to sag off him and keep him from getting to the basket. That will make it hard for Ebanks to be any kind of offensive threat in the half court.

Ebanks should have a much easier adjustment at the defensive end. He's got an NBA body, including a 7-foot wingspan. Ebanks was a key part of an athletic Mountaineers defense that gave Kentucky fits in the NCAA Tournament, and he's got stopper potential if he puts his mind to being an elite defender. Ebanks is also a plus on the glass and a quality transition player. Comparisons with Trevor Ariza are inevitable, because Ariza's skill set was very similar when he came out of UCLA early and was drafted in the second round. If Ebanks puts in the work Ariza did to get better, his potential is enormous.

PG 2	Derek Fisher		Hght: 6'1" Wght: 210 2011-12 status:	Exp: 14 From: Arkansas-Little Rock guaranteed contract for $3.4 million		Salary: $1.8 million								**SKILL RATINGS**						
														TOT	OFF	DEF	REB	PAS	HND	SHT	ATH
														-2	0	-3	-4	-3	+1	-3	-2
Year	Team	Age	G	MPG	Usg	3PA%	FTA%	INS	2P%	3P%	FT%	TS%	Reb%	Ast%	TO%	BLK%	STL%	PF%	oRTG	dRTG	Win%	WARP
07-08	LAL	33.7	82	27.4	.187	.291	.087	.796	.453	.406	.883	.556	.041	.047	.095	.001	.017	.037	106.0	106.9	.472	2.6
08-09	LAL	34.7	82	29.8	.148	.370	.070	.700	.446	.397	.846	.546	.043	.047	.088	.002	.019	.034	106.3	107.3	.469	2.7
09-10	LAL	35.7	82	27.2	.140	.323	.084	.761	.401	.348	.856	.499	.042	.041	.112	.003	.021	.041	103.8	106.7	.405	-0.6
10-11p	LAL	36.7	76	25.0	.147	.309	.084	.775	.408	.349	.869	.505	.041	.045	.115	.003	.018	.042	103.8	107.1	.391	-1.0
Most similar to: David Wesley (98.0), John Starks, Tyrone Corbin, Derek Harper																	IMP: 32%		BRK: 10%		COP: 10%	

Derek Fisher's 2009-10 season was essentially his 2008-09 in reverse. The shooting slump that began in the 2009 postseason continued throughout the entire regular season (by which point, presumably, it ceased to become a slump and became the new reality). This time around, Fisher bounced back in the playoffs, making 36.0 percent of his threes and an improbable 50.9 percent of his shots inside the arc. Once again, Fisher delivered in a key moment, scoring 11 crucial points in the fourth quarter of Game Three of the NBA Finals, highlighted by an end-to-end layup that might have been the least likely score of the season.

At age 36, Fisher is unlikely to see his shooting numbers rebound much. As an undersized point guard with little remaining athleticism, he's one of the league's worst finishers, so his best hope is a return to form beyond the arc. Fisher is also an enormous defensive liability in most matchups, though he plays better against shooting guards and did a credible job against Ray Allen in the Finals.

After some retirement talk, Fisher signed a new three-year contract. Expect him to gradually give up more minutes and responsibility to Steve Blake.

PF 16	Pau Gasol		Hght: 7'0" Wght: 250 2011-12 status:	Exp: 9 From: Barcelona, Spain guaranteed contract for $18.7 million		Salary: $17.8 million								**SKILL RATINGS**						
														TOT	OFF	DEF	REB	PAS	HND	SHT	ATH
														+4	+3	0	+2	+5	+4	+3	0
Year	Team	Age	G	MPG	Usg	3PA%	FTA%	INS	2P%	3P%	FT%	TS%	Reb%	Ast%	TO%	BLK%	STL%	PF%	oRTG	dRTG	Win%	WARP
07-08	LAL	27.8	66	35.6	.221	.014	.136	1.122	.539	.250	.807	.594	.129	.040	.106	.030	.006	.026	107.4	104.6	.592	8.6
08-09	LAL	28.8	81	37.0	.205	.001	.138	1.137	.567	.500	.781	.617	.146	.042	.113	.021	.009	.025	109.3	105.5	.623	12.9
09-10	LAL	29.8	65	37.0	.215	.004	.139	1.135	.539	.000	.790	.593	.170	.041	.125	.035	.008	.028	108.8	103.7	.663	12.3
10-11p	LAL	30.8	73	37.0	.209	.007	.129	1.122	.533	.177	.782	.584	.143	.041	.119	.028	.007	.028	107.0	104.7	.575	9.0
Most similar to: Brad Miller (96.8), Larry Nance, Kevin McHale, Mychal Thompson																	IMP: 24%		BRK: 0%		COP: 10%	

Any remaining vestige of the notion that Pau Gasol's softness is a problem for the Lakers was eradicated when Gasol outplayed Kevin Garnett, his nemesis during the 2008 Finals, in last spring's rematch. Gasol was the best player on the floor in the deciding game, grabbing 18 rebounds. After moving past early hamstring issues, Gasol put together another excellent season, grabbing a career-high 17.0 percent of all available rebounds. He also improved his block rate as compared to his first two years with the Lakers.

Gasol has established himself as the league's most skilled post player, and on another team he'd have the ability to be a dominant low-block scorer who touched the ball on virtually every possession. Getting the ball in Gasol's hands is always a good idea because he is a fine decision-maker with the court vision to find teammates. Often, Gasol's best decision is to keep the ball himself and set up a hook he shoots accurately with either hand. SCHOENE does suggest we've already seen the best of Gasol, especially on the glass.

PF 7	Lamar Odom	Hght: 6'10" Wght: 230 2011-12 status: guaranteed contract for $8.9 million	Exp: 11 From: Rhode Island	Salary: $8.2 million		**SKILL RATINGS**						
					TOT	OFF	DEF	REB	PAS	HND	SHT	ATH
					+2	+1	+5	+3	+5	+4	0	+1

Year	Team	Age	G	MPG	Usg	3PA%	FTA%	INS	2P%	3P%	FT%	TS%	Reb%	Ast%	TO%	BLK%	STL%	PF%	oRTG	dRTG	Win%	WARP
07-08	LAL	28.5	77	37.9	.166	.103	.132	1.029	.566	.274	.698	.582	.153	.041	.142	.018	.011	.033	105.9	104.3	.553	8.3
08-09	LAL	29.5	78	29.7	.182	.108	.119	1.011	.522	.320	.623	.542	.155	.039	.145	.033	.017	.045	105.9	104.1	.559	6.9
09-10	LAL	30.5	82	31.5	.170	.186	.091	.905	.510	.319	.693	.533	.173	.046	.153	.017	.015	.040	106.0	103.9	.569	8.2
10-11p	LAL	31.5	76	30.0	.164	.140	.097	.958	.508	.314	.665	.530	.153	.043	.152	.021	.014	.042	104.6	104.3	.510	4.5

Most similar to: Mychal Thompson (97.5), Brad Miller, P.J. Brown, Maurice Lucas   IMP: 29% BRK: 0% COP: 10%

The unsung hero of the Lakers' back-to-back championships, Lamar Odom was once again reliable for the Lakers as both a starter and a reserve. Because of injuries to Andrew Bynum and Pau Gasol, he split his regular season almost evenly between the two roles before coming off the bench throughout the postseason. A quality rebounder who peaked on the glass last year, Odom is an underrated defender with the ability to handle a variety of challenging matchups. The Lakers have been noticeably better on defense with Odom on the floor each of the last three seasons.

At the offensive end, the southpaw is solid from midrange but has never been able to consistently hit from beyond the arc, which has limited his True Shooting Percentage. Odom's three-point attempts nearly doubled last season while he got to the foul line less frequently, a bad recipe for his efficiency. Still, Odom's ability to handle the basketball on the perimeter and find teammates makes him a productive cog in the triangle offense.

C 50	Theo Ratliff	Hght: 6'10" Wght: 235 2011-12 status: free agent	Exp: 15 From: Wyoming	Salary: $0.9 million		**SKILL RATINGS**						
					TOT	OFF	DEF	REB	PAS	HND	SHT	ATH
					-3	-2	-1	-3	-4	-3	-3	-1

Year	Team	Age	G	MPG	Usg	3PA%	FTA%	INS	2P%	3P%	FT%	TS%	Reb%	Ast%	TO%	BLK%	STL%	PF%	oRTG	dRTG	Win%	WARP
07-08	DET	35.0	26	16.7	.136	.008	.151	1.143	.488	.000	.674	.534	.122	.015	.168	.069	.008	.065	101.9	103.4	.447	0.3
08-09	PHI	36.0	46	12.6	.074	.000	.165	1.165	.531	.000	.600	.560	.133	.007	.150	.066	.015	.061	102.3	103.6	.455	0.5
09-10	CHA	37.0	49	16.5	.124	.000	.102	1.102	.461	-	.760	.511	.116	.014	.191	.060	.008	.050	101.2	104.2	.400	-0.3
10-11p	LAL	38.0	76	5.0	.104	.003	.120	1.116	.456	.000	.679	.496	.113	.011	.187	.063	.010	.064	100.5	103.9	.385	-0.2

Most similar to: Alton Lister (97.1), Herb Williams, Dikembe Mutombo, Caldwell Jones   IMP: 36% BRK: 0% COP: 21%

Theo Ratliff experienced an abrupt change of fortune at midseason. Having been buried in San Antonio by a deep frontcourt rotation, Ratliff was dealt to Charlotte and became the Bobcats' starting center down the stretch. Reunited with his former coach in Philadelphia, Larry Brown, Ratliff anchored a defense that finished the season as the league's best. Nearing age 40, Ratliff is still one of the league's better shot blockers thanks to his long arms and excellent timing.

Offensively, Ratliff was never much more than passable, and now he's a liability. Age has caught up to him on the glass as well. That's why the starting job was a stretch. Ratliff will be back in a more appropriate role this season after signing with the Lakers as a free agent. He'll battle Derrick Caracter for the job of fourth big man and could see some spot minutes as a defensive specialist.

LOS ANGELES LAKERS

SG 18	Sasha Vujacic	Hght: 6'7" Wght: 205 2011-12 status: free agent	Exp: 6 From: Maribor, Slovenia	Salary: $5.5 million	SKILL RATINGS						
					TOT	OFF	DEF	REB	PAS	HND	SHT	ATH
					0	--	-4	--	--	--	--	--

Year	Team	Age	G	MPG	Usg	3PA%	FTA%	INS	2P%	3P%	FT%	TS%	Reb%	Ast%	TO%	BLK%	STL%	PF%	oRTG	dRTG	Win%	WARP
07-08	LAL	24.1	72	17.8	.198	.470	.070	.599	.476	.437	.835	.605	.065	.025	.091	.003	.012	.037	107.5	106.8	.523	2.9
08-09	LAL	25.1	80	16.2	.160	.475	.071	.596	.416	.363	.921	.531	.058	.039	.075	.004	.030	.052	106.8	106.3	.516	2.7
09-10	LAL	26.1	67	8.6	.153	.414	.074	.660	.494	.309	.848	.518	.077	.032	.087	.005	.018	.052	106.0	107.1	.466	0.6
10-11p	LAL	27.1	76	--	.169	.553	.071	.518	.479	.358	.885	.555	.065	.034	.085	.004	.020	.049	--	--	.445	--

Most similar to: Tim Legler (97.7), Lucious Harris, Trent Tucker, Anthony Peeler   IMP: 57%   BRK: 10%   COP: 7%

Sasha Vujacic had a memorable postseason, though not really because of his own production. After returning from a severe ankle sprain that sidelined him the first two rounds, Vujacic harassed Goran Dragic during the Western Conference Finals. The rivalry between the two Slovenians was evidently personal and may have had its roots in Vujacic being cut from his national team last summer before the European Championships. The feisty back-and-forth thrust The Machine back into the NBA nation's collective consciousness, though he was a bit player during the Lakers' run.

Before the playoffs, Vujacic's season was most memorable for a run-in with Assistant Coach Brian Shaw that led to his benching. Vujacic hasn't played well enough to justify the extracurricular activities. Since he made 43.7 percent of his threes in 2007-08, Vujacic has been far less efficient. As a shooter first and foremost, Vujacic has to make shots. He figures to be the odd man out of a suddenly crowded Lakers perimeter rotation, and the team would gladly trade him to reduce its luxury-tax bill if the right deal materialized.

SF 4	Luke Walton	Hght: 6'8" Wght: 235 2011-12 status: guaranteed contract for $5.7 million	Exp: 7 From: Arizona	Salary: $5.3 million	SKILL RATINGS						
					TOT	OFF	DEF	REB	PAS	HND	SHT	ATH
					-2	--	+2	--	--	--	--	--

Year	Team	Age	G	MPG	Usg	3PA%	FTA%	INS	2P%	3P%	FT%	TS%	Reb%	Ast%	TO%	BLK%	STL%	PF%	oRTG	dRTG	Win%	WARP
07-08	LAL	28.1	74	23.4	.160	.134	.077	.942	.475	.333	.706	.509	.092	.056	.160	.007	.015	.034	104.1	105.8	.443	0.9
08-09	LAL	29.1	65	17.9	.152	.142	.063	.920	.468	.298	.719	.491	.087	.067	.172	.007	.014	.040	104.8	107.3	.419	0.1
09-10	LAL	30.1	29	9.4	.162	.174	.018	.844	.343	.412	.500	.402	.078	.066	.123	.003	.019	.031	103.3	106.4	.396	-0.1
10-11p	LAL	31.1	68	--	.151	.205	.040	.835	.401	.383	.614	.456	.083	.062	.145	.006	.016	.036	--	--	.403	--

Most similar to: Eric Williams (96.7), Bill Hanzlik, Ernie Grunfeld, Billy Owens   IMP: 44%   BRK: 8%   COP: 3%

A pinched nerve in Luke Walton's lower back required a surgical procedure (a facet rhizotomy) and limited him to just 29 games during the regular season. He was active throughout the postseason and played 16 games, though only limited minutes. Walton's production has slid each of the last two seasons, and last year's numbers reflect a player who was never healthy. It's not clear that Walton will ever be 100 percent again. Having added Matt Barnes and Devin Ebanks, the Lakers no longer have to count on Walton. Still, he can contribute in a spot role by coming in to get the team into the triangle when its execution is off. That has always been the strength of Walton's game.

C --	DJ Mbenga	Hght: 7'0" Wght: 255 2011-12 status: free agent	Exp: 6 From: Kinshasa, DRC	Salary: --	SKILL RATINGS						
					TOT	OFF	DEF	REB	PAS	HND	SHT	ATH
					-3	-2	0	-2	-3	-3	-2	-3

Year	Team	Age	G	MPG	Usg	3PA%	FTA%	INS	2P%	3P%	FT%	TS%	Reb%	Ast%	TO%	BLK%	STL%	PF%	oRTG	dRTG	Win%	WARP
07-08	LAL	27.3	42	7.7	.138	.000	.052	1.052	.464	.000	.417	.465	.122	.014	.118	.058	.009	.095	101.0	105.1	.362	-0.4
08-09	LAL	28.3	23	7.9	.179	.014	.048	1.034	.482	.000	.875	.504	.096	.022	.177	.102	.028	.080	100.8	101.0	.493	0.3
09-10	LAL	29.3	49	7.2	.160	.000	.066	1.066	.466	--	.474	.471	.137	.010	.119	.062	.007	.068	101.4	104.3	.403	-0.1
10-11p	AVG	30.3	76	7.3	.148	.002	.057	1.055	.473	.000	.471	.477	.125	.012	.127	.058	.008	.077	101.0	104.9	.369	-0.5

Most similar to: Calvin Booth (97.3), Adonal Foyle, Duane Causwell, Clemon Johnson   IMP: 48%   BRK: 10%   COP: 6%

As the Lakers' third center the last three seasons, DJ Mbenga's playing time has strictly depended on the injuries ahead of him in the frontcourt. In 2009-10, Mbenga played a career-high 49 games. His production was essentially the same as it's always been. Mbenga is a strong shot blocker, but none of his other skills are even NBA average. Mbenga is a non-factor on offense and a subpar rebounder for a 7-footer. Mbenga won't hurt a team too badly, but the Lakers had the chance to upgrade and did so with the addition of Theo Ratliff. Mbenga will search for another home for training camp.

Memphis Grizzlies

"We're committed to putting a contending team on the floor," Heisley said, "and the target is three years. I'm looking for--three years from today Memphis to have a team than contends and then turning that team into a team that competes for championships."

Grizzlies owner Michael Heisley to the *Commercial Appeal* on June 29, 2008.

Year three is here. Can the Grizzlies take the next step? If there are to be further gains, where will they come from?

Pro Basketball Prospectus was considerably more bullish on the Grizzlies last season, despite the usual refrain that Memphis was just a team that wouldn't spend enough money to compete. We projected the Grizzlies to have a big bump in the win column. They did just that, though there are still developmental concerns surrounding a number of their young players. And almost all their players are young, as Memphis projects to have a weighted average age of 25.3 years old, 26th in the NBA.

The main thing that went right for Memphis, however, concerned a veteran. Power forward Zach Randolph enjoyed the best season of his career. He played hard and focused his game on what he does well, pushing some of the inefficient parts of his arsenal to the wayside in the process. His big-man counterpart, Marc Gasol, morphed into a top-10 center, giving the Grizzlies a dynamic offensive rebounding duo on the interior to go with an exciting troop of high-wire walkers on the perimeter. Under promising coach Lionel Hollins, the Grizzlies jumped from 28th to 17th in Offensive Rating despite finishing 18th in effective field-goal percentage and 24th in turnover rate. Memphis was able to overcome these deficiencies thanks to the league's best offensive rebound rate.

Unfortunately, a heavy emphasis on second shots can have an adverse effect on team defense, especially in transition. Despite so many athletic, young legs, the Grizzlies gave up the sixth-highest rate of transition opportunities in the league and only the Timberwolves allowed a higher average of points per play on such possessions. Overall, Memphis sank to 24th in Defensive Rating. Worse, the team seemed to recognize this potential shortcoming before the season, when Memphis spent its three draft picks on defensive-minded players, headlined by ultra-long center Hasheem Thabeet. It's too soon to draw firm conclusions, but it seems like the Grizzlies were more miss than hit on those picks.

Thabeet couldn't get on the court and when he did, he appeared to be a one-trick pony. He even spent time the D-League, becoming the highest-drafted player ever to spend time in that circuit. His block rate was predictably astronomical, but he rated in the bottom fifth in the league defensively in points allowed per play in key areas like

GRIZZLIES IN A BOX

Last year's record	40-42
Last year's Offensive Rating	109.1 (17)
Last year's Defensive Rating	112.1 (24)
Last year's point differential	-1.5 (17)
Team pace	92.3 (8)
SCHOENE projection	39-43 (11)
Projected Offensive Rating	110.5 (14)
Projected Defensive Rating	111.3 (22)
Projected team weighted age	25.3 (26)
Projected '10-11 payroll	$60.1 (20)
Est. payroll obligations, '11-12	$48.8 (23)

Head coach: Lionel Hollins

Lionel Hollins enjoyed a new experience last fall: overseeing a training camp as head coach. Previously, Hollins had taken over the Grizzlies on an interim basis at midseason on three separate occasions. Memphis gave Hollins the job on a full-time basis last summer and he delivered a 16-game increase in the team's win total. Hollins relied heavily on his starting lineup, which played more minutes than any other fivesome in the league. The Memphis second unit was far less successful, so one of the keys for Hollins this season will be successfully expanding the rotation. If Hollins can get his players to buy in at the defensive end and cobble together a league-average defense, Memphis has the chance to build on last season's success.

isolations, post-ups and pick-and-rolls. Offensively, he proved to be extremely limited in all areas except in finishing opportunities created other people at the rim. His usage rate was an almost incredibly low .107. Fellow rookie DeMarre Carroll lived up to his billing as a hard-working player and good defender, but he's similarly limited on the offensive end. Sam Young displayed a fair amount of athleticism, but had little luck applying that to useful on-court activities. Worse, Carroll and Young were on the old end of the age spectrum for rookies. Memphis improved despite, not because of, its rookie class.

Unfortunately, the poor play of the rookie trio put bad ideas into the head of Heisley. We defended the outspoken owner last season, noting that it's sound strategy to tear down a team in order to build it back up. This was despite the dismissal of the team's entire scouting staff and Heisley's comments that the Grizzlies were profitable as a franchise, mostly due to their low payroll. This summer, Heisley added to his reputation as a tight-fisted owner by squeezing Memphis' first-round picks for relative peanuts. It's the industry standard to pay rookies at the maximum allowable 120 percent of the salary scale listed in the Collective Bargaining Agreement, though teams will frequently make first-year players achieve some easy-to-reach performance incentives to earn that extra 20 percent. San Antonio and Denver have been exceptions to that rule. Suddenly, Heisley got it into his head to reinvent the rookie scale. He insisted that Xavier Henry and Greivis Vasquez, Memphis' first-round picks this year, sign deals for the base scale and be held to much more difficult incentives than are commonly given. Henry and Vasquez remained unsigned into mid-September before league officials explained the "spirit" of the CBA to Heisley.

There is a fine line between perceived fiscal discipline and skinflintiness, and Heisley seems to confirm fears that he's a latter-day Ted Septien, the infamously tight owner of the Cleveland Cavaliers in the early 1980s. Perception is everything in this situation. It's not a matter of whether of not it's fair for an owner to incent his rookies in this manner, given his right to do so under the CBA. The problem is that the incentives were reportedly unheard of in the standard rookie contract. It's not illegal by the CBA, but is well beyond the bounds of standard practice in the industry. The collateral costs of this move by Heisley far outweigh the 20 percent that Henry and Vasquez ended up getting. Heisley is making it that much more unlikely that quality free agents will ever want to sign with the Grizzlies. Plus, for the second straight year, prospects snubbed Memphis when invited to work out for the team before the draft. Word gets around.

That said, the Grizzlies did spend some money this past offseason, re-signing forward Rudy Gay to a five-year max contract for $82 million. Was the re-signing of Gay the right move? That's not an easy question to answer. We just wrote about perception and not bucking up to sign Gay would have been yet another PR hit for the franchise. Plus, Gay is one of the league's most exciting players. At the same time, he hasn't really improved much the last couple of years and doesn't do much to make his teammates better. He's also a big reason the Grizzlies were atrocious defensively on the wings. Does this sound like a max player to you? The deal could work out for Memphis, particularly if Gay improves on defense, where his athleticism may not translate into production because of shortcomings elsewhere on that end of the court. Right now, the first thing you'd like to see from Gay is an improved willingness to share the ball on offense.

This is a big problem for the Memphis offense overall. At 47.8 percent, the Grizz's assist percentage was again the lowest in the NBA, and they were the only team to assist on less than half of their made field goals. The offense was largely comprised of ineffective isolations and reasonably effective post-ups. Point guard play is lacking in the Memphis attack, as Michael Conley continues to fall short as a playmaker while ball-dominators Randolph, Gay and O.J. Mayo all tend to look for their own shot first. Because of the strength in offensive rebounding, the Grizzlies could have still been a playoff team if they could have translated their collective physical skills into a top-10 defensive performance, but that didn't happen. Memphis improved from 24 wins to 40, and was nominally a playoff contender for much of the season. Nevertheless, the team is going to have to plug some of these offensive holes to maintain that progress.

Without top point guard play, the Grizzlies will likely remain a disorganized bunch. This year's draft offered little help in that regard, as the incoming crop was a little weak in lead guards beyond top pick John Wall. That makes last year's selection of Thabeet that much more galling, though it wasn't particularly panned at the time. There is a strong possibility that Memphis would have gone a different direction had the team known just how much better Gasol would get in the pivot. Last year's draft was loaded at the point guard position, and Memphis could have had its pick of Brandon Jennings, Stephen Curry and Jonny Flynn, not to mention Ricky Rubio or Tyreke Evans. Conley did get better and remains the team's best hope at the position. However, he's got to defend well enough to stay on the floor or much of his time could be usurped by free-agent addition Tony Allen. Allen is far from a natural point, but he is a dogged defender and could share playmaking duties with Mayo. Memphis could also further exploit the fine passing skills of Gasol. However he does it, Hollins has got to get more consistency and continuity from his offense.

Perhaps Memphis could start Allen at the point and alternate him and Mayo as the offense initiators, depending upon matchups, while running lots of sets through Gasol, who is probably their best passer. Allen is a good passer as well, though he doesn't handle the ball well enough to be a pure point. Meanwhile, Conley and Henry could give the second unit some much-needed scoring punch.

Mayo had a largely disappointing second season in the league, not so much because he got worse but because he failed to improve. Randolph's presence led to a more deferential Mayo taking on a lighter share of the offensive load, but instead of focusing his considerable talents in complementary areas like defense and playmaking, he simply disappeared at times. He then spent some time in summer league trying to learn the point guard position. That's to his credit, but the results weren't particularly promising. He did nominally improve his shooting percentages while working off the ball more than he did as a rookie. Still, for Memphis' offense to make a significant improvement, you'd like to see Mayo with the ball in his hands more often and making good decisions. He has the raw skills of a player that can elevate the play of his teammates; he just has to learn to put those skills to use.

A big story in the coming season will be Randolph's expiring contract. Can it be flipped for a top point guard with multiple years on his deal? Should it? Thabeet could answer these questions for Memphis because if he comes along, Gasol could slide over to the four position. However, Thabeet seems a long ways from being starter-quality at the NBA level. Also a possibility is that the well-liked Randolph could have another good season and thus sucker Heisley into another new contract. Fan sentiment will be heavily in favor of retaining Randolph.

Because the Grizzlies did not address their biggest shortcomings, a similar bottom-line performance as last season seems in the offing. SCHOENE sees almost a carbon copy of last season, with the roster merely getting another year older and more expensive. That's not a good sign for a team with so many young players. And if the Grizzlies do find themselves mired in a stagnant season, expect Heisley to be reminded early and often about his three-year plan.

Bradford Doolittle

From the Blogosphere

Who: Chris Herrington
What: Beyond the Arc
Where: http://www.memphisflyer.com/blogs/BeyondtheArc/

The emergence of Marc Gasol made the drafting of project center Hasheem Thabeet even worse than it would have otherwise been. But, oddly enough, Gasol could also be the key to helping Thabeet become a useful piece for the team. Last season, the Grizzlies were very good with all five starters on the floor (+7.3 per 48 minutes) and very bad when any starter came out (-6.7 per 48). The biggest, most surprising, exception: when the team paired Gasol and Thabeet. The Grizzlies performed very well using the "twin towers" approach and very poorly in more conventional-- and more common--lineups where Thabeet was paired with Zach Randolph. Credit Gasol, whose slimmed-down physique prompted a defensive transformation, allowing him to guard power forwards. Offensively, Gasol's passing and hoops IQ seemed to help out the generally overwhelmed Thabeet, while the pairing also funneled more touches toward the efficient Gasol. Finding minutes for that pairing without wearing down Gasol will be an interesting challenge for the Grizzlies this season.

MEMPHIS GRIZZLIES

GRIZZLIES FIVE-YEAR TRENDS

Season	AGE	W-L	POW	PYTH	SEED	ORTG	DRTG	PT DIFF	PACE
05-06	28.1	49-33	52.3 (5)	52.4	5	107.3 (16)	103.3 (2)	3.7 (6)	85.0 (30)
06-07	26.2	22-60	24.7 (30)	27.4	---	108.7 (11)	114.3 (30)	-5.1 (30)	92.0 (8)
07-08	24.4	22-60	23.4 (24)	24.8	---	107.2 (22)	114.3 (28)	-6.2 (24)	93.1 (7)
08-09	23.3	24-58	24.7 (26)	25.6	---	105.1 (28)	111.2 (20)	-5.5 (26)	88.8 (21)
09-10	24.7	40-42	38.7 (17)	36.8	---	109.1 (17)	112.1 (24)	-1.5 (17)	92.3 (8)

		OFFENSE				DEFENSE			
Season	PAY	eFG	oREB	FT/FGA	TO	eFG	oREB	FT/FGA	TO
05-06	$64.6	.496 (8)	.258 (21)	.241 (20)	.161 (21)	.469 (4)	.720 (21)	.237 (10)	.172 (3)
06-07	$47.1	.504 (9)	.259 (21)	.285 (2)	.175 (25)	.529 (30)	.711 (23)	.237 (12)	.164 (19)
07-08	$54.5	.500 (13)	.237 (24)	.225 (17)	.157 (23)	.521 (29)	.734 (16)	.196 (3)	.137 (26)
08-09	$55.1	.486 (23)	.258 (20)	.249 (9)	.171 (27)	.515 (27)	.735 (15)	.247 (19)	.163 (8)
09-10	$57.6	.494 (18)	.313 (1)	.235 (12)	.163 (24)	.520 (25)	.733 (20)	.205 (3)	.152 (20)

(league rankings in parenthesis)

SG 9 — Tony Allen

Hght: 6'4" Wght: 213 Exp: 6 From: Oklahoma State Salary: $3.0 million
2011-12 status: guaranteed contract for $3.2 million

SKILL RATINGS

TOT	OFF	DEF	REB	PAS	HND	SHT	ATH
0	-1	+5	+3	0	-3	-1	+5

Year	Team	Age	G	MPG	Usg	3PA%	FTA%	INS	2P%	3P%	FT%	TS%	Reb%	Ast%	TO%	BLK%	STL%	PF%	oRTG	dRTG	Win%	WARP
07-08	BOS	26.3	75	18.4	.196	.099	.138	1.039	.456	.316	.762	.528	.070	.039	.189	.013	.021	.056	102.1	105.4	.391	-0.7
08-09	BOS	27.3	46	19.3	.216	.066	.117	1.051	.510	.222	.725	.541	.070	.035	.188	.021	.032	.052	102.3	104.7	.420	0.1
09-10	BOS	28.3	54	16.5	.198	.013	.141	1.128	.520	.000	.605	.540	.099	.038	.178	.017	.034	.058	103.3	104.2	.469	1.0
10-11p	MEM	29.3	70	15.0	.193	.062	.131	1.070	.509	.140	.671	.527	.081	.038	.177	.016	.029	.055	103.0	104.8	.439	0.5

Most similar to: Ruben Patterson (95.2), Randy Brown, Quinn Buckner, Bonzi Wells   IMP: 54% BRK: 5% COP: 5%

Tony Allen played a valuable role on the contending Celtics, but decided to take on more responsibility with the Grizzlies. Allen will be the first guard off the bench behind O.J. Mayo and Mike Conley and should see 25 minutes or so per night. His per-game numbers will surely rise, but perhaps not his per-minute figures. Allen is a dangerous man off the dribble and in transition who has been relatively indifferent to passing the ball. If he decides a "bigger role" means "shooting more often," his efficiency will plummet and he won't help the Grizzlies. If he accepts a combo guard role and defers to the many scorers in the Memphis rotation, his perimeter defense will be a godsend for a Grizzlies team that has been exceedingly weak in that area.

PF 00 — Darrell Arthur

Hght: 6'9" Wght: 235 Exp: 2 From: Kansas Salary: $1.1 million
2011-12 status: team option for $2.0 million

SKILL RATINGS

TOT	OFF	DEF	REB	PAS	HND	SHT	ATH
-2	-2	-2	+2	-2	-1	-3	+2

Year	Team	Age	G	MPG	Usg	3PA%	FTA%	INS	2P%	3P%	FT%	TS%	Reb%	Ast%	TO%	BLK%	STL%	PF%	oRTG	dRTG	Win%	WARP
08-09	MEM	21.1	76	19.3	.164	.004	.052	1.048	.440	.000	.667	.456	.146	.014	.092	.029	.019	.066	102.0	105.4	.389	-0.8
09-10	MEM	22.1	32	14.3	.175	.006	.073	1.067	.434	.000	.567	.449	.141	.014	.121	.023	.015	.058	101.3	105.5	.363	-0.5
10-11p	MEM	23.1	68	15.0	.169	.010	.066	1.056	.458	.006	.625	.472	.142	.016	.107	.027	.017	.061	101.6	104.9	.390	-0.5

Most similar to: Kris Humphries (98.2), Gerald Wallace, Tony Battie, Johan Petro   IMP: 67% BRK: 15% COP: 2%

Darrell Arthur enjoyed a fairly promising rookie season, logging nearly 1,500 minutes as Memphis' primary power forward in 2008-09. His second year was a loss, as pectoral surgery kept him out until February and he never did quite get into shape. Arthur enters his third season hoping to reestablish himself. He'll likely be the top big man off the bench behind Marc Gasol and Zach Randolph, and if he has a big season, the Grizzlies may think twice about throwing a lot of money at free-agent-to-be Randolph. Ideally, the Grizzlies would like to see Hasheem Thabeet come on, which would allow them to slide Gasol over to power forward, so Arthur may be

MEMPHIS GRIZZLIES

playing to prove he can provide quality long-term depth. Arthur is a face-up, midrange kind of big who needs to upgrade the accuracy on his shot to carve an offensive niche for himself. He shows promise as a physical rebounder and defender.

SF 1	DeMarre Carroll	Hght: 6'8" Wght: 212 2011-12 status: team option for $1.2 million		Exp: 1 From: Missouri		Salary: $1.1 million			**SKILL RATINGS**							
									TOT	OFF	DEF	REB	PAS	HND	SHT	ATH
									-4	-2	+1	+3	-2	+1	-4	+1

Year	Team	Age	G	MPG	Usg	3PA%	FTA%	INS	2P%	3P%	FT%	TS%	Reb%	Ast%	TO%	BLK%	STL%	PF%	oRTG	dRTG	Win%	WARP
09-10	MEM	23.7	71	11.2	.149	.022	.087	1.064	.407	.000	.623	.426	.110	.018	.089	.009	.018	.059	101.2	106.8	.319	-1.6
10-11p	MEM	24.7	76	2.6	.141	.044	.090	1.046	.423	.000	.664	.442	.107	.020	.089	.012	.019	.058	101.5	106.2	.349	-0.3

Most similar to: Ed O'Bannon (97.4), Ronald Dupree, Jud Buechler, Scott Burrell IMP: 76% BRK: 18% COP: 4%

DeMarre Carroll was drafted to help the Grizzlies on the defensive end. He did that, but he's got to find some kind of offensive role or his hopes for being more than an 8- to 10-minute player will disappear. As for the defense, Carroll is strong and athletic despite not having great leaping ability and has the size and versatility to guard either forward position. What he probably needs to do is strive for a Dennis Rodman-type status, where he chases down every rebound, steps in and takes charges (he drew just six in his rookie season) and gets in everybody's face. Carroll took 64 percent of his shots from midrange, but he lacks touch and the chances of him developing into a reliable shooter are slim. Carroll needs to focus his efforts on everything else--including passing the ball, which he was very good at in college--and restrict his shots to layups and stick-backs.

PG 11	Mike Conley	Hght: 6'1" Wght: 185 2011-12 status: due qualifying offer of $6.5 million		Exp: 3 From: Ohio State		Salary: $4.9 million			**SKILL RATINGS**							
									TOT	OFF	DEF	REB	PAS	HND	SHT	ATH
									+2	+4	-5	-1	+1	+1	+1	0

Year	Team	Age	G	MPG	Usg	3PA%	FTA%	INS	2P%	3P%	FT%	TS%	Reb%	Ast%	TO%	BLK%	STL%	PF%	oRTG	dRTG	Win%	WARP
07-08	MEM	20.5	53	26.1	.189	.156	.092	.937	.453	.330	.732	.502	.057	.072	.152	.001	.014	.027	104.7	106.8	.431	0.4
08-09	MEM	21.5	82	30.6	.181	.226	.090	.864	.458	.406	.817	.548	.068	.067	.149	.003	.019	.027	106.7	106.8	.498	4.3
09-10	MEM	22.5	80	32.1	.186	.196	.076	.880	.464	.387	.743	.526	.043	.073	.157	.004	.021	.031	105.8	106.9	.463	2.5
10-11p	MEM	23.5	76	32.0	.191	.228	.093	.865	.476	.390	.786	.551	.053	.075	.145	.002	.018	.026	107.0	106.6	.514	5.0

Most similar to: Jason Terry (98.0), Wes Matthews, Dee Brown, Raymond Felton IMP: 67% BRK: 3% COP: 3%

Mike Conley finished the 2009-10 season strong and enters his fourth NBA campaign slated to remain the Grizzlies' starting point guard. Conley enters what may be a make-or-break season. He's eligible to receive an extension to his rookie contract by the Oct. 31 deadline, but a deal is unlikely, so he will probably be on the market next summer as a restricted free agent. Conley has turned into a good three-point shooter, but he's got to improve inside the arc. With his athleticism, he should get to the rim more often and draw more fouls. Like most of Memphis' primary players, he has no trouble creating his own shot, but might improve his efficiency if he focused more on distributing the ball and serving as a catch-and-shoot option when the rock comes back around his way. Defensively, he remains a mess, and there really is no good reason for him to be so bad on that end of the floor. If he doesn't improve his defense, he could see his minutes cut in favor of new Grizzly Tony Allen.

C 33	Marc Gasol	Hght: 7'1" Wght: 265 2011-12 status: due qualifying offer of $4.5 million		Exp: 2 From: Barcelona, Spain		Salary: $3.6 million			**SKILL RATINGS**							
									TOT	OFF	DEF	REB	PAS	HND	SHT	ATH
									+3	+3	-1	0	+3	+3	+4	+4

Year	Team	Age	G	MPG	Usg	3PA%	FTA%	INS	2P%	3P%	FT%	TS%	Reb%	Ast%	TO%	BLK%	STL%	PF%	oRTG	dRTG	Win%	WARP
08-09	MEM	24.2	82	30.7	.185	.001	.167	1.166	.530	.000	.733	.590	.148	.027	.166	.029	.013	.050	106.0	105.6	.515	5.2
09-10	MEM	25.2	69	35.8	.170	.001	.174	1.173	.582	.000	.670	.617	.151	.029	.142	.034	.014	.045	106.9	104.7	.573	8.0
10-11p	MEM	26.2	74	36.0	.169	.002	.171	1.169	.568	.002	.697	.612	.145	.029	.146	.031	.013	.046	106.2	104.7	.548	7.4

Most similar to: Brendan Haywood (96.2), LaSalle Thompson, Larry Nance, Emeka Okafor IMP: 44% BRK: 5% COP: 0%

MEMPHIS GRIZZLIES

Marc Gasol built upon a nice rookie season and emerged as one of the 10 best centers in the league. Looming over his third year will be his expiring contract. Next summer, the Grizzlies will have to choose between Gasol or Zach Randolph for a new contract calling for eight figures annually, because it's unlikely they'll cough up the money for both players. Not even Michael Heisley would be crazy enough to choose Randolph in that scenario. Gasol is terrific in the post and is deadly from 10 feet and in. He's strong and is not afraid to bang, a trait illustrated by his premier foul-drawing rate. Gasol is also an excellent rebounder and is probably the best passer among Memphis' frontline players. He's slow afoot and doesn't have great leaping ability, which renders him merely average on the defensive end. In a perfect world, Gasol would put his full range of skills to use at the power forward position, where his defensive shortcomings would be erased by a developing Hasheem Thabeet. However, Thabeet has a long way to go to fill his role in that scenario.

SF 22 — Rudy Gay

Hght: 6'8" Exp: 4 Salary: $13.6 million
Wght: 230 From: Connecticut
2011-12 status: guaranteed contract for $15.0 million

SKILL RATINGS

TOT	OFF	DEF	REB	PAS	HND	SHT	ATH
+3	+3	-5	-1	-1	-3	+2	+3

Year	Team	Age	G	MPG	Usg	3PA%	FTA%	INS	2P%	3P%	FT%	TS%	Reb%	Ast%	TO%	BLK%	STL%	PF%	oRTG	dRTG	Win%	WARP
07-08	MEM	21.7	81	37.0	.251	.230	.083	.853	.507	.346	.785	.546	.093	.024	.113	.019	.016	.034	106.0	105.3	.523	6.7
08-09	MEM	22.7	79	37.3	.259	.150	.094	.944	.477	.351	.767	.528	.092	.022	.126	.016	.017	.035	104.6	106.2	.447	1.9
09-10	MEM	23.7	80	39.7	.227	.124	.108	.984	.492	.327	.753	.535	.087	.021	.103	.015	.019	.028	104.5	105.8	.459	2.8
10-11p	MEM	24.7	76	38.0	.241	.219	.099	.880	.506	.361	.789	.558	.081	.024	.109	.017	.018	.029	106.0	105.4	.518	6.2

Most similar to: Jason Richardson (98.0), John Long, Glenn Robinson, Shane Battier

IMP: 52% BRK: 6% COP: 5%

It was a bit of an upset that Rudy Gay returned to the Grizzlies after testing the market as a restricted free agent. There was enough interest in the sky-walking forward that it took a max contract to bring him back to Memphis. Is Gay a max player? On one hand, no one who plays defense so poorly can be a max player. On the other hand, there is no physical reason why Gay shouldn't be a plus defender. If the Grizzlies can concoct a better defensive scheme, Gay may start looking a whole lot better. For what it's worth, his metrics are headed in the right direction. There are no questions about most of Gay's offensive arsenal as a scorer. His usage rate dropped last season, but part of that was because he cut his turnover rate. He started to draw more fouls and generally took shots closer to the basket. Gay can score, but everything else in his skill set could be better, including helping out on the defensive glass, being a more willing passer and improving his long-distance shot. Gay has the talent to do all of these things with average or better proficiency. If he doesn't focus on improving his all-around game, Gay runs the risk of becoming Allan Houston without the range when his athleticism starts to ebb.

C 15 — Hamed Haddadi

Hght: 7'2" Exp: 2 Salary: $1.6 million
Wght: 265 From: Ahvaz, Iran
2011-12 status: due qualifying offer of $2.0 million

SKILL RATINGS

TOT	OFF	DEF	REB	PAS	HND	SHT	ATH
+1	--	+1	--	--	--	--	--

Year	Team	Age	G	MPG	Usg	3PA%	FTA%	INS	2P%	3P%	FT%	TS%	Reb%	Ast%	TO%	BLK%	STL%	PF%	oRTG	dRTG	Win%	WARP
08-09	MEM	23.9	19	6.3	.209	.000	.248	1.248	.484	.000	.600	.543	.241	.031	.169	.081	.004	.079	107.8	102.5	.671	0.6
09-10	MEM	24.9	36	6.7	.166	.033	.093	1.059	.407	.000	.737	.441	.182	.018	.221	.044	.002	.105	101.1	106.5	.326	-0.5
10-11p	MEM	25.9	76	-	.157	.041	.098	1.057	.404	.015	.581	.416	.186	.017	.236	.098	.013	.069	-	-	.486	-

Most similar to: Alton Lister (87.8), Jim McIlvaine, DeSagana Diop, Calvin Booth

IMP: - BRK: - COP: -

Hamed Haddadi's per-minute numbers, compiled in very limited action, indicate a guy that can block a lot of shots and, probably, be a plus rebounder. He's just too slow and unathletic to be much of a factor at either end of the floor, and his skill set is redundant to Hasheem Thabeet's without the latter's room for growth. Haddadi had a nice showing in the FIBA World Championship, but that only proves that his rightful place is overseas. This will likely be his last year in the NBA.

MEMPHIS GRIZZLIES

SG 13	Xavier Henry	Hght: 6'6" Exp: R Salary: $1.7 million						
		Wght: 220 From: Kansas	**SKILL RATINGS**					
		2011-12 status: free agent	TOT	OFF	DEF	REB	PAS	HND	SHT	ATH
			-2	-1	-1	+1	-3	-4	-2	0

Year	Team	Age	G	MPG	Usg	3PA%	FTA%	INS	2P%	3P%	FT%	TS%	Reb%	Ast%	TO%	BLK%	STL%	PF%	oRTG	dRTG	Win%	WARP
10-11p	MEM	20.1	76	10.0	.170	.275	.080	.804	.411	.368	.768	.498	.071	.023	.144	.009	.020	.043	103.0	106.2	.396	-0.3

Most similar to: Thaddeus Young (98.7), Luol Deng, Gilbert Arenas, Eric Gordon IMP: - BRK: - COP: -

With the summer's rookie-scale scandal behind Henry, it's now time to figure out what he has to offer on the court. He enters the NBA with a reputation as a deadeye shooter, but could be lost in a wing player logjam that includes O.J. Mayo, Rudy Gay, DeMarre Carroll and Tony Allen. What Henry has going for him is that, unlike Gay, Mayo and Mike Conley, he functioned at Kansas as an off-the-ball player. He didn't shoot lights-out during his lone season at KU, but he had his moments and could emerge as a prime option on kick-outs. The contract issue kept Henry from playing in the NBA Summer League, where we might have gotten a glimpse of how well he can adapt to the NBA three-point line. As it is, he'll get plenty of run in the exhibition season. Henry has the athleticism to be an effective wing defender, and if he adapts quickly at the defensive end, he could earn significant minutes as a rookie. He's got the versatility to play either wing position and will be a good fit when playing alongside any combination of Conley, Mayo or Gay because he is a threat without the ball in his hands.

PG 2	Acie Law	Hght: 6'3" Exp: 3 Salary: $0.9 million						
		Wght: 202 From: Texas A&M	**SKILL RATINGS**					
		2011-12 status: free agent	TOT	OFF	DEF	REB	PAS	HND	SHT	ATH
			-2	+1	+1	-1	0	+2	-3	-3

Year	Team	Age	G	MPG	Usg	3PA%	FTA%	INS	2P%	3P%	FT%	TS%	Reb%	Ast%	TO%	BLK%	STL%	PF%	oRTG	dRTG	Win%	WARP
07-08	ATL	23.2	56	15.4	.167	.108	.067	.959	.433	.206	.792	.455	.038	.060	.181	.000	.015	.039	101.1	107.4	.299	-2.1
08-09	ATL	24.2	55	10.2	.163	.149	.136	.987	.391	.310	.817	.490	.061	.072	.149	.004	.010	.036	104.6	107.9	.393	-0.3
09-10	CHI	25.2	26	9.0	.217	.141	.190	1.049	.508	.313	.776	.585	.041	.050	.150	.003	.023	.031	106.2	106.3	.496	0.4
10-11p	MEM	26.2	76	5.0	.156	.156	.106	.950	.430	.312	.820	.508	.051	.067	.151	.002	.011	.035	104.3	107.5	.394	-0.2

Most similar to: Doug Overton (98.7), Anthony Johnson, David Wingate, Jeff McInnis IMP: 67% BRK: 13% COP: 0%

Given the composition of their roster, you'd think the Grizzlies would want to fill out their squad with a few pass-first types. Instead, they signed three-year veteran Acie Law to back up Mike Conley at point guard--though his minutes might be limited if O.J. Mayo proves capable of operating the point for stretches or if rookie Greivis Vasquez develops quickly. Law is a bit of a gunner, typical of a contemporary college combo guard who isn't able to carve out a specific role for himself at the NBA level. To claim any kind of a significant rotation spot, Law needs to greatly improve his three-point shooting. He is quick with the ball in his hands and gets to the rim, where he finishes well for a small player and draws a lot of fouls. Law's defense is tough to read because of his sporadic playing time, but he looks like he can hold his own on that end of the floor.

SG 32	O.J. Mayo	Hght: 6'4" Exp: 2 Salary: $4.5 million						
		Wght: 210 From: USC	**SKILL RATINGS**					
		2011-12 status: team option for $5.6 million	TOT	OFF	DEF	REB	PAS	HND	SHT	ATH
			+2	+3	-5	-1	+1	-1	+3	-1

Year	Team	Age	G	MPG	Usg	3PA%	FTA%	INS	2P%	3P%	FT%	TS%	Reb%	Ast%	TO%	BLK%	STL%	PF%	oRTG	dRTG	Win%	WARP
08-09	MEM	21.5	82	38.0	.247	.232	.076	.844	.461	.384	.879	.539	.061	.040	.138	.003	.015	.031	105.8	107.6	.441	1.6
09-10	MEM	22.5	82	38.0	.209	.241	.078	.837	.490	.383	.809	.551	.058	.034	.119	.004	.016	.025	105.6	107.2	.447	2.0
10-11p	MEM	23.5	76	36.0	.218	.283	.087	.804	.500	.398	.845	.577	.060	.040	.126	.004	.014	.024	106.9	106.9	.500	4.8

Most similar to: Jason Richardson (98.6), Ray Allen, Latrell Sprewell, Hersey Hawkins IMP: 70% BRK: 9% COP: 2%

There are only so many possessions to go around, and when the Grizzlies added Zach Randolph to their mix of high-usage players, no one was impacted more than O.J. Mayo. The effect on Mayo's efficiency was interesting, but in the end, he really didn't grow much from his rookie season. He operated a little less frequently in the midrange and attacked the basket more often and with great success, though he hasn't yet learned how to draw contact in the lane. Mayo's three-point shooting was a mirror image of his first year, establishing a nice baseline for that skill. Also, it should be noted that while his usage rate fell by nearly four percent, a chunk of that came from close to a two-percent improvement in his turnover percentage. Mayo wants to take on the role of backup point guard and seems intent on working his way into that mix, to his credit. His performance in that role in two summer-league games was kind of scary, as he put up just six assists against 15 turnovers. Mayo is talented enough that if he wants to take on more of a playmaking role, then it's within his grasp to make it happen. As with so many of the Grizzlies' young players, Mayo is a poor defender and there is no earthly reason why that should be the case.

PF 50 — Zach Randolph
Hght: 6'9" Exp: 9 Salary: $17.7 million
Wght: 260 From: Michigan State
2011-12 status: free agent

SKILL RATINGS — TOT +2, OFF +2, DEF 0, REB +4, PAS +2, HND 0, SHT -1, ATH +1

Year	Team	Age	G	MPG	Usg	3PA%	FTA%	INS	2P%	3P%	FT%	TS%	Reb%	Ast%	TO%	BLK%	STL%	PF%	oRTG	dRTG	Win%	WARP
07-08	NYK	26.8	69	32.6	.276	.058	.093	1.034	.474	.275	.772	.513	.183	.028	.136	.006	.012	.040	104.7	104.8	.497	3.8
08-09	LAC	27.8	50	35.1	.283	.089	.098	1.009	.494	.330	.734	.531	.165	.027	.104	.007	.012	.034	107.2	106.0	.537	4.4
09-10	MEM	28.8	81	37.7	.248	.030	.119	1.089	.496	.288	.778	.546	.182	.022	.101	.008	.013	.033	107.8	105.6	.571	9.8
10-11p	MEM	29.8	74	37.0	.243	.048	.101	1.053	.487	.318	.756	.529	.165	.025	.112	.007	.013	.037	105.8	105.6	.505	5.1

Most similar to: Terry Cummings (97.5), Bison Dele, Dino Radja, Loy Vaught   IMP: 32%   BRK: 6%   COP: 10%

The way Zach Randolph performed, you would have thought that last season was his contract year. Randolph has reportedly sought an extension from the Grizzlies, but as camps opened, no offer had materialized. Michael Heisley has suggested he wanted to extend Randolph, but the forward ran into some off-court trouble during the offseason. That probably won't be the leading factor in whether or not he remains in Memphis. It's really all about money. Randolph is more of a $9-10 million dollar player than a max player, and he turns 30 next summer. With Memphis also facing decisions on Mike Conley and Marc Gasol, it may all come down to how Randolph and his representatives view his place in the current marketplace. There is no doubt that Randolph was a boon to the Grizzlies last season. He improved his shot selection, shedding low-percentage three-point shots in exchange for more looks in the post as well as leading the team's league-best charge on the offensive glass. Randolph even turned in a passable job as a post defender, though he'll never have the reach to be a basket protector. If Randolph continues to focus his game on what he does best, perhaps he'll earn that extension after all. If he decides that an inflated scoring average is the best route to another mega-contract, then it could be a long season for the Grizzlies.

C 34 — Hasheem Thabeet
Hght: 7'3" Exp: 1 Salary: $4.8 million
Wght: 267 From: Connecticut
2011-12 status: team option for $5.1 million

SKILL RATINGS — TOT +2, OFF 0, DEF +1, REB +1, PAS -5, HND -5, SHT +5, ATH +1

Year	Team	Age	G	MPG	Usg	3PA%	FTA%	INS	2P%	3P%	FT%	TS%	Reb%	Ast%	TO%	BLK%	STL%	PF%	oRTG	dRTG	Win%	WARP
09-10	MEM	23.2	68	13.0	.107	.000	.190	1.190	.588	—	.581	.605	.161	.005	.200	.077	.009	.081	103.1	103.4	.488	1.3
10-11p	MEM	24.2	76	17.0	.115	.000	.204	1.204	.598	.000	.588	.617	.160	.006	.197	.073	.009	.077	103.3	103.4	.498	2.2

Most similar to: Theo Ratliff (93.2), John Salley, Michael Stewart, Duane Causwell   IMP: 65%   BRK: 4%   COP: 4%

Hasheem Thabeet needs to show significant progress this season, or Memphis fans will not be able to look at him without thinking about the players they could have had in the 2009 Draft, like Stephen Curry or Brandon Jennings. The shot blocking and rebounding are already there for Thabeet, but there are plenty of DeSagana Diop-types who have sat on the end of NBA benches. First of all, Thabeet must improve his defensive footwork. Despite averaging four blocks for every 40 minutes he played, Thabeet ranked in the lower fifth of the league against isolations, post-ups and pick-and-rolls. In Europe, you can be a guy that just stands at the basket and sends back shots. In the NBA, that doesn't play. On offense, Thabeet's weak hands led to an

MEMPHIS GRIZZLIES

unsightly turnover rate. He showed no offensive arsenal to speak of, as 101 of his 131 field-goals attempts came at the rim. Few of those shots came off post-ups, but Thabeet did show some promise with his back to the basket. Unfortunately, the Grizzlies can't run any plays for him because there is a 20 percent chance he'll turn the ball over. Thabeet looks like he's going to post a high foul-drawing rate, so it's essential that he improve his accuracy from the line.

PF 24 — Kenny Thomas

Hght: 6'7" Exp: 11 Salary: --
Wght: 261 From: New Mexico
2011-12 status: free agent

SKILL RATINGS
TOT	OFF	DEF	REB	PAS	HND	SHT	ATH
-4	--	-1	--	--	--	--	--

Year	Team	Age	G	MPG	Usg	3PA%	FTA%	INS	2P%	3P%	FT%	TS%	Reb%	Ast%	TO%	BLK%	STL%	PF%	oRTG	dRTG	Win%	WARP
07-08	SAC	30.7	23	12.3	.097	.000	.036	1.036	.421	.000	.000	.398	.126	.021	.343	.003	.009	.059	98.0	107.2	.222	-1.2
08-09	SAC	31.7	8	7.8	.065	.000	.000	1.000	.375	.000	.000	.375	.142	.007	.111	.012	.048	.065	99.8	102.7	.400	0.0
09-10	SAC	32.7	26	12.0	.082	.000	.092	1.092	.486	-	.583	.509	.158	.021	.297	.023	.016	.060	101.9	105.3	.388	-0.2
10-11p	MEM	33.7	76	-	.073	.006	.071	1.065	.462	.000	.411	.459	.140	.020	.311	.017	.014	.061	-	-	.351	-

Most similar to: Larry Smith (90.0), Cadillac Anderson, Malik Rose, Corie Blount   IMP: -   BRK: -   COP: -

Kenny Thomas' contract that wouldn't end finally ended, and now he's shopping around to see if he can score a few more veteran's minimum dollars. He worked out for the Grizzlies and will head to camp in Memphis.

SG 21 — Greivis Vasquez

Hght: 6'6" Exp: R Salary: --
Wght: 200 From: Maryland
2011-12 status: free agent

SKILL RATINGS
TOT	OFF	DEF	REB	PAS	HND	SHT	ATH
-1	+1	-2	-1	+5	+3	-4	-1

Year	Team	Age	G	MPG	Usg	3PA%	FTA%	INS	2P%	3P%	FT%	TS%	Reb%	Ast%	TO%	BLK%	STL%	PF%	oRTG	dRTG	Win%	WARP
10-11p	MEM	24.3	76	10.0	.214	.216	.075	.858	.387	.308	.837	.456	.059	.079	.160	.005	.017	.038	104.8	106.8	.433	0.3

Most similar to: Keith Bogans (94.6), Francisco Garcia, Courtney Alexander, Willie Solomon   IMP: -   BRK: -   COP: -

The knock against Greivis Vasquez is that he's too slow for the NBA, and summer surgery to remove a bone spur from his ankle won't help. He's expected to be ready for camp, but will be working himself back into shape. Vasquez is a multi-talented guard who can play either off the ball or with it in his hands. His long-range shooting will be important because he may not be athletic enough to take guys off the dribble if they don't have to crowd him at the three-point line. We've criticized the Grizzlies for collecting too many shoot-first types, so we have to acknowledge that Vasquez's best attribute is his passing ability. The key will be how well he defends, because Memphis can't afford to give another defensive sieve a rotation spot. Along the lines of recent Grizzlies picks DeMarre Carroll and Sam Young, Vazquez is old for his draft class.

SF 3 — Damien Wilkins

Hght: 6'6" Exp: 6 Salary: --
Wght: 225 From: Georgia
2011-12 status: free agent

SKILL RATINGS
TOT	OFF	DEF	REB	PAS	HND	SHT	ATH
-3	--	-3	--	--	--	--	--

Year	Team	Age	G	MPG	Usg	3PA%	FTA%	INS	2P%	3P%	FT%	TS%	Reb%	Ast%	TO%	BLK%	STL%	PF%	oRTG	dRTG	Win%	WARP
07-08	SEA	28.3	76	24.3	.194	.188	.077	.889	.427	.323	.736	.474	.072	.035	.108	.007	.015	.030	103.1	106.3	.394	-0.9
08-09	OKC	29.3	41	15.5	.189	.266	.075	.808	.355	.375	.804	.467	.064	.026	.137	.008	.017	.038	102.7	107.2	.353	-0.8
09-10	MIN	30.3	80	19.8	.142	.119	.110	.992	.459	.295	.798	.515	.089	.037	.148	.012	.021	.040	103.4	105.9	.418	0.0
10-11p	MEM	31.3	76	-	.153	.246	.086	.840	.421	.347	.775	.496	.078	.034	.139	.012	.017	.038	-	-	.378	-

Most similar to: Eric Williams (98.7), Ernie Grunfeld, Mike Sanders, Bill Hanzlik   IMP: 36%   BRK: 7%   COP: 4%

Damien Wilkins made the most important shot of the Timberwolves' season, beating the New Jersey Nets with a banker on opening night. The win helped send the Nets spiraling to an 0-18 shot, while Minnesota got off to a good start. A trade from the Thunder to the Timberwolves gave Wilkins the chance to play rotation minutes all season long, and he was adequate. Wilkins is a solid defender on the wing who can body up opponents, which makes him slightly

MEMPHIS GRIZZLIES

more valuable than the replacement-level contributor his statistics suggest. Wilkins' offensive game has stagnated, however. He's never been able to consistently hit NBA three-pointers and he generally relies far too much on a diet of midrange jumpers. Wilkins saw the five-year contract he signed with the Seattle SuperSonics after a solid rookie season come to an end, and he'll be in a more appropriate tax bracket this year. He can still help, but it's tough to see where he fits in Memphis. The Grizzlies are flush with young wing players.

Sam Young — SF #4

Hght: 6'6" Wght: 220 Exp: 1 From: Pittsburgh Salary: $0.9 million
2011-12 status: team option for $0.9 million

SKILL RATINGS

TOT	OFF	DEF	REB	PAS	HND	SHT	ATH
-2	0	-2	0	-3	-4	-2	0

Year	Team	Age	G	MPG	Usg	3PA%	FTA%	INS	2P%	3P%	FT%	TS%	Reb%	Ast%	TO%	BLK%	STL%	PF%	oRTG	dRTG	Win%	WARP
09-10	MEM	24.9	80	16.5	.223	.084	.115	1.031	.483	.196	.777	.518	.089	.017	.141	.012	.013	.035	103.3	106.9	.382	-1.0
10-11p	MEM	25.9	76	10.0	.213	.099	.117	1.018	.488	.223	.787	.526	.087	.019	.136	.012	.014	.036	103.5	106.4	.402	-0.2

Most similar to: Tariq Abdul-Wahad (99.0), Felipe Lopez, Doug West, Shandon Anderson

IMP: 61% BRK: 12% COP: 6%

Sam Young was drafted to provide physical play and defense, but it's unclear if he's going to fill any kind of consistent role in the NBA. He did show a penchant for hot streaks every so often, but the overall picture is of a guy that needs to become more efficient. Young fits in with the Grizzlies in that he's far more interested in getting his own shot than setting up a teammate. He was physical enough to be a factor in the lane, but shot the ball poorly from every distance away from the rim. Young's mission, should he choose to accept it, is to forget about the midrange, improve his long-range shooting, continue to attack off of close-outs and become the defender he was drafted to become.

Trey Gilder — SF

Hght: 6'9" Wght: 185 Exp: 1 From: Northwestern State Salary: --
2011-12 status: free agent

SKILL RATINGS

TOT	OFF	DEF	REB	PAS	HND	SHT	ATH
0	0	0	+1	-1	-2	0	+3

Year	Team	Age	G	MPG	Usg	3PA%	FTA%	INS	2P%	3P%	FT%	TS%	Reb%	Ast%	TO%	BLK%	STL%	PF%	oRTG	dRTG	Win%	WARP
09-10	MEM	25.2	2	2.5	.088	.000	.000	1.000	1.000	-	-	1.000	.117	.000	.000	.000	.101	.000	105.6	94.4	.828	0.0
10-11p	AVG	26.2	76	2.5	.172	.156	.110	.954	.478	.377	.705	.533	.097	.023	.143	.024	.018	.043	103.1	105.0	.438	0.1

Most similar to: Felipe Lopez (96.9), Buck Johnson, Craig Ehlo, Joe Bryant

IMP: 57% BRK: 10% COP: 10%

D-League stud Trey Gilder started last season with the Grizzlies, but only played in two games before getting released. He projects as a rangy three-point threat and wing defender if he can catch on with a team, which he was still trying to do at press time. He hadn't earned a camp invite yet, but worked out for the Spurs.

Steven Hunter — C

Hght: 7'0" Wght: 240 Exp: 8 From: DePaul Salary: --
2011-12 status: free agent

SKILL RATINGS

TOT	OFF	DEF	REB	PAS	HND	SHT	ATH
--	--	--	--	--	--	--	--

Year	Team	Age	G	MPG	Usg	3PA%	FTA%	INS	2P%	3P%	FT%	TS%	Reb%	Ast%	TO%	BLK%	STL%	PF%	oRTG	dRTG	Win%	WARP
07-08	DEN	26.5	18	6.6	.158	.000	.201	1.201	.536	.000	.450	.530	.132	.000	.160	.036	.000	.071	101.1	106.7	.318	-0.2
09-10	MEM	28.5	21	7.5	.189	.000	.233	1.233	.395	-	.528	.450	.155	.000	.133	.048	.003	.028	102.1	104.4	.423	0.0

Steven Hunter hurt his knee towards the end of last season, then spent the summer healing up. In September, he was working out in Phoenix, hoping to earn a camp invite that apparently never came. Hunter remains a shot-blocking/defense specialist and can help a team in a pinch.

MEMPHIS GRIZZLIES

PG	Jamaal Tinsley	Hght: 6'3"	Exp: 8	Salary: --	SKILL RATINGS
--		Wght: 185	From: Iowa State		TOT OFF DEF REB PAS HND SHT ATH
		2011-12 status: free agent			-3 -1 +2 +2 +3 -2 -5 +3

Year	Team	Age	G	MPG	Usg	3PA%	FTA%	INS	2P%	3P%	FT%	TS%	Reb%	Ast%	TO%	BLK%	STL%	PF%	oRTG	dRTG	Win%	WARP
07-08	IND	30.1	39	33.3	.213	.221	.069	.848	.422	.284	.720	.458	.060	.109	.204	.006	.022	.032	105.1	105.3	.492	2.0
09-10	MEM	32.1	38	15.5	.161	.181	.055	.874	.446	.179	.815	.438	.065	.081	.293	.006	.028	.050	101.6	105.8	.363	-0.7
10-11p	AVG	33.1	76	15.5	.162	.210	.057	.847	.433	.211	.786	.436	.063	.086	.274	.008	.027	.048	101.9	105.2	.390	-0.6

Most similar to: Foots Walker (91.6), Rick Brunson, Robert Pack, Lester Conner IMP: 54% BRK: 18% COP: 4%

This may be the end of the line for Jamaal Tinsley. For what it's worth, Tinsley was a pretty good player on some pretty good teams during his prime. In Memphis last year, he struggled to get shots and make them, though remnants of his solid floor game were still intact. Combine what Tinsley has to offer with the perception that he comes with baggage and he may have to head overseas to keep playing.

PG	Marcus Williams	Hght: 6'3"	Exp: 4	Salary: --	SKILL RATINGS
--		Wght: 205	From: Connecticut		TOT OFF DEF REB PAS HND SHT ATH
		2011-12 status: free agent			+2 +3 -4 +2 +2 0 -2 -2

Year	Team	Age	G	MPG	Usg	3PA%	FTA%	INS	2P%	3P%	FT%	TS%	Reb%	Ast%	TO%	BLK%	STL%	PF%	oRTG	dRTG	Win%	WARP
07-08	NJN	22.4	53	16.2	.209	.365	.053	.688	.377	.380	.787	.499	.069	.075	.193	.003	.013	.028	105.0	106.3	.455	0.7
08-09	GSW	23.4	9	5.9	.191	.254	.112	.858	.182	.333	.333	.305	.041	.105	.169	.013	.009	.049	101.5	108.3	.287	-0.1
09-10	MEM	24.4	62	14.1	.187	.219	.066	.846	.421	.296	.673	.456	.062	.081	.200	.001	.019	.022	103.8	106.4	.412	-0.1
10-11p	AVG	25.4	76	14.1	.195	.347	.061	.715	.414	.365	.704	.501	.064	.082	.181	.001	.018	.023	105.9	106.0	.497	1.8

Most similar to: John Bagley (98.7), Derek Fisher, Greg Anthony, Larry Drew IMP: 62% BRK: 17% COP: 10%

Even on a team desperate for playmaking, Marcus Williams could not carve out a major role on the Grizzlies last season. His three-point percentage dipped under .300, which didn't help; nor did his high turnover rate. If Williams' offensive game lags, he's not going to stick, as he offers little defensive value. He signed with Enisey Krasnoyarsk in Russia during the offseason.

Miami Heat

In poker, it's called going "all in." This is when you put all the money on the table and bet your survival on the cards in your hand. That may be an overly dramatic way to define Miami's offseason, especially given that the franchise's survival wasn't actually at stake, but the Heat had an awful lot on the line during the summer of 2010.

As we noted last year, Heat president Pat Riley had the chance to literally hit the reset button for his organization. He nearly did. His plan was to clear as much cap space as possible, then leverage his salary flexibility to convince a superstar free agent (or two) to join his franchise player, Dwyane Wade. The only problem was that Wade himself was a free agent, and there was no overt guarantee that he'd return to Miami. If Wade had chosen to leave, Riley's plan could have collapsed. Worse, the Heat, unlike the other major players in the free-agent market, did not have a core group of young players to fall back upon. It was a high-stakes game, and Riley made out like Chris Moneymaker.

We know now how it played out. Riley traded Daequan Cook to Oklahoma City on the eve of the draft, shedding Miami's first-round pick in the process. Doing so cleared enough cap space that Riley could fit, or very nearly fit, three max players onto his roster. A week or so later, after Wade flirted with hometown Chicago Bulls, the best player in Heat history made a joint announcement with fellow prized free agent Chris Bosh that the duo would team up in South Beach. Two days later, in the infamous "The Decision", they were joined by the crown jewel of the free agency market, LeBron James.

So Riley gambled and won, and thus is born the era of the super team. At this point, the story of how this all came together for Miami has pretty much been told. Other players reportedly have made noises about trying to join forces on other teams, but no one is really in position to make it happen. Even if they were, none of them can get LeBron James and it is his presence that makes this such a unique circumstance. For all the noise about James' decision to join "Wade's team," let's face facts: Any team that has LeBron on it is *LeBron*'s team, as LeBron himself might say.

That leaves us with two general questions about this great basketball experiment. How will Wade and James fit together? And is the supporting cast good enough for a championship team?

Let's start with what we know. Last year, the Heat's base offense was dependent upon pick-and-rolls, primarily involving Wade, and spot-up shooting coming off that base. Wade was at the epicenter of everything, using over 35 percent of Miami's possessions when he was on the floor--more than 36 minutes per game, which was actually down a couple of minutes from previous seasons. The Heat was 16.5 points per 100 possessions better offensively when Wade was on the floor. That

HEAT IN A BOX

Last year's record	47-35
Last year's Offensive Rating	108.9 (19)
Last year's Defensive Rating	105.1 (4)
Last year's point differential	2.3 (13)
Team pace	88.2 (28)
SCHOENE projection	60-22 (1)
Projected Offensive Rating	113.9 (3)
Projected Defensive Rating	106.0 (1)
Projected team weighted age	29.1 (5)
Projected '10-11 payroll	$64.5 (17)
Est. payroll obligations, '11-12	$67.8 (5)

Head coach: Erik Spoelstra

Erik Spoelstra is the league's youngest head coach, but he finds himself with a unique opportunity as the leader of the Heat's super team. The pressure is on Spoelstra, who has legendary team president Pat Riley looming in the front office. Riley mused over the summer that he was open to a return to the sidelines if asked to coach by one of the free agents the team was recruiting. Dwyane Wade has pledged his support, but as soon as Miami struggles, the media will question Spoelstra's job security. He deserves better. With limited defensive talent, Spoelstra guided the Heat to the league's fourth-best Defensive Rating in 2009-10. His teams have been as slow-paced as Riley's, but Spoelstra may want to increase the tempo to take advantage of the talent Miami has collected.

152

dynamic is going to change, but how much?

Neither Wade and James scored as much out of isolations as you'd think, though it's unclear from Synergy data whether there were actually a lot of those sets called that ended up in kick-outs against double-teams. Miami's high rate of spot-ups suggests this might have happened frequently, as does Wade's assist rate. Cleveland didn't have a high frequency of spot-ups in its offense. Instead, its attack worked off of LeBron by having bigs cut to the basket--the Cavaliers were second in shots coming off of cuts. That being the case, it's not surprising that Cleveland's LeBroncentric offense was considerably more efficient than Miami's Wadecentric offense.

You'd like to see a system in Miami that has more ball movement and more back screens and cuts than the Heat offense featured in past seasons. If defenses are constantly forcing the ball out of James' and/or Wade's hands for spot-up shots, then the defense wins. The focus that opponents will give to the perimeter super duo will surely open up all sorts of holes in the defense. The Heat will fall short of its potential efficiency if supporting players are merely spotting up or standing at the three-point line, though floor stretchers like Mike Miller and Mario Chalmers will play important roles.

How Bosh fits into all of this remains to be seen, but it's likely that he'll take the biggest usage hit of the new group of core players. Nearly a fifth of Bosh's offense came off of isolations last season and less than half of his baskets came off of assists. (The league standard is 56.3 percent. By the way, Wade was at 28 percent, and James at 36 percent.) Bosh is now going to be working off of Wade and James, with a lot of two-man basketball resulting when one of them is on the bench. That'll be a perfect fit for Bosh, who was in the league's 93rd percentile working off pick-and-roll sets in Toronto. So he might not use 29 percent of his team's possessions again; it'll probably be more like 22 or 23 percent. However, his True Shooting Percentage could skyrocket. Indeed, SCHOENE foresees his True Shooting Percentage creeping over the 60 percent mark. Also, Bosh's passing skills could be put to the test. He's always had a decent assist rate for his position, though his skill rating (+3) in this area might be overstating things given Bosh's large role in the Toronto offense, not to mention the outside shooters surrounding him with the Raptors.

One of the big things that pairing Wade and James accomplishes is that you can have at least one of the two on the floor at all times. That fact in itself alleviates much of Miami's lack of quality depth. Is there really such a thing as a "second unit" when it's led by Dwyane Wade or LeBron James? Despite the good reputation of so many of the reserves Riley signed during the summer, depth could still be an issue because a lot of those guys are aging (Miller, Eddie House, Juwan Howard, Jamaal Magloire, Zydrunas Ilgauskas) and project as below replacement level. (See the chart comparing the benches of Miami and Chicago in the Bulls chapter.)

And, yes, that means we're saying Jeff Van Gundy is wrong. Initially skeptical of the Miami Experiment, Van Gundy changed his tune after Riley filled out his roster, predicting the Heat would break every record for success in the books. If the players comprising the supporting roster were in their primes, Miami might well project as a 70-win team. That would be amazing since projections merely contextualize past performance, which involves regressing a player's statistical record to the mean to calculate a reasonable baseline expectation for future performance. You just don't see 70 wins as a "reasonable" projection when constructed by objective methods. However, Miami could have gotten there with a slightly better plan at the middle and back end of its roster. As it is, it feels like Riley should have limited himself to two or three of these replacement-level veterans, like Miller, Udonis Haslem and House, and gone young to fill out the rest of the squad. Yes, the presence of the big three could raise the level of play of some of these guys. In fact, it surely will because the role players are going to have wide-open spaces in which to work. However, aren't we better off assessing the supporting group based on what they did in less-than-ideal settings? Under that light, most of the four through 15 spots on the Miami roster aren't markedly better than an upper-tier group of D-Leaguers. However, the core trio is going to plaster over an awful lot of those roster holes.

The most interesting dynamic of the Miami Experiment will be what sort of lineup head coach Erik Spoelstra deploys when the big three are together on the floor. Will the Heat's best lineup throw traditional positions out the window? (Most certainly yes.) If so, how does that lineup fare defensively? Will it be vulnerable to quick, smallball configurations? Will it be so good on offense that it won't matter?

In early September, a salty-talking Riley suggested that James may function as the Heat's primary point guard. That's an exciting idea and might be the best

From the Blogosphere

Who: Couper Moorhead
What: Heat.com
Where: http://www.nba.com/heat/

Everyone expects something of the Heat, but nobody knows quite what that is. Maybe that's why reactions to, and projections for, this deus ex machina--really, what is Miami's collection of talent other than a deviation from established NBA logic?--have favored the extreme. We have ideas, but with three players that offer possibilities we have never even had to consider, thinking up schemes and styles is little more than loose conjecture. The stars will certainly be stars, judged on their jewelry, but the burden will fall on the support columns. Can the role players space the floor? Will they hedge and help consistently enough for Erik Spoelstra's defense? Can it blend into a playoff brand? Toss out the Freudian crutches used for the pessimistic side of the discussion. Passing and playmaking abilities alone will make it work. Beyond that, patience is a virtue.

---

will look like the 2008 American Olympic team. (Which, of course, almost lost.) There is another question that could play a bigger role than anything we've discussed so far: How fast will Miami play?

Since Pat Riley arrived in Miami for the 1995-96 season, the Heat has finished in the bottom half of the league in tempo in every season except one, when it finished 14th out of 30. Miami has finished in the bottom three of the league six times, including last season when it was 28th. Before going to South Beach, Riley lorded over a slow crawl in New York, where the Knicks finished 21st or lower in possessions per game in all four of his seasons. Even in Los Angeles, where Riley coached the Magic-led Lakers of the Showtime era, the Lakers gradually slid from third to 17th in tempo during his nine seasons. The man is a control freak, so much so that we're discussing the subject of team tempo by looking at the history of the team president rather than the head coach because, let's face it, whatever system Spoelstra installs is going to bear Riley's stamp of approval. Is it possible that a team with James and Wade will play at an average tempo or slower? If so, that's great news for the other 29 teams in the NBA. If there is one sure-fire way Miami can consistently overwhelm its competition, it's by pressuring the ball, pushing it down the floor and cleaning up the defensive boards. For what it's worth, Miami had the lowest rate of shots off transition last season. That shouldn't and couldn't happen again. Right?

When you think of Miami Heat basketball, you think of a plodding tempo. This is a new and potentially golden era in Miami basketball, and Riley would do well to let his horses run.

Theoretically, Wade, James and Bosh will be together for the next six seasons. This season may represent their *worst* chance at a title, with the Lakers still holding the label of favorites, the Celtics capable of another run and other contenders rising up from coast to coast. Miami still needs to work on its roster and may not be able to do much in that regard until the next offseason. So the coronations and celebrations that ensued after the free-agent news hit South Beach might have been worth it, because it might be awhile before they get to party for real, if ever. It's not just because of the reasons noted so far. While many call this offseason of 2010 the summer that changed everything, next summer may turn out to be really be the season that deserves that label, because the negotiations for a new Collective Bargaining Agreement could result in the Miami Experiment turning into a one-and-done proposition.

---

option for Spoelstra. Steve Nash may be the only current NBA player that sees the court as well as James, and he's unselfish by nature. If he plays off the ball too often alongside two All-Star-level alpha dogs like Wade and Bosh, there is the danger of James becoming overly deferential. It's not that he's going to turn into Marvin Williams. It's just that, in James, Miami now has in its grasp the world's best player. And no matter how good the talent is around him, he's got to be the focal point of everything. Using him as the offense's organizer and distributor is stupefyingly fascinating from a basketball standpoint. If ever there is a situation when a player could average a triple-double in today's game, this could be it. For most of James' career, he's stood up well to the Michael Jordan comparisons, but he's always been considered a hybrid of Jordan and Magic Johnson. This season, we could see James' inner Magic flourishing like never before.

All of these questions and speculations about complementary skills and players, who is going to play what role and how the usage/efficiency graphs of the big three are going to change--these may merely be tiny degrees of concern. In other words, the frontline talent on the Heat could be so overwhelming that it

We have no idea what the NBA's next CBA is going to look like. At this point, we don't even have a firm grasp at how legitimate the owners' cry of massive losses may be, and we don't know how steadfast they are going to be in going after a hard salary cap. However, if a hard cap is what the owners want, a work stoppage is a near certainty. When they are finally able to shove the hard cap down the players' throats, the Heat may find that the super team they've constructed simply can't be held together unless the big three want to make financial sacrifices well beyond the ones they made when taking their less-than-max deals in 2010. In fact, it is the very creation of the Heat's super team that may steel the owners' will, as the next labor deal may well be structured to prevent the Miami model from becoming an epidemic.

The Heat will be both successful and disappointing this season. Miami will be one of the best teams in the league, perhaps the best, and is a bona fide title contender. However, depth issues and lack of shooting make this team vulnerable. Right now, the Heat is the objective favorite to win it all, but the gap between Miami and the other top contenders in the East, much less the West, is not that large. The expectations are through the roof, perhaps higher than any team could possibly hope to reach.

Bradford Doolittle

HEAT FIVE-YEAR TRENDS

Season	AGE	W-L	POW	PYTH	SEED	ORTG	DRTG	PT DIFF	PACE
05-06	29.2	52-30	51.4 (6)	52.0	2	110.8 (6)	105.9 (10)	3.9 (5)	90.1 (12)
06-07	29.3	44-38	40.2 (15)	38.2	4	106.9 (18)	106.3 (8)	-0.9 (17)	88.4 (26)
07-08	27.4	15-67	15.6 (30)	18.0	---	102.9 (29)	112.6 (26)	-8.7 (29)	88.1 (25)
08-09	25.6	43-39	42.9 (14)	41.7	5	109.5 (18)	109.1 (13)	0.3 (14)	88.6 (22)
09-10	27.7	47-35	46.5 (13)	47.8	5	108.9 (19)	105.1 (4)	2.3 (13)	88.2 (28)

Season	PAY	OFFENSE eFG	oREB	FT/FGA	TO	DEFENSE eFG	oREB	FT/FGA	TO
05-06	$59.7	.517 (2)	.267 (17)	.254 (15)	.160 (16)	.477 (10)	.764 (1)	.251 (17)	.143 (29)
06-07	$78.2	.506 (6)	.249 (25)	.222 (25)	.164 (14)	.485 (8)	.733 (14)	.232 (9)	.162 (20)
07-08	$74.7	.482 (24)	.221 (30)	.218 (21)	.158 (24)	.510 (24)	.719 (24)	.245 (20)	.152 (10)
08-09	$50.0	.500 (16)	.246 (24)	.212 (26)	.139 (3)	.502 (16)	.729 (19)	.251 (21)	.169 (4)
09-10	$72.8	.496 (16)	.261 (20)	.223 (17)	.148 (9)	.480 (2)	.749 (6)	.246 (22)	.162 (8)

(league rankings in parenthesis)

C 50 — Joel Anthony
Hght: 6'9" Exp: 3 Salary: $3.3 million
Wght: 245 From: Nevada-Las Vegas
2011-12 status: guaranteed contract for $3.5 million

SKILL RATINGS
TOT	OFF	DEF	REB	PAS	HND	SHT	ATH
-2	-2	+2	-4	-5	-4	+1	-2

Year	Team	Age	G	MPG	Usg	3PA%	FTA%	INS	2P%	3P%	FT%	TS%	Reb%	Ast%	TO%	BLK%	STL%	PF%	oRTG	dRTG	Win%	WARP
07-08	MIA	25.7	24	20.7	.095	.000	.219	1.219	.467	.000	.592	.521	.113	.003	.172	.050	.008	.052	100.9	104.7	.373	-0.5
08-09	MIA	26.7	65	16.1	.081	.000	.113	1.113	.483	.000	.652	.521	.113	.012	.229	.072	.010	.063	101.7	104.5	.405	-0.2
09-10	MIA	27.7	80	16.5	.088	.000	.166	1.166	.478	-	.717	.546	.111	.004	.184	.067	.008	.057	102.0	104.3	.423	0.2
10-11p	MIA	28.7	75	20.0	.076	.002	.165	1.163	.515	.002	.706	.570	.112	.007	.193	.058	.008	.059	101.5	104.7	.393	-0.7

Most similar to: Duane Causwell (96.8), Andrew Lang, Adonal Foyle, Eric Riley   IMP: 65%   BRK: 15%   COP: 5%

Joel Anthony doesn't get the minutes to qualify for the shot-block title, but he may be the game's best basket protector. Anthony still has no offensive game to speak of, with usage rates that you need a magnifying glass to spot. He ordinarily finishes a high rate of his stick-backs and scores off of other people's penetration, though he slumped in that regard last season. Anthony is a physical marvel, with a powerful build and long arms, who gets off the court as quickly as any player in the league. Nevertheless, he's unskilled to the extent he can kill the ordinary offense--though that may not be an issue if he's sharing the court with LeBron James, Dwyane Wade and Chris Bosh. Anthony will stay on the court as long as his foul rate allows.

MIAMI HEAT

PG	Carlos Arroyo	Hght: 6'2"	Exp: 8	Salary: $0.9 million	SKILL RATINGS							
8		Wght: 202	From: Florida International		TOT	OFF	DEF	REB	PAS	HND	SHT	ATH
		2011-12 status: free agent			-3	0	+3	-2	0	+4	-1	-4

Year	Team	Age	G	MPG	Usg	3PA%	FTA%	INS	2P%	3P%	FT%	TS%	Reb%	Ast%	TO%	BLK%	STL%	PF%	oRTG	dRTG	Win%	WARP
07-08	ORL	28.7	62	20.4	.171	.181	.095	.915	.485	.341	.853	.546	.050	.080	.164	.001	.009	.030	105.8	107.2	.452	0.9
09-10	MIA	30.7	72	22.0	.140	.053	.085	1.031	.489	.280	.844	.529	.048	.067	.115	.003	.012	.031	104.6	107.4	.410	-0.2
10-11p	MIA	31.7	74	11.7	.127	.097	.080	.983	.482	.310	.830	.527	.048	.069	.138	.003	.011	.033	103.3	107.5	.363	-1.0

Most similar to: Bimbo Coles (98.2), Anthony Johnson, Antonio Daniels, Kevin Ollie — IMP: 32% BRK: 4% COP: 12%

Carlos Arroyo starts the season trying to recover from a deep bruise in his left quad, an injury bad enough that it may limit his workload in the early part of training camp. He's slated to battle Mario Chalmers for the starting point guard position in Miami. Chalmers was also injured in late summer, so the duo may be starting from the same point. Arroyo isn't as good of a catch-and-shoot player as Chalmers, which puts him at a disadvantage because whoever wins the point guard job isn't likely to do a whole lot of playmaking. Arroyo's three-point shot is shaky, but he does defend well, albeit without Chalmers' high steal rate. Even if he doesn't start, Arroyo is a solid backup point guard. Ordinarily, his ability to get his own shot is an important quality. However, that may not matter as much with the Heat always keeping one of its stars on the floor.

PG	Patrick Beverley	Hght: 6'1"	Exp: R	Salary: $0.5 million	SKILL RATINGS							
2		Wght: 181	From: Arkansas		TOT	OFF	DEF	REB	PAS	HND	SHT	ATH
		2011-12 status: guaranteed contract for $0.8 million			--	--	--	--	--	--	--	--

Patrick Beverley is the rare NBA player who is going into camp with a guaranteed contract yet is still a long shot to make the opening-night roster. The Heat has 15 players with guaranteed deals entering camp, but that doesn't include rehabbing second-round pick Da'Sean Butler, who is believed to be the favorite for the last spot on Miami's roster. Beverley has a reputation as a defensive stopper, which is what enticed Pat Riley to sign him up to begin with. If he really defends that well, he'll find a spot elsewhere even if there isn't room on the Heat.

PF	Chris Bosh	Hght: 6'10"	Exp: 7	Salary: $14.5 million	SKILL RATINGS							
1		Wght: 230	From: Georgia Tech		TOT	OFF	DEF	REB	PAS	HND	SHT	ATH
		2011-12 status: guaranteed contract for $16.0 million			+4	+4	+1	+2	+3	+2	+2	+2

Year	Team	Age	G	MPG	Usg	3PA%	FTA%	INS	2P%	3P%	FT%	TS%	Reb%	Ast%	TO%	BLK%	STL%	PF%	oRTG	dRTG	Win%	WARP
07-08	TOR	24.1	67	36.2	.279	.018	.172	1.155	.496	.400	.844	.588	.143	.033	.107	.022	.012	.030	108.5	104.3	.636	11.1
08-09	TOR	25.1	77	38.0	.270	.029	.159	1.130	.497	.245	.817	.569	.154	.030	.102	.020	.012	.030	108.2	105.2	.597	11.0
09-10	TOR	26.1	70	36.1	.288	.014	.164	1.150	.521	.364	.797	.592	.175	.030	.107	.021	.009	.031	109.6	104.8	.652	12.4
10-11p	MIA	27.1	74	36.0	.251	.023	.168	1.145	.524	.362	.823	.601	.145	.031	.101	.020	.010	.030	107.5	104.7	.591	9.7

Most similar to: Vin Baker (97.7), Karl Malone, Derrick Coleman, Antonio McDyess — IMP: 43% BRK: 0% COP: 6%

Chris Bosh became a whole lot more famous through his summer free-agent saga, but he's been a well-known figure among NBA fans for several years. He's one of the best offensive post players in the league, but can also step out and knock down a high percentage of midrange shots. Bosh uses his quickness and mobility to get by bigger defenders and his length to shoot over the smaller ones. He draws fouls and makes his free throws, pounds the boards and is an excellent passer. Bosh's lack of strength has made him a shaky defensive player at center, but he's been much better when guarding power forwards, which he will do most of his time in Miami. Bosh's skill set is above average across the board and his versatility makes him an ideal third wheel to the LeBron James/Dwyane Wade super duo.

MIAMI HEAT

SG	Da'Sean Butler	Hght: 6'7"	Exp: R	Salary: $0.5 million	SKILL RATINGS						
34		Wght: 230	From: West Virginia		TOT	OFF	DEF	REB	PAS	HND	SHT	ATH
		2011-12 status: due qualifying offer of $1.0 million			0	--	--	--	--	--	--	--

Year	Team	Age	G	MPG	Usg	3PA%	FTA%	INS	2P%	3P%	FT%	TS%	Reb%	Ast%	TO%	BLK%	STL%	PF%	oRTG	dRTG	Win%	WARP
10-11p	MIA	23.3	46	-	.171	.237	.106	.869	.385	.314	.771	.465	.086	.040	.099	.006	.011	.043	-	-	.438	-

Most similar to: Chris Jefferies (97.5), Jason Kapono, Adam Morrison, Desmond Mason   IMP: -   BRK: -   COP: -

The last we saw of Da'Sean Butler, he was in tears on the floor during the Final Four being consoled by his coach, Bob Huggins, after blowing out his knee in West Virginia's semifinal loss to Duke. The injury probably cost Butler a slot in the draft's first round and the two years of guaranteed dollars that go along with it. However, like Smash Williams, this story can have a happy ending. Butler is still rehabbing from the injury and probably won't be ready for training camp. While Miami will have a bloated camp roster, the Heat is reportedly leaning towards keeping Butler around, even though he probably won't be ready until January or so. Before he was injured, Butler projected as a long, multi-skilled wing with potential as an ATRBTL player (at the rim and behind the line) with the ability to get to the basket. Most importantly, he'd bring with him the hard-nosed defense he learned at West Virginia.

PG	Mario Chalmers	Hght: 6'1"	Exp: 2	Salary: $0.9 million	SKILL RATINGS						
15		Wght: 190	From: Kansas		TOT	OFF	DEF	REB	PAS	HND	SHT	ATH
		2011-12 status: free agent			+2	+2	+1	-3	+1	+1	+2	+2

Year	Team	Age	G	MPG	Usg	3PA%	FTA%	INS	2P%	3P%	FT%	TS%	Reb%	Ast%	TO%	BLK%	STL%	PF%	oRTG	dRTG	Win%	WARP
08-09	MIA	22.9	82	32.0	.164	.341	.093	.752	.467	.367	.767	.548	.052	.072	.181	.002	.032	.043	106.9	106.0	.528	6.1
09-10	MIA	23.9	73	24.8	.164	.377	.077	.700	.491	.318	.745	.519	.044	.065	.197	.005	.026	.046	105.2	106.0	.473	2.1
10-11p	MIA	24.9	74	28.0	.148	.372	.083	.710	.492	.365	.747	.553	.044	.071	.181	.005	.026	.042	105.4	105.7	.493	3.3

Most similar to: Earl Watson (96.5), Larry Drew, Pearl Washington, Darwin Cook   IMP: 60%   BRK: 5%   COP: 5%

Mario Chalmers took a step backwards in his second pro season, almost entirely because of a decline in his three-point percentage. That was huge for Chalmers, because threes accounted for more than half of his shot attempts. Perhaps equally troubling is that the high turnover rate he posted as a rookie actually went up. Since Chalmers plays off the ball so much, it's imperative that he take care of the ball. He has the leg up to start in the Miami backcourt, but will be even more of a stand-still shooter this season playing alongside LeBron James and Dwyane Wade. If he again fails to shoot the ball well--and maybe even if he does--he may sit during crunch time in favor of veteran Mike Miller. Chalmers will be counted upon to defend the small guards throughout the league. He's a mixed bag on the defensive end. His quick hands and excellent anticipation allow him to get a lot of steals, but he tends to gamble too often. He also doesn't play very good one-on-one defense, as his success in stopping isolations ranked in the bottom quarter of the league. This is a huge season for Chalmers, who will be a restricted free agent next summer. He can gain international fame as a starter for the Miami super team, but he could also get buried and find himself in Minnesota next season. Complicating matters is the high ankle sprain Chalmers suffered in July, which may limit his time in the early part of training camp.

SG	Kenny Hasbrouck	Hght: 6'3"	Exp: R	Salary: $0.8 million	SKILL RATINGS						
4		Wght: 190	From: Siena		TOT	OFF	DEF	REB	PAS	HND	SHT	ATH
		2011-12 status: non-guaranteed contract for $0.9 million			--	--	--	--	--	--	--	--

Will Kenny Hasbrouck ever actually see the court for the Miami Heat in a regular-season game? He signed with the Heat back in March, but never appeared in a game. Then he played for the Heat in summer league and performed very well, leading to an offer of a non-guaranteed deal to go to camp. Unfortunately, there doesn't seem to be room for Hasbrouck on the roster. Even if he makes the team, he'll sit out two games after being suspended for a DWI. The former Siena star is a shoot-first combo/tweener guard with a promising three-point stroke.

MIAMI HEAT

PF 40	Udonis Haslem	Hght: 6'8" Wght: 235 2011-12 status: guaranteed contract for $3.8 million	Exp: 7 From: Florida	Salary: $3.5 million							
					SKILL RATINGS						
					TOT	OFF	DEF	REB	PAS	HND	SHT	ATH
					-3	-1	0	+2	-3	0	0	-4

Year	Team	Age	G	MPG	Usg	3PA%	FTA%	INS	2P%	3P%	FT%	TS%	Reb%	Ast%	TO%	BLK%	STL%	PF%	oRTG	dRTG	Win%	WARP
07-08	MIA	27.9	49	36.8	.168	.000	.098	1.098	.467	.000	.810	.517	.148	.018	.105	.008	.010	.037	102.2	105.5	.392	-0.9
08-09	MIA	28.9	75	34.1	.148	.000	.094	1.094	.518	.000	.753	.553	.145	.016	.103	.008	.009	.038	103.6	106.6	.402	-0.8
09-10	MIA	29.9	78	27.9	.173	.000	.107	1.107	.494	-	.762	.538	.169	.011	.095	.009	.007	.038	103.8	105.5	.442	1.2
10-11p	MIA	30.9	75	28.0	.144	.003	.095	1.092	.503	.000	.754	.539	.146	.014	.098	.008	.008	.040	101.9	106.0	.365	-2.2

Most similar to: Loy Vaught (98.3), Joe Smith, Tony Massenburg, Derek Strong   IMP: 39%   BRK: 2%   COP: 7%

Udonis Haslem remained with the Heat, signing on as a free agent for a deal worth less than half of what he was previously making per year. He goes from being grossly overpaid to just overpaid. Haslem is a highly respected player whose offensive game consists of knocking down long two-point shots. He's a hard-working defender whose lack of length means he's no better than average on that end. Haslem makes up for his lack of steals and blocks by drawing a lot of charges. Miami needs low-usage, high-efficiency role players, and Haslem fits the bill. He shoots well from his spots, finishes at the rim and does his part to help hold down the opposition. The worrisome part, however, is that he's on the wrong side of 30, and the Heat has given five guaranteed years to a player our projection system thinks is going to hit the skids. Miami really can't afford to tie up unproductive money.

PG 55	Eddie House	Hght: 6'1" Wght: 175 2011-12 status: guaranteed contract for $1.4 million	Exp: 10 From: Arizona State	Salary: $1.4 million							
					SKILL RATINGS						
					TOT	OFF	DEF	REB	PAS	HND	SHT	ATH
					-1	0	+3	0	-4	-1	0	-4

Year	Team	Age	G	MPG	Usg	3PA%	FTA%	INS	2P%	3P%	FT%	TS%	Reb%	Ast%	TO%	BLK%	STL%	PF%	oRTG	dRTG	Win%	WARP
07-08	BOS	29.9	78	19.0	.197	.478	.025	.547	.431	.393	.917	.535	.064	.048	.124	.006	.018	.036	106.3	105.3	.531	3.5
08-09	BOS	30.9	81	18.3	.202	.533	.037	.504	.445	.444	.792	.592	.062	.029	.086	.004	.021	.036	108.3	106.2	.569	4.7
09-10	NYK	31.9	68	17.9	.201	.432	.044	.611	.412	.348	.923	.495	.053	.033	.090	.004	.017	.031	104.4	106.6	.426	0.2
10-11p	MIA	32.9	74	10.0	.173	.433	.037	.605	.434	.377	.878	.520	.053	.035	.096	.003	.017	.036	104.0	106.6	.413	0.0

Most similar to: Mike Evans (96.5), Lindsey Hunter, Anthony Peeler, Darrell Griffith   IMP: 42%   BRK: 3%   COP: 6%

With a big three like Miami's, you need shooters, and Eddie House has filled that role as a hired gun for nine teams in 10 years. House returns for his second stint with the Heat, the franchise for whom he played his first three years in the league. House showed serious signs of slippage last season, which was why the Celtics sent him to New York for Nate Robinson. While he rates as a solid defender against other small players, House's primary calling card is streak shooting from three-point range. If he doesn't recover some of last season's decline, he won't see many minutes in Miami. House turns 33 during the next postseason, so there is no guarantee that last year's dip in long-range accuracy will regress towards his career mark.

C 5	Juwan Howard	Hght: 6'9" Wght: 253 2011-12 status: free agent	Exp: 16 From: Michigan	Salary: $0.9 million							
					SKILL RATINGS						
					TOT	OFF	DEF	REB	PAS	HND	SHT	ATH
					-5	--	-4	--	--	--	--	--

Year	Team	Age	G	MPG	Usg	3PA%	FTA%	INS	2P%	3P%	FT%	TS%	Reb%	Ast%	TO%	BLK%	STL%	PF%	oRTG	dRTG	Win%	WARP
07-08	DAL	35.2	50	7.0	.116	.000	.071	1.071	.359	.000	.786	.406	.132	.023	.195	.004	.007	.082	99.2	107.9	.235	-1.3
08-09	CHA	36.2	42	11.2	.189	.000	.080	1.080	.510	.000	.676	.534	.099	.026	.138	.011	.008	.071	103.4	108.9	.325	-0.9
09-10	POR	37.2	73	22.4	.140	.002	.064	1.062	.511	.000	.786	.538	.127	.018	.151	.005	.009	.056	102.2	107.3	.333	-2.8
10-11p	MIA	38.2	74	-	.120	.002	.062	1.059	.470	.000	.747	.496	.106	.019	.158	.005	.008	.070	-	-	.303	-

Most similar to: Tony Massenburg (98.8), Bill Cartwright, Stacey Augmon, James Edwards   IMP: 38%   BRK: 0%   COP: 29%

Juwan Howard has played his Solid Veteran card one more time and will return for his 17th NBA season. Was the Fab Five really that long ago? Howard played a much bigger role than expected last season in Portland because of the injuries to Greg Oden and Joel Przybilla. If he plays 22 minutes a game this season for the Heat,

MIAMI HEAT

something will be seriously wrong. Howard is reasonably efficient with the scraps he gets off other people's offense and he's got a dependable midrange shot. As you'd expect for a 38 year old, he's lost his athleticism. That has made him much worse at the defensive end, where he was never that great to begin with.

C 11	Zydrunas Ilgauskas	Hght: 7'3"	Exp: 12	Salary: $1.4 million		**SKILL RATINGS**						
		Wght: 260	From: Kaunas, Lithuania			TOT	OFF	DEF	REB	PAS	HND	SHT	ATH
		2011-12 status: player option or ETO for $1.4 million				-2	-1	+5	0	0	+1	-2	-4

Year	Team	Age	G	MPG	Usg	3PA%	FTA%	INS	2P%	3P%	FT%	TS%	Reb%	Ast%	TO%	BLK%	STL%	PF%	oRTG	dRTG	Win%	WARP
07-08	CLE	32.9	73	30.5	.230	.001	.095	1.095	.475	.000	.802	.522	.176	.021	.121	.042	.007	.052	105.4	104.1	.542	5.8
08-09	CLE	33.9	65	27.2	.240	.044	.086	1.042	.477	.385	.799	.523	.163	.017	.101	.038	.008	.049	105.7	104.6	.535	4.3
09-10	CLE	34.9	64	20.9	.191	.042	.081	1.039	.441	.478	.743	.491	.151	.017	.116	.029	.005	.064	103.1	106.1	.401	-0.4
10-11p	MIA	35.9	72	15.0	.183	.024	.082	1.058	.470	.254	.760	.506	.146	.019	.115	.036	.007	.063	102.7	105.6	.402	-0.3

Most similar to: Olden Polynice (95.6), Kevin Willis, Derrick Coleman, Herb Williams   IMP: 38%   BRK: 8%   COP: 0%

The Heat cornered the market on both top players and old centers in the 2010 free-agent class. Zydrunas Ilgauskas is chasing a ring by coming to Miami, but he deserves one as much as anybody. Ilgauskas hit just 35 percent on his midrange shots, but did knock down nearly half of his 23 three-point attempts. The small sample means that probably doesn't indicate a whole lot, but he's shot threes well for two years now. Ilgauskas is still capable of defending the post, though as he's grown more immobile, his foul rate has soared. That's not really a problem because he won't be counted for heavy minutes anyway. Ilgauskas is just a piece of what shapes up to be a very complicated puzzle in Miami, but to be a useful piece he's got to regain the touch on his stand-still jumper.

SF 6	LeBron James	Hght: 6'8"	Exp: 7	Salary: $14.5 million		**SKILL RATINGS**						
		Wght: 250	From: St. Vincent-St. Mary HS (OH)			TOT	OFF	DEF	REB	PAS	HND	SHT	ATH
		2011-12 status: guaranteed contract for $16.0 million				+5	+5	+5	+2	+5	+5	+3	+5

Year	Team	Age	G	MPG	Usg	3PA%	FTA%	INS	2P%	3P%	FT%	TS%	Reb%	Ast%	TO%	BLK%	STL%	PF%	oRTG	dRTG	Win%	WARP
07-08	CLE	23.3	75	40.4	.338	.160	.152	.991	.531	.315	.712	.568	.114	.081	.114	.021	.021	.026	112.8	103.3	.773	22.5
08-09	CLE	24.3	81	37.7	.341	.175	.153	.978	.535	.344	.780	.591	.117	.091	.110	.024	.024	.022	115.7	102.8	.839	26.9
09-10	CLE	25.3	76	39.0	.337	.182	.160	.978	.560	.333	.767	.604	.107	.103	.123	.020	.022	.019	115.5	103.3	.828	25.4
10-11p	MIA	26.3	75	38.0	.303	.229	.152	.923	.553	.315	.752	.584	.101	.099	.118	.022	.020	.020	112.7	103.4	.770	21.0

Most similar to: Dwyane Wade (93.1), Grant Hill, Michael Jordan, Kobe Bryant   IMP: 43%   BRK: 0%   COP: 9%

LeBron James has existed in the celebrity netherworld for a long time now, and perhaps he drank some of the same crazy juice that is served to child actors. That explains "The Decision" as well as anything. Whether or not LeBron exists in the same reality as the rest of us, once the ball goes in the air, he's the best player on the planet. That's the only reason any of us cares about the rest of this stuff. You have to look real close to see any flaws in James' game. Given his success rate, he probably shoots a few too many long shots inside the arc and out, but if he shot the ball like Steve Nash, it wouldn't even be fun to play the games. It will be fascinating to see James operate the point in Miami with a pair of elite players around him. He'll likely eschew some of the forced shots he took in Cleveland, which will drive up his effective field-goal percentage. James may also focus more on cleaning off the defensive boards, or help out some on the offensive glass. What we're getting at is that he has a chance to put up +5 skill ratings across the board in next year's book. It's not likely James can average a triple-double, not in today's game and not at Miami's pace, but it will be fun to watch him try. There is nothing he can't do on the court. If the Heat doesn't win a title, it won't be James' fault, just like it wasn't his fault when the Cavaliers fell short in the last two playoffs.

MIAMI HEAT

SF 22 — James Jones

Hght: 6'8"	Exp: 7	Salary: $2.4 million	
Wght: 220	From: Miami (Fla.)		
2011-12 status: guaranteed contract for $2.9 million			

SKILL RATINGS

TOT	OFF	DEF	REB	PAS	HND	SHT	ATH
-2	+1	0	-5	-4	+2	+4	-5

Year	Team	Age	G	MPG	Usg	3PA%	FTA%	INS	2P%	3P%	FT%	TS%	Reb%	Ast%	TO%	BLK%	STL%	PF%	oRTG	dRTG	Win%	WARP
07-08	POR	27.5	58	22.0	.149	.515	.108	.593	.426	.444	.878	.625	.074	.013	.070	.009	.009	.036	107.6	106.8	.526	2.9
08-09	MIA	28.5	40	15.8	.131	.550	.078	.528	.415	.344	.839	.520	.059	.015	.069	.018	.010	.043	105.1	107.6	.421	0.1
09-10	MIA	29.5	36	14.0	.134	.632	.087	.454	.207	.411	.821	.556	.052	.016	.077	.006	.011	.042	105.9	107.5	.447	0.3
10-11p	MIA	30.5	74	10.0	.118	.651	.080	.429	.315	.404	.834	.572	.054	.015	.074	.010	.010	.042	104.6	107.3	.410	-0.1

Most similar to: Kevin Grevey (93.5), Bruce Bowen, Tracy Murray, Dennis Scott   IMP: 31%   BRK: 14%   COP: 3%

James Jones is typical of the role players the Heat has filled its roster out with in that he's not as productive as his reputation. Jones is a mono-skilled spot-up shooter. Actually, that description doesn't even do him justice. Last season, James took 119 shots from the field. Of those, 113 were either long twos or three-point attempts. He's taken seven out of 268 shots at the rim the last two years. You have to love a guy who knows what he's good at doing. Jones is a quality three-point threat who can be counted upon to hit around the 40 percent mark. Jones is a decent defender, which makes him a logical player for the 14- to 15-minute role he plays.

C 21 — Jamaal Magloire

Hght: 6'11"	Exp: 10	Salary: $0.9 million	
Wght: 255	From: Kentucky		
2011-12 status: free agent			

SKILL RATINGS

TOT	OFF	DEF	REB	PAS	HND	SHT	ATH
-4	-2	+2	+2	-5	-5	-1	-1

Year	Team	Age	G	MPG	Usg	3PA%	FTA%	INS	2P%	3P%	FT%	TS%	Reb%	Ast%	TO%	BLK%	STL%	PF%	oRTG	dRTG	Win%	WARP
07-08	DAL	29.9	31	9.2	.172	.000	.182	1.182	.333	.000	.465	.384	.176	.012	.298	.028	.002	.082	96.0	105.8	.205	-1.3
08-09	MIA	30.9	55	12.9	.126	.000	.139	1.139	.496	.000	.483	.505	.188	.015	.169	.029	.008	.081	103.5	106.5	.403	-0.2
09-10	MIA	31.9	36	10.0	.131	.000	.262	1.262	.500	-	.356	.470	.198	.001	.172	.025	.013	.078	101.8	105.2	.388	-0.2
10-11p	MIA	32.9	76	5.0	.122	.002	.192	1.190	.476	.000	.423	.484	.167	.007	.190	.023	.009	.082	100.6	106.3	.317	-0.8

Most similar to: Corie Blount (96.0), Brian Skinner, Greg Kite, Francisco Elson   IMP: 33%   BRK: 8%   COP: 22%

The Heat brought back Jamaal Magloire for his defense and rebounding. He's an excellent percentage rebounder and his per-play numbers in post defense rank in the 94th percentile. He's not counted upon to do much, or anything, at the offensive end except to dunk the ball when the defense breaks down. Last year, Magloire had one assist in 359 minutes. That is probably nothing more than a statistical oddity, but we thought you'd like to know. Magloire won't likely log more than 8-10 minutes per night, which is a good thing since he usually averages about seven fouls per 40 minutes.

SF 13 — Mike Miller

Hght: 6'8"	Exp: 10	Salary: $5.0 million	
Wght: 218	From: Florida		
2011-12 status: guaranteed contract for $5.4 million			

SKILL RATINGS

TOT	OFF	DEF	REB	PAS	HND	SHT	ATH
+1	+2	-4	+2	+5	+4	+5	-5

Year	Team	Age	G	MPG	Usg	3PA%	FTA%	INS	2P%	3P%	FT%	TS%	Reb%	Ast%	TO%	BLK%	STL%	PF%	oRTG	dRTG	Win%	WARP
07-08	MEM	28.2	70	35.3	.198	.327	.085	.758	.558	.432	.774	.626	.107	.043	.166	.005	.006	.026	107.6	106.5	.535	6.1
08-09	MIN	29.2	73	32.3	.146	.297	.086	.790	.554	.378	.732	.588	.123	.063	.191	.010	.007	.027	106.9	106.5	.514	4.8
09-10	WAS	30.2	54	33.4	.148	.292	.064	.772	.515	.480	.824	.623	.108	.054	.196	.005	.011	.033	106.7	106.3	.515	3.7
10-11p	MIA	31.2	71	28.0	.136	.328	.071	.743	.543	.435	.775	.618	.102	.052	.186	.007	.008	.032	105.2	106.3	.466	2.1

Most similar to: Mario Elie (94.1), Craig Ehlo, Rick Fox, Rodney McCray   IMP: 35%   BRK: 4%   COP: 9%

Pat Riley called Mike Miller the "finest perimeter shooter in the NBA." He might be right, but Miller is more than just a spot-up shooter. He has always been able to put the ball on the floor when the defense crowds him and finishes at the rim at a very high percentage. He's also a terrific passer from either wing position. Miller is weak defensively, very weak, and that's hampered the teams he's been on in recent seasons. In Miami, the Heat will probably surround Miller with four good defenders at all times, which should paper over his lack of point-prevention skills. Miller will play a major role with the Heat this season. He may even justify the guaranteed five-year deal Riley gave him this summer, or at least a couple of years of it.

MIAMI HEAT

PF 45	Dexter Pittman	Hght: 6'10" Exp: R Salary: $0.5 million						
		Wght: 290 From: Texas	**SKILL RATINGS**					
		2011-12 status: non-guaranteed contract for $0.8 million	TOT	OFF	DEF REB PAS HND SHT ATH			
			0	--	-- -- -- -- -- --			

Year	Team	Age	G	MPG	Usg	3PA%	FTA%	INS	2P%	3P%	FT%	TS%	Reb%	Ast%	TO%	BLK%	STL%	PF%	oRTG	dRTG	Win%	WARP
10-11p	MIA	23.1	76	--	.157	.000	.131	1.132	.548	.000	.543	.559	.131	.010	.177	.042	.006	.085	--	--	.453	--

Most similar to: David Harrison (97.0), Ike Diogu, Jamaal Magloire, Emeka Okafor   IMP: -   BRK: -   COP: -

The Heat nabbed burly Dexter Pittman in the second round of this year's draft, hoping he can carve out a Kevin Duckworth-like role for himself in the NBA ... eventually. Pittman will be hard-pressed to earn regular minutes in his first season--if he does make the opening-night roster, which seems probable. Conditioning will be important, of course. Pittman really struggled in three summer-league games, shooting .313 from the field and committing 15 fouls in 58 minutes. He'll most likely log some D-League time this year and will not see meaningful minutes unless Erik Spoelstra needs somebody to come in and knock somebody into the first row. Pittman can't get complacent because only the first year of his contract is guaranteed.

PF 42	Shavlik Randolph	Hght: 6'10" Exp: 5 Salary: $1.0 million						
		Wght: 236 From: Duke	**SKILL RATINGS**					
		2011-12 status: non-guaranteed contract for $1.1 million	TOT	OFF	DEF REB PAS HND SHT ATH			
			--	--	-- -- -- -- -- --			

Year	Team	Age	G	MPG	Usg	3PA%	FTA%	INS	2P%	3P%	FT%	TS%	Reb%	Ast%	TO%	BLK%	STL%	PF%	oRTG	dRTG	Win%	WARP
07-08	PHI	24.4	9	3.1	.260	.000	.000	1.000	.286	.000	.000	.286	.232	.049	.125	.085	.017	.083	106.8	103.0	.625	0.1
08-09	POR	25.4	10	3.7	.266	.048	.085	1.037	.583	1.000	.250	.610	.301	.000	.289	.021	.000	.051	109.4	106.4	.597	0.1
09-10	POR	26.4	6	8.8	.196	.000	.040	1.040	.333	--	1.000	.371	.156	.009	.137	.015	.010	.081	100.2	107.7	.268	-0.2

Shavlik Randolph is unlikely to make the Miami roster as he enters camp with a partially guaranteed contract. For the Heat, Randolph is always just a phone call away. He's played 25 games in three years, which makes him the prototype of an NBA fringer. When he does get on the court, Randolph is strictly a banger. He rebounds, gives a few fouls and, like Ollie in *Hoosiers*, has been ordered not to shoot unless he's wide open under the basket.

SG 3	Dwyane Wade	Hght: 6'4" Exp: 7 Salary: $14.2 million						
		Wght: 220 From: Marquette	**SKILL RATINGS**					
		2011-12 status: guaranteed contract for $15.7 million	TOT	OFF	DEF REB PAS HND SHT ATH			
			+5	+5	+3 +2 +5 +3 +1 +5			

Year	Team	Age	G	MPG	Usg	3PA%	FTA%	INS	2P%	3P%	FT%	TS%	Reb%	Ast%	TO%	BLK%	STL%	PF%	oRTG	dRTG	Win%	WARP
07-08	MIA	26.3	51	38.2	.334	.056	.151	1.095	.485	.286	.759	.549	.066	.087	.164	.015	.021	.033	108.3	105.1	.603	7.6
08-09	MIA	27.3	79	38.6	.364	.118	.144	1.026	.524	.317	.765	.574	.078	.091	.116	.028	.030	.028	114.1	103.7	.792	23.8
09-10	MIA	28.3	77	36.3	.352	.117	.149	1.032	.509	.300	.761	.562	.078	.085	.122	.024	.027	.031	112.7	103.7	.761	20.0
10-11p	MIA	29.3	75	36.0	.311	.130	.145	1.015	.512	.321	.766	.568	.073	.090	.129	.023	.024	.029	110.3	103.8	.699	15.9

Most similar to: Michael Jordan (94.0), Scottie Pippen, Kobe Bryant, Clyde Drexler   IMP: 50%   BRK: 0%   COP: 8%

While everyone seems to want to call the Heat "Dwyane Wade's team," he's the one that's going to have to learn to play second fiddle. No player, LeBron James included, has been more responsible for his team's success than Wade the last couple of years. At first, the lightened load will probably feel like a big relief. The metric to follow for Wade is the percentage of his field goals that are assisted. He's consistently in the 25-29 percent range, which is getting close to the most ball-dominant point guards in the league. That number may skyrocket as Wade works off of James. It's not that he's going to turn into a catch-and-shoot player. Wade is a below-average shooter outside of 10 feet. If defenses can get him to shoot from out there, they win. However, he is probably going to have to learn to use his athleticism to get himself open without the ball in his hands, a task that depends upon desire and offensive design. Don't read between the lines of any of this and think there are concerns about Wade's game. There is merely fascination about how his game is going to change. The only worry about Wade is his health, but since an injury-plagued 2007-08 season in which people started comparing him to Penny Hardaway, he's gone right back to absorbing the pounding he took before he was hurt. All the while, Wade has played the best basketball of his career over the last two years.

MIAMI HEAT

PF	**Jarvis Varnado**	Hght: 6'9" Exp: R Salary: --					SKILL RATINGS						
		Wght: 230 From: Mississippi State					TOT	OFF	DEF	REB	PAS	HND	SHT	ATH
--		2011-12 status: free agent					+2	--	--	--	--	--	--	--

Year	Team	Age	G	MPG	Usg	3PA%	FTA%	INS	2P%	3P%	FT%	TS%	Reb%	Ast%	TO%	BLK%	STL%	PF%	oRTG	dRTG	Win%	WARP
10-11p	MIA	23.1	76	-	.139	.000	.139	1.139	.477	.000	.596	.510	.130	.012	.149	.066	.008	.050	-	-	.492	-

Most similar to: Emeka Okafor (95.0), Justin Williams, Channing Frye   IMP: -   BRK: -   COP: -

The Heat picked up Jarvis Varnado with the 41th overall pick in the second round and will hope he develops a game more appropriate to his body type in the Italian League, where he signed with second-division squad Carmatic Pistoia over the summer. At Mississippi State, Varnado was a defensive anchor extraordinaire, finishing as the leading shot blocker in NCAA history. However, he's far too slender to be a center in the NBA, so he's got to flesh out at least a couple of other usable traits in his game. Length and athleticism aren't bad starting points.

PG	**Rafer Alston**	Hght: 6'2" Exp: 11 Salary: --					SKILL RATINGS						
		Wght: 171 From: Fresno State					TOT	OFF	DEF	REB	PAS	HND	SHT	ATH
--		2011-12 status: free agent					-1	0	+4	-1	-1	0	-4	0

Year	Team	Age	G	MPG	Usg	3PA%	FTA%	INS	2P%	3P%	FT%	TS%	Reb%	Ast%	TO%	BLK%	STL%	PF%	oRTG	dRTG	Win%	WARP
07-08	HOU	31.7	74	34.1	.208	.356	.053	.697	.427	.351	.715	.492	.057	.071	.140	.005	.018	.026	105.7	105.2	.517	5.3
08-09	ORL	32.7	77	31.8	.200	.315	.087	.772	.417	.338	.750	.494	.052	.077	.133	.003	.023	.026	106.9	106.2	.524	5.5
09-10	MIA	33.7	52	27.3	.190	.291	.062	.770	.349	.345	.728	.443	.054	.058	.165	.005	.018	.034	102.6	106.5	.372	-1.3
10-11p	AVG	34.7	76	27.3	.181	.349	.064	.714	.387	.344	.731	.475	.053	.061	.156	.006	.018	.031	104.0	106.2	.428	0.5

Most similar to: Lindsey Hunter (96.7), Randy Smith, Derek Fisher, Damon Stoudamire   IMP: 44%   BRK: 5%   COP: 3%

Rafer Alston is hoping for another NBA season, but he may no longer be worth the trouble. Alston seemed largely disengaged last season, then bolted on the Heat after his sister attempted suicide. The problem wasn't that he left the team. It was that he didn't tell them why he left. Alston didn't tell them anything. He just left, and it coincided with getting benched during a game. Alston tumbled to well below replacement level last year, with a decline inside the arc that doesn't bode well for the 34-year-old.

SF	**Yakhouba Diawara**	Hght: 6'7" Exp: 4 Salary: --					SKILL RATINGS						
		Wght: 225 From: Pepperdine					TOT	OFF	DEF	REB	PAS	HND	SHT	ATH
--		2011-12 status: free agent					-2	+1	+2	-5	-2	+4	0	-5

Year	Team	Age	G	MPG	Usg	3PA%	FTA%	INS	2P%	3P%	FT%	TS%	Reb%	Ast%	TO%	BLK%	STL%	PF%	oRTG	dRTG	Win%	WARP
07-08	DEN	25.6	54	10.0	.129	.403	.083	.680	.500	.318	.710	.518	.062	.029	.098	.004	.006	.047	104.6	108.5	.375	-0.5
08-09	MIA	26.6	63	13.5	.134	.675	.035	.359	.463	.313	.526	.473	.058	.015	.066	.006	.008	.042	105.2	108.7	.387	-0.5
09-10	MIA	27.6	6	7.3	.140	.462	.000	.538	.250	.167	-	.250	.053	.032	.231	.000	.012	.086	98.0	109.5	.175	-0.2
10-11p	AVG	28.6	76	7.3	.127	.650	.047	.396	.490	.327	.607	.507	.054	.021	.080	.004	.006	.043	105.0	108.4	.391	-0.3

Most similar to: Rafael Addison (93.6), Michael Curry, Keith Bogans, Rasual Butler   IMP: 45%   BRK: 10%   COP: 10%

Yakhouba Diawara had a nice run, hanging around the NBA for four seasons despite being a wing player with no offensive ability whatsoever. He signed to play for Enel Brindisi in the Italian League next season.

Milwaukee Bucks

Under the regime of general manager John Hammond and head coach Scott Skiles, the Bucks are building a nice little basketball operation in the Upper Midwest. However, in light of the rise of several teams within Milwaukee's conference, how much will it ultimately matter?

Let's not begin there. The Bucks have done a lot of things right over the last couple of years, not the least of which was hiring Skiles, who has instilled his brand of tough-as-nails, in-your-face defense in Milwaukee and given the franchise a style of play to call its own. In two seasons, Skiles has taken the Bucks from 30th to third in Defensive Rating and 26 to 46 in victories. Anybody that thinks coaching doesn't matter in the NBA just isn't paying attention. The Bucks won 29 of 42 games to finish the season and made the playoffs as a six-seed, earning their first postseason berth since 2006. Once there, Milwaukee narrowly missed knocking off the favored Hawks in the first round despite the absence of injured center Andrew Bogut, the victim of a nasty fall during an early April game against the Suns.

It's not all Skiles, of course. The Bucks hit a home run in the 2009 Draft with their selection of point guard Brandon Jennings. The pick might not have been a grand slam, but was at least a three-run shot. Jennings exploded on the NBA scene with a 55-point game against the Warriors early in the season, then spent the rest of the campaign trying to live up to the expectations created by that stunning performance.

The kid has some rough edges to iron out. His herky-jerky jump shot was inconsistent during his rookie season and he posted just a .475 True Shooting Percentage. However, Jennings played in every game, averaged nearly 33 minutes of court time, held his own on defense, posted a solid assist percentage, took care of the ball and even proved adept on the defensive glass for a player his size. More than anything else, Jennings has that intangible "it" factor that you can't really describe or quantify, but you know if you see it. (If Bill James were dead, he would have just rolled over in his grave.) If Jennings can become a more consistent shooter, he will become the superstar that the Bucks can build around for the next decade--the first home-grown, elite foundation player the Bucks have gotten their hands on since Sidney Moncrief.

Last year, we noted a tuning-out effect in the teams Skiles coached before Milwaukee. In Phoenix, it hit in year three. In Chicago, it didn't come until year five. Things feel different this time around, but entering his third season in Milwaukee, this is a situation that bears watching. The telltale sign in the past is a sudden slip in Defensive Rating. There is hardly anywhere to go but down in that respect for the Bucks, but a stark drop would be a surprise and perhaps indicative of a problem. If Skiles is no longer getting through to his charges, we'll see it on the defensive end of the floor. Right now, if the opposition doesn't share the ball and keep players moving away from the

BUCKS IN A BOX

Last year's record	46-36
Last year's Offensive Rating	106.2 (23)
Last year's Defensive Rating	105.1 (3)
Last year's point differential	1.7 (14)
Team pace	90.3 (21)
SCHOENE projection	**42-40 (6)**
Projected Offensive Rating	108.7 (22)
Projected Defensive Rating	108.4 (9)
Projected team weighted age	27.4 (16)
Projected '10-11 payroll	$69.2 (10)
Est. payroll obligations, '11-12	$53.1 (17)
Head coach: Scott Skiles	

Last year's Bucks were a quintessential Scott Skiles team. Playing his unorthodox brand of aggressive pressure defense, Milwaukee ranked fourth in the league in Defensive Rating. The Bucks finished in the NBA's top 10 in three of the four defensive Four Factors but were 29th in terms of putting opponents on the free throw line. Skiles did a nice job of integrating newcomers into the Milwaukee lineup and was especially effective handling Brandon Jennings' adjustment to the NBA. Skiles earned Basketball Prospectus' vote for Coach of the Year and ranked second in the media voting for the award.

ball, they are going to have a hard time scoring against the Bucks, who are terrific at defending the pick-and-roll, winning isolations and contesting spot-up shots. The only real weak link is their transition defense. The Skiles profile is to take care of the ball on offense and force turnovers on the other end while disrupting the flow of the opponent's attack with a physical defensive stance. Milwaukee defended well across the board last season, but at the cost of committing a lot of fouls. Under Skiles, that's not going to change. However, you can commit fouls because of laziness or lack of lateral quickness or you can commit them because you're playing balls-out defense. If the Bucks' high foul rate is accompanied by a spike in opponent effective field-goal percentage, look out.

In last year's book, we were very wrong about the Bucks, in terms of their selection of Jennings, their outlook for last season and the overall direction of the franchise. The feeling was that they'd overachieved, mostly by the grace of their coach, and the talent hadn't been upgraded enough to maintain the charge. The Jennings pick was a wild card and felt questionable, especially given the fact that former Bucks Luke Ridnour and Ramon Sessions made point guard a position of strength. The Bucks got it right, but Jennings wasn't their only feel-good story last season.

Before getting hurt, Bogut had established himself as one of the best post players in the league. To maintain their progress, the Bucks need Bogut to recover, stay healthy and resume the level of play he was playing at when he was hurt. If he hadn't been injured, the Bucks would probably have gotten by Atlanta in the first round and surely would have been a tougher opponent for Orlando than the Hawks proved to be in the conference semifinals. As training camp approached, it sounded like Bogut's early-season availability was very much up in the air, and he hasn't been able to shoot with his natural form since having surgery on his elbow. If he's good to go, you'd like to see an element of the Milwaukee offense with more Princeton or flex principles, utilizing cutters and Bogut's ability to pass the ball out of the high post. If he's back to 100 percent, Bogut will remain Milwaukee's best player no matter what Jennings does.

Elsewhere, Ersan Ilyasova showed the potential to be the third wheel in this machine. You have to credit former Bucks general manager Larry Harris for drafting Ilyasova back in 2005 as well as crediting Hammond for bringing him back after two seasons overseas at just the right time. Perhaps Hammond pays close attention to SCHOENE, because our projections system pretty much nailed Ilyasova based on his European translations. Ilyasova is a gifted face-up player who just needs to become a little more consistent behind the arc. He's also a good passer, a lengthy defender and a legit rebounder from the four position. If he can improve his average defense, he can win Skiles' confidence and become a 30-minute player. He needs to do that, though, because the competition will be fierce with Drew Gooden, Luc Richard Mbah a Moute, Jon Brockman and Larry Sanders all capable of logging minutes at the four position.

John Salmons played inspired ball after coming over from Chicago in a deadline deal that sent Hakim Warrick and Joe Alexander to the Bulls. (The Bucks also swapped first-round picks in the trade, which allowed them to draft Sanders.) In just four more minutes per game, Salmons upped his scoring average from 12.7 points with Chicago to 19.9 points with Milwaukee. It wasn't just raw numbers, either; his efficiency also jumped. Despite increasing his usage rate by 4.6 percent after the move, Salmons upped his True Shooting Percentage from .530 to .581. As a result, the Bucks handed him a long-term deal during the offseason. Salmons should remain a solid player this season, but he'll be 31 in December and the Bucks are looking at three guaranteed seasons beyond this one. At $8 million per annum, it's not a total cap-wrecker, but the Bucks are already on the books for roughly a third of a salary cap five years down the line, a figure likely to grow larger when Jennings is eventually given an extension. The Bucks are going to wish the money due Salmons was freed up at some point, sooner rather than later.

The Bucks' record of drafting has been hit or miss recently, but they've been able to improve anyway by recognizing the mistakes quickly, and turning their underachievers into usable assets. Sure, they nailed the Jennings pick and deserve credit for the fact that his selection was far from being a no-brainer at the time. There is still Yi Jianlian and Joe Alexander for which to answer. However, Yi was eventually turned into Carlos Delfino, while Alexander was a small part of the deal that brought back Salmons. Those were some nice recoveries by Hammond. Still, when he took Alexander, he could have had either of the Lopez twins; instead of Yi, Harris could have had Joakim Noah. Teams of Milwaukee's market size can't whiff on lottery picks and get away with it for very long.

The Bucks' plan this offseason was to add some firepower to the offense, which fell off so drastically after Bogut was injured, and add some size to cover themselves from further absences from their star center.

First, Milwaukee added Corey Maggette from Golden State in a trade for Dan Gadzuric and Charlie Bell. The series against the Hawks showed that the Bucks were short a scorer or two, but how do they integrate Maggette? Does Maggette really make them better? Does he conflict with Salmons? Can Maggette continue last season's trend for better shot selection? Where he helps them is in his ability to get to the line. Milwaukee had the league's worst foul-drawing rate last season, which will happen when your offense is so stagnant and ineffective. Only San Antonio ran more pick-and-rolls than Milwaukee, but the Bucks were 24th on a points-per-play basis. Like San Antonio, Milwaukee also had a high rate of spot-up shots (third), presumably off of pick-and-pop plays); here, the success rate was better (11th). Still, there is not much motion in this offense and not much transition, which is disappointing considering the presence of Jennings. At the very least, Maggette should give them someone who can put the ball on the floor, get to the line and run the court.

First-round pick Sanders is potentially a great fit. He is a long, shot-blocking four with a good face-up jumper who can run the pick-and-roll with Jennings and also get down the floor with him in transition. That's the scouting angle. His initial statistical translations aren't quite that optimistic and he must prove himself against heightened competition after coming out of Virginia Commonwealth. Drew Gooden may yet become the first player to play for every franchise. He's oft-acquired because of what he is: a good scorer and fine rebounder. He's oft-traded because of what he isn't: a long big man with good athleticism. He'll help the Bucks in a limited role, proving additional punch for the second unit unless his defense is so poor that Skiles refuses to put him on the court.

The loss of Ridnour is tough. He had a tremendous season in 2009-10 and, while he will likely regress, he still would have helped cover the Bucks against further inconsistency from the still-developing Jennings. Can offseason acquisitions Keyon Dooling and/or Earl Boykins make up for the loss of Ridnour, who signed with Minnesota over the summer? Perhaps in tandem they can, but it's not likely.

What is the ceiling here? That's the key question, the one with which we began this chapter. The Bucks have built a nice team and have continued to massage

> **From the Blogosphere**
>
> **Who:** Frank Madden
> **What:** Brew Hoop
> **Where:** http://www.brewhoop.com/
>
> The obvious concern is the health of Andrew Bogut. His right arm injury may make him even more dependent on the lefty hook he already favored (off two feet, not running), though the Bucks can ill afford to be missing their MVP and defensive anchor for long. Next to Bogut, Ersan Ilyasova may be a chucker with some of the worst post instincts ever seen in a 6'10" player, but he and Luc Richard Mbah a Moute are crucial glue guys. John Salmons is destined to be a cap albatross in a couple years, but he still has a gravity-defying knack for absorbing contact and finishing while on the way down from his not-so-majestic heights. That helped make him the Bucks' top scoring option down the stretch, though perhaps that's faint praise. Fortunately, Salmons will also get much-needed wing scoring help from free throw machine Corey Maggette and his new apprentice, Chris Douglas-Roberts.

the roster to maintain their progress. However, is there a championship core here? Jennings could develop into that kind of a player. Bogut could be the third-best player on an elite team. That's really about it. The Bucks are probably still one upper-crust player away from hanging with the big boys. Unless Ilyasova and/or Sanders develop in unforeseen ways, it's difficult to see how they are going to come up with one--especially now that they've improved to the point that picking in the lottery probably won't happen in the foreseeable future.

This season could reveal whether or not the Bucks still have some upward mobility with this group, which you'd hope for given that their second-best player is just 21 years old. They may settle into a dangerous period of being locked into the 42-47 win range, health permitting. That might sound good for fans of a team that has been down for awhile, but it gets old really fast. There is little growth left from the defensive improvements Skiles has made, so the offense has to get better for Milwaukee to even maintain its plateau.

SCHOENE sees a slip for the Bucks this season, which isn't surprising when you consider where Milwaukee was just two years ago on the defensive end of the floor. Perhaps Skiles can maintain the defensive standing, but more troubling is the fact that they don't project to improve much on the offensive end, even though that's what the focus was in the off-season.

Overall, we see the Bucks as finishing on the right side of .500, but again on a tier below the big boys in the East, which now means Miami, Orlando and Chicago.

Bradford Doolittle

BUCKS FIVE-YEAR TRENDS

Season	AGE	W-L	POW	PYTH	SEED	ORTG	DRTG	PT DIFF	PACE
05-06	25.5	40-42	38.0 (16)	38.0	8	107.6 (15)	109.4 (25)	-1.0 (16)	89.8 (13)
06-07	26.0	28-54	27.2 (28)	29.0	—	108.3 (13)	113.6 (29)	-4.4 (28)	91.0 (10)
07-08	25.8	26-56	22.7 (26)	22.7	—	107.2 (23)	115.1 (30)	-6.9 (27)	89.6 (16)
08-09	26.3	34-48	36.1 (19)	38.2	—	108.2 (23)	109.2 (15)	-1.0 (18)	91.4 (11)
09-10	27.1	46-36	45.2 (14)	46.0	6	106.2 (23)	105.1 (3)	1.7 (14)	90.3 (21)

		OFFENSE				DEFENSE			
Season	PAY	eFG	oREB	FT/FGA	TO	eFG	oREB	FT/FGA	TO
05-06	$56.5	.492 (14)	.273 (11)	.238 (22)	.161 (19)	.504 (23)	.746 (6)	.262 (21)	.159 (17)
06-07	$54.6	.504 (8)	.276 (15)	.209 (30)	.165 (15)	.522 (29)	.681 (30)	.234 (11)	.171 (7)
07-08	$62.3	.482 (23)	.300 (3)	.215 (23)	.158 (25)	.524 (30)	.730 (18)	.250 (21)	.146 (16)
08-09	$70.2	.484 (25)	.279 (7)	.241 (11)	.154 (16)	.502 (17)	.741 (11)	.312 (30)	.178 (1)
09-10	$68.3	.482 (25)	.262 (18)	.181 (30)	.144 (4)	.486 (8)	.764 (3)	.266 (29)	.167 (4)

(league rankings in parenthesis)

Andrew Bogut — C, 6

Hght: 7'0" Exp: 5 Salary: $11.0 million
Wght: 260 From: Melbourne, Australia
2011-12 status: guaranteed contract for $12.0 million

SKILL RATINGS

TOT	OFF	DEF	REB	PAS	HND	SHT	ATH
+4	+2	+4	+2	+4	+2	+3	0

Year	Team	Age	G	MPG	Usg	3PA%	FTA%	INS	2P%	3P%	FT%	TS%	Reb%	Ast%	TO%	BLK%	STL%	PF%	oRTG	dRTG	Win%	WARP
07-08	MIL	23.4	78	34.9	.203	.006	.116	1.110	.515	.000	.587	.532	.168	.033	.142	.039	.011	.043	104.6	103.8	.526	6.2
08-09	MIL	24.4	36	31.2	.179	.000	.097	1.097	.577	.000	.571	.586	.197	.029	.193	.027	.010	.052	105.2	104.7	.516	2.3
09-10	MIL	25.4	69	32.3	.234	.002	.091	1.089	.521	.000	.629	.540	.182	.026	.114	.062	.009	.045	105.4	101.8	.619	9.4
10-11p	MIL	26.4	72	32.0	.204	.004	.101	1.097	.548	.004	.614	.563	.172	.030	.140	.042	.009	.045	105.3	103.3	.567	7.3

Most similar to: Emeka Okafor (98.6), Benoit Benjamin, Dikembe Mutombo, Larry Nance IMP: 50% BRK: 2% COP: 2%

One of the more unfortunate moments of the 2009-10 season happened in Milwaukee on April 3, when Andrew Bogut took off on a run out against Phoenix. He beat everyone down the floor, took a long outlet pass from Carlos Delfino and dunked the ball with two hands. Amar'e Stoudemire, who was trailing the play, gave Bogut a light shove with his left hand, knocking Bogut off balance. He attempted to hang on the rim to recompose himself, but he was going too fast and his hands slipped off, sending his feet flying in front of him. Bogut's right arm wrapped around his back and he crashed to the floor on top of it. He suffered a broken index finger, a broken wrist and a severely dislocated elbow, ending his season. He's lucky it didn't end his career. The Bucks played spirited basketball once Bogut went down, but after Milwaukee dropped a seven-game series in the first round against Atlanta, you have to think having their best player would have gotten them over the hump. Bogut didn't resume shooting the ball until the latter stages of summer, and before camp opened, Bucks general manager John Hammond said that Bogut is likely going to be playing through pain all season. The Bucks need Bogut at or near his previous level, which was All-Star caliber. He's become one of the more prolific post players in the league and remains a terrific passer for his position. His defense is easily above average and last season his shot blocks soared to a career-high 2.54 swats per game. Bogut takes 89 percent of his shots within 10 feet of the basket, so the hope is that he can remain an effective interior scoring threat even if he doesn't initially regain full range of motion in the elbow.

MILWAUKEE BUCKS

PG 11	Earl Boykins	Hght: 5'5" Exp: 11 Salary: $1.4 million						
		Wght: 133 From: Eastern Michigan						
		2011-12 status: free agent						

SKILL RATINGS

TOT	OFF	DEF	REB	PAS	HND	SHT	ATH
-3	+1	-4	-5	0	+1	-4	-4

Year	Team	Age	G	MPG	Usg	3PA%	FTA%	INS	2P%	3P%	FT%	TS%	Reb%	Ast%	TO%	BLK%	STL%	PF%	oRTG	dRTG	Win%	WARP
07-08	CHA	31.9	36	15.9	.192	.184	.109	.925	.367	.318	.831	.467	.034	.077	.172	.000	.010	.017	103.7	107.5	.378	-0.5
09-10	WAS	33.9	67	16.7	.209	.117	.077	.959	.446	.317	.865	.498	.039	.070	.135	.002	.011	.020	104.8	107.6	.409	-0.2
10-11p	MIL	34.9	73	5.0	.185	.176	.080	.904	.413	.335	.878	.489	.034	.066	.141	.002	.010	.020	104.2	107.6	.387	-0.2

Most similar to: Charlie Criss (95.1), Damon Stoudamire, Chucky Atkins, Kenny Anderson   IMP: 32%   BRK: 0%   COP: 5%

The Bucks are hoping that some combination of Earl Boykins and Keyon Dooling will make up for the departure of Luke Ridnour, one of the top backup point guards in the league. Boykins isn't quite as much of an unconscious gunner as he once was, but he's still not an efficient shooter. Perhaps because of his size, the 5'5" Boykins has trouble hitting three-point shots consistently, though he's never been shy about taking them. Most of his looks come off the dribble, which freezes out his teammates. He's also not a great distributor of the ball. Boykins is quick down the floor and can help teams when they want to push the pace, which doesn't happen a whole lot in Milwaukee. As you'd expect, Boykins is a defensive cipher and doesn't even provide a high steal rate to help compensate. Boykins turns 35 during the next postseason, which makes the guaranteed deal Milwaukee gave him this summer a little hard to fathom.

PF 40	Jon Brockman	Hght: 6'7" Exp: 1 Salary: $1.0 million						
		Wght: 255 From: Washington						
		2011-12 status: guaranteed contract for $1.0 million						

SKILL RATINGS

TOT	OFF	DEF	REB	PAS	HND	SHT	ATH
+1	--	-2	--	--	--	--	--

Year	Team	Age	G	MPG	Usg	3PA%	FTA%	INS	2P%	3P%	FT%	TS%	Reb%	Ast%	TO%	BLK%	STL%	PF%	oRTG	dRTG	Win%	WARP
09-10	SAC	23.1	52	12.6	.104	.000	.178	1.178	.534	-	.597	.564	.187	.015	.150	.006	.011	.078	106.0	107.6	.448	0.4
10-11p	MIL	24.1	72	-	.100	.000	.175	1.175	.527	.000	.605	.560	.169	.018	.151	.006	.012	.075	-	-	.483	-

Most similar to: Reggie Evans (97.0), Reggie King, Tyrone Hill, Adam Keefe   IMP: 46%   BRK: 10%   COP: 8%

Anyone that grew up playing Statis-Pro basketball has a soft spot for rebounding specialists. Those old-school table-top guys would love Jon Brockman--who, for the record, would have had a rebound rating of 33 for his rookie season. Statis-Pro players would have also loved Brockman's field-goal percentage (11-52!), but his stamina and secondary ratings would have been low. Brockman became the odd man out in a post numbers game in Sacramento after the Kings acquired Samuel Dalembert and drafted DeMarcus Cousins and Hassan Whiteside. Brockman is the kind of dirty-work player that Scott Skiles will appreciate. He commits seven fouls per 40 minutes, which will fit right in on the league's most foul-prone team. Brockman lacks the mobility or length to be a quality on-ball defender, and he's got to develop a face-up shot to have any use on offense beyond an astronomical offensive rebound rate.

SF 10	Carlos Delfino	Hght: 6'6" Exp: 5 Salary: $3.5 million						
		Wght: 230 From: Santa Fe, Argentina						
		2011-12 status: partially-guaranteed contract for $3.5 million						

SKILL RATINGS

TOT	OFF	DEF	REB	PAS	HND	SHT	ATH
+2	+2	+3	+1	+3	+3	+1	-2

Year	Team	Age	G	MPG	Usg	3PA%	FTA%	INS	2P%	3P%	FT%	TS%	Reb%	Ast%	TO%	BLK%	STL%	PF%	oRTG	dRTG	Win%	WARP
07-08	TOR	25.6	82	23.5	.191	.405	.088	.684	.412	.382	.744	.527	.111	.036	.097	.005	.017	.043	106.2	105.5	.523	4.3
09-10	MIL	27.6	75	30.4	.181	.404	.058	.654	.450	.367	.782	.526	.102	.040	.132	.007	.018	.028	105.3	104.7	.522	5.0
10-11p	MIL	28.6	75	24.0	.168	.423	.061	.639	.443	.377	.775	.534	.096	.040	.129	.006	.017	.031	105.6	105.2	.512	3.6

Most similar to: Walt Williams (97.8), Morris Peterson, Fred Hoiberg, Scott Burrell   IMP: 37%   BRK: 2%   COP: 10%

After starting six games in four previous NBA seasons, Carlos Delfino started 66 in 2009-10 and became an important part of the Bucks' rotation. All it really took was a coach to value what he had to offer, because on a per-minute and per-possession basis, he was pretty much the same player he has always been. Delfino takes half of his shots from behind the three-point line and can be counted upon to knock down an above-average percentage, so that's a big part of his game. He doesn't mess with the midrange stuff, which makes sense because he shoots poorly there. Delfino isn't particularly athletic and doesn't finish well at the rim, though his percentage there was better last season. He's an unselfish player and a good passer who rebounds well on the defensive end, though he's too far away from the basket to be a factor on the offensive glass. On defense, Delfino is above average, with solid marks in most on-ball metrics and a decent steal rate. Still, the Bucks were better defensively when he went to the bench.

PG 55	Keyon Dooling	Hght: 6'3" Wght: 195 2011-12 status: guaranteed contract for $2.2 million	Exp: 10 From: Missouri	Salary: $2.1 million							
					SKILL RATINGS						
					TOT	OFF	DEF	REB	PAS	HND	SHT	ATH
					+1	+3	+3	-5	-1	+1	+1	-2

Year	Team	Age	G	MPG	Usg	3PA%	FTA%	INS	2P%	3P%	FT%	TS%	Reb%	Ast%	TO%	BLK%	STL%	PF%	oRTG	dRTG	Win%	WARP
07-08	ORL	28.0	72	18.5	.197	.114	.149	1.035	.492	.338	.845	.572	.042	.046	.107	.003	.012	.044	105.3	107.4	.432	0.4
08-09	NJN	29.0	77	26.9	.175	.305	.088	.783	.446	.421	.825	.562	.045	.061	.136	.003	.018	.031	107.2	107.5	.490	3.2
09-10	NJN	30.0	53	18.3	.195	.383	.065	.682	.419	.376	.770	.519	.033	.064	.144	.000	.018	.039	106.4	107.7	.457	0.8
10-11p	MIL	31.0	71	15.0	.181	.366	.083	.716	.440	.394	.800	.548	.036	.061	.131	.001	.016	.039	106.8	107.2	.487	1.6

Most similar to: Allen Leavell (99.0), Mike James, Juan Dixon, Mike Bratz   IMP: 44%   BRK: 8%   COP: 5%

Keyon Dooling will most likely be the primary backup to Brandon Jennings in his first season with the Bucks. Dooling has turned into a good catch-and-shoot player with range and is a solid on-ball defender. The high foul-drawing rates he used to post have gone by the wayside as he's become more perimeter oriented. Where he comes up short of Luke Ridnour, whose job he is inheriting, is in his ability to run an offense. Even 10 years into his pro career, Dooling still plays like a natural two-guard learning to play the point. Dooling is a decent backup option, but a clear downgrade from Ridnour.

SF 17	Chris Douglas-Roberts	Hght: 6'7" Wght: 210 2011-12 status: due qualifying offer of $1.1 million	Exp: 2 From: Memphis	Salary: $0.9 million							
					SKILL RATINGS						
					TOT	OFF	DEF	REB	PAS	HND	SHT	ATH
					-2	--	+2	--	--	--	--	--

Year	Team	Age	G	MPG	Usg	3PA%	FTA%	INS	2P%	3P%	FT%	TS%	Reb%	Ast%	TO%	BLK%	STL%	PF%	oRTG	dRTG	Win%	WARP
08-09	NJN	22.3	44	13.3	.189	.051	.116	1.065	.476	.250	.823	.531	.051	.042	.132	.010	.011	.027	103.8	107.8	.371	-0.5
09-10	NJN	23.3	67	25.8	.198	.073	.093	1.020	.464	.259	.847	.512	.068	.025	.131	.008	.016	.027	101.8	106.4	.350	-2.4
10-11p	MIL	24.3	73	-	.189	.126	.102	.975	.475	.282	.873	.527	.059	.034	.124	.010	.013	.025	-	-	.398	-

Most similar to: Willie Burton (98.9), Todd Lichti, Lucious Harris, Alvin Williams   IMP: 61%   BRK: 13%   COP: 11%

Chris Douglas-Roberts had a chance to establish himself as a legitimate scorer during last year's debacle in New Jersey, but he's still trying to figure out what kind of offensive player he's going to be at the NBA level. Douglas-Roberts does not yet have three-point range on his jump shot, which stifles his efficiency because he has draws fouls at only an average rate and shoots a low percentage from the midrange. Douglas-Roberts' first step is not quick enough to create quality looks of his own, and his inconsistent stroke makes him a poor fit as a catch-and-shot option. As Douglas-Roberts tried to become more aggressive as a scorer, his assist rate dropped, which dented his Offensive Rating that much more. As bad as the Nets were on offense last season, they were 4.5 points worse per 100 possessions with Douglas-Roberts on the floor. Douglas-Roberts does appear to be a plus defender, which is likely what attracted the Bucks' attention. He'll have a lot more stability around him in Milwaukee and the hope is that he'll improve his stroke and find a niche for himself on offense.

PF 23	Tiny Gallon	Hght: 6'9" Wght: 290 2011-12 status: free agent	Exp: R From: Oklahoma	Salary: $0.5 million							
					SKILL RATINGS						
					TOT	OFF	DEF	REB	PAS	HND	SHT	ATH
					-2	--	--	--	--	--	--	--

Year	Team	Age	G	MPG	Usg	3PA%	FTA%	INS	2P%	3P%	FT%	TS%	Reb%	Ast%	TO%	BLK%	STL%	PF%	oRTG	dRTG	Win%	WARP
10-11p	MIL	20.3	76	-	.173	.042	.088	1.046	.478	.209	.684	.503	.158	.015	.208	.016	.011	.079	-	-	.391	-

Most similar to: J.J. Hickson (91.8), DeAndre Jordan, Spencer Hawes   IMP: -   BRK: -   COP: -

MILWAUKEE BUCKS

The Bucks took a flier on Tiny Gallon, who is of course anything but. Gallon's deal with Milwaukee isn't guaranteed and the Bucks are going to camp with 15 guaranteed contracts, so you can draw your own conclusions. There is nothing in Gallon's translated college stats that marks him as an interesting player. What he has going for him is size, youth and perhaps the fleeting hope he's going to be a good face-up shooter.

PF 0	Drew Gooden	Hght: 6'10" Exp: 8 Salary: $5.8 million				SKILL RATINGS								
		Wght: 250 From: Kansas				TOT	OFF	DEF	REB	PAS	HND	SHT	ATH
		2011-12 status: guaranteed contract for $6.1 million				0	0	-4	+3	-3	-4	-2	0

Year	Team	Age	G	MPG	Usg	3PA%	FTA%	INS	2P%	3P%	FT%	TS%	Reb%	Ast%	TO%	BLK%	STL%	PF%	oRTG	dRTG	Win%	WARP
07-08	CHI	26.6	69	30.8	.201	.006	.099	1.092	.451	.000	.753	.494	.159	.017	.127	.020	.010	.043	102.0	104.7	.408	-0.4
08-09	SAS	27.6	51	24.8	.237	.006	.105	1.099	.472	.000	.840	.526	.165	.017	.117	.011	.012	.052	104.9	106.3	.455	1.0
09-10	LAC	28.6	70	25.1	.211	.010	.118	1.108	.483	.125	.861	.547	.178	.012	.134	.025	.012	.051	105.2	105.0	.506	3.3
10-11p	MIL	29.6	72	25.0	.205	.009	.104	1.095	.478	.069	.827	.529	.152	.015	.132	.020	.011	.050	103.7	105.3	.449	1.3

Most similar to: Lorenzen Wright (98.7), Kevin Willis, Armon Gilliam, Tyrone Hill   IMP: 34% BRK: 7% COP: 9%

Drew Gooden is not a bad player, even though the Bucks will be his 10th organization in nine NBA seasons. He's not yet 30 years old and he's worked in more cities than George Clooney's character in *Up in the Air.* Wherever he goes, he plays a significant role until his team finds somebody they think is better. Through it all, Gooden has remained remarkably consistent. He's an excellent rebounder on both ends of the floor, but the rest of his skill set is average or worse. Gooden is not a rebounding specialist, per se, but he has never shot a high enough percentage to be an efficient offensive player. He doesn't pass the ball well and is overly reliant on long twos. Gooden has always used plays at an above-average rate, but maybe it's time for him to stop trying to be more than he is. On defense, his metrics are poor. He's a little slow and doesn't have much leaping ability. He is strong and knows how to position himself, so he can function adequately when playing alongside a good help defender. The Bucks gave him an unwieldy five-year, $32 million deal, which they are going to regret sooner rather than later. Gooden will serve as a placeholder at center as long as Andrew Bogut is unable to play full time during his recovery from elbow surgery.

SG 9	Darington Hobson	Hght: 6'7" Exp: R Salary: $0.5 million				SKILL RATINGS								
		Wght: 210 From: New Mexico				TOT	OFF	DEF	REB	PAS	HND	SHT	ATH
		2011-12 status: free agent				0	–	–	–	–	–	–	–

Year	Team	Age	G	MPG	Usg	3PA%	FTA%	INS	2P%	3P%	FT%	TS%	Reb%	Ast%	TO%	BLK%	STL%	PF%	oRTG	dRTG	Win%	WARP
10-11p	MIL	23.6	76	-	.183	.136	.099	.963	.373	.302	.638	.428	.119	.058	.170	.007	.014	.039	-	-	.438	-

Most similar to: Luke Walton (95.7), Chris Jefferies, Joey Graham, DeMarcus Nelson   IMP: - BRK: - COP: -

The odds are stacked against Darington Hobson, the 37th pick of the most recent draft. The lefty is a tweener forward in style, but has a wing player's body. He has excellent passing skills, but will struggle to find a defensive niche. Worst of all for Hobson, he injured his groin, which is likely going to keep him out of training camp. Hobson may need to have surgery, which would knock him out for his rookie year. Only the first season of his deal is guaranteed, so there is little preventing the Bucks from eating those dollars and giving Hobson's roster spot to Tiny Gallon.

PF 7	Ersan Ilyasova	Hght: 6'10" Exp: 2 Salary: $2.3 million				SKILL RATINGS								
		Wght: 235 From: Eskisehir, Turkey				TOT	OFF	DEF	REB	PAS	HND	SHT	ATH
		2011-12 status: partially-guaranteed contract for $2.5 million				+3	+3	0	+2	+1	+3	0	0

Year	Team	Age	G	MPG	Usg	3PA%	FTA%	INS	2P%	3P%	FT%	TS%	Reb%	Ast%	TO%	BLK%	STL%	PF%	oRTG	dRTG	Win%	WARP
09-10	MIL	22.9	81	23.4	.209	.277	.080	.803	.496	.336	.715	.526	.158	.020	.082	.010	.014	.060	106.8	105.6	.541	4.9
10-11p	MIL	23.9	76	20.0	.208	.306	.078	.773	.501	.338	.728	.531	.142	.022	.083	.010	.014	.056	107.0	105.7	.541	4.0

Most similar to: Charlie Villanueva (98.4), Gene Banks, Paul Thompson, Mike Brooks   IMP: 53% BRK: 5% COP: 2%

MILWAUKEE BUCKS

From time to time, you'd hear Ersan Ilyasova referred to as a rookie because people forgot he had played for the Bucks in the 2006-07 season before heading back overseas for a couple of years. Ilyasova returned to the NBA much more mature, both in body and game. He played a key role in the Bucks' improvement and now looks like he can be a foundation player for Milwaukee. The only thing holding Ilyasova back last season offensively was an iffy three-point percentage, but he's got an easy stroke from downtown and shot the ball much better from deep in his rookie campaign. At 6'10", he has a chance to be a premier spot-up shooter. His usage rate was above average even though more than three-quarters of his field goals came off assists. Ilyasova doesn't spend a lot of time in the middle, but gets to the rim and gets a fair share of putbacks. He's a good passer and takes care of the ball. Defensively, he defended the pick-and-roll very well and excelled when teams tried to take him in isolation. Not the strongest guy in the world, Ilyasova was vulnerable to post-ups. Overall, he rated as an average defender. Ilyasova should be a fixture in Milwaukee for many years to come.

PG 3 — Brandon Jennings

Hght: 6'1" Exp: 1 Salary: $2.3 million
Wght: 169 From: Oak Hill Academy (Mouth of Wilson, VA)
2011-12 status: team option for $2.5 million

SKILL RATINGS

TOT	OFF	DEF	REB	PAS	HND	SHT	ATH
+3	+4	+4	+1	+2	+1	-4	+2

Year	Team	Age	G	MPG	Usg	3PA%	FTA%	INS	2P%	3P%	FT%	TS%	Reb%	Ast%	TO%	BLK%	STL%	PF%	oRTG	dRTG	Win%	WARP
09-10	MIL	20.6	82	32.6	.262	.253	.078	.826	.370	.374	.817	.475	.062	.080	.130	.005	.020	.033	106.2	105.6	.518	5.6
10-11p	MIL	21.6	76	34.0	.257	.262	.078	.816	.377	.392	.826	.491	.058	.081	.126	.004	.020	.031	107.0	105.7	.543	6.8

Most similar to: Isiah Thomas (95.4), Stephon Marbury, Sebastian Telfair, Mike Bibby

IMP: - BRK: - COP: -

Brandon Jennings exceeded all expectations last season and you can craft a good argument that he should have been the NBA Rookie of the Year. A glance at Jennings' skill ratings confirms what you've heard about the flashy lefty. He's good across the board, but won't reach All-Star level until he raises his shooting percentages. Jennings' three-point percentage was fine, though was he streaky from that range. It was in between where the real problem could be found. Jennings shot .340 on long twos (league average .401), .229 from 10-15 feet (.391), .375 between the rim and 10 feet (.430) and just .427 at the rim (.608). He's reportedly been focusing his summer efforts on getting better from midrange and improving his right hand, the latter of which would help him finish a better percentage of his attempts at the basket. His shooting form is really long and he's been trying to shore that up in search of a more consistent release. The rest of Jennings' game looks great. He's a flashy and willing passer, a good, aggressive on-ball defender who buys into what Scott Skiles preaches and he rebounds very well for his size. The one thing that concerns you about Jennings is his off-court behavior. He's not a troublemaker; it's just that he has yet to learn the art of diplomacy. Jennings is an affable, accessible kid, but still has a tendency to say things that could get him in hot water.

SF 5 — Corey Maggette

Hght: 6'6" Exp: 11 Salary: $9.6 million
Wght: 225 From: Duke
2011-12 status: guaranteed contract for $10.3 million

SKILL RATINGS

TOT	OFF	DEF	REB	PAS	HND	SHT	ATH
0	+2	-4	0	+1	-3	0	+2

Year	Team	Age	G	MPG	Usg	3PA%	FTA%	INS	2P%	3P%	FT%	TS%	Reb%	Ast%	TO%	BLK%	STL%	PF%	oRTG	dRTG	Win%	WARP
07-08	LAC	28.4	70	35.7	.278	.136	.200	1.065	.477	.384	.812	.595	.091	.035	.130	.002	.013	.038	107.8	106.5	.541	6.5
08-09	GSW	29.4	51	31.1	.253	.101	.195	1.094	.497	.253	.824	.582	.097	.025	.128	.003	.013	.052	106.5	107.7	.460	1.4
09-10	GSW	30.4	70	29.7	.268	.039	.187	1.148	.531	.260	.835	.615	.100	.036	.130	.001	.012	.048	108.3	107.4	.527	4.8
10-11p	MIL	31.4	72	32.0	.239	.087	.178	1.091	.502	.288	.819	.582	.090	.030	.130	.002	.012	.051	105.9	107.0	.463	2.3

Most similar to: Marques Johnson (97.5), Juwan Howard, Billy Knight, Matt Harpring

IMP: 25% BRK: 2% COP: 11%

Scott Skiles and John Hammond have built the Bucks around defense, but when they found themselves starved for points in their tight first-round series with Atlanta, it looked like Milwaukee might have tipped the scale too far towards that end of the court. That explains acquisition of Corey Maggette. He fills an important role for the Bucks, though he'll do so at a prohibitive $10.2 million per season over the next three years. The Bucks were too perimeter oriented last season, especially once Andrew Bogut was injured, and finished last in the league in

MILWAUKEE BUCKS

foul-drawing rate. Maggette is one of the best slashers in the league, with a perennially high rate of fouls drawn and high-percentage finishing at the rim. The other parts of his game lag, though he's not a bad passer when he chooses to be. Maggette's defense has never been very good and cratered in Golden State. However, he always draws a lot of charges, and he will have plenty of support with the Bucks. Maggette shoots well from midrange, but his three-point game has disappeared the last two seasons. In recognition of this, he's cut his three attempts from 203 in 2007-08 to 50 last year. The Bucks don't need another long-range shooter, so Maggette is not likely to start planting himself behind the arc now that he's in Milwaukee. One concern at the season's outset is that Maggette is still recovering from ankle surgery. That may hamper his availability and mobility in camp and early in the season.

PF 12	Luc Richard Mbah a Moute	Hght: 6'8" Wght: 230 2011-12 status: due qualifying offer of $1.1 million	Exp: 2 From: UCLA	Salary: $0.9 million							
					SKILL RATINGS						
					TOT	OFF	DEF	REB	PAS	HND	SHT	ATH
					-1	-1	+4	-2	0	+1	-1	+1

Year	Team	Age	G	MPG	Usg	3PA%	FTA%	INS	2P%	3P%	FT%	TS%	Reb%	Ast%	TO%	BLK%	STL%	PF%	oRTG	dRTG	Win%	WARP
08-09	MIL	22.6	82	25.8	.144	.006	.125	1.119	.466	.000	.729	.516	.138	.019	.148	.018	.021	.043	103.2	105.0	.439	1.0
09-10	MIL	23.6	73	25.6	.121	.034	.118	1.083	.486	.353	.699	.530	.123	.020	.141	.016	.017	.044	103.3	105.3	.431	0.5
10-11p	MIL	24.6	74	25.0	.131	.039	.120	1.081	.489	.210	.729	.527	.115	.021	.143	.015	.017	.041	103.0	105.2	.425	0.4

Most similar to: Anthony Bonner (97.8), Grant Long, Horace Grant, Adam Keefe   IMP: 56%   BRK: 7%   COP: 3%

Luc Richard Mbah a Moute took another step towards becoming the neo-Bruce Bowen in 2009-10. His defense remained excellent. He's one of the best combo forwards in the game at that end, capable of guarding threes and fours, though he's vulnerable against good post players. On offense, Mbah a Moute used fewer plays, shooting effectively only at the basket. He did begin to show an inkling of a three-point shot. He took fewer long twos, a trend you'd like to see continue. He's a better rebounder than Bowen ever was, but of course Mbah a Moute is a little taller and about 50 pounds heavier than the retired Spurs stopper. If Mbah a Moute can find a consistent offensive role to play, he can keep his court time at 25 minutes a night.

SG 22	Michael Redd	Hght: 6'6" Wght: 215 2011-12 status: free agent	Exp: 10 From: Ohio State	Salary: $18.3 million							
					SKILL RATINGS						
					TOT	OFF	DEF	REB	PAS	HND	SHT	ATH
					0	+2	-4	-2	0	+1	-3	-1

Year	Team	Age	G	MPG	Usg	3PA%	FTA%	INS	2P%	3P%	FT%	TS%	Reb%	Ast%	TO%	BLK%	STL%	PF%	oRTG	dRTG	Win%	WARP
07-08	MIL	28.7	72	37.5	.274	.218	.131	.913	.475	.363	.820	.559	.069	.041	.110	.004	.011	.021	107.7	107.0	.522	6.0
08-09	MIL	29.7	33	36.5	.251	.285	.106	.821	.503	.366	.814	.566	.054	.033	.079	.001	.015	.017	108.0	107.0	.531	2.9
09-10	MIL	30.7	18	27.3	.238	.233	.113	.880	.373	.300	.712	.444	.064	.036	.058	.003	.020	.022	103.3	105.9	.416	0.0
10-11p	MIL	31.7	22	10.0	.231	.293	.105	.813	.422	.333	.764	.505	.057	.035	.078	.003	.015	.022	105.4	106.5	.464	0.2

Most similar to: John Long (98.1), Mike Woodson, Purvis Short, Junior Bridgeman   IMP: 22%   BRK: 7%   COP: 15%

A poster of Michael Redd should hang on the wall of every NBA general manager, bearing the caption, "Beware the max contract." Few people in any line of work will earn more for doing less than Redd, who will make $18.3 million for the coming season even though he's not likely to play until February, if at all. Redd is not a bad guy by any stretch. He's just a player that never had the kind of impact on a game that merits max dollars. Redd enters the last season of his contract in rehab mode after tearing his ACL for the second time in as many seasons. The Bucks can't count on him this season, but what about after that? If Redd can get the knee back to some degree of health, he would surely be able to find work as an off-the-bench gunner playing 15-20 minutes a night. When he's right, Redd is perfect for the role. That said, even before his season ended prematurely last year, he struggled mightily with his shot and was unable to even make free throws at the league rate. Redd's career might be over, but at least we know he's not going to retire to the poorhouse.

MILWAUKEE BUCKS

SF 15 — John Salmons

Hght: 6'6" | Exp: 8 | Salary: $8.0 million
Wght: 207 | From: Miami (Fla.)
2011-12 status: guaranteed contract for $8.0 million

SKILL RATINGS

TOT	OFF	DEF	REB	PAS	HND	SHT	ATH
+1	+2	0	-4	+3	+2	+2	-1

Year	Team	Age	G	MPG	Usg	3PA%	FTA%	INS	2P%	3P%	FT%	TS%	Reb%	Ast%	TO%	BLK%	STL%	PF%	oRTG	dRTG	Win%	WARP
07-08	SAC	28.4	81	31.0	.194	.111	.106	.995	.504	.325	.823	.556	.081	.037	.157	.010	.016	.030	104.0	105.6	.448	1.6
08-09	CHI	29.4	79	37.5	.215	.214	.108	.894	.493	.417	.830	.580	.065	.038	.117	.006	.014	.028	107.0	107.3	.491	4.6
09-10	MIL	30.4	81	34.9	.200	.248	.108	.860	.468	.382	.830	.553	.054	.036	.099	.007	.018	.027	105.5	105.9	.488	4.2
10-11p	MIL	31.4	76	37.0	.187	.238	.102	.864	.477	.394	.827	.561	.059	.036	.119	.007	.015	.029	105.1	106.0	.470	3.2

Most similar to: Stephen Jackson (98.4), Reggie Williams, Bryon Russell, Mike Woodson | IMP: 27% | BRK: 7% | COP: 7%

It was a tale of two seasons for John Salmons, who struggled in Chicago and chafed at his inconsistent role under Vinny Del Negro, then went to Milwaukee and sparked the Bucks' late-season run. Milwaukee decided the latter represented the "real" Salmons and bestowed upon him a five-year, $40 million deal even though he turns 31 in December. Contracts this long and for this much money for 6'6" wing players are never a good idea, and Bucks fans can shudder about the prospect of paying Salmons and Corey Maggette for another half-decade. For the second consecutive year, Salmons increased his rate of three attempts without sacrificing trips to the line. That's made him as efficient on the offensive end as he's ever been, but he does become increasingly perimeter oriented with each passing season. Salmons has learned to play off the ball more at this stage of the career, which is a good thing because he's not going to dominate the rock playing alongside Brandon Jennings. Salmons has a solid floor game, with good passing skills, a low turnover rate and average defensive indicators.

PF 8 — Larry Sanders

Hght: 6'11" | Exp: R | Salary: $1.7 million
Wght: 235 | From: Virginia Commonwealth
2011-12 status: guaranteed contract for $1.9 million

SKILL RATINGS

TOT	OFF	DEF	REB	PAS	HND	SHT	ATH
-2	-1	+1	+1	-2	-3	-4	0

Year	Team	Age	G	MPG	Usg	3PA%	FTA%	INS	2P%	3P%	FT%	TS%	Reb%	Ast%	TO%	BLK%	STL%	PF%	oRTG	dRTG	Win%	WARP
10-11p	MIL	22.4	76	13.9	.176	.026	.103	1.078	.430	.206	.627	.459	.138	.015	.122	.040	.010	.068	101.9	105.2	.390	-0.6

Most similar to: Jason Thompson (96.3), Channing Frye, Josh Boone, Othello Hunter | IMP: - | BRK: - | COP: -

Hey now! Larry Sanders is taking his show to the NBA after the Bucks took him with the 15th pick in the first round of this summer's draft. Sanders has a chance to make an immediate impact on the defensive end, though the Bucks are deep at the big-man positions. Sanders is very athletic and will be a plus rebounder right out of the gate. He's still raw offensively, as he didn't start playing basketball until he was 16 years old, but Sanders made great strides during his time at Virginia Commonwealth. If the Bucks choose to push the tempo at times, Sanders will be a perfect running mate for Brandon Jennings or Earl Boykins. Sanders is going to have to get a lot stronger to score close to the basket in the league; his jump shot is very much a work in progress, but it's getting better fast.

PF — Brian Skinner

Hght: 6'9" | Exp: 12 | Salary: --
Wght: 255 | From: Baylor
2011-12 status: free agent

SKILL RATINGS

TOT	OFF	DEF	REB	PAS	HND	SHT	ATH
-2	--	-2	--	--	--	--	--

Year	Team	Age	G	MPG	Usg	3PA%	FTA%	INS	2P%	3P%	FT%	TS%	Reb%	Ast%	TO%	BLK%	STL%	PF%	oRTG	dRTG	Win%	WARP
07-08	PHX	31.9	66	12.8	.141	.011	.105	1.093	.462	.667	.524	.485	.154	.008	.147	.059	.011	.056	100.5	102.4	.434	0.3
08-09	LAC	32.9	51	16.5	.146	.007	.077	1.070	.453	.000	.638	.474	.140	.015	.160	.046	.010	.051	101.5	104.8	.387	-0.5
09-10	LAC	33.9	16	7.7	.132	.000	.099	1.099	.400	-	.750	.456	.127	.000	.197	.024	.012	.074	98.9	106.3	.267	-0.4
10-11p	MIL	34.9	74	-	.121	.013	.084	1.071	.434	.262	.579	.456	.133	.010	.160	.055	.011	.059	-	-	.399	-

Most similar to: Chris Dudley (97.4), Tree Rollins, Wayne Cooper, Tony Massenburg | IMP: 50% | BRK: 3% | COP: 10%

With DeAndre Jordan's development and the addition of Craig Smith, Brian Skinner was pushed to the end of the bench. He ended up playing just 123 minutes, the lowest total of his NBA career. Skinner is still competent as a rebounder and a shot blocker. On offense, he no longer has enough athleticism to compensate for giving

MILWAUKEE BUCKS

up an inch or more to most opponents he faces in the middle. At best, he's a third center at this point. Skinner signed with the Bucks early in training camp and has a chance to earn the 15th spot on the roster, especially if Milwaukee wants more size because of concerns over Andrew Bogut's health.

C	Primoz Brezec	Hght: 7'1" Exp: 8 Salary: --	SKILL RATINGS							
		Wght: 255 From: Postojna, Slovenia	TOT	OFF	DEF	REB	PAS	HND	SHT	ATH
--		2011-12 status: free agent	-5	-2	0	-5	-4	-4	-3	-5

Year	Team	Age	G	MPG	Usg	3PA%	FTA%	INS	2P%	3P%	FT%	TS%	Reb%	Ast%	TO%	BLK%	STL%	PF%	oRTG	dRTG	Win%	WARP
07-08	TOR	28.6	50	9.5	.135	.000	.130	1.130	.468	.000	.600	.502	.101	.011	.177	.014	.003	.082	100.1	108.7	.240	-1.7
09-10	MIL	30.6	21	4.5	.147	.000	.086	1.086	.346	-	.167	.332	.152	.005	.065	.025	.005	.091	100.0	107.9	.256	-0.3
10-11p	AVG	31.6	76	4.5	.129	.009	.121	1.111	.472	.000	.573	.488	.094	.009	.170	.013	.003	.086	99.9	109.2	.222	-1.4

Most similar to: Greg Foster (95.7), Joe Wolf, Marc Iavaroni, Ken Bannister   IMP: 48%   BRK: 12%   COP: 8%

Primoz Brezec played quality minutes for Slovenia during the FIBA World Championship, which is more than you can say about the 91 minutes he played for the 76ers and Bucks last season. Finding only tepid interest in his services as a free agent, Brezec returned to Europe, signing with BC Krasnye Krylya Samara of the Russian Superleague.

SG	Jerry Stackhouse	Hght: 6'6" Exp: 15 Salary: --	SKILL RATINGS							
		Wght: 218 From: North Carolina	TOT	OFF	DEF	REB	PAS	HND	SHT	ATH
--		2011-12 status: free agent	-3	0	+1	0	+1	-2	-2	-3

Year	Team	Age	G	MPG	Usg	3PA%	FTA%	INS	2P%	3P%	FT%	TS%	Reb%	Ast%	TO%	BLK%	STL%	PF%	oRTG	dRTG	Win%	WARP
07-08	DAL	33.5	58	24.3	.225	.272	.096	.824	.447	.326	.892	.523	.054	.048	.127	.005	.009	.027	105.6	107.0	.454	1.1
08-09	DAL	34.5	10	16.2	.205	.264	.043	.779	.317	.158	1.000	.333	.060	.034	.125	.005	.013	.017	98.9	107.3	.242	-0.6
09-10	MIL	35.5	42	20.4	.220	.315	.074	.758	.452	.346	.797	.517	.069	.037	.160	.008	.013	.030	103.9	106.5	.416	0.0
10-11p	AVG	36.5	76	20.4	.203	.316	.076	.760	.432	.331	.824	.502	.064	.042	.168	.008	.012	.032	103.5	106.9	.388	-0.9

Most similar to: Byron Scott (97.2), Johnny Newman, Mitch Richmond, Steve Smith   IMP: 30%   BRK: 7%   COP: 11%

Jerry Stackhouse has entered the Roger Clemens phase of his career, where he sits out training camp and the early part of the season, waiting until some team that needs an infusion of offense comes calling. Stackhouse positioned himself as a possible role player for the Miami Heat, but no offer came his way. He was useful in spurts for Scott Skiles in Milwaukee last season and played some important minutes. When you add it all up, however, he was merely filling space. If Stackhouse wants to play in the NBA this season, he probably will, but fans of whichever team he ends up with shouldn't expect much.

PG	Roko Ukic	Hght: 6'5" Exp: 2 Salary: --	SKILL RATINGS							
		Wght: 183 From: Split, Croatia	TOT	OFF	DEF	REB	PAS	HND	SHT	ATH
--		2011-12 status: free agent	-3	0	+2	-2	+1	+1	-5	-3

Year	Team	Age	G	MPG	Usg	3PA%	FTA%	INS	2P%	3P%	FT%	TS%	Reb%	Ast%	TO%	BLK%	STL%	PF%	oRTG	dRTG	Win%	WARP
08-09	TOR	24.9	72	12.4	.214	.151	.064	.913	.427	.177	.733	.430	.049	.080	.146	.002	.017	.040	103.8	108.1	.362	-1.0
09-10	MIL	25.9	13	7.5	.192	.294	.119	.825	.611	.250	.818	.574	.018	.056	.147	.000	.005	.028	106.1	109.0	.406	0.0
10-11p	AVG	26.9	76	7.5	.212	.188	.067	.879	.436	.201	.730	.439	.047	.077	.136	.001	.015	.040	103.9	107.5	.382	-0.4

Most similar to: Negele Knight (97.4), Jeff McInnis, Alvin Williams, Keyon Dooling   IMP: 56%   BRK: 14%   COP: 10%

Roko Ukic expected to step into Jose Calderon's shoes in Toronto after coming over from Croatia two years ago. Dealt to Milwaukee last summer, he found that the NBA was a lot tougher than it looked and headed back overseas after negotiating a buyout with the Bucks. While Ukic's playmaking skills are solid, his defense is not, and there isn't anything about the rest of his game to entice an NBA team to bring him back stateside.

Minnesota Timberwolves

In barely a year as the president of basketball operations for the Minnesota Timberwolves, David Kahn has established himself as the laughingstock of the NBA. It's hard to say now which aspect of Kahn's tenure has drawn more guffaws--his selection of multiple players at the same position in the draft, his outlandish public comments or his infatuation with another NBA punchline, Darko Milicic.

Look a little more closely and Kahn has accomplished some things since taking over the Timberwolves. Minnesota's core group of talent is far deeper now than it was when predecessor Kevin McHale exited at the end of the 2008-09 season, and Kahn has made some value pickups in that time. The biggest problem remains that the pieces don't fit together. There is little internal consistency to Kahn's moves, which frequently contradict each other.

This is not quite the same as the repeated criticism that Kahn does not have a plan. Plans are overrated. Most every terrible general manager of the last decade has had a plan, or at least offered the appearance of one in dealing with the media. Ultimately, talent triumphs, and Kahn mostly seems to understand that--except when he inexplicably doesn't.

Take this summer's two biggest additions for the Timberwolves. Kahn put the team's hard-earned cap space to work in a trade with the Miami Heat, which was desperate to offload the contract of Michael Beasley in order to sign its trio of max players while still leaving room to add Mike Miller and re-sign Udonis Haslem. In exchange for the No. 2 overall pick of the 2008 Draft, a 21-year-old forward with immense talent who has performed decently though not to expectations during his first two pro seasons, all Minnesota gave up was a pair of second-round picks.

The Beasley deal was just the kind of calculated risk in which the Timberwolves should be engaging. If he pans out, Beasley's upside is immense. If he fails, Minnesota has risked little. Yet Kahn's thought process in dealing for Beasley stands in marked contrast to his approach to the No. 4 overall pick in June's NBA Draft. In terms of pure talent, Kentucky big man DeMarcus Cousins was unquestionably the best player available. Like Beasley, Cousins came accompanied by plenty of baggage, most notably a reputation for letting his temper get the best of him.

Instead of taking what was admittedly a larger gamble on Cousins, Kahn made an ultra-conservative pick, selecting Syracuse forward Wesley Johnson. Johnson is basically everything Cousins (and Beasley) is not: a reliable player with limited upside (he turned 23 this summer, making him a year and a half older than Beasley) who should fit perfectly into Minnesota's triangle offense. Later, Kahn served up another baffling move, dealing the No. 16 pick and forward Ryan Gomes (valuable because of his contract, which was only partially guaranteed) to Portland in exchange for middling veteran Martell Webster--who, yes, happens to play the same position as Johnson.

TIMBERWOLVES IN A BOX

Last year's record	15-67
Last year's Offensive Rating	103.0 (29)
Last year's Defensive Rating	113.8 (28)
Last year's point differential	-9.6 (30)
Team pace	94.5 (3)
SCHOENE projection	30-52 (14)
Projected Offensive Rating	107.6 (23)
Projected Defensive Rating	111.7 (24)
Projected team weighted age	24.5 (29)
Projected '10-11 payroll	$45.1 (29)
Est. payroll obligations, '11-12	$48.6 (24)

Head coach: Kurt Rambis

Given the roster he was handed, Rambis can't be graded on wins and losses. Where he failed during his first season at the helm in Minnesota was at the far more important task of developing talent. Corey Brewer and Wayne Ellington came around over the course of the season, but the triangle offense Rambis brought with him from the Lakers stifled point guards Jonny Flynn and Ramon Sessions. Meanwhile, Rambis buried Kevin Love behind Al Jefferson. Good NBA coaches adapt their system to suit the talent they're given, and Rambis has yet to show that ability.

174

If there's one word that best describes Kahn's tenure at the helm of the Timberwolves, it's unfocused. One minute, Kahn is stockpiling talent, which is a sensible approach for a team as far away from contention as the Timberwolves. The next, he's adding veterans (Minnesota's big addition in free agency was Luke Ridnour, a 29-year-old point guard coming off a career year). One minute, he's dealing players who make little sense in Minnesota's offense (like Ramon Sessions). The next, he's picking up multiple players who cannot coexist with each other.

All told, Kahn has made 14 trades, a pace of nearly one a month, during his tenure with the Timberwolves. He's signed five notable free agents and made five first-round picks (not counting the ones, like Ty Lawson, selected for other teams). Make so many moves and it is inevitable there will be winners and losers. Kahn seems to hit both extremes on a regular basis.

Arguably, Kahn's most harmful move thus far has come off the court. The selection of Kurt Rambis as head coach made sense at the time, and was even considered something of a coup because Rambis was believed to be the heir apparent to Phil Jackson with the Los Angeles Lakers. However, the triangle offense Rambis brought with him from L.A. proved to be a poor fit for Minnesota's talent.

In particular, the triangle's emphasis on sharing the basketball makes a ball-dominant point guard something of a liability. Naturally, Kahn hired Rambis months after selecting a pair of point guards in the lottery. While Ricky Rubio continues to ply his trade in Spain, waiting for his move to the NBA to make sense financially, rookie Jonny Flynn was asked to learn the triangle. That worked about as well as you'd expect. Flynn's strength is creating off the dribble, not playing off the basketball, and he struggled in an offense that played to his weaknesses. At least Flynn had more luck than Sessions, who not only had to adjust to the triangle but had to do so in limited minutes because Rambis was unwilling to play the two point guards together.

Meanwhile, the triangle also worked against the Timberwolves' centerpiece player, center Al Jefferson. Already hampered by his recovery from a torn ACL suffered midway through the 2008-09 season, Jefferson was asked to be more of a passer and spend more time away from the basket. Making matters worse, Jefferson and second-year forward Kevin Love had a tough time coexisting at the defensive end of the floor because both are undersized for their positions and neither is especially effective as a help defender. Even though Love might have been the Minnesota player whose skills fit best within the triangle--he's a fine passer--he spent most of the year coming off the bench behind Jefferson.

Things were little better on the wing, where the Timberwolves gave nearly 2,500 minutes to replacement-level veterans Sasha Pavlovic and Damien Wilkins. However, one of the season's few bright spots was the emergence of shooting guard Corey Brewer, coming back from a torn ACL of his own. Always effective at the defensive end of the floor, Brewer showed signs of improving his offensive game.

Still, it was a dismal season for the Timberwolves. They managed the remarkable feat of having the worst point differential in a league where the New Jersey Nets threatened the NBA record for single-season futility and finished with 12 wins. Thanks to a handful of close wins, including a one-point victory over New Jersey on opening night that proved prophetic, Minnesota avoided such ignominy. That was little consolation down the stretch, as the Timberwolves won just two of their last 29 games and finished with 15 victories, tying the worst record in franchise history.

Because of Kahn's moves, Minnesota's roster for 2010-11 bears relatively little resemblance to the group that took the floor last season. Just two teams (the New Jersey Nets and New York Knicks) project to have fewer minutes played by returning players. The most important change might be in the middle, where the Timberwolves resolved the Jefferson-Love dilemma by dumping Jefferson and his contract on the Utah Jazz. In return, Minnesota got relatively little in terms of assets--young center Kosta Koufos and a pair of future first-round picks. The primary yield from the trade was significant cap space. Considering Jefferson was playing at an All-Star level before his knee injury in 2008-09, the haul was disappointing. However, it was unclear Jefferson was ever going to return to that level and choosing Love over him was the right move.

Stepping into the middle is Milicic, who played decently after being acquired from New York at the trade deadline. Milicic is neither as bad as has been advertised nor as good as Kahn has made him out to be. (Most infamously, he told NBA TV during the NBA Summer League that Milicic was the league's best passer among big men.) He'll be pushed by rookie Nikola Pekovic, a 2008 McHale selection who has good size for the position and is very skilled offensively but weak defensively and on the glass. Love

From the Blogosphere

Who: Nate Arch
What: Canis Hoopus
Where: http://www.canishoopus.com/

The elephant in Target Center is the oversized personality of David Kahn. Thankfully, his comments about Michael Beasley crossed a line that cost him some money and his future actions should be accompanied by a more reasonable press strategy and a wider recognition that he is following a fairly obvious and reasonable rebuilding path. The Wolves are all-in on Ricky Rubio. They are assembling a team of athletic wingmen who can defend and shoot, along with a bunch of European-style bigs who can run the pick-and-roll and pass the ball in Rambis' quasi-triangle. Despite all of his failings, Kahn seems to understand something that the national sports press does not: Rubio stayed in Europe because of money and his road to the NBA always has, does, and will go through Minny. This year's team won't win many games, but it will be one step closer to a Rubio-led future.

---

may also get some minutes at center, making room at power forward for Beasley and newcomer Anthony Tolliver, who was effective as a starter in Golden State after being called up from the D-League.

Beasley should also see some time at small forward, where the competition is also crowded. Johnson and Webster figure to share most of the minutes, while the Timberwolves added another rookie small forward at the end of the first round, Marquette product Lazar Hayward. Shooting guard is the one position essentially unchanged from last season, with Brewer and sophomore Wayne Ellington combining to give Minnesota outside shooting.

At the point, Flynn will be coming back from summer surgery to repair a torn left hip labrum. He's got a new backup, as Kahn sent Sessions and center Ryan Hollins (two of last year's most prominent additions in free agency) to Cleveland in a salary dump, getting back the non-guaranteed contract of guard Delonte West (since waived) and former Timberwolves point guard Sebastian Telfair. To replace Sessions, Minnesota signed veteran Ridnour, whose shooting makes him a slightly better fit for the triangle offense than his predecessors at the point.

Going through that group, the upside is there is far more credible NBA talent on hand than there was a year ago. Tolliver's performance last season makes him overqualified to be a fifth big man, and Minnesota goes two deep at every position. That should help the Timberwolves take a solid step forward from last year's disastrous finish. The issue is now a lack of top-tier talent. Love is the only player on the roster who is solidly better than league average. Most everyone else in the rotation resides somewhere between replacement level and average.

Looking down the road, the Timberwolves can hope that Beasley develops into that kind of contributor, though whether he can coexist with Love or is simply trade bait remains to be seen. Despite the team's youth, no one else on the roster has that kind of upside. Minnesota could add another star-caliber prospect when and if Rubio comes stateside, but Kahn's focus needs to be on acquiring stars, not role players. If he can somehow pull that off, the NBA will find a new source for front-office humor. More likely, the joke will remain on Kahn.

Kevin Pelton

MINNESOTA TIMBERWOLVES

TIMBERWOLVES FIVE-YEAR TRENDS

Season	AGE	W-L	POW	PYTH	SEED	ORTG	DRTG	PT DIFF	PACE
05-06	26.7	33-49	34.1 (24)	35.2	---	103.8 (27)	105.9 (9)	-1.9 (21)	87.6 (22)
06-07	27.7	32-50	31.6 (24)	30.5	---	105.3 (25)	109.7 (22)	-3.7 (25)	89.6 (17)
07-08	24.3	22-60	22.1 (28)	22.7	---	105.5 (27)	114.0 (27)	-6.8 (26)	90.0 (13)
08-09	25.4	24-58	26.5 (25)	27.5	---	106.9 (25)	113.7 (27)	-4.9 (25)	90.4 (15)
09-10	24.8	15-67	16.2 (29)	17.5	---	103.0 (29)	113.8 (28)	-9.6 (30)	94.5 (3)

		OFFENSE				DEFENSE			
Season	PAY	eFG	oREB	FT/FGA	TO	eFG	oREB	FT/FGA	TO
05-06	$54.3	.480 (23)	.252 (28)	.226 (25)	.164 (22)	.475 (7)	.713 (24)	.236 (9)	.157 (19)
06-07	$66.7	.490 (20)	.252 (24)	.231 (21)	.171 (22)	.498 (14)	.721 (19)	.226 (7)	.156 (26)
07-08	$51.1	.484 (20)	.275 (11)	.183 (30)	.154 (21)	.513 (26)	.736 (14)	.269 (27)	.144 (21)
08-09	$63.5	.482 (27)	.277 (13)	.222 (24)	.156 (19)	.515 (26)	.750 (5)	.254 (24)	.138 (28)
09-10	$62.7	.478 (27)	.267 (15)	.207 (24)	.171 (28)	.525 (27)	.736 (16)	.220 (15)	.151 (21)

(league rankings in parenthesis)

PF 8 — Michael Beasley
Hght: 6'10" Exp: 2 Salary: $5.0 million
Wght: 235 From: Kansas State
2011-12 status: team option for $6.3 million

SKILL RATINGS

TOT	OFF	DEF	REB	PAS	HND	SHT	ATH
+2	+1	-2	-1	+1	-1	-1	+3

Year	Team	Age	G	MPG	Usg	3PA%	FTA%	INS	2P%	3P%	FT%	TS%	Reb%	Ast%	TO%	BLK%	STL%	PF%	oRTG	dRTG	Win%	WARP
08-09	MIA	20.3	81	24.8	.278	.068	.090	1.021	.478	.407	.772	.528	.131	.020	.102	.015	.011	.043	104.9	106.3	.454	1.6
09-10	MIA	21.3	78	29.8	.260	.080	.083	1.003	.469	.275	.800	.505	.125	.020	.103	.017	.018	.045	103.6	104.7	.464	2.3
10-11p	MIN	22.3	75	26.0	.273	.094	.090	.996	.483	.337	.819	.530	.120	.024	.098	.017	.015	.042	105.1	105.4	.489	3.0

Most similar to: Cliff Robinson (98.2), Drew Gooden, Luol Deng, Joe Smith

IMP: 66% BRK: 11% COP: 0%

Just two years after there was a legitimate debate about whether Michael Beasley was a deserving No. 1 overall pick, the Miami Heat could barely give Beasley away this summer. With the additions of Chris Bosh and LeBron James, Beasley no longer fit into the Heat's plans, and understandably so. He's hardly the kind of role player you'd want alongside Miami's Big Three. It's baffling why none of the other teams with cap space were willing to take a chance on Beasley, however. At age 21, he's put up two seasons of essentially league-average play. Beasley no longer projects as a superstar, and the concerns about him off the court appear well-founded despite David Kahn's assurance that he no longer smokes weed. Still, Beasley is a contributor at worst and at best a solid starter down the road.

After splitting time at both forward positions as a rookie, Beasley largely settled in at the four last season. This did not do much to help his statistics. He continues to spend too much time on the perimeter, which has hurt both his True Shooting Percentage and his rebounding. The Heat often isolated Beasley on the wing, but he was unable to use his quickness to beat power forwards off the dribble and too often ended up shooting midrange jumpers. The most troubling aspect of Beasley's offensive statistics might be the distinct lack of free throw attempts that could prop up his efficiency. Beasley tends to get lost defensively, limiting his value as a help defender. Per BasketballValue.com, Miami allowed 5.2 more points per 100 possessions when he was on the floor last season. Beasley will have to improve at the defensive end to earn his coaches' trust.

MINNESOTA TIMBERWOLVES

SG 22 — Corey Brewer

Hght: 6'9" Wght: 188 Exp: 3 From: Florida Salary: $3.7 million
2011-12 status: due qualifying offer of $5.0 million

SKILL RATINGS

TOT	OFF	DEF	REB	PAS	HND	SHT	ATH
-1	0	-4	+2	0	-1	-1	+4

Year	Team	Age	G	MPG	Usg	3PA%	FTA%	INS	2P%	3P%	FT%	TS%	Reb%	Ast%	TO%	BLK%	STL%	PF%	oRTG	dRTG	Win%	WARP
07-08	MIN	22.1	79	22.8	.157	.058	.078	1.020	.389	.194	.800	.429	.095	.028	.143	.011	.019	.048	100.1	105.6	.321	-3.6
08-09	MIN	23.1	15	20.5	.165	.108	.075	.967	.410	.417	.737	.473	.094	.037	.117	.008	.025	.055	103.7	106.4	.409	0.0
09-10	MIN	24.1	82	30.3	.216	.193	.092	.899	.459	.346	.648	.502	.063	.034	.134	.009	.023	.039	103.4	106.2	.406	-0.6
10-11p	MIN	25.1	73	28.0	.185	.218	.084	.866	.435	.391	.713	.508	.074	.035	.131	.010	.022	.045	104.0	106.0	.434	0.8

Most similar to: Walter McCarty (96.6), Jiri Welsch, Mitchell Wiggins, Mark Macon   IMP: 59% BRK: 9% COP: 4%

Corey Brewer needed to make strides in his third season to remain part of the Timberwolves' plans, and he did just that despite coming back from a torn ACL that ended his 2008-09 campaign prematurely. Starting all 82 games, he scored enough to keep defenses honest, which was a major upgrade from his disappointing rookie year. Brewer never figures to be anything better than average offensively. He showed the ability to create his own shot at the NBA level last season, a pleasant surprise, but creating efficient shots remains a different story. Brewer also needs to continue improving from beyond the arc. He went from attempting just 19 threes his first two seasons to 237 last year, but made them at only an average clip.

Minnesota can live with Brewer being average offensively because of his defensive potential. Last year's poor counterpart numbers, as reflected by Brewer's -4 defense skill rating, are largely attributable to the poor defenders around him. In one-on-one situations, Brewer was much more effective, using his size to keep a hand in the face of opposing wings. Brewer showed few ill effects of his ACL injury, other than his drop in rebound percentage, and he should take another step forward in his development this season. He needs the rest of the Timberwolves to improve enough that a defensive specialist on the wing is more than a luxury.

SG 19 — Wayne Ellington

Hght: 6'4" Wght: 200 Exp: 1 From: North Carolina Salary: $1.1 million
2011-12 status: team option for $1.2 million

SKILL RATINGS

TOT	OFF	DEF	REB	PAS	HND	SHT	ATH
-2	+1	+3	0	-3	-3	+3	-4

Year	Team	Age	G	MPG	Usg	3PA%	FTA%	INS	2P%	3P%	FT%	TS%	Reb%	Ast%	TO%	BLK%	STL%	PF%	oRTG	dRTG	Win%	WARP
09-10	MIN	22.4	76	18.2	.175	.293	.056	.763	.441	.395	.871	.527	.065	.023	.134	.003	.007	.023	103.5	107.8	.363	-1.5
10-11p	MIN	23.4	75	15.0	.175	.319	.060	.741	.462	.419	.869	.559	.064	.024	.127	.003	.008	.022	104.5	107.4	.405	-0.2

Most similar to: Sasha Pavlovic (96.4), Casey Jacobsen, Daniel Gibson, Jeff Malone   IMP: 69% BRK: 31% COP: 4%

As a rookie, Wayne Ellington had two very different seasons. He couldn't buy a three-pointer in 2009, making them at a 24.6 percent clip. Given Ellington's reputation as a sharpshooter, the Timberwolves had to be wondering whether they drafted the wrong player by mistake. Then Ellington rediscovered his stroke, and he shot 47.6 percent from the arc the rest of the way.

Ellington will have to be a lights-out shooter because the rest of his game is not up to NBA standards. He's a poor ballhandler for a two-guard and rarely created much separation off the dribble. The vast majority of his unassisted shot attempts came from midrange, where Ellington shot poorly. At the defensive end, his statistics were impressive. That doesn't match the subjective impression. Ellington gives up size to most of the players he defends and is not especially athletic.

There's a little Jason Kapono in Ellington's game in that his ratio of three attempts is relatively low for a player who makes them at such a high percentage. He needs to cut on the long twos and focus on the shots that are worth the extra point.

MINNESOTA TIMBERWOLVES

PG 10	Jonny Flynn	Hght: 6'0" Exp: 1 Salary: $3.2 million									SKILL RATINGS							
		Wght: 185 From: Syracuse									TOT	OFF	DEF	REB	PAS	HND	SHT	ATH
		2011-12 status: team option for $3.4 million									0	+1	-5	-2	0	-3	-2	+1
Year	Team	Age	G	MPG	Usg	3PA%	FTA%	INS	2P%	3P%	FT%	TS%	Reb%	Ast%	TO%	BLK%	STL%	PF%	oRTG	dRTG	Win%	WARP
09-10	MIN	21.2	81	28.9	.244	.165	.091	.926	.434	.358	.826	.511	.046	.067	.179	.001	.017	.018	104.3	106.9	.413	-0.2
10-11p	MIN	22.2	66	30.0	.240	.162	.094	.932	.435	.379	.828	.518	.046	.067	.170	.001	.018	.018	104.7	106.5	.440	1.0
Most similar to: Sebastian Telfair (98.1), Wes Matthews, Isiah Thomas, Mike Bibby																IMP: 46%		BRK: 11%			COP: 14%	

Five years ago, nobody would have blinked at Jonny Flynn's rookie season, since first-year point guards were once expected to struggle in the league. In large part because of the limitations placed on hand-checking on the perimeter, that has changed dramatically. Three point guards and combo guard Tyreke Evans placed on last year's All-Rookie First Team, and by comparison to them Flynn's campaign fell short. In particular, what separated them from Flynn was their ability to use their quickness to get into the paint and create shots for themselves and teammates. Flynn has similar tools, so the lingering question is how much of the problem was the shackles placed on him within the triangle offense.

Two red flags stand out on Flynn's shot breakdown from Hoopdata.com. First, he attempted too many mid-range jumpers (2.9 a night) for someone who made them at just a 35.0 percent clip. Flynn was slightly more accurate from beyond the arc, and his ability to make the NBA three was probably the best aspect of his rookie season. Second, Flynn made just 53.4 percent of his attempts when he did get to the rim. It's possible to thrive without good finishing ability by sheer volume of attempts at the rim (Russell Westbrook, who shot 52.7 percent at the rim, is proof of this), but this is a sign that Flynn's issues go beyond the offense. If that's the case, he's keeping the point guard position warm for Ricky Rubio.

Flynn underwent surgery on his hip during the offseason. The injury should not be a big issue in the long term, but Flynn will likely miss training camp and could be sidelined at the start of the regular season. His projection was docked 10 games to account for this possibility.

PG —	Jason Hart	Hght: 6'3" Exp: 9 Salary: --									SKILL RATINGS							
		Wght: 185 From: Syracuse									TOT	OFF	DEF	REB	PAS	HND	SHT	ATH
		2011-12 status: free agent									-4	--	+2	--	--	--	--	--
Year	Team	Age	G	MPG	Usg	3PA%	FTA%	INS	2P%	3P%	FT%	TS%	Reb%	Ast%	TO%	BLK%	STL%	PF%	oRTG	dRTG	Win%	WARP
07-08	UTA	30.0	57	10.6	.169	.136	.087	.951	.315	.355	.844	.413	.055	.064	.123	.004	.023	.057	101.2	106.2	.337	-1.0
08-09	DEN	31.0	39	8.9	.166	.048	.080	1.033	.341	.000	.783	.375	.077	.063	.174	.009	.018	.051	100.7	107.3	.291	-0.9
09-10	NOH	32.0	5	4.4	.103	.000	.000	1.000	.500	--	.500	.500	.054	.124	.600	.034	.046	.083	99.9	102.8	.400	0.0
10-11p	MIN	33.0	76	--	.144	.089	.076	.987	.335	.144	.797	.374	.067	.067	.168	.009	.019	.056	--	--	.329	--
Most similar to: Moochie Norris (97.0), Randy Brown, David Wingate, Jacque Vaughn																IMP: 68%		BRK: 32%			COP: 0%	

Jason Hart had brief stints with both Minnesota and New Orleans last season, meaning he's now played for nine teams in as many seasons in the NBA. Hart went to camp with the Timberwolves but played just one game as an emergency option at the point before being traded to Phoenix for Alando Tucker. The Suns were simply dumping Tucker's guaranteed contract and immediately waived Hart to get luxury-tax relief. He then signed a 10-day contract with the Hornets, playing four games. A heady, pass-first point guard, Hart can probably extend his NBA career one 10-day deal at a time if he prefers not to go overseas.

SF 32	Lazar Hayward	Hght: 6'6" Exp: R Salary: $1.0 million									SKILL RATINGS							
		Wght: 225 From: Marquette									TOT	OFF	DEF	REB	PAS	HND	SHT	ATH
		2011-12 status: guaranteed contract for $1.1 million									-2	-1	-1	+5	-1	-3	-5	+2
Year	Team	Age	G	MPG	Usg	3PA%	FTA%	INS	2P%	3P%	FT%	TS%	Reb%	Ast%	TO%	BLK%	STL%	PF%	oRTG	dRTG	Win%	WARP
10-11p	MIN	24.4	76	8.2	.231	.219	.065	.846	.386	.293	.815	.437	.129	.022	.100	.007	.021	.072	102.9	106.1	.392	-0.3
Most similar to: Al Thornton (93.5), Keith Bogans, Joey Graham, J.R. Giddens																IMP: -		BRK: -			COP: -	

Lazar Hayward was a surprise first-round pick as a four-year NCAA player who was good, not great, in college (he wasn't even a First Team All-Big East pick as a senior). Hayward spent last year as the de facto center for a tiny Marquette team that started no player bigger than 6'6". This had its benefits at the offensive end, where Hayward was usually matched up against bigger defenders unaccustomed to chasing opponents around the perimeter. Mostly a volume shooter, Hayward ranked 10th in the country in the percentage of his team's shots he took while on the floor.

In the NBA, Hayward will primarily be a small forward. His rebounding is an asset at the position, but his shooting range has gone from a strength to a weakness. As compared to that projection, Hayward will surely use fewer plays and score more efficiently, but it's hard to find any reason to believe he'll be much better than replacement level as a rookie. Given that Hayward will be 24, his growth potential is limited. As a first-round pick, he looks like a reach.

SF 4 — Wesley Johnson

Hght: 6'7" Exp: R Salary: $3.7 million
Wght: 205 From: Syracuse
2011-12 status: guaranteed contract for $4.0 million

SKILL RATINGS

TOT	OFF	DEF	REB	PAS	HND	SHT	ATH
0	0	+2	+3	0	-1	-2	+2

Year	Team	Age	G	MPG	Usg	3PA%	FTA%	INS	2P%	3P%	FT%	TS%	Reb%	Ast%	TO%	BLK%	STL%	PF%	oRTG	dRTG	Win%	WARP
10-11p	MIN	23.8	76	30.0	.158	.174	.084	.910	.443	.355	.755	.502	.106	.027	.146	.028	.016	.037	103.2	104.8	.446	1.5

Most similar to: J.R. Giddens (97.2), David West, Desmond Mason, Terence Morris IMP: - BRK: - COP: -

A four-year college player drafted in the top five picks, Wesley Johnson is a throwback to a different era. Technically, Johnson did enter the draft early because he sat out a year for his transfer from Iowa State to Syracuse, but he was still the oldest player drafted in the top 10 in the last decade. Had Minnesota passed, however, another team would have quickly snapped Johnson up. Within his first month of playing for the Orange, he had established Syracuse as a contender and won over NBA scouts with his well-rounded game.

Johnson's translated stat line is less effusive about his game. While he is polished and has no obvious weaknesses, he also lacks the special skill that usually separates elite NBA players. That could be defense, since Johnson blocked a lot of shots in the Syracuse zone, but his one-on-one ability needs development. Johnson does look like a good fit for the Timberwolves' offense. He's a solid three-point shooter who could develop into a dangerous threat from beyond the arc, and he'll be able to move the basketball and attack the glass from the weak side. Johnson stands a good chance of being one of the league's better rookies this season. The issue is how many of his peers will grow past him in years to come.

C 41 — Kosta Koufos

Hght: 7'0" Exp: 2 Salary: $1.3 million
Wght: 265 From: Ohio State
2011-12 status: team option for $2.2 million

SKILL RATINGS

TOT	OFF	DEF	REB	PAS	HND	SHT	ATH
+3	--	+1	--	--	--	--	--

Year	Team	Age	G	MPG	Usg	3PA%	FTA%	INS	2P%	3P%	FT%	TS%	Reb%	Ast%	TO%	BLK%	STL%	PF%	oRTG	dRTG	Win%	WARP
08-09	UTA	20.2	48	11.8	.186	.000	.096	1.096	.508	.000	.706	.540	.146	.016	.111	.043	.011	.056	104.2	105.1	.468	0.6
09-10	UTA	21.2	36	4.8	.180	.000	.096	1.096	.468	-	.600	.494	.154	.016	.219	.019	.006	.068	100.6	107.1	.294	-0.4
10-11p	MIN	22.2	76	-	.198	.010	.098	1.088	.520	.018	.747	.551	.140	.019	.113	.038	.010	.050	-	-	.542	-

Most similar to: Al Jefferson (98.2), Jermaine O'Neal, Andray Blatche, Kwame Brown IMP: 56% BRK: 9% COP: 0%

A telling bit of commentary on Kosta Koufos' time in Utah: When Mehmet Okur ruptured his Achilles tendon in the opening game of the playoffs, the Jazz was desperate for any kind of size in the middle. Still, Koufos played 31 minutes in the entire postseason because Jerry Sloan did not trust him at all. Now Koufos is the Timberwolves' project after he was included in the Al Jefferson deal, and he might have to play well in training camp just to get Minnesota to pick up the final year of his rookie contract.

Bizarrely, Jefferson shows up as the best comp for Koufos, whose ridiculously optimistic projection is based on his solid performance in limited action as a rookie. When he did see the floor last season, he regressed. There's talent here--Koufos also played well in the D-League--but whether it can be harnessed into actual production remains to be seen.

MINNESOTA TIMBERWOLVES

PF 42	Kevin Love	Hght: 6'10" Exp: 2 Salary: $3.6 million				SKILL RATINGS								
		Wght: 260 From: UCLA				TOT	OFF	DEF	REB	PAS	HND	SHT	ATH
		2011-12 status: team option for $4.6 million				+5	+4	+1	+5	+4	+1	-3	+2

Year	Team	Age	G	MPG	Usg	3PA%	FTA%	INS	2P%	3P%	FT%	TS%	Reb%	Ast%	TO%	BLK%	STL%	PF%	oRTG	dRTG	Win%	WARP
08-09	MIN	20.6	81	25.3	.211	.020	.155	1.135	.469	.105	.789	.538	.212	.019	.124	.019	.009	.045	107.2	105.5	.555	5.9
09-10	MIN	21.6	60	28.6	.226	.120	.137	1.017	.474	.330	.815	.549	.216	.035	.132	.010	.012	.035	109.2	104.7	.643	8.1
10-11p	MIN	22.6	72	30.0	.224	.107	.152	1.045	.486	.200	.808	.539	.206	.033	.128	.013	.010	.038	108.1	104.9	.604	8.5

Most similar to: Elton Brand (94.1), Clark Kellogg, Terry Cummings, Amare Stoudemire   IMP: 57% BRK: 9% COP: 6%

The Al Jefferson trade sends a clear message that this is Kevin Love's team. His first two seasons suggest that Love is up to the task. Despite his inconsistent role, he made solid strides as a sophomore, developing the range to hit the occasional three-pointer and substantially improving his assist rate while handling the ball more frequently in the triangle offense. A gifted passer who sees the floor well, Love has the ability to fill the Pau Gasol role for the Timberwolves. He'll never match Gasol as a scorer, but his decision-making allows Minnesota to funnel a lot of its offense through Love.

Defensively, Love has been acceptable, which is better than critics expected he would be. Guarding smaller and more athletic power forwards can be a challenge for him, but Minnesota defended better with Love on the floor last season. It helps that he's a very good defensive rebounder in addition to his excellent work on the offensive glass.

Expect Love to beat that prediction, which suggests based on the combination of his first two years of statistics that Love will shoot a lot of three-pointers (120) while making very few of them. He'll either be more accurate from the perimeter or stop heaving up threes at some point.

C 31	Darko Milicic	Hght: 7'0" Exp: 7 Salary: $4.3 million				SKILL RATINGS								
		Wght: 275 From: Novi Sad, Serbia				TOT	OFF	DEF	REB	PAS	HND	SHT	ATH
		2011-12 status: guaranteed contract for $4.8 million				-1	-1	0	-2	+3	+3	-1	+2

Year	Team	Age	G	MPG	Usg	3PA%	FTA%	INS	2P%	3P%	FT%	TS%	Reb%	Ast%	TO%	BLK%	STL%	PF%	oRTG	dRTG	Win%	WARP
07-08	MEM	22.8	70	23.8	.176	.002	.081	1.080	.440	.000	.554	.457	.143	.016	.154	.050	.009	.049	100.4	103.7	.386	-1.1
08-09	MEM	23.8	61	17.0	.164	.000	.128	1.128	.515	.000	.562	.533	.158	.016	.133	.040	.011	.061	103.8	105.1	.457	0.9
09-10	MIN	24.8	32	21.4	.161	.004	.049	1.045	.493	.000	.536	.497	.124	.030	.139	.037	.016	.053	102.4	104.5	.428	0.2
10-11p	MIN	25.8	75	25.0	.163	.005	.074	1.068	.494	.005	.551	.502	.130	.025	.139	.040	.012	.053	102.2	104.6	.419	0.1

Most similar to: Jon Koncak (97.8), Rick Mahorn, Kent Benson, John Salley   IMP: 48% BRK: 5% COP: 6%

The number one thing that David Kahn can do to help his public perception is to shut up, to put it bluntly. He's hardly helped his cause by openly and hyperbolically championing Darko Milicic since acquiring the former No. 2 pick at last year's trade deadline. Milicic has generally played competent NBA basketball when he's gotten minutes, so suggesting that Milicic just needs a chance to play and a team that believes in him is reasonable. Calling him "manna from heaven" and comparing his passing skill to that of fellow Serbian Vlade Divac is not.

Milicic is a fairly average rebounder and shot blocker whose 7-foot size makes him useful at the defensive end. He proved a good partner in the middle for Kevin Love, whose defensive limitations require him to play next to a longer, more athletic center. In fact, Love-Milicic lineups allowed 5.8 fewer points per 100 possessions than the Timberwolves' Defensive Rating over the course of the season. Milicic's biggest weakness has been his underdeveloped offense. The versatile game he flashed as a teenager never really materialized, and at this point Milicic's range doesn't extend much beyond about five feet.

Nobody else in the league would have offered Milicic anywhere near the money he got from the Timberwolves, who evidently had to overpay to keep Milicic from giving up on the NBA and heading back to Europe.

MINNESOTA TIMBERWOLVES

C 14	**Nikola Pekovic**	Hght: 6'11" Exp: R Salary: $4.3 million
		Wght: 243 From: Montenegro
		2011-12 status: guaranteed contract for $4.5 million

SKILL RATINGS

TOT	OFF	DEF	REB	PAS	HND	SHT	ATH
+2	+4	-3	-4	-1	-4	+3	+3

Year	Team	Age	G	MPG	Usg	3PA%	FTA%	INS	2P%	3P%	FT%	TS%	Reb%	Ast%	TO%	BLK%	STL%	PF%	oRTG	dRTG	Win%	WARP
10-11p	MIN	25.3	76	10.0	.248	.006	.166	1.160	.546	.006	.770	.607	.112	.016	.152	.021	.009	.065	107.3	107.5	.496	1.3

Most similar to: Brian Grant (96.8), Walter Berry, Billy Owens, Orlando Woolridge   IMP: 40% BRK: 0% COP: 8%

Nikola Pekovic should be one of the NBA's most interesting rookies this season. A skilled center who slipped to the second round of the 2008 Draft largely because of his problematic buyout, Pekovic is headed stateside after winning a Euroleague title in 2008-09 and putting together two highly effective seasons for Greek power Panathinaikos.

Pekovic's translated statistics are fascinating. Scouting reports indicate he's much better on offense than defense, but his Euroleague numbers suggest that might be an understatement. In particular, Pekovic has been abysmal on the defensive glass. He's actually rebounded a higher percentage of misses on the offensive glass, which is extraordinarily unusual. His defensive rebounding rates would be below average for a small forward, let alone a center. Kevin Love might be able to cover up that weakness up to some extent, but Pekovic won't offer much assistance in the way of help defense.

Pekovic's transition should be much easier at the offensive end, where he's a high-percentage finisher in the paint who frequently gets to the foul line and makes his free throws at a high percentage. The unusual package of skills for a center produces a bizarre set of comparable players.

PG 13	**Luke Ridnour**	Hght: 6'2" Exp: 7 Salary: $4.0 million
		Wght: 175 From: Oregon
		2011-12 status: guaranteed contract for $4.0 million

SKILL RATINGS

TOT	OFF	DEF	REB	PAS	HND	SHT	ATH
+1	+3	-2	-2	+2	+3	-1	0

Year	Team	Age	G	MPG	Usg	3PA%	FTA%	INS	2P%	3P%	FT%	TS%	Reb%	Ast%	TO%	BLK%	STL%	PF%	oRTG	dRTG	Win%	WARP
07-08	SEA	27.2	61	20.0	.174	.145	.082	.937	.424	.296	.857	.482	.042	.086	.164	.008	.013	.043	104.4	107.2	.408	-0.2
08-09	MIL	28.2	72	28.2	.181	.192	.082	.890	.420	.350	.869	.500	.065	.081	.157	.007	.023	.044	105.7	106.2	.482	2.8
09-10	MIL	29.2	82	21.5	.221	.212	.072	.860	.513	.381	.907	.570	.048	.084	.124	.003	.016	.047	109.2	107.3	.561	5.3
10-11p	MIN	30.2	75	22.0	.185	.199	.072	.873	.462	.358	.884	.525	.049	.084	.147	.006	.016	.047	106.5	107.3	.476	2.1

Most similar to: Johnny Dawkins (99.1), Kenny Anderson, Travis Best, Moochie Norris   IMP: 33% BRK: 4% COP: 12%

At the age of 29 and in his seventh NBA season, Luke Ridnour finally made good on the promise he flashed as a young point guard. Playing an entirely different, more confident brand of basketball, Ridnour teased defenses with his ability to score off the dribble, knock down threes or set up teammates depending on the situation. Ridnour crushed his previous career highs in both usage rate (.202) and True Shooting Percentage (.509) during his best NBA season. What made the performance especially odd was that Ridnour had previously struggled coming off the bench, yet he thrived playing behind and often alongside rookie Brandon Jennings.

Ridnour timed the performance well, since he hit the open market as a free agent for the first time this summer and signed a four-year, $16 million contract to join the Timberwolves. It's not clear Ridnour will fit in the triangle much better than his predecessors. Last season aside, he's been an average spot-up jump shooter at best. Like Ramon Sessions, who made the same move from Milwaukee to Minnesota as a free agent, Ridnour is strongest with the ball in his hands, especially operating out of the pick-and-roll. No matter where he went, Ridnour would have been hard-pressed to match last year's performance. The triangle offense figures to exaggerate his regression this season.

MINNESOTA TIMBERWOLVES

PG 3	Sebastian Telfair	Hght: 6'0"	Exp: 6	Salary: $2.7 million	SKILL RATINGS						
		Wght: 175	From: Abraham Lincoln HS (Brooklyn, NY)		TOT	OFF	DEF	REB	PAS	HND	SHT	ATH
		2011-12 status: free agent			0	+2	-3	-4	+2	+2	-2	-1

Year	Team	Age	G	MPG	Usg	3PA%	FTA%	INS	2P%	3P%	FT%	TS%	Reb%	Ast%	TO%	BLK%	STL%	PF%	oRTG	dRTG	Win%	WARP
07-08	MIN	22.9	60	32.2	.167	.160	.065	.905	.432	.281	.743	.462	.041	.083	.156	.005	.014	.041	103.8	107.4	.383	-1.3
08-09	MIN	23.9	75	27.9	.198	.231	.077	.846	.399	.346	.819	.481	.036	.074	.160	.004	.018	.040	105.1	108.0	.405	-0.5
09-10	CLE	24.9	43	15.3	.185	.210	.061	.851	.483	.232	.784	.479	.040	.087	.187	.006	.019	.049	104.1	107.4	.394	-0.3
10-11p	MIN	25.9	76	3.9	.182	.223	.066	.843	.461	.308	.779	.503	.037	.083	.156	.005	.017	.044	105.8	107.1	.454	0.2

Most similar to: Darrick Martin (99.2), Wes Matthews, Travis Best, Troy Hudson — IMP: 65% BRK: 9% COP: 4%

The David Kahn era can fairly neatly be summarized by this fact. Last summer, the Timberwolves traded Craig Smith to the L.A. Clippers in order to shed the last year of Sebastian Telfair's contract. This summer, Minnesota reacquired Telfair as the price for sending Ryan Hollins and Ramon Sessions to the Cleveland Cavaliers. The Timberwolves ultimately dumped Telfair on … themselves. Good luck trying to figure that sequence out.

SCHOENE is inexplicably fond of Telfair's game, suggesting that a breakout season is just around the corner. Telfair provided little indication last season that he's ready to make the leap. After two seasons as a stopgap starter in Minnesota, he backed up Baron Davis for the first half before being sent packing in a three-way trade and landing in Cleveland, where a groin injury limited him to four games.

PF 44	Anthony Tolliver	Hght: 6'9"	Exp: 2	Salary: $2.4 million	SKILL RATINGS						
		Wght: 243	From: Creighton		TOT	OFF	DEF	REB	PAS	HND	SHT	ATH
		2011-12 status: guaranteed contract for $2.4 million			+3	+3	0	-1	+3	+5	-1	-1

Year	Team	Age	G	MPG	Usg	3PA%	FTA%	INS	2P%	3P%	FT%	TS%	Reb%	Ast%	TO%	BLK%	STL%	PF%	oRTG	dRTG	Win%	WARP
08-09	SAS	23.9	19	10.9	.179	.537	.058	.521	.417	.220	.500	.375	.117	.040	.092	.004	.013	.037	104.6	106.9	.424	0.0
09-10	GSW	24.9	46	31.0	.167	.274	.106	.832	.481	.329	.769	.531	.126	.026	.083	.017	.011	.039	105.9	105.8	.504	2.6
10-11p	MIN	25.9	76	15.0	.165	.328	.107	.778	.477	.334	.777	.535	.120	.027	.083	.017	.010	.038	106.4	105.8	.520	2.5

Most similar to: Donyell Marshall (97.2), Danny Granger, Dan Majerle, Greg Ballard — IMP: 39% BRK: 3% COP: 12%

On the cusp of breaking into the NBA for good the last two seasons, Anthony Tolliver got his opportunity on an injury-decimated Golden State team and took full advantage, becoming the Warriors' starting center down the stretch and proving he can contribute in the NBA. A power forward by trade, shooting is the strength of Tolliver's game. He shot just 32.9 percent from three-point range, but took enough triples to make defenses respect him. That floor-spacing ability is a big reason Tolliver rated as well as he did last season.

Defensively, Tolliver was overmatched against many centers. He's an average defensive rebounder who is less of a factor on the offensive glass because of the time he spends on the perimeter. Tolliver's floor spacing is a unique attribute in the Timberwolves frontcourt, which should help him carve out a role despite the large group of players battling for playing time.

SF 5	Martell Webster	Hght: 6'7"	Exp: 5	Salary: $4.8 million	SKILL RATINGS						
		Wght: 235	From: Seattle Prep HS (WA)		TOT	OFF	DEF	REB	PAS	HND	SHT	ATH
		2011-12 status: guaranteed contract for $5.3 million			+3	+4	0	-2	-3	-1	+4	-1

Year	Team	Age	G	MPG	Usg	3PA%	FTA%	INS	2P%	3P%	FT%	TS%	Reb%	Ast%	TO%	BLK%	STL%	PF%	oRTG	dRTG	Win%	WARP
07-08	POR	21.4	75	28.4	.182	.390	.090	.700	.454	.388	.735	.548	.082	.020	.102	.010	.009	.035	105.0	106.2	.460	1.9
08-09	POR	22.4	1	5.0	.095	1.000	.000	.000	.000	.000	.000	.000	.000	.000	.000	.000	.000	.000	97.0	109.7	.151	0.0
09-10	POR	23.4	82	24.5	.183	.433	.089	.656	.440	.373	.813	.543	.083	.015	.078	.016	.012	.037	105.6	106.1	.485	2.8
10-11p	MIN	24.4	72	25.0	.182	.552	.091	.539	.454	.383	.813	.575	.079	.018	.085	.015	.012	.034	107.5	106.3	.539	4.6

Most similar to: Vladimir Radmanovic (96.8), Morris Peterson, Rod Higgins, Quentin Richardson — IMP: 57% BRK: 9% COP: 4%

Martell Webster is trapped in a catch-22: He's been much more effective as a starter, but isn't quite good enough to justify a regular job. Because of the difference in production in the two roles, Webster is something of a liability as either a starter or a reserve. With Corey Brewer and Wesley Johnson likely to start on the wings, Webster will have to embrace coming off the bench in Minnesota after being dealt to the Timberwolves on the night of the draft.

Healthy after a broken bone in his foot limited him to one game in 2008-09, Webster got the chance to start at the outset of the season because Nicolas Batum was sidelined by shoulder surgery. Webster was up and down in the role, occasionally playing lockdown defense. He made 42 three-pointers during a superb month of January that saw him average 15.5 points per game. Batum eventually reclaimed his job, and Webster was the invisible man before bouncing back when other injuries opened up more regular playing time. Because he's so dependent on his outside shot falling, Webster will always be a streaky player. He has more control of his consistency at the defensive end of the floor, where he has all the tools to be a stopper. He shut down Kevin Durant during an early-season matchup, but the Blazers could not rely on him to play at that level on a nightly basis.

SF	**Nemanja Bjelica**	Hght: 6'10"	Exp: R	Salary: --			SKILL RATINGS						
		Wght: 224	From: Serbia			TOT	OFF	DEF	REB	PAS	HND	SHT	ATH
--		2011-12 status: free agent				+1	--	--	--	--	--	--	--

Year	Team	Age	G	MPG	Usg	3PA%	FTA%	INS	2P%	3P%	FT%	TS%	Reb%	Ast%	TO%	BLK%	STL%	PF%	oRTG	dRTG	Win%	WARP
10-11p	MIN	23.0	76	--	.163	.246	.091	.846	.422	.261	.642	.446	.167	.041	.144	.009	.014	.049	--	--	.472	--

Most similar to: Jared Jeffries (94.7), J.R. Reid, Richard Anderson, Tony Battie   IMP: 75%   BRK: 25%   COP: 4%

One of the smartest things David Kahn has done at the helm of the Timberwolves was hiring respected European expert Tony Ronzone, formerly of the Detroit Pistons, as assistant GM in charge of player personnel. Ronzone's voice was surely prominent in Minnesota's pair of international second-round selections, led by No. 35 pick Nemanja Bjelica. A member of the Serbian National Team who shined in the World Championship, Bjelica is another European oddball. He's a 6'10" wing described as a point forward whose strongest skill in EuroCup play was his rebounding.

The point forward label is probably hype, but Bjelica's assist rate suggests he could successfully play a Luke Walton-type role for the Timberwolves on the wing in the triangle, keeping the ball moving. The big area of improvement for Bjelica will be his scoring efficiency. He lacks three-point range and isn't especially accurate inside the arc either. Bjelica has a couple of years to improve before coming to the NBA. He signed a five-year deal with defending ACB champ Caja Laboral over the summer, with a buyout he can exercise in the summer of 2012.

C	**Paulao Prestes**	Hght: 6'11"	Exp: R	Salary: --		SKILL RATINGS						
		Wght: 260	From: Brazil		TOT	OFF	DEF	REB	PAS	HND	SHT	ATH
--		2011-12 status: free agent			--	--	--	--	--	--	--	--

With the No. 45 pick, Minnesota went back to Europe to select Brazilian big man Paulão Prestes, who spent last season playing in Spain for CB Murcia. A physical center who uses his size in the paint, Prestes was highly effective on the glass, averaging an ACB-leading 12.1 rebounds per 40 minutes. Offensively, Prestes operates primarily out of the post and was a high-percentage shooter last season. He may have difficulty translating his game to the NBA at the defensive end, where his bulk limits his mobility and he is not a big-time shot blocker. Prestes will turn 23 during the season and may have a couple more years of development ahead of him before the Timberwolves bring him over.

MINNESOTA TIMBERWOLVES

C	**Nathan Jawai**	Hght: 6'10"	Exp: 2	Salary: --	**SKILL RATINGS**							
		Wght: 280	From: Australia		TOT	OFF	DEF	REB	PAS	HND	SHT	ATH
--		2011-12 status: free agent			-3	0	0	-1	+3	+1	-3	0

Year	Team	Age	G	MPG	Usg	3PA%	FTA%	INS	2P%	3P%	FT%	TS%	Reb%	Ast%	TO%	BLK%	STL%	PF%	oRTG	dRTG	Win%	WARP
08-09	TOR	22.5	6	3.2	.146	.000	.000	1.000	.250	.000	.000	.250	.062	.000	.333	.000	.000	.073	92.9	111.3	.073	-0.1
09-10	MIN	23.5	39	10.6	.164	.006	.108	1.102	.445	.000	.684	.485	.141	.025	.175	.016	.012	.062	103.4	106.8	.389	-0.2
10-11p	AVG	24.5	76	10.6	.169	.009	.110	1.101	.455	.000	.678	.489	.135	.026	.165	.018	.012	.060	103.2	106.5	.390	-0.4

Most similar to: Jason Collins (97.9), Olden Polynice, Kevin Duckworth, Dickey Simpkins — IMP: 57% BRK: 20% COP: 12%

Behemoth Aussie Nathan Jawai got a chance to show his wares at the NBA level last season, and the results were mixed at best. Jawai's size makes him intriguing as a prospect, but it doesn't appear he's athletic enough to make use of it. Jawai is earthbound, and since he's not exceptionally tall, he had a tough time finishing in the paint. According to Hoopdata.com, 16.2 percent of his shot attempts were blocked last season, which explains his poor two-point shooting. Jawai doesn't move well enough to defend in the modern NBA, where centers are required to spend time on the perimeter based on matchups or to defend the pick-and-roll. Jawai signed to play in Euroleague for Partizan, and his weaknesses should be less problematic in the European game.

SG	**Sasha Pavlovic**	Hght: 6'8"	Exp: 7	Salary: --	**SKILL RATINGS**							
		Wght: 220	From: Montenegro		TOT	OFF	DEF	REB	PAS	HND	SHT	ATH
--		2011-12 status: free agent			-3	0	+2	+1	-2	-2	0	-4

Year	Team	Age	G	MPG	Usg	3PA%	FTA%	INS	2P%	3P%	FT%	TS%	Reb%	Ast%	TO%	BLK%	STL%	PF%	oRTG	dRTG	Win%	WARP
07-08	CLE	24.4	51	23.3	.190	.233	.069	.836	.386	.296	.688	.432	.063	.032	.111	.004	.011	.046	101.4	107.5	.307	-2.7
08-09	CLE	25.4	66	16.0	.157	.337	.069	.731	.430	.410	.463	.510	.070	.033	.138	.012	.011	.055	104.4	107.8	.390	-0.6
09-10	MIN	26.4	71	12.4	.182	.324	.031	.708	.407	.297	.385	.422	.076	.029	.145	.005	.013	.042	100.5	107.0	.293	-2.3
10-11p	AVG	27.4	75	12.3	.171	.447	.052	.605	.422	.364	.486	.490	.070	.030	.129	.008	.012	.046	103.6	107.1	.385	-0.6

Most similar to: Bostjan Nachbar (98.0), Walter McCarty, Rod Higgins, Brian Scalabrine — IMP: 64% BRK: 28% COP: 8%

Three years removed from starting for the Cleveland Cavaliers in the NBA Finals, Sasha Pavlovic had a hard time finding big minutes for the Timberwolves last season. Pavlovic has both fallen off and been found out. He was never much better than replacement level because his efficiency was poor for a role player, but even replacement level has looked like a stretch the last three seasons. Sometimes, it's as simple as making shots, and Pavlovic can't do it. He figures to have a tough time finding NBA work this season.

C	**Oleksiy Pecherov**	Hght: 7'0"	Exp: 3	Salary: --	**SKILL RATINGS**							
		Wght: 234	From: Donetsk, Ukraine		TOT	OFF	DEF	REB	PAS	HND	SHT	ATH
--		2011-12 status: free agent			+2	+3	0	0	-4	-4	-1	0

Year	Team	Age	G	MPG	Usg	3PA%	FTA%	INS	2P%	3P%	FT%	TS%	Reb%	Ast%	TO%	BLK%	STL%	PF%	oRTG	dRTG	Win%	WARP
07-08	WAS	22.4	35	9.2	.224	.386	.088	.702	.415	.283	.645	.451	.122	.010	.109	.013	.009	.044	103.3	106.2	.402	-0.1
08-09	WAS	23.4	32	8.7	.204	.347	.103	.756	.431	.326	.828	.510	.162	.003	.081	.009	.011	.056	108.3	107.4	.529	0.6
09-10	MIN	24.4	44	10.2	.229	.222	.060	.838	.463	.269	.906	.487	.157	.011	.137	.024	.010	.054	102.9	105.3	.420	0.0
10-11p	AVG	25.4	76	10.2	.223	.361	.080	.719	.452	.342	.839	.523	.145	.009	.111	.018	.011	.050	106.0	105.7	.508	1.5

Most similar to: Pete Chilcutt (97.1), Donyell Marshall, Wayne Cooper, Brad Lohaus — IMP: 64% BRK: 20% COP: 10%

On paper, Oleksiy Pecherov's skill set sounds pretty good. He's a 7-footer with occasional three-point range who is strong on the glass. When the lights come on, however, Pecherov has been unable to put those various attributes together on a consistent basis and earn regular playing time. Last season's 447 minutes were a career high. Pecherov is still young enough to get it, but if that happens this year it's going to be in Europe. Pecherov is headed back to the continent and will play for Armani Jeans Milano.

MINNESOTA TIMBERWOLVES

										SKILL RATINGS							
SF	Alando Tucker		Hght: 6'6"	Exp: 3		Salary: --				TOT	OFF	DEF	REB	PAS	HND	SHT	ATH
--			Wght: 205	From: Wisconsin						0	+3	-1	-4	-2	-3	0	-3
			2011-12 status: free agent														

Year	Team	Age	G	MPG	Usg	3PA%	FTA%	INS	2P%	3P%	FT%	TS%	Reb%	Ast%	TO%	BLK%	STL%	PF%	oRTG	dRTG	Win%	WARP
07-08	PHX	24.2	6	8.0	.231	.162	.107	.945	.389	.250	.833	.446	.095	.000	.000	.014	.000	.018	103.7	107.4	.378	0.0
08-09	PHX	25.2	30	9.4	.234	.154	.097	.943	.449	.348	.788	.509	.065	.019	.094	.003	.009	.022	105.3	108.6	.395	-0.1
09-10	MIN	26.2	15	6.4	.245	.131	.174	1.042	.500	.143	.762	.529	.059	.018	.094	.000	.000	.028	105.7	109.5	.377	-0.1
10-11p	AVG	27.2	76	6.4	.226	.242	.100	.858	.462	.370	.786	.532	.062	.019	.094	.003	.008	.022	106.2	108.0	.440	0.2

Most similar to: Ron Anderson (96.2), Charles Davis, Bobby Hansen, Terry Teagle   IMP: 62% BRK: 13% COP: 9%

Phoenix's 2007 first-round pick, Alando Tucker never could carve out playing time for himself, and when the Suns put together a solid young reserve core, Tucker became expendable. A trade to Minnesota figured to give Tucker more opportunity to prove himself on the floor, but he played even more sparingly before being waived in March. The biggest factor that worked against Tucker in the NBA was his lack of three-point range, which made it easy for opponents to play him for the drive. Tucker is headed to Russia to play with Lokomotiv Kuban, which will play in the third-tier EuroChallenge.

New Jersey Nets

For everyone who entered save the Miami Heat, this summer's free-agency sweepstakes proved a disappointment. In terms of the gap between expectation and reality, however, the New Jersey Nets had things worst. The aggressive "Blueprint for Success" billboard the Nets purchased across from Madison Square Garden proved symbolic, but not for the reasons the team hoped. Instead of heralding the Nets' arrival as a player in the New York market, the billboard proved fleeting. By the start of August, when the Nets were setting their sights lower for 2010-11 and beyond, it had been painted over.

The Nets' brash confidence stood in stark contrast to their complete lack of success on the court last season. With a team composed of washed-up veterans on expiring contracts and young prospects, New Jersey set an NBA record by losing its first 18 games. As late as mid-March, the Nets were still threatening the worst record in league history before three wins in a four-game stretch allowed them to surpass the 9-73 1972-73 Philadelphia 76ers. The Nets would finish with 12 wins, the league's lowest total in the 2000s.

Still, the Nets had reason to hope they could attract one or more of the best free agents on the market. Their pitch, as neatly summarized by the "Blueprint" billboard, focused not on players or coaches but instead the team's owners, Russian billionaire Mikhail Prokhorov and minority partner Jay-Z. The May approval of Prokhorov's purchase of the team from Bruce Ratner heralded a new era in Nets history, one that will take place in Brooklyn.

The highlight of the 2009-10 season for the Nets might have been the team finally breaking ground on the site of their new arena, the Barclays Center, at the Atlantic Yards in Brooklyn. The arena, Ratner's brainchild, has been in the works for more than six years. It took that long to secure funding and fend off a series of lawsuits aimed at preventing the arena from being built. With the last legal challenge dismissed, the Nets broke ground in March and expect to move across state lines into their new home in time for the 2012-13 season.

While the Nets will still be in New Jersey for the next two seasons (which they will play at the Prudential Center in Newark after moving from their long-time home in East Rutherford, the Izod Center), the prospect of playing in New York was also a key part of their presentation to LeBron James and other marquee free agents. As in 2009-10 the Nets came up short on the court, where they could not offer the chance to compete immediately. They may have been more compelling as a destination had they parlayed the league's worst record into the top pick in the draft and a chance to add Kentucky's John Wall. Instead, the Nets dropped to third and settled for Georgia Tech freshman Derrick Favors.

Favors presented another problem in free agency. Adding him to third-year center Brook Lopez completed the Nets' frontcourt of the future, but with the best of the second-tier free agents all big men, the team would

NETS IN A BOX

Last year's record	12-70
Last year's Offensive Rating	102.1 (30)
Last year's Defensive Rating	112.5 (25)
Last year's point differential	-9.1 (29)
Team pace	89.9 (24)
SCHOENE projection	40-42 (7)
Projected Offensive Rating	110.4 (15)
Projected Defensive Rating	110.9 (21)
Projected team weighted age	25.6 (24)
Projected '10-11 payroll	$55.5 (23)
Est. payroll obligations, '11-12	$40.8 (28)

Head coach: Avery Johnson

After two years as an analyst for ESPN, Johnson returns to an NBA sideline in New Jersey, which gives us a chance to see what he's learned from his first job as a head coach in Dallas. Johnson was an instant success, winning Coach of the Year and reaching the NBA Finals in his first full season at the helm, but players slowly began to tune out his shrill voice. This season, expect Johnson to slow the pace and get results at the defensive end of the floor. With a younger team, he will need to be patient and tone down his style to have sustained success.

have had to bury Favors behind a veteran to sign a name free agent. They considered Carlos Boozer and David Lee before ultimately deciding to go a different direction and spread out their money on younger, cheaper players--guards Jordan Farmar and Anthony Morrow (acquired from Golden State in a sign-and-trade deal), forward Travis Outlaw and center Johan Petro.

Understandably, the newcomers look underwhelming compared to the dream of adding James or another marquee free agent. In terms of value, they were a mixed bag. The Nets overpaid for Outlaw, giving him a lavish five-year deal that suggests they expect him to be a long-term solution as a starter at small forward. Outlaw is better suited for a reserve role and has performed much better when playing as an undersized power forward. Petro, meanwhile, did little in Denver to suggest that he was worth much more than the minimum, making his three-year, $10 million deal a curious one. The Nets did better in the backcourt, where the sharpshooting Morrow was one of the summer's best signings at $4 million a year and Farmar has the chance to make good on his promise outside the spotlight of Los Angeles.

The deals marked the end of Rod Thorn's tenure with the Nets after a decade as team president, during which he turned around a moribund franchise and took New Jersey to back-to-back NBA Finals. Thorn stepped down in the middle of July, but wasn't out of the league for long, taking the same position in Philadelphia alongside former Nets executive Ed Stefanski. Fittingly, to replace Thorn the Nets turned to former 76ers GM Billy King, whose good drafting in Philadelphia was undone by his fondness for long-term deals for mediocre players like Willie Green and Kenny Thomas.

Before leaving his role, Thorn hired Avery Johnson as the Nets' new head coach. Lawrence Frank, the longest-tenured coach in the Eastern Conference, was dismissed after 16 losses to start the season, and general manager Kiki Vandeweghe coached the balance of the campaign before being fired from both roles. In Johnson, the Nets got the most coveted coach on the market. Johnson won big in his first head-coaching job in Dallas before apparently losing the team during his last year with the Mavericks.

The Nets had one last big move in store after King took over the team midway through the summer. He involved the team in a four-team trade with Houston, Indiana and New Orleans, sending out third-year shooting guard Courtney Lee and using the remaining cap space to take on the larger contract of forward Troy Murphy. Adding a veteran starter at power forward relieves some of the pressure on the raw Favors to contribute immediately without sacrificing much in terms of flexibility because Murphy will be a free agent at season's end.

Despite the shopping spree, the Nets are in good shape financially for next summer, with less than $40 million committed. Predicting what the NBA's salary cap might look like under what will likely be a new Collective Bargaining Agreement is an inexact science, but the Nets should have enough room to make another max offer. By the end of the season, they may be able to present a more compelling case to free agents that they can win.

One of SCHOENE's more surprising projections for 2010-11 is that the Nets will return to the postseason, more than tripling their win total from a year ago. In truth, the Nets don't have quite as far to go as their record suggests. One of the biggest reasons New Jersey threatened the worst record in league history was the team's complete inability to win a close game. The Nets were 1-13 in games decided by five points or fewer, which was historic futility. No other team in the last nine seasons has been anywhere near that poor in close games (Table 1).

Table 1: Worst Record in Close Games, 2001-10

Year	Team	Close Wins	Close Losses	Close Win%
2009-10	New Jersey	1	13	.071
2008-09	Sacramento	5	21	.192
2007-08	Memphis	5	15	.250
2009-10	Golden State	5	15	.250
2006-07	Boston	7	20	.259

Another factor working in the Nets' favor is clearing the dreck that inhabited the end of the roster a year ago. Nine players who saw action for the Nets last season rated below replacement level. Combined, these players cost New Jersey nearly nine games as compared to freely available talent. Of the nine, only Terrence Williams--who made huge strides over the course of his rookie season and is projected comfortably above replacement level this year--remains on the roster. Most of the players were veterans finishing up long-term guaranteed contracts that kept them in the NBA. Compared to this group, the new free agents represent a massive infusion of talent.

The Nets can count on some improvement from within. In addition to Williams, Lopez should take another step forward in his steady development and could emerge as an All-Star center as quickly as this season. Point guard Devin Harris is the second-oldest player in the Nets' rotation after Murphy, but he figures to bounce back after he followed up a breakthrough All-Star campaign with a nightmarish 2009-10 season.

Coaching will also be a factor. Harris played at an All-Defensive level under Johnson in Dallas before turning into a sieve in New Jersey. His effort level, which was nonexistent much of last season, should turn around in a hurry. Johnson will be a major upgrade at the defensive end over Vandeweghe, who was miscast as a head coach.

Even a win total in the 30s may be enough to convince free agents that joining up with the Nets' youngsters would be a worthwhile endeavor. Like everyone else with cap space next summer, the Nets will be aiming for Denver forward Carmelo Anthony, who would give them scoring punch on the wing they currently lack. If they strike out on Anthony, the summer of 2011 need not be the Nets' last foray into free agency. By limiting the contracts they handed out during the upcoming offseason, they should be able to get back under the cap after the 2012-13 season.

At that point, the Nets' makeover will be closer to completion. The team will be in Brooklyn with a new name. The organization filed paperwork to change its name in conjunction with the move, though it is unclear whether the nickname will change when the team drops the New Jersey designation. The Nets will market themselves as the younger, hipper alternative to the Knicks. If they can sell a big-name free agent on that proposition, they might just be able to make good on Prokhorov's stated desire to compete for the New York market--both on and off the court.

Kevin Pelton

From the Blogosphere

Who: Shane Patel
What: Nets Daily
Where: http://www.netsdaily.com/

Is it possible for a 12-win team to have any bright spots? Surprisingly, yes. Surely center Brook Lopez didn't get his share of the NBA limelight, but Terrence Williams' season of ups and downs was even less appreciated. At first glance, he looks like a prototypical "million-dollar talent, 10-cent head" shooting guard. His raw season stats did nothing to rectify this perception. Yet as the season matured, Williams did as well. He rose above countless distractions and posted an eye-opening 14-7-5 line in March and April, dropping 27, 13 and 10 on the Bulls in the final week of the season. At times, he seemed like the most natural rebounder and distributor on the Nets, giving him a ceiling few players possess. Williams is the rare four-year college player with a great body, great instincts, and great talent, who came out of school unpolished. The hope here is that Avery Johnson can harness that talent going forward.

NETS FIVE-YEAR TRENDS

Season	AGE	W-L	POW	PYTH	SEED	ORTG	DRTG	PT DIFF	PACE
05-06	28.6	49-33	46.4 (10)	45.2	3	105.7 (22)	104.0 (3)	1.4 (13)	88.4 (20)
06-07	28.2	41-41	38.8 (17)	38.8	6	108.0 (15)	107.8 (14)	-0.8 (16)	89.9 (16)
07-08	28.4	34-48	29.3 (22)	26.8	---	106.3 (25)	111.5 (20)	-5.1 (23)	89.6 (17)
08-09	25.7	34-48	34.0 (21)	34.0	---	109.8 (14)	112.7 (23)	-2.4 (21)	88.6 (23)
09-10	25.6	12-70	14.3 (30)	17.3	--	102.1 (30)	112.5 (25)	-9.1 (29)	89.9 (24)

		OFFENSE				DEFENSE			
Season	PAY	eFG	oREB	FT/FGA	TO	eFG	oREB	FT/FGA	TO
05-06	$61.6	.478 (25)	.240 (29)	.262 (10)	.154 (9)	.476 (9)	.763 (2)	.266 (25)	.162 (11)
06-07	$63.8	.504 (7)	.246 (26)	.245 (15)	.163 (12)	.490 (10)	.744 (9)	.266 (23)	.160 (22)
07-08	$65.4	.481 (25)	.265 (18)	.255 (10)	.159 (27)	.496 (11)	.737 (11)	.272 (29)	.143 (22)
08-09	$62.0	.497 (17)	.252 (22)	.236 (15)	.146 (10)	.510 (21)	.735 (16)	.272 (29)	.151 (19)
09-10	$61.0	.458 (30)	.251 (21)	.240 (11)	.160 (20)	.517 (23)	.718 (28)	.229 (17)	.155 (15)

(league rankings in parenthesis)

NEW JERSEY NETS

Jordan Farmar — PG #2

Hght: 6'2" | Exp: 4 | Salary: $3.8 million
Wght: 180 | From: UCLA
2011-12 status: guaranteed contract for $4.0 million

SKILL RATINGS

TOT	OFF	DEF	REB	PAS	HND	SHT	ATH
+1	+3	+3	-2	-2	-1	+2	-1

Year	Team	Age	G	MPG	Usg	3PA%	FTA%	INS	2P%	3P%	FT%	TS%	Reb%	Ast%	TO%	BLK%	STL%	PF%	oRTG	dRTG	Win%	WARP
07-08	LAL	21.4	82	20.6	.203	.397	.044	.647	.546	.371	.679	.563	.059	.059	.140	.002	.020	.027	107.3	105.8	.551	4.7
08-09	LAL	22.4	65	18.3	.197	.274	.064	.790	.421	.336	.584	.466	.055	.057	.163	.006	.024	.039	103.5	106.5	.402	-0.4
09-10	LAL	23.4	82	18.0	.191	.367	.060	.693	.483	.376	.671	.535	.049	.039	.115	.006	.018	.033	105.2	106.5	.458	1.3
10-11p	NJN	24.4	75	15.0	.193	.336	.057	.721	.489	.369	.653	.533	.046	.053	.129	.005	.019	.029	106.0	106.5	.485	1.6

Most similar to: Steve Colter (98.9), Luther Head, Byron Scott, B.J. Armstrong

IMP: 66%   BRK: 8%   COP: 4%

A change of scenery might do wonders for Jordan Farmar, who went from the Lakers' point guard of the future to lightning rod for criticism during the last two seasons. Farmar's shooting did rebound after a fluky 2008-09 saw his True Shooting Percentage sink dramatically, but the Lakers opted to part ways at season's end and Farmar ended up signing in New Jersey. He'll have more freedom with the Nets, though not necessarily more playing time unless he and Devin Harris end up playing together in the backcourt.

The triangle offense worked well for Farmar because he is unexceptional as a passer. Playing a more traditional point guard role will mean increased playmaking responsibility. It should give Farmar the chance to create more frequently off the dribble, an aspect of his game he subjugated with the Lakers in favor of scoring most of his points in spot-up situations. Opinions on Farmar's defense remain mixed. Lakers fans were less than thrilled with Farmar, who should have been the superior defensive option at the point as Derek Fisher aged. However, Farmar has generally posted good defensive statistics.

Derrick Favors — PF #14

Hght: 6'10" | Exp: R | Salary: $4.1 million
Wght: 246 | From: Georgia Tech
2011-12 status: guaranteed contract for $4.4 million

SKILL RATINGS

TOT	OFF	DEF	REB	PAS	HND	SHT	ATH
-2	-1	+1	0	-2	-4	+1	0

Year	Team	Age	G	MPG	Usg	3PA%	FTA%	INS	2P%	3P%	FT%	TS%	Reb%	Ast%	TO%	BLK%	STL%	PF%	oRTG	dRTG	Win%	WARP
10-11p	NJN	19.8	76	25.0	.163	.003	.106	1.103	.514	.005	.619	.537	.131	.016	.198	.036	.012	.060	102.5	105.4	.405	-0.4

Most similar to: Chris Bosh (97.3), Spencer Hawes, Anthony Randolph

IMP: -   BRK: -   COP: -

For a top-three pick, Derrick Favors was relatively unaccomplished in college. However, his age, his natural gifts and the skills he did flash in his lone year at Georgia Tech make him a potential star. Paul Hewitt's disorganized offense did little to help Favors, who often found himself reduced to trying to get the ball on the offensive glass. That aside, Favors' post-up game is very raw, and he'll need to work to refine his footwork. Developing 12- to 15-foot range will also be critical to the success of a frontcourt partnership with Brook Lopez that will require Favors to play the high post much of the time.

Favors is closer to being a finished product at the defensive end of the floor, where he figures to be an excellent shot blocker for a power forward. He's got legitimate size and long arms, and it's possible he could grow into the center position down the line. Favors' athleticism allows him to step out and defend the pick-and-roll. He will have to add some strength to battle in the post.

The addition of Troy Murphy sets a clear timeline for Favors. He'll come off the bench next season, likely seeing action at both the four and the five, before inheriting the starting job in 2011-12.

NEW JERSEY NETS

SG #26 Stephen Graham

Hght: 6'6" Exp: 5 Salary: $1.0 million
Wght: 215 From: Oklahoma State
2011-12 status: team option for $1.1 million

SKILL RATINGS

TOT	OFF	DEF	REB	PAS	HND	SHT	ATH
-3	0	+3	+3	-5	-5	+2	-3

Year	Team	Age	G	MPG	Usg	3PA%	FTA%	INS	2P%	3P%	FT%	TS%	Reb%	Ast%	TO%	BLK%	STL%	PF%	oRTG	dRTG	Win%	WARP
07-08	IND	25.9	22	5.9	.251	.187	.094	.907	.614	.500	.750	.669	.093	.030	.133	.006	.013	.047	108.9	106.3	.583	0.5
08-09	IND	26.9	52	13.2	.210	.201	.083	.882	.453	.303	.806	.498	.078	.021	.137	.004	.007	.052	102.5	108.7	.306	-1.6
09-10	CHA	27.9	70	11.5	.178	.164	.094	.930	.542	.320	.646	.551	.100	.013	.118	.010	.013	.055	102.7	106.6	.373	-0.7
10-11p	NJN	28.9	76	4.9	.180	.230	.084	.855	.507	.339	.702	.546	.080	.016	.128	.008	.011	.055	103.2	107.3	.368	-0.4

Most similar to: Jeff Grayer (98.0), Mike Sanders, Raja Bell, Greg Buckner   IMP: 46% BRK: 11% COP: 14%

Larry Brown quickly took a shine to Stephen Graham, who played a career-high 70 games for the Bobcats, including a handful of starts. By virtue of his high two-point percentage, Graham was a useful role player. He's always had the physical tools to be an effective wing defender, making the marriage with Brown's defensive scheme a successful one. Charlotte allowed 6.3 points fewer per 100 possessions with Graham on the floor, per BasketballValue.com. The biggest limitation for Graham is that he is largely invisible on offense. Since the Bobcats were already low on creators, that was a major problem for them. Graham latched on with New Jersey, but he will have a tough time beating out one of the Nets' younger wing players for regular minutes.

PG #34 Devin Harris

Hght: 6'3" Exp: 6 Salary: $9.0 million
Wght: 190 From: Wisconsin
2011-12 status: guaranteed contract for $9.3 million

SKILL RATINGS

TOT	OFF	DEF	REB	PAS	HND	SHT	ATH
+3	+4	-5	-2	+2	0	-2	+3

Year	Team	Age	G	MPG	Usg	3PA%	FTA%	INS	2P%	3P%	FT%	TS%	Reb%	Ast%	TO%	BLK%	STL%	PF%	oRTG	dRTG	Win%	WARP
07-08	NJN	25.1	64	31.6	.225	.169	.134	.965	.504	.335	.824	.573	.050	.084	.163	.004	.020	.043	107.5	106.3	.541	5.2
08-09	NJN	26.1	69	36.1	.286	.145	.175	1.030	.477	.291	.820	.563	.056	.090	.140	.004	.024	.031	110.4	106.5	.623	10.7
09-10	NJN	27.1	64	34.7	.257	.176	.138	.962	.444	.276	.798	.512	.055	.088	.147	.006	.018	.037	107.2	106.8	.514	4.5
10-11p	NJN	28.1	72	35.0	.251	.197	.142	.945	.470	.298	.811	.540	.046	.085	.150	.005	.019	.035	108.1	106.7	.542	6.7

Most similar to: Steve Francis (98.5), Isiah Thomas, Eddie Johnson Jr., Robert Pack   IMP: 40% BRK: 2% COP: 6%

A strained groin cost Devin Harris 10 games early in the season, and by the time he returned the Nets were 0-12 and on their way to dubious history. More than any other Nets player, Harris seemed to be affected by the general malaise hanging over the team, taking a significant step back from his All-Star 2008-09 campaign. New Jersey badly needs Harris to turn it around, and getting him back on track will be one of the key tasks for new coach Avery Johnson. It was Johnson who gave a young Harris the keys to the Mavericks in 2006-07 and was rewarded with a 67-win season, so there should be a level of trust between player and coach.

The most obvious change in Harris' game last year was that he attacked the basket less frequently. His percentage of shot attempts at the rim, per Hoopdata.com, dropped from 39.2 percent to 34.2 percent. Harris' two-point percentage suffered, as did his free throw rate, and his True Shooting Percentage followed suit. It's also hard to believe that Harris used a far lower percentage of the Nets' plays after the team replaced Vince Carter with role players at shooting guard. Even during 2008-09, Harris was a major liability at the defensive end of the floor, watching point guards blow by him off the dribble. In Dallas, Harris had been a very effective defender at the point, so the issue is apparently one of focus. Expect Johnson to get Harris' attention at the defensive end.

NEW JERSEY NETS

PF 43	Kris Humphries	Hght: 6'9" Wght: 235 2011-12 status: free agent	Exp: 6 From: Minnesota	Salary: $3.2 million							

SKILL RATINGS

TOT	OFF	DEF	REB	PAS	HND	SHT	ATH
+1	0	-1	+2	-3	-3	-3	+3

Year	Team	Age	G	MPG	Usg	3PA%	FTA%	INS	2P%	3P%	FT%	TS%	Reb%	Ast%	TO%	BLK%	STL%	PF%	oRTG	dRTG	Win%	WARP
07-08	TOR	23.2	70	13.3	.221	.005	.126	1.121	.488	.000	.605	.514	.166	.014	.108	.025	.013	.054	103.6	104.6	.468	1.0
08-09	TOR	24.2	29	9.1	.208	.000	.177	1.177	.422	.000	.792	.513	.155	.017	.067	.018	.015	.054	105.8	105.9	.496	0.4
09-10	NJN	25.2	69	17.7	.211	.002	.150	1.148	.442	.000	.668	.495	.180	.012	.118	.029	.015	.055	103.2	104.1	.471	1.4
10-11p	NJN	26.2	74	9.1	.204	.008	.150	1.142	.460	.006	.705	.515	.145	.014	.098	.023	.014	.051	104.2	105.1	.469	0.7

Most similar to: Nazr Mohammed (98.9), Alan Henderson, David West, Lorenzen Wright — IMP: 41% BRK: 7% COP: 9%

Had the Nets been able to enlist two max players, they were prepared to dump Kris Humphries to clear the necessary cap space, but New Jersey's strikeout in free agency proved a reprieve for Humphries. Acquired from Dallas in January, Humphries played a career-high 20.6 minutes per night the rest of the way, giving the Nets solid production off the bench.

The burly Humphries is at his best on the glass. Among non-centers, he ranked ninth in the league by grabbing 25.1 percent of available defensive rebounds. He could probably help himself by focusing more single-mindedly on the glass and forgetting about trying to be a scorer. Humphries has used plays at an above-average rate most of his NBA career despite never posting a True Shooting Percentage better than .516. Humphries' lack of height works against him in the paint, and he frequently has his shot rejected, limiting his shooting percentages.

SF 10	Damion James	Hght: 6'7" Wght: 220 2011-12 status: guaranteed contract for $1.2 million	Exp: R From: Texas	Salary: $1.2 million				

SKILL RATINGS

TOT	OFF	DEF	REB	PAS	HND	SHT	ATH
0	0	+1	+5	-4	-5	-3	+3

Year	Team	Age	G	MPG	Usg	3PA%	FTA%	INS	2P%	3P%	FT%	TS%	Reb%	Ast%	TO%	BLK%	STL%	PF%	oRTG	dRTG	Win%	WARP
10-11p	NJN	23.5	76	15.0	.189	.128	.127	.998	.441	.330	.659	.493	.137	.013	.117	.016	.019	.060	103.6	105.4	.440	0.6

Most similar to: David West (97.3), Morris Peterson, Tayshaun Prince, Leon Powe — IMP: - BRK: - COP: -

An effective stretch four at Texas, Damion James will make the move to the wing as a pro. His shooting range will be an asset in the transition, as he was a dangerous three-point shooter at the NCAA level and should eventually be able to hit the NBA three. James' biggest adjustment will be in terms of handling the basketball, something he rarely did in college. When teams press, he'll have to be able to help out with ballhandling.

James should be capable of defending on the perimeter. A good athlete who is strong for a small forward, James will contribute the occasional blocked shot to the Nets' cause. His best asset is his rebounding. James averaged double-figure rebounds twice as a Longhorn and has the ability to crash the glass from the perimeter if opponents fail to box him out. The battle for playing time on the wings in New Jersey is crowded, but James should find a spot for himself.

C 11	Brook Lopez	Hght: 7'0" Wght: 265 2011-12 status: team option for $3.1 million	Exp: 2 From: Stanford	Salary: $2.4 million				

SKILL RATINGS

TOT	OFF	DEF	REB	PAS	HND	SHT	ATH
+4	+3	-4	-2	+3	+1	+2	+2

Year	Team	Age	G	MPG	Usg	3PA%	FTA%	INS	2P%	3P%	FT%	TS%	Reb%	Ast%	TO%	BLK%	STL%	PF%	oRTG	dRTG	Win%	WARP
08-09	NJN	21.1	82	30.5	.205	.002	.088	1.086	.532	.000	.793	.568	.159	.016	.135	.050	.009	.048	105.2	104.5	.523	5.5
09-10	NJN	22.1	82	36.9	.238	.001	.144	1.143	.500	.000	.817	.570	.137	.029	.131	.034	.009	.038	106.8	105.1	.555	8.7
10-11p	NJN	23.1	76	37.0	.233	.005	.131	1.126	.525	.005	.806	.581	.130	.027	.133	.037	.009	.041	106.6	104.9	.555	8.2

Most similar to: Pau Gasol (97.5), Vin Baker, Elton Brand, Al Jefferson — IMP: 62% BRK: 0% COP: 2%

During his summer rankings of the league's best players by position at the Yahoo! Ball Don't Lie blog, the esteemed Kelly Dwyer ranked Brook Lopez as the league's third-best center. At first blush, that sounds crazy, but as long as you consider Tim Duncan a power forward, the argument is a sound one. Lopez has put together two excellent seasons by age 22, and is likely to be one of the NBA's top big men for the next decade. What Lopez did last season was largely obscured by the fact that the Nets were so pitiful, but he was able to maintain the efficiency he showed as a rookie while playing a larger role in the New Jersey offense and heavier minutes, an important step in his development.

Lopez is a tough matchup in the post, where he can turn to a half hook, face up or shoot little fadeaways. His footwork in the paint is very sound. Lopez made major strides last season in terms of getting to the free throw line, and he figures to continue improving as he gets more respect from referees. Lopez should be even more dangerous this season because of the addition of Troy Murphy, who will make opponents think twice about doubling Lopez with another big. Meanwhile, a future pairing with Derrick Favors will help Lopez at the defensive end. He saw both his block and rebound rates decrease last season, and putting him alongside another player with length should compensate for the fact that Lopez is only average as a help defender.

SG 22	Anthony Morrow	Hght: 6'5" Wght: 210 2011-12 status: guaranteed contract for $4.0 million	Exp: 2 From: Georgia Tech	Salary: $4.0 million		SKILL RATINGS						
					TOT	OFF	DEF	REB	PAS	HND	SHT	ATH
					+2	+4	-1	-1	-3	0	+4	-4

Year	Team	Age	G	MPG	Usg	3PA%	FTA%	INS	2P%	3P%	FT%	TS%	Reb%	Ast%	TO%	BLK%	STL%	PF%	oRTG	dRTG	Win%	WARP
08-09	GSW	23.6	67	22.6	.177	.294	.065	.771	.483	.467	.870	.588	.071	.023	.083	.005	.011	.037	107.8	108.2	.486	2.2
09-10	GSW	24.6	69	29.2	.178	.367	.060	.693	.477	.456	.886	.597	.072	.022	.100	.006	.015	.034	106.7	106.9	.495	3.3
10-11p	NJN	25.6	73	28.0	.174	.370	.064	.694	.481	.439	.887	.590	.063	.024	.089	.006	.012	.034	107.1	107.3	.493	3.3

Most similar to: Wesley Person (98.0), Hubert Davis, Glen Rice, Tracy Murray   IMP: 42%   BRK: 5%   COP: 5%

It was reasonable to believe that Anthony Morrow would be unable to sustain his league-leading three-point percentage from his rookie campaign, and indeed that was the case. He dropped all the way from 46.7 percent to 45.6 percent. Clearly, the man can shoot. Seeing increased action because of the Warriors' injuries on the wings, Morrow led the NBA in total three-pointers during a second season that was more or less a carbon copy of his first.

Morrow has likely maxed out his skill set, and SCHOENE agrees there is little room for him to continue growing. Still, he's a very valuable contributor on the wing who should prove a bargain for the Nets. His shooting ability will help space the floor and is a nice complement to the more athletic wings New Jersey has accumulated. For a specialist, Morrow is fairly effective at the defensive end. He contributes on the glass, has legitimate size and competed on a team where defense was anything but a priority.

PF 7	Troy Murphy	Hght: 6'11" Wght: 245 2011-12 status: free agent	Exp: 9 From: Notre Dame	Salary: $12.0 million		SKILL RATINGS						
					TOT	OFF	DEF	REB	PAS	HND	SHT	ATH
					+4	+4	-5	+3	+3	+4	+2	0

Year	Team	Age	G	MPG	Usg	3PA%	FTA%	INS	2P%	3P%	FT%	TS%	Reb%	Ast%	TO%	BLK%	STL%	PF%	oRTG	dRTG	Win%	WARP
07-08	IND	28.0	75	28.1	.184	.264	.119	.855	.485	.398	.797	.574	.142	.034	.107	.011	.010	.045	106.9	105.3	.554	6.0
08-09	IND	29.0	73	34.0	.170	.372	.084	.712	.496	.450	.826	.614	.192	.030	.119	.010	.011	.040	108.9	104.8	.632	11.1
09-10	IND	30.0	72	32.6	.189	.334	.085	.751	.533	.384	.798	.585	.172	.028	.100	.010	.015	.033	107.8	103.9	.628	10.3
10-11p	NJN	31.0	74	30.0	.172	.365	.085	.720	.506	.368	.794	.564	.156	.029	.106	.009	.012	.039	107.0	105.2	.560	6.7

Most similar to: Bill Laimbeer (95.7), Keith Van Horn, Steve Hawes, Maurice Lucas   IMP: 32%   BRK: 2%   COP: 15%

Troy Murphy is exhibit A in the argument for considering multiple statistics to evaluate a player. Based simply on his individual advanced numbers, Murphy looks like a star. He's a strong rebounder who is supremely efficient on offense because of his three-point range. Murphy ranked 21st in the league in WARP last season. Alas, Murphy's inept defense gives back much of that value. The Pacers were 6.9 points worse per 100 possessions with Murphy on the floor last season, per BasketballValue.com, and they've been substantially worse at the defensive end when Murphy has played each of the last three seasons.

As a band-aid solution, Murphy should be good for the Nets, who can milk his floor-spacing ability for a season before letting him walk as a free agent. Murphy could be described as a rich man's version of the player he's replacing in the New Jersey lineup, Yi Jianlian. Avery Johnson will also have the ability to spot Murphy with Derrick Favors against tougher defensive matchups. His effort is OK defensively, but Murphy has very slow feet and disdains physical play, leaving him overmatched against power forwards of all varieties.

NEW JERSEY NETS

SF 21 — Travis Outlaw

Hght: 6'9" | Exp: 7 | Salary: $7.0 million
Wght: 207 | From: Starkville HS (MS)
2011-12 status: guaranteed contract for $7.0 million

SKILL RATINGS

TOT	OFF	DEF	REB	PAS	HND	SHT	ATH
+1	+2	-1	0	-1	-2	0	0

Year	Team	Age	G	MPG	Usg	3PA%	FTA%	INS	2P%	3P%	FT%	TS%	Reb%	Ast%	TO%	BLK%	STL%	PF%	oRTG	dRTG	Win%	WARP
07-08	POR	23.6	82	26.6	.262	.083	.108	1.024	.438	.400	.741	.500	.101	.023	.089	.022	.013	.038	103.3	104.8	.451	1.5
08-09	POR	24.6	81	27.7	.222	.225	.101	.877	.482	.377	.723	.541	.092	.018	.089	.020	.011	.035	105.3	106.3	.468	2.4
09-10	LAC	25.6	34	21.5	.215	.310	.077	.767	.398	.381	.831	.503	.098	.022	.094	.018	.013	.027	104.8	105.6	.475	0.9
10-11p	NJN	26.6	69	28.0	.222	.247	.089	.842	.444	.392	.784	.527	.087	.023	.093	.020	.013	.031	105.3	105.7	.488	2.9

Most similar to: Hedo Turkoglu (98.3), Todd Day, Al Wood, Chris Mills | IMP: 61% | BRK: 7% | COP: 5%

Travis Outlaw carved out a successful role for himself as a sixth man in Portland in 2007-08 and 2008-09, but the Blazers realized they didn't really need Outlaw when he suffered a stress fracture of the fifth metatarsal in his right foot last November. By the time Outlaw was ready to return to the court, he had been traded to the L.A. Clippers as part of the package for center Marcus Camby. Outlaw helped solidify the Clippers' bench the rest of the way, supplying similar production to his previous two seasons.

While most of the league sees Outlaw as a quality reserve, the Nets apparently view him as their answer at small forward. This presents a problem because Outlaw has been better at the four position, where he can use his quickness to beat defenders off the dribble or make open threes against players who are reluctant to defend him on the perimeter. Since Outlaw is not strong enough to take smaller defenders into the post, against better athletes he's forced to settle for contested attempts on the perimeter. Outlaw's size will be beneficial on the perimeter at the defensive end. He's got solid timing as a shot blocker and does a good job of contesting shots when he's focused on defense.

C 27 — Johan Petro

Hght: 7'0" | Exp: 5 | Salary: $3.3 million
Wght: 247 | From: Paris, France
2011-12 status: guaranteed contract for $3.3 million

SKILL RATINGS

TOT	OFF	DEF	REB	PAS	HND	SHT	ATH
-3	-1	0	0	-2	-2	-1	+2

Year	Team	Age	G	MPG	Usg	3PA%	FTA%	INS	2P%	3P%	FT%	TS%	Reb%	Ast%	TO%	BLK%	STL%	PF%	oRTG	dRTG	Win%	WARP
07-08	SEA	22.2	72	18.1	.184	.002	.070	1.068	.420	.000	.736	.453	.155	.011	.133	.024	.012	.058	100.0	104.8	.340	-2.1
08-09	DEN	23.2	49	11.4	.173	.009	.059	1.050	.420	.000	.552	.429	.163	.013	.129	.021	.017	.085	100.2	106.1	.310	-1.2
09-10	DEN	24.2	36	12.1	.136	.008	.069	1.062	.540	.000	.667	.553	.170	.014	.173	.022	.011	.082	102.1	105.8	.377	-0.4
10-11p	NJN	25.2	76	15.0	.157	.012	.067	1.055	.496	.005	.649	.507	.150	.015	.145	.024	.014	.076	101.6	105.6	.369	-1.1

Most similar to: Olden Polynice (98.7), Jon Koncak, Donald Hodge, Shelden Williams | IMP: 65% | BRK: 18% | COP: 4%

The three-year, $10 million deal the Nets gave Johan Petro isn't big enough to do any real damage, but it was still among the more unexpected contracts of the summer given that Petro has not been a rotation player since coming off the bench for the 20-win 2007-08 Sonics. An athletic 7-footer, Petro has developed into a productive rebounder, but his instincts are poor at the defensive end of the floor, which explains why he has played nearly as much power forward as center over the course of his career.

Petro was able to improve his two-point percentage last season by cutting down considerably on his attempts from midrange. The tradeoff was the lowest usage percentage of his career, so even with a 55.3 percent True Shooting Percentage Petro was a below-average offensive contributor. His 54.0 percent shooting on twos also reflects some good luck around the basket, where Petro was far more accurate than ever before in his career.

NEW JERSEY NETS

SG 13 — Quinton Ross

Hght: 6'6" | Exp: 6 | Salary: $1.1 million
Wght: 193 | From: Southern Methodist
2011-12 status: free agent

SKILL RATINGS

TOT	OFF	DEF	REB	PAS	HND	SHT	ATH
-5	--	+4	--	--	--	--	--

Year	Team	Age	G	MPG	Usg	3PA%	FTA%	INS	2P%	3P%	FT%	TS%	Reb%	Ast%	TO%	BLK%	STL%	PF%	oRTG	dRTG	Win%	WARP
07-08	LAC	27.0	76	19.8	.121	.054	.067	1.014	.387	.429	.667	.429	.066	.027	.074	.016	.013	.040	100.4	106.3	.309	-3.4
08-09	MEM	28.0	68	17.1	.127	.281	.059	.778	.386	.375	.810	.478	.067	.019	.115	.010	.014	.046	102.6	107.6	.339	-1.9
09-10	WAS	29.0	52	10.8	.105	.164	.048	.884	.400	.190	.571	.393	.050	.010	.086	.008	.012	.056	99.3	108.2	.231	-2.2
10-11p	NJN	30.0	75	-	.109	.240	.048	.808	.399	.302	.649	.431	.051	.017	.094	.010	.013	.049	-	-	.277	-

Most similar to: Bruce Bowen (97.4), Trenton Hassell, Tony Brown, Clint Richardson
IMP: 57% | BRK: 27% | COP: 3%

The Mavericks signed Quinton Ross last summer to be their defensive specialist on the perimeter, but they had to include him in their midseason trade with Washington to acquire Caron Butler and Brendan Haywood. Ross played rotation minutes the rest of the way before moving on again when the Wizards dumped him on the Nets in exchange for taking back Yi Jianlian's contract. Ross doesn't have much value to a non-contending team because he is so one-dimensional as a player, and he is unlikely to see regular action in New Jersey. A smart player with quick feet, Ross is very good as a defender, but his impotent offense makes it difficult for him to put those skills to use.

During his best days with the L.A. Clippers, Ross made enough midrange jumpers to hold his own, but his shooting percentages have slipped badly the last three seasons. Ross' adjusted True Shooting Percentage (accounting for his small role on offense) was second-worst in the NBA among players with at least 500 minutes last season. The only player below him, DeShawn Stevenson, went the other direction in the Dallas-Washington trade.

PF 8 — Joe Smith

Hght: 6'10" | Exp: 15 | Salary: $0.9 million
Wght: 225 | From: Maryland
2011-12 status: free agent

SKILL RATINGS

TOT	OFF	DEF	REB	PAS	HND	SHT	ATH
-2	0	+1	0	-1	+2	-3	-4

Year	Team	Age	G	MPG	Usg	3PA%	FTA%	INS	2P%	3P%	FT%	TS%	Reb%	Ast%	TO%	BLK%	STL%	PF%	oRTG	dRTG	Win%	WARP
07-08	CLE	32.7	77	22.4	.216	.004	.110	1.107	.480	.000	.755	.524	.134	.018	.087	.021	.009	.051	104.9	105.9	.466	1.8
08-09	CLE	33.7	57	19.3	.163	.018	.092	1.074	.469	.429	.720	.507	.139	.017	.063	.029	.008	.051	104.3	106.2	.437	0.5
09-10	ATL	34.7	64	9.3	.185	.030	.089	1.060	.409	.143	.813	.453	.155	.016	.093	.024	.005	.074	103.4	107.0	.379	-0.5
10-11p	NJN	35.7	75	5.0	.173	.024	.092	1.068	.448	.170	.747	.493	.128	.017	.086	.029	.007	.068	103.9	106.6	.409	-0.1

Most similar to: Scott Williams (97.8), Terry Cummings, Kurt Thomas, Herb Williams
IMP: 42% | BRK: 10% | COP: 0%

Age appeared to catch up with Joe Smith last season. The NBA's most generically named player fell out of Atlanta's rotation by the postseason and slipped below replacement level for the first time since 1997-98. Despite the fact that Smith turned 35 over the summer, he has a chance to bounce back. His athleticism markers, especially his rebound percentage, remained strong. The biggest difference in his stat line was a drop from 39.0 percent to 30.0 percent on long two-point attempts. Since Smith mostly plays on the perimeter now, his inaccuracy from 16-23 feet doomed his shooting percentage. If he can regain his touch, Smith has a chance to carve out some playing time in the frontcourt after signing with New Jersey as a free agent. The Nets will be Smith's 11th team during a 16-year NBA career.

PG 18 — Ben Uzoh

Hght: 6'3" | Exp: R | Salary: $0.5 million
Wght: 205 | From: Tulsa
2011-12 status: due qualifying offer of $1.0 million

SKILL RATINGS

TOT	OFF	DEF	REB	PAS	HND	SHT	ATH
-1	--	--	--	--	--	--	--

Year	Team	Age	G	MPG	Usg	3PA%	FTA%	INS	2P%	3P%	FT%	TS%	Reb%	Ast%	TO%	BLK%	STL%	PF%	oRTG	dRTG	Win%	WARP
10-11p	NJN	23.1	76	-	.161	.205	.087	.882	.412	.285	.748	.461	.053	.059	.151	.009	.010	.033	-	-	.413	-

Most similar to: Acie Law (96.9), Chris Jefferies, Royal Ivey, Joe Crawford
IMP: - | BRK: - | COP: -

The Nets traded their second-round pick to move up and get Damion James, but they added depth by aggressively pursuing undrafted rookies. Tulsa point guard Ben Uzoh was one of two players who got a token guarantee to join New Jersey for the NBA Summer League in Orlando and training camp. A big guard who averaged 4.7 rebounds and 4.7 assists as a senior, Uzoh will have to improve as a shooter to find a home in the NBA. He was a career 34.9 percent shooter from the NCAA's three-point line. Uzoh isn't quick enough off the bounce to get to the rim regularly in the NBA, so he's going to have a tough time scoring efficiently. Still, he's got the inside track on being New Jersey's third point guard.

SG 1	Terrence Williams	Hght: 6'6" Wght: 220 2011-12 status: team option for $2.4 million	Exp: 1 From: Louisville	Salary: $2.2 million													
					SKILL RATINGS												
					TOT	OFF	DEF	REB	PAS	HND	SHT	ATH					
					+1	+2	+1	+5	+4	+2	-1	-2					

Year	Team	Age	G	MPG	Usg	3PA%	FTA%	INS	2P%	3P%	FT%	TS%	Reb%	Ast%	TO%	BLK%	STL%	PF%	oRTG	dRTG	Win%	WARP
09-10	NJN	22.8	78	22.6	.220	.119	.076	.956	.417	.310	.715	.459	.118	.059	.148	.004	.013	.033	102.7	106.0	.391	-1.0
10-11p	NJN	23.8	75	24.0	.214	.206	.077	.871	.439	.369	.749	.505	.104	.063	.145	.005	.013	.030	105.3	106.0	.478	2.3

Most similar to: Elston Turner (96.7), Doug Smith, Willie Burton, Vern Fleming   IMP: 72%   BRK: 23%   COP: 2%

If there was an award for the player who improved the most from the start of the season to the end, Terrence Williams would have been a lock to win as a rookie. Williams struggled badly at the start of the year and was out of the rotation by midseason, but after the All-Star break he averaged 11.9 points, 5.8 rebounds and 4.4 assists per game, providing the kind of versatile production the Nets expected when they took him in the lottery.

The knock on Williams has always been his difficulty scoring efficiently, and even after the break Williams' True Shooting Percentage of 49.6 percent was poor. However, he makes up for it with his myriad skills. Avery Johnson has said he views Williams strictly as a shooting guard, and he's a great rebounder for the position as well as a good enough ballhandler to step in and run the point at times. Williams also has the tools to be a very good defensive player, and he was one of New Jersey's best defenders as a rookie.

Even without knowing about the progress Williams made within his rookie season, SCHOENE pegs him to take a huge leap forward this year, suggesting he'll be much more accurate from long distance. If he keeps his production up over an entire season, Williams might be in line for some non-mythical hardware.

C 55	Brian Zoubek	Hght: 7'1" Wght: 260 2011-12 status: due qualifying offer of $1.0 million	Exp: R From: Duke	Salary: $0.5 million													
					SKILL RATINGS												
					TOT	OFF	DEF	REB	PAS	HND	SHT	ATH					
					+1	--	--	--	--	--	--	--					

Year	Team	Age	G	MPG	Usg	3PA%	FTA%	INS	2P%	3P%	FT%	TS%	Reb%	Ast%	TO%	BLK%	STL%	PF%	oRTG	dRTG	Win%	WARP
10-11p	NJN	23.0	76	-	.110	.000	.115	1.115	.533	.000	.539	.545	.189	.023	.212	.019	.014	.126	-	-	.481	-

Most similar to: Chris Richard (89.2), David Lee, Jamaal Magloire   IMP: -   BRK: -   COP: -

Haddonfield, N.J. native Brian Zoubek was the Nets' other undrafted pickup. The difference between the first and second halves of Zoubek's senior season dwarves even Terrence Williams' improvement. Zoubek went from a foul-prone stiff to one of the key contributors to Duke's national championship. A light apparently went on at midseason, as Zoubek figured out how to use his immense size to his advantage without drawing the attention of referees.

At 7'1", Zoubek is big and strong even as an NBA center, and he can muscle his way into position on the offensive glass. His offensive rebounding last season approached the previously unprecedented heights reached by DeJuan Blair the previous year. Zoubek's other primary contribution on offense is his screen-setting. He'll have to be careful to make sure he's stationary to avoid getting called for offensive fouls, but Zoubek is a brick wall when he sets a pick, freeing up his teammates. Zoubek's ability to contribute in the NBA will depend heavily on whether he can defend against the steady stream of pick-and-rolls he is likely to face. Zoubek's size will always work against him when it comes to moving laterally, and that might doom him as a regular in the pros.

NEW JERSEY NETS

Josh Boone — C

- Hght: 6'10"
- Wght: 240
- Exp: 4
- From: Connecticut
- Salary: --
- 2011-12 status: free agent

SKILL RATINGS

TOT	OFF	DEF	REB	PAS	HND	SHT	ATH
0	-1	-2	+1	-2	+1	+2	0

Year	Team	Age	G	MPG	Usg	3PA%	FTA%	INS	2P%	3P%	FT%	TS%	Reb%	Ast%	TO%	BLK%	STL%	PF%	oRTG	dRTG	Win%	WARP
07-08	NJN	23.4	70	25.3	.156	.000	.160	1.160	.547	.000	.456	.542	.167	.014	.114	.027	.009	.040	103.9	104.5	.479	2.3
08-09	NJN	24.4	62	16.0	.134	.000	.132	1.132	.528	.000	.376	.513	.155	.015	.110	.039	.012	.050	104.0	105.1	.461	0.9
09-10	NJN	25.4	63	16.6	.126	.000	.089	1.089	.525	-	.328	.509	.176	.013	.130	.034	.015	.049	103.3	104.0	.475	1.3
10-11p	AVG	26.4	72	16.6	.135	.003	.115	1.112	.532	.005	.376	.517	.158	.015	.122	.032	.012	.045	103.0	104.4	.451	0.9

Most similar to: Tony Battie (98.4), Cherokee Parks, Anderson Varejao, Cadillac Anderson

IMP: 45% BRK: 7% COP: 5%

All of Josh Boone's statistics, both at the individual and the plus-minus level, suggest he's a perfectly competent NBA backup center. For whatever reason, Boone has failed to inspire much enthusiasm from New Jersey or any other suitors now that he is an unrestricted free agent. To preserve their cap space, the Nets chose not to tender Boone a qualifying offer and renounced his Bird rights. At press time, Boone was still looking for a new home.

In four years in the NBA, Boone has yet to show any real development. Nearing 26, it's hard to anticipate any growth ahead of him. Still, Boone is a very good rebounder who blocks the occasional shot and can finish at the rim. Given the state of backup big men in the league, that skill set should be enough to earn Boone steady employment somewhere.

Trenton Hassell — SF

- Hght: 6'5"
- Wght: 227
- Exp: 9
- From: Austin Peay
- Salary: --
- 2011-12 status: free agent

SKILL RATINGS

TOT	OFF	DEF	REB	PAS	HND	SHT	ATH
-5	-2	-3	-3	-1	0	-4	-4

Year	Team	Age	G	MPG	Usg	3PA%	FTA%	INS	2P%	3P%	FT%	TS%	Reb%	Ast%	TO%	BLK%	STL%	PF%	oRTG	dRTG	Win%	WARP
07-08	NJN	29.1	63	12.4	.096	.055	.027	.972	.433	.222	.700	.438	.062	.024	.135	.003	.008	.053	99.1	108.2	.224	-3.1
08-09	NJN	30.1	53	20.6	.100	.034	.047	1.013	.459	.250	.800	.480	.080	.022	.129	.012	.010	.040	101.2	107.7	.295	-2.8
09-10	NJN	31.1	52	21.3	.124	.017	.102	1.086	.421	.000	.754	.465	.080	.021	.159	.006	.008	.038	100.4	107.9	.268	-3.4
10-11p	AVG	32.1	70	21.3	.105	.040	.068	1.029	.440	.112	.760	.463	.073	.022	.148	.009	.009	.042	100.1	107.6	.268	-4.6

Most similar to: Doug West (98.1), Calbert Cheaney, Michael Curry, Mike Sanders

IMP: 47% BRK: 15% COP: 12%

Trenton Hassell's now-completed six-year contract might have been the single worst in NBA history in terms of WARP over the life of the deal. Hassell rung up a total of 22.0 Wins Below Replacement while pocketing $26.1 million. Hassell's hype as the next Bruce Bowen expired about six months after the Timberwolves matched Portland's offer to him during the summer of 2004, and he's spent the last six years playing out the string on a series of teams ranging from mediocre to worse.

On offense, Hassell's only contributions come in the form of midrange jumpers, the game's least efficient shot. As a result, his True Shooting Percentage has been below 50 percent each of the last three years. That might be acceptable if Hassell were truly an elite defender, but he's an average one who had some good outings in the 2004 playoffs. The Nets have been no better defensively with Hassell on the floor the last three seasons, and his net plus-minus ratings (-9.2 points per 100 possessions in 2007-08, -8.0 in 2008-09 and -7.8 last season) confirm WARP's dim view of his contributions. Without a guaranteed contract, Hassell will have a tough time finding another NBA job.

Jarvis Hayes — SF

- Hght: 6'8"
- Wght: 228
- Exp: 7
- From: Georgia
- Salary: --
- 2011-12 status: free agent

SKILL RATINGS

TOT	OFF	DEF	REB	PAS	HND	SHT	ATH
-1	+1	+3	-3	-3	0	+2	-3

Year	Team	Age	G	MPG	Usg	3PA%	FTA%	INS	2P%	3P%	FT%	TS%	Reb%	Ast%	TO%	BLK%	STL%	PF%	oRTG	dRTG	Win%	WARP
07-08	DET	26.7	82	15.7	.213	.336	.046	.710	.465	.376	.750	.520	.083	.023	.081	.004	.018	.052	104.5	106.1	.447	0.8
08-09	NJN	27.7	74	24.8	.167	.376	.035	.659	.489	.385	.692	.537	.088	.014	.076	.003	.015	.042	104.3	107.2	.406	-0.4
09-10	NJN	28.7	45	22.9	.163	.492	.022	.530	.523	.335	.778	.521	.063	.018	.077	.006	.015	.041	104.2	107.0	.409	-0.2
10-11p	AVG	29.7	70	22.9	.163	.472	.028	.556	.500	.357	.726	.530	.072	.018	.080	.005	.015	.044	104.3	106.7	.419	0.1

Most similar to: Pat Garrity (97.6), Bobby Hansen, Devean George, Maurice Evans

IMP: 38% BRK: 11% COP: 2%

NEW JERSEY NETS

It's a testament to the Nets' horrendous depth last season that so many of their rotation players became free agents and drew crickets in response from the rest of the league. Jarvis Hayes has at least contributed to winning teams in the past, though his individual statistics have long suggested that teams overrated his shooting ability. Hayes is a pretty good shooter, not a great one, and his True Shooting Percentages have consistently been average at best. Hayes is still considered a shooting specialist because he's not very good at anything else. Last year saw him go from passable to liability on the glass, and he's a poor defender. Hayes' name still carries enough weight that he'll likely latch on somewhere, but expect his minutes per game to drop considerably.

PF	Sean May	Hght: 6'9"	Exp: 4	Salary: $0.1 million				SKILL RATINGS					
		Wght: 266	From: North Carolina		TOT	OFF	DEF	REB	PAS	HND	SHT	ATH
--		2011-12 status: free agent			-3	--	+1	--	--	--	--	--

Year	Team	Age	G	MPG	Usg	3PA%	FTA%	INS	2P%	3P%	FT%	TS%	Reb%	Ast%	TO%	BLK%	STL%	PF%	oRTG	dRTG	Win%	WARP
08-09	CHA	25.0	24	12.5	.210	.008	.066	1.059	.392	1.000	.700	.435	.141	.016	.196	.011	.009	.051	98.8	107.0	.247	-1.1
09-10	SAC	26.0	37	8.9	.194	.028	.098	1.070	.477	.000	.656	.492	.122	.023	.132	.015	.018	.062	102.0	105.8	.376	-0.3
10-11p	NJN	27.0	76	--	.186	.038	.089	1.051	.453	.423	.684	.495	.120	.021	.152	.017	.015	.054	--	--	.384	--

Most similar to: Tom Tolbert (97.8), Jack Haley, Mike Brown, Frank Brickowski   IMP: 71%   BRK: 33%   COP: 2%

Fully healthy after spending the 2008-09 season battling his way back from microfracture knee surgery, Sean May dealt with a far bigger problem last year in Sacramento: he wasn't very good. May was healthy and in far better shape than at the end of his tenure in Charlotte, but it failed to translate into results on the floor, leaving May's NBA career in jeopardy.

At North Carolina, May excelled because he combined his enormous girth with exceptional athleticism for a player of his size. The knee problems have cost May that quickness, and he's been unable to compensate. Once a deft finisher in the paint, May's shooting percentage at the rim last season (29.4 percent, per Hoopdata.com) is so low it looks like a misprint. He's also no longer a plus on the glass. The Nets guaranteed May $100,000 to get him to come to training camp for a look, but he suffered a stress fracture of a bone in his left foot during an offseason workout at the University of North Carolina and was subsequently waived. It is unlikely May will be back on the floor in time for training camp.

PF	Sean Williams	Hght: 6'10"	Exp: 3	Salary: --				SKILL RATINGS					
		Wght: 235	From: Boston College		TOT	OFF	DEF	REB	PAS	HND	SHT	ATH
--		2011-12 status: free agent			-2	-1	+1	+1	-2	-4	-2	0

Year	Team	Age	G	MPG	Usg	3PA%	FTA%	INS	2P%	3P%	FT%	TS%	Reb%	Ast%	TO%	BLK%	STL%	PF%	oRTG	dRTG	Win%	WARP
07-08	NJN	21.6	73	17.5	.157	.000	.135	1.135	.538	.000	.609	.563	.146	.010	.163	.065	.010	.070	102.4	103.3	.469	1.4
08-09	NJN	22.6	33	11.1	.136	.000	.133	1.133	.417	.000	.625	.465	.129	.017	.189	.065	.010	.093	101.8	105.7	.371	-0.3
09-10	NJN	23.6	20	11.4	.158	.013	.108	1.095	.438	.000	.526	.453	.117	.002	.259	.062	.018	.084	98.6	103.9	.324	-0.4
10-11p	AVG	24.6	76	11.4	.156	.009	.135	1.126	.477	.010	.608	.504	.136	.016	.173	.055	.010	.079	102.0	104.8	.405	-0.2

Most similar to: Keon Clark (99.2), Michael Stewart, Ryan Hollins, Adonal Foyle   IMP: 50%   BRK: 6%   COP: 6%

The Nets finally cut ties with Sean Williams when they waived him in January. Williams fell rapidly from center of the future to underachieving troublemaker. He played just 593 minutes total over the last two seasons and was ineffective when he did get on the floor. During his rookie season, Williams was a terrific shot blocker who finished enough dunks to shoot 53.8 percent. Williams is still 6'10" and athletic, so it's possible someone will take a flyer on him. More likely, his history of off-court troubles (he was kicked off the team at Boston College and arrested while playing in the D-League for the Nets' affiliate) will keep teams away. Williams finished last season playing in the Chinese CBA, where he won the league's Slam Dunk Contest.

New Orleans Hornets

Throughout the history of the NBA, there have been plenty of players who have earned the nickname "Franchise," either because of their importance to the team or, in the case of Steve Francis, because of their surname. It's hard to imagine a situation where the term was more apt than in the case of Chris Paul and the New Orleans Hornets.

Playing in a football town opposite the defending NFL champs and in a city still dealing with the effects of Hurricane Katrina, the Hornets' future remains tenuous at best. Local minority partner Gary Chouest has been in talks to purchase the team from long-time owner George Shinn, but to date nothing has materialized from those negotiations. To capture the city's attention and remain viable, New Orleans needs Paul. For better or worse, the franchise knows it.

The Hornets got a look at life without Paul during the 2009-10 season. Arthroscopic surgery on his left knee along with a couple of minor ailments cost Paul 37 games, during which New Orleans went 14-23 to kill any hopes of making the postseason. Rookie Darren Collison acquitted himself nicely in Paul's stead, averaging 18.8 points and 9.1 assists per game, but he wasn't Paul. The Hornets were 6.2 points better per 100 possessions with Paul on the floor.

Before Paul's injury, New Orleans' season had already gotten off to a ruinous start. Byron Scott entered the season with shaky job security because of the way the Denver Nuggets mopped the floor with the Hornets in the 2009 postseason. Against that backdrop, a change was inevitable after the Hornets started the season 3-6. Scott's last stand was a dispirited 20-point loss at Phoenix on national TV.

New Orleans told general manager Jeff Bower to take over coaching duties. An assistant coach for the Hornets under Tim Floyd in 2003-04, Bower brought Floyd back to be his lead assistant. On the sidelines, Bower's faith in his own 2009 draft picks would be rewarded. Collison and Marcus Thornton had been buried under Scott, who favored shoot-first point guard Bobby Brown and journeyman Devin Brown in the backcourt. Given more minutes, the youngsters thrived and New Orleans was able to right the ship. At the time of Paul's injury, the Hornets were 25-21. While a playoff trip was unlikely because of the depth of the Western Conference, New Orleans was competitive when healthy.

The problem is that being competitive is not good enough to justify a payroll that entered the offseason in luxury-tax territory. It also might not be good enough for Paul. Before the draft, whispers suggested that the Hornets were pondering offers for their superstar point guard in a massive trade that would also allow them to get out from the last three years of Emeka Okafor's contract.

The draft did provide some salary relief when New Orleans traded its lottery pick, along with Morris Peterson, to Oklahoma City for two selections later in the first round. The Hornets saved the $6.7 million

HORNETS IN A BOX

Last year's record	37-45
Last year's Offensive Rating	109.4 (16)
Last year's Defensive Rating	111.8 (22)
Last year's point differential	-2.5 (20)
Team pace	91.0 (16)
SCHOENE projection	49-33 (5)
Projected Offensive Rating	114.2 (2)
Projected Defensive Rating	110.7 (19)
Projected team weighted age	27.6 (14)
Projected '10-11 payroll	$67.9 (13)
Est. payroll obligations, '11-12	$51.8 (18)

Head coach: Monty Williams

Just seven years removed from the end of his playing career in the NBA, Williams rapidly became one of the league's most coveted young assistant coaches before being hired by the Hornets in June. Stylistically, Williams is a bit of a blank slate. Like many coaches, he vowed to push the pace when he was introduced, but his experience on the sidelines has been under two of the league's slowest-tempo coaches, Gregg Popovich and Nate McMillan. Williams did gain some experience running a team during games when he acted as McMillan's surrogate after a torn Achilles left the Blazers coach tethered to the bench.

owed to Peterson in the last year of his contract, one of several generous long-term deals Bower handed out to declining veteran wings.

The trade would be Bower's last big move before he was fired as general manager. The curious timing of his dismissal--right during the middle of free agency--lent credence to whispers that part of the reason Bower was pushed out was his willingness to consider trading Paul, while ownership wanted to make the star guard untouchable.

The situation only got stranger in July, when word leaked that Paul was planning to demand or had already demanded a trade. The explanation had it that Paul--who reportedly signed with LRMR, the marketing firm run by LeBron James' childhood friend Maverick Carter--wanted to join another superstar like James did by signing in Miami. James didn't help matters with a cryptic tweet from his official account, @KingJames, telling Paul to, "Do what's best for You (sic) and your family."

New Orleans responded by hastily calling a meeting between Paul and his agent, Leon Rose (who is also James' agent), team president Hugh Weber and the new leaders of the Hornets' basketball staff, general manager Dell Demps and head coach Monty Williams. Everyone emerged from the meeting with assurances that things had been patched up, and with two years left on his contract Paul has little leverage to force a trade. Still, the message is clear--to keep its superstar happy, New Orleans must win.

That puts a lot of pressure on Demps and Williams, both up-and-coming young basketball minds not far removed from their playing careers (they were actually teammates in San Antonio in 1995-96) who have been promoted to their respective top jobs for the first time. Demps must seek out short-term upgrades without sacrificing the Hornets' long-term vision while keeping an eye on the payroll. Williams will have little time to find his way as a rookie head coach and must have New Orleans competitive from day one.

Demps' blockbuster summer move to improve the Hornets received mixed reviews. Using Collison as trade bait because he is stuck behind Paul, New Orleans was involved in a three-way deal that sent Collison and veteran James Posey (owner of another of the team's dubious contracts) to the Indiana Pacers and returned Trevor Ariza from the Houston Rockets. Ariza is an immediate upgrade at small forward, where Peja Stojakovic has aged considerably and is entering the walk year of his contract, but he came at a price--he has four years and almost $28 million left on his deal--and the team might have sold low on the promising Collison.

On the court, Ariza is a great fit. He will be the Hornets' best wing defender, which had been an area of need in the starting lineup. Should Williams push the pace in New Orleans, as promised, Ariza can be a great wingman for Paul. Ariza's role as the team's fourth option on offense is much more appropriate for his skills than the Rockets' attempt to make him into a go-to player. And at 26, Ariza is just entering his prime.

The trade left the Hornets needing to rebuild their bench, which figures to be a weakness. Stojakovic shifts into the role of sixth man and go-to scorer for the second unit. New Orleans re-signed center Aaron Gray, but the rest of the reserves are new to the roster. Score-first guards Jannero Pargo and Willie Green are both projected below replacement level. Pargo has struggled since leaving New Orleans after a successful run as Paul's backup. Green was acquired from Philadelphia with Jason Smith just before training camp in exchange for first-round pick Craig Brackins and veteran Darius Songaila. The move left the Hornets thin up front. Pops Mensah-Bonsu might be the Hornets' best backup big man, while rookie Quincy Pondexter may have to play out of position at power forward to find a spot in the rotation.

SCHOENE suggests that New Orleans will be much improved on offense with Ariza taking minutes that had been going to two less productive players, Peterson and Posey, and with a full season of Thornton starting at shooting guard. Thornton, nicknamed Lil' Buckets by HornetsHype.com, lived up to the name with big-time scoring production down the stretch, averaging better than 20 points per game in March and April. If Thornton keeps up that kind of pace and maintains his efficiency, a leap from 16th in the league to second in Offensive Rating might be realistic for the Hornets.

There are more questions at the defensive end of the floor, where New Orleans took a step back by replacing Tyson Chandler in the middle with Okafor. The Hornets were 22nd in the league in Defensive Rating a year ago. Ariza will help, as will a healthy Paul, but the onus is also on Williams to put together a more effective defensive system. As an assistant in Portland, Williams had first-hand experience with a variety of zone defenses, which could help cover the lack of interior defense on the second unit.

With reasonable health, New Orleans should be in the mix for one of the last playoff spots in the Western Conference. It's a little harder to see the Hornets competing with the conference's best teams. In the past three years, they've been caught and passed by several younger teams in addition to the existing contenders like Dallas, the L.A. Lakers and San Antonio.

If New Orleans has another first-round exit, or even worse fails to make the playoffs altogether, convincing Paul to stick it out will become even more difficult. The Hornets get some financial breathing room next summer with the expiration of Stojakovic's contract, but will be limited in free agency to the mid-level exception. New Orleans figures to be able to make some incremental improvements to the bench, but with Ariza in place the starting lineup is essentially set.

Looking ahead, forward David West, the team's second-best player, is entering his 30s. There's also this ticking time bomb: Paul's surgery cost him a significant chunk of the meniscus in his left knee, which could become a problem at some point down the road. Further trouble is hardly imminent, and knee wear and tear can be difficult to project, but the Hornets can't count on Paul staying healthy forever. At some point, New Orleans will have to consider rebuilding, and that might mean preparing for life without Paul.

Kevin Pelton

From the Blogosphere

Who: Rohan
What: At the Hive
Where: http://www.atthehive.com/

For a team that's been rather untrusting of youth in recent years, the New Orleans Hornets have become really young, really fast. There were the success stories of Darren Collison and Marcus Thornton in 2009-10. Collison has been traded, but first-round pick Quincy Pondexter will challenge for a spot in the rotation. And to top it all off, the team also hired a rookie GM, a rookie head coach and appears on the verge of handing the reins to a rookie owner. The logic is clear: If Chris Paul does eventually leave, various secondary building blocks will already be in place. For now, this is the youngest, most athletic collection of guys Paul has had around him in New Orleans. For the first time in a while, despite a summer of stale rumors, fans will be treated to something fresh.

HORNETS FIVE-YEAR TRENDS

Season	AGE	W-L	POW	PYTH	SEED	ORTG	DRTG	PT DIFF	PACE
05-06	26.3	38-44	35.8 (20)	32.5	---	104.8 (26)	108.8 (20)	-2.8 (24)	87.7 (21)
06-07	26.4	39-43	38.5 (18)	36.3	---	106.1 (23)	108.4 (16)	-1.6 (18)	88.9 (23)
07-08	27.2	56-26	57.6 (6)	55.7	2	114.3 (4)	107.8 (7)	5.3 (6)	87.9 (26)
08-09	28.2	49-33	47.4 (11)	45.7	7	110.6 (13)	108.4 (9)	1.5 (13)	86.4 (28)
09-10	28.1	37-45	35.7 (20)	34.1	--	109.4 (16)	111.8 (22)	-2.5 (20)	91.0 (16)

		OFFENSE				DEFENSE			
Season	PAY	eFG	oREB	FT/FGA	TO	eFG	oREB	FT/FGA	TO
05-06	$43.6	.464 (30)	.269 (15)	.257 (13)	.151 (4)	.502 (22)	.734 (10)	.243 (15)	.165 (8)
06-07	$53.2	.479 (27)	.291 (6)	.215 (28)	.161 (10)	.499 (16)	.747 (7)	.212 (4)	.152 (29)
07-08	$60.3	.512 (6)	.270 (13)	.193 (29)	.128 (2)	.501 (17)	.754 (3)	.184 (1)	.150 (12)
08-09	$67.0	.501 (14)	.246 (25)	.232 (18)	.145 (7)	.496 (12)	.749 (7)	.230 (16)	.153 (14)
09-10	$69.6	.506 (12)	.248 (23)	.189 (29)	.147 (7)	.523 (26)	.738 (14)	.205 (5)	.156 (14)

(league rankings in parenthesis)

NEW ORLEANS HORNETS

SF 11	Joe Alexander	Hght: 6'8" Wght: 230 2011-12 status: free agent	Exp: 2 From: West Virginia	Salary: --						

SKILL RATINGS

TOT	OFF	DEF	REB	PAS	HND	SHT	ATH
0	--	-1	--	--	--	--	--

Year	Team	Age	G	MPG	Usg	3PA%	FTA%	INS	2P%	3P%	FT%	TS%	Reb%	Ast%	TO%	BLK%	STL%	PF%	oRTG	dRTG	Win%	WARP
08-09	MIL	22.3	59	12.1	.210	.138	.109	.972	.432	.348	.699	.494	.096	.026	.156	.034	.011	.067	103.1	107.0	.374	-0.6
09-10	CHI	23.3	8	3.6	.114	.137	.180	1.044	.200	.000	.667	.273	.096	.031	.000	.026	.017	.140	101.1	108.6	.270	-0.1
10-11p	NOH	24.3	76	-	.195	.193	.117	.924	.469	.351	.713	.528	.097	.028	.143	.031	.011	.059	-	-	.441	-

Most similar to: Hakim Warrick (97.7), Buck Johnson, Peter Thibeaux, Detlef Schrempf
IMP: 71% BRK: 29% COP: 4%

A lottery pick just two years ago, Joe Alexander sure looks like a washout at this point. Some of his trouble has come from injuries, but he's had a hard time finding work this offseason, which tells you what teams think of his abilities. Alexander is headed to camp with New Orleans, where he will try to earn a spot on a roster with a couple of open slots.

SF 1	Trevor Ariza	Hght: 6'8" Wght: 210 2011-12 status: guaranteed contract for $6.8 million	Exp: 6 From: UCLA	Salary: $6.3 million						

SKILL RATINGS

TOT	OFF	DEF	REB	PAS	HND	SHT	ATH
+3	+2	+2	+1	+3	+3	0	+4

Year	Team	Age	G	MPG	Usg	3PA%	FTA%	INS	2P%	3P%	FT%	TS%	Reb%	Ast%	TO%	BLK%	STL%	PF%	oRTG	dRTG	Win%	WARP
07-08	LAL	22.8	35	15.7	.155	.094	.172	1.078	.542	.278	.653	.568	.107	.036	.120	.014	.025	.036	104.9	103.9	.534	1.3
08-09	LAL	23.8	82	24.4	.167	.252	.098	.846	.526	.319	.710	.544	.099	.032	.115	.009	.034	.037	106.1	104.4	.555	5.8
09-10	HOU	24.8	72	36.5	.213	.323	.080	.757	.436	.334	.649	.488	.090	.047	.128	.011	.024	.027	104.8	104.5	.507	4.9
10-11p	NOH	25.8	74	32.0	.177	.319	.106	.788	.488	.339	.679	.530	.093	.040	.118	.011	.025	.031	105.6	104.6	.531	5.7

Most similar to: Sonny Parker (98.0), Robert Reid, James Posey, Don Collins
IMP: 46% BRK: 5% COP: 11%

Trevor Ariza's conversion from a role player for the L.A. Lakers to leading man in Houston went worse than expected, though not quite as badly as conventional wisdom would have you believe. Ariza's True Shooting Percentage plummeted as the shots he created for himself turned out to be low-percentage ones, but he maintained a low turnover rate and managed to hand out a few more assists. The overall package wasn't all that different in terms of value from what Ariza offered in L.A., though it was less aesthetically pleasing.

It might have been difficult for Ariza to accept a smaller role with the Rockets, but in New Orleans his role in the pecking order is much clearer. Ariza is the most athletic wing starter the Hornets have ever put alongside Chris Paul, and the combination should result in more easy baskets for Ariza. He'd help his cause by easing up on the threes (having only shot a high percentage from downtown during the 2009 playoffs) and entirely doing away with long two-point attempts, which he makes at a lower percentage than threes. Ariza has the tools to be an impact defender and plays the passing lanes well, but his new role as New Orleans' top wing defender will require increased focus against the opposition's best perimeter scorer.

SG 8	Marco Belinelli	Hght: 6'5" Wght: 200 2011-12 status: due qualifying offer of $3.4 million	Exp: 3 From: Bologna, Italy	Salary: $2.4 million						

SKILL RATINGS

TOT	OFF	DEF	REB	PAS	HND	SHT	ATH
+1	+3	+4	-4	+2	+1	+3	-1

Year	Team	Age	G	MPG	Usg	3PA%	FTA%	INS	2P%	3P%	FT%	TS%	Reb%	Ast%	TO%	BLK%	STL%	PF%	oRTG	dRTG	Win%	WARP
07-08	GSW	22.1	33	7.3	.190	.376	.036	.660	.385	.390	.778	.490	.032	.026	.110	.000	.009	.026	103.1	108.0	.343	-0.4
08-09	GSW	23.1	42	21.0	.194	.328	.057	.729	.473	.397	.769	.547	.044	.043	.148	.001	.019	.035	105.6	107.6	.433	0.3
09-10	TOR	24.1	66	17.0	.202	.321	.108	.787	.425	.380	.835	.543	.049	.036	.122	.003	.019	.033	105.4	106.8	.453	0.8
10-11p	NOH	25.1	71	10.0	.180	.375	.090	.715	.459	.404	.797	.570	.046	.043	.127	.002	.018	.033	106.0	106.8	.473	0.8

Most similar to: Danny Ainge (98.5), Tony Delk, Steve Colter, Hubert Davis
IMP: 53% BRK: 13% COP: 4%

Marco Belinelli enjoyed the best season of his three-year career in Toronto, and will try to build on the effort after being dealt to New Orleans in exchange for forward Julian Wright. Belinelli's ability is tantalizing. He has good size for a shooting guard, can handle the ball and is a good shooter. Squint hard enough and you can see him developing into a Brent Barry type.

Belinelli has primarily been held back by his shot selection, as well as his inability to be effective inside the three-point line in the half-court offense. He takes too many difficult shots instead of focusing on the stand-still jumpers he makes at a higher percentage. Belinelli attempted 1.5 shots a game from 16 to 23 feet last season, per Hoopdata.com, and that's far too many.

Aaron Gray — C #34

Hght: 7'0" Exp: 3 Salary: $0.9 million
Wght: 270 From: Pittsburgh
2011-12 status: guaranteed contract for $0.9 million

SKILL RATINGS

TOT	OFF	DEF	REB	PAS	HND	SHT	ATH
+1	+2	+1	+3	+4	+4	+1	+2

Year	Team	Age	G	MPG	Usg	3PA%	FTA%	INS	2P%	3P%	FT%	TS%	Reb%	Ast%	TO%	BLK%	STL%	PF%	oRTG	dRTG	Win%	WARP
07-08	CHI	23.4	61	10.0	.222	.003	.143	1.140	.507	.000	.566	.529	.156	.030	.187	.021	.016	.087	104.1	106.0	.439	0.3
08-09	CHI	24.4	56	12.8	.146	.004	.111	1.107	.488	.000	.576	.508	.176	.029	.172	.018	.010	.085	104.6	107.3	.411	-0.1
09-10	NOH	25.4	32	9.7	.166	.000	.110	1.110	.512	—	.714	.551	.199	.032	.160	.027	.015	.080	106.8	105.3	.549	0.9
10-11p	NOH	26.4	76	10.0	.158	.007	.118	1.111	.515	.004	.656	.541	.176	.034	.161	.023	.013	.077	105.2	105.9	.478	1.0

Most similar to: Nenê Hilario (98.0), Will Perdue, Jeff Foster, Scott Williams
IMP: 52% BRK: 7% COP: 3%

Desperate for any kind of size in the middle, New Orleans picked up Aaron Gray from Chicago in late January in exchange for Devin Brown. Gray had fallen out of favor with Vinny Del Negro, but got semi-regular playing time as a backup center for the Hornets. He remains the only true center on the team's bench after signing a new two-year contract, which should help him find a role.

Gray is a legit 7-footer who is rock solid in the middle. His size has been most useful on the glass, and only Jon Brockman had a higher offensive rebound percentage last season among players with at least 250 minutes. Gray gets enough putbacks and easy looks in the paint to keep his True Shooting Percentage respectable. He struggles at the defensive end, where he is effective defending the post but simply isn't quick enough to keep up with almost anyone in the league. Despite his size, Gray isn't much of a shot blocker, and he needs an athletic player alongside him in the frontcourt.

Willie Green — SG #33

Hght: 6'3" Exp: 7 Salary: $4.0 million
Wght: 201 From: Detroit Mercy
2011-12 status: free agent

SKILL RATINGS

TOT	OFF	DEF	REB	PAS	HND	SHT	ATH
-2	+1	+1	-4	+2	+4	+1	-3

Year	Team	Age	G	MPG	Usg	3PA%	FTA%	INS	2P%	3P%	FT%	TS%	Reb%	Ast%	TO%	BLK%	STL%	PF%	oRTG	dRTG	Win%	WARP
07-08	PHI	26.7	74	26.6	.241	.171	.062	.891	.475	.285	.757	.492	.056	.035	.104	.009	.013	.028	102.8	106.5	.379	-1.5
08-09	PHI	27.7	81	22.6	.191	.212	.049	.837	.473	.317	.729	.493	.041	.040	.084	.006	.015	.039	104.1	108.0	.373	-1.7
09-10	PHI	28.7	73	21.3	.195	.206	.076	.870	.494	.346	.833	.538	.049	.045	.101	.006	.011	.040	105.1	108.1	.401	-0.5
10-11p	NOH	29.7	74	13.4	.180	.227	.060	.834	.498	.350	.789	.533	.047	.043	.097	.006	.013	.037	104.4	107.3	.403	-0.3

Most similar to: Raja Bell (98.3), Gordan Giricek, John Long, Kevin Gamble
IMP: 56% BRK: 17% COP: 2%

Willie Green was one of the few Sixers that actually improved last season. He became more effective from beyond the arc, which could a one-year blip, but he also was better at attacking the rim and shot really well on long twos. He's not a bad passer, takes good care of the ball and is an above-average perimeter defender despite being undersized. Alas, just when he started to see the light, the Sixers dumped Green on the Hornets as part of a four-player deal before the start of training camp. Green should see regular playing time in New Orleans, where he will battle Jannero Pargo for minutes in the second unit. Hornets GM Dell Demps indicated after the deal that he believes Green can play either guard position, meaning he could emerge as the backup to Chris Paul in addition to playing two-guard.

NEW ORLEANS HORNETS

C 50	Emeka Okafor	Hght: 6'10" Exp: 6 Salary: $11.5 million
		Wght: 255 From: Connecticut
		2011-12 status: guaranteed contract for $12.5 million

SKILL RATINGS

TOT	OFF	DEF	REB	PAS	HND	SHT	ATH
+1	0	-1	+3	-3	-4	+3	0

Year	Team	Age	G	MPG	Usg	3PA%	FTA%	INS	2P%	3P%	FT%	TS%	Reb%	Ast%	TO%	BLK%	STL%	PF%	oRTG	dRTG	Win%	WARP
07-08	CHA	25.6	82	33.2	.202	.000	.138	1.138	.534	.000	.570	.552	.185	.012	.138	.039	.010	.040	103.7	103.1	.522	6.0
08-09	CHA	26.6	82	32.8	.191	.000	.151	1.151	.561	.000	.593	.581	.190	.009	.134	.042	.010	.044	105.5	103.9	.555	7.8
09-10	NOH	27.6	82	28.9	.172	.000	.136	1.136	.530	-	.562	.547	.185	.011	.125	.041	.012	.042	104.2	103.6	.521	5.2
10-11p	NOH	28.6	76	29.0	.172	.003	.130	1.128	.537	.002	.561	.552	.178	.012	.135	.038	.010	.043	103.5	103.9	.489	3.4

Most similar to: Dale Davis (98.2), Alton Lister, Tyrone Hill, Nazr Mohammed

IMP: 26%   BRK: 0%   COP: 9%

Emeka Okafor's NBA career has been defined more by what he is not than what he actually is. Okafor is not a franchise player, which the Bobcats thought they were getting when they picked him No. 2 overall as the team's first draft pick. He's not worth a $10 million annual salary, which is what the Bobcats eventually gave Okafor when he became a restricted free agent. The contract has turned Okafor into a hot potato. Charlotte dealt him to New Orleans for Tyson Chandler last summer, and the Hornets have been trying to move Okafor's salary for some time now.

On the floor, Okafor remains a useful contributor. He has consistently been one of the league's better rebounders, and at times Okafor has been a dominant defender in the paint. As he's aged and lost his quickness, Okafor has become less effective on defense, one big reason he's been unable to live up to the contract. For a center, Okafor is skilled on offense. He's got a rudimentary post game and hits the occasional midrange jumper. SCHOENE does see Okafor's productivity beginning to fade rather quickly this season. Similar players have not held their value into their late 20s and early 30s.

PG 2	Jannero Pargo	Hght: 6'1" Exp: 7 Salary: $0.9 million
		Wght: 175 From: Arkansas
		2011-12 status: free agent

SKILL RATINGS

TOT	OFF	DEF	REB	PAS	HND	SHT	ATH
-3	-1	0	0	-2	-1	-4	-3

Year	Team	Age	G	MPG	Usg	3PA%	FTA%	INS	2P%	3P%	FT%	TS%	Reb%	Ast%	TO%	BLK%	STL%	PF%	oRTG	dRTG	Win%	WARP
07-08	NOH	28.6	80	18.7	.244	.237	.046	.809	.405	.351	.877	.468	.051	.060	.119	.003	.016	.039	104.5	106.9	.404	-0.4
09-10	CHI	30.6	63	13.1	.246	.306	.044	.738	.387	.275	.933	.429	.052	.049	.111	.002	.018	.037	102.3	106.9	.349	-1.2
10-11p	NOH	31.6	76	10.0	.217	.312	.042	.730	.393	.304	.876	.445	.055	.053	.122	.002	.017	.040	102.8	107.0	.364	-0.8

Most similar to: Kevin Edwards (94.0), John Long, Derek Fisher, Doug Overton

IMP: 35%   BRK: 4%   COP: 8%

Jannero Pargo continues to hover on the fringes of NBA existence. He had a disappointing season in Chicago, which was hoping Pargo would supply a consistent dose of instant offense off the bench. Unfortunately, he just never found his stroke working under Vinny Del Negro's inconsistent usage patterns. Pargo was reportedly close to landing in Golden State, but that didn't pan out. Instead, it's back to New Orleans, where Pargo enjoyed his best NBA campaigns. He'll battle Willie Green for the right to back up and play alongside Chris Paul.

PG 3	Chris Paul	Hght: 6'0" Exp: 5 Salary: $14.9 million
		Wght: 175 From: Wake Forest
		2011-12 status: guaranteed contract for $16.4 million

SKILL RATINGS

TOT	OFF	DEF	REB	PAS	HND	SHT	ATH
+5	+5	-1	+4	+5	+5	+4	+5

Year	Team	Age	G	MPG	Usg	3PA%	FTA%	INS	2P%	3P%	FT%	TS%	Reb%	Ast%	TO%	BLK%	STL%	PF%	oRTG	dRTG	Win%	WARP
07-08	NOH	23.0	80	37.6	.259	.150	.103	.953	.516	.369	.851	.576	.063	.144	.121	.001	.034	.029	115.0	104.0	.803	24.2
08-09	NOH	24.0	78	38.5	.278	.103	.134	1.032	.525	.364	.868	.599	.087	.139	.135	.003	.039	.034	116.2	104.0	.825	25.6
09-10	NOH	25.0	45	38.0	.224	.153	.100	.948	.514	.409	.847	.584	.066	.129	.135	.004	.029	.032	112.4	105.2	.715	10.6
10-11p	NOH	26.0	70	38.0	.243	.187	.114	.927	.528	.409	.879	.608	.071	.140	.127	.003	.030	.031	115.1	104.6	.791	20.8

Most similar to: Isiah Thomas (93.7), Kevin Johnson, Tim Hardaway, Johnny Moore

IMP: 53%   BRK: 6%   COP: 0%

The numbers back up the NBA conventional wisdom that it rarely works out for a team to trade a superstar player in his prime, even when the player has requested or demanded a trade. As a result, it makes sense for the Hornets to do everything they can to try to keep Chris Paul happy. Don't read much into Paul's apparent statistical decline last season. A significant chunk of the drop-off is due to the seven games Paul played after coming back from knee surgery; take those out and his winning percentage leaps to .755. The most encouraging development of Paul's season was his 40-percent shooting from beyond the arc. SCHOENE thinks that Paul should be able to maintain that improvement, and if Paul is making the three regularly he will become nearly impossible to defend.

Already, stopping Paul is a major challenge because of his quickness, shooting touch and court vision. The Hornets offense has run through Paul his entire career, and his ability to balance looking for his own shot and setting up his teammates has made him an elite point guard. Paul's defensive statistics have fluctuated from great to terrible to average. He was down last year, when opposing point guards scored well against him. His arthroscopic knee surgery could hurt him at the defensive end going forward if it costs him some of his lateral mobility.

Quincy Pondexter — SF #20

- Hght: 6'6" Exp: R Salary: $1.1 million
- Wght: 225 From: Washington
- 2011-12 status: guaranteed contract for $1.2 million

SKILL RATINGS

TOT	OFF	DEF	REB	PAS	HND	SHT	ATH
-2	0	-2	+3	-1	-1	-2	-1

Year	Team	Age	G	MPG	Usg	3PA%	FTA%	INS	2P%	3P%	FT%	TS%	Reb%	Ast%	TO%	BLK%	STL%	PF%	oRTG	dRTG	Win%	WARP
10-11p	NOH	23.1	76	15.0	.174	.064	.115	1.051	.453	.305	.809	.516	.106	.022	.108	.008	.014	.048	103.8	106.9	.398	-0.4

Most similar to: Desmond Mason (97.7), Alan Anderson, Ronald Dupree, Brandon Roy   IMP: -   BRK: -   COP: -

Quincy Pondexter capped an up-and-down college career with a fine senior season, emerging as Washington's do-everything leader and guiding the Huskies to the Sweet Sixteen. Pondexter thrived as an undersized power forward. At 6'6", he's too small to see anything more than spot minutes at the four in the NBA, though he may have to play the position at times this season because of the Hornets' needs. The key to Pondexter's development will be the ability to make the NBA three-pointer. He improved his accuracy from the college line as his senior season went on and will put in the necessary work, but the lack of NBA range ultimately doomed comparables Desmond Mason and Ronald Dupree.

There are no such worries about Pondexter's ability to defend small forwards. He's a protypical athlete for the three position and guarded a variety of different players last season depending on matchups. After seeing himself as a star during his first two years on campus, Pondexter humbled himself to accept a role as a stopper during his junior season. As a small forward, Pondexter should also be effective as a rebounder, and he can use his experience in his paint to post up smaller defenders at times.

Mustafa Shakur — PG #22

- Hght: 6'3" Exp: R Salary: $0.5 million
- Wght: 190 From: Arizona
- 2011-12 status: free agent

SKILL RATINGS

TOT	OFF	DEF	REB	PAS	HND	SHT	ATH
+1	--	--	--	--	--	--	--

Year	Team	Age	G	MPG	Usg	3PA%	FTA%	INS	2P%	3P%	FT%	TS%	Reb%	Ast%	TO%	BLK%	STL%	PF%	oRTG	dRTG	Win%	WARP
10-11p	NOH	26.7	76	-	.180	.223	.107	.884	.451	.359	.691	.515	.061	.060	.143	.004	.027	.039	-	-	.469	-

Most similar to: Lester Conner (97.2), Darwin Cook, Darrell Walker, Darnell Valentine   IMP: 52%   BRK: 7%   COP: 9%

Mustafa Shakur spent most of the final month of last season on Oklahoma City's roster, but he's still awaiting his NBA debut. The Thunder signed Shakur to keep his rights and allow him to continue playing for the D-League's Tulsa 66ers, owned by Oklahoma City. Shakur delivered a strong campaign in the D-League and parlayed it into a contract with the Hornets that is partially guaranteed.

Shakur was more scorer than distributor for the 66ers, averaging 19.2 points and 6.9 assists per game. Inevitably, he'll find a little more balance at the NBA level. He should be able to score enough to set up the pass. The big addition to Shakur's game in the three years since he finished up at the University of Arizona has been three-point range. He knocked down long-range attempts at a 38.2 percent clip last year in the D-League and figures to be able to keep defenses honest with his shooting. Shakur has legit NBA size at the defensive end and generates plenty of steals.

NEW ORLEANS HORNETS

C 14 — Jason Smith

Hght: 7'0" | Exp: 2 | Salary: $2.2 million
Wght: 240 | From: Colorado State
2011-12 status: due qualifying offer of $3.1 million

SKILL RATINGS

TOT	OFF	DEF	REB	PAS	HND	SHT	ATH
-1	-1	0	-3	+1	+2	0	+2

Year	Team	Age	G	MPG	Usg	3PA%	FTA%	INS	2P%	3P%	FT%	TS%	Reb%	Ast%	TO%	BLK%	STL%	PF%	oRTG	dRTG	Win%	WARP
07-08	PHI	22.1	76	14.5	.163	.035	.091	1.056	.461	.286	.659	.490	.124	.009	.121	.036	.009	.060	101.3	105.3	.369	-1.1
09-10	PHI	24.1	56	11.8	.159	.127	.081	.954	.448	.345	.690	.491	.121	.023	.154	.034	.016	.077	103.2	105.9	.411	-0.1
10-11p	PHI	25.1	72	5.0	.147	.130	.087	.956	.480	.371	.668	.520	.117	.020	.136	.035	.015	.070	103.0	105.5	.416	0.0

Most similar to: Chris Anstey (98.0), Brad Lohaus, Scott Hastings, Cherokee Parks

IMP: 62% BRK: 12% COP: 5%

Jason Smith was once considered a promising player for the Sixers, but he missed an entire season after tearing his left ACL, then came back last year with no apparent growth in his game. Smith tried to fashion himself as a face-up big man, but he doesn't shoot the ball well enough to justify the 48 percent of his shots that came away from the rim. He was actually very effective in the paint, exacerbating the issue. Smith is also a decent shot blocker, but doesn't rebound well for his size; nor is he an effective defender in the post. The Sixers gave up on developing Smith any further and sent him to the Hornets in a trade just before the start of camp. New Orleans is badly in need of size, so Smith has a chance to be a rotation player if he demonstrates improvement.

SF 16 — Peja Stojakovic

Hght: 6'10" | Exp: 12 | Salary: $14.3 million
Wght: 229 | From: Belgrade, Serbia
2011-12 status: free agent

SKILL RATINGS

TOT	OFF	DEF	REB	PAS	HND	SHT	ATH
-1	+1	+1	-3	-3	+3	+1	-4

Year	Team	Age	G	MPG	Usg	3PA%	FTA%	INS	2P%	3P%	FT%	TS%	Reb%	Ast%	TO%	BLK%	STL%	PF%	oRTG	dRTG	Win%	WARP
07-08	NOH	30.9	77	35.3	.198	.456	.054	.597	.438	.441	.929	.581	.072	.017	.053	.003	.010	.022	107.6	106.7	.530	6.4
08-09	NOH	31.9	61	34.2	.190	.471	.056	.585	.424	.378	.894	.531	.076	.017	.063	.001	.013	.023	106.4	107.0	.478	2.7
09-10	NOH	32.9	62	31.4	.187	.445	.060	.615	.435	.375	.897	.533	.069	.022	.071	.002	.013	.020	105.7	106.9	.460	1.7
10-11p	NOH	33.9	72	25.0	.172	.439	.050	.611	.440	.374	.864	.526	.072	.019	.062	.002	.011	.023	104.8	107.0	.427	0.4

Most similar to: Michael Finley (97.9), Kiki Vandeweghe, Rod Higgins, Robert Reid

IMP: 38% BRK: 0% COP: 4%

Every Peja Stojakovic three-pointer during the 2008 playoffs was accompanied by oversized cutouts of Stojakovic's head being run through the aisles of New Orleans Arena so that they appeared to be floating across the bottom of your television screen. The Peja heads still exist, but now the biggest point of celebration for the Hornets with Stojakovic will be the expiration of his contract at season's end and the cap relief that entails. 2007-08 was, as it turned out, Stojakovic's last hurrah. Since then, recurring back problems have sapped his energy and athleticism, leaving him a shell of himself.

The biggest difference has been in terms of Stojakovic's trademark three-point shooting. A 40 percent shooter or better seven times in the eight-year span from 2000-01 through 2007-08, Stojakovic has slipped below that mark the last two seasons. He's also no longer capable of expending the energy necessary to create separation with the off-ball movement that once seemed to produce a layup a game. One of last season's biggest surprises was Stojakovic's outstanding individual defensive statistics. He has proven crafty as a defender while battling his declining athleticism, and his size helps him against smaller opponents. Still, these numbers likely overstated Stojakovic's effectiveness on defense.

With the addition of Trevor Ariza, Stojakovic moves into a more appropriate role as the Hornets' sixth man. He could enjoy a second career as a reserve sharpshooter, preserving his back by playing fewer minutes.

SG 5 — Marcus Thornton

Hght: 6'4" | Exp: 1 | Salary: $0.8 million
Wght: 205 | From: Louisiana State
2011-12 status: free agent

SKILL RATINGS

TOT	OFF	DEF	REB	PAS	HND	SHT	ATH
+3	+4	-2	0	-2	0	+3	0

Year	Team	Age	G	MPG	Usg	3PA%	FTA%	INS	2P%	3P%	FT%	TS%	Reb%	Ast%	TO%	BLK%	STL%	PF%	oRTG	dRTG	Win%	WARP
09-10	NOH	22.9	73	25.6	.255	.302	.075	.773	.493	.374	.814	.550	.067	.028	.073	.004	.016	.031	107.7	107.1	.520	4.0
10-11p	NOH	23.9	74	32.0	.247	.336	.081	.745	.503	.381	.809	.564	.066	.030	.072	.005	.015	.029	108.1	106.8	.541	6.2

Most similar to: Quentin Richardson (97.0), Chris Mullin, Todd Day, Kerry Kittles

IMP: 63% BRK: 2% COP: 6%

NEW ORLEANS HORNETS

Marcus Thornton is a classic shooting guard, a pure scorer who proved a second-round steal as a rookie. All Thornton needed, it turned out, was the opportunity--first to play rotation minutes, then to serve as the Hornets' go-to guy on the perimeter with Chris Paul sidelined. Thornton's usage rate was fourth among rookies (behind Tyreke Evans, Brandon Jennings and Tyler Hansbrough), yet he still managed a True Shooting Percentage slightly better than league average.

Thornton is an effective scorer in part because he can score in multiple ways. He was a dangerous three-point shooter as a rookie and figures to improve in this regard. He was also able to create for himself on the dribble, getting to the rim regularly (4.4 times per game, according to Hoopdata.com) and finishing well there (59.2 percent). Thornton can help himself by drawing more trips to the line in the future, while midrange shooting is the only aspect of his scoring that really needs work. At the defensive end, Thornton was below average. He's on the small side for a shooting guard and struggled when isolated one-on-one with opponents. The arrival of Trevor Ariza will takes away some of the pressure on him to defend high scorers.

The lone downside for the Hornets is that they only have Thornton locked up through this season. If he hits his SCHOENE projection, which calls for 18.1 points per game, Thornton could be a coveted restricted free agent next summer.

PF 30	David West	Hght: 6'9" Exp: 7 Salary: $8.3 million								SKILL RATINGS							
		Wght: 240 From: Xavier (Ohio)								TOT	OFF	DEF	REB	PAS	HND	SHT	ATH
		2011-12 status: player option or ETO for $7.5 million								0	+1	0	-1	+3	+2	0	0

Year	Team	Age	G	MPG	Usg	3PA%	FTA%	INS	2P%	3P%	FT%	TS%	Reb%	Ast%	TO%	BLK%	STL%	PF%	oRTG	dRTG	Win%	WARP
07-08	NOH	27.6	76	37.8	.265	.015	.096	1.080	.487	.240	.850	.535	.139	.029	.102	.027	.010	.034	105.1	104.3	.527	6.6
08-09	NOH	28.6	76	39.2	.267	.015	.112	1.096	.477	.240	.884	.540	.131	.028	.100	.019	.009	.034	105.9	105.9	.499	5.2
09-10	NOH	29.6	81	36.4	.242	.017	.097	1.080	.510	.259	.865	.560	.121	.037	.112	.015	.013	.036	106.0	105.8	.504	5.4
10-11p	NOH	30.6	76	36.0	.231	.020	.093	1.074	.500	.246	.841	.546	.124	.030	.103	.018	.011	.038	104.5	105.7	.462	2.7

Most similar to: Terry Cummings (98.9), Tom Gugliotta, Shareef Abdur-Rahim, Marques Johnson IMP: 39% BRK: 5% COP: 5%

David West's star lost a little of its luster last season. In 2008-09, West's value was propped up by his average of 39.2 minutes per game. Playing more typical minutes for a starter in 2009-10, West dropped below 20 points per game, and his rebounding average (7.5 a night) made it clear that he's nothing better than average on the glass for his position. So despite the fact that West actually improved on a per-minute basis, largely because he was more accurate from the field in a smaller role in the offense, there were no All-Star accolades this time around.

West has carved out a niche for himself as one of the league's most versatile offensive power forwards. He can score with his back to the basket, but is probably best running the pick-and-pop. West shot 45.0 percent from 16 to 23 feet last season, per Hoopdata.com, and is as efficient a player as you'll find from this spot on the floor with his flat-footed jumper. West's accuracy extended to the free throw line, where he's close to automatic for a big man. West moves well defensively and can play on the perimeter, making up for the fact that he often gives up size to his opposing number.

West turns 30 this year, and SCHOENE sees him beginning to decline. West has the chance to become a free agent next summer, and could really help himself by maintaining his value--especially in terms of per-game stats--to get a last big payday.

New York Knicks

Okay, New York, open your eyes and exhale. The free-agent bonanza of 2010 is over. LeBron James went to South Beach and not even Tony Soprano could steer him to the Big Apple. Oh, Dwyane Wade and Chris Bosh are in Florida, too, so that your retired parents can at least enjoy some world-class basketball. In their place, you've got Amar'e Stoudemire and Ray Felton. The Knicks insist they aren't done and that's almost certainly true, but after selling the riches of 2010 to fans for two years of relative non-competitiveness on the court, this offseason has to be considered a disappointment for general manager Donnie Walsh and head coach Mike D'Antoni.

The bright side of this is that all the work Walsh did to clean up the mess he inherited from Isiah Thomas has left the Knicks in a much, much better place than they were on April 2, 2008, when Walsh became New York's president of basketball operations. To turn around a franchise, the first thing you need is wiggle room under the salary cap, and Walsh cleared the decks of every salary albatross except for Eddy Curry. When Walsh took over, Thomas was still manning the New York sidelines as coach and the roster included the following players making $5 million or more per year: Stephon Marbury, Zach Randolph, Curry, Quentin Richardson, Jamal Crawford, Jerome Williams, Malik Rose, Jerome James and Jared Jeffries. Those nine players accounted for $83.5 million in salary that season, and to get from there to a position to make a legitimate run at two max free agents just two years later is one of more impressing bits of team rebuilding we've seen in the NBA.

Through the decadence, despair and hopelessness of the last decade, Knicks fans continued to sell out Madison Square Garden nearly every night, with less than one percent of seats going unsold over the last nine years. The Knicks have the luxury of toiling in front the biggest fan base in sports, and an affluent one at that, but there are a lot of entertainment options in New York. Through thick and thin, sports fans in the Big Apple continued to spend their dough on basketball tickets. They continued to come the last two years though Walsh had done everything but hang an "Under Construction" sign on the front door of the Garden. Insofar as any fan base "deserves" a winning team, Knicks fans ought to get a better product to consume.

Indeed, the team has gotten better and will likely return to the playoffs this season. However, it looks like the Knicks have landed in the second tier of their own conference, still short of Orlando and Boston (unless SCHOENE is right about a sudden Celtic decline, which is entirely possible), and now passed by Chicago and Miami. So there is still work to do, because the Knicks haven't won an NBA title since well before Walt Frazier touched his first tube of Just for Men.

The Knicks' stay in the dreaded NBA middle class

KNICKS IN A BOX

Last year's record	29-53
Last year's Offensive Rating	109.5 (15)
Last year's Defensive Rating	113.7 (27)
Last year's point differential	-3.8 (23)
Team pace	92.3 (9)
SCHOENE projection	**44-38 (4)**
Projected Offensive Rating	113.6 (4)
Projected Defensive Rating	112.5 (29)
Projected team weighted age	25.5 (25)
Projected '10-11 payroll	$57.8 (22)
Est. payroll obligations, '11-12	$48.1 (25)

Head coach: Mike D'Antoni

2009-10 was a trying season for Mike D'Antoni. After surpassing expectations during his first campaign in New York, D'Antoni found that last year's transitory roster was ill-suited for his coaching style. He put the brakes on his trademark up-tempo attack, which dropped from second in the league in pace all the way to ninth. On a per-possession basis, the Knicks' offense actually improved, but the defense ranked 27th in the league. That's now in the past, and the remade New York lineup should allow D'Antoni's system to thrive. The biggest improvement might come in the pick-and-roll, which now features Amar'e Stoudemire screening for Raymond Felton with plenty of shooters on the wings.

may be a short one. Curry, the last legacy of Isiah's mad spending reign, comes off the books after this season, which will put the Knicks in position to make another run at a free agent. New York enjoys an advantage over the other teams that will have money to spend in 2011, a group that right now appears to include the likes of Indiana, Sacramento, New Jersey and possibly Oklahoma City and Houston, in that almost every player views the Knicks as an attractive situation. The Nets are emerging as a solid free-agent destination, but the Thunder isn't likely to make a free-agent splash and the Rockets' cap space would be quickly eaten up by re-signing Yao Ming. The Pacers and Kings have no chance to out-recruit the Knicks for a top-tier free agent and probably wouldn't try. Even with Curry leaving, the Knicks will probably need to renounce Wilson Chandler, but it looks like it'll be the Knicks and Nets vying for the best free agent next summer.

Who are the possibilities for that market? It won't be anything like this past summer. Everybody knows about Carmelo Anthony, but his situation may well be resolved before he hits the open market. The Nuggets are under the gun to trade Anthony and no team is going to acquire him without an agreement in place to sign an extension. That route will be attractive to Anthony, who would like to get some guaranteed dollars in hand before the Collective Bargaining Agreement expires next July. The Knicks continue to be a part of any Anthony trade chatter, but as of mid-September, it didn't sound like Walsh has the pieces to get a deal done. If the Knicks can't land Anthony, the free-agent class will be headlined by Tony Parker, who is not an elite player at this point in his career. So the best option for Walsh may be to add another big piece through a trade, and you never know who could pop up and become available. Every disgruntled star looking for a new address is going to have the Knicks at or near the top of his wish list. Sooner or later, you'd think, something is going to happen.

Here we are, at it again, looking ahead when there is a season to be played. The Knicks will have a very different team this season, a better team, and if a few things go right, the pressing need for another star-caliber player may not seem so urgent after all.

Let's start with last season, because the Knicks did manage to build a foundation the last two years while keeping their eyes squarely focused on the future. Though the Knicks had no post-up game last season, they did have an excellent pick-and-roll attack despite lacking a starting-caliber NBA point guard. Now they have Stoudemire, one of the game's best at finishing in the pick-and-roll and increasingly adept at the pick-and-pop. Stoudemire isn't an elite player with his back to the basket, but he's well above average and can exploit matchups down on the block, which was something lacking from the game of former power forward David Lee. As a foundation player, Stoudemire's game has its warts. He's probably a better defender than his metrics give him credit for, but he's not great, and his shot blocking has regressed the last couple of years from really good to just above average. He's also the kind of player that is the perfect complement for a playmaker, such as he was in Phoenix alongside Steve Nash, but he's not someone who is going to necessarily raise the play of those around him.

That makes Felton a key player for the Knicks. Their investment in the former Bobcats point guard is negligible--two years for $14.6 million. It's really a make-good kind of contract for Felton as the Knicks bide time until Chris Paul's free agency in two years or, perhaps, Parker next summer. D'Antoni's offense is super-friendly to point guard performance, as illustrated by the uptick Chris Duhon's game took the last two years. The key will be Felton's shooting. He's always been inefficient in that regard, but last season shot a career-best .385 from three-point range. That's way above where he was before, so a regression can be expected. If, however, the improvement proves to be real, that will make him a viable candidate for a three-man game involving Felton, Stoudemire and Danilo Gallinari working the perimeter. It could be a dynamic not unlike what Paul had in New Orleans with David West and Peja Stojakovic a couple of years ago. SCHOENE sees the Knicks as the league's fourth most efficient offense for the coming season, which would be an 11-place jump in Offensive Rating.

While ending up with Stoudemire and Felton might have felt like a letdown for Knicks fans hoping for James, Wade, Bosh or some combination of all the above, it's really the best Walsh could have done under the circumstances. He may have overpaid a little for Stoudemire, but the Knicks desperately needed a player like him and the contract should work out okay--health permitting. Let's not forget that Stoudemire had microfracture surgery not so long ago. Anyway, while these signings in themselves represented a small bit of face-saving for Walsh, the sign-and-trade deal that sent Lee to Golden State has the potential to salvage the entire summer.

From the Blogosphere

Who: Mike Kurylo
What: KnickerBlogger
Where: http://www.knickerblogger.net/

When the Knicks drafted a teenage Danilo Gallinari in 2008, it was expected that it would take a few years for him to develop. In Gallo's first two seasons, he has shown the ability to score at a high rate (58.0 percent True Shooting Percentage) but has struggled with volume (15.9 pts/36). Gallinari has no post game to speak of, and at times he is unwilling or unable to beat his man off the dribble. However, players in their early 20s tend to improve their scoring. Using my similarity scores, I found a resemblance between him and another jump shooting European: Dirk Nowiztki. Both players increased their scoring volume in their first two seasons, and Nowitzki continued improving his third (20.6 pts/36) and fourth (22.2 pts/36) seasons. A Dirk-like transformation would be Gallinari's ceiling, but even a modest increase would make him similar to Rashard Lewis (circa 2005) or a Kings-era Peja Stojakovic.

Lee is a fine player whose presence was rendered unnecessary by the acquisition of Stoudemire. Since they were over the cap, the Warriors had to work a sign-and-trade to acquire Lee. Golden State coughed up Anthony Randolph, a lottery talent who makes up for the Knicks' lack of a first-round pick this year, plus Ronny Turiaf, a terrific glue player who might emerge as the team's starting center in lieu of better options, and Kelenna Azubuike, who should be a good fit in the Knicks' system but is recovering from a knee injury. That's an awfully big haul for a sign-and-trade. The move improves the Knicks' depth considerably and the versatility of all those players gives D'Antoni a whole slew of additional lineup options. Randolph can play all three frontcourt positions and is a fine passer and athlete who only needs to find a base offensive arsenal to become an efficient offensive player. Turiaf will be a fan favorite at the Garden, giving the team toughness, leadership and defense. Azubuike can shoot the three, and you can never have enough of those types in D'Antoni's system, but is also a capable wing defender.

The Knicks will have some fascinating lineups, with Felton and his backup, Toney Douglas, working with long players like Stoudemire, Gallinari, Randolph, Chandler and Bill Walker who can be swapped in and out at several positions as dictated by the opponent and game. There was some talk that the Knicks may start a huge lineup, with Gallinari at two and Randoph at three. That would be interesting. The roster has some bulk in Turiaf and Russian rookie Timofey Mozgov, who was impressive in the FIBA World Championship. Second-round rookie Landry Fields looked like a keeper in the NBA Summer League, and the Knicks added veteran combo guard Roger Mason for added depth in the backcourt. The roster isn't a finished product, but it's light years ahead of where it was when Walsh took over.

As for the bad news ... Jim Dolan is still the Chairman of Madison Square Garden, Inc., because apparently that company doesn't believe in performance reviews. In a shocking development, Knicks honcho Dolan tried to bring Thomas back into the organization in July, but luckily the arrangement to which the dynamic due agreed was too seedy for the tastes of the NBA. The idea was that Thomas would become a special consultant to the team while remaining as head coach at Florida International. Thomas ultimately withdrew himself from the situation, but the door still seems open for Thomas to work his way back into a position of power at MSG once Walsh retires. The notion has to make Knicks fans shudder and makes you wonder just what is the root of this magical hold that Isiah has over Dolan. It makes you question whether the Knicks can ever really get back to prominence as long as Dolan is on board. Indeed, Dolan's continued presence casts something of a pall over the entire organization. Walsh's contract option must be renewed by April 1, 2011, and the Thomas saga reportedly had him considering resigning in August. Seriously, it would be interesting to see who would win an battle of wits between Dolan and Michael Heisley. ESPN's Ric Bucher wrote that that former Knick Allan Houston is being groomed as Walsh's successor. Hopefully, one of the key tidbits in Houston's mentorship is that he should never dole out a max contract to somebody like him. In any event, if Walsh does step down, it will be a huge relief for New Yorkers if it's Houston that takes over and not Isiah. (Let's not forget about some of the quality front office guys out of work right now, like Kevin Pritchard and Mark Warkentien.)

That's more off-the-court news, however, and for one season at least, perhaps the basketball gods will allow Knicks fans to simply immerse themselves in the action on the court. There are so many questions and possibilities for the franchise now that you don't want to get mired in negativity. Here's a basketball thought: It doesn't always have to be Felton orchestrating things for the offense. Randolph is a terrific passer and if Gallinari can become a better ballhandler, his shooting could make him a deadly partner in pick-and-roll sets with Stoudemire. D'Antoni was able to find a way to use Boris Diaw's full range of skills in Phoenix, so you know he's creative enough to make this work. More good basketball news: SCHOENE actually sees a bit of a breakout season for Chandler, which would be icing on the cake for D'Antoni. Finally, everyone is excited about Walker, but he hasn't performed consistently in a featured role since high school. His top comp is Reggie Miller, but that's merely a statistical match, of course. Still, Walker demonstrated some serious upside after coming over from Boston, and this is a big season for him.

It's a big season for the Knicks, the season in which New York could begin to move back toward the center of the basketball universe. LeBron? That was so last year. Carmelo? Something will have to be done, with Curry's money coming off the books. Parker, and perhaps more importantly Eva Longoria, may also have their eyes on the Big Apple. And then there's Paul. There is always drama in New York beyond the arena, and even after a turbulent summer, that's not going to change. However, a little on-court success would go a long way towards restoring a little buzz around the franchise and establishing enough forward momentum that the Knicks will be able to compete with the young and potentially dominant cores in Chicago and Miami, not to mention a more established Orlando team that isn't going anywhere.

The Knicks will still be very young next year. The offense promises to be a whole lot more efficient because of the additions of a real point guard and Stoudemire, plus some growth from within. The Knicks should be right in the mix in the battle for middling seeds in the East, which would be their best season in years. Then we'll see what the next chapter brings.

Bradford Doolittle

KNICKS FIVE-YEAR TRENDS

Season	AGE	W-L	POW	PYTH	SEED	ORTG	DRTG	PT DIFF	PACE
05-06	25.6	23-59	22.1 (29)	23.6	---	105.3 (24)	112.9 (27)	-6.4 (29)	89.5 (16)
06-07	25.4	33-49	31.8 (23)	32.8	---	107.0 (17)	110.7 (25)	-2.9 (21)	89.4 (21)
07-08	25.7	23-59	22.1 (27)	23.9	---	106.4 (24)	114.7 (29)	-6.4 (25)	89.7 (14)
08-09	25.7	32-50	33.1 (23)	34.0	---	109.7 (17)	113.0 (24)	-2.6 (22)	95.0 (2)
09-10	26.2	29-53	29.0 (22)	30.7	--	109.5 (15)	113.7 (27)	-3.8 (23)	92.3 (9)

		OFFENSE				DEFENSE			
Season	PAY	eFG	oREB	FT/FGA	TO	eFG	oREB	FT/FGA	TO
05-06	$92.9	.481 (22)	.312 (4)	.303 (1)	.195 (30)	.511 (26)	.728 (13)	.294 (28)	.155 (23)
06-07	$81.7	.494 (16)	.310 (2)	.270 (7)	.189 (29)	.504 (23)	.740 (11)	.246 (16)	.151 (30)
07-08	$92.8	.475 (27)	.287 (10)	.226 (16)	.152 (17)	.517 (28)	.725 (21)	.227 (15)	.135 (27)
08-09	$97.1	.503 (12)	.244 (27)	.210 (28)	.150 (13)	.521 (28)	.727 (20)	.215 (7)	.151 (18)
09-10	$84.6	.509 (9)	.235 (27)	.200 (28)	.150 (12)	.526 (29)	.721 (27)	.207 (7)	.155 (16)

(league rankings in parenthesis)

SF	Kelenna Azubuike	Hght: 6'5" Exp: 4 Salary: $3.3 million						SKILL RATINGS							
		Wght: 220 From: Kentucky						TOT	OFF	DEF	REB	PAS	HND	SHT	ATH
7		2011-12 status: free agent						+1	+3	+1	-1	-2	0	+3	-2
Year	Team	Age	G	MPG	Usg	3PA%	FTA%	INS	2P%	3P%	FT%	TS%	Reb%	Ast%	TO%	BLK%	STL%	PF%	oRTG	dRTG	Win%	WARP
07-08	GSW	24.3	81	21.4	.172	.276	.086	.810	.485	.364	.717	.534	.101	.018	.082	.014	.011	.039	105.3	106.1	.474	2.1
08-09	GSW	25.3	74	32.1	.188	.202	.097	.895	.469	.448	.808	.562	.085	.021	.091	.015	.011	.033	106.2	107.2	.468	2.6
09-10	GSW	26.3	9	25.7	.200	.252	.115	.863	.623	.370	.679	.623	.099	.019	.065	.028	.010	.030	108.7	105.4	.607	0.9
10-11p	NYK	27.3	64	25.0	.179	.268	.088	.820	.475	.432	.776	.567	.085	.021	.087	.015	.010	.035	106.1	106.5	.487	2.4

Most similar to: Chris Mills (98.9), Al Wood, Gordan Giricek, Mark Alarie   IMP: 48%   BRK: 7%   COP: 7%

NEW YORK KNICKS

If healthy, Kelenna Azubuike could emerge as the starting shooting guard for the Knicks this season. He seems like an ideal fit for Mike D'Antoni's system because of his accurate stroke from three-point range and a good first step that allows him to get to the rim and draw a decent amount of fouls. He's not as proficient from mid-range. Azubuike is going to look for his own shot first, but doesn't have to do it off the dribble. A fine athlete, Azubuike is a physical defender with a good mix of steals, blocks and on-ball defense that could give him the nod over other Knicks wings like Bill Walker and Wilson Chandler. Unfortunately, he is still recovering from the ruptured patella tendon that limited him to nine games in 2009-10. Azubuike just started running and jumping in late August and probably won't play during camp, though the team was hopeful he might be ready by the start of the regular season. Even if he is, it's likely that he'll be worked in slowly.

SG 21	Wilson Chandler	Hght: 6'8" Wght: 225 2011-12 status: due qualifying offer of $3.1 million	Exp: 3 From: DePaul	Salary: $2.1 million			**SKILL RATINGS**						
							TOT	OFF	DEF	REB	PAS	HND	SHT	ATH
							+1	+2	-1	+4	-2	-1	+1	-2

Year	Team	Age	G	MPG	Usg	3PA%	FTA%	INS	2P%	3P%	FT%	TS%	Reb%	Ast%	TO%	BLK%	STL%	PF%	oRTG	dRTG	Win%	WARP
07-08	NYK	21.0	35	19.6	.192	.102	.081	.979	.458	.300	.630	.480	.107	.022	.092	.018	.010	.056	102.7	106.3	.380	-0.5
08-09	NYK	22.0	82	33.4	.206	.244	.073	.830	.475	.328	.795	.515	.091	.027	.108	.020	.013	.040	104.5	106.4	.439	1.3
09-10	NYK	23.0	65	35.7	.203	.144	.068	.923	.524	.267	.806	.534	.086	.027	.104	.016	.010	.036	104.1	106.8	.412	-0.3
10-11p	NYK	24.0	73	32.0	.204	.242	.074	.831	.509	.332	.782	.538	.094	.028	.103	.019	.011	.038	105.5	106.2	.477	3.0

Most similar to: Sean Elliott (98.2), Michael Finley, Kenny Walker, Joe Johnson   IMP: 59%   BRK: 14%   COP: 0%

We watch Wilson Chandler and think, "Boy, that guy is athletic." But he doesn't get steals, doesn't rebound, doesn't draw fouls. He does block a few shots, but doesn't it seem like a player with his physical gifts should do more? After showing progress in 2008-09, Chandler dropped back below replacement level last season. During the summer, Chandler was reportedly offered to Portland for disgruntled Spaniard Rudy Fernandez, but the Blazers turned their thumbs down on that idea. Chandler has attempted 464 three-pointers the last two seasons while making them just 31 percent of the time. Wonder why he's below replacement level? There's Exhibition A. He's an excellent finisher at the rim, but doesn't leverage that ability or his athleticism to get to the foul line. His midrange shot remains spotty, though he can knock down the foul-line jumper. On defense, Chandler has the attributes to guard any wing, but his indicators are mostly average to poor. The one mark in his favor is that the Knicks were 5.3 points per 100 possessions better defensively when he was on the floor last season. There is a lot to work with here and SCHOENE is optimistic that Chandler will begin to find himself this season with better talent alongside him.

C 34	Eddy Curry	Hght: 7'0" Wght: 295 2011-12 status: free agent	Exp: 9 From: Thornwood HS (IL)	Salary: $11.3 million			**SKILL RATINGS**						
							TOT	OFF	DEF	REB	PAS	HND	SHT	ATH
							-1	--	-4	--	--	--	--	--

Year	Team	Age	G	MPG	Usg	3PA%	FTA%	INS	2P%	3P%	FT%	TS%	Reb%	Ast%	TO%	BLK%	STL%	PF%	oRTG	dRTG	Win%	WARP
07-08	NYK	25.4	59	25.9	.237	.000	.165	1.165	.546	.000	.623	.578	.103	.009	.157	.015	.004	.047	103.9	107.4	.385	-1.0
08-09	NYK	26.4	3	4.0	.194	.000	.248	1.248	1.000	.000	.333	.753	.189	.000	.376	.000	.000	.182	98.6	110.8	.164	-0.1
09-10	NYK	27.4	7	8.9	.304	.000	.180	1.180	.381	-	.588	.456	.120	.000	.313	.012	.000	.095	93.7	109.3	.103	-0.4
10-11p	NYK	28.4	61	-	.227	.009	.164	1.155	.561	.007	.633	.587	.101	.010	.157	.015	.004	.048	-	-	.429	-

Most similar to: Kevin Duckworth (96.2), Othella Harrington, Ike Austin, Maurice Taylor   IMP: 56%   BRK: 12%   COP: 8%

We have no idea what Eddy Curry's personal finances are like*, but doesn't he just seem like a player who is going to end up flat-ass broke within a couple of years after leaving the league? We won't print the words here, but Curry would have done well to heed Niedermeyer's advice to Flounder in *Animal House*. He's played 10 games over the last few years, finding so many ways to be unavailable that new stories about him read like pieces from *The Onion*. What does he have to offer on the court? We forget. Mercifully, the Knicks will be rid of Curry's contract after the season. How was his summer? Who knows? The Knicks didn't hear from him in the three months before camp opened. What do they expect? The guy only makes $11 million. (* Googled this after writing and found that, apparently, EC's finances are not good.)

NEW YORK KNICKS

PG 23	Toney Douglas	Hght: 6'1"	Exp: 1	Salary: $1.1 million	SKILL RATINGS							
		Wght: 200	From: Florida State		TOT	OFF	DEF	REB	PAS	HND	SHT	ATH
		2011-12 status: team option for $1.1 million			+3	+5	-3	0	-2	0	+3	-1

Year	Team	Age	G	MPG	Usg	3PA%	FTA%	INS	2P%	3P%	FT%	TS%	Reb%	Ast%	TO%	BLK%	STL%	PF%	oRTG	dRTG	Win%	WARP
09-10	NYK	24.1	56	19.4	.199	.368	.063	.695	.514	.389	.809	.571	.057	.047	.116	.002	.019	.048	108.2	107.5	.523	2.4
10-11p	NYK	25.1	76	20.0	.197	.406	.065	.660	.509	.379	.817	.567	.053	.049	.113	.003	.018	.046	108.7	107.3	.545	4.1

Most similar to: Kyle Macy (98.4), Byron Scott, Steve Colter, Leandro Barbosa — IMP: 46% BRK: 6% COP: 8%

The Knicks went out and signed veteran Ray Felton to man the point guard position, but their investment in the former Bobcat is limited and it's not out of the realm of possibility that Felton gets outplayed by second-year guard Toney Douglas. In his rookie season, Douglas proved he could put the ball in the hoop and stroke it from every distance on the court. He takes care of the ball and can shoot off the dribble and in catch-and-shoot situations. However, to be the leading man in Mike D'Antoni's scheme, Douglas has to become a far more proficient playmaker. On defense, Douglas was poor as a rookie, with nothing really that stands out as an encouraging sign.

SF 20	Patrick Ewing Jr.	Hght: 6'8"	Exp: R	Salary: $0.5 million	SKILL RATINGS							
		Wght: 240	From: Georgetown		TOT	OFF	DEF	REB	PAS	HND	SHT	ATH
		2011-12 status: due qualifying offer of $1.0 million			-1	--	--	--	--	--	--	--

Year	Team	Age	G	MPG	Usg	3PA%	FTA%	INS	2P%	3P%	FT%	TS%	Reb%	Ast%	TO%	BLK%	STL%	PF%	oRTG	dRTG	Win%	WARP
10-11p	NYK	26.9	76	-	.166	.150	.126	.976	.447	.252	.714	.488	.123	.028	.141	.036	.020	.054	-	-	.432	-

Most similar to: Earl Cureton (94.3), Malik Rose, Shelden Williams, Monty Williams — IMP: 56% BRK: 10% COP: 12%

It seems like Patrick Ewing Jr. will finally earn a place on the Knicks' regular-season roster, though things could change if Donnie Walsh continues New York's roster makeover. Ewing is a face-up forward with three-point range whose defense is his calling card. Even if Ewing breaks camp with the team, it will likely be as the last guy on the roster, so it's hard to say when, or if, he'll see any regular-season action.

PG 2	Raymond Felton	Hght: 6'1"	Exp: 5	Salary: $7.0 million	SKILL RATINGS							
		Wght: 198	From: North Carolina		TOT	OFF	DEF	REB	PAS	HND	SHT	ATH
		2011-12 status: guaranteed contract for $7.6 million			+3	+3	+4	+2	+2	+2	-1	+1

Year	Team	Age	G	MPG	Usg	3PA%	FTA%	INS	2P%	3P%	FT%	TS%	Reb%	Ast%	TO%	BLK%	STL%	PF%	oRTG	dRTG	Win%	WARP
07-08	CHA	23.8	79	37.7	.210	.148	.105	.958	.447	.280	.802	.501	.046	.090	.158	.003	.015	.028	105.6	106.9	.456	2.5
08-09	CHA	24.8	82	37.6	.220	.145	.084	.939	.437	.285	.805	.483	.062	.085	.159	.008	.022	.029	105.3	106.0	.476	3.8
09-10	CHA	25.8	80	33.0	.193	.143	.070	.927	.475	.385	.763	.525	.065	.079	.154	.007	.024	.030	105.9	105.3	.522	5.8
10-11p	NYK	26.8	76	33.0	.197	.205	.078	.873	.467	.365	.796	.527	.061	.080	.148	.007	.020	.030	106.8	106.0	.527	5.8

Most similar to: Rod Strickland (98.1), Larry Drew, Luke Ridnour, Norm Nixon — IMP: 50% BRK: 4% COP: 4%

Raymond Felton has a golden opportunity the next two years to prove he's a top-flight point guard in the NBA. If 2009-10 was any indicator, he'll be a great fit for the Knicks' system. The problem is that we don't know if last season's numbers can be relied upon, because a sudden 100-point spike in three-point percentage screams for regression. However, SCHOENE is optimistic Felton can keep most of that gain and he'll shoot a lot more threes this year playing for Mike D'Antoni. Felton isn't Steve Nash when it comes to running the point, but he is an above-average playmaker. Felton is also a solid defensive point guard who won't often have to guard bigger twos as he did on occasion when playing alongside D.J. Augustin in Charlotte. The assumption when Felton signed with New York was that he was a stopgap, and the Knicks only signed him to a two-year deal to set themselves up for a run at Chris Paul in 2012. That may prove the case, but in a system as conducive to gaudy point guard numbers as any, Felton will be playing for a big contract beyond the next two years, whether or not it's in New York.

NEW YORK KNICKS

SF	Landry Fields	Hght: 6'7"	Exp: R	Salary: $0.5 million	SKILL RATINGS							
6		Wght: 210	From: Stanford		TOT	OFF	DEF	REB	PAS	HND	SHT	ATH
		2011-12 status: non-guaranteed contract for $0.5 million			-1	0	+1	+4	+2	0	-4	+3

Year	Team	Age	G	MPG	Usg	3PA%	FTA%	INS	2P%	3P%	FT%	TS%	Reb%	Ast%	TO%	BLK%	STL%	PF%	oRTG	dRTG	Win%	WARP
10-11p	NYK	22.8	76	5.0	.222	.098	.117	1.019	.426	.288	.681	.473	.119	.034	.119	.010	.016	.038	103.5	105.4	.436	0.2

Most similar to: Brandon Roy (97.3), Leon Powe, Caron Butler, Chris Douglas-Roberts IMP: - BRK: - COP: -

Landry Fields excited the Knicks with an outstanding performance while playing for their summer-league team and landed a two-year contract, the first of which is guaranteed. Fields has the potential to be an excellent wing defender. He's strong, athletic and long-armed, plus he's as smart and cagey as you'd expect a Stanford grad to be. In college, Fields was a big-time scorer, but in the NBA--especially in the Knicks' system--he needs to show more range and consistency on his outside shot. As good as he was in summer league, he shot just 3-of-13 behind the arc. In any event, the Knicks might have found a keeper with the 39th pick of the draft. The Knicks have a lot of options at the wing positions, so it may be difficult for Fields to get on the court as a rookie, but he can earn some minutes if he proves to have a stopper mentality.

SF	Danilo Gallinari	Hght: 6'10"	Exp: 2	Salary: $3.3 million	SKILL RATINGS							
8		Wght: 225	From: Sant'Angelo Lodigiano, Italy		TOT	OFF	DEF	REB	PAS	HND	SHT	ATH
		2011-12 status: team option for $4.2 million			+4	+4	+4	-1	-1	0	+4	+1

Year	Team	Age	G	MPG	Usg	3PA%	FTA%	INS	2P%	3P%	FT%	TS%	Reb%	Ast%	TO%	BLK%	STL%	PF%	oRTG	dRTG	Win%	WARP
08-09	NYK	20.7	28	14.7	.161	.474	.078	.604	.453	.444	.963	.621	.074	.016	.099	.007	.017	.051	107.8	107.4	.511	0.8
09-10	NYK	21.7	81	33.9	.194	.416	.115	.699	.469	.381	.818	.575	.083	.022	.094	.016	.014	.032	106.9	106.0	.529	6.4
10-11p	NYK	22.7	76	34.0	.185	.425	.112	.686	.469	.406	.897	.602	.085	.023	.093	.013	.013	.039	107.9	106.2	.555	7.5

Most similar to: Mike Miller (97.0), Peja Stojakovic, J.R. Smith, Rashard Lewis IMP: 56% BRK: 4% COP: 0%

It's hard not to compare Danilo Gallinari to Toronto's Andrea Bargnani. They're both tall. They're both Italian. They were both high lottery picks. They both like to shoot a long ways from the basket. Whereas Bargnani has developed in fits and starts, Gallinari's second year showed a clear progression over his first. He looks like a legit starter in the NBA with the potential for more to come. Gallinari is already one of the NBA's deadliest perimeter shooters, and last year's .381 mark from behind the arc could prove to be on the low end of what he shoots from long range. However, he is more than just a spot-up shooter. Gallinari attacked the basket to get a fifth of his shots at the rim, where he converted at near the league average despite lacking strength. Gallinari also drew fouls at an above-average rate. 21 percent of his shot attempts were long twos, and while the .380 he shot there isn't terrible, you'd like to see him get that up to a Korver-esque .460 or so. Otherwise, he needs to cut down on that portion of his game. Gallinari's passing skills improved as well, but they're still not quite as good as they need to be, particularly if he ends up playing a lot of shooting guard this season. On defense, Gallinari is way better than expected. He moves well and uses his length to bother shots. Teams look at him and drool like he's a New York strip, so 20 percent of his defensive possessions came against isolations. (And why wouldn't you isolate him? He looks like a tall 12-year-old.) He responded by allowing .860 points per play in those situations, which puts him right at the league average. If he plays more twos, however, he'll probably suffer against isos. The rest of Gallinari's defensive profile looks solid. He's a future All-Star.

SG	Roger Mason	Hght: 6'5"	Exp: 6	Salary: $1.4 million	SKILL RATINGS							
18		Wght: 212	From: Virginia		TOT	OFF	DEF	REB	PAS	HND	SHT	ATH
		2011-12 status: free agent			0	+3	0	-2	+1	+2	+2	-5

Year	Team	Age	G	MPG	Usg	3PA%	FTA%	INS	2P%	3P%	FT%	TS%	Reb%	Ast%	TO%	BLK%	STL%	PF%	oRTG	dRTG	Win%	WARP
07-08	WAS	27.6	80	21.3	.190	.467	.045	.578	.498	.398	.873	.573	.046	.036	.099	.009	.011	.039	107.2	107.4	.493	2.7
08-09	SAS	28.6	82	30.4	.190	.405	.053	.649	.428	.421	.890	.554	.059	.034	.103	.004	.009	.031	106.2	107.7	.452	1.8
09-10	SAS	29.6	79	19.2	.173	.463	.026	.563	.453	.333	.794	.490	.062	.042	.104	.007	.010	.030	104.5	106.8	.423	0.2
10-11p	NYK	30.6	75	10.0	.176	.492	.036	.543	.448	.373	.836	.531	.058	.039	.105	.006	.010	.034	106.1	107.3	.461	0.7

Most similar to: Wesley Person (98.6), Raja Bell, Eldridge Recasner, Dennis Scott IMP: 48% BRK: 9% COP: 3%

Though Roger Mason Jr. dropped to near replacement level in his second season with the Spurs, the Knicks might have found an important bench piece by picking him up on a one-year contract over the summer. Mason shot just 31 percent from the floor after the 2009-10 All-Star break. In February, he tore a ligament in his right hand, which required surgery after the season. Prior to the injury, Mason's percentages were right in line with his recent career baseline. The injury doesn't really explain why Mason's already low foul-drawing rate dropped to almost nothing, but he's strictly a catch-and-shoot specialist with limited athletic ability. Mason is an average defender in most respects, but struggles against isolations, so you have to monitor his matchups.

C 25	Timofey Mozgov	Hght: 7'1" Exp: R Salary: $3.6 million									
		Wght: 270 From: Russia									
		2011-12 status: guaranteed contract for $3.3 million									

SKILL RATINGS

TOT	OFF	DEF	REB	PAS	HND	SHT	ATH
-1	-1	+2	+3	-5	-5	-2	+1

Year	Team	Age	G	MPG	Usg	3PA%	FTA%	INS	2P%	3P%	FT%	TS%	Reb%	Ast%	TO%	BLK%	STL%	PF%	oRTG	dRTG	Win%	WARP
10-11p	NYK	24.8	76	15.0	.204	.000	.099	1.099	.474	.000	.628	.504	.179	.006	.187	.062	.009	.110	102.7	105.1	.419	0.1

Most similar to: Rony Seikaly (96.8), Michael Olowokandi, Erick Dampier, Adonal Foyle   IMP: 58%   BRK: 13%   COP: 3%

Timofey Mozgov had already signed with the Knicks when the FIBA World Championship was played, but his showing in that tournament had to whet the collective appetite of fans in the Big Apple. He's also the latest product of Mike D'Antoni's one-man hype machine. One year after calling Danilo Gallinari the greatest shooter he's ever seen, D'Antoni told reporters that Mozgov is "maybe our most athletic guy." Mind you, Mozgov is massive--tall, long-armed and built like a power forward. You could see in the World Championship how well he moves; that in itself sets Mozgov apart from most oversized European imports. He's going to be a factor on defense right away and may turn into one of the best per-minute rebounders in the league. Offensively, he's got little touch beyond the immediate vicinity of the rim, but he should be an efficient finisher of putbacks and his mobility will make him a viable screener on pick-and-rolls. Mozgov is definitely one of the more interesting newcomers to the NBA this season.

PF 4	Anthony Randolph	Hght: 6'10" Exp: 2 Salary: $2.0 million									
		Wght: 210 From: Louisiana State									
		2011-12 status: team option for $2.9 million									

SKILL RATINGS

TOT	OFF	DEF	REB	PAS	HND	SHT	ATH
+4	+2	-1	+3	+3	0	-3	+5

Year	Team	Age	G	MPG	Usg	3PA%	FTA%	INS	2P%	3P%	FT%	TS%	Reb%	Ast%	TO%	BLK%	STL%	PF%	oRTG	dRTG	Win%	WARP
08-09	GSW	19.8	63	17.9	.218	.007	.108	1.101	.466	.000	.716	.506	.175	.019	.140	.045	.018	.054	104.5	103.6	.532	2.7
09-10	GSW	20.8	33	22.7	.240	.012	.143	1.131	.447	.200	.801	.521	.160	.024	.117	.049	.018	.053	105.4	103.0	.578	2.5
10-11p	NYK	21.8	68	25.0	.241	.018	.129	1.111	.466	.127	.801	.526	.159	.028	.119	.046	.018	.048	105.6	102.8	.593	6.3

Most similar to: Tracy McGrady (96.5), Kevin Garnett, Joe Smith, Josh Smith   IMP: 63%   BRK: 4%   COP: 4%

Everyone is excited to see what Anthony Randolph can do in the Knicks' system. In Phoenix, Mike D'Antoni turned Boris Diaw into a solid NBA starter by leveraging his versatile skill set, and Diaw doesn't have nearly as much raw ability as Randolph. Randolph is coming off a nasty ankle injury, which saw him tear three ligaments and cost him the final 49 games of 2009-10. Before getting hurt, Randolph's statistics were right in line with his rookie performance. He was doing it in a slightly bigger chunk of playing time, though Don Nelson severely underutilized him in Golden State. Randolph is a gifted passer and rebounder, and will someday be an elite-level defensive player if he's willing to commit to being one. The offensive ability is also there. Randolph draws fouls, hits his free throws and shoots well close to the basket. He's not a good midrange shooter, but still took about 40 percent of his shots from 10-23 feet, which was a blight on his Offensive Rating. D'Antoni is reportedly projecting Randolph as his starting small forward, where he could be a matchup nightmare for opponents, because he's athletic enough to guard opposing threes. Randolph should be able to take small forwards on the blocks on the offensive end, though his post game is still developing. SCHOENE loves this guy, and Randolph could be one of the breakout players in the NBA this season.

NEW YORK KNICKS

SG 11	Andy Rautins	Hght: 6'4"	Exp: R	Salary: $0.5 million	SKILL RATINGS							
		Wght: 194	From: Syracuse		TOT	OFF	DEF	REB	PAS	HND	SHT	ATH
		2011-12 status: due qualifying offer of $1.0 million			0	+1	-1	-4	+4	+3	0	-1

Year	Team	Age	G	MPG	Usg	3PA%	FTA%	INS	2P%	3P%	FT%	TS%	Reb%	Ast%	TO%	BLK%	STL%	PF%	oRTG	dRTG	Win%	WARP
10-11p	NYK	24.5	76	4.7	.130	.436	.060	.624	.468	.347	.796	.525	.045	.063	.229	.004	.021	.042	104.8	106.5	.446	0.2

Most similar to: Steve Blake (92.0), Keith Bogans, Lionel Chalmers   IMP: -   BRK: -   COP: -

Andy Rautins has a chance to be a nice fit with the Knicks, who spread the floor and create open looks for spot-up shooters. Rautins was an outstanding three-point shooter in college and has the stroke to translate that to the next level. He's limited athletically, enough so that he probably won't even hold down a Kyle Korver-type role in the NBA. However, as a 5-8 minute shooting specialist, he can carve out a nice career for himself. Rautins is a good passer, so he should be able make plays off of aggressive close-outs.

PF 1	Amar'e Stoudemire	Hght: 6'10"	Exp: 8	Salary: $16.5 million	SKILL RATINGS							
		Wght: 249	From: Cypress Creek (Orlando, FL)		TOT	OFF	DEF	REB	PAS	HND	SHT	ATH
		2011-12 status: guaranteed contract for $18.2 million			+4	+4	-3	+1	-1	-4	+4	+2

Year	Team	Age	G	MPG	Usg	3PA%	FTA%	INS	2P%	3P%	FT%	TS%	Reb%	Ast%	TO%	BLK%	STL%	PF%	oRTG	dRTG	Win%	WARP
07-08	PHX	25.4	79	33.9	.284	.018	.180	1.162	.601	.161	.805	.656	.146	.020	.103	.040	.010	.047	110.1	103.5	.702	16.0
08-09	PHX	26.4	53	36.8	.242	.007	.159	1.153	.540	.429	.835	.617	.127	.024	.140	.021	.012	.037	107.1	105.8	.542	5.1
09-10	PHX	27.4	82	34.6	.275	.003	.158	1.155	.559	.167	.771	.615	.143	.013	.121	.021	.009	.044	107.9	105.5	.578	9.5
10-11p	NYK	28.4	75	35.0	.261	.010	.155	1.145	.557	.264	.795	.617	.133	.019	.126	.024	.010	.043	107.9	105.7	.572	8.5

Most similar to: Larry Nance (96.9), Dino Radja, Christian Laettner, Shareef Abdur-Rahim   IMP: 33%   BRK: 0%   COP: 4%

Amar'e Stoudemire has been a well-known player in the NBA for a long time, but now that he's in New York, he's going to get really famous, really fast. The danger here, in terms of perception by fans and what is ultimately written about him by the New York media, is that Stoudemire shouldn't be expected to be any more or less than what he was in Phoenix. He's the same player in the same system, but without Steve Nash, the key component of said system for the Suns. SCHOENE sees a status quo season for Stoudemire, which makes sense and should allow him to keep his superficial numbers at a level that will keep the dogs at bay. Stoudemire's defense is an issue, which is why it's important that he be paired with a decent defensive center. Decent is about what describes Ronny Turiaf at that end; Timofey Mozgov is probably too raw for the first unit, but if he emerges, it will be because of his defense, which would make him a good partner for Stoudemire. On offense, it wouldn't be a surprise to see a nice little bump in assists from Stoudemire. He actually sees the floor pretty well, but has always been asked to be a finisher for Nash's creative passes. The one area where Stoudemire probably doesn't get enough credit is shooting. Sure, he dunks the ball a lot and is one of the best finishers in basketball. However, he shoots a high percentage all the way out to the three-point line and is as much of a pick-and-pop option as he is a pick-and-roll wizard. As long as Stoudemire maintains his current level of play, his five-year, $99.8 million contract won't be a problem. If injuries come into play, a problem for Stoudemire in the past, then the Knicks will be stuck, but that's a worst-case scenario. Chances are that Stoudemire is going to be a megastar in Madison Square Garden.

C 14	Ronny Turiaf	Hght: 6'10"	Exp: 5	Salary: $4.0 million	SKILL RATINGS							
		Wght: 250	From: Gonzaga		TOT	OFF	DEF	REB	PAS	HND	SHT	ATH
		2011-12 status: player option or ETO for $4.4 million			+1	0	-1	-3	+5	+5	+3	-1

Year	Team	Age	G	MPG	Usg	3PA%	FTA%	INS	2P%	3P%	FT%	TS%	Reb%	Ast%	TO%	BLK%	STL%	PF%	oRTG	dRTG	Win%	WARP
07-08	LAL	25.3	78	18.7	.167	.004	.149	1.145	.477	.000	.753	.540	.115	.039	.131	.053	.008	.060	104.2	104.2	.497	2.5
08-09	GSW	26.3	79	21.5	.124	.006	.111	1.105	.512	.000	.790	.559	.115	.042	.143	.069	.010	.061	104.1	104.0	.505	3.1
09-10	GSW	27.3	42	20.8	.113	.004	.150	1.145	.586	.000	.474	.574	.123	.044	.214	.044	.012	.048	103.2	104.3	.466	0.9
10-11p	NYK	28.3	70	20.0	.126	.006	.131	1.125	.544	.002	.643	.568	.115	.042	.172	.051	.010	.055	103.7	104.5	.475	1.7

Most similar to: John Salley (97.2), Andrew Lang, Duane Causwell, Brendan Haywood   IMP: 45%   BRK: 6%   COP: 8%

NEW YORK KNICKS

For the big lineup that Mike D'Antoni wants to play to work, Ronny Turiaf is going to have to play a bigger role than he's ever played. His numbers don't suggest a 25- to 30-minute player on the offensive end, where he averaged just 9.5 points per 40 minutes last season. However, it's his post defense that will determine how much Turiaf stays on the court. He's an excellent shot blocker and help defender, always willing to step in and take a charge. Turiaf is undersized, which could hurt the Knicks against the top teams in the league despite their overall length. (The Knicks may start a shooting guard that is taller than their center.) Turiaf's play-by-play data suggests that he is an average defender in the post, so we'll see. On offense, he's one of the best-passing big men in the game. He can't do much scoring-wise other than finish at the basket, where he shot nearly 80 percent last season. Turiaf will be fine in a low-usage role if he ratchets up his rebound percentages. He's been below average on the boards for his position during his career, but the Knicks need him to chip in as part of what promises to be a team effort off the glass.

SG 5	Bill Walker	Hght: 6'6" Wght: 220 2011-12 status: guaranteed contract for $0.9 million	Exp: 2 From: Kansas State	Salary: $0.9 million	SKILL RATINGS TOT +3	OFF +4	DEF -3	REB +1	PAS -2	HND 0	SHT +5	ATH -2

Year	Team	Age	G	MPG	Usg	3PA%	FTA%	INS	2P%	3P%	FT%	TS%	Reb%	Ast%	TO%	BLK%	STL%	PF%	oRTG	dRTG	Win%	WARP
08-09	BOS	21.5	29	7.4	.187	.012	.118	1.106	.632	.000	.696	.646	.080	.028	.209	.007	.014	.111	103.9	109.7	.318	-0.4
09-10	NYK	22.5	35	21.9	.167	.412	.077	.665	.603	.431	.796	.649	.066	.024	.099	.003	.015	.049	107.6	107.4	.504	1.4
10-11p	NYK	23.5	76	10.3	.174	.357	.088	.731	.601	.426	.810	.648	.069	.028	.099	.003	.015	.047	108.1	107.1	.534	1.9

Most similar to: Reggie Miller (96.5), J.R. Smith, Peja Stojakovic, Mike Miller   IMP: 59% BRK: 5% COP: 5%

This is a huge season for Bill Walker, who got little playing time in Boston but impressed the Knicks in an extended audition after being traded to New York. Walker does not fudge around with midrange shots, even though he's been pretty good from there in a limited sample size. Last season, 83 percent of his shots came at the rim or from behind the three-point arc. If he can shoot 43 percent from downtown as he did last season, or something close to that, he's going to play a major role for the Knicks. At one time, it was widely believed that Walker was the favorite to start at the two for the Knicks this season, but later reports seemed to indicate otherwise. Walker's athletic and defensive indicators are disappointing for someone with his raw ability, but improved conditioning could help him; he reportedly lost 27 pounds over the summer. If Walker can recover the elite-level explosiveness he had in high school before tearing his ACL twice, he'll become one of the most exciting players in the league. Walker could go a lot of ways at this point. He may still end up as the Knicks' starting shooting guard. He could also end up buried on the bench.

C --	Jerome Jordan	Hght: 7'0" Wght: 253 2011-12 status: free agent	Exp: R From: Tulsa	Salary: --	SKILL RATINGS TOT -2	OFF --	DEF --	REB --	PAS --	HND --	SHT --	ATH --

Year	Team	Age	G	MPG	Usg	3PA%	FTA%	INS	2P%	3P%	FT%	TS%	Reb%	Ast%	TO%	BLK%	STL%	PF%	oRTG	dRTG	Win%	WARP
10-11p	NYK	24.6	76	-	.174	-.001	.149	1.150	.435	.000	.671	.494	.132	.018	.157	.034	.006	.062	-	-	.398	-

Most similar to: Dan Gadzuric (97.2), Melvin Ely, Rob Kurz, Britton Johnsen   IMP: - BRK: - COP: -

Jerome Jordan was taken by the Bucks with the 44th pick of the draft and sent to the Knicks on the same day. He ended up signing with KK Hemofarm in Serbia, where he will try to develop his skills. Jordan didn't start playing basketball until his junior year of high school, when he moved from Jamaica, so he's worth a flier as a high-ceiling prospect. He's got an NBA body, so New York will sit on his rights and monitor his progress overseas with great interest.

NEW YORK KNICKS

C — Earl Barron

Hght: 7'0"	Exp: 4	Salary: --
Wght: 250	From: Memphis
2011-12 status: free agent

SKILL RATINGS

TOT	OFF	DEF	REB	PAS	HND	SHT	ATH
-5	-2	-1	-2	-2	-3	-5	-1

Year	Team	Age	G	MPG	Usg	3PA%	FTA%	INS	2P%	3P%	FT%	TS%	Reb%	Ast%	TO%	BLK%	STL%	PF%	oRTG	dRTG	Win%	WARP
07-08	MIA	26.7	46	19.4	.221	.032	.093	1.061	.417	.077	.701	.446	.134	.016	.114	.007	.010	.060	100.8	106.8	.308	-2.0
09-10	NYK	28.7	7	33.1	.180	.000	.139	1.139	.441	-	.759	.508	.189	.016	.120	.013	.009	.047	105.0	105.9	.473	0.3
10-11p	AVG	29.7	76	33.1	.207	.050	.083	1.032	.427	.075	.688	.442	.127	.015	.125	.006	.010	.062	100.2	107.3	.278	-7.2

Most similar to: Larry Krystkowiak (97.1), Kevin Duckworth, Predrag Drobnjak, Malik Allen
IMP: 46% BRK: 10% COP: 10%

Journeyman Earl Barron played well for the Knicks in a snippet of playing time at the end of last season, but he was still looking for work at press time. Barron is an offense-first center who has a nice face-up shot on long twos. Unfortunately, it's tough to build a career out of that if you don't defend well, which appears to be the case for Barron. Barron's rebound percentages were excellent for New York, far better than his below-average career norms. If he has legitimately improved his rebounding, he can still find a job.

PF — Jonathan Bender

Hght: 7'0"	Exp: 8	Salary: --
Wght: 230	From: Picayune HS (MS)
2011-12 status: free agent

SKILL RATINGS

TOT	OFF	DEF	REB	PAS	HND	SHT	ATH
-4	-2	0	-4	+2	-4	-4	-4

Year	Team	Age	G	MPG	Usg	3PA%	FTA%	INS	2P%	3P%	FT%	TS%	Reb%	Ast%	TO%	BLK%	STL%	PF%	oRTG	dRTG	Win%	WARP
09-10	NYK	29.2	25	11.7	.217	.280	.082	.802	.426	.359	.923	.529	.102	.025	.201	.043	.003	.051	103.5	105.8	.425	0.0
10-11p	AVG	30.2	70	11.7	.220	.243	.084	.840	.434	.246	.910	.478	.097	.025	.196	.038	.004	.051	101.4	106.1	.348	-1.2

Most similar to: Ralph Sampson (89.3), Kurt Nimphius, Edgar Jones, James Bailey
IMP: 47% BRK: 27% COP: 7%

Surprisingly, Jonathan Bender resurfaced last season after basically missing a half-decade because of chronic knee problems. He wasn't in the best of shape, which was to be expected given the layoff, but showed potential for a nice face-up shot from downtown. Bender worked out with a fitness expert over the summer, hoping to recover some mobility, but was unsigned at press time.

PG — Sergio Rodriguez

Hght: 6'3"	Exp: 4	Salary: --
Wght: 176	From: Tenerife, Spain
2011-12 status: free agent

SKILL RATINGS

TOT	OFF	DEF	REB	PAS	HND	SHT	ATH
+3	+4	0	-1	+3	0	+1	+1

Year	Team	Age	G	MPG	Usg	3PA%	FTA%	INS	2P%	3P%	FT%	TS%	Reb%	Ast%	TO%	BLK%	STL%	PF%	oRTG	dRTG	Win%	WARP
07-08	POR	21.9	72	8.8	.200	.218	.063	.845	.377	.293	.658	.423	.054	.093	.199	.000	.018	.043	103.2	106.8	.381	-0.5
08-09	POR	22.9	80	15.3	.187	.237	.070	.834	.428	.325	.792	.491	.066	.111	.247	.001	.024	.051	106.9	107.3	.487	1.8
09-10	NYK	23.9	66	15.9	.217	.180	.081	.901	.519	.352	.731	.554	.049	.091	.225	.004	.024	.036	106.5	106.4	.504	1.9
10-11p	AVG	24.9	76	15.9	.204	.247	.073	.826	.472	.381	.745	.540	.053	.103	.217	.002	.023	.039	107.3	106.3	.536	3.0

Most similar to: Allen Leavell (97.8), Raul Lopez, Micheal Williams, Cory Alexander
IMP: 58% BRK: 15% COP: 6%

When the Knicks acquired Sergio Rodriguez last season, it really felt like the passing specialist could fit as an exciting option in Mike D'Antoni's offense. His per-minute numbers were very good, he shot the ball well and even seemed to rise above the level of sieve at the defensive end. Rodriguez signed a three-year deal to return home to Spain with Real Madrid, so we've seen the last of him in the NBA for awhile--maybe forever.

Oklahoma City Thunder

A sold-out Ford Center on its feet, drawing comparisons to the league's best crowds. A legitimate superstar, Kevin Durant, leading the Thunder on offense while a team defensive effort helped contain Kobe Bryant. And Oklahoma City playing the eventual champions, the Los Angeles Lakers, to a draw through six hotly contested games before seeing the series end on the narrowest of margins, a putback in the closing seconds of Game Six. The conclusion of the 2009-10 season was everything the Oklahoma City Thunder had imagined it would be, only it was way ahead of schedule.

It was easy to forget, by year's end, that this same Thunder squad was two years removed from winning 20 games in its final season in Seattle and just a year away from starting the 2008-09 campaign 2-24. By the end of that first year in Oklahoma City, it was clear that the pieces were in place to build something special. It just seemed far more likely that the bright future was at least a couple of seasons away.

The Thunder began 2009-10 as the league's youngest team, with one of its youngest coaches on the sideline, but coalesced quickly into a formidable foe. Oklahoma City surpassed the previous season's Portland Trail Blazers squad as the youngest in league history to win at least 50 games and also displaced the Blazers as the NBA's new "it" team.

In the center of it all was Durant, one of the league's brightest young stars. Durant took his lumps during his rookie season but began blossoming after Scott Brooks replaced P.J. Carlesimo early in 2008-09. By year three, Durant's hard work had paid off. Forget just becoming an All-Star. Durant skipped right past that level of play and reached the All-NBA First Team, finishing second in MVP voting.

As good as Durant was on offense--he became the youngest scoring champion in league history, and did so while posting an impressive 60.7 percent True Shooting Percentage--his bigger strides came at the defensive end of the floor. Durant's focus was more consistent, and he learned how to use his length to make life difficult for opposing wings. One of the highlights of Durant's season was the way he shut down Kobe Bryant late in Game Three of the Thunder's series with the Lakers.

The willingness of their best player to work on his defense set the tone for Oklahoma City's progress at that end, which began during the second half of the 2008-09 season. A pair of imports from Chicago played key roles. Assistant coach Ron Adams, who helped Scott Skiles mold some of the league's best defenses with the Bulls, joined the coaching staff midseason and tightened up the Thunder's defensive schemes. Meanwhile, Oklahoma City GM Sam Presti landed long-limbed defensive specialist Thabo Sefolosha at the trade deadline and plugged him in as the starter at shooting guard.

Having both Adams and Sefolosha for an entire season made the Thunder one of the league's most improved defenses. Oklahoma City jumped from 21st in the league in Defensive Rating to eighth and

THUNDER IN A BOX

Last year's record	50-32
Last year's Offensive Rating	110.2 (12)
Last year's Defensive Rating	105.9 (8)
Last year's point differential	3.5 (10)
Team pace	91.8 (11)
SCHOENE projection	48-34 (6)
Projected Offensive Rating	110.0 (18)
Projected Defensive Rating	107.0 (2)
Projected team weighted age	24.3 (30)
Projected '10-11 payroll	$51.0 (28)
Est. payroll obligations, '11-12	$45.1 (26)

Head coach: Scott Brooks

In his first full season as a head coach, Scott Brooks earned Coach of the Year honors for his role in Oklahoma City's surprising playoff run. Brooks did an excellent job of keeping the league's youngest team focused and mature beyond its years. Offensively, the Thunder initially relied heavily on Kevin Durant and improved over the course of the year as other options stepped up. Oklahoma City was especially effective at the defensive end of the floor. However, the Thunder will miss Ron Adams, the assistant coach who was in charge of the defense before rejoining the Bulls as an assistant to Tom Thibodeau.

finished fifth in terms of opponent effective field-goal percentage. With a trio of quality defenders on the perimeter (Durant, Sefolosha and physical point guard Russell Westbrook), Jeff Green's versatility at power forward and two good defensive big men coming off the bench (veteran Nick Collison and rookie Serge Ibaka), the Thunder was difficult to score against much of the time.

On offense, Oklahoma City could be predictable in terms of getting the ball to Durant and isolating him and Westbrook. The scoring attack improved as the season went along, however. One reason for that was the development of rookies Ibaka and James Harden, the latter the No. 3 overall pick in the 2009 Draft. The raw Ibaka began the season as strictly an asset on defense before expanding his offensive repertoire as he got more comfortable and more confident. Because of his role off the bench, Harden was streaky, but his three-point shooting was a welcome addition to a team that was lacking in terms of floor spacing the previous season.

Presti added to the second unit in December, making use of the Thunder's room under the salary cap. Oklahoma City absorbed the contract of Matt Harpring from the Utah Jazz, helping Utah reduce its luxury-tax burden, in return for getting rookie point guard Eric Maynor. Already, Maynor is one of the league's better backup point guards, and he has a friendly rookie contract for the next three seasons.

A nine-game winning streak in January and February helped the Thunder separate itself from the pack of contenders for the last playoff seeds in the Western Conference, and Oklahoma City put itself in position to compete for the Northwest Division title before fading a bit down the stretch with four losses in the last six games. Despite 50 wins, the Thunder finished in the eighth and final playoff spot, getting an unenviable first-round matchup against the Lakers.

The contrast between the experience of the defending champions and Oklahoma City's youth was stark. Just three of the Thunder's nine rotation players had previously appeared in the postseason--Collison, Sefolosha and starting center Nenad Krstic--and none got as far as the conference finals. That didn't stop Oklahoma City from putting a legitimate scare in the Lakers by taking Games Three and Four at home, the latter in lopsided fashion. Had the Thunder boxed out Pau Gasol on the final possession of Game Six, the series would have been forced to a deciding seventh game in L.A.

Given the way Oklahoma City exceeded expectations, it was impossible to be disappointed about the way the season ended. Instead, the focus was on what lies ahead for the Thunder. Summer prognostication has put the team as high as second in the West, which is reasonable at face value given how compact the conference was a year ago (just five games separated Oklahoma City and second-place Dallas) and the likelihood of continued improvement from the young core of players.

There are a couple of factors working against the Thunder, however. By far the most significant of these is health, the hidden factor in Oklahoma City's surprise run. Four of the Thunder's five starters played all 82 games; the other, Krstic, missed six games. None of Oklahoma City's key reserves dealt with any major injuries either. Collison was the rotation player the team missed the most often; he sat out seven games all year. Being able to write the same starters on the lineup every night, backed up by the same rotation, was a huge luxury for Brooks.

In terms of players, the Thunder had no notable defections during the offseason. On the sidelines, the loss of Adams--who returned to Chicago to serve as an assistant to Tom Thibodeau--could be significant. The defensive principles Adams put in place will still aid Oklahoma City, but he won't be around to reinforce them on a daily basis.

Those issues suggest that much of the Thunder's development next season will be devoted not to taking steps forward but to ensuring the team does not slip back from last year's win total. Oklahoma City will do it with virtually the same group of players. Veteran center Etan Thomas, who played almost all of his 321 minutes in the season's first month, was the most-used Thunder player no longer on the roster.

Oklahoma City entered the offseason with cap space, but Presti continued to use the space on absorbing other teams' bad contracts rather than making a splash in free agency. The Thunder made a pair of such trades connected to the draft. The day before the draft, Miami sent wing Daequan Cook and its first-round pick, No. 18 overall, to Oklahoma City in exchange for the Thunder's No. 32 pick in the second round. Cook was expendable because the Heat was desperate to clear cap space, but he is a useful young player with a reasonable final year of his contract, while Oklahoma City also moved up 14 spots in the draft order.

During the draft, the Thunder moved up again, packaging two picks later in the round (No. 21 and No. 26) to move up to the 11th selection, taking on the last year of Morris Peterson's deal in the process. Presti's target was Kansas center Cole Aldrich, who becomes Oklahoma City's latest center of the future. The deep frontcourt rotation means Aldrich might play sparingly this season, but both Collison and Krstic become free agents at season's end, so Aldrich could move up quickly.

The Thunder remained busy throughout the draft, sending the 18th pick to the L.A. Clippers for a conditional future first-round pick and ending up with three players selected in the second round. None figures to play a key role in Oklahoma City next season, but stashing German center Tibor Pleiss to continue his development in Europe is another example of Presti stockpiling assets.

Next season might be a mild disappointment in that the Thunder looks more likely to remain in the bottom four seeds of the Western Conference playoffs rather than seriously competing for the conference title. Such a result should take nothing away from Oklahoma City's prospects for contending in the future. The Thunder still projects to be the league's youngest team next season, and with Aldrich likely to wrest playing time away from one of the veteran centers in 2011-12, the Thunder's lineup could get even younger.

In the big picture, far and away the most important development of the summer was Oklahoma City quickly locking up Durant, who signed a maximum five-year extension rather than considering his options as a restricted free agent next summer. Durant would not have been able to get away until the summer of 2012, when he could have become an unrestricted free agent, and never showed any interest in doing so. Durant is the perfect superstar for the low-key OKC market, and with a strong young core around him, he had no need to go elsewhere.

There is one big decision left for Presti, and that's Green's future in a Thunder uniform. Green has been there alongside Durant since day one, but his track record on the court is decidedly more mixed. It may be difficult for the two sides to come to agreement on an extension. Deferring a Green decision until next summer leaves Oklahoma City open to another team making a big offer to the restricted free agent. At the same time, it would give the Thunder a sizeable chunk of cap space, probably the last time the team will be significantly under the cap for a while (presuming that a Westbrook extension will kick in during the summer of 2012). Oklahoma City could use the money to sign a replacement for Green or promote the promising Ibaka and look for help elsewhere.

With other teams in the West loading up on veterans, the conference is wide open for the Thunder and a handful of other young contenders like Portland to battle over later this decade. The moves Presti makes over the next 12 months to complete Oklahoma City's core will determine whether the Thunder's ceiling is mere contender or as an odds-on favorite in the West.

Kevin Pelton

From the Blogosphere

Who: Royce Young
What: Daily Thunder
Where: http://www.dailythunder.com/

Everyone knows about Kevin Durant. Most folks were introduced to Russell Westbrook during last season's playoff series against the Lakers. And Jeff Green is well known as KD's sidekick. But if you don't know who Serge Ibaka is, you're totally missing out. The man dubbed Chewblocka, Air Congo and Dr. Nasty has muscle that's probably made of adamantium. He's as athletic as any player in the league and here's the best part about Ibaka--he's only 20 and has played organized basketball for only a few years. Whether the Thunder can challenge for the Western Conference crown in the future will hinge largely on Air Congo's development. Ibaka is a high-energy, high-excitement type of player. He blocked seven shots against the Lakers last postseason and introduced himself to the basketball world. But 2010-11 might be his breakout season. As Yahoo!'s Kelly Dwyer said so perfectly, Serge Ibaka is your favorite player. You just don't know it yet.

OKLAHOMA CITY THUNDER

THUNDER FIVE-YEAR TRENDS

Season	AGE	W-L	POW	PYTH	SEED	ORTG	DRTG	PT DIFF	PACE
05-06	25.6	35-47	34.3 (23)	32.8	---	111.9 (4)	115.9 (30)	-3.0 (26)	90.7 (9)
06-07	25.9	31-51	32.2 (22)	32.9	---	108.5 (12)	112.0 (27)	-2.9 (22)	90.6 (14)
07-08	24.7	20-62	19.3 (29)	18.9	---	102.5 (30)	112.0 (24)	-8.8 (30)	94.3 (5)
08-09	24.5	23-59	23.3 (27)	24.5	---	104.1 (29)	111.4 (21)	-6.1 (27)	92.2 (8)
09-10	23.8	50-32	50.8 (10)	50.8	8	110.2 (12)	105.9 (8)	3.5 (10)	91.8 (11)

Season	PAY	OFFENSE eFG	oREB	FT/FGA	TO	DEFENSE eFG	oREB	FT/FGA	TO
05-06	$46.9	.504 (5)	.304 (5)	.246 (18)	.161 (20)	.527 (29)	.690 (29)	.260 (20)	.159 (16)
06-07	$56.6	.499 (14)	.278 (14)	.228 (23)	.169 (18)	.515 (27)	.709 (27)	.243 (15)	.165 (17)
07-08	$52.6	.467 (29)	.268 (14)	.204 (26)	.160 (28)	.503 (19)	.737 (13)	.215 (11)	.133 (29)
08-09	$61.5	.471 (30)	.286 (4)	.242 (10)	.175 (29)	.514 (25)	.739 (13)	.216 (8)	.150 (21)
09-10	$55.2	.494 (19)	.286 (3)	.268 (2)	.162 (23)	.483 (5)	.736 (17)	.229 (18)	.163 (5)

(league rankings in parenthesis)

C 45 — Cole Aldrich
Hght: 6'11" Exp: R Salary: $1.8 million
Wght: 245 From: Kansas
2011-12 status: guaranteed contract for $1.9 million

SKILL RATINGS — TOT +2, OFF -1, DEF +4, REB +2, PAS -2, HND -2, SHT -2, ATH +1

Year	Team	Age	G	MPG	Usg	3PA%	FTA%	INS	2P%	3P%	FT%	TS%	Reb%	Ast%	TO%	BLK%	STL%	PF%	oRTG	dRTG	Win%	WARP
10-11p	OKC	22.5	76	6.9	.139	.000	.132	1.132	.468	.000	.665	.511	.166	.014	.142	.061	.010	.062	102.8	103.1	.491	0.8

Most similar to: Emeka Okafor (96.7), Brendan Haywood, Roy Hibbert   IMP: -   BRK: -   COP: -

Thanks to a bulky frame and a buzzcut that evokes Eric Montross and Greg Ostertag, Cole Aldrich looks like a stiff from NBA central casting. NBA fans who rarely saw him play at Kansas may therefore be surprised by Aldrich's athleticism. He's unlikely to win many footraces, but Aldrich is agile in the paint and finishes well at the rim, which explains his above-average Athleticism score.

Aldrich is the new Oklahoma City center of the future, but with Nenad Krstic and Nick Collison in place he'll be the Thunder's fifth post this season, giving him an opportunity to make the adjustment to the NBA. Aldrich will need to work on his footwork and ability to defend on the perimeter, especially against the pick-and-roll. In the paint, he should be just fine. Aldrich uses his wingspan to full effect as a shot blocker and is good on the glass at both ends of the floor. Offensively, Aldrich is unlikely to ever be a go-to option. He'll get his points on putbacks and with the ability to post up when he faces undersized defenders. As long as Aldrich doesn't flop in practice and limited playing time, he's on track to be Oklahoma City's starting center as soon as 2011-12.

C 4 — Nick Collison
Hght: 6'10" Exp: 6 Salary: $6.8 million
Wght: 255 From: Kansas
2011-12 status: free agent

SKILL RATINGS — TOT -1, OFF 0, DEF +2, REB 0, PAS -1, HND +1, SHT +4, ATH -1

Year	Team	Age	G	MPG	Usg	3PA%	FTA%	INS	2P%	3P%	FT%	TS%	Reb%	Ast%	TO%	BLK%	STL%	PF%	oRTG	dRTG	Win%	WARP
07-08	SEA	27.5	78	28.5	.164	.004	.088	1.085	.504	.000	.737	.536	.179	.022	.142	.019	.009	.049	104.4	105.1	.476	2.7
08-09	OKC	28.5	71	25.8	.136	.004	.107	1.103	.570	.000	.721	.599	.155	.016	.130	.020	.014	.058	105.3	106.2	.468	2.0
09-10	OKC	29.5	75	20.8	.122	.010	.112	1.103	.593	.250	.692	.616	.141	.011	.150	.023	.012	.067	104.4	106.2	.442	0.8
10-11p	OKC	30.5	74	20.0	.124	.005	.100	1.094	.564	.103	.705	.588	.144	.016	.144	.021	.012	.062	103.8	105.9	.431	0.5

Most similar to: Brian Skinner (97.7), Michael Cage, Clarence Weatherspoon, Rick Mahorn   IMP: 43%   BRK: 0%   COP: 12%

His individual statistics don't reflect it, but Nick Collison put together his best NBA campaign in 2009-10, emerging as the leader of the Thunder's young second unit and anchoring the Oklahoma City defense. Collison thrived in the more disciplined style taught by Ron Adams. Knowing where his teammates would funnel opposing perimeter players allowed Collison to be in the right position to take charges. He ended up drawing

57 of them in all, according to Hoopdata.com, more than any other player in the league. Collison's heads-up defense had an impact at the team level. BasketballValue.com showed Collison ranking third in the NBA in net defensive plus-minus. The Thunder allowed 7.6 fewer points per 100 possessions with Collison on the floor.

While Collison started just five games, his lowest total since his rookie season, he was often part of Oklahoma City's lineup to close games because of his defensive presence. Hardly a zero on offense, Collison also shot a career-best 59.3 percent on twos. He's cut back heavily on midrange jumpers the last two seasons, scoring primarily around the basket, where he is more efficient. Collison is due to drop off as he enters his 30s, but he's a consummate role player who should be able to extend his career by compensating for declining athleticism with his experience. Though the Thunder has plenty of bigs in the pipeline, the team would miss Collison's veteran presence if he heads elsewhere next summer.

SG 14 — Daequan Cook

Hght: 6'5" Exp: 3 Salary: $2.2 million
Wght: 210 From: Ohio State
2011-12 status: due qualifying offer of $3.1 million

SKILL RATINGS

TOT	OFF	DEF	REB	PAS	HND	SHT	ATH
-1	+1	+1	+1	-2	+1	-2	-4

Year	Team	Age	G	MPG	Usg	3PA%	FTA%	INS	2P%	3P%	FT%	TS%	Reb%	Ast%	TO%	BLK%	STL%	PF%	oRTG	dRTG	Win%	WARP
07-08	MIA	21.0	59	24.5	.199	.395	.042	.646	.424	.332	.825	.480	.075	.025	.105	.005	.007	.051	102.8	107.7	.345	-2.2
08-09	MIA	22.0	75	24.4	.183	.555	.035	.480	.356	.387	.875	.512	.062	.018	.059	.004	.011	.032	105.9	107.7	.442	1.0
09-10	MIA	23.0	45	15.4	.198	.438	.038	.601	.323	.317	.840	.422	.069	.030	.083	.012	.011	.034	102.7	106.6	.371	-0.7
10-11p	OKC	24.0	70	10.0	.196	.467	.043	.576	.384	.358	.861	.486	.070	.027	.078	.010	.011	.033	104.4	106.4	.434	0.3

Most similar to: Jeff Malone (95.9), Terry Teagle, Trent Tucker, Allan Houston   IMP: 76% BRK: 41% COP: 7%

Daequan Cook's business is long-distance shooting, and business was very bad last season. Cook started slowly, shooting 26.5 percent beyond the arc in the month of November, and never really recovered. By the All-Star break, he was out of the rotation for good, and he played just 15 minutes combined in March and April. Based on that performance, sacrificing Cook in the name of cap space was an easy call for Pat Riley, and he was bundled with a first-round pick and sent to Oklahoma City in exchange for a second-rounder the day before the draft.

For the Thunder, Cook is a free lottery ticket. If he rediscovers his three-point stroke, terrific. If not, Oklahoma City can cut ties at season's end. In James Harden, the Thunder already has one shooter off the bench, but spacing the floor remains the team's biggest weakness, so Cook could be a nice fit as the team's fourth wing. He'd help his cause by showing more versatility. Cook was a big-time rebounder in his lone season at Ohio State, but this skill has not followed him to the NBA, and he's been inconsistent at the defensive end of the floor. If he's going to play for the Thunder, he'll have to be up to speed on defense.

SF 35 — Kevin Durant

Hght: 6'9" Exp: 3 Salary: $6.1 million
Wght: 230 From: Texas
2011-12 status: guaranteed contract for $13.6 million

SKILL RATINGS

TOT	OFF	DEF	REB	PAS	HND	SHT	ATH
+5	+5	-2	+1	+3	-2	+2	+4

Year	Team	Age	G	MPG	Usg	3PA%	FTA%	INS	2P%	3P%	FT%	TS%	Reb%	Ast%	TO%	BLK%	STL%	PF%	oRTG	dRTG	Win%	WARP
07-08	SEA	19.6	80	34.6	.283	.114	.110	.996	.455	.288	.873	.520	.068	.030	.129	.020	.012	.019	103.3	105.4	.431	0.8
08-09	OKC	20.6	74	39.0	.285	.125	.125	1.000	.486	.422	.863	.577	.097	.032	.122	.014	.017	.021	107.1	105.6	.551	8.1
09-10	OKC	21.6	82	39.5	.322	.152	.160	1.008	.506	.365	.900	.607	.108	.032	.117	.019	.017	.024	110.0	104.0	.688	18.3
10-11p	OKC	22.6	76	39.0	.303	.139	.145	1.006	.502	.363	.888	.592	.095	.036	.115	.016	.016	.021	108.4	104.5	.625	12.9

Most similar to: Kobe Bryant (97.7), Carmelo Anthony, Shareef Abdur-Rahim, Tracy McGrady   IMP: 50% BRK: 8% COP: 4%

A complete list of players younger than 22 with more valuable seasons in terms of WARP than Kevin Durant's 2009-10 campaign: LeBron James and Shaquille O'Neal. End of list. Durant surpassed a who's who of NBA stars:

Table 1: Best Seasons, NBA Players Under 22

Player	Age	Season	Win%	WARP
LeBron James	20.3	2005	0.750	23.4
LeBron James	21.3	2006	0.741	22.6
Shaquille O'Neal	21.1	1993	0.710	18.4
Kevin Durant	21.6	2010	0.688	18.3
Tracy McGrady	21.9	2001	0.696	17.8
Tim Duncan	22.0	1998	0.671	16.7
Chris Paul	21.0	2006	0.688	15.7
Magic Johnson	20.7	1980	0.673	14.6
Dwight Howard	21.4	2007	0.646	14.4
Kevin Garnett	21.9	1998	0.618	13.2

In year three, Durant not only surpassed the hype but shattered it to pieces, delivering a superstar campaign. SCHOENE is still a tad suspicious of Durant's rapid rise, but there are a couple of reasons to believe it underrates Durant's potential. First, a projection system inevitably has to assume average development. Durant's work ethic is superhuman and has allowed him to refine his game each season. Second, it has become increasingly obvious that Durant's performance as a rookie was held back by P.J. Carlesimo's uninspired coaching. Take away the 2007-08 season and Durant's projection would be far more optimistic. (That the league's sixth-best WARP total could be considered negative shows just how incredible expectations are.)

Durant has emerged as the NBA's anti-superstar. He forgot to demand a trade this offseason and instead quietly signed a long-term extension to stay in Oklahoma City. He also didn't realize he was supposed to take the summer off, so he ended up the centerpiece of the USA team in the FIBA World Championship, winning MVP honors by leading the team to victory. Next season could see Durant go from League Pass hero to legitimate superstar and one of the NBA's most popular players.

PF 22 — Jeff Green

Hght: 6'9" Exp: 3 Salary: $4.5 million
Wght: 235 From: Georgetown
2011-12 status: due qualifying offer of $5.9 million

SKILL RATINGS

TOT	OFF	DEF	REB	PAS	HND	SHT	ATH
+2	+2	-5	-4	+1	0	+1	+1

Year	Team	Age	G	MPG	Usg	3PA%	FTA%	INS	2P%	3P%	FT%	TS%	Reb%	Ast%	TO%	BLK%	STL%	PF%	oRTG	dRTG	Win%	WARP
07-08	SEA	21.6	80	28.1	.196	.075	.104	1.028	.446	.276	.744	.492	.091	.023	.156	.015	.009	.038	101.1	106.4	.328	-4.1
08-09	OKC	22.6	78	36.8	.213	.179	.098	.919	.463	.389	.788	.536	.105	.024	.126	.008	.014	.031	104.7	106.6	.439	1.3
09-10	OKC	23.6	82	37.1	.193	.239	.075	.836	.503	.333	.740	.530	.091	.020	.104	.018	.017	.033	104.3	105.0	.476	3.8
10-11p	OKC	24.6	76	36.0	.201	.281	.090	.809	.493	.372	.776	.553	.089	.024	.117	.015	.015	.031	105.2	105.4	.493	4.4

Most similar to: Shane Battier (98.5), Danny Granger, Derrick McKey, Armon Gilliam

IMP: 64% BRK: 7% COP: 2%

This might be a make-or-break season for Jeff Green, who will likely be playing for a new contract. Unless he agrees to an extension, Green will be a restricted free agent at season's end, giving him the opportunity to translate a breakthrough campaign into a lucrative long-term deal. If Green struggles, however, he could be on his way out of Oklahoma City. Green's third NBA campaign failed to provide much clarity about the direction of his career. He made incremental strides and compensated for a drop in three-point percentage by shooting more accurately inside the arc. However, Green's rebounding slipped and he played a smaller role in the Thunder's offense. Both are troubling indicators.

Part of the issue might be that Green is more naturally a wing player with the ability to slide to the four. He's been used in exactly the opposite pattern in Oklahoma City, moving to small forward only when Kevin Durant is resting. As a power forward, Green is a major liability on the glass. To make up for that, he needs to be a dangerous threat on offense, and right now he is not. After a strong season beyond the arc in 2008-09, Green was below average from three-point range last season. That did not stop him from attempting more triples while getting to the free throw line less frequently. Green's athleticism is a plus at power forward in certain matchups, and he blocked more shots last season. Still, the Thunder was far better defensively with Serge Ibaka on the floor, and Oklahoma City improved by 9.2 points per 100 possessions overall when Green hit the bench. Given those numbers, it will be hard for the Thunder to justify spending big money on him.

SG 13	James Harden	Hght: 6'5" Exp: 1 Salary: $4.3 million						
		Wght: 220 From: Arizona State		**SKILL RATINGS**				
		2011-12 status: team option for $4.6 million	TOT	OFF	DEF	REB	PAS	HND	SHT	ATH
			+4	+4	+4	+2	0	-1	+3	+4

Year	Team	Age	G	MPG	Usg	3PA%	FTA%	INS	2P%	3P%	FT%	TS%	Reb%	Ast%	TO%	BLK%	STL%	PF%	oRTG	dRTG	Win%	WARP
09-10	OKC	20.7	76	22.9	.205	.314	.134	.820	.424	.375	.808	.551	.079	.036	.134	.009	.023	.052	106.2	105.8	.515	3.5
10-11p	OKC	21.7	75	24.0	.202	.338	.130	.792	.445	.413	.818	.585	.075	.038	.123	.011	.023	.051	107.5	105.5	.565	5.6

Most similar to: Ron Artest (95.8), J.R. Smith, Monta Ellis, C.J. Miles IMP: 69% BRK: 11% COP: 6%

Ordinarily, a No. 3 overall pick who did not start a single game during his rookie season despite good health would be considered a disappointment. In the case of James Harden, it was perfectly understandable. Thabo Sefolosha proved the better fit with the Oklahoma City starting lineup because of his exceptional defense, while the Thunder needed Harden's scoring punch coming off the bench. He still finished seventh among rookies in WARP in a solid debut campaign that suggested Harden should be a nice complementary player for Oklahoma City.

Harden has a complete offensive game. He answered any questions about his shooting range by knocking down 37.5 percent of his three-pointers, but was far more than just a spot-up shooter. In particular, Harden is very good at getting to the free throw line off the dribble. He has a knack for beating defenders without having exceptional burst, finding angles and using his size to make his way to the paint. Harden figures to take on more ballhandling duties as he matures and becomes more sure-handed. Defensively, Harden benefited from the good group of athletes around him. He plays the passing lanes well and has good instincts, but can be beaten by quicker players.

Year two should see Harden ramp up his minutes and finish more games. As good as Sefolosha is defensively, it's only a matter of time before Harden forces his way into the starting lineup.

C 9	Serge Ibaka	Hght: 6'10" Exp: 1 Salary: $1.2 million						
		Wght: 235 From: Brazzaville, Republic of Congo		**SKILL RATINGS**				
		2011-12 status: team option for $1.3 million	TOT	OFF	DEF	REB	PAS	HND	SHT	ATH
			+1	0	+1	+2	-5	-5	+4	-1

Year	Team	Age	G	MPG	Usg	3PA%	FTA%	INS	2P%	3P%	FT%	TS%	Reb%	Ast%	TO%	BLK%	STL%	PF%	oRTG	dRTG	Win%	WARP
09-10	OKC	20.6	73	18.1	.163	.004	.085	1.080	.543	.500	.630	.562	.171	.003	.142	.055	.010	.066	103.6	103.7	.497	2.2
10-11p	OKC	21.6	74	24.0	.164	.004	.083	1.079	.547	.542	.664	.567	.164	.004	.137	.050	.011	.062	103.3	103.7	.484	2.5

Most similar to: Tyson Chandler (97.0), Andris Biedrins, Al Jefferson, Jermaine O'Neal IMP: 50% BRK: 0% COP: 7%

It's been a remarkable ascent for Serge Ibaka. Two years removed from playing in the second division of the Spanish ACB, Ibaka played big minutes during his rookie season with the Thunder. Ibaka won a spot in the rotation early in the regular season and never relinquished it, developing his game from week to week and month to month. By the postseason, Ibaka saw the second-most minutes of any Oklahoma City post player, an indication of what lies in store for him.

In the early going, Ibaka was very raw, trying to block every shot and quickly racking up fouls. By the end of the year, he was much more confident and had improved his decision making. Offensively, Ibaka expanded his game, displaying 15- to 18-foot range on his jumper and even contributing the occasional post-up score. Ibaka is a very good shot blocker and rebounder, though he's better as a power forward at this stage of his career because he struggles badly defending one-on-one down low. The Thunder wisely used an unconventional platoon with Ibaka and Nick Collison, assigning Collison to the opposition's superior post scorer while allowing Ibaka to use his athleticism on the perimeter.

Ibaka is already knocking on the door of the starting lineup. The question is whether he'll ultimately settle in at the four, displacing Jeff Green, or improve his strength and play the center position.

OKLAHOMA CITY THUNDER

PG 7	Royal Ivey	Hght: 6'4" Wght: 215 2011-12 status: guaranteed contract for $1.2 million	Exp: 6 From: Texas	Salary: $1.1 million							
					SKILL RATINGS						
					TOT	OFF	DEF	REB	PAS	HND	SHT	ATH
					-2	0	-3	0	-4	+2	-4	0

Year	Team	Age	G	MPG	Usg	3PA%	FTA%	INS	2P%	3P%	FT%	TS%	Reb%	Ast%	TO%	BLK%	STL%	PF%	oRTG	dRTG	Win%	WARP
07-08	MIL	26.3	75	19.1	.159	.212	.102	.890	.422	.327	.726	.488	.049	.050	.151	.004	.014	.053	103.3	107.9	.353	-1.9
08-09	PHI	27.3	71	12.1	.133	.456	.076	.620	.319	.342	.791	.465	.053	.023	.092	.007	.022	.040	103.9	107.0	.399	-0.3
09-10	MIL	28.3	44	7.4	.139	.353	.053	.701	.438	.400	.750	.527	.062	.038	.111	.005	.030	.055	104.5	105.8	.458	0.3
10-11p	OKC	29.3	76	1.0	.124	.426	.065	.639	.417	.382	.750	.464	.055	.037	.115	.000	.023	.049	103.3	106.4	.399	0.0

Most similar to: Tony Brown (95.0), Lucious Harris, Bruce Bowen, Scott Burrell   IMP: 57% BRK: 9% COP: 0%

The Milwaukee Bucks wanted Royal Ivey back so badly after a season and a half with the Philadelphia 76ers that they worked out a four-player deadline deal. In truth, the Bucks were just looking for a third point guard after Roko Ukic agreed to a midseason buyout to go back to Europe, and Ivey fit the bill. He'll play the same role in Oklahoma City, giving the Thunder some depth in the backcourt and ensuring the position will be solid defensively in case of injuries.

Ivey has struggled to score efficiently throughout his NBA career. He's primarily a three-point shooter, yet is not especially accurate beyond the arc, so last season's .527 True Shooting Percentage in limited playing time was the best of his NBA career. As a point guard, Ivey is a stopgap. He's capable of getting teams into their offense, but isn't going to set up his teammates very frequently. Ivey is in the league primarily because of his defense. He can match up against either backcourt position thanks to his good size and quickness.

C 12	Nenad Krstic	Hght: 7'0" Wght: 240 2011-12 status: free agent	Exp: 6 From: Kraljevo, Serbia	Salary: $5.5 million							
					SKILL RATINGS						
					TOT	OFF	DEF	REB	PAS	HND	SHT	ATH
					-3	-1	-1	-2	-3	0	-2	-3

Year	Team	Age	G	MPG	Usg	3PA%	FTA%	INS	2P%	3P%	FT%	TS%	Reb%	Ast%	TO%	BLK%	STL%	PF%	oRTG	dRTG	Win%	WARP
07-08	NJN	24.7	45	18.0	.211	.005	.082	1.076	.413	.000	.754	.451	.143	.015	.110	.016	.005	.063	98.9	106.2	.271	-2.5
08-09	OKC	25.7	46	24.8	.190	.000	.071	1.071	.469	.000	.797	.504	.128	.011	.092	.032	.009	.044	102.9	105.8	.403	-0.3
09-10	OKC	26.7	76	22.9	.172	.008	.070	1.063	.505	.200	.717	.527	.125	.013	.087	.019	.009	.046	103.5	106.1	.415	-0.1
10-11p	OKC	27.7	75	22.0	.175	.012	.072	1.060	.476	.097	.747	.501	.125	.013	.095	.023	.008	.053	102.0	106.0	.369	-1.6

Most similar to: Malik Allen (98.6), Jason Collier, Cherokee Parks, Blair Rasmussen   IMP: 35% BRK: 6% COP: 6%

Nenad Krstic started all 76 games he played last season, but that overstates his role in a timeshare at center with Nick Collison. The two players ended up playing nearly equally, and Collison appears more likely to be re-signed next summer when both centers become free agents. Krstic's contribution to the Thunder's frontcourt rotation is his ability to knock down the midrange jumper. According to Hoopdata.com, Krstic shot an excellent 44.0 percent between 16 and 23 feet. He's effective in the pick-and-pop. The rest of Krstic's game is not up to par for a starting NBA center. He's adequate defensively and on the glass and rarely does much damage in the paint on offense. Uncomfortable banging with bigger players, Krstic made more long twos than shots at the rim last season.

Krstic made headlines over the summer while playing for the Serbian National Team. In a pre-World Championship "friendly," Krstic was involved in a wild melee against the Greek National Team that saw him punch the gargantuan Sofoklis Schortsanitis from behind before fleeing to the endline and attempting to defend himself by throwing a chair at Schortsanitis. Fortunately, Krstic's aim was poor, and the only minor damage he did was to teammate Ioannis Bouroussis. Krstic was suspended for the first two games of the World Championship, but the more severe punishment will surely come in the form of ribbing from teammates and opposing fans all season long.

OKLAHOMA CITY THUNDER

PG	Eric Maynor	Hght: 6'3"	Exp: 1	Salary: $1.4 million	SKILL RATINGS						
		Wght: 175	From: Virginia Commonwealth		TOT	OFF	DEF	REB	PAS	HND	SHT	ATH
6		2011-12 status: team option for $1.5 million			+1	+3	+3	0	+3	+4	-2	-1

Year	Team	Age	G	MPG	Usg	3PA%	FTA%	INS	2P%	3P%	FT%	TS%	Reb%	Ast%	TO%	BLK%	STL%	PF%	oRTG	dRTG	Win%	WARP
09-10	OKC	22.9	81	15.7	.173	.146	.065	.919	.444	.310	.722	.478	.058	.095	.175	.006	.016	.041	104.9	106.9	.435	0.5
10-11p	OKC	23.9	76	17.0	.175	.176	.072	.896	.452	.337	.741	.497	.057	.098	.159	.006	.016	.038	106.2	106.7	.485	1.9

Most similar to: Jason Terry (97.6), Dee Brown, Bimbo Coles, Luke Ridnour   IMP: 62%   BRK: 20%   COP: 2%

Oklahoma City turned backup point guard from a weakness to a strength with the addition of Eric Maynor in December. As a rookie, Maynor proved to be a quick study, posting the highest assist percentage of any backup point guard. Of the nine players with superior assist rates, six were All-Stars. He handed out assists at a high rate for both the Jazz and the Thunder, so his skill as a distributor appears to be legitimate. Maynor was also effective at the defensive end of the floor, where he has a size advantage against most of his opponents.

Development for Maynor will come mostly as a scorer, which is odd given that he averaged 22.4 points per game as a senior at Virginia Commonwealth. A volume scorer in college, Maynor was able to create shots at a good rate for a backup point guard but needs to find more ways to score efficiently. Improving his accuracy from beyond the arc would help in this regard. Maynor made up to 39.4 percent of his threes in college, but struggled with the NBA line. SCHOENE sees him bolstering his shooting percentages and cutting down his turnovers. If he makes good on that projection, he may quickly become overqualified for the limited minutes Oklahoma City has available behind starter Russell Westbrook.

C	Byron Mullens	Hght: 7'0"	Exp: 1	Salary: $1.2 million	SKILL RATINGS						
		Wght: 275	From: Ohio State		TOT	OFF	DEF	REB	PAS	HND	SHT	ATH
23		2011-12 status: team option for $1.3 million			-4	--	-1	--	--	--	--	--

Year	Team	Age	G	MPG	Usg	3PA%	FTA%	INS	2P%	3P%	FT%	TS%	Reb%	Ast%	TO%	BLK%	STL%	PF%	oRTG	dRTG	Win%	WARP
09-10	OKC	21.2	13	4.2	.192	.000	.000	1.000	.368	-	.368	.105	.008	.174	.000	.019	.109	96.0	108.6	.149	-0.3
10-11p	OKC	22.2	76	-	.203	.117	.082	.966	.413	.408	.668	.473	.124	.012	.145	.021	.010	.050	-	-	.343	-

Most similar to: Jeff Green (94.7), Jerrod Mustaf, Samaki Walker, Dirk Nowitzki   IMP: 69%   BRK: 25%   COP: 0%

Byron Mullens essentially took a redshirt season as a rookie, playing just 54 minutes for the Thunder. Oklahoma City utilized the D-League franchise it owns, the Tulsa 66ers, to get Mullens more game action. He played 27 games for the 66ers with mixed results. Most assigned players are more dominant in the D-League than Mullens was, and his translation suggests he is not yet ready to contribute at the NBA level.

The big red flag in Mullens' projected stat line is a conspicuous lack of blocked shots for a 7-footer. The same was true in his lone season at Ohio State. Mullens made up for it as a collegian by shooting a high percentage from the field, something he did not do in Tulsa. The Thunder knew all along that Mullens was going to be a project, but the addition of Cole Aldrich suggests Oklahoma City does not see him developing into a starter. Based on the results to date, Mullens might not even become a rotation player.

SG	Morris Peterson	Hght: 6'7"	Exp: 10	Salary: $6.7 million	SKILL RATINGS						
		Wght: 220	From: Michigan State		TOT	OFF	DEF	REB	PAS	HND	SHT	ATH
42		2011-12 status: free agent			-3	--	-4	--	--	--	--	--

Year	Team	Age	G	MPG	Usg	3PA%	FTA%	INS	2P%	3P%	FT%	TS%	Reb%	Ast%	TO%	BLK%	STL%	PF%	oRTG	dRTG	Win%	WARP
07-08	NOH	30.7	76	23.6	.155	.483	.063	.580	.445	.394	.765	.549	.068	.017	.069	.003	.012	.033	105.3	106.7	.453	1.4
08-09	NOH	31.7	43	12.0	.195	.412	.041	.629	.408	.388	.632	.499	.098	.015	.073	.003	.016	.048	104.7	107.0	.424	0.1
09-10	NOH	32.7	46	21.2	.166	.486	.068	.581	.415	.363	.611	.503	.077	.020	.077	.004	.013	.038	106.6	107.0	.486	1.4
10-11p	OKC	33.7	75	-	.155	.485	.056	.570	.421	.373	.647	.512	.079	.018	.074	.003	.012	.041	-	-	.379	-

Most similar to: Robert Reid (98.1), Scott Wedman, Anthony Peeler, Wesley Person   IMP: 45%   BRK: 2%   COP: 7%

OKLAHOMA CITY THUNDER

With Chris Bosh's defection to the Miami Heat, Morris Peterson's claim to fame as the all-time leader in games played in a Toronto Raptors uniform (542) is safe for the immediate future. The nearest active contender, Jose Calderon, is 183 games away. Andrea Bargnani is the most likely to surpass Peterson, but not for at least another three seasons.

Like many wing players, Peterson saw his game erode quickly once he hit his 30s. After one productive season in New Orleans, he spent 2008-09 battling injuries and was simply ineffective last year. Once an above-average wing defender, Peterson now gets torched. According to Synergy Sports, no wing player allowed opponents more points per play. On offense, Peterson contributes only via the three-pointer, and his accuracy dropped beyond the arc last season. The Hornets were thrilled to be rid of the last year of Peterson's contract. He's got an outside chance of carving out regular minutes on the wing for the Thunder, but his primary value to Oklahoma City will be as an expiring contract to offer at the trade deadline. If he contributes in the locker room before then, all the better.

SG 2 — Thabo Sefolosha

Hght: 6'7" Exp: 4 Salary: $3.3 million
Wght: 215 From: Vevey, Switzerland
2011-12 status: guaranteed contract for $3.6 million

SKILL RATINGS

TOT	OFF	DEF	REB	PAS	HND	SHT	ATH
+1	0	+2	+4	-1	+1	0	+3

Year	Team	Age	G	MPG	Usg	3PA%	FTA%	INS	2P%	3P%	FT%	TS%	Reb%	Ast%	TO%	BLK%	STL%	PF%	oRTG	dRTG	Win%	WARP
07-08	CHI	24.0	69	20.8	.173	.155	.082	.926	.452	.333	.721	.497	.102	.040	.166	.016	.019	.040	102.2	104.5	.423	0.2
08-09	OKC	25.0	66	22.0	.140	.192	.071	.879	.474	.276	.836	.500	.096	.034	.141	.023	.026	.032	103.3	104.2	.471	1.6
09-10	OKC	26.0	82	28.6	.110	.230	.069	.839	.494	.313	.674	.509	.093	.028	.158	.015	.021	.030	102.4	104.6	.425	0.4
10-11p	OKC	27.0	75	28.0	.127	.312	.067	.755	.488	.336	.741	.524	.091	.034	.147	.020	.022	.032	103.6	104.1	.482	2.9

Most similar to: Aaron McKie (97.7), Craig Ehlo, Bryon Russell, James Posey   IMP: 56% BRK: 13% COP: 5%

There tends to be a lag of a year or two between an NBA player's defensive performance and the perception of his defense. It's typically difficult for a player to break into the stopper category, as Thabo Sefolosha did last season.

Sefolosha rightly got much of the credit for Oklahoma City's defensive transformation, earning All-Defensive Second Team honors, and it helped that his size and Go-Go-Gadget arms made him an elite defensive prospect when he first entered the league. Sefolosha's defense slipped a bit down the stretch, and it was Kevin Durant who supplied the definitive defensive effort on Bryant during the series with the Lakers, but Sefolosha had already done enough to be considered the league's premier defender at the shooting guard position. On offense, Sefolosha is nothing better than adequate. His usage rate tanked as he became largely a spot-up shooter for the Thunder, which is not an ideal use of his skills. Sefolosha is best getting out in transition. He's a poor three-point shooter without the skills to create, which left him missing most of the shots he did take. Ultimately, Sefolosha's offensive limitations figure to put him behind James Harden in Oklahoma City's rotation. Still, his four-year, $13.8 million extension that kicks in this year will be a bargain for the Thunder.

PG 0 — Russell Westbrook

Hght: 6'3" Exp: 2 Salary: $4.0 million
Wght: 187 From: UCLA
2011-12 status: team option for $5.1 million

SKILL RATINGS

TOT	OFF	DEF	REB	PAS	HND	SHT	ATH
+4	+4	-3	+4	+3	0	-4	+4

Year	Team	Age	G	MPG	Usg	3PA%	FTA%	INS	2P%	3P%	FT%	TS%	Reb%	Ast%	TO%	BLK%	STL%	PF%	oRTG	dRTG	Win%	WARP
08-09	OKC	20.4	82	32.5	.260	.083	.121	1.038	.416	.271	.815	.490	.086	.073	.176	.004	.021	.032	106.2	106.9	.475	3.2
09-10	OKC	21.4	82	34.3	.259	.064	.115	1.051	.438	.221	.780	.491	.081	.105	.166	.009	.019	.033	107.9	105.8	.569	8.9
10-11p	OKC	22.4	76	34.0	.252	.090	.115	1.025	.444	.242	.799	.499	.079	.093	.155	.009	.019	.031	107.5	105.8	.558	7.7

Most similar to: Isiah Thomas (96.7), Allen Iverson, Stephon Marbury, Gilbert Arenas   IMP: 52% BRK: 13% COP: 9%

Russell Westbrook's stat lines in his first two seasons were virtually identical, but with one crucial difference: Westbrook pushed his assist percentage from average for a point guard to elite. He was one of eight players in the league to record an assist on at least 10 percent of his team's possessions. Suddenly, Westbrook no longer had to deal with questions about whether his long-term future was at shooting guard. He is a point guard, and one of the league's best young players at the position.

Westbrook's quickness ensures him a steady stream of trips to the paint, so the opportunities to set up teammates were always there and he did a better job of finding them in his second year. That helped because Westbrook is a volume driver, if there is such a thing. He gets to the rim constantly, but struggles badly to finish there. Per Hoopdata.com he made 52.7 percent of his at-rim attempts, up from 47.0 percent as a rookie but still far below average. Oklahoma City is better off when those drives turn into dishes or trips to the free throw line. To become a complete offensive player, Westbrook will also have to develop some semblance of a perimeter shot. The Lakers may have given other teams a template for defending him with the way they used Kobe Bryant to dare Westbrook to take 20-foot jumpers.

At UCLA, Westbrook was known primarily for his defense, but his numbers at that end of the floor were poor across the board last season. Playing with the Thunder's starting bigs, who were weaker defensively, does not entirely explain away these statistics. Westbrook will have to use his tools at both ends of the floor on a more regular basis.

C 3 — D.J. White

- Hght: 6'9" Exp: 2 Salary: $1.1 million
- Wght: 251 From: Indiana
- 2011-12 status: team option for $2.0 million

SKILL RATINGS

TOT	OFF	DEF	REB	PAS	HND	SHT	ATH
+1	--	0	--	--	--	--	--

Year	Team	Age	G	MPG	Usg	3PA%	FTA%	INS	2P%	3P%	FT%	TS%	Reb%	Ast%	TO%	BLK%	STL%	PF%	oRTG	dRTG	Win%	WARP
08-09	OKC	22.6	7	18.6	.201	.000	.097	1.097	.520	.000	.769	.556	.143	.021	.051	.028	.012	.034	106.6	105.0	.553	0.4
09-10	OKC	23.6	12	8.5	.214	.000	.091	1.091	.610	-	.900	.650	.129	.018	.062	.022	.025	.053	110.4	104.7	.676	0.6
10-11p	OKC	24.6	73	-	.166	.008	.080	1.072	.533	.000	.787	.561	.143	.011	.131	.026	.009	.045	-	-	.467	-

Most similar to: Victor Alexander (99.0), Stacey King, Michael Cage, Samaki Walker

IMP: 49% BRK: 12% COP: 5%

After jaw surgery cost D.J. White nearly all of his rookie season, he was mostly healthy in 2009-10, missing nine games due to a fractured right thumb. White simply could not crack the deep Oklahoma City frontcourt rotation, and his only contributions came at the D-League level. The addition of Cole Aldrich pushes White further down the Thunder depth chart, and his best hope of getting a chance to play NBA minutes is the possibility of a trade.

All the available evidence suggests White can play in the pros. His projection is based on his D-League translation and shows White to be a reasonably efficient scorer and good rebounder. He provided the same kind of play at Indiana University and has fared well in the extremely limited chances he has gotten in the NBA. White is a classic undersized post, compensating for his lack of height with a wide frame and good touch around the basket. He's also a decent athlete who can block the occasional shot.

C — — Tibor Pleiss

- Hght: 7'1" Exp: R Salary: --
- Wght: 242 From: Germany
- 2011-12 status: free agent

SKILL RATINGS

TOT	OFF	DEF	REB	PAS	HND	SHT	ATH
--	--	--	--	--	--	--	--

Sam Presti seems to favor a volume approach to the center position, taking chances on a high number of longshots in the hope of one or two panning out. 20-year-old German Tibor Pleiss is the latest gamble on a 7-footer. The Thunder took Pleiss with the first pick of the second round, purchased from Atlanta. He's likely to spend another year or two playing for Brose Baskets, which will compete in Euroleague this season, before coming to the NBA. Nicknamed "the Octopus," Pleiss saw solid minutes in EuroCup play last year, though not quite enough to generate a projection. His EuroCup numbers suggest he's got a lot of work to do as a scorer, but he was very impressive on the glass.

Pleiss, who played for the German National Team in the World Championship, gained some measure of NBA notoriety when an interview he conducted with sprox.com was translated by europeanprospects.com. The highlight: "I did not know anyone of all those college players; also this guy called Wall, I have never heard of him before."

OKLAHOMA CITY THUNDER

PF	Ryan Reid	Hght: 6'8" Wght: 232 2011-12 status: free agent	Exp: R From: Florida State Salary: --	SKILL RATINGS							
				TOT	OFF	DEF	REB	PAS	HND	SHT	ATH
				-5	--	--	--	--	--	--	--

Year	Team	Age	G	MPG	Usg	3PA%	FTA%	INS	2P%	3P%	FT%	TS%	Reb%	Ast%	TO%	BLK%	STL%	PF%	oRTG	dRTG	Win%	WARP
10-11p	OKC	24.5	76	-	.103	.033	.097	1.064	.517	.200	.673	.537	.112	.012	.134	.032	.011	.070	-	-	.303	-

Most similar to: Brian Scalabrine (96.4), Britton Johnsen, Luke Walton, Hanno Mottola   IMP: -   BRK: -   COP: -

Arguably the most obscure American draft pick this decade, Ryan Reid was picked 57th overall despite averaging just 6.8 points and 4.0 rebounds per game as a senior at Florida State. There is little in his statistics to suggest he can be an NBA contributor, but Reid's ability as an individual defender was intriguing to the Thunder. He played for the NCAA's best defensive team as a senior at Florida State. Reid will play in Tulsa next season while Oklahoma City retains his rights.

SF	Latavious Williams	Hght: 6'8" Wght: 195 2011-12 status: free agent	Exp: R From: Life Center Academy (MS) Salary: --	SKILL RATINGS							
				TOT	OFF	DEF	REB	PAS	HND	SHT	ATH
				+2	--	--	--	--	--	--	--

Year	Team	Age	G	MPG	Usg	3PA%	FTA%	INS	2P%	3P%	FT%	TS%	Reb%	Ast%	TO%	BLK%	STL%	PF%	oRTG	dRTG	Win%	WARP
10-11p	OKC	22.1	76	-	.147	.035	.091	1.055	.486	.072	.585	.489	.191	.012	.128	.027	.016	.062	-	-	.511	-

Most similar to: Dorell Wright (95.3), Lorenzen Wright, Kwame Brown, Stromile Swift   IMP: 68%   BRK: 13%   COP: 0%

Latavious Williams is the first of his kind, a player who was ineligible to play college basketball (he was committed to Memphis) and chose to make his way to the NBA through the D-League. The Tulsa 66ers selected Williams in the D-League Draft, and the big club surely kept a close eye on his development. Lo and behold, when he became eligible for the draft Oklahoma City selected Williams with a second-round pick purchased from Miami. Williams is expected to return to Tulsa to continue his development.

Williams has the frame of a small forward, but his forte in the D-League was cleaning the glass. His projection suggests he would be one of the NBA's top 15 rebounders immediately. Williams also put his athleticism to use at the defensive end, racking up blocks and steals at good rates. Williams will have to work to become a more efficient offensive player. He shot a decent percentage on two-point attempts, but since he does not have three-point range and was inaccurate when he got to the line, it's an empty field-goal percentage. While Williams is inexperienced, he's not exactly young; he'll be 22 during the season, so his upside is probably limited to becoming a solid role player.

SF	Ryan Bowen	Hght: 6'7" Wght: 215 2011-12 status: free agent	Exp: 10 From: Iowa Salary: --	SKILL RATINGS							
				TOT	OFF	DEF	REB	PAS	HND	SHT	ATH
				-4	-1	+1	-1	-3	+3	-1	+3

Year	Team	Age	G	MPG	Usg	3PA%	FTA%	INS	2P%	3P%	FT%	TS%	Reb%	Ast%	TO%	BLK%	STL%	PF%	oRTG	dRTG	Win%	WARP
07-08	NOH	32.4	53	12.4	.091	.008	.100	1.092	.495	.000	.552	.505	.089	.018	.117	.013	.023	.055	102.0	105.8	.376	-0.6
08-09	NOH	33.4	21	10.4	.100	.000	.049	1.049	.579	.000	.600	.585	.066	.020	.111	.019	.034	.082	102.6	106.1	.383	-0.2
09-10	OKC	34.4	1	8.0	.106	.000	.468	1.468	1.000	-	1.000	1.064	.144	.000	.000	.000	.063	.113	116.0	103.6	.828	0.1
10-11p	AVG	35.4	76	8.0	.080	.017	.091	1.074	.484	.000	.544	.491	.082	.016	.117	.013	.024	.060	101.7	106.2	.353	-0.8

Most similar to: Stacey Augmon (94.8), Derrick McKey, Grant Long, Jerome Kersey   IMP: 51%   BRK: 3%   COP: 6%

Veteran overachiever Ryan Bowen made the Thunder's roster out of training camp but was gone by the end of November, having played only one game for Oklahoma City. A quintessential effort and energy player, Bowen has put together a 10-year NBA career despite limited athleticism and poor shooting. Most likely, this is the end of the line for him.

OKLAHOMA CITY THUNDER

PG — Kevin Ollie

Hght: 6'2" Wght: 195 Exp: 13 From: Connecticut Salary: --
2011-12 status: free agent

SKILL RATINGS: TOT --, OFF --, DEF --, REB --, PAS --, HND --, SHT --, ATH --

Year	Team	Age	G	MPG	Usg	3PA%	FTA%	INS	2P%	3P%	FT%	TS%	Reb%	Ast%	TO%	BLK%	STL%	PF%	oRTG	dRTG	Win%	WARP
07-08	PHI	35.3	40	7.5	.122	.012	.082	1.069	.426	.000	.800	.463	.038	.058	.062	.000	.016	.044	102.3	107.5	.333	-0.5
08-09	MIN	36.3	50	17.0	.121	.004	.187	1.182	.409	.000	.833	.525	.053	.062	.150	.004	.012	.042	103.6	108.4	.346	-1.2
09-10	OKC	37.3	25	10.5	.094	.018	.065	1.046	.409	.000	1.000	.453	.053	.034	.110	.000	.017	.027	100.1	106.8	.289	-0.7

Respected veteran point guard Kevin Ollie signed with the Thunder in hopes of serving as Russell Westbrook's backup, but the addition of Eric Maynor pushed Ollie to third string when he returned from arthroscopic surgery that sidelined him from November through January. While he played sparingly, Ollie still served as a leader in the young Oklahoma City locker room before deciding to call it a career at season's end. Ollie played for 12 teams in 13 years and made himself a fixture despite entering the league as an undrafted rookie. He'll put his experience to use as an assistant coach under Jim Calhoun at his alma mater. Expect Ollie to become a rising star in the coaching ranks.

PG — Mike Wilks

Hght: 5'10" Wght: 185 Exp: 7 From: Rice Salary: --
2011-12 status: free agent

SKILL RATINGS: TOT --, OFF --, DEF --, REB --, PAS --, HND --, SHT --, ATH --

Year	Team	Age	G	MPG	Usg	3PA%	FTA%	INS	2P%	3P%	FT%	TS%	Reb%	Ast%	TO%	BLK%	STL%	PF%	oRTG	dRTG	Win%	WARP
07-08	SEA	29.0	15	12.5	.107	.175	.038	.864	.500	.375	1.000	.543	.055	.033	.175	.000	.021	.030	102.0	106.1	.366	-0.2
09-10	OKC	31.0	4	14.8	.136	.169	.099	.930	.444	.667	.500	.581	.038	.031	.225	.000	.000	.038	102.2	109.7	.270	-0.2

When backup point guards Shaun Livingston and Kevin Ollie were both sidelined by injuries prior to the arrival of Eric Maynor, Oklahoma City put in a call to veteran Mike Wilks to spell Russell Westbrook. The well-traveled guard played four games during his third separate tour of duty with the organization. Wilks is a nice stopgap option at the point; he's heady and has decent scoring punch for a third point guard. He played well when he got extended minutes in Seattle. Wilks' size has worked against him throughout his career. Instead of waiting around for another 10-day contract, Wilks signed with Polish champion Asseco Prokom for the upcoming season.

Orlando Magic

Through the first two rounds of the 2010 playoffs, the Orlando Magic was the league's best team. Orlando won 59 games and the Southeast Division, posted the NBA's best point differential and swept the first two rounds of the playoffs, embarrassing the Atlanta Hawks in a semifinal matchup of 50-win teams. Unfortunately, they don't give out trophies for the first two rounds. In the Eastern Conference Finals, the Magic fell victim to the same kind of upset they'd pulled off against the Cleveland Cavaliers in the conference finals the year before, losing 4-2 to the Boston Celtics.

There should be little shame in coming up short against the Celtics, who upset the 61-win Cavaliers before taking the Los Angeles Lakers a full seven games in the NBA Finals. However, Orlando has to feel like its best chance for winning a championship slipped away at the hands of the Celtics. Had LeBron James gone to New York or New Jersey, the Magic would have been the favorites to win the East. Now, the team has become something of an afterthought behind the Miami Heat's power trio of James, Chris Bosh and Dwyane Wade.

The 2009-10 season was not entirely smooth from start to finish. Orlando began the year trying to adjust to major changes on the perimeter. The team got Jameer Nelson back in the lineup after shoulder surgery had sidelined him for the second half of the regular season and the run to the 2009 NBA Finals. Nelson returned to play off the bench against the Lakers in the Finals before reclaiming his job as the starter at the point when he was fully healthy for the start of training camp.

Meanwhile, the Magic's boldest move of the offseason sent two expiring contracts (guard Rafer Alston and center Tony Battie) with second-year guard Courtney Lee to New Jersey for veteran guard Vince Carter. The idea was that Carter would replace forward Hedo Turkoglu, whom Orlando general manager Otis Smith let walk because of the outlandish contract offers he got as an unrestricted free agent.

Carter's combination of ballhandling, passing and shooting skills allowed him to fill Turkoglu's role as a creator on the wing, while newly-signed Matt Barnes stepped into the starting spot at small forward and replaced Lee as a perimeter stopper.

It took some time for the Magic to adjust to the new combination, a process that was slowed when Nelson missed nearly the entire month of December after undergoing arthroscopic knee surgery. Actually, Orlando played quite well without Nelson. Backup Jason Williams capably stepped into the lineup and led the Magic to a 14-4 record in a starting role. Orlando struggled in January, when Nelson was working his way back from surgery and Carter slumped badly, going 9-8 in the month.

By the start of February, the issues were forgotten and the Magic was the league's hottest team over the last two months of the season, finishing the campaign on a 30-7 tear. The run continued unabated into

MAGIC IN A BOX

Last year's record	59-23
Last year's Offensive Rating	114.0 (2)
Last year's Defensive Rating	104.4 (2)
Last year's point differential	7.5 (1)
Team pace	90.4 (18)
SCHOENE projection	52-30 (2)
Projected Offensive Rating	112.3 (8)
Projected Defensive Rating	107.7 (4)
Projected team weighted age	29.0 (6)
Projected '10-11 payroll	$95.7 (1)
Est. payroll obligations, '11-12	$99.1 (1)
Head coach: Stan Van Gundy	

Van Gundy added another standout line to one of the league's best coaching résumés in 2009-10, leading the Magic to 59 wins for the second consecutive season. Orlando was the NBA's most balanced team, ranking second in both Offensive and Defensive Rating. Van Gundy is a phenomenal defensive coach who has been able to get the most out of a unique set of offensive parts. He also showed his adaptability last season, toning down his complaining to his team after Dwight Howard asked him to ease up. Being able to motivate the Magic without losing the team will be Van Gundy's challenge in years to come.

the postseason, where Orlando was the only team to sweep its first-round matchup (against Charlotte) and then outscored Atlanta by an average of 25.3 points per game during an embarrassingly lopsided sweep.

Boston quickly served notice that the Magic would not have things so easy during the Eastern Conference Finals, stealing Game One of the series on the road against a flat Orlando squad and following it up with another narrow win in Game Two. A blowout loss back at the TD Garden in Game Three left the Magic on the verge of suffering a sweep, but Orlando rallied to win Game Four in overtime and put together by far its best effort of the series back home for Game Five. By that point, the Magic could envision becoming the first team in league history to come back from a 3-0 deficit, but the Celtics crushed that dream and ended the series with a win in Game Six.

What cost Orlando in the series was its inability to produce beyond the arc. The Magic set a new NBA record with 841 three-pointers during the regular season, an average of more than 10 per game, and tied for third in the league by hitting threes at a 37.5 percent clip. Boston emphasized staying at home and held Orlando to 33.8 percent shooting from long distance. Had the Magic hit at its regular-season percentage, the two teams would have been separated by just two points over the course of the series. Forward Rashard Lewis, who was rendered invisible by Kevin Garnett, was the worst culprit. Lewis shot 4-of-23 (17.4 percent) from downtown and averaged just 8.2 points per game in the conference finals.

Wisely, Orlando resisted the temptation to overreact to the disappointing series. Though the Magic made some changes during the offseason, they were mostly tweaks to the established core. Orlando solidified the franchise's direction by signing head coach Stan Van Gundy to a contract extension and promoting Smith, who is now president of basketball operations.

On the court, the biggest change is at small forward, where Barnes was allowed to leave for the L.A. Lakers as a free agent. The Magic filled his spot in the lineup by signing Quentin Richardson away from the Miami Heat to a four-year, $10.8 million contract. Orlando used the rest of its mid-level exception to sign Chris Duhon for four years and $15 million to have a long-term backup for Nelson. Williams ended up re-signing and will become an overqualified third-stringer.

The Magic's other notable free agent was shooting guard J.J. Redick, who became coveted after a strong postseason. Chicago offered Redick, a restricted free

From the Blogosphere

Who: Evan Dunlap
What: Orlando Pinstriped Post
Where: http://www.orlandopinstripedpost.com/

Remarkably, the Orlando Magic fielded the league's second-most efficient offense despite seeing its highest-usage player, Vince Carter, ending plays ineffectively. A failure to adapt to Orlando's drive-and-kick offense marred his November and December--still looking for his shot first, he averaged 18.3 shooting possessions per game--while nagging injuries to his left shoulder and both ankles made his January miserable, to the tune of a 38.7 percent True Shooting Percentage and 8.7 points per game. A more balanced approach helped him play at an All-Star level from February to the end of the regular season, but he still had a down year overall, ranking second to last on the team in True Shooting; his backcourt-mate, Jameer Nelson, was a mere one one-thousandth of a percent worse. If Carter can duplicate his late-season form, Orlando could lead the league in offense. Defense shouldn't be a concern here. A return to the Finals is not out of the question.

Who: Eddy Rivera
What: MagicBasketball.net
Where: http://www.magicbasketball.net/

In the state of Florida, all eyes will be on the Miami Heat. But if there's somebody that is worth keeping tabs on for the Orlando Magic, it's Dwight Howard. After losing to the Boston Celtics in the 2010 NBA Eastern Conference Finals, Howard enlisted the help of Hakeem Olajuwon during the summer so that he could continue to expand and improve his low-post game. Given what's at stake for the Magic, Howard must take his skills to the next level if he wants to lead his team to the promised land. Howard is the best defensive player in the NBA, but there's no question that he needs to be equally as dominant on offense for Orlando to win a championship. Olajuwon's wisdom is invaluable, in this case, because he's been telling Howard not to be afraid to use his full arsenal of moves and not to hesitate from doing anything on the floor. Can Howard fully evolve into a devastating two-way player? We'll find out soon enough.

agent, a three-year, $20 million deal (with just two years guaranteed). The Magic matched, taking the team's payroll past the $90 million mark. Though the Bulls envisioned Redick as a starter at shooting guard, he will remain a backup in Orlando, making the price awfully steep.

Orlando should benefit financially from moving into the brand-new Amway Center this fall. (Not to be confused with Amway Arena, the Magic's old home. In something less than a coincidence, Orlando owner Rich DeVos is the co-founder of Amway.) Nonetheless, having one of the league's highest payrolls puts the onus on the Magic to win and win big. The biggest threat to that objective lies south along Florida's Turnpike. SCHOENE's projections agree with the conventional wisdom that Orlando and Miami are headed for a blockbuster collision in the Eastern Conference Finals, with the Heat as the favorite in that series.

The Magic's hopes for winning such a matchup would rest on the team's continuity, shooting and superior team defense. This offseason reinforced all three attributes. Orlando brings back 10 of the 12 players that saw action last season, and newcomers Duhon and Richardson fit in to the Magic's system nicely. Both players are capable three-point shooters. Duhon will be an upgrade defensively over Williams, who has become a liability at that end of the floor.

What is less clear is Orlando's long-term plan, especially if Miami establishes itself as the favorite to win championships as long as Bosh, James and Wade play together. The Magic will have to decide at the ownership level how long it can sustain exorbitant payrolls in the name of maintaining one of the league's deepest rosters.

Carter's contract offers a possible out. Since his salary for 2011-12 is only partially guaranteed, it is unlikely Orlando will be content to pay him $19 million for his age-35 season. Players similar to Carter were worth an average of just 2.5 WARP at the same age. The Magic must then choose whether to waive Carter and take advantage of the savings or use his contract as a valuable trade chip. Should Redick continue to play well enough in a reserve role to indicate he's ready to take on more minutes as a starter, Orlando will have few needs to fill in a trade. Magic fans will continue to dream of using Carter's contract and Nelson as part of a trade to land Chris Paul in Orlando.

A trade is also likely at some point in the next year or two in the frontcourt, which is flush with talent behind the starting duo of Lewis and Dwight Howard. The Magic added Ryan Anderson as part of the Carter trade last summer and signed Brandon Bass while also matching an offer to center Marcin Gortat, creating a logjam for playing time. Bass was the odd man out in 2009-10. He could see more playing time this season with Lewis shifting to small forward against certain matchups, but making room for five regulars in the frontcourt is all but impossible. The most probable scenario is a trade involving either Bass or Gortat, which could provide salary relief.

Orlando has built one of the strongest teams possible around Howard using the old NBA model of a single superstar and a supporting cast. Under ordinary circumstances, the Magic would be one of the favorites to win this year's championship. Unfortunately for Orlando, the Heat changed the game this summer. The Magic will be there if Miami falters, but the window is starting to close ever so slightly. Smith will need to navigate the next couple of seasons expertly to maintain Orlando's chances of capping what has been a very successful three-year run with a championship.

Kevin Pelton

ORLANDO MAGIC

MAGIC FIVE-YEAR TRENDS

Season	AGE	W-L	POW	PYTH	SEED	ORTG	DRTG	PT DIFF	PACE
05-06	25.5	36-46	35.6 (22)	37.8	---	107.9 (14)	109.0 (22)	-1.1 (17)	87.0 (23)
06-07	25.6	40-42	40.5 (14)	43.4	8	106.3 (22)	105.9 (7)	0.8 (11)	88.5 (25)
07-08	26.7	52-30	52.2 (11)	55.7	3	114.1 (5)	107.5 (5)	5.5 (5)	91.3 (9)
08-09	27.3	59-23	58.3 (4)	59.3	3	111.7 (9)	103.0 (1)	6.7 (4)	90.8 (12)
09-10	28.7	59-23	59.4 (1)	60.9	2	114.0 (2)	104.4 (2)	7.5 (1)	90.4 (18)

		OFFENSE				DEFENSE			
Season	PAY	eFG	oREB	FT/FGA	TO	eFG	oREB	FT/FGA	TO
05-06	$52.9	.496 (9)	.285 (9)	.270 (6)	.172 (25)	.490 (15)	.725 (16)	.264 (24)	.152 (26)
06-07	$60.5	.500 (13)	.293 (4)	.276 (5)	.191 (30)	.480 (6)	.737 (13)	.286 (29)	.169 (12)
07-08	$61.8	.537 (2)	.234 (27)	.256 (9)	.151 (14)	.484 (6)	.749 (6)	.217 (14)	.139 (24)
08-09	$69.7	.520 (3)	.240 (28)	.251 (6)	.153 (15)	.466 (1)	.760 (2)	.209 (4)	.144 (25)
09-10	$82.1	.536 (2)	.246 (25)	.246 (7)	.155 (17)	.477 (1)	.774 (1)	.205 (4)	.141 (26)

(league rankings in parenthesis)

PF 35 — Malik Allen
Hght: 6'10" Exp: 9 Salary: $1.2 million
Wght: 255 From: Villanova
2011-12 status: free agent

SKILL RATINGS: TOT -5 | OFF -- | DEF 0 | REB -- | PAS -- | HND -- | SHT -- | ATH --

Year	Team	Age	G	MPG	Usg	3PA%	FTA%	INS	2P%	3P%	FT%	TS%	Reb%	Ast%	TO%	BLK%	STL%	PF%	oRTG	dRTG	Win%	WARP
07-08	DAL	29.8	73	15.0	.163	.008	.029	1.021	.483	.333	.920	.501	.102	.019	.118	.021	.008	.063	101.4	106.6	.331	-2.0
08-09	MIL	30.8	49	11.8	.155	.005	.046	1.041	.432	.000	.476	.435	.107	.027	.100	.017	.006	.069	101.1	108.3	.277	-1.7
09-10	DEN	31.8	51	8.9	.140	.042	.040	.998	.409	.167	.923	.431	.104	.016	.153	.008	.012	.066	100.5	107.9	.270	-1.4
10-11p	ORL	32.8	76	-	.143	.023	.038	1.015	.428	.146	.806	.443	.097	.020	.130	.014	.010	.069	-	-	.305	-

Most similar to: Greg Foster (98.5), Marc Iavaroni, Joe Wolf, Jerome Whitehead

IMP: 49% BRK: 18% COP: 16%

Malik Allen has carved out a nine-year NBA career despite rating above replacement level just once--his rookie 2002-03 campaign in Miami, when he played 161 minutes. In its own way, that is quite an impressive feat. Whatever skills Allen once had, they have deteriorated now that he is in his 30s. Allen is inefficient, does not create his own shot and is a poor rebounder and defender for his position. Allen signed on with Orlando for training camp, reuniting him with Stan Van Gundy, his coach in Miami. However, Allen will have a tough time cracking the deep Magic roster.

PF 33 — Ryan Anderson
Hght: 6'10" Exp: 2 Salary: $1.4 million
Wght: 240 From: California
2011-12 status: guaranteed contract for $2.2 million

SKILL RATINGS: TOT +4 | OFF +5 | DEF +3 | REB 0 | PAS +1 | HND -2 | SHT +1 | ATH +1

Year	Team	Age	G	MPG	Usg	3PA%	FTA%	INS	2P%	3P%	FT%	TS%	Reb%	Ast%	TO%	BLK%	STL%	PF%	oRTG	dRTG	Win%	WARP
08-09	NJN	21.0	66	19.9	.187	.363	.098	.735	.417	.365	.845	.532	.142	.019	.121	.012	.018	.056	107.1	106.3	.527	3.0
09-10	ORL	22.0	63	14.4	.246	.440	.075	.636	.514	.370	.866	.574	.127	.019	.117	.011	.014	.041	109.8	105.9	.625	4.0
10-11p	ORL	23.0	75	15.0	.239	.385	.091	.706	.488	.356	.861	.559	.129	.023	.117	.009	.014	.044	108.5	105.8	.587	4.0

Most similar to: Vladimir Radmanovic (96.0), Rashard Lewis, Quentin Richardson, Tim Thomas

IMP: 57% BRK: 7% COP: 3%

The most valuable player in the Vince Carter trade just might end up being "throw-in" Ryan Anderson. A perfect fit for Orlando's three-happy offense, Anderson enjoyed a strong campaign off the bench and looks like the eventual replacement for Rashard Lewis at power forward. Anderson is a shooter first and foremost, attempting more threes than twos a year ago. Although Anderson still has yet to knock down threes at an elite clip over the course of a season, his frequent attempts force opposing defenders to respect him and think twice before helping in the paint.

Anderson is much more than just a specialist, however. He's got enough size to match up with fours at the defensive end and he more than holds his own on the defensive glass. Anderson's individual defense is the weakest aspect of his game, since he is slow laterally. Still, the Magic will look past that to take advantage of Anderson's offensive production. He used nearly a quarter of Orlando's plays while on the floor last season, providing volume on offense to go with his efficiency, and was able to create his own offense at times. Only the Magic's depth up front is keeping Anderson from playing more minutes.

PF 30	Brandon Bass	Hght: 6'8" Wght: 250 2011-12 status: guaranteed contract for $4.0 million	Exp: 5 From: Louisiana State	Salary: $4.0 million	SKILL RATINGS							
					TOT	OFF	DEF	REB	PAS	HND	SHT	ATH
					0	+1	0	-2	-2	-3	0	-1

Year	Team	Age	G	MPG	Usg	3PA%	FTA%	INS	2P%	3P%	FT%	TS%	Reb%	Ast%	TO%	BLK%	STL%	PF%	oRTG	dRTG	Win%	WARP
07-08	DAL	23.0	79	19.7	.200	.006	.131	1.125	.503	.000	.822	.564	.128	.017	.124	.023	.007	.045	104.6	105.6	.466	1.6
08-09	DAL	24.0	81	19.4	.201	.009	.135	1.126	.502	.000	.867	.571	.134	.013	.125	.026	.009	.041	105.2	106.0	.472	1.8
09-10	ORL	25.0	50	13.0	.210	.000	.095	1.095	.511	-	.825	.556	.113	.014	.106	.031	.009	.050	105.0	105.9	.470	0.7
10-11p	ORL	26.0	76	11.0	.205	.010	.106	1.096	.507	.006	.849	.556	.114	.015	.111	.027	.008	.044	104.5	105.9	.454	0.7

Most similar to: Lorenzen Wright (98.0), Brian Grant, Alan Henderson, Antoine Carr   IMP: 40%   BRK: 5%   COP: 13%

Brandon Bass became a favorite of traditionalist Orlando fans who blame the Magic's small lineup for the team's shortcomings. Any time something went wrong, those fans cried out for Stan Van Gundy to move Rashard Lewis to small forward and play Bass at power forward. The wailing intensified during the Eastern Conference Finals, when Bass played well in limited action. Essentially, Bass was the beloved backup quarterback, and that story usually ends with the player being exposed when they do get a chance. Bass is strictly an average reserve, and his poor rebounding undercuts the notion that playing him would really strengthen the Magic's weaknesses.

Bass is certainly overqualified for his current role as Orlando's fifth big man. He's a productive offensive player who gets frequent second-chance scores and has become an accurate midrange shooter. Defensively, Bass' lack of height works against him. He'll block shots thanks to his long arms, but his average vertical makes him a poor defensive rebounder. Bass is OK as a power forward, but when teams have tried to use him as a center they have been burned.

SG 15	Vince Carter	Hght: 6'6" Wght: 220 2011-12 status: partially-guaranteed contract for $18.9 million	Exp: 12 From: North Carolina	Salary: $17.5 million	SKILL RATINGS							
					TOT	OFF	DEF	REB	PAS	HND	SHT	ATH
					+3	+4	+1	+1	+3	+3	-1	-1

Year	Team	Age	G	MPG	Usg	3PA%	FTA%	INS	2P%	3P%	FT%	TS%	Reb%	Ast%	TO%	BLK%	STL%	PF%	oRTG	dRTG	Win%	WARP
07-08	NJN	31.2	76	39.0	.258	.165	.114	.949	.482	.359	.816	.550	.089	.061	.109	.009	.014	.038	107.8	105.9	.564	9.1
08-09	NJN	32.2	80	36.8	.270	.232	.107	.875	.459	.385	.817	.545	.084	.060	.098	.011	.015	.037	109.4	107.0	.578	9.9
09-10	ORL	33.2	75	30.8	.253	.258	.107	.849	.456	.367	.840	.541	.071	.048	.084	.006	.012	.038	107.7	106.7	.534	5.6
10-11p	ORL	34.2	75	30.0	.245	.243	.100	.856	.462	.357	.821	.534	.071	.052	.098	.008	.012	.039	107.2	106.5	.522	5.0

Most similar to: Walter Davis (97.8), Ricky Pierce, Rolando Blackman, Mitch Richmond   IMP: 37%   BRK: 2%   COP: 4%

Despite going from a lottery team to a championship contender, Vince Carter actually maintained a higher usage rate throughout the first half of last season. Somewhere along the line, Carter noticed that he had a variety of talented offensive teammates and decided to defer to them. After the All-Star break, Carter's usage rate declined from 27.2 percent of Orlando's plays to 22.3 percent, while his True Shooting Percentage went the opposite direction--skyrocketing from 50.7 percent to 60.9 percent.

Carter remains skilled enough to be dangerous as a secondary weapon, but he can no longer carry an offense by himself because the drives of his youth have turned into contested jumpers. The former Air Canada had just 28 dunks last season, per CBSSports.com, putting him just behind Rasual Butler (29). Needless to say, Carter's athleticism isn't coming back, and the track record for wings at his age is very poor. Working in Carter's favor is his versatility. His continued success will depend on him maintaining the same kind of restraint he showed in the second half of the season. Since his 2011-12 contract is only partially guaranteed, Carter will have plenty of motivation to play well this season.

ORLANDO MAGIC

PG 25 — Chris Duhon

Hght: 6'1" Wght: 190 Exp: 6 From: Duke Salary: $3.5 million
2011-12 status: guaranteed contract for $3.7 million

SKILL RATINGS

TOT	OFF	DEF	REB	PAS	HND	SHT	ATH
+2	+4	-3	-3	+2	+3	+1	-4

Year	Team	Age	G	MPG	Usg	3PA%	FTA%	INS	2P%	3P%	FT%	TS%	Reb%	Ast%	TO%	BLK%	STL%	PF%	oRTG	dRTG	Win%	WARP
07-08	CHI	25.6	66	22.6	.134	.344	.078	.734	.418	.348	.813	.508	.045	.078	.158	.001	.014	.028	105.6	106.9	.459	1.3
08-09	NYK	26.6	79	36.8	.149	.327	.093	.765	.451	.391	.856	.570	.047	.085	.223	.002	.012	.019	107.2	107.8	.481	3.9
09-10	NYK	27.6	67	30.9	.132	.428	.069	.641	.404	.349	.716	.501	.049	.083	.182	.001	.014	.018	106.3	107.2	.471	2.3
10-11p	ORL	28.6	73	16.7	.142	.457	.080	.623	.423	.374	.794	.547	.044	.081	.186	.001	.013	.020	107.3	106.9	.512	2.5

Most similar to: Steve Blake (97.9), Phil Ford, Bimbo Coles, John Bagley

IMP: 57%   BRK: 13%   COP: 2%

There was plenty of blame to go around for the Knicks' disappointing 2009-10 campaign, and much of it got showered on Chris Duhon despite the fact that he essentially played at his usual level of performance. Mike D'Antoni got credit for turning Duhon's career around during his first year of New York, when the Suns were flailing and D'Antoni looked like a mastermind. As it turned out, Duhon's improvement was a case of fluky shooting combined with the pace inflation that comes with the Seven Seconds or Less offense. Reality hit hard last season, as Duhon shot worse than 28 percent from the field in October and November. By the end of the campaign, his numbers were right back at their usual level, but the damage had been done.

At the conclusion of his two-year contract with the Knicks, Duhon will step into a more appropriate reserve role in Orlando, and he's a nice fit for the Magic's system. A projected rebound in his three-point percentage will help Duhon space the floor on offense, and he's become proficient at running the pick-and-roll. Defensively, Duhon will be a major upgrade from Jason Williams. He was very effective defensively as part of a defined system in Chicago and should enjoy the same success in Orlando thanks to his ability to physically defend bigger players.

C 13 — Marcin Gortat

Hght: 6'11" Wght: 240 Exp: 3 From: Lodz, Poland Salary: $6.3 million
2011-12 status: guaranteed contract for $6.8 million

SKILL RATINGS

TOT	OFF	DEF	REB	PAS	HND	SHT	ATH
+1	0	-1	+3	-5	-4	+3	-2

Year	Team	Age	G	MPG	Usg	3PA%	FTA%	INS	2P%	3P%	FT%	TS%	Reb%	Ast%	TO%	BLK%	STL%	PF%	oRTG	dRTG	Win%	WARP
07-08	ORL	24.2	6	6.7	.234	.000	.065	1.065	.471	.000	.667	.491	.231	.023	.098	.018	.011	.045	109.0	104.8	.634	0.2
08-09	ORL	25.2	63	12.6	.135	.004	.085	1.081	.570	1.000	.578	.583	.201	.008	.108	.048	.012	.065	105.6	103.5	.569	2.5
09-10	ORL	26.2	81	13.4	.131	.010	.108	1.098	.540	.000	.680	.563	.179	.007	.150	.048	.008	.059	103.3	103.6	.488	1.6
10-11p	ORL	27.2	76	15.0	.130	.008	.102	1.093	.547	.163	.643	.564	.175	.008	.137	.043	.009	.059	103.4	104.0	.478	1.5

Most similar to: Etan Thomas (97.8), Kelvin Cato, Duane Causwell, Keon Clark

IMP: 50%   BRK: 2%   COP: 11%

It was a disappointing season for Marcin Gortat, who failed to build on the momentum created by his outstanding 2009 postseason. Gortat was hoping to play a larger role or possibly even start in Dallas, but Orlando unexpectedly matched the Mavericks' offer sheet. Playing behind the league's best center in a deep frontcourt, Gortat has little hope of ever seeing big minutes for the Magic, and he played much of the season with that weight on his shoulders. Gortat did rebound with a solid playoff run.

At the defensive end, Gortat is solid in the middle. He's a capable shot blocker with the strength to hold off big men as well as a plus rebounder. For a player whose small role allows him to take chances, Gortat's foul rate is certainly not excessive. Considering he's splitting minutes with the two-time reigning Defensive Player of the Year, Gortat's net defensive plus-minus numbers have been very good. At the offensive end, Gortat has no range whatsoever, so he's limited to finishing at the rim, often on putbacks. He was effective out of the pick-and-roll during the 2009 playoffs, but he tended to fumble paint catches more often last season, explaining his increased turnover rate.

Gortat's combination of salary and playing time make him a luxury for the Magic. Ultimately Otis Smith is going to have to get value for him in a trade.

ORLANDO MAGIC

Dwight Howard — C #12

Hght: 6'11" | Wght: 265 | Exp: 6 | From: SW Atlanta Christian Academy (GA) | Salary: $16.6 million
2011-12 status: guaranteed contract for $18.1 million

SKILL RATINGS

TOT	OFF	DEF	REB	PAS	HND	SHT	ATH
+5	+4	+5	+4	+2	-3	+5	+5

Year	Team	Age	G	MPG	Usg	3PA%	FTA%	INS	2P%	3P%	FT%	TS%	Reb%	Ast%	TO%	BLK%	STL%	PF%	oRTG	dRTG	Win%	WARP
07-08	ORL	22.4	82	37.7	.244	.002	.242	1.239	.601	.000	.590	.619	.213	.016	.162	.041	.011	.040	107.1	101.4	.681	17.0
08-09	ORL	23.4	79	35.7	.262	.001	.235	1.233	.573	.000	.594	.600	.216	.018	.151	.059	.014	.044	109.0	101.0	.745	19.3
09-10	ORL	24.4	82	34.7	.240	.005	.245	1.240	.617	.000	.592	.630	.217	.024	.187	.060	.013	.047	107.9	100.7	.724	18.2
10-11p	ORL	25.4	76	35.0	.256	.009	.241	1.232	.605	.006	.604	.622	.201	.023	.168	.056	.012	.043	107.9	101.2	.711	16.4

Most similar to: David Robinson (94.2), Hakeem Olajuwon, Shawn Kemp, Tim Duncan

IMP: 45%   BRK: 0%   COP: 0%

Dwight Howard put together another strong effort that earned him a fourth-place finish in MVP voting for the second consecutive season. Howard has firmly established himself as the league's best center and single most dominant defender. Howard's single-season adjusted plus-minus rating of +25.0 per 100 possessions was the best mark in the NBA, according to BasketballValue.com.

For a player whose offensive flaws are regularly dissected, Howard puts up impressive scoring numbers. Last year's 63.0 percent True Shooting Percentage was a career high. Howard might have benefited from playing a slightly smaller role in the offense with Vince Carter's arrival. More than almost any other post player in the league, Howard's success is dependent on his ability to establish early position. His touch diminishes rapidly the farther he is away from the basket, so centers who can battle to keep him out of the paint and force him to make up ground after catching an entry pass can limit Howard. Boston's Kendrick Perkins does this better than anyone in the league.

Howard won his second Defensive Player of the Year award in as many seasons by maintaining the new standard in terms of block percentage that he established in 2008-09. His traditional defensive statistics are the best in the league, and Howard anchors an Orlando defense that came within a hair of repeating atop the league. The Magic allowed 104.40 points per 100 possessions; Charlotte was at 104.39.

Rashard Lewis — PF #9

Hght: 6'10" | Wght: 230 | Exp: 12 | From: Alief Elsik HS (TX) | Salary: $19.6 million
2011-12 status: guaranteed contract for $21.1 million

SKILL RATINGS

TOT	OFF	DEF	REB	PAS	HND	SHT	ATH
+3	+3	+3	-5	+2	+2	+3	0

Year	Team	Age	G	MPG	Usg	3PA%	FTA%	INS	2P%	3P%	FT%	TS%	Reb%	Ast%	TO%	BLK%	STL%	PF%	oRTG	dRTG	Win%	WARP
07-08	ORL	28.7	81	38.0	.208	.398	.082	.684	.498	.409	.838	.591	.080	.029	.101	.009	.015	.031	108.1	105.4	.590	11.1
08-09	ORL	29.7	79	36.2	.221	.406	.087	.681	.482	.397	.836	.580	.088	.033	.116	.013	.014	.031	108.8	105.7	.601	11.0
09-10	ORL	30.7	72	32.9	.195	.426	.080	.653	.476	.397	.806	.573	.076	.021	.109	.009	.017	.035	106.7	105.9	.527	5.4
10-11p	ORL	31.7	74	33.0	.195	.427	.079	.652	.477	.387	.822	.568	.078	.025	.112	.011	.015	.035	106.6	105.8	.529	5.7

Most similar to: Dan Majerle (96.7), Danny Ferry, Dale Ellis, Bryon Russell

IMP: 37%   BRK: 5%   COP: 8%

Rashard Lewis' season got off to a poor start when he was suspended for the first 10 games because he tested positive last summer for what he claimed was a banned stimulant purchased over the counter. Lewis never truly got back on track. While his shooting statistics were virtually identical to his 2008-09 All-Star campaign, Lewis played a far smaller role in the Orlando offense and was less effective defensively and on the glass. Ultimately, Lewis shouldered a fair amount of the blame for the Magic's Eastern Conference Finals loss because of his quiet series.

At best, Lewis is a dangerous offensive weapon whose ability to space the floor helps make the Magic's offense effective. As a power forward, he's finished in the league's top five in three-pointers during each of his three seasons in Orlando. When confronted with an athletic opponent comfortable on the perimeter, like Garnett, Lewis is less effective. Post-ups against smaller defenders, a big component of his success as a small forward in Seattle, have nearly been purged from his game. According to Synergy Sports, post-ups accounted for just 12 percent of Lewis' plays last season despite the fact that he was very effective when he did go to the block. Lewis has worked to improve his strength, enabling him to battle bigger players at the defensive end, but his rebounding is increasingly becoming a weakness.

ORLANDO MAGIC

PG 14 — Jameer Nelson

Hght: 6'0" | Exp: 6 | Salary: $7.8 million
Wght: 190 | From: Saint Joseph's
2011-12 status: guaranteed contract for $7.8 million

SKILL RATINGS

TOT	OFF	DEF	REB	PAS	HND	SHT	ATH
+4	+5	+2	0	+3	+1	+3	-3

Year	Team	Age	G	MPG	Usg	3PA%	FTA%	INS	2P%	3P%	FT%	TS%	Reb%	Ast%	TO%	BLK%	STL%	PF%	oRTG	dRTG	Win%	WARP
07-08	ORL	26.2	69	28.4	.190	.190	.082	.892	.488	.416	.828	.564	.069	.090	.174	.001	.014	.038	107.4	106.3	.536	4.9
08-09	ORL	27.2	42	31.2	.232	.276	.065	.789	.529	.453	.887	.612	.061	.080	.126	.002	.020	.044	111.9	107.0	.652	6.4
09-10	ORL	28.2	65	28.6	.224	.252	.057	.805	.481	.381	.845	.540	.059	.088	.155	.001	.013	.037	108.2	107.2	.532	4.5
10-11p	ORL	29.2	71	30.0	.219	.296	.061	.765	.491	.412	.837	.568	.056	.087	.154	.001	.015	.039	109.1	107.0	.569	6.8

Most similar to: Sleepy Floyd (98.0), Damon Stoudamire, Tim Hardaway, Kenny Anderson | IMP: 39% | BRK: 4% | COP: 5%

At first glance, Jameer Nelson regressed last season after a career 2008-09 campaign. Much of the difference can be explained by midseason arthroscopic surgery on his left knee. Before the All-Star break, Nelson posted a below-.500 winning percentage. The rest of the year, he boosted his winning percentage to .593--down from where he was the previous season, but still good enough to power Orlando to the league's best record after the break. Expect Nelson to maintain that second-half level of play this year.

Defending Nelson in the high pick-and-roll is difficult because of his broad skill set. He's quick enough to beat defenders off the dribble and finds open teammates when he draws a trap. If the defense backs off, Nelson is an excellent three-point shooter. Nelson's pick-and-roll game was more important to the Magic last season because Vince Carter wasn't the same kind of threat in the two-man game as his predecessor, Hedo Turkoglu. Defensively, Nelson is undersized--the biggest reason he slipped in the 2004 Draft--but a competitor with good strength and a low center of gravity.

C 21 — Daniel Orton

Hght: 6'10" | Exp: R | Salary: $1.0 million
Wght: 255 | From: Kentucky
2011-12 status: guaranteed contract for $1.1 million

SKILL RATINGS

TOT	OFF	DEF	REB	PAS	HND	SHT	ATH
-4	--	--	--	--	--	--	--

Year	Team	Age	G	MPG	Usg	3PA%	FTA%	INS	2P%	3P%	FT%	TS%	Reb%	Ast%	TO%	BLK%	STL%	PF%	oRTG	dRTG	Win%	WARP
10-11p	ORL	20.7	76	-	.112	.011	.130	1.119	.441	.003	.515	.459	.109	.013	.245	.050	.015	.110	-	-	.346	-

Most similar to: Robin Lopez (91.0), JaVale McGee, Cedric Simmons | IMP: - | BRK: - | COP: -

Daniel Orton's draft stock skyrocketed during the month and a half after he wrapped up his lone season at Kentucky, leading him to leave his name in the draft despite the fact that he did not start a single college game. Orton peaked at No. 13 in the DraftExpress.com mock draft before tumbling. When draft night rolled around, Orton nearly slipped to the second round before Orlando took him with the 30th and final pick in the first round.

Orton was picked in the correct spot for a player whose numbers indicate he is a major project. Defensively, Orton could be competent right away. He's a quality shot blocker with strength who moves well. His biggest statistical shortcoming--a prodigious foul rate--is explained in part by his small role, which allowed him to take risks. On the offensive end, Orton is extremely raw. Most of his scoring was set up by his talented teammates, allowing him to focus on finishing at the rim. Orton has the touch to eventually develop a post-up game, but must polish his skills. His turnover rate was abysmal. Fortunately, the Magic has zero need for Orton to play right away. He'll be able to develop in practice before being tested as part of an NBA rotation.

SF 20 — Mickael Pietrus

Hght: 6'6" | Exp: 7 | Salary: $5.3 million
Wght: 215 | From: Les Abymes, Guadeloupe
2011-12 status: player option or ETO for $5.3 million

SKILL RATINGS

TOT	OFF	DEF	REB	PAS	HND	SHT	ATH
+2	+2	-1	-3	-3	-3	+3	-2

Year	Team	Age	G	MPG	Usg	3PA%	FTA%	INS	2P%	3P%	FT%	TS%	Reb%	Ast%	TO%	BLK%	STL%	PF%	oRTG	dRTG	Win%	WARP
07-08	GSW	26.2	66	19.9	.154	.380	.090	.710	.505	.363	.673	.547	.101	.016	.100	.024	.021	.064	105.1	104.9	.509	2.5
08-09	ORL	27.2	54	24.6	.185	.420	.091	.671	.473	.359	.709	.538	.074	.023	.106	.013	.012	.044	106.2	107.1	.472	1.5
09-10	ORL	28.2	75	22.5	.181	.466	.073	.607	.502	.379	.633	.555	.072	.014	.105	.014	.016	.038	105.4	105.9	.484	2.3
10-11p	ORL	29.2	73	25.0	.171	.519	.075	.556	.492	.368	.651	.547	.074	.017	.103	.016	.015	.044	105.7	106.0	.491	2.9

Most similar to: Keith Bogans (98.2), Bobby Simmons, Devean George, James Posey | IMP: 39% | BRK: 5% | COP: 2%

ORLANDO MAGIC

While Mickaël Pietrus was signed by Orlando in the summer of 2008 with the expectation that he would become the team's starting shooting guard, the Magic seems to be comfortable with Pietrus as a backup wing. Courtney Lee beat him out for the starting job in 2008-09, Matt Barnes played ahead of him last year and now Quentin Richardson is the likely starter alongside Vince Carter. That's not to say Pietrus has been a disappointment. He played crucial minutes in the 2009 playoffs and has been a capable role player.

Defensively, Pietrus is best against bigger opponents. He shined as Orlando's top defensive option against LeBron James in the 2009 Eastern Conference Finals. He's physical and likes to put a lot of pressure on the basketball. That means taking some risks, but overall Pietrus has been very effective. As a three-point shooter, Pietrus is good enough to force teams to respect him. He's more effective offensively in the open court, where his combination of speed and size makes him tough to stop.

SG 7 — J.J. Redick

Hght: 6'4" Wght: 190 Exp: 4 From: Duke Salary: $7.3 million
2011-12 status: guaranteed contract for $6.7 million

SKILL RATINGS: TOT +1, OFF +4, DEF -3, REB -4, PAS 0, HND +1, SHT +3, ATH -3

Year	Team	Age	G	MPG	Usg	3PA%	FTA%	INS	2P%	3P%	FT%	TS%	Reb%	Ast%	TO%	BLK%	STL%	PF%	oRTG	dRTG	Win%	WARP
07-08	ORL	23.8	34	8.1	.230	.312	.108	.797	.477	.395	.794	.569	.046	.027	.109	.000	.007	.047	105.7	108.4	.411	0.0
08-09	ORL	24.8	64	17.4	.164	.454	.104	.649	.408	.374	.871	.559	.054	.030	.137	.001	.010	.030	105.7	107.9	.429	0.3
09-10	ORL	25.8	82	22.0	.184	.384	.137	.753	.473	.405	.860	.606	.048	.041	.088	.002	.008	.030	108.6	107.8	.526	4.1
10-11p	ORL	26.8	76	24.0	.187	.396	.118	.722	.464	.398	.846	.586	.047	.035	.105	.001	.009	.032	107.0	107.8	.476	2.3

Most similar to: Jason Kapono (97.2), Tim Legler, Rex Chapman, B.J. Armstrong   IMP: 57%   BRK: 7%   COP: 9%

After making strides in the 2008-09 season and showing his potential during Orlando's playoff run, J.J. Redick put it all together during his fourth NBA campaign. He was in the Magic's rotation throughout the year and was the team's fourth-leading scorer in the loss to the Celtics. The timing was right for Redick, who cashed in with a new three-year offer sheet from the Chicago Bulls that Orlando chose to match. With another strong season, Redick has a chance to convince Orlando that he can replace Vince Carter in the starting lineup.

Redick's shooting talent is obvious, but largely because of his inconsistent role he had never shot the ball especially well before last year, when he posted career highs in three-point percentage and True Shooting Percentage. Since his time at Duke, Redick has broadened his skills. He has been the Magic's best matchup defensively against Ray Allen the last two postseasons. Being undersized can work against Redick at times, but he executes Orlando's sound defensive scheme. Redick has also become an asset as a ballhandler and developed the ability to find teammates. SCHOENE is wary of Redick's overnight improvement last season, but his skills suggest he can match or beat his 2009-10 effort.

SF 5 — Quentin Richardson

Hght: 6'6" Wght: 228 Exp: 10 From: DePaul Salary: $2.3 million
2011-12 status: guaranteed contract for $2.4 million

SKILL RATINGS: TOT +1, OFF +2, DEF -2, REB +1, PAS -1, HND +1, SHT +2, ATH -4

Year	Team	Age	G	MPG	Usg	3PA%	FTA%	INS	2P%	3P%	FT%	TS%	Reb%	Ast%	TO%	BLK%	STL%	PF%	oRTG	dRTG	Win%	WARP
07-08	NYK	28.0	65	28.3	.163	.321	.058	.737	.380	.324	.682	.444	.099	.028	.104	.006	.011	.038	102.5	106.3	.377	-1.5
08-09	NYK	29.0	72	26.3	.183	.415	.065	.650	.420	.365	.761	.510	.094	.027	.093	.003	.012	.030	105.9	107.2	.459	1.7
09-10	MIA	30.0	76	27.4	.149	.547	.048	.501	.493	.397	.732	.572	.105	.021	.095	.007	.018	.039	106.8	105.4	.546	5.6
10-11p	ORL	31.0	74	25.0	.159	.528	.052	.525	.438	.366	.739	.528	.097	.024	.099	.005	.014	.038	105.6	106.0	.487	2.8

Most similar to: James Posey (98.5), Ime Udoka, Morris Peterson, Tim Thomas   IMP: 38%   BRK: 7%   COP: 8%

Having battled back problems and inaccurate shooting throughout his tenure in New York, Quentin Richardson was revitalized after a busy offseason saw him get traded four times before he landed in Miami. Playing alongside Dwyane Wade, Richardson emerged as a long-range specialist, attempting more than half his shots from beyond the arc. He spent so little time doing anything but shooting threes that he did not take a free throw until Dec. 3 despite playing regular minutes. The role worked, as Richardson made nearly 40 percent of his three-pointers and posted far and away the best True Shooting Percentage of his 10-year NBA career.

The fondness for the three-ball will certainly serve Richardson well now that he's gone upstate to sign with the Magic as an unrestricted free agent. The bigger challenge for Richardson will be at the defensive end, where he'll have to take on the most difficult matchups while playing alongside Vince Carter. Despite playing in a very good Heat defense, Richardson's counterpart numbers were below average. It remains to be seen whether his motivation will wane now that he is not playing for a new contract.

SF 24 — Stanley Robinson

Hght: 6'9" | Exp: R | Salary: $0.5 million
Wght: 210 | From: Connecticut
2011-12 status: due qualifying offer of $1.0 million

SKILL RATINGS

TOT	OFF	DEF	REB	PAS	HND	SHT	ATH
-3	--	--	--	--	--	--	--

Year	Team	Age	G	MPG	Usg	3PA%	FTA%	INS	2P%	3P%	FT%	TS%	Reb%	Ast%	TO%	BLK%	STL%	PF%	oRTG	dRTG	Win%	WARP
10-11p	ORL	22.8	76	-	.164	.122	.063	.941	.473	.296	.615	.485	.100	.013	.151	.016	.009	.029	-	-	.390	-

Most similar to: Ronald Dupree (96.6), Othello Hunter, Antoine Wright, Nick Young | IMP: - | BRK: - | COP: -

The Magic made UConn forward Stanley Robinson the penultimate pick of the 2010 NBA Draft. Robinson is talented for a player drafted so late and has a chance to develop into an NBA contributor, but he faces an uphill battle to make Orlando's roster in training camp because the team is over the luxury tax. Suspended for the first semester of his junior year, Robinson bounced back with a strong senior campaign. At the pro level, the biggest factor working against him is a shaky jumper. Robinson is a good athlete, but not good enough to survive without defenses respecting his outside shooting. Odds are he'll get a chance to work on it overseas or in the D-League.

PG 44 — Jason Williams

Hght: 6'1" | Exp: 11 | Salary: $1.4 million
Wght: 180 | From: Florida
2011-12 status: free agent

SKILL RATINGS

TOT	OFF	DEF	REB	PAS	HND	SHT	ATH
+1	+2	-3	-4	+1	+3	+1	-4

Year	Team	Age	G	MPG	Usg	3PA%	FTA%	INS	2P%	3P%	FT%	TS%	Reb%	Ast%	TO%	BLK%	STL%	PF%	oRTG	dRTG	Win%	WARP
07-08	MIA	32.4	67	28.1	.171	.406	.052	.646	.415	.354	.863	.503	.042	.078	.135	.002	.021	.023	106.5	106.0	.517	4.0
09-10	ORL	34.4	82	20.8	.145	.416	.034	.618	.512	.380	.756	.555	.041	.082	.164	.001	.016	.018	107.3	106.5	.526	3.9
10-11p	ORL	35.4	76	5.0	.140	.388	.034	.646	.459	.364	.765	.521	.038	.075	.164	.002	.017	.021	105.8	106.5	.475	0.5

Most similar to: Terry Porter (97.0), Brad Davis, Derek Harper, Rickey Green | IMP: 32% | BRK: 0% | COP: 16%

Jason Williams returned from a one-year retirement to give the Magic a solid campaign as Jameer Nelson's backup at the point. Williams was especially effective in a starting role when Nelson was sidelined in the month of December, averaging 8.6 points and 5.1 assists as the team went 14-4. Williams has become more selective and more accurate as a shooter in his 30s, and last year's three-point percentage was a career high. No longer the flashy passer who earned the nickname "White Chocolate," Williams takes fewer chances now, which also means fewer plays made for his teammates. Stan Van Gundy surely accepts the tradeoff.

At this stage of his career, Williams has become a defensive liability. He's too slow to keep most point guards in front of him and is undersized against bigger opponents. That's where Chris Duhon will be an upgrade behind Nelson. Orlando brought Williams back to serve as the league's premier third point guard.

C — Adonal Foyle

Hght: 6'10" | Exp: 12 | Salary: --
Wght: 270 | From: Colgate
2011-12 status: free agent

SKILL RATINGS

TOT	OFF	DEF	REB	PAS	HND	SHT	ATH
--	--	--	--	--	--	--	--

Year	Team	Age	G	MPG	Usg	3PA%	FTA%	INS	2P%	3P%	FT%	TS%	Reb%	Ast%	TO%	BLK%	STL%	PF%	oRTG	dRTG	Win%	WARP
07-08	ORL	33.1	82	9.5	.120	.005	.074	1.069	.458	.000	.471	.462	.153	.011	.159	.042	.009	.055	100.9	104.0	.396	-0.3
08-09	ORL	34.1	10	6.2	.124	.000	.159	1.159	.636	.000	.500	.623	.235	.007	.180	.093	.000	.038	106.1	100.5	.681	0.3

After 13 seasons in the NBA and more than $63 million in salary, per Basketball-Reference.com, Adonal Foyle called it quits over the summer. He did so in typically thoughtful fashion, sharing a poem about his career on

ESPN's TrueHoop blog. Foyle eased his way into retirement as the Magic's fourth center last season, never setting foot on the floor. A member of the Sports Humanitarian Hall of Fame thanks to his work with his Kerosene Lamp Foundation, Foyle surely has a rich second act ahead of him now that his playing days are through. In September, Orlando named him the team's director of player development.

PG	Anthony Johnson	Hght: 6'3"	Exp: 13	Salary: --	SKILL RATINGS						
		Wght: 195	From: Charleston (SC) || TOT	OFF	DEF	REB	PAS	HND	SHT	ATH
--		2011-12 status: free agent			-2	+1	+2	+1	0	0	-2	-4

Year	Team	Age	G	MPG	Usg	3PA%	FTA%	INS	2P%	3P%	FT%	TS%	Reb%	Ast%	TO%	BLK%	STL%	PF%	oRTG	dRTG	Win%	WARP
07-08	SAC	33.6	69	22.2	.135	.200	.041	.841	.432	.457	.814	.519	.052	.077	.183	.005	.015	.033	104.7	106.7	.436	0.6
08-09	ORL	34.6	80	18.5	.156	.267	.071	.805	.411	.391	.753	.505	.055	.063	.164	.002	.016	.035	105.1	107.3	.430	0.4
09-10	ORL	35.6	31	13.1	.167	.267	.060	.793	.500	.333	.950	.543	.067	.072	.178	.002	.014	.037	106.1	107.1	.467	0.4
10-11p AVG		36.6	76	13.1	.145	.262	.061	.799	.444	.352	.869	.511	.058	.068	.195	.003	.013	.038	104.3	107.3	.402	-0.3

Most similar to: Brian Shaw (97.5), Brad Davis, Rickey Green, Derek Harper — IMP: 39% BRK: 7% COP: 14%

Jason Williams beat out Anthony Johnson for the backup point guard job, leaving Johnson to pick up a series of DNP-CDs. When he did play, mostly during Jameer Nelson's absence, Johnson was reasonably effective. He's still just two years removed from providing good minutes off the bench during Orlando's run to the NBA Finals and can run a team while knocking down the occasional shot. At age 36, however, Johnson has had a hard time finding work this summer and might be almost ready to call it a career.

Philadelphia 76ers

The Sixers' theme song should be "Stuck in the Middle With You" because that's exactly your situation if you're a Philly hoops fan. Somehow or another, Michael Madsen dancing around and cutting off some dude's ear would seem to figure into all this, but we don't want to be grotesque. Last year, we wrote about how the Sixers had become the living embodiment of a .500-level franchise, as they'd hovered around break even for a half-decade. They were average while clearing cap space, blew that space on Elton Brand and stayed average. Finally, in 2009-10, general manager Ed Stefanski found a way to break away from the mediocrity: He hired Eddie Jordan as his head coach.

It was really a lost season in Philadelphia. Jordan's system fit the Sixers about as well as a size-two dress fits Rosie O'Donnell. Brand was completely lost in the Princeton offense, then got hurt again. Andre Iguodala's interpretation of the offense was to shoot more three-pointers. Samuel Dalembert as a high-post center ... let's not even go there. Desperate for some cachet, Stefanski brought former Sixers legend Allen Iverson back to town. He might as well have brought back 60-year-old Julius Erving for all the good it did. After the season, Jordan was gone, as was Dalembert, and Stefanski ended up with Rod Thorn looking over his shoulder just like in the good old days back in New Jersey.

To be fair, the Jordan hire didn't seem as obviously disastrous as it turned out when he took the job. There was always the possibility that installing a few Princeton principles would add life to the attack by getting a few players to improve some dormant aspects of their games. Anyway, Jordan talked about wanting to run and not get bogged down in half-court sets. The Sixers could still play pressure defense and run the floor while becoming more efficient in the half court. None of that came together, as the Jordan system proved to be the worst possible scheme for Philadelphia's roster, and was ultimately scrapped *in medias res*. At the same time, the things that had made the Sixers competitive--forcing turnovers on defense and getting to the foul line on offense--sagged, especially the latter. The Sixers missed former point guard Andre Miller immensely. Things just didn't work out.

To replace Jordan, Stefanski tore a page from happier days in the franchise's history and brought in former Sixers All-Star Doug Collins for his fourth crack at an NBA coaching job. Collins may be a better coach than Jordan, but is his style any better suited to Philly's roster? That's the big question as we enter the 2010-11 season, and it's a fair one. Collins enters with a reputation as a good defensive coach who preaches a methodical style and has always been a bit of a control freak. The hyper-intense Collins coached the Bulls, Pistons and Wizards for a total of eight seasons from 1986-2002, which illustrates his tendency to flame out quickly. All of his

76ERS IN A BOX

Last year's record	27-55
Last year's Offensive Rating	107.7 (20)
Last year's Defensive Rating	112.1 (23)
Last year's point differential	-3.9 (24)
Team pace	90.2 (22)
SCHOENE projection	33-49 (11)
Projected Offensive Rating	105.4 (28)
Projected Defensive Rating	108.9 (11)
Projected team weighted age	25.0 (28)
Projected '10-11 payroll	$68.4 (12)
Est. payroll obligations, '11-12	$62.2 (7)

Head coach: Doug Collins

The last time Doug Collins coached a playoff team, his 1996-97 Detroit Pistons featured Michael Curry, Joe Dumars and Kenny Smith. Needless to say, it's been a while for Collins, who is seven years removed from his most recent coaching gig in Washington. Nonetheless, hopes are high as Collins returns to the team he played for throughout his entire eight-year career. Collins has produced instant defensive improvements everywhere he has gone, but he will be challenged to produce immediate results without any quality interior defenders on the roster. Look for Philadelphia to play at one of the league's slowest paces, which could stifle the open-court ability of the Sixers' young perimeter players.

teams in Chicago and Detroit finished in the top 11 of the league in Defensive Rating. All of his teams have been near the bottom of the NBA in tempo. With a Sixers team full of good athletes, one that got even younger and more athletic during the offseason, let's hope that Collins' seven-year sabbatical in the broadcast business has softened his approach to the game. At least we know he won't neglect the defense, which happened under Jordan.

That the Sixers were able to improve at all is a minor miracle, further proof of just how much rides on the crapshoot that is the NBA draft lottery. There is a large variance in the quality and depth of the year-to-year draft classes. We don't know how the 2010 draftees are going to pan out, but in any given season the closer you get to the top, the better is the chance you're going to land a franchise-changing player. There is often a huge difference between the second pick, which is where the Sixers landed Ohio State's Evan Turner, and the sixth or seventh pick, which is where they would have selected had the slots lined up with last season's final standings. SCHOENE tabs Turner's top comp as Portland's Brandon Roy. If Turner can reach that level, this year's lottery could prove to be just the kind of a break a franchise needs to escape middle-class malaise.

Hitting a lottery homer is also a more effective way to climb the ladder than what the Sixers tried in the summer of 2008. The Sixers were in a similar situation to that of the Bulls, Knicks, Heat, Nets, Clippers, et al. this past offseason. They had money to spend only, unlike 2010, there weren't really any top free agents to spend it on. The top unrestricted guys were Baron Davis, Elton Brand, Corey Maggette and Gilbert Arenas. So the Sixers gave Brand an $80 million deal with which they are now stuck. In fairness, most people applauded the move at the time, even though Brand was coming off a ruptured Achilles tendon. Many picked the Sixers to make a leap towards the top of the Eastern Conference in 2008-09, but Brand proved to be a poor fit and even if he hadn't been, he isn't the player he was before the leg problems that limited his time with the Clippers. You can't be too hard on the Sixers, because somebody was going to overpay Brand. It wasn't just the Sixers bidding on him--Golden State offered Brand $90 million. Supply and demand is a bitch. Chances are one of the teams that spent freely this summer will end up in the Sixers' predicament a year from now. Teams set themselves up for a splash, dive in, and ram their head on the bottom of the pool.

Brand didn't fit with the up-tempo attack that was successful under Maurice Cheeks, then abandoned when Brand came aboard. He was an even worse fit under the doomed Princeton offense experiment of Jordan. Under Jordan, ball and player movement were supposed to become prevalent. Instead, the Sixers' offense devolved into harried isolations, second-chance shots and a little transition--just as it had in past seasons, only Jordan didn't know how to coach that style. Brand was really a non-factor. Collins quickly identified him as a reclamation project and reached out to him over the summer, saying he wanted Brand to rediscover his joy for the game, or some such touchy-feely thing. That doesn't necessarily mean Collins will repeat Cheeks' mistake of engineering his half-court offense around Brand, but that outcome is possible. Collins has suggested that Brand will start at center, which makes a lot of sense. Brand remains a good defender; while he won't be confused with Dwight Howard, he'll be solid enough to allow Collins to allot his power forward minutes to Marreese Speights and Thaddeus Young. He can also use a Utah-like lineup with Brand at four and Spencer Hawes as a face-up five.

Whichever way Collins decides to deploy his big men, the offense will likely be focused around a wing player, which was the model he used with Michael Jordan in Chicago and Grant Hill in Detroit. Of course, that may have been because he *had* Jordan and Hill and any other offensive structure would have been just plain silly. Collins also had Jordan in Washington. In Philadelphia, his hope will likely be that Turner becomes the face of the franchise and takes on a Hill-type role. Hill played his rookie season under Don Chaney in Detroit and averaged 19.9 points, 6.4 rebounds and 5.0 assists. His role was firmly established when Collins took over the next season. SCHOENE is projecting Turner to get 12.5 points, 7.0 rebounds and 5.7 assists. He's got the playmaking skills to be Collins' initiator, and if he shoots the ball better than he's projected, Turner can emerge as the Sixers' feature player in his first NBA season.

However, Turner will have to pry the go-to player role out of the cold, dead hands of Iguodala. Iguodala should have found his calling during the FIBA World Championship, when he excelled as a role player and defensive stopper for the U.S. squad that won gold. Unfortunately, his post-tournament comments sounded like those of a guy ready to get back to pounding the rock for entire possessions at a time. Iguodala's name will likely continue to pop up on the trade rumor mill, but assuming he stays in Philly, Collins will have to handle Iguodala very carefully. In the right role, Iguodala is an All-Star player. In the wrong role, he's an inefficient ball dominator. Hopes for significant improvement for this team are dependent upon Turner transitioning to the pro game and becoming the impact talent the Sixers so desperately need. For that to happen, Collins must find a way for Turner and Iguodala to co-exist, because Iggy's contract isn't going to be easy to move.

One thing that Collins has never really worked with is a traditional, starting-caliber point guard. Reading through summer stories on the Sixers, it sounds like he's prepared to cast his lot with second-year guard Jrue Holiday. That would push Lou Williams to the bench, where he can be a top-tier sixth man. He excelled as a reserve scorer when Miller was still with the Sixers, and Collins should be able to convince Williams of the importance of returning to the bench.. As for Holiday, it sure looks like the Sixers nailed that pick. He was better than he was in college and more NBA-ready than most of us thought. While Holiday looks like he'll be a long-term solution at the point, the offense suffered in the short term after Miller left as a free agent. In Chicago, John Paxson was Collins' point guard; in Detroit, it was Lindsey Hunter. Both of those players served as kick-out options for superstars. Holiday looks like he's going to be a fine shooter, but it remains to be seen if can play off the ball consistently. Last season, 39 percent of Holiday's field goals were assisted. That puts him right smack in the middle of the spectrum between Mike Bibby, who is strictly a catch-and-shoot point guard, and Steve Nash, who gets almost all of his own offense. In any event, it looks like Holiday can function without having to dominate the ball, but can also run a team's attack when needed.

After all the summer's major free-agent business was settled, Thorn made the move from New Jersey to Philadelphia. He's the team president, while Stefanski drops that title and becomes the Sixers' general manager. The pair worked well together in New Jersey, so there is a positive history there, but Thorn's presence still changes the dynamic of the team's front office. Ultimately, the buck stops with Thorn. Collins also brought in Quin Snyder as a player development assistant. With some good work in the D-League, Snyder has rebuilt the once-promising career he wrecked

> **From the Blogosphere**
>
> **Who:** Jordan Sams
> **What:** Liberty Ballers
> **Where:** http://www.libertyballers.com/
>
> The Sixers had an eventful offseason. They replaced Eddie Jordan with Doug Collins. They selected Evan Turner with the No. 2 overall pick. Andre Iguodala has finally received national buzz for starting during the World Championship for the U.S. National Team. The one guy still flying under everyone's radar--who shouldn't be--is second-year point guard Jrue Holiday. Last season, Holiday was the lone bright spot for a Sixers team run into the ground by Eddie Jordan. He averaged 13.3 points, 6.5 assists and 4.0 rebounds per 36 in March and April, and shot 50 and 43 percent from the field and three, respectively. However, not even those numbers do Holiday justice, nor do advanced statistics. In order to fully appreciate Holiday, you have to witness his innate court vision, or his flashes of dominant man-to-man defense. With his rookie season behind him and significant upgrades at both head coach and shooting guard, expect Holiday to have a breakout 10-11 campaign.

at the University of Missouri. He's once again a bit of a rising star in coaching circles, and will likely come to be viewed as Collins' heir apparent, especially if Philly's young players blossom under Snyder's tutelage. Everything in Philadelphia depends upon the development of a young core, because the long-term cap situation is murky. The cap woes weren't helped when Stefanski dealt Dalembert's expiring deal, bringing back Hawes from Sacramento, a nice get, but also Andres Nocioni, an aging, replacement-level forward with two more years guaranteed on his deal.

As for that young core, what will it be? Iguodala is still just 26 as the season opens, but he is a rough-and-tumble player whose game is very dependent upon his athleticism. His performance, while still excellent, has been declining, though you almost have to throw out last season because of Eddie Jordan. The Sixers have seen what an Iggy-dominated team looks like. If he can thrive as the third wheel along with Holiday and Turner, that would help, but at some point, a big man is going to have to emerge as the third component of a big three. It's not going to be the aging Brand, Hawes

PHILADELPHIA 76ERS

looks like a solid role player but not much more than that, Young still has a good ceiling but is only 6'8" and Speights doesn't play defense. The cap situation being what it is, Thorn will have to turn to the trade market to fill out his team's foundation. Iguodala could be the piece that makes a trade work, but Thorn had better move before Iggy's contract becomes a Brand-like anchor.

You have to give the Sixers a mulligan for last season. Jordan is gone. Stefanski has been effectively emasculated by the hiring of Thorn. So Philadelphia gets a clean slate for Collins, who should prove to be a well-loved coach in a city that can be hard on its sports figures. However, even if you throw out last season, the Sixers are still a team mired in the middle muck of professional basketball. There are some nice pieces here, some young pieces that can grow together and become something better than average. The franchise could really go in just about any direction, or it could continue to run in place. This will be a season of getting a better picture of what the future of Philadelphia basketball looks like.

Bradford Doolittle

76ERS FIVE-YEAR TRENDS

Season	AGE	W-L	POW	PYTH	SEED	ORTG	DRTG	PT DIFF	PACE
05-06	26.5	38-44	35.8 (21)	35.5	---	108.0 (13)	109.2 (24)	-2.0 (22)	91.3 (6)
06-07	26.2	35-47	32.4 (21)	32.1	---	105.2 (26)	108.3 (15)	-3.0 (23)	89.4 (20)
07-08	26.4	40-42	39.9 (17)	42.2	7	108.1 (20)	108.6 (11)	0.4 (14)	88.6 (21)
08-09	26.1	41-41	41.1 (15)	41.2	6	109.1 (20)	109.1 (14)	0.1 (15)	88.9 (20)
09-10	26.2	27-55	28.8 (24)	30.0	--	107.7 (20)	112.1 (23)	-3.9 (24)	90.2 (22)

		OFFENSE				DEFENSE			
Season	PAY	eFG	oREB	FT/FGA	TO	eFG	oREB	FT/FGA	TO
05-06	$59.7	.487 (17)	.256 (22)	.270 (5)	.153 (8)	.500 (21)	.713 (23)	.240 (12)	.168 (5)
06-07	$44.4	.480 (26)	.272 (16)	.255 (12)	.170 (19)	.501 (19)	.708 (28)	.221 (6)	.173 (4)
07-08	$57.8	.482 (22)	.318 (1)	.227 (15)	.152 (16)	.504 (20)	.720 (23)	.205 (7)	.168 (3)
08-09	$67.2	.485 (24)	.312 (2)	.253 (4)	.158 (21)	.507 (19)	.714 (25)	.216 (9)	.175 (2)
09-10	$64.5	.496 (17)	.276 (9)	.204 (27)	.160 (22)	.518 (24)	.732 (21)	.231 (19)	.160 (10)

(league rankings in parenthesis)

C 4 — Tony Battie

Hght: 6'11" Exp: 12 Salary: $0.9 million
Wght: 240 From: Texas Tech
2011-12 status: free agent

SKILL RATINGS

TOT	OFF	DEF	REB	PAS	HND	SHT	ATH
-2	--	+1	--	--	--	--	--

Year	Team	Age	G	MPG	Usg	3PA%	FTA%	INS	2P%	3P%	FT%	TS%	Reb%	Ast%	TO%	BLK%	STL%	PF%	oRTG	dRTG	Win%	WARP
08-09	ORL	33.2	77	15.6	.156	.022	.089	1.067	.497	.222	.659	.518	.129	.012	.114	.015	.011	.043	103.0	106.3	.394	-0.6
09-10	NJN	34.2	15	8.9	.164	.084	.093	1.008	.361	.250	.700	.405	.102	.010	.063	.011	.015	.066	99.2	106.6	.269	-0.4
10-11p	PHI	35.2	76	-	.131	.028	.083	1.055	.491	.232	.639	.509	.117	.011	.114	.017	.011	.046	-	-	.396	-

Most similar to: Aaron Williams (97.8), Mark Bryant, Scott Williams, Mychal Thompson

IMP: 43% BRK: 2% COP: 7%

Tony Battie should have "frontcourt depth" engraved on his tombstone. The Sixers signed him up to be a defensive option from the end of their bench. Battie may or may not provide defense at this stage of his career. He doesn't block shots like he used to, and his on-ball metrics are unimpressive. In a small, 134-minute sample from last season, he ranked in just the 18th percentile of all players in post defense. On offense, Battie can kill you with long twos if you let him.

PHILADELPHIA 76ERS

PF 33	Craig Brackins	Hght: 6'10"	Exp: R	Salary: $1.3 million	SKILL RATINGS								
		Wght: 230	From: Iowa State		TOT	OFF	DEF	REB	PAS	HND	SHT	ATH
		2011-12 status: guaranteed contract for $1.4 million			-5	-2	-1	-3	+2	+3	-5	-4

Year	Team	Age	G	MPG	Usg	3PA%	FTA%	INS	2P%	3P%	FT%	TS%	Reb%	Ast%	TO%	BLK%	STL%	PF%	oRTG	dRTG	Win%	WARP
10-11p	PHI	23.5	76	10.0	.174	.115	.084	.969	.372	.270	.743	.420	.108	.026	.114	.015	.008	.037	100.3	106.3	.307	-1.7

Most similar to: Chris Jefferies (96.6), Brian Cook, Rob Kurz, Hakim Warrick | IMP: - | BRK: - | COP: -

A poor junior season cost Craig Brackins' stock in the draft. As a sophomore, Brackins was one of the national leaders in usage rate, and he had lottery buzz going into 2009-10. With Iowa State adding JC transfer Marquis Gilstrap, Brackins had more help, yet his efficiency sunk even lower than it had been in 2008-09. He made just 44.6 percent of his two-point attempts and had a True Shooting Percentage below 50 percent.

There have been few players in recent memory who have succeeded while being as inefficient as Brackins was as a collegian, and since he was already 22 throughout his junior year, he doesn't have age on his side. Brackins needs to score, and score efficiently, because the rest of his game is underwhelming. He's a poor rebounder and is not a major factor at the defensive end of the floor. As a result, it's tough to see Brackins panning out for the Sixers, who acquired him just before training camp.

PF 42	Elton Brand	Hght: 6'9"	Exp: 11	Salary: $16.0 million	SKILL RATINGS								
		Wght: 254	From: Duke		TOT	OFF	DEF	REB	PAS	HND	SHT	ATH
		2011-12 status: guaranteed contract for $17.1 million			-2	-1	+4	0	0	-1	-2	0

Year	Team	Age	G	MPG	Usg	3PA%	FTA%	INS	2P%	3P%	FT%	TS%	Reb%	Ast%	TO%	BLK%	STL%	PF%	oRTG	dRTG	Win%	WARP
07-08	LAC	29.1	8	34.3	.259	.000	.135	1.135	.452	.000	.787	.520	.135	.027	.111	.041	.005	.035	104.6	104.3	.508	0.5
08-09	PHI	30.1	29	31.7	.240	.000	.099	1.099	.447	.000	.676	.484	.166	.018	.142	.039	.010	.039	102.5	104.3	.439	0.4
09-10	PHI	31.1	76	30.2	.218	.001	.094	1.093	.481	.000	.738	.518	.119	.022	.120	.027	.018	.046	103.7	105.4	.443	1.3
10-11p	PHI	32.1	72	28.0	.198	.004	.095	1.091	.464	.000	.728	.501	.127	.021	.124	.035	.012	.043	102.0	104.7	.409	-0.3

Most similar to: Mychal Thompson (97.8), Joe Barry Carroll, Armon Gilliam, Kurt Thomas | IMP: 36% | BRK: 3% | COP: 9%

The preseason news on Elton Brand is all good. He's slimmed down in an effort to recapture some of his old quickness. He was embraced by new coach Doug Collins, who believes Brand is a key player for the Sixers. And no matter what system Collins installs, it's got to be a better fit for Brand than Eddie Jordan's Princeton offense. Brand used to be a bruiser who made a living at the foul line, but that's changed over the last two seasons, a surefire indicator that Brand doesn't move like he used to. His rebounding percentages tumbled last season, as well, though some of that may have been Jordan's system. Brand is still effective around the basket, but was merely average at converting his post-ups. That will be a point of emphasis for Collins. Brand remains a fine defender and a good shot blocker. His prowess on that end might be best illustrated by how infrequently opponents attempted to post him up. However, he doesn't move as well in space as he used to, so quicker fours can give him trouble in isolations. This is a huge year for Brand. If he doesn't recover his value this year, it's never going to happen.

C 31	Spencer Hawes	Hght: 7'1"	Exp: 3	Salary: $3.0 million	SKILL RATINGS								
		Wght: 245	From: Washington		TOT	OFF	DEF	REB	PAS	HND	SHT	ATH
		2011-12 status: due qualifying offer of $4.1 million			0	0	-4	-1	+4	+4	+1	-3

Year	Team	Age	G	MPG	Usg	3PA%	FTA%	INS	2P%	3P%	FT%	TS%	Reb%	Ast%	TO%	BLK%	STL%	PF%	oRTG	dRTG	Win%	WARP
07-08	SAC	20.0	71	13.1	.193	.053	.064	1.011	.478	.190	.655	.486	.145	.021	.140	.033	.007	.061	102.3	105.4	.396	-0.4
08-09	SAC	21.0	77	29.3	.204	.113	.059	.946	.486	.348	.662	.509	.142	.030	.157	.031	.010	.050	103.8	105.8	.435	0.9
09-10	SAC	22.0	72	26.4	.197	.103	.055	.952	.494	.299	.689	.507	.132	.037	.155	.032	.008	.047	104.2	105.3	.462	1.8
10-11p	PHI	23.0	74	25.0	.190	.111	.061	.950	.519	.334	.684	.535	.136	.035	.146	.033	.009	.049	103.8	105.2	.453	1.4

Most similar to: Nenad Krstic (97.9), Kwame Brown, Tony Battie, Chris Mihm | IMP: 69% | BRK: 11% | COP: 2%

PHILADELPHIA 76ERS

Spencer Hawes has gotten gradually better in his three NBA seasons, but the Kings dealt him to Philadelphia in anticipation of landing DeMarcus Cousins and Hassan Whiteside in the draft. The addition of Hawes gives Doug Collins a lot of options for deploying his big men. Hawes is a good passer and an average rebounder, but beyond that he still needs to upgrade his game. His shot-block rate is fine, if not dominant. However, he plays soft, with a miniscule foul-drawing rate and too many long shots. His three-point shooting can be a weapon, but it doesn't help the team if he's only hitting 30 percent from behind the arc. Hawes will likely come off the bench behind Elton Brand, but will also play alongside Brand in certain configurations. He's sworn to improve his weak post game and poor defense. If that happens, the Sixers will be thrilled to have landed a quality big man still in his developmental seasons.

PG 11	Jrue Holiday	Hght: 6'4" Wght: 180 2011-12 status: team option for $1.7 million	Exp: 1 From: UCLA		Salary: $1.6 million				**SKILL RATINGS**							
									TOT +1	OFF +1	DEF -4	REB +2	PAS +1	HND -1	SHT +2	ATH 0

Year	Team	Age	G	MPG	Usg	3PA%	FTA%	INS	2P%	3P%	FT%	TS%	Reb%	Ast%	TO%	BLK%	STL%	PF%	oRTG	dRTG	Win%	WARP
09-10	PHI	19.9	73	24.2	.185	.223	.053	.830	.465	.390	.756	.526	.064	.073	.219	.008	.023	.040	105.0	106.4	.454	1.4
10-11p	PHI	20.9	74	30.0	.173	.232	.053	.821	.480	.415	.765	.547	.062	.074	.211	.007	.023	.038	105.0	105.9	.472	2.6

Most similar to: Tony Parker (96.5), Gilbert Arenas, Shaun Livingston, Ricky Davis   IMP: -   BRK: -   COP: -

Doug Collins has already churned up the hype machine on Jrue Holiday, and it's easy to see why he loves his new point guard. Holiday's game is deceptively solid in that he doesn't pound the rock for long stretches just to get a shot of his own like so many very young point guards. And he's young--last season he became the first NBA player born in the 1990s. Holiday has surprisingly good catch-and-shoot skills and excellent range. He needs to gain more confidence in attacking the rim to up his foul-drawing rate and improve his percentage at the basket. As a playmaker, he's a work in progress. He commits too many turnovers and isn't yet great at setting up teammates, though he does play unselfishly. Some of these qualities might be shored up simply by playing in a better system. Holiday was pretty bad on the defensive end as a rookie, and that will likely be point of emphasis for the coming season.

SF 9	Andre Iguodala	Hght: 6'6" Wght: 207 2011-12 status: guaranteed contract for $13.5 million	Exp: 6 From: Arizona		Salary: $12.3 million				**SKILL RATINGS**							
									TOT +4	OFF +3	DEF +5	REB 0	PAS +5	HND +4	SHT +1	ATH +3

Year	Team	Age	G	MPG	Usg	3PA%	FTA%	INS	2P%	3P%	FT%	TS%	Reb%	Ast%	TO%	BLK%	STL%	PF%	oRTG	dRTG	Win%	WARP
07-08	PHI	24.2	82	39.6	.240	.179	.130	.951	.496	.329	.721	.543	.082	.055	.125	.012	.025	.027	106.7	104.2	.581	11.1
08-09	PHI	25.2	82	39.9	.224	.163	.143	.980	.521	.307	.724	.560	.087	.061	.139	.009	.021	.021	107.7	105.6	.568	10.3
09-10	PHI	26.2	82	38.9	.219	.198	.124	.925	.492	.310	.733	.535	.099	.068	.143	.014	.023	.021	106.8	104.8	.564	9.8
10-11p	PHI	27.2	76	37.0	.209	.222	.129	.908	.502	.328	.745	.553	.087	.062	.134	.012	.021	.022	106.4	104.7	.558	8.3

Most similar to: Ron Harper (98.4), Gary Payton, Bonzi Wells, Steve Francis   IMP: 44%   BRK: 0%   COP: 13%

It seems like Andre Iguodala's name finds a way into every NBA trade rumor, even if the Sixers aren't initially involved. AI2 is still around, and coming off an excellent showing for the U.S. team in the FIBA World Championship. If he sticks around Philadelphia, buys what Doug Collins is selling and learns to share the offensive focus with young stars Jrue Holiday and Evan Turner, then Iguodala can be an All-Star as a role player supreme. Iguodala is miscast as an offensive focal point because he's just not a good enough outside shooter. However, he's one of the game's best at driving to the hoop and getting fouled. Iguodala is also one of the two or three best passing wing players in the NBA. He's elite on defense, a wing player who does it all, which is why he'd be so valuable if he'd only trim back on the jump shots. Even though Iguodala is always popping up in rumors, it's not like the Sixers are trying to dump him. He's always mentioned in megadeals, including one rumor that would have sent him to Denver in exchange for Carmelo Anthony. However, the best-case scenario for Sixers fans is that Iguodala stays around and doesn't act like an alpha dog around his young teammates, who can help him get to where he wants to go.

PHILADELPHIA 76ERS

Jason Kapono — SF #72

Hght: 6'8" Exp: 7 Salary: $6.6 million
Wght: 215 From: UCLA
2011-12 status: free agent

SKILL RATINGS

TOT	OFF	DEF	REB	PAS	HND	SHT	ATH
-5	--	-3	--	--	--	--	--

Year	Team	Age	G	MPG	Usg	3PA%	FTA%	INS	2P%	3P%	FT%	TS%	Reb%	Ast%	TO%	BLK%	STL%	PF%	oRTG	dRTG	Win%	WARP
07-08	TOR	27.2	81	18.9	.178	.206	.033	.827	.491	.483	.860	.562	.046	.020	.101	.001	.010	.040	103.1	107.9	.345	-2.3
08-09	TOR	28.2	80	22.9	.175	.331	.027	.696	.435	.428	.810	.525	.052	.027	.101	.001	.006	.036	104.1	109.0	.343	-2.8
09-10	PHI	29.2	57	17.1	.161	.501	.019	.519	.485	.368	.600	.527	.040	.018	.100	.005	.011	.038	104.2	108.2	.372	-0.9
10-11p	PHI	30.2	72	-	.149	.482	.022	.540	.465	.423	.705	.564	.044	.022	.103	.003	.010	.038	-	-	.301	-

Most similar to: Pat Garrity (98.0), Hubert Davis, Bobby Hansen, Raja Bell

IMP: 44% BRK: 10% COP: 4%

You can be a $6 million shooting specialist and still be a solid value, but Jason Kapono isn't. The difference between Kapono and someone like Chicago's Kyle Korver is that Kapono doesn't do anything but shoot. Korver has that reputation, but he's a very good passer, chips in on the boards and holds his own on the defensive end. None of these descriptions apply to Kapono. He'll probably be a 10- to 15-minute player for Doug Collins who is used to space the floor in certain lineups.

Jodie Meeks — SG #20

Hght: 6'4" Exp: 1 Salary: $0.8 million
Wght: 208 From: Kentucky
2011-12 status: non-guaranteed contract for $0.9 million

SKILL RATINGS

TOT	OFF	DEF	REB	PAS	HND	SHT	ATH
0	+1	-2	+4	-2	+1	+1	-3

Year	Team	Age	G	MPG	Usg	3PA%	FTA%	INS	2P%	3P%	FT%	TS%	Reb%	Ast%	TO%	BLK%	STL%	PF%	oRTG	dRTG	Win%	WARP
09-10	PHI	22.7	60	12.0	.197	.426	.055	.630	.456	.318	.795	.493	.082	.025	.081	.005	.013	.033	104.1	106.4	.425	0.1
10-11p	PHI	23.7	76	5.0	.189	.452	.059	.607	.477	.346	.814	.527	.082	.027	.082	.007	.014	.032	104.7	106.1	.454	0.3

Most similar to: Mike Woodson (97.4), Dell Curry, J.J. Redick, Terry Teagle

IMP: 66% BRK: 26% COP: 5%

Jodie Meeks showed potential as an off-the-bench scorer as a rookie, but was still dealt in-season from the Bucks to the Sixers, probably because Scott Skiles didn't see plus defense in Meeks' makeup. Meeks needs improvements across the board. He operated most of the time as a spot-up player, but must considerably upgrade the range on his shot. Over half his shots were threes, but he shot just 31 percent from behind the arc. That's not what teams look for in a shooting specialist. Meeks has potential as a finisher at the rim and needs to learn when to attack the basket. The pre-camp trade that sent Willie Green to New Orleans could present a rotation opportunity for Meeks--if he shows growth in his game.

Andres Nocioni — SF #5

Hght: 6'7" Exp: 6 Salary: $6.9 million
Wght: 225 From: Santa Fe, Argentina
2011-12 status: guaranteed contract for $6.7 million

SKILL RATINGS

TOT	OFF	DEF	REB	PAS	HND	SHT	ATH
-1	+1	-4	+1	-2	-2	+2	-4

Year	Team	Age	G	MPG	Usg	3PA%	FTA%	INS	2P%	3P%	FT%	TS%	Reb%	Ast%	TO%	BLK%	STL%	PF%	oRTG	dRTG	Win%	WARP
07-08	CHI	28.4	82	24.6	.246	.309	.095	.786	.476	.365	.809	.549	.098	.021	.119	.017	.006	.055	104.8	106.7	.439	1.0
08-09	SAC	29.4	76	26.2	.202	.348	.090	.742	.449	.399	.792	.555	.105	.023	.126	.012	.010	.059	105.8	107.4	.450	1.4
09-10	SAC	30.4	75	19.7	.210	.357	.062	.705	.408	.386	.717	.504	.087	.023	.096	.013	.011	.048	104.3	106.7	.421	0.1
10-11p	PHI	31.4	75	16.8	.184	.413	.070	.657	.437	.393	.761	.541	.096	.021	.111	.016	.009	.055	104.3	106.8	.417	0.0

Most similar to: Tim Thomas (98.7), Scott Wedman, Danny Ferry, Sean Elliott

IMP: 30% BRK: 8% COP: 9%

There is always a cost to getting rid of a contract like Samuel Dalembert's, and in Philadelphia, that cost is named Andres Nocioni. The problem is that Nocioni may be the kind of gritty, gutty rabble-rouser whom Doug Collins will love. Nocioni has resided barely above replacement level in recent seasons despite shooting solid percentage from three-point range. Unfortunately, he isn't accurate anywhere else, but shoots frequently and burns through possessions. Nocioni has a reputation as a scrappy defender, but you can't find any evidence of that in the numbers. Most likely, Nocioni will get 20 or so minutes per night this season. Those will be 20 or so minutes Sixer fans will wish they could get back.

PHILADELPHIA 76ERS

PG 1	Chris Quinn		Hght: 6'2" Wght: 175 2011-12 status: free agent	Exp: 4 From: Notre Dame		Salary: --			**SKILL RATINGS**						
									TOT	OFF	DEF	REB	PAS	HND	SHT	ATH
									+1	--	0	--	--	--	--	--

Year	Team	Age	G	MPG	Usg	3PA%	FTA%	INS	2P%	3P%	FT%	TS%	Reb%	Ast%	TO%	BLK%	STL%	PF%	oRTG	dRTG	Win%	WARP
07-08	MIA	24.6	60	22.4	.167	.337	.092	.754	.439	.403	.867	.559	.053	.063	.117	.002	.016	.032	106.9	106.5	.514	2.7
08-09	MIA	25.6	66	14.6	.171	.394	.073	.679	.408	.409	.810	.539	.047	.065	.095	.002	.013	.039	109.1	108.2	.528	2.2
09-10	NJN	26.6	25	8.9	.142	.466	.038	.572	.417	.313	1.000	.477	.043	.060	.146	.003	.021	.031	104.8	106.5	.445	0.1
10-11p	PHI	27.6	76	-	.156	.408	.080	.672	.445	.406	.830	.564	.048	.065	.101	.002	.012	.035	-	-	.482	-

Most similar to: Chris Whitney (98.0), Travis Diener, Shammond Williams, Steve Blake   IMP: 46% BRK: 7% COP: 7%

Unlike many of the former Nets cast off to the Island of the Misfit Toys, Chris Quinn has a decent NBA résumé. He was effective off the bench in Miami when he was making better than 40 percent of his three-pointers. Last season saw Quinn's shooting percentage slump, and he also turned the ball over far more frequently. There's no obvious explanation for Quinn's downturn, so he's likely to bounce back and is a solid fit for teams looking for a third point guard who can shoot the basketball. The 76ers appear to fit that bill.

C 25	Darius Songaila		Hght: 6'9" Wght: 248 2011-12 status: free agent	Exp: 7 From: Wake Forest		Salary: $4.8 million			**SKILL RATINGS**						
									TOT	OFF	DEF	REB	PAS	HND	SHT	ATH
									-3	--	+3	--	--	--	--	--

Year	Team	Age	G	MPG	Usg	3PA%	FTA%	INS	2P%	3P%	FT%	TS%	Reb%	Ast%	TO%	BLK%	STL%	PF%	oRTG	dRTG	Win%	WARP
07-08	WAS	30.2	80	19.4	.174	.003	.055	1.052	.460	.000	.918	.496	.103	.040	.146	.009	.016	.055	102.3	106.4	.367	-1.6
08-09	WAS	31.2	77	19.8	.172	.002	.069	1.068	.533	.000	.889	.570	.089	.028	.130	.011	.022	.060	104.0	107.3	.394	-0.7
09-10	NOH	32.2	75	18.8	.196	.010	.054	1.044	.498	.167	.811	.522	.097	.023	.135	.008	.022	.067	101.5	106.5	.338	-2.3
10-11p	PHI	33.2	75	-	.160	.011	.058	1.048	.506	.088	.858	.533	.088	.028	.137	.009	.020	.065	-	-	.378	-

Most similar to: Tom Gugliotta (97.5), Tyrone Corbin, Matt Harpring, Duane Ferrell   IMP: 44% BRK: 7% COP: 15%

The Hornets got away with Darius Songaila as their primary big man off the bench last season, but new GM Dell Demps dealt Songaila to Philadelphia as part of a four-player trade. The Lithuanian is a total finesse player who fares poorly against bigger opponents. A liability at power forward, his rebounding--which would be average for a small forward--became untenable when he moved over to center. Songaila is also a poor help defender who lacks the ability to block shots.

Songaila is in the league primarily because of his soft touch on offense. When he's going well, as in 2008-09 in Washington, Songaila is an efficient scorer who can make defenses pay for ignoring him. Per Hoopdata.com, Songaila's shooting percentages did not really change much in any particular area. The reason for the drop in his two-point percentage was primarily tied to attempting fewer shots at the rim and more long twos. Songaila also saw a decline in his free throw percentage, historically a strength.

C 16	Marreese Speights		Hght: 6'10" Wght: 245 2011-12 status: team option for $2.7 million	Exp: 2 From: Florida		Salary: $1.8 million			**SKILL RATINGS**						
									TOT	OFF	DEF	REB	PAS	HND	SHT	ATH
									+1	+1	-5	-1	-1	+1	0	+1

Year	Team	Age	G	MPG	Usg	3PA%	FTA%	INS	2P%	3P%	FT%	TS%	Reb%	Ast%	TO%	BLK%	STL%	PF%	oRTG	dRTG	Win%	WARP
08-09	PHI	21.7	79	16.0	.220	.013	.096	1.083	.506	.250	.773	.543	.139	.011	.076	.036	.011	.066	106.3	106.3	.500	2.2
09-10	PHI	22.7	62	16.4	.252	.009	.114	1.105	.483	.000	.745	.524	.147	.016	.091	.026	.015	.069	105.0	105.7	.475	1.2
10-11p	PHI	23.7	76	20.0	.216	.014	.104	1.090	.501	.089	.795	.542	.138	.017	.085	.029	.013	.062	104.4	105.4	.467	1.6

Most similar to: Channing Frye (98.3), Kris Humphries, LaMarcus Aldridge, Drew Gooden   IMP: 53% BRK: 7% COP: 5%

If Marreese Speights ever learns that there are two ends on a standard basketball court, the Sixers may really have something. The kid can score. He faces up effectively inside the arc and operates well in the post, though his percentage at the rim dropped off last season, which put a dent in his True Shooting Percentage. Speights is a bit of a black hole on offense; once he gets the rock, it's going towards the basket, which is why his usage rate is so high. That doesn't make him a bad player; it just makes him a role player. But even that role will be limited if Speights doesn't start defending. The Sixers were 7.2 points per 100 possessions worse with Speights on the floor during his rookie season; last year the figure rose (dropped?) to 8.4. If he doesn't become a more accomplished stopper under Doug Collins, it won't bode well for his career. That's a shame, because a player that can score like Speights should be able to earn more than 16 minutes a night.

SF 12 — Evan Turner

Hght: 6'7" Exp: R Salary: $4.6 million
Wght: 205 From: Ohio State
2011-12 status: guaranteed contract for $4.9 million

SKILL RATINGS

TOT	OFF	DEF	REB	PAS	HND	SHT	ATH
0	0	+1	+4	+5	+3	-3	+2

Year	Team	Age	G	MPG	Usg	3PA%	FTA%	INS	2P%	3P%	FT%	TS%	Reb%	Ast%	TO%	BLK%	STL%	PF%	oRTG	dRTG	Win%	WARP
10-11p	PHI	22.5	76	35.0	.220	.065	.087	1.022	.448	.317	.742	.494	.127	.079	.200	.014	.019	.054	104.1	105.3	.461	2.5

Most similar to: Brandon Roy (91.7), George Hill, Jared Dudley   IMP: -   BRK: -   COP: -

The real problem with Evan Turner's poor showing in summer league was that people are going to read too much into his mediocre play and the fact that he wasn't in great shape. That just adds another layer or two of pressure to the expectations that already come within being picked No. 2 overall. Turner should be fine. He can't afford further lapses in conditioning, as he's an average athlete for an NBA player as it is. Still, Turner is one of the most skilled rookies coming into the league this season, a gifted passer and an excellent shooter. He's also committed on the defensive end, which is the key to playing big minutes in his first year. Once Turner hits his stride, with the comfort of NBA teammates and an NBA system around him, he should excel. Chances are he'll be the Sixers' best player within three years.

PG 23 — Louis Williams

Hght: 6'1" Exp: 5 Salary: $5.0 million
Wght: 175 From: South Gwinnett HS (Snellville, GA)
2011-12 status: guaranteed contract for $5.2 million

SKILL RATINGS

TOT	OFF	DEF	REB	PAS	HND	SHT	ATH
+4	+4	0	0	0	+1	+1	+3

Year	Team	Age	G	MPG	Usg	3PA%	FTA%	INS	2P%	3P%	FT%	TS%	Reb%	Ast%	TO%	BLK%	STL%	PF%	oRTG	dRTG	Win%	WARP
07-08	PHI	21.5	80	23.4	.244	.152	.127	.975	.441	.359	.783	.523	.053	.062	.124	.006	.020	.032	106.2	106.0	.505	3.4
08-09	PHI	22.5	81	23.7	.278	.189	.145	.957	.438	.286	.790	.513	.052	.058	.130	.006	.023	.031	106.4	106.6	.495	3.1
09-10	PHI	23.5	64	29.9	.212	.233	.116	.883	.527	.340	.824	.576	.058	.064	.120	.006	.022	.026	108.1	106.2	.562	5.8
10-11p	PHI	24.5	73	28.0	.221	.239	.129	.891	.500	.357	.818	.572	.055	.064	.118	.007	.020	.026	107.7	105.9	.559	6.1

Most similar to: Jason Terry (97.5), Terrell Brandon, Derek Anderson, Devin Harris   IMP: 65%   BRK: 9%   COP: 0%

It looks like Louis Williams is headed back to the bench to fill the instant offense role he filled so well two years ago. Williams became more of a playmaker working with the first unit and his usage rate dropped. The good news is that his efficiency went way up, even more than you'd expect. Williams became a dangerous man off the dribble, posting a finishing percentage at the rim you'd expect from a quality big man while maintaining his high foul-drawing rate. He also shot the ball better from long range, but remains a below-average shooter from beyond the arc. One of the reasons Williams is probably better suited to a sixth-man role is that he's not a very good defender. Williams should go back to a higher-usage role this season working with the second unit. Even though his name won't be called when the lineup is introduced, Williams will remain a value member of the Sixers' rotation.

PHILADELPHIA 76ERS

PF 21	Thaddeus Young	Hght: 6'8" Exp: 3 Salary: $2.9 million						
		Wght: 220 From: Georgia Tech						
		2011-12 status: due qualifying offer of $4.0 million						

SKILL RATINGS

TOT	OFF	DEF	REB	PAS	HND	SHT	ATH
0	+1	+2	-4	0	0	+3	+1

Year	Team	Age	G	MPG	Usg	3PA%	FTA%	INS	2P%	3P%	FT%	TS%	Reb%	Ast%	TO%	BLK%	STL%	PF%	oRTG	dRTG	Win%	WARP
07-08	PHI	19.8	74	21.0	.175	.032	.076	1.044	.548	.316	.738	.570	.120	.017	.107	.004	.022	.038	104.6	105.2	.480	2.1
08-09	PHI	20.8	75	34.4	.207	.141	.072	.930	.526	.341	.735	.549	.088	.015	.102	.007	.020	.029	104.9	106.4	.452	1.9
09-10	PHI	21.8	67	32.0	.216	.136	.072	.935	.495	.348	.691	.523	.097	.021	.125	.006	.019	.028	103.9	106.3	.419	0.1
10-11p	PHI	22.8	73	30.0	.195	.160	.076	.916	.540	.360	.726	.563	.093	.021	.107	.005	.020	.029	104.5	105.8	.457	1.9

Most similar to: Ron Mercer (97.4), Rudy Gay, Josh Childress, Luol Deng   IMP: 63%   BRK: 5%   COP: 3%

The Sixers asked Thaddeus Young to put on weight and add strength, so it looks like the days of him flipping between the forward spots are over. Young has gradually backslid since his promising rookie season, but one thing you can hang your hat on is the fact that the Sixers have been consistently better with him on the floor. Last season, Young became a little less perimeter oriented, but he's yet to leverage his solid interior skills into a good foul-drawing rate. As a face-up shooter, he's increasingly poor, and Doug Collins will probably discourage him from taking so many midrange jump shots. He does shoot the deep ball well enough to be deployed as a floor-spacing four. Young could stand to polish his playmaking skills and if he indeed gets stronger, perhaps he can do something about his disappointing rebound percentages. Young was a lower-usage, higher-efficiency player as a rookie, and the Sixers would like to see him get back to that. Young couldn't do any shooting over the summer because he was recovering from the broken thumb that sidelined him towards the end of last season. Don't expect that shaky jumper to suddenly become a weapon.

PG —	Allen Iverson	Hght: 6'0" Exp: 14 Salary: --						
		Wght: 165 From: Georgetown						
		2011-12 status: free agent						

SKILL RATINGS

TOT	OFF	DEF	REB	PAS	HND	SHT	ATH
-2	0	+4	-1	-1	-2	-3	+1

Year	Team	Age	G	MPG	Usg	3PA%	FTA%	INS	2P%	3P%	FT%	TS%	Reb%	Ast%	TO%	BLK%	STL%	PF%	oRTG	dRTG	Win%	WARP
07-08	DEN	32.9	82	41.8	.268	.128	.163	1.035	.482	.345	.809	.567	.038	.073	.114	.002	.020	.013	108.7	106.2	.582	11.8
08-09	DET	33.9	57	36.7	.259	.087	.135	1.047	.435	.283	.781	.504	.049	.065	.129	.002	.023	.020	105.1	106.2	.464	2.1
09-10	PHI	34.9	28	30.9	.231	.057	.132	1.075	.436	.360	.794	.515	.054	.060	.146	.002	.011	.025	104.2	107.6	.388	-0.5
10-11p	AVG	35.9	75	30.9	.220	.091	.130	1.039	.444	.326	.777	.515	.050	.057	.140	.002	.015	.023	104.0	106.7	.410	-0.3

Most similar to: Vinnie Johnson (94.8), Avery Johnson, Dennis Johnson, Nate Archibald   IMP: 21%   BRK: 0%   COP: 17%

The sad thing is that Allen Iverson still doesn't recognize how far his skills have fallen, which makes him a pitiable figure. He's probably sitting at home right now completely befuddled why no NBA team has signed him up to be their starting two-guard, or point guard, or whatever he is. The 28 games Iverson played last season were probably the last of his NBA career, which will eventually land him in the Hall of Fame.

Phoenix Suns

The Phoenix Suns finished a resurgent 2009-10 season two wins shy of the NBA Finals. That recent success stands in contrast to a future that looks much bleaker. A poor offseason has left Phoenix trailing the pack in the Western Conference with an aging group of core players that will make it difficult for the Suns to contend in the near future.

2009-10 marked a return for the Suns to the Seven Seconds or Less philosophy that led the team to back-to-back conference finals in the middle of the decade and 177 wins in a three-year span. As befits a franchise that has the fourth-best winning percentage in NBA history yet has never won a championship, Phoenix was unable to break through. The two best Suns teams fell to the San Antonio Spurs in 2005 and 2007 despite the benefit of home-court advantage, fueling the belief that Phoenix's run-and-gun system could not win during the postseason.

With the blessing of owner Robert Sarver, Suns general manager Steve Kerr set about remaking the team with more of a half-court mindset. Midway through Kerr's first season on the job, 2007-08, Phoenix sent forward Shawn Marion to Miami with guard Marcus Banks for center Shaquille O'Neal, making the Suns bigger and slower. After another playoff loss to San Antonio, this time in the opening round, the team and coach Mike D'Antoni decided to part ways. With an eye toward improving Phoenix's defense, Kerr hired Terry Porter as D'Antoni's replacement.

The Porter era was short-lived. Not only did he frustrate the Suns' stars, the team's defense actually got worse. By the All-Star break of the 2008-09 season, Kerr pushed reset by firing Porter and promoting assistant Alvin Gentry, a holdover from D'Antoni's staff, to return Phoenix to its old ways. Any chance Gentry had of turning things around during the second half ended when Amar'e Stoudemire was lost for the year with a detached retina just two games after the break.

By the start of last year, the Suns much more closely resembled the D'Antoni-era roster. O'Neal was gone, having been dealt to Cleveland in a salary dump. He was replaced by Channing Frye, a floor-spacing big man more in the Phoenix tradition. The results were immediate. The Suns reintroduced themselves as contenders by starting the season 8-1, survived a midseason swoon (they went 12-18 between the start of December and late January) and finished the season strong with 28 wins in their last 35 games to claim the third playoff seed in the West.

The results were familiar for Phoenix, which led the NBA in Offensive Rating for the fifth time in six seasons and shot 41.2 percent from beyond the arc, the second-best mark in league history. The Suns were 19th in Defensive Rating, near where most of the D'Antoni-era teams ranked at that end of the floor.

There were a couple of important changes for Phoenix. Gentry played much bigger than D'Antoni did, with Stoudemire spending most of the season at power forward instead of as an undersized center. Frye spaced

SUNS IN A BOX

Last year's record	54-28
Last year's Offensive Rating	117.4 (1)
Last year's Defensive Rating	111.4 (19)
Last year's point differential	4.9 (5)
Team pace	94.0 (4)
SCHOENE projection	37-45 (12)
Projected Offensive Rating	110.8 (12)
Projected Defensive Rating	112.4 (28)
Projected team weighted age	30.2 (4)
Projected '10-11 payroll	$64.0 (18)
Est. payroll obligations, '11-12	$51.2 (20)

Head coach: Alvin Gentry

A veteran of NBA sidelines, Gentry enjoyed his finest season as a head coach in 2009-10, leading the Suns to 54 wins and the Western Conference Finals. Gentry showed that Mike D'Antoni's system could succeed even without D'Antoni himself, but he wasn't exactly a carbon copy of the man he formerly assisted. The biggest difference was Gentry's willingness to open up the bench, showing a tremendous amount of trust in a youthful reserve corps. They repaid Gentry with several big playoff performances.

the floor when he started alongside Stoudemire, but the combination of Stoudemire and second-year center Robin Lopez was surprisingly conventional. Gentry did not turn to smallball until the postseason, when the Suns had to cover for the absence of Lopez (sidelined with a back injury) during the first two rounds.

The more notable change was in Phoenix's depth. D'Antoni tended to favor a seven- or eight-man rotation, and part of the reason the Suns regularly sold or traded their first-round picks was that these players were unlikely to see any action. By contrast, Gentry relied heavily on the young players Kerr acquired through the draft and value signings, often using five reserves at a time. The Phoenix bench ranked fifth in the league by producing a total of 10.9 Wins Above Replacement Player, and the all-reserve lineup outscored opponents by 11 points per 48 minutes.

After beating a Portland team with a hobbled Brandon Roy in six games to open the playoffs, the Suns faced their long-time nemesis, San Antonio. The Spurs' first-round upset over Dallas gave Phoenix home-court advantage, and this time the Suns made it pay off. Phoenix won two close games at home, then rode the improbable fourth-quarter heroics of backup point guard Goran Dragic to a 3-0 lead before sweeping San Antonio out of the playoffs.

The Suns' reward was a matchup in the Western Conference Finals with the Los Angeles Lakers. After two ugly road losses, Phoenix's offense was reinvigorated at home, and a zone defense helped the Suns even the series at two. Phoenix was inches away from overtime at the Staples Center in Game Five before Ron Artest rebounded Kobe Bryant's airball and scored the game-winner. Bryant hit a series of difficult shots down the stretch of Game Six to finish the Suns off.

The end of the season meant the expiration of a pair of important contracts--Stoudemire's and Kerr's. Talks on a new deal for Kerr to stay on as general manager and president of basketball operations broke down in mid-June, and Kerr announced he would not return. The move was unexpected, in that Kerr and Sarver had been close confidants, which was the reason Kerr took the position in the first place. Despite the work Kerr put in stocking the bench with talent, Sarver apparently wanted him to take a pay cut. With his old role as a color analyst for TNT open because Doug Collins was hired as coach of the Philadelphia 76ers, Kerr decided to return to TV.

The loss of Kerr and senior vice president of basketball operations David Griffin left Phoenix to make critical decisions for the franchise's future in the middle of a transition period. By the time Sarver hired Lon Babby as the team's new president of basketball operations, the Suns' roster was nearly complete. Phoenix's offseason moves were made long before Cleveland assistant GM Lance Blanks was hired as general manager and the team's lead talent evaluator.

Phoenix faced a big decision on Stoudemire, who had nearly been traded at the trade deadline in 2009 and again in 2010 before finishing out his contract with the Suns. After the deadline came and passed, Stoudemire rebounded from a disappointing first half of the season to play some of the best basketball of his career down the stretch. Combined with the number of teams with cap space exceeding the number of max players available, Stoudemire's strong finish made him a coveted free agent.

Phoenix's final offer to Stoudemire was fully guaranteed for three years with the last two becoming guaranteed based on playing time and Stoudemire staying healthy. It was a reasonable offer from the Suns' perspective, limiting their exposure in case Stoudemire's surgically-repaired left knee became problematic in the future. However, other teams were more bullish on Stoudemire, and he broke off negotiations with Phoenix before signing a five-year max contract in New York.

The Suns moved quickly in free agency, agreeing to a new five-year, $30 million deal with Frye on the opening day and signing Hakim Warrick to help replace Stoudemire. The athletic Warrick makes perfect sense as a Phoenix four, but the price--$17.9 million over four years, with the last year at the team's option--was high because of an inflated market early in the summer.

More big moves were in store. On consecutive days, the Suns announced a pair of trades. They sent backup guard Leandro Barbosa and center Dwayne Jones to Toronto for forward Hedo Turkoglu, then dealt a second-round pick to Atlanta in a sign-and-trade in exchange for forward Josh Childress, who is returning to the NBA after a two-year sojourn in Greece. Notably, both players were former Babby clients, suggesting he might have had a hand in their acquisition (because he had already begun talking with Phoenix about a position, Babby recused himself as Turkoglu's agent before the deal).

More important from the Suns' perspective, Childress and Turkoglu both play the small forward position, which was already flush in Phoenix with veteran Grant Hill and young Jared Dudley. Hill, who will turn 38 early in training camp, could be headed for a smaller role and Dudley is possible trade bait. Still, adding two wings suggests the Suns could be thinking about a return to increased smallball to replace Stoudemire.

From a value perspective, the two deals were a mixed bag at best. Childress signed for $34 million over five years, which is a reasonable amount per year but an awfully long contract. The Turkoglu deal is even more dangerous to Phoenix's bottom line. He's due $39 million guaranteed and up to $45 million total over the next four years, an amount the Raptors were happy to shed after one frustrating season in Toronto where Turkoglu failed to be the kind of difference-maker the Raptors hoped he would be. Turkoglu also clashed with management after he was allegedly caught out on the town after a game he missed due to illness. Turkoglu doesn't figure to age well, and the last couple of years of his contract could get ugly.

SCHOENE's projections show the Suns taking a major step back. On defense, Phoenix is projected to drop to 28th in the league on a per-possession basis. Defensive rebounding will be a major issue with Warrick (who grabbed 13.9 percent of available defensive rebounds last season) and Turkoglu (15.2 percent) replacing Stoudemire (18.9 percent) and Amundson (19.9 percent). Stoudemire's awareness and focus have been fairly maligned, but the Suns will still miss his size and athleticism at the defensive end if they go small.

The more surprising projection is Phoenix slipping out of the top 10 in Offensive Rating. Here, age is a major factor. The Suns are projected to be the league's fourth-oldest team next season, with four of their five starters in their 30s and Hill and Nash (37) both well past their prime. Phoenix may benefit here from a training staff that has helped keep veteran players healthy and productive. Nash in particular has a good chance to outplay his projection, which calls for his productivity to decline by 5.4 percent this season.

At the same time, SCHOENE still expects the Suns to shoot the ball very well (third in the league in projected effective field-goal percentage). The big difference could be in terms of getting to the line, where Stoudemire will be missed, and turning the ball over. With shooters at every position and multiple ballhandlers (including Turkoglu as a possible point power forward, an extreme example of the NBA's positional revolution), Phoenix should still be a very good offensive team. The problem is, to make up for their lack of size in the frontcourt, the Suns will need to be great. With Nash as the last remaining link on the floor to the start of the Seven Seconds or Less era, Phoenix no longer appears to have that ability.

Kevin Pelton

From the Blogosphere

Who: Seth Pollack
What: SB Nation Arizona
Where: http://arizona.sbnation.com/

The Suns will carry forward several of their key strengths from the amazing 2009-10 season: chemistry, three-point shooting, depth, versatility. The beauty of the offense has long been the willingness to share the ball to create and hit open shots. The team has done a good job taking some of that pressure off Steve Nash by adding two solid ballhandlers (Hedo Turkoglu, Josh Childress) to keep that going. Amar'e Stoudemire's scoring ability will be missed, but the addition of more passers and finishers should offset that with drive-and-kick opportunities. And don't count out Robin Lopez's low-post and pick-and-roll offensive potential. Defensively, the Suns should be much better on the perimeter with a variety of versatile players who can switch screens. Beyond Lopez there's a lack of size that is very much a concern on the glass. This team may not get back to the Western Conference Finals, but nor is it a lottery team either.

PHOENIX SUNS

SUNS FIVE-YEAR TRENDS

Season	AGE	W-L	POW	PYTH	SEED	ORTG	DRTG	PT DIFF	PACE
05-06	27.5	54-28	56.4 (4)	55.4	2	113.9 (1)	107.2 (16)	5.5 (4)	94.2 (1)
06-07	27.6	61-21	62.2 (3)	59.3	2	116.1 (1)	107.7 (13)	7.3 (2)	94.2 (3)
07-08	29.3	55-27	56.3 (8)	54.0	6	116.5 (1)	109.9 (16)	5.0 (7)	94.5 (4)
08-09	29.5	46-36	45.6 (13)	46.1	---	115.8 (1)	113.0 (25)	1.9 (11)	94.5 (4)
09-10	29.2	54-28	53.7 (6)	53.6	3	117.4 (1)	111.4 (19)	4.9 (5)	94.0 (4)

		OFFENSE				DEFENSE			
Season	PAY	eFG	oREB	FT/FGA	TO	eFG	oREB	FT/FGA	TO
05-06	$59.7	.537 (1)	.221 (30)	.166 (30)	.139 (2)	.490 (17)	.721 (19)	.200 (2)	.156 (22)
06-07	$82.4	.551 (1)	.227 (29)	.215 (27)	.152 (4)	.492 (12)	.719 (20)	.206 (3)	.159 (23)
07-08	$71.2	.551 (1)	.224 (29)	.228 (14)	.146 (11)	.488 (8)	.709 (29)	.191 (2)	.135 (28)
08-09	$75.4	.545 (1)	.277 (14)	.250 (8)	.166 (26)	.511 (23)	.717 (22)	.233 (17)	.150 (20)
09-10	$74.9	.546 (1)	.276 (10)	.240 (10)	.157 (18)	.491 (11)	.708 (29)	.224 (16)	.138 (29)

(league rankings in parenthesis)

PG 17 — Chucky Atkins

Hght: 5'11" Exp: 11 Salary: –
Wght: 185 From: South Florida
2011-12 status: free agent

SKILL RATINGS

TOT	OFF	DEF	REB	PAS	HND	SHT	ATH
-5	--	0	--	--	--	--	--

Year	Team	Age	G	MPG	Usg	3PA%	FTA%	INS	2P%	3P%	FT%	TS%	Reb%	Ast%	TO%	BLK%	STL%	PF%	oRTG	dRTG	Win%	WARP
07-08	DEN	33.7	24	14.6	.165	.581	.029	.448	.395	.316	.444	.449	.047	.057	.074	.002	.011	.032	105.5	107.4	.440	0.2
08-09	OKC	34.7	32	12.9	.154	.398	.049	.651	.339	.263	.938	.408	.033	.064	.161	.004	.012	.029	103.5	108.3	.346	-0.6
09-10	DET	35.7	40	16.1	.145	.363	.059	.696	.417	.301	.926	.477	.029	.066	.159	.000	.015	.038	104.5	108.2	.380	-0.5
10-11p	PHX	36.7	76	-	.159	.397	.056	.659	.374	.268	.847	.426	.036	.062	.156	.002	.012	.038	-	-	.310	-

Most similar to: David Wesley (92.5), Brian Shaw, Lindsey Hunter, Rickey Green

IMP: 48% BRK: 14% COP: 14%

Chucky Atkins remains a fringe NBA player because of a skill set that is increasingly difficult to ascertain. Atkins is attending training camp with the Suns. He's battling Zabian Dowdell and Matt Janning for one spot in the backcourt. Atkins is a veteran leader while the other two competitors have no NBA experience, but Phoenix cannot count on him contributing if he is forced to play.

SF 1 — Josh Childress

Hght: 6'8" Exp: 4 Salary: $6.5 million
Wght: 209 From: Stanford
2011-12 status: guaranteed contract for $6.7 million

SKILL RATINGS

TOT	OFF	DEF	REB	PAS	HND	SHT	ATH
+2	+3	-3	+1	-1	-1	+5	+1

Year	Team	Age	G	MPG	Usg	3PA%	FTA%	INS	2P%	3P%	FT%	TS%	Reb%	Ast%	TO%	BLK%	STL%	PF%	oRTG	dRTG	Win%	WARP
07-08	ATL	24.8	76	29.9	.159	.076	.153	1.077	.595	.367	.807	.647	.096	.023	.124	.014	.014	.026	106.8	105.8	.531	5.4
10-11p	PHX	27.8	76	28.0	.170	.107	.140	1.033	.577	.396	.822	.637	.093	.025	.126	.014	.013	.026	106.4	105.9	.516	4.4

Most similar to: Gene Banks (97.5), Cedric Maxwell, Calvin Natt, Cliff Levingston

IMP: 31% BRK: 3% COP: 8%

Josh Childress' two-year Greek odyssey has come to an end, and he will return to the NBA with the Suns. When translated, Childress' Euroleague performance with Olympiakos was fairly similar to his track record of production in Atlanta. Childress took on a slightly larger role in the offense, and wasn't quite as effective a two-point shooter considering the level of defense.

Childress will be an interesting fit in Phoenix. His ability to run the floor will be an asset, but in the half-court offense Childress could struggle. Despite an optimistic SCHOENE projection of improved three-point shooting, Childress is lacking in range. Grant Hill isn't much of a shooter from long range either, but Hill has an effective 20-foot jumper. Childress is no more effective a step inside the line than he is beyond it. Most of Childress' points come at the rim thanks to off-ball movement. Those opportunities will be there for him, especially alongside Steve Nash, but opponents are unlikely to respect him on the perimeter. That could compromise the Suns' spacing.

SF	Earl Clark	Hght: 6'10"	Exp: 1	Salary: $1.9 million	SKILL RATINGS							
		Wght: 225	From: Louisville		TOT	OFF	DEF	REB	PAS	HND	SHT	ATH
55		2011-12 status: team option for $2.0 million			-3	--	0	--	--	--	--	--
Year	Team	Age	G	MPG	Usg	3PA%	FTA%	INS	2P%	3P%	FT%	TS%	Reb%	Ast%	TO%	BLK%	STL%	PF%	oRTG	dRTG	Win%	WARP
09-10	PHX	22.3	51	7.5	.220	.026	.083	1.057	.370	.400	.722	.420	.089	.024	.121	.024	.009	.029	99.4	105.9	.294	-1.0
10-11p	PHX	23.3	76	-	.238	.019	.090	1.071	.400	.415	.771	.453	.099	.027	.125	.025	.010	.027	-	-	.377	-
Most similar to: Kirk Snyder (96.4), Sly Williams, Randy White, DeShawn Stevenson														IMP: 84%		BRK: 42%		COP: 3%		

Earl Clark took a redshirt rookie season, playing more than 20 minutes in a game just three times all year. Alvin Gentry used a large rotation, but it rarely included Phoenix's first-round pick. Clark's overall numbers are poor, though he was more effective in the rare extended stints of action he saw. More damning is the fact that the Suns opted to bring in two small forwards rather than give Clark the opportunity to win more playing time.

At 6'10", Clark might be able to develop into a stretch four for Phoenix. His athleticism makes him effective in an up-tempo system, and Clark could become an accurate outside shooter with work. To be able to play up front, Clark will have to improve his rebounding and become stronger to defend bigger players. Clark doesn't have forever to develop, so it will be important for him to demonstrate at some point this season how he can help the Suns. There's no more time for orange slices and juiceboxes on the bench.

PG	Goran Dragic	Hght: 6'3"	Exp: 2	Salary: $2.0 million	SKILL RATINGS							
		Wght: 190	From: Ljubljana, Slovenia		TOT	OFF	DEF	REB	PAS	HND	SHT	ATH
2		2011-12 status: team option for $2.1 million			+3	+4	+2	+4	+1	-2	+1	+1
Year	Team	Age	G	MPG	Usg	3PA%	FTA%	INS	2P%	3P%	FT%	TS%	Reb%	Ast%	TO%	BLK%	STL%	PF%	oRTG	dRTG	Win%	WARP
08-09	PHX	23.0	55	13.2	.197	.166	.088	.922	.400	.370	.769	.487	.082	.067	.224	.003	.020	.053	104.1	107.6	.388	-0.4
09-10	PHX	24.0	80	18.0	.212	.274	.102	.828	.488	.394	.736	.566	.065	.074	.183	.004	.016	.040	107.6	106.9	.522	3.2
10-11p	PHX	25.0	76	21.0	.217	.305	.098	.793	.449	.402	.745	.555	.076	.075	.190	.004	.017	.042	107.3	106.5	.525	3.6
Most similar to: Sam Cassell (98.8), Khalid Reeves, Bimbo Coles, Larry Drew														IMP: 55%		BRK: 11%		COP: 8%		

In terms of sheer, visceral improvement, Goran Dragic might have taken the NBA's largest leap last season. A disaster much of his rookie campaign, Dragic came on after Phoenix's coaching change and took a major step forward during his second season. A national audience saw during the postseason what Dragic is capable of doing, and he has established himself as the heir apparent when Steve Nash someday decides to call it a career.

A confident player who used plays at an average rate even during his rookie season, Dragic had the results to back up that attitude in year two. Like Nash, he has the ability to beat the defense in a variety of manners. A threat beyond the arc, Dragic is most effective driving hard to the basket with his dominant left hand. Dragic's biggest area for improvement is taking care of the basketball. He constantly turned the ball over as a rookie and his turnover rate remained problematic last season.

SF	Jared Dudley	Hght: 6'7"	Exp: 3	Salary: $2.2 million	SKILL RATINGS							
		Wght: 225	From: Boston College		TOT	OFF	DEF	REB	PAS	HND	SHT	ATH
3		2011-12 status: due qualifying offer of $3.1 million			+2	+3	+2	+1	0	+1	+3	+3
Year	Team	Age	G	MPG	Usg	3PA%	FTA%	INS	2P%	3P%	FT%	TS%	Reb%	Ast%	TO%	BLK%	STL%	PF%	oRTG	dRTG	Win%	WARP
07-08	CHA	22.8	73	19.0	.149	.091	.115	1.024	.502	.220	.737	.528	.118	.027	.111	.006	.018	.042	104.7	105.8	.461	1.3
08-09	PHX	23.8	68	17.0	.146	.198	.123	.926	.507	.392	.676	.562	.105	.022	.115	.005	.025	.041	105.9	106.2	.492	1.8
09-10	PHX	24.8	82	24.3	.138	.423	.098	.675	.461	.458	.754	.612	.079	.026	.110	.006	.020	.036	107.4	106.2	.539	5.1
10-11p	PHX	25.8	75	16.8	.154	.351	.107	.756	.472	.394	.738	.564	.097	.025	.113	.005	.019	.039	106.1	105.9	.507	2.4
Most similar to: James Posey (97.7), Scott Burrell, Paul Graham, Mike O'Koren														IMP: 44%		BRK: 5%		COP: 10%		

Jared Dudley put together his best year as a pro by consistently producing for Phoenix off the bench while playing big minutes for a reserve. Dudley's reward? An uncertain future after the Suns loaded up at his position. Dudley's upside is limited; he's a role player whose contract expires at season's end. Still, he's overqualified to be the odd man out if that is indeed the case.

2009-10 saw Dudley embrace what Mark Travis of the But The Game is On blog has termed the "3/D" role, which describes wing players who specialize in defending high scorers and shooting threes. The addition of the longball changed Dudley's offensive game and allowed him to post the best True Shooting Percentage of his career. Defensively, Dudley is stronger than most opposing wings and has good length, which makes him effective defending multiple positions. That versatility will pay off for Dudley and is his ticket to playing time this season.

C 8	Channing Frye	Hght: 6'11" Wght: 245 2011-12 status: guaranteed contract for $5.6 million	Exp: 5 From: Arizona	Salary: $5.2 million							**SKILL RATINGS**						
											TOT	OFF	DEF	REB	PAS	HND	SHT	ATH
											0	+1	-3	-3	+1	+3	0	0
Year	Team	Age	G	MPG	Usg	3PA%	FTA%	INS	2P%	3P%	FT%	TS%	Reb%	Ast%	TO%	BLK%	STL%	PF%	oRTG	dRTG	Win%	WARP
07-08	POR	24.9	78	17.2	.197	.016	.086	1.070	.492	.333	.780	.530	.154	.020	.099	.016	.010	.073	104.1	106.0	.436	0.5
08-09	POR	25.9	63	11.8	.198	.106	.051	.945	.436	.333	.722	.465	.117	.015	.093	.017	.012	.067	102.2	107.2	.337	-1.2
09-10	PHX	26.9	81	27.0	.168	.473	.064	.591	.466	.439	.810	.598	.106	.023	.088	.024	.014	.053	107.5	105.2	.576	7.2
10-11p	PHX	27.9	76	28.0	.189	.308	.060	.752	.456	.389	.772	.528	.122	.021	.094	.019	.012	.062	104.5	105.8	.454	1.7
Most similar to: Danny Ferry (97.5), Scott Padgett, Matt Bonner, Austin Croshere																IMP: 39%		BRK: 5%			COP: 11%	

A few feet turned around Channing Frye's entire career. During his first four NBA seasons, Frye's favorite shot on the court was from 18 to 20 feet. He was effective at times running the pick-and-pop, but shooting long twos limited his efficiency, which ranged from acceptable (in 2007-08) to atrocious (in 2008-09). Frye spent last summer working to add another few feet to his range, stepping back behind the three-point line with the Suns' full encouragement. Improbably, Frye began the year with a career total of 20 three-pointers and finished it as the league's leader in triples with 172 in 2009-10.

Instead of using him to pick-and-pop, Phoenix put Frye on the weak side while running pick-and-rolls for Amar'e Stoudemire and Robin Lopez. When opponents had to help, that left Frye all alone, and he made them pay time and again. Little else changed about Frye's game. His rebounding numbers have sunk as he has spent more time on the perimeter, but he blocked more shots while playing primarily center instead of his natural power forward position. Frye is a liability defensively, but as long as he's knocking down the three he's a net positive. Last season, the Suns were 6.0 points better per 100 possessions with Frye on the floor, per BasketballValue.com.

SF 33	Grant Hill	Hght: 6'8" Wght: 225 2011-12 status: free agent	Exp: 15 From: Duke	Salary: $3.2 million							**SKILL RATINGS**						
											TOT	OFF	DEF	REB	PAS	HND	SHT	ATH
											-2	-1	+1	+1	+2	+2	0	-1
Year	Team	Age	G	MPG	Usg	3PA%	FTA%	INS	2P%	3P%	FT%	TS%	Reb%	Ast%	TO%	BLK%	STL%	PF%	oRTG	dRTG	Win%	WARP
07-08	PHX	35.5	70	31.8	.181	.116	.096	.980	.535	.317	.867	.576	.086	.041	.107	.016	.012	.029	105.1	105.3	.492	3.5
08-09	PHX	36.5	82	29.8	.175	.078	.102	1.023	.547	.316	.808	.584	.094	.034	.130	.016	.018	.033	104.6	105.8	.460	2.2
09-10	PHX	37.5	81	30.0	.169	.087	.120	1.033	.483	.438	.817	.561	.100	.035	.117	.010	.012	.030	104.2	105.7	.451	1.7
10-11p	PHX	38.5	76	28.0	.170	.090	.096	1.005	.486	.360	.811	.539	.096	.034	.127	.012	.013	.032	102.8	105.6	.406	-0.4
Most similar to: Detlef Schrempf (96.9), Otis Thorpe, Buck Williams, Terry Cummings																IMP: 33%		BRK: 0%			COP: 19%	

The Valley of the Sun remains a fountain of youth for Grant Hill, who has now played in 163 out of a possible 164 games during his age-36 and age-37 seasons while starting and averaging 30 minutes a night. The Phoenix training staff has kept Hill on the floor and his heady play has allowed him to remain productive at an age where most players, even ones who did not suffer through years of ankle injuries like Hill, are considering retirement.

SCHOENE does suspect this might be the year Hill tumbles off the cliff. He saw a sharp decline in his two-point percentage last season because he struggled to finish at the rim, and only his improvement beyond the arc allowed Hill to maintain an above-average True Shooting Percentage. Hill never previously made more than 35 percent of threes, so the accuracy was likely a case of Small Sample Size Theatre (Hill attempted just 80 three-pointers all year). Hill has been an effective defender and his ability to find teammates from the wing is an asset, but a decline in his shooting would rob him of much of his value. The Suns already seem to be preparing for a future without Hill, whose contract is up at season's end.

SG 22	Matt Janning	Hght: 6'4" Wght: 175 2011-12 status: due qualifying offer of $1.0 million	Exp: R From: Northeastern	Salary: $0.5 million			SKILL RATINGS						
						TOT	OFF	DEF	REB	PAS	HND	SHT	ATH
						-4	--	--	--	--	--	--	--

Year	Team	Age	G	MPG	Usg	3PA%	FTA%	INS	2P%	3P%	FT%	TS%	Reb%	Ast%	TO%	BLK%	STL%	PF%	oRTG	dRTG	Win%	WARP
10-11p	PHX	22.8	76	-	.202	.223	.080	.857	.361	.271	.736	.416	.058	.041	.132	.002	.017	.032	-	-	.354	-

Most similar to: Acie Law (96.6), Sonny Weems, Eric Maynor, Daniel Ewing   IMP: -   BRK: -   COP: -

As a senior at Northeastern, Matt Janning averaged 15.4 points, 3.9 rebounds and 3.1 assists per game, numbers that look considerably better when accounting for the fact that the other other Huskies ranked 334th out of 347 D-I teams in pace of play. In particular, Janning's translated statistics emphasize his ability to handle the basketball. That's part of what caught the Suns' eye over the summer. They're looking for a third point guard, but wouldn't mind one like Janning who can play both backcourt positions. As a result, they invited him to training camp early in the summer, offering a small guarantee. Still, there's a distinct lack of standout skills in Janning's stat line, and he wasn't on anyone's radar prior to the draft. He'll have to shoot the ball much better than he did in college to stick. His competition includes Zabian Dowdell, a long-time favorite of the Phoenix organization who is primarily a point guard.

C 0	Dwayne Jones	Hght: 6'11" Wght: 250 2011-12 status: free agent	Exp: 5 From: Saint Joseph's	Salary: $1.0 million			SKILL RATINGS						
						TOT	OFF	DEF	REB	PAS	HND	SHT	ATH
						0	--	-1	--	--	--	--	--

Year	Team	Age	G	MPG	Usg	3PA%	FTA%	INS	2P%	3P%	FT%	TS%	Reb%	Ast%	TO%	BLK%	STL%	PF%	oRTG	dRTG	Win%	WARP
07-08	CLE	24.9	56	8.4	.086	.011	.288	1.277	.556	.000	.483	.545	.169	.010	.192	.042	.010	.088	103.9	105.5	.446	0.3
08-09	CHA	25.9	6	8.7	.125	.000	.194	1.194	.571	.000	.667	.622	.143	.000	.293	.016	.000	.055	102.9	108.7	.318	-0.1
09-10	PHX	26.9	2	3.5	.000	.000	.000	1.000	-	-	-	.152	.000	.000	.000	.000	.064	97.4	107.2	.208	0.0
10-11p	PHX	27.9	76	-	.091	.013	.267	1.254	.536	.008	.496	.536	.169	.010	.194	.040	.009	.086	-	-	.462	-

Most similar to: Jon Koncak (96.5), Don Reid, Brian Skinner, Kelvin Cato   IMP: 34%   BRK: 3%   COP: 14%

Despite putting up monster numbers in the D-League, Dwayne Jones was repeatedly passed over for call-ups before the Suns finally signed him late in the season. He was dealt to Toronto with Leandro Barbosa, but returned to Phoenix after being waived by the Raptors and has a good chance to make the Suns' roster to provide some needed size.

Jones has always been able to rebound and defend, as he demonstrated while playing a career-high 473 minutes for Cleveland in 2007-08. He's especially effective on the offensive glass, and putbacks are responsible for a good portion of his offense. What Jones showed in the D-League was the ability to score on a regular basis. Translated to the NBA environment, his usage rate of 14.8 percent of his team's plays was nearly double Jones' involvement with the Cavaliers' offense. Backup big men with the ability to contribute at both ends are a rare commodity. Jones' statistics suggest he might be one.

PF 31	Gani Lawal	Hght: 6'9" Wght: 234 2011-12 status: guaranteed contract for $0.8 million	Exp: R From: Georgia Tech	Salary: $0.5 million			SKILL RATINGS						
						TOT	OFF	DEF	REB	PAS	HND	SHT	ATH
						-2	--	--	--	--	--	--	--

Year	Team	Age	G	MPG	Usg	3PA%	FTA%	INS	2P%	3P%	FT%	TS%	Reb%	Ast%	TO%	BLK%	STL%	PF%	oRTG	dRTG	Win%	WARP
10-11p	PHX	22.5	76	-	.210	.002	.146	1.144	.435	.000	.560	.469	.162	.007	.157	.027	.006	.052	-	-	.397	-

Most similar to: Jamaal Magloire (97.5), D.J. White, Josh Boone, Jason Smith   IMP: -   BRK: -   COP: -

PHOENIX SUNS

During his third and final season at Georgia Tech, Gani Lawal teamed with Derrick Favors to make up one of the nation's most athletic frontcourts. Phoenix likes Lawal's ability to run the court and be a factor at the defensive end. As a second-round pick, he signed a three-year contract with a full guarantee for this season and partial guarantees the next two.

The strength of Lawal's game at the NCAA level was rebounding. Despite playing alongside another big-time rebounder, his translated rebounding percentage ranks third among college players who were selected in the draft. Lawal has enough size to defend power forwards and is an above-average shot blocker for the position. The Georgia Tech offense did Lawal few favors, forcing him to create a lot of his own offense. As a result, his two-point percentage tanked. Expect to see him outshoot that projection while playing a much smaller role in the Phoenix offense. He'll rely primarily on second chances and transition buckets to score in the NBA.

C 15 — Robin Lopez

Hght: 7'0" Wght: 255 Exp: 2 From: Stanford Salary: $1.9 million
2011-12 status: team option for $2.9 million

SKILL RATINGS

TOT	OFF	DEF	REB	PAS	HND	SHT	ATH
0	+1	+1	-1	-5	-5	+4	0

Year	Team	Age	G	MPG	Usg	3PA%	FTA%	INS	2P%	3P%	FT%	TS%	Reb%	Ast%	TO%	BLK%	STL%	PF%	oRTG	dRTG	Win%	WARP
08-09	PHX	21.1	60	10.2	.140	.005	.153	1.148	.522	.000	.691	.566	.112	.006	.144	.049	.009	.070	103.5	106.3	.408	-0.1
09-10	PHX	22.1	51	19.3	.174	.000	.142	1.142	.588	-	.704	.621	.141	.003	.106	.038	.005	.053	106.2	105.7	.519	2.1
10-11p	PHX	23.1	71	25.0	.182	.004	.148	1.144	.555	.002	.697	.593	.136	.005	.129	.043	.006	.059	104.3	105.3	.465	1.8

Most similar to: Brendan Haywood (97.1), Josh Boone, LaMarcus Aldridge, Jermaine O'Neal   IMP: 53% BRK: 8% COP: 5%

It was a big year for the Suns' 2008 draft class. Like Goran Dragic, first-round pick Robin Lopez returned for his sophomore campaign as a totally different player. A broken bone in his left foot sidelined Lopez at the start of the year, but by the middle of January he had replaced Channing Frye as Phoenix's starting center. The Suns played their best basketball with Lopez in the lineup before a bulging disc in his lower back kept him out late in the regular season and through the first two rounds of the playoffs.

Lopez has always been an NBA-caliber defender, and Phoenix allowed six fewer points per 100 possessions with him on the floor, per BasketballValue.com. Lopez is a good shot blocker who holds his ground in the post, but his true strength is his agility when defending on the perimeter, especially against the pick-and-roll.

To become an NBA starter, Lopez had to improve as an offensive player. He did so in a big way. Creating offense through dives to the basket out of pick-and-rolls and finishing at the rim when set up by teammates, Lopez shot one of the league's better percentages on two-point attempts. He's got the raw tools to score occasionally in the post, so there is more room for him to explore on offense. The other big change in Lopez's game was on the glass, where he was a liability as a rookie but improved to average for a center last season.

PG 13 — Steve Nash

Hght: 6'3" Wght: 178 Exp: 14 From: Santa Clara Salary: $10.3 million
2011-12 status: guaranteed contract for $11.7 million

SKILL RATINGS

TOT	OFF	DEF	REB	PAS	HND	SHT	ATH
+5	+5	-3	0	+5	+2	+4	-4

Year	Team	Age	G	MPG	Usg	3PA%	FTA%	INS	2P%	3P%	FT%	TS%	Reb%	Ast%	TO%	BLK%	STL%	PF%	oRTG	dRTG	Win%	WARP
07-08	PHX	34.2	81	34.3	.221	.279	.079	.800	.527	.470	.906	.641	.054	.145	.216	.001	.008	.017	113.1	107.1	.684	15.5
08-09	PHX	35.2	74	33.6	.212	.206	.078	.871	.529	.439	.933	.615	.051	.127	.208	.003	.011	.019	111.4	107.8	.611	10.1
09-10	PHX	36.2	81	32.8	.230	.211	.072	.861	.540	.426	.938	.615	.055	.149	.214	.003	.008	.018	113.1	107.2	.679	14.5
10-11p	PHX	37.2	75	32.0	.222	.227	.068	.841	.513	.405	.915	.586	.054	.139	.223	.002	.008	.021	110.5	107.4	.598	9.1

Most similar to: Mark Jackson (91.9), John Stockton, Sam Cassell, Rod Strickland   IMP: - BRK: - COP: -

Deep into his mid-30s, Steve Nash continues to stack together outstanding seasons. 2009-10 was his 10th consecutive year with double-figure WARP; only Tim Duncan and Jason Kidd (13) and Kobe Bryant (11) have longer streaks. (Nash's former teammate Dirk Nowitzki is also at a decade and counting.) Nash bounced back from a rough first half in 2008-09, when he clashed with Terry Porter, to put up similar numbers to his peak years in Phoenix. If there's any evidence that Nash is aging, it does not show up statistically.

Alvin Gentry has suggested that Nash's role could be slightly different this season with the arrival of Hedo

Turkoglu. Because Turkoglu is so good on the ball, Nash may spend more time spotting up. While Nash is perfectly effective as a catch-and-shoot player, that almost seems like a waste of his skills unless it helps keep Nash fresh. Already, the emergence of Goran Dragic has allowed the Suns to limit Nash's minutes. It makes more sense to keep Turkoglu on the floor whenever Nash is resting, allowing him to split ballhandling duties with Dragic.

SG 23 — Jason Richardson

Hght: 6'6" Exp: 9 Salary: $14.4 million
Wght: 225 From: Michigan State
2011-12 status: free agent

SKILL RATINGS

TOT	OFF	DEF	REB	PAS	HND	SHT	ATH
+3	+3	-4	+4	-2	-1	+3	-1

Year	Team	Age	G	MPG	Usg	3PA%	FTA%	INS	2P%	3P%	FT%	TS%	Reb%	Ast%	TO%	BLK%	STL%	PF%	oRTG	dRTG	Win%	WARP
07-08	CHA	27.3	82	38.4	.261	.337	.082	.746	.466	.406	.750	.554	.081	.038	.093	.013	.017	.035	107.8	105.5	.577	10.6
08-09	PHX	28.3	72	33.5	.216	.281	.076	.795	.518	.397	.769	.571	.077	.027	.082	.009	.016	.027	107.3	106.8	.518	5.1
09-10	PHX	29.3	79	31.5	.209	.342	.069	.728	.528	.393	.739	.574	.089	.026	.079	.009	.013	.030	107.3	106.0	.544	6.6
10-11p	PHX	30.3	75	32.0	.240	.370	.069	.699	.493	.384	.753	.554	.089	.028	.085	.010	.014	.031	106.8	105.8	.530	5.7

Most similar to: Glen Rice (98.8), Byron Scott, George McCloud, Morris Peterson

IMP: 33% BRK: 5% COP: 6%

The vision the Suns had for Jason Richardson was fully realized during the 2010 playoffs, when he torched Portland and San Antonio for better than 20 points per game and 50 percent-plus shooting beyond the arc. Fed a steady stream of open three-point attempts created by Phoenix's pick-and-roll, Richardson was nearly automatic. As a result, Richardson could be affected as much as anyone else if the Suns' pick-and-roll no longer has the same teeth without Amar'e Stoudemire as the roll man. SCHOENE expects Richardson to pick up a bigger share of the offense and give back some of his efficiency.

Because he gets few steals, Richardson scores poorly in terms of statistical athleticism. However, he's still largely the same high-flyer who won a pair of Slam Dunk Contests during his Golden State days. Richardson is a major contributor on the glass from the perimeter and is one of the league's best finishers in transition. In the half-court offense, Richardson is primarily a spot-up specialist. Phoenix does like to put him in the post at times against smaller defenders. Richardson has never put his athletic gifts to the same use at the defensive end of the floor, where he is below average.

SF 19 — Hedo Turkoglu

Hght: 6'10" Exp: 10 Salary: $10.2 million
Wght: 220 From: Istanbul, Turkey
2011-12 status: guaranteed contract for $11.0 million

SKILL RATINGS

TOT	OFF	DEF	REB	PAS	HND	SHT	ATH
+2	+3	0	0	+5	+3	0	0

Year	Team	Age	G	MPG	Usg	3PA%	FTA%	INS	2P%	3P%	FT%	TS%	Reb%	Ast%	TO%	BLK%	STL%	PF%	oRTG	dRTG	Win%	WARP
07-08	ORL	29.1	82	36.9	.249	.254	.105	.852	.485	.400	.829	.576	.087	.062	.150	.006	.011	.036	108.5	105.9	.585	10.6
08-09	ORL	30.1	77	36.6	.231	.269	.122	.854	.445	.356	.807	.541	.080	.062	.146	.005	.012	.036	107.3	106.7	.522	6.2
09-10	TOR	31.1	74	30.7	.181	.322	.111	.789	.436	.374	.774	.540	.087	.061	.139	.011	.012	.044	106.7	106.7	.499	3.9
10-11p	PHX	32.1	74	32.0	.208	.363	.103	.740	.438	.368	.783	.540	.090	.060	.150	.008	.012	.042	106.3	106.4	.500	4.1

Most similar to: Reggie Theus (97.0), Jalen Rose, Steve Smith, Craig Ehlo

IMP: 39% BRK: 5% COP: 5%

The single biggest problem for Hedo Turkoglu during his lone season north of the border was the expectation that he would be a difference-maker for the Raptors. Turkoglu's role in Orlando's run to the NBA Finals made him a coveted free agent, but his statistics from the previous three seasons painted a much more pedestrian view of Turkoglu's game. Lo and behold, Turkoglu performed at about that level. Turkoglu certainly did not help his own cause. Often uninterested at the defensive end of the floor, Turkoglu went through the motions at times after the Raptors were effectively eliminated, and he burned bridges on his way out of town.

Turkoglu will no longer bear the weight of high hopes in Phoenix, where it's understood that he is a piece on a successful team. Most likely, Turkoglu will step into the power forward spot vacated by Amar'e Stoudemire, creating an entirely different set of matchup problems for defenses. Turkoglu should be able to beat slower defenders off the dribble, and his passing ability will help keep the ball moving. However, Turkoglu creates equally large matchup problems at the other end of the floor. Though he's 6'10", Turkoglu has never defended power forwards on a regular basis and figures to struggle in this role. He will also be a major liability on the defensive glass.

The Suns need Turkoglu to produce now because similar wings have crashed quickly in their early- to mid-30s. As his production declines, Turkoglu's salary will continue to increase. Despite giving up part of the guaranteed money in the final year of his contract, Turkoglu is still due a full $11.8 million in 2012-13, when he'll turn 34.

PF 21	Hakim Warrick	Hght: 6'9" Wght: 219 2011-12 status:	Exp: 5 From: Syracuse guaranteed contract for $4.4 million	Salary: $4.3 million		SKILL RATINGS							
						TOT	OFF	DEF	REB	PAS	HND	SHT	ATH
						-1	0	-3	-1	-2	-3	-1	+1

Year	Team	Age	G	MPG	Usg	3PA%	FTA%	INS	2P%	3P%	FT%	TS%	Reb%	Ast%	TO%	BLK%	STL%	PF%	oRTG	dRTG	Win%	WARP
07-08	MEM	25.8	75	23.4	.217	.056	.134	1.078	.521	.271	.704	.555	.114	.013	.099	.012	.009	.040	105.1	106.5	.452	1.3
08-09	MEM	26.8	82	24.7	.222	.024	.172	1.148	.500	.217	.711	.554	.123	.015	.103	.016	.012	.040	105.8	106.5	.476	2.5
09-10	CHI	27.8	76	20.5	.219	.009	.161	1.151	.486	.143	.737	.547	.114	.015	.107	.009	.008	.037	104.9	106.8	.437	0.6
10-11p	PHX	28.8	75	20.0	.230	.030	.155	1.125	.488	.185	.732	.541	.124	.015	.108	.012	.009	.039	103.9	106.3	.422	0.2

Most similar to: Lawrence Funderburke (99.1), Alan Henderson, Terry Catledge, Ken Norman IMP: 43% BRK: 6% COP: 8%

After bouncing around the last 18 months, Hakim Warrick figures to stick in Phoenix with a new long-term contract. Warrick's Memphis career ended last summer when the Grizzlies rescinded their qualifying offer to him, making him an unrestricted free agent. Warrick signed in Milwaukee, then ended the season in Chicago after a deadline deal.

It's obvious why the Suns were attracted to Warrick, who runs the floor very well for a power forward and can finish above the rim. Expect him to boost his two-point percentage thanks to more plentiful easy baskets. Still, Warrick is nothing special as a player. The tradeoff to using him at power forward is that he is weak on the glass and a mediocre defender in the post.

PF —	Dwayne Collins	Hght: 6'8" Wght: 240 2011-12 status:	Exp: R From: Miami (Fla.) free agent	Salary: --		SKILL RATINGS							
						TOT	OFF	DEF	REB	PAS	HND	SHT	ATH
						-1	--	--	--	--	--	--	--

Year	Team	Age	G	MPG	Usg	3PA%	FTA%	INS	2P%	3P%	FT%	TS%	Reb%	Ast%	TO%	BLK%	STL%	PF%	oRTG	dRTG	Win%	WARP
10-11p	PHX	23.0	76	-	.195	.000	.144	1.145	.480	.000	.556	.508	.159	.021	.208	.023	.009	.063	-	-	.428	-

Most similar to: Ike Diogu (96.2), Jamaal Magloire, David Lee, Othello Hunter IMP: - BRK: - COP: -

The Suns drafted a pair of power forwards in the second round of the draft, and Dwayne Collins profiles as a fairly similar player to Gani Lawal. In part because of this duplication, Phoenix asked Collins to start his career overseas. He'll play for Cimberio Varese in Italy this season. A touch short for a power forward, though certainly not small, Collins is a quality defensive rebounder. He has the chance to become an effective defender, having blocked shots on a regular basis at Miami. Collins was a high-percentage shooter, though his True Shooting Percentage was held back by his poor accuracy at the foul line. The last pick of the draft, Collins was the NBA's Mr. Irrelevant and had the description tattooed on his left hand.

SF —	Taylor Griffin	Hght: 6'7" Wght: 238 2011-12 status:	Exp: 1 From: Oklahoma free agent	Salary: --		SKILL RATINGS							
						TOT	OFF	DEF	REB	PAS	HND	SHT	ATH
						-3	-2	0	+2	0	-2	-5	+4

Year	Team	Age	G	MPG	Usg	3PA%	FTA%	INS	2P%	3P%	FT%	TS%	Reb%	Ast%	TO%	BLK%	STL%	PF%	oRTG	dRTG	Win%	WARP
09-10	PHX	24.0	8	4.0	.177	.157	.138	.981	.500	.000	.500	.425	.033	.014	.078	.044	.000	.056	98.8	107.2	.241	-0.1
10-11p	AVG	25.0	76	4.0	.136	.221	.115	.894	.421	.210	.671	.437	.101	.026	.173	.013	.022	.044	100.9	104.8	.370	-0.3

Most similar to: Thabo Sefolosha (96.3), Anthony Bonner, Tyrone Corbin, Elston Turner IMP: 65% BRK: 19% COP: 6%

PHOENIX SUNS

During his rookie season, Taylor Griffin saw just 32 minutes of NBA action. He got more run in the D-League, but his statistics there suggest that Griffin is not an NBA-caliber player. The Suns surprised prognosticators by taking Blake Griffin's elder brother during the second round of last year's draft, hoping to turn him into a small forward. His three-point shooting and ballhandling numbers from the D-League indicate that process is going to take a long time if it ever comes to fruition. Since Griffin was 24 by the end of the season, it doesn't make sense to wait around. Phoenix waived Griffin over the summer.

Portland Trail Blazers

In the time it took you to read this sentence, the 2009-10 Portland Trail Blazers just suffered another injury. From start to finish, the Blazers saw a season that began with great expectations hampered by key players on the sidelines. The most significant of the injuries:

• Late in training camp, Nicolas Batum's torn shoulder labrum worsened to the point that he had to undergo surgery. Batum, Portland's starting small forward throughout his rookie season, missed the season's first 45 games.

• Sixth man Travis Outlaw, one of the players counted on to help fill Batum's minutes, suffered a stress fracture of the fifth metatarsal in his left foot during a game in Charlotte on Nov. 14. Outlaw would not return until February.

• While playing the best basketball of his abbreviated NBA career, starting center Greg Oden suffered a fractured left patella when he rose to block a shot against the Houston Rockets on Dec. 5. The injury ended Oden's season.

• Oden's replacement in the lineup, Joel Przybilla, suffered his own patella injury less than a month later, rupturing his right patella tendon on Dec. 22 at Dallas. Like Oden, Przybilla would miss the remainder of the season, and his rehabilitation was set back when he re-ruptured the tendon in the shower at home in March.

• Backup wing Rudy Fernandez underwent microdiscectomy surgery to relieve pressure on his sciatic nerve, sitting out 19 games.

• Star guard Brandon Roy missed 14 games in late December and early January with a strained right hamstring and was never fully healthy the rest of the year. With three games left in the regular season, Roy tore the meniscus in his left knee. The subsequent surgery figured to end his playoff run, but Roy unexpectedly made an inspirational return for Game Four of the team's opening-round series with Phoenix. Productive in that game, Roy was badly limited the rest of the way.

• Even head coach Nate McMillan fell victim to the injury bug in December. While participating in a scrimmage to give the Blazers enough healthy bodies, McMillan ruptured his right Achilles tendon. McMillan missed a road trip after undergoing surgery and spent an extended period tethered to the bench, with assistant Monty Williams roaming to provide instructions.

Had Portland packed things in and blamed a disappointing season on the injuries, it would have been impossible to blame them. Instead, the Blazers won 50 games and made their second consecutive trip to the playoffs. Despite Roy being limited, Portland won a pair of playoff games against the Suns, who would sweep San Antonio in the following round.

That outcome was a testament to the depth built by the Blazers. The injuries actually solved, to some extent, the problem of distributing playing time among several qualified contenders on the wing. Up front,

TRAIL BLAZERS IN A BOX

Last year's record	50-32
Last year's Offensive Rating	112.5 (7)
Last year's Defensive Rating	108.3 (13)
Last year's point differential	3.3 (11)
Team pace	86.6 (30)
SCHOENE projection	**55-27 (1)**
Projected Offensive Rating	114.2 (1)
Projected Defensive Rating	108.3 (8)
Projected team weighted age	27.2 (17)
Projected '10-11 payroll	$73.4 (7)
Est. payroll obligations, '11-12	$75.3 (3)

Head coach: Nate McMillan

It was a challenging season for McMillan, who began the year trying to figure out how to integrate Andre Miller into the lineup, then spent much of the schedule dealing with a series of injuries. McMillan's steady leadership kept the team focused, and he filled holes with reserves stepping into larger roles. He was rewarded with a third-place finish in Coach of the Year voting. McMillan's staff saw heavy turnover this summer. Monty Williams got the top job in New Orleans, while the contracts of Dean Demopoulos and Joe Prunty were not renewed. They'll be replaced by Bernie Bickerstaff, Bob Ociepka and Blazers legend Buck Williams.

second-round pick Dante Cunningham gave Portland solid rotation minutes during a year in which he was mostly expected to watch and learn. In the backcourt, Jerryd Bayless got a chance to play extended minutes at shooting guard and demonstrated conclusively that he can score and draw fouls at the NBA level.

The biggest problem the injuries created for the Blazers was at center, where both Oden and Przybilla were lost to the team for good by New Year's Day. That forced McMillan to start 37-year-old Juwan Howard in the middle. Howard offered a game effort and was better than expected on offense thanks to his solid midrange jumper, but he is not a center by nature and provided little shot blocking in the middle.

To fill the hole, Portland acquired veteran center Marcus Camby from the L.A. Clippers just before the trade deadline. The 36-year-old Camby hardly made the Blazers younger in the middle, but his rebounding and shot blocking were just what Portland needed from the position. The Blazers were able to pull off the trade because Outlaw and point guard Steve Blake, whom they sent to L.A. in a swap involving three players with expiring contracts, had become expendable.

Blake was involved in the season's early drama, a battle at the point. The incumbent starter, Blake had a solid 2008-09 season, but Portland wanted more creativity at the point to reduce the burden on Roy to create his own offense. The Blazers got experienced Andre Miller on a reasonable three-year contract after striking out with their first two targets in free agency, forwards Hedo Turkoglu and Paul Millsap.

The front office wanted Miller to start, but McMillan was more reluctant, while Roy was also more comfortable playing alongside Blake. Batum's absence offered a temporary solution, with both point guards starting together and Roy sliding to small forward in a smaller lineup. The unit was surprisingly successful, going 7-2, but it only delayed a decision between Blake and Miller. A January shouting match at practice between Miller and McMillan seemed like it might mark the end for Miller. Instead, it proved a turning point. Later in the month, Miller exploded for a franchise-record 52 points at Dallas in a game Roy sat out, and he established himself as the starter before Blake was traded.

After the deal for Camby, Portland played its best basketball, winning 19 of its last 27 games to reach the 50-win mark. The defense picked up immediately with Camby in the middle, and he was actually the most successful of the Blazers' centers in terms of how the team played with him on the floor (Table 1).

Table 1: Portland Centers, 2009-10

Center	Ortg	Drtg	Net
Camby	116.3	103.9	12.3
Oden	114.5	105.7	8.8
Aldridge*	115.9	108.2	7.8
Pryzbilla	103.9	101.1	2.8
Howard*	109.0	108.6	0.4
Pendergraph*	111.5	117.7	-6.2
Total	111.0	107.0	4.0

* Stats only from minutes at center

Had Roy been healthy, Portland's series against Phoenix might have been interesting. As it was, a big night from Miller led the Blazers to a Game One win on the road. The Suns were able to contain Miller by putting the bigger Grant Hill on him, and Portland had a tough time consistently generating enough offense to keep up with Phoenix. Roy's gutsy return produced the Hollywood ending of a Game Four victory at a raucous Rose Garden, but it proved to be the Blazers' last hurrah of the season.

When the action ended on the floor, it picked up in the front office. During March, Portland unexpectedly fired assistant GM Tom Penn, the right-hand man to general manager Kevin Pritchard. It's unclear exactly what precipitated Penn's dismissal, but the likely explanation involves office politics gone wrong. Warren LeGarie, the agent for both Penn and Pritchard, tied the move to Pritchard, calling it "a drive-by." It soon became clear that Pritchard was on the way out, but the timing of the move was baffling. Owner Paul Allen fired Pritchard the day of the draft, having him complete the Blazers' selections as his final act as GM.

The draft had always been Pritchard's favorite time of the year, and he was busy again. He dealt backup wing Martell Webster to Minnesota in exchange for forward Ryan Gomes (whom the team would soon waive, taking advantage of a contract that was minimally guaranteed) and the No. 16 pick, used on Nevada forward Luke Babbitt. Portland drafted Memphis guard Elliot Williams at No. 22 and another Nevada product, point guard Armon Johnson, in the second round with the 34th overall pick.

The Blazers would stabilize the circus in the front office the next month, hiring Oklahoma City assistant GM Rich Cho to replace Pritchard. A salary-cap ex-

From the Blogosphere

Who: Benjamin Golliver
What: Blazersedge
Where: http://www.blazersedge.com/

2010 is an audit year for the Blazers, as they pick up the pieces from a 2009 season that taught them nothing can be taken for granted. Not Greg Oden, who is perpetually rehabbing; not general manager Kevin Pritchard, who was fired unceremoniously on draft night; not even Brandon Roy, who, limited by injuries, couldn't lead the team out of the first round. New GM Rich Cho, who boasts legal and engineering degrees and a decade-plus of NBA experience, seems tailor-made to carry out the reassessment. Cho's story is enchanting and unprecedented, combining a Burmese immigrant rags-to-riches biography, an accountant's hard-line data-centric approach and a hope-selling fresh face. Please, call him "H and R Barack." While Portland fans are eager to turn the page after a drama-filled summer, they, like owner Paul Allen, are even more anxious to advance in the playoffs now. Cho seems poised to fulfill that mandate.

---

pert with a background as an engineer that has helped him embrace statistical analysis, Cho's steady presence starkly contrasts with Pritchard's outgoing, media- and fan-friendly personality and figures to suit Allen better. Like any first-time GM, however, Cho must demonstrate the ability to lead a front office.

Portland struck in free agency prior to Cho's hiring, when team president Larry Miller was running the front office with assistance from scouts Mike Born and Chad Buchanan. Taking an aggressive approach, Portland front-loaded a five-year mid-level offer to Utah guard Wesley Matthews, a restricted free agent, with the largest signing bonus possible. The Jazz, already in luxury-tax territory, chose not to match. Matthews' ability as a shooter and individual defender makes him an ideal role player, but he'll be well paid for playing a reserve role behind established starters Batum and Roy.

Other than Matthews playing the backup wing minutes that went to Webster and Fernandez (who threatened a holdout through his agent and wishes to return to Europe), the Blazers' rotation will be largely the same as it was a year ago. The difference? Having a full complement of players available at the same time.

Portland cannot count on perfect health. Oden's history of injuries, which have limited him to one full season--precisely 82 games--in three years as a pro, is well documented. The history of players in their 30s returning from patella tendon injuries is limited, and the re-injury makes it all the more unlikely Przybilla will be able to contribute next season. Roy is an injury risk in his own right, having missed extended periods twice in four NBA seasons. In the long term, the series of scopes he has endured on both knees is a concern.

Still, it is exceedingly unlikely that the Blazers will be as battered by injuries as they were a year ago, and that makes a major difference in projecting Portland in 2010-11 and beyond. The Oklahoma City Thunder usurped the Blazers' title as up-and-coming Western Conference contender by matching their 50 wins with an even younger roster, but the role of health in the two teams' campaigns cannot be ignored. The Thunder's rotation players missed a total of 20 games all season; five different Portland players missed that many or more.

If SCHOENE is to be believed, a healthy Blazers squad will be very dangerous this season. It is Portland, not the Lakers or Orlando, that owns the second-best projection in the league after the star-studded Miami Heat. The Blazers are projected to rise to the top of the league in Offensive Rating, near where they finished in 2008-09 (when they were second behind Phoenix) while also improving incrementally to eighth in the league in Defensive Rating with a full season from Camby.

If Oden stays on the court and continues the progress he made last season toward being a force at both ends of the floor, and if the other core pieces stay healthy, Portland is as deep and as talented as anyone in the league.

Kevin Pelton

PORTLAND TRAIL BLAZERS

TRAIL BLAZERS FIVE-YEAR TRENDS

Season	AGE	W-L	POW	PYTH	SEED	ORTG	DRTG	PT DIFF	PACE
05-06	24.6	21-61	17.9 (30)	16.0	---	102.0 (30)	113.9 (28)	-9.5 (30)	86.5 (28)
06-07	24.4	32-50	30.9 (25)	28.6	---	105.9 (24)	111.8 (26)	-4.3 (27)	87.2 (29)
07-08	24.5	41-41	40.5 (15)	38.1	---	109.4 (15)	110.4 (17)	-1.0 (17)	86.3 (29)
08-09	24.0	54-28	55.2 (5)	56.1	4	115.4 (2)	109.0 (12)	5.3 (5)	85.6 (29)
09-10	27.4	50-32	50.0 (11)	50.6	6	112.5 (7)	108.3 (13)	3.3 (11)	86.6 (30)

		OFFENSE				DEFENSE			
Season	PAY	eFG	oREB	FT/FGA	TO	eFG	oREB	FT/FGA	TO
05-06	$51.1	.474 (26)	.266 (18)	.214 (28)	.169 (24)	.507 (25)	.682 (30)	.231 (7)	.149 (27)
06-07	$64.8	.483 (23)	.282 (12)	.241 (16)	.170 (20)	.508 (25)	.730 (15)	.267 (24)	.155 (27)
07-08	$57.2	.490 (18)	.267 (15)	.216 (22)	.139 (7)	.491 (9)	.718 (25)	.212 (8)	.139 (25)
08-09	$56.2	.511 (8)	.326 (1)	.233 (17)	.148 (11)	.500 (15)	.750 (6)	.224 (10)	.153 (15)
09-10	$58.2	.499 (14)	.282 (4)	.249 (5)	.141 (3)	.502 (17)	.748 (7)	.219 (14)	.154 (18)

(league rankings in parenthesis)

PF 12 — LaMarcus Aldridge
Hght: 6'11" Exp: 4 Salary: $11.2 million
Wght: 240 From: Texas
2011-12 status: guaranteed contract for $12.4 million

SKILL RATINGS
TOT	OFF	DEF	REB	PAS	HND	SHT	ATH
+2	+2	+3	-1	+2	+3	0	+1

Year	Team	Age	G	MPG	Usg	3PA%	FTA%	INS	2P%	3P%	FT%	TS%	Reb%	Ast%	TO%	BLK%	STL%	PF%	oRTG	dRTG	Win%	WARP
07-08	POR	22.8	76	34.9	.255	.005	.092	1.088	.485	.143	.762	.522	.128	.022	.089	.028	.010	.043	105.0	104.9	.503	4.8
08-09	POR	23.8	81	37.1	.239	.019	.097	1.079	.489	.250	.781	.529	.125	.025	.080	.020	.014	.033	106.3	105.7	.520	6.5
09-10	POR	24.8	78	37.5	.231	.011	.095	1.084	.498	.313	.757	.535	.133	.026	.074	.013	.012	.038	105.6	105.6	.500	5.0
10-11p	POR	25.8	75	37.0	.239	.018	.095	1.077	.494	.285	.777	.533	.120	.026	.077	.018	.013	.036	105.5	105.5	.498	4.8

Most similar to: Vin Baker (98.6), Charles D. Smith, Antawn Jamison, Dominique Wilkins

IMP: 47% BRK: 4% COP: 4%

At 25, LaMarcus Aldridge seems to have established who he is as an NBA player. In terms of both advanced and traditional statistics, Aldridge's numbers have been extremely consistent the last three seasons. That has made Aldridge a polarizing figure in Portland. Supporters point to his consistent, reliable production, while critics focus on Aldridge's lack of development and tendency to struggle against top opposition. Both arguments have their merits.

From a statistical perspective, the strength of Aldridge's game is his ability to avoid turnovers. Among players who used plays at an average rate or better, Aldridge's turnover rate was the fourth-lowest in the league. When he posts up, his size allows him to keep the ball high and away from pesky defenders. Aldridge utilizes a variety of turnarounds and fadeaways to get shots from midrange, yet still gets to the free throw line at a reasonable rate, keeping his True Shooting Percentage at an acceptable level. Aldridge will yield ground defensively in the post, but his length allows him to contest shots and he defends well on the perimeter after switching screens.

SF 11 — Luke Babbitt
Hght: 6'9" Exp: R Salary: $1.6 million
Wght: 225 From: Nevada-Reno
2011-12 status: guaranteed contract for $1.8 million

SKILL RATINGS
TOT	OFF	DEF	REB	PAS	HND	SHT	ATH
-3	-1	-2	+2	-1	-2	-3	-3

Year	Team	Age	G	MPG	Usg	3PA%	FTA%	INS	2P%	3P%	FT%	TS%	Reb%	Ast%	TO%	BLK%	STL%	PF%	oRTG	dRTG	Win%	WARP
10-11p	POR	21.8	76	9.1	.189	.119	.101	.982	.416	.349	.898	.505	.099	.024	.123	.008	.010	.042	102.8	106.9	.367	-0.7

Most similar to: Troy Murphy (97.4), Antoine Wright, Malik Hairston, Bill Walker

IMP: - BRK: - COP: -

Luke Babbitt's combination of size and shooting skill made him a coveted player in the draft. The Blazers landed him via the trade that sent Martell Webster to Minnesota. Babbitt shot better than 40 percent from beyond the arc in both of his seasons at Nevada and was above 90 percent at the line, showing his pure shooting ability. His translation, which accounts for the relatively low level of play in the WAC, suggests it will take a year or two for Babbitt to become an efficient NBA scorer, but his ability to get to the free throw line and score from the perimeter should help him.

Babbitt has more work to do defensively, where he will make the adjustment from playing in the post to defending on the perimeter. His quickness should allow him to match up with wings, and Babbitt's size will be a plus in terms of contesting shots. Way down the road, he could develop into a stretch four like his best comp, Troy Murphy.

SF 88	Nicolas Batum	Hght: 6'8" Exp: 2 Salary: $1.2 million									**SKILL RATINGS**						
		Wght: 200 From: Lisieux, France									TOT	OFF	DEF	REB	PAS	HND	SHT	ATH
		2011-12 status: team option for $2.2 million									+4	+4	0	0	0	+2	+5	-1
Year	Team	Age	G	MPG	Usg	3PA%	FTA%	INS	2P%	3P%	FT%	TS%	Reb%	Ast%	TO%	BLK%	STL%	PF%	oRTG	dRTG	Win%	WARP
08-09	POR	20.4	79	18.4	.142	.387	.053	.666	.513	.369	.808	.555	.094	.024	.115	.022	.019	.045	106.5	106.0	.516	3.0
09-10	POR	21.4	37	24.8	.166	.416	.071	.655	.625	.409	.843	.646	.095	.023	.085	.022	.014	.043	108.5	105.6	.594	3.4
10-11p	POR	22.4	69	28.0	.167	.344	.073	.729	.589	.394	.852	.620	.090	.027	.095	.023	.015	.042	107.5	105.4	.569	6.2
Most similar to: Rashard Lewis (96.7), Mike Miller, Quentin Richardson, Dirk Nowitzki																IMP: 67%		BRK: 7%		COP: 4%		

At 21, Nicolas Batum has only scratched the surface of his immense talents, but his performance thus far suggests a bright future ahead of him. After returning from shoulder surgery, Batum delivered an impressive second half. He increased his involvement in the Blazers' offense from his rookie season, when he was mostly a bystander in the half court. Batum became a dangerous three-point shooter and was even better inside the arc. His two-point percentage ranked third among players with at least 500 minutes. The other leaders were 7-footers who rarely shoot outside the paint.

The way Batum glides around the court belies his explosiveness. This is most evident in transition at both ends. Batum is a superb finisher at the rim who had to wear a brace on his shoulder in part to keep him from cocking back too far on his dunks. At the other end, the chasedown block has become Batum's signature play. Blazersedge.com counted five of them in Batum's abbreviated season. His length and quickness make him potentially lethal as a defender, and he made major strides in his development as a stopper in year two. Batum has been asked to create offense for the French National Team in international play. Portland's depth might not allow him that kind of responsibility in the NBA, but the experience can help him make defenses pay for devoting too much attention elsewhere.

PG 4	Jerryd Bayless	Hght: 6'3" Exp: 2 Salary: $2.3 million									**SKILL RATINGS**						
		Wght: 200 From: Arizona									TOT	OFF	DEF	REB	PAS	HND	SHT	ATH
		2011-12 status: team option for $3.0 million									-1	+2	-2	0	0	-2	-4	+1
Year	Team	Age	G	MPG	Usg	3PA%	FTA%	INS	2P%	3P%	FT%	TS%	Reb%	Ast%	TO%	BLK%	STL%	PF%	oRTG	dRTG	Win%	WARP
08-09	POR	20.7	53	12.4	.210	.093	.156	1.063	.383	.259	.806	.487	.055	.056	.193	.002	.013	.059	102.4	108.7	.302	-1.6
09-10	POR	21.7	74	17.6	.251	.135	.156	1.021	.437	.315	.831	.534	.057	.063	.138	.003	.011	.056	106.1	108.2	.431	0.4
10-11p	POR	22.7	75	15.0	.231	.136	.158	1.022	.434	.305	.840	.535	.056	.068	.157	.004	.011	.055	105.6	108.0	.422	0.1
Most similar to: Maurice Williams (96.0), Sebastian Telfair, Marcus Williams, Derrick Chievous																IMP: 71%		BRK: 23%		COP: 3%		

Portland's project of turning Jerryd Bayless into a point guard is akin to making an attack dog a house pet. Bayless has the ballhandling ability to play the position and has shown the court vision at times, but his mentality is simply incompatible with the point. Bayless is always thinking about getting to the paint and scoring. He demonstrated he could do so at the NBA level when asked to play shooting guard following injuries, but there simply aren't regular minutes available off the ball in Portland.

The Blazers need Bayless to play the point, and he struggled in that role down the stretch. He has a tendency to overdribble while the shot clock ticks down and too often settled for a pull-up jumper when no driving lane was available. Bayless was more effective defending point guards. His strength gives him an advantage over most backup ones. His aggressive style resulted in a high foul rate, but also helped disrupt opponents at times.

PORTLAND TRAIL BLAZERS

C	Marcus Camby	Hght: 6'11"	Exp: 14	Salary: $11.7 million	SKILL RATINGS							
		Wght: 235	From: Massachusetts		TOT	OFF	DEF	REB	PAS	HND	SHT	ATH
23		2011-12 status: guaranteed contract for $12.9 million			+4	0	+4	+4	+4	+5	-2	+3

Year	Team	Age	G	MPG	Usg	3PA%	FTA%	INS	2P%	3P%	FT%	TS%	Reb%	Ast%	TO%	BLK%	STL%	PF%	oRTG	dRTG	Win%	WARP
07-08	DEN	34.1	79	34.9	.130	.024	.105	1.082	.456	.300	.708	.499	.201	.040	.140	.074	.013	.033	103.5	99.9	.622	11.8
08-09	LAC	35.1	62	31.0	.159	.006	.120	1.114	.514	.250	.725	.556	.211	.030	.139	.051	.014	.031	105.0	101.7	.608	7.7
09-10	POR	36.1	74	31.3	.129	.011	.083	1.072	.478	.286	.639	.501	.223	.037	.141	.048	.021	.032	104.6	100.6	.631	10.3
10-11p	POR	37.1	74	28.1	.122	.016	.091	1.075	.471	.253	.665	.500	.198	.034	.147	.054	.016	.035	103.3	101.0	.578	7.0

Most similar to: David Robinson (91.5), Dikembe Mutombo, Hakeem Olajuwon, Robert Parish   IMP: -   BRK: -   COP: -

The ageless Marcus Camby continues to play at a high level as he approaches his 37th birthday. Since turning 30, Camby has totaled more than 59 WARP and posted three of his four double-digit seasons in terms of WARP. Players similar to Camby aged very well for understandable reasons. Their size and length never atrophied, allowing them to remain effective at the defensive end. Camby is still a premier shot blocker and enjoyed his best season on the glass in 2009-10. As a result, Portland can feel comfortable with the two-year extension Camby signed in April.

Camby's True Shooting Percentage spiked upward in 2008-09 because of a fluke performance in terms of his two-point percentage. His finishing at the rim returned to normal last season and his two-point percentage followed suit. Camby spent most of his time in Portland on the perimeter, which explains the drop in his free throw rate. His unorthodox long jumper (really more of a set shot) is moderately effective, but Camby does his best work crashing the glass and tipping the ball back to teammates. He is a very good passer from the high post, something that helped the Blazers after his arrival.

PF	Dante Cunningham	Hght: 6'8"	Exp: 1	Salary: $0.8 million	SKILL RATINGS							
		Wght: 230	From: Villanova		TOT	OFF	DEF	REB	PAS	HND	SHT	ATH
33		2011-12 status: free agent			-1	-1	-1	-1	-4	+1	0	+1

Year	Team	Age	G	MPG	Usg	3PA%	FTA%	INS	2P%	3P%	FT%	TS%	Reb%	Ast%	TO%	BLK%	STL%	PF%	oRTG	dRTG	Win%	WARP
09-10	POR	23.0	63	11.2	.169	.008	.084	1.076	.500	.000	.646	.517	.140	.009	.060	.025	.018	.066	103.4	105.1	.443	0.4
10-11p	POR	24.0	76	10.0	.170	.011	.081	1.070	.504	.000	.677	.524	.124	.011	.061	.022	.018	.062	103.1	105.3	.428	0.2

Most similar to: Brian Cook (98.4), Terry Mills, Kris Humphries, Travis Outlaw   IMP: 42%   BRK: 6%   COP: 4%

When injuries cleared the way for Dante Cunningham to play rotation minutes, he responded with consistent production and established himself as a bona fide NBA player. Portland played better with Cunningham on the floor, a nice accomplishment for a rookie taken in the second round.

Cunningham left Villanova with a polished game. On offense, his primary contribution was accurate midrange shooting. Per Hoopdata.com, Cunningham shot an impressive 48.0 percent on long two attempts. The Blazers utilized that skill by running pick-and-pop plays to set up Cunningham, who also knocked down shots when defenses doubled off of him. Cunningham was very good on the glass and never turned the ball over. Nate McMillan was hesitant to give Cunningham more minutes in part because of his lack of size, but he held his own defensively and is fine as long as he's got a true center alongside him. The next step for Cunningham is extending his range to the three-point line, which would boost his True Shooting Percentage.

SG	Rudy Fernandez	Hght: 6'6"	Exp: 2	Salary: $1.2 million	SKILL RATINGS							
		Wght: 185	From: Palma de Mallorca, Spain		TOT	OFF	DEF	REB	PAS	HND	SHT	ATH
5		2011-12 status: team option for $2.2 million			+4	+4	+4	0	+1	+2	+2	0

Year	Team	Age	G	MPG	Usg	3PA%	FTA%	INS	2P%	3P%	FT%	TS%	Reb%	Ast%	TO%	BLK%	STL%	PF%	oRTG	dRTG	Win%	WARP
08-09	POR	24.0	78	25.6	.185	.511	.081	.570	.470	.399	.839	.588	.065	.038	.110	.005	.019	.026	109.0	106.7	.575	6.6
09-10	POR	25.0	62	23.2	.179	.494	.080	.586	.395	.368	.867	.540	.071	.042	.134	.006	.023	.029	106.8	105.5	.544	3.8
10-11p	POR	26.0	72	10.0	.179	.511	.086	.576	.432	.378	.865	.565	.065	.042	.124	.008	.020	.027	107.6	105.6	.566	2.3

Most similar to: Luther Head (97.1), Mike Bratz, Trent Tucker, Brent Barry   IMP: 57%   BRK: 8%   COP: 3%

PORTLAND TRAIL BLAZERS

The Rudy Fernandez experience in Portland fell apart so quickly it is difficult to understand what went wrong. An immediate fan favorite upon his arrival from Spain, Fernandez was a valuable contributor as a rookie. Year two saw an unhappy and unhealthy Fernandez lose his confidence. His statistics don't do justice to how poorly Fernandez played, especially during the playoffs. With the Blazers badly in need of offensive punch, Fernandez scored double-figures just twice in six games.

The Fernandez-Nate McMillan marriage was always one of convenience. Fernandez is at his best in transition, where his risk-taking results in big plays and turnovers. The cautious McMillan wanted nothing of that flair, which left Fernandez largely as a spot-up shooter in the half-court offense. He was perfectly effective in that role in 2008-09, but moped his way through last season and saw his shooting percentages plummet both inside and outside the arc.

With the arrival of Wesley Matthews, Fernandez no longer has a role in Portland and desperately wants out. He was fined $25,000 by the league after his agent, Andy Miller, said Fernandez would consider choosing not to report to training camp. Rich Cho wants to extract value for Fernandez, but there's little to gain from having him sulk on the bench or hold out. A trade is inevitable sooner rather than later.

PG 1	Armon Johnson	Hght: 6'3" Exp: R Salary: $0.5 million											
		Wght: 195 From: Nevada-Reno											
		2011-12 status: due qualifying offer of $1.0 million											

SKILL RATINGS

TOT	OFF	DEF	REB	PAS	HND	SHT	ATH
-5	-2	-4	-4	0	-2	-4	-5

Year	Team	Age	G	MPG	Usg	3PA%	FTA%	INS	2P%	3P%	FT%	TS%	Reb%	Ast%	TO%	BLK%	STL%	PF%	oRTG	dRTG	Win%	WARP
10-11p	POR	22.2	76	5.0	.181	.091	.061	.970	.434	.201	.664	.445	.040	.068	.194	.004	.008	.032	101.3	108.2	.285	-1.0

Most similar to: Ramon Sessions (96.7), Deron Williams, Richard Jefferson, Kirk Snyder   IMP: -   BRK: -   COP: -

Portland bought its way into the early second round with an eye toward selecting Armon Johnson, Luke Babbitt's teammate at Nevada. Johnson impressed during the NBA Summer League and enters training camp with an outside chance of unseating Jerryd Bayless as the backup point guard. Johnson's ability as a distributor and his pressure defense potentially make him a better fit for the role.

The numbers are divided on Johnson's long-term potential. His projected winning percentage suggests he has no business on an NBA court next season, but similar players have fared well in the league. Ramon Sessions is an especially interesting match. Johnson's predecessor at Nevada overcame similar weaknesses (poor outside shooting and a tendency to turn the ball over) to become a quality NBA point guard. Johnson will have to show some modicum of shooting ability to get defenses to respect him.

SG 2	Wesley Matthews	Hght: 6'5" Exp: 1 Salary: $5.8 million
		Wght: 220 From: Marquette
		2011-12 status: guaranteed contract for $6.1 million

SKILL RATINGS

TOT	OFF	DEF	REB	PAS	HND	SHT	ATH
+1	+3	-1	-3	-2	-1	+4	-1

Year	Team	Age	G	MPG	Usg	3PA%	FTA%	INS	2P%	3P%	FT%	TS%	Reb%	Ast%	TO%	BLK%	STL%	PF%	oRTG	dRTG	Win%	WARP
09-10	UTA	23.5	82	24.7	.166	.222	.114	.892	.525	.382	.829	.592	.055	.028	.125	.006	.016	.034	104.5	106.9	.421	0.2
10-11p	POR	24.5	76	25.0	.170	.276	.112	.836	.518	.409	.851	.606	.052	.029	.121	.006	.016	.032	106.0	106.7	.476	2.4

Most similar to: Jim Paxson (97.5), Aaron McKie, Kevin Martin, Byron Scott   IMP: 58%   BRK: 5%   COP: 6%

Wesley Matthews was one of last season's best stories. Undrafted out of Marquette, Matthews worked his way into a starting job in Utah and ended up across from Kobe Bryant in the playoffs. Matthews never gave the impression that the situation was too big for him, confidently filling his role at both ends of the floor. Matthews cashed in with a front-loaded five-year offer sheet from the Blazers that the Jazz chose not to match.

Matthews' skill set is ideal for a role player. He's an example of the 3/D concept (see Jared Dudley comment for more), having shot 38.2 percent from beyond the arc as a rookie and handled the toughest defensive assignments in Utah. Matthews makes few mistakes and will rarely hurt the team while he's on the floor. Still, Portland's five-year offer is troubling because of the poor track record of long-term mid-level contracts for reserves. Matthews' age also limits his upside. He'll be 24 this season, and though SCHOENE projects a solid step forward, this may be as good as Matthews gets while his cap hit continues to escalate.

PORTLAND TRAIL BLAZERS

PG 24	Andre Miller	Hght: 6'2" Exp: 11 Salary: $7.3 million					
		Wght: 200 From: Utah					
		2011-12 status: non-guaranteed contract for $7.8 million					

SKILL RATINGS

TOT	OFF	DEF	REB	PAS	HND	SHT	ATH
+1	+2	-1	+2	+2	+1	-3	+1

Year	Team	Age	G	MPG	Usg	3PA%	FTA%	INS	2P%	3P%	FT%	TS%	Reb%	Ast%	TO%	BLK%	STL%	PF%	oRTG	dRTG	Win%	WARP
07-08	PHI	32.1	82	36.7	.227	.023	.097	1.075	.504	.088	.772	.537	.064	.085	.136	.002	.016	.028	107.2	106.6	.521	6.6
08-09	PHI	33.1	82	36.3	.219	.037	.127	1.089	.483	.283	.826	.548	.074	.082	.140	.004	.019	.030	108.4	106.9	.546	8.0
09-10	POR	34.1	82	30.5	.240	.064	.138	1.074	.469	.200	.821	.530	.066	.085	.138	.003	.020	.032	107.7	106.4	.542	6.5
10-11p	POR	35.1	76	32.0	.219	.057	.108	1.051	.469	.200	.806	.514	.062	.080	.143	.003	.017	.032	105.8	106.7	.472	2.8

Most similar to: Rod Strickland (97.7), Maurice Cheeks, Dennis Johnson, Sedale Threatt   IMP: 39%   BRK: 0%   COP: 6%

The concerns about how Andre Miller would fit with the Blazers expressed in this space a year ago proved largely unfounded. There was an adjustment period as Nate McMillan figured out how to use Miller alongside Brandon Roy with only one basketball available for two players who like to handle it, but Miller proved indispensable late in the season. The addition of a second player capable of creating offense from the perimeter made Portland less predictable and Miller stepped up when Roy was out of the lineup.

At this stage of his career, Miller's craftiness masks his declining quickness. He has a unique knack for finding open spots on the floor, helping cover up for the fact that he has virtually no range whatsoever. At times, this weakness limited the Blazers' ability to space the floor, but Miller was generally too good to take off the floor. At the defensive end, Miller's strength is his biggest advantage. Portland was able to get away with Miller defending off-guards at times when Nicolas Batum slid over to the point to provide more length on the ball. Miller is a very good rebounder for a guard.

PG 8	Patrick Mills	Hght: 6'0" Exp: 1 Salary: --
		Wght: 185 From: St. Mary's (CA)
		2011-12 status: free agent

SKILL RATINGS

TOT	OFF	DEF	REB	PAS	HND	SHT	ATH
--	--	--	--	--	--	--	--

Year	Team	Age	G	MPG	Usg	3PA%	FTA%	INS	2P%	3P%	FT%	TS%	Reb%	Ast%	TO%	BLK%	STL%	PF%	oRTG	dRTG	Win%	WARP
09-10	POR	21.7	10	3.8	.392	.129	.099	.970	.400	.500	.571	.480	.033	.063	.129	.000	.000	.076	104.7	111.3	.299	-0.1

The Blazers wanted to send second-round pick Patty Mills overseas, but he chose to sign the tender teams are required to offer second-round picks. Despite a broken bone in his right foot, Mills made the roster as Portland's 15th man. After Mills returned to the floor, he saw garbage time in a handful of games and played well in brief D-League stints.

Lightning quick off the dribble, Mills gave the USA team fits during the 2008 Beijing Olympics and has the potential to live in the lane thanks to the NBA's restrictions on contact on the perimeter. However, Mills' score-first mentality limits him because he is too small to play anywhere but point guard in the NBA. Armon Johnson's skills are a better contrast to those of current backup Jerryd Bayless, and Mills would have to convince the Blazers to keep four point guards to make the roster. He spent the summer shopping for a better deal than the qualifying offer Portland extended before ultimately deciding to go to camp with the Blazers.

C 52	Greg Oden	Hght: 7'0" Exp: 2 Salary: $6.8 million
		Wght: 285 From: Ohio State
		2011-12 status: due qualifying offer of $8.8 million

SKILL RATINGS

TOT	OFF	DEF	REB	PAS	HND	SHT	ATH
+5	+4	0	+4	0	-4	+5	+2

Year	Team	Age	G	MPG	Usg	3PA%	FTA%	INS	2P%	3P%	FT%	TS%	Reb%	Ast%	TO%	BLK%	STL%	PF%	oRTG	dRTG	Win%	WARP
08-09	POR	21.2	61	21.5	.194	.000	.185	1.185	.564	.000	.637	.599	.201	.011	.162	.042	.010	.086	107.2	105.4	.557	3.9
09-10	POR	22.2	21	23.9	.209	.000	.128	1.128	.605	-	.766	.647	.220	.018	.178	.077	.009	.080	108.3	102.1	.693	2.9
10-11p	POR	23.2	61	24.0	.220	.004	.151	1.146	.601	.006	.729	.638	.193	.019	.168	.062	.009	.076	107.8	103.2	.647	7.1

Most similar to: Hakeem Olajuwon (93.6), Yao Ming, Dwight Howard, Tim Duncan   IMP: 63%   BRK: 0%   COP: 0%

The shame of the fractured patella that ended Greg Oden's season was how well the big man was playing at the start of his second NBA campaign. Oden made strides over his rookie year in virtually every category. He was dominant as a rebounder and shot blocker, allowing Portland to play a small backcourt during the month of November. Oden also showed his potential as a scorer, increasing his usage rate with more touches in the post while shooting a very high percentage from the field.

Given the way he played last season, it's hard to say the injuries have slowed Oden's development. However, they have made it difficult for the Blazers to learn how to play with him. Adding another post-up threat to LaMarcus Aldridge and finding enough touches for Brandon Roy and Andre Miller on the perimeter is a challenge for Nate McMillan, though a happy one. Oden also needs time on the court to improve his defensive instincts and cut down on his foul rate, which has impeded him from logging heavier minutes.

As of the start of training camp, Oden was still not able to participate in 5-on-5 action. He told reporters on media day that he will not play on opening night, which will be nearly 11 months removed from his injury. Oden is dealing with patella tendinitis, which is common for players who suffer patella injuries.

C #31 Jeff Pendergraph

Hght: 6'9" Exp: 1 Salary: $0.8 million
Wght: 240 From: Arizona State
2011-12 status: partially-guaranteed contract for $0.9 million

SKILL RATINGS

TOT	OFF	DEF	REB	PAS	HND	SHT	ATH
-2	-1	-3	0	-5	-5	+5	-3

Year	Team	Age	G	MPG	Usg	3PA%	FTA%	INS	2P%	3P%	FT%	TS%	Reb%	Ast%	TO%	BLK%	STL%	PF%	oRTG	dRTG	Win%	WARP
09-10	POR	23.0	39	10.4	.101	.000	.103	1.103	.662	-	.900	.705	.150	.001	.140	.032	.009	.090	103.1	106.1	.403	-0.1
10-11p	POR	24.0	71	6.7	.105	.000	.103	1.103	.643	.000	.928	.685	.145	.001	.133	.034	.010	.083	102.8	105.5	.409	-0.1

Most similar to: Clifford Rozier (94.6), Dale Davis, David Lee, Bo Outlaw IMP: 61% BRK: 11% COP: 0%

Out of necessity, Jeff Pendergraph was thrown on the court shortly after returning in December from surgery to correct an impingement in his left hip. Pendergraph was able to translate his high-percentage shooting from the NCAA ranks to the pro game, but despite his impressive True Shooting Percentage, the Blazers were far worse with Pendergraph on the court.

Pendergraph's problems were at the defensive end of the floor. He's undersized for a center and is also not exceptionally quick. This resulted in frequent fouls and poor help defense. Per BasketballValue.com, Portland allowed 11.8 more points per 100 possessions with Pendergraph in the game. Since he's too slow of foot to defend power forwards, Pendergraph might not have an NBA position on defense. The rest of Pendergraph's game was sound. He rebounded the ball well at both ends and finished very well at the rim. Expect Pendergraph's shooting percentage to come slightly back to earth this season. He can offset that by improving his defensive instincts.

C #10 Joel Przybilla

Hght: 7'1" Exp: 10 Salary: $7.4 million
Wght: 245 From: Minnesota
2011-12 status: free agent

SKILL RATINGS

TOT	OFF	DEF	REB	PAS	HND	SHT	ATH
0	-1	+5	+4	-5	-5	+5	-3

Year	Team	Age	G	MPG	Usg	3PA%	FTA%	INS	2P%	3P%	FT%	TS%	Reb%	Ast%	TO%	BLK%	STL%	PF%	oRTG	dRTG	Win%	WARP
07-08	POR	28.5	77	23.6	.104	.003	.136	1.133	.581	.000	.680	.614	.209	.007	.240	.039	.003	.061	102.5	103.9	.455	1.5
08-09	POR	29.5	82	23.8	.102	.002	.176	1.174	.627	.000	.663	.652	.229	.007	.185	.039	.009	.052	104.6	103.3	.543	5.2
09-10	POR	30.5	30	22.7	.104	.000	.152	1.152	.523	-	.647	.567	.217	.006	.265	.051	.006	.067	102.0	103.4	.453	0.5
10-11p	POR	31.5	32	10.0	.103	.005	.151	1.146	.565	.000	.658	.609	.198	.006	.237	.046	.006	.064	102.5	104.1	.447	0.2

Most similar to: Ervin Johnson (93.1), Will Perdue, Marvin Webster, Greg Ostertag IMP: 56% BRK: 4% COP: 15%

The Blazers were able to rely on Joel Przybilla as their Greg Oden insurance until Przybilla suffered a serious patella injury of his own just before Christmas. The combination of the two injuries was devastating for Portland. Having re-injured his patella tendon during the rehabilitation process, Przybilla now faces an uphill battle to get back on the court and be productive again. The track record for players suffering ruptured patella tendons is ugly, especially among players in their 30s. Przybilla is not expected to be ready for the start of training camp. We've gone with a conservative projection that has him barely playing this season.

When healthy, Przybilla is one of the league's top rebounders. He puts his size to good use on the offensive glass, establishing position early and tracking the basketball well. Also a good shot blocker, Przybilla controls the paint at the defensive end. Mostly an observer on offense, Przybilla shoots the ball at a high percentage during his rare offensive chances. Przybilla will still be 7'1" when he gets back on the court, so he should have some value. The loss of mobility might limit him to being a third option at center, however.

SG 7	Brandon Roy	Hght: 6'6" Exp: 4 Salary: $13.6 million									SKILL RATINGS							
		Wght: 211 From: Washington									TOT	OFF	DEF	REB	PAS	HND	SHT	ATH
		2011-12 status: guaranteed contract for $15.0 million									+5	+5	+1	+1	+4	+4	+1	+1
Year	Team	Age	G	MPG	Usg	3PA%	FTA%	INS	2P%	3P%	FT%	TS%	Reb%	Ast%	TO%	BLK%	STL%	PF%	oRTG	dRTG	Win%	WARP
07-08	POR	23.7	74	37.7	.251	.146	.112	.965	.480	.340	.753	.531	.073	.073	.093	.004	.013	.025	108.4	105.9	.579	9.5
08-09	POR	24.7	78	37.2	.277	.130	.131	1.001	.501	.377	.824	.573	.080	.065	.090	.006	.016	.021	111.2	106.5	.649	14.1
09-10	POR	25.7	65	37.2	.269	.162	.142	.980	.512	.330	.780	.568	.073	.060	.095	.005	.013	.027	109.8	106.6	.603	9.4
10-11p	POR	26.7	73	36.0	.269	.199	.130	.930	.494	.347	.786	.557	.070	.068	.094	.005	.013	.024	109.9	106.5	.607	10.5
Most similar to: Michael Finley (97.2), Penny Hardaway, Corey Maggette, Kobe Bryant															IMP: 43%		BRK: 2%		COP: 9%			

After a breakthrough 2008-09 season left him on the cusp of superstardom, Brandon Roy took a slight step back last year. It's hard to point to any one specific area where Roy dropped off besides games played, but he was slightly less effective across the board. It's possible that 2008-09 represented a high-water mark for Roy, who will be 26 this season and has battled a series of nagging injuries while undergoing multiple arthroscopies on his knees.

Certainly, the level at which Roy played last season was very good in its own right. Like many of his Blazer teammates, Roy is remarkably sure-handed with the basketball. Combined with his ability to penetrate off the dribble for high-percentage scores and trips to the free throw line, the turnover-free play makes Roy efficient for a go-to option on offense. Roy runs an offense well enough to play point guard at times when Portland goes to a big lineup, and he's an above-average rebounder from the perimeter. Besides a three-point shot that comes and goes, the biggest weakness in Roy's game is up-and-down effort at the defensive end of the floor.

SG 9	Elliot Williams	Hght: 6'5" Exp: R Salary: $1.3 million									SKILL RATINGS							
		Wght: 180 From: Memphis									TOT	OFF	DEF	REB	PAS	HND	SHT	ATH
		2011-12 status: guaranteed contract for $1.3 million									-2	--	--	--	--	--	--	--
Year	Team	Age	G	MPG	Usg	3PA%	FTA%	INS	2P%	3P%	FT%	TS%	Reb%	Ast%	TO%	BLK%	STL%	PF%	oRTG	dRTG	Win%	WARP
10-11p	POR	21.8	76	-	.191	.223	.133	.910	.416	.304	.742	.495	.052	.049	.174	.002	.014	.039	-	-	.407	-
Most similar to: Maurice Williams (98.0), Ramon Sessions, Ben Gordon, Antoine Wright															IMP: -		BRK: -		COP: -			

One of a number of transfers who were selected in the first round of last June's draft, Elliot Williams was unique because of the reason behind his move from Duke to Memphis. Williams started for the Blue Devils at the end of his freshman season and could have been part of a national championship, but he wanted to be near his ill mother. The NCAA granted Williams a waiver, making him immediately eligible, and he boosted his NBA stock by playing well in a leading role for a young Tigers team.

An effective slasher, Williams attempted nearly eight free throws a game last season. Williams needs to improve his finishing when he gets to the rim and does not draw fouls, which limited his two-point percentage. He'll also have to develop his range to get defenses to honor his first step. A good ballhandler capable of finding teammates, Williams might ultimately fit alongside Jerryd Bayless in a second-team backcourt where both players share responsibility for initiating the offense. Unlikely to play much this season, Williams will focus on developing in practice. He missed the NBA Summer League because of a bruised right knee.

PORTLAND TRAIL BLAZERS

																	SKILL RATINGS						
PG	Travis Diener		Hght: 6'1" Wght: 175 2011-12 status: free agent		Exp: 5 From: Marquette			Salary: --					TOT +3	OFF +4	DEF -3	REB 0	PAS +1	HND +5	SHT 0	ATH -4			
--																						

Year	Team	Age	G	MPG	Usg	3PA%	FTA%	INS	2P%	3P%	FT%	TS%	Reb%	Ast%	TO%	BLK%	STL%	PF%	oRTG	dRTG	Win%	WARP
07-08	IND	26.1	66	20.5	.166	.451	.061	.609	.431	.318	.901	.494	.047	.081	.107	.002	.011	.034	107.7	107.4	.508	2.6
08-09	IND	27.1	55	13.1	.126	.571	.032	.461	.459	.390	.800	.555	.066	.074	.102	.005	.018	.026	108.9	106.4	.581	2.5
09-10	POR	28.1	9	5.7	.106	.595	.150	.554	.333	.143	.250	.255	.034	.072	.000	.000	.040	.018	103.6	104.1	.483	0.1
10-11p	AVG	29.1	71	5.7	.137	.550	.039	.489	.456	.354	.844	.515	.055	.077	.111	.004	.014	.030	107.8	106.8	.531	1.0

Most similar to: Damon Jones (97.0), Mike Dunleavy, Steve Kerr, Chris Whitney IMP: 35% BRK: 5% COP: 5%

November surgery on his left big toe sidelined Travis Diener for a month and a half. By the time he returned, he found himself buried on the Indiana Pacers' depth chart at point guard, and he was waived at his request in early March. Diener latched on in Portland, giving the Blazers a veteran reserve option at the point, but saw sparing action. The sure-handed sharpshooter is headed to Italy, where he will play for Dinamo Sassari.

Sacramento Kings

The sad truth for many rebuilding teams is that no matter how well they manage their salary cap, no matter how well they scout amateur and overseas talent and no matter how well they develop the talent they bring in and fit them into a logical, well-rendered basketball system, they aren't going to win a championship without a superstar.

We hear that term--superstar--bandied around quite a bit in basketball, probably too often. There are only a handful of real superstars in the league at any one time, perhaps 8-10 at most, guys that can be or have been the cornerstone of a championship team. Teams lose, bob up to the top of the draft board, and select a touted player whom they hope will be a superstar, but they just don't come around very often. Once they do, they tend to dominate the league for a long time. That's why when you look back at the title teams over the last two decades, you see the names of Duncan, Jordan, Bryant, O'Neal and Olajuwon pop up again and again. The exceptions are few and far between. The Pistons won a title with defense and balance; the Celtics won with an aging core that featured one-time superstar Kevin Garnett in his last go-round as a top-five player.

In Tyreke Evans, the Kings just may have found their superstar.

We wrote a pretty positive assessment of the Kings organization in last year's book. The selection of Tyreke Evans with the fourth pick in last year's draft gave the Kings a young player with upside at every position, and it was easy to muse about the team climbing the ladder with a starting five of Evans, Kevin Martin, Spencer Hawes, Jason Thompson and one of a trio of young wing players (Francisco Garcia, Omri Casspi and Donté Greene). The Kings generated solid buzz early in the season, winning nine of their first 17 and standing 13-14 at one point. From there, Sacramento went 11-44, proving not only that the future had not yet arrived but also that it may in fact not be as rosy as once thought. As a result, general manager Geoff Petrie continued to shake things up, not content to merely collect another high lottery pick.

The changes started at the trade deadline, when Petrie sent Martin to the Rockets for Carl Landry. Martin hadn't been healthy and was having a subpar season, but more than anything, he hadn't meshed with Evans on the floor during the handful of games they played together when Martin was in the lineup. When it became apparent the Kings were going to be Evans' team going forward, Petrie seized the chance to unload the three years, $34.5 million left on Martin's contract. Landry gave the Kings an inside scoring threat that had been lacking, but his effectiveness sagged when surrounded by so much inexperience. However, the Kings' investment in Landry is limited and he can become a free agent after the season.

Petrie struck again before the draft, sending Hawes and Andres Nocioni to Philadelphia for center Samuel

KINGS IN A BOX

Last year's record	25-57
Last year's Offensive Rating	106.6 (22)
Last year's Defensive Rating	111.6 (21)
Last year's point differential	-4.4 (25)
Team pace	92.7 (7)
SCHOENE projection	43-39 (9)
Projected Offensive Rating	112.3 (9)
Projected Defensive Rating	111.4 (23)
Projected team weighted age	25.2 (27)
Projected '10-11 payroll	$43.4 (30)
Est. payroll obligations, '11-12	$29.2 (30)

Head coach: Paul Westphal

Nearly a decade removed from his previous NBA head-coaching assignment, Paul Westphal made a successful return to the sidelines in Sacramento. Westphal deserves a lot of the credit for guiding the Kings' defense to a nine-spot improvement in Defensive Rating, where the team finished last in the league in 2008-09. The defensive turnaround was out of character for Westphal, whose NBA teams have historically been better on offense than defense. From a long-term perspective, Westphal's willingness to turn his young stars loose should speed up Sacramento's rebuilding process. That doesn't figure to change now that the Kings have added DeMarcus Cousins to their new core.

Dalembert. Doing so ridded the roster of Nocioni's bad contract, and brought back a potential defensive anchor in Dalembert. Losing Hawes can be chalked up to the price of doing business. He was a developing player, but far from irreplaceable. Plus Dalembert's contract expires after the season, reducing the Kings' payroll obligations to under $30 million for the 2011-12 season. By then, Petrie should have a firm idea what the ceiling is for the young group he's assembled. Also, if raw rookie center Hassan Whiteside develops, he might be able to replace much of the skill set lost by Dalembert's departure.

A key piece of Petrie's core group will be DeMarcus Cousins, a stathead favorite who fell to the Kings at No. 5 in the 2010 Draft. Cousins immediately becomes the Kings' second-best player, the Robin to Evans' Batman. Cousins projects as a five-win player right out of the gate; if he shoots the ball well, he will be even better. He'll give the Kings, who were 23rd in blocked shots last season, a second back-line defender to play alongside Dalembert. Cousins can also man the center position, opening the four for a jump shooter like Thompson, a second post threat like Landry or a floor spacer like Greene or Casspi. Kings head coach Paul Westphal will have a lot of options at his disposal in the frontcourt.

Evans headlines the backcourt, of course. Look, the comparables that SCHOENE generates are not meant to tell you that Player X is going to be just like Player Y. Instead, the system suggests the most likely path a player's career is going to follow and says a lot about how much upside he possesses. Evans' top two comps are about as promising as any Kings fan could dream of: Kobe Bryant and LeBron James. Evans has a long road to travel before he gets to the level those two megastars have reached in their maturity. Right now, all we're saying is that at 20 years old, Evans, James and Bryant shared a fairly similar starting point. You have to admit, though, that's a pretty damned good starting point.

The next major to-do item for Petrie and Westphal is to figure out what kind of a player fits best alongside Evans, who really isn't a one or a two but just a guard. It may not even be accurate to call him a combo guard, because that label suggests a player that mixes in a little bit of the skills of both positions. Evans does everything, and he does it well with one exception--his jump shot. Like Derrick Rose before him and, quite probably, John Wall after him, Evans is a John Calipari-mentored guard who just needs to develop some outside shooting touch to be a truly unguardable player. He shot .255 from three-point range last season and just 32 percent on long twos. If Evans can get above league average in those sectors, he'll be an MVP-caliber player. Right now, it seems like the best bet for the Kings is to find a catch-and-shoot guard who can defend smaller players.

That player doesn't seem to be on the roster right now. Beno Udrih is a solid, but not great, spot-up shooter and gets a fair amount of his offense off the dribble. He's also a below-average defender, and is best suited to a reserve role. The other issue is that when Udrih and Evans are on the floor together, it takes the ball out of Evans' hands too often. The Kings' offense is going to run through Evans for better or worse, and you want him to become the team's primary decision maker. It'll be up to him to ensure that his teammates don't become innocent bystanders. You can accomplish that by playing Evans alongside one of the Kings' long wing players like Garcia, Casspi or Greene. This gives the Kings a tall lineup and a lot of good kick-out options. However, that forces Evans to play the other team's quickest guard and is a weak defensive configuration overall. Or at least it was last season. Perhaps having Dalembert and Cousins at the back of the defense will help paper some of that over. The best option at the moment would seem to be an Evans/Garcia starting backcourt, with Udrih serving as the third guard and primary playmaker when Evans is out of the game. Newcomer Pooh Jeter can potentially help in spurts by guarding some of the league's small, quick guards. After the season, the Kings can use some of their cap space to find the Steve Blake-type that they currently lack.

Garcia is an interesting player whose 2009-10 season was derailed by a forearm injury that limited him to 25 games. He's a good athlete and a long 6'7" at the wing positions, but he's very thin, which might explain his poor defensive metrics. When in rhythm, Garcia is a dangerous perimeter shooter. Even with his sporadic court time last season, he still hit 39 percent of his three-pointers, a success rate that he keeps churning out season after season. In 2008-09, Garcia became more assertive on the offensive end. His usage rate climbed to near league average and a greater percentage of his made field goals were unassisted, indicators that he was becoming more adept at getting his own shot. His True Shooting Percentage fell a bit, but was still above league average. In his limited time last season, Garcia became a statue on the perimeter. His foul-drawing rate plummeted, nearly 80 percent of his field goals were assisted and his usage rate dropped. Just 16 percent of his shots came at the rim, down 10 percent from the season before. Through the change in his game, Evans' presence and his physical problems, Garcia continued to stroke it--the guy can shoot. If he can stay healthy for a season and if he proves that he can be an adequate defender of both backcourt decisions, it's not out of the realm of possibility that Garcia can prove to be more than a stopgap answer as Evans' backcourt partner.

Why are we so concerned about Evans guarding opposing point guards? Didn't we write last year about how the super athletic, long-armed Evans had the potential to be a game-changing defender? Did he do anything to change that perception during his rookie season? No, he didn't and his defense got better and better as the season progressed. Here's the thing: Upper-crust stars don't draw difficult defensive assignments most of the time. James and Bryant are excellent defensive players who often become the stoppers for their respective teams during crunch time. However, if you sift through the treasure trove of data from Synergy, Inc., and look at just the sheer number of defensive plays those kinds of players are involved in, you discover that their defensive usage rates are very low. Most of the time, those players are hidden against the opponent's worst offensive player. Consider this: Synergy credited James with 2,396 offensive plays last season. On defense, he had 727 plays. It's not an apples-to-apples comparison because certain plays are credited to team defense (like cuts and transition plays), but that doesn't account for a shortfall of more than 1,600 plays. By comparison, take a defensive specialist like Oklahoma City's Thabo Sefolosha. He had 599 plays on offense and 1,097 plays on defense, where he typically guarded the opponent's best perimeter player until the time they needed a crunch time stop, when Kevin Durant slid over to take the other team's star. That's what happened when the Thunder played the Lakers in the playoffs.

The reasons star players don't draw the tough defensive assignments are fairly obvious. You don't want them expending too much energy on defense because they are so valuable at creating offense on the other end, and those skill sets are rarer than is good defense. You also don't want them getting into foul trouble. If we're right about Evans and he is destined to become a elite offensive creator, then he's not going to be able to guard the Chris Pauls and Deron Williamses of the league for entire games. So the defensive prowess and versatility of the partner or partners you match with Evans in the Kings' backcourt are key ingredients.

In any event, aren't these kinds of issues a lot more fun to discuss for Kings fans than what faced the franchise a couple of years ago, when the bulk of the payroll was going to descending veterans like Mike Bibby, Ron Artest, Brad Miller, Kenny Thomas and Shareef Abdur-Rahim? You'd think so. You'd think there is a lot of excitement in Sacramento and perhaps there is. However, despite a young roster showing signs of a hoops renaissance in Sacramento, the attendance failed to rebound, though it is headed in the right direction. The Kings sold out Arco Arena to the tune of 100 percent of capacity for over half of the last decade. That fell to 81.7 percent in 2007-08, then 72.6 percent the season before last. In 2009-10, the figure climbed to 76.5 percent in an environment where the league was down overall. The arena situation in Sacramento is murky. Pretty much everybody agrees that the Kings need a new venue. There have been ongoing negotiations to get one built, possibly downtown. However, it's tenuous and wholly dependent upon a national economy that is unlikely to improve significantly any time soon. The Kings' owners, the Maloof

---

From the Blogosphere

Who: Tom Ziller
What: Sactown Royalty
Where: http://www.sactownroyalty.com/

The most striking thing about Tyreke Evans isn't that he can get to the rim; many NBA players do that both frequently and well. It's the lack of mystery in Evans' intentions that knocks you off-kilter after watching him for a few months. So many great penetrators play off a counterbalance, either their own perimeter game or the gravity (and defensive attention) of a teammate. Evans had neither as a rookie. He shot worse from outside than most of the league and, until the late-season trade for Carl Landry, had no post presence alongside him. Everyone knew Evans would be dropping his head and barreling to the rim. And no one could stop him. If he adds a Derrick Rose-style pull-up or Brandon Roy's hesitation moves, watch out.

brothers, have softened their public comments due to the current economic climate, but the team's future in Sacramento is not assured.

What helps is what is happening on the court. The Kings have talent, no large long-term contracts and the lowest payroll in the league. They'll nearly have room for two max free agents after the season, which will allow them to take on a key player through trade or extend their young players as they mature and prove themselves worthy of the investment. As always, the arena issue looms large, but the Kings will establish themselves as one of the league's up-and-coming squads in the coming season, finishing on the right side of .500 and making a push for the playoffs.

Bradford Doolittle

KINGS FIVE-YEAR TRENDS

Season	AGE	W-L	POW	PYTH	SEED	ORTG	DRTG	PT DIFF	PACE
05-06	27.2	44-38	45.8 (11)	45.5	8	108.2 (11)	106.5 (13)	1.5 (12)	90.7 (10)
06-07	27.3	33-49	35.0 (19)	36.0	---	107.9 (16)	109.6 (21)	-1.8 (19)	93.3 (4)
07-08	27.4	38-44	37.1 (18)	34.8	---	109.7 (14)	112.3 (25)	-2.3 (20)	92.7 (8)
08-09	26.3	17-65	17.9 (30)	19.4	---	106.9 (24)	116.6 (30)	-8.8 (29)	92.9 (7)
09-10	24.9	25-57	26.8 (25)	29.1	---	106.6 (22)	111.6 (21)	-4.4 (25)	92.7 (7)

		OFFENSE				DEFENSE			
Season	PAY	eFG	oREB	FT/FGA	TO	eFG	oREB	FT/FGA	TO
05-06	$60.5	.492 (12)	.254 (26)	.262 (11)	.160 (17)	.488 (13)	.722 (18)	.210 (3)	.160 (15)
06-07	$61.1	.491 (19)	.231 (28)	.289 (1)	.155 (5)	.513 (26)	.725 (17)	.240 (13)	.173 (3)
07-08	$50.5	.503 (11)	.252 (22)	.276 (1)	.164 (30)	.510 (25)	.717 (27)	.256 (24)	.157 (7)
08-09	$68.7	.491 (22)	.245 (26)	.252 (5)	.164 (25)	.526 (29)	.699 (29)	.269 (27)	.153 (17)
09-10	$60.7	.491 (22)	.278 (6)	.207 (25)	.160 (21)	.505 (19)	.735 (18)	.244 (21)	.146 (23)

(league rankings in parenthesis)

SF 18 — Omri Casspi
Hght: 6'9" Exp: 1 Salary: $1.3 million
Wght: 225 From: Yavne, Israel
2011-12 status: team option for $1.3 million

SKILL RATINGS — TOT +2, OFF +2, DEF +4, REB +2, PAS -1, HND -2, SHT +2, ATH 0

Year	Team	Age	G	MPG	Usg	3PA%	FTA%	INS	2P%	3P%	FT%	TS%	Reb%	Ast%	TO%	BLK%	STL%	PF%	oRTG	dRTG	Win%	WARP
09-10	SAC	21.8	77	25.1	.195	.240	.090	.851	.480	.369	.672	.529	.104	.022	.116	.006	.014	.029	104.3	105.9	.446	1.2
10-11p	SAC	22.8	75	28.0	.197	.272	.095	.823	.495	.379	.678	.547	.103	.024	.113	.007	.014	.028	105.5	105.8	.491	3.3

Most similar to: Joe Johnson (97.8), Dirk Nowitzki, Jason Richardson, Sean Elliott — IMP: 63% BRK: 7% COP: 2%

Either Omri Casspi or Donté Greene will likely start at small forward for the Kings this season. Casspi looks like the better player, through Greene might have more raw ability. Casspi has the potential to be one of the game's best deep-ball threats, with a consistent stroke and the size to get clean looks with a hand in his face. He's not strictly a stand-still shooter, though, and operated well in the lane as a rookie. The Kings were considerably better defensively when Casspi was on the floor, and his individual defensive metrics are impressive. He ranked in the 92nd percentile when it came to getting stops against isolations. If Casspi demonstrates any growth in his game whatsoever, it's tough to see how Greene could get the starting nod.

C 15 — DeMarcus Cousins
Hght: 6'11" Exp: R Salary: $3.4 million
Wght: 270 From: Kentucky
2011-12 status: guaranteed contract for $3.6 million

SKILL RATINGS — TOT +2, OFF +2, DEF +1, REB +3, PAS 0, HND -3, SHT -3, ATH +5

Year	Team	Age	G	MPG	Usg	3PA%	FTA%	INS	2P%	3P%	FT%	TS%	Reb%	Ast%	TO%	BLK%	STL%	PF%	oRTG	dRTG	Win%	WARP
10-11p	SAC	20.7	76	30.0	.221	.009	.153	1.144	.463	.146	.593	.499	.183	.018	.138	.035	.015	.086	105.7	105.3	.514	4.7

Most similar to: Michael Beasley (95.1), Kevin Love, Chris Bosh, Patrick O'Bryant — IMP: - BRK: - COP: -

SACRAMENTO KINGS

DeMarcus Cousins is the latest statistical darling of the rookie class, like DeJuan Blair before him. It's not that Cousins was completely overlooked in the draft; the fifth slot isn't bad. It's just that opinions of him were more divided than they should have been. Of course, much of that stemmed from concerns about Cousins' maturity, but you can't deny his productivity on the court. Cousins will be a dynamite rebounder and interior scorer as a rookie. He will also be more physical and get to the line more than the usual timid young big man. Cousins is versatile enough to take smaller players on the blocks, but can burn slower defenders with his face-up game. He needs to improve his free throw shooting, and his foul rate could be a concern. Still, Cousins will become the second-best young player on a team full of talented young players.

C 10	Samuel Dalembert	Hght: 6'11" Exp: 8 Salary: $13.4 million										SKILL RATINGS							
		Wght: 250 From: Seton Hall										TOT	OFF	DEF	REB	PAS	HND	SHT	ATH
		2011-12 status: free agent										+2	-1	+3	+4	-4	-5	+2	-1
Year	Team	Age	G	MPG	Usg	3PA%	FTA%	INS	2P%	3P%	FT%	TS%	Reb%	Ast%	TO%	BLK%	STL%	PF%	oRTG	dRTG	Win%	WARP
07-08	PHI	27.0	82	33.2	.155	.001	.124	1.123	.513	.000	.707	.555	.186	.007	.166	.056	.007	.046	103.5	103.0	.517	5.7
08-09	PHI	28.0	82	24.8	.136	.003	.090	1.087	.500	.000	.734	.535	.207	.004	.193	.058	.008	.056	102.5	103.2	.477	2.6
09-10	PHI	29.0	82	25.9	.152	.000	.083	1.083	.545	-	.729	.573	.219	.014	.175	.056	.010	.054	104.1	102.7	.549	5.8
10-11p	SAC	30.0	76	20.0	.141	.002	.090	1.088	.525	.000	.747	.559	.193	.010	.187	.052	.009	.053	102.9	102.9	.501	2.7

Most similar to: Alton Lister (98.6), Ervin Johnson, Kelvin Cato, Rasho Nesterovic   IMP: 36%   BRK: 3%   COP: 8%

Samuel Dalembert made noises over the summer about becoming a factor in the Kings' offense, but he's fine in a low-usage role. Plus, he has neither the post game nor the face-up jumper to be more than that. Dalembert's strengths are on defense, where he's an above-average post defender and one of the game's best shot blockers. He's also a top-notch rebounder who can get his points by crashing the offensive glass. Dalembert is surprisingly effective as a finisher in the pick-and-roll, so you can't just stick a lead-footed banger on him, but he took over a quarter of his shots from outside of 10 feet and spent even more time on the perimeter in the past. Perhaps he's getting the idea. One of the reasons Dalembert will never be a featured player on offense is that he never passes the ball once he gets it, but still manages to commit an extremely high rate of turnovers.

SG 13	Tyreke Evans	Hght: 6'6" Exp: 1 Salary: $3.9 million										SKILL RATINGS							
		Wght: 220 From: Memphis										TOT	OFF	DEF	REB	PAS	HND	SHT	ATH
		2011-12 status: team option for $4.2 million										+5	+5	+4	+3	+5	+2	-1	+4
Year	Team	Age	G	MPG	Usg	3PA%	FTA%	INS	2P%	3P%	FT%	TS%	Reb%	Ast%	TO%	BLK%	STL%	PF%	oRTG	dRTG	Win%	WARP
09-10	SAC	20.6	72	37.2	.264	.089	.129	1.040	.485	.255	.748	.529	.082	.069	.136	.007	.020	.034	106.6	105.7	.530	6.3
10-11p	SAC	21.6	73	37.0	.281	.092	.124	1.031	.498	.273	.778	.544	.078	.074	.128	.008	.021	.032	108.3	105.3	.599	10.3

Most similar to: Kobe Bryant (95.0), LeBron James, Carmelo Anthony, Mike Bibby   IMP: 67%   BRK: 3%   COP: 3%

It wasn't the best of summers for Tyreke Evans. First, he was caught driving over 120 miles per hour on a California freeway, a transgression that got him suspended for the Kings' first game this season. Then he nursed a bum ankle during U.S. practices for the FIBA World Championship and didn't make the final roster. Evans isn't a problem guy; he's just young, and the ankle was a bit of bad timing. Evans should be fine. More than fine, actually. SCHOENE sees a major breakout for Evans in his second season, one that will put him among the league's elite players. And why not? Evans is outstanding on both ends of the court. He does need to work on his playmaking and selectivity, especially when it comes to taking three-point shots. Evans is dangerous off the dribble and has a knack for getting to the line, especially when the Kings most need points. His jump shot is a work in progress and, hopefully, was an area of focus over the offseason. It is troubling that the Kings were better with Evans off the court last season. You don't want to read too much into one-year plus-minus numbers, but Evans clearly needs to master the art of raising the level of his teammates. That is why Basketball Prospectus picked Milwaukee's Brandon Jennings, not Evans, for Rookie of the Year.

SACRAMENTO KINGS

SG 32	Francisco Garcia	Hght: 6'7" Wght: 195 2011-12 status: guaranteed contract for $5.8 million	Exp: 5 From: Louisville	Salary: $5.5 million		SKILL RATINGS							
						TOT	OFF	DEF	REB	PAS	HND	SHT	ATH
						+2	+3	-4	-1	-1	+1	+3	-2

Year	Team	Age	G	MPG	Usg	3PA%	FTA%	INS	2P%	3P%	FT%	TS%	Reb%	Ast%	TO%	BLK%	STL%	PF%	oRTG	dRTG	Win%	WARP
07-08	SAC	27.3	79	26.5	.209	.296	.094	.798	.506	.392	.779	.576	.073	.027	.132	.018	.020	.049	105.9	105.3	.520	4.5
08-09	SAC	28.3	65	30.4	.195	.258	.092	.833	.466	.398	.820	.554	.065	.034	.131	.025	.020	.045	105.9	106.1	.492	3.1
09-10	SAC	29.3	25	23.0	.158	.289	.037	.748	.504	.390	.882	.550	.066	.035	.103	.024	.009	.038	104.9	106.4	.451	0.4
10-11p	SAC	30.3	67	23.0	.171	.359	.060	.702	.492	.388	.826	.560	.063	.034	.116	.023	.012	.043	105.9	106.1	.493	2.5

Most similar to: Anthony Bowie (98.2), Blue Edwards, James Posey, Rod Higgins IMP: 40% BRK: 5% COP: 5%

There are a lot of ways Francisco Garcia's season could go. He could start at two or three for the Kings, or he could come off the bench. Given the current roster, it seems like Garcia fits best starting in the backcourt beside Tyreke Evans, but the word as camps opened was that Beno Udrih held the edge for that role. However the chips fall for Garcia, he'll be an important part of Paul Westphal's rotation. Garcia has become increasingly perimeter oriented. He still finishes extremely well, shooting .786 at the rim last season, but on just 28 attempts. Garcia took 27 percent of his shots at the basket three years ago. Last season, it was down to 16 percent. His foul-drawing rate has fallen from just below league average to non-existent. It's not that Garcia has become a three-point specialist. He's very consistent at hitting 39-40 percent from behind the line, and the portion of his shots there has held fairly steady. Instead of attacking the basket when he gets the ball on the elbow, Garcia has become more prone to launching a long two-point shot. He hit a decent percentage there, but that's not the point. The inefficiency of long twos is killing his overall game. Garcia's bad habits may well be a product of all the injury problems he's had, and if healthy maybe he'll recover his aggression. However, Garcia also turns 30 on Dec. 31. Even though it doesn't seem like he's been in the league very long, it's possible that Garcia is already suffering an irretrievable loss of athleticism. In that respect, this is a huge season for him.

SF 8	J.R. Giddens	Hght: 6'5" Wght: 215 2011-12 status: free agent	Exp: 2 From: New Mexico	Salary: --		SKILL RATINGS							
						TOT	OFF	DEF	REB	PAS	HND	SHT	ATH
						0	--	-1	--	--	--	--	--

Year	Team	Age	G	MPG	Usg	3PA%	FTA%	INS	2P%	3P%	FT%	TS%	Reb%	Ast%	TO%	BLK%	STL%	PF%	oRTG	dRTG	Win%	WARP
08-09	BOS	24.2	6	1.3	.235	.000	.000	1.000	.667	.000	.000	.667	.232	.000	.250	.000	.065	.059	110.7	102.0	.759	0.1
09-10	NYK	25.2	32	7.5	.168	.115	.116	1.001	.560	.000	.565	.492	.125	.025	.195	.006	.019	.056	101.7	106.1	.356	-0.3
10-11p	SAC	26.2	76	-	.165	.117	.076	.960	.525	.265	.644	.526	.084	.027	.129	.039	.016	.032	-	-	.448	-

Most similar to: Buck Johnson (96.5), Antoine Carr, Greg Buckner, Billy Thompson IMP: 50% BRK: 6% COP: 13%

J.R. Giddens has started the merry-go-round of non-guaranteed contracts and camp invites without really ever getting a shot to show his skills on a consistent basis in the NBA. He's a long-range shooter, yet amazingly enough is still looking for his first three-point shot in an NBA game. He goes to Kings camp facing an uphill battle for a role as an off-the-bench shooting specialist.

SF 20	Donté Greene	Hght: 6'11" Wght: 226 2011-12 status: team option for $1.7 million	Exp: 2 From: Syracuse	Salary: $0.9 million		SKILL RATINGS							
						TOT	OFF	DEF	REB	PAS	HND	SHT	ATH
						0	+1	-1	-1	-2	-3	+1	0

Year	Team	Age	G	MPG	Usg	3PA%	FTA%	INS	2P%	3P%	FT%	TS%	Reb%	Ast%	TO%	BLK%	STL%	PF%	oRTG	dRTG	Win%	WARP
08-09	SAC	21.2	55	13.2	.179	.347	.052	.705	.375	.260	.853	.416	.070	.019	.128	.014	.011	.042	101.2	107.5	.299	-1.8
09-10	SAC	22.2	76	21.4	.193	.259	.087	.828	.473	.377	.643	.526	.083	.019	.131	.024	.013	.041	103.5	105.8	.424	0.2
10-11p	SAC	23.2	75	21.0	.193	.313	.076	.763	.466	.369	.743	.530	.081	.022	.126	.023	.012	.039	104.3	105.8	.452	1.2

Most similar to: Marcus Liberty (97.5), Sasha Pavlovic, Andrea Bargnani, Joe Johnson IMP: 83% BRK: 33% COP: 2%

We haven't been high on Donté Greene since he left Syracuse after his freshman year, because he seemed far too reliant on jump shots that he didn't hit with a lot of regularity. Plus, he really didn't do anything else that would stake a role in an NBA rotation. This was all despite being a 6'11" player who can play the wing and who possesses superior physical gifts. We have to admit, though--Greene got a heck of a lot better last season. He's still not good, mind you, but he's getting closer to average, with a bullet. He became more aggressive, upping his foul-drawing rate and getting more shots at the hoop, which he did a better job of finishing. He cut the number of forced three-pointers and his accuracy rose above the league-average line. Most importantly, he began to demonstrate a modicum of defensive ability, though he still struggles when isolated against smaller players. It looks like Greene may yet become something. He entered camp locked in a battle with Omri Casspi and Francisco Garcia for a starting spot on the wing.

SG 9	Luther Head	Hght: 6'3" Wght: 185 2011-12 status: free agent	Exp: 5 From: Illinois	Salary: --		**SKILL RATINGS**						
						TOT	OFF	DEF	REB	PAS	HND	SHT	ATH
						-2	--	+1	--	--	--	--	--

Year	Team	Age	G	MPG	Usg	3PA%	FTA%	INS	2P%	3P%	FT%	TS%	Reb%	Ast%	TO%	BLK%	STL%	PF%	oRTG	dRTG	Win%	WARP
07-08	HOU	25.4	73	18.9	.194	.387	.061	.674	.506	.351	.815	.544	.055	.046	.120	.005	.015	.025	105.9	105.9	.500	2.4
08-09	MIA	26.4	32	15.6	.169	.301	.059	.758	.389	.370	.792	.482	.061	.055	.139	.003	.018	.035	104.4	107.1	.411	-0.1
09-10	IND	27.4	47	17.3	.213	.269	.065	.796	.481	.352	.828	.530	.054	.039	.138	.008	.011	.029	103.9	106.9	.402	-0.3
10-11p	SAC	28.4	70	-	.185	.384	.056	.672	.463	.376	.808	.537	.052	.045	.130	.007	.013	.030	-	-	.396	-

Most similar to: Tony Smith (98.6), James Robinson, Clint Richardson, Mike James   IMP: 47%   BRK: 11%   COP: 7%

Luther Head is a pretty consistent player. You know what you're going to get from him; it's just a matter of him finding a team that can employ his skill set. Head is a good defender and can check players at either guard spot. He doesn't have the playmaking skills to run the point, but can play alongside ball-dominant off guards like the Kings' Tyreke Evans. Head's three-point shooting is his bread-and-butter, but his accuracy too often hovers around the league average. If he could hit 40 percent beyond the arc, he'd have much less trouble sticking with a team. Head is a smart player who is usually favored by his coaches, so it wouldn't be a shock to see him make the Kings' opening-night roster. A complicating factor for Head is an ankle issue that reportedly spurred the Hornets to yank a two-year contract offer from the table over the summer.

PF 41	Darnell Jackson	Hght: 6'9" Wght: 253 2011-12 status: free agent	Exp: 2 From: Kansas	Salary: $0.9 million		**SKILL RATINGS**						
						TOT	OFF	DEF	REB	PAS	HND	SHT	ATH
						-4	--	-2	--	--	--	--	--

Year	Team	Age	G	MPG	Usg	3PA%	FTA%	INS	2P%	3P%	FT%	TS%	Reb%	Ast%	TO%	BLK%	STL%	PF%	oRTG	dRTG	Win%	WARP
08-09	CLE	23.5	51	8.4	.128	.017	.133	1.116	.440	.000	.686	.483	.119	.009	.121	.007	.012	.085	102.1	108.6	.296	-1.1
09-10	MIL	24.5	28	4.4	.175	.088	.058	.970	.308	.250	.667	.352	.106	.015	.285	.025	.008	.081	96.6	107.6	.182	-0.6
10-11p	SAC	25.5	75	-	.129	.028	.134	1.106	.457	.009	.684	.492	.118	.010	.117	.008	.012	.084	-	-	.350	-

Most similar to: Mark Bryant (98.4), Jarron Collins, Michael Doleac, Jeff Turner   IMP: 66%   BRK: 20%   COP: 5%

Darnell Jackson looks like he's headed for a career as basketball's version of a AAAA player. He'll put up big numbers in the D-League, but never really find any job security at the NBA level. The Kings picked him up in the sign-and-trade deal that send Jon Brockman to Milwaukee. Jackson hasn't shown the ability to get his own shot, nor hit the ones that others create for him. He doesn't have a dominant rebound rate, nor are his play-by-play numbers on defense encouraging. You have to think he'll end up overseas.

PG 5	Pooh Jeter	Hght: 5'11" Wght: 175 2011-12 status: due qualifying offer of $1.0 million	Exp: R From: Portland	Salary: $0.5 million		**SKILL RATINGS**						
						TOT	OFF	DEF	REB	PAS	HND	SHT	ATH
						-1	+2	-3	+2	-2	+2	-3	-3

Year	Team	Age	G	MPG	Usg	3PA%	FTA%	INS	2P%	3P%	FT%	TS%	Reb%	Ast%	TO%	BLK%	STL%	PF%	oRTG	dRTG	Win%	WARP
10-11p	SAC	27.4	76	10.0	.157	.314	.111	.798	.390	.356	.840	.516	.063	.048	.111	-.001	.012	.042	105.8	107.8	.435	0.3

Most similar to: Lindsey Hunter (95.7), Tyronn Lue, James Robinson, Jerry Sichting   IMP: 49%   BRK: 5%   COP: 13%

SACRAMENTO KINGS

The Kings decided to give Pooh Jeter a look-see after he fared well for Cleveland's summer league team. He's a mighty-mite of a point guard who could offer a change of pace as Sacramento's third point guard. Jeter has been playing overseas, but has excellent quickness, is a good shooter and has the makeup of a guy that will be fan favorite as he moves back stateside. He's not Chris Paul, but the Kings gave him a guaranteed contract to prove he's an NBA player.

PF 24 — Carl Landry

Hght: 6'9" Exp: 3 Salary: $3.0 million
Wght: 248 From: Purdue
2011-12 status: free agent

SKILL RATINGS

TOT	OFF	DEF	REB	PAS	HND	SHT	ATH
+2	+3	-1	-1	-3	-4	+4	+1

Year	Team	Age	G	MPG	Usg	3PA%	FTA%	INS	2P%	3P%	FT%	TS%	Reb%	Ast%	TO%	BLK%	STL%	PF%	oRTG	dRTG	Win%	WARP
07-08	HOU	24.6	42	16.9	.190	.003	.164	1.160	.619	.000	.661	.641	.165	.014	.089	.007	.011	.064	109.5	106.7	.592	2.6
08-09	HOU	25.6	69	21.3	.182	.005	.149	1.143	.576	.333	.813	.634	.135	.012	.119	.015	.009	.053	107.0	106.9	.504	2.7
09-10	SAC	26.6	80	30.9	.226	.002	.150	1.147	.537	.333	.806	.600	.109	.012	.108	.019	.011	.042	106.3	106.3	.500	4.2
10-11p	SAC	27.6	75	32.0	.200	.007	.148	1.141	.557	.265	.777	.610	.118	.013	.109	.015	.010	.051	106.7	106.8	.499	4.2

Most similar to: Dino Radja (98.3), Armon Gilliam, Brian Grant, Loy Vaught   IMP: 32% BRK: 1% COP: 8%

Carl Landry is a prolific post scorer. We've seen that on a per-minute basis in each of his three NBA seasons. He's quick and physical, posts a high finishing rate despite getting a lot of shots blocked and also earns plenty of free throw attempts. His efficiency diminished when he came over to Sacramento from Houston last season, which might be a red flag that the Kings need to keep a lasso on his usage rate. Perhaps more importantly, Landry has shown a decreasing interest in rebounding, but he's got to help on the boards if he's going to be a 30-minute power forward at the NBA level. Defensively, Landry is average. He's fine as a stationary defender, but has trouble when opponents get him on the move. The biggest concern about Landry entering this season is that since he's entering a contract year, he might become too enamored of his superficial numbers and will hurt the Kings in an effort to put up a 20-point scoring average. Sacramento already has one ball-dominant player in Tyreke Evans; the Kings can't afford another one toiling in the post.

SF 42 — Marcus Landry

Hght: 6'7" Exp: 1 Salary: --
Wght: 230 From: Wisconsin
2011-12 status: free agent

SKILL RATINGS

TOT	OFF	DEF	REB	PAS	HND	SHT	ATH
-3	--	0	--	--	--	--	--

Year	Team	Age	G	MPG	Usg	3PA%	FTA%	INS	2P%	3P%	FT%	TS%	Reb%	Ast%	TO%	BLK%	STL%	PF%	oRTG	dRTG	Win%	WARP
09-10	BOS	24.5	18	6.2	.210	.547	.043	.496	.467	.321	.600	.487	.098	.000	.117	.013	.005	.057	103.5	107.7	.363	-0.1
10-11p	SAC	25.5	76	-	.178	.508	.075	.567	.385	.353	.517	.484	.088	.024	.108	.027	.015	.058	-	-	.375	-

Most similar to: Devean George (96.6), Bostjan Nachbar, Reggie Williams, Sasha Pavlovic   IMP: 63% BRK: 24% COP: 4%

Marcus Landry will try to team up with brother Carl this season, as he's going to camp with the Kings. Frankly, Marcus didn't show a whole lot in his stints with the Knicks and Celtics last season. He's more perimeter oriented than his brother, but showed limited ability to do anything inside the arc and did not shoot particularly well outside it. There is little to go on as far as defensive performance, but his showing at that end will inform the Kings whether he might develop into a wing-defense/spot-shooting specialist.

SG 23 — Donald Sloan

Hght: 6'3" Exp: R Salary: $0.5 million
Wght: 205 From: Texas A&M
2011-12 status: due qualifying offer of $1.0 million

SKILL RATINGS

TOT	OFF	DEF	REB	PAS	HND	SHT	ATH
-4	--	--	--	--	--	--	--

Year	Team	Age	G	MPG	Usg	3PA%	FTA%	INS	2P%	3P%	FT%	TS%	Reb%	Ast%	TO%	BLK%	STL%	PF%	oRTG	dRTG	Win%	WARP
10-11p	SAC	23.3	76	-	.213	.162	.116	.954	.399	.317	.758	.475	.053	.029	.131	.001	.007	.038	-	-	.324	-

Most similar to: Joe Crawford (98.1), Jason Kapono, Nick Young, Ronald Dupree   IMP: - BRK: - COP: -

SACRAMENTO KINGS

Donald Sloan is a skilled player who has been stricken with a combo-guard body. He's got potential as a drive-and-shoot role player, as he was a prolific scorer at Texas A&M and has the athleticism to work in the lane and get to the line. He's going to have to prove he can hit the NBA three-point shot or show he can run the point guard position, which wasn't really his bread-and-butter in college. More than anything, Sloan is going to have to prove he can guard somebody. The numbers he put up in summer league (he shot .222 from the field) aren't at all encouraging.

PF 34	Jason Thompson	Hght: 6'11" Exp: 2 Salary: $2.2 million
		Wght: 250 From: Rider
		2011-12 status: team option for $3.0 million

SKILL RATINGS

TOT	OFF	DEF	REB	PAS	HND	SHT	ATH
0	+1	+2	+2	+1	-1	-1	+1

Year	Team	Age	G	MPG	Usg	3PA%	FTA%	INS	2P%	3P%	FT%	TS%	Reb%	Ast%	TO%	BLK%	STL%	PF%	oRTG	dRTG	Win%	WARP
08-09	SAC	22.8	82	28.1	.194	.008	.127	1.119	.502	.000	.692	.540	.154	.018	.148	.019	.010	.062	104.9	107.1	.428	0.5
09-10	SAC	23.8	75	31.4	.197	.010	.117	1.107	.477	.100	.715	.518	.155	.023	.133	.023	.009	.053	104.3	105.8	.451	1.7
10-11p	SAC	24.8	75	18.2	.196	.011	.126	1.115	.498	.061	.706	.535	.146	.024	.138	.022	.009	.055	104.7	106.0	.459	1.2

Most similar to: Sean Rooks (99.1), Troy Murphy, Tom Chambers, Kevin Willis | IMP: 53% BRK: 14% COP: 1%

Jason Thompson has gotten heavy minutes during his first two NBA seasons, so we have a pretty clear picture of what he is. He's a plus rebounder who does good work off the offensive glass in particular. He's a good passer for his size, and a good defender as long as he's not playing a skilled post center. Thompson's biggest issue is his lack of ability to get quality shots other than face-up jumpers, which he's not special at converting. He has a good finishing rate around the rim and gets to the line when he's being aggressive. However, he became increasingly prone to settling for the long two in his second year, which is why his Offensive Rating actually fell. Thompson is a solid NBA player, above average or average with his skill set across the board. Right now, it doesn't look like he's a star.

PG 19	Beno Udrih	Hght: 6'3" Exp: 6 Salary: $6.5 million
		Wght: 205 From: Sempeter, Slovenia
		2011-12 status: guaranteed contract for $6.9 million

SKILL RATINGS

TOT	OFF	DEF	REB	PAS	HND	SHT	ATH
+1	+3	-2	-1	0	0	+1	-2

Year	Team	Age	G	MPG	Usg	3PA%	FTA%	INS	2P%	3P%	FT%	TS%	Reb%	Ast%	TO%	BLK%	STL%	PF%	oRTG	dRTG	Win%	WARP
07-08	SAC	25.8	65	32.0	.199	.149	.070	.921	.482	.387	.850	.540	.061	.061	.161	.004	.012	.029	104.9	106.8	.438	0.9
08-09	SAC	26.8	73	31.1	.183	.123	.072	.949	.491	.310	.820	.525	.057	.068	.172	.004	.018	.038	105.0	107.7	.411	-0.2
09-10	SAC	27.8	79	31.4	.187	.192	.060	.868	.530	.377	.837	.566	.051	.067	.131	.003	.018	.030	106.9	106.8	.504	4.5
10-11p	SAC	28.8	75	31.0	.183	.194	.065	.871	.506	.366	.829	.549	.050	.064	.145	.005	.016	.031	106.0	106.8	.475	2.9

Most similar to: Larry Drew (98.6), Rory Sparrow, Bimbo Coles, Vinny Del Negro | IMP: 46% BRK: 8% COP: 4%

Beno Udrih is the kind of player that you're always trying to replace, but he's just solid enough that you can't seem to keep him out of your lineup. Udrih shot the ball extremely well last season, putting up sparkling percentages from every sector on the shot chart. He still is more comfortable getting his shot off the bounce, which makes him an awkward partner for Tyreke Evans in the Kings' backcourt. Udrih is just average as a playmaker, but is miscast playing off the ball. Defensively, he's not going to put the fear of God in anybody, but he's not awful. If he's in the lineup, teams will look to get him on an island, where he has trouble staying with quicker players. Udrih is a good player whom the Kings seem intent on wedging into their starting lineup. He's better suited to a second-unit spot at guard.

SACRAMENTO KINGS

C 33 — Hassan Whiteside

- Hght: 7'0" Exp: R Salary: $0.7 million
- Wght: 235 From: Marshall
- 2011-12 status: guaranteed contract for $0.8 million

SKILL RATINGS

TOT	OFF	DEF	REB	PAS	HND	SHT	ATH
-1	-2	+4	-1	-5	-5	-5	0

Year	Team	Age	G	MPG	Usg	3PA%	FTA%	INS	2P%	3P%	FT%	TS%	Reb%	Ast%	TO%	BLK%	STL%	PF%	oRTG	dRTG	Win%	WARP
10-11p	SAC	21.9	76	5.0	.176	.009	.125	1.116	.412	.497	.576	.445	.134	.005	.144	.084	.007	.055	100.3	102.4	.425	0.1

Most similar to: Brendan Haywood (89.4), Sean Williams, Joel Przybilla   IMP: -   BRK: -   COP: -

Hassan Whiteside is a 7-footer with an exceptional wingspan who moves well, draws fouls, blocks shots at an extremely high rate and even has a semblance of a face-up jumper. Sure, he's raw and is going to have to get a lot stronger, but how does this package of skills fall into the second round? Whiteside could prove to be the steal of the 2010 Draft. Of course, there may be a reason why so many teams passed on him. The Kings are deep enough that Whiteside won't be rushed into a major role, but they aren't so deep that he won't ever see the floor. Whiteside is one of the more intriguing prospects in this year's draft class. He should be a game-changing basket protector right off the bat.

SF 3 — Antoine Wright

- Hght: 6'7" Exp: 5 Salary: $0.9 million
- Wght: 215 From: Texas A&M
- 2011-12 status: free agent

SKILL RATINGS

TOT	OFF	DEF	REB	PAS	HND	SHT	ATH
-1	+1	-2	-4	0	+1	0	-2

Year	Team	Age	G	MPG	Usg	3PA%	FTA%	INS	2P%	3P%	FT%	TS%	Reb%	Ast%	TO%	BLK%	STL%	PF%	oRTG	dRTG	Win%	WARP
07-08	DAL	24.2	56	22.0	.155	.269	.072	.803	.470	.291	.687	.485	.068	.030	.122	.012	.011	.048	102.8	106.8	.369	-1.2
08-09	DAL	25.2	65	23.9	.157	.283	.079	.797	.475	.302	.747	.501	.050	.023	.103	.013	.015	.051	103.2	107.7	.353	-2.0
09-10	TOR	26.2	67	20.8	.162	.352	.069	.717	.460	.335	.688	.502	.079	.023	.118	.006	.011	.044	103.5	107.4	.371	-1.3
10-11p	SAC	27.2	73	10.0	.160	.413	.080	.668	.466	.346	.722	.520	.064	.025	.109	.010	.012	.049	104.9	107.2	.424	0.1

Most similar to: Bobby Hansen (98.3), DeShawn Stevenson, Bill Willoughby, Rod Higgins   IMP: 64%   BRK: 24%   COP: 4%

Antoine Wright is part of a crowded mix of wing players on the Kings, and it's hard to see what he's has going for him that will win a rotation role. Wright doesn't have one standout skill. He doesn't create his own shot, yet only shoots a consistently good percentage on long twos. Wright doesn't get to the line, is a poor rebounder and a below-average defender. He handles the ball well and is a willing passer, but he's been overexposed in recent seasons nevertheless. This is not a 20-minute player. There are flashes of defensive ability in Wright's profile, so if he's going to find a niche, it looks like it will be on that end of the floor.

SF -- — Desmond Mason

- Hght: 6'7" Exp: 10 Salary: --
- Wght: 224 From: Oklahoma State
- 2011-12 status: free agent

SKILL RATINGS

TOT	OFF	DEF	REB	PAS	HND	SHT	ATH
-5	-2	+2	-1	-1	-2	-3	-3

Year	Team	Age	G	MPG	Usg	3PA%	FTA%	INS	2P%	3P%	FT%	TS%	Reb%	Ast%	TO%	BLK%	STL%	PF%	oRTG	dRTG	Win%	WARP
07-08	MIL	30.5	59	28.9	.169	.000	.120	1.120	.482	.000	.659	.519	.090	.032	.130	.014	.011	.029	102.2	106.1	.370	-1.7
08-09	OKC	31.5	39	27.3	.158	.008	.099	1.091	.440	.000	.541	.456	.086	.019	.148	.021	.007	.040	99.9	107.2	.269	-3.3
09-10	SAC	32.5	5	13.2	.120	.000	.099	1.099	.417	-	.750	.472	.113	.013	.225	.011	.008	.034	99.5	106.6	.277	-0.2
10-11p	AVG	33.5	74	13.2	.150	.009	.100	1.091	.453	.000	.581	.472	.080	.023	.150	.021	.009	.037	99.7	106.4	.286	-2.6

Most similar to: Calbert Cheaney (96.8), Chucky Brown, Michael Curry, Sam Mitchell   IMP: 59%   BRK: 11%   COP: 11%

Desmond Mason says he's not ready to retire, but he may not have any choice at this point. It takes two to tango, so they say. His athleticism has waned to the point where there is just not enough defensive payoff for his complete lack of offensive skills.

SACRAMENTO KINGS

SG — **Ime Udoka**
Hght: 6'5" Wght: 220
Exp: 6 From: Portland State
Salary: --
2011-12 status: free agent

SKILL RATINGS

TOT	OFF	DEF	REB	PAS	HND	SHT	ATH
-2	-1	+5	+5	-3	-2	-3	-1

Year	Team	Age	G	MPG	Usg	3PA%	FTA%	INS	2P%	3P%	FT%	TS%	Reb%	Ast%	TO%	BLK%	STL%	PF%	oRTG	dRTG	Win%	WARP
07-08	SAS	30.7	73	18.1	.168	.360	.056	.696	.467	.370	.759	.528	.101	.023	.126	.010	.020	.046	103.7	104.6	.470	1.5
08-09	SAS	31.7	67	15.4	.163	.362	.059	.697	.426	.328	.609	.470	.107	.025	.110	.009	.019	.040	103.3	105.7	.423	0.1
09-10	SAC	32.7	69	13.7	.145	.295	.081	.786	.433	.286	.737	.470	.117	.027	.136	.005	.018	.039	103.4	105.8	.421	0.1
10-11p	AVG	33.7	75	13.7	.148	.329	.062	.733	.432	.324	.696	.478	.104	.025	.131	.008	.017	.042	102.7	105.6	.404	-0.3

Most similar to: M.L. Carr (98.6), Bryon Russell, Tyrone Corbin, George Lynch

IMP: 40%   BRK: 2%   COP: 12%

Ime Udoka is looking to land one more gig as a defensive specialist. He worked out for the Bulls, among other teams, in late September, but had not secured a camp invite at press time.

San Antonio Spurs

Far removed from the San Antonio Spurs' 2009-10 season, it is still a challenge to figure out just what to make of the year. Expected to return to championship contention at the outset of the season, San Antonio started slowly at 9-9. The Spurs were better down the stretch, though they never delivered their trademark dominant month, instead building slowly to a 50-32 finish that tied them for sixth in the Western Conference.

Point differential provided a very different view of San Antonio's regular season. By virtue of an uncharacteristic number of blowouts (including 22 wins by 15-plus points, the league's second-highest total), the Spurs' 54.8 expected wins far surpassed their actual total. In fact, San Antonio underperformed its point differential by the largest amount of any team in the league. Going strictly by differential, the Spurs were the conference's second-best team, trailing only the Utah Jazz.

The first-round matchup between Dallas and San Antonio matched two teams with very different expected records (the Mavericks outperformed their differential by more than any other team), so in some sense the Spurs' six-game victory should not have been considered an upset.

Had the season ended there, it would have been easy to suggest that San Antonio lived up to expectations but was victimized by misfortune in close games. That position became more difficult to argue in the wake of a four-game sweep in the conference semifinals at the hands of the Phoenix Suns. The outcome was no fluke; Phoenix was simply the better team.

Along the way, the Spurs had a few key players fall short of expectations. Their biggest offseason addition, forward Richard Jefferson, was a disappointment. The hope was that Jefferson would provide San Antonio another player capable of creating his own offense while sliding into a smaller role spotting up on the perimeter when the Spurs' stars were on the floor. With his skills in decline, Jefferson wasn't up to the first task, and his three-point percentage slid after a career year in 2008-09 in Milwaukee.

Meanwhile, a variety of ailments conspired to make sure one of those stars--Tony Parker--was absent from the court for extended periods. Parker missed 26 games and was never fully healthy. The influence of the injuries shows up all over Parker's stat line, which declined in basically every category from his excellent 2008-09 campaign. Most notably, Parker's usage rate dropped from a career-high 31.9 percent to 25.9 percent, his lowest involvement in the offense since 2004-05. Ordinarily, the smaller role would translate into improved efficiency, but in Parker's case it only served to keep his True Shooting Percentage from declining further because of his health.

The silver lining to Parker's lost season was the opportunity it provided second-year guard George Hill

SPURS IN A BOX

Last year's record	50-32
Last year's Offensive Rating	111.7 (9)
Last year's Defensive Rating	106.2 (9)
Last year's point differential	5.1 (4)
Team pace	90.3 (20)
SCHOENE projection	49-33 (2)
Projected Offensive Rating	113.1 (6)
Projected Defensive Rating	109.6 (15)
Projected team weighted age	28.8 (9)
Projected '10-11 payroll	$70.0 (9)
Est. payroll obligations, '11-12	$63.6 (6)

Head coach: Gregg Popovich

The greatest testament to Popovich's tenure at the helm of the Spurs might not be his four championships or the second-best winning percentage of any NBA coach with at least 1,000 games (behind only Phil Jackson). Instead, Popovich should take credit for the spreading network of former Spurs on sidelines and in front offices around the league. This summer, Monty Williams joined Mike Brown and P.J. Carlesimo as former Spurs assistants turned head coaches, while two ex-San Antonio execs, Lance Blanks and Dell Demps, were hired as general managers. Add in Danny Ferry, Kevin Pritchard and Sam Presti (who cut their teeth with the Spurs) and players Popovich coached (Vinny Del Negro, Avery Johnson, Steve Kerr, Terry Porter) and his immense influence is obvious.

to see more action at the point. Hill was one of the league's most improved players, boosting his True Shooting Percentage from 50.2 percent to 57.2 percent. The three-point shooting and size on defense he provided allowed the Spurs to play nearly as well with him at the point as they did with Parker.

As Parker was dealing with health issues, shooting guard Manu Ginobili was bouncing back from his prior injury-plagued campaign. Through the All-Star break, Ginobili was essentially playing as well as ever, though his limited minutes and a poor field-goal percentage kept people from taking notice. Down the stretch, it was impossible to miss Ginobili, who averaged 21.4 points, 5.6 assists and 4.2 rebounds per game after the break. In April, San Antonio took Ginobili off the free-agent market, agreeing to a three-year, $39 million extension. Despite Ginobili's advancing age, the deal was a fair one given his continued high level of play.

While Parker's health and Jefferson's play hurt them, what ultimately cost the Spurs was the same thing that was once their trademark: defense. Over the first 11 seasons of Tim Duncan's career, San Antonio never finished worse than third in the league in Defensive Rating and was best in the NBA six times. The last two years, the Spurs' defense has not had the same teeth. San Antonio fell to sixth in the league in 2008-09, then ninth a year ago.

The biggest problem for the Spurs has been a lack of size in the frontcourt. They long loved to pair Duncan with another 7-footer. Progressively, San Antonio has been getting smaller. Last year, Duncan started alongside 6'9" veteran Antonio McDyess. The Spurs brought a pair of poor interior defenders off the bench in 6'10" Matt Bonner and 6'7" DeJuan Blair. The reserves brought their own strengths to the table--Bonner's ability to space the floor and Blair's super-human offensive rebounding--but San Antonio suffered on defense.

The deficiencies were on full display in the playoffs against the Suns. Phoenix posted a 117.6 Offensive Rating in the four-game sweep, actually surpassing its league-leading regular-season rating (117.4). The Suns' ability to score in the paint was the biggest difference from San Antonio's three series wins over Phoenix between 2005 and 2008.

Fortunately for the Spurs, help is on the way. Over the three years since San Antonio drafted Tiago Splitter late in the first round of the 2007 NBA Draft, the Brazilian has developed into arguably the best player

From the Blogosphere

Who: Timothy Varner
What: 48 Minutes of Hell
Where: http://www.48minutesofhell.com/

With the rhythm of a drum you'll hear that the Spurs championship window is closing. Tim Duncan is old. Manu Ginobili is old. Tony Parker wants to be traded. They're done. You'll hear wrong. Sure, age is a factor. And no one is sure where Tony Parker will be after the trade deadline in February. But know this: the San Antonio Spurs began renovations before it was time to rebuild. George Hill enters his third year after finishing second in the NBA's Most Improved Player voting, and is the reason Parker turned into a valuable trade chip. DeJuan Blair is a stud, with or without crucial knee ligaments. And Tiago Splitter is the best big man lining up with Duncan since The Admiral. Splitter could be good enough to carry the load when Duncan's gone. Either way, don't expect these San Antonio Spurs to be forgotten when the current championship window closes.

in Europe. Because of the time that has elapsed since his selection, the Spurs were able to exceed the first-round salary scale to sign Splitter to a three-year, $10.9 million contract that was still a great bargain.

A skilled shot blocker with legitimate size at 6'11", Splitter should immediately slide in next to Duncan up front. He has a chance to be San Antonio's best all-around big man besides Duncan since David Robinson retired in 2003. Adding Splitter also improves the Spurs' frontcourt depth, with McDyess joining Blair and Bonner on the bench to give the team five big men whom they can feel comfortable having in the rotation.

Before free agency started, Jefferson delivered a surprise by opting out of the final year of his contract, which called for him to make $15 million. He wound up re-signing with San Antonio for $40 million over four years, a deal that helps both him and the team. Jefferson gets the security of locking in a long-term contract before the Collective Bargaining Agreement expires, which might have made it difficult for him to secure a deal anywhere near as lucrative next summer. The Spurs were happy to commit more money down the road because the $6.6 million drop in Jefferson's salary this season should allow them to stay under the luxury tax.

As notable as the moves San Antonio made was one the team chose not to make--a trade involving Parker. As the French point guard enters the last year of his deal, trading him is a possibility. Teams like New York could bid up Parker's salary next summer, and in Hill the Spurs already have a replacement on hand. Still, it seems unlikely that San Antonio could get equal value for Parker in a trade, and Hill is an asset as a backup at both guard positions. All signs point toward Parker rebounding next season, which will help the Spurs.

San Antonio's other changes were minor. The Spurs' second unit will have a different look on the wing after the team drafted Oklahoma State's James Anderson in the first round of the draft and signed Gary Neal from Europe as a free agent. Anderson offers size, while Neal is a superior ballhandler whose best comparable per SCHOENE is the player he's replacing, Keith Bogans. San Antonio will have less experience behind Ginobili and Jefferson, but potentially more talent.

The new backups are the latest examples of the Spurs continually churning their role players and getting younger around the aging core duo of Duncan and Ginobili. Having gotten dangerously old a couple of seasons ago, San Antonio is now closer to the middle of the pack in terms of team age. Coach Gregg Popovich has also done a masterful job of managing the minutes of his veterans, helping keep Duncan fresh.

The system won't work forever, because at some point the Spurs are going to need to find go-to replacements for Duncan (who will turn 35 in April), Ginobili (now 33) and possibly even Parker. The best of the players San Antonio has developed and added, Hill and Splitter, aren't quite at that level. For now, the reinforcements are upgrade enough that the Spurs have to be considered among the teams battling for the chance to knock off the Los Angeles Lakers in the Western Conference.

San Antonio will enter this season with far less hype than a year ago, when the Spurs were considered to be the clear-cut second-best team in the West. For whatever reason, the addition of Splitter has failed to generate much buzz. It impresses SCHOENE, however, which puts the team behind only Portland. The takeaway is clear: Don't write off the Spurs just yet.

Kevin Pelton

SPURS FIVE-YEAR TRENDS

Season	AGE	W-L	POW	PYTH	SEED	ORTG	DRTG	PT DIFF	PACE
05-06	29.8	63-19	63.6 (1)	60.5	1	109.6 (9)	100.9 (1)	6.8 (1)	87.0 (24)
06-07	30.4	58-24	62.7 (2)	63.8	3	111.1 (4)	101.5 (2)	8.4 (1)	88.3 (27)
07-08	31.5	56-26	58.0 (5)	55.2	3	109.9 (13)	104.3 (3)	4.8 (8)	86.6 (28)
08-09	30.4	54-28	51.8 (8)	52.0	3	110.7 (12)	106.2 (6)	3.8 (7)	86.8 (27)
09-10	29.7	50-32	53.4 (8)	55.2	7	111.7 (9)	106.2 (9)	5.1 (4)	90.3 (20)

		OFFENSE				DEFENSE			
Season	PAY	eFG	oREB	FT/FGA	TO	eFG	oREB	FT/FGA	TO
05-06	$79.6	.513 (3)	.260 (20)	.209 (29)	.157 (13)	.457 (1)	.742 (8)	.220 (4)	.158 (18)
06-07	$65.6	.521 (2)	.242 (27)	.235 (20)	.156 (6)	.471 (2)	.757 (3)	.201 (1)	.162 (21)
07-08	$72.5	.504 (10)	.234 (25)	.210 (24)	.138 (6)	.477 (5)	.771 (1)	.201 (4)	.142 (23)
08-09	$68.4	.513 (5)	.221 (30)	.191 (30)	.134 (1)	.487 (7)	.780 (1)	.191 (1)	.133 (30)
09-10	$78.8	.515 (7)	.268 (14)	.219 (20)	.150 (11)	.483 (4)	.763 (4)	.214 (10)	.139 (28)

(league rankings in parenthesis)

SG 25 — James Anderson

Hght: 6'6" Exp: R Salary: $1.4 million
Wght: 215 From: Oklahoma State
2011-12 status: guaranteed contract for $1.5 million

SKILL RATINGS

TOT	OFF	DEF	REB	PAS	HND	SHT	ATH
0	+2	-2	+3	-1	-2	-2	+1

Year	Team	Age	G	MPG	Usg	3PA%	FTA%	INS	2P%	3P%	FT%	TS%	Reb%	Ast%	TO%	BLK%	STL%	PF%	oRTG	dRTG	Win%	WARP
10-11p	SAS	22.1	76	20.0	.210	.255	.122	.867	.458	.299	.793	.516	.081	.032	.112	.009	.015	.052	105.2	106.8	.446	1.0

Most similar to: Chris Douglas-Roberts (96.4), Malik Hairston, Antoine Wright, Bill Walker

IMP: - BRK: - COP: -

SAN ANTONIO SPURS

The Big 12 Player of the Year as a junior, James Anderson ranked third nationally in scoring at 22.3 points per game before leaving for the NBA. Anderson has big-time offensive potential. At 6'6", he's got good size for the shooting guard position and is a better shooter than his projection indicates. Anderson made just 34.1 percent of his threes last season after hitting them at a 40.8 percent clip during his sophomore campaign.

As a rookie, Anderson will primarily function in the spot-up shooter role the Spurs prefer for their wings. As he develops, Anderson should be able to add responsibility because he can score off the dribble. Anderson was especially effective at getting to the free throw line from the wing in college, and his size helps him finish at the rim. San Antonio will have to get Anderson up to speed at the defensive end. He could coast there in college, but the Spurs won't tolerate that kind of effort. Anderson is a contributor on the glass.

DeJuan Blair — C #45

Hght: 6'7" Exp: 1 Salary: $0.9 million
Wght: 265 From: Pittsburgh
2011-12 status: partially-guaranteed contract for $1.0 million

SKILL RATINGS

TOT	OFF	DEF	REB	PAS	HND	SHT	ATH
+4	+3	-3	+4	+2	-1	+4	+3

Year	Team	Age	G	MPG	Usg	3PA%	FTA%	INS	2P%	3P%	FT%	TS%	Reb%	Ast%	TO%	BLK%	STL%	PF%	oRTG	dRTG	Win%	WARP
09-10	SAS	21.0	82	18.2	.209	.003	.105	1.102	.558	.000	.547	.564	.206	.020	.165	.019	.017	.069	106.1	104.7	.548	4.1
10-11p	SAS	22.0	76	18.0	.198	.003	.107	1.103	.565	.000	.576	.574	.198	.023	.155	.018	.017	.064	106.0	104.5	.550	3.8

Most similar to: Mike Sweetney (97.7), Carlos Boozer, Shawn Kemp, Al Jefferson IMP: 59% BRK: 10% COP: 3%

In a development that came as no surprise to Basketball Prospectus readers, DeJuan Blair ranked fourth among rookies in WARP after being selected with the 37th pick of the draft. It took all of a couple of weeks for other teams to realize they had made a mistake by allowing Blair to slip to the second round of the draft because he does not have a functional ACL in either knee. Turned loose from the bench, Blair was one of the league's top rebounders (he ranked seventh in the league in rebound percentage) and shot a high percentage on two-point attempts.

The question now is where Blair can go from here. San Antonio strictly played Blair as a center and asked him to serve as a primary help defender. Blair's lack of height and vertical lift works against him in this role, and the Spurs were weaker defensively with him on the floor. To graduate to a larger role, Blair will need to improve his help defense--taking more charges could work to his advantage--or be paired with a longer defender who also has the ability to spread the floor while Blair works the paint. Even if that never happens, Blair is already a steal.

Matt Bonner — PF #15

Hght: 6'10" Exp: 6 Salary: $3.1 million
Wght: 240 From: Florida
2011-12 status: guaranteed contract for $3.4 million

SKILL RATINGS

TOT	OFF	DEF	REB	PAS	HND	SHT	ATH
+2	+3	+4	-2	0	+4	+4	-4

Year	Team	Age	G	MPG	Usg	3PA%	FTA%	INS	2P%	3P%	FT%	TS%	Reb%	Ast%	TO%	BLK%	STL%	PF%	oRTG	dRTG	Win%	WARP
07-08	SAS	28.0	68	12.6	.197	.394	.055	.661	.487	.333	.864	.524	.131	.018	.111	.015	.008	.062	105.6	106.3	.479	1.1
08-09	SAS	29.0	81	23.8	.147	.460	.017	.558	.552	.440	.739	.611	.119	.021	.063	.010	.013	.048	108.4	106.4	.562	5.9
09-10	SAS	30.0	65	17.9	.171	.535	.049	.514	.539	.390	.729	.581	.107	.027	.090	.015	.013	.043	108.3	105.8	.581	4.0
10-11p	SAS	31.0	73	18.0	.146	.500	.039	.539	.535	.378	.767	.568	.109	.021	.087	.012	.011	.051	106.3	106.3	.499	2.3

Most similar to: Raef Lafrentz (96.8), Rod Higgins, Danny Ferry, Pete Chilcutt IMP: 28% BRK: 5% COP: 13%

For a totally different look in the frontcourt, Gregg Popovich had the ability to insert Matt Bonner to space the floor. The "Red Rocket" saw his three-point percentage drop from a career-high 44.0 percent in 2008-09, but he was still a dangerous threat from beyond the arc. For a shooting specialist, Bonner maintains a high usage rate and is also surprisingly accurate when he steps inside the line, making him valuable.

Bonner has developed into a competent defensive player, though not the standout his defensive skill rating would indicate. He has added strength and competes well in the post. Bonner is weakest as a help defender because he does not cover ground quickly and is not a shot blocker, which presented an issue when he was paired with DeJuan Blair up front. Bonner is also subpar on the glass. Those weaknesses make Bonner a role player, but his other skills make him valuable off the bench.

SAN ANTONIO SPURS

C 21 — Tim Duncan

Hght: 6'11"	Exp: 13	Salary: $18.8 million		
Wght: 260	From: Wake Forest			
2011-12 status: player option or ETO for $21.2 million				

SKILL RATINGS

TOT	OFF	DEF	REB	PAS	HND	SHT	ATH
+5	+4	+4	+3	+5	+5	+1	+2

Year	Team	Age	G	MPG	Usg	3PA%	FTA%	INS	2P%	3P%	FT%	TS%	Reb%	Ast%	TO%	BLK%	STL%	PF%	oRTG	dRTG	Win%	WARP
07-08	SAS	32.0	78	34.0	.284	.003	.131	1.128	.498	.000	.730	.546	.195	.040	.114	.043	.010	.034	107.7	101.5	.696	15.5
08-09	SAS	33.0	75	33.6	.287	.001	.143	1.142	.505	.000	.692	.549	.188	.051	.111	.037	.008	.033	109.2	103.2	.687	14.2
09-10	SAS	34.0	78	31.3	.262	.008	.119	1.111	.522	.182	.725	.560	.188	.046	.101	.035	.009	.029	109.1	102.8	.698	14.3
10-11p	SAS	35.0	75	31.0	.234	.007	.123	1.116	.513	.073	.715	.552	.174	.043	.109	.033	.009	.033	107.0	103.5	.616	9.7

Most similar to: David Robinson (95.9), Patrick Ewing, Moses Malone, Hakeem Olajuwon — IMP: 14% BRK: 0% COP: 0%

By reinforcing the frontcourt, the Spurs were able to cut Tim Duncan's minutes to a career-low 31.3 per game, helping him stay healthy for the full 82 games. At 34, Duncan posted the third-best two-point percentage of his entire career, and overall his statistics were remarkably consistent with his previous two campaigns. Duncan's offensive game has scarcely changed in a decade. He still favors that beloved left block, frequently facing up and using the backboard when he attempts the midrange jumper. Duncan hasn't gotten enough credit for his passing ability from the post. Among big men, Boris Diaw and Josh Smith were the only players with superior assist rates last season.

Duncan has lost a step at the defensive end of the floor, as Phoenix exposed during a playoff sweep of San Antonio. In part, Duncan is a victim of the expectations he created as the league's best defender in his prime. Duncan once had the ability to step out to defend the pick-and-roll and control the paint in the same play. Now, he needs a bit more help. Tiago Splitter should provide it.

SG 23 — Alonzo Gee

Hght: 6'6"	Exp: 1	Salary: $0.8 million		
Wght: 220	From: Alabama			
2011-12 status: due qualifying offer of $1.1 million				

SKILL RATINGS

TOT	OFF	DEF	REB	PAS	HND	SHT	ATH
-2	--	+1	--	--	--	--	--

Year	Team	Age	G	MPG	Usg	3PA%	FTA%	INS	2P%	3P%	FT%	TS%	Reb%	Ast%	TO%	BLK%	STL%	PF%	oRTG	dRTG	Win%	WARP
09-10	WAS	22.9	11	16.5	.205	.110	.156	1.046	.420	.778	.621	.564	.105	.018	.122	.004	.020	.033	106.4	106.1	.510	0.4
10-11p	SAS	23.9	76	-	.178	.202	.131	.929	.469	.377	.671	.536	.086	.012	.135	.011	.017	.039	-	-	.391	-

Most similar to: Willie Burton (98.7), Ronald Dupree, Scott Burrell, Cedric E. Henderson — IMP: 64% BRK: 17% COP: 7%

After Alonzo Gee's strong 11-game audition for the Wizards, the Spurs swooped in, signing him for the remainder of the season and through 2010-11. Gee returned to San Antonio's D-League affiliate in Austin, where he had previously starred, and finished as the D-League's Rookie of the Year. He'll compete for a roster spot in training camp with a small amount of his contract guaranteed.

Despite Gee's D-League accolades, his translated statistics result in an unimpressive projection. When adjusted for the level of play, his efficiency was mediocre. Gee gets to the free throw line on a regular basis but shoots poorly there, and his three-point accuracy has to be considered suspect given that he was a poor three-point shooter at the NCAA level. Gee is a very good rebounder from the wing and has the potential to develop into a plus defender.

SG 20 — Manu Ginobili

Hght: 6'6"	Exp: 8	Salary: $11.9 million		
Wght: 205	From: Bahia Blanca, Argentina			
2011-12 status: guaranteed contract for $13.0 million				

SKILL RATINGS

TOT	OFF	DEF	REB	PAS	HND	SHT	ATH
+5	+5	+5	+3	+5	+3	+3	+4

Year	Team	Age	G	MPG	Usg	3PA%	FTA%	INS	2P%	3P%	FT%	TS%	Reb%	Ast%	TO%	BLK%	STL%	PF%	oRTG	dRTG	Win%	WARP
07-08	SAS	30.7	74	31.1	.289	.282	.141	.860	.499	.402	.860	.612	.090	.070	.145	.011	.023	.036	111.9	104.0	.737	15.4
08-09	SAS	31.7	44	26.8	.273	.315	.126	.811	.546	.330	.884	.594	.099	.065	.133	.010	.029	.037	111.1	104.3	.708	7.2
09-10	SAS	32.7	75	28.7	.260	.288	.129	.840	.481	.377	.870	.584	.077	.079	.127	.008	.025	.033	111.7	105.0	.705	12.9
10-11p	SAS	33.7	73	28.0	.226	.301	.127	.826	.519	.357	.864	.594	.082	.071	.136	.010	.024	.037	109.8	104.7	.661	10.4

Most similar to: Clyde Drexler (96.2), Scottie Pippen, Darrell Armstrong, Gary Payton — IMP: 26% BRK: 0% COP: 9%

SAN ANTONIO SPURS

It took an out-of-character play for Manu Ginobili to remind the league that he was back after a 2008-09 season hampered by injuries. Just after the All-Star break, Ginobili acrobatically leaped high to block a Kevin Durant dunk attempt in transition. Ginobili blocked just 24 shots all year, but the play did show the return of his athleticism. Ginobili's per-minute numbers were strong throughout the season. When he ramped up his playing time down the stretch, it was obvious that Ginobili is still one of the league's top shooting guards.

SCHOENE is incredibly optimistic about Ginobili's prospects for aging well. The biggest reason is his versatility. Players who contribute in a variety of areas tend to compensate better than specialists. Last season saw Ginobili embrace a larger role as a playmaker with Tony Parker in and out of the lineup; his assist percentage was a career high. Ginobili also pumps up his True Shooting Percentage with a steady dose of makes from three-point range as well as regular trips to the free throw line.

PG 3	George Hill	Hght: 6'2" Wght: 180 2011-12 status: team option for $1.5 million	Exp: 2 From: IUPUI	Salary: $0.9 million		SKILL RATINGS							
						TOT	OFF	DEF	REB	PAS	HND	SHT	ATH
						+1	+3	+3	+1	-2	0	+2	+2
Year	Team	Age	G	MPG	Usg	3PA%	FTA%	INS	2P%	3P%	FT%	TS%	Reb%	Ast%	TO%	BLK%	STL%	PF%	oRTG	dRTG	Win%	WARP
08-09	SAS	23.0	77	16.5	.196	.143	.126	.983	.421	.329	.781	.502	.074	.052	.145	.012	.019	.058	104.2	106.7	.416	0.0
09-10	SAS	24.0	78	29.2	.191	.199	.111	.911	.505	.399	.772	.572	.052	.046	.107	.008	.016	.045	106.2	106.9	.478	2.9
10-11p	SAS	25.0	75	30.0	.178	.240	.120	.880	.479	.406	.773	.568	.057	.050	.119	.012	.016	.048	106.0	106.6	.483	3.2
Most similar to: Sleepy Floyd (98.6), B.J. Armstrong, Delonte West, Vernon Maxwell																IMP: 58%		BRK: 2%		COP: 4%		

George Hill used an old Spurs favorite as the fuel for his breakout season: the corner three-pointer. Nearly 80 percent of Hill's three-point attempts came from the corner, and he made them at an impressive 44.6 percent clip. (When Hill shot from the top of the key or the wings, his accuracy dropped to 23.7 percent.) Buoyed by his improvement beyond the arc, Hill's True Shooting Percentage rocketed upward, making him an above-average scorer.

As a rookie, Hill earned his keep at the defensive end. He's got a 6'9" wingspan, which helps him defend both guard positions and smother smaller guards. Hill is also physical enough to deal well with on-ball screens. Hill will likely come off the bench to start 2009-10, but could force his way into the lineup at some point before Tony Parker's contract ends. He is not a natural point guard, but Manu Ginobili can assist with the ballhandling duties when the two are in the backcourt together. The Ginobili-Hill backcourt is San Antonio's best option in terms of defense and shooting.

SF 24	Richard Jefferson	Hght: 6'7" Wght: 225 2011-12 status: guaranteed contract for $9.3 million	Exp: 9 From: Arizona	Salary: $8.4 million		SKILL RATINGS							
						TOT	OFF	DEF	REB	PAS	HND	SHT	ATH
						-1	+1	-4	-3	+1	+1	+1	-1
Year	Team	Age	G	MPG	Usg	3PA%	FTA%	INS	2P%	3P%	FT%	TS%	Reb%	Ast%	TO%	BLK%	STL%	PF%	oRTG	dRTG	Win%	WARP
07-08	NJN	27.8	82	39.0	.263	.117	.164	1.047	.487	.362	.798	.571	.062	.036	.109	.005	.011	.032	106.3	107.0	.477	4.0
08-09	MIL	28.8	82	35.8	.248	.181	.141	.960	.453	.397	.805	.554	.078	.031	.102	.004	.011	.039	106.0	107.2	.463	2.9
09-10	SAS	29.8	81	31.1	.184	.186	.125	.940	.515	.316	.735	.551	.082	.029	.104	.011	.009	.033	104.4	106.3	.437	1.1
10-11p	SAS	30.8	76	31.0	.191	.193	.133	.939	.496	.353	.759	.558	.072	.029	.103	.008	.010	.037	104.6	106.9	.423	0.4
Most similar to: Chris Mills (98.5), Rolando Blackman, Tony Campbell, Mike Mitchell																IMP: 33%		BRK: 5%		COP: 9%		

The corner three was not kind to Richard Jefferson last year. During his lone season in Milwaukee, Jefferson made 45.8 percent of his corner three attempts, part of the reason the Spurs figured he would be a good fit for them. Instead, Jefferson slipped to 36.0 percent from the corners and was wildly ineffective overall from beyond the arc. The poor shooting negated the benefit Jefferson derived from becoming a third or fourth option on offense after years as a go-to scorer. Jefferson's two-point percentage was his best since 2005-06, yet he was still a major disappointment on offense.

Publicly, San Antonio is hoping that Jefferson will be more comfortable during his second year with the team. However, Jefferson's advancing age suggests that optimistic outcome is unlikely. Jefferson hasn't been an average player by win percentage since 2005-06, and players don't typically bounce back from that once they hit their 30s. Wings who are not great shooters tend to age especially quickly. As it is, Jefferson contributes little besides scoring. He's an average defender and is poor on the glass.

PG 5	Curtis Jerrells	Hght: 6'1" Wght: 195 2011-12 status: due qualifying offer of $1.1 million	Exp: R From: Baylor	Salary: $0.8 million							
					SKILL RATINGS						
					TOT	OFF	DEF	REB	PAS	HND	SHT	ATH
					-1	--	--	--	--	--	--	--

Year	Team	Age	G	MPG	Usg	3PA%	FTA%	INS	2P%	3P%	FT%	TS%	Reb%	Ast%	TO%	BLK%	STL%	PF%	oRTG	dRTG	Win%	WARP
10-11p	SAS	24.2	76	-	.169	.246	.102	.856	.443	.367	.725	.519	.052	.050	.138	.004	.020	.032	-	-	.418	-

Most similar to: David Wingate (98.0), Jim Thomas, Bimbo Coles, George Hill   IMP: 62% BRK: 12% COP: 8%

Curtis Jerrells took the Austin-San Antonio express last season. He went to training camp with the Spurs before spending the entire season with the Toros. San Antonio signed Jerrells to a contract through 2010-11 in March, but he never played a game for the big club, staying in Austin instead. Jerrells will take another shot at the roster during training camp, battling Garrett Temple to be the third point guard.

Jerrells scored as similar to George Hill based on both college statistics and his D-League translation. The big difference is Jerrells lacks the size to be an above-average defender. At the offensive end, Jerrells can hold his own. He's shown some three-point range and has the quickness to get in the paint. As a passer, Jerrells is only average, though he takes good care of the basketball.

PF 34	Antonio McDyess	Hght: 6'9" Wght: 245 2011-12 status: partially-guaranteed contract for $5.2 million	Exp: 14 From: Alabama	Salary: $4.9 million							
					SKILL RATINGS						
					TOT	OFF	DEF	REB	PAS	HND	SHT	ATH
					-2	-1	-3	+3	+1	+3	0	-2

Year	Team	Age	G	MPG	Usg	3PA%	FTA%	INS	2P%	3P%	FT%	TS%	Reb%	Ast%	TO%	BLK%	STL%	PF%	oRTG	dRTG	Win%	WARP
07-08	DET	33.6	78	29.3	.154	.003	.092	1.090	.490	.000	.622	.511	.174	.018	.101	.018	.013	.052	103.1	104.2	.462	2.2
08-09	DET	34.6	62	30.1	.158	.000	.062	1.062	.510	.000	.698	.529	.194	.021	.083	.021	.012	.049	105.2	104.8	.513	3.7
09-10	SAS	35.6	77	21.0	.152	.004	.047	1.043	.481	.000	.632	.492	.164	.024	.148	.014	.014	.042	102.5	104.9	.421	0.1
10-11p	SAS	36.6	74	10.0	.126	.005	.055	1.050	.500	.000	.644	.509	.156	.022	.135	.016	.013	.048	102.4	105.3	.406	-0.2

Most similar to: Kurt Thomas (98.8), Buck Williams, P.J. Brown, Mychal Thompson   IMP: 26% BRK: 0% COP: 15%

Signed by San Antonio after a big 2008-09 season in Detroit, Antonio McDyess took a major step backward that could signal the beginning of the end for him. McDyess turned 36 in September, making it unlikely that he will entirely bounce back. McDyess has relied heavily on long two-pointers in his 30s. He's very good from this range, but it is difficult to be efficient on a steady diet of twos. McDyess rarely gets to the free throw line, so his True Shooting Percentage has long been mediocre. McDyess was also far more prone to turnovers last season, both as a passer and a ballhandler.

At the defensive end, McDyess is still solid. He was the Spurs' best defensive option alongside Tim Duncan. McDyess can execute a defensive scheme despite the fact that he is not much of a shot blocker at this stage of his career, and he rarely commits fouls. Still, he might be the odd man out of the San Antonio frontcourt with the addition of Tiago Splitter.

SG 31	Gary Neal	Hght: 6'4" Wght: 210 2011-12 status: guaranteed contract for $0.8 million	Exp: R From: Towson	Salary: $0.5 million							
					SKILL RATINGS						
					TOT	OFF	DEF	REB	PAS	HND	SHT	ATH
					0	+1	-1	+2	0	+2	-1	0

Year	Team	Age	G	MPG	Usg	3PA%	FTA%	INS	2P%	3P%	FT%	TS%	Reb%	Ast%	TO%	BLK%	STL%	PF%	oRTG	dRTG	Win%	WARP
10-11p	SAS	26.5	76	16.7	.183	.361	.083	.722	.434	.349	.738	.510	.075	.037	.103	.000	.019	.037	105.1	106.3	.461	1.2

Most similar to: Keith Bogans (97.9), Morris Peterson, Tyrone Nesby, Anthony Peeler   IMP: 61% BRK: 11% COP: 5%

SAN ANTONIO SPURS

Gary Neal is hardly a household name in the U.S., even among basketball die-hards. He wrapped up his college career at tiny Towson on a team that went below .500 his senior season. Neal quickly proved his bona fides overseas, however, and was a coveted European player before deciding to take his shot at the NBA. On the strength of a solid performance in Las Vegas, the Spurs guaranteed Neal a three-year contract.

In Europe, Neal had the ball in his hands on a regular basis and operated out of a lot of pick-and-rolls. His role will be different for the Spurs, who will primarily ask him to spot up. He was inconsistent from the shorter international line, shooting 44.7 percent from three-point range in EuroCup play during 2008-09 before slipping to 34.6 percent last season. He should get better looks opposite San Antonio's stars than he did as a go-to scorer overseas. In addition to making shots, Neal will have to commit to the defensive end to earn playing time for the Spurs. If he does that, he might be a bargain at the league minimum.

PG 9 — Tony Parker

Hght: 6'2" Wght: 180 Exp: 9 From: Paris, France Salary: $13.7 million
2011-12 status: free agent

SKILL RATINGS

TOT	OFF	DEF	REB	PAS	HND	SHT	ATH
+2	+3	+1	-2	+3	+1	0	0

Year	Team	Age	G	MPG	Usg	3PA%	FTA%	INS	2P%	3P%	FT%	TS%	Reb%	Ast%	TO%	BLK%	STL%	PF%	oRTG	dRTG	Win%	WARP
07-08	SAS	25.9	69	33.5	.284	.049	.112	1.064	.510	.258	.715	.542	.056	.086	.121	.003	.011	.019	107.8	106.2	.555	6.7
08-09	SAS	26.9	72	34.1	.319	.040	.099	1.059	.518	.292	.782	.556	.054	.098	.116	.001	.015	.022	110.7	107.0	.618	10.3
09-10	SAS	27.9	56	30.9	.259	.035	.111	1.076	.497	.294	.756	.542	.045	.085	.153	.003	.009	.026	106.0	107.4	.452	1.3
10-11p	SAS	28.9	71	28.0	.249	.056	.105	1.049	.508	.308	.756	.547	.047	.086	.131	.003	.010	.022	106.8	107.1	.490	3.1

Most similar to: World B. Free (95.1), Johnny Davis, Steve Francis, Kevin Johnson
IMP: 43% BRK: 3% COP: 8%

A year removed from the best season of his career, Tony Parker suffered through a miserable 2009-10 campaign that put his future in San Antonio in jeopardy. With Tim Duncan and Manu Ginobili ailing in 2008-09, Parker stepped up his involvement in the Spurs offense without sacrificing any efficiency and helped keep the team afloat during the second half of the season. At 27, Parker seemed to be establishing a new level of play. Instead, he found himself unable to create good shots nearly as frequently last year, seeing his usage rate tumble badly while his True Shooting Percentage and assist percentage also declined. Parker also turned the ball over more frequently than he had in five seasons.

Parker took the summer off from international play (as did Ginobili) to focus on getting healthy for a crucial campaign. A free agent at season's end, Parker has the chance to earn a big contract with a bounceback performance. When healthy, his quickness makes it nearly impossible to keep him out of the paint. One positive last season was that Parker's free throw rate was strong, showing he still had the ability to get to the rim at times. Parker has made strides as a passer the last three years and emerged as one of the league's assist leaders in 2008-09. He's unlikely to repeat that performance, but expect him to return to his previous form and beat his SCHOENE projection.

SF 1 — Bobby Simmons

Hght: 6'6" Wght: 230 Exp: 8 From: DePaul Salary: --
2011-12 status: free agent

SKILL RATINGS

TOT	OFF	DEF	REB	PAS	HND	SHT	ATH
-4	--	+4	--	--	--	--	--

Year	Team	Age	G	MPG	Usg	3PA%	FTA%	INS	2P%	3P%	FT%	TS%	Reb%	Ast%	TO%	BLK%	STL%	PF%	oRTG	dRTG	Win%	WARP
07-08	MIL	27.9	70	21.7	.180	.283	.051	.768	.458	.351	.757	.504	.089	.024	.129	.003	.015	.043	103.3	106.7	.387	-0.9
08-09	NJN	28.9	71	24.4	.144	.496	.048	.553	.453	.447	.741	.596	.096	.025	.117	.005	.015	.051	107.4	107.5	.497	2.9
09-10	NJN	29.9	23	17.2	.170	.435	.061	.626	.407	.317	.900	.485	.095	.018	.131	.006	.020	.061	103.1	106.5	.391	-0.2
10-11p	SAS	30.9	67	--	.144	.501	.051	.550	.432	.368	.839	.531	.089	.021	.127	.004	.016	.057	--	--	.347	--

Most similar to: Devean George (98.1), Jaren Jackson, James Posey, Walter McCarty
IMP: 39% BRK: 5% COP: 7%

Usually, Most Improved Players parlay their improvement (whether real or imagined based on increased minutes) into a strong NBA career. For Bobby Simmons, winning the award in 2004-05 proved to be a high point. The Milwaukee Bucks rewarded Simmons with a five-year, $47 million contract, but he was unable to repeat his performance during his first season in Milwaukee before a pair of surgeries on his right ankle and foot cost him the entire 2006-07 campaign and left him a shadow of his former self.

Simmons has still been decent when he's knocked down his three-pointers at a strong clip, as during his first year with the Nets. When his accuracy beyond the arc slipped badly last season, however, Simmons was worthless. If his shooting bounces back, Simmons could be a bargain at the minimum. That's what the Spurs are hoping after inviting Simmons to their training camp. He has a chance to claim the backup spot behind Richard Jefferson, but he is not guaranteed a spot on the roster.

PF 22 — Tiago Splitter

Hght: 6'11" Exp: R Salary: $3.4 million
Wght: 232 From: Brazil
2011-12 status: guaranteed contract for $3.7 million

SKILL RATINGS

TOT	OFF	DEF	REB	PAS	HND	SHT	ATH
+2	+2	+1	-1	+4	+4	+4	+2

Year	Team	Age	G	MPG	Usg	3PA%	FTA%	INS	2P%	3P%	FT%	TS%	Reb%	Ast%	TO%	BLK%	STL%	PF%	oRTG	dRTG	Win%	WARP
10-11p	SAS	26.3	76	28.0	.191	.009	.168	1.159	.556	.006	.646	.585	.120	.037	.119	.028	.010	.057	105.9	105.5	.513	4.3

Most similar to: Rasheed Wallace (97.5), Billy Owens, Cadillac Anderson, Chris Wilcox

IMP: 47% BRK: 3% COP: 2%

The word that best describes Tiago Splitter's game is complete. While not necessarily outstanding anywhere, he is solid across the board, which should make him a very effective NBA player and a perfect complement to Tim Duncan. Splitter has proven his value at the game's highest levels outside the U.S. He led his Caja Laboral team to a sweep over Euroleague champs Regal FC Barcelona to win last year's Spanish ACB title, then played very well in the FIBA World Championship. Splitter's summer was highlighted by his strong performance in a near-upset of the United States.

Caja Laboral used Splitter in every way conceivable for a big man. He ran the pick-and-roll, got post-up opportunities and isolated on the perimeter. His passing is an underrated strength that should help him feed Duncan from the high post at times. Inside, Splitter is an excellent finisher who shot far better than 60 percent on twos in both 2007-08 and 2008-09. Splitter has enough length and shot-blocking ability to play the center in the NBA, yet is also athletic enough to step out and defend power forwards. If there's one minor quibble with his game, it's that Splitter is slightly below average on the glass. Still, he figures to be one of the league's best newcomers and will probably have more impact on the postseason than any other rookie.

SG 2 — Garrett Temple

Hght: 6'6" Exp: 1 Salary: $0.8 million
Wght: 190 From: Louisiana State
2011-12 status: due qualifying offer of $1.1 million

SKILL RATINGS

TOT	OFF	DEF	REB	PAS	HND	SHT	ATH
0	+1	0	-3	-1	-4	+4	+3

Year	Team	Age	G	MPG	Usg	3PA%	FTA%	INS	2P%	3P%	FT%	TS%	Reb%	Ast%	TO%	BLK%	STL%	PF%	oRTG	dRTG	Win%	WARP
09-10	SAS	24.0	27	12.4	.204	.247	.147	.900	.484	.351	.700	.553	.054	.029	.180	.013	.020	.057	103.4	106.7	.394	-0.2
10-11p	SAS	25.0	76	5.0	.182	.311	.149	.838	.493	.395	.711	.591	.053	.031	.172	.016	.020	.058	104.8	106.3	.450	0.3

Most similar to: Greg Graham (97.4), LaBradford Smith, Thabo Sefolosha, Milt Palacio

IMP: 61% BRK: 9% COP: 7%

Garrett Temple is another product of the D-League, but he played with the Houston Rockets' affiliate, Rio Grande Valley, after being cut by the Rockets during the preseason. Temple had 10-day contracts with both Houston and Sacramento before landing in San Antonio. When injuries sidelined George Hill and Tony Parker, Temple started four games late in the regular season and held his own, averaging 11.2 points per game.

That experience aside, Temple is really a shooting guard, which explains his inflated turnover percentage when asked to be the Spurs' primary ballhandler. Temple was a much better shooter at the NBA level than his D-League statistics suggested, so it will be interesting to see whether he can maintain that level of efficiency going forward. He'll have to play well to hold off Alonzo Gee and Curtis Jerrells, though his performance last season gives him a leg up in that race.

SAN ANTONIO SPURS

PF	Ryan Richards	Hght: 6'11"	Exp: R	Salary: --	SKILL RATINGS						
		Wght: 230	From: England		TOT	OFF	DEF	REB	PAS	HND	SHT	ATH
--		2011-12 status: free agent			--	--	--	--	--	--	--	--

Nobody has mined Europe like San Antonio, but England is new ground for the Spurs. Most Englishmen in the NBA came through the NCAA ranks. Richards has played professionally in Europe. ACB club Gran Canaria holds his rights, though he spent last year on loan to Swiss club BBC Monthey to get some court time. At 19, Richards is far from a finished product, but his combination of height and athleticism makes him an intriguing prospect. The Spurs nabbed him late in the second round and will hope for another European success story in a few years.

SG	Malik Hairston	Hght: 6'6"	Exp: 2	Salary: --	SKILL RATINGS
		Wght: 220	From: Oregon		TOT OFF DEF REB PAS HND SHT ATH
--		2011-12 status: free agent			-3 0 -1 +4 -3 0 0 -2

Year	Team	Age	G	MPG	Usg	3PA%	FTA%	INS	2P%	3P%	FT%	TS%	Reb%	Ast%	TO%	BLK%	STL%	PF%	oRTG	dRTG	Win%	WARP
08-09	SAS	22.2	15	10.3	.201	.016	.048	1.032	.500	.000	.286	.480	.107	.041	.187	.033	.021	.060	102.2	105.1	.404	0.0
09-10	SAS	23.2	47	6.7	.146	.110	.132	1.022	.585	.182	.567	.555	.090	.023	.110	.020	.006	.042	103.3	106.6	.392	-0.2
10-11p	AVG	24.2	76	6.7	.149	.185	.125	.941	.571	.172	.591	.515	.087	.025	.106	.021	.007	.039	103.1	106.7	.384	-0.3

Most similar to: Danny Vranes (96.8), Chucky Brown, Mark Alarie, Greg Minor   IMP: 54% BRK: 13% COP: 2%

Malik Hairston spent his rookie year going back and forth between Austin and San Antonio before graduating to a full-time spot on the Spurs' roster in year two. Playing time was still hard to find for the Oregon product, who played decently in limited opportunities thanks to a high two-point percentage. Hairston would have had a chance to compete for a rotation spot this season, but instead chose to be released from his contract to sign a two-year deal with Italian team Montepaschi Siena. According to TheHoopsMarket.com, the Italian club dissolved the contract due to a back injury, but may re-sign Hairston after he rehabilitates.

Hairston is an athletic wing with good potential as a defender. The biggest impediment to his success on the perimeter is his lack of NBA three-point range. Hairston shot 2-of-11 beyond the arc last season.

PF	Marcus Haislip	Hght: 6'10"	Exp: 4	Salary: --	SKILL RATINGS
		Wght: 230	From: Tennessee		TOT OFF DEF REB PAS HND SHT ATH
--		2011-12 status: free agent			-- -- -- -- -- -- -- --

Year	Team	Age	G	MPG	Usg	3PA%	FTA%	INS	2P%	3P%	FT%	TS%	Reb%	Ast%	TO%	BLK%	STL%	PF%	oRTG	dRTG	Win%	WARP
09-10	SAS	29.3	10	4.4	.274	.191	.084	.893	.438	.600	.400	.539	.133	.000	.115	.033	.000	.052	105.5	106.6	.465	0.0

The Spurs hoped Marcus Haislip could contribute for them last season as a stretch power forward, but his declining Euroleague statistics suggested he would be overmatched in his return to the NBA after a lengthy absence. Score this one for the numbers. Haislip never found a role and was let out of his contract in January to sign with Greek power Panathinaikos. Haislip will be 30 this year and is probably back in Europe for good.

Toronto Raptors

It's been a repetitive cycle in the history of the Toronto Raptors. Draft an athletic phenom. Develop him into an star. See him get sucked into the NBA marketing machine. Watch him leave town. Start again. Vince Carter, Tracy McGrady, Chris Bosh--there's the franchise's story in a nutshell.

It might be a stretch to include McGrady in that small group of elite Raptors. He only played three seasons in Toronto and was just emerging as a star when he left for Orlando as a free agent, ostensibly to get out of Carter's shadow. Still, you get the picture. It's got to be tough to be a Raptors fan, an underrated group that has supported their team through all the waywardness and melodrama surrounding their favorite franchise.

There have been two occasions when it appeared that the Raptors were going to turn the corner and become a serious player in the Eastern Conference. The first came when Lenny Wilkens was the coach. The Raps won 47 games and advanced to the Eastern Conference semifinals, where they lost a seven-game series to eventual conference champ Philadelphia. Carter had blown up into a full-blown sensation, but the Raptors also featured two starters (Mark Jackson and Charles Oakley) who were 35 or older, plus another (Antonio Davis) who was 32. Toronto slipped back into mediocrity, got even worse, then Carter grew disenchanted and was sent to run with Jason Kidd in New Jersey. McGrady, who had become one of the league's best players in Orlando, drew the ire of Raptors fans whenever he visited Toronto, as visions of a fully-mature McGrady running on the wing with Carter filled many a Canadian night.

Bosh was drafted the year before Carter forced his way out of town. By his second year, he had already shown enough that he became the face of the franchise when Carter was traded 20 games into the season. A couple of years later, Bosh was a two-time All-Star at the age of 22, and the Raptors won the Atlantic Division, matching the franchise apex of 47 wins. This time, the future looked more promising. Bosh played alongside what appeared to be a dynamic point guard combo in T.J. Ford and Jose Calderon, and the top pick of the 2006 draft, Andrea Bargnani, was just getting his feet wet. The Raptors needed a top-flight wing player to complete the foundation and the role players on that 2006-07 team were a fairly nondescript group, but it felt like the Raptors were right there.

That team was also the first Toronto roster assembled by general manager Bryan Colangelo. At the time, he received a lot of praise for bringing in the likes of Ford, Kris Humphries, Anthony Parker and Jorge Garbajosa. Really, there was nothing wrong with those acquisitions, even if his overall vision for the franchise seemed to include a preoccupation with European basketball that was almost bizarre. With the benefit of hindsight, you can pinpoint the selection of Bargnani as the move that sent the wheels churning in the wrong direction. That certainly wasn't all Colangelo's fault, as 2006 was

RAPTORS IN A BOX

Last year's record	40-42
Last year's Offensive Rating	113.1 (6)
Last year's Defensive Rating	114.8 (30)
Last year's point differential	-1.8 (19)
Team pace	91.6 (13)
SCHOENE projection	**35-47 (9)**
Projected Offensive Rating	111.1 (11)
Projected Defensive Rating	113.3 (30)
Projected team weighted age	25.7 (22)
Projected '10-11 payroll	$61.3 (19)
Est. payroll obligations, '11-12	$56.3 (15)

Head coach: Jay Triano

During Jay Triano's first full season as head coach, the Raptors bounced back on offense but cratered on defense. Toronto's Defensive Rating was the worst in the league. While he wasn't given much defensive talent to work with, Triano certainly shares the blame for the team's shortcomings at that end of the floor. Now, Triano is tasked with rebuilding the Raptors after the departure of Chris Bosh. The biggest challenge will be finding a go-to player on offense. Triano hopes increased ball movement will be a plus; the more buckets Toronto can create out of its offense rather than one-on-one play, the better. Triano has also vowed that the team will be more aggressive on defense.

a pretty weak draft class. There was no clear top pick, and if you look at mock drafts produced at the time, the other leading contenders to be picked No. 1 were LaMarcus Aldridge and Tyrus Thomas, neither of whom would have made a whole lot of sense next to Bosh. The top wing players were Brandon Roy, Rudy Gay and Adam Morrison, with Roy probably being the most coveted at the time, though even that's debatable. Ford wasn't brought in for Charlie Villanueva until two days after the draft, so if they went with Roy, chances are the Ford deal doesn't get done. Then you end up with a probable lineup of Calderon, Roy, Bosh, Villanueva and Rasho Nesterovic. Is that really any better? Not really, and anyway nobody viewed Roy as the top pick. If you really want to employ hindsight, you can maybe say that Colangelo should have traded the pick, but all you can really say for certain is that it was unfortunate timing for Toronto to win that particular draft lottery.

We know what happened next. The Raptors struggled to get near the .500 mark and annually competed for the last seed in the East playoff bracket. Bosh's contract ran out and he skipped off for a South Beach party with his Olympic buddies. Hedo Turkoglu came in as a prized free agent and alienated everyone in town. He's now in Phoenix, and no one north of the border is shedding any tears over that. What's left is a franchise that is starting over--once again, and with little to show for the rebuilding efforts of the past.

Let's sort out the aftermath.

The first task for Colangelo, who still reportedly has the support of his overseers in Toronto, is to determine which--if any--members of the current roster are foundation players. That evaluation begins with Bargnani, whose development has been uneven, painfully slow and downright disappointing. Dirk Nowitzki he is not. Bargnani has gradually become a more polished offensive player, albeit one lacking in consistency. He's become more efficient in the post, which has made him something more than the neo-Brad Lohaus. What concerns you about him becoming the focal point of the attack, which will happen this season, is that he relies so heavily on others to get him the ball in the right spots. He's not a player who is going to create a lot of his own offense, which can be a problem if he spends too much time on the perimeter. However, you want him to play above the three-point line frequently, because his clear-cut strength is his ability to drain the long-range shot. Perhaps now that he's out of Bosh's shadow, he can become the passer that many thought he'd be at the time we was drafted. SCHOENE's projection for Bargnani this season feels right: higher usage, a dip in shooting percentage inside the arc, but a higher foul-drawing rate. If he can add a higher assist rate to that package, then the Raptors have themselves a passable No. 2 option on offense.

The problem is that there is no No. 1. Offseason signee Linas Kleiza, like Bargnani, is itching to show what he can do when not overshadowed by an All-Star teammate. In Denver, Carmelo Anthony was to Kleiza what Bosh was to Bargnani. Kleiza looked pretty good in the FIBA World Championship. Though he was relegated to being a stand-still shooter in Denver, he has the ability to put the ball onto the floor. Kleiza can also be very physical and should get to the foul line often. He'll also up his assist rate, though it remains to be seen how much. Once upon a time, when he was first recruited by the University of Missouri, Kleiza's hype machine included such phrases as "the Lithuanian Larry Bird." Admittedly, that's laying it on a bit thick, and Kleiza is probably also best suited to be the second or third option in a quality offense. As with Bargnani, Kleiza also must prove he can play defense, as the Raptors would like to improve upon last season's league-worst Defensive Rating. Part of the answer there will be whoever emerges as the starting big alongside Bargnani, who cannot continue to be looked upon as the backline of the defense, but there are no obvious solutions on the current roster. In any event, there are four reasons to watch the Raptors this season, and two of them are to see what Bargnani and Kleiza can do as featured players.

The third reason is second-year guard DeMar DeRozan, who remains a divisive figure. It's not because of any attitude or behavioral problems. He seems likable enough. The problem is that the numbers that disliked DeRozan so much when he left USC for the pros still aren't particularly high on him. Fans of raw athletes, both in the stands and in the scouting community, remain enamored of DeRozan, who has been referred to in some circles as the next Vince Carter. Gulp. High among his comps are Gerald Green and Joe Johnson. He's probably going to end up somewhere between those extremes; if you root for the Raptors, you hope he's closer to a more physically gifted version of the latter. DeRozan is talented, there is no question about that. He already gets to the line at an above-average rate, which is a nice starting point. However, his usage rate was below average during his rookie season, a result of DeRozan being unwilling to shoot outside of about 10 feet. (Though, he shot very well inside that range.) Sixty-eight percent of his made field goals

From the Blogosphere

Who: Scott Carefoot
What: RaptorBlog
Where: http://www.raptorblog.com/

After hating LeBron James, the second-most popular fan activity this off-season was ridiculing the contracts given out to so-called "max players" like Joe Johnson as well as reputed "scrubs" like Amir Johnson. Amir's five-year, $28 million deal was evidence to some that Raptors President/GM Bryan Colangelo had officially lost his mind. While it's unclear whether Johnson will claim the starting power forward role vacated by Chris Bosh, there's evidence that the 23 year old could prove to be underpaid if he can reduce last season's rate of 6.3 fouls per 36 minutes. He was easily the Raptors' best defensive big man in 2009-10 (faint praise, I know), and in the 12 games where he played at least 25 minutes, Johnson averaged 13.0 points, 8.7 rebounds and 1.5 blocks while shooting 71.1 percent from the field. The field-goal percentage is unsustainable, but I believe the other numbers can be duplicated--as long as Johnson can stay on the court.

were assisted, which suggests a player that has trouble getting his own offense. You just don't expect that of a player with DeRozan's physical abilities. You more expect a guy with a bloated usage rate and a low efficiency. In any event, DeRozan has a long way to go. He's got to improve his range, become a better and more willing passer and upgrade about three rungs on the defensive ladder. He put up startlingly good numbers in the summer league, so perhaps he's headed in the right direction. DeRozan will never have a better opportunity to establish himself as a rising star than he will have in Toronto this season.

The last player to watch this season is rookie big man Ed Davis, the Raptors' first-round pick out of North Carolina in June. Davis has the statistical profile of a center, but he sure doesn't have the body of one. He projects as a good rebounder and shot blocker out of the gate. On offense, he didn't stray far from the basket for Carolina, and won't do much more than finish off of cuts and putbacks for the Raptors during the early part of his career. He's something of a wild card. If he adds bulk and a base offensive skill set, you could envision a frontcourt combo where Davis could actually team with Bargnani, and the pair could swap offensive and defensive assignments depending upon the opposition. As it is, this will be a getting-to-know-you season for Davis. A potential red flag for him is availability. He broke his wrist last winter and missed a good portion of his sophomore season as a Tar Heel. Then he hurt his knee in mid-September and, at press time, it was unclear whether the injury would linger into his rookie season. Also, it bears noting that, yes, Davis is raw and he's young, but he's actually older than DeRozan.

To reiterate, this season will be about finding out if there are foundation players on the Raptors' current roster. If all goes well, the team would head into the 2011 offseason feeling good about a Bargnani/Kleiza/DeRozan/Davis core. Not likely, but it could happen. If so, then the next step for Colangelo is to position Toronto to add to said foundation.

The Raptors do have a lot of assets with which to work. There is the $14.5 million trade exception created by the Bosh sign-and-trade that extends to July 9, 2011. That gives Colangelo a full season to shop for a fit, plus enough time to swing something before the next draft. (Though, as with all musings about the future NBA, this is complicated by the looming CBA stalemate.) The Raptors' immediate salary-cap position isn't all that flexible, unless Colangelo can find a taker for Calderon. As such, bringing in a player at or near the value of the Bosh exception would mean getting into luxury-tax territory for a roster that really doesn't merit it. At least Colangelo has some options. The Raptors will also have two first-round picks in the next draft (unless the Heat somehow miss the playoffs, in which case Miami would send cash to Toronto instead of its first pick). The Raptors' own pick could potentially end up very high in the lottery.

SCHOENE's projection for 35 wins seems a little high. If that's the range Toronto is in, however, then Colangelo has some serious work to do. The team was in the middle class with Bosh and it can't be there without him unless the team's core is expected to develop into contending status. This one may not. In fact, this roster may turn out to be completely devoid of foundation players. If that's the case, then this franchise is in a mess. However, if the youngsters develop in the brighter light that will be shining on them this season, then perhaps the Raptors can finally set about establishing a core group of players that actually want to stay in Toronto for the long term.

Bradford Doolittle

TORONTO RAPTORS

RAPTORS FIVE-YEAR TRENDS

Season	AGE	W-L	POW	PYTH	SEED	ORTG	DRTG	PT DIFF	PACE
05-06	25.9	27-55	29.0 (26)	32.8	---	111.2 (5)	114.3 (29)	-3.0 (25)	89.7 (15)
06-07	26.0	47-35	44.6 (10)	43.9	3	109.4 (8)	107.5 (12)	1.0 (10)	90.9 (11)
07-08	26.3	41-41	43.9 (13)	49.3	6	112.8 (10)	109.4 (14)	2.9 (12)	88.2 (24)
08-09	27.0	33-49	33.3 (22)	33.1	---	108.7 (22)	111.6 (22)	-2.8 (23)	90.6 (14)
09-10	26.0	40-42	37.7 (19)	36.2	--	113.1 (6)	114.8 (30)	-1.8 (19)	91.6 (13)

Season	PAY	OFFENSE eFG	oREB	FT/FGA	TO	DEFENSE eFG	oREB	FT/FGA	TO
05-06	$34.6	.500 (6)	.254 (27)	.249 (17)	.144 (3)	.530 (30)	.733 (11)	.263 (23)	.156 (20)
06-07	$42.2	.504 (10)	.222 (30)	.239 (17)	.147 (2)	.503 (22)	.745 (8)	.219 (5)	.166 (15)
07-08	$63.8	.511 (8)	.234 (26)	.200 (28)	.126 (1)	.505 (22)	.750 (4)	.205 (6)	.150 (13)
08-09	$73.2	.494 (20)	.240 (29)	.230 (21)	.146 (9)	.511 (22)	.737 (14)	.202 (3)	.146 (23)
09-10	$67.7	.521 (6)	.247 (24)	.244 (9)	.146 (6)	.513 (22)	.729 (23)	.247 (23)	.138 (30)

(league rankings in parenthesis)

C 50 — Solomon Alabi
Hght: 7'1" Exp: R Salary: $0.8 million
Wght: 251 From: Florida State
2011-12 status: guaranteed contract for $0.8 million

SKILL RATINGS
TOT	OFF	DEF	REB	PAS	HND	SHT	ATH
-1	--	--	--	--	--	--	--

Year	Team	Age	G	MPG	Usg	3PA%	FTA%	INS	2P%	3P%	FT%	TS%	Reb%	Ast%	TO%	BLK%	STL%	PF%	oRTG	dRTG	Win%	WARP
10-11p	TOR	23.1	76	-	.179	.000	.119	1.120	.432	.000	.777	.497	.120	.008	.168	.049	.009	.061	-	-	.425	-

Most similar to: Jason Thompson (95.8), David Harrison, Channing Frye, Emeka Okafor
IMP: -   BRK: -   COP: -

Solomon Alabi was the backline anchor on the nation's best defensive team last season at Florida State. He's a first-round talent who dropped to No. 50 in the draft over concerns about his Hepatitis-B condition, which has plagued him since birth. It's never bothered Alabi on the court in the past, so there is no reason to think it will hamper him in the future. He's also extremely smart, reportedly scoring the best-ever IQ score on a pre-draft test given by the Celtics. Alabi is raw offensively, but he's got a legitimate NBA body for a big man, a long reach and could be a game-changing defender at the pro level. As a player looking for a chance to prove his defensive prowess, he's come to the right place in Toronto.

C 13 — David Andersen
Hght: 6'11" Exp: 1 Salary: $2.5 million
Wght: 247 From: Frankston, Australia
2011-12 status: guaranteed contract for $2.7 million

SKILL RATINGS
TOT	OFF	DEF	REB	PAS	HND	SHT	ATH
-2	0	0	-1	+1	+2	-3	-2

Year	Team	Age	G	MPG	Usg	3PA%	FTA%	INS	2P%	3P%	FT%	TS%	Reb%	Ast%	TO%	BLK%	STL%	PF%	oRTG	dRTG	Win%	WARP
09-10	HOU	29.8	63	14.1	.203	.192	.073	.881	.458	.346	.687	.497	.136	.022	.091	.010	.008	.059	104.1	106.8	.411	-0.1
10-11p	TOR	30.8	73	5.2	.207	.190	.072	.882	.452	.321	.676	.489	.139	.021	.097	.010	.009	.065	103.8	106.7	.407	-0.1

Most similar to: Jeff Wilkins (98.3), LaPhonso Ellis, Tom McMillen, Malik Allen
IMP: 44%   BRK: 8%   COP: 8%

David Andersen's game didn't translate quite as well from Europe as we hoped, but he does have his good traits. Andersen is a bit more of a gunner than you'd think, though he does have good passing skills. He simply needs to be more selective so that he can up his shooting percentages, or he's not helping his team. Andersen appears to be an average defender, which makes him a useable player in Toronto. The Raptors' system should be a good fit for him. However, Andersen's skill set is redundant to Andrea Bargnani's. Even if Andersen proves to be better at those skills than Bargnani, he's still not going to steal Bargnani's role. The main thing you'd like to see from Andersen this season is for him to get his three-point accuracy above league average.

TORONTO RAPTORS

PG 3 — Marcus Banks

Hght: 6'2" Exp: 7 Salary: $4.8 million
Wght: 205 From: Nevada-Las Vegas
2011-12 status: free agent

SKILL RATINGS

TOT	OFF	DEF	REB	PAS	HND	SHT	ATH
-1	--	-1	--	--	--	--	--

Year	Team	Age	G	MPG	Usg	3PA%	FTA%	INS	2P%	3P%	FT%	TS%	Reb%	Ast%	TO%	BLK%	STL%	PF%	oRTG	dRTG	Win%	WARP
07-08	MIA	26.4	36	15.8	.204	.417	.064	.647	.517	.396	.771	.582	.048	.051	.153	.018	.012	.053	106.9	106.9	.500	1.0
08-09	TOR	27.4	22	9.4	.180	.241	.100	.860	.474	.158	.611	.431	.052	.064	.177	.008	.028	.059	102.1	106.5	.356	-0.3
09-10	TOR	28.4	22	11.1	.199	.227	.121	.894	.653	.292	.828	.635	.055	.049	.189	.006	.025	.056	106.4	106.4	.498	0.4
10-11p	TOR	29.4	76	--	.209	.467	.058	.591	.512	.387	.772	.575	.046	.051	.160	.026	.011	.054	--	--	.420	--

Most similar to: Mike Dunleavy (96.5), Shammond Williams, Allen Leavell, Steve Kerr   IMP: 42% BRK: 2% COP: 4%

Marcus Banks was ill, injured and mostly ineffective last season, but still will likely stick as the Raptors' third point guard because of his $4.8 million guaranteed deal. He took a third of his shots from three-point range last year, but hit just 29 percent of them. That's too bad, because he was very effective inside the arc, albeit in very small samples. Banks seems to become less of a playmaker each season and is loose with the ball. He gambles a lot on defense and is below average overall on that end. He'll get a taste of life on the fringe after this season.

SG 28 — Leandro Barbosa

Hght: 6'3" Exp: 7 Salary: $7.1 million
Wght: 202 From: Sau Paulo, Brazil
2011-12 status: player option or ETO for $7.6 million

SKILL RATINGS

TOT	OFF	DEF	REB	PAS	HND	SHT	ATH
+2	+3	-3	-3	+1	0	+1	0

Year	Team	Age	G	MPG	Usg	3PA%	FTA%	INS	2P%	3P%	FT%	TS%	Reb%	Ast%	TO%	BLK%	STL%	PF%	oRTG	dRTG	Win%	WARP
07-08	PHX	25.4	82	29.5	.229	.343	.076	.733	.514	.388	.822	.575	.051	.040	.095	.005	.013	.034	107.2	106.9	.512	4.8
08-09	PHX	26.4	70	24.4	.243	.256	.091	.835	.532	.375	.881	.588	.061	.042	.099	.003	.024	.030	108.7	106.5	.570	5.4
09-10	PHX	27.4	44	17.9	.251	.307	.072	.766	.485	.324	.877	.526	.048	.036	.104	.011	.014	.040	105.4	107.0	.448	0.5
10-11p	TOR	28.4	70	25.0	.251	.309	.074	.765	.497	.351	.867	.547	.052	.040	.105	.008	.015	.036	107.0	106.8	.506	3.3

Most similar to: Rex Chapman (98.8), Dell Curry, Anthony Peeler, Tim Legler   IMP: 36% BRK: 0% COP: 4%

The problem with Leandro Barbosa is one of self-recognition. You get the feeling that he wants to hold down a 35-minute role, but it's unclear that he would help a team given that much of a leash. Jay Triano says he's going to stress ball movement this season, and Barbosa is well suited to play in a balanced system, as he can score both off the dribble and when spotting up. He's always been a big per-minute scorer who uses a lot of possessions, but his efficiency is going to tumble if he tries to become The Man. As it is, the Raptors are leaning towards starting DeMar DeRozan at the two-guard anyway. Barbosa was hobbled for much of last season, and a return to health should be accompanied by a rebound in his shooting percentage behind the arc. If so, he'll be a valuable part of the Raptors' rotation, though it's tough to say that he'll be contributing to anything great. If the season goes poorly for Toronto, Barbosa could turn into a gunner, which would be good for fantasy owners, not so much for Raptors fans.

PF 7 — Andrea Bargnani

Hght: 7'0" Exp: 4 Salary: $8.5 million
Wght: 250 From: Rome, Italy
2011-12 status: guaranteed contract for $9.3 million

SKILL RATINGS

TOT	OFF	DEF	REB	PAS	HND	SHT	ATH
+3	+3	-5	-4	-1	-1	+1	-3

Year	Team	Age	G	MPG	Usg	3PA%	FTA%	INS	2P%	3P%	FT%	TS%	Reb%	Ast%	TO%	BLK%	STL%	PF%	oRTG	dRTG	Win%	WARP
07-08	TOR	22.5	78	23.8	.227	.294	.084	.790	.409	.345	.840	.495	.092	.023	.099	.016	.006	.054	103.3	106.9	.383	-1.3
08-09	TOR	23.5	78	31.4	.229	.240	.097	.856	.468	.409	.831	.559	.099	.018	.112	.031	.007	.046	105.2	106.4	.463	2.4
09-10	TOR	24.5	80	35.0	.224	.238	.075	.837	.509	.372	.774	.552	.102	.015	.088	.030	.005	.035	105.3	106.0	.477	3.5
10-11p	TOR	25.5	75	36.0	.242	.347	.084	.736	.466	.392	.820	.555	.098	.019	.096	.030	.005	.040	106.8	105.9	.530	6.4

Most similar to: Thurl Bailey (97.8), Mel Turpin, Danny Granger, Tom Chambers   IMP: 53% BRK: 11% COP: 11%

With Chris Bosh gone, this is the season for Andrea Bargnani to establish himself as the Raptors' franchise player. It's not likely to happen. Bargnani is a top-notch deep threat as a big man and has greatly improved his efficiency at the rim. He's an above-average shooter all over the court, but doesn't use his big body enough to draw contact. Bargnani does not set up teammates well and his rebounding is abysmal for a player with his talent. Concerning the former, he admitted to reporters that he struggles with double-teams, so he could be in trouble this year without Bosh around to attract attention. On defense, Bargnani might be one of the worst regulars in the league. He's not bad in the post, but because he's played so much power forward, teams have been able to draw him out of the lane, where he gets into trouble. The Raptors were 9.1 points per 100 possessions better on defense when Bargnani was resting. There is so much pressure on Bargnani to be the featured performer in Toronto that this could turn out to be a very frustrating season for him. Who knows? Maybe he'll turn a corner. What might help is if he were paired with a true defensive center, someone who could protect the basket rather than Bargnani playing the role himself. Perhaps rookie Solomon Alabi can develop into that player, but probably not this season. In the long term, the Raptors would likely prefer that Bargnani start alongside young power forward Ed Davis.

PG 8 — Jose Calderon

Hght: 6'3" Exp: 5 Salary: $9.0 million
Wght: 210 From: Villanueva de la Serena, Spain
2011-12 status: guaranteed contract for $9.8 million

SKILL RATINGS

TOT	OFF	DEF	REB	PAS	HND	SHT	ATH
+5	+5	-5	-1	+4	+4	+4	-3

Year	Team	Age	G	MPG	Usg	3PA%	FTA%	INS	2P%	3P%	FT%	TS%	Reb%	Ast%	TO%	BLK%	STL%	PF%	oRTG	dRTG	Win%	WARP
07-08	TOR	26.6	82	30.3	.169	.207	.060	.852	.551	.429	.908	.607	.056	.129	.143	.002	.016	.025	111.3	106.2	.658	12.5
08-09	TOR	27.6	68	34.3	.170	.236	.079	.843	.538	.406	.981	.613	.049	.120	.167	.002	.016	.023	111.0	107.3	.618	9.8
09-10	TOR	28.6	68	26.7	.180	.240	.064	.824	.519	.398	.798	.569	.045	.102	.139	.003	.013	.034	109.4	107.7	.553	5.1
10-11p	TOR	29.6	73	27.0	.184	.253	.064	.811	.515	.405	.852	.576	.049	.113	.156	.003	.014	.028	110.3	107.1	.602	7.7

Most similar to: Brad Davis (96.6), Mark Jackson, Sleepy Floyd, Steve Nash

IMP: 36% BRK: 2% COP: 9%

Reports out of Toronto say that the Raptors have cast their lot with Jarrett Jack at point guard, so it's no surprise that they've been shopping Jose Calderon around so aggressively. It's too bad, because Calderon is a very productive player. He's one of the best assist men in the game and a wizard at orchestrating the pick-and-roll. He's always going to be a pass-first player, but shoots the ball extremely well. His defense is poor, to terrible, but might not look so bad if he had better defensive support from his frontline. Jack is a nice third guard, but Calderon is the better player. Yes, he makes a lot of money, and has two more years guaranteed after this, but he's a legit starting lead guard. The team that finally pries Calderon away from the Raptors will be pleased. Calderon has had frequent problems with his hamstring and continues to struggle with that malady into late summer. He's expected to be ready for camp, but will have to be watched carefully.

PF 32 — Ed Davis

Hght: 6'10" Exp: R Salary: $1.9 million
Wght: 215 From: North Carolina
2011-12 status: guaranteed contract for $2.1 million

SKILL RATINGS

TOT	OFF	DEF	REB	PAS	HND	SHT	ATH
0	-1	+3	+3	-3	-4	-2	-1

Year	Team	Age	G	MPG	Usg	3PA%	FTA%	INS	2P%	3P%	FT%	TS%	Reb%	Ast%	TO%	BLK%	STL%	PF%	oRTG	dRTG	Win%	WARP
10-11p	TOR	21.9	76	25.0	.171	.000	.146	1.146	.473	.001	.646	.519	.156	.014	.156	.046	.005	.040	102.3	104.1	.440	1.0

Most similar to: Cedric Simmons (96.1), Al Horford, Marreese Speights, Charlie Villanueva

IMP: - BRK: - COP: -

Ed Davis has the kind of long, active body that makes the hearts of traditional NBA scouts go pitter-patter. He looks like he's going to have some true strengths right off the bat. He should be a good rebounder and his shot blocking should make him a valuable help defender. Davis needs to get stronger and his offensive arsenal is very raw. However, he did a great job of getting to the line in college, and if that skill translates to the NBA level as his projection suggests it will, Davis will have a nice starting point to craft his offensive repertoire. Meanwhile, he can crash the boards, run the floor and finish off of alley-oops on backcuts. Sadly, Davis' rookie season will get off to a belated start, as he had surgery for a torn meniscus in his right knee in September. He'll likely be out until late November.

TORONTO RAPTORS

SG 10	DeMar DeRozan	Hght: 6'7" Wght: 220 2011-12 status: guaranteed contract for $2.6 million	Exp: 1 From: USC	Salary: $2.5 million		SKILL RATINGS							
						TOT	OFF	DEF	REB	PAS	HND	SHT	ATH
						-2	0	-4	+2	-4	-4	+1	+1
Year	Team	Age	G	MPG	Usg	3PA%	FTA%	INS	2P%	3P%	FT%	TS%	Reb%	Ast%	TO%	BLK%	STL%	PF%	oRTG	dRTG	Win%	WARP
09-10	TOR	20.7	77	21.6	.182	.024	.129	1.105	.506	.250	.763	.554	.078	.015	.094	.008	.013	.049	103.1	107.4	.361	-1.9
10-11p	TOR	21.7	75	28.0	.197	.034	.131	1.097	.508	.279	.803	.564	.076	.016	.089	.009	.014	.048	104.1	107.0	.405	-0.5
Most similar to: Marvin Williams (97.4), Wilson Chandler, Joe Johnson, Gerald Green																			IMP: 71%	BRK: 13%	COP: 0%

Our numbers still don't like DeMar DeRozan, but the Raptors do, which is probably more important for his career prospects. For now, anyway. DeRozan is an impressive athlete, there's no denying that. He attacks the rim, runs the floor, finishes well and draws contact. His jumper was unreliable in his rookie season and he didn't have a three-point shot, but his entire offseason workout regimen was reportedly built around adding range and accuracy to his distance shooting. If DeRozan can become a threat from the perimeter, his numbers will start looking a whole lot better. Defensively, he grades poorly, but this is the Raptors we're talking about, and there is no physical reason why he can't be a plus on the defensive end. Even statheads no longer consider DeRozan a surefire bust. Instead, he appears to be just a couple of upgrades away from becoming a truly interesting player.

C 9	Joey Dorsey	Hght: 6'8" Wght: 268 2011-12 status: due qualifying offer of $1.1 million	Exp: 2 From: Memphis	Salary: $0.9 million		SKILL RATINGS							
						TOT	OFF	DEF	REB	PAS	HND	SHT	ATH
						+3	--	0	--	--	--	--	--
Year	Team	Age	G	MPG	Usg	3PA%	FTA%	INS	2P%	3P%	FT%	TS%	Reb%	Ast%	TO%	BLK%	STL%	PF%	oRTG	dRTG	Win%	WARP
08-09	HOU	25.3	3	2.0	.156	.000	.000	1.000	.500	.000	.000	.500	.093	.078	.000	.000	.000	.000	105.7	107.1	.452	0.0
09-10	SAC	26.3	15	7.1	.131	.000	.169	1.169	.450	-	.417	.455	.234	.008	.192	.014	.014	.088	102.6	105.6	.401	0.0
10-11p	TOR	27.3	76	-	.185	.000	.127	1.127	.553	.000	.465	.549	.220	.017	.240	.027	.016	.068	-	-	.537	-
Most similar to: Kurt Rambis (94.3), Bison Dele, Reggie Evans, Michael Smith																			IMP: 48%	BRK: 0%	COP: 8%

Two years into his NBA career, Joey Dorsey is already a journeyman. There really is not enough evidence to go on with his numbers to date. Based on his D-League and summer-league performances, it certainly appears that Dorsey is a beast on the boards, particularly on the offensive glass. If he proves he can defend and finish his putback opportunities, he might carve out an end-of-the-bench niche for himself.

PF 30	Reggie Evans	Hght: 6'8" Wght: 245 2011-12 status: free agent	Exp: 8 From: Iowa	Salary: $5.1 million		SKILL RATINGS							
						TOT	OFF	DEF	REB	PAS	HND	SHT	ATH
						-2	-2	+2	+5	-3	-5	-3	+5
Year	Team	Age	G	MPG	Usg	3PA%	FTA%	INS	2P%	3P%	FT%	TS%	Reb%	Ast%	TO%	BLK%	STL%	PF%	oRTG	dRTG	Win%	WARP
07-08	PHI	27.9	81	23.2	.137	.002	.199	1.198	.438	1.000	.467	.463	.194	.016	.190	.003	.021	.053	102.3	104.5	.424	0.3
08-09	PHI	28.9	79	14.4	.130	.003	.238	1.235	.446	.000	.594	.514	.190	.010	.213	.006	.019	.065	103.4	106.2	.407	-0.2
09-10	TOR	29.9	28	11.1	.173	.000	.225	1.225	.493	-	.450	.498	.197	.012	.187	.010	.023	.065	102.1	104.4	.420	0.0
10-11p	TOR	30.9	68	8.3	.147	.004	.208	1.204	.462	.107	.499	.488	.192	.013	.207	.007	.021	.061	101.5	104.4	.402	-0.2
Most similar to: Antonio McDyess (94.9), Kenny Thomas, Corie Blount, Andrew DeClercq																			IMP: 41%	BRK: 0%	COP: 3%

A poll of his peers named Reggie Evans as the NBA's dirtiest player, but foot trouble meant he didn't get to do a whole lot of shoving and undercutting last season. When Evans did play, he did what he always does: Grab about one of every five available rebounds and play extremely hard on the defensive end. The Raptors were 9.1 points per 100 possessions worse defensively when Andrea Bargnani was on the floor; with Evans, they were 9.7 points better. Evans finished at the rim better than he has in the past. He is typically poor in the lane because he doesn't have any touch, can't really get off the ground and gets a ton of shots blocked. That's why Evans can't hold down a full-time role. But he fills his niche as well as any player in the league.

TORONTO RAPTORS

PG 1	Jarrett Jack	Hght: 6'3" Exp: 5 Salary: $4.6 million										SKILL RATINGS							
		Wght: 197 From: Georgia Tech										TOT	OFF	DEF	REB	PAS	HND	SHT	ATH
		2011-12 status: guaranteed contract for $5.0 million										+2	+4	-3	+1	+1	-1	+2	-1

Year	Team	Age	G	MPG	Usg	3PA%	FTA%	INS	2P%	3P%	FT%	TS%	Reb%	Ast%	TO%	BLK%	STL%	PF%	oRTG	dRTG	Win%	WARP
07-08	POR	24.5	82	27.2	.194	.210	.120	.910	.470	.340	.867	.557	.062	.067	.196	.000	.013	.027	105.2	106.5	.457	1.9
08-09	IND	25.5	82	33.1	.186	.192	.100	.909	.487	.353	.852	.554	.056	.054	.160	.005	.016	.029	105.5	107.2	.442	1.4
09-10	TOR	26.5	82	27.4	.192	.212	.113	.901	.511	.412	.842	.599	.057	.085	.173	.002	.014	.031	108.3	107.4	.531	5.3
10-11p	TOR	27.5	76	27.0	.204	.243	.110	.867	.490	.391	.857	.582	.058	.071	.170	.003	.012	.029	107.5	107.1	.512	4.1

Most similar to: Jameer Nelson (98.7), Sam Vincent, Rory Sparrow, Bimbo Coles   IMP: 41% BRK: 2% COP: 6%

Jarrett Jack was deadly from three-point range last season, which fueled his career-best performance. He's the favorite to start at point guard for Toronto this season, and if he can repeat last season's efficiency, he'll be okay. However, Jack isn't a great playmaker and commits a lot of turnovers. Since he can play either guard position, he's really an ideal third guard. Jack tends to look for his own shot first, a trait that became more acute last year as his confidence in his shot rose. He's a very good one-on-one player, so you can bring him in to exploit matchups against an opponent featuring a weak defender in the backcourt. Jack isn't great defensively, but appears more solid than he is, perhaps because Jose Calderon is so much worse. Jack's season last year was probably a career year. However, if he's able to maintain that progress, then he could be looking at a multi-year run as a starting guard. Jack will also be an attractive asset on the trade market thanks to his skills and a reasonable contract.

PF 15	Amir Johnson	Hght: 6'9" Exp: 5 Salary: $5.0 million										SKILL RATINGS							
		Wght: 210 From: Westchester HS (Los Angeles, CA)										TOT	OFF	DEF	REB	PAS	HND	SHT	ATH
		2011-12 status: guaranteed contract for $5.5 million										+3	+2	+5	+4	-1	-2	+5	+2

Year	Team	Age	G	MPG	Usg	3PA%	FTA%	INS	2P%	3P%	FT%	TS%	Reb%	Ast%	TO%	BLK%	STL%	PF%	oRTG	dRTG	Win%	WARP
07-08	DET	21.0	62	12.4	.141	.000	.106	1.106	.558	.000	.673	.584	.183	.018	.171	.084	.015	.089	104.4	101.2	.605	3.0
08-09	DET	22.0	62	14.7	.111	.000	.073	1.073	.595	.000	.657	.608	.151	.011	.156	.051	.012	.090	104.5	105.6	.465	0.9
09-10	TOR	23.0	82	17.7	.146	.009	.142	1.133	.630	.000	.638	.639	.160	.015	.136	.035	.015	.081	106.4	105.4	.531	3.5
10-11p	TOR	24.0	76	25.0	.144	.005	.115	1.110	.599	.007	.666	.617	.160	.017	.152	.051	.014	.083	105.4	104.3	.534	4.7

Most similar to: Sam Williams (97.6), Bo Outlaw, Dale Davis, Bill Garnett   IMP: 45% BRK: 7% COP: 3%

Amir Johnson continues to add versatility to his offensive arsenal and is efficient enough in the post that you'd like to see the Raptors run a few more plays for him. He's a terrific finisher, a top rebounder and is gradually developing touch as he steps out of the immediate vicinity of the basket. Johnson's shot-blocking has fallen off in recent seasons, but his overall defensive indicators are really impressive. With Chris Bosh out of the picture, Johnson should get a solid chance to prove he can hold down a full-time role in the NBA. The Raptors demonstrated their faith in Johnson by giving him a five-year, $30.25 million contract over the summer.

SF 11	Linas Kleiza	Hght: 6'8" Exp: 4 Salary: $5.0 million										SKILL RATINGS							
		Wght: 245 From: Missouri										TOT	OFF	DEF	REB	PAS	HND	SHT	ATH
		2011-12 status: guaranteed contract for $4.8 million										+2	+4	-3	+2	-3	-3	+2	-2

Year	Team	Age	G	MPG	Usg	3PA%	FTA%	INS	2P%	3P%	FT%	TS%	Reb%	Ast%	TO%	BLK%	STL%	PF%	oRTG	dRTG	Win%	WARP
07-08	DEN	23.3	79	23.9	.189	.329	.110	.781	.568	.339	.768	.584	.094	.021	.106	.007	.010	.040	106.5	106.9	.486	2.7
08-09	DEN	24.3	82	22.2	.200	.327	.110	.783	.533	.326	.725	.552	.103	.016	.100	.006	.008	.038	106.3	107.6	.460	1.7
10-11p	TOR	26.3	76	25.0	.217	.371	.107	.736	.534	.336	.750	.558	.101	.019	.098	.006	.009	.037	107.1	106.9	.505	3.5

Most similar to: Matt Bonner (97.1), Brian Cook, Mickael Pietrus, Mark Alarie   IMP: 53% BRK: 8% COP: 9%

After a one-year Greek adventure, Linas Kleiza is back in North America and is bucking to become a featured player in the NBA. Kleiza was a spot-up shooting specialist during his time with the Nuggets, but has always had the talent base to be more than that. He's big, strong and moves well for a guy his size. The shooting touch has been inconsistent, but Kleiza will get more chances to hock his wares inside the arc in Toronto, which should help his efficiency. He can take players off the dribble and is a strong finisher at the rim, though it remains to be seen if his strength will get him by defenders now that he'll be playing small forward. However, what you might see is a spike in his already solid foul-drawing rate and a nice little bump in his assist rate. Kleiza has excellent court vision and sense; he's just never been asked to create plays for others. That is a necessary part of the arsenal of a quality NBA three. On defense, he's probably going to be a step slow, so he's going to have to commit himself to being at least average. There is a good chance that the Raptors got a steal by landing Kleiza for a four-year, $18.8 million deal, and he could be one of the breakout players in the NBA this season.

SG 24	Sonny Weems	Hght: 6'6" Wght: 203 2011-12 status: due qualifying offer of $1.1 million	Exp: 2 From: Arkansas	Salary: $0.9 million							
					SKILL RATINGS						
					TOT	OFF	DEF	REB	PAS	HND	SHT	ATH
					-2	-1	-1	+4	0	-1	+1	-2

Year	Team	Age	G	MPG	Usg	3PA%	FTA%	INS	2P%	3P%	FT%	TS%	Reb%	Ast%	TO%	BLK%	STL%	PF%	oRTG	dRTG	Win%	WARP
08-09	DEN	22.8	12	4.6	.281	.087	.102	1.015	.364	.000	.375	.333	.041	.024	.174	.000	.009	.065	92.5	109.7	.084	-0.4
09-10	TOR	23.8	69	19.8	.185	.027	.051	1.024	.528	.133	.688	.533	.082	.034	.118	.014	.014	.042	102.6	106.4	.376	-1.2
10-11p	TOR	24.8	74	20.0	.197	.044	.052	1.008	.524	.149	.712	.526	.082	.036	.122	.016	.015	.040	102.9	105.9	.402	-0.4

Most similar to: Mitchell Butler (97.8), Aaron McKie, Greg Buckner, Cedric E. Henderson   IMP: 62% BRK: 10% COP: 4%

Athletic Sonny Weems had some nice moments for the Raptors in his second NBA season. Unlike last year, he didn't have to sweat out his 2010-11 destination into the late summer. Weems is very effective off the dribble and close to the rim, with a developing midrange game. He passes the ball pretty well and has potential as a perimeter defender. The Raptors have plenty of options on the wing, but Weems was an effective player for them last season and should get minutes on a nightly basis again this year. Like DeMar DeRozan, Weems worked on his three-point shot over the summer, and if he can become consistent from behind the arc, he could be headed for a nice career.

SF 14	Julian Wright	Hght: 6'8" Wght: 225 2011-12 status: due qualifying offer of $4.0 million	Exp: 3 From: Kansas	Salary: $2.9 million							
					SKILL RATINGS						
					TOT	OFF	DEF	REB	PAS	HND	SHT	ATH
					0	0	+2	+2	0	-2	+2	+2

Year	Team	Age	G	MPG	Usg	3PA%	FTA%	INS	2P%	3P%	FT%	TS%	Reb%	Ast%	TO%	BLK%	STL%	PF%	oRTG	dRTG	Win%	WARP
07-08	NOH	20.9	57	11.2	.165	.106	.101	.995	.552	.417	.635	.581	.108	.029	.151	.015	.021	.032	104.2	104.1	.502	1.1
08-09	NOH	21.9	54	14.3	.183	.072	.045	.973	.502	.095	.567	.479	.119	.027	.148	.021	.024	.031	102.1	104.3	.427	0.2
09-10	NOH	22.9	68	12.8	.155	.020	.061	1.041	.504	.333	.610	.518	.097	.022	.150	.016	.017	.024	102.0	105.5	.384	-0.6
10-11p	TOR	23.9	76	13.0	.183	.106	.061	.954	.518	.302	.633	.526	.104	.028	.144	.017	.019	.025	103.4	104.6	.458	0.9

Most similar to: Bryon Russell (98.6), Jared Dudley, Mitchell Butler, Gerald Wallace   IMP: 58% BRK: 12% COP: 4%

Julian Wright has underachieved since coming into the NBA and groused his way out of New Orleans, complaining about playing time and refusing to play in summer league. He comes to Toronto with one season to turn things around before hitting restricted free agency, so the Raptors may have found themselves with a very talented, motivated player. Wright has a small forward's body, but a power forward's game, and has struggled to find a role at the offensive end. He finishes well at the basket and is reluctant to stray outside the paint. That was even more the case last season as he lost confidence in his outside shot. He rebounds well for his position and is a quality, playmaking defender. If Wright has his head on straight, he's definitely a player the Raptors can use.

Rasho Nesterovic

C	Hght: 7'0"	Exp: 12	Salary: --
--	Wght: 255	From: Ljubljana, Slovenia
2011-12 status: free agent	

SKILL RATINGS

TOT	OFF	DEF	REB	PAS	HND	SHT	ATH
-1	0	0	-3	+4	+5	+1	-2

Year	Team	Age	G	MPG	Usg	3PA%	FTA%	INS	2P%	3P%	FT%	TS%	Reb%	Ast%	TO%	BLK%	STL%	PF%	oRTG	dRTG	Win%	WARP
07-08	TOR	31.9	71	20.9	.175	.005	.039	1.034	.552	.333	.755	.565	.137	.026	.109	.029	.006	.042	104.7	105.4	.476	1.8
08-09	IND	32.9	70	17.3	.185	.002	.027	1.025	.514	.000	.781	.524	.109	.039	.123	.023	.012	.062	104.8	107.1	.424	0.2
09-10	TOR	33.9	42	9.8	.186	.000	.013	1.013	.544	-	.200	.539	.127	.028	.096	.032	.012	.060	105.1	105.8	.475	0.5
10-11p	AVG	34.9	75	9.8	.168	.003	.020	1.017	.520	.051	.485	.518	.113	.031	.104	.027	.012	.061	103.6	106.1	.418	0.0

Most similar to: Mychal Thompson (97.2), Olden Polynice, Danny Manning, Antoine Carr | IMP: 37% | BRK: 5% | COP: 7%

Rasho Nesterovic signed to play in Greece during the summer, which probably means we've seen the last of him in the NBA. Nesterovic had a nice 12-year run as backup center, and was sometimes even a little better than that. There really didn't appear to be any slippage in his game last year in Toronto, so he must have been looking for more money or a bigger role.

Patrick O'Bryant

C	Hght: 7'0"	Exp: 4	Salary: --
--	Wght: 250	From: Bradley
2011-12 status: free agent	

SKILL RATINGS

TOT	OFF	DEF	REB	PAS	HND	SHT	ATH
-3	-2	0	0	+2	-2	+2	-1

Year	Team	Age	G	MPG	Usg	3PA%	FTA%	INS	2P%	3P%	FT%	TS%	Reb%	Ast%	TO%	BLK%	STL%	PF%	oRTG	dRTG	Win%	WARP
07-08	GSW	21.8	24	4.3	.151	.000	.059	1.059	.571	.000	.600	.579	.146	.016	.188	.063	.012	.110	102.5	104.4	.435	0.0
08-09	TOR	22.8	39	6.5	.210	.017	.077	1.059	.549	.000	.550	.544	.152	.020	.192	.058	.010	.112	101.3	105.3	.368	-0.3
09-10	TOR	23.8	11	4.6	.204	.044	.117	1.072	.571	.000	.500	.539	.125	.009	.221	.060	.020	.108	99.5	103.9	.352	-0.1
10-11p	AVG	24.8	76	4.6	.212	.019	.068	1.049	.546	.005	.548	.541	.146	.023	.173	.051	.010	.103	101.5	105.1	.383	-0.2

Most similar to: Elmore Spencer (97.2), Brad Lohaus, Hilton Armstrong, Carlos Rogers | IMP: 52% | BRK: 16% | COP: 4%

The lackadaisical ways of Patrick O'Bryant may have finally left him on the outside of the NBA circle looking in. He certainly looks like an NBA player standing still in his uniform, and he's put up some interesting per-minute numbers. Despite that, at the age of 24, O'Bryant finds himself home waiting by the phone.

Utah Jazz

In many ways, the Utah Jazz is a model for a certain kind of NBA franchise. Like the Spurs and Magic, among others, they thrive in a small market with no competition from one of the other major professional sports leagues. They've done well through good scouting, shrewd management and an iconic coach. What they haven't done is win a championship.

Fans in Utah aren't as patient as you'd think. There is a common perception that the Jazz is only willing to commit to winning up to a certain level, that winning records and playoff appearances are enough but championships are beyond the franchise's reach. They recognize the team's shortage of interior defense and, with Cole Aldrich still on the boards when the Jazz picked, the crowd gathered at EnergySolutions Arena booed on draft night when the selection of Gordon Hayward was announced. Sure, the Miller family, which owns the Jazz, has time and again been willing to pay the luxury tax, but can't they afford it when Jazz fans so consistently sell out the home court?

In a way, this attitude of a significant portion of the fan base in Salt Lake City is a residue from the John Stockton/Karl Malone glory days. The best of those teams were among the NBA's elite and they made it to the Finals on two occasions, only to fall to the Bulls. In that respect, Utah was merely a victim of bad timing. The two squads that reached the Finals were almost certainly of championship quality and, in fact, the 64-win team of 1996-97 is one of the best non-title teams in league history. There were a lot of quality teams and players that didn't win rings under Michael Jordan's watch.

The Jazz of recent seasons have been similar. Utah has again featured a point guard/power forward combo as its foundation in Deron Williams and Carlos Boozer. The team is still coached by the ageless Jerry Sloan. The Jazz is again planted firmly in the middle of the NBA's second tier, with a quality and entertaining team, but one that really hasn't seriously challenged the Lakers in the West. And, really, that's where things stand as we enter the 2010-11 season. The chronically overlooked Jazz appears to still be among the top eight or nine teams in the West, but firmly outside of the NBA's top tier.

Last season, the Jazz bounced back from an off year in 2008-09, but a few key losses prevented the team from landing the No. 2 seed in the pack behind the Lakers in the West. That led to a lousy postseason draw. Utah survived the Nuggets in the first round, but the Jazz was flattened by the Lakers once again in the conference semifinals.

After the season, the long-rumored departure of Boozer from Utah finally came to pass when the too-vocal forward signed with the Bulls in free agency. The Jazz had plenty of time to concoct a plan for Boozer's exit and, sure enough, the organization reacted with impressive swiftness.

JAZZ IN A BOX

Last year's record	53-29
Last year's Offensive Rating	112.2 (8)
Last year's Defensive Rating	107.2 (11)
Last year's point differential	5.3 (3)
Team pace	92.2 (10)
SCHOENE projection	41-41 (10)
Projected Offensive Rating	109.5 (20)
Projected Defensive Rating	109.4 (13)
Projected team weighted age	27.8 (13)
Projected '10-11 payroll	$78.5 (5)
Est. payroll obligations, '11-12	$61.7 (8)

Head coach: Jerry Sloan

Another year, another 50 wins for Jerry Sloan and the Jazz. Ho hum. The consistent success has moved Sloan up to fourth on the league's all-time coaching wins leaderboard. Barring a return to the sidelines by Pat Riley, he will surely climb to third this season, with all-time leader Don Nelson just 145 wins away and apparently headed into retirement. Sloan doesn't care about the records, of course, but he's got the chance to amass them nonetheless. Sloan doesn't get enough credit for his willingness to trust young players. How many other coaches would have started Wesley Matthews as an undrafted rookie? Sloan also was rewarded with a game-winning three-pointer by a rookie on a 10-day contract (Sundiata Gaines). Nobody gets more out of the talent on their roster than Sloan.

First, Utah turned the Boozer move into a sign-and-trade, sending a second-round pick to Chicago and creating a $13 million trade exception. Second, the Jazz turned around and dealt young big man Kosta Koufos and a pair of future first-round picks to Minnesota for power forward Al Jefferson. Voila! Boozer's spot is filled.

There are a couple of concerns here. First, you have to wonder what the move means for Jazz forward Paul Millsap. Millsap has shined as Boozer's caddie and the Jazz's top frontcourt reserve during his four NBA seasons. He hasn't produced at Boozer's level, but Millsap was close enough that it was assumed that he would move into the starting four position once Boozer left. At first, he will. With Jazz center Mehmet Okur recovering from a ruptured Achilles tendon and likely out until January, Jefferson is slated to open the season as the starting center. Millsap has developed a solid face-up game and good range, which will allow him to play effectively alongside Jefferson. Both are capable of finishing on the pick-and-roll while working with Williams, so Sloan will have some options. The Jazz should continue to sport one of the league's most efficient offenses. The problem the last few years has been on the other end, and therein lies the issue. Millsap is a good defender who will hold his own at the four. But Jefferson, who is skilled but short-armed and unathletic, has consistently rated as one of the league's worst-defending big men. Perhaps his mobility will be improved now that he's another year removed from a 2009 knee surgery, but you have to expect Utah's interior defense to once again be a major problem. The Jazz is solid on the perimeter defensively and few teams defend the pick-and-roll as well. However, if you can't defend the interior in the Western Conference, you aren't going to be able to get past the Lakers.

Really, though, there are no concerns about the offense. A lot of that has to do with Sloan, who just keeps running the same simple system season after season, yet no one can consistently shut it down. Sloan's flex attack utilizes very few isolations. It also doesn't run pick-and-roll sets quite as often as people usually believe, but is highly effective when it does. The ball-handler on those sets rarely looks for his own shot--it's almost always pick-and-roll or pick-and-pop, which is why it's so essential to have a capable and versatile big man to pair with Williams. No offense produces more shots coming off screens. Everybody is in motion, and no scheme creates more easy baskets off of cuts, the root of an efficient offense. The flex produces cut opportunities at nearly twice the league rate. Beyond that, Sloan doesn't get enough credit for his belief in the transition game, espousing that the best half-court offense is no half-court offense. The Jazz was middle of the pack in transition plays, but no team was more efficient on them. That won't change without Boozer, as long as the defensive rebound percentage doesn't crater.

The Jazz also lost a key part this summer when sharpshooter Kyle Korver left via free agency, also to Chicago. That's where Hayward comes in. Like Korver, Hayward initially projects as a low-usage shooter who will depend upon his teammates to create his shots. His focus will be on developing his stroke for the NBA game. Neither he nor anyone else can be counted upon to hit open shots with Korver's proficiency, but Hayward has the length to be a more frequent option and the technique to be a very efficient player. He's also a superior athlete to Korver, with a solid range of all-around skills to chip in on the boards and in the passing game. He can be a poor man's Korver, but he's got the base to become much more than that. His short-term task might be to replace Korver. However, with Andrei Kirilenko's contract expiring after the coming season, Hayward's long-term role may be as the Jazz' starting small forward.

Another Utah departure was guard Wesley Matthews. Matthews played so well as a rookie after going undrafted in 2009 that he was signed to an offer sheet by Portland that the Jazz simply could not afford to match. In a way, Jazz general manager Kevin O'Connor fell victim to its own excellence at spotting young talent for Sloan's system. He'd cast his lot with Matthews by dealing former starting two-guard Ronnie Brewer to Memphis in a deal that was more a cost-cutting measure than anything. When Matthews also left, it put O'Connor in a bit of a pickle. He ended up signing veteran two Raja Bell, who was limited to six games last season because of surgery to repair a ligament in his left wrist. Bell is a good fit for Utah's system with his three-point shooting and prowess on defense, but he's also old. If he isn't healthy or his performance seriously declines, the Jazz will be short a starter.

While O'Connor continues to keep an excellent flow of talent coming into Salt Lake City, the team's cap situation has put the squeeze on his maneuverability. Late in the summer, the roster was woefully thin at center. Meanwhile, inexplicably unsigned big man Lou Amundson was still dangling on the free-agent

From the Blogosphere

Who: Basketball John
What: SLC Dunk
Where: http://www.slcdunk.com/

Though it will likely take a lifetime of convincing, and perhaps Jerry Sloan's retirement, I'm here to tell you that the Jazz is not a half-court, pick-and-roll team. Even in the half-court set, the Jazz will run the flex offense, which allows for some beautiful passing, hard cuts, hard screens, and easy buckets as defenders' heads are turned about as if on a swivel. It's a refreshing change from the iso sets that seem so prevalent in the NBA today. The spacing and timing that is required to execute the offense carries over to the team's fast-break game. Led by the best point guard in the NBA, the Jazz provide some of the best fast breaks in the league with otherworldly passes from Deron Williams to a cutting wing or a running big man for the easy two.

market. No dice. The Jazz's own free-agent, promising Kyrylo Fesenko, was also searching for a better deal with only Utah's qualifying offer sitting on the table. To cover himself, O'Connor signed veteran center Francisco Elson, a less-than-inspiring move. Utah remains hamstrung by Kirilenko's contract, an example of the dangers of giving max or close-to-max deals to players that don't make elite impact on both ends of the floor. Kirilenko has and always will be limited offensively. Even Kirilenko seems to realize this, saying that he'd like to stay in Utah but realizes to do so, he'll have to take a deal for far less money than he and wife Masha have become accustomed. Kirilenko is a tremendously valuable player--at the right price.

The Jazz still has about $2.7 million left of its mid-level exception plus a $2.1 bi-annual exception, not to mention the $6.3 million trade exception created by trading Matt Harpring to Oklahoma City last season. Unfortunately, each dollar counts twice in luxury-tax land. The Miller family has been generous, but there are limits, especially considering what you'd be paying for. Amundson was reportedly looking for about $3 million per year guaranteed. He signed for two years and $5 million with Golden State. The Jazz could surely have landed him with a back-loaded deal, giving him more in the last two or three years of a multi-year deal when the cap situation is more tenable. He's exactly the kind of backline defender Utah needs. O'Connor could have closed the money gap by renouncing Fesenko and added a minimum salary rookie big man rather than Elson. O'Connor has been so good at his job for so long that it's tough to criticize anything he does. However, defending the paint has been a problem for so long now that's it difficult to understand how O'Connor hasn't found a solution.

Sloan will be back for another season, but he's year-to-year at this point. O'Connor was given a multi-year contract extension, so the Jazz will remain of paragon of stability in the stormy seas of the NBA. Overall, you have to like the position of the team. However, if you're an unimpressed Jazz fan who feels like you've seen this all before, what do you see to suggest Utah is going to get over the championship hump? Also, if things don't go well, will Williams' thinly veiled discontent become a bigger issue? Williams has just two more seasons left on his deal before a final year at player option that, right now, seems like a long shot to be exercised. With minimal flexibility, the Jazz had better impress Williams with some upward mobility.

For a team that seems so solid, there are plenty of questions. How long can Jazz ownership spend at the level they've been spending at, especially with no rings to show for the investment? Will Utah ever find an interior defender that can help them with the top big men in the West? How long will Sloan stay around? How about Williams? Without shoring up the defense, the Jazz again looks like a team that will score often and efficiently while allowing opponents to do the same. Utah will be in the chase for the playoffs, but will be a fringe candidate to advance beyond the first round.

Bradford Doolittle

UTAH JAZZ

JAZZ FIVE-YEAR TRENDS

Season	AGE	W-L	POW	PYTH	SEED	ORTG	DRTG	PT DIFF	PACE
05-06	25.6	41-41	37.8 (17)	33.0	---	105.0 (25)	108.8 (21)	-2.6 (23)	86.7 (26)
06-07	25.9	51-31	51.9 (5)	49.1	5	111.1 (3)	109.1 (19)	2.9 (8)	90.3 (15)
07-08	25.7	54-28	59.5 (3)	58.9	4	115.9 (2)	108.9 (12)	6.9 (4)	91.3 (11)
08-09	25.5	48-34	48.0 (10)	48.3	8	111.7 (8)	109.0 (11)	2.6 (9)	91.7 (10)
09-10	26.4	53-29	55.1 (4)	55.5	5	112.2 (8)	107.2 (11)	5.3 (3)	92.2 (10)

		OFFENSE				DEFENSE			
Season	PAY	eFG	oREB	FT/FGA	TO	eFG	oREB	FT/FGA	TO
05-06	$57.8	.467 (28)	.324 (1)	.286 (2)	.180 (28)	.490 (14)	.732 (12)	.303 (30)	.162 (9)
06-07	$60.3	.502 (11)	.317 (1)	.283 (3)	.171 (23)	.496 (13)	.751 (4)	.314 (30)	.165 (16)
07-08	$54.7	.528 (3)	.295 (5)	.265 (4)	.156 (22)	.501 (16)	.741 (9)	.294 (30)	.168 (2)
08-09	$66.3	.506 (9)	.282 (5)	.271 (2)	.159 (22)	.505 (18)	.727 (21)	.260 (26)	.174 (3)
09-10	$71.9	.524 (4)	.268 (13)	.252 (4)	.164 (27)	.492 (13)	.756 (5)	.269 (30)	.163 (7)

(league rankings in parenthesis)

SG 19 — Raja Bell
Hght: 6'5" Exp: 10 Salary: $3.0 million
Wght: 215 From: Florida International
2011-12 status: guaranteed contract for $3.2 million

SKILL RATINGS
TOT	OFF	DEF	REB	PAS	HND	SHT	ATH
-3	0	+4	-2	-3	+1	+1	-5

Year	Team	Age	G	MPG	Usg	3PA%	FTA%	INS	2P%	3P%	FT%	TS%	Reb%	Ast%	TO%	BLK%	STL%	PF%	oRTG	dRTG	Win%	WARP
07-08	PHX	31.6	75	35.3	.146	.511	.047	.536	.449	.402	.868	.561	.056	.029	.076	.007	.009	.036	105.7	107.3	.446	1.6
08-09	CHA	32.6	67	34.6	.164	.333	.055	.723	.448	.421	.853	.548	.063	.029	.106	.003	.011	.033	104.9	107.8	.406	-0.5
09-10	GSW	33.6	6	30.0	.173	.401	.020	.619	.471	.444	1.000	.570	.076	.033	.074	.009	.011	.039	107.2	107.0	.507	0.3
10-11p	UTA	34.6	64	28.0	.148	.440	.047	.608	.427	.384	.848	.529	.056	.026	.098	.005	.010	.035	104.0	107.4	.389	-1.0

Most similar to: Anthony Peeler (97.8), Bruce Bowen, Michael Finley, Jim Jackson

IMP: 45% BRK: 11% COP: 8%

The Jazz will be looking for Raja Bell to play good defense and hit the three-point shot, and really nothing more than that. Luckily, those are the two skills that have kept him in the NBA for 10 seasons. He's coming off wrist surgery, which limited him to six games, but it probably works to Utah's advantage that Bell didn't spend a full season picking up bad habits from Don Nelson. Bell is a solid option for the role he's being asked to fill, but there are a couple of concerns. First, he just turned 34 and his athletic indicators have already cratered. If you remove threes from the "3/D" equation, you really don't have much. Also, the Jazz is hoping that Al Jefferson can help keep the offense clicking as efficiently as it did with Carlos Boozer, but there is no guarantee that will be the case. As such, Utah might need more from a starting two than what Bell has to offer at this point, which could in turn lead to premature clamoring for rookie Gordon Hayward.

C 16 — Francisco Elson
Hght: 7'0" Exp: 7 Salary: $0.9 million
Wght: 240 From: California
2011-12 status: free agent

SKILL RATINGS
TOT	OFF	DEF	REB	PAS	HND	SHT	ATH
-5	-2	-2	-2	-3	-3	-4	+1

Year	Team	Age	G	MPG	Usg	3PA%	FTA%	INS	2P%	3P%	FT%	TS%	Reb%	Ast%	TO%	BLK%	STL%	PF%	oRTG	dRTG	Win%	WARP
07-08	SEA	32.1	63	12.9	.161	.003	.054	1.051	.390	.000	.703	.415	.134	.013	.157	.018	.008	.052	98.4	105.8	.265	-2.6
08-09	MIL	33.1	59	16.6	.108	.017	.073	1.056	.497	.250	.846	.537	.140	.015	.205	.031	.019	.066	102.7	105.6	.405	-0.2
09-10	PHI	34.1	12	5.5	.126	.000	.121	1.121	.333	-	.400	.349	.122	.014	.055	.000	.008	.048	100.1	108.0	.258	-0.2
10-11p	UTA	35.1	75	8.3	.116	.025	.058	1.033	.438	.171	.774	.464	.124	.013	.202	.024	.014	.064	99.9	105.9	.305	-1.4

Most similar to: Corie Blount (97.4), Aaron Williams, Tom Gugliotta, LaSalle Thompson

IMP: 57% BRK: 0% COP: 9%

The Jazz was apparently nostalgic for the Jarron Collins era, when Jerry Sloan could always deploy a player with no apparent statistical value, so the team went out and signed Francisco Elson. Suffice to say that the more you see of Elson, the worse it will be for the Jazz. Besides, at the time, Collins himself was available.

UTAH JAZZ

PF 40 — Jeremy Evans

Hght: 6'9"	Exp: R	Salary: $0.5 million
Wght: 196	From: Western Kentucky
2011-12 status: non-guaranteed contract for $0.8 million

SKILL RATINGS

TOT	OFF	DEF	REB	PAS	HND	SHT	ATH
-1	--	--	--	--	--	--	--

Year	Team	Age	G	MPG	Usg	3PA%	FTA%	INS	2P%	3P%	FT%	TS%	Reb%	Ast%	TO%	BLK%	STL%	PF%	oRTG	dRTG	Win%	WARP
10-11p	UTA	23.5	76	-	.136	-.001	.099	1.100	.399	.000	.583	.432	.084	.022	.205	.012	.009	.044	-	-	.414	-

Most similar to: Othello Hunter (97.4), Terence Morris, Channing Frye, James Johnson   IMP: -   BRK: -   COP: -

Jeremy Evans is a long, unpolished combo forward who will likely stick as a project player on Utah's opening-night roster. He's very thin, and really has no offensive skills other than to dunk off alley-oops, but he does make most of the dunks that present themselves. Evans looked pretty good in summer league, so maybe he's well suited for the pro game. Jerry Sloan, never one to be effusive with praise, said a lot of nice things about Evans, which certainly won't hurt his chances of sticking.

C 44 — Kyrylo Fesenko

Hght: 7'1"	Exp: 3	Salary: --
Wght: 300	From: Dnepropetrovsk, Ukraine
2011-12 status: free agent

SKILL RATINGS

TOT	OFF	DEF	REB	PAS	HND	SHT	ATH
-3	-1	+2	-2	0	-1	+4	0

Year	Team	Age	G	MPG	Usg	3PA%	FTA%	INS	2P%	3P%	FT%	TS%	Reb%	Ast%	TO%	BLK%	STL%	PF%	oRTG	dRTG	Win%	WARP
07-08	UTA	21.3	9	7.9	.163	.000	.068	1.068	.375	.000	.500	.394	.215	.013	.311	.034	.000	.122	101.1	108.4	.273	-0.2
08-09	UTA	22.3	21	7.4	.157	.000	.170	1.170	.583	.000	.333	.542	.142	.012	.166	.076	.023	.101	104.5	103.4	.536	0.4
09-10	UTA	23.3	49	8.3	.159	.007	.174	1.167	.553	.000	.421	.533	.130	.017	.167	.037	.007	.086	102.2	106.8	.351	-0.6
10-11p	UTA	24.3	76	15.0	.162	.004	.175	1.171	.560	.000	.423	.540	.126	.019	.160	.042	.007	.080	102.5	106.1	.380	-0.8

Most similar to: Elmore Spencer (96.0), Eric Leckner, Clifford Rozier, Kevin Duckworth   IMP: 66%   BRK: 24%   COP: 10%

Kyrylo Fesenko received a qualifying offer from the Jazz, then waited all summer for a multi-year offer as a restricted free agent. He ended up signing the q.o. with Utah just before camp. It was his in-limbo status that helped stir the Jazz to sign Francisco Elson, so there was collateral damage from Fesenko's long wait. His free agency was lot of trouble for a below-replacement player who plays decent defense and dunks the ball successfully at the basket as long as no one gets in his way.

PG 15 — Sundiata Gaines

Hght: 6'1"	Exp: 1	Salary: $0.8 million
Wght: 195	From: Georgia
2011-12 status: due qualifying offer of $1.1 million

SKILL RATINGS

TOT	OFF	DEF	REB	PAS	HND	SHT	ATH
+3	--	0	--	--	--	--	--

Year	Team	Age	G	MPG	Usg	3PA%	FTA%	INS	2P%	3P%	FT%	TS%	Reb%	Ast%	TO%	BLK%	STL%	PF%	oRTG	dRTG	Win%	WARP
09-10	UTA	24.0	32	6.8	.242	.224	.174	.950	.554	.269	.500	.518	.078	.081	.120	.000	.028	.035	107.7	105.4	.574	0.7
10-11p	UTA	25.0	76	-	.215	.294	.141	.847	.523	.287	.579	.514	.058	.061	.117	.006	.026	.031	-	-	.522	-

Most similar to: Darwin Cook (97.2), Marquis Daniels, Devin Harris, Earl Watson   IMP: 60%   BRK: 4%   COP: 8%

Sundiata Gaines emerged as a poster child for why the D-League exists when he went from the Idaho Stampede to hitting a game-winning three-pointer to lift the Jazz past LeBron James' Cavaliers on TNT. That was exciting, but now comes the hard part: sticking in the NBA. Gaines showed good playmaking skills, but he's a shoot-first point guard. Too much of his game is predicated on the midrange, so it's essential that he improve his stroke from behind the arc. Gaines' contract for this season isn't fully guaranteed, and his chances to make the final roster were hurt when Utah signed veteran Earl Watson.

UTAH JAZZ

SF 20	Gordon Hayward	Hght: 6'9" Exp: R Salary: $2.4 million				SKILL RATINGS							
		Wght: 207 From: Butler				TOT	OFF	DEF	REB	PAS	HND	SHT	ATH
		2011-12 status: guaranteed contract for $2.5 million				-1	0	+1	+4	-1	-3	-3	+1

Year	Team	Age	G	MPG	Usg	3PA%	FTA%	INS	2P%	3P%	FT%	TS%	Reb%	Ast%	TO%	BLK%	STL%	PF%	oRTG	dRTG	Win%	WARP
10-11p	UTA	21.1	76	22.0	.188	.235	.126	.892	.481	.252	.813	.517	.128	.024	.156	.014	.013	.045	103.4	105.6	.430	0.5

Most similar to: Marcus A. Williams (97.8), Mike Miller, Jeff Green, Bill Walker — IMP: - BRK: - COP: -

Gordon Hayward comes into the league as kind of a wild card because it's just not known how well his level of athleticism is going to translate to the professional level. In part, those concerns are rooted in the level of competition Hayward generally faced at Butler, but the Bulldogs did pretty well against the big guys, too. Hayward will have to be a knock-down shooter to be an asset. His summer-league performance could be an indicator of what to expect. He scored 54 points in five games, but needed only 21 shots to get there. Hayward is not strictly an outside shooter, as he's got a nice crossover dribble and the ability to draw contact. He's a very smart player who works hard, and that offers hope that he can be an average defender. Hayward is the kind of player that is always looking to make the right play, and so he has the ability to raise the level of his teammates. He enters the NBA with only Raja Bell standing ahead of him on the Jazz's depth chart, but he's not a natural two and could be hurt by having to play against quicker guards. Is Hayward a legit prospect, or did the Jazz simply get fooled by Butler's spirited run in the NCAA Tournament? Could go either way.

SF 6	Othyus Jeffers	Hght: 6'5" Exp: 1 Salary: $0.8 million				SKILL RATINGS							
		Wght: 210 From: Robert Morris (Ill.)				TOT	OFF	DEF	REB	PAS	HND	SHT	ATH
		2011-12 status: due qualifying offer of $1.1 million				-3	--	0	--	--	--	--	--

Year	Team	Age	G	MPG	Usg	3PA%	FTA%	INS	2P%	3P%	FT%	TS%	Reb%	Ast%	TO%	BLK%	STL%	PF%	oRTG	dRTG	Win%	WARP
09-10	UTA	24.7	14	5.1	.272	.000	.193	1.193	.414	-	.684	.495	.156	.006	.138	.000	.028	.063	103.1	105.6	.417	0.0
10-11p	UTA	25.7	76	-	.223	.070	.085	1.015	.435	.284	.635	.463	.100	.028	.137	.007	.024	.052	-	-	.384	-

Most similar to: Walter Bond (96.8), Mark Macon, Kevin Edwards, Malik Sealy — IMP: 61% BRK: 16% COP: 7%

Othyus Jeffers was a virtual non-entity when the Jazz picked up him from the D-League. He got just 72 minutes of playing time with Utah, so we still don't really know that much about him. In the D-League, Jeffers was explosive athletically, more of a slasher than a jump shooter, and a good defender. Even in the small sample size of his court time last year, some of those qualities came through. He's headed to camp with the Jazz, hoping to make his first opening-night roster. He is something of a project and there may not be room on the squad for another one of those besides rookie Jeremy Evans, but Jeffers could certainly stick if he keeps impressing in his limited opportunities.

C 25	Al Jefferson	Hght: 6'10" Exp: 6 Salary: $13.0 million				SKILL RATINGS							
		Wght: 265 From: Prentiss HS (MS)				TOT	OFF	DEF	REB	PAS	HND	SHT	ATH
		2011-12 status: guaranteed contract for $14.0 million				+3	+1	-5	+1	+1	+1	0	+2

Year	Team	Age	G	MPG	Usg	3PA%	FTA%	INS	2P%	3P%	FT%	TS%	Reb%	Ast%	TO%	BLK%	STL%	PF%	oRTG	dRTG	Win%	WARP
07-08	MIN	23.3	82	35.5	.277	.003	.097	1.095	.502	.000	.721	.535	.183	.018	.094	.032	.012	.035	106.6	103.6	.598	11.0
08-09	MIN	24.3	50	36.7	.291	.003	.094	1.091	.499	.000	.738	.532	.177	.020	.078	.035	.011	.035	107.1	104.1	.596	6.9
09-10	MIN	25.3	76	32.4	.245	.003	.085	1.082	.500	.000	.680	.524	.161	.024	.099	.030	.013	.036	104.7	104.2	.517	5.2
10-11p	UTA	26.3	73	34.0	.269	.007	.092	1.085	.506	.005	.717	.534	.162	.022	.090	.032	.012	.035	104.7	103.6	.535	6.2

Most similar to: Vin Baker (97.2), Charles D. Smith, Terry Cummings, Jermaine O'Neal — IMP: 45% BRK: 0% COP: 3%

Al Jefferson gets a new lease on life as he goes from, in his words, "a Toyota to a Bentley." Jefferson worked hard on his conditioning over the summer, dropped weight and pledged to improve his defense. That's good, but no matter how hard he works, the Jazz is still going to have a gaping defensive hole in the middle as long as Jefferson is starting in the pivot, which is the plan until Mehmet Okur gets right. Jefferson should be a solid fit in Utah's offensive scheme, as he does most of the same good things as Carlos Boozer. He's probably better in the post, though he's more of a finesse post player in the Bill Cartwright mold and thus doesn't put up a great foul-drawing rate. Jefferson is an underrated passer, but doesn't have Boozer's face-up game. He shoots from midrange plenty, probably way too often. He's just not efficient from there. As for the defense, let's just say there is nowhere to go but up for Jefferson, so it's good to see him committed to getting better.

Andrei Kirilenko — SF #47

Hght: 6'9" Wght: 225 Exp: 9 From: St. Petersburg, Russia Salary: $17.8 million
2011-12 status: free agent

SKILL RATINGS
TOT	OFF	DEF	REB	PAS	HND	SHT	ATH
+4	+2	+5	0	+4	+3	0	+5

Year	Team	Age	G	MPG	Usg	3PA%	FTA%	INS	2P%	3P%	FT%	TS%	Reb%	Ast%	TO%	BLK%	STL%	PF%	oRTG	dRTG	Win%	WARP
07-08	UTA	27.2	72	30.8	.162	.146	.142	.996	.540	.379	.770	.603	.094	.058	.176	.040	.018	.034	106.6	103.7	.596	8.3
08-09	UTA	28.2	67	27.3	.204	.088	.165	1.077	.475	.274	.785	.549	.104	.043	.146	.033	.023	.031	105.3	103.9	.548	5.0
09-10	UTA	29.2	58	29.0	.178	.134	.155	1.021	.555	.292	.744	.588	.092	.042	.119	.034	.025	.027	106.2	103.3	.597	6.3
10-11p	UTA	30.2	71	29.0	.184	.133	.148	1.014	.510	.295	.750	.557	.089	.045	.135	.036	.021	.030	105.2	103.4	.560	6.2

Most similar to: Bobby Jones (96.6), Jerome Kersey, Alvan Adams, Robert Horry   IMP: 28% BRK: 4% COP: 10%

It was apparent several years ago that the back end of the contract Andrei Kirilenko signed with the Jazz in 2004 wasn't going to be a good value. Well, here we are. Kirilenko remains very good at the things he does well. He's one of the most disruptive help defenders in basketball, a load as an on-ball defender, an excellent passer and a fine finisher at the rim on offense. His efforts at becoming more efficient from the perimeter have been mixed, and at this point you have to accept that Kirilenko is better off getting his looks off the work of others. He's now carrying the "expiring contract" label and that makes him a candidate to be traded at some point in the season. He was involved in a four-way trade headlined by Carmelo Anthony that fell apart just before the start of training camp. If Kirilenko makes it through the season with the Jazz, he has stated that he'd like to stay in Utah and realizes it will be for a significantly reduced contract. So this may not be his last year under Jerry Sloan after all.

C.J. Miles — SF #34

Hght: 6'6" Wght: 227 Exp: 5 From: Skyline HS (Dallas, TX) Salary: $3.7 million
2011-12 status: team option for $3.7 million

SKILL RATINGS
TOT	OFF	DEF	REB	PAS	HND	SHT	ATH
+1	+2	-4	-4	+2	+2	+3	-1

Year	Team	Age	G	MPG	Usg	3PA%	FTA%	INS	2P%	3P%	FT%	TS%	Reb%	Ast%	TO%	BLK%	STL%	PF%	oRTG	dRTG	Win%	WARP
07-08	UTA	21.1	60	11.5	.187	.269	.080	.811	.522	.390	.788	.574	.069	.035	.094	.009	.021	.065	105.5	106.3	.476	0.8
08-09	UTA	22.1	72	22.5	.185	.269	.059	.790	.509	.352	.876	.546	.061	.030	.096	.007	.014	.052	105.1	108.1	.403	-0.5
09-10	UTA	23.1	63	23.8	.206	.317	.061	.744	.484	.341	.695	.515	.066	.032	.118	.009	.020	.057	103.8	106.8	.401	-0.5
10-11p	UTA	24.1	72	28.0	.206	.367	.064	.696	.496	.378	.782	.554	.063	.034	.105	.008	.017	.051	105.8	106.7	.472	2.3

Most similar to: Byron Scott (98.7), Dion Glover, Sasha Pavlovic, Rashad McCants   IMP: 53% BRK: 7% COP: 9%

C.J. Miles had been gradually improving, but his development seemed to plateau last season. Miles fancies himself a three-point gunner, but he's inconsistent from behind the line. He's got tremendous athleticism and does a great job of running the floor and attacking the rim. He's still learning how to make plays for teammates, and his defensive performance falls well short of his physical skills. The makeup of the Jazz roster ensures that Miles will get another season to find the right side of replacement level.

Paul Millsap — PF #24

Hght: 6'8" Wght: 250 Exp: 4 From: Louisiana Tech Salary: $7.6 million
2011-12 status: guaranteed contract for $8.1 million

SKILL RATINGS
TOT	OFF	DEF	REB	PAS	HND	SHT	ATH
+3	+2	+4	+2	+2	+1	+2	+3

Year	Team	Age	G	MPG	Usg	3PA%	FTA%	INS	2P%	3P%	FT%	TS%	Reb%	Ast%	TO%	BLK%	STL%	PF%	oRTG	dRTG	Win%	WARP
07-08	UTA	23.2	82	20.7	.182	.006	.146	1.140	.507	.000	.677	.547	.165	.021	.126	.034	.019	.072	104.7	104.0	.526	3.9
08-09	UTA	24.2	76	30.1	.201	.004	.140	1.137	.537	.000	.699	.576	.170	.027	.126	.025	.017	.057	107.2	105.2	.567	7.2
09-10	UTA	25.2	82	27.8	.188	.009	.123	1.113	.543	.111	.693	.573	.144	.026	.122	.035	.014	.056	105.0	104.7	.513	4.5
10-11p	UTA	26.2	76	30.0	.198	.009	.129	1.120	.532	.054	.702	.565	.148	.025	.121	.030	.015	.057	105.3	104.6	.523	5.1

Most similar to: Cadillac Anderson (97.4), Cliff Levingston, Kenny Carr, LaSalle Thompson   IMP: 37% BRK: 2% COP: 3%

UTAH JAZZ

The Jazz got in a luxury-tax bind by matching Portland's offer sheet to Paul Millsap in the summer of 2009, but the actual deal itself is a tremendous value for the team. Millsap is as solid as they come, with an above-average skill set across the board and the work ethic to improve each season. Last year, he remained solid on defense; he is the Jazz' second-best weak-side shot-blocker behind Andrei Kirilenko. His rebound percentages dropped on the offensive end last year, and you can't help but point to the increase of midrange shots as the reason. Millsap shot the ball very well on long twos, particularly along the baseline, and his tendency to hang out there may well have been by design. The Jazz' team standing in offensive rebounding dropped eight rungs, but the overall Offensive Rating was pretty much the same. So the tradeoff must have been worth it. Millsap will start alongside Al Jefferson to begin the season, and chances are he will need to focus his efforts on defense and rebounding.

Mehmet Okur — C #13

Hght: 6'11" Exp: 8 Salary: $9.9 million
Wght: 263 From: Yalova, Turkey
2011-12 status: guaranteed contract for $10.9 million

SKILL RATINGS

TOT	OFF	DEF	REB	PAS	HND	SHT	ATH
+3	+2	-3	-2	+2	+2	+1	0

Year	Team	Age	G	MPG	Usg	3PA%	FTA%	INS	2P%	3P%	FT%	TS%	Reb%	Ast%	TO%	BLK%	STL%	PF%	oRTG	dRTG	Win%	WARP
07-08	UTA	28.9	72	33.2	.197	.281	.097	.816	.474	.388	.804	.555	.141	.027	.099	.010	.011	.045	106.3	105.6	.525	5.4
08-09	UTA	29.9	72	33.5	.218	.173	.126	.953	.497	.446	.817	.592	.138	.022	.113	.017	.011	.041	106.9	105.8	.538	6.1
09-10	UTA	30.9	73	29.4	.212	.211	.104	.893	.486	.385	.820	.561	.140	.025	.126	.030	.009	.047	105.7	105.0	.524	4.8
10-11p	UTA	31.9	55	25.0	.206	.236	.102	.866	.473	.417	.814	.567	.131	.024	.117	.026	.010	.047	105.8	105.2	.520	3.0

Most similar to: Bill Laimbeer (97.9), Mike Gminski, Sam Perkins, Maurice Lucas   IMP: 43% BRK: 8% COP: 4%

Mehmet Okur went down with a ruptured Achilles tendon during the playoffs and isn't expected to return to action until December. However, players don't often bounce right back from Achilles injuries, so he might not be right until well after that, if at all. Okur hasn't really derived his value from athleticism anyway, and his face-up game should come back pretty fast. The rest of his skill set might lag behind, and his defense in particular could be an even bigger problem than usual. Okur is a solid rebounder whose overall percentage in that area is dragged down because he spends so much time around the three-point line. An underrated part of his game is his ability to put the ball on the floor against close-outs, and that's something that may be diminished until he gets completely healthy. Okur is on the wrong side of 30, and you have to wonder if he's entering a new, lower plateau as a supporting player rather than as the third part of a core trio, as he's been in recent years in Utah.

Ronnie Price — PG #17

Hght: 6'2" Exp: 5 Salary: $1.4 million
Wght: 184 From: Utah Valley University
2011-12 status: free agent

SKILL RATINGS

TOT	OFF	DEF	REB	PAS	HND	SHT	ATH
0	+1	+3	-1	0	-1	-2	+4

Year	Team	Age	G	MPG	Usg	3PA%	FTA%	INS	2P%	3P%	FT%	TS%	Reb%	Ast%	TO%	BLK%	STL%	PF%	oRTG	dRTG	Win%	WARP
07-08	UTA	24.8	61	9.6	.192	.299	.067	.768	.481	.347	.684	.516	.048	.060	.120	.004	.025	.065	105.0	106.5	.452	0.4
08-09	UTA	25.8	52	14.2	.173	.215	.070	.855	.408	.311	.756	.465	.056	.066	.215	.005	.027	.045	102.5	106.4	.371	-0.7
09-10	UTA	26.8	60	13.4	.181	.194	.080	.886	.447	.286	.695	.476	.054	.069	.173	.013	.025	.061	103.8	106.5	.411	-0.1
10-11p	UTA	27.8	76	5.0	.184	.282	.070	.788	.451	.335	.719	.500	.050	.066	.170	.013	.023	.056	104.4	106.1	.446	0.2

Most similar to: Kelvin Upshaw (98.6), Randy Brown, Gerald Henderson, Anthony Johnson   IMP: 51% BRK: 15% COP: 9%

Ronnie Price had injury issues last season, and was nudged out of the rotation at times by upstart D-Leaguer Sundiata Gaines. His bottom line was below replacement, and it appears his is a roster spot the Jazz would be able to upgrade fairly easily. Price is a poor perimeter shooter, but also doesn't draw the fouls or post the high finishing percentage that you'd like to see from a slasher. He's a decent, but not special, playmaker. Price's decent defensive metrics offer hope, but the Jazz' second unit has generally been better on that end of the court in recent seasons anyway. Price isn't a bad player, just one that's easily replaced--hence the term "replacement level." The signing of Earl Watson drops him to third on the depth chart at the point, a spot that he'll fight over with Gaines during camp.

UTAH JAZZ

PG 11	Earl Watson	Hght: 6'1" Wght: 185 2011-12 status: free agent	Exp: 9 From: UCLA	Salary: 0.854		SKILL RATINGS						
					TOT	OFF	DEF	REB	PAS	HND	SHT	ATH
					-2	0	-2	0	+3	0	-3	-1

Year	Team	Age	G	MPG	Usg	3PA%	FTA%	INS	2P%	3P%	FT%	TS%	Reb%	Ast%	TO%	BLK%	STL%	PF%	oRTG	dRTG	Win%	WARP
07-08	SEA	28.9	78	29.1	.189	.134	.065	.931	.470	.371	.766	.516	.054	.102	.178	.003	.013	.030	106.5	106.9	.486	3.3
08-09	OKC	29.9	68	26.1	.164	.130	.071	.941	.418	.235	.755	.448	.060	.098	.238	.005	.014	.034	103.9	107.7	.374	-1.6
09-10	IND	30.9	79	29.4	.148	.238	.096	.858	.500	.288	.710	.517	.057	.076	.226	.005	.022	.035	104.6	106.0	.452	1.7
10-11p	UTA	31.9	75	15.0	.153	.213	.073	.860	.454	.289	.708	.484	.056	.086	.237	.006	.017	.037	103.6	106.6	.402	-0.3

Most similar to: Chris Childs (97.6), Moochie Norris, Foots Walker, Mark Jackson   IMP: 31%   BRK: 5%   COP: 18%

Earl Watson will continue to find work as long as he can defend opposing point guards and run a second-unit offense. Last season, he played heavy minutes and performed reasonably well, though he had an unsightly turnover rate. He's basically a layup or three-pointer guy at this juncture of his career, but his three-point percentage has cratered the last two seasons, undermining his value. Watson hooked on with the Jazz during the late summer, where his numbers will improve in Jerry Sloan's system if he can hold off Ronnie Price and Sundiata Gaines for minutes behind Deron Williams.

PG 8	Deron Williams	Hght: 6'3" Wght: 207 2011-12 status: guaranteed contract for $16.4 million	Exp: 5 From: Illinois	Salary: $14.9 million		SKILL RATINGS						
					TOT	OFF	DEF	REB	PAS	HND	SHT	ATH
					+5	+5	-4	0	+4	+3	+2	+1

Year	Team	Age	G	MPG	Usg	3PA%	FTA%	INS	2P%	3P%	FT%	TS%	Reb%	Ast%	TO%	BLK%	STL%	PF%	oRTG	dRTG	Win%	WARP
07-08	UTA	23.8	82	37.3	.231	.133	.115	.982	.533	.395	.803	.595	.048	.127	.177	.006	.013	.030	110.6	106.6	.625	13.3
08-09	UTA	24.8	68	36.8	.248	.164	.122	.959	.518	.310	.849	.573	.046	.130	.165	.006	.015	.024	111.7	107.2	.640	11.6
09-10	UTA	25.8	76	36.9	.240	.174	.124	.950	.501	.371	.801	.574	.063	.129	.169	.005	.017	.034	111.1	106.4	.646	13.4
10-11p	UTA	26.8	74	37.0	.241	.183	.117	.934	.510	.359	.831	.578	.054	.126	.169	.006	.014	.029	111.1	106.6	.641	12.9

Most similar to: Kevin Johnson (98.2), Andre Miller, Isiah Thomas, Jason Kidd   IMP: 45%   BRK: 0%   COP: 10%

Deron Williams was as good as ever last season, and remains a top-five NBA point guard. His game was really steady in every respect from 2008-09. He displayed a slightly increased tendency to settle for the jump shot, but he was shooting well from the perimeter, so it didn't dent his efficiency. Williams commits a lot of turnovers, but that sort of goes along with him making plays and may also be a byproduct of Jerry Sloan's system. There is no reason to think that Williams is going to tail off any time soon. He was reportedly miffed over the offseason exodus of former teammates to the Chicago Bulls, so the Jazz is on the clock for showing some forward momentum. Williams is under contract this year and next, but then he's got a player option he can exercise. If he's unhappy with the team's direction, the trade rumors could start to kick in as soon as next summer.

C --	Ante Tomic	Hght: 7'2" Wght: 220 2011-12 status: free agent	Exp: -- From: Croatia	Salary: --		SKILL RATINGS						
					TOT	OFF	DEF	REB	PAS	HND	SHT	ATH
					--	--	--	--	--	--	--	--

Ante Tomic showed promise playing for Croatia in the FIBA World Championship, but opted to remain overseas for another season. He's got potential as a back-to-the-basket scorer.

Washington Wizards

In sports, there is something nice about the idea of starting fresh. In the Wizards' case, it couldn't have come soon enough.

2009-10 was about as disastrous of a season a franchise can have. The Wizards entered the campaign hoping that the combination of a healthy Gilbert Arenas and the acquisitions of veterans Randy Foye and Mike Miller would propel them to the top of the Eastern Conference. It wasn't just the Wizards who were hopeful; many (not us, mind you) picked Washington as a sleeper team to contend in the conference. Instead, the team fell apart. Washington lost seven of its first nine games and was never a factor in the playoff race. Arenas was suspended for bringing weapons into the Wizards' locker room in one of the more thickheaded maneuvers by an athlete in recent memory. Wizards general manager Ernie Grunfeld, whose professional life teetered on extinction, began cleaning house of the key components of the recent Eddie Jordan-led teams. Caron Butler, DeShawn Stevenson and Brendan Haywood went to Dallas. Antawn Jamison went to Cleveland. No one would dare take on Arenas' contract, so he's still around. The Wizards finished with 26 wins.

With so much turbulence around the team's locker room, the ownership transition from the family of the late Abe Pollin to Capitals/Mystics owner Ted Leonsis received relatively little national fanfare. However, that transaction may turn out to have a bigger effect on the franchise's future than anything Grunfeld has done. Leonsis will be an out-front owner and replaces Dallas' Mark Cuban as the most prolific blogger among NBA stewards. He'll have likely have a lower threshold for mediocrity than did Pollin, a beloved civic figure in Washington, D.C. but something less than that as a sport owner who tended to be loyal to key team personnel to a fault. Leonsis brings energy, money and a fresh perspective to the picture, and his acquisition of the team is perfectly timed with the next era of D.C. basketball.

The Wizards--and Grunfeld--desperately needed something good to happen and that break came on lottery night, when Washington landed the top pick in the draft. Kentucky freshman John Wall was a clear-cut consensus as the No. 1 pick and the night the Wizards won the lottery, Grunfeld was able to start plotting the future of the franchise around his dynamic new point guard.

Wall becomes the new face of a franchise that badly needed one, but his presence isn't likely to immediately boost the Wizards into the playoffs. It's entirely reasonable to point at the career tracks of the last two elite guards to move from John Calipari's roster to the NBA, Derrick Rose and Tyreke Evans. In both cases, the raw point guards flashed jaw-dropping athleticism and only cemented their team's faith that the right plan was to build around them. However, as young point guards tend to be, they were largely inefficient. Wall projects as below replacement level this season, with some seriously shaky shooting percentages.

WIZARDS IN A BOX

Last year's record	26-56
Last year's Offensive Rating	105.6 (25)
Last year's Defensive Rating	111.2 (18)
Last year's point differential	-4.8 (26)
Team pace	90.3 (19)
SCHOENE projection	**22-60 (15)**
Projected Offensive Rating	101.9 (30)
Projected Defensive Rating	109.7 (16)
Projected team weighted age	25.9 (21)
Projected '10-11 payroll	$55.5 (24)
Est. payroll obligations, '11-12	$57.7 (13)

Head coach: Flip Saunders

Flip Saunders suddenly finds himself in a very different role than the one he signed up for in the summer of 2009. Back then, the optimistic belief was that a healthy Wizards squad could contend in the Eastern Conference. Those hopes quickly evaporated, leaving Saunders to oversee a rebuilding process in Washington. That's an unfamiliar position for Saunders, who last coached a young team when he was building the Timberwolves into a contender in the late 1990s. Fortunately, Saunders has always done his best work with point guards. He and assistant coach Sam Cassell should help No. 1 overall pick John Wall make a smooth transition to the NBA.

Don't let that fool you. It's the process. Just remember that three years ago, Kevin Durant was barely above replacement level. Last season, he was 18 wins above it. Wall will be a star. Just give him time.

In hindsight, it really is unfortunate that Grunfeld traded the No. 5 pick in 2009 for Foye and Miller. He was trying to add the final pieces to a core that was not of championship caliber. The Arenas/Butler/Jamison core had been together for several years, had barely gotten above .500 and only once got out of the first round of the playoffs. Five years into that group playing together, and with all three already at or nearing 30 years of age, what made Grunfeld think that adding an average combo guard and a shooting specialist was going to be enough to get the team over the hump? The Wizards were beset with injury problems in 2008-09, but Grunfeld passed on the chance to begin the rebuilding process during that 63-loss debacle. Instead, he decided to use the injuries as an excuse, and the result was Washington's Hindenburg of a season last year. Grunfeld could have had Stephen Curry. He could have had Ricky Rubio or Brandon Jennings. Instead, he opted for Randy Foye and Mike Miller.

Grunfeld also brought in the solid Flip Saunders as his head coach. That did seem like an upgrade, though it seemed unfair to can Jordan after such an injury-marred season. It remains to be seen how Saunders is going to work out, but it was to his credit that despite everything else going on with the team, he was able to improve the club's Defensive Rating from 29th to 18th in the league. The offense was just 26th, but the Wizards managed to win seven more games than the year before. Saunders implemented the matchup zone that he likes to mix in and made his team more consistent at contesting shots. The Wizards were the league's worst transition team, but now they have Wall and Saunders has pledged to push the pace. Even if the results aren't great at first, at least the style of play will be more aesthetically pleasing.

The Wizards' roster beyond Wall consists of a hodgepodge of stopgap veterans, raw talents that may or may not develop and end-of-the-roster wishcasts.

Arenas is still around. Whether or not he fits with Wall, it's tough to envision him being moved, not with four more years and $80.1 million still left on his contract. In the 32 games Arenas played last season before getting suspended, he was more or less the same old Gil, both in the good and bad parts of his game. He was creating offense as much as he did pre-injury, but remained a sinkhole in the Wizards' attack. This season, he will have to learn to play off the ball much more than he's accustomed to doing. His catch-and-shoot skills are so-so, but he can stroke the ball and remains athletic enough to defend if he so chooses. Saunders needs to keep the ball in Wall's hands for development purposes, but in the end of close games, it will likely still be Arenas to whom he turns as a closer. Washington will likely showcase Arenas as much as possible in hopes of finding some sucker, er, team that feels like a scorer can get them over the hump. The sooner the Wizards find a taker for Arenas, the better. His $17.7 million salary for this season is bad enough, but it continues to ramp up from here.

Kirk Hinrich was brought in from Chicago to provide stability to the backcourt situation. If Wall really struggles, then Hinrich can play alongside Arenas. Or he can play alongside Wall if Arenas proves to be a disruptive presence or gets injured again. Hinrich can play either backcourt position on offense and guard either position on defense. He's kind of expensive for the role he plays, but he's a solid, solid player and only has two more years left on his deal.

The backcourt situation is actually pretty rosy when viewed against what Saunders has to work with in the frontcourt. The key piece is Andray Blatche, who can play inside or outside, can handle all three frontcourt positions and is your basic wildly talented, but undisciplined, young player. Blatche was pretty much the only show left in town once Grunfeld gutted the roster last season. Not only did he up his usage rate by a large margin, he also became more efficient. He's an excellent passer and a playmaking defender. If Saunders can keep Blatche pointed in the right direction, then the Wizards have the second part of their future big three already in house.

The Wizards continue to have high hopes for young center JaVale McGee, who actually went to camp for USA Basketball prior to the summer's FIBA World Championship, though his presence was mostly a result of a shortage of big men and he didn't make the final roster. McGee is a top-flight shot blocker and finisher at the basket. He still needs to become stronger and to develop a post game, but he does display a decent touch within 10 feet. Hilton Armstrong's high hopes aside, McGee doesn't have any competition at the center position, so he'll get as much playing time as his high foul rate allows. It's a key campaign for him.

A similar talent is Yi Jianlian, who comes to his third team in four seasons. He looked awfully good playing for China this summer, but has yet to perform consistently in the NBA. He really can't defend anyone, and has the most value as a potential floor-spacing big forward. You'd like to see Yi be more than that, but he struggles to make half of his shots at the rim, so until he get stronger, he needs to be a face-up forward off the bench. He's a good rebounder, though, and it's too early to write off Yi's chances to become an NBA starter.

Wall, Blatche, McGee and Yi could serve as nice starting points for Washington's next good roster. They'll have plenty of time to develop, because the Wizards won't likely have cap room this year or next to improve the roster with veterans--though an Arenas or Hinrich trade could alter that somewhat. Failing that, the best chance for Washington to get better in the future is to be bad in the present. That's a bullet the former Bullets have never been willing to bite, and if there is one positive result from last season's mess, it's that finally the Wizards can make the break from mediocrity.

This year's key questions are worth following. What do the Wizards have in Blatche? He can put up big counting numbers, but how does he fit into the team concept? Can McGee begin to move beyond his "project" label? If so, he could lift the Wizards into the league's top 10 defenses. Is Nick Young as much of a head case as has been suggested? If so, there is no reason for him to be around. As pointed out in last year's book, point guards in Saunders' system carry a lot of responsibility, so this will be Wall's team from the get-go. Can Arenas, after all the physical problems and the relatively light workload the last three years or so, adapt to being a pure two? Can Saunders sort out what Yi does well and take advantage of situations in which you can hide his defense? After all, the guy still won't even be 24 by the end of next season.

With a raw rookie having so much control, Washington projects as the league's worst offensive team and as the worst overall team. However, there is nowhere to go but up, especially if Wall is efficient and productive right away and some good things happen with Blatche and McGee. There will be no playoffs this year, but Grunfeld has gotten the Wizards back into reasonable shape much quicker than one would have thought possible after the Arenas incident. That doesn't excuse Grunfeld for his misreadings of rosters past, but it does buy him another year in the front office.

Bradford Doolittle

From the Blogosphere

Who: Mike Prada
What: Bullets Forever
Where: http://www.bulletsforever.com/

Washington was an elite offensive team for years, but that trend came to a screeching halt last season. The Wizards finished 25th in Offensive Rating and struggled to adjust from Eddie Jordan's Princeton offense to Flip Saunders' pro-style Hawk system. Saunders' system calls for rigid positional differences, and that was an issue with a Wizards roster stocked with combination players. Gilbert Arenas and Caron Butler, in particular, struggled to adjust to their new roles. Before his suspension, Arenas was uncomfortable being a pure point guard, while Butler could never learn how to be more of a catch-and-shoot player. The Wizards ultimately settled for too many poor perimeter jump shots--only the Bulls took more attempts per game from 16-23 feet. With John Wall coming in and Andray Blatche's emergence, Saunders now has a group of players better suited for his style. The Wizards should eventually be able to reclaim their place as one of the league's offensive juggernauts.

WASHINGTON WIZARDS

WIZARDS FIVE-YEAR TRENDS

Season	AGE	W-L	POW	PYTH	SEED	ORTG	DRTG	PT DIFF	PACE
05-06	26.5	42-40	43.2 (13)	46.3	5	110.4 (7)	109.1 (23)	1.9 (10)	91.1 (7)
06-07	26.8	41-41	39.2 (16)	39.6	7	111.1 (5)	112.5 (28)	-0.5 (15)	92.9 (5)
07-08	27.5	43-39	40.4 (16)	40.0	5	111.1 (12)	111.9 (23)	-0.3 (15)	87.7 (27)
08-09	26.9	19-63	19.9 (28)	21.3	---	106.6 (26)	115.8 (29)	-7.5 (28)	89.6 (17)
09-10	28.7	26-56	26.6 (26)	27.6	--	105.6 (25)	111.2 (18)	-4.8 (26)	90.3 (19)

		OFFENSE				DEFENSE			
Season	PAY	eFG	oREB	FT/FGA	TO	eFG	oREB	FT/FGA	TO
05-06	$50.2	.484 (21)	.295 (6)	.284 (4)	.152 (5)	.504 (24)	.709 (26)	.256 (18)	.176 (2)
06-07	$61.9	.491 (18)	.281 (13)	.272 (6)	.148 (3)	.517 (28)	.710 (24)	.249 (18)	.168 (13)
07-08	$61.1	.489 (19)	.289 (9)	.233 (11)	.142 (8)	.514 (27)	.728 (20)	.217 (12)	.152 (11)
08-09	$70.6	.480 (29)	.277 (10)	.224 (22)	.155 (17)	.533 (30)	.714 (26)	.227 (13)	.155 (11)
09-10	$73.6	.481 (26)	.276 (8)	.216 (22)	.163 (25)	.502 (18)	.724 (25)	.239 (20)	.149 (22)

(league rankings in parenthesis)

PG 9 — Gilbert Arenas
Hght: 6'4" Exp: 9 Salary: $17.7 million
Wght: 215 From: Arizona
2011-12 status: guaranteed contract for $19.3 million

SKILL RATINGS
TOT	OFF	DEF	REB	PAS	HND	SHT	ATH
+4	+4	-1	+4	+2	-2	-2	+4

Year	Team	Age	G	MPG	Usg	3PA%	FTA%	INS	2P%	3P%	FT%	TS%	Reb%	Ast%	TO%	BLK%	STL%	PF%	oRTG	dRTG	Win%	WARP
07-08	WAS	26.3	13	32.6	.315	.271	.147	.876	.471	.282	.771	.527	.072	.072	.170	.002	.026	.033	107.0	104.9	.570	1.4
08-09	WAS	27.3	2	31.5	.225	.226	.227	1.001	.250	.286	.750	.433	.086	.145	.032	.013	.000	.029	111.9	107.8	.626	0.3
09-10	WAS	28.3	32	36.5	.322	.220	.111	.891	.437	.348	.739	.511	.066	.090	.142	.006	.018	.037	108.6	106.4	.572	3.8
10-11p	WAS	29.3	72	35.0	.288	.268	.116	.847	.445	.339	.745	.519	.070	.081	.147	.004	.020	.036	107.3	105.8	.549	7.0

Most similar to: Ray Williams (98.1), Baron Davis, Isiah Thomas, Robert Pack   IMP: 35% BRK: 0% COP: 9%

It will be a different kind of season for Gilbert Arenas, who is trying to maintain a low profile by being reserved around the media and wearing a bushy beard. He's no longer the focal point of the Wizards, both in terms of attention and in getting to dominate the ball. Those are now the domain of rookie John Wall. Arenas will be playing off the ball, and it will be interesting to see what happens to his efficiency. He has always gotten most of his offense off the dribble, but it seems like he has the skill set to thrive as a catch-and-shoot option who can drive the ball against close-out defenders. Certainly his turnovers should fall, and he still will be able to set up teammates who will no longer have to stand around and watch him dribble. It might not work, but if it does, the switch may help the Wizards cut out some of Arenas' bad habits and isolate the things he does well. He may also improve defensively since he won't have to defend opposing point guards and won't have to expend as much energy as the offense's initiator. It'll be interesting to see how it works out, because it's not too late for Arenas to reinvent himself, and he's smart enough to realize that.

C 24 — Hilton Armstrong
Hght: 6'11" Exp: 4 Salary: $0.9 million
Wght: 235 From: Connecticut
2011-12 status: free agent

SKILL RATINGS
TOT	OFF	DEF	REB	PAS	HND	SHT	ATH
-4	-2	+1	-2	+1	-1	-4	+4

Year	Team	Age	G	MPG	Usg	3PA%	FTA%	INS	2P%	3P%	FT%	TS%	Reb%	Ast%	TO%	BLK%	STL%	PF%	oRTG	dRTG	Win%	WARP
07-08	NOH	23.4	65	11.2	.153	.000	.130	1.130	.453	.000	.629	.498	.131	.015	.248	.037	.010	.084	100.3	106.0	.318	-1.5
08-09	NOH	24.4	70	15.6	.164	.005	.117	1.111	.566	.000	.633	.585	.108	.013	.217	.035	.013	.081	102.7	107.0	.358	-1.3
09-10	SAC	25.4	33	10.2	.157	.009	.122	1.114	.359	.000	.469	.381	.142	.029	.191	.027	.023	.080	99.6	104.9	.324	-0.6
10-11p	WAS	26.4	75	5.0	.147	.012	.127	1.115	.446	.005	.565	.474	.129	.021	.190	.030	.016	.078	100.4	105.5	.334	-0.6

Most similar to: Donald Hodge (96.0), Loren Woods, Frank Brickowski, Paul Mokeski   IMP: 51% BRK: 15% COP: 8%

WASHINGTON WIZARDS

Hilton Armstrong fancies himself a potential starter and, indeed, Washington is one of the few places above the D-League where that could ever possibly happen. Still, as he proved with three teams last season, he's got a long way to go to translate his athleticism into useful basketball production. 2009-10 was lost because Armstrong kept getting traded and never found anything close to consistent minutes. The year before, he showed excellent finishing abilities and the knack for getting to the foul line. He has nothing in his arsenal beyond the immediate vicinity of the basket. Armstrong's rebounding is nothing to write home about, but he actually passes the ball pretty well, though he has Kwame Brown-esque hands and has the turnover rate to prove it. While he's not a great shot blocker, Armstrong's defensive indicators show promise. The opportunity is there for Armstrong to show he can be a rotation player at the NBA level in Washington this season.

PF 7 — Andray Blatche

Hght: 6'11" Exp: 5 Salary: $3.3 million
Wght: 260 From: South Kent Prep (CT)
2011-12 status: guaranteed contract for $3.5 million

SKILL RATINGS

TOT	OFF	DEF	REB	PAS	HND	SHT	ATH
+1	0	+2	+1	+4	+1	-1	+4

Year	Team	Age	G	MPG	Usg	3PA%	FTA%	INS	2P%	3P%	FT%	TS%	Reb%	Ast%	TO%	BLK%	STL%	PF%	oRTG	dRTG	Win%	WARP
07-08	WAS	21.7	82	20.5	.198	.018	.095	1.077	.480	.231	.695	.512	.150	.025	.156	.056	.015	.072	103.7	103.8	.497	2.8
08-09	WAS	22.7	71	24.0	.220	.026	.087	1.061	.479	.238	.704	.508	.132	.032	.143	.035	.016	.057	104.0	105.6	.446	1.1
09-10	WAS	23.7	81	27.9	.260	.034	.080	1.046	.487	.295	.744	.519	.131	.034	.142	.024	.019	.044	104.5	104.4	.503	4.0
10-11p	WAS	24.7	75	32.0	.222	.033	.087	1.054	.498	.243	.728	.526	.136	.034	.144	.032	.017	.054	103.7	104.2	.482	3.3

Most similar to: Christian Laettner (97.6), Darius Miles, Charles D. Smith, Kenyon Martin

IMP: 46% BRK: 8% COP: 10%

One of the saving graces from Washington's dismal 2009-10 season was the emergence of Andray Blatche as a potential core talent with a dazzling array of skills. He clashed with coach Flip Sanders at times, but they seemed to come to some sort of détente by the end of the season, and Blatche negotiated a three-year extension for himself during the summer without the help of an agent. His per-40 minute averages tell the story: 20.3 points, 9.0 rebounds, 3.0 assists, 1.5 steals, 1.3 blocks. Blatche's True Shooting Percentage is held back by his tendency to float on the perimeter, and he doesn't have three-point range yet. He makes up for some of that by being a very good playmaker and rebounder who can run the floor with any big man in the game. Blatche is a capable defender who can shut down guys in the post and make plays off the weak side. At this point, he's only an upgrade in shot selection away from being an All-Star-caliber player. Playing alongside offensive talents like John Wall and Gilbert Arenas could help him take that next step. Blatche had a broken bone in his foot, but declared himself ready to go as camps opened.

PF 35 — Trevor Booker

Hght: 6'7" Exp: R Salary: $1.2 million
Wght: 240 From: Clemson
2011-12 status: guaranteed contract for $1.3 million

SKILL RATINGS

TOT	OFF	DEF	REB	PAS	HND	SHT	ATH
0	-1	+2	+1	+4	+4	-3	+2

Year	Team	Age	G	MPG	Usg	3PA%	FTA%	INS	2P%	3P%	FT%	TS%	Reb%	Ast%	TO%	BLK%	STL%	PF%	oRTG	dRTG	Win%	WARP
10-11p	WAS	23.4	76	18.0	.169	.054	.112	1.057	.456	.230	.577	.474	.137	.035	.123	.023	.016	.042	102.8	104.6	.441	0.7

Most similar to: David West (98.5), Craig Smith, Nick Fazekas, Ryan Humphrey

IMP: - BRK: - COP: -

There are a few undersized fours that have stuck in the NBA, but it's not an ideal situation. You'd be hard-pressed to find one that was more productive in college than Trevor Booker. Booker is longer-armed than you'd expect of a 6'7" guy and has a lot of skill in the post, though it's hard to imagine him making a living on the blocks in the league. He should be able to contribute as a rebounder, and he passes the ball really well for a big guy. If Booker succeeds, it will be a victory for stats over the scouts.

WASHINGTON WIZARDS

SG 12 — Kirk Hinrich

Hght: 6'3" Exp: 7 Salary: $9.0 million
Wght: 190 From: Kansas
2011-12 status: guaranteed contract for $8.0 million

SKILL RATINGS

TOT	OFF	DEF	REB	PAS	HND	SHT	ATH
0	+2	+1	-2	+4	+5	0	-1

Year	Team	Age	G	MPG	Usg	3PA%	FTA%	INS	2P%	3P%	FT%	TS%	Reb%	Ast%	TO%	BLK%	STL%	PF%	oRTG	dRTG	Win%	WARP
07-08	CHI	27.3	75	31.7	.190	.236	.062	.826	.442	.350	.826	.502	.059	.085	.154	.006	.017	.043	105.6	106.3	.476	3.0
08-09	CHI	28.3	51	26.3	.182	.311	.070	.759	.456	.408	.791	.551	.052	.066	.160	.010	.025	.042	106.8	106.2	.519	2.9
09-10	CHI	29.3	74	33.5	.167	.306	.054	.749	.431	.371	.752	.501	.058	.060	.123	.007	.017	.037	105.0	106.3	.456	2.0
10-11p	WAS	30.3	73	28.0	.157	.308	.056	.748	.438	.387	.786	.520	.057	.068	.144	.009	.018	.041	105.1	106.3	.463	2.0

Most similar to: Mike James (98.4), Rafer Alston, Gerald Henderson, Lindsey Hunter
IMP: 40% BRK: 5% COP: 9%

It was the lure of cap space and the possibility of LeBron James or Dwyane Wade that spurred the Bulls to send steady Kirk Hinrich to the Wizards for basically nothing. Hinrich had emerged as a nice complement to Derrick Rose in the Bulls' backcourt, as he developed his catch-and-shoot skills and did the dirty work on the defensive end. Hinrich's drop in True Shooting Percentage can be traced back to a percentage at the rim (.477) that was way below his past level, and you may as well blame on the offensive design of Vinny Del Negro. Hinrich may be declining athletically, though, because his foul-drawing rate was also down. Nevertheless, he'll be a perfect fit in Washington, where he can spell both John Wall and Gilbert Arenas and also play alongside them in smallball lineups.

SF 5 — Josh Howard

Hght: 6'7" Exp: 7 Salary: $3.0 million
Wght: 210 From: Wake Forest
2011-12 status: free agent

SKILL RATINGS

TOT	OFF	DEF	REB	PAS	HND	SHT	ATH
-1	0	+3	0	-1	-1	-2	+1

Year	Team	Age	G	MPG	Usg	3PA%	FTA%	INS	2P%	3P%	FT%	TS%	Reb%	Ast%	TO%	BLK%	STL%	PF%	oRTG	dRTG	Win%	WARP
07-08	DAL	28.0	76	36.2	.261	.137	.110	.973	.482	.319	.813	.534	.110	.028	.075	.009	.010	.034	106.2	105.6	.520	5.9
08-09	DAL	29.0	52	32.0	.269	.173	.100	.927	.480	.345	.782	.532	.090	.023	.092	.013	.017	.037	105.6	106.2	.479	2.2
09-10	WAS	30.0	35	26.2	.249	.174	.124	.950	.444	.267	.784	.496	.078	.024	.093	.009	.014	.046	103.5	106.8	.390	-0.5
10-11p	WAS	31.0	68	25.0	.234	.181	.113	.933	.467	.309	.782	.520	.091	.023	.087	.011	.014	.044	104.0	106.2	.425	0.3

Most similar to: Tony Campbell (99.1), Terry Teagle, Chris Mills, Mike Mitchell
IMP: 40% BRK: 7% COP: 7%

The Wizards gave veteran Josh Howard a one-year guaranteed deal even though he tore his ACL last season and probably won't be playing until December. Prior to the injury, Howard's performance had sagged considerably, as he's dropped off the NBA map with startling rapidity. Before getting hurt, he had shown that he could still finish at the rim when he chose to visit there, and could get to the line. However, Howard used far too many possessions for such an inefficient scorer. When he returns, he's got to adapt to being a supporting player. He will be asked play defense off the bench and stay out of the way of the frontline scorers ahead of him.

PG 3 — Lester Hudson

Hght: 6'3" Exp: 1 Salary: $0.5 million
Wght: 190 From: Tennessee-Martin
2011-12 status: due qualifying offer of $1.0 million

SKILL RATINGS

TOT	OFF	DEF	REB	PAS	HND	SHT	ATH
+2	--	0	--	--	--	--	--

Year	Team	Age	G	MPG	Usg	3PA%	FTA%	INS	2P%	3P%	FT%	TS%	Reb%	Ast%	TO%	BLK%	STL%	PF%	oRTG	dRTG	Win%	WARP
09-10	MEM	25.7	25	5.2	.254	.220	.079	.859	.432	.313	.846	.494	.082	.045	.193	.018	.031	.042	103.7	104.4	.477	0.2
10-11p	WAS	26.7	76	--	.203	.414	.082	.669	.400	.367	.789	.520	.122	.051	.142	.010	.021	.054	--	--	.491	--

Most similar to: Erick Strickland (96.3), John Starks, Lindsey Hunter, Doug Christie
IMP: 56% BRK: 7% COP: 7%

We were hoping that former small-college scoring star Lester Hudson would carve out a regular role last season, but even though he showed the ability to create shots, it's looking like he's a fringe player. Hudson showed scant recognition of sharing the court with four other players when he stepped on the floor, and shot poor percentages everywhere but at the rim. Washington is giving him a shot in camp, but the Wizards can probably do better. Hudson is already 26, so there doesn't seem to be much of a ceiling here.

WASHINGTON WIZARDS

C 4	Sean Marks	Hght: 6'10" Wght: 250 2011-12 status: free agent	Exp: 10 From: California	Salary: --	SKILL RATINGS						
					TOT	OFF	DEF	REB	PAS	HND	SHT	ATH
					-4	--	+1	--	--	--	--	--

Year	Team	Age	G	MPG	Usg	3PA%	FTA%	INS	2P%	3P%	FT%	TS%	Reb%	Ast%	TO%	BLK%	STL%	PF%	oRTG	dRTG	Win%	WARP
07-08	PHX	32.7	19	6.8	.206	.067	.141	1.073	.564	.250	.632	.574	.151	.014	.135	.050	.010	.076	104.1	103.7	.511	0.3
08-09	NOH	33.7	60	14.0	.127	.046	.088	1.043	.503	.200	.682	.521	.135	.008	.160	.033	.004	.070	102.1	107.0	.340	-1.3
09-10	NOH	34.7	14	5.4	.075	.000	.180	1.180	.500	-	.400	.490	.179	.012	.164	.030	.000	.104	105.3	108.8	.389	0.0
10-11p	WAS	35.7	76	-	.109	.044	.083	1.039	.508	.184	.656	.519	.136	.007	.167	.038	.004	.080	-	-	.350	-

Most similar to: Aaron Williams (97.4), Tony Massenburg, Chris Dudley, Caldwell Jones — IMP: 57% BRK: 10% COP: 10%

Sean Marks put up one of last season's most impressive statistics. You'll find it in the experience column of the table above. 2009-10 marked a decade in the league for the affable Kiwi, who has made a career out of being a good guy to have around. Marks has played 2,068 career minutes, a number exceeded by 124 players last season alone. This total is historic. Over the past three decades, no NBA player has played as few minutes as Marks during the first 10 years of their career. (10-day contract specialist Randy Livingston came closest, playing 2,658 minutes.)

Marks might have added to that total last season had he not missed 33 games due to injury (he finished the year on the shelf due to a shoulder injury that lingered and kept him out of this summer's FIBA World Championship). When he was pressed into duty during the 2008-09 season, however, Marks was ineffective, struggling defensively and showing no skills league average or better. He saw just 75 minutes of action when he was healthy for a team that was perilously thin in the frontcourt last year. Still, the *Washington Post* reported in September that Marks was headed to training camp with the Wizards.

SF 20	Cartier Martin	Hght: 6'7" Wght: 220 2011-12 status: free agent	Exp: 2 From: Kansas State	Salary: $0.5 million	SKILL RATINGS						
					TOT	OFF	DEF	REB	PAS	HND	SHT	ATH
					-3	--	+2	--	--	--	--	--

Year	Team	Age	G	MPG	Usg	3PA%	FTA%	INS	2P%	3P%	FT%	TS%	Reb%	Ast%	TO%	BLK%	STL%	PF%	oRTG	dRTG	Win%	WARP
08-09	CHA	24.4	33	8.1	.173	.340	.113	.773	.409	.303	.800	.489	.076	.023	.093	.012	.016	.059	104.1	107.4	.393	-0.1
09-10	WAS	25.4	18	21.7	.189	.291	.078	.787	.379	.347	.800	.473	.098	.018	.113	.002	.014	.054	103.8	107.6	.377	-0.3
10-11p	WAS	26.4	76	-	.167	.323	.089	.766	.411	.345	.798	.499	.093	.021	.105	.007	.015	.056	-	-	.367	-

Most similar to: Devean George (98.4), Jarvis Hayes, Walter Bond, Keith Bogans — IMP: 65% BRK: 19% COP: 7%

The Wizards will have a lot of make-good players in camp, a description that fits perennial fringe player Cartier Martin. Martin can defend, which works in his favor as Flip Sanders tries to find the optimum mix of complementary talents. Martin has tried to fashion himself as a three-point specialist, but he's not consistent from behind the arc. If he gets on a hot streak during preseason, and continues to impress on the defensive end, there may be room for him on the Wizards' roster.

C 34	JaVale McGee	Hght: 7'0" Wght: 252 2011-12 status: team option for $2.5 million	Exp: 2 From: Nevada-Reno	Salary: $1.6 million	SKILL RATINGS						
					TOT	OFF	DEF	REB	PAS	HND	SHT	ATH
					+3	0	-3	0	-4	-4	+2	+2

Year	Team	Age	G	MPG	Usg	3PA%	FTA%	INS	2P%	3P%	FT%	TS%	Reb%	Ast%	TO%	BLK%	STL%	PF%	oRTG	dRTG	Win%	WARP
08-09	WAS	21.3	75	15.2	.208	.000	.137	1.137	.494	.000	.660	.534	.152	.009	.117	.054	.015	.062	104.9	104.6	.509	2.2
09-10	WAS	22.3	60	16.1	.193	.002	.125	1.122	.510	.000	.638	.539	.145	.007	.125	.080	.009	.058	103.6	102.5	.538	2.4
10-11p	WAS	23.3	76	25.0	.188	.006	.132	1.127	.530	.003	.647	.558	.147	.010	.121	.067	.010	.055	103.4	102.8	.519	4.1

Most similar to: Jermaine O'Neal (97.1), Elden Campbell, Darko Milicic, Stromile Swift — IMP: 57% BRK: 6% COP: 3%

This could be a breakout season for JaVale McGee, who has compiled some tantalizing indicators in limited court time the last two seasons. First, he was diagnosed with asthma, which had prevented him from ever getting in really good shape. That taken care of, he added weight and strength and even grew another inch. McGee got to practice with the U.S. National Team prior to their departure for the World Championship, which had to

WASHINGTON WIZARDS

be a good experience for him. He's long and really athletic, which should make him a force on the boards. If he can stay out of foul trouble, he will challenge for the league title in shot blocking. McGee is penciled in as the Wizards' starting center as camp opens, so this is his time to shine.

SF 6	Adam Morrison	Hght: 6'8" Wght: 205 2011-12 status: free agent	Exp: 3 From: Gonzaga	Salary: --					SKILL RATINGS						
									TOT	OFF	DEF	REB	PAS	HND	SHT	ATH
									-5	--	-2	--	--	--	--	--

Year	Team	Age	G	MPG	Usg	3PA%	FTA%	INS	2P%	3P%	FT%	TS%	Reb%	Ast%	TO%	BLK%	STL%	PF%	oRTG	dRTG	Win%	WARP
08-09	LAL	24.8	52	13.7	.176	.362	.038	.676	.378	.333	.739	.448	.069	.027	.121	.004	.007	.051	102.6	108.9	.303	-1.7
09-10	LAL	25.8	31	7.8	.184	.213	.036	.823	.422	.238	.625	.418	.074	.034	.102	.006	.006	.032	101.6	107.7	.307	-0.6
10-11p	WAS	26.8	76	--	.158	.351	.039	.688	.408	.378	.752	.492	.075	.026	.120	.006	.006	.051	--	--	.303	--

Most similar to: Bostjan Nachbar (97.0), Jeff Judkins, Rod Higgins, Yakhouba Diawara IMP: 89% BRK: 37% COP: 0%

At the conclusion of his rookie contract, Adam Morrison finds himself at a crossroads. There's still enough cachet left from his stellar career at Gonzaga that Morrison drew some interest in free agency. However, it's hard to trade in potential when you're 26 years old. Morrison has to demonstrate to an NBA team that he can contribute immediately, and nothing in his stat line testifies to that possibility. In college, Morrison thrived on making difficult shots, which became impossible ones against NBA defenders. Morrison just doesn't have the ability to get easy points, whether in the paint or at the line, leaving him to rely on shooting around 40 percent on two-pointers. Morrison's best hope for relevance as a pro is developing a three-point shot. SCHOENE thinks that might happen, but still pegs Morrison well south of replacement level. Morrison will go to training camp with the Wizards. This might be his last chance to prove himself in the NBA.

C 55	Hamady Ndiaye	Hght: 7'0" Wght: 235 2011-12 status: free agent	Exp: R From: Rutgers	Salary: --					SKILL RATINGS						
									TOT	OFF	DEF	REB	PAS	HND	SHT	ATH
									-3	-2	+3	-3	-5	-4	-2	-4

Year	Team	Age	G	MPG	Usg	3PA%	FTA%	INS	2P%	3P%	FT%	TS%	Reb%	Ast%	TO%	BLK%	STL%	PF%	oRTG	dRTG	Win%	WARP
10-11p	WAS	24.3	76	10.0	.110	-.001	.129	1.130	.473	.000	.602	.509	.115	.006	.160	.069	.005	.064	100.3	104.3	.367	-0.8

Most similar to: Loren Woods (89.0), Taj Gibson, Dan Gadzuric IMP: -- BRK: -- COP: --

Second-round pick Hamady Ndiaye never got a solid offer from the team and settled for going to camp on a non-qualifying tender. Ndiaye is a cheap, defense-first big man and the Wizards have room for someone like that. He's going to block shots, but the rest of his game is suspect.

PF 13	Kevin Seraphin	Hght: 6'9" Wght: 264 2011-12 status: guaranteed contract for $1.7 million	Exp: R From: French Guyana	Salary: $1.6 million					SKILL RATINGS						
									TOT	OFF	DEF	REB	PAS	HND	SHT	ATH
									--	--	--	--	--	--	--	--

Kevin Seraphin was acquired by the Wizards as part of the deal that brought Kirk Hinrich to Washington and left the Bulls with more cap space. He's a tremendous physical specimen--long, muscular and athletic. He's a late comer to basketball, so his ceiling would seem to be high. Seraphin will likely start as a board crasher and floor runner, then work up from there.

WASHINGTON WIZARDS

	SF · 14	Al Thornton	Hght: 6'8"	Exp: 3	Salary: $2.8 million				SKILL RATINGS				
			Wght: 235	From: Florida State		TOT	OFF	DEF	REB	PAS	HND	SHT	ATH
			2011-12 status: due qualifying offer of $3.9 million			-3	-1	-4	-1	-2	-3	-1	-2

Year	Team	Age	G	MPG	Usg	3PA%	FTA%	INS	2P%	3P%	FT%	TS%	Reb%	Ast%	TO%	BLK%	STL%	PF%	oRTG	dRTG	Win%	WARP
07-08	LAC	24.4	79	27.4	.241	.116	.113	.997	.447	.331	.743	.504	.096	.021	.114	.015	.010	.041	102.7	106.3	.382	-1.5
08-09	LAC	25.4	71	37.4	.228	.060	.104	1.045	.462	.253	.754	.502	.081	.018	.099	.017	.011	.039	102.8	107.5	.348	-3.8
09-10	WAS	26.4	75	27.7	.191	.036	.107	1.071	.479	.355	.725	.523	.082	.020	.117	.013	.011	.045	102.8	107.4	.351	-2.9
10-11p	WAS	27.4	74	28.0	.193	.081	.106	1.024	.476	.369	.737	.525	.082	.020	.108	.017	.011	.044	102.5	106.6	.366	-2.2

Most similar to: Calbert Cheaney (98.0), Desmond Mason, Eric Williams, Matt Harpring   IMP: 56%   BRK: 9%   COP: 6%

It's hard to be so consistently bad and yet get so many minutes, but Al Thornton seems to manage the trick every season. He's below average at every skill on the board, a clean sweep few players with any sizable statistical record can match. On offense, Thornton has some scoring ability, even though he burns through possessions. The rest of his game is lackluster. He doesn't rebound, isn't a skilled passer, and is poor on defense. Thornton is headed for restricted free agency, and it would be a huge upset if the Wizards try to extend him. First, they need to figure out what he does well, then put him in a position to focus on those things. He's got natural ability, but he's a role player, not a star, so it's time to find Thornton a niche.

	PG · 2	John Wall	Hght: 6'4"	Exp: R	Salary: $5.1 million				SKILL RATINGS				
			Wght: 195	From: Kentucky		TOT	OFF	DEF	REB	PAS	HND	SHT	ATH
			2011-12 status: guaranteed contract for $5.5 million			-2	-1	-1	+1	+2	-1	-4	+1

Year	Team	Age	G	MPG	Usg	3PA%	FTA%	INS	2P%	3P%	FT%	TS%	Reb%	Ast%	TO%	BLK%	STL%	PF%	oRTG	dRTG	Win%	WARP
10-11p	WAS	20.6	76	36.0	.176	.134	.109	.975	.423	.285	.740	.481	.057	.078	.215	.007	.018	.035	102.9	106.2	.390	-1.4

Most similar to: Derrick Rose (97.5), Jordan Farmar, Russell Westbrook, Javaris Crittenton   IMP: -   BRK: -   COP: -

John Wall is the top prospect from this year's draft class and has already been embraced by the Wizards as the new face of their franchise. His natural ability is off the charts, but he's got some rough edges to smooth over before he becomes an NBA star. Wall is a killer off the dribble, a pure playmaker who will raise the level of play of his teammates. He's quick to the basket and down the floor, so he'll get to the line a lot. Wall is also a solid defender who will commit to making a difference on that end of the floor. As he learns the pro game, the turnover count promises to be frightening. Also, his number one area of focus for future improvement will be his jump shot, which lacks consistency inside the arc and the range to be a factor outside of it. Wall has more length than some of the other exciting point guards that have come into the league in recent years, which gives him the added value of being able to guard both backcourt positions. Judging by the stir his games in summer league caused, he's going to be a rallying point for Washington fans looking forward to a new era.

	PF · 31	Yi Jianlian	Hght: 7'0"	Exp: 3	Salary: $4.1 million				SKILL RATINGS				
			Wght: 250	From: Shenzhen, China		TOT	OFF	DEF	REB	PAS	HND	SHT	ATH
			2011-12 status: due qualifying offer of $5.4 million			-1	-1	-2	+1	-1	-1	-3	+1

Year	Team	Age	G	MPG	Usg	3PA%	FTA%	INS	2P%	3P%	FT%	TS%	Reb%	Ast%	TO%	BLK%	STL%	PF%	oRTG	dRTG	Win%	WARP
07-08	MIL	20.5	66	25.0	.184	.031	.095	1.064	.427	.286	.841	.485	.125	.015	.131	.027	.010	.043	101.2	105.3	.365	-1.8
08-09	NJN	21.5	61	23.3	.207	.224	.087	.862	.397	.343	.772	.474	.138	.020	.112	.021	.011	.052	103.3	106.1	.407	-0.3
09-10	NJN	22.5	52	31.8	.203	.057	.117	1.061	.406	.366	.798	.481	.132	.013	.106	.023	.012	.048	102.4	105.6	.394	-0.8
10-11p	WAS	23.5	70	18.0	.187	.111	.102	.992	.436	.356	.815	.505	.137	.018	.113	.026	.011	.046	102.5	104.9	.419	0.1

Most similar to: Doug Smith (97.4), Kiki Vandeweghe, Joe Smith, Donyell Marshall   IMP: 68%   BRK: 16%   COP: 5%

If you saw Yi Jianlian in the FIBA World Championship, you saw why he was so coveted three years ago when he was drafted by the Bucks. Yi was a 20-10 player in that international setting as the top player on the Chinese team. He's had trouble with the physical nature of the NBA. Yi doesn't really create much for himself; nor does he create opportunities for others. It's like he just sort of stands around and waits for chances to shoot. He needs to carry the aggressiveness he had in FIBA over to the NBA. Last season, he improved his foul-drawing rate, which is a good sign. Defensively, he's hurt by his lack of strength, but he's long and makes plays as a help defender. For Yi, it's really all about adding strength, because a 7-footer shouldn't finish as poorly as he does. Let's not forget that Yi is still very young, and his recent performance suggests he may be on the upswing. It would be an ideal situation for the Wizards to fit Yi alongside Andray Blatche and an improved JaVale McGee in a revamped frontline full of young, high-ceiling talents.

SG 1 — Nick Young
Hght: 6'7" Wght: 210 Exp: 3 From: USC Salary: $2.6 million
2011-12 status: due qualifying offer of $3.7 million

SKILL RATINGS: TOT -4, OFF -1, DEF +3, REB -3, PAS -3, HND -3, SHT 0, ATH -2

Year	Team	Age	G	MPG	Usg	3PA%	FTA%	INS	2P%	3P%	FT%	TS%	Reb%	Ast%	TO%	BLK%	STL%	PF%	oRTG	dRTG	Win%	WARP
07-08	WAS	22.9	75	15.4	.251	.160	.087	.927	.450	.400	.815	.527	.059	.025	.150	.005	.014	.053	102.6	107.4	.344	-1.7
08-09	WAS	23.9	82	22.4	.232	.176	.091	.915	.473	.341	.850	.530	.049	.024	.099	.009	.011	.035	104.2	108.5	.365	-2.0
09-10	WAS	24.9	74	19.2	.216	.253	.085	.832	.423	.406	.800	.519	.042	.015	.083	.004	.010	.047	103.7	108.4	.351	-1.9
10-11p	WAS	25.9	75	7.3	.210	.203	.089	.886	.453	.398	.823	.531	.050	.022	.098	.007	.012	.045	103.0	107.4	.356	-0.7

Most similar to: Johnny Newman (98.3), Keith Herron, Kareem Rush, Sasha Pavlovic   IMP: 54% BRK: 15% COP: 7%

Nick Young's development has floundered in his three NBA seasons. He can score, but not efficiently, and shows little inclination for helping boost the level of his teammates. Young is a good athlete and hits a good percentage from the three-point line, so if he would commit to a "3/D" role, he could still help his team. Unfortunately, Young seems hung up on big superficial numbers. He'll be fourth in the Wizards' backcourt rotation for the upcoming season, but with Kirk Hinrich's durability and ability to play both positions, Young will have a smaller role.

C — Paul Davis
Hght: 6'11" Wght: 270 Exp: 4 From: Michigan State Salary: --
2011-12 status: free agent

SKILL RATINGS: TOT -3, OFF -1, DEF +1, REB -3, PAS 0, HND +2, SHT -4, ATH +3

Year	Team	Age	G	MPG	Usg	3PA%	FTA%	INS	2P%	3P%	FT%	TS%	Reb%	Ast%	TO%	BLK%	STL%	PF%	oRTG	dRTG	Win%	WARP
07-08	LAC	23.8	22	9.0	.185	.000	.056	1.056	.369	.000	.600	.389	.138	.024	.115	.023	.014	.077	101.5	106.4	.339	-0.3
08-09	LAC	24.8	27	11.9	.181	.008	.119	1.111	.412	.000	.794	.474	.122	.017	.103	.007	.016	.063	103.0	107.6	.353	-0.4
09-10	WAS	25.8	2	4.0	.278	.000	.180	1.180	.500	-	.500	.512	.000	.171	.000	.095	.000	.000	118.0	103.0	.871	0.1
10-11p	AVG	26.8	76	4.0	.170	.026	.117	1.091	.430	.006	.787	.484	.121	.019	.105	.008	.014	.061	102.6	106.7	.366	-0.3

Most similar to: Michael Doleac (97.3), Mark Bryant, Jayson Williams, Jack Haley   IMP: 65% BRK: 24% COP: 8%

Paul Davis was dropped by the Wizards early last season and hasn't found another NBA gig. There really isn't anything he can provide a team at this point other than giving a few fouls here and there. He's headed to Spain to play this season for Cajasol Sevilla.

PG — Mike James
Hght: 6'2" Wght: 188 Exp: 9 From: Duquesne Salary: --
2011-12 status: free agent

SKILL RATINGS: TOT -4, OFF -1, DEF -1, REB -1, PAS -3, HND -2, SHT -5, ATH -4

Year	Team	Age	G	MPG	Usg	3PA%	FTA%	INS	2P%	3P%	FT%	TS%	Reb%	Ast%	TO%	BLK%	STL%	PF%	oRTG	dRTG	Win%	WARP
07-08	NOH	32.8	54	13.3	.226	.279	.061	.782	.361	.320	.813	.436	.057	.039	.103	.002	.014	.037	102.1	107.0	.341	-1.1
08-09	WAS	33.8	61	27.0	.179	.286	.056	.770	.388	.375	.829	.483	.048	.056	.146	.003	.014	.030	104.4	108.2	.378	-1.3
09-10	WAS	34.8	4	11.5	.283	.210	.123	.913	.286	.333	.500	.383	.038	.050	.175	.000	.034	.030	98.7	105.5	.283	-0.1
10-11p	AVG	35.8	75	11.5	.179	.330	.051	.721	.359	.319	.777	.434	.049	.047	.141	.004	.012	.035	102.2	107.4	.333	-1.5

Most similar to: Kendall Gill (94.5), Vernon Maxwell, Bobby Jackson, David Wesley   IMP: 36% BRK: 4% COP: 28%

It's been a long run for Mike James, but it might be over as camps open with him still out of work. James got only four games in last year, which sort of looks like a final-season line.

WASHINGTON WIZARDS

C	Fabricio Oberto	Hght: 6'10" Exp: 5 Salary: --								SKILL RATINGS							
--		Wght: 245 From: Las Varillas, Argentina								TOT	OFF	DEF	REB	PAS	HND	SHT	ATH
		2011-12 status: free agent								-5	-1	0	-4	+4	+5	+5	-5

Year	Team	Age	G	MPG	Usg	3PA%	FTA%	INS	2P%	3P%	FT%	TS%	Reb%	Ast%	TO%	BLK%	STL%	PF%	oRTG	dRTG	Win%	WARP
07-08	SAS	33.1	82	20.1	.109	.003	.072	1.069	.610	.000	.607	.615	.154	.028	.134	.009	.011	.060	104.8	105.9	.462	1.5
08-09	SAS	34.1	54	12.5	.113	.006	.098	1.091	.592	.000	.571	.595	.125	.042	.241	.012	.006	.068	104.9	108.6	.381	-0.5
09-10	WAS	35.1	57	11.4	.070	.000	.075	1.075	.625	-	.765	.654	.094	.036	.362	.011	.009	.085	101.3	108.6	.274	-1.9
10-11p	AVG	36.1	76	11.4	.077	.007	.074	1.067	.601	.000	.663	.611	.107	.034	.287	.011	.008	.077	102.0	108.3	.302	-2.1

Most similar to: Aaron Williams (90.0), Bo Outlaw, Kurt Rambis, Ervin Johnson   IMP: -   BRK: -   COP: -

It's been a steep fall for Fabricio Oberto, who was a rotation player and part-time starter for a championship team just a few years ago. Oberto was out of work when camps opened, but it was expected that he'd land somewhere. As usual, he shot a high percentage close to the rim last season, but he has no ability to get shots for himself. Ninety-four percent of Oberto's made field goals were assisted last season, which is a testament to his lack of offensive skill and his decline on the offensive glass. Oberto's athletic indicators are in the toilet, and if he can't be counted up to at least provide solid defense, then his passing skills really don't mean that much. Oberto will probably get a few games in with somebody this season but, at 35, the end is nigh.

PF	James Singleton	Hght: 6'8" Exp: 4 Salary: --								SKILL RATINGS							
--		Wght: 230 From: Murray State								TOT	OFF	DEF	REB	PAS	HND	SHT	ATH
		2011-12 status: free agent								0	0	+3	+3	-3	-3	-3	+1

Year	Team	Age	G	MPG	Usg	3PA%	FTA%	INS	2P%	3P%	FT%	TS%	Reb%	Ast%	TO%	BLK%	STL%	PF%	oRTG	dRTG	Win%	WARP
08-09	DAL	27.8	62	14.3	.152	.137	.118	.981	.575	.325	.859	.615	.162	.009	.124	.023	.015	.057	106.8	105.5	.543	2.3
09-10	WAS	28.8	57	17.1	.155	.112	.083	.971	.415	.189	.855	.452	.163	.015	.148	.033	.015	.053	102.9	104.4	.448	0.6
10-11p	AVG	29.8	76	17.1	.155	.088	.096	1.008	.477	.167	.832	.508	.153	.013	.140	.028	.015	.054	103.3	104.8	.451	1.0

Most similar to: Scott Williams (97.5), Edgar Jones, James Bailey, Aaron Williams   IMP: 49%   BRK: 3%   COP: 7%

James Singleton is an undersized, physical combo forward who hasn't been able to get over the hump and stick in a team's rotation. He's tried to improve his midrange game to no avail, but is a solid rebounder and defender against second-unit types. Singleton signed to play this season in China.

Fantasy 2010-11

'The Decision" has implications that have rippled throughout this book and the fantasy section is no exception. Playing together will influence the statistics of Chris Bosh, LeBron James and Dwyane Wade. All three were among SCHOENE's top 10 fantasy players entering last season, with James and Wade both in the top five. Since there are only so many points to go around, all three players figure to be less valuable in 2010-11. This is offset by improved efficiency, and James and Wade may benefit from something SCHOENE is unable to project--increased assist numbers. In fact, it is Bosh who figures to take the biggest hit because he will sacrifice not only points but also rebounds now that he is playing alongside several good rebounders instead of Andrea Bargnani.

SCHOENE offers the most comprehensive fantasy projections available. Like the core SCHOENE projections, they consider to some extent player interaction and roles in addition to aging patterns. They also take into account team pace and feature full projected stat lines. While the player stat boxes solely offer advanced statistics, here you can find the traditional per-game numbers that come into play in fantasy sports.

Before getting down to the rankings, let's look at SCHOENE's consensus top 10 picks, 10 players SCHOENE likes and 10 players who might be overrated. The top 10 is based on a 12-team league, using the average of eight-category scoring (no turnovers) and nine-category scoring (with turnovers). The projections that follow are based on a nine-category league.

TOP 10 PICKS

1. Chris Paul, New Orleans
(ESPN rank: 3; Yahoo! average draft position: 2)

Now that he's healthy, Chris Paul's stat line should look more like his 2007-08 and 2008-09 efforts than last year's performance. The arthroscopic knee surgery that cost Paul an extended period last spring is a minor concern, but hardly a red flag. With an improved wing duo of Trevor Ariza and Marcus Thornton alongside him, Paul should lead the league in assists while scoring 20-plus points per game.

2. Kevin Durant, Oklahoma City
(ESPN rank: 1; Yahoo! average draft position: 1)

Last fall, I took Paul with the top overall pick in my fantasy league. If I landed in the same spot this time around, I'd defy SCHOENE and go with Durant. A poor rookie season still limits Durant's projection. Last year's performance is more indicative of what we can expect in 2010-11. Drafting Durant practically guarantees first place in free throw percentage; he's projected to shoot nearly 90 percent from the line while attempting almost nine foul shots a game.

3. LeBron James, Miami
(ESPN rank: 4; Yahoo! average draft position: 3)

Even if his scoring average takes a hit--and SCHOENE sees him dipping to fourth in the league, closer to Monta Ellis than Durant--James will remain a hugely valuable fantasy contributor because of his breadth of skills. James is above average in every category save free throw percentage and turnovers. He stands an excellent chance of beating the projection of 7.8 assists per game.

4. Dirk Nowitzki, Dallas
(ESPN rank: 5; Yahoo! average draft position: 4)

While Nowitzki might not belong among the league's elite talents any longer, he remains a standout fantasy producer. Nowitzki's accurate free throw shooting and balanced stat line make him a top pick. In a 12-team, nine-category league, he shoots ahead of James to third thanks to his turnover-free play.

5. Stephen Curry, Golden State
(ESPN rank: 11; Yahoo! average draft position: 7)

SCHOENE pegs the Warriors' sophomore guard for a breakout campaign. As a result, even his current lofty draft status may slightly underrate Curry's potential. Count on efficient shooting and a decent assist total. If Curry develops into a go-to scorer as well, he'll be the most valuable guard in fantasy this side of Paul.

6. Kobe Bryant, L.A. Lakers
(ESPN rank: 6; Yahoo! average draft position: 6)

Bryant is projected to rank a close second to Durant in the league in scoring. However, he doesn't offer the well-rounded contributions needed to be one of the league's best fantasy players. Bryant is a below-average rebounder and is only average for a guard when it comes to racking up steals.

7. Danny Granger, Indiana
(ESPN rank: 7; Yahoo! average draft position: 8)

Granger has emerged as the best of the versatile forwards, making him a legitimate fantasy star. One factor that could work in his favor in fantasy terms is the unsettled power forward position in Indiana. If Granger spends more time at the four, he'll likely pile up more rebounds and might get more three-point opportunities against slower defenders.

8. Dwyane Wade, Miami
(ESPN rank: 12; Yahoo! average draft position: 5)

There is a disconnect between where ESPN's fantasy experts rank Wade and where he has been selected by users in early Yahoo! leagues. SCHOENE about splits the difference. Wade's scoring average will take a hit, but he'll get his points slightly more efficiently while handing out assists. He's still a sure-fire first-round pick.

9. David Lee, Golden State
(ESPN rank: 22; Yahoo! average draft position: 13)

Lee won a lot of fantasy leagues last year with his All-Star campaign. His versatility makes him useful in fantasy terms. Lee is one of the NBA's best big men when it comes to assists. He's perennially outstanding on the glass and added high scoring to his arsenal last season without sacrificing much in terms of efficiency. Believe it or not, going to the Warriors means Lee will likely play at a faster pace than he did last season under Mike D'Antoni.

10. Brook Lopez, New Jersey
(ESPN rank: 19; Yahoo! average draft position: 18)

Though not an especially sexy fantasy pick, Lopez's steady development should make him the league's most valuable center under most fantasy scoring systems. Lopez will contribute high-percentage shooting, rebounding and blocks without the turnovers and poor foul shooting that plague many other top centers.

UNDER THE RADAR

Nicolas Batum, Portland
(SCHOENE rank: 62.5; ESPN rank: 118; Yahoo! average draft position: 114)

The Blazers' third-year forward owns one of this year's most optimistic projections, thanks in part to the fact that last year was a relatively small sample--Batum shot the ball exceedingly well after returning from shoulder surgery that cost him the first half of the schedule. Even if his percentages go down, Batum is improving rapidly and enters the season established as Portland's starting small forward.

Andrew Bynum, L.A. Lakers
(SCHOENE rank: 27; ESPN rank: 90; Yahoo! average draft position: 65)

Bynum is outstanding in two categories thanks to his high-percentage shooting and his regular blocked shots. His health is a bit of a risk, especially after news broke that he will miss the start of the regular season following summer arthroscopic surgery on his right knee. Still, Bynum is worth the chance around the fourth or fifth round.

Danilo Gallinari, New York
(SCHOENE rank: 24; ESPN rank: 55; Yahoo! average draft position: 52)

The influx of talent in the Big Apple should help Il Gallo as he develops into a quality wing producer. Gallinari's scoring average might not jump because of the other options, but they'll help out his shooting percentage and make him more efficient.

Kevin Garnett, Boston
(SCHOENE rank: 26; ESPN rank: 72; Yahoo! average draft position: 57)

Rumors of Garnett's demise are greatly exaggerated. Playing at less than 100 percent most of last season, he still contributed in multiple categories. Garnett's high shooting percentage helps make up for declining per-game averages.

Amir Johnson, Toronto
(SCHOENE rank: 67; ESPN rank: NR; Yahoo! average draft position: NR)

Johnson goes to training camp with a chance, and possibly even the inside track, to claim Bosh's old spot in the Raptors' starting lineup. If he can play consistently and stay on the floor--the big key, given his propensity for picking up fouls—Johnson will provide blocked shots and high-percentage shooting, a nice pickup in the late rounds.

Carl Landry, Sacramento

(SCHOENE rank: 56.5; ESPN rank: 87; Yahoo! average draft position: 95)

Hey, remember when Landry was a co-favorite for the Sixth Man Award? Landry was forgotten after he was dealt to the Kings at the trade deadline despite averaging 18.0 points on 52.0 percent shooting, numbers that would look good in the fifth or sixth rounds.

Shawn Marion, Dallas

(SCHOENE rank: 81.5; ESPN rank: NR; Yahoo! average draft position: 120)

Granted, we didn't exactly spew optimism about Marion in his player comment. There's a difference between real value and fantasy value, however, and Marion's poor outside shooting matters less online. He continues to provide rebounds, steals and blocks in good measure.

Greg Oden, Portland

(SCHOENE rank: 60.5; ESPN rank: 150; Yahoo! average draft position: 91)

The term "red light" health risk was practically invented to describe Oden, who has played just 82 games total through three seasons. Oden will not be back from his fractured patella for the start of the season. If you can wait, he'll rack up rebounds and blocks with a high percentage when he's in the lineup.

Tiago Splitter, San Antonio

(SCHOENE rank: 142; ESPN rank: NR; Yahoo! average draft position: NR)

Splitter is more valuable on the court than in fantasy, but he's worth a flier in the late rounds of a deep draft. Even with a conservative projection that he will play 28 minutes a night, Splitter comes out worthy of a draft pick. He's got a chance to outperform expectations if he makes the adjustment to the NBA quickly.

Reggie Williams, Golden State

(SCHOENE rank: 72; ESPN rank: NR; Yahoo! average draft position: NR)

Williams is emphatically not a pick based on potential. We've already seen him average 15.2 points, 4.6 rebounds and 2.8 assists over a two-month stretch. All Williams needs is the playing time. If for some reason Dorell Wright beats him out for the small forward job with the Warriors, Wright becomes a sleeper in his own right.

OVERRATED

Samuel Dalembert

(SCHOENE rank: 145.5; ESPN rank: 98; Yahoo! average draft position: 88)

Evaluating Dalembert's fantasy prospects really means evaluating DeMarcus Cousins, as the two centers will be competing for playing time in the Sacramento frontcourt. We like Cousins to be one of the leading contenders for Rookie of the Year, which translates into Dalembert watching from the bench instead of blocking shots.

Blake Griffin

(SCHOENE rank: 145.5; ESPN rank: 83; Yahoo! average draft position: 72)

The biggest thing working against the 2009 No. 1 overall pick is his terrible free throw shooting. Griffin is projected to make just 57.6 percent from the charity stripe. Since he draws fouls prolifically, Griffin will have plenty of chances to drag down a fantasy team's free throw percentage.

Dwight Howard

(SCHOENE rank: 50.5; ESPN rank: 9; Yahoo! average draft position: 10)

Howard has replaced Shaquille O'Neal as the most divisive fantasy player. Teams willing to punt the free throw category can get value out of Howard, especially in eight-category leagues where his frequent turnovers are not an issue. Everyone else ought to stay away. First-round picks should not have two glaring weaknesses.

Antawn Jamison

(SCHOENE rank: 106; ESPN rank: 38; Yahoo! average draft position: 53)

Most fantasy players seem to view Jamison as the All-Star we saw in Washington who might be Cleveland's best scorer next season. However, J.J. Hickson's emergence could cut into Jamison's playing time, and he simply isn't the player he once was.

Steve Nash

(SCHOENE rank: 67.5; ESPN rank: 14; Yahoo! average draft position: 19)

Turnovers are Nash's Achilles' heel, at least in fantasy terms. In eight-category leagues, he's only a slight reach in the second round. In nine-category leagues, it's best to stay away. Nash also generates few steals for a point guard.

Tony Parker

(SCHOENE rank: 170; ESPN rank: 75; Yahoo! average draft position: 90)

SCHOENE usually tends to favor players trying to come back from down seasons, but Parker is the exception that proves the rule in large part because he wasn't especially good as a fantasy player before his disappointing 2009-10 campaign. Parker is a poor rebounder and free throw shooter who rarely contributes steals.

Luis Scola

(SCHOENE rank: 125.5; ESPN rank: 73; Yahoo! average draft position: 77)

Yes, Scola put up some impressive numbers last season, but a full year of Kevin Martin coupled with Yao Ming's return to the lineup means he will have fewer opportunities on offense this year. Expect Scola to perform more like he did in 2007-08 and 2008-09, making him a late-round fantasy option.

John Wall

(SCHOENE rank: 191.5; ESPN rank: 48; Yahoo! average draft position: 50)

As exciting as Wall is as a prospect, he's a year or two away from playing winning basketball. That translates to fantasy, where Wall's dismal turnover rate and low shooting percentage doom his chances of contributing. He's better than his SCHOENE ranking, especially in eight-category leagues, but will be overdrafted.

Russell Westbrook

(SCHOENE rank: 86.5; ESPN rank: 26; Yahoo! average draft position: 36)

Westbrook is another player whose value fluctuates dramatically depending on whether turnovers are included in league settings. He ranks 61 spots higher in eight-category leagues than nine-category ones. Besides turnovers, Westbrook's low shooting percentage is another reason to avoid drafting him.

Terrence Williams

(SCHOENE rank: 216; ESPN rank: 94; Yahoo! average draft position: 127)

Because he is versatile and finished 2009-10 on a roll, Williams has become a fantasy sleeper. SCHOENE sharply disagrees. In part, Williams may have a tough time finding big minutes in a crowded New Jersey wing rotation. Beyond that, Williams remains a liability in terms of field-goal percentage and turnovers despite an optimistic projection.

Kevin Pelton

Fantasy Rankings

Player	Team	PS	V12	MPG	PPG	RPG	APG	SPG	BPG	TOPG	3MPG	FG%	FT%	Imp	Break	Cop
Chris Paul	noh	PG	10.7	38	21.4	4.4	11.6	2.5	0.1	2.5	1.5	0.500	0.879	0.53	0.06	0.00
Kevin Durant	okc	SG,SF	9.2	39	27.3	6.4	3.1	1.4	0.8	3.0	1.3	0.476	0.888	0.50	0.08	0.04
Dirk Nowitzki	dal	PF	8.2	37	24.0	7.1	2.6	0.8	0.9	1.8	1.0	0.479	0.891	0.35	0.00	0.07
LeBron James	mia	SF	7.6	38	24.8	6.4	7.8	1.6	1.1	2.8	1.7	0.478	0.751	0.43	0.00	0.09
Danny Granger	ind	SG,SF,PF	6.9	37	22.9	5.5	2.8	1.4	1.1	2.4	2.6	0.436	0.855	0.42	0.00	0.04
Stephen Curry	gsw	PG,SG	6.7	36	20.3	4.4	6.3	2.1	0.2	3.1	2.4	0.468	0.887	0.75	0.04	0.04
Kobe Bryant	lal	SG	6.5	39	27.0	4.9	4.8	1.5	0.4	2.9	1.5	0.467	0.838	0.26	0.00	0.00
David Lee	gsw	PF,C	6.1	36	18.7	10.6	3.0	1.1	0.4	2.1	0.0	0.547	0.797	0.37	0.02	0.00
Chris Bosh	mia	PF,C	6.0	36	20.4	8.7	2.4	0.7	0.9	1.9	0.2	0.519	0.822	0.43	0.00	0.06
Dwyane Wade	mia	PG,SG	5.7	36	23.2	4.4	6.8	1.8	1.0	3.0	1.0	0.478	0.767	0.50	0.00	0.08
Brook Lopez	njn	PF,C	5.5	37	18.9	8.0	2.2	0.7	1.8	2.5	0.0	0.521	0.807	0.62	0.00	0.02
Pau Gasol	lal	PF,C	5.3	37	17.5	9.3	3.3	0.6	1.4	2.0	0.0	0.530	0.783	0.24	0.00	0.10
Amare Stoudemire	nyk	PF,C	5.2	35	21.8	7.9	1.5	0.7	1.1	2.5	0.1	0.553	0.796	0.33	0.00	0.04
Gerald Wallace	cha	SF,PF	5.2	40	18.5	8.2	2.7	1.7	1.0	2.5	1.0	0.475	0.773	0.37	0.02	0.03
Al Jefferson	uta	PF,C	4.8	34	19.6	9.6	1.6	0.9	1.4	1.8	0.0	0.504	0.718	0.45	0.00	0.03
Danilo Gallinari	nyk	SF	4.8	34	15.2	4.9	1.7	1.0	0.6	1.3	2.4	0.435	0.896	0.56	0.04	0.00
Al Horford	atl	PF,C	4.8	35	13.1	9.7	2.4	0.9	1.1	1.6	0.0	0.541	0.770	0.47	0.03	0.02
Rudy Gay	mem	SF,PF	4.7	38	20.4	5.3	2.0	1.5	0.8	2.2	1.6	0.466	0.789	0.52	0.06	0.05
Kevin Garnett	bos	PF	4.6	30	13.5	7.3	2.7	1.1	0.9	1.4	0.0	0.521	0.832	0.19	0.00	0.04
Chauncey Billups	den	PG	4.5	34	16.7	2.8	5.9	1.3	0.2	2.2	1.8	0.428	0.905	0.46	0.00	0.00
Andrea Bargnani	tor	PF,C	4.3	36	19.1	6.2	1.5	0.4	1.4	1.8	2.6	0.434	0.819	0.53	0.11	0.11
David West	noh	PF	4.3	36	17.8	7.4	2.4	0.9	0.8	1.9	0.1	0.495	0.843	0.39	0.05	0.05
Carmelo Anthony	den	SF	4.3	38	25.3	6.5	3.5	1.3	0.4	3.0	1.2	0.459	0.811	0.43	0.00	0.09
Andrew Bynum	lal	C	4.2	30	15.4	8.0	1.5	0.5	1.7	1.8	0.0	0.579	0.728	0.63	0.00	0.03
Deron Williams	uta	PG	4.0	37	18.9	3.5	10.4	1.2	0.3	3.3	1.3	0.473	0.832	0.45	0.00	0.10
LaMarcus Aldridge	por	PF,C	3.9	37	18.3	7.2	2.0	1.0	0.8	1.4	0.1	0.490	0.779	0.47	0.04	0.04
Marc Gasol	mem	C	3.8	36	14.3	8.9	2.3	1.1	1.5	2.0	0.0	0.566	0.698	0.44	0.05	0.00
Tyreke Evans	sac	PG,SG	3.8	37	22.6	5.0	6.3	1.7	0.4	3.1	0.6	0.470	0.779	0.67	0.03	0.03
Manu Ginobili	sas	SG	3.7	28	14.1	3.8	4.3	1.4	0.4	1.9	1.5	0.454	0.865	0.26	0.00	0.09
Monta Ellis	gsw	PG,SG	3.7	40	24.3	4.0	4.7	2.0	0.4	3.2	0.9	0.464	0.794	0.60	0.03	0.06
Carlos Boozer	chi	PF,C	3.5	34	18.8	10.0	2.8	1.2	0.4	2.5	0.0	0.531	0.731	0.44	0.04	0.04
Tim Duncan	sas	PF,C	3.4	31	15.5	9.0	2.9	0.6	1.4	1.7	0.0	0.509	0.715	0.14	0.00	0.00
Rajon Rondo	bos	PG	3.3	37	13.8	4.6	9.3	2.3	0.2	2.7	0.3	0.518	0.647	0.61	0.00	0.00
Marcus Thornton	noh	PG,SG	3.2	32	18.1	3.5	2.1	1.1	0.2	1.2	2.2	0.455	0.809	0.63	0.02	0.06
Paul Pierce	bos	SG,SF	3.2	34	16.5	4.4	3.2	1.1	0.4	2.2	1.9	0.459	0.837	0.22	0.00	0.12
Josh Smith	atl	SF,PF	3.2	35	15.4	8.0	3.7	1.6	2.1	2.4	0.1	0.485	0.630	0.37	0.00	0.02
Marcus Camby	por	PF,C	3.2	28	6.1	9.0	2.0	0.9	1.9	1.1	0.0	0.467	0.664	-	-	-
Nenê Hilario	den	PF,C	3.1	34	12.8	8.1	2.3	1.3	1.1	1.8	0.0	0.565	0.678	0.40	0.00	0.04
Jason Richardson	pho	SG,SF	3.0	32	17.4	5.1	2.0	1.0	0.4	1.5	2.4	0.445	0.754	0.33	0.05	0.06
Joe Johnson	atl	PG,SG	3.0	38	19.3	4.2	5.0	1.1	0.1	2.0	2.1	0.436	0.822	0.30	0.05	0.05

FANTASY RANKINGS

Player	Team	PS	V12	MPG	PPG	RPG	APG	SPG	BPG	TOPG	3MPG	FG%	FT%	Imp	Break	Cop
Brandon Roy	por	PG,SG	3.0	36	20.5	4.1	5.1	1.0	0.2	1.9	1.4	0.457	0.785	0.43	0.02	0.09
Nicolas Batum	por	SG,SF	2.8	28	11.0	4.1	1.6	0.9	0.8	0.9	1.3	0.508	0.850	0.67	0.07	0.04
Zach Randolph	mem	PF,C	2.8	37	18.9	10.4	2.1	1.0	0.4	2.3	0.3	0.477	0.757	0.32	0.06	0.10
Kevin Martin	hou	SG	2.8	35	21.2	3.4	2.4	1.0	0.1	2.3	1.8	0.419	0.869	0.38	0.00	0.02
O.J. Mayo	mem	SG	2.8	36	17.7	3.7	3.2	1.2	0.2	2.2	2.0	0.463	0.845	0.70	0.09	0.02
Jeff Green	okc	SF,PF	2.7	36	15.5	5.5	1.9	1.2	0.7	1.9	1.7	0.450	0.777	0.64	0.07	0.02
Andrew Bogut	mil	C	2.7	32	13.9	9.3	2.1	0.6	1.7	2.0	0.0	0.546	0.614	0.50	0.02	0.02
Carl Landry	sac	SF,PF	2.7	32	15.9	6.6	0.9	0.7	0.6	1.6	0.0	0.554	0.778	0.32	0.01	0.08
Andre Iguodala	phi	SG,SF	2.7	37	15.2	5.1	4.7	1.6	0.5	2.1	1.2	0.451	0.746	0.44	0.00	0.13
Paul Millsap	uta	SF,PF	2.6	30	13.0	7.8	1.7	1.0	1.1	1.6	0.0	0.527	0.701	0.37	0.02	0.03
Anthony Randolph	nyk	PF	2.5	25	12.4	6.8	1.5	1.0	1.5	1.6	0.0	0.459	0.801	0.63	0.04	0.04
Amir Johnson	tor	SF,PF	2.5	25	8.3	6.9	0.9	0.8	1.6	1.2	0.0	0.595	0.669	0.45	0.07	0.03
Ray Allen	bos	SG	2.5	34	14.0	3.2	2.5	0.8	0.3	1.4	1.9	0.461	0.911	0.45	0.06	0.15
Andray Blatche	was	PF,C	2.5	32	13.8	7.4	2.4	1.2	1.3	2.2	0.1	0.487	0.727	0.46	0.08	0.10
Baron Davis	lac	PG	2.5	34	14.9	3.4	7.4	1.8	0.6	2.5	1.6	0.398	0.785	0.46	0.03	0.03
Maurice Williams	cle	PG	2.4	34	17.7	2.9	4.9	0.9	0.2	2.7	2.5	0.443	0.904	0.47	0.02	0.07
Kevin Love	min	PF,C	2.4	30	14.6	11.0	2.3	0.7	0.5	2.0	0.3	0.443	0.809	0.57	0.09	0.06
Andrei Kirilenko	uta	SF,PF	2.4	29	11.4	4.5	2.9	1.4	1.3	1.6	0.5	0.472	0.749	0.28	0.04	0.10
Greg Oden	por	C	2.4	24	11.8	7.5	1.0	0.5	1.8	1.9	0.0	0.598	0.728	0.63	0.00	0.00
Tyrus Thomas	cha	SF,PF	2.4	28	12.2	6.9	1.4	1.4	1.7	1.9	0.0	0.469	0.739	0.55	0.11	0.05
Jason Kidd	dal	PG	2.3	32	7.3	4.9	7.9	1.7	0.4	2.1	1.4	0.389	0.803	-	-	-
Rashard Lewis	orl	SF,PF	2.3	33	13.9	4.5	1.8	1.1	0.5	1.5	2.3	0.429	0.825	0.37	0.05	0.08
Dorell Wright	gsw	SG,SF	2.2	25	9.9	4.1	1.7	1.0	0.8	1.0	1.0	0.472	0.893	0.59	0.09	0.05
Troy Murphy	njn	PF,C	2.2	30	11.3	7.7	1.9	0.8	0.4	1.2	1.5	0.444	0.794	0.32	0.02	0.15
John Salmons	mil	SG,SF	2.2	37	15.0	3.7	2.9	1.2	0.4	1.8	1.4	0.452	0.828	0.27	0.07	0.07
Rodrigue Beaubois	dal	PG,SG	2.2	22	13.7	2.4	2.5	1.0	0.5	1.6	1.5	0.519	0.822	0.76	0.05	0.05
Chris Kaman	lac	C	2.1	34	15.3	9.1	1.8	0.6	1.6	2.8	0.0	0.509	0.734	0.51	0.05	0.04
Josh Childress	pho	SG, SF	2.1	28	11.8	4.6	1.5	0.8	0.5	1.3	0.4	0.551	0.822	0.31	0.03	0.08
Shawn Marion	dal	SF,PF	2.0	30	10.7	6.4	1.6	1.1	0.8	1.2	0.2	0.486	0.762	0.37	0.02	0.08
Joakim Noah	chi	PF,C	2.0	30	10.2	8.7	2.0	0.7	1.4	1.7	0.0	0.506	0.728	0.52	0.04	0.02
Luol Deng	chi	SG,SF	2.0	35	16.5	5.9	2.0	1.0	0.6	1.7	0.4	0.465	0.795	0.53	0.05	0.07
Reggie Williams	gsw	SG, SF	2.0	25	12.8	3.2	2.4	0.8	0.2	1.0	1.4	0.483	0.853	0.59	0.04	0.06
Jason Terry	dal	PG,SG	2.0	32	14.7	1.9	3.4	1.2	0.2	1.3	1.7	0.438	0.852	0.25	0.00	0.15
Dwight Howard	orl	C	1.9	35	19.8	12.3	1.7	0.9	2.6	3.2	0.0	0.596	0.605	0.45	0.00	0.00
Yao Ming	hou	C	1.7	24	14.1	6.5	1.2	0.3	1.3	2.3	0.0	0.528	0.855	0.31	0.00	0.07
Roy Hibbert	ind	C	1.7	28	13.1	6.5	2.1	0.5	1.8	1.8	0.0	0.495	0.708	0.50	0.06	0.13
Wilson Chandler	nyk	SG,SF	1.7	32	13.9	5.1	2.0	0.8	0.8	1.5	1.2	0.457	0.784	0.59	0.14	0.00
Michael Beasley	min	SF,PF	1.7	26	15.6	5.5	1.4	0.9	0.6	1.6	0.5	0.466	0.820	0.66	0.11	0.00
Javale McGee	was	PF,C	1.6	25	10.0	6.3	0.5	0.6	2.1	1.2	0.0	0.526	0.647	0.57	0.06	0.03
Marvin Williams	atl	SF,PF	1.6	30	11.4	4.9	1.3	0.9	0.5	1.0	0.8	0.447	0.840	0.59	0.12	0.02
Caron Butler	dal	SG,SF	1.6	32	13.9	5.0	2.5	1.4	0.3	1.9	0.6	0.439	0.849	0.26	0.05	0.11
Aaron Brooks	hou	PG	1.5	34	18.1	2.6	4.5	0.8	0.2	2.4	2.4	0.431	0.854	0.63	0.04	0.02
Channing Frye	pho	PF,C	1.5	28	11.3	6.1	1.3	0.7	0.7	1.1	1.4	0.432	0.772	0.39	0.05	0.11
Jamario Moon	cle	SF	1.5	28	8.0	5.0	1.2	1.0	0.8	0.7	1.0	0.424	0.810	0.27	0.00	0.15
Raymond Felton	nyk	PG,SG	1.5	33	12.9	3.4	5.8	1.5	0.3	2.1	1.1	0.440	0.794	0.50	0.04	0.04
Charlie Villanueva	det	SF,PF	1.5	25	12.5	5.7	1.1	0.6	0.7	1.2	1.3	0.444	0.818	0.56	0.00	0.06
Trevor Ariza	noh	SF	1.4	32	11.6	4.9	2.8	1.7	0.4	1.5	1.3	0.428	0.679	0.46	0.05	0.11
Darren Collison	ind	PG,SG	1.4	30	14.9	3.0	6.6	1.3	0.1	2.9	0.8	0.480	0.868	0.54	0.03	0.05

FANTASY RANKINGS

Player	Team	PS	V12	MPG	PPG	RPG	APG	SPG	BPG	TOPG	3MPG	FG%	FT%	Imp	Break	Cop
Serge Ibaka	okc	C	1.3	24	8.5	6.8	0.2	0.6	1.6	1.2	0.0	0.547	0.661	0.50	0.00	0.07
Mehmet Okur	uta	PF,C	1.3	25	11.3	5.7	1.3	0.5	0.8	1.3	1.1	0.457	0.814	0.43	0.08	0.04
Eric Gordon	lac	SG	1.2	36	17.7	2.5	3.4	1.2	0.4	2.4	1.7	0.458	0.784	0.57	0.04	0.04
Brandon Jennings	mil	PG	1.2	34	16.4	3.3	6.0	1.5	0.2	2.4	2.0	0.382	0.826	-	-	-
Louis Williams	phi	PG,SG	1.2	28	12.8	2.4	3.7	1.2	0.2	1.5	1.1	0.454	0.817	0.65	0.09	0.00
Derrick Rose	chi	PG	1.1	37	20.7	3.3	6.6	0.8	0.3	2.8	0.3	0.487	0.779	0.64	0.06	0.03
Lamar Odom	lal	SF,PF	1.1	30	9.8	8.1	2.9	0.9	0.8	1.6	0.5	0.472	0.665	0.29	0.00	0.10
Anthony Morrow	njn	SG,SF	1.1	28	11.4	2.9	1.4	0.7	0.2	0.9	1.7	0.464	0.884	0.42	0.05	0.05
Antawn Jamison	cle	SF,PF	1.1	32	17.3	6.9	1.2	1.0	0.3	1.3	1.2	0.444	0.701	0.23	0.00	0.03
Vince Carter	orl	SG,SF	1.1	30	15.1	3.7	3.4	0.8	0.3	1.5	1.4	0.430	0.820	0.37	0.02	0.04
James Harden	okc	PG,SG	1.1	24	10.9	3.1	2.0	1.2	0.3	1.3	1.5	0.432	0.817	0.69	0.11	0.06
Stephen Jackson	cha	SG,SF	1.0	39	18.3	4.5	4.2	1.5	0.5	3.1	1.8	0.411	0.795	0.36	0.02	0.13
Steve Nash	pho	PG	1.0	32	14.4	3.1	9.9	0.6	0.1	3.5	1.5	0.477	0.918	-	-	-
Brandan Wright	gsw	SF,PF	1.0	22	10.3	4.8	0.8	0.5	1.1	0.8	0.0	0.535	0.739	0.48	0.05	0.05
Jamal Crawford	atl	PG,SG	0.9	32	15.7	2.4	3.3	0.8	0.2	1.7	1.7	0.429	0.856	0.32	0.08	0.05
Jameer Nelson	orl	PG	0.9	30	13.5	2.9	5.5	0.9	0.0	2.2	1.7	0.461	0.833	0.39	0.04	0.05
Devin Harris	njn	PG	0.9	35	17.6	2.6	6.5	1.4	0.2	2.9	1.1	0.422	0.810	0.40	0.02	0.06
C.J. Miles	uta	SG,SF	0.9	28	12.6	3.1	2.1	1.1	0.3	1.3	1.8	0.446	0.779	0.53	0.07	0.09
Rodney Stuckey	det	PG,SG	0.9	34	15.1	3.8	5.0	1.4	0.2	2.1	0.4	0.422	0.837	0.72	0.04	0.04
Al Harrington	den	PF,C	0.9	29	14.6	5.3	1.3	0.9	0.3	1.5	1.8	0.431	0.760	0.28	0.02	0.19
Jose Calderon	tor	PG	0.8	27	10.6	2.3	6.7	0.8	0.1	1.7	1.1	0.478	0.853	0.36	0.02	0.09
Mike Conley	mem	PG	0.8	32	12.9	2.9	5.4	1.3	0.1	2.0	1.2	0.450	0.786	0.67	0.03	0.03
Thabo Sefolosha	okc	SG,SF	0.8	28	7.0	4.4	2.1	1.3	0.7	1.1	0.8	0.430	0.742	0.56	0.13	0.05
Martell Webster	min	SG,SF	0.8	25	11.0	3.5	1.0	0.7	0.5	0.9	2.2	0.408	0.814	0.57	0.09	0.04
Wesley Johnson	min	SF	0.8	30	9.3	5.7	1.9	1.1	1.1	1.6	0.7	0.423	0.753	-	-	-
Thaddeus Young	phi	SF,PF	0.8	30	12.1	4.4	1.3	1.2	0.2	1.3	0.7	0.504	0.724	0.63	0.05	0.03
George Hill	sas	PG	0.7	30	11.5	2.9	3.3	1.0	0.5	1.4	1.1	0.455	0.771	0.58	0.02	0.04
Shane Battier	hou	SF	0.7	30	7.0	4.1	2.0	0.8	0.9	0.9	1.4	0.400	0.767	0.43	0.06	0.03
Russell Westbrook	okc	PG	0.7	34	15.9	4.6	7.0	1.4	0.4	2.9	0.4	0.419	0.798	0.52	0.13	0.09
Chris Andersen	den	PF,C	0.6	20	4.9	5.7	0.4	0.6	1.8	0.7	0.0	0.570	0.694	0.41	0.00	0.06
Corey Maggette	mil	SF,PF	0.6	32	17.0	4.8	2.1	0.8	0.1	2.2	0.4	0.475	0.820	0.25	0.02	0.11
J.R. Smith	den	SG,SF	0.6	28	15.1	3.2	2.5	1.2	0.2	1.8	2.3	0.428	0.731	0.47	0.04	0.06
Travis Outlaw	njn	SF,PF	0.6	28	13.0	4.0	1.4	0.8	0.7	1.3	1.3	0.429	0.783	0.61	0.07	0.05
Beno Udrih	sac	PG	0.6	31	12.2	2.7	4.6	1.1	0.2	1.9	0.9	0.471	0.832	0.46	0.08	0.04
Anderson Varejao	cle	PF,C	0.5	28	8.8	7.3	1.2	0.9	0.8	1.2	0.0	0.526	0.632	0.42	0.07	0.04
Tayshaun Prince	det	SF,PF	0.5	32	11.6	5.0	2.8	0.6	0.5	1.0	0.6	0.465	0.732	0.37	0.06	0.08
Robin Lopez	pho	PF,C	0.5	25	10.5	6.0	0.3	0.4	1.5	1.3	0.0	0.552	0.698	0.53	0.08	0.05
Jermaine O'Neal	bos	C	0.4	28	11.6	5.8	1.6	0.4	1.5	1.8	0.0	0.489	0.736	0.38	0.04	0.11
Hedo Turkoglu	pho	SG,SF	0.4	32	13.6	5.2	4.2	0.8	0.4	2.2	2.0	0.403	0.781	0.39	0.05	0.05
Brendan Haywood	dal	C	0.4	27	8.2	7.1	0.6	0.3	1.6	1.2	0.0	0.539	0.658	0.40	0.00	0.15
DeMar DeRozan	tor	SG,SF,PF	0.4	28	12.4	3.7	1.0	0.9	0.3	1.1	0.1	0.499	0.804	0.71	0.13	0.00
Leandro Barbosa	tor	PG,SG	0.4	25	13.4	2.3	2.2	0.8	0.2	1.4	1.5	0.441	0.870	0.36	0.00	0.04
Luis Scola	hou	PF,C	0.4	30	13.3	7.7	1.6	0.8	0.2	1.7	0.0	0.503	0.712	0.40	0.02	0.09
Ron Artest	lal	SG,SF	0.4	32	12.4	4.2	2.7	1.5	0.4	1.7	1.6	0.406	0.709	0.29	0.03	0.13
Emeka Okafor	noh	PF,C	0.3	29	10.4	8.5	0.8	0.6	1.4	1.5	0.0	0.536	0.563	0.26	0.00	0.09
Gilbert Arenas	was	PG	0.3	35	19.3	4.2	6.1	1.5	0.2	3.2	2.0	0.407	0.745	0.35	0.00	0.09
Grant Hill	pho	SG,SF	0.2	28	10.0	4.8	2.1	0.9	0.4	1.3	0.3	0.471	0.811	0.33	0.00	0.19

FANTASY RANKINGS

Player	Team	PS	V12	MPG	PPG	RPG	APG	SPG	BPG	TOPG	3MPG	FG%	FT%	Imp	Break	Cop
Boris Diaw	cha	SF,PF	0.1	32	11.3	4.7	3.5	0.8	0.7	2.1	0.9	0.487	0.724	0.57	0.10	0.02
Samuel Dalembert	sac	C	0.1	20	5.9	6.7	0.4	0.4	1.4	1.2	0.0	0.523	0.750	0.36	0.03	0.08
Kelenna Azubuike	nyk	SG,SF	0.1	25	10.3	3.6	1.2	0.6	0.5	0.9	1.2	0.463	0.780	0.48	0.07	0.07
Ronnie Brewer	chi	SG,SF	0.0	28	10.4	2.8	2.2	1.5	0.3	1.0	0.3	0.493	0.697	0.50	0.04	0.11
Tiago Splitter	sas	PF	0.0	28	12.0	5.6	2.3	0.6	1.1	1.4	0.0	0.549	0.647	0.47	0.03	0.02
Drew Gooden	mil	PF,C	0.0	25	10.3	6.5	0.8	0.6	0.7	1.5	0.0	0.473	0.827	0.34	0.07	0.09
Evan Turner	phi	SG, SF	0.0	35	12.5	7.0	5.7	1.4	0.6	3.2	0.3	0.437	0.741	-	-	-
J.J. Hickson	cle	SF,PF	-0.1	28	12.9	6.5	0.6	0.6	0.8	1.9	0.0	0.532	0.705	0.65	0.17	0.02
Francisco Garcia	sac	SG,SF	-0.1	23	8.9	2.5	1.8	0.6	0.7	1.0	1.3	0.448	0.829	0.40	0.05	0.05
Elton Brand	phi	PF,C	-0.1	28	10.0	5.6	1.2	0.7	1.2	1.4	0.0	0.462	0.729	0.36	0.03	0.09
Kyle Korver	chi	SG,SF	-0.2	24	9.4	2.6	1.9	0.6	0.4	1.1	1.5	0.455	0.838	0.35	0.05	0.09
Brad Miller	hou	C	-0.2	26	9.1	5.5	2.4	0.7	0.5	1.5	0.4	0.442	0.829	0.31	0.02	0.08
Kirk Hinrich	was	PG,SG	-0.3	28	8.5	2.7	4.1	1.1	0.3	1.4	1.1	0.419	0.787	0.40	0.05	0.09
Jrue Holiday	phi	PG,SG	-0.3	30	9.2	2.9	4.5	1.4	0.3	2.2	1.0	0.460	0.768	-	-	-
Mario Chalmers	mia	PG	-0.3	28	7.9	2.1	4.2	1.5	0.2	1.6	1.2	0.428	0.744	0.60	0.05	0.05

A Primer on the CBA Crisis

More now than ever, the NBA feels like a year-round league. Interest in professional hoops, post-Finals, has never been higher--fans follow the draft, the summer leagues, free agency and international tournaments. More basketball is available to us than ever before, and it seems like we can't get enough.

Despite all of that, dark times may lie ahead. The current Collective Bargaining Agreement between NBA owners and the players' union expires on June 30, 2011. If no new agreement is reached, pro basketball fans will find their League Pass channels dark come next October.

That's been the situation since the league declined last December an option to keep the current agreement in place for another season. As with any negotiation of this sort, there are myriad levels of complexity. However, at the heart of the looming dispute is this: It's not so much how the pie between the players and owners is divided now, but how it must be divided in the future amid uncertain economic times.

"We are at a revenue percentage right now with our players that is simply too high to power a sustainable business model," commissioner David Stern said on Bill Simmons' podcast last February.

The first proposal in this process put together by the owners was reportedly more of a call to arms than it was a starting point for good-faith negotiations.

"This [new proposal] has gone too far," player representative Adonal Foyle told ESPN in February. "It wants a hard cap, it basically will create no middle class and which, in effect, means none of the Bird rules would apply."

According to the *Associated Press*, the owners' initial proposal called for a true shift in the economic structure in the game. Among other things, the owners wanted:
• draft picks to have starting salaries cut by a third
• the minimum salary to be slashed by as much as 20 percent
• the total value of maximum contracts to be held under $60 million
• contracts to be guaranteed for half their value, or less
• the dreaded "hard cap" that would eliminate all those nifty little CBA exceptions that we track so diligently
• total player compensation to fall to around 45 percent of Basketball-Related Income, down from the current 57 percent of BRI

After an indignant response by the players and Billy Hunter, their union chief, the owners tore up that initial proposal, but we're left with the flavor of what they're after. No has come out and stated that the league is seeking a hard cap. Well, at least no one was supposed to.

"In a salary-cap era--and soon a hard salary cap in the NBA like it's in the NHL--if everyone can pay the same amount to the same amount of players, its the small nuanced differences that matter," Wizards owner Ted Leonsis told a group of Northern Virginia businessmen in late September.

As you'd expect, Stern was not pleased, and the statement isn't going to do much in terms of winning of the trust of the union.

"We're negotiating and that was one of our negotiating points," Stern told the AP. "But collective bargaining is a negotiating process, and that was not something that Ted was authorized to say and he will be dealt with for that lapse in judgment."

Leonsis was relieved of $100,000 from his outsized wallet by Stern the day after his comments, but the cat was out of the bag. The owners want a hard cap, or something like it. However, before discussions on the payout structure can even begin, the two sides have to find some sort of common ground on a very fundamental issue: How much, if any, money are the owners losing? If they can't even agree on that, how can they agree on how to split up the bounty?

"That's the biggest issue that still has to be resolved," said Hunter after the last meeting. "In terms of the revenue split between players and owners, there has not been any progress on that front."

The players put together a proposal of their own in July, but it reportedly only tweaked the current system, calling for more revenue sharing among teams. Really, that's the line in the sand. The owners want change; the players want the status quo.

The owners say they collectively lost over $400 million last season. The union isn't buying it, saying that the 57 percent of BRI model still works for both sides. You might think it should merely be a matter of the sides agreeing to an independent financial audit, but apparently it's not that simple. It's an age-old problem. The owners cry poor, yet go out and spend countless millions of dollars on player salaries. Then, at negotiating time, they come back and ask the players to help protect them from themselves.

That said, if the industry-wide losses the owners are claiming are accurate, something has to be done. The two sides are so far apart that they can't even be properly identified as sides. The rhetoric coming out of the negotiating sessions has softened, which is mildly encouraging. However, there is a lot of ground to cover for the owners and players to agree to a new CBA, and the time to get there is running out fast.

The players will cling to the argument that the luxury-tax system in place is a mechanism that already protects the owners and assures the profitability of the teams as a group, though individual franchises might suffer through mismanagement. The degree to which this is true, and the degree to which it can be proven to be true, will decide how amicable the negotiations will be going forward.

The Issues

1. Competitive balance and the cost of winning. The current system does little to enhance parity, though smart teams can and do succeed within the current structure. Paying the luxury tax can almost be viewed as the cost of winning. The more you can afford, the longer you can remain a contender. The Lakers' payroll this season, including the luxury tax, will more than double that of the teams on the other end of the scale. However, though this isn't the case with the profitable Lakers, some of the bottom feeders are the ones actually making money. As long as they don't overspend, teams can chug along on shared revenue. Just don't go ordering those championship t-shirts.

The other part of this is the chess game created by cap management. Teams like the Knicks were willing to punt one or even two seasons in order to position themselves for the 2010 free-agent market. It's not that the strategy is unsound. It's just not fair to the fans. Plus, last time we checked, teams were still charging full price for their tickets.

2. Reduction in players' share of BRI, likely to somewhere below 50 percent, perhaps into the mid-40s. This is a question of overhead. The salary cap is a standard percentage of the BRI, which means that the biggest chunk on the expense side of the owners' ledgers is fixed. So if labor costs are accounted for, and the owners are still losing money, where is that other 43 percent going? This is where creative accounting comes into the mix, the deft touch bean-counters have with depreciation and interest costs, the kind of practices that once led Hunter to refer to the owners' claim of massive losses "baloney." This is the smokescreen that needs to be cleared away before the two sides can agree to a new revenue split. Everything proceeds from this.

3. Fewer, or no, cap exceptions, which in plain English is a hard salary cap. We know why the owners want such a system, and it's easy to understand why the players don't. What are the other problems with a hard cap? First of all, as Foyle has pointed out, it eliminates the middle class of players. You know all that analysis we do about the folly of giving multi-year deals to $6-7 million players? Have you read the one about the ills of the mid-level exception? Don't worry: those guys are going away under a hard cap. Owners know it's the max-contract guys who make the real difference, and they're going to get the vast majority of the money. Everyone else will be fighting for the scraps. Plus, with only so many max contracts to go around, players will go to the cities where they can get them, which will be good for competitive balance. It will also mean fewer stars in key markets as well as higher roster turnover. Cohesiveness is a key benefit to owners of the Larry Bird Exception that allows teams to re-sign their own players while over the cap.

4. Reduction in the length and amount of max contracts. The max contract you sign today might not look so good tomorrow, as the Hawks will find out a couple of years into their deal with Joe Johnson. Under the current system, Atlanta will be hamstrung by that contract until halfway through the new decade. And yes, this is clearly another case of the owners seeking protection against themselves.

5. Protection against bad contracts in the form of less guaranteed money. There have been too many instances of non-performing players like Eddy Curry and Raef LaFrentz occupying space on an NBA roster, earning millions, while being physically unable to play. The owners want to go the NFL route of guaranteeing less money, which in turn would theoretically help keep players motivated.

6. Another year added to the minimum age limit. Teams are still concerned about the investment made in amateur players who are not ready for the NBA, on or off the court. Another year at the college level means one more year for accurate evaluation and one less year of player development on the NBA's dime. The league will also likely want a more team-friendly rookie salary scale.

7. Enhanced revenue sharing among the teams. This will be a familiar refrain on the players' side. Some teams are profitable. Others aren't. If the owners haven't figured out a way to split revenue among themselves, how can they ask the players to cover for the inequities? This problem is that this stance doesn't address the industry-wide shortfall the owners are claiming. If the league as a whole is hemorrhaging money, it doesn't really matter how the teams are splitting up their revenue. That's a big if, however.

8. A more dynamic escrow account. Under the current system, a certain percentage of player salaries is held in escrow to help the owners cover for revenue shortfalls. This is in effect the players giving the owners back some of their salaries, and in the aggregate, we're not talking about token amounts. You better believe the owners would be in favor of expanding this practice.

9. NFL-style franchise tags. This was an idea bandied about by, among others, Kyle Stack of *Slam Magazine*. In his piece on the subject, former Phoenix general manager Steve Kerr said that the franchise tag "would be a huge hit for the owners." The effect would be to delay a player's free agency for a year, giving teams more time to work out extensions. You'd have fewer situations like the current one with Carmelo Anthony, because Denver could simply slap a franchise tag on him and say, "You ain't going anywhere, big guy."

10. A more costly luxury tax, with a lower threshold for payouts. If the current system doesn't tax owners of rich teams enough to prevent them from going deep into luxury-tax waters, perhaps more corrective standards would do the trick. Doing so also reallocates more money to the teams on the other end of the spectrum. The problem? See item No. 1 on this list. It's also worth noting that the teams with money to throw around would like to retain that competitive advantage, even if it cuts into their profitability. Maintaining a united front will be tricky for Stern.

11. A stricter salary scale. Tweaks to the current salary schedule like lower minimums, lower annual raises, etc., which are just more manifestations of cost control.

Likely Outcomes

What happens really depends on just how firmly the owners believe they need a hard cap. If they've got to have it, a work stoppage is probable. If they're flexible on that issue, then once the disagreement over the BRI split is resolved, everything else can fall into place. However, that could go a lot of ways, including the union decertifying itself in order to put all of the previous tenets of the Collective Bargaining Agreement under the scrutiny of antitrust laws. If that happens, we could be in for a long haul.

In the interim, don't expect non-impact players to be getting extensions this season, as owners don't want to tie up long-term money without knowing what kind of roster they'll be able to afford. Next year's draft could be dominated by seniors more than any in a long time, as players won't want to abandon their scholarships and jump into a work stoppage. And, of course, the headlines will become increasingly dominated by the back-and-forth between David Stern and Billy Hunter, which is tiresome for those who just like three-pointers and slam dunks.

Chances are, there is going to be a lockout next season. The lockout, as these things tend to do, will extend into the season. If players aren't faced with the reality of losing game checks, what is really the point? In the meantime, you could see the existence of the NBA become ever more precarious in markets that are already struggling like Indianapolis, Memphis, Charlotte, Sacramento and New Orleans. The global economy hovers over all of this, as whispers about a second recession are becoming shouts. There is little reason to hope things will improve in a nation that some time ago ceased to produce things of tangible value.

There is still time to head off this battle between millionaires and billionaires. However, when the owners and players can't even agree about what's real, what difference will time make? That's the sad reality for NBA fans, who don't care about BRIs or MLEs and just want to see LeBron James charging down an open court. Eventually, the owners and the players alike will make out fine, though there will be players who mismanage their fortunes and end up in bankruptcy court. Still, the real losers in all of this will be the rest of us. You now, the people who actually pay the bills.

Bradford Doolittle

Second Best: Ranking the Other Leagues

As ESPN's international expert, Fran Fraschilla has a difficult job: convincing skeptical Americans of the value of overseas basketball. It's impossible to ignore the talent that now comes out of Europe, South America and parts of Asia. Still, Brandon Jennings' decision to head to Italy after he failed to qualify to play at the University of Arizona shed light on the true perception of European basketball. When Jennings predictably struggled while competing against veteran professionals, his draft stock slipped.

Fraschilla has turned to baseball's organized system of minor leagues to help explain the level of play in the Euroleague, the competition featuring the premier teams on the continent. As ESPN's analyst for U.S. games during this summer's FIBA World Championship, Fraschilla explained that the Euroleague was equivalent to AAA and compared major college basketball to double-A competition.

The minor-league analogy helps us introduce statistics into the equation. Clay Davenport, our colleague at Baseball Prospectus, advanced analysis of minor-league baseball by using the performance of players at multiple levels of play to translate minor-league statistics into their major-league equivalents. The Davenport Translations have also been used to project how players who come to MLB from Cuba and Japan will perform stateside.

In much the same way, Basketball Prospectus has developed methods to translate player performance at the college, D-League, Euroleague and EuroCup levels to the NBA. These translations are an integral part of the SCHOENE projection system and produce the projections for rookies and other newcomers that appear throughout this book. These translations also offer the chance to compare the quality of play in each "minor" league against a consistent standard. While the progression from A-ball up to the majors is relatively clear and linear, it is more difficult to objectively compare the D-League and the EuroCup. Statistics can help quantify these distinctions.

Let's back up briefly to explain the process in a little more detail. The translation for each other basketball league to the NBA is slightly different. As a pseudo-minor league, the D-League offers the closest comparison to the baseball model. Players go back and forth between the NBA and the D-League on a regular basis, so our translations compare player performance within the same season.

In-season movement is less common between Europe and the NBA, so for Euroleague and EuroCup translations we rely on players going back and forth in consecutive years. Since the movement runs both directions, aging evens out and is not a factor. That's not the case with the NCAA because players cannot go from the NBA back to college, no matter how much Adam Morrison might like to do so. Our college translations are strictly forward-looking, so for these purposes we had to adjust them to take out a year's worth of player development.

The results (Table 1):

Table 1: Drop Off For NBA Players, By League

League	Drop Off
Euroleague	-12.8%
D-League	-20.8%
NCAA - Georgetown	-24.4%
NCAA - Average Pro	-25.3%
EuroCup	-25.4%
NCAA - Harvard	-36.2%

As expected, the Euroleague is the closest competitor to the NBA. The typical Euroleague player loses about 12.8 percent of their value on a per-minute basis when they make the trip across the pond. More surprising is the fact that the D-League rates second. Because D-League salaries are so much lower than what top European teams offer, many of the best fringe players end up heading overseas. However, the lure of a possible call-up and the presence of players assigned to the D-League by their NBA teams have helped improve the quality of play in the top American minor league.

Because strength of schedule is an important component in the NCAA translations, we have to consider college basketball from multiple perspectives. The "average" strength of schedule, via KenPom.com, is actually the mean among players who have reached the NBA. We can consider that a fair approximation of the typical BCS conference. The numbers show the level of play there to be very similar to the EuroCup, the second-tier European competition. The very hardest schedule in the country (Georgetown earned that honor last year) is slightly more difficult. Harvard's Jeremy Lin played the easiest slate of opponents of any rookie entering the league this year, and the level of play in the Ivy League was dramatically lower than what we see in bigger conferences.

As interesting as these average adjustments are, they do not actually come into play in our translations. Instead, we consider 14 different component statistics individually to account for the fact that not all players can translate their games equally. Different categories carry over more consistently. Rebounding tends to be relatively unaffected by the level of competition, but usage rates plunge when players reach the NBA. Newcomers also get less respect from officials, drawing fewer trips to the foul line while being whistled for more fouls themselves. As a result, players who depend on free throws to score can face a more difficult adjustment.

The different rules by which each league plays add a layer of complexity that has no baseball equivalent. Yes, park factors affect the way the game is played and certain leagues tend to favor hitting or pitching (like the Pacific Coast League, with a number of high-altitude stadiums that make it friendly to hitters), but the rules are the same. The biggest point of differentiation in basketball is the three-point line, which is far closer in the college game (20'9") as well as Europe prior to this season (20'6"). FIBA has now moved the line back to 22'2"--closer to the NBA distance of 23'9" at the top of the key and 22' in the corners.

Let's compare the drop-offs (or occasionally gains) in each of the component statistics between the leagues (Table 2).

A handful of differences in style and scorekeeping are evident looking at the European leagues. Players coming from the Euroleague to the NBA actually increase their assist and block percentages, while players in the EuroCup see relatively little decline. The difference in assist rates is explained by a much more stringent-- and probably more accurate--standard for recording an assist in Europe. Meanwhile, D-League scorekeepers seem to be just as generous as their NBA peers.

Scorekeeping could also serve to deflate block percentages, which additionally seem to be limited by the style of play overseas. Most European guards prefer the floater to venturing deep into the paint, cutting down on shot-blocking opportunities. Meanwhile, defensive rebounding tends to be stronger internationally. However, FIBA refs are apparently far more generous with whistles, which explains why players coming from Europe do not see their foul rates skyrocket.

Predictably, some of the most interesting differences are in the ratios of three-point attempts. College players cut down heavily on their long-distance offerings as they adjust to the longer line. However, their D-League counterparts tend to let loose more than ever. The D-League plays with the same three-point line in the NBA, but that doesn't necessarily explain why players would attempt more triples. Instead, this seems to be a function of D-League stars becoming role players and spot-up shooters in the NBA. One factor that is consistent across the board is that players use far fewer plays once they arrive in the NBA no matter where they were previously playing.

These statistics have meaningful implications for teams. While they have generally treated the D-League as the basketball equivalent of A-ball or rookie level, these numbers and the growing ranks of former D-Leaguers in the NBA suggest that the NBA's minor league has improved its level of play to something

Table 2: Statistical Dropoffs To NBA, By League

League	2P%	3P%	FT%	OR%	DR%	Ast%	Stl%	Blk%	Usage	2A%	3A%	FTA%	TO%	PF%
Euroleague	-9.1%	-11.0%	1.7%	4.9%	-7.5%	19.0%	-30.2%	4.6%	-17.9%	12.0%	-6.3%	-12.9%	-2.9%	-1.9%
D-League	-13.4%	-15.3%	-8.4%	-6.5%	-12.1%	-25.9%	-7.3%	-13.8%	-18.8%	-1.2%	26.5%	-18.6%	-3.7%	26.8%
NCAA	-14.6%	-17.3%	-3.1%	-6.5%	-13.3%	-14.1%	-26.5%	-16.5%	-27.2%	13.1%	-29.2%	-25.6%	2.1%	34.1%
EuroCup	-20.2%	-12.3%	-3.0%	8.4%	-10.8%	-8.6%	-34.8%	-2.2%	-26.9%	15.0%	-11.1%	-20.3%	-2.6%	8.2%

closer to double-A.

Four NBA teams now own or operate their D-League affiliates, moving us toward a true minor-league system where teams control the development of their young players and have replacements on call in case of injury. Until D-League salaries improve to the point where players no longer have to sacrifice financially to stay in the U.S., European teams are going to have superior top-end talent. At least the competition is close enough that teams should know that their young players can get something out of going down to the D-League to get more playing time.

The numbers definitely bear out Fraschilla's conclusion about international basketball. While Ricky Rubio and Milos Teodosic may not have Dick Vitale hyping them on your television each weekend, the Euroleague is second only to the NBA when it comes to quality of play. The NCAA simply cannot compare.

Kevin Pelton

The WARP Hall of Fame

The Naismith Memorial Basketball Hall of Fame is a relatively new entrant among the ubiquitous American sports museums that dot our continental landscape. The first inductees were announced in 1959. The physical structure in Springfield, Mass. that houses the Hall didn't open until 1985. In many respects, the BHOF is still sorting out what it is, and those who vote on new members are still figuring out exactly what defines a Hall of Famer.

You've heard the term--Hall of Famer--thrown around a lot lately because of the creation of Miami's super team. This has happened before, people say. The Celtics in the 1980s had four Hall of Famers, five when they had Bill Walton. That's certainly true. You also hear that the Lakers of the late '60s and early '70s had Wilt Chamberlain, Elgin Baylor and Jerry West. True that. It was a super team, no doubt about it. However, that Lakers group didn't win a championship. Seriously, you can look it up. The Lakers didn't win their first title on the West Coast until the 1971-72 season. Baylor retired nine games into that campaign because of chronic knee problems that limited him to 11 games in his last two years. He never won a ring.

This is the kind of story the Hall, or any sports museum, is built to tell. We see the Hall as the preferred eventual destination for the NBA's elite, but it's more than that. Perhaps because basketball has such a well-chronicled evolution--we know who created the game, when he created it and why he did it--the BHOF exists as much to honor the game's pioneers as it does the stars of the NBA. There is no specific NBA Hall of Fame, and perhaps that's for the best. A good hall of fame is as much a history museum as it is a pantheon. There have been 304 enshrinees in the BHOF, if you double-count John Wooden, Bill Sharman and Lenny Wilkens, who made it as both as coaches and players. Of those, you can really point to just 90 members who are there primarily on the merits of their NBA performance, or who at least enjoyed a significant NBA career.

As we expand our offerings at Basketball Prospectus, we hope to enhance the historical aspect to our content. At the center of that will be our core metric, WARP (Wins Above Replacement), created by Kevin Pelton and explained earlier in the book. What we want to do now is take a look at how this performance metric can be used to help us prune the list of potential Hall members. The number, of course, is just a jumping-off point.

Over the last half-century, the NBA has nearly quadrupled in size, from eight teams in 1960-61 to the current total of 30. The expansion hasn't watered down the level of play, either, as the popularity of the game at the youth level has never been higher and the league has expanded its reach into just about every corner of the globe. It can easily be argued that there are more outstanding basketball players in the world today than at any point in history. From there you can also extrapolate that there are more Hall of Fame-worthy players than ever, many of them playing in the NBA right now. Let's try to flash forward a few years and figure out if, for example, the Miami Heat does indeed boast a core of three future Hall of Famers in LeBron James, Dwyane Wade and Chris Bosh.

The WARP era only stretches back to the advent of the three-point line at this time, so our focus will be on the last three decades in the NBA. For the purposes of this discussion, that's fine, because the BHOF has already done a pretty comprehensive job of honoring those who flourished in the early days of the league.

Who's already there?

Let's start by looking at the career WARP totals of players in the Hall. We list everyone who registered any WARP totals at all, even though the guys lower on the list played most or all of their career during the era in which we don't have WARP (Table 1).

We include an estimate of peak-season WARP to give us a better picture of those who burned brightly during a relatively short career, such as Magic Johnson. We also include WARP compiled outside of peak seasons to reflect not just the player's longevity, but how effective players were (or weren't) during their waning years. For our purposes here, we're going to be extremely liberal in what we're going to refer to as

THE WARP HALL OF FAME

Table 1: Highest WARP, Hall of Fame Players

PLAYER	WARP2	WYRS	W/S	PEAK	oPEAK	PLAYER	WARP2	WYRS	W/S	PEAK	oPEAK
John Stockton	302	19	15.9	167	135	Adrian Dantley	98	12	8.1	94	4
Karl Malone	285	19	15.0	150	135	Alex English	95	12	7.9	77	19
Hakeem Olajuwon	267	18	14.9	190	77	James Worthy	64	12	5.3	61	3
Michael Jordan	264	15	17.6	176	88	Joe Dumars	59	14	4.2	35	24
Charles Barkley	261	16	16.3	194	68	Dan Issel	54	6	9.1	23	31
David Robinson	247	14	17.7	165	82	Dennis Johnson	48	11	4.3	40	8
Magic Johnson	228	13	17.5	198	30	George Gervin	46	7	6.6	44	3
Larry Bird	209	13	16.1	175	34	Bob Lanier	31	5	6.1	10	21
Clyde Drexler	196	15	13.0	144	52	Bill Walton	26	6	4.4	20	6
Moses Malone	189	16	11.8	135	54	Elvin Hayes	16	5	3.2	0	16
Scottie Pippen	174	17	10.2	129	45	David Thompson	14	5	2.9	14	0
Patrick Ewing	169	17	10.0	121	48	Wes Unseld	12	2	6.1	0	12
Robert Parish	147	18	8.2	72	75	Drazen Petrovic	10	4	2.4	10	0
Dominique Wilkins	140	15	9.4	110	31	Bob McAdoo	9	7	1.3	7	2
Isiah Thomas	129	13	9.9	110	19	Dave Cowens	4	2	2.2	4	1
Kareem Abdul-Jabbar	109	10	10.9	0	109	Rick Barry	4	1	4.3	0	4
Kevin McHale	108	13	8.3	95	12	Calvin Murphy	4	4	1.1	3	1
Julius Erving	105	8	13.1	57	48						

KEY -- WARP: wins above replacement; WYRS: WARP-era seasons played; W/S: WARP per WARP season; PEAK: WARP during peak seasons; oPEAK: WARP outside of peak seasons.

a "peak" season, so we're flagging all WARP compiled from a player's age-23 campaign through his age-32 campaign for a nice round figure of 10 peak seasons. This penalizes Michael Jordan to a certain extent, because he missed all of his age-30 season and most of his age-31 season while toiling for the Birmingham Barons. Also, we include an average seasonal WARP total as another data point, one that will help us compare these players to those in the league today.

As we mentioned, there are 90 Hall of Fame members selected in large part because of their performance as NBA players. There have been 1,091 players who have logged five or more NBA seasons. From that, you can extrapolate that you need to reach about the 93rd percentile on the career WARP list. That will at least get a player into the conversation. As it turns out, that corresponds directly with right about 100 career WARP. In other words, once you hit 100 WARP, you can begin to be discussed as a Hall candidate. That doesn't get you in--there are a number of non-statistical criteria that can get a player into the Hall of Fame, or keep one out. It also doesn't shut you out if you don't hit 100 WARP, though your inclusion may lead to some head scratching. Once you get up to about 170 WARP or so, you're a no-brainer for a future trip to Springfield.

Here are some thoughts about a few players on this first list:

Kareem Abdul-Jabbar: What an amazing career. His 20-year NBA journey is split perfectly between the WARP and non-WARP era. Not a single one of his peak seasons carries a WARP total, yet his 109 non-peak WARP are enough in themselves to merit Hall of Fame discussion.

James Worthy: Worthy retired at 32, so nearly all of his WARP came in his peak seasons. Worthy was never named First or Second Team All-NBA. He received votes for only one MVP award, in 1985-86. He didn't make All-Rookie. He never made All-Defense. Worthy's career WARP total can serve as the basis for a serious argument that he wasn't obviously better than some of his contemporary small forwards such as Bernard King and Marques Johnson. That's not how we remember Worthy, though. He was a spectacular figure in the open court. He also had an outstanding college career, which we have to remind ourselves figures into all of this. However, based strictly on his NBA career, Worthy is a reach as a Hall of Famer, a guy that rode the coattails of Magic Johnson on the championship Lakers teams of the 1980s. Worthy did make for an imposing Klingon, which is a feather in his cap.

Table 2: Highest WARP, non-Hall of Fame Players

PLAYER	WARP2	WYRS	W/S	PEAK	oPEAK	PLAYER	WARP2	WYRS	W/S	PEAK	oPEAK
Tim Hardaway	149	13	11.4	112	36	Buck Williams	90	17	5.3	72	19
Mark Jackson	139	17	8.2	85	53	Terrell Brandon	90	11	8.2	89	1
Terry Porter	135	17	7.9	96	38	Sam Perkins	87	17	5.1	51	36
Larry Nance	131	13	10.1	103	28	Hersey Hawkins	87	13	6.7	80	7
Mookie Blaylock	129	13	9.9	114	15	Bill Laimbeer	86	14	6.2	69	18
Jack Sikma	113	12	9.4	95	18	Sidney Moncrief	86	11	7.9	86	0
Shawn Kemp	112	14	8.0	92	20	Alvin Robertson	85	10	8.5	83	3
Kevin Johnson	112	12	9.3	107	4	Terry Cummings	83	18	4.6	69	14
Chris Mullin	108	16	6.8	79	29	Doc Rivers	82	13	6.3	79	4
Jeff Hornacek	107	14	7.6	69	38	Horace Grant	82	17	4.8	75	7
Derek Harper	106	16	6.6	89	17	Dennis Rodman	80	14	5.7	55	26
Mark Price	101	12	8.4	92	9	Artis Gilmore	79	9	8.8	6	73
Maurice Cheeks	98	14	7.0	83	14	Mitch Richmond	77	14	5.5	60	17
Fat Lever	93	11	8.5	90	3	Michael Adams	77	11	7.0	75	1
Detlef Schrempf	92	16	5.7	59	32	Dan Majerle	74	14	5.3	57	17

Joe Dumars: Dumars was never a statistical darling, and you can make some of the same arguments against him as you do for Worthy. However, with Dumars, you don't have the benefit of a high-profile college career. (Though if he weren't already in the Hall, his career as an NBA executive would be a talking point.) Strictly on the court, Dumars wasn't as good as, for example, Sidney Moncrief, who isn't yet in the Hall and isn't likely to get there.

Bill Walton: Walton is a perfect illustration of the type of player that transcends this type of cold, objective approach to evaluating a Hall of Famer. His best seasons weren't in the WARP era, but even if they were, his career total would be held down by his injury woes. However, he was the best player on an iconic championship team with the 1977 Portland Trail Blazers. He was the sixth man on another title team, the 1986 Boston Celtics, which was one of the best teams of all time. Of course, even if Walton had never stepped foot on an NBA court, he'd probably get into the Hall as one of the best-ever college basketball players.

Who should be there?

These are the 30 Hall-eligible non-Hall of Famers with the highest career WARP totals (Table 2).

You can see some overlap in the totals of the first two lists, and you can see some obvious non-Hall of Famers in this second set of players. Despite what we titled this section, we're not saying that all of these players should be in the Hall. In particular, WARP seems to be far too fond of point guards who peaked in the 1990s. No one considers Mookie Blaylock a Hall of Famer. However, some of the other players on this list should be. Let's comment on a few of the latter:

Tim Hardaway: Does Hardaway seem like a Hall of Famer to you? Probably not, but his career numbers are compelling. He's in the upper crust of the gray area. A good comparison is Dominique Wilkins. Neither player won a championship. Wilkins made All-Rookie and was once on the First Team All-NBA squad. So was Hardaway, though Wilkins made the Second Team once more. Both players played their entire careers in the WARP era. Hardaway finished with 149 WARP, Wilkins with 140. That's not a significant difference and could be dismissed as methodology, except that Hardaway played two fewer seasons. Their peak totals (112-110 in favor of Hardaway) were virtually identical. Clearly, Wilkins was the more iconic player, but if he's in the Hall, then you have to give Hardaway serious consideration.

Jack Sikma: Sikma's career totals are missing his first two seasons, which would paint him in an even better light and boost him close to 130 WARP. He was a key player on a championship team, but didn't make any All-NBA teams. However, Sikma was one of the greatest NAIA-level college players ever, and if you're putting together a comprehensive basketball hall of fame, Sikma's got to be in there somewhere.

Kevin Johnson: Johnson has been the subject of much debate. His career was short--he recorded just four non-peak WARP. However, his peak total ranks in the 96th percentile of all players. If you do a player-to-player comparison of second-tier Hall point guards, Johnson is going to come out pretty well. He never won a title, but you can say the same thing about a lot of Johnson's contemporaries, who were at their peak when Michael Jordan was at his. Johnson made the All-NBA Second Team four times, so he was an elite player for a good period of time. His case isn't clear-cut, but you can make an argument in his favor.

Chris Mullin: Mullin is on the fringe for his NBA career, but when you couple that with his time at St. John's, he's a solid candidate.

Artis Gilmore: Come on, now. This one has to be rectified. Gilmore had a long, solid career in the NBA, the first part of which was pre-WARP. Otherwise, he'd be over 100 WARP for the NBA portion of his career. However, with Gilmore, that's just the starting point because of his phenomenal ABA career. He won an ABA MVP award in 1971-72, and was First Team All-Defense four times. Gilmore ranks 17th in all-time ABA scoring, second in rebounding and tops in blocks. Prior to that, he enjoyed a storied college career, averaging 24.2 points and 22.7 rebounds in his two seasons with Jacksonville, where he nearly led the Dolphins to the NCAA title. Gilmore is the Hall's biggest current omission, and not just because of his size.

Who's next?

Here are the 10 retired players who are in the 93rd percentile or better in career WARP, but are not yet Hall-eligible (Table 3).

Payton and Miller are in, with the latter likely to be inducted next year. The others ... let's just say we probably need more perspective. Mutombo is an interesting case as a dominant defender who should also get a huge boost for his humanitarian work off the court (something that ought to be considered and should eventually give rise to a movement to have Manute Bol enshrined as a contributor). Just in terms of his NBA career, Mutombo falls short in peak value. He never played on a title team. He was, however, a four-time Defensive Player of the Year. Tough call.

What about the guys still playing?

Let's finish off with a look at the 30 active players who are either in the 93rd percentile of career WARP, or at that level in WARP per season, with a minimum

Table 3: Highest WARP, not yet eligible for HOF

PLAYER	WARP2	WYRS	W/S	PEAK	oPEAK
Gary Payton	184	17	10.8	126	58
Reggie Miller	172	18	9.6	106	66
Dikembe Mutombo	141	18	7.8	84	57
Chris Webber	136	15	9.1	104	33
Alonzo Mourning	123	15	8.2	112	12
Vlade Divac	120	16	7.5	88	32
Rod Strickland	119	17	7.0	89	30
Stephon Marbury	116	13	8.9	88	28
Eddie Jones	114	14	8.1	89	25
Sam Cassell	105	15	7.0	62	43

of five seasons in the league.

Indeed, there are some future Hall of Famers already toiling in the league. Shaquille O'Neal is on the cusp of finishing in the top five in career WARP, and may get to third. He had 2.5 WARP last season, but is at an age when a below-replacement total looms as a possibility, in which case he might drop behind Charles Barkley. In any event, Shaq is a no-brainer, a first-ballot Hall of Famer. So is Jason Kidd, who had 15.4 WARP last season and seems kind of ageless. He may end up in the top five. You can see the other players that are first-ballot guys, still adding to their totals: Kevin Garnett, Tim Duncan, Kobe Bryant and Dirk Nowitzki.

After that, you have four guys that will almost certainly get in Paul Pierce, Ray Allen, Steve Nash and LeBron James. James, of course, may well top the all-time list in a few years. He had 25.4 WARP last season, and can probably be counted up to tack on wins in at that range for another 7-8 years at a minimum. Pierce and Allen are interesting in that they might have been considered more borderline just a couple of years ago, but the Celtics' success has probably cemented their candidacy. Nash is a two-time MVP who is compiling a ton of post-peak WARP. He'll get in.

Beyond that, it gets murky. Tracy McGrady? Geez, that's a tough one. The guy has never won a playoff series. Allen Iverson? He seems like an obvious yes, but after a few years, will he come to be perceived as overrated? Maybe, but every former MVP eligible for the Hall of Fame is in there, which also bodes well for Nash. Of the others, you have to like the chances of Chauncey Billups. Grant Hill might have missed too much time, but also had a great college career. Vince Carter's stock is plummeting. As of today, he's probably out. Ben Wallace will have some support be-

Table 4: Highest WARP, Active Players

PLAYER	WARP2	WYRS	W/S	PEAK	oPEAK	PLAYER	WARP2	WYRS	W/S	PEAK	oPEAK
Shaquille O'Neal	263	18	14.6	178	85	Elton Brand	115	11	10.4	94	21
Jason Kidd	236	16	14.7	148	88	Grant Hill	111	15	7.4	95	16
Kevin Garnett	233	15	15.6	194	39	Baron Davis	111	11	10.0	95	15
Tim Duncan	226	13	17.4	181	45	Ben Wallace	110	14	7.9	89	21
Kobe Bryant	181	14	12.9	154	27	Dwyane Wade	103	7	14.7	98	5
Dirk Nowitzki	164	12	13.7	157	7	Marcus Camby	102	14	7.3	61	41
Paul Pierce	151	12	12.5	131	20	Pau Gasol	97	9	10.8	88	9
Ray Allen	149	14	10.7	122	27	Jason Terry	95	11	8.6	89	6
Steve Nash	149	14	10.7	91	58	Andrei Kirilenko	92	9	10.2	69	22
LeBron James	146	7	20.9	75	72	Dwight Howard	88	6	14.6	38	50
Tracy McGrady	146	13	11.2	105	41	Manu Ginobili	86	8	10.8	73	13
Allen Iverson	139	14	9.9	116	23	Amar'e Stoudemire	68	8	8.5	42	26
Vince Carter	130	12	10.8	116	14	Chris Bosh	67	7	9.6	46	21
Shawn Marion	128	11	11.6	124	4	Andre Iguodala	52	6	8.6	41	11
Chauncey Billups	124	13	9.5	98	26	Josh Smith	51	6	8.4	20	31

cause of the unique ways he made his contributions. Pau Gasol and Manu Ginobili are both adding to their totals and have multiple championship rings apiece. Don't forget their international résumés when considering them. Amar'e Stoudemire could get there if he helps get the Knicks turned around.

That leaves us with our Miami super trio. James quite likely would get into the Hall if he walked away from the game tomorrow. It might take a couple of years for the sting to wear off, but the numbers are overwhelming. Dwyane Wade has a ring, may get more, and he has several peak seasons remaining. Bosh is behind the other duo, but he could enjoy a Worthy-like ride on the coattails of his running mates. More than the other two, Bosh needs a ring or two on his résumé to get serious consideration. Otherwise, in the end, we could very well come to view the Miami super friends in a similar light to the West/Chamberlain/Baylor teams--not for their greatness as individuals, but for their lack of championships.

Bradford Doolittle

2010-11 NBA Schedule

(All times EST)

Oct. 26
Mia @ Bos, 7:30
Phx @ Por, 10
Hou @ LAL, 10:30

Oct. 27
Mia @ Phi, 7
NYK @ Tor, 7
Det @ NJN, 7
Bos @ Cle, 7
Atl @ Mem, 8
Sac @ Min, 8
Chi @ OKC, 8
Mil @ NWO, 8
Ind @ SAS, 8:30
Cha @ Dal, 8:30
Uta @ Den, 9
Hou @ GSW, 10:30
Por @ LAC, 10:30

Oct. 28
Was @ Orl, 8
Phx @ Uta, 10:30

Oct. 29
Atl @ Phi, 7
Sac @ NJN, 7
Ind @ Cha, 7
Cle @ Tor, 7
NYK @ Bos, 7:30
Den @ NWO, 8
Orl @ Mia, 8
OKC @ Det, 8
Mil @ Min, 8
Mem @ Dal, 8:30
LAL @ Phx, 10:30
LAC @ GSW, 10:30

Oct. 30
Was @ Atl, 7
Sac @ Cle, 7:30
Por @ NYK, 7:30
Phi @ Ind, 8
Min @ Mem, 8
Det @ Chi, 8
NWO @ SAS, 8:30
Cha @ Mil, 8:30
Den @ Hou, 8:30

Oct. 31
Mia @ NJN, 1
Dal @ LAC, 3:30
Uta @ OKC, 7
GSW @ LAL, 9:30

Nov. 1
Por @ Chi, 8
Tor @ Sac, 10
SAS @ LAC, 10:30

Nov. 2
Phi @ Was, 7
Atl @ Cle, 7
Min @ Mia, 7:30
Bos @ Det, 7:30
Orl @ NYK, 7:30
Por @ Mil, 8
Mem @ LAL, 10:30

Nov. 3
Min @ Orl, 7
Cha @ NJN, 7
Ind @ Phi, 7
Det @ Atl, 7
Mil @ Bos, 8
NWO @ Hou, 8:30
Dal @ Den, 9
Tor @ Uta, 9
SAS @ Phx, 10
LAL @ Sac, 10:30
OKC @ LAC, 10:30
Mem @ GSW, 10:30

Nov. 4
NYK @ Chi, 8
OKC @ Por, 10:30

Nov. 5
Mil @ Ind, 7
Cle @ Phi, 7
NJN @ Orl, 7
Cha @ Det, 7:30
Was @ NYK, 7:30
Chi @ Bos, 8
Atl @ Min, 8
Mia @ NWO, 8
Mem @ Phx, 10
Uta @ GSW, 10:30
Tor @ LAL, 10:30
LAC @ Den, 10:30

Nov. 6
NJN @ Mia, 7
Cle @ Was, 7
Orl @ Cha, 7
Hou @ SAS, 8:30
NWO @ Mil, 8:30
LAC @ Uta, 9
Den @ Dal, 9
Mem @ Sac, 10
Tor @ Por, 10

Nov. 7
Phi @ NYK, 12
Phx @ Atl, 5
GSW @ Det, 6
Min @ Hou, 7
Bos @ OKC, 7
Por @ LAL, 9:30

Nov. 8
SAS @ Cha, 7
GSW @ Tor, 7
Atl @ Orl, 7
Phx @ Mem, 8
Den @ Chi, 8
Bos @ Dal, 8:30

Nov. 9
Cle @ NJN, 7
Den @ Ind, 7
Uta @ Mia, 7:30
LAC @ NWO, 8
NYK @ Mil, 8
Det @ Por, 10
Min @ LAL, 10:30

Nov. 10
Uta @ Orl, 7
Cha @ Tor, 7
Hou @ Was, 7
Mil @ Atl, 7
GSW @ NYK, 7:30
NJN @ Cle, 7:30
Phi @ OKC, 8
Dal @ Mem, 8
LAC @ SAS, 9:30
Min @ Sac, 10

Nov. 11
Bos @ Mia, 8
GSW @ Chi, 8
LAL @ Den, 10:30

Nov. 12
Hou @ Ind, 7
Tor @ Orl, 7
Uta @ Atl, 7
Cha @ Was, 7
NYK @ Min, 8
Phi @ Dal, 8:30
Sac @ Phx, 9
Por @ OKC, 9:30
Det @ LAC, 10:30

Nov. 13
Uta @ Cha, 7
Orl @ NJN, 7
Ind @ Cle, 7:30
Tor @ Mia, 7:30
Was @ Chi, 8
Bos @ Mem, 8
Por @ NWO, 8
GSW @ Mil, 8:30
Phi @ SAS, 8:30

Nov. 14
Min @ Atl, 2
Det @ Sac, 6
SAS @ OKC, 7
Hou @ NYK, 7:30
Phx @ LAL, 9:30

Nov. 15
Min @ Cha, 7
Mem @ Orl, 7
NWO @ Dal, 8:30
OKC @ Uta, 9
Den @ Phx, 9
Det @ GSW, 10:30
NJN @ LAC, 10:30

Nov. 16
Tor @ Was, 7
Atl @ Ind, 7
Phi @ Cle, 7
LAL @ Mil, 8
Por @ Mem, 8
Chi @ Hou, 8:30
NYK @ Den, 9

Nov. 17
Tor @ Phi, 7
Phx @ Mia, 7:30
LAL @ Det, 7:30
Was @ Bos, 7:30
LAC @ Min, 8
Dal @ NWO, 8
Hou @ OKC, 8
NJN @ Uta, 9
Chi @ SAS, 9:30
NYK @ Sac, 10

Nov. 18
LAC @ Ind, 7
Phx @ Orl, 8
Den @ Por, 10:30

Nov. 19
OKC @ Bos, 7
Hou @ Tor, 7
Mil @ Phi, 7
Mem @ Was, 7
Cha @ Mia, 7:30
Cle @ NWO, 8
LAL @ Min, 8
SAS @ Uta, 9
Chi @ Dal, 9:30
NJN @ Sac, 10
NYK @ GSW, 10:30

Nov. 20
Phx @ Cha, 7
Orl @ Ind, 7
Mia @ Mem, 8
Dal @ Atl, 8
OKC @ Mil, 8:30
Cle @ SAS, 8:30
NJN @ Den, 9
Uta @ Por, 10
NYK @ LAC, 10:30

Nov. 21
Bos @ Tor, 1
Was @ Det, 6
NWO @ Sac, 6
GSW @ LAL, 9:30

Nov. 22
Bos @ Atl, 7
Ind @ Mia, 7:30
Min @ OKC, 8
Phx @ Hou, 8:30
Orl @ SAS, 8:30
Sac @ Uta, 9
NWO @ LAC, 10:30
Den @ GSW, 10:30

Nov. 23
Phi @ Was, 7
Atl @ NJN, 7
Cle @ Ind, 7
Cha @ NYK, 7:30
Det @ Dal, 8:30
Chi @ LAL, 10:30

Nov. 24
NYK @ Cha, 7
Phi @ Tor, 7
Mil @ Cle, 7
Mia @ Orl, 7:30
NJN @ Bos, 7:30
Det @ Mem, 8
SAS @ Min, 8
Dal @ OKC, 8
GSW @ Hou, 8:30
NWO @ Uta, 9
Chi @ Phx, 9

Nov. 25
Was @ Atl, 8
Sac @ LAC, 10:30

Nov. 26
Cle @ Orl, 7
Hou @ Cha, 7
Phi @ Mia, 7:30
Mil @ Det, 7:30
Tor @ Bos, 7:30
OKC @ Ind, 8
Dal @ SAS, 8:30
LAL @ Uta, 9
Chi @ Den, 9
LAC @ Phx, 9
GSW @ Mem, 9:30
NWO @ Por, 10

345

2010-11 NBA SCHEDULE

Nov. 27
Atl @ NYK, 1
Orl @ Was, 7
NJN @ Phi, 7:30
Mem @ Cle, 7:30
GSW @ Min, 8
Mia @ Dal, 8:30
Cha @ Mil, 9
Chi @ Sac, 10

Nov. 28
Atl @ Tor, 1
NYK @ Det, 1:30
SAS @ NWO, 3
Uta @ LAC, 3:30
OKC @ Hou, 7
Por @ NJN, 7
Phx @ Den, 8
Ind @ LAL, 9:30
Nov. 29
Was @ Mia, 7:30
NWO @ OKC, 8
Hou @ Dal, 8:30
Mil @ Uta, 9

Nov. 30
Det @ Orl, 7
Bos @ Cle, 7
NJN @ NYK, 7:30
Por @ Phi, 7:30
LAL @ Mem, 8
Ind @ Sac, 10
SAS @ GSW, 10:30
December

Dec. 1
OKC @ NJN, 7
Was @ Tor, 7
Mem @ Atl, 7
Det @ Mia, 7:30
Por @ Bos, 7:30
Orl @ Chi, 8
Cha @ NWO, 8
Min @ Dal, 8:30
LAL @ Hou, 8:30
Mil @ Den, 9
Ind @ Uta, 9
SAS @ LAC, 10:30

Dec. 2
Mia @ Cle, 8
Phx @ GSW, 10:30

Dec. 3
NJN @ Cha, 7
OKC @ Tor, 7
Por @ Was, 7
Phi @ Atl, 7:30
Orl @ Det, 7:30
Chi @ Bos, 8
NYK @ NWO, 8
Hou @ Mem, 8
Min @ SAS, 8:30
LAC @ Den, 9
Ind @ Phx, 9
Sac @ LAL, 10:30
Dal @ Uta, 10:30

Dec. 4
Atl @ Mia, 7:30
Cha @ Phi, 7:30
Cle @ Min, 8
Hou @ Chi, 8
Orl @ Mil, 8:30
Dal @ Sac, 10

Dec. 5
NYK @ Tor, 1
Bos @ NJN, 1
Cle @ Det, 6
GSW @ OKC, 7
NWO @ SAS, 7
Mem @ Den, 8
Was @ Phx, 8
LAC @ Por, 8

Dec. 6
Tor @ Ind, 7
Atl @ Orl, 7
Min @ NYK, 7:30
OKC @ Chi, 8
Mia @ Mil, 8
Mem @ Uta, 9
Sac @ LAC, 10:30

Dec. 7
Den @ Cha, 7
Cle @ Phi, 7
NJN @ Atl, 7
GSW @ Dal, 8:30
Det @ Hou, 8:30
Phx @ Por, 10
Was @ LAL, 10:30

Dec. 8
Den @ Bos, 7
Chi @ Cle, 7
Tor @ NYK, 7:30
OKC @ Min, 8
Ind @ Mil, 8
Det @ NWO, 8
GSW @ SAS, 8:30
Mem @ Phx, 9
Mia @ Uta, 9
Was @ Sac, 10
LAL @ LAC, 10:30

Dec. 9
Bos @ Phi, 8
NJN @ Dal, 8:30
Orl @ Por, 10:30

Dec. 10
Cha @ Ind, 7
NYK @ Was, 7
Den @ Tor, 7
OKC @ NWO, 8
LAL @ Chi, 8
Det @ Min, 8
Atl @ SAS, 8:30
Hou @ Mil, 8:30
Por @ Phx, 9
Orl @ Uta, 9
Mia @ GSW, 10:30

Dec. 11
Mem @ LAC, 3:30
Ind @ Atl, 7
Bos @ Cha, 7
Tor @ Det, 7:30
Min @ Chi, 8
Uta @ Dal, 8:30
Cle @ Hou, 8:30
Mia @ Sac, 10

Dec. 12
NWO @ Phi, 12
Den @ NYK, 12
LAL @ NJN, 1
Por @ SAS, 7
Cle @ OKC, 7
Orl @ LAC, 9:30

Dec. 13
NWO @ Mia, 7:30
Ind @ Chi, 8
Por @ Mem, 8
Mil @ Dal, 8:30
GSW @ Uta, 9

Dec. 14
Phi @ NJN, 7
LAL @ Was, 7
Tor @ Cha, 7
Atl @ Det, 7:30
Sac @ Hou, 8:30
Orl @ Den, 9
Min @ GSW, 10:30

Dec. 15
LAL @ Ind, 7
Chi @ Tor, 7
LAC @ Phi, 7
Bos @ NYK, 7
Cle @ Mia, 7:30
Cha @ Mem, 8
Sac @ NWO, 8
Hou @ OKC, 8
Mil @ SAS, 8:30
Min @ Phx, 9
Por @ Dal, 9:30

Dec. 16
Was @ NJN, 7
Atl @ Bos, 8
SAS @ Den, 10:30

Dec. 17
Mia @ NYK, 7
LAL @ Phi, 7
NJN @ Tor, 7
Cle @ Ind, 7
Cha @ Atl, 7:30
LAC @ Det, 7:30
Sac @ OKC, 8
Uta @ NWO, 8
Mem @ Hou, 8:30
Phx @ Dal, 9:30
Min @ Por, 10

Dec. 18
Mia @ Was, 7
Phi @ Orl, 7
NYK @ Cle, 7:30
LAC @ Chi, 8
Mem @ SAS, 8:30
Uta @ Mil, 8:30
Min @ Den, 9
GSW @ Por, 10

Dec. 19
Ind @ Bos, 1
Atl @ NJN, 1
LAL @ Tor, 1
NWO @ Det, 6
Hou @ Sac, 6
Phx @ OKC, 7

Dec. 20
NWO @ Ind, 7
Uta @ Cle, 7
Cha @ Was, 7
Orl @ Atl, 7
Dal @ Mia, 7:30
Phx @ SAS, 8:30
Mil @ Por, 10
Hou @ GSW, 10:30
Min @ LAC, 10:30

Dec. 21
OKC @ Cha, 7
Dal @ Orl, 7
NJN @ Mem, 8
Phi @ Chi, 8
GSW @ Sac, 10
Mil @ LAL, 10:30

Dec. 22
Chi @ Was, 7
Cle @ Atl, 7
Det @ Tor, 7
OKC @ NYK, 7:30
Phi @ Bos, 7:30
Uta @ Min, 8
NJN @ NWO, 8
Den @ SAS, 8:30
Hou @ LAC, 10:30

Dec. 23
SAS @ Orl, 8
Mil @ Sac, 10
Mia @ Phx, 10:30

Dec. 25
Chi @ NYK, 12
Bos @ Orl, 2:30
Mia @ LAL, 5
Den @ OKC, 8
Por @ GSW, 10:30

Dec. 26
Phx @ LAC, 3
Min @ Cle, 6
Chi @ Det, 6
Mem @ Ind, 7
Was @ SAS, 7
Atl @ NWO, 7
Phi @ Den, 8

Dec. 27
Orl @ NJN, 7
Det @ Cha, 7
Atl @ Mil, 8
Tor @ Mem, 8
Dal @ OKC, 8
NWO @ Min, 8
Was @ Hou, 8:30
Por @ Uta, 9
LAC @ Sac, 10
Phi @ GSW, 10:30

Dec. 28
Bos @ Ind, 7
Orl @ Cle, 7
NYK @ Mia, 7:30
Mil @ Chi, 8
LAL @ SAS, 8:30
Tor @ Dal, 8:30
Por @ Den, 9

Dec. 29
GSW @ Atl, 7
Cle @ Cha, 7
Ind @ Was, 7
Bos @ Det, 7:30
Den @ Min, 8
NJN @ OKC, 8
LAL @ NWO, 8
Mia @ Hou, 8:30
Phi @ Phx, 9
Mem @ Sac, 10
Uta @ LAC, 10:30

Dec. 30
NYK @ Orl, 7
SAS @ Dal, 9:30
Uta @ Por, 10

Dec. 31
NWO @ Bos, 3
NJN @ Chi, 3
Was @ Ind, 3
GSW @ Cha, 3
Tor @ Hou, 7
Atl @ OKC, 8
Det @ Phx, 9
Phi @ LAL, 10:30

Jan. 1
NWO @ Was, 7
Cle @ Chi, 7
GSW @ Mia, 7:30
NJN @ Min, 8
OKC @ SAS, 8:30
Dal @ Mil, 9
Sac @ Den, 8:30
Mem @ Uta, 8:30

Jan. 2
Ind @ NYK, 1
Atl @ LAC, 3:30
Bos @ Tor, 6
Dal @ Cle, 7
Hou @ Por, 9
Phx @ Sac, 9
Mem @ LAL, 9:30

2010-11 NBA SCHEDULE

Jan. 3
Mia @ Cha, 7
GSW @ Orl, 7
Min @ Bos, 7:30
Phi @ NWO, 8
Hou @ Den, 8:30
Det @ Uta, 8:30

Jan. 4
Mil @ Mia, 7:30
SAS @ NYK, 7:30
Tor @ Chi, 8
OKC @ Mem, 8
Por @ Dal, 8:30
Atl @ Sac, 10
Det @ LAL, 10:30

Jan. 5
Tor @ Cle, 7
Chi @ NJN, 7
Mil @ Orl, 7
Was @ Phi, 7
SAS @ Bos, 7:30
Cha @ Min, 8
GSW @ NWO, 8
Por @ Hou, 8:30
Atl @ Uta, 8:30
LAL @ Phx, 10:30
Den @ LAC, 10:30

Jan. 6
OKC @ Dal, 8
Den @ Sac, 10:30

Jan. 7
SAS @ Ind, 7
Chi @ Phi, 7
NJN @ Was, 7
Tor @ Bos, 7:30
Hou @ Orl, 8
Uta @ Mem, 8
Por @ Min, 8
Mia @ Mil, 8:30
NYK @ Phx, 10:30
Cle @ GSW, 10:30
NWO @ LAL, 10:30

Jan. 8
Ind @ Atl, 7
Was @ Cha, 7
Mil @ NJN, 7
Phi @ Det, 7:30
Bos @ Chi, 8
Mem @ OKC, 8
Orl @ Dal, 8:30
Uta @ Hou, 8:30

Jan. 9
Sac @ Tor, 1
GSW @ LAC, 3:30
Min @ SAS, 7
Cle @ Phx, 8
NWO @ Den, 8:30
Mia @ Por, 9
NYK @ LAL, 9:30

Jan. 10
Mem @ Cha, 7
Hou @ Bos, 7:30
Det @ Chi, 8

Jan. 11
Mil @ Atl, 7
Ind @ Phi, 7
Sac @ Was, 7
SAS @ Min, 8
Phx @ Den, 8:30
NYK @ Por, 10
Cle @ LAL, 10:30

Jan. 12
Chi @ Cha, 7
Dal @ Ind, 7
Atl @ Tor, 7
Sac @ Bos, 7:30
Mem @ Det, 7:30
SAS @ Mil, 8
Orl @ NWO, 8
OKC @ Hou, 8:30
NJN @ Phx, 8:30
NYK @ Uta, 8:30
LAL @ GSW, 10:30
Mia @ LAC, 10:30

Jan. 13
Was @ Min, 8
Orl @ OKC, 8
Mia @ Den, 10:30

Jan. 14
Chi @ Ind, 7
Mil @ Phi, 7
Det @ Tor, 7
Cha @ Bos, 7:30
Sac @ NYK, 7:30
Dal @ SAS, 8
NWO @ Hou, 8:30
Cle @ Uta, 8:30
Por @ Phx, 10:30
LAC @ GSW, 10:30
NJN @ LAL, 10:30

Jan. 15
Hou @ Atl, 7
NWO @ Cha, 7
Tor @ Was, 7
Sac @ Det, 7:30
Mia @ Chi, 8
Dal @ Mem, 8
Orl @ Min, 8
Cle @ Den, 8:30
NJN @ Por, 10

Jan. 16
LAL @ LAC, 3:30
Den @ SAS, 9

Jan. 17
Phx @ NYK, 1
Uta @ Was, 1
Chi @ Mem, 1
Cha @ Phi, 2
Mil @ Hou, 3
Tor @ NWO, 3
Dal @ Det, 3:30
Ind @ LAC, 3:30
Sac @ Atl, 4
NJN @ GSW, 4
Orl @ Bos, 8
Min @ Por, 10
OKC @ LAL, 10:30

Jan. 18
Atl @ Mia, 7:30
Cha @ Chi, 8

Jan. 19
Phx @ Cle, 7
Uta @ NJN, 7
Phi @ Orl, 7
Det @ Bos, 7:30
Was @ Mil, 8
Mem @ NWO, 8
NYK @ Hou, 8:30
Tor @ SAS, 8:30
LAL @ Dal, 9
OKC @ Den, 8:30
Por @ Sac, 10
Ind @ GSW, 10:30
Min @ LAC, 10:30

Jan. 20
Phi @ Cha, 7
Dal @ Chi, 8
LAC @ Por, 10:30

Jan. 21
Det @ NJN, 7
Tor @ Orl, 7
NWO @ Atl, 7:30
Uta @ Bos, 7:30
Mil @ Cle, 7:30
Phx @ Was, 8
Hou @ Mem, 8
NYK @ SAS, 8:30
LAL @ Den, 10:30
Sac @ GSW, 10:30

Jan. 22
Atl @ Cha, 7
Dal @ NJN, 7
Bos @ Was, 7
Phx @ Det, 7:30
Tor @ Mia, 7:30
Uta @ Phi, 7:30
Cle @ Chi, 8
SAS @ NWO, 8
NYK @ OKC, 8
Orl @ Hou, 8:30
Mem @ Mil, 8:30
Ind @ Por, 10
GSW @ LAC, 10:30

Jan. 23
Ind @ Den, 8

Jan. 24
Cle @ NJN, 7
Det @ Orl, 7
Phx @ Phi, 7
Mem @ Tor, 7
Was @ NYK, 7:30
Mil @ Chi, 8
Hou @ Min, 8
OKC @ NWO, 8
Sac @ Por, 10
SAS @ GSW, 10:30

Jan. 25
Den @ Was, 7
Cle @ Bos, 7:30
LAC @ Dal, 8:30
Cha @ Sac, 10
Uta @ LAL, 10:30

Jan. 26
Orl @ Ind, 7
Mem @ NJN, 7
Phi @ Tor, 7
Den @ Det, 7:30
Atl @ Mil, 8
OKC @ Min, 8
LAC @ Hou, 8:30
Cha @ Phx, 8:30
SAS @ Uta, 9:30
NWO @ GSW, 10:30

Jan. 27
Mia @ NYK, 8
Hou @ Dal, 8:30
Bos @ Por, 10:30

Jan. 28
NJN @ Ind, 7
Mem @ Phi, 7
Mil @ Tor, 7
NYK @ Atl, 7:30
Den @ Cle, 7:30
Det @ Mia, 7:30
Orl @ Chi, 8
Was @ OKC, 8
Min @ Uta, 8:30
Bos @ Phx, 10:30
Cha @ GSW, 10:30
Sac @ LAL, 10:30

Jan. 29
Ind @ Chi, 8
Was @ Mem, 8
Tor @ Min, 8
Atl @ Dal, 8:30
NJN @ Mil, 8:30
Hou @ SAS, 8:30
NWO @ Sac, 10
Cha @ LAC, 10:30

Jan. 30
Mia @ OKC, 1
Bos @ LAL, 3:30
Cle @ Orl, 6
Den @ Phi, 6
Det @ NYK, 7:30
NWO @ Phx, 8
Uta @ GSW, 10

Jan. 31
Tor @ Ind, 7
Den @ NJN, 7
Cle @ Mia, 7:30
Orl @ Mem, 8
Was @ Dal, 8:30
Cha @ Uta, 8:30
Mil @ LAC, 10:30

Feb. 1
Was @ NWO, 8
SAS @ Por, 10
Bos @ Sac, 10
Hou @ LAL, 10:30

Feb. 2
Tor @ Atl, 7
Ind @ Cle, 7
Phi @ NJN, 7
Cha @ Det, 7:30
Dal @ NYK, 7:30
Mem @ Min, 8
NWO @ OKC, 8
Por @ Den, 8:30
Mil @ Phx, 8:30
Hou @ Uta, 8:30
Chi @ LAC, 10:30

Feb. 3
Mia @ Orl, 8
Mil @ GSW, 10:30
SAS @ LAL, 10:30

Feb. 4
Mia @ Cha, 7
Por @ Ind, 7
NYK @ Phi, 7
Min @ Tor, 7
Orl @ Was, 7
LAC @ Atl, 7:30
NJN @ Det, 7:30
Dal @ Bos, 8
Cle @ Mem, 8
OKC @ Phx, 8:30
SAS @ Sac, 10
Uta @ Den, 10:30

Feb. 5
Dal @ Cha, 7
Atl @ Was, 7
Por @ Cle, 7:30
LAL @ NWO, 8
Mem @ Hou, 8:30
Det @ Mil, 8:30
Den @ Min, 8:30
OKC @ Uta, 8:30
Chi @ GSW, 10:30

Feb. 6
LAC @ Mia, Noon
Ind @ NJN, Noon
Phi @ NYK, Noon
Orl @ Bos, 2:30

Feb. 7
Bos @ Cha, 7
LAL @ Mem, 8
Min @ NWO, 8
Cle @ Dal, 8:30
Hou @ Den, 8:30
Chi @ Por, 10
Uta @ Sac, 10
Phx @ GSW, 10:30

347

2010-11 NBA SCHEDULE

Feb. 8
Phi @ Atl, 7
LAC @ Orl, 7
SAS @ Det, 7:30
Ind @ Mia, 7:30
Tor @ Mil, 8
Mem @ OKC, 8 @ 8
Min @ Hou, 8:30

Feb. 9
Det @ Cle, 7
Cha @ Ind, 7
NWO @ NJN, 7
Orl @ Phi, 7
SAS @ Tor, 7
Mil @ Was, 7
LAC @ NYK, 7:30
Chi @ Uta, 8:30
Dal @ Sac, 10
Den @ GSW, 10:30

Feb. 10
LAL @ Bos, 8
GSW @ Phx, 8:30
Dal @ Den, 10:30

Feb. 11
NJN @ Cha, 7
Min @ Ind, 7 @ 7
NWO @ Orl, 7
SAS @ Phi, 7
Por @ Tor, 7
LAC @ Cle, 7:30
Mia @ Det, 7:30
LAL @ NYK, 8
Mil @ Mem, 8
Phx @ Uta, 10:30

Feb. 12
Cha @ Atl, 7
NYK @ NJN, 7
SAS @ Was, 8
Phi @ Min, 8
Chi @ NWO, 8
Dal @ Hou, 8:30
Ind @ Mil, 8:30
OKC @ Sac, 10

Feb. 13
Mia @ Bos, 1
LAL @ Orl, 3:30
Was @ Cle, 6
Por @ Det, 6
LAC @ Tor, 6
Den @ Mem, 6
Sac @ Phx, 8
OKC @ GSW, 8

Feb. 14
LAL @ Cha, 7
SAS @ NJN, 7
Atl @ Det, 7:30
LAC @ Mil, 8
Por @ Min, 8
Den @ Hou, 8:30

Feb. 15
Mia @ Ind, 7
Cha @ Chi, 8
Phi @ Mem, 8
Sac @ OKC, 8
Uta @ Phx, 8:30
NWO @ GSW, 10:30

Feb. 16
Was @ Orl, 7
Mia @ Tor, 7
NJN @ Bos, 7:30
LAL @ Cle, 7:30
Ind @ Det, 7:30
Atl @ NYK, 7:30
LAC @ Min, 8
Sac @ Dal, 8:30
Phi @ Hou, 8:30
Den @ Mil, 9
GSW @ Uta, 8:30
NWO @ Por, 10

Feb. 17
SAS @ Chi, 8
Dal @ Phx, 10:30
Tor @ Cha, 7
Ind @ Was, 7
Hou @ Det, 7:30
Sac @ Mia, 7:30
Min @ Mil, 8
LAC @ OKC, 8
Mem @ Den, 8:30
Bos @ GSW, 10:30
Atl @ LAL, 10:30

Feb. 23
Hou @ Cle, 7
Det @ Ind, 7
Sac @ Orl, 7
Was @ Phi, 7
Chi @ Tor, 7
Mil @ NYK, 7:30
Mem @ Min, 8
LAC @ NWO, 8
OKC @ SAS, 8
Uta @ Dal, 8:30
Atl @ Phx, 8:30
LAL @ Por, 10:30

Feb. 24
Mia @ Chi, 8
Bos @ Den, 10:30

Feb. 25
Sac @ Cha, 7
Uta @ Ind, 7
Det @ Phi, 7
Phx @ Tor, 7
NYK @ Cle, 7:30
Was @ Mia, 7:30
OKC @ Orl, 8
NWO @ Min, 8
NJN @ SAS, 8:30
Atl @ GSW, 10:30
LAC @ LAL, 10:30
Den @ Por, 10:30

Feb. 26
Dal @ Was, 8
Uta @ Det, 7:30
Sac @ Mem, 8
NJN @ Hou, 8:30
Chi @ Mil, 8:30
Bos @ LAC, 10:30

Feb. 27
Phx @ Ind, Noon
LAL @ OKC, 2:30
Phi @ Cle, 5
GSW @ Min, 5
Cha @ Orl, 6
Dal @ Tor, 6
Hou @ NWO, 7
Mem @ SAS, 7
NYK @ Mia, 8
Atl @ Por, 10:30

Feb. 28
Phx @ NJN, 7
Chi @ Was, 7
Atl @ Den, 8:30
Bos @ Uta, 8:30
LAC @ Sac, 10

March 1
GSW @ Ind, 7
NYK @ Orl, 7
Dal @ Phi, 7
NWO @ Tor, 7
SAS @ Mem, 8
Det @ Mil, 8
LAL @ Min, 8
Hou @ Por, 10

March 2
Chi @ Atl, 7
SAS @ Cle, 7
GSW @ Was, 7
Phx @ Bos, 7:30
Min @ Det, 7:30
NWO @ NYK, 7:30
Ind @ OKC, 8
Cha @ Den, 8:30
Por @ Sac, 10
Hou @ LAC, 10:30

March 3
Orl @ Mia, 8
Den @ Uta, 10:30

March 4
Tor vs. NJN @ London, 3
Chi @ Orl, 7
Min @ Phi, 7
OKC @ Atl, 7:30
GSW @ Bos, 7:30
Cle @ NYK, 7:30
NWO @ Mem, 8
Ind @ Dal, 8:30
Phx @ Mil, 8:30
Mia @ SAS, 9:30
Cha @ LAL, 10:30

March 5
Tor vs. NJN @ London, 3
Min @ Was, 7
Ind @ Hou, 8:30
Sac @ Uta, 8:30
Cha @ Por, 10
Den @ LAC, 10:30

March 6
Chi @ Mia, 1
LAL @ SAS, 3:30
NYK @ Atl, 6
Was @ Det, 6
GSW @ Phi, 6
NWO @ Cle, 6:30
Phx @ OKC, 7
Mem @ Dal, 7:30
Bos @ Mil, 9

March 7
LAC @ Cha, 7
Por @ Orl, 7
Uta @ NYK, 7:30
NWO @ Chi, 8
OKC @ Mem, 8
Dal @ Min, 8
Hou @ Sac, 10

March 8
LAL @ Atl, 7
GSW @ Cle, 7
Phi @ Ind, 7
Mil @ Was, 7
Por @ Mia, 7:30
Hou @ Phx, 8:30

March 9
Chi @ Cha, 7
GSW @ NJN, 7
OKC @ Phi, 7
Uta @ Tor, 7
LAC @ Bos, 7:30
NYK @ Mem, 8
Cle @ Mil, 8
Ind @ Min, 8
Dal @ NWO, 8
Det @ SAS, 8:30
Orl @ Sac, 10

March 10
LAL @ Mia, 8
NYK @ Dal, 8:30
Den @ Phx, 10:30

March 11
Por @ Cha, 7
LAC @ NJN, 7
Bos @ Phi, 7
Ind @ Tor, 7
Atl @ Chi, 8
Uta @ Min, 8
Det @ OKC, 8
Sac @ SAS, 8:30
Orl @ GSW, 10:30

March 12
Mem @ Mia, 3:30
Por @ Atl, 7
LAC @ Was, 7
Uta @ Chi, 8
Phi @ Mil, 8
Sac @ NWO, 8
LAL @ Dal, 8:30
SAS @ Hou, 8:30
Det @ Den, 8:30

March 13
OKC @ Cle, 1
Cha @ Tor, 1
Orl @ Phx, 3:30
Mil @ Bos, 6
Ind @ NYK, 6
Min @ GSW, 9

March 14
Bos @ NJN, 7
OKC @ Was, 7
SAS @ Mia, 8
LAC @ Mem, 8
Den @ NWO, 8
Phx @ Hou, 8:30
Phi @ Uta, 8:30
GSW @ Sac, 10
Orl @ LAL, 10:30:30

March 15
NYK @ Ind, 7
Was @ Chi, 8
Dal @ Por, 10

March 16
Den @ Atl, 7
Ind @ Bos, 7:30
Tor @ Det, 7:30
OKC @ Mia, 8
Orl @ Mil, 8
Phx @ NWO, 8
Cha @ Hou, 8:30
Min @ Uta, 8:30
Cle @ Sac, 10
Dal @ GSW, 10:30
Phi @ LAC, 10:30

March 17
Chi @ NJN, 7
Mem @ NYK, 7:30
Cle @ Por, 10

March 18
Chi @ Ind, 7
Den @ Orl, 7
Was @ Tor, 7
Mia @ Atl, 7:30
NYK @ Det, 7:30
Cha @ OKC, 8
SAS @ Dal, 8:30
Bos @ Hou, 8:30
NJN @ Mil, 8:30
GSW @ Phx, 10
Phi @ Sac, 10
Min @ LAL, 10:30

March 19
Cle @ LAC, 3:30
Den @ Mia, 7:30
Ind @ Mem, 8
Bos @ NWO, 8
Cha @ SAS, 8:30
Phi @ Por, 10

March 20
NJN @ Was, 1
Det @ Atl, 2
NYK @ Mil, 3
Sac @ Min, 3:30
Phx @ LAC, 3:30
Uta @ Hou, 7
Tor @ OKC, 7
GSW @ Dal, 7:30
Por @ LAL, 9:30

2010-11 NBA SCHEDULE

March 21
Orl @ Cle, 7
Ind @ NJN, 7
Bos @ NYK, 7:30
Sac @ Chi, 8
Uta @ Mem, 8
GSW @ SAS, 8:30
Tor @ Den, 8:30

March 22
Chi @ Atl, 8
Was @ Por, 10
Phx @ LAL, 10:30

March 23
Ind @ Cha, 7
NJN @ Cle, 7
Atl @ Phi, 7
Mem @ Bos, 7:30
Mia @ Det, 7:30
Orl @ NYK, 8
Sac @ Mil, 8
Uta @ OKC, 8
GSW @ Hou, 8:30
Tor @ Phx, 10
SAS @ Den, 10:30
Was @ LAC, 10:30

March 24
Min @ Dal, 8:30
NWO @ Uta, 8:30

March 25
Sac @ Ind, 7
NJN @ Orl, 7
Cha @ Bos, 7:30
Det @ Cle, 7:30
Phi @ Mia, 7:30
Mil @ NYK, 7:30
Mem @ Chi, 8
Min @ OKC, 8
Was @ Den, 8:30
NWO @ Phx, 10
SAS @ Por, 10
Tor @ GSW, 10:30
LAC @ LAL, 10:30

March 26
NJN @ Atl, 7
NYK @ Cha, 7
Ind @ Det, 7:30
Chi @ Mil, 8:30
Dal @ Uta, 8:30
Tor @ LAC, 10:30

March 27
Sac @ Phi, Noon
Atl @ Cle, 6
Hou @ Mia, 6
SAS @ Mem, 6
Bos @ Min, 7
Por @ OKC, 8
Was @ GSW, 9
NWO @ LAL, 9:30
Dal @ Phx, 10:30

March 28
Mil @ Cha, 7
Bos @ Ind, 7
Phi @ Chi, 8
Por @ SAS, 8:30
Was @ Uta, 8:30

March 29
Mia @ Cle, 7
Hou @ NJN, 7
GSW @ OKC, 8
Phx @ Sac, 10

March 30
Orl @ Atl, 7
Cle @ Cha, 7
Det @ Ind, 7
Hou @ Phi, 7
Mil @ Tor, 7
Mia @ Was, 7
NJN @ NYK, 7:30
GSW @ Mem, 8
Chi @ Min, 8
Por @ NWO, 8
Sac @ Den, 8:30
OKC @ Phx, 10
Dal @ LAC, 10:30

March 31
Bos @ SAS, 8
Dal @ LAL, 10:30

April 1
Mil @ Ind, 7
Cha @ Orl, 7
NJN @ Phi, 7
Cle @ Was, 7
Chi @ Det, 7:30
Bos @ Atl, 8
Mia @ Min, 8
Mem @ NWO, 8
SAS @ Hou, 8:30
LAC @ Phx, 10
OKC @ Por, 10
Den @ Sac, 10
LAL @ Uta, 10:30

April 2
Tor @ Chi, 8
Min @ Mem, 8
Phi @ Mil, 8:30
Dal @ GSW, 10:30
OKC @ LAC, 10:30

April 3
Phx @ SAS, 1
Den @ LAL, 3:30
Det @ Bos, 6
Was @ Cha, 6
Mia @ NJN, 6
Cle @ NYK, 6
Orl @ Tor, 6
Uta @ Sac, 6
Atl @ Hou, 7
Ind @ NWO, 7
Dal @ Por, 9

April 5
SAS @ Atl, 7
Cha @ Cle, 7
Min @ NJN, 7
Mil @ Orl, 7
Det @ Was, 7
Phi @ Bos, 7:30
Tor @ NYK, 7:30
Phx @ Chi, 8
LAC @ Mem, 8
Sac @ Hou, 8:30
OKC @ Den, 8:30
GSW @ Por, 10
Uta @ LAL, 10:30

April 6
Orl @ Cha, 7
Was @ Ind, 7
Mil @ Mia, 7
NYK @ Phi, 7
Cle @ Tor, 7
NJN @ Det, 7:30
Phx @ Min, 8
Hou @ NWO, 8
LAC @ OKC, 8
Sac @ SAS, 8:30
Den @ Dal, 9:30
LAL @ GSW, 10:30

April 7
Bos @ Chi, 8
Por @ Uta, 10:30

April 8
Atl @ Ind, 7
NYK @ NJN, 7
Tor @ Phi, 7
Was @ Bos, 7:30
Chi @ Cle, 7:30
Mil @ Det, 7:30
Cha @ Mia, 7:30
Sac @ Mem, 8
Phx @ NWO, 8
Den @ OKC, 8
LAC @ Dal, 8:30
LAL @ Por, 10

April 9
Atl @ Was, 7
LAC @ Hou, 8:30
Cle @ Mil, 8:30
Uta @ SAS, 8:30
Min @ Den, 8:30

April 10
Chi @ Orl, 1
Bos @ Mia, 3:30
Det @ Cha, 6
NJN @ Tor, 6
NWO @ Mem, 6
NYK @ Ind, 7
Phx @ Dal, 7:30
Sac @ GSW, 9
OKC @ LAL, 9:30

April 11
Mia @ Atl, 7
Cha @ NJN, 7
Orl @ Phi, 7
Bos @ Was, 7
Cle @ Det, 7:30
Tor @ Mil, 8
Uta @ NWO, 8
Dal @ Hou, 8:30
GSW @ Den, 8:30
Min @ Phx, 10
OKC @ Sac, 10

April 12
Chi @ NYK, 8
Mem @ Por, 10
SAS @ LAL, 10:30

April 13
NYK @ Bos, 8
Atl @ Cha, 8
Was @ Cle, 8
Ind @ Orl, 8
Det @ Phi, 8
Mia @ Tor, 8
NJN @ Chi, 8
NWO @ Dal, 8
Hou @ Min, 8
Mil @ OKC, 8
Den @ Uta, 8
Por @ GSW, 10:30
Mem @ LAC, 10:30
SAS @ Phx, 10:30
LAL @ Sac, 10:30

Acknowledgments

- Thanks to everyone who helped out with data, either specifically or via invaluable websites. Justin Kubatko of Basketball-Reference.com goes above and beyond time and again. Aaron Barzilai of BasketballValue.com supplied a spreadsheet with net and adjusted plus-minus data that was very helpful.

Hoopdata.com provided extraordinarily useful numbers on shooting by distance and charges drawn. Thanks to Eli Witus for offering adjusted plus-minus for 2007-08 as well as cracking the code on the NBA's HotSpots feature. Thanks to Jeff of storytellerscontracts.com, whose awesome database of NBA contracts and salary-cap information served as the foundation for our financial data. ShamSports.com was also a useful salary resource.

Thanks to Synergy Sports Technology for providing us with subscriptions to My Synergy Sports. The analysis of play types and league percentile rankings you see in the player capsules come from Synergy. Visit http://www.mysynergysports.com to sign up for video.

- Thanks to Nathaniel Friedman, Mark Haubner and Nate Parham from the SSSBDA, Scott Carefoot, Laura Sgrecci, Tom Ziller and especially Benjamin Golliver for proofreading.
- Thanks to all our blogger contributors--please check out their blogs.
- Thanks to Anthony Macri and John Perrotto for their contributions to our online NBA coverage and our NCAA colleagues John Gasaway and Ken Pomeroy for commiserating.
- Thanks to Kevin Goldstein, David Pease and Jeffrey Pease of PEV for their support in making this book reality.
- Thanks to Dean Oliver and John Hollinger for helping pave the way.
- Thanks to friends in other sports: Bill Barnwell, Will Leitch, Joe Posnanski, Aaron Schatz and Joe Sheehan.
- Thanks to Will Carroll for his helpfulness in shedding light on injuries throughout the year.
- Thanks to Henry Abbott, Kevin Arnovitz, Tommy Craggs, Kelly Dwyer, Chad Ford, Paul Forrester, Eric Freeman, Jonathan Givony, Trey Kerby, David Locke, Tas Melas, Eric Neel, Neil Paine, J.E. Skeets, Bill Simmons, Marc Stein and Chris Villani for promotion.
- Kevin wants to thank his real family (especially Mom, Tristan, Keayleen and Katie), his Storm family (Aaron, Amanda, Chauntelle, Derek, Gentry, Jennifer, Kelly M., Kelly N., Matt and others) and former Sonics coworkers (too many to name).
- Bradford wants to thank his wife Amy for her never-ending support, patience and understanding, his dog Hunter for keeping him company through the long process of writing and his parents, Bruce and Karen. He'd especially like to thank his brother Brian for being the world's biggest NBA junkie, an invaluable sounding board and the father of Samantha, the cutest niece on the planet.
- Most important, thanks to all our readers for helping spread the word. We couldn't do it without you.

Author Bios

Bradford Doolittle is a fiction writer and freelance sports journalist who writes for Baseball Prospectus, MLB.com and the Associated Press, and has written for Slate, ESPN, *Sports Illustrated*, *The Kansas City Star*, Deadspin, The Hardball Times and other outlets. He's been with Basketball Prospectus since November 2007, and is the creator of the NBAPET basketball analysis system. He is a member of the Pro Basketball Writers Association, SABR and the Baseball Writers' Association of America. You may have surmised from numerous shameless drop-ins that he attended the University of Missouri. He is based in the Uptown/Edgewater area of Chicago, where he lives with his wife, Amy. You can follow him on Twitter under the handle of @bbdoolittle.

Kevin Pelton has served as an author for Basketball Prospectus since the site's inception in October 2007. His NBA commentary has appeared on Hoopsworld.com, 82games.com, SI.com, CourtsideTimes.Net and ESPN Insider. Pelton also moderates the APBRmetrics discussion forum for statistical analysis and is the co-host of the Dontonio Wingcast on Blazersedge.com. He spent four seasons as the beat writer for supersonics.com and has covered the WNBA's Seattle Storm for the team's official site, stormbasketball.com, since 2003. The Storm's recent victory in the 2010 WNBA Finals gives Pelton two more championship rings than Charles Barkley, Patrick Ewing, LeBron James, Karl Malone and John Stockton combined and ties him with Adam Morrison. His Twitter account is @kpelton.

Vince Verhei is a freelance writer, editor, and podcast host based out of Seattle. He is a featured writer for Football Outsiders and author of the Any Given Sunday column published on ESPN.com. A graduate of the journalism program at Western Washington University, he also co-hosts podcasts covering professional wrestling and other silliness at figurefouronline.com.

Player Index

Afflalo, Arron: 70
Ajinca, Alexis: 59
Alabi, Soloman: 299
Aldrich, Cole: 222
Aldridge, Lamarcus: 267
Alexander, Joe: 202
Allen, Malik: 235
Allen, Ray: 15
Allen, Tony: 144
Alston, Rafer: 162
Amundson, Louis: 90
Andersen, Chris: 70
Andersen, David: 299
Anderson, Antonio: 100
Anderson, James: 288
Anderson, Ryan: 235
Anthony, Carmelo: 71
Anthony, Joel: 155
Arenas, Gilbert: 318
Ariza, Trevor: 202
Armstrong, Hilton: 318
Arroyo, Carlos: 156
Artest, Ron: 133
Arthur, Darrell: 144
Asik, Omer: 39
Atkins, Chucky: 256
Augustin, D.J.: 27
Azubuike, Kelenna: 211
Babbitt, Luke: 267
Balkman, Renaldo: 71
Banks, Marcus: 300
Barbosa, Leandro: 300
Barea, Jose: 60
Bargnani, Andrea: 300
Barnes, Matt: 134
Barron, Earl: 218
Bass, Brandon: 236
Battie, Tony: 246
Battier, Shane: 100
Batum, Nicolas: 268
Bayless, Jerryd: 268
Beasley, Michael: 177

Beaubois, Rodrigue: 60
Belinelli, Marco: 202
Bell, Charlie: 90
Bell, Raja: 309
Bender, Jonathan: 218
Beverley, Patrick: 156
Bibby, Mike: 5
Biedrins, Andris: 90
Billups, Chauncey: 72
Bjelica, Nemanja: 184
Blair, Dejuan: 289
Blake, Steve: 134
Blakely, Marqus: 122
Blatche, Andray: 319
Bledsoe, Eric: 122
Bogans, Keith: 39
Bogut, Andrew: 166
Bonner, Matt: 289
Booker, Trevor: 319
Boone, Josh: 197
Boozer, Carlos: 40
Bosh, Chris: 156
Bowen, Ryan: 230
Boykins, Earl: 167
Brackins, Craig: 247
Bradley, Avery: 15
Brand, Elton: 247
Brewer, Corey: 178
Brewer, Ronnie: 40
Brezec, Primoz: 173
Brockman, Jon: 167
Brooks, Aaron: 101
Brown, Bobby: 128
Brown, Derrick: 27
Brown, Devin: 45
Brown, Kwame: 28
Brown, Shannon: 135
Bryant, Kobe: 135
Budinger, Chase: 101
Butch, Brian: 76
Butler, Caron: 60
Butler, Dasean: 157

Butler, Rasual: 122
Bynum, Andrew: 136
Bynum, Will: 80
Calderon, Jose: 301
Camby, Marcus: 269
Caracter, Derrick: 136
Cardinal, Brian: 61
Carney, Rodney: 91
Carroll, Demarre: 145
Carroll, Matt: 28
Carter, Anthony: 72
Carter, Vince: 236
Casspi, Omri: 278
Chalmers, Mario: 157
Chandler, Tyson: 61
Chandler, Wilson: 212
Childress, Josh: 256
Clark, Earl: 257
Collins, Dwayne: 262
Collins, Jarron: 123
Collins, Jason: 5
Collins, Mardy: 128
Collins, Sherron: 28
Collison, Darren: 113
Collison, Nick: 222
Conley, Mike: 145
Conroy, Will: 107
Cook, Brian: 123
Cook, Daequan: 223
Cousins, Demarcus: 278
Crawford, Jamal: 5
Crawford, Jordan: 6
Cunningham, Dante: 269
Curry, Eddy: 212
Curry, Jameson: 128
Curry, Stephen: 91
Dalembert, Samuel: 279
Dampier, Erick: 33
Daniels, Marquis: 15
Davis, Baron: 124
Davis, Ed: 301
Davis, Glen: 16

Davis, Paul: 324
Davis, Ricky: 129
Daye, Austin: 80
Delfino, Carlos: 167
Deng, Luol: 41
Derozan, Demar: 302
Diaw, Boris: 29
Diawara, Yakhouba: 162
Diener, Travis: 274
Diogu, Ike: 81
Diop, Desagana: 29
Dooling, Keyon: 168
Dorsey, Joey: 302
Douglas, Toney: 213
Douglas-Roberts, Chris: 168
Dragic, Goran: 257
Dudley, Jared: 257
Duhon, Chris: 237
Duncan, Tim: 290
Dunleavy Jr., Mike: 113
Durant, Kevin: 223
Ebanks, Devin: 136
Ellington, Wayne: 178
Ellis, Monta: 92
Elson, Francisco: 309
Erden, Semih: 16
Evans, Jeremy: 310
Evans, Maurice: 6
Evans, Reggie: 302
Evans, Tyreke: 279
Ewingjr., Patrick: 213
Eyenga, Christian: 50
Farmar, Jordan: 190
Favors, Derrick: 190
Felton, Raymond: 213
Fernandez, Rudy: 269
Fesenko, Kyrylo: 310
Fields, Landry: 214
Finley, Michael: 22
Fisher, Derek: 137
Flynn, Jonny: 179

PLAYER INDEX

Ford, T.J.: 113
Foster, Jeff: 114
Foye, Randy: 124
Foyle, Adonal: 241
Frye, Channing: 258
Gadzuric, Dan: 92
Gaffney, Tony: 17
Gaines, Sundiata: 310
Gallinari, Danilo: 214
Gallon, Keith: 168
Garcia, Francisco: 280
Garnett, Kevin: 17
Gasol, Marc: 145
Gasol, Pau: 137
Gay, Rudy: 146
Gee, Alonzo: 290
George, Devean: 96
George, Paul: 114
Gibson, Daniel: 50
Gibson, Taj: 41
Giddens, J.R.: 280
Gilder, Trey: 150
Ginobili, Manu: 290
Gladyr, Sergiy: 11
Gomes, Ryan: 125
Gooden, Drew: 169
Gordon, Ben: 81
Gordon, Eric: 125
Gortat, Marcin: 237
Graham, Joey: 51
Graham, Stephen: 191
Granger, Danny: 114
Gray, Aaron: 203
Green, Danny: 51
Green, Jeff: 224
Green, Willie: 203
Greene, Donte: 280
Griffin, Blake: 126
Griffin, Taylor: 262
Haddadi, Hamed: 146
Hairston, Malik: 295
Haislip, Marcus: 295
Hamilton, Richard: 81
Hansbrough, Tyler: 115
Harangody, Luke: 17
Harden, James: 225
Harrington, Al: 73
Harris, Devin: 191
Harris, Mike: 102

Hart, Jason: 179
Hasbrouck, Henny: 157
Haslem, Udonis: 158
Hassell, Trenton: 197
Hawes, Spencer: 247
Hayes, Chuck: 102
Hayes, Jarvis: 197
Hayward, Gordon: 311
Hayward, Lazar: 179
Haywood, Brendan: 62
Head, Luther: 281
Hendersonjr, Gerald: 30
Henry, Xavier: 147
Hibbert, Roy: 115
Hickson, J.J.: 51
Hilario, Nenê: 73
Hill, George: 291
Hill, Grant: 258
Hill, Jordan: 102
Hinrich, Kirk: 320
Hobson, Darington: 169
Holiday, Jrue: 248
Hollins, Ryan: 52
Horford, Al: 7
House, Eddie: 158
Howard, Dwight: 238
Howard, Josh: 320
Howard, Juwan: 158
Hudson, Lester: 320
Hughes, Larry: 33
Humphries, Kris: 192
Hunter, Chris: 96
Hunter, Lindsey: 46
Hunter, Othello: 10
Hunter, Steven: 150
Ibaka, Serge: 225
Iguodala, Andre: 248
Ilgauskas, Zydrunas: 159
Ilungambenga, Didier: 139
Ilyasova, Ersan: 169
Iverson, Allen: 252
Ivey, Royal: 226
Jack, Jarrett: 303
Jackson, Cedric: 52
Jackson, Darnell: 281
Jackson, Stephen: 30
James, Damion: 192
James, Lebron: 159
James, Mike: 324

Jamison, Antawn: 52
Janning, Matt: 259
Jawai, Nathan: 185
Jeffers, Othyus: 311
Jefferson, Al: 311
Jefferson, Richard: 291
Jeffries, Jared: 103
Jennings, Brandon: 170
Jerebko, Jonas: 82
Jerrells, Curtis: 292
Jeter, Pooh: 281
Jianlian, Yi: 323
Johnson, Alexander: 103
Johnson, Amir: 303
Johnson, Anthony: 242
Johnson, Armon: 270
Johnson, James: 42
Johnson, Joe: 7
Johnson, Wesley: 180
Jones, Dahntay: 116
Jones, Dominique: 62
Jones, Dwayne: 259
Jones, James: 160
Jones, Solomon: 116
Jordan, Deandre: 126
Jordan, Jerome: 217
Kaman, Chris: 126
Kapono, Jason: 249
Karl, Coby: 76
Kidd, Jason: 63
Kirilenko, Andrei: 312
Kleiza, Linas: 303
Korver, Kyle: 42
Koufos, Kosta: 180
Krstic, Nenad: 226
Lafayette, Oliver: 22
Landry, Carl: 282
Landry, Marcus: 282
Law, Acie: 147
Lawal, Gani: 259
Lawson, Ty: 74
Lee, Courtney: 104
Lee, David: 93
Lewis, Rashard: 238
Lin, Jeremy: 93
Livingston, Shaun: 30
Lopez, Brook: 192
Lopez, Robin: 260
Love, Kevin: 181

Lowry, Kyle: 104
Lucasiii, John: 42
Maggette, Corey: 170
Magloire, Jamaal: 160
Mahinmi, Ian: 63
Marion, Shawn: 64
Marks, Sean: 321
Martin, Cartier: 321
Martin, Kenyon: 74
Martin, Kevin: 105
Mason, Desmond: 284
Mason, Roger: 214
Matthews, Wesley: 270
Maxiell, Jason: 82
May, Sean: 198
Maynor, Eric: 227
Mayo, O.J.: 147
Mbahamoute, Luc: 171
Mcdyess, Antonio: 292
Mcgee, Javale: 321
Mcgrady, Tracy: 83
Mcguire, Dominic: 31
Mcroberts, Josh: 117
Meeks, Jodie: 249
Miles, C.J.: 312
Miles, Darius: 31
Milicic, Darko: 181
Miller, Andre: 271
Miller, Brad: 105
Miller, Mike: 160
Mills, Patrick: 271
Millsap, Paul: 312
Mohammed, Nazr: 32
Monroe, Greg: 83
Moon, Jamario: 53
Moore, Mikki: 96
Morris, Randolph: 11
Morrison, Adam: 322
Morrow, Anthony: 193
Mozgov, Timofey: 215
Mullens, Byron: 227
Murphy, Troy: 193
Murray, Ronald: 46
Najera, Eduardo: 32
Nash, Steve: 260
Ndiaye, Hamady: 322
Neal, Gary: 292
Nelson, Jameer: 239
Nesterovic, Rasho: 305

PLAYER INDEX

Nichols, Demetris: 314
Noah, Joakim: 43
Nocioni, Andres: 249
Novak, Steve: 64
Nowitzki, Dirk: 65
Oberto, Fabricio: 325
O'Bryant, Patrick: 305
Oden, Greg: 271
Odom, Lamar: 138
Okafor, Emeka: 204
Okur, Mehmet: 313
Ollie, Kevin: 231
O'Neal, Jermaine: 18
O'Neal, Shaquille: 18
Orton, Daniel: 239
Outlaw, Travis: 194
Pachulia, Zaza: 8
Pargo, Jannero: 204
Parker, Anthony: 53
Parker, Tony: 293
Patterson, Patrick: 105
Paul, Chris: 204
Pavlovic, Sasha: 185
Pecherov, Oleksiy: 185
Pekovic, Nikola: 182
Pendergraph, Jeff: 272
Perkins, Kendrick: 19
Peterson, Morris: 227
Petro, Johan: 194
Pierce, Paul: 19
Pietrus, Mickael: 239
Pittman, Dexter: 161
Pleiss, Tibor: 229
Pondexter, Quincy: 205
Posey, James: 117
Powe, Leon: 54
Powell, Josh: 8
Prestes, Paulao: 184
Price, A.J.: 117
Price, Ronnie: 313
Prince, Tayshaun: 83
Przybilla, Joel: 272
Quinn, Chris: 250
Radmanovic, Vladimir: 94

Randolph, Anthony: 215
Randolph, Shavlik: 161
Randolph, Zach: 148
Ratliff, Theo: 138
Rautins, Andy: 216
Redd, Michael: 171
Redick, J.J.: 240
Reid, Ryan: 230
Richard, Chris: 43
Richards, Ryan: 295
Richardson, Jason: 261
Richardson, Quentin: 240
Ridnour, Luke: 182
Robinson, Nate: 20
Robinson, Stanley: 241
Rodriguez, Sergio: 218
Rolle, Magnum: 118
Rondo, Rajon: 20
Rose, Derrick: 43
Ross, Quinton: 195
Roy, Brandon: 273
Rush, Brandon: 118
Rush, Kareem: 129
Salmons, John: 172
Samuels, Samardo: 54
Sanders, Larry: 172
Scalabrine, Brian: 44
Scola, Luis: 106
Sefolosha, Thabo: 228
Seraphin, Kevin: 322
Sessions, Ramon: 55
Shakur, Mustafa: 205
Simmons, Bobby: 293
Singleton, James: 325
Skinner, Brian: 172
Sloan, Donald: 282
Smith, Craig: 127
Smith, Ishmael: 106
Smith, J.R.: 75
Smith, Jason: 206
Smith, Joe: 195
Smith, Josh: 8
Songaila, Darius: 250
Speights, Marreese: 250

Splitter, Tiago: 294
Stackhouse, Jerry: 173
Stephenson, Lance: 118
Stevenson, DeShawn: 65
Stiemsma, Greg: 55
Stojakovic, Peja: 206
Stoudemire, Amare: 216
Stuckey, Rodney: 84
Summers, Dajuan: 84
Sy, Pape: 9
Taylor, Jermaine: 107
Teague, Jeff: 9
Telfair, Sebastian: 183
Temple, Garrett: 294
Terry, Jason: 66
Thabeet, Hasheem: 148
Thomas, Etan: 10
Thomas, Kenny: 149
Thomas, Kurt: 44
Thomas, Tim: 66
Thomas, Tyrus: 32
Thompson, Jason: 283
Thornton, Al: 323
Thornton, Marcus: 206
Tinsley, Jamaal: 151
Tolliver, Anthony: 183
Tucker, Alando: 186
Turiaf, Ronny: 216
Turkoglu, Hedo: 261
Turner, Evan: 251
Udoh, Epke: 94
Udoka, Ime: 285
Udrih, Beno: 283
Ukikc, Roko: 173
Uzoh, Ben: 195
Varejao, Anderson: 55
Varnado, Jarvis: 162
Vasquez, Greivis: 149
Villanueva, Charlie: 85
Vujacic, Sasha: 139
Wade, Dwyane: 161
Wafer, Von: 20
Walker, Bill: 217
Wall, John: 323

Wallace, Ben: 85
Wallace, Gerald: 33
Wallace, Rasheed: 22
Walton, Luke: 139
Warren, Willie: 127
Warrick, Hakim: 262
Watson, C.J.: 45
Watson, Earl: 314
Weaver, Kyle: 45
Webster, Martell: 183
Weems, Sonny: 304
West, David: 207
West, Delonte: 21
West, Mario: 21
Westbrook, Russell: 228
White, D.J.: 229
White, Terrico: 85
Whiteside, Hassan: 284
Wilcox, Chris: 86
Wilkins, Damien: 149
Wilks, Mike: 231
Williams, Deron: 314
Williams, Elliot: 273
Williams, Jason: 241
Williams, Jawad: 56
Williams, Latavious: 230
Williams, Lou: 251
Williams, Marcus: 151
Williams, Marvin: 10
Williams, Maurice: 56
Williams, Reggie: 94
Williams, Sean: 198
Williams, Shelden: 75
Williams, Terrence: 196
Wright, Antoine: 284
Wright, Brandan: 95
Wright, Dorell: 95
Wright, Julian: 304
Yao, Ming: 107
Young, Nick: 324
Young, Sam: 150
Young, Thaddeus: 252
Zoubek, Brian: 196

Made in the USA
Lexington, KY
29 October 2010